CENTRE PANEL OF THE ARTISTS' RIFLES WAR MEMORIAL
AT HEADQUARTERS, DUKE'S ROAD.

THE REGIMENTAL
ROLL OF HONOUR

AND

WAR RECORD

OF THE

ARTISTS' RIFLES

(1/28th, 2/28th and 3/28th BATTALIONS
THE LONDON REGIMENT T.F.)

COMMISSIONS, PROMOTIONS, APPOINTMENTS

AND

REWARDS FOR SERVICE IN THE FIELD

OBTAINED BY MEMBERS OF THE CORPS

Since 4th August, 1914.

THIRD EDITION.

LONDON:
HOWLETT & SON,
10, FRITH STREET, SOHO SQUARE, W. 1.

1922.

CONTENTS.

	PAGE.
FOREWORD BY COLONEL MAY	vii.
EDITOR'S PREFACE	ix.
SUMMARY OF HONOURS, CASUALTIES, ETC.	xviii.
A CALENDAR OF REGIMENTAL NUMBERS	xix.
THE FIRST FIFTY	xxii.
WITH THE ROYAL NAVAL DIVISION	xxiii.
ADDENDA TO SECTIONS I. TO VI.	xli.
SECTION I. THE ROLL OF HONOUR	1
SECTION II. V.C.: D.S.O.: D.S.C.: M.C.: A.F.C. ...	43
OTHER HONOURS AND DECORATIONS ...	148
FOREIGN ORDERS AND MEDALS	150
MENTIONED IN DESPATCHES	152
BROUGHT TO NOTICE OF SECRETARY OF STATE	159
SECTION III. ROLL OF COMMISSIONS	161
SUPPLEMENTAL LIST	427
ANALYSIS OF COMMISSIONS	430
SECTION IV. ROLL OF "OTHER RANKS"	433
SECTION V. PAST MEMBERS	487
SECTION VI. THE 104TH (ARTISTS' RIFLES) V.A.D. ...	495
INDEX TO ROLL OF HONOUR, COMMISSIONS, REGIMENTS AND HONOURS	497
CORRIGENDA	593

NOTE.

In searching for a name reference should be made both to the Index and to the alphabetical Roll of Other Ranks (p. 433). To save space, names in the latter are not repeated in the Index (except in the case of Deaths, Honours, and M-G Instructors at G.H.Q.).

ILLUSTRATIONS

BY PAST AND PRESENT MEMBERS OF THE CORPS AND PHOTOGRAPHS.

	PAGE.
CENTRE PANEL OF WAR MEMORIAL AT HEADQUARTERS. (Designed and wrought by *Capt. Alwyn Carr*)	*Frontispiece.*
EMBRYO OFFICERS AT ST. OMER	xvi.
EMBRYO OFFICERS AT ROMFORD	xvii.
THE "FALL-IN" AND "CEASE-FIRE" (*facsimiles*)	xx.
NOTRE DAME DE BREBIÈRE, ALBERT. (*Col. W. C. Horsley*)	17
BAILLEUL, 1914. (*Capt. W. Lee-Hankey*)	32
BAILLEUL IN 1918	33
DEFEAT OF THE PRUSSIAN GUARD. (*Capt. W. B. Wollen*, R.I., R.O.I.)	97
RECAPTURE OF BRITISH TANK AT SERANVILLERS. (*Capt. H. M. Paget*)	113
CAVALRY OF THE AIR. (*Capt. W. B. Wollen*)	177
ARRAS (LITTLE SQUARE). (*Capt. E. Handley-Read*)	192
GETTING THE GUNS AWAY. (*Capt. W. B. Wollen*)	193
JOINT ROAD-CONTROL POST (French Troops and Artists)	241
MACHINE-GUN INSTRUCTION, G.H.Q. SCHOOL	241
A SHELL-PITTED AREA (Aeroplane photograph)	256
RECAPTURE OF SANCTUARY WOOD, 1916. (*Capt. W. B. Wollen*)	257
A GERMAN TANK AND A BRITISH. (*Capt. E. Handley-Read*)	305
TERRITORIALS AT POZIÈRES. (*Capt. W. B. Wollen*)	320
CADETS SELECTING AND CUTTING BRUSHWOOD, France, 1915	321
THE RUNNER. (*Lieut. J. M. Watt*)	385
THE ORIGINAL ARTISTS' BADGE	400
SKETCH OF THE BATTLE FOR NIERGNIES. (*Capt. H. M. Paget*)	401
THE LAST STAND OF THE 2ND DEVONS. (*Capt. W. B. Wollen*)	465
OVER THE TOP : THE ARTISTS AT MARCOING. (*Sgt. John Nash*)	480
TAMBOUR DU BATAILLON "ARTIST-RIFLES." (*By Georges Scott*)	481

ILLUSTRATIONS—*continued.*

PORTRAITS.

	PAGE.
Capt. E. P. BENNETT, V.C.	240
2/Lieut. G. E. CATES, V.C.	304
Capt. G. ST.G. S. CATHER, V.C.	464
Lieut. D. J. DEAN, V.C.	384
Lieut. A. J. T. FLEMING-SANDES, V.C.	112
2/Lieut. R. P. HALLOWES, V.C.	16
Capt. Rev. E. N. MELLISH, V.C.	176
Lt.-Col. B. W. VANN, V.C.	196

FOREWORD

BY

COLONEL H. A. R. MAY, C.B., V.D.,
recently Commanding the Artists' Rifles.

As one who has been intimately connected with the Corps for nearly forty years, and who yields place to none in his interest in, and love for, his old Regiment, I have awaited the publication of this Roll of Honour of the Artists' Rifles with an eagerness that I would find it hard to describe. For it is a Record of which, not only every past or present member of the Regiment, but everyone who values the proved possibilities of the Territorial Force may rightly be proud.

The story it tells is one of alert and patriotic acceptance of the responsibilities cast upon us by the war, of many thousands of officers trained for service in the field, of duty nobly done, of gallant service rendered—even unto death. And in no boasting rhetoric is the tale related: the narrative unfolds itself, modestly and simply, in columns of names and figures which speak more eloquently perhaps than any letterpress that could accompany them. Every line records good service voluntarily rendered: one in every seven lines denotes the splendid tragedy of a promising young life sacrificed for his country.

The book contains a complete record of all whose names have been inscribed in our Muster Roll since August, 1914; of Commissions obtained; of honours and decorations awarded (with particulars, where published, of the deeds by which they were gained); and of casualties suffered.

This colossal work, although I know it has been a labour of love, has been compiled and edited with immense and continuous care, spread over some years, by Major S. Stagoll Higham, V.D., assisted by a devoted band of willing and enthusiastic helpers, to all of whom the gratitude of every comrade is due—and is given, It is issued with pride to preserve for future generations the memory of men who, when the occasion arose voluntarily served their country and their Regiment in the greatest emergency.

The time has almost come when the feelings with which we regard the greatest possible Sacrifice made by our best and bravest during the awful days of 1914-18 begin to be free from regret and longing and sadness. And my earnest wish and hope is that when the relatives and friends of those Artists who were then called upon to give up all turn the pages of this book, they will be strengthened to do so with pride and thankfulness only.

Despite the gloom that may sometimes come to us at happenings in these present times, my firm conviction is that so long as we can produce men of the quality of those whose names and deeds are enshrined in this Roll of Honour we can go forward joyfully and with every confidence into the unknown future. And may we all be inspired to carry out our present obligations and duties patriotically, and to live henceforth lives worthy of the example of those 2,003 Artists who died for us that we as an Empire might live. This would be the best War Memorial of all.

November 11th, 1921.

EDITOR'S PREFACE.

At an Army examination in 1913 the candidates, who included a few Officers of the Artists in pursuit of the coveted "Q," were confronted with the following conundrum:—

"Supposing a war continues—What machinery exists in England for supplying the wastage in Officers?"

Little did any of those candidates dream how soon this question would insist on an immediate answer: that within the next twelve months the old regular Army, hopelessly out-gunned, would have been sacrificed: and that the nation would be called upon to provide, and would eventually succeed in producing, from civilians, upwards of a quarter of a million new Officers.

Still less did any member of the Artists then imagine that the quota of such new Officers furnished by his own Battalion of amateur soldiers—one of the original Rifle Volunteer Corps that was raised by Painters and Art students in post-Crimean days and incorporated in 1908 in the new Territorial Force as the "28th London (Artists Rifles)"—would run into five figures. Or that within a few months of the outbreak of hostilities ex-Artists (over 1,000 in number) would have been gazetted to every regular infantry regiment in the British Army including all the Foot Guards.

There is no more striking incident in the whole history of the Corps, since the day when in beards and shakos our ancestors made their first appearance on parade, than the story of the first little batch of men suddenly called out of our ranks to replace, in the field, Army Officers who had become casualties.

From this small beginning, extemporised to meet an emergency, sprang the huge organisation which in the words of Earl French may be said to have laid the foundation of that Officers' School of War whose ramifications were soon to extend, not only behind all the fighting lines, but throughout the United Kingdom. By the end of the war this Territorial unit had furnished over 10,000 Officers to our big Armies, as chronicled in detail in the following pages, and had also trained in its schools in France and in England several thousand cadets from other Regiments, in addition to maintaining latterly a fighting Battalion in the line.

X.

THE FIRST BATTALION.

On the 2nd August, 1914, the 2nd London Division T.F. to which the Artists were allocated as Army Troops, assembled on Salisbury Plain for their annual camp. At midnight the Division was recalled post-haste to London and on the 5th August was mobilised for active service and placed on duty the same day. Within a fortnight it moved out to its War Station in Hertfordshire, minus the Artists, who were left behind, much to their chagrin "to help in the defence of London." Quartered successively at Manchester Street Schools, Lord's Cricket Ground, and the Tower, they presently rejoined their Division in the country but had not been there a week when at less than 48 hours' notice the Battalion was embarked overseas, landing in the critical period at the end of October, 1914.

On their way up to Ypres they were dramatically halted at Bailleul by a Staff-Officer (as it happened, an old Artists Adjutant, Col. Romer) with an urgent message from the Commander-in-Chief who wished to see them. They de-bussed and were visited by him there. The result of an historic interview between him and Colonel May was that a few days later some 50 "other ranks," public school and University men who had taken to heart Lord Roberts' warning and trained in peace time, were rapidly given some practical tips, promoted to Second Lieutenant and the next day went straight into action (still wearing their Territorial private's uniform and Artists badge with the addition of a "pip") against some of Germany's most famous Regiments, in command of seasoned regular soldiers of the immortal Seventh Division.*

The experiment of thus attaching Artists to the Old Contemptibles as "Probationary Officers" having proved successful, a further batch was called for and orders were issued by the G.O.C. directing the Battalion to be transformed into an Officers' Training Corps to be drawn on from time to time to supply Officers, the remainder being retained as a fighting unit to be used as occasion demanded. He thus refers to the matter in his first Despatch.

> "I established the Battalion as a Training Corps for officers in the field. The cadets pass through a course, which includes some thoroughly practical training as all cadets do a tour of 48 hours in the trenches, and afterwards write a report on what they see and notice. They also visit an observation post of a battery or group of batteries, and spend some hours there. A Commandant has been appointed, and he arranges and supervises the work, sets schemes for practice, administers the school, delivers lectures, and reports on the candidates. The cadets are instructed in all branches of military training suitable for platoon commanders. Machine-gun tactics, a knowledge of which

---

*Their names should be placed on record and will be found at page xxii.

is so necessary for all junior officers, is a special feature of the course of instruction. When first started the school was able to turn out officers at the rate of 75 a month. This has since been increased to 100. Reports received from Divisional and Army Corps Commanders on officers who have been trained at the school are most satisfactory."

Earl French has since on several occasions written and spoken on this subject in generous terms and in particular at a recent reunion of survivors, when he said:—

"I shall never, never forget the first visit I paid to the Artists after they landed in France, or the wonderful impression they left on my mind of the possibilities which were in that Corps of furnishing a want which was so terrible to all of us at that time, the supply of officers. What really influenced me in trying the experiment I had to try was the appreciation I had of the splendid material of which I saw you were composed, and of the marked aptitude of Colonel May and those who helped him for organizing and commanding such a Corps. Just at the period I am speaking of we had suffered fearful casualties, and the proportion of losses in officers was higher than in any other rank, and it was going on every day. I was really positively at my wits' end, suffering almost agony, to know where I could get officer reinforcements. You all know how any fighting force must deteriorate, and deteriorate badly, unless this supply of officers is kept up properly and regularly.

Well, in this trouble and difficulty the Artists came to my help, and I shall never forget as long as I live the courage, the determination, the skill, the organizing power which they displayed in trying to meet my wishes. By day and by night, almost under the enemy's guns, and very often under close rifle-fire in the trenches, they commenced, they carried on, and they developed this work to the very highest standard of efficiency, and they showed clearly what men of energy and skill could do in this direction when they knew how. They taught us, indeed, a very great lesson, among the many lessons which all we regular soldiers had to learn in the war. We never knew what the possibilities were before. We used to talk about it taking two years to train an artillery driver, and, above all things, we said we could not turn out officers under a certain considerable length of time. Well the Artists showed us we made a mistake there, because they turned out a most efficient body of officers, and kept up everything they said they would. From that moment they became the model for and an example to that large number of training establishments all over France, which to the end of the war turned out officers with the utmost speed and the utmost efficiency. What they suffered in doing it is recorded in this book which I now hold in my hand (Artists

Rifles Regimental Roll of Honour, 1914-1919), and I may recall at this moment, without frivolity, the fact that these boys, all of them, looked death straight in the face, laughing and smiling, and that the Artists earned at that time the sobriquet of 'The Suicide Club.' That, perhaps, is the highest honour that could be paid to them."

The School in France was originally run entirely by Colonel May and his Officers and Sergeants, but presently, as the enemy pressure relaxed, he had the advantage of the assistance of Regular Officers (one of whom was appointed "Commandant of School") and gradually as additional candidates for commissions began to arrive from other regiments, the two units were worked as separate organisations.

In April, 1915, quarters were changed from Bailleul to St. Omer and a new Commandant to the school was appointed, which from that date became "G.H.Q. School." Thereafter Artists who came out in drafts, together with selected N.C.O's. from Cavalry, Artillery, Canadian and other units sent up for instruction in Infantry work, were first trained in "the Colonel's Class" and on passing out went on to this School until July, 1916, when the Battalion was specially authorised by Earl Haig to send candidates approved by their C.O. direct to Commissions.

Another branch of their early activities was the staffing of the Machine Gun School at Visques, near G.H.Q., which was started by a Hythe Instructor (Major Baker-Carr), who had one Hythe Sergeant to assist him. They trained as assistants 16 men from the Artists, who in their turn trained others of their comrades, until eventually multitudes of little groups (each of eight Officers or N.C.O's. temporarily withdrawn from the trenches) were daily to be seen dotted all over the parade ground keenly studying the intricacies and tactics of the weapon, expounded to them by an Artists' Sergeant who had specialised in the subject. A large proportion of such Instructors afterwards passed on to Commissions in the M.G. Corps, Tanks, R.F.C., and other units where their expert knowledge was invaluable.*

Reinforced from time to time by strong drafts, the special task of supplying and training Officers thus undertaken by the Artists kept them at G.H.Q. (where as "Headquarters Battalion" they were also entrusted with multifarious other and responsible duties) for about $2\frac{1}{2}$ years. During this period there were of course considerable changes in personnel. The bulk of the original N.C.O's. and men had soon obtained Commissions, while senior Captains had been promoted to command Battalions in the field, and many junior Officers had been attached or transferred to regular Regiments. In December, 1915, Col. May was invalided home. On recovering from a

---

*Vide p. 313.

severe illness he was appointed to the important post, which he held till the end of the War, of Commandant at Tidworth of the Southern Command School of Instruction for Infantry Officers, where over 14,000 Officers (including 5,000 Australians) passed through his curriculum. He was succeeded in France by his Second-in-command, Lt. Col. Chatfeild-Clarke, who carried on until the summer of 1917, when the authorities decided to close down Cadet Schools in France and to send all future candidates for Commissions back to England for training. Thereupon the remaining Officers and men, less 200 cadets whose training was on the point of completion, at last had an opportunity of fulfilling the role for which the Artists had volunteered in 1914 (the reason they then went to France), of going into action together as a fighting unit, and they were allotted to the 190th Brigade in the Royal Naval Division (63rd).

There was nothing very nautical about the 190th, the explanation being that there were not enough naval men available at that time to make up an entire Division, so the Army was called in to complete it by adding four Battalions.

Appended to this Preface is an abridged account of their adventures in the line for which the Editor is indebted to Captains Money and Hewitt and to Col. Goldthorp, whose contribution is of especial value as shewing the impressions, necessarily unbiassed by preconceived Regimental associations, of a "foreign" C.O. when in command of a Battalion of the Artists. His very live account of a modern battle will be of absorbing interest, both to those who have shared this experience and to those who have not been through the mill.

THE SECOND BATTALION.

Prior to the departure of the original Battalion overseas, a second (Reserve) Battalion, distinguished as "2/28th London," had been raised under the command of Col. Horsley, the late Commanding Officer of the Artists, who was assisted by Officers transferred from the First Battalion (1/28th) or promoted from the ranks. Enrolment started on the 31st August, 1914, and within a week 5,000 would-be recruits had applied for admission, 'Varsity Blues, rowing men and athletes of every description, mostly without any previous military training. Uniforms and arms were for a time unobtainable, but soon every one of the 1,000 selected recruits had succeeded in purchasing a khaki outfit at ruinous prices, from somewhere, and presently the authorities unearthed a large supply of ancient Martini-Henry carbines. The sole equipment then provided was a regulation water-bottle for each man but with no means of attaching the same to the person of the soldier. Mufti overcoats were worn en banderole and rations were carried in neat brown paper packets tied on to waist-belts of every hue and shape.

After three or four months recruit training with only 50 modern rifles available, interspersed with daily journeys into Kent of strong working parties to assist in the construction of "the last ditch," the Battalion was properly equipped and armed and moved to Roehampton, thence to camp in Richmond Park where they also initiated a valuable machine gun school.

Like many similar units this Reserve Battalion was eventually drained dry in supplying drafts to its 1st Battalion overseas. It also furnished Officers for the New Armies and some other Territorial Units. Col. Horsley was then appointed to the command of the 104th Provisional Battalion for Home Defence, stationed at the Tower of London, and eventually finished up his 42 years service in the Artists by proceeding overseas to a Staff appointment as Area Commandant at Englebelmer in France.

The Third Battalion and No. 15 (Artists' Rifles) O.C.B.

Meanwhile on the 1st January, 1915, by which date old Artists and others were beginning to arrive from the Colonies for training as Officers, a third Battalion, "3/28th London" had been started (at first severely restricted to two Companies under a Major), in which all subsequent recruits had to be enrolled. It was placed under the command of Lt.-Col. William Shirley, an old friend of the Corps, recently retired from the Indian Army, who had been acting as Second-in-command of 2/28th. He brought very special qualifications to the post, having been for some years an Army Instructor in India, at Sandhurst, and at Cambridge University, where on the outbreak of war he was holding the appointment of Director of Military Studies. On occasions this Battalion, which was principally officered in the first instance by senior N.C.O's sent home for the purpose from 1/28th in France, was over 3,000 strong and in $3\frac{1}{2}$ years had passed 9,352 recruits through its ranks. After a period of recruit training in London, which included the construction at Kenwood of a series of entrenchments and dug-outs on the most up-to-date Continental models, it also went into camp in Richmond Park, whence it was moved in July, 1915, to High Beech in Epping Forest, thence to Hare Hall, Romford, and finally to Berkhampstead, and on the absorption of the original 2nd Battalion by the 1st it was re-numbered 2/28th.*

In May, 1915, instructions were issued for the formation within this Battalion of a separate School of Instruction for newly gazetted Officers of other Territorial regiments on similar lines to the School in France and during the next few months upwards of 1,500 such Officers passed through the School courses and examinations.

---

*To avoid confusion in this book, Col. Shirley's Battalion is throughout referred to as 3/28th, and Col. Horsley's as 2/28th, notwithstanding the re-numbering.

In November, 1915, the Regiment was officially recognised by Army Order* as an Officers' Training Corps, and the Home Battalion became the 2nd Artists Rifles O.T.C.

In March, 1916, its separate School, then at Gidea Park, was converted into four Companies of cadets to which recruits were passed on for training as Officers after receiving a preliminary military training in the ranks of the other four Companies, the whole being under the command of Colonel Shirley and run by Artists' Officers and Sergeant Instructors. In August, 1916, by which date the organisation of Officer Cadet Battalions throughout the United Kingdom had been perfected, the four Cadet Companies were separated from Colonel Shirley's Battalion and transformed into "No. 15 (Artists Rifles), O.C.B." which was placed under the command of Lt.-Col. E. St. L. Shaw (1st East Surrey) an invalided Regular Officer, with a Staff of Artists and other Officers and Sergeant Instructors. Thenceforth recruits enrolled in 3/28th were sent, on completion of their preliminary training, indiscriminately to No. 15 or to any other O.C.B. in which there were vacancies at the moment, while No. 15 as part of the general scheme of these O.C.B.'s received Cadets from other units besides the Artists.

In 1918 Colonel Shaw was succeeded by Colonel Gascoigne who retained command of this O.C.B. until the end of the War.

In July, 1918, Colonel Shirley was compelled by ill-health to relinquish the command of 3/28th, and was succeeded by Lt.-Col. Ostle (an Artists Officer who went out in October, 1914, as a junior Captain, rose to be Second-in-command of the 2nd Border Regiment, and subsequently commanded two different Battalions in the Field before being sent home to Hospital.

The history of this publication is shortly as follows:—

Early in 1915, the Editor, as an Officer who had served in all three Battalions, was deputed by the three Commanding Officers to keep a record of Commissions and Honours then being obtained by members of the Regiment and of casualties suffered, there being in the nature of things no provision in Official regimental documents or T.F. Records for following up the career of a man after he had been struck off the Artists on obtaining a Commission in another unit. Correspondents were appointed in each Battalion to assist the Editor, and on the first anniversary of the Declaration of War the first Edition of the present work, containing 1508 names, was published.

The intention was to re-issue the pamphlet periodically until the end of

---

* No. 429 of 1915.

the War, and on the second anniversary a second Edition brought up to date, containing 3434 Commissions, was printed and on the point of distribution when the Press Bureau Order was issued, which prohibited any reference to places, numbers of Battalions and other details in which the book abounded.

These copies were accordingly sealed up, but monthly supplemental lists were published in the Regimental Journal for a time, the publicity thus obtained being a valuable check against error. Presently the Journal itself was also suspended for some months, but eventually it was allowed to reappear, and the supplemental lists were resumed after being shorn of all offending details, and were continued until the Armistice.

It then became necessary to dig out from every available source the particulars which had not been previously obtainable, such as dates and places of deeds and deaths, and this research has occupied an unconscionable time. Still it has been done, and the result is a much more complete and reliable record than was previously obtainable.

With regard to the plan of the book, the original scheme was to make it a record only of Commissions and Honours, with a list of casualties in all ranks, but whilst this final edition was in the press a very strong desire was expressed for a complete Roll comprising every one of the 15,000 Artists who at one time or another during the War had served in the Regiment in any capacity. An additional Section No. IV has therefore been compiled and added containing the names of all N.C.O.'s and privates who are not known to have taken Commissions. Here, however, the Editor came up against an insurmountable difficulty. It soon became evident that this Section not having been, like the rest of the book, entered up from day to day, it would now be absolutely impossible to ascertain what had happened to a very large number of men who had been discharged or transferred to other Regiments since August, 1914. In these circumstances it has not been practicable to make Section IV more than an alphabetical list of some 4,800 "other ranks" not included in the Roll of Commissions, with the addition of reference letters and symbols indicating those who are known to have served overseas with the 1st Battalion or in other units, or to have been killed, wounded, etc.

It is probable that there may be discovered in this Section the names of many men who had in fact obtained Commissions, some further casualties, and possibly a hidden D.S.O. or other Honour.

In these circumstances it will be realised, and the Editor desires to emphasize the fact, that the absence of any reference letter against a man's name in Section IV is no reflection upon him. It simply means that the news of his promotion, reward or other event has not reached the Regiment. And the list includes the very large number of cadets who were under instruction in England on the cessation of hostilities, at least 2,000; also men discharged during the War as medically unfit.

EMBRYO OFFICERS.
Cadets leaving Barracks at St. Omer, on completion of Course, 1915.

EMBRYO OFFICERS.
Passing-out Inspection of Cadets at Romford, 1917.

The Editor much regrets that he is compelled strictly to limit this Section IV to those who enlisted originally in the Artists, as recruits. He recognises that this means the exclusion of those members of other units who were transferred or attached to the 1st Battalion in France, wore their regimental badge, fought and died with them. Probably they are included in their own Regimental War Records, but they were all so thoroughly imbued with the spirit and traditions of their new unit, that he would willingly have inserted in this book every one of the hundreds of additional names had the exigencies of space and expense permitted. He has, however, been sufficiently inconsistent to include their Officers, together with their Military Crosses and other Honours if gained whilst serving with the Artists.

In conclusion, the Editor warmly acknowledges his very great indebtedness to his hosts of correspondents in every theatre of war, to sympathetic Record Officers at home and abroad, and to the patient and painstaking members of his constantly changing staff, without whose meticulous care in the laborious daily task of searching Gazettes and Casualty Lists against their ever-growing Card Index, the compilation of this gigantic record would have fallen through. To enumerate all those who during a period of nearly five years lent a hand in this way, invalids and light duty men at home, Officers and men on leave, cadets awaiting Gazette, and other keen helpers would fill pages, and it is useless to attempt it.

In the mass of detail dealt with in this work and the circumstances under which it was collected, there are no doubt mistakes and omissions: possibly a considerable number. To meet such cases the copy of the book which is to be deposited in the War Memorial recently erected at Headquarters will be interleaved and if short particulars of any serious error that may be discovered are forwarded to "The Hon. Secretary, Roll of Honour," Artists Rifles, Duke's Road, Euston Road, W.C.2, it shall be rectified in such Headquarters copy. Arrangements may also be made for periodical publication of lists of corrections in the Regimental Journal.

SUMMARY OF WAR HONOURS,
1914—1919.

Victoria Cross	8
C.B.	1
C.M.G.	1
M.V.O.	3
Order of the British Empire	K.B.E., 1 ; C.B.E., 2
" " " "	O.B.E., 43 ; M.B.E., 37
Distinguished Service Order	52 ; Bars, 4
Distinguished Service Cross	4 ; Bars, 1
Military Cross	822 ; Bars, 63 ; 2nd Bars, 6
Distinguished Flying Cross	23 ; Bars, 3
Air Force Cross	15
Royal Victorian Medal	4
Distinguished Conduct Medal	6
Military Medal	15
Meritorious Service Medal	14
Foreign Decorations	90
Mentioned in Despatches	564
Brought to notice of Secretary of State	70

STRENGTH.

Numbers on Mobilization	621
Recruits during the War (including past members rejoined)	14,401
Total of Muster Roll	15,022
Gazetted to Commissions (so far as ascertained)	10,256

CASUALTIES.

Nature.	As Officers.	As Rank and File.	Total.
Killed in action or died	1,614	389	2,003
Wounded or gassed	2,816	434	3,250
Missing	418	114	532
Prisoners of War	256	30	286
			6,071

NOTE.—The above figures include only enlisted Artists, not officers or men transferred or attached from other Regiments.

A CALENDAR OF REGIMENTAL NUMBERS.

showing at a glance the approximate date on which any recruit joined, or old member rejoined, by reference to his Regimental Number*

Date.	Highest No.		Date.	Highest No.		Date.	Highest No.
	1st Battalion.			**3rd Battalion.**			**3rd Bn.**
	Old style	New† style	**1916**	Old style	New† style	**1917**	
1908	{1 to 425}	{760001 760032}	Jan. 1	6400	761300	Jan. 11	764517
1909	787	48	,, 14	6600	... 400	,, 13	... 700
1910	940	57	,, 27	6900	... 500	,, 16	... 900
1911	1037	64	Feb. 1	7000	... 570	Feb. 1	765000
1912	1137	75	,, 7	7100	... 600	,, 7	... 200
1913	1281	98	,, 17	7300	... 720	,, 21	... 300
Aug. 3/14	1345	760111	Mch. 1	7600	... 860	Mch. 27	... 400
,, 30 ,,	1749	... 165	,, 7	7700	... 920	Apr. 19	... 500
			Apl. 27	7800	... 970	,, 26	... 600
1914	**2nd Battalion.**		May 7	7850	... 944	May 7	... 700
Aug. 31	1907	760188	June 8	7900	762000	,, 25	... 900
Sep. 1	2000	... 200	,, 14	8000	... 100	June 7	766000
,, 15	2500	... 276	July 1	8100	... 150	,, 29	... 200
Oct. 30	2800	... 300	Aug. 24	8200	... 200	July 20	... 400
Nov. 24	3000	... 375	Sep. 13	8300	... 300	,, 31	... 500
Dec. 31	3063	... 391	,, 20	8400	... 400	Aug. 9	... 600
			,, 26	8500	... 500	,, 30	... 800
1915	**3rd Battalion.**		Oct. 4	8600	... 600	Sep. 25	767000
Jan. 5	3100	760400	,, 17	8800	... 800	Oct. 26	... 200
Feb. 2	3300	... 455	,, 25	9000	763000	Nov. 16	... 300
Mch. 16	3500	... 500	,, 30	9100	... 100	Dec. 7	... 400
Apr. 20	3700	... 552	Nov. 6	9200	... 200	**1918**	
May 27	3900	... 580	,, 11	9400	... 400	Jan. 24	... 600
June 21	4100	... 600	,, 20	9600	... 600	Feb. 20	... 800
July 13	4200	... 612	,, 27	9700	... 700	Apl. 5	... 900
Aug. 20	4400	... 643	Dec. 11	9800	... 800	,, 24	768000
Sep. 23	4500	... 700	,, 14	9900	... 900	May 29	... 200
Oct. 29	4800	... 760	,, 18	10000	764000	June 15	... 400
Nov. 12	5000	... 800	,, 29	10200	... 200	,, 28	... 500
,, 29	5500	761000	**1917**			July 10	... 700
Dec. 6	5800	... 100	Jan. 6	10400	... 400	,, 27	... 900
,, 10	6000	... 180	,, 8	10515	764516	Aug. 7	769000
,, 13	6100	... 200	End of re-numbering.†			Sep. 4	... 200
,, 28	6300	... 290				Oct. 2	... 400
						,, 21	... 600
						Nov. 11	769703

*Example.—No. 760777 joined in 1915, between Oct. 29 and Nov. 12.

†Explanation.—In January, 1917, the 4,516 Cadets then serving (bearing numbers between 1 and 10515) were consecutively re-numbered 760001 to 764516. Subsequent recruits were numbered from 764517 onwards. Men transferred, or attached, to the Artists were distinguished by special numbering and are not included in the above Table.—Ed.

THE "FALL-IN."
August 4th, 1914.
(*facsimile.*)

No. 1   Army Form E. 635.

Territorial Force.

EMBODIMENT.

NOTICE TO JOIN.

No., Rank and Name } Capt. Hon Major S. S. Higham

28th. (COUNTY OF LONDON) BATTN THE LONDON REGIMENT (ARTISTS RIFLES) Regt. or Corps.

Whereas the Army Council, in pursuance of His Majesty's Proclamation, have directed that the 28th. (COUNTY OF LONDON) BATTN THE LONDON REGIMENT (ARTISTS RIFLES) be embodied on the 5th day of August 1914.

You are hereby required to attend at Head Quarters not later than ~~midday~~ 12 o'clock ~~o'clock~~ that day. Should you not present yourself as ordered you will be liable to be proceeded against.

O. F. Blackwood Capt
~~28th. (COUNTY OF LONDON) BATTN~~ Adjutant.
THE LONDON REGIMENT
(ARTISTS RIFLES)

Date Aug 4 -1914

THE "CEASE FIRE."
November 11th, 1918.
(*facsimile*.)

O.C. A Coy
    B
    C
    D

OC no.3 Sect. M.G.C. (Matta Artists)

URGENT

Hostilities will cease at 11 a.m. to-day.
Form up and march back independently to the Château, HARVENG at once. Do not forget to bring the cookers with you.

09.30 hrs
11.11.18.

G. Paterson
Lt. & A/adj.

xxii

THE FIRST FIFTY.

Roll of N.C.O.'s and men of the Overseas Battalion who went into action in November, 1914, as Probationary 2nd Lieutenants in the 7th Division.

20th INFANTRY BRIGADE.

1st Grenadier Guards.
1076 Cpl. CRISP, F. E. F.
1634 Pte.*EDLMANN, F. J.
1464 „ *HILLAS-DRAKE, R. F.
1186 „ MOLLER, A. A.

2nd Border.
392 Cpl.*CLOSE, M. A.
1614 Pte. CUTHBERTSON, F. T.
1551 „ SAMPSON, H. F.
1613 „ *WORNUM, T. H.

2nd Gordon Highlanders.
691 Cpl. CHATER, A. D.
1437 Pte. HORSLEY, O.
1436 „ HORSLEY. S. M.
997 L/Cpl. MULOCK, E. R.

21st INFANTRY BRIGADE.

2nd Yorkshire.
2220 Pte. CROSSE, M. E. B.
1167 „ CUTTLE, G.
2255 „ HOLLIS, H. L.
1794 „ PICKUP, A. J.

2nd Bedfordshire.
1260 Pte. BREWER, C. H.
1929 „ DABELL, N. V.
1033 L/Cpl. DE BURIATTE, H.
1030 Pte. WILLANS, H.

2nd Royal Scots Fusiliers.
1760 Pte.*RAYMOND-BARKER, C.L.
1755 „ STEWART, J.
1578 „ WALLACE, J. R.
1573 „ *WHITE, L. S.

2nd Wiltshire.
1823 Pte. CARDEN, R. H.
1138 „ KITCAT, A. J.
1536 „ SHEPHERD, W. S.
1725 „ STRAWSON, F. M.

22nd INFANTRY BRIGADE.

2nd Royal Warwickshire.
1101 Pte. HERBAGE, P. F. W.
1285 „ MONK, G. B.
539 „ PEACE, G. V.
787 Sgt. STANDRING, B. A

2nd Royal West Surrey.
693 Sgt. AUSTIN, C. F.
1372 Pte. HUMPHREYS, D. F.
1390 Cpl. MESSOM, H.
1371 Pte. ROUGHT, C. G.

1st Royal Welsh Fusiliers.
954 Cpl. JONES, L.
608 L/Cpl. PARKES, H. F.
1429 Pte. REES, J. T.
1934 „ WINTERS, J. W.

1st South Staffordshire.
706 Cpl.*FROST, K.
1744 „ MACKINTOSH, H. L.
1087 L/Cpl. SILCOCK, A.
1399 Pte.*WEST, F.

ROYAL ENGINEERS.
1150 *HUNTER, J. W.
1491 *HUTT, H. V.

[This Roll does not entirely agree with the Army List, as some of the above Officers were killed, and others (marked *) had been transferred to other Battalions before a belated Gazette recognised the appointment of the remainder to Commissions as above.—ED.]

WITH THE ROYAL NAVAL DIVISION.

A SHORT HISTORY OF 1/ARTISTS IN THE LINE.
FROM JULY 1917, TO THE ARMISTICE.

Oppy Wood.
Passchendaele.
On the Somme (Marcoing).
Withdrawal to Metz and Beaulencourt.
Advance to Couillet Wood Sector.
Retirement from Havrincourt Wood to Forceville.
To Aveluy Wood Sector.
Attack on Hindenburg Line.
Rest at Bailleulval.
Capture of Hindenburg Line.
Fall of Cambrai.
First British troops in at Blaugies and Sars-la-Bruyere.
Pursuit to Harvengt and Harmignies.
Mons.

63rd (ROYAL NAVAL) DIVISION.

188th Inf. Bde.	189th Inf. Bde.	190th Inf. Bde.
1/R.M.L.I.	" Drake " Bn.	1/Artists.
2/R.M.L.I.	" Hawke " Bn.	4/Bedford.
" Anson " Bn.	" Hood " Bn.	7/R. Fusiliers.
" Howe " Bn.	" Nelson " Bn.	4/Shropshire L.I.

From July to Sept. 1917, the Division was in the front line ("R3" and "R4" Sectors, Oppy and Gavrelle) and with the exception of a few casualties, nothing of special note occurred during this period so far as the Artists' were concerned. After a normal tour, the Division was relieved by the 47th (formerly 2/London) Division, the Artists themselves being replaced by the 22/London, commanded by Lt. Col. C. F. H. Greenwood, an Artists' Officer, and moved to La Comté.

On coming out of the line inexorable Anno Domini deprived us of our Commanding Officer, Col. Chatfeild-Clarke, while our esprit de corps was momentarily ruffled by the appearance of a reinforcing draft composed not of Artists, but of 119 men from another unit.

It was recognised however that pooling, not only of reinforcements but of C.O's. was now inevitable: that as no other Battalion overseas was being exclusively fed from its own Regiment, the Artists could not expect different treatment.

During the ensuing twelve months they had five new Commanding Officers, all drawn from other Regiments.

October, 1917.

In October, the Division was ordered to the Ypres front: we journeyed to Houtkerque, thence to Reigersburgh and on the 28th left camp for our first big fight, the C.O. Major Edlmann, bringing news, that owing to the impossible state of the ground the Divisional front had not been advanced so far as had been expected, so that what was to have been our jumping off line would now be our objective. During the next thirty hours we suffered a good many casualties from long range artillery fire, D Co. losing their C.S.M., C. W. W. King.

The story of the battle for the Passchendaele Ridge, so far as the Artists are concerned, is soon told. Other Divisions before us had been taking their share in the slow process of gaining ground in this water-logged area, at tremendous cost. The 188th was the first Brigade of the 63rd Division to attack; and advancing under a terrific artillery and machine-gun barrage they, too, made some headway, but suffered severely. Early on the 30th our Brigade attacked, also under a very heavy barrage: the British artillery averaged one gun to every 9 yards of front. To reach our objective we had to cross the Paddebeeke, on the map an insignificant streamlet, but in fact by this time a wide and almost impassable swamp.

ORDER OF BATTLE
{
B Co. (*Capt. Bare*). A Co. (*Capt. Mieville*).
C Co. (*Capt. Chetwood*) Support.
D Co. (*Capt. Royds*) Reserve.
}

The instant our attack started, the forward troops came under intense machine-gun fire from an almost invisible enemy who had taken refuge in their "pill boxes" during our bombardment, and were now posted in carefully chosen tactical positions. Simultaneously our supporting troops suffered heavy casualties from enemy artillery, while the ground to be traversed was a deep sea of mud, which drowned wounded men and clogged rifles and Lewis guns in the first few minutes, rendering them entirely useless. Consequently it was not long before the attack was brought to a complete standstill, and the very attenuated Battalions proceeded to consolidate as best they could on our side of the Paddebeeke.* On our

---

*In his book, "From Bapaume to Passchendaele," Sir Phillip Gibbs thus depicts the situation. Ed.

"It is idle for me to try to describe this ground over which the London men and the Artists had to attack. Nothing that I can write will convey remotely the look of such ground and the horror of it. Unless one has seen vast fields of barren earth, blasted for miles by shell-fire, pitted by deep craters so close that they are like holes in a sieve, and so deep that the tallest men can drown in them when they are filled with water, as they are now filled, imagination cannot conceive the picture of this slough of despond. The London men had to wade and haul out one leg after the other from deep sucking bog as though in glue, and sank above their waists. A rescue party led by a Sergeant-Major could not haul out men, breast-high in the bog, until they had surrounded them with duck-boards and fastened ropes to them. Our barrage went ahead, the enemy's barrage came down, and from the German block-houses came a chattering fire of machine guns, and in the great stretch of swamp they struggled.

And not far away from them, but invisible in their own trouble among the pits, the Artists' Rifles, Bedfords, and Shropshires were trying to get forward to other blockhouses on the way to the rising ground beyond the Paddebeeke. The Artists and

right the Canadians continued to advance: being on higher and drier ground they were able to get on, so that presently there was a dangerous gap between their left and our right. This was closed by sending up the Shropshires from our Brigade reserve.

On this day the Artists went into action about 500 strong and suffered 350 casualties, amongst those killed being Captains Bare, Chetwood and Gordon Williams, Lieuts. Haslam and Howe, and our splendid Padre, Capt. Harry Dickinson. The toll of deaths would have been still higher but for the untiring efforts of our M.O., Capt. Matthew, who for 72 hours hardly rested from the work of collecting and dressing the wounded.*

The task set the Division appeared to be an impossible one, and no doubt would not have been attempted but for the urgent necessity of those tremendous attacks in this sector, which drew away all the enemy's reserves from other points where it was of the utmost importance to prevent his attacking in force. It was not a case of lives being fruitlessly thrown away, but of sacrifices which enabled the whole Allied line to remain intact at a time when the Russian débacle was straining to the utmost our resources on the Western Front.

The next day the remains of the Battalion moved out of the line to refit, and while at Eringhem received a special message of sympathy in respect of their losses, and congratulations on the part they had played in the battle, brought direct to them from Earl Haig. They learned also from the Canadians (who were loud in their praises of the way in which our men had pressed forward) that several Artists had succeeded in actually crossing the Paddebeeke before being killed.

DECEMBER, 1917.

After a period of rest and reorganisation (during which Lt.-Col. John Harington, 3/Rifle Brigade, took over the command, Major Edlmann was appointed O.C. 63rd Divisional Wing, and substantial reinforcements arrived, including 6 Officers and a draft from 3/28th), the Battalion was on its way back to the Passchendaele sector, when the successful British offensive before Cambrai was checked and the Boche began to press back the wedge that had been driven into his line there. Thereupon the 63rd

---

their comrades were more severely tried by shell-fire than the Londons. No doubt the enemy had been standing at his guns through the night ready to fire at the first streak of dawn, which might bring an English attack. A light went up and instantly there roared a great sweep of fire from heavy batteries and field guns; 4.2's and 5.9's fell densely and in depth and this bombardment did not slacken for hours. It was a tragic time for our men, struggling in the slime with their feet dragged down. They suffered but did not retreat: no man turned back but either fell under the shell-fire or went on."

And in a subsequent letter he wrote:—

"The London Regiment and the Royal Fusiliers fought this battle, and not far from them were the Artists' Rifles—the dear old 'Artists,' who, in the old volunteer days, looked so dandy in their grey and silver across the lawns of Wimbledon. They suffered yesterday in hellish fire, and made heavy sacrifices to prove their quality. It was a fight against the elements, in league with the German explosives, and it was a frightful combination for the boys of London and the clean-shaven fellows of the Naval Brigade.

* Awarded M.C. See p. 104. Ed.

Division was sent to the Somme district, and at the end of December moved into the front line in the Marcoing salient (Couillet Wood sector).

On the 30th the enemy launched a terrific attack and succeeded in penetrating the front line to the east of the Welsh Ridge salient. The Artists who were in support at this point were detailed for a counter-attack which had to be made without artillery support. It was pressed for all we were worth but resulted in very heavy casualties without the achievement of our object. However, we heard subsequently that our efforts were not in vain as the enemy, deceived as to the strength of our available reserves by the promptitude and determination with which the counter-attack was delivered, refrained from exploiting their initial success. Had they done so, it is conceivable that their object in driving us from the Welsh Ridge might have been attained.

ORDER OF BATTLE
{
   A Co. (Capt. Pike)————*B Co. (Lieut. Shinner).*
   D Co. (Capt. Barnett) Support.
   C Co. (Capt. Lepingwell) Reserve.
}

A very gruelling night followed, consolidation work having to be carried out in ground which was frozen hard. Sufficient praise cannot be given to the Medical Staff under Capt. Mathew, M.C., who were again working all day at high pressure and at night did much to assist in the recovery of the wounded men who were lying out in front of our line. Excellent work was accomplished by D Co. under Capt. Barnett in forming a defensive left flank, by Capt. Mieville in reconnaissance, and by Lt. Holland, these officers gaining on that occasion very hard-earned M.C's.* Lt. Margetson also earned recognition for good work in the maintenance of signal communication† and R.S.M. Emslie did much to keep things going by the organisation of carrying parties to get hot food up during the night. One Corporal did yeoman service to his Company by going back under heavy fire, crossing a gas-filled valley and bringing up the Company water supply which had had to be abandoned in the rush of the morning.

Our casualties were nine Officers and 110 other ranks. Lieuts. Salisbury, English, Shinner and Lightfoot, with our M.G. Officer (Groom) and Intelligence Officer (Godfrey) were killed, while Pike, Lepingwell and Holland were wounded, and from this date the Battalion ceased to be exclusively officered by Artists. But although Officers and men came to us from many other Regiments the spirit and traditions of the Corps were maintained to the end: one of the most striking features in connection with the arrival of reinforcements from other units was the rapidity with which our new comrades assimilated Artists' ideas and methods of getting things done.

JANUARY—MARCH, 1918.

During January and February, 1918, we put in further tours of duty in the front line (during one of which both the Boche and ourselves lived on top behind our respective parados, the trenches having become nothing but ditches of liquid mud several feet deep), while Col. Harrington left us to command the 2/Rifle Brigade (eventually becoming a Brigadier-General), and Major Lathom who had been temporarily in command of the Fusiliers was appointed acting C.O. of the Artists.

---

*Vide pp. 57, 106 and 91.   †Vide p. 103.   Ed.

The Brigade was then withdrawn to Divisional Reserve at Beaulencourt where we were joined by Major F. S. B. Johnson, 1/Royal Lancaster, as our own new C.O. and our strength was brought up to 28 Officers and 766 other ranks by the addition of a complete half Battalion of the 2nd Bn. London Rifle Brigade which had been broken up on the formation of 3-Battalion Brigades.

In March we returned to the Couillet Wood sector, and on the 21st had our first experience of the anxious times experienced by the Allies during the Spring of 1918. Shortly after day-break, while in camp in Havrincourt Wood, we were aroused by a violent bombardment. A dense gas and smoke cloud passed through the Wood as we moved to our battle positions. On the way up Lt. Lintott, L.R.B. (formerly an Artist Sergeant), was killed. The next night we were ordered back to Havrincourt Wood as the enemy had gained a considerable amount of ground on our right (the Fifth Army Front). During the withdrawal, Lt. J. I. Royds was killed in Trescault. We started to dig in, but the next morning were retired to a defence line east of Ytres. There we again made ready to fight a rear-guard action, but we were again disappointed as we were directed to withdraw on a line Ytres—Bus-le-Transloy. That night the whole Brigade withdrew into Ytres, and as communication with both Brigade and Divisional H.Q. was lost, a meeting of all the C.O.'s in the Brigade was called, and it was arranged that the Brigade should form a defensive flank extending East-West, to conform with the withdrawal of the 2nd Division on our left. The Brigade was then taken over by Lt.-Col. Collings Wells of the 4th Bedfords, who for his good work during the withdrawal was awarded the V.C.*

We moved to our new position about midnight, the route taken leading us past the vast ammuniton and petrol dump which was being destroyed. Here a shell splinter from the dump wounded Major Lathom, who was carried back to Beaulencourt. C Co., under Lt. Eric Willis, was also unfortunate in running into a Boche M.G. post and suffering severe casualties. Good work was done by Sergt. A. Coviello, who succeeded in penetrating the enemy lines in rear of us and establishing communication.†
Next morning the retirement continued through Barastre with heavy casualties (amongst whom was Lt. Dow, our American M.O.) to Beaulencourt, where we found Brigade H.Q. Then back through Gueudecourt, Flers, Bazentin-le-Grand, Bazentin-le-Petit to Courcelette, and the next day's trek took us through Pozieres to Thiepval. On the slopes in that neighbourhood we had an opportunity of checking the Boche, great work being done by a Lewis Gun team, for whom the Brigade Major was spotting. During the night orders came to cross at Authuille to the west bank of the river before daybreak, when the R.E.'s were to destroy the bridges. On reaching the other side we found the 12th Division waiting to take over from us. To celebrate the conclusion of our long innings, Bn. H.Q. indulged in a game of stump cricket which was rather spoilt by the arrival of a Hun H.V. shell. It ruined the pitch and scattered the field, but fortunately no one retired hurt. We then marched through Martinsart to Englebelmer, and the same evening moved to Millencourt for an attack on another Divisional front on the outskirts of Albert. This attempt to

---

And Col. Johnson (Artists) the D.S.O. Vide p. xlii.   †Awarded D.C.M.   Ed.

dislodge the Boche proved fruitless and resulted in somewhat serious casualties, chief among which was the loss of Lt. Eric Willis.

The Battalion was then withdrawn (via Senlis and Mailly Maillet) to Forceville for a complete rest over Easter. Our total casualties during the retirement amounted to 17 officers and 300 other ranks.

April—August, 1918.

During April and May we performed tours of duty in the new line established after the retreat north of Mesnil and in Aveluy Wood sector. We lost Capt. Neighbour (who had rejoined us in March) through sickness and Col. Johnson was wounded in Aveluy Wood. Thereupon Capt. Wilkinson (L.R.B.) assumed command. In June the Battalion went into Corps reserve at Toutencourt Wood and was attached to the "flying" Corps, kept for operations on any front, and throughout July we were engaged in line holding alternately between Acheux Wood south of Auchonvillers and the line north of Mesnil.

In August, on the eve of the Australian offensive before Amiens, we went to Beaucourt-sur-l'Hallue. After their attack had been successfully launched the Division marched north again via Famechon to Souastre, whence we moved out via Fonquevillers to take our part in the commencement of that vast movement which resulted in the eventual overthrow of the enemy. The Division attacked on the 21st in heavy mist supported by a very intense artillery barrage and at the end of the day the Artists found themselves in the front line, having passed unconsciously through the Battalion we were supporting who had lost direction to a certain extent and moved too far to the right.

The next morning the C.O. and Adjt. (Capt. Barnett) were wounded and we sustained our most deeply regretted casualty in the death of R.S.M. Peter Emslie, who was ever a magnificent stand-by in the line, where his courageous efficiency rendered him at all times invaluable. The Battalion was brought out by Lieuts. Bayne and Besch.

On the 24th at Achiet-le-Petit we went over in close support of the 188th Brigade in a heavy ground mist intermingled with gas and smoke. Objectives were carried and the attack turned south-east towards Warlencourt and Ligny-Thilloy where stout opposition was encountered and the attack delivered on the following morning in conjunction with the Canadians failed. The Division was then withdrawn via Irles, Miraumont, Achiet-le-Petit, Bucquoy, Ayette to Boiry St. Rictrude.

The next day we moved into trenches at Boiry-Becquerelle, and on the 26th we followed up the attack as Division in reserve, the attacking waves passing through Fontaine and Hendecourt to Caignicourt, and so on to the Hindenburg line between Inchy and Moeuvres.

September, 1918.

Early in September the Division was withdrawn by stages to Bailleulval on the Arras-Doullens road, where we remained for a period of rest and "fattening." On leaving we received an address from the Mayor thanking us on behalf of the population for our considerate treatment of them and their belongings.

We then marched back again to the Croisilles area, the Artists finding a home in tents and shelters on the high ground south-east of St. Leger near L'Homme Mort Wood. Here we were joined by our new C.O., Lt. Col. Goldthorp (4/West Riding), who shall now continue the narrative.

I think that my story, such as it is, had better take the form of a sort of letter. It was late on the night of 18/19th September, 1918, when I reached the 63rd R.N.D. Wing, then at Boisleux-au-Mont, where I was welcomed by Major Edlmann, the O.C. Wing, and Capt. Baillie-Hamilton, the Adjutant, who informed me that I was either for the Artists or the Bedfords, who were both without C.O.'s.

The following morning I was taken forward to Divisional H.Q. in dug-outs between St. Leger and Ecoust, and I was officially told that I was to take over the command of the Artists. After reporting to the Brigadier, General Lesslie, who proceeded to tell me all he knew about the Artists as a Regiment and about the officers individually, I set out on my lonely journey across a little valley to their H.Q. to "take over." I can imagine their Officers watching me come along, and wondering what sort of a "blighter" they were getting this time. Well, my feelings were much the same, but I had learned from the Brigadier some of their good points, and they did not know even my bad ones then, so I started "one up" on them anyhow.

I took over from Acting-Captain Hermelin, who was then in command; Besch was the Intelligence Officer; Morris, Signalling Officer; Nelson, the "Doc."; Hewitt, Acting Adjutant; Light, Quarter-Master; Prentice, Transport Officer; Robinson, Padre; and Wyler our Interpreter.

Very early a batch of officer-reinforcements arrived, and it became obvious we were in for a show the nature of which we could only guess, but for my part I should like to say that from the very first I had every help from Officers, N.C.O.'s and men, and my work was made easy by the spirit they all showed of welcoming me as one of themselves from the start. I shall never forget those first few days and the solid foundation of trust and comradeship they laid for what was before us.

On the 26th September we left our Camp for the old trenches just outside Queant, where we were to assemble prior to a march on to our "tape" between Moeuvre and Inchy, and we knew when we left (having received all the barrage tables, etc.) that we were in for one of the biggest battles fought by the British Armies during the whole of the War, as the Division had to cross the Canal du Nord and take the Hindenburg Line in conjunction with the Canadians on our left, and the Guards on our right. This was only to be the first phase, and as far as the Naval Division was concerned, the 190th Brigade was the first to kick off. Afterwards, the other Brigades were to go through us and capture Anneux and get on as far as they could.

I was rather pleased to find that it fell to the Artists to do the lion's share of the work of our Brigade, i.e., we had to capture the Hindenburg Line after the Fusiliers and the Bedfords had crossed the Canal, a very delicate and involved movement which required a great deal of preparation and explanation.

We arrived at our Assembly Point without trouble and at midnight started off—a pitch black night, in a deluge of rain. We made very slow progress; it was a difficult job keeping in touch and following the line, which was marked out by whitewashed posts, most of which had either been knocked down by the Artillery, or obliterated by the rain. Without Hewitt and Goacher we should have found it very difficult indeed, and might easily have had the same misfortune as was experienced by another Battalion who missed the track somewhere outside Pronville and got too much to the left. But these two officers did splendidly and we eventually arrived at a trench which marked our then front line. I halted the Battalion and they laid down and soon went to sleep. We waited about, hoping against hope that the other troops would arrive, but finally gave up all expectation of seeing them and got the Battalion out into shell holes slightly in advance of our previous position.

Seeing that the situation was exceedingly vague, I decided to put every available man on the line, and issued orders to the Company Commanders telling them that unless the missing Battalion turned up, we should have to tackle their job as well as our own on our immediate front, and that in the advance up the Hindenburg Line we would take half their objective, and the Canadians would look after the other half.

About 4.30 a.m. everything was ready as far as we could foresee, and there was nothing further to be done then but wait, and what a long time the last half hour before zero seems! However the time arrived at last and so did the Boche attempt at retaliation. It seemed to come down on our trench for some reason or other, and soon the doctors were very busy, and after what seemed an age Morris arrived back to say that all was going well, that the Battalion was in the Canal taking a lot of prisoners, that our barrage was as near perfection as anything he had ever dreamed of, and that the Boche barrage was falling well behind our men—all of which was good news. With my H.Q. and runners I started off at once.

What a change from the night before! It was a lovely morning, and once out in the open, going towards the Canal, it was a wonderful sight to see our barrage and the men following it up. I cannot describe the feeling I had watching the Artists in action—to me the first time. From behind it looked as near drill-perfect as you could wish for. We were not long in getting across the Canal, where we saw one of our tanks stuck, and met many wounded coming back, amongst them being Fergus Young, who was supported by a Boche prisoner about twice his size. He was very worried about his Company, though as it turned out he had no need to be—they were carrying on all right, away on in front. As we got nearer the front line things seemed to get very busy. There were crowds of prisoners coming down—batches of 200 at a time in charge of one or two men—all their officers wanting to go down into dug-outs to collect their belongings, but I do not suppose they found many, because the ground was literally on fire, and after walking a short distance between the Hindenburg Line one's feet were quite hot from the heat of the earth. Soon messages began to come back—that the first objective had been taken—then the barrage moved on again, so did our men, and our messages came fast—"Cannot get on for machine gun fire;" "No sign of the Bedfords on the right flank," and with like messages from the left.

It then appeared that things were sticking a bit, so we pushed on up to see what really was happening, and found things pretty well mixed up—our men short of bombs, having used everything they had and everyone doing his level best. We discovered that both our flanks were well in the air, and getting forward was out of the question until matters righted themselves on the flanks. By this time we had lost the barrage for our second objective, and it had become a question of holding on to what we had until the position cleared up. Being shot at from three sides is never a very pleasant experience but the men stuck it out wonderfully. I saw that we should need every single available man to hold on, so I went down the line a bit to collect any oddments I could find. It is surprising the number one comes across in a big show like this. There were Bedfords and Fusiliers who were beginning to come along in large batches. They were all gathered into parties and sent up straight away. The Fusiliers had had a pretty rough time trekking about all night, and had just arrived in time to go over with the Canadians, where they were soon doing their share "good and hard" as the Brigadier, who had spent his time cheering up the men, would say. I found the Signallers fixing up communications to the Companies and we got news of the poor Bedfords too who had had a very rough crossing, but had come through all right. We knew then that our right flank was in touch though it was thrown back very considerably, and we seemed to catch the whole attention of the Boche.

Presently orders came through that the attack preceded by heavy barrage on one or two selected places—a sugar factory on the Bapaume-Cambrai Road being one—would be resumed at 2.15.

Everything up the line was as good as we could hope for, and the 188th Brigade was getting ready to carry on. They were to go through us, and on to Anneux and as much further as they could get. We then returned to Brigade H.Q. where we found Prentice and his transport—all safe and sound, and rather surprised to be so near the battle. Thoughts of hot food for the men seemed to be within the range of possibility provided the resumed attack went off all right. I saw the Brigadier again, told him that we were all ready for our original third objective, but he said we need not move at all, as the 188th were going through us, where we were, to their objective. The rest had been cut out and was being dealt with by the Artillery alone, so I went back post-haste, but was not in time to stop many men getting on, especially those at the front, who had numerous scores to pay off by this time.

The 2.15 show was a complete success, so much so, that the 188th were able to move right up to Anneux without any trouble: then they bumped into plenty, I believe, but that is outside the story of the Artists. Shortly afterwards the Divisional General came round our line, thanking the men for the splendid victory, and still more for the magnificent resistance they had made when checked. I had been told beforehand that if we got the crest of the hill—which was our first objective—and stuck to it, we should have won the day whatever happened. As it was we got beyond and held on, against Machine-Gun fire, Trench Mortars, and Bombing, for hours, until the whole situation cleared all along the line; a hard enough test for any troops and an achievement in itself that would have made any Battalion's reputation.

Late in the evening we got orders to spend the night on our battle positions. Besch and I took a look round the places where we had been held up earlier in the day and in every case there was no lack of evidence of the supreme courage of our men. Before settling down we buried all our dead: there seemed to us to be a lot, but in comparison to the total casualties of the day, and in relation to the value of the work accomplished, there were really few. So ended one of the greatest days in this War and my first experience of the Artists in action. I, for one, shall never forget the 27th September, 1918, and I can only pray to be forgiven if I in any way failed them during that day, or subsequently: they never failed me once.*

There were one or two incidents in the battle which are, perhaps, worth noting. One was the wonderful view we got from our first objective—how we could see right across the Bapaume-Cambrai Road the Germans directing their fire, both field and machine-guns, and watching the battle. From one of the forward posts we actually saw the officer-in-charge and one of the guns knocked out, and we could see the Guards trying to get forward and being held up, as we were.

As a matter of interest in training, I found in a large square hole (which had probably been intended for a concrete shelter) Capt. Hall with several men, including a Lewis Gun team. It was a very warm corner, and there he was directing the fire of his men and the Lewis Gun team as if he was carrying out a Range Practice in the most approved Hythe manner. It is a point which is so apt to be forgotten in training, that if your instruction has been good, you will unconsciously do the right thing in a tight corner. The mere fact of real good fire-orders at such a time had a most wonderfully steadying effect.

What struck me largely about the Boche prisoners was that they did not seem to be a bit sorry to be captured, that they worked well and hard in helping the wounded, and that a large number of them spoke English very well. Our attack along the Hindenburg Line in a southerly direction must have been an entire surprise to the enemy, as we found their machine-guns were mounted facing west, and that when our attack down the line developed from the north they had had to dismantle all their guns.

I think that a large portion of our success should be attributed to the Artillery; the barrage was marvellous, especially the swing to enable us to change our direction. This took 79 minutes, and it was not particularly pleasant for us to wait the time, but it obviously fooled the Boche.

Another thing which came to our help that day (which has rarely happened in connection with the English) was that the wind and the weather were perfect for us, and as for our smoke barrages, the smoke went just where it should have gone. But by far and away the greatest satisfaction to me was to know that whatever happened afterwards, I could depend absolutely upon the Battalion in every conceivable circumstance. To take a new Battalion into an action of that size, without ever having been in the line at all with them before, is a very anxious job.

ORDER OF BATTLE
{ C Co. (Capt. Young)——A Co. (Capt. Goacher).
D Co. (Lieut. Elliott)——B Co. (Lieut. Ashford).
Hd.-Qrs. Co. (Lieut. Morris).

The Artists were detailed to follow the front-line troops and then swing with the Artillery on to the Hindenburg Line.

Next morning (28th) we were on the move again and reached the sugar factory on the Bapaume-Cambrai Road. There we waited until the afternoon—had a sleep and were off again via Graincourt to Cantaing. This

---

*Col. Goldthorp omits to mention that he was awarded the D.S.O. for this day's work. (Vide p. 47). Ed.

xxxiii.

was well behind the Boche lines, and we were going towards the Canal de l'Escaut, which was obviously the next obstacle that was before us. We halted rather to the north-west of the village and dug in. We were not troubled very much during the night. We could quite easily see the towers of the town of Cambrai, and watched some large fires which the Germans had started there.

Early in the morning (29th) I went round the lines—if you could call them such. It was most encouraging to find the men so cheerful after what they had been through, a testament of their excellent training, and of the wonderful esprit de corps which I always found with the Artists, and it was no joke camping out in a beastly little hole all night long. It was very cold indeed and there were no nice Army blankets to help matters. Still, they were Artists—and they were winning—so what did it matter?

We were not wanted that morning and made the most of it, whilst the other Brigades had the pleasure of forcing a crossing over the Canal. It was Naval Division against Naval Division that day, so our fellows were all out for it, somewhat enlivened by the success on the 27th. From where we were it did not sound a big show when it started, but one could see we were not getting things without paying the price. Many good fellows were coming back, some badly wounded to a Dressing Station near our Headquarters and lots of prisoners.

Later in the day we moved up to the east of Cantaing and had just got nicely settled down hoping to get a decent night's rest when we got orders to cross the Canal de l'Escaut and form up on a road running south from Cambrai near a farm called La Marliere. So off we went cursing the old Boche and the War in general through some gun positions round to a place where a pontoon bridge had been thrown across the Canal. It was a very noisy journey as far as the Canal, and then the fun began. As usual it started to rain—real rain—and it was as black as ink as we plodded along. After a good deal of trekking about we found our road well to the right of the place where we should have hit it—so far so good. We had to put up with a ditch where there were far more machine-gun bullets flying about than was exactly pleasant and had just settled down to sleep when I was sent for by Brigade, and learned there was a 'show' hatching. We were to attack at 5.30 in the morning, and were given three objectives. Our attack was roughly due east, and the final objective was a place called Niergnies. The difficulty in the show was the barrage arrangements. No guns up to then had been brought across the Canal, and Niergnies was 5,000 yards away from the nearest gun, also they were in low country, and angles for shooting all wrong. Anyway we were to go on and push the Boche back, and the second Corps on our right was to co-operate with us.

About 1.30 a.m. (Sept. 30th) all was settled so far as we could arrange it, and the horrible time of waiting started, we trying to sleep. Zero arrived, our men started off and I sent Hewitt and a few runners on to select a new H.Q. just to the rear of our first objective. Presently one of them came back with the information that the party had arrived all right, having gone through very heavy machine gun fire. He also stated that there was no sign of the Battalion, that it was a very bad place and that one of Hewitt's men had been hit. We did not like this news, so we went to find out what had happened. It soon became only too evident that the attack was held up, and we had not even been able to reach our first objective. I made my way up to the Battalion who were digging-in under very heavy machine gun fire, about 300 yards east of the road and found they could not get any further forward; they were in some sort of line in the open and in a trench, but in a poor position, under machine-gun fire all the time and it was a case of sitting tight again. Meanwhile, our right flank was thrown back a bit, and the Second Corps Troops who ought to have gone over with us came up but were quite unable to push forward.

An anxious morning passed somehow, and then we got orders to resume the attack—in other words, to try again. We tried but only to fail. This meant a lot of reorganising for the Company Commanders, and a tremendous extra strain on the men, but they stuck it and we had to stay where we were.

A long night came to an end and presently to my relief Hewitt turned up. Afterwards we got his story out of him. The poor fellow who had been hit had died, and they had to bury him as best they could. If they showed their heads above the top they were at once shot at. Hewitt had sent no further messages back as it was too risky, and he decided to wait until dark and then get back as best he could. He did so, and luck was with him—they found their way eventually to our present place. They had had a dreadful time, and a really terrible experience, but like all good soldiers, they hated to talk about it, so we left it at that.

OCTOBER, 1918.

In the evening (Oct. 1st) the Division was relieved and we went back again to the west of Cantaing into trenches with improvised shelters. The next day or two we spent in reorganising, quite a difficult job as we were very weak, and cleaning up.

We now felt fairly certain that we were going out for a rest, as we had had a pretty stiff time since the 26th and had lost a lot of very fine fellows, mostly wounded, thank goodness. We needed a rest, and felt somehow that we had earned it, but on October 6th a message came before breakfast that we were to have another go for Niergnies, this time jumping off from Rumilly. It was to be an "in-and-out show," just a day's hard fighting and then out again, and if we were successful it would ensure the fall of Cambrai.

Our reconnaissances and plans having been made we moved (7th) to Noyelles, and so to a field where we tried to sleep a bit, to the accompaniment of a neighbouring 6-inch naval gun, and crossed the canal after dark and slowly made our way to our assembling place.

Soon the show started and we found that a sunken road, where our H.Q. dug-out was, came in for considerable attention from the Boche. Quite a lot of people were wounded just outside, my signalling officer (Bayne) amongst them.† Then the two Intelligence Officers—my own (Besch) and the Bedfords—went to find us a new H.Q. The latter was hit before he got across the road, Besch escaped and got on all right. Soon all the rest of us followed. The shelling did not seem to be so bad when we got out—it never does—dug-outs are beastly, and things sound much worse in them than they are. It was nice to be out and following up the Battalion, of which we could see nothing at first, but we soon got up to them, found they had managed to keep together, and were in good order

---

†On this occasion Lieut. Nelson (M.O.) was awarded M.C. Vide p. 143. Ed.

and busy digging in. Things seemed to be going very well. "A" Co. were very pleased with themselves, as they got 105 prisoners and 12 machine guns in one trench on the way. Soon there was unusual activity up at the front, and one of our tanks came back chased by a 5.9 all the way. It was a wonderful sight, and rather funny, but poor sport for the men in the tank. It was extraordinary how near the shells fell round it and yet never once hit it, and I heard afterwards that it got home.

We were conscious of a lot of extra firing, and a number of little shells which seemed to come very low. All at once I saw the line to our south begin to move back—this gave one a very uncomfortable feeling, to say the least of it. We heard that the Germans were counter-attacking with tanks—so I went forward, and found that the Commanding Officer of the Battalion in front of us had gone to retrieve the position, and could quite easily see the German Tanks—which really were our own captured in November, 1917 (or even later during the retreat in 1918) and were equipped with German and Belgian Guns. The nearest one to us was burning away, as it had been hit and set on fire. Another one we were firing at from a Boche anti-tank gun. In passing, it is interesting to note that out of five (possibly seven) tanks that attacked us, two were knocked out by German weapons we captured that day: one by a Boche anti-tank gun and the other by one of their anti-tank rifles. The other tanks, seeing the fate of two of their companions and that the Boche infantry did not support them, decided it was wiser to go back where they came from. It was really quite an exciting hour until the situation became normal again.

Nothing more happened for a bit. The situation seemed vague on the left flank and in the village of Niergnies, so I sent up an officer (McKinley) to make a reconnaissance for the Brigade, which he did, and telephoned the result back, and later went up again just to make certain that everything was still. The information he got was of the greatest assistance to the Brigade, and the reconnaissance was very well done indeed.*

Shortly before dusk we were warned that a counter-attack was expected on our left flank, and I was told that should it assume a serious nature, the Artists would be required to carry out the counter-counter-attack and restore the position. However, it was no good looking for trouble before it came, so we just kept a special look-out on this flank, and moved a few more Lewis Guns there in case anything occurred. Nothing happened, and later in the evening I heard we were to be relieved by a Battalion who we could see coming up. It seemed an interminable time before we got the word to go home. We were all ready for it, watching the valley behind us, which was receiving continous attention from the Boche who was using gas and H.E., mixed with instantaneous fuses, very freely, and when we finally got the order to go the gassing was really quite bad. Between where we were and Rumilly, it was a sort of nightmare going back. We had to use our gas-masks and fortunately all got through safely to our billets outside Cantaing. The attack had been a great success and a surprise for the Boche—Cambrai fell the next day, as a direct result of our work. To show how we had suffered, and to what small units we had descended, it is interesting to note that the Battalion which relieved us, relieved the whole of the Division. It was a strong Battalion of over 800, but all the same it is not often that a Battalion can relieve a Division.

---

*Awarded M.C. Vide p. 101. Ed.

This time we were fairly certain to be taken out of the line, for the obvious reason that we were no longer a real fighting force. We had been at it since the 26th September, and had suffered very heavily. The Division soon got orders to go North out of the 3rd Army into the 1st, in places round St. Pol where we were to refit, get our drafts, train hard, and get back as soon as possible, as it was now Division against Division, and no one could be spared out of the line for long.

We were soon on our way by stages via Vaulx-Vraucourt to Brias where we settled down to the work of reorganising. We were a small Battalion now, but a very cheerful one. We started giving each other dinners, and on the night the Brigadier dined with us Croft reported to the Battalion.

One dinner which I shall not forget was the fourth anniversary (Oct. 28th) of the Artists coming out to France, when all those who were left, amounting I think to 26, met at a little estaminet in Avesnes-le-Comte. I took it as a great compliment to be the only guest asked.

These good times soon come to an end. After various alarms and excursions, we finally marched off and embussed, our destination being a place called Le Forest, just outside Douai. It was rather a wonderful ride, and a lovely day. We went via Lens, which was a pitiable sight. I do not think I have ever seen any place of its size so completely and deliberately destroyed. There were a lot of refugees coming back, both east and west, carrying their worldly belongings with them. There was no possibility of anyone finding anything habitable when they got to Lens. One family struck me as a particularly bad case, even amongst so many. They had come goodness knows how far, and consisted of an old man, his wife, their daughter, and son-in-law, and their child in a tumbled down old perambulator, piled up with all kinds of other things. They had just arrived, and were standing on a heap of bricks, which they realized was the site of their old home. I shall never forget the look of utter desolation on their faces—they were beyond crying. There must have been many, many cases like this, and they would all either have to settle there, or face the journey back from where they had come, a case of 7 or 8 miles at the least, on roads that only bore the name out of courtesy. I saw some of our men crying when they saw these people. There is something about a Frenchman's love of his home that appeals to us. With dog-like faith they tramp for miles to start all over again in a place rendered more than desolate, which seems to me the highest form of patriotism imaginable.

At Henin-Lietard we had to get out, as the bridges across the Canal were blown up, and trekked to Le Forest. The Artists got an old Boche hospital and after the usual spring clean was not too bad a home. Headquarter Mess was in a nice little house in the main Street—at least the bottom part of it was nice, the staircase having been burnt out, and the upstairs rooms were rather a muddle. Here we gave a concert and some conjuring exhibitions to the inhabitants, who hardly seemed to realise that they were actually free and allowed to do more or less as they liked. Some rumours of moves began to come along, and we realised that it would not be very long before we were off again—this time to some purpose.

NOVEMBER, 1918: THE LAST PHASE OF THE WAR.

On November 5th our rest at Le Forest came to an end and we

journeyed back via Auby and Douai to Thiant. The next morning we marched on to Saultain, movement being slow owing to the congestion on the roads and their state, and we got completely blocked up in a village (Aulnoy) which showed signs of recent fighting, a good many dead lying about outside.

On the 7th we were off again to Sebourquiaux. By this time the Brigade that we were following were in action, and we were moving up in readiness to go through it when ordered, and that evening reached Angré.

Early the next day (8th) we reached Audregnies, where we went through the other Brigade, and had three objectives assigned, but it was obviously impossible that we should accomplish them in the time that was left to us in the day. Near Wiheries there was a fair amount of indiscriminate shelling on forward slopes and we lost some men. However, we moved on in artillery formation, keeping pretty well closed up and halted in the outskirts of Blaugies where we managed to get on the line of our first objective without further trouble and had to pass the night there as we could not overcome the Boche machine-gun fire.

November 9th was a day which I do not think any Artists who were then with us are ever likely to forget. We advanced in all 15,000 yards, as the crow flies, which of course meant considerably more trekking, and a good bit had to be done through woods and across country. We started off something like a triumphal procession, as we were the first English troops to enter Blaugies, and we were met by the inhabitants, who rushed out and kissed us, old and young alike, and offered us coffee, liqueurs, and anything they could lay their hands on. It was really pathetically sad, and yet very funny, and it was with difficulty one refrained from crying, by the necessity of laughing.

Passing through Blaugies, we ran into our own barrage, which eventually I got stopped, as it was falling amongst the cavalry and was holding up our advance. From that moment we were not bothered with any more barrages, the artillery being attached to us, which is really far the most sensible way in going through open country, as we were. It gives one the means of visible retaliation, which is always lacking when dependent entirely on artillery behind you, whose doings, except barrage work you know nothing about. We next had to go through the Wood of Sars-la-Bruyere and on to the village of the same name, where again we were welcomed by the inhabitants in like manner. I was presented with a large bouquet of flowers, tied up with Belgian ribbon and had to walk through the village carrying the beastly thing. The centre of this village had been our last objective, and we had no sooner got through than we had orders to move on again to a railway embankment on the other side of the wood to the east of Sars-la-Bruyere. Further orders came extending this objective right up to the Mons-Maubeuge Road in front of Quevy-le-Petit, so we packed up once more and started off. Then taking two runners with me, I started off straight through the wood, arrived in the village before the Battalion and took up my H.Q. in the Burgomaster's house, which had only been left a few hours earlier by a General of the German Army, who had stopped to watch our advance and then gone off in a motor car. At last the Battalion was in possession of their objective and settled down for a few hours rest.

The next morning (10th) I got orders to 'side-slip' to the north, take up a position on the Mons-Maubeuge Road to the west of the village of Harvengt and support the Fusiliers and Bedfords. This was the first time that the Artists had been in support to either of the other Battalions since coming north from the Cambrai Sector, but it only lasted half a day. I met my Company Commanders at a Chateau on the Mons-Maubeuge Road, just below a bridge, which the Germans had blown up. We had a short conference in a delightful room placed at our disposal by the owner of the Chateau, then marched on up the road and we were in our place almost as soon as the cavalry had gone out.

I noticed going up the road that there was a Boche Observation Balloon up—the last one we saw during the War—and the only one which had been visible since our start on the 5th. Unfortunately, it saw the other Brigade, which was coming up to go through us, and this drew a considerable amount of fire round our H.Q. in the village of Asquillies.

Just after they had gone, I got the news by runner, that poor old Croft had been killed. It is no use trying to tell you what that meant to the Battalion, or to me personally. He had not been back with us very long after a prolonged absence, and I know he felt like coming home when he rejoined us at Brias. He was always like a ray of sunshine if there was anything doing. With him were two other good fellows, 2/Lt. King and Sergt. Garbutt; also a Lancer with whom they were talking at the time; a stray shell fell in the sunken road and killed all four of them.

We were anxiously expecting rations and orders to return to Asquillies for the rest we were all wanting, but were sent forward to Harvengt where there seemed to be a good deal of confusion, so I halted the Battalion and had a look round. I found from the 56th Division who were there that they had been held up just outside the village by heavy machine gun fire and that it would be quite impossible to go forward that night. Eventually it was arranged that the Artists should relieve the 1st London and we moved forward again as far as we could get.

November 11th. At daybreak I started off up the line, having received information that the Battalion had commenced to move and that the Boche had 'hooked it.' Reaching Harmignies, I found that our men had been in within less than half an hour after the departure of the Germans, and our patrols reported that at two of the villages in front there were no signs of the enemy. We had orders to take up our position and remain at Harmignies, and that the 188th Brigade would go through us early in the morning. I went round, saw everybody and waited until the other Brigade had started to move forward and then set off to return. On my way back I met a whole lot of the Lancers, all formed up ready to go through. It was a fine sight seeing them all on their horses anxious to be off. On getting back I was met by a Doctor who said that he owed me some money (he had made a bet with me; that there would be no armistice or peace this year). For a moment I could not quite make out what he meant, until I noticed that everybody seemed pleased and then I learned the news of the Armistice which had come through a few minutes previously. I saw the Brigadier, got confirmation of the Armistice news, sent it up to the Companies, scrounged round making arrangements for baths for the men, got them all back again, and they had their baths and went to bed.

xxxix.

In the afternoon the Band arrived, after a somewhat chequered journey from England, very sorry for themselves. Also British prisoners, who had been left behind by the enemy, began to trickle through; they were in a most pitiable state. And so came the Armistice to the Artists—in the line to the very last. It will always be a satisfaction to us when we come to look back upon things that we were there when the end came and that the efforts of our Division contributed in no small degree to the final collapse of the Boche.

After the Armistice.

Of course we could hardly realise things at first and there was still an awful lot to do. The silence seemed almost uncanny at times.

I do not know if I can describe the funeral of Ben Croft, King and Garbutt, but of course it was the first thing we did. As they were killed just outside the village, we decided to bury them at the side of the road where they fell, with such Military Honours as we could, their own Company finding the firing party, and the buglers sounded the Last Post. It was a sad little party that gathered round the graves of the last Artists to fall in action. A large number of Officers and men came and the Brigadier found time to be present. I think these three were the last casualties of the War in our Brigade. It seemed so very hard, that it was only a matter of 24 hours, and all would have been well. The inhabitants of the village had given us some oak to make a cross from and someone else thought of flowers—and after doing all we could we returned to our billets.

We soon heard stories of going on to the Rhine and were selected for this, but owing to the heavy fighting, and our additional wastage through sickness, our strength was so far short that finally it was decided we should not go. So we had to accept the hard fact and see another Division put in our place. At the time we were generally disappointed, but on looking back now I think it was just as well, and possibly most Artists will agree.

On the 15th, a cold, clear November day, we took part in the official entry of the First Army into Mons, lined the street, and after hours of waiting marched past the Army Commander in the square. We did not exactly enjoy it, but now that distance is lending its enchantment we can regard it as a thing to have done.

Soon we got permission to move back to Harmignies to better billets, thence to Athis, where we started Education Classes and a Debating Society. We also had to practice for a Review by the First Army Commander, had two full-dress rehearsals, and then the show was put off, but I suppose a little ceremonial drill did not do any of us much harm; anyway it provided a certain amount of amusement. Next we were moved back to Blaugies where we were not long in getting ready for our Christmas plans. We decided to have Company dinners, three in one day was the maximum reached, and we came safely through the lot. It was really a great Christmas taking it all round. There was not one of us who did not want to be home for it, but as we could not, we put our backs into it, and made the most of it under the circumstances, and now it is all over I do not think one of us regrets having spent it in Blaugies.

All this time we were slowly getting smaller, and one day we were sent to our final destination, St. Ghislain. It was an eye-opener for the men when they arrived there—almost like going home, without the home—real beds and sheets for every man, it must have been the first bed that most of them had seen for many, many months.

I soon found that the men preferred their own time to organised amusements, which so long as all went well was really much better for them, and I am more than glad to know that it did go well. It was a very good change for them to get into some sort of civilisation, and demobilisation started quicker when we got to St. Ghislain.

One day I got special leave, as I had been applied for at this end. I do not know exactly how to describe what I felt: I knew that this special leave was tantamount to saying "Farewell" to the Artists. However, it was unavoidable and would have had to come sooner or later, and perhaps it was as well that it was hurried a bit at the end. I got all packed up, and then went on to the Mess, where I found some villain had collected most of the Battalion to see me off. I think it takes nearly as much courage to go round and say "Good-bye" to people as it does to go over the top.

Soon after this I went down for the first time to the Artists Headquarters in Duke's Road, where I met a lot of people whom I had often heard of, but never before seen. They one and all made me so welcome, that I almost felt I was going to my own home. I shall never forget Colonel May coming up to me, and saying that he would like to thank me for all I had done for the Artists, but that he did not quite know how to do so, so he thought perhaps he had better repeat to me what one of the men had said to him. When asked something about their new Commanding Officer, this man had replied, "Well, Sir, he might have been an Artist himself."

I think that if I have earned those words, honestly spoken, it is as much as anyone could have wished.

R. H. G.

P.S.—I have said very little about the organisation and interior working of the Battalion because I do not consider it would be a compliment to go into such details. I think the secret of the Artists' success was very largely the wonderful amount of material always at hand. When Adjutants, Scouts, Signallers, Runners, Pioneers, and all these people were ever ready, and there was always somebody fit to step into someone else's shoes if anything happened, it really was very easy work for a stranger, once he realised this. Then there was old Freddy Light, with his 40 years service in the Corps, and R.Q.M.S. Hack, a veteran of the Boer War times. They always worked quietly without any fuss or bother, always had what was wanted, and would have done anything in the world which was humanly possible, that the men should be comfortable, and that the Battalion should always have the best of everything. There were few Territorial Regiments who had the services of one of their own Quarter-Masters, and the Artists have been extremely lucky in theirs.

Then you will find in my notes that the names of the Officers are nearly always the same. I have avoided using names at all except where I thought it would simplify matters, but I do not wish to convey the impression that these are the only names worthy of note, as it is not so. I should not know where to begin, or end, if I had to tell you what I thought about individuals. I see that R.S.M. Fox is not mentioned—there again we were singularly fortunate, and had to do a great deal of "wangling" to keep him. As you know, any man who occupied that position after Peter Emslie had gone, had a very tough proposition before him.

ADDENDA TO SECTIONS I. TO VI.

Particulars received whilst this Edition was in the Press—

Add to ROLL OF HONOUR (pp. 2 to 42).

1917	Dec.	22.	ABEL, 2/Lt. James Edgar,* 6/R. West Kent	*Died as Prisoner of war*
1918	Nov.	4.	ATKINSON, Edward Arthur, 14/London (late 2/Lt. 1/London)	[*Dublin*
1920	Nov.	22.	BAGGALLAY, Capt. Geoffrey Thomas, 1/Welch (A.P.M.)	*Assassinated in*
1920	Nov.	28.	BAYLEY, Lieut. Cyril Dunstan Wakefield, R.F.C.	*Kilmichael, Ireland*
1917	Dec.	3.	BEVAN, 2/Lt. Wilfred, 20th Squadron, R.F.C.	*Belgium*
1920	Aug.	13.	BUCHANAN, Capt. Edward Laurie, R.F.A. & R.A.F.	*Baghdad*
1920	Oct.	9.	CORFIELD, Lieut. Frederick John Arthur, Bucks Bn. O.B.L.I.	
1919	Nov.	2.	FLEET, Pte. Charles Arthur, 2/Artists	*Died*
1919	Sept.	20.	GERHARDI, 2/Lt. Charles, R.A.F.	
1920	Dec.	3.	GOLDING, Lieut. Harold Gordon Lancelot, 35/Sikhs	*Palestine*
1919	Feb.	9.	GRASSICK, 2/Lt. William Henderson, R.F.A.	*Died, Wimereux*
1919	Sept.	22.	HIGGINSON, Capt. John Victor, 2/R. Welch Fusiliers	*Gas poisoning*
1918	Oct.	23.	HILDITCH, 2/Lt. Charles Henry, 27th Bde. R.F.A.	
1917	July	31.	HOPKINS, 2/Lt. George Henry Stanton, 45/Machine Gun Corps	
1917	Dec.	20.	HUMPHREYS, Pte. Albert Brent, 1/Artists	*Died*
1917	Nov.	5.	LORIMER, Capt. John Scott, 1/Norfolk	
1917	June	18.	LOWRIE, 2/Lt. John Edward, Household Battalion	
1918	Mar.	21.	RICHARDSON, 2/Lt. Arthur Balfour, 8/Royal West Kent	
1917	June	22.	RUDGE, Lieut. Arthur Edgar, R.A.F.	*Combat near La Bassée*
1918	April	21.	SHERLOCK, 2/Lt. Gerald,* 55/Machine Gun Corps	
1915	Aug.	9.	SHUFFREY, Lieut. Gilbert, 6/South Lancashire	*Gallipoli*
1920	May	7.	SPILLER, L/Cpl. Herbert George, 1/Artists	
1919	Aug.	13.	TAYLOR, Lieut. Norman Samuel, R.A.F.	*In Russia*
1916	Jan.	1.	VERNON, Cpl. Harold, R.E. (Meteorological)	*Mailly Maillet*
1918	May	31.	VIVIAN, Lieut. Vincent, 22/Durham L.I.	
1918	Feb.	27.	WARD, 2/Lt. Eric,* 10/R. Fusiliers	
1919	Mar.	2.	WEBB, 2/Lt. Bernard Hugh, S.B./Middlesex	*Died (septic pneumonia)*
1916	Sept.	26.	WENDT, Pte. George Norman, 13/London	
1918	Sept.	6.	WHARTON, Pte. Ernest Philip, 1/Artists	*Accident*

* *Died of Wounds.*

xlii

ADDENDA—*continued.*

Add to DISTINGUISHED SERVICE ORDER (pp. 46 & 47).

CLARK, Capt. Philip Lindsay ... ... 11/Royal Sussex
 E. of YPRES, 25th to 27th October, 1917. For conspicuous gallantry and devotion to duty when in command of the left flank company of the battalion. When the enemy broke through on his left he organised a defensive flank. Finding a gap on his left he filled and held it with some of his own men and of the unit on his left. He personally led a charge against the advancing enemy and dispersed them, and later repelled another attack. He was wounded by a piece of shrapnel in the head, but though dazed, continued in command of his company for two days until relieved.
  [3712

FAGAN, Capt. Herbert Archer, *M.C.* (*bar*) ... 9/Gurkha Rifles (late 5/Yorkshire)
 In SOUTH RUSSIA. For conspicuous gallantry and determination on several occasions, particularly at SORAROGHA, on the 18th January, and at MAKIN, on the 19th February, 1920. In the first instance he was in charge of a company ordered to establish a piquet in a position which was much exposed and commanded by fire. He set a fine example in beating off attacks and in attempting to establish the piquet. Subsequently he withdrew his company with great skill. In the second instance he again showed gallantry and leadership when troops on the left were ordered to withdraw.
  [3635

FIELD, 2/Lt. Edward ... ... Machine Gun Corps
 ROUPY, near ST. QUENTIN, 21st March, 1918. For conspicuous gallantry and devotion to duty when in charge of a section of guns during repeated enemy attacks. For eight hours he fired his guns with great judgment under heavy machine-gun and artillery fire. The enemy poured out of a valley in large numbers, and the guns fired with terrific effect. The enemy was held for seven hours. Then, reinforced, they advanced to within 100 yards of the guns and bombed the positions from the right rear. He ordered his guns to cut their way to new positions while he helped their retirement by throwing the remainder of the bombs. In getting back he was shot through the body. His determination and fearlessness were magnetic. Throughout the day he fought magnificently.
  [763848

JOHNSON, Lt.-Col. Francis Shand Byam ... R. of O., Royal Lancaster (1/Artists)
 POZIERES RIDGE, 24th March, 1918. For conspicuous gallantry and devotion to duty. When his battalion became isolated during an enemy attack and both flanks were exposed, by his courage and skill he succeeded in withdrawing his battalion without serious loss. The successful withdrawal was entirely due to his splendid leadership and determination.

Add to MILITARY CROSSES (pp. 55, 89 & 117).

ASTBURY, 2/Lt. Alec ... ... R.F.A. (D/286 Brigade, R.F.A. (T.F.)
 Near BOYELLES, 22nd August, 1918. For conspicuous gallantry and devotion to duty. He brought his battery into action under very heavy fire, and got his ammunition wagons up to the battery position in spite of congested traffic. Later, he was instrumental in laying telephone wires from a very advanced post to the battery over open country under heavy machine-gun fire. The information which he sent back was of great value in enabling the enemy line to be driven back.
  [765207

HEY, 2/Lt. Percy ... ... R.G.A.
 Near VILLERS BRETONNEUX, 7th August, 1918. For conspicuous gallantry and devotion to duty. When a number of tanks filled with bombs and explosives close to his battery position had been set alight by enemy shell fire, he led a small party and successfully extinguished the burning camouflage covering his own and neighbouring guns, and dragged into safety all exposed cartridges. His determined courage saved the loss of ammunition and stores.
  [765448

xliii.

ADDENDA—*continued.*

RICHARD, 2/Lt. Stanley ... ... Machine Gun Corps
    Near LES RUES VERTES, 3rd December, 1917. For conspicuous gallantry and devotion to duty. During an enemy attack, and whilst under intense artillery fire, he performed magnificent work, keeping his guns in action, being with one gun himself in an exposed position until gun and team were blown up. Being the only one remaining unwounded, on his own initiative he moved up to his other three guns, which he continued to keep in action and supplied with ammunition, until these also were put out of action and he was wounded. Throughout he set a fine example of courage, and was of great assistance in checking the hostile attack. [6352

WHITE, 2/Lt. Lawrence Arthur ... ... R.F.A.
    Awarded 3rd June, 1918. [2786

Add to MENTIONED IN DESPATCHES (p. 152–158).

3383	BARNES, Lieut. R. C.	...	*Haig*
760549	DAWSON, Capt. F. A.	...	*Haig*
2256	SAVORY, Major K. S.	...	*Hamilton*
598	THORNE, Lieut. A. J. P.	...	*Haig*
766235	TAYLOR, Capt. P. S.	...	*Murray*
—	TYER, Capt. A. A.	...	*Haig*

Add to BROUGHT TO NOTICE (p. 159).

    557 IRWIN, CSM H. G., Artists (M-G. School).

Add the following to G.H.Q. MACHINE GUN SCHOOL (p. 313), and in Section IV. (p. 434) insert the symbols *a* or *f* as below against their names.

3591	DUCLOS, Henri François	26/ 6/16	*f*
3637	FIELDING, Percy Arthur	3/ 9/16	*a, f*
5685	FLEMING, Ernest	3/ 9/16	*f*
7194	JACQUES, George	26/ 6/16	*f*
3643	LAND, Leo Frederick	3/ 9/16	*f*
1728	MORGAN, Hugh T.	15/12/15	*To 2/Lt. M.G.C.*
6189	NEWTON, William McIntosh	3/ 9/16	*a, f*
3145	SEYMOUR, Bernard Gilbert	26/ 6/16	*To 2/Lt. 4/East Lancs.*
3645	TAYLOR, Bertram Walter	26/ 6/16	*a, f*
3112	TUCKER, Richard Stuart	21/11/15	*f*
2862	WEBB, Francis Rands	2/ 1/16	*f*
3648	WILLIS, William Stephen	26/ 6/16	*f*

Add to FURTHER COMMISSIONS (p. 427).

    2364 BEALE, William Piere ... ... 7/ 9/15 *R.A.S.C. Capt.*

SECTION I.

THE ARTISTS RIFLES'
Roll of Honour.

At the call of King and Country, those of our comrades whom this Roll commemorates left all that was dear to them, endured hardships, faced danger, and finally passed out of the sight of men by the path of duty and self-sacrifice, giving up their own lives that others might live in freedom.

Let those that come after see to it that their names are not forgotten.

CHRONOLOGICAL ROLL OF HONOUR.
KILLED IN ACTION, DIED OF WOUNDS, etc.
(Alphabetical Index at end of Book.)

1914.

1914.			
Nov. 27.	WARREN, Sgt. Walter, 1/Artists	...	At Lindenhoek
,, ,,	THOMPSON, Pte. William John, 1/Artists	...	,,
Dec. 11.	RAWLINS, Cpl. Glenrowan Edward Champion, 1/Artists		On Messines Ridge
,, 18.	PEARCE, 2/Lt. Geoffrey Vincent, 2/R. Warwick		Rouges-Bancs, Armentières
,, 19.	MONK, 2/Lt. George Bertram,* 2/R. Warwick		,, ,,
,, ,,	STANDRING, 2/Lt. Benjamin Arthur,* 2/R. Warwick		,, ,,

1915.

1915.			
Jan. 5.	CRISP, 2/Lt. Francis Edward Fitzjohn, 1/GrenadierGuards		Near Cuinchy
,, 22.	REES, 2/Lt. John Trevor, 1/R. Welch Fusiliers	...	Near Armentières
,, 25.	THOMPSON, 2/Lt. John Cecil Caster, 1/Scots Guards		Near Cuinchy
,, ,,	WELD, 2/Lt. Hugh Edward, 1/Scots Guards	...	,, ,,
,, 26.	HUTT, 2/Lt. Harold Vernon, 2/R. Sussex	...	,, ,,
Feb. 1.	CLIFTON, 2/Lt. Harold Norton,* 1/Coldstream Guards...		Near Cuinchy (Jan. 25)
,, 21.	DAVIS, Pte. Alexander Herbert, Artists	...	Died
,, 22.	FROST, 2/Lt. Kenneth, 1/R. West Kent	...	Near Ypres
Mar. 5.	MACKINTOSH, 2/Lt. Harry Leith,* 1/South Stafford	...	Sailly-sur-Lys
,, 9.	HAMLEN, Pte. Percy, Artists	...	Died
,, 10.	AUSTEN, 2/Lt. Cyril Frederick, 2/R. West Surrey	..	Near Laventie
,, ,,	BENNINGFIELD, 2/Lt. Maurice Victor, 1/Worcester		...Battle of Neuve-Chapelle
,, ,,	HARE, 2/Lt. Evan Amyas Alfred, 2/Middlesex	...	,, ,,
,, ,,	HOLLAND, 2/Lt. Basil Thomas, 2/R. Highlanders	...	,, ,,
,, ,,	KIRKALDY, 2/Lt. Charles Henry, 1/Seaforth	...	,, ,,
,, ,,	WINDSOR, 2/Lt. Mark Gilham, 2/Devon	...	,, ,,
,, 11.	CUTTLE, 2/Lt. Geoffrey, 2/Yorks	...	,, ,,
,, ,,	GOTCH, 2/Lt. Duncan Hepburn, 1/Worcester	...	,, ,,
,, ,,	MULOCK, 2/Lt. Edward Ross, 2/Gordon Highlanders...		,, ,,
,, 12.	CLOSE, 2/Lt. Max Arthur, 1/Highland L.I.		,, ,,
,, ,,	DE BURIATTE, 2/Lt. John Philip, 2/East Surrey	...	Near Lindenhoek
,, ,,	LORD, 2/Lt. Frank Samuel, 2/Devon	...	Battle of Neuve-Chapelle
,, ,,	MANN, 2/Lt. Fredk. Christmas, 1/North Stafford	...	
,, ,,	PARKES, 2/Lt. Horace Frederick, 1/R. Welch Fus.		...Battle of Neuve-Chapelle
,, ,,	PAYNE, 2/Lt. Charles Geraint, 1/Highland L.I.	...	,, ,,
,, ,,	CROSSE, 2/Lt. Marlborough Evelyn, 2/Yorks		,, ,,
,, 14.	CARDEN, 2/Lt. Ronald Hugh, 2/Wilts	...	,, ,,
,, 15.	COLLEY, 2/Lt. Archibald, 2/D.C.L.I.	...	Near St. Eloi
,, ,,	FORD, 2/Lt. Royston Dearmer, 1/Royal Irish	...	,, ,,

* Died of Wounds.

ARTISTS' RIFLES, 1915.

1915.			
Mar. 15.	WHITE, 2/Lt. Leslie Spencer, 1/R. West Kent	...	*Accident near Ypres*
Apr. 13.	WHITTLE, 2/Lt. Walter Victor Patrick C., 1/Worcester		*Near Bois Grenier*
,, 14.	WHITEHEAD, 2/Lt. Henry Montague, 2/East Surrey		*Near Zonnebeke*
,, 18.	CRASTON, 2/Lt. John,* 3/R. West Kent	... ...	*On Hill 60*
,, 19.	KELLIE, 2/Lt. Esmond Lawrence, 1/Bedford	...	,, ,,
,, ,,	KIRCH, 2/Lt. Charles Sidney, 1/Bedford	...	,, ,,
,, 22.	WALLACE, 2/Lt. John Roger, 2/R. Scots Fusiliers	...	*2nd Battle of Ypres*
,, 23.	WHITFELD, 2/Lt. Fredk. Ashburnham Hooker, 3/Middx.		,, ,,
,, 25.	BLACK, 2/Lt. Francis Henry, 1/R. Warwick	...	,, ,,
,, ,,	NEELEY, 2/Lt. Hugh Bertram, 3(1)Suffolk	...	,, ,,
,, ,,	PAYNE, 2/Lt. John Oswald, 4(1)R. Warwick	...	*On Hill 60*
,, ,,	SHARPE, 2/Lt. Charles Lancelot Arnot, 3/Middlesex		*2nd Battle of Ypres*
,, 26.	ROBINSON, 2/Lt. Arthur Hine, 1/Manchester	...	*At St. Julian*
,, 28.	PARKER, 2/Lt. Frederick Neville, 1/K.R.R.C.	...	*Died at Bethune*
,, 29.	CAREW, 2/Lt. Cyril Joseph Theodore,* 2/East Yorks		*2nd Battle of Ypres*
,, 30.	BERRY, Pte. Percy Hamilton, 1/Artists	...	*Died at St. Omer*
May 5.	LONGUET-HIGGINS, 2/Lt. Kenneth Aislabie, R.M.L.I.		*At the Dardanelles*
,, 8.	CROFT-SMITH, 2 Lt. Edwin Spencer, 4/K.R.R.C.	...	
,, 9.	COPLAND, 2/Lt. Dudley Charles James, 1/Notts & Derby		*Aubers Ridge*
,, ,,	DAY, 2/Lt. Morris, 2/R. Berks		,, ,,
,, ,,	DENNYS, 2/Lt. Kenneth Rose, 2/R. Munster Fusiliers		*Nr. Richebourg L'Avoue*
,, ,,	DICK, 2/Lt. Geo. Frederick Graeme, 1/Notts & Derby		*Aubers Ridge*
,, ,,	FAZAN, 2/Lt. Roy, 5/R. Sussex ...		*Near Richebourg L'Avoue*
,, ,,	HORSFALL, 2/Lt.Arthur Mendelssohn, 2/R. Munster Fus.		*Nr.Richebourg L'Avoue*
,, ,,	HOWELL, 2/Lt. Herbert Edgar, 2/East Lancashire	...	*Aubers Ridge*
,, ,,	MARSHALL, 2/Lt. Augustus de la Poer, 2/East Lancs.		,, ,,
,, ,,	MARVIN, 2/Lt. Donald, 1/Seaforth Highlanders		*Near Richebourg L'Avoue*
,, ,,	MORRIS, 2/Lt. Clive Wilson, 2/K.R.R.C.	... ,,	,, ,,
,, ,,	NORTON, 2/Lt. Alfred George, 2/East Lancashire	...	*Aubers Ridge*
,, ,,	ORTON, 2/Lt. Ernest Henry, 2/Scottish Rifles		*...Fromelles, Aubers Ridge*
,, ,,	PAGE, 2/Lt. Francis Trafford, 2/R. Munster Fusiliers		*Nr. Richebourg L'Avoue*
,, ,,	PARKER, 2/Lt. Wilfred Horsley, 2/R. Munster Fusiliers	,,	,, ,,
,, ,,	RANDALL, 2/Lt. Reginald Wigmore Sancroft, 2/Northampton		*Aubers Ridge*
,, ,,	TIGAR, 2/Lt. Harold Walter, 3/Middlesex ...	...	*Near Klein Zillebeke*
,, ,,	WEBB, 2/Lt. John Timms, 6/London	...	
,, ,,	WINDUS, 2/Lt. Charles Eric, 1/R. Irish Rifles	...	*Aubers Ridge*
,, 11.	HELLMERS, 2/Lt. Alfred,* 1/R. Irish Rifles ...		*Aubers Ridge (9th)*
,, ,,	PEAKE, 2/Lt. John Thelwall,* 2/Northampton	...	*Aubers Ridge (9th)*
,, 13.	BALES, 2/Lt. Keith, 2/Border	...	*Battle of Festubert*
,, 15.	BROWN, 2/Lt. Harold Atherton, 2/Leicester		*...Nr. Richebourg L'Avoue*
,, 16.	BYNG, 2/Lt. Harry,* 2/Border	...	*Battle of Festubert*
,, ,,	DE ROUGEMONT, 2/Lt. Maurice Henry, 2/R. West Surrey		,, ,,
,, ,,	HUDSON, 2/Lt. Charles Herbert, 1/Liverpool	...	,, ,,
,, ,,	HUMPHREYS, 2/Lt. Dudley Francis,* 2/R. West Surrey		,, ,,
,, ,,	JAMES, 2/Lt. John Stephen Harvey, 1/K.R.R.C.	...	,, ,,
,, ,,	JONES, 2/Lt. Leonard, 1/R. Welch Fusiliers	...	,, ,,
,, ,,	KROHN, 2/Lt. Nicholas Adolph, 2/Border	...	,, ,,

* *Died of Wounds.*

1915.

May	16.	MESSOM, 2/Lt. Harold, ✠ 2/R. West Surrey...	Battle of Festubert
,,	,,	MORTEN, 2/Lt. Galbraith, 1/Liverpool	,, ,,
,,	,,	SIMPSON, 2/Lt. William Robert Carde, 2/Border	,, ,,
,,	,,	WILLIAMSON, 2/Lt. John Maurice, 2/Gordon	,, ,,
,,	17.	APPS, 2/Lt. Reginald Denman, 2/R. Berks	,, ,,
,,	,,	CASSIDY, 2/Lt. Cyril Martin,* 1/K.R.R.C.	,, ,,
,,	,,	FISHER, 2/Lt. Edward Humbert, 2/Yorks	,, ,,
,,	,,	GOODMAN, 2/Lt. Reginald Moon, 2/Border	,, ,,
,,	23.	BRIDGE, 2/Lt. Donald Gerald Clive, 2/R. Berks	,, ,,
,,	24.	PRICE, 2/Lt. Harold Strachan, 3/Royal Fusiliers	Near Ypres
,,	,,	JUDD, 2/Lt. Frederick George, 2/R. Dublin Fusiliers...	,, Wieltje
,,	,,	YOUNG, 2/Lt. Henry Harman, 3/Royal Fusiliers	Belleward Lake, Ypres
,,	25.	MACEY, 2/Lt. Clifford James, 1/Dorset	On Hill 60
,,	29.	BALLARD, 2/Lt. Maurice Arnold,* 23/London	Battle of Festubert (26th)
June	2.	MEAD, 2/Lt. Bernard Wallace, 4/Royal Fusiliers	Near Ypres
,,	4.	HARLEY, 2/Lt. John, 13/Worcester	Gallipoli
,,	,,	PARKER, 2/Lt. Edward Thompson, 13/Yorks (1/Lancs. Fus.)	,, ,,
,,	16	GREEN, 2/Lt. Frank Clifford, 1/Lincoln	Near Ypres
,,	,,	PEARSON, 2/Lt. Reginald Oswald, 1/Lincoln	,, ,,
,,	,,	SIMPSON, 2/Lt. Henry Gordon, 9/D.C.L.I. (1/R. Inniskg. Fus.)	Gallipoli
,,	,,	TRINDER, 2/Lt. Arnold James, 7/Northumberland Fus.	Near Hooge
,,	18.	DUFF, 2/Lt. John Crerar, 2/Gordon Highlanders	Near Givenchy
,,	19.	LLARENA, 2/Lt. Eustace Fernando, 2/Suffolk	Near Ypres
,,	20.	BARFOOT, 2/Lt. George Allan, 3/Worcester	At Hooge
,,	,,	FAIRBAIRN, 2/Lt. George Eric,* 10/Durham L.I.	
,,	,,	WINDSOR, 2/Lt. Leslie St. Lawrence, 2/Suffolk	Near Ypres
July	1.	WILLIAMS, 2/Lt. Theodore Edward, 1/Somerset L.I. ...	At Pilkem
,,	9.	STANWELL, 2/Lt. William Alexander,* 2/Lancs. Fusiliers	,, ,,
,,	14.	CUXSON, 2/Lt. Basil Pryce, 2/R. Scots	
,,	15.	PEMBERTON, Pte. Algernon George, Artists...	Died
,,	30.	DEWES, 2/Lt. Bryan Osmond, 1/Middlesex	Near Laventie
,,	,,	ELBOROUGH, Capt. Alfred Charles Ernest,* 6/Yorkshire L.I.	Near Ypres
Aug.	6.	STEARNS, 2/Lt. Eric Gordon,* 4/R. Fusiliers	
,,	7.	BROWN, 2/Lt. Frederick Charles, 9/Notts & Derby	On Gallipoli
,,	,,	PEARKES, Capt. Andre Mellard, 9/West Yorks	,, ,,
,,	9.	FOULGER, 2/Lt. Maurice, 1/Shropshire L.I.	• At Hooge
,,	,,	GOODALE, 2/Lt. Arthur William, 1/Shropshire L.I.	,, ,,
,,	,,	ISAAC, 2/Lt. Frank Philip, 1/Shropshire L.I.	,, ,,
,,	,,	KAY, 2/Lt. George Alexander, 2/Notts & Derby	
,,	10.	HIGGINS, Capt. Herbert Edward Powell, 6/R. Lancaster	At the Dardanelles
,,	,,	SILCOCK, 2/Lt. Bertram Baber, 7/R. Welch Fusiliers...	At Suvla Bay
,,	12.	ADAMS, 2/Lt. Robert, 5/Norfolk	,, ,,
,,	,,	OLIPHANT, 2/Lt. Marcus Francis, 5/Norfolk	,, ,,
,,	16.	BARNETT, Lieut. Denis Oliver,* 2/Leinster	At Hooge
,,	17.	JURGENS, 2/Lt. Sydney George,* 6/R. Lancaster	At the Dardanelles
,,	19.	TIPPET, 2/Lt. Alexander Arnold,* 2/Shropshire L.I.	Chapelle d'Armentières
,,	21.	CURREY, Capt. George Grafton, 6/Yorkshire	On Gallipoli

* Died of Wounds.

1915			
Aug. 21.	RABONE, 2/Lt. Maxwell, 2/R. Munster Fusiliers	...	*On Gallipoli*
,, 22.	WESTON, 2/Lt. Wilfred James, 6/York & Lancaster	...	,, ,,
,, 23.	COX, 2/Lt. Norman John, 7/R. Sussex	...	*Near Houplines*
,, 24.	MILES, 2/Lt. Alfred Crosfield Vernon, 2/Welch	..	*Near Cambrin*
,, 25.	NORRIS, 2/Lt. William Forbes, 5/Norfolk (A.C.C.)	...	*At Suvla Bay*
Sept. 1.	PULVERMAN, 2/Lt. Oscar Percy,* 1/Suffolk		*In Flanders*
,, 7.	MARTIN, 2/Lt. Frederick Arthur,* 2/Notts & Derby	...	
,, 22.	KOCH, 2/Lt. Marcus Addison, 2/Shropshire L.I.	...	*Near Cappy-sur-Somme*
,, 25.	BEAUMONT, 2/Lt. Wilfred Newton, 2/Border	...	*Battle of Loos*
,, ,,	BERRY, 2/Lt. John Anthony, 2(1)Gordon	...	,, ,,
,, ,,	BROMLEY, 2/Lt. Hugh Frederick, 2/R. Sussex	...	,, ,,
,, ,,	BROWN, 2/Lt. Arthur Lyster, 2/R. West Surrey	...	,, ,,
,, ,,	BUDIBENT, 2/Lt. Cecil, 2/Lincoln	...	,, ,,
,, ,,	GOLDIE, 2/Lt. Paul, 1/Loyal N. Lancashire	...	,, ,,
,, ,,	HARE, 2/Lt. Bernard Urmston, 1/Middlesex	...	,, ,,
,, ,,	HILL, 2/Lt. Arthur Lionel, 1/Middlesex	...	,, ,,
,, ,,	HILLIAR, 2/Lt. Gordon Edward, 3/S. Lancs. (2/E. Lancs.)		*At Bois-Grenier*
,, ,,	HOWELL, 2/Lt. John, 9/K.R.R.C.	...	*In Flanders*
,, ,,	HULM, 2/Lt. Wynne Odverne, 8/Devon	...	*Battle of Loos*
,, ,,	JONES, 2/Lt. Charles Taylor, 2/R. West Surrey	...	,, ,,
,, ,,	LEE, 2/Lt. Walton Noel Olliff, 1/South Stafford	...	,, ,,
,, ,,	MELLISH, 2/Lt. Richard Coppin, 1/Middlesex	...	,, ,,
,, ,,	PLANT, 2/Lt. Frederick George, 1/R. West Surrey	...	,, ,,
,, ,,	RAYMOND-BARKER, 2/Lt. Cecil Langton, 12/Rifle Brigade		,, ,,
,, ,,	REYNARD, 2/Lt. Henry Corner, 1/South Stafford	...	,, ,,
,, ,,	VANN, Capt. Arthur Allard Harrison, 12/West Yorks		,, ,,
,, ,,	WALCH, 2/Lt. James Bernard Millard, 2/R. West Surrey		,, ,,
,, ,,	WEBB, Lieut. Cyril Francis, 2/Yorks	...	,, ,,
,, ,,	WILKINSON, 2/Lt. Ernest Alexander, 2/Leicester	...	
,, ,,	WILSON, Lieut. William Clement, 1/Worcester	...	*Near Fleurbaix*
,, 26.	PICKUP, 2/Lt. Alfred James, 2/Yorks	...	*Battle of Loos*
,, ,,	SAUNDERS, 2/Lt. Louis Desormeaux, 1/S. Wales Bdrs.		,, ,,
,, ,,	STEPHENSON, 2/Lt. Kenneth Langton, 2/Bedford	...	,, ,,
,, 27.	ALLEN, 2/Lt. Frederick John,* 9/Devon	...	,, ,,
,, ,,	BOOTH, 2/Lt. Frederick Atkins, 2/East Kent	...	,, ,,
,, 29.	CHANDLER, 2/Lt. Charles Robert, 2/East Surrey	...	,, ,,
,, ,,	FRIEND, 2/Lt. Frank Howard, 2/Wilts	...	,, ,,
,, 30.	HALLOWES, 2/Lt. Rupert Price, **V.C.**✠ 4/Middlesex		,, ,,
,, ,,	LAW, 2/Lt. Charles Lindsay Gwyder, 2/Suffolk	...	*At Hooge*
Oct. 1.	HOBLYN, 2/Lt. Walter Frederick, 4/Coldstream Gds.		*Battle of Loos*
,, ,,	GATES, 2/Lt. Douglas Leslie, 1/Suffolk	...	,, ,,
,, 2.	HARTLEY, 2/Lt. William Edwin, 2/Cheshire	...	,, ,,
,, 3.	AKERMAN, 2/Lt. Ralph Portland,* 11/London	...	,, ,,
,, 4.	WILKINS, 2/Lt. Geoffrey,* 2/Northumberland Fusiliers		
,, 6.	TRIER, 2/Lt. Norman Ernest,* 2/East Yorks	...	
,, 8.	LUMB, 2/Lt. Herbert, R.F.A.	...	*Died*
,, 13.	ADDY, 2/Lt. Kenneth James Balguy, 1/K.R.R.C.	...	*Battle of Loos*

* *Died of Wounds.*   ✠ = *Military Cross.*

ROLL OF HONOUR

1915.
Oct. 13. TWEEDIE-SMITH, 2/Lt. Alan, 1/R. West Surrey
„ 20. TALLENTIRE, 2/Lt. Arthur Tom, 1/Artists (R.F.C.) ... *Near Abeele*
„ 23. CHRISTMAS, Capt. Dudley Vyvyan, 5/Suffolk (Staff) ... *Accident*
„ 29. CROMPTON, Pte. Thomas Sherwood, Artists ... *Died*
Nov. 19. GILL, 2/Lt. Jack Woodward, 6/Yorkshire L.I. ...
Dec. 4. SNOW, 2/Lt. Richard Aslin, 4/York & Lancaster ... *Near Ypres*
„ 15. HINES, 2/Lt. Austin,* 10/Durham L.I. ... ...
„ 22. GREIFFENHAGEN, 2/Lt. Norman,* 1/East Kent ... *Near Ypres*
„ „ SMITH, 2/Lt. Ernest Kennedy,* 1/East Kent ... „ „
„ 25. DARRELL, 2/Lt. Albert, 1/East Surrey ... ...

1916.

1916.
Jan. 5. WHITE, 2/Lt. Esmonde Ricarde Burke, 6/Northumberland Fus.
„ 6. HUTCHINSON, 2/Lt. Innes Owen, 2/R. Highlanders *Near Ypres*
„ „ WILSON, Capt. Harold Algar, 1/Shropshire L.I. ... „ „
„ 15. GEARY, 2/Lt. Ronald Fitzmaurice, 21/London ... „ *Loos*
„ 21. OKEY, 2/Lt. William Ewart, 1/Connaught Rangers *Shaikh-Said, Mesopotamia*
„ 29. DAVIES, 2/Lt. William Edward, 5/Cheshire ... *In France*
„ 31. BUTLAND, 2/Lt. William Henry,* 10/Durham L.I. ... *Near Ypres*
Feb. 6. ARNOLD, 2/Lt. Bernard Marcus,* 7/K.R.R.C. *Near Ypres (2nd)*
„ 11. HAKEWILL, 2/Lt. Thomas George, 11/N. Stafford (R.F.C.) *In Egypt*
„ 14. HILL, 2/Lt. Douglas Charles Lucas, 9/R. Sussex ... *Near Ypres*
„ 17. WYATT-SMITH, Pte. Hugh Hargreaves, 2/Artists ... *Died*
„ 20. RADCLIFFE, 2/Lt. Ernest John, R.F.C. ... ... *Accident at Brooklands*
„ 25. CARPENTER, 2/Lt. Hubert Granville,* Army Cyclist Corps
„ 28. LAILY, 2/Lt. Eric Lillywhite, 7/D.C.L.I. ... ... *Near Ypres*
Mar. 3. MADAN, Lieut. Nigel Cornwallis, 8/R. Lancaster ... „ „
„ 5. BURTON, Pte. William Edgar Bowness, Artists ... *Died*
„ 8. D'OMBRAIN, 2/Lt. Rowland Maund, 5/East Kent (53/Sikhs) *Battle of Dajailah*
„ 11. LLOYD-JONES, Capt. John, ✠ 2/Yorks ... *Died*
„ 13. FORTUNE, 2/Lt. Stanley Welsh, 10/Rifle Brigade ...
„ 16. RAINFORTH, Pte. Gray Victor, 1/Artists ... ... *Died at Rouen*
„ „ SINCLAIR, Pte. William Kenneth, 1/Artists ... „ „
„ „ WISEMAN, Pte. Charles, 1/Artists ... ... „ „
„ 19. ELLIS, 2/Lt. Shirley Duncan, ✠ R. Engineers ... *Died*
„ 20. PYCOCK, Sgt. Herbert Richard Holmes, 2/Artists ... „
Apr. 4. PASSMORE, 2/Lt. Arthur William, 9/R. West Surrey ...
„ „ SIMCOX, Pte. Charles Grosvenor, 1/Artists . ... *Died at Rouen*
„ 5. WHEATE, 2/Lt. Arthur,* 1/East Lancashire ... *Near Hannah, Mesopotamia*
„ 9. WILLIAMS, 2/Lt. Donald Matthew, 12(9)R. Warwick
„ 18. MOSSE, 2/Lt. Philip Godfrey, 13/R. Warwick (East Lancs.)
„ 19. JOHNSON, 2/Lt. Wilfred Lloyd, 2/Border ... ... *Near Mametz*
„ 21. HITCHCOCK, 2/Lt. Cyril Augustus, 1/Shropshire L.I. *Near Ypres*
„ 22. JOHNSTON, 2/Lt. Alec, 1/Shropshire L.I. *On Ypres-Langemarch Road*

* *Died of Wounds.*

ARTISTS' RIFLES, 1916.

1916.			
Apr. 24.	MAYBROOK, 2/Lt. Walter Richard, 1/Wilts		*On Vimy Ridge*
,, 29.	READING, 2/Lt. John Francis, 7/Worcester		*Near Hebuterne*
May 3.	MORLAND, 2/Lt. Leonard Mark, 10/West Yorks		
,, 4.	WYATT, 2/Lt. William Herbert, 1/East Yorks		*Near Fricourt*
,, 9.	BRACHER, Pte. William Victor Allen, Artists		*Died*
,, 10.	JENSEN, 2/Lt. Cyril Thornton, 25/Manchester (T.M.B.)		*Near Vaux*
,, 12.	FISCHER, 2/Lt. Alexander William, 1/Devon		
,, 13.	GOULD, 2/Lt. Arthur, 13/Cheshire		
,, 18.	CHRISTMAS, Capt. Bernard Lovell, 3/London		*On Vimy Ridge*
,, 19.	YOUNG, 2/Lt. Leonard Geo. Birmingham, 10/Cheshire		
,, 21.	MILLER, Lieut. John Lockhart, 8/London		*On Vimy Ridge*
,, ,,	POTTER, 2/Lt. Frederick John, 8/London		
,, 22.	HILLYER, Capt. William Harold, ✠ R. Engineers		*On Vimy Ridge*
,, 23.	HUNTER, 2/Lt. Alexander Forbes, 21/London		
,, 25.	RUCK, 2/Lt. John Arthur, R.F.C.		*Accident*
,, 28.	HALLWARD, 2/Lt. Kenneth Leslie, 3/Worcester		
June 1.	SKERRY, 2/Lt. James Beadnell, 17/Middlesex		*On Vimy Ridge*
,, 2.	STREET, 2/Lt. Edmund Algar, 22/Manchester		*Near Mametz*
,, 3.	THOMPSON, 2/Lt. Charles Henry, 2/Durham L.I.		,, *Ypres*
,, ,,	DICKENS, Pte. Aubrey John Edward, 1/Artists		*Died in France*
,, 4.	MADDOCKS, Lieut. John Anslow, 15/R. Warwick		*Near Arras*
,, ,,	TOWNSEND, 2/Lt. Thomas, 1/East Yorks		,, *Fricourt*
,, 13.	DODDS, 2/Lt. Herbert Alex. Christopher, 5/York & Lancs.		*Died*
,, 17.	MONTGOMERY, 2/Lt. Norman Stevenson, 2/Coldstream Gds.		
,, 27.	LANGFORD, 2/Lt. Wallace George,* 18/K.R.R.C.		
,, 28.	GETHIN, 2/Lt. Percy Francis, 3/Devon		*Near Mametz*
,, 30.	BURNETT, 2/Lt. Charles Guy Arbouin, 7/Northumb. Fus.		*Near Wytschaete*
July 1.	ALLEN, 2/Lt. Geoffrey Austin, 2/Essex		
,, ,,	BROCKLEHURST, Capt. Thomas Pownall, 2/R. West Surrey		*Near Mametz*
,, ,,	BURTON, 2/Lt. Cyril Henry, 7/Notts & Derby		
,, ,,	CHURCHFIELD, 2/Lt. Sidney Percival, 4/Middlesex		
,, ,,	ELLIOTT, 2/Lt. Philip Maurice, 3/Middlesex		*Near La Boiselle*
,, ,,	GILES, 2/Lt. Geoffrey, 2/Gordon Highlanders		*Battle of Somme*
,, ,,	GODFREY, 2/Lt. Victor, 2/R. Scots Fusiliers		*Near Montauban*
,, ,,	GOODCHILD, 2/Lt. Stanley Cecil, 2/Essex		*Battle of Somme*
,, ,,	HORSNELL, 2/Lt. Alick George, 7/Suffolk		
,, ,,	HOWE, 2/Lt. Charles Kingsley, 6/R. Berks		*Battle of Somme*
,, ,,	JEFFCOCK, Capt. Robert Salisbury, 6/S. Stafford		,, ,,
,, ,,	JONES, 2/Lt. Kenneth Champion, 1/East Lancashire		*Near Beaumont-Hamel*
,, ,,	MALLET, 2/Lt. Eric Sydney, 1/East Lancashire		,, ,,
,, ,,	MIDDLEDITCH, Lieut. Archibald Milne, 12/Essex		
,, ,,	MUSGROVE, Lieut. G. H. Stuart, 8/East Surrey		*Near Montauban*
,, ,,	NEWCOMBE, Lieut. Richard Clyde Davies, 1/E.Lancs. (M.G.C.)		*Battle of Somme*
,, ,,	PILGRIM, 2/Lt. Henry Bastick, 13/London		
,, ,,	RUSHTON, 2/Lt. Frank Gregson, 8/Wilts (T.M.B.)		*Near Fricourt*
,, ,,	SPATZ, 2/Lt. Walter Rudolph, 2/Middlesex		*Near La Boiselle*
,, ,,	THOMAS, Capt. Henrich William Max, 1/East Lancs.		*Near Beaumont-Hamel*

* *Died of Wounds.*

ROLL OF HONOUR

1916.

July	1.	WARNER, 2/Lt. Archibald, 5/London	...	...	*Near Hebuterne*
"	"	WILSON, 2/Lt. John, 2/Middlesex	...	...	*Near La Boiselle*
"	"	YATES, 2/Lt. Arthur Gerald Vavasour, 16/London	...		
"	2.	COY, 2/Lt. Alfred Reginald, 7/West Yorks	...	...	*Near Pozieres Wood*
"	"	DICKINSON, Capt. George Sidney, 7/Lincoln	...	...	*" Fricourt Wood*
"	"	EAMES, Lieut. Arthur H., 1/East Yorks	...	...	*Battle of Somme*
"	"	FLINT, 2/Lt. Charles William, 26/Northumb. Fusiliers			
"	"	ROGERS, 2/Lt. Robert Murray, 8/K.R.R.C.	...		
"	"	SPINNEY, Lieut. Ronald Henry,* 2/Coldstream Guards			*Near Abeele*
"	3.	WRIGHT, 2/Lt. Edwin Stanley, 7/Suffolk	...	...	
"	4.	REACHER, Capt. Stanley William,* 11/R. Warwick (16/R.B.)			*Near Festubert*
"	6.	COOMBES, 2/Lt. Claude Stuart,* 6/R. West Kent		...	*Battle of Somme*
"	7.	CONWAY, 2/Lt. Joseph Michael, 7/R. Lancaster		...	*Near La Boiselle*
"	"	CULLING, 2/Lt. Harold William, 9/W. Riding		...	*Battle of Somme*
"	"	HARRISON, 2/Lt. Wm. Stanford Bennett, 9/L. N. Lancs.			*Near La Boiselle*
"	"	LONGSTAFF, 2/Lt. Jack Campbell, 5/York & Lancaster			
"	"	MOORE, 2/Lt. Kenneth Hartley, 6/Dorset		...	*Near Mametz Wood*
"	"	PEECOCK, 2/Lt. Edward Gordon, 9/R. Fusiliers		...	
"	8.	STRIBLING, 2/Lt. Frederick George,* 1/Notts & Derby			*Battle of Somme*
"	9.	HAEFFNER, 2/Lt. Frederick Wilfred, R.F.A.		...	*" "*
"	"	HUNTER, 2/Lt. James Whitaker, 5/Northampton		...	*" "*
"	10.	SNOWDEN, Lieut. Reginald Wallace, 8/S. Stafford		...	*Near Mametz Wood*
"	"	VOKINS, 2/Lt. Kean Esse, 11/R. Warwick		...	*Battle of Somme*
"	11.	HORNE, 2/Lt. James Anthony, 16/London		...	*Near Gommecourt*
"	"	JOB, Capt. Ernest Dalzel, 1/Artists (M.G.C.)		...	*Near Mametz Wood*
"	14.	HAMILTON, 2/Lt. Noel Crawford, 6/Northampton		...	*Battle of Somme*
"	"	SAMUEL, Capt. Gerard Steuart, 8/East Yorks		...	*" "*
"	16.	DEEDES, Capt. Herbert Philip, 16/K.R.R.C.		...	*" "*
"	"	SIMPKIN, 2/Lt. Reginald John Henry, 5/R. Warwick			
"	20.	ALLANSON, 2/Lt. Henry Peter, 1/Suffolk		...	
"	"	MURRAY, 2/Lt. Edward Douglas,* 11/R. Highlanders			*At Longueval (14th)*
"	21.	BROWN, 2/Lt. Francis Arthur Noel, 7/Worcester		...	*Near Ovillers*
"	22.	FLEMING, 2/Lt. John Allister,* 1/R. West Kent		...	*At High Wood*
"	"	LEATHERDALE, 2/Lt. Donald Ryan, 1/R. West Kent			*" "*
"	"	SANDERSON, 2/Lt. Gerald Stanley, 11/London		...	
"	23.	BALDERSON, 2/Lt. Henry Leslie Paxton, 8/Devon (Gloucester)			*Near Pozieres*
"	"	FOX, 2/Lt. Douglas Charles, 1/Northumberland Fusiliers			*Near Longueval*
"	"	VINCENT, 2/Lt. Basil Britten, 8/Gloucester		...	
"	"	WOOD, 2/Lt. David Cardale, 8/Gloucester	...		
"	27.	CHAMPNESS, Pte. Bernard, Artists (13/London)		...	
"	"	HELLICAR, 2/Lt. Geoffrey Theodore, 20/London		...	*Near Arras*
"	"	MARTIN, 2/Lt. Ernest William, 1/Norfolk	...		*Near Longueval*
"	28.	BAKER, 2/Lt. Arthur William, 5/Yorkshire L.I.		...	
"	"	DICKINSON, 2/Lt. Colin James Henry, 15/Cheshire		...	
"	30.	BALLARD, 2/Lt. Robert Francis Cooper, 2/Bedford		...	*At Trones Wood*
"	"	PLESTED, 2/Lt. Horace George, 4/Manchester		...	
"	31.	SHARPE, 2/Lt. Gerald Norman, 4/York & Lancaster		...	

* *Died of Wounds.*

1916.			
Aug.	4.	TODD, 2/Lt. Charles Leslie Morgan,* 4/S. Lancashire	*In France (3rd)*
,,	,,	MILES, 2/Lt. Harold Gordon, 10/D.C.L.I. ...	
,,	7.	WILSON, Lieut. Robert Philip, 6/East Yorks ...	
,,	8.	BISHOP, 2/Lt. Keith Ford, R.G.A.	
,,	9.	WALKER, 2/Lt. Richard, 5/Lancashire Fusiliers ...	
,,	10.	THACKERAY, L/Cpl. Lance, Artists	*Died*
,,	11.	WARD, 2/Lt. Norman John, 11/R. Warwick ...	*Near Bazentin-le-Petit*
,,	12.	GUMNER, 2/Lt. Basil Austin, 9/Liverpool	*Near Pozieres*
,,	,,	POOLEY, 2/Lt. Robin Mark, 9/Liverpool	,, ,,
,,	14.	PHILLIPS, 2/Lt. Sydney Vernon, 10(7)Leicester ...	*Near Arras*
,,	,,	ROEBER, 2/Lt. David Arnold, 3(7)Bedford ..	*Near Armentières*
,,	15.	TURNER, 2/Lt. Ronald, 5/Essex	
,,	16.	DOVE, 2/Lt. Sydney Ernest, 6/R. West Kent ...	
,,	17.	FORBES, Lieut. Alexander Stuart, 10/Seaforth (M.G.C.)	
,,	18.	MORRISH, 2/Lt. Donald Bernard, 6/Yorkshire L.I. (T.M.B.)	
,,	20.	BIRD, 2/Lt. Stanley Treadgold,* 7/K.R.R.C. ...	*On the Ancre*
,,	24.	FARRAN, 2/Lt. Charles, 9/K.R.R.C.	*Near Longueval*
,,	,,	WARING, 2/Lt. Frank,* 5/York & Lancaster	*At Rouen*
,,	27.	FARQUHARSON, 2/Lt. Hugh Joseph, 1/Norfolk	*Died at Basra, Mesopotamia*
,,	28.	JARVIS, Capt. Ernest Cory, 6/S. Lancashire	*Near Thiepval*
Sept.	1.	HOOD, 2/Lt. Oswald, 10/R. Sussex	
,,	3.	FISH, 2/Lt. Barrow Edmondson, 11/R. Sussex ...	
,,	,,	FORBES, Capt. Alec, 2/R. Warwick	
,,	,,	HAWTREY, Lieut. Ralph, 8/Northampton (R.E.)	
,,	,,	MILES, Capt. Herbert Francis, 2/K.O.S.B.	
,,	,,	PENNY, 2/Lt. George, 8/West Yorks	
,,	9.	APERGIS, 2/Lt. Tasso Scott, 10/London	
,,	,,	BOWERMAN, Lieut. Arthur James, 8/Somerset L.I. (R.F.C.)	
,,	,,	ESSEX, 2/Lt. Percy Clifford, 5/Lancashire Fusiliers ...	*Ginchy, on Somme*
,,	,,	FALBY, 2/Lt. Edward Frederick, 4/L. N. Lancashire	
,,	,,	GODFREY, 2/Lt. Henry, 5/Lancashire Fusiliers ...	
,,	,,	HENNA, 2/Lt. John Ramsay, 3(6)R. Irish ...	
,,	,,	JACKSON, 2/Lt. John Henry, 5/Lancashire Fusiliers ...	
,,	,,	WAKELEY, 2/Lt. John Eric Stanley,* 1/Gloucester ...	
,,	13.	ALLEN, 2/Lt. Maurice Reginald, 2/Notts & Derby ...	*Battle of Somme*
,,	,,	REYNOLDS, 2/Lt. Frank, 2/Notts & Derby (T.M.B.) ...	,, ,,
,,	14.	KENNEDY, 2/Lt. John Gilbert, 1/Leicester ...	*Near Ginchy*
,,	,,	MALLOCH, 2/Lt. David, R. Engineers	*Battle of Somme*
,,	,,	SIM, 2/Lt. Lancelot George Earle. 1/Grenadier Guards	*Near Flers*
,,	15.	ARBUTHNOT, Lieut. John, 2/Grenadier Guards ...	*Battle of Somme*
,,	,,	DICKINSON, 2/Lt. Lionel St. Clair, 1/London ...	*Near High Wood*
,,	,,	GRISSELL, 2/Lt. Francis, 5/Coldstream Guards ...	
,,	,,	HILLS, 2/Lt. Malcolm Arthur, 1/East Kent ...	*Battle of Somme*
,,	,,	HOOLE, 2/Lt. Geoffrey,* 15/London	*Near High Wood*
,,	,,	JOHNSON, 2/Lt. Francis Hugh, 19/London ...	,, ,,
,,	,,	KENNEDY, 2/Lt. Lancelot R. A. E., 8/London ...	,, ,,
,,	,,	LANGFORD, 2/Lt. John Joseph, 18/K.R.R.C. ...	*Near Flers*

* *Died of Wounds.*

ROLL OF HONOUR

1916.
Sept. 15.	LIVERMORE, 2/Lt. Ernest Bernard, 24/London ...		*Battle of Somme*
,, ,,	NELSON, 2/Lt. Harry, 20/London		
,, ,,	NIVISON, 2/Lt. Robert Butler, 21/K.R.R.C. ...		*Near Flers*
,, ,,	ROWSON, 2/Lt. Tom Hollingworth, 19/London ..		*Near High Wood*
,, ,,	TERRY, Capt. John Norman, 6/London		*Near Flers*
,, ,,	TOWSE, Capt. William Norman, 4/London ...		*Near High Wood*
,, 16.	BAXTER, 2/Lt. Rowland Percival, 5/Border		,, *Martinpuich*
,, ,,	HOBBS, 2/Lt. Geoffrey Harold Chapman, 7/Dorset (6/Somerset L.I.)		
,, ,,	MAIDEN, 2/Lt. Albert Augustus, 6/Yorkshire L.I. ...		
,, ,,	MATTHEWS, 2/Lt. Edward Philip,* 8/Rifle Brigade ...		
,, ,,	MAXWELL, 2/Lt. Wellwood,* 20/London		*Near High Wood*
,, ,,	PETLEY, Capt. Hugh, 1/London		*Battle of Somme*
,, 18.	FELTHAM, 2/Lt. Alan, 5/Border		
,, 19.	MUNRO, Lieut. Ronald George,* ✠ 18/London (1/Irish Gds)		*B. of Somme (15th)*
,, 22.	STONE, 2/Lt. Oliver John, R.F.A.		*In France*
,, 25.	FLOWER, Lieut. Alfred Chegwin,* 4/Grenadier Guards		
,, ,,	GRIMSDELL, 2/Lt. Reginald Edward, 4/London ...		
,, ,,	LOCK, 2/Lt. James Alexander, 31(10)Northumb. Fusiliers		
,, 26.	CARD, 2/Lt. Arthur Henry, ✠ 12/Middlesex ...		
,, ,,	WILKINSON, 2/Lt. Ambrose Joseph, 6(12)Middlesex ...		
,, 27.	GIBSON, 2/Lt. Alewyn Morland,* 6/West Yorks ...		*Near Thiepval*
,, ,,	RICHARDS, 2/Lt. Charles Walker, 8/Liverpool ...		,, *Flers*
,, ,,	ROBERTS, 2/Lt. Thomas William, 7/R. West Kent ...		*At Schwaben Redoubt*
,, 28.	BENTON, 2/Lt. John Walford, 11/Notts & Derby ...		
,, ,,	BLISS, 2/Lt. Francis Kennard, R.F.A.		*Near Thiepval*
,, 29.	FRICKER, 2/Lt. Edwin, 7/R. West Kent		*At Schwaben Redoubt*
,, 30.	BARTRUM, 2/Lt. Arthur Alan, 8/East Surrey ...		
,, ,,	CLARKE, 2/Lt. Thomas Purcell, 6/York & Lancaster ...		
Oct. 1.	BULL, 2/Lt. Joseph William,* 2/East Lancashire (R.E.)		*Died at Rouen*
,, ,,	CLARKE, 2/Lt. Edwin Alfred,* 20/London		
,, 2.	GUTTERIDGE, 2/Lt. Richard Howard, 9/London ...		
,, ,,	SPINNEY, 2/Lt. Frank,* 2/R. Scots		*Near Salonika*
,, 3.	LLOYD, 2/Lt. Francis Burrows, 2/Devon		
,, 5.	COOK, Capt. Percy Mellows, 18/K.R.R.C. ...		*Near Flers*
,, ,,	GOLDS, 2/Lt. Frank, 11/East Surrey (R. Sussex) ...		,, ,,
,, 7.	BATH, 2/Lt. Reginald Frederick, 10/London ...		*Near le Transloy*
,, ,,	CHRISTMAS, 2/Lt. Edwin Cecil Russell, 18/K.R.R.C.		
,, ,,	DURSTON, 2/Lt. Charles Giles, 12/London ...		
,, ,,	HALL, 2/Lt. Norman de Havilland,* 1/Suffolk ...		*Near Salonika*
,, ,,	LAYCOCK, 2/Lt. Joseph Harris, 18/K.R.R.C. ...		
,, ,,	MADDOCK, 2/Lt. Owen Loftus, 9/London ...		*Near Les Bœufs*
,, ,,	MOSS, 2/Lt. Reginald Barnes Newton, 8/East Kent ...		,, *Guedecourt*
,, ,,	PURVER, Capt. Bernard Arthur, 11/R. West Kent		...*Near Eaucourt L'Abbaye*
,, ,,	RIDGEWAY, 2/Lt. Henry Collinson, 7/London ...		*Near Warlencourt*
,, ,,	RIDGWAY, 2/Lt. William, 18/K.R.R.C. ...		
,, ,,	STUART, 2/Lt. William Esme Montague, 6/R. West Kent		*Near Guedecourt*
,, ,,	WILLIAMS, 2/Lt. Harold Edward, 1/London ...		

* *Died of Wounds.*

ARTISTS' RIFLES, 1916.

1916.			
Oct.	7.	WILLIS, 2/Lt. Cyril Louis, 12/London	*Near Les Bœufs*
,,	8.	GLOVER, 2/Lt. Cyril John,* 10/London	,, ,,
,,	,,	GLUCKMAN, Lieut. Philip, 25/London	
,,	,,	KILNER, 2/Lt. Charles Usher,* 1/Suffolk	*Near Salonica (7th)*
,,	,,	LUDLOW, 2/Lt. Lionel, 9/London	,, ,,
,,	,,	OAKENFULL, 2/Lt. Herbert Joseph, 10/London	
,,	,,	TURNER, Pte. Penrhyn Godfrey, 22/London	*Eaucourt L'Abbaye*
,,	,,	WARREN, 2/Lt. Alan Rowland, 9/London	
,,	9.	MANN, 2/Lt. Robert Leonard, 3(16)R. Welch Fusiliers	
,,	10.	PARSLOW, 2/Lt. Albert Jack,* 9/London	*Near Les Bœufs*
,,	11.	SANDERSON, Capt. Sydney Charles, 18/London	*…Near Neuville-St.-Vaast*
,,	12.	CLARKE, 2/Lt. Vincent Charles,* 10/Durham L.I.	*Wounded 7th*
,,	13.	COBB, 2/Lt. Reginald, 9/R. Berks	*Near Flers*
,,	,,	PHILLIPS, 2/Lt. Fenton Ellis Stanley, ✠ 3/Devon (R.F.C.)	
,,	16.	CARRÉ, Lieut. Edward Mervyn, 8/Lincoln (R.F.C.)	
,,	18.	PAGE, 2/Lt. John Canler, 9/Norfolk	*Near Guedecourt*
,,	,,	PALMER, 2/Lt. John Stanley,* 2/Durham L.I.	
,,	19.	PAGE, 2/Lt. Thomas Spencer, 9/Norfolk (T.M.B.)	*In France*
,,	,,	MEACOCK, 2/Lt. Robert Hugh,* 19/Durham L.I.	
,,	23.	MARSHALL, 2/Lt. John Hamilton, 2/East Lancashire	
,,	25.	HOARE, Capt. Walter John Gerald, D.S O., 11/S. Fus.	
,,	26.	PEART, Pte. Robert Eustace, 1/Artists	*Accident in France*
,,	27.	JAMES, 2/Lt. Meredith Charles Clifton,* 1/Worcester…	*Near Guedecourt*
Nov.	1.	PERRY, 2/Lt. Kenneth George,* 3/R. Sussex	
,,	3.	ELTHAM, Lieut. Charles William, 1/R. West Surrey	
,,	,,	STYER, Pte. Wilfred Henry, 1/Artists	*Accident in France*
,,	6.	BENNETT, Lieut. Albert Henry, 6/Notts & Derby	
,,	,,	HARRIS, Lieut. Henry James Lawrence, 14/Hampshire	*In France*
,,	7.	COWPER, 2/Lt. Leonard Harris,* 32(20)Northumb. Fus.	*Died*
,,	8.	OPPENHEIMER, Lieut. Lehman James, 23/London	*Accident*
,,	,,	VERNON, 2/Lt. Frank Lawson, 12/Loyal N. Lancs.	*Died on the Doiran Front*
,,	9.	STOODLEY, 2/Lt. Percy Ballard, 2/Wilts.	*Near Givenchy*
,,	10.	ANDERSON, 2/Lt. William Wallace, R.F.A.	
,,	11.	DUDLEY, 2/Lt. Noel Montague Charles,* 5/Liverpool…	
,,	13.	REDDICK, Sub-Lt. George Adam, R.N.V.R.	*Near Beaumont-Hamel*
,,	,,	STEDMAN, 2/Lt. William Walter Thomas, 18/London	*In France*
,,	,,	WAGNER, Sub-Lt. Caspar Henry Granville, R.N.V.R.	
,,	14.	BOYS, Lieut. Richard Harvey, 2/Bedford	
,,	,,	WILKINSON, 2/Lt. William Donald, 5/Essex (13/R. B.)	
,,	17.	WALTON, 2/Lt. Leon Maitland, 4/Loyal N. Lancs.	*In Flanders*
,,	18.	BARTHOLOMEW, 2/Lt. Benjamin James, 4/Cameron H.	
,,	,,	BOLTON, 2/Lt. Gilbert Benson, 8/N. Stafford	*Near Grandcourt*
,,	,,	JAMES, 2/Lt. Samuel Forest, 8/Gloucester…	
,,	22.	HORSEY, 2/Lt. Cyril James, 7/S. Lancashire	
,,	23.	KERR, 2/Lt. Robert Thomas, 4/York & Lancaster	*In France*
,,	26.	COX, Pte. Francis Daulman,* 1/Artists	,, ,,
,,	27.	DESLANDES, 2/Lt. Denis George, 7/East Surrey	

* Died of Wounds.

ROLL OF HONOUR

1916.
Nov. 27.	HEDGECOCK, Pte. Samuel, Artists			*Died*
,, 29.	COLLEY, 2/Lt. Douglas James, 6/Liverpool			
,, 30.	BREDE, Pte. Charles Robert, 1/Artists			*Died*
Dec. 2.	WATKINS, Pte. James Henry, 1/Artists (R. W. Kent)			
,, 18.	MERRETT, 2/Lt. Arthur Edwin, 3/Hampshire			*In France*
,, 20.	CALLANAN, 2/Lt. Michael, 3/R. Munster Fusiliers			
,, ,,	KING-STEPHENS, 2/Lt. Lionel Eustace,* 8/Notts & Derby			
,, ,,	READ, 2/Lt. Leonard St. Clair, 11/Essex			*Died while P.O.W.*
,, 23.	CARNE, 2/Lt. Maxwell Halford,* 2/D.C.L.I.			
,, 26.	DAWS, 2/Lt. Harold, 10/Durham L.I.			*Near Arras*
,, 30.	SMITH, 2/Lt. John Richard Gutteridge,* 8/Northumb. Fus.			

1917.

Jan. 10.	ANNAND, Capt. Alan Young, 1/Highland L.I.			*At Kut-el-Amara*
,, ,,	LOFTING, 2/Lt. Charles Edgar, 8/Northumb. Fusiliers			*In France*
,, 11.	WOOD, Capt. John Patrick Hamilton, 22/Manchester			
,, 12.	THIERRY, 2/Lt. Frederick George, R.F.C.			,, ,,
,, 13.	THOMPSON, 2/Lt. Frank Dickinson, 15/London			*In France*
,, 16.	THOMPSON, 2/Lt. Richard Seward, 18/London			
,, 21.	BALL, 2/Lt. Thomas Harold, General List			*Accident*
,, ,,	WILLIAMS, 2/Lt. Harold Osborne, 13/Middlesex			
,, 24.	STIVEN, 2/Lt. Albert, 2/R. Scots Fusiliers			*Near Martinpuich*
,, 25.	CALLENDER, Capt. George Wilfred, 13/Worcester			*At Kut-el-Amara*
,, 26.	FERGUSON, 2/Lt. Douglas Chalmers,* 10/Highland L.I.			*At Rouen*
,, ,,	PHILLIPS, 2/Lt. Reginald Gurwen, 8/East Kent			
,, ,,	SHARPE, 2/Lt. Henry Norman, 3/Leicester (R.F.C.)			*At Croydon*
,, 30.	ELLEN, Capt. Eric Adrian, 2/East Lancashire			
Feb. 4.	UNDERWOOD, 2/Lt. Cyril Charles, 7/Worcester (8/R. Warwick)			
,, 6.	O'MEARA, 2/Lt. Leon Alfred, 3(6)East Lancashire			*At Kut-el-Amara*
,, ,,	THOMPSON, 2/Lt. Cecil Victor, 6/East Lancashire			,, ,,
,, 7.	DRAPER, 2/Lt. Mark Denman, R.F.C.			*Accident*
,, ,,	JACKSON, 2/Lt. Arthur, R.F.C.			*Accident at Netheravon*
,, 10.	LAWRENCE, Pte. Evan Ernest, Artists			*Died*
,, 11.	RIX, Capt. Leslie Gordon, 4/London			*Near Merville*
,, 12.	CURTIS, 2/Lt. Henry Thomas, 24/London			*Near Serre*
,, ,,	GLYNN, 2/Lt. Alfred Henry,* 15/London (Yorkshire L.I.)			,, ,,
,, 14.	TURNER, Pte. Edward Ricketts, Artists			*Died*
,, 15.	VOKES, 2/Lt. Basil, Bucks Bn./Oxford & Bucks L.I.			*Near Peronne*
,, 17.	BIRCH, 2/Lt. Arthur, 6/R. Berks			*Near Grandcourt*
,, ,,	BIRD, 2/Lt. Charles Edwin, 5/Essex (8/Suffolk)			,, *Mireaumont*
,, ,,	COOPER, 2/Lt. George Spencer, 6/Northampton			*In France*
,, 21.	TUCKER, Pte. John d'Anter, Artists (K.O.S.B.)			*Roelincourt, Arras*
,, 23.	SAMSON, Sgt. Clyde Alfred, 1/Artists			*Died*
,, 27.	ADAMS, Lieut. John Bernard Pye,* 1/R. Welch Fusiliers			*At Puisieux-le-Mont*

* *Died of Wounds.*

1917.			
Feb. 27.	BULKELEY-HUGHES, Capt. Geo. Montagu Warren, 12/K.R.R.C.	Near Ginchy
,, ,,	MACKAIN, 2/Lt. Henry Fergus, R.F.C.	
,, 28.	ASTINGTON, 2/Lt. Thomas Jeffery, 3/East Surrey	Near Irles
,, ,,	SILMON, 2/Lt. William Osman de Weld, 8/West York	Near Achiet-le-Petit
Mar. 2.	SHIELD, 2/Lt. William James, 6/Liverpool	
,, 4.	BIRTLES, Capt. Rowland Powell, 1/Worcester	Near Bouchavesnes
,, ,,	MAHONEY, Lieut. James,* 9/R. West Surrey	
,, 6.	WHIDBOURNE, Pte. George Warren, 1/Artists	Died at Etaples
,, 7.	MORTER, Pte. Alan Gordon, 1/Artists	Died
,, 9.	CATES, 2/Lt. George Edward, V.C., 2/Rifle Brigade	Near Ham
,, 10.	BRAZIER, 2/Lt. Anthony David Cecil, 1/R. Berks	Near Grevillers
,, 11.	SMITH, 2/Lt. Colin, R.F.C.	Over South Carlton
,, 13.	CURRIE, 2/Lt. James Alexander Vance, 10/London	In France
,, 14.	TAYLOR, 2/Lt. Leonard Frank, 5/S. Stafford	Near Bucquoy
,, 17.	JOHNSON, 2/Lt. William Stanley,* 3(7)East Surrey	,, Arras
,, 21.	LANDER, Pte. John Herbert, 1/Artists	Died
,, 24.	BOUIE, 2/Lt. Jean Augustine Andre, R.F.C.	
,, 25.	CHUTER, Lieut. Harry Athelstan, 2/R. Fusiliers (R.F.C.)	
,, 26.	FRANKENSTEIN, 2/Lt. Oscar Reginald, 5/Welch	At Gaza, Palestine
,, ,,	SPICER, Capt. Robert William, 4/R. West Surrey	,, ,,
,, 30.	DAVIS, 2/Lt. Percy Warren Theo, 1/East Kent	
,, 31.	COATES, Pte. Bertram Nöel, Artists	Died
,, ,,	RATCLIFF, 2/Lt. Sydney Arthur, R.F.A.	
Apr. 1.	COLLINS, 2/Lt. Arthur Duppa, R.F.C.	Near Meaulte
,, 2.	MARGOLIOUTH, 2/Lt. Alfred Henry, 5/Yorkshire L.I. (R.F.C.)	Near Cambrai
,, ,,	MINSHULL, Capt. John Lewis, 3/London	Near Agny
,, ,,	PAPWORTH, 2/Lt. Alfred Wyatt, R.E.	
,, ,,	RICHARDS, 2/Lt. Ernest Harry, 21/Manchester	
,, ,,	TOWERS, 2/Lt. Wilfred Goodwin, 4/Manchester	Near Croisilles
,, ,,	WRIGHT, 2/Lt. Edward Frank Macer, 4/Northumb. Fus.	,, Arras
,, 5.	BLACKBURN, Lieut. Harry Dudley, 1/R. Berks (R.F.C.)	Near La Bassee
,, ,,	HEPPELL, 2/Lt. Henry Denby, 4/R. Berks...	,, Roussoy
,, ,,	MEADE, 2/Lt. Cyril, 5/Gloucester	
,, 6.	DADSWELL, Pte. James Arnold, 1/Artists	Died in France
,, ,,	DAVIES, 2/Lt. Robert Wm. Marengwyn, 22/Northumb. Fus. (R.F.C.)	
,, ,,	DAY, Lieut. William Leonard, 2/Border (R.F.C.)	Near Bois-Bernardi
,, 7.	WILSON, 2/Lt. Harold Benjamin, 18/London	In Ypres Salient
,, 9.	ABERCASIS, 2/Lt. Arthur, 6/Somerset L.I.	Battle of Arras
,, ,,	BARTON, 2/Lt. George Frank, 7/Norfolk	,, ,,
,, ,,	BOLITIIO, 2/Lt. Victor Ayling, Household Battalion	,, ,,
,, ,,	BROWNE, 2/Lt. Langford Kyffin, 25/Northumb. Fusiliers	
,, ,,	CALKIN, 2/Lt. John Ernest, 22/Northumb. Fusiliers	,, ,,
,, ,,	GRIFFEN, 2/Lt. Harold Samuel,* 9/Shropshire L.I.	
,, ,,	HOLLOWAY, Lieut. Leonard, 20/Northumb. Fusiliers	
,, ,,	ISAACS, 2/Lt. Henry Roland, 4/Suffolk	
,, ,,	LEE, 2/Lt. Percy William, 5/Shropshire L.I.	
,, ,,	NOWELL, 2/Lt. Wilfred James, R.F.A.	Battle of Arras

Died of Wounds.

ROLL OF HONOUR

1917.
Apr.	9.	PARKER, 2/Lt. Geoffrey, 10/Loyal N. Lancashire	...	*Near Metz-en-Couture*
,,	,,	PEEBLES, 2/Lt. Percy Norman, 12/London...	...	*Battle of Arras*
,,	,,	PENROSE, Capt. George Alwyn, 8/R. West Surrey	...	*On Vimy Ridge*
,,	,,	PROBERT, 2/Lt. Arthur James, 25/Northumb. Fusiliers		*Battle of Arras*
,,	,,	ROSS, 2/Lt. James Kenneth,* R.F.C. ...	...	*Died while P.O.W.*
,,	,,	THOMAS, 2/Lt. Philip Edward, R.G.A. ...	...	*Battle of Arras*
,,	,,	WEBB, 2/Lt. Arthur Pelham, 5/Shropshire L.I.	...	,, ,,
,,	,,	WILSON, 2/Lt. Charles George Gordon, 9/Scottish Rifles		
,,	10.	McCLARENCE, 2/Lt. Stanley, 27/Northumb. Fusiliers...		*Battle of Arras*
,,	,,	WATERHOUSE, 2/Lt. Gilbert Wilmot,* 6/R. West Kent		
,,	11.	BENNETT, 2/Lt. William Henry, 8/Notts & Derby		
,,	,,	BROUGHTON, 2/Lt. Thomas Dugdale, 7/Yorkshire L I.		*Near Bray*
,,	,,	COPPIN, Capt. Richard Alfred, 6/R. West Surrey	...	*Near Monchy-le-Preux*
,,	,,	GOODMAN, 2/Lt. Joseph, 5/R. Lancaster (L.N. Lancs.)		*Near Bullecourt*
,,	,,	McKIE, 2/Lt. Douglas Hamlin,* 27/Northumb. Fusiliers		
,,	12.	LEMON, 2/Lt. Lionel Theodore, 6/Dorset ...	...	*Battle of Arras*
,,	,,	MACOUART, 2/Lt. John, 12/Royal Scots ...	...	
,,	,,	MOORE, 2/Lt. Albert Reginald, 8/West Yorks	...	
,,	,,	SHAVE, 2/Lt. Leslie Harrie, 6/Dorset ...	...	*Near Arras*
,,	13.	BEADELL, 2/Lt. Alfred George, 4/Gloucester	...	
,,	,,	CROUCH, 2/Lt. William Ballard, R.G.A. ...	...	*Battle of Arras*
,,	,,	GILLESPIE, 2/Lt.Gordon Wood, 9/Middlesex (R.F.C.)		*Presumed K/A on Somme*
,,	,,	TWEEDY, 2/Lt. Gerald Vincent, 11/Border		*At Fayet, near St. Quentin*
,,	14.	BAKER, 2/Lt. Thomas Sidney, 16/London	...	*Near Wancourt*
,,	,,	BENSTEAD, 2/Lt Henry Edwin, 7/London		
,,	,,	BOULTING, 2/Lt. Stanley Ernest, 4/Suffolk (T.M.B.)		*Accident near Ypres*
,,	,,	FENNELL, Pte. Linton Albert Ramsay, Artists		*Died*
,,	,,	GRAY, 2/Lt. Cyrus Keswick, 18/London ...	...	*Battle of Arras*
,,	,,	HARVEY-JAMES, Capt. Arthur Keedwill, 1/East Kent		*Near Loos*
,,	,,	HOBSON, 2/Lt. Geoffrey Hamilton,* 1/Hampshire	...	*Battle of Arras (9th)*
,,	,,	PICKLES, 2/Lt. Harry, 4/Border	...	
,,	,,	RICHENS, Lieut. Richard Ivor,* 18/London	...	*Near Wancourt*
,,	,,	YEATES, Lieut. Stanley Charles, 16/London	...	,, ,,
,,	15.	MITCHELL, Pte. Herbert Arnold, 1/Artists	...	*Died*
,,	,,	PRESCOTT, 2/Lt. Reginald Julius, 18/Lancashire Fusiliers		*Battle of Arras*
,,	16.	DAVIS, 2/Lt. Uriah Philip, 10/London ...	...	*Near Heninel*
,,	17.	SIDDALL, 2/Lt. Thomas Arthur,* 25/London	...	*Battle of Arras (16th)*
,,	,,	TWEDDLE, 2/Lt. William John, 7/Essex (T.M.B)	...	*Near Vermelles*
,,	,,	UNDERWOOD, 2/Lt. John,* 8/Leicester		
,,	,,	VAUGHAN, 2/Lt. Richard Cresswell, 8/R. West Kent		
,,	,,	WILSON, 2/Lt. Cecil Eustace, R.F.C. ...	...	*In France*
,,	18.	HARDIE, 2/Lt. William,* 4(13)Lancashire Fusiliers	...	
,,	19.	DEHN, 2/Lt. Thomas George Rudolph,* 3/Wilts (2/R. Berks)		*Wounded 4th*
,,	,,	GRICE, 2/Lt. Leslie Clark,* R.F.A. ...	...	
,,	,,	WILLIAMSON, 2/Lt. Kenneth Harper,* 7/K.R.R.C.	...	*At Etaples*
,,	20.	RODNEY, 2/Lt. Burnett William, 11/R. West Kent	...	
,,	22.	BESWICK, 2/Lt. John Charles,* 11/R. Lancaster	...	*Died while P.O.W.*

* *Died of Wounds.*

1917.				
Apr.	22.	HEBDEN, 2/Lt. George Spencer, 12/Leicester	..	
,,	,,	O'SULLIVAN, 2/Lt. Horace Alexander, R.G.A.	...	
,,	23.	BRUNSKILL, 2/Lt. John Jesmond, 12(4)Worcester	...	
,,	,,	CHATFIELD-CLARKE, 2/Lt. Horace Y., 2/S. Wales B'drs		*Near Monchy*
,,	,,	CORRIE, 2/Lt. William Ronald, 1/East York	...	*Battle of Arras*
,,	,,	DICKINSON, 2/Lt. Walter Stanley, 8/Leicester	...	
,,	,,	HALCROW, Lieut. Arthur Palmer, 2/Hampshire	...	*Battle of Arras*
,,	,,	JAMES, 2/Lt. Henry Stoddart, 5/Border	... ...	
,,	,,	JOSEPH, 2/Lt. John Rhys, R.F.C.	... ...	*Died*
,,	,,	KARSLAKE, 2/Lt. Harry Howard, 7/Devon (D.C.L.I.)		
,,	,,	OWEN, Capt. John Morris, 2/R. Welch Fusiliers	...	
,,	,,	PEER, 2/Lt. Edmund Faithfull, 4/East Yorks	...	
,,	,,	PHILLIPS, 2/Lt. Reginald, 3(2)S. Wales Borderers	...	*Near Monchy*
,,	,,	SCOTT, 2/Lt. James Francis, 13/Royal Scots	...	*In France*
,,	,,	SHAW, Lieut. Bernard Lynton, 4/R. Welch Fus. (2/S.W.B.)		*Near Monchy*
,,	,,	SNYDER, 2/Lt. Lorne, 2/Hampshire	... ...	
,,	24.	HOWARD, 2/Lt. William Aloysius, 7/K.O.S.B.	...	
,,	,,	LUCKHURST, 2/Lt. William Heartfield, 4/Yorkshire	...	
,,	,,	PEARS, 2/Lt. Norman, 6/Gloucester	... ...	
,,	,,	SCOTT, 2/Lt. Alexander, 13/Highland L.I.	...	
,,	,,	SEATH, Lieut. Douglas Ambrose, 2/Scottish Rifles	...	
,,	25.	BIRD, 2/Lt. Eric James,* 4/Worcester	... ...	
,,	,,	CHAFFEY, Pte. George Frederick, 1/Artists	...	*In France*
,,	,,	GILBERT, Pte. Ernest Alfred, 1/Artists	...	*At Ypres*
,,	,,	HAZEL, 2/Lt. Dudley David Fraser, 6/West Riding	...	*At Ecoust (18th)*
,,	26.	MOORE, Lieut. Francis William,* ✠ 10/Devon	...	
,,	27.	BARTON, 2/Lt. Edwin William, 5/Lancashire Fusiliers		*Died*
,,	,,	CROKER, 2/Lt. Frederick Reginald, 6/Lanc. Fus. (R.F.C.)		*Combat over Lens*
,,	,,	STONIER, Lieut. William John, 2/Bedford (R.F.C.)	...	*Near Lens*
,,	,,	TUFT, Capt. Gerald Hugh, 6/Notts & Derby	...	*Near Hargicourt*
,,	,,	WARRY, 2/Lt. John Lucas,* 8/Notts & Derby	..	
,,	28.	BELL, Lieut. Guy Bayford, 5/Lanc. Fusiliers (M.G.C.)		*Battle of Arras*
,,	,,	ELSOM, 2/Lt. Harold, 1/Lincoln	...	
,,	,,	STONEHOUSE, 2/Lt. Robert Alfred, 4/Loyal N. Lancashire		*Near Gavrelles*
,,	,,	TAYLOR, 2/Lt. Herbert Samuel, Bucks Bn./Oxford & Bucks L.I.		
,,	29.	GIBBS, 2/Lt. Horace Austin, 1/R. Berks	...	
,,	,,	HAYES, Capt. Mortimer Frederick, 8/East Yorks	...	*Near Monchy-le-Preux*
,,	,,	OLVER, Lieut. John Dennis Circuit,✠ R.F.A.	...	*On Vimy Ridge*
,,	30.	HICKSON, Capt. Reginald Davis,* ✠ 9/Essex	...	*Near Monchy-le-Preux*
May	2.	CHOWNE, Capt. Gerald Henry Tilson* 9/East Lancashire		
,,	3.	CLIVELY, 2/Lt. John Harold, 4/York & Lancaster	...	
,,	,,	LAMBERT, Lieut. Philip Felix, ✠ 2/W. Riding	...	*Near Bullecourt*
,,	,,	LOWDER, 2/Lt. Noel Reginald, 1/R. Warwick	...	
,,	,,	MARLOR, Lieut. Eric, 6/W. Riding	... ...	
,,	,,	McGIBNEY, 2/Lt. Francis George, 1/R. Irish Fusiliers		
,,	,,	PASSINGHAM, Lieut. Edward George,✠ 1/Northumb. Fus.		
,,	,,	PATON, 2/Lt. Edward Kesson,* M.G.C.		

* *Died of Wounds.*

ROLL OF HONOUR

1917.
May	3.	SHEEN, 2/Lt. Cyril,* 12/Suffolk	*Wounded 2nd*
,,	,,	SLATER, 2/Lt. John Elwyn, 5/East Lancashire	
,,	,,	STOCK, 2/Lt. John Lancelot Walmesley,* 3/Dorset (Som. L.I.)	*Near Wancourt*
,,	,,	WADE, 2/Lt. George Edward Ahern, 9/Rifle Brigade	
,,	,,	WELSH, 2/Lt. Alexander Thorburn, 4/R. Welch Fus.	
,,	4.	FAUNCH, 2/Lt. Ernest Alfred, R.G.A.	
,,	,,	FOOT, 2/Lt. David Victor, R.F.C.	*Accident over Montrose*
,,	,,	GIBSON, 2/Lt. Cecil Mervyn, 5/York & Lancaster	
,,	,,	HALL, 2/Lt. Joseph Stanley,* 12/East Yorks	
,,	,,	MASON, 2/Lt. George, R.F.C.	*Accident*
,,	,,	SYRETT, 2/Lt. Alfred Montague, 1/R. Welch Fusiliers	*In France*
,,	,,	THEAK, 2/Lt. Horace Leonard,* 11/Essex	
,,	,,	WHITAKER, 2/Lt. Foster, 5/Argyll & Suth'd Highlanders	
,,	6.	SANDFORD, 2/Lt. Charles J. Vavasour, 8/Middlesex	
,,	7.	WARHAM, 2/Lt. Joseph,* 5(8)K.R.R.C.	*Battle of Arras*
,,	8.	MASSIE, 2/Lt. Sidney Edward, 1/Somerset L.I.	
,,	,,	McCORMICK, 2/Lt. Harry,* 5/East Lancs. (M.G.C.)	*Died while P.O.W.*
,,	,,	SANDOE, 2/Lt. Montague William A., 11/Devon	*Near Bullecourt*
,,	,,	STEPHENSON, 2/Lt. Hubert Victor, 1/D.C.L.I.	
,,	9.	SMITH, 2/Lt. Gordon Hamilton, 8/Devon	*Near Bullecourt*
,,	,,	TREADWAY, 2/Lt. Harold Ligouer, 15/R. Warwick	*Near Oppy*
,,	12.	KNIGHT, 2/Lt. Edward James, 7/Lan. Fusiliers	
,,	13.	BARKER, 2/Lt. Theodore, 22/Manchester	
,,	,,	MERCHANT, 2/Lt. Arthur Douglas, R.F.C.	*Accident*
,,	14.	HOLM, Lieut. Frank Diederick, R.E.	
,,	15.	COSSAR, 2/Lt. Norman Thomson, 7/Rifle Brigade	
,,	19.	ARMSTRONG, 2/Lt. Leonard William, 3/Border	*Near Monchy-le-Preux*
,,	,,	BENNETT, 2/Lt. John Nichol, R.G.A.	
,,	,,	MACDONALD, 2/Lt. Alan Leslie, 8/Manchester	*Near La Bassee*
,,	,,	WARNER, Lieut. Bernard Oldershaw, 3(1)Essex	*Near Monchy-le-Preux*
,,	20.	BEAUMONT, 2/Lt. Charles Leslie, R.F.C.	
,,	,,	LISTER, 2/Lt. John Curtis, R.F.A.	*Battle of Arras*
,,	,,	SMITH, 2/Lt. Harold Benjamin,* 7/London	
,,	22.	KELLER, Lieut. Francis Frederick,* 6/London	
,,	,,	WILLIAMS, Lieut. Henry Evan Vincent,* 2/London	*Near Bullecourt*
,,	23.	CLARK, Capt. Walter Llewellyn, 15/Middlesex (R.F.C.)	
,,	,,	GOODYEAR, 2/Lt. Frederick,* 2/Essex	*Near Fampoux (3rd)*
,,	24.	COPE, 2/Lt. Gerald Quin,* 9/Manchester	*Wounded 5th*
,,	,,	GARDNER, Pte. Richard Percy,* 1/Artists	*In France*
,,	25.	JOHNSON, 2/Lt. Stanley Morrell, R.F.C.	*Accident over Dover*
,,	26.	CAMPBELL, Capt. Guy, ✠ M.G.C.	*Died*
,,	,,	COCK, Pte. Edward Millar, 1/Artists	*In France*
,,	,,	MACANDREW, Pte. William Forsyth, 2/Artists	*Died*
,,	,,	SIMPSON, 2/Lt. Rolf, 6(18)K.R.R.C.	*Near Ypres*
,,	27.	COATES, 2/Lt. Sidney, R.F.C.	
,,	29.	WALKER, 2/Lt. Vernon Lee, 8/East Lancashire	
,,	,,	WAY, 2/Lt. Robert Edward Allen,* 10/Loyal N. Lancs.	*In France*

* Died of Wounds.

R. P. HALLOWES, V.C. [pp. 44, 319.

Copyright.] [Col. WALTER C. HORSLEY.
NOTRE DAME DE BREBIÈRE, ALBERT, 1917.

1917.				
May 31.		HUGHES, 2/Lt. Ronald Baskerville, R.F.C.		*Accident at South Carlton*
,,	,,	JOHNSON, 2/Lt. Frederick Blacktin, 13/Rifle Brigade		*Battle of Arras*
June	1.	ROWLAND, 2/Lt. William Ronand, 17/London	...	*In the Ypres Salient*
,,	,,	THUELL, 2/Lt. William Johnson, R.F.C.	...	
,,	2.	LEAKE, Capt. Geo. Ernest Arthur, D.S.O.,* 4/London		*Bullecourt (May 15)*
,,	,,	SAYERS, Lieut. Horace Geo. David, 23/London	...	*Drowned at Sea*
,,	,,	SIMMONDS, 2/Lt. Austin Gundry, R.F.A.	... ...	*Acc. Drowned*
,,	3.	FOSTER, 2/Lt. Frank Hawley, R.F.C.	... ...	
,,	,,	WARNER, 2/Lt. Henry James, 6/Northampton	...	*Near Cherisy*
,,	4.	MITCHELL, Lieut. John Leishman,* 18/London	...	
,,	,,	PRICE, 2/Lt. Frank Maurice, 5/Lincoln	... ...	*Near Arras*
,,	,,	TYNDALL, 2/Lt. James, 19(10)London	... ...	
,,	5.	DONALDSON, 2/Lt. William, 12/R. Scots	... ...	
,,	,,	ELIAS, 2/Lt. Hywel James, 31/Northumberland Fusiliers		*Near Rouex*
,,	,,	WILLIAMS, 2/Lt. Roland Vaughan, R.F.C.	...	
,,	6.	ARBERRY, 2/Lt. Ernest Edward, R.F.C.	...	*Near Dunkirk*
,,	,,	MACFAYDEN, 2/Lt. John Craig, R.F.A.	... ...	*On the Messines Ridge*
,,	,,	SCATTERGOOD, 2/Lt. Tom Victor,* 21/Northumb. Fus.		,, ,,
,,	7.	BOLLAND, 2/Lt. Fredk. William Henry, 26/R. Fusiliers		
,,	,,	CROOM, 2/Lt. William Charles, 10(6)London	...	
,,	,,	DEAN, 2/Lt. Reginald Evan, 10/London	... ...	*Battle of Messines*
,,	,,	FARADAY, 2/Lt. Roy, 6/London (M G.C.)	...	,, ,,
,,	,,	HENDERSON, 2/Lt. Eric, 8/London	... ...	,, ,,
,,	,,	SILVESTER, 2/Lt. Reginald, 20/London	... ...	,, ,,
,,	,,	UPTON, 2/Lt. Roger Maitland, 4/Durham L.I.	...	,, ,,
,,	8.	STONE, 2/Lt. Harold, 23/London	... ...	,, ,,
,,	9.	ADDIS, 2/Lt. David Malcolm,* 6/R. Fusiliers	...	
,,	10.	DUNN, 2/Lt. Ernest George, 10/Liverpool (M.G.C.)	...	*Near Arras*
,,	,,	STEPHENS, 2/Lt. Llewellyn, R.F.C.	... ...	*Accident*
,,	11.	ANDERSON, 2/Lt. Richard Wm. Lawrence, R.F.C.	...	
,,	,,	ROOTS, 2/Lt Percy William, 7/London	... ...	
,,	12.	O'DONNELL, 2/Lt. Anthony Patrick, 4/York & Lancs.		
,,	14.	CALDER, 2/Lt. William Paul, 18/K.R.R.C.	...	
,,	16.	HARRIS, 2/Lt. Harold Maltby, 3/London Yeomanry	...	
,,	,,	MARGETSON, 2/Lt. Emil Alexander, R.F.C.	...	*Accident*
,,	,,	QUARRELL, 2/Lt. Charles Hubert, 13/Northumb. Fusiliers		
,,	,,	SAVAGE, 2/Lt. William Leslie, R.F.C.	... ...	*Accident*
,,	17.	BAILEY, 2/Lt Louis John, R.F.C.	... ...	*In France*
,,	18.	NEWTON, Lieut. Murray Edell, 17/London (R.F.C.)		*Battle of Messines*
,,	,,	WELTER, 2/Lt. Leslie Dingman, 17/K R.R.C.	...	
,,	19.	HALSEY, 2/Lt. Eric Charles, 7/London	... ...	
,,	20.	BRADFIELD, Cpl. William Leslie,* 1/Artists	... ...	*In France*
,,	21.	HARRINGTON, 2/Lt. Walter, 5/Welch	... ...	
,,	26.	GRACE, 2/Lt. Alexander A. G., R.F.C.	... ...	*Accident*
,,	,,	ROSS, 2/Lt. Peter C., R.F.C.	... ...	
,,	27.	RICHARDS, 2/Lt. Arthur,* 1/Monmouth	... ...	*At Lievin*
,,	28.	HUNSTONE, 2/Lt. George Neil, R.F.C.	... ...	

* *Died of Wounds.*

ROLL OF HONOUR

1917.
June 28.	Rew, 2/Lt. Douglas Jolland, 11/Essex			Near Loos
,,	,,	Rumilly, 2/Lt. Alfred Henry R.,* 7/Worcester (R. Warwick)		
July	1.	Cowley, 2/Lt. Alexander, 8/Notts & Derby		Near Lens
,,	3.	Frampton, 2/Lt. John Reginald, 13/Gloucester		,, Ypres
,,	,,	Littler, 2/Lt. Tom, R.F.C.		Combat over Bailleul
,,	4.	Newton, Lieut. Walter Claude, 4/Loyal N. Lancashire		
,,	5.	Moss, 2/Lt. William Thomas Gregory, R.F.C.		Accident
,,	6.	Lawson, 2/Lt. Arthur Cyril,* 7/Rifle Brigade		
,,	7.	Fairbairn, 2/Lt. Maurice, 11/R. Lancaster		
,,	,,	Tardugo, 2/Lt. Ray, 17/R. Welch Fusiliers (R.F.C.)		
,,	,,	Wright, 2/Lt. Cecil Lawrence, R.G.A.		
,,	,,	Young, 2/Lt. John Edward Rostron, R.F.C.		Combat over London
,,	9.	Elliot, 2/Lt. Nichol, 1/Northampton (T.M.B.)		Near Lombartzyde
,,	,,	Forbes, 2/Lt. Lawrence,* 5/London		Near Bullecourt
,,	,,	Thornton, 2/Lt. Herbert Boucher, 9/London (M.G.C.)		
,,	10.	Lockhart, 2/Lt. Reginald Frank,* 13/London (M.G.C.)		
,,	,,	Smith, 2/Lt. Geoffrey Harold,* 1/Northampton		Near Lombartzyde
,,	12.	Bishop, 2/Lt. Frank Ernest, R.F.C.		Near Ypres
,,	,,	Ellis, 2/Lt. Guy Stuart, R.F.C.		,, ,,
,,	,,	Wager, 2/Lt. Wilson Stanley, 16/Northumberland Fusiliers		
,,	13.	Bull, Capt. Ronald John Howard, 16/London (R.E.)		Accident
,,	14.	Smith, 2/Lt. Thomas Edmund,* R.F.C.		At Douai
,,	16.	Cayford, 2/Lt. George Everitt, R.F.C.		
,,	17.	Dodd, Lieut. Ernest John, R.F.A.		Near Ypres
,,	18.	Owen, 2/Lt. Herbert Ernest Malcolm, R.F.C.		At Scampton
,,	20.	Shipstone, L/Cpl. Francis Edgar, 1/Artists		Oppy Wood
,,	21.	Ping, 2/Lt. Alan Roy, 3/Worcester		Near Ypres
,,	22.	King, Lieut. Eric George Lauder, 1/Grenadier Guards	Bluett Farm, Ypres	
,,	,,	Morton, Lieut. William Cattell,* ✠ R.F.A.		
,,	23.	Littler, 2/Lt. Frank, 3(8)South Lancashire		
,,	,,	Morris, 2/Lt. Tom Bernard, 5/R. Welch Fusiliers		Near Ypres
,,	,,	Noakes, 2/Lt. Harold Thomas, R.F.C.		In Belgium
,,	24.	Collins, Pte. Arthur Leslie, 1/Artists		Oppy Wood
,,	,,	Dunn, Pte. Henry Adolphus, 1/Artists		,, ,,
,,	,,	Spinks, Pte. Sidney Morris, 1/Artists		,, ,,
,,	25.	Curtis, 2/Lt. Henry Neville, R.F.C.		In France
,,	27.	Froud, Lieut. Harold William,* 5/Durham L.I.		
,,	28.	Fowler, Capt. Francis Archibald, R.G.A.		Near Armentieres
,,	,,	Ottley, 2/Lt. Raymon Gasgoyne, 3/Leicester (R.A F.)		
,,	30.	Trevarthen, Pte. John Marshall, Artists		Died
,,	31.	Andrews, 2/Lt. Reginald, 7/Lancashire Fusiliers		
,,	,,	Bailey, 2/Lt. Herbert Packer, ✠ 12/East Surrey		Near Hollebeke
,,	,,	Betts, 2/Lt. Thomas Walter, 17/Notts and Derby		
,,	,,	Cottle, Lieut. Walter Edward Worsdale, Grenadier Gds.(M.G.C.)	Pilkem Ridge	
,,	,,	Davies, 2/Lt. William Lloyd, 13/R. Welch Fusiliers		,, ,,
,,	,,	Eaton, 2/Lt. Harold, 13/Gloucester		3rd Battle of Ypres
,,	,,	Edgar, 2/Lt. Bernard Ray, M.G.C.		,, ,,

* Died of Wounds.

1917.			
July 31.		FORD, 2/Lt. Clement William, 4/R. Lancaster	*3rd Battle of Ypres*
,,	,,	KENT, Lieut. Lionel Victor,* 3(5)S. Wales Borderers	*Near Oostaverne*
,,	,,	KIRKUS, Capt. Cuthbert Hayward, R.G.A.	
,,	,,	MARTIN, 2/Lt. William Howard, 2/R. Welch Fusiliers	*On Pilkem Ridge*
,,	,,	MATHER, 2/Lt. Volney, 12/Loyal N. Lancashire	
,,	,,	SCOTT, 2/Lt. Cecil, 7/Essex	*3rd Battle of Ypres*
,,	,,	SOWERBY, 2/Lt. Victor Holgate* 2/Lincoln	,, ,,
,,	,,	TARRANT, 2/Lt. Henry Geoffrey Nelson, ✠ 6/R. Berks	
,,	,,	THRUPP, 2/Lt. Maurice, 1/Grenadier Guards	*On Pilkem Ridge*
,,	,,	WATERSON, 2/Lt. Frederick Paris, 17/Notts & Derby	*3rd Battle of Ypres*
Aug. 1.		DOHERTY 2/Lt. Patrick,* 1/R. Irish Rifles	
,,	,,	JONES, 2/Lt. Clifford, 15/R. Welch Fusiliers	*Near Ypres*
,,	,,	KILVERT, 2/Lt. Harry,* 9/R. Welch Fusiliers	
,,	,,	WILSON, Capt. George Andrew Glanville, 6/R. Sussex (K.R.R.C.)	*Nr. Hollebeke*
,,	2.	ALLEN, 2/Lt. Mervyn Richard William, 7/Norfolk	*Near Monchy*
,,	4.	DENNY, 2/Lt. Ernest, 15/London (K.R.R.C.)	
,,	,,	KENT, 2/Lt. Harold,* 3(8)S. Wales Borderers	
,,	7.	MILLARD, 2/Lt. Alfred George, 3(9)East Surrey	*Near Klein Zillebeke*
,,	8.	DICKSON, Pte. James,* 1/Artists	*Oppy Wood (July 30)*
,,	,,	GJEMS, 2/Lt. Albert Ole Moller, 2/R. Fusiliers	*Near Boesinghe*
,,	,,	REID, 2/Lt. Archibald David,* 5(4)Middlesex	*In France (2nd)*
,,	9.	SMITH, 2/Lt. Sydney Newman, 7/Suffolk	*Near Monchy-le-Preux*
,,	10.	DIX, 2/Lt. Cyril Bernard, 8/East Surrey	*Zillebeke*
,,	11.	BASELEY, 2/Lt. Albert Laurence, 6/Lancashire Fusiliers	*3rd Battle of Ypres*
,,	,,	HOSKEN, 2/Lt. Henry Richard, M.G.C.	
,,	12.	BIRD, 2/Lt. Eric Stephen, 8/R. Irish Fusiliers	*Monchy-le-Preux*
,,	14.	CHAPMAN, 2/Lt. Montague Gerald H. 10/Rifle Brigade	*Near Langemarcke*
,,	,,	HIBBERT, 2/Lt. Arthur James, R.F.A.	*Drowned, Boulogne*
,,	15.	HARGREAVES, 2/Lt. Cyril Augustus,* R.F.C.	
,,	16.	BILBY, 2/Lt. Eustace John, 6(2)Middlesex	
,,	,,	BOWMAN, 2/Lt. Claude Herbert, 4/Oxford & Bucks L.I.	*3rd Battle of Ypres*
,,	,,	CAHILL, Capt. John Archibald, ✠ 2/R. Berks	*Near Zonnebeke*
,,	,,	COX, 2/Lt. George Beckett, 7/London	*Near Langemarcke*
,,	,,	CRISP, 2/Lt. Cyril Bright,* 7/Somerset L.I.	
,,	,,	CROSLAND, 2/Lt. William Philip, 2/West Yorks	
,,	,,	ENNIS, 2/Lt. Reginald Joseph, 1/R. Irish Rifles	
,,	,,	GRANGER, Capt. Ernest Everys Wyatt, 9/Lancs. Fusiliers	*3rd Battle of Ypres*
,,	,,	MACKAY, 2/Lt. Gordon, 24/Middlesex (M.G.C.)	*In France*
,,	,,	MOLYNEUX, 2/Lt. James Herbert, 12/K.R.R.C.	
,,	,,	MUNSEY, 2/Lt. William Frederick, 12/K.R.R.C.	
,,	,,	RAVENSCROFT, 2/Lt. Richard Birkbeck, 1/Herts (8th Middlesex)	
,,	,,	STEEL, 2/Lt. Norman, 5/Gloucester	*3rd Battle of Ypres*
,,	17.	BRANSON, Pte. Arthur Henry, 1/Artists	*Oppy Wood*
,,	,,	BROWN, 2/Lt. Edward John, R.F.C.	
,,	,,	FITZSIMMONS, Pte. Cyril Hugh, 1/Artists	*Oppy Wood*
,,	,,	GARRAWAY, Pte. William Gloster, 1/Artists	,, ,,
,,	,,	MARLOW, 2/Lt. Charles Dwyer, 8/R. Dublin Fusiliers	*Langemarcke*

* Died of Wounds.

ROLL OF HONOUR

1917.
Aug. 17.	NEWCOMBE, 2/Lt. Clarke Charles Upham,	5(10) Worcester		*3rd Battle of Ypres*
,, 18.	ABBOTT, 2/Lt. Thomas Walker, R.F.C.	...	...	
,, ,,	CLAYDON, Pte. Douglas Christie, 1/Artists		...	*Oppy Wood*
,, ,,	HAREL, 2/Lt. Louis Octave, R.F.C.	...	...	
,, ,,	PENNY, 2/Lt. Bernard Willoughby,	2/R. Fusiliers	...	*3rd Battle of Ypres*
,, 19.	GREEN, 2/Lt. Alan, 21/West Yorks	...	...	*Near Arras*
,, ,,	MORGAN, 2/Lt. George Elton,* 15/Welch	...	...	
,, 20.	FAIRBAIRNS, 2/Lt. Joseph Maurice. ✠ R.F.A.		...	*Near Ypres*
,, ,,	TRESTRAIL, Pte. Edward Mitchell,* 1/Artists		...	*Oppy Wood*
,, ,,	WINSER, 2/Lt. Frank Edwards, R.F.C.	...	...	*Near Lens*
,, 21.	AFFLECK, Cpl. Bertrand Percy,* 1/Artists	...	...	*Oppy Wood*
,, ,,	GILL, 2/Lt. William Rey, Bucks Bn./Oxford & Bucks L.I.			*Near Wieltje*
,, 22.	TYSON, 2/Lt. Claude Richmond, Bucks Bn./Oxford & Bucks L.I.			*In Flanders*
,, 23.	BARRETT, 2/Lt. Arthur Edward, 8(21)K.R.R.C.		...	*Near Sanctuary Wood*
,, ,,	BECKINGSALE, 2/Lt. John Edgar, 4/D.C.L.I.		...	*Near Ypres*
,, ,,	COLLEY, 2/Lt. Ernest Vincent,* 16/R. Fusiliers (Tank Corps)			
,, ,,	DUDLEY, 2/Lt. Herbert Edward, 9(16)Somerset L.I.		...	*Near Inverness Copse*
,, ,,	FOSTER, 2/Lt. Franklin James, R.F.C.	...	...	
,, ,,	McCALL, 2/Lt. Archibald,* ✠ 4/K.O.S.B.	...	...	*3rd Battle of Ypres*
,, ,,	WRIGHT, 2/Lt. Walter Whitmore, R.G.A.	...	...	*In Belgium*
,, 24.	BOURDILLON, Major Thomas Louis, ✠ 8/K.R.R.C.		...	*Near Sanctuary Wood*
,, ,,	DALE, Pte. Owen Brownlow, 1/Artists		...	*Oppy Wood*
,, ,,	WILLS, Pte. Cuthbert Hugh Clement, 1/Artists		...	*,, ,,*
,, 25.	JONES, 2/Lt. Reginald Rees, *D.S.O.*, 1/Welsh Guards			*Near Langemarcke*
,, ,,	LEWIS, Pte. David,* 1/Artists	...	...	*Oppy Wood (July 28)*
,, ,,	POCOCK, 2/Lt. Raglan Lionel Alfred, 8/East Lancashire			*Near Wytschaete*
,, 27.	BEAVON, 2/Lt. Donald James, 4/Gloucester		...	
,, ,,	HADLEY, 2/Lt. Ernest Sydney, 4/Gloucester		...	
,, ,,	HEMMING, 2/Lt. Jesse Clifford, 8/Worcester		...	
,, ,,	TURNER, 2/Lt. William Ernest, 7/Worcester		...	*Near St. Julian*
,, 30.	BAKER, 2/Lt. Herbert Norman, 1/Herts (2/Nigerian R.)			*d. Wuranzi, E. Africa*
,, 31.	FORSYTH, 2/Lt. James Carson, 1/Worcester		...	
,, ,,	MASTERS, 2/Lt. Charles William, 5(8)R. Fusiliers		...	*Near Monchy*
Sept. 2.	LARCOMBE, 2/Lt. Harry Reginald R., 6/R. Fusiliers		...	*At Dover*
,, 4.	BARBER, Capt. Bradley King Bell, 1/Northumb. Fus. (R.F.C.)			
,, ,,	WIGHTMAN, 2/Lt. John Francis, R.F.C.	...	...	*Near Bapaume*
,, 6.	BIRD, 2/Lt. Arthur Leonard, 5/R. Warwick		...	*,, Wieltje*
,, ,,	PROCTOR, Lieut. George Henry Vincent, 8/Lancashire Fus.			*,, Westhoek*
,, ,,	RUSHMORE, 2/Lt. Ernest Reginald, 4(11)Lancashire Fus.			*,, ,,*
,, 13.	HILL, 2/Lt. Alfred, 5/N Stafford	...	...	
,, 14.	BRIGGS, 2/Lt. William Lonsdale,* 1/R. Lancaster (Lancs. Fus.)			*In Belgium*
,, ,,	GENT, 2/Lt. George Edward, R.F.A.	...	...	*3rd Battle of Ypres*
,, 15.	ALBURY, 2/Lt. Norman Howard, R.F.C.	...	...	*In France*
,, ,,	DANN, 2/Lt. Henry Norman Groves, R.F.C.		...	*Near St. Omer*
,, ,,	MOORE, 2/Lt. Kenneth James, 3(11)Essex	...	...	*,, Loos*
,, ,,	PALMER, 2/Lt. William Samuel Hudson, R.F.C.		...	*Accident*
,, 16.	HUMPHRIES, 2/Lt. Leslie Glendower, R.F.C.		...	*Near Ypres*

* *Died of Wounds.*

ARTISTS' RIFLES, 1917.

1917.			
Sept. 16.	LASCELLES, Pte. Richard Mark, 1/Artists ...	...	*Oppy Wood*
,, 19.	CROCKER, Lieut. Joseph, 5/West Riding ...	...	*In France*
,, ,,	WILLIAMS, 2/Lt. Maxwell Henry, 17/London	...	
,, ,,	WILLIAMS, 2/Lt. William James, ✠ 16/R. Welch Fus.	*Near Erquinghem, Lys*	
,, 20.	ADAMS, 2/Lt. Arthur Marston,* ✠ 9/Liverpool	...	*In Flanders*
,, ,,	ADAMS, 2/Lt. Caleb Henry, 10/R. West Surrey	..	*3rd Battle of Ypres*
,, ,,	EDWARDS, 2/Lt. Griffith Oliver, ✠ 11/Northumb. Fusiliers		
,, ,,	FULLER, 2/Lt. Ernest Paget, 4/R. West Surrey	...	
,, ,,	GREEVES, 2/Lt. Arthur F. Wellesley,* 8/North Stafford...	*3rd Battle of Ypres*	
,, ,,	HUGH-JONES, Capt. Kenneth Herbert, 12/Rifle Brigade	*Near Langemarcke*	
,, ,,	JONES, 2/Lt. Llewellyn Price, 9/Welch ...	...	*Near the Menin Road*
,, ,,	MATTHEWS, 2/Lt. Richard Malcolm, 9/Yorks	...	
,, ,,	OATES, 2/Lt. Herbert Prudent, 5/Liverpool	..	*Near the Menin Road*
,, ,,	THOMAS, 2/Lt. Lionel G. Theophilus, 5/Welch (M.G.C.)	,,	,,
,, ,,	WARD, 2/Lt. Dudley Theophilus, 5/London	..	*Near Langemarcke*
,, ,,	WILLIAMS, Lieut. Francis Stanley, 17(8)Notts & Derby	*3rd Battle of Ypres*	
,, 21.	BRACEWELL, 2/Lt. Harry, 17/Notts & Derby	...	,, ,,
,, ,,	CAVE, 2/Lt. Joseph,* 11/West Yorks	...	,, ,,
,, ,,	Low, Pte. Howard St. John, 1/Artists	...	*Died*
,, 22.	WILDE, Pte. Charles, 1/Artists ...	...	*Oppy Wood (17th)*
,, 23.	GARVIN, 2/Lt. William Miles, 1/Essex		
,, ,,	McGIBBON, 2/Lt. William Patrick, 4/Durham L.I.	...	*3rd Battle of Ypres*
,, 25.	CHARMAN, 2/Lt. John Ewart,* 4/R. Sussex ...		*(P.O.W.)*
,, ,,	CROOK, Capt. Leslie Arthur, ✠ 2/R. West Surrey	...	
,, ,,	RAPLEY, 2/Lt. William Godfrey, 1/Middlesex	...	
,, ,,	WORSTENHOLME, 2/Lt. John, R.F.C.	...	
,, 26.	BATCHELOR, 2/Lt. Edward, 24/London	...	*In Belgium*
,, ,,	MORGAN, 2/Lt. Daniel Phillips, 1/Worcester	...	*In France*
,, ,,	RATHBONE, 2/Lt. Thomas Ford, 5/N. Stafford	...	
,, ,,	ROBERTS, 2/Lt. Gavern Brooke, R.F.C.	...	
,, ,,	THOMPSON, 2/Lt. Harold Victor, R.F.C.	...	
,, ,,	WOOD, 2/Lt. Edwin Leonard, 3(1)R. Scots Fusiliers	*Near Zonnebeke*	
,, 27.	BARBER, Lieut. John, 4/Essex (R.E.)	...	
,, ,,	BARRATT, 2/Lt. John Leslie, 13/Liverpool ...	...	*Near Zonnebeke*
,, 28.	BRAND, 2/Lt. Percy Alfred E., 12/Rifle Brigade	...	*Near Langemarcke*
,, ,,	BROADHURST, 2/Lt. Thomas Clifford, R.F.C.	...	*Accident at Catterick*
,, ,,	HOOD, 2/Lt. Ronald Paton, R.F.C.	...	*Near Wingles*
,, 30.	WEBBERLEY, 2/Lt. Reginald Selwyn,* 1/North Stafford	*Near Broodstein (28th)*	
Oct. 4.	BARNES, 2/Lt. Arthur Randall, 3/Somerset L.I.	...	
,, ,,	BALL, Capt. Leslie Alfred, 10/Middlesex ...	...	
,, ,,	BAYNE, Lieut. Edward Gordon, 2/East Surrey	...	
,, ,,	CRANE, 2/Lt. Reginald Hooper, 1/East Yorks	...	*Near Polygon Wood*
,, ,,	CROALL, Capt. John James, 5/R. Scots Fus.(R.Warwick)	,, *Poelcapelle*	
,, ,,	DANIEL, 2/Lt. Archibald Morris, 1/R. West Kent	...	, *Broodseinde*
,, ,,	GREGORY, 2/Lt. Percy John, 12/Northumberland Fus.	,, *Passchendaele*	
,, ,,	HEYWOOD, 2/Lt. Albert Bertine, 10/Yorkshire L.I. ...	., *Reutel*	
,, ,,	JONES, Capt. Lawrence, 2/East Surrey ...	...	,, *Polygon Wood*

* *Died of Wounds.*

ROLL OF HONOUR

1917.

Oct.	4.	Lyons, 2/Lt. Edward Thomas, 1/East Lancashire	...	*In Flanders*
,,	,,	Martin, 2/Lt. Charles Stanley, 6/Leicester	...	*Near Ypres*
,,	,,	Perrin, 2/Lt. Alfred John, 10/Yorkshire L.I.	...	,, *Reutel*
,,	,,	Phillips, 2/Lt. Mark Hibbert, 4(1) South Stafford	...	*Near Passchendaele*
,,	,,	Rae, 2/Lt. James, 2/Seaforth Highlanders	...	
,,	,,	Rowland, Lieut. Maurice, 10/Yorkshire L.I.	...	*Near Reutel (Accident)*
,,	,,	Tarbet, 2/Lt. Victor, 4/Devon ...	...	,, *Polygon Wood*
,,	5.	Nash, 2/Lt. Philip Geoffrey, 21/Manchester	...	,, *Passchendaele*
,,	,,	Parkes, Capt. Theodore David, 1/South Stafford	...	,, ,,
,,	7.	Grew, 2/Lt. Walter Ernest, 16/R. Warwick	...	*Near Ypres*
,,	,,	Young, 2/Lt. Leslie Duncan, 7/Manchester	...	*Near Passchendaele*
,,	8.	Long, 2/Lt. John Thomas, R.F.C.	...	*Accident near Bailleul*
,,	,,	Wattson, 2/Lt. Cyril Benson, R.F.C. ...	...	
,,	9.	Ainsworth, 2/Lt. Herbert Green, 9/Manchester	...	
,,	,,	Baxter, 2/Lt. Gerald William, 10/Manchester	...	*Near Passchendaele*
,,	,,	Beacham, 2/Lt. Cecil James, 8/Worcester	...	*Near Ypres*
,,	,,	Boswell, 2/Lt. Claude Oliver, 5/East Lancashire	...	*In Belgium*
,,	,,	Chapman, 2/Lt. Henry Randal, 10/Manchester	...	
,,	,,	Cranmer, 2/Lt. Guy Patterson, 5/Yorkshire L.I.	...	
,,	,,	Fanshawe, 2/Lt. Harvey Vernon, 1/Irish Guards	...	*Near Passchendaele*
,,	,,	Ferris, 2/Lt. Henry Norman, 4/Gloucester	...	
,,	,,	Glass, 2/Lt. Leonard George, 2/Lancashire Fusiliers		
,,	,,	Hampshire, 2/Lt. Stanley, 4/East Lancashire	...	*Near Passchendaele*
,,	,,	Mottershall, 2/Lt. Herbert Stanley, 3/Manchester		,, *Zonnebeke*
,,	,,	Quarterman, 2/Lt. Percy Harold, 23/London	...	,, *Passchendaele*
,,	,,	Sharpe, 2/Lt. William Dalton Colombo, 1/Norfolk ...		
,,	,,	Speight, Lieut. James Leslie,* 6/West Yorks	...	
,,	,,	Storm, Capt. William George, ✠ 5/York & Lancaster		
,,	,,	Tetley, Capt. John Charles Dodsworth, 3/Grenadier Gds.		*Nr. Houlthurst Forest*
,,	,,	Tweedy, Lieut. Charles Francis, 5/Lancashire Fusiliers		*Near Passchendaele*
,,	,,	Tyrrell, 2/Lt. Leonard Collin, 5/West Yorks	...	
,,	,,	Wells, 2/Lt. Alfred Langton, 1/Irish Guards	...	*Near Passchendaele*
,,	,,	Williamson, 2/Lt. Gerald Coutts, 4/Essex	...	,, *Poelcapelle*
,,	10.	†Crow, Pte. (late Capt. L.N. Lancs.) Arthur Arnold, Essex		
,,	,,	Greenhill, 2/Lt. Frederick Wm. Ridge, 3/Grenadier Gds.		*Near Poelcapelle*
,,	,,	Riley, 2/Lt. Paul, 8/Lancashire Fusiliers	...	*Near Ypres*
,,	11.	Arnold, 2/Lt. Thomas Sorrell Dight,* 3/E. Surrey (Lancs. Fus.)		*Zonnebeke (9th)*
,,	,,	Milne, 2/Lt. John Archibald Dickie, 1/Scots Guards		*Near Houlthurst Forest*
,,	,,	Roper, 2/Lt. William Horace Stanley, 3/Grenadier Gds		,, ,,
,,	12.	Brenchley, 2/Lt. John, ✠ 4/Coldstream Guards	...	,, ,,
,,	,,	Fearn, 2/Lt. Herbert, 8/East Surrey	...	*Near Poelcapelle*
,,	,,	Hicks, 2/Lt. Harry Ronald, R.F.C.	...	
,,	,,	Michell, 2/Lt. Arthur Charles, 7/R. West Kent	...	*Near Passchendaele*
,,	,,	Pearce, 2/Lt. Norman, 1/R. Lancaster	...	,, ,,
,,	,,	Sidey, 2/Lt. William Hepburn,* R.G.A.	...	

* *Died of Wounds.*

† *Capt. A. A. Crow (Loyal N. Lancashire Regt.) resigned his commission owing to ill-health, on recovering he joined the Essex Regt. as a Private.* [*Ed.*]

1917.			
Oct. 13.	BARKER, 2/Lt. Frederick Ernest, 10/West Yorks	...	
,, ,,	COLE, 2/Lt. Cecil Clarke,* R.G.A.	... ...	
,, ,,	CRYER, 2/Lt. Harold James, R.F.C.	... ...	
,, ,,	ELVIN, 2/Lt. Arthur George, 4/Suffolk	... ...	*Died*
,, ,,	SHUTE, 2/Lt. George Francis, 4/Gloucester	...	*Died (P.O.W.)*
,, ,,	TIGAR, 2/Lt. Geoffrey Herbert, 6/R. Bucks	...	*Near Poelcapelle*
,, 14.	WARR, 2/Lt. Thomas Edward,* 6/Dorset	... ...	
,, 15.	ABLETT, 2/Lt. Leslie Wallace, 11/Northumberland Fusiliers		*Near Reutel*
,, 17.	FROST, Capt. Alan, 1/Artists (M.G.C.)	... ...	*In East Africa*
,, ,,	STANLEY, 2/Lt. Sidney Edgar, R.F.C.	... ...	*Died*
,, 18.	HEARN, 2/Lt. Leonard Webb, 6/D.C.L.I. ...	...	
,, ,,	MICHELSON, 2/Lt. Arthur Conrad, R.F.A. ...	...	*Near Gravenstafel*
,, 23.	LEWIS, 2/Lt. Harold Lockwood, 24/Northumberland Fus.		*,, Poelcapelle*
,, 26.	BARTON, 2/Lt. Clarence Henry, R.F.C.	... ...	*Near Gheluvelt*
,, ,,	BONNET, Lieut. Ernest Charles, Royal Marines	...	*Near Passchendaele*
,, ,,	BROCK, 2/Lt. Algernon Bertram,* 9/Devon ...	...	*Near Gheluvelt*
,, ,,	MARVIN, 2/Lt. Henry Leslie, R.F.C.	... ...	*Ypres*
,, ,,	PARK, 2/Lt. Herbert Sidney, 1/Border	... ...	
,, ,,	SHAW, Lieut. Philip, 6/Northumberland Fusiliers	...	
,, ,,	WALLACE, 2/Lt. George Douglas, 21/Manchester	...	*In Belgium*
,, 27.	BENTON, 2/Lt. Sydney, 3(1)Norfolk	... ...	*,, ,,*
,, ,,	LEWIS, 2/Lt. Thomas William,* 1/R. Welch Fusiliers ...		
,, ,,	VALIANT, 2/Lt. James,* 7/R. Welch Fusiliers	...	*In Palestine*
,, 28.	BRYANS, Lieut. John,* 5/Loyal North Lancashire	...	
,, ,,	HARDMAN, Lieut. William Frederick K. ✠ R.E.	...	*Near Zonnebeke*
,, ,,	KING, C.-S.-M. Charles William Wykeham, 1/Artists ...		*Near Passchendaele*
,, ,,	RETFORD, Pte. Harry Hector, 1/Artists	... ...	*,, ,,*
,, 29.	HUNT, Pte. George Albert, 1/Artists	... ...	*,, ,,*
,, ,,	WOOD, Sgt. Frederick Raymon, 1/Artists ...	...	*,, ,,*
,, ,,	WRIGHT, Pte. Thomas Alfred,* 1/Artists	...	*,, ,,*
,, 30.	BALL, Capt. Arthur Hugh, ✠ R.G.A.	... ...	*,, ,,*
,, ,,	DUNCAN, 2/Lt. Philip Courtenay, 8/London	...	*Near Ypres*
,, ,,	WAKEMAN, Lieut. Philip Trevor, 5/R. Warwick (R.F.C).		*In France*

Oct. 30. Officers, N.C.Os. and Men, 1/Artists, killed in action or died of wounds received in attack on *Passchendaele*.

      BARE, Capt. Arnold Edwin, *M.V.O.*
      CHETWOOD, Capt. Ernest Stanley
      DICKINSON, Capt. Rev. Harry, *C.F.* (R.A.C.D. attached)
      HASLAM, Lieut. James
      HOWE, 2/Lt. Arnold Ewart
      WILLIAMS, Capt. Gordon, *R.V.M.*

ABURN, Pte. Edward Mark	AMOS, Pte. Alfred Reginald
ADAMS, Cpl. Leslie Robert	ANDERSON, Pte. Henry Campbell
ALDOUS, Pte. Harold Edward	ANTILL, L/Cpl. Thomas Tabrah
ALEXANDER, Pte. Thomas Henry	ARMES, Pte. Frederick William
ALLUM, Pte. John	ASHBY, Pte. William Ewart

* *Died of Wounds.*

1917.
Oct. 30.   Casualties in 1/Artists at *Passchendaele*—continued.

ASHFORD, Pte. Reginald Edwin
BAILEY, L/Cpl. John Arthur
BAKER, Pte. Frank Farmer
BARCLAY, L/Cpl. Robert Herman
BARKER, Pte. Ernest
BARNACLE, Pte. Herbert Frederick
BAUGH, Pte. Arthur William
BEARNE, L/Cpl. Aubrey Duncan
BELL, L/Cpl. Samuel Frederick
BENBOW, Pte. John Henry
BILLINGTON, Pte. George
BOWEN-ROWLANDS, Pte. Cyril Francis Wogan
BROWN, L/Cpl. Harold Burgess
BROWN, Pte. Walter Ralfe
BRUNT, Pte. Edgar
BUTLER, Pte. Ottiwell Hastings Stanhope
BRYNE, L/Cpl. Paul Stanislaus
CALDER, Pte. Gilbert James
CHAPMAN, L/Cpl. Robert Leonard
CHISHOLM, Pte. Douglas Wilson
CHITTY, Pte. Alfred Charles
COLBORNE, Pte. Reginald
COMMON, L/Cpl. Thomas
CONINGSBY, Pte. Herbert Arthur
COX, Pte. George Percy Linford
CRAWFORD, Pte. Ernest George
CROWDER, Pte. Robert Ashley
CUMMINGS, Pte. Alexander Gordon
DALZIEL, Sgt. Thomas
DAVIS, Pte. Jeffery Osborn
DAWES, Pte. Harold Henry
DAWS, Sgt. Arthur
DIXON, Pte. Clement Arthur
EDWARDS, Pte. Harry
EGERTON, Pte. John Howard
EVERETT, Pte. Stanley
FARR, Pte. Frederick James
FENNER, Pte. Percy Geddes
FISK, Pte. Herbert Hemming
FLINDERS, Pte. John James
FORDE, Pte. James Herbert
FREAKER, Sgt. Allan Lionel
GERRARD, L/Cpl. Frederick William
GETHING, Pte. Stanley
GODSON, Pte. Stanley Frederick Thomas
GOODING, Pte. Richard John

GRACE, Cpl. William Henry
GREEN, Pte. Arthur Bowden
HAMMOND, Pte. Lionel Goodesham
HARTLEY, L/Cpl. William Cecil
HAY, Pte. Robert McDonald
HAYDON, Pte. Frederick William
HENDERSON, Pte. Ernest Spring
HENLEY, Pte. Frank James
HERON, Pte. Victor Hampden
HEWITT, Pte. Alexander Horn
HILL, Pte. Joseph Alfred
HORROCKS, Pte. James George
HOUSDEN, L/Cpl. Arthur Thomas
HUMPLEBY, Pte. Ernest Stuart
HUTT, Pte. Hugh Richard
JACKSON, Sgt. Kenneth Stuart
JEFFERSON, Pte. Henry
JOHNSON, L/Cpl. Charles Eric
JOHNSTON, Pte. Duncan Charles Bain
JOHNSTON, Pte. William
KEILY, Pte. Robert Edward
KELLY, Pte. Cecil Urban Fleetwood
KENNETT, L/Cpl. Percy William
KERRIDGE, Pte. Charles Duncan
KING, Pte. James William
LAFFORD, Sgt. Wilfred John
LLEWELLYN, Pte. Thomas George
MALSOM, Pte. Frederick George
MANBY, Cpl. Cyril John
MASKREY, Pte. Harold
MAUDSLEY, Cpl. Harry Dean
McLAREN, Pte. Andrew Charles
MERTENS, Pte. Edgar Herbert
MESSERVY, L/Sgt. Edmund Sydney
MILLER, Pte. William Erin
MILLS, Pte. Leonard George Edwin
MILNE, L/Cpl. Norman
MOORE, Pte. Joseph Arthur
MOORE, Pte. Reginald Frank
MORRIS. L/Cpl. James Outram
MOSS, Pte. Montague Alfred
MOUNTCASTLE, Pte. Herbert William
MURPHY, Pte. George Maurice
MURRAY, Pte. Edward Frank
NOEL, Pte. Henry William Edgar
O'DONOGHUE, L/Cpl. Dennis Alfred

1917.
Oct. 30.   Casualties in 1/Artists at *Passchendaele*—continued.

O'Donoghue, L/Cpl. Reginald Charles
Ongley. Pte. Reginald Douglas
Palmer, L/Cpl. Edward Durcarel
Paradise, Pte. John
Peerless, Pte. Charles Leonard
Perkins, Pte. William Edward
Phillips, Sgt. Norman
Phillips, L/Cpl. William Henry
Priestly, L/Cpl. Donald Lacey
Purnell, Pte. Stanley
Ream, Pte. Norman Scholes
Redman, Pte. Claude Stansfield
Renshaw, Pte. Eric Glyn
Sharman, Pte. Bertie Thomas
Shea, Pte. William Devereux
Sorrell, Pte. Clarence Edward
Spencer, Pte. Edwin Dowsing
Springthorpe, Pte. William Francis
Staines, Pte. William James
Sturges, Pte. Montague Edgar
Taylor, Cpl. Philip Herbert
Trenbath, Pte. Frederick Taylor
Tully, Cpl. Patrick Joseph
Walker, Pte. Thomas Foskett
Weavill, Pte. Edward Kilner
Whichelow, Pte. Thomas
Wildsmith, Pte. George Frederick
Wilkins, Pte. Sidney Ernest
Willcox, Pte. Alfred Octavius
Williams, Pte. Harry Percy Garrons
Williams, Sgt. Henry Bancroft
Williams, Pte. Thomas Howard
Wright, Cpl. Ernest William*

Oct.	31.	Foard, Pte. Basil Horace, 1/Artists	*Passchendaele*
,,	,,	Hodge, 2/Lt. Frederick George, 21/London	*Near Beersheba*
,,	,,	Morse, 2/Lt. Gerald Ernest, 4/R. Welch Fusiliers (R.F.C.)	*Accident*
Nov.	1.	Essex, Pte. Richard Allister York,* 1/Artists	*Passchendaele*
,,	,,	Singer, Pte. John Marshall Laing,* 1/Artists	,,
,,	2.	Bell, 2/Lt. Robert James, 3(4)Northampton	*Near Gaza*
,,	,,	Pickering, 2/Lt. George Anthony Raymond, 3(4)Northampton	,, ,,
,,	,,	Taylor, 2/Lt. George Thomas, 7/Essex	
,,	,,	Wilson, Pte. James Henry,* 1/Artists	*Passchendaele*
,,	3.	Cunningham, Pte. Virden Edward Barry,* 1/Artists	*Passchendaele (Oct. 30)*
,,	,,	Williams, 2/Lt. Arthur Jones, 4/Welch	*In Palestine*
,,	4.	Bispham, 2/Lt. David Charles, R.F.C.	*Accident*
,,	,,	Niven, 2/Lt. Alan Scott, R. Lancaster (9/Yorkshire L.I.)	*Passchendaele*
,,	5.	Brown, 2/Lt. Herbert James, 7/R. Welch Fusiliers	*Tel-el-Kulweilfeh, Palestine*
,,	,,	Hunter, 2/Lt. Harry,* R.F.C.	
,,	,,	Wood, L/Cpl. Charles Bertram,* 1/Artists	*Passchendaele*
,,	6.	Hamilton, Capt. Claude William, 10/K.R R.C. (R.G.A.)	,,
,,	,,	Laidlaw, Capt. James Clelland, 3/Scottish Rifles (Border)	,,
,,	,,	Mallalieu, 2/Lt. Joseph,* 6/West Riding	*Wounded May 24*
,,	,,	Richardson, 2/Lt. Robert Harold, 18/London	*Near Dickebusch*
,,	,,	Taylor, Major Bruce Mitchell, D.S O., ✠✠ 1/D.C.L.I.	
,,	7.	Dyke, 2/Lt. Cyril John, 24/London	*Tel-el-Sheria, Syria*
,,	,,	Sterndale-Bennett, Cdr. Walter, D.S.O., R.N. Div., R.N.V.R.	*Passchendaele*
,,	8.	Livock, Lieut. Eric Stuart, 4/R. West Surrey (R.F.C.)	*Near Ypres*
,,	10.	Bullock, Pte. Alec Stuart,* 1/Artists	*Passchendaele (1st)*
,,	,,	Davies, 2/Lt. Harry Harding, 3/S. Wales Borderers	
,,	,,	Taylor, Pte. Francis Lawrie Vincent, Artists	*Died*
,,	,,	Walker, 2/Lt. Gordon Henry, 6/Northampton	*Near Houlthurst Forest*

* *Died of Wounds.*

ROLL OF HONOUR

1917.

Nov. 11.	COATS, 2/Lt. William Evans,* 17/R. Scots	...	...	*Passchendaele (Oct. 24)*
,, ,,	HEWITSON, 2/Lt. John, 23/Northumberland Fusiliers			
,, ,,	MILLS, 2/Lt. Kenneth le Gaye, R.F.C.	...	...	
,, ,,	WEST, 2/Lt. Mortimer Sackville, R.F.C.	...	...	*Accident in France*
,, ,,	WOOD, Lieut. Walter Bertram, 8/Hampshire (R.F.C.)			*Over Ilford*
,, 12.	LOVELL, 2/Lt. Edward Cator, 5/Lancashire Fusiliers	...		*Near Zonnebeke*
,, ,,	SYMONDS, 2/Lt. Spencer Leslie Hatton, R.F.C.	...		*In France*
,, 13.	THOMAS, Pte. Robert James,* 1/Artists	...	...	*Wounded 10th*
,, 14.	DEANE, Lieut. Arthur Reginald,* 5/Sussex	...	...•	*Passchendaele (13th)*
,, 15.	BARNETT, 2/Lt. William Augustus, R.F.C.	...	...	*Near Ypres*
,, 16.	GIRARD, 2/Lt. Geoffrey Marcus Erskine, 7/Leinster	...		*Accident*
,, 18.	COLES, 2/Lt. Herbert, 5/Rifle Brigade	...	...	
,, ,,	MABEY, Capt. John Hume,* 23/London	...	...	*Tel-el-Sheria (7th)*
,, 19.	STURROCK, Pte. George Holmes,* 1/Artists	...	...	*Passchendaele (Oct. 30)*
,, 20.	ADDIE, 2/Lt. Robert Leatham, 5/Lancashire Fusiliers			*Battle of Cambrai*
,, ,,	APPS, 2/Lt. Jack Harry Mason, 1/Northumb. Fusiliers			*Near Bourlon Wood*
,, ,,	FRASER, 2/Lt. Eldred Leslie, Tank Corps	...	...	*Near Ribecourt*
,, ,,	HOWE, Capt. Claude Arthur, 4/R. Welch Fusiliers	...		
,, ,,	JONES, Lieut. Cyril Gordon, 9/Norfolk	...	...	*Battle of Cambrai*
,, ,,	PAUL, 2/Lt. Herbert James, 12/K.R.R.C.	...	...	*,, ,,*
,, ,,	SMITH, Lieut. William Travers, 4/R. Warwick (R.E.)	...		*Near Croisilles*
,, ,,	WICKETT, 2/Lt. Thomas Penberthy,* 5/R. Berks	...		*Battle of Cambrai*
,, 21.	WILSON, Pte. Charles Tillotson,* 1/Artists	...	...	*Passchendaele (Oct. 30)*
,, 22.	BROOKES, 2/Lt. Percy, 6/Cheshire	...	..	*Near Gheluvelt*
,, 23.	COLLIS, L/Cpl. Albert Brandreth,* 1/Artists	...	...	*Passchendaele (Oct. 30)*
,, ,,	GREEN, 2/Lt. Joseph George Airey, Tank Corps	...		*Battle of Cambrai*
,, ,,	HANAFY, 2/Lt. Sydney Reginald, R.F.C.	...	...	*,, ,,*
,, ,,	HANNAFORD, 2/Lt. William Alan, 3(5)Somerset L.I.	...		*In Palestine*
,, ,,	HOWELLS, 2/Lt. George James, R.F.C.	...	...	*Near Cambrai*
,, ,,	LEAROYD, 2/Lt. Ernest Smith, 20/Middlesex	...		
,, 24.	BAILEY, 2/Lt. Hubert Percy Andrew, 17/Welch	...		*Near Bourlon Wood*
,, ,,	MONAGHAN, Capt. Denis Lawrence, Tank Corps	...		*,, ,,*
,, ,,	THOMAS, 2/Lt. Reginald Ivor Victor Charles, 3/S. Wales Bdrs.			
,, 25.	FILMER, 2/Lt. Vivian Reginald Royal, 2/Dragoons	...		*Battle of Cambrai*
,, ,,	THOMAS, 2/Lt. Tudor, 19/R. Welch Fusiliers	...		
,, 27.	HARRISON, Lieut. Charles Geoffrey, 4/York & Lancaster			
,, ,,	HUGHES, 2/Lt. George William Victor, 5/Yorkshire L.I.			
,, ,,	SUTTON, 2/Lt. Geoffrey Alfred, 3/R. Irish Rifles	...		*Near Bourlon Wood*
,, 28.	BELL, 2/Lt. Cecil Charles, 16/Lancashire Fusiliers	...		
,, ,,	DAVIES, 2/Lt. John Rhys,* 23/London	...	...	
,, ,,	MANN, 2/Lt. William George, R.F.C.	...	...	
,, 29.	JACOB, 2/Lt. Cecil Otway Reed, 2/Devon	...	...	
,, ,,	WARD, Capt. Harold Frederick, ✠✠ 2/East Surrey	...		*Near Zonnebeke*
,, 30.	BULLMAN, 2/Lt. Haddon Robert Horsley, 3/R. West Kent (M.G.C.)			*Nr. Marcoing*
,, ,,	CAWSON, 2/Lt. George Adrian, R.F.C.	...	...	
,, ,,	GOLDS, Capt. Ingram Thomas, 7/East Surrey	...		*Near Gouzeaucourt*
,, ,,	HODGE, 2/Lt. Lionel Clifford, 6/R. West Kent	...		

* Died of Wounds.

1917.			
Nov. 30.	LAING, Lieut. Ivan, ✠ 2/Coldstream Guards...	...	*Near Gouzeaucourt*
,, ,,	MARCHANT, 2/Lt. Charles Victor, 15/London	...	*,, Bourlon Wood*
,, ,,	MOLYNEUX, Capt. Eric Seymour, 1/Worcester	...	*,, Gouzeaucourt*
,, ,,	PRYKE, 2/Lt. Edgar, R.F.C.		*Accident in France*
,, ,,	SMART, Lieut. Edgar Herbert, 6/London	...	
,, ,,	WYKES, 2/Lt. Ernest Arthur Innes, 5/R. Berks	...	*Battle of Cambrai*
,, ,,	YATES, 2/Lt. Frederick, 2/Hampshire	...	
Dec. 2.	GILLESPIE, Flt.-Sub-Lt. Leslie Herbert Guy, R.N.A.S.		*Drowned (Ægean Sea)*
,, ,,	ORRELL, 2/Lt. John Turton, R.F.C.	...	
,, 3.	BENNETT, 2/Lt. George Arthur, 6/R. Warwick	...	*Battle of Cambrai*
,, ,,	BINER, 2/Lt. Frank Armden, R.F.C.	...	*In France*
,, ,,	DAWSON, 2/Lt. Wilfred Leedham, 6/R. Warwick		*Near La Vacquerie*
,, ,,	KEIGHLY, 2/Lt. Lindon Rayner,* 4/R. Lancaster	...	
,, ,,	WATSON, 2/Lt. Clifford Thomas,* 7/London	...	
,, 4.	GIBBINS, Capt. Roland Bevington, 8/R. Warwick	...	*Battle of Cambrai*
,, ,,	SPENCER, Lieut. George, Artists (Rifle Brigade)	...	
,, ,,	WHYTE, 2/Lt. George Henry, R.F.C.	...	*In France*
,, 5.	LAUGHTON, 2/Lt. Geoffrey, 26/Northumberland Fusiliers		
,, ,,	LEFROY, Major Tracy Edward, Artists (8/R. Warwick)		*Battle of Cambrai*
,, ,,	RUNNELS-MOSS, 2/Lt. Cyril Gower Vincent, R.F.C. ...		*Died*
,, 8.	FENNER, 2/Lt. Alan Thomas, 3(6)North Stafford	...	
,, ,,	SUTHERLAND, 2/Lt. John Alexander, 24/London	...	*Capture of Jerusalem*
,, ,,	TOMS, Lieut. Stanley Muir,* 18/London	...	*,, ,,*
,, 9.	RICHMOND, Lieut. Hugh Bowten, 21/London	...	*In France*
,, 10.	RUNDELL, Capt. Leslie Eric,* ✠ ✠ 7/London		
,, ,,	SMITH, 2/Lt. Frederick Herbert Corbitt Douglas, R.G.A.	...	*In France*
,, ,,	WRIGHT, 2/Lt. Alfred Kyrle Terrett.* 16/London	...	*,, ,,*
,, 11.	BYLES, Capt. Arthur Benzeville,* 2/Notts & Derby	...	*Near Marcoing*
,, 13.	ALLCHIN, 2/Lt. Sidney Milton,* 3/R. West Kent		*(While P.O.W.)*
,, ,,	CORRY, 2/Lt. Frank Moring,* 8/Notts & Derby (R.F.C.)		*Near Ypres (12th)*
,, 17.	GURNEY, 2/Lt. Kenneth Gerard,* 5/Gloucester	...	*(While P.O.W.)*
,, 18.	RAWBONE, 2/Lt. Charles Robert, R.F.C.	...	*Accident in England*
,, ,,	SAGE, 2/Lt. Douglas Michael, R.F.C.	...	
,, 20.	GRAY, 2/Lt. Eric Balfour, R.F.A.	...	
,, 21.	BIRD, 2/Lt. John Woodall, Household Battalion	...	*Near Monchy, Arras*
,, 22.	LITTLEBOY, Sub-Lt. Vernon Hatherton, R.N.A.S.	...	*Accident*
,, 23.	BRAYDON, 2/Lt. Kevin, 18/London	...	
,, ,,	BUCKLEY, Capt. Joseph Michael, 9/Rifle Brigade	...	*Near Passchendaele*
,, 24.	CAPPER, Capt. Ernest Raphael,* ✠ 3/Essex	...	
,, ,,	TAYLOR, 2/Lt. John Birley, 4/East Lancashire	...	*Near Bethune*
,, 25.	HARVEY, 2/Lt. Robert George Bosworth, 5/Lincoln	...	*,, Cambrai*
,, ,,	MACDONALD, Pte. Ronald Francis Keith, Artists		*Died*
,, 27.	JEPHSON, Lieut. Charles Mitchell W., 4/R. West Surrey		*In Palestine*
,, ,,	PATTISON, Capt. Robert, 10/London	...	
,, ,,	RIDPATH, Lieut. Frederick Cecil Lacey, 4/R. West Surrey		*In Palestine*
,, 28.	PAUL, Capt. Edgar Newton, 6/K.R.R.C.	...	*Near Cambrai*
,, ,,	ROGERS, 2/Lt. Cecil Walter,* 7/R. West Surrey	...	

* *Died of Wounds.*

ROLL OF HONOUR

1917.

Dec. 30. Officers, N.C.Os. and Men, 1/Artists, killed in action or died of wounds received at *Welsh Ridge, Cambrai,* on this date.

    ENGLISH, 2/Lt. Alfred Cecil
    GODFREY, 2/Lt. Stephen Mervyn
    GROOM, Lieut. Cyril
    LIGHTFOOT, 2/Lt. Francis Bertram
    SALISBURY, 2/Lt. Walter Frederick*
    SHINNER, Lieut. William Goodwin Blake* (*d. Nov. 2*)

AMOORE, Pte. Ralph Hannam*
CLELAND, Pte. Alan Ian Henry
CRAMOND, Pte. William*
DEAN, Sgt. Alfred Henry
DEAN, Sgt. Louis Sandbach
DEWEY, Sgt. Francis Cecil
DYSON, Pte. Gamm
GARE, L/Sgt. John Henry
GOLLE, Cpl. Claude Victor
HOLLYMAN, Pte. William Henry
HUMPHREY, Pte. Harold George
JARVIS, Pte. David Frederick Charles
JUMP, Pte. Stanley
LE BAS, Pte. Albert Olavasia
LEY, Pte. John William
MARTIN, Pte. Alfred Edgar
NEILL, Pte. Robert
NORRIS, Pte. Robert
O'VASTON, Pte. Adalia Daniel
PAINE, Pte. James Horace
PARSONS, Pte. Charles Warden* (*d. 31st*)
PHILLIPS, Pte. George Edward
PRESSNELL, Pte. Charles Edgar
PULFORD, Pte. John Charles
SCHOFIELD, Pte. James Leach
SIMPSON, Pte. James Arthur
STAPLETON, L/Cpl. Walter Richard
TAYLOR, L/Cpl. Douglas Clifton
THORP, Pte. Albert Ernest
TREVENEN, Pte. Samuel
TURPIN, Pte. Walter Frank
WOODHEAD, Pte. Frederick Gordon* (*d. 31st*)

Dec. 31.   MEASURES, Capt. Percy,   5/Leicester   ...   ...   *Near La Bassée*

1918.

1918.

Jan.	1.	MEW, Pte. Ronald,* 1/Artists	...	*Welsh Ridge (Dec. 30)*
,,	,,	POLLOCK, Pte. John,* 1/Artists		,, ,, ,,
,,	,,	WILLIAMSON, 2/Lt. Gerald Douglas, R.F.C.	...	
,,	2.	ALLEN, Pte. Lionel Edward,* 1/Artists ...	...	*Welsh Ridge (Dec. 30)*
,,	3.	DAVIS, Pte. Sidney James George,* 1/Artists		,, ,, ,,
,,	4.	BUTT, 2/Lt. Alfred, 10/Bedford (R.F.C.) ...	...	*Near Djenin, Palestine*
,,	,,	WOODHEAD, L/Cpl. Frederick Gordon,* 1/Artists	...	*Cambrai*
,,	5.	BROWN, Pte. Alfred Hughes,* 1/Artists	...	*Welsh Ridge (Dec. 30)*
,,	6.	REEDER, Capt. Robert, 10/Manchester	...	*In France*
,,	,,	RATA, Sgt. Samuel,* 1/Artists		*Welsh Ridge (Dec. 30)*
,,	9.	BECK, Pte. Jack, 1/Artists	...	*Died*
,,	13.	BALFOUR, 2/Lt. Alan Scott, R.F.A. (R.F.C.)	...	
,,	17.	STURT, Lieut. Humphrey Morriston, 8/Lancashire Fusiliers		*Died*
,,	,,	THOMPSON, Pte. Sidney Reginald,* 1/Artists	...	*Welsh Ridge*
,,	18.	FENN-SMITH, 2/Lt. Warren Kemp, R.F.C.	...	*In France*
,,	,,	STEVENS, 2/Lt. Gorham Venton, 5/Lincoln	...	*Died*

* *Died of Wounds.*

1918.			
Jan. 22.	PAUL, 2/Lt. Arthur Reginald, R.F.C.		
,, 25.	SMALLWOOD, 2/Lt. William Spencer, R.F.C.		
,, 31.	DALE, Lieut. Robert Jacomb Norris, 9/Manchester (R.F.C.)		
Feb. 1.	EDEY, 2/Lt. William John, 1/Essex		*Near Wieltje*
,, 2.	LOCK, 2/Lt. James Palmer,* R.F.A.		
,, ,,	QUAIL 2/Lt. Henry Charles, R.E.		
,, 4.	DEDMAN, Lieut. William Albert, 8/West Yorks		*Died in France*
,, 5.	HUGHES, Lieut. Thomas McKinney, 2/K.R.R.C. (R.F.C.)		
,, 6.	GREENE, Sub-Lt. David Wilson,* R.N.V.R.		
,, 9.	WINTER, Flt.-Comd. Rupert Randolph, R.N.A.S.		
,, 11.	SHARP, 2/Lt. Matthew, ✠ 7/London		*Near Arras*
,, 13.	DAWE, Capt. Sydney Charles, ✠ 5/Lincoln		*Accident*
,, 15.	DUNCAN, 2/Lt. James Athol Gordon, R.F.C.		*Accident at Montrose*
,, ,,	TALL, 2/Lt. John Jeffrey, 4/Devon		*In France*
,, 17.	EVANS, 2/Lt. Francis Bernard, R.F.C.		*Accident at Sedgeford*
,, 18.	WHITEHEAD, 2/Lt. Eric Wilfred, R.F.C.		*Accident*
,, 19.	MALCOLM, Lieut. Kenneth James, 20/London		*Near Jerusalem*
,, ,,	WEATHERLEY, Lieut. Laurence Edwin M., 20/London		,, ,,
,, ,,	WILSON, 2/Lt. Humphrey Hamilton, R.F.C.		*In France*
,, 20.	BUNNEY, Pte. Vincent Henry, 1/Artists		*Highland Ridge, Marcoing*
,, 21.	HARGREAVES, 2/Lt. Willoughby Frankland, R.F.C.		*Accident*
,, 23.	ROBERTS, 2/Lt. Lawrie Paterson, R.F.C.		*In France*
,, 28.	HOWELLS, 2/Lt. George Davey, 1/Monmouth (15/Cheshire)		*Langemarcke*
,, ,,	PURSER, 2/Lt. Norman Frederick, R.F.C.		
Mar. 3.	ELLIS, 2/Lt. Frederick William, 13/London		*Near Arras*
,, 5.	FEAR, 2/Lt. Robert S.,* /Worcester (R.F.C.)		*In France*
,, 8.	FERGUSON, Pte. Bernard Vincent, 1/Artists		*Passchendaele (Oct. 26)*
,, ,,	HEWITT, Pte. Guy Stevenson, 1/Artists		*Highland Ridge*
,, ,,	WARREN, 2/Lt. Ivan John,* 3(1)Gloucester		*Near Furnes*
,, 9.	BYRNE, 2/Lt. Thomas Edmund, 1/Welsh Guards		
,, 10.	FRANCIS, 2/Lt. William George, R.F.C.		*Near Treviso, Italy*
,, 11.	IKIN, 2/Lt. Alfred Edward, R.F.C.		*Near Auchel*
,, ,,	KITCHEN, Cpl. Arthur, Artists		
,, 13.	ALLEN, 2/Lt. Cyrus, R.F.C.		
,, 15.	CRANE, 2/Lt. Lancelot, R.G.A.		*Died*
,, 17.	SMITH, 2/Lt. Herbert Dudley, 7/Lancashire Fusiliers		*Near Hargicourt*
,, ,,	VAUGHAN, Lieut. Francis Seymour, 5/R. West Kent (R.F.C.)		*Near Salonika*
,, 18.	TILBURY, 2/Lt. Robert William, R.F.C.		*Died*
,, 21.	ADAMS, 2/Lt. Arthur Charles Henry, 5(8)Worcester		*Near St. Quentin*
,, ,,	BASSETT, Lieut. Geoffrey Edward, R.A.S.C. (Ox. & Bucks L.I.)		
,, ,,	BATTOCK, Lieut. Thomas William, 5/East Lancashire		*Near Hesbecourt*
,, ,,	BEGG, Capt. Arthur, 4/Norfolk		*Died*
,, ,,	BOYCOTT, Lieut. Harold Charlton, 4/Coldstream Guards		*Near Arras*
,, ,,	CAREFULL, Capt John Holt, 12/Liverpool		
,, ,,	CARMICHAEL, 2/Lt. Gilbert, 10/Manchester		*Near St. Quentin*
,, ,,	CATTERALL, Lieut. Albert, 7/Notts & Derby		
,, ,,	CHAPLIN, Lieut. Sydney Stanger, 5/Manchester		

* *Died of Wounds.*

ROLL OF HONOUR

1918.
Mar. 21.	CLAYTON, Capt. Arthur Oliver, 2/Wiltshire ...		*L'Epine de Dallon*
,,	,,	COOK, 2/Lt. Horace Montague,* 7/London ...	*Near St. Quentin*
,,	,,	CROUCH, Capt. Frank Harris, 5/Lancashire Fusiliers	
,,	,,	FAWCETT, 2/Lt. Woodford, 5/Oxford & Bucks L.I. ...	*Near Essigny*
,,	,,	FELLOWES, 2/Lt. Cyril Walter, 3/N. Stafford	
,,	,,	GITTINGS, 2/Lt. Charles, 3(5)East Lancashire	*Near Hargicourt*
,,	,,	GREEN, 2/Lt. Arthur Fairbrother, 6/N. Stafford	*At Ecoust*
,,	,,	HAWKESWORTH, 2/Lt. Henry Charles H., ✠ 10/Essex ...	*Near La Fere*
,,	,,	JACKSON, 2/Lt. Stewart Spiers, ✠ 1(8)Worcester	
,,	,,	JERWOOD, Major John Hugh, ✠ 10/Durham L I. (Somerset L.I.)	
,,	,,	NEWCOMBE, 2/Lt. John Carr, R. Engineers...	*Near Morchies*
,,	,,	PRIME, 2/Lt. Arnold, 4/Manchester	
,,	22.	BAKER, 2/Lt. Frank Vincent, 6/K.R.R.C. ...	*Near St. Quentin*
,,	,,	BROAD, Lieut. Walter Victor Mantach, 13/London ...	
,,	,,	CASE, Lieut. Geoffrey, 2/S. Lancashire	
,,	,,	CHAMBERS, 2/Lt. Philip Carlisle, Tank Corps	*Near Maricourt Wood*
,,	,,	EDGE, Lieut. Edward Holden,* 8/London ...	*Near Tergnier*
,,	,,	ELKINGTON, 2/Lt. Walter Henry, 3/Hampshire	,, *Peronne*
,,	,,	FRASER, 2/Lt. Charles Douglas, 3/London ...	,, *Tergnier*
,,	,,	HAMMOND, 2/Lt. Kenneth Lawton C., 23/Northumb. Fus.	,, *Croisilles*
,,	,,	LEE, Lieut. Frank Stanley, 13/Rifle Brigade	,, *Peronne*
,,	,,	LINTOTT, Lieut. Harry Chamen,* 5/London ...	
,,	,,	ROBBINS, Capt. Arthur Hodder, 7/R. Inniskg. Fusiliers.	*Near St. Emilie*
,,	,,	ROYDS, Lieut. John Iltid, 1/Artists	*Near Havrincourt Wood*
,,	,,	THIRLBY, 2/Lt. Stuart Longston, 6/Leicester	
,,	,,	THOMSON, 2/Lt. George Vallance Bruce, 10/R. Scots	
,,	,,	WOOLNOUGH, Capt. Frederick Ullathorne,* 3/Dorset (6/Somerset L.I.)	
,,	23.	AREND, 2/Lt. Ronald Sydney, 12/R. Scots	
,,	,,	BATCHELAR, 2/Lt. Robert Thomas, 7/R. West Surrey	
,,	,,	BROAD, 2/Lt. John Eric, 1/Hertford	
,,	,,	COCKBURN, 2/Lt. George Percival, 6/Suffolk	*Near Tergnier*
,,	,,	FRANCIS, 2/Lt. William Joseph, 5(11)Royal Fusiliers	*Near Jussy*
,,	,,	HAMMOND, Capt. Hugh Jerrold,* 2/Gloucester	*Salonika (18th)*
,,	,,	HUTTON, 2/Lt. Lorne de Hutton, M.G.C. ...	*Near Bufvillers*
,,	,,	LIDGETT, Lieut. John Cuthbert, 3/South Lancashire ...	*Near Ham*
,,	,,	MC.ILROY, Pte. James, 1/Artists ...	*Trescault*
,,	,,	MEDLAND, 2/Lt. James Edward Percy, Royal Engineers	
,,	,,	MORRALL, 2/Lt. John Bernard, 10/R. Warwick	
,,	,,	OWEN, Pte. Wilfred Ernest, 1/Artists	*Trescault*
,,	,,	SMITH, 2/Lt. Norman Havelock, 20/London	*Near Fins*
,,	,,	STEAD, 2/Lt. Horace Stuart, 3/Lancashire Fusiliers	
,,	,,	WALLEY, Lieut. John Clifford, 5/Leicester	*Near Epehy*
,,	,,	WRIGLEY, 2/Lt. Percy Bernard, R. Engineers	
,,	24.	BAILEY, 2/Lt. Arnold, 8/R. Lancaster	*Near Arras*
,,	,,	BUCKLEY, Lieut. Sidney James, 5/South Stafford	*Haplincourt*
,,	,,	CHEVERTON, Major Thomas Bird, ✠ R.F.A. (T.F.)	
,,	,,	CLARK, 2/Lt. Ronald Hope,* 16/Rifle Brigade	

* *Died of Wounds.*

ARTISTS' RIFLES, 1918.

1918.			
Mar. 24.	CUMNER, 2/Lt. Cyril William, 4/London	...	
,, ,,	DENT, 2/Lt. Reginald Teesdale, 6/Rifle Brigade	...	*Near Pargny, Somme*
,, ,,	ELEY, 2/Lt. Ralph Corban, 19/London	...	
,, ,,	GRAHAM, 2/Lt. Thomas Eric, ✠ 2/Scottish Rifles	...	
,, ,,	HADDOCK, 2/Lt. Joseph Henry, 14/R. Irish Rifles	..	
,, ,,	HAND, Pte. John William,* 1/Artists	...	*Ytres*
,, ,,	KIDD, Capt. Claud Bernard, ✠ 15/Cheshire	...	*Near Mericourt*
,, ,,	LAST, Capt. Ernest Reginald, ✠ ✠ 1/Liverpool	...	
,, ,,	MCKIE, 2/Lt. Eric, 6(11)K.R.R.C.	...	*Near Voyennes, Somme*
,, ,,	MATHESON, 2/Lt. Herbert, 13(15)London	...	*Near Le Cateau*
,, ,,	MAXWELL, Pte. John Humphrey, 1/Artists ...	..	*Ytres*
,, ,,	MOORHOUSE, Pte. Allen, 1/Artists	...	,,
,, ,,	MORGAN, Pte. James Roland, 1/Artists	...	,,
,, ,,	SIMPSON, L/Cpl. William Donovan, 1/Artists	...	,,
,, ,,	TERRY, Capt. Sidney Frederic, ✠ 1/Wilts	...	*Near Bapaume*
,, ,,	TINCKLER, Pte. Eric Harrison, 1/Artists	...	*Ytres*
,, ,,	WARD, Pte. Dudley Grant, 1/Artists	...	,,
,, 25.	DAVIES, Pte. Geo. Edwin Carlton,* 1/Artists	...	
,, ,,	HILLIER, 2/Lt. Sidney Napier, 6/S. Wales Borderers		*Near Achiet-le-Grand*
,, 26.	EVANS, Lieut. Hugh Elwyn, ✠ 5/Yorkshire	...	*Near Peronne*
,, ,,	GRELLIER, 2/Lt. Arthur Berteau, 7/Lancashire Fusiliers		
,, ,,	READING, 2/Lt. Vernon Jack, R.F.C.	...	*Combat over Parvillers*
,, ,,	SCOLDING, 2/Lt. George Henry, 5/Norfolk ...	...	*In France*
,, 27.	ANCELL, L/Cpl. Horace, 1/Artists	...	*Aveluy Wood*
,, ,,	CLARKE, 2/Lt. Alfred Lord, 3/Lancashire Fusiliers	...	
,, ,,	FINNEMORE, 2/Lt. Henry James,* 7/R. Sussex (R.F.C.)		
,, ,,	HARVEY, Lieut. Douglas, 2/Grenadier Guards	...	
,, ,,	HENDRY, 2/Lt. Charles Arthur, 5(9) R. Fusiliers	...	*Near Aveluy Wood*
,, ,,	JACKSON, Pte. James Herbert, 1/Artists	...	*Near Albert*
,, ,,	MACKLIN, 2/Lt. David Harold, 5/Bedford ...	...	
,, ,,	MATTHEWS, 2/Lt. Joseph Henry, 5/R. Berks	...	
,, ,,	PAINE, Capt. George Gordon,* ✠ 2/R. Berks		*Near Aveluy Wood (26th)*
,, ,,	PENTECOST, 2/Lt. Charles Gordon, R.F.C....	...	*Near Amiens*
,, ,,	WILLIS, Lieut. Eric FitzGeorge, 1/Artists ...	...	*Near Albert*
,, 28.	ADAMS, Sgt.-Inst. Arthur Cyril, 1/Artists ...	...	*In France*
,, ,,	CAMPKIN, 2/Lt. Reginald Ernest,* 4/London	...	*Near Oppy Wood*
,, ,,	DAVIES, 2/Lt. Evan Jones, 1/Welsh Guards	..	*Boiry-Becquerelle*
,, ,,	EDWARDS, Capt. William,* R.A.S.C. (Shropshire L.I.)		
,, ,,	FORBES, 2/Lt. Duncan, 13/R. Scots	...	*Near Monchy*
,, ,,	GOODCHILD, 2/Lt. Stewart John, 3/Shropshire L.I.	...	*Near Henin*
,, ,,	GROWSE, Capt. John Hartley,* 2/Northampton	...	
,, ,,	HUGO, Lieut. Reginald Graeff,* 11/Highland L.I.	...	*In France*
,, ,,	PARTINGTON, Capt. Leigh, 1/Northumberland Fusiliers		
,, ,,	ROSE, Lieut. Stewart Alan, 2/Northumberland Fusiliers		
,, ,,	SMITH, 2/Lt. George William, 8/R. Lancaster	...	
,, ,,	WELLS, 2/Lt. Maurice Godfrey, R.F.A.	...	
,, ,,	WOODHOUSE, 2/Lt. Percy Wilfred, R.F.C. ...	...	

* *Died of Wounds.*

1918.
Mar. 29. JONES, 2/Lt. Herbert Joaquim,* 4(7)R. Irish ... (*While P.O.W.*)
,, ,, MALEHAM, 2/Lt. Edgar Hubert,* 9/York & Lancaster...
,, ,, PALMER, 2/Lt. Henry John, 5/D.C.L.I. ... ...*Near Villers-Brettoneux*
,, ,, POWELL, Pte. Philip George,* 1/Artists ... ...*P.O.W. (Missing 25th)*
,, 30. CHANDLER, Capt. Cecil William, ✠ 8/R. Munster Fusiliers
,, ,, DUXBURY, Capt. Andrew Marshall, ✠ Bucks Bn./Ox. & Bucks L.I.
,, ,, HARDING, Pte. Stanley Whittall,* 1/Artists ... ... *Wounded Nov. 3*
,, ,, LINDREA, 2/Lt. Wilfred George, 4/Gloucester ... *Warfusse-Abancourt*
,, ,, MARTIN, Lieut. Cyril Basnett, 21/London ... ...
,, ,, SERVICE, 2/Lt. George Brown, M.G.C.
,, ,, WHITWORTH, 2/Lt. Arthur Geo. Richard,* 19/Northumb. Fus.
,, 31. PREEDY, 2/Lt. Lawrence Jack, 4(1)R. Warwick ... *Near Arras*
Apr. 1. MULLANE, 2/Lt. Bernard Patrick,* 6(9)R. Fusiliers ... *Wounded Mar. 26*
,, ,, OSBORN, 2/Lt. Edward Bertram,* 5/E. Lancs.... ... *Hargicourt (Mar. 21)*
,, ,, SMITH, L/Cpl. George Herbert,* 1/Artists ... ... *Forceville*
,, 2. JOHNS, Pte. Thomas,* 1/Artists ... ... ,,
,, ,, MOORE, 2/Lt. Jack Greville, R.A.F. ... ... *Accident at Scampton*
,, 3. JAMIESON, 2/Lt. John, 9(16)Lancashire Fusiliers ... *Near Arras*
,, 4. ANDREW, 2/Lt. Frank Douglas,* 7/Manchester *Died in Bohain (Mar. 31)*
,, ,, HALL, Capt. Albert Loader, 8/East Surrey ... ...*Near Villers-Brettoneux*
,, ,, NEWELL, Capt. Arthur Francis, 8/Rifle Brigade ...
,, ,, NICHOLLS, Capt. Henry King, 5/East Surrey ...*Near Villers-Brettoneux*
,, ,, PARKES, 2/Lt. Percy Reginald,* 18/London ... (*While P.O.W.*)
,, 5. ASKEY, 2/Lt. Cecil Harry Leonard.* 3/Lincoln ...
,, ,, BOYER, 2/Lt. Ernest Alexander, 7/London... ... *Near Aveluy Wood*
,, ,, EWEN, Lieut. Henry Spencer, ✠ 23/London... ...
,, ,, FULLAGER, Sgt. Charles Ernest, 1/Artists ... ... *Mesnil*
,, ,, HOYLE, Pte. James William, 1/Artists ... ... ,,
,, ,, KEMBLE, Pte Colin Stuart, 1/Artists ... ... ,,
,, ,, ROBERTSON, L/Cpl. David Whitelaw, 1/Artists ... ,,
,, ,, ROSE, 2/Lt. Eric William, ✠ 2/Lancashire Fusiliers ... *Near Bucquoy*
,, 6. CORNWELL, Pte. William Henry Arthur,* 1/Artists ... *Mesnil*
,, ,, CROSIER, 2 Lt. Vernon Swann, 7/London (R. W. Surrey) *Near Doullens (5th)*
,, ,, HALLPIKE, 2/Lt. Christopher George, R.G.A. ...
,, 9. BEAK, Lieut. Frank Leslie. R.F.A. ... ...
,, ,, BROOKE, 2/Lt. Leonard, ✠ 4/Loyal N. Lancashire ... *Near Givenchy*
,, ,, LEAVER, 2/Lt. Stanley Horace, 5(17)Middlesex ... *Near Sailly-Lys*
,, ,, LOWRY, Lieut. Vyvyan Charles, M.G.C. ... *Near Bailleul*
,, ,, SMITH, 2/Lt. Charles Frederick, 12 Suffolk (T.M.B.)
,, ,, WALKER, 2/Lt. William Francis, 9/Northumberland Fusiliers
,, 10. COPPOCK, Lieut. Hugh Searle, 2/S. Lancashire ... *Near Ploegsteert*
,, ,, DUDDY, 2/Lt. Geo. Lionel Alfred, 11/Suffolk ...
,, ,, SEWELL, 2/Lt. Edward John,* R.G.A. ... ... *Near Neuve-Chapelle*
,, 11. ARNOLD, 2/Lt. Hedley Graham, 3(2)S. Wales Borderers
,, ,, COXON, Capt. William Basil, 23/Northumberland Fusiliers *Pont de Nieppe*
,, ,, MORGAN, 2/Lt. William Hugh, 12/S. Wales Bdrs. (Welch)
,, ,, THOMAS, 2/Lt. William Hope, 1/Leicester (T.M.B.)

* *Died of Wounds.*

[Capt. W. Lee-Hankey.

BAILLEUL IN 1914.

BAILLEUL IN 1918.

The Pâtisserie, Bailleul.

Rue de la Gare, Bailleul.

Church and Town Hall, Bailleul.

Artists' Graves at Neuve Eglise
(The first two casualties).

1918.		
April 11.	THOMPSON, 2/Lt. Ronald William, 1/Monmouth (4/S. Lancs.)	*Festubert*
,, 12.	BALL, 2/Lt. Gerald Harman, ✠ M.G.C.	*Near Vieux-Bercquin*
,, ,,	BOLTER, 2/Lt. Charles Albert, M.G.C.	*Near Bailleul*
,, ,,	CROOKSTON, 2/Lt. William John, 4/Scottish R. (8/Border)	*Near Neuve-Eglise*
,, ,,	LEECH, Lieut. Arthur William,* ✠ 6/Northumberland Fus.	*On the Somme*
,, ,,	METCALFE, 2/Lt. George,* 10/R. Scots	
,, ,,	SMITH, 2/Lt. Leon Walter, 4/D.C.L.I.	*Near Estaires*
,, 13.	BINGHAM, Lieut. Montague Hearfield, 5/Yorkshire L.I.	*Near Forêt de Nieppe*
,, ,,	SANGER, 2/Lt. Henry Keith, 10/East Yorks	
,, 14.	ALLEN, Capt. Norman, 14/R. Warwick	*Near Merville*
,, ,,	CHALLIS, 2/Lt. Ivor James. 11/Lancashire Fusiliers	
,, ,,	DAVIES, Capt. Geraint,* 9/Northumberland Fusiliers	*Near Neuve-Eglise*
,, ,,	GEORGE, 2/Lt. Alan Lee.* 15/R. Warwick	*Near Thiennes*
,, ,,	McCARTHY, 2/Lt. Thadeus Francis, ✠ 4/Loyal N. Lancs.	,, *Givenchy*
,, 15.	EDGEHILL, 2/Lt. Ashley Gay,* ✠ 15/Lancs. Fus. (T.M.B.)	*Near Ayette (14th)*
,, ,,	GOULD, 2/Lt. James Robertson Sabiston,* M.G.C.	*Nr. Ablonzeville (Mar. 27)*
,, ,,	HESKETT, 2/Lt. John, 2/West Riding	*Near La Bassee Canal*
,, ,,	LEFTWICH, Lieut. Nigel George, 2/Cheshire	*Barakli, Salonika*
,, ,,	MASON, 2/Lt. George, 1/North Stafford	*Near Bailleul*
,, ,,	SMITH, Capt. William Leslie,* ✠ 2/Worcester	
,, 17.	BARKER, 2/Lt. Henry Watson, 4/Lincoln	*Near Kemmel*
,, ,,	CHEERS, 2/Lt. Donald Heriot Anson, R.A F.	*Accident at Gullane*
,, ,,	HEATLEY, 2/Lt. Charles Frederick, 3/R. Welch Fusiliers	*Armentieres (7th)*
,, ,,	ROWE, 2/Lt. Gilbert James Burberry, 5/R. Berks	*Near Armentieres*
,, ,,	YOUNG, 2/Lt. James Cecil,* 7/R. Fusiliers	*Wounded 6th*
,, 18.	COX, 2/Lt. Lupton James, 1/Gloucester	*Near Festubert*
,, ,,	GORDON, 2/Lt. Arthur Forbes,* 1/Cameron Highlanders	,, *Givenchy*
,, 20.	WILKES, 2/Lt. George Lionel, 7/London	,, *Amiens*
,, 22.	HALLIWELL, 2/Lt. Frederick, 11/Manchester	
,, 23.	ROLFE, Lieut. Raymond Harold, 4/Grenadier Guards	*Near Hazebrouck*
,, 24.	MILLER, Lieut. Frederick Charles, 6/Gloucester	
,, ,,	RAWF, 2/Lt. Charles Henry, R.F.A. (R.G.A.)	
,, ,,	THOMAS, 2/Lt. Arthur Lewis, 2/Northampton	
,, 25.	EASTERBROOK, Lieut. Henry George,* 9/London	
,, ,,	MOSSMAN, 2/Lt. Harold Alexander, ✠ 1/Grenadier Guards	*Near Warlencourt*
,, 26.	CHAPLYN, 2/Lt. Cyril Edward, 10/Essex	
,, ,,	KING, 2/Lt. Henry Garfield, 10/Essex	
,, ,,	NICHOLSON, 2/Lt. Paul Chessum, 9/Yorkshire L.I.	*Mount Kemmel*
,, ,,	O'NEILL, 2/Lt. Douglas Quirk, 10/R. Warwick	*Near Reninghelst*
,, 27.	CARR, Capt. Leslie George,✠✠ 1/London (4/S. Stafford)	*Near Kemmel*
,, ,,	TEDDER, 2 Lt. Oswald Stanley, 3/Lincoln	
,, 28.	HUNT, 2/Lt. Arthur Warner,* 11/Essex	
,, ,,	ROBINSON, 2/Lt. Cyril Charles Edward, R.A.F.	*Near Doullens*
,, 30.	DIXON, 2/Lt. William Swanston, 5/Lincoln	
,, ,,	McHARDY, 2/Lt. Stewart John, 7/London	*In Syria*
May 1.	ALDRICH, 2/Lt. Arnold, 1(8)Worcester	*Died*
,, 2.	CARO, 2/Lt. Jacob Pisa, 17/London	

* *Died of Wounds.*

ROLL OF HONOUR

1918.

May	2.	HEPPENSTALL, L/Cpl. Robert Archibald,* 1/Artists	...	*Albert (Mar. 28)*
,,	,,	MOORE, 2/Lt. George Alexander, 14/R. Warwick	...	
,,	,,	UNDERWOOD, Capt. Cyril Henry, 17/London	...	*Palestine*
,,	3.	PARRY, 2/Lt. Samuel, R. Engineers (R.A.F.)	...	*Over German Lines*
,,	8.	BOWIE, 2/Lt. Alan Stuart Hunter,* R.G.A. ...	...	
,,	14.	NASH, 2/Lt. Henry Alfred, R.A.F.	...	...
,,	15.	HARRIS, 2/Lt. Sydney Ernest, 3(4)Loyal N. Lancashire		*Wounded 11th*
,,	,,	JONES, Lieut. Harry, 4/London	...	*Accident (bombing)*
,,	16.	HEYNES, 2/Lt. Dudley Hugo, R.F.A.	...	*...Near Villers-Brettoneux*
,,	,,	HOLWILL, 2/Lt. William Bertram,* M.G.C....		*Near St. Quentin (Mar. 21)*
,,	18.	FLEET, 2/Lt. William Alexander, 1/Grenadier Guards		*Near Warlencourt*
,,	,,	WOODS, 2/Lt. Eric Evelyn,* 12/Liverpool	...	...
,,	19.	KELLAND, Sub-Lt. Robert Sydney, R.N.V.R.		...
,,	,,	TAYLOR, Pte. William, 1/Artists ..	...	*Aveluy Wood*
,,	,,	TUDOR, Pte. Adrian de Roy, 1/Artists	...	,, ,,
,,	20.	KITCHIN, Pte. Arthur, 1/Artists ...	...	,, ,,
,,	21.	BUTLAND, Lieut. George, 2/York & Lancaster	...	
,,	22.	BURFOOT, 2/Lt. William Martin, 3/Dorset (R.A.F.) ...		
,,	,,	HEATH, 2/Lt. Gerard Bower, 2/Coldstream Guards ...		*At Ayette*
,,	,,	MOTT, L/Cpl. Charles,* 1/Artists ...	...	*Aveluy Wood*
,,	24.	COLVILLE-JONES, Capt. Thomas,* R.A.F.	...	*While P.O.W.*
,,	25.	GILLIAT, Lieut. Robert Vincent,* 10/Manchester	...	,, ,,
,,	27.	BOWE, 2/Lt. Eric Arthur, Durham L.I.	...	
,,	,,	COUNSELL, 2/Lt. Henry Cecil, R.F.A.	...	
,,	,,	PELLS, 2/Lt. Cyril Elmore, 3/Devon	...	
,,	,,	PLATT, 2/Lt. Claud Lucien Francis, R.F.A.	...	
,,	,,	ROBERTS, Pte. Lionel William,* 1/Artists ...	...	*At Doullens*
,,	,,	SARGENT, Lieut. Ernest Malcolm, 5/Northumb. Fusiliers		
,,	,,	SMITH, 2/Lt. Donovan Richardson McC.,* 4/Manchester (1/Worcester)		
,,	,,	TAYLOR, Lieut. Leslie Francis, ✠ 1/K.R.R.C. (M.G.C.)		
,,	28.	BRAY, 2/Lt. Frank Hugh, 3(9)R. Sussex ...	...	*Near Loos*
,,	,,	DONAGHY, 2/Lt. Robert Andrews, R.G.A. ...	...	*In France*
,,	,,	HARTREE, 2/Lt. Cyril, R.G.A. ...	...	*Near Hazebrouck*
,,	,,	JACOB, Pte. Edmund, 1/Artists ...	...	*Aveluy Wood*
,,	,,	SLATER, Lieut. Harry,* 6/South Stafford	...	*...Near Gorre Wood (21st)*
,,	29.	BOWLY, Lieut. Reginald Walter, 20/Manchester	... ,,	*Forêt de Nieppe*
,,	,,	DAVIES, 2/Lt. Melville Allen Duff, ✠ 9/K.R.R.C.	...	*Died*
,,	,,	MOORE, Lt.-Col. Robert Frank, *D.S.O.*, ✠ 1/Notts & Derby		
,,	,,	STAFFORD-BADGER, Pte. Herbert Pearson, 1/Artists ..		*Aveluy Wood*
,,	30.	MILLS, Capt. Henry Jackson, M.G.C. ...	*On the Champagne Front*	
,,	,,	MORETON, 2/Lt. Norman Houghton, R.A.F.	...	
,,	,,	NOTLEY, 2/Lt. Albert Carr, 5/R. Lancaster (5/S. Lancs.)		
,,	31.	LEANING, 2/Lt. Reginald William, 9/Liverpool	...	*Accident*
June	1.	AYLES, Lieut. Francis Powell, Grenadier Guards (R.A.F.)	*Accident at Scampton*	
,,	,,	FIRTH, Pte. Edwin, 1/Artists ...	...	*Aveluy Wood*
,,	,,	KEMP, 2/Lt. George Hubert, 15/Durham L.I. (R.A.F.)		
,,	,,	PRINGLE, Pte. Hugh Frederick D., 1/Artists	...	*Aveluy Wood*

* *Died of Wounds.*

ARTISTS' RIFLES, 1918.

1918.			
June	3.	PAILTHORPE, Pte. Lawrence Stewart,* 1/Artists	Aveluy Wood
,,	,,	PARKHURST, 2/Lt. George Henry, 3/Manchester (8/Worcester)	
,,	4.	CAPPER, 2/Lt. Harold Kent, R.A.F.	Accident at Stamford
,,	8.	LOUDOUN, 2/Lt. Thomas, 3/R. Highlanders	
,,	13.	FAIRTLOUGH, Capt. Gerard Howard,* ✠ 1/Artists (R.E.)	Wounded May 25
,,	,,	HAMILTON, Capt. Herbert James, ✠ R.A.F.	Accident at Tadcaster
,,	,,	WHITESIDE, Lieut. Miles Bruce Dalzell, 1/Highland L.I. (R.A.F.)	Accident
,,	15.	BUTTERY, 2/Lt. Robert Arthur, 3(4)Oxford & Bucks L.I.	Asiago Plateau, Italy
,,	,,	CHUTTER, Lieut. George Philip, 3/Gloucester	,, ,, ,,
,,	16.	HARLAND, 2/Lt. Richard, R.G.A.	
,,	,,	LEVICK, 2/Lt. Cyril, R.A.F.	Near St. Omer
,,	17.	BIRDSALL, Pte. Geoffrey, 1/Artists	In France
,,	19.	CARTMAN, 2/Lt. James Victor, 5/Liverpool	
,,	20.	COLE, 2/Lt. William Maurice,* ✠ 5/Leicester	Near Essars, Bethune
,,	,,	PERRY, 2/Lt. Arthur Ernest Cecil,* R.G.A.	Near Albert
,,	,,	SESSIONS, Lieut. Donald Humphrey, ✠ R.A.F.	Over New Romney
,,	21.	REDLER, Lieut. Harold Bolton, ✠ R.A.F.	Accident
,,	25.	CARTER, 2/Lt. Alan, R.A.F.	Near Abbeville
,,	,,	MATTHEWS, Capt. Thomas, M.B.E.,* R.G.A.	At Aire
,,	29.	FIELD, Pte. Roy Hammersley,* 1/Artists	In France
July	1.	BALLS, Lieut. Frank William, 3/Suffolk (R.A.F.)	Died in Arabia
,,	,,	WHITELEY, Lieut. Charles Taylor,* 8/R. Warwick	Near Merville (June 29)
,,	2.	HARTMANN, Lieut. Charles Herbert, 5/R. West Kent	Near Bouzincourt
,,	4.	BURT, Pte. Horace Christopher, Artists	Died
,,	,,	MACKENZIE, Capt. Frederick Boyce, R.G.A.	Accident
,,	5.	BURNS, Pte. William Alfred, 1/Artists	Auchonvillers
,,	,,	WALTERS, Pte. Robert Ernest, 1/Artists	
,,	14.	HUGHES, 2/Lt. William,* ✠ 8/Bedford	Near Albert (3rd)
,,	15.	GRAY, Lieut. Harry Albert,✠ R. West Kent	Wounded 10th
,,	16.	HAYES, Pte. Thomas Frederick, 1/Artists	Auchonvillers
,,	,,	ROGERS, 2/Lt. Arthur Forbes, R.A.F.	Accident at Lydd
,,	,,	WALKER, Pte. John Thomas, 1/Artists	Auchonvillers
,,	17.	DOWSETT, 2/Lt. Henry George, R.A.F.	Over Nether Wallop, Hants.
,,	,,	MILLER, Pte. Frank, 1/Artists	Died while P.O.W.
,,	20.	BRAY, 2/Lt. Sidney Herbert,* 8/West Yorks	
,,	,,	CORNELIUS, 2/Lt. Herbert Walter, 1/Bedford	Near Forêt de Nieppe
,,	21.	HICKS, Lieut. Charles Hubert, 8/Notts & Derby	Near Hazebrouck
,,	22.	STREATER, 2/Lt. John Wenham,* 15/R. Warwick	Forêt de Nieppe (June 28)
,,	25.	DANSEY, 2/Lt. Felix Ramon Arthur, 7/London	Near Albert
,,	27.	GREENWOOD, Lieut. James Hurst,* ✠ 11/R. West Kent	Aveluy Wood (April 6)
,,	29.	CHEESMAN, Pte. Daniel Gordon, Artists	Died
,,	,,	DULIN, Lieut. William Walker Motta, R.A.F.	Accident
,,	30.	BLAKE, Major Charles Edwin Norman, ✠ R.F.A.	
,,	,,	BRISLEY, Major Cuthbert Everard, R.A.F.	Accident, Market Drayton
,,	,,	KING, Lieut. Kenneth Vivian, R.A.F.	Combat over German lines
Aug.	2.	NUTCOMBE, 2/Lt. Thomas Arthur, 3/East Lancashire (R.A.F.)	
,,	,,	SWEETING, 2/Lt. Alan Ernest, R.A.F.	Accident at Biggin Hill

* *Died of Wounds.*

ROLL OF HONOUR

1918.
Aug.	4.	Moss, 2/Lt. Herbert Stanley, 2/R. Regt. Cavalry (1/Lond. Yeomanry)		*Died.*
,,	6.	Dawson, Capt. Frederick Albert, ✠ 8/East Surrey	...	*Near Albert*
,,	,,	Mummery, Capt. Harry Norman,* 1(14)Highland L.I.		*d. in German hands*
,,	7.	Baines, Capt. Ellis Eyton A.O.D.	... ...	*Died*
,,	,,	Nicholls, Lieut. Harold, 3/East Surrey	... ...	*Morlancourt (6th)*
,,	,,	Pearson, 2/Lt. Robert,* 1/Yorks (8/W. Yorks)	*d. in German hands, Rethel, Aisne*	
,,	,,	Selfe, Capt. Edgar Donald, 9/Norfolk	...	
,,	,,	Stevens, 2/Lt. Douglas Harcourt, 4/East Kent	...	*Near Morlancourt*
,,	8.	Anderson, Capt. David Wilson, ✠✠ 6/London	...	*Near the Ancre*
,,	,,	Barber, 2/Lt. Harry Mason, 3(8)East Surrey	...	*Near the Somme*
,,	,,	Claydon, Pte. Douglas Christie, Artists	...	
,,	,,	Murray, 2/Lt. Arthur, 7/R. Sussex.	...	
,,	,,	Roberts, 2/Lt. Francklin Alexander, 7/London	...	*Near Albert*
,,	,,	Thorley, Lieut. Horace William, 17/Lancers	...	*Near Cayeux*
,,	9.	Constance, 2/Lt. William Ernest, 7/London	...	*Near Chipilly*
,,	,,	Dickinson, Lieut. Henry Waite,* 12/Northumb. Fusiliers		*(While P.O.W.)*
,,	,,	Mansel-Howe, Lieut. Charles Iorworth, 23/London		
,,	,,	Perring, Lieut. Charles Richard, R.A.F. ...	...	*Accident*
,,	,,	Sampson, Capt. Charles Alexander, ✠ 25/London	...	*Near Bois Celestine*
,,	10.	Moss, 2/Lt. Gerald Alec, 2/Manchester	... ...	*Near Bois-en-Equerre*
,,	11.	Taylor, Capt. Ernest Reginald, ✠ 7/Essex	...	
,,	,,	Tee, 2/Lt. Clifford Vernon,* R.G.A.	... ...	*Hamel*
,,	13.	Fattorini, Lieut. Thomas, R.A.F.	...	*Over Parvillers*
,,	15.	Wright, 2/Lt. Arthur Samuel, 3(8)East Yorks	...	*Forêt de Nieppe*
,,	17.	Merrett, 2/Lt. Harold Edmund,* 10/Notts & Derby	...	
,,	18.	Emslie, Staff-Sgt.-Major Peter, *D.C.M.*, 1/Artists	...	
,,	,,	Thomas, 2/Lt. Cyril Reynard, 11/S. Wales Borderers		*Near Outersteene*
,,	19.	Horsley, Capt. Oswald, ✠✠ 2/Gordon H'drs. (R.A.F.)	*Accident over Reading*	
,,	,,	Knox, 2/Lt. Thomas Cowe, 7/Liverpool	...	...
,,	,,	Whyte, 2/Lt. Mark Gilchrist, 6/R. Fusiliers		...
,,	20.	Buttery, 2/Lt. Walter, 5/East Yorks	... ...	*Near Vieux Berquin*
,,	,,	Wolstenholme, 2/Lt. James Benjamin W., R.A.F.	...	
,,	21.	Traynor, Pte. Francis Edward, 1/Artists ...		*Near Fonquevillers*
,,	22.	Evershed, Lieut. Philip Douglas, 7/London		*Near Bray*
,,	,,	Lakeman, 2/Lt. Harold Leslie, R.A.S.C. (7/Lancs. Fus.)		
,,	,,	Nelson, Pte. Frederick Andrew Johnston,* 1/Artists	...	*Near Logeast Wood*
,,	,,	Schell, 2/Lt. Frederick Stanley, R.G.A.	...	
,,	,,	Tyler, Capt. Guy Cromwell, 1/Norfolk	...	*Near Achiet-le-Petit*
,,	,,	Webber, Pte. William Kingsbury, 1/Artists	...	*In Logeast Wood*
,,	23.	Chippington, 2/Lt. Horace Leonard,* 3/Suffolk (16/R. Warwick)		
,,	,,	Edinger, 2/Lt. Valentine, 1(4)R. Warwick	...	
,,	,,	Hewlett, Capt. Harold Alcester Tom, 4/London	...	
,,	,,	Palmer, Lieut. Arthur Baillie Bentinck, R.A.F.	...	*Accident at Thetford*
,,	,,	Thompson, 2/Lt. Leonard, R.A.F.	...	
,,	,,	Watson, Lieut. Henry James Arthur, 5/Bedford	...	*Near Achiet-le-Petit*
,,	,,	Baker, Pte. Albert George. 1/Artists	... ...	*Logeast—Achiet Area*
,,	,,	Evans, Pte. Jenkin Evan,* 1/Artists	... ...	,, ,, ,,

* *Died of Wounds.*

ARTISTS' RIFLES, 1918.

1918.			
Aug. 23.	HARRIS, Pte. Ernest Beach,* 1/Artists	(P.O.W.)	Achiet Area
,, ,,	JONES, Pte. John Humphrey Ernest,* 1/Artists		In France (Jan. 1)
,, ,,	REEVE, Pte. Claud Harold,* 1/Artists		Logeast Wood
,, 24.	BELL, 2/Lt. Oliver, R.A.F.		
,, ,,	GUY, 2/Lt. Reginald Churchill, 8/R. Berks		
,, ,,	KEEPING, Capt. Claude Jeffery, 8/Middlesex		Near Croisilles
,, ,,	OWEN, 2/Lt. Henry James, 16/R. Welch Fusiliers		Near Mametz Wood
,, ,,	WATT, Lieut. Hugo Burn Craig, ✠ 8/Durham L.I.		
,, 25.	BACKHOUSE, 2/Lt. Herbert Frankland, 4/Middlesex		Near Achiet-le-Grand
,, ,,	GIBBON, 2/Lt. Frederick William, 1/Northumb. Fusiliers		
,, ,,	MACMILLAN, Pte. Charles Ellis,* 1/Artists		Loupart Wood
,, ,,	MURPHY, Lieut. John, 6/Northumberland Fusiliers		
,, 26.	ATHOL, Lieut. Charles Colbourne, M.G.C.		
,, ,,	HOUGHTON, 2/Lt. George, 3/West Yorks (6/Dorset)		Near Martinpuich
,, ,,	STAPLETON, 2/Lt. William Howell, 3/Bedford (5/R. Berks)		Near Carnoy
,, 27.	ALLISON, Lieut. Harry, 3/R. Welch Fusiliers		Near Longueval
,, ,,	EDWARDS-TROLLIP, 2/Lt. John, 7/London		,, Albert
,, ,,	LANGLEY, 2/Lt. Francis Jasper, 2/Grenadier Guards		
,, ,,	MAULE-FFINCH, 2/Lt. Eric Herbert J., 7/London		Near Bray
,, ,,	TYLER, 2/Lt. William Alfred, 7/London		,, Albert
,, ,,	WILSON, 2/Lt. Alexander Gordon, 12(13)R. Inniskg. Fus.		Near Vieux-Berquin
,, ,,	COLLINS, Pte. Arthur Leslie, 1/Artists		Thilloy
,, ,,	DAVIDSON, Pte. Eric Harry Lucas, 1/Artists		,,
,, ,,	GRAY, Pte. Oswald, 1/Artists		,,
,, ,,	HARLAND, Pte. Morgan Lewis, 1/Artists		,,
,, ,,	HORTON, Pte. Alan Moncrieff, 1/Artists		,,
,, ,,	HUTCHINSON, Pte. William Laurence, 1/Artists		,,
,, ,,	MILES, Pte. Frank David,* Artists		,,
,, 28.	NORMAN, Pte. Eric William,* Artists		,,
,, ,,	NORTH, Pte. Charles Edward P. J.,* Artists		,,
,, 29.	HUGGINS, Capt. Douglas Frank, 1/London		
,, ,,	WALLIS, Pte. Charles F., Artists (13/London)		
,, 30.	DUNN, 2/Lt. Harold Black, 5/Devon		Near Vaux-Vraicourt
,, ,,	EDE, Capt. Edwin William, ✠ 11/R. Fusiliers		
,, ,,	GREENWOOD, 2/Lt. Arthur Donald, 2/Bedford		
,, ,,	MADDOX, 2/Lt. Leonard George, ✠✠ 22/London		Accident
,, ,,	THORP, 2/Lt. Charles Evans, R.A.F.		In France
,, ,,	PEARSON, Pte. Kenneth Herbert,* 1/Artists		,, ,,
,, 31.	CURLING, Capt. Frank Trevor, 18/London		Near Maurepas
,, ,,	DAVIES, Pte. John,* 1/Artists		In France
,, ,,	FRASER, 2/Lt. Alan Cuming, ✠ 7/London		Bouchavesnes
,, ,,	HEWAT, Lieut. Richard Alexander, R.A.F.		
,, ,,	MOSES, Lieut. Frank Samuel, R.G.A.		Near Monchy
,, ,,	STEVENSON, 2/Lt. Ralph Tapley, 5/London (R.F.C.)		Near Bullecourt
,, ,,	YOUNG, Pte. Sidney Mountford,* 1/Artists		In France
Sept. 1.	EDWARDS, 2/Lt. Arthur Ernest, 8(7) East Yorks		Near Guedecourt
,, ,,	NELSON, Pte. William W., 1/Artists		Cagnicourt

* Died of Wounds.

ROLL OF HONOUR

1918.

Sept.	1	REEVE, Lieut. Garnet Norman Bray, 9/Manchester ...		*Near Bapaume*
,,	2.	GARRETT, 2/Lt. Maurice Humphries, 15/London ...		
,,	,,	HALLMARK, 2/Lt. Percy Harold, 3/York & Lancaster		
,,	,,	KIRK, 2/Lt. Ronald Leslie, 7/London	...	
,,	3.	BOSWOOD, Lieut. Leslie John, R.A.F. ...	...	*Accident, New Romney*
,,	,,	RICE, Pte. Albert George,* 1/Artists ...	...	*Inchy—Mœuvres*
,,	,,	STARK, 2/Lt. James Duncan,* 6/K.O.S.B. ...	...	*While P.O.W.*
,,	,,	THOROGOOD, Lieut. Edward Linford, 8/Lancashire Fus.		
,,	,,	WEISS, 2/Lt. Hubert Foveanse,* 8/London ...	...	
,,	4.	LEYBOURNE, Capt. Philip Edwin, ✠ ✠ 8/Hampshire ...		*Near Kemmel*
,,	,,	MACADAM, Lieut. Arthur Charles,* R.M.L.I.	...	
,,	,,	MARTIN, 2/Lt. Edwin John, 1/London ...	...	*Messines Ridge*
,,	5.	CABLE, 2/Lt. James Sydney, R.G.A. (S/R) ...	...	*Died*
,,	,,	MUNRO, Lieut. William Pearce,* R.F.A. ...	...	*Near Arras*
,,	,,	SPEAKMAN, 2/Lt. Alan Edwards, 2/R. Fusiliers	...	
,,	,,	WALTERS, L/Cpl. Robert Ernest, 1/Artists ...	...	*Inchy—Mœuvres*
,,	6.	HUCKLE, 2/Lt. Henry Wilson, 1/Cambridge	...	*Near Nurlu*
,,	7.	GAUNT, Lieut. Benjamin William, 3/York & Lanc. (T.M.B.)		*Havrincourt Wood*
,,	8.	RITSON, Pte. Charles Roy,* 1/Artists ...	...	*Inchy – Mœuvres*
,,	10.	SPURGEON, Lieut. Donald Frank Parker, 20/London ...		
,,	12.	HOLLIS, Lieut. Arthur Reginald, 10/D.C.L.I.		*Near Hermies*
,,	14.	WHITWORTH, 2/Lt. Walter Haworth,* 7/Lancashire Fus.		*Wounded 12th*
,,	16.	GRIFFIN, Lieut. Edward William, 6/Gloucester (R.A.F.)		*Near Le Cateau*
,,	18.	DAWSON, 2/Lt. Roger Graham, 3(6)Northampton		
,,	,,	GOTELEE, Capt. Geoffrey Harris, 1/S. Wales Borderers		*Near Salonika*
,,	,,	HOWARD, Lieut. Albert Leonard, 1/Loyal N. Lancs.		*Near Fresnoy-la-Petite*
,,	,,	KILSBY, 2/Lt. George Alfred, 4/Northampton	...	*Near Roussoy*
,,	19.	COMBER, Capt. Turner, ✠ 9/Essex ...	..	,, *Epehy*
,,	,,	CROCKETT, Lieut. Wallace John, R.A.F. ...	...	
,,	,,	EVANS, 2/Lt. Hugh Robert, 9/Welch	...	
,,	,,	STOTT, Lieut. Walter Goodwin, 4/Manchester (15/Cheshire)		*Near Ypres*
,,	20.	LONGTHORPE, 2/Lt. Frederick,* Tank Corps	...	
,,	,,	MILES, Pte. Frank David,* 1/Artists	...	...	*In France*
,,	21.	ISAACS, 2/Lt. Vincent Harcourt, 5(9) R. Fusiliers	...	*Near Epehy*
,,	,,	LARKEN, 2/Lt. John Savage, 2(1)West Kent Yeomanry		
,,	22.	COX, Lieut. William George, R. Engineers ...	...	*Died at Baghdad*
,,	,,	HIGGS, 2/Lt. Reginald Frank, 1/R. West Surrey	...	*Near Epehy*
,,	,,	SEDGELEY, Lieut. Henry Frederick, 9/London	...	
,,	23.	HARGER, 2/Lt. Edwyn Oscar,* R. Engineers	...	
,,	,,	SIMMONS, 2/Lt. Robert Dewdney, 7/London	...	
,,	24.	LAMBDIN, Lieut. John Reginald,* ✠ 7/West Yorks	...	*Near Cambrai*
,,	25.	UNDERWOOD, Lieut. Roy Gaton, R.A.F. ...		*Accident at North Weald*
,,	26.	CRUICKSHANK, Major Eric,* R.F.A. ...	...	
,,	27.	BALDWIN, 2/Lt. Austin Provost, 2/Suffolk ...	...	*Near Cambrai*
,,	,,	DRUMMOND, Lieut. Joseph Rayson, R.A.F.		
,,	,,	EVANS, 2/Lt. John Ewart, 3/Devon	...	*Near Marcoing*
,,	,,	HUGHESDON, 2/Lt. Arthur Hamilton, R.F.A.	...	,, *Cambrai*

* *Died of Wounds.*

1918.			
Sept. 27.	STEPHENS, Lieut. Robert Miller, 5/R. West Kent		Near Gouzeaucourt
,, ,,	ADAMS, Pte. Edgar Lawson, 1/Artists		Canal du Nord, Bourlon Wood
,, ,,	BAGOT, Pte. Christopher Whitehead,* 1/Artists		,, ,, ,, ,,
,, ,,	CROXON, Pte. Abraham Belcham, 1/Artists		,, ,, ,, ,,
,, ,,	MAGSON, Pte. Walter, 1/Artists		,, ,, ,, ,,
,, ,,	MAINGOT, Pte. Edmund, 1/Artists		,, ,, ,, ,,
,, ,,	POPKIN, Pte. Roland Gilbert, 1/Artists		,, ,, ,, ,,
,, ,,	RICKARD, Pte. William Charles,* 1/Artists		,, ,, ,, ,,
,, ,,	REYNOLDS, Pte. William Halliday, 1/Artists		,, ,, ,, ,,
,, ,,	SELBY, Pte. Michael George, 1/Artists		,, ,, ,, ,,
,, ,,	TIMMS, Pte. William Frederick, 1/Artists		,, ,, ,, ,,
,, ,,	WHITE, Cpl. Frederick, 1/Artists		,, ,, ,, ,,
,, ,,	WILLIAMS, Pte. Maxwell James, 1/Artists		,, ,, ,, ,,
,, 29.	BOWLING, 2/Lt. Arthur Henry, R.G.A.		...d. on service (Cambrai)
,, ,,	GIRLING, Lieut. Stephen Easthaugh, 9/D.C.L.I.		Near Villers-Pluich
,, ,,	LAUGHTON, 2/Lt. Joseph Thornton, 1/Bedford		,, Cambrai
,, ,,	PARKER, 2/Lt. Leslie Rowland, 3(1)S. Wales Borderers		
,, 30.	BEATON, 2/Lt. Grover Cleveland,* ✠ R.G.A.		
,, ,,	BOWYER, Pte. Frederick William Snell, 1/Artists		S. of Cambrai
,, ,,	HARTY, 2/Lt. William, 4/Shropshire L.I.		Aubers Ridge
,, ,,	HARVEY, Capt. Eric Howard, ✠✠ 5/Gloucester		
,, ,,	LEECH, 2/Lt. Robert Edward Holt, 4/Shropshire L.I.		Near Bethune
,, ,,	WIDDOP, Lieut. Arthur Norman, 4/East Kent		
,, ,,	EDMONDS, Lieut. Edward Peregrin Pell, R.A.F.		Died
,, ,,	SAWYER, Lieut. Robert Henry, R.A.F.		Died
Oct. 1.	BARTLETT, Lieut. Leonard, 2/Oxford & Bucks L.I.		. Near Cambrai
,, ,,	PENDEREL-BRODHURST, 2/Lt. Bernard R., R. Engineers		Near Neuve-Chapelle
,, ,,	ROBERTS, Pte. George,* 1/Artists		S. of Cambrai
,, ,,	TINNISWOOD, 2/Lt. Alfred, R. Engineers		
,, ,,	WILSON, Pte. Percy Gordon,* 1/Artists		S. of Cambrai
,, 2.	GRIFFITHS, Pte. Garnet,* 1/Artists		,, Died
,, ,,	SAULL, 2/Lt. Harold Truscott, /King's Liverpool		
,, ,,	SKELTON, 2/Lt. Henry, 11/Lancashire Fusiliers		
,, 3.	ADAMS, 2/Lt. Percy Horace, 1/Notts & Derby		
,, ,,	CHARLTON, 2/Lt. Frank Tysoe,* 3/South Lancashire		Near Bethune
,, ,,	CHRISTY, 2/Lt. John George, 1(5)Leicester		Near St. Quentin
,, ,,	COLLINGS, Lieut. Lionel Lapidge, Durham L.I. (R.A.F.)		Died at Netley
,, ,,	LAING, Major James Gordon, 1/Artists (M.G.C.)		Near Estaires
,, ,,	VANN, Lt.-Col. Bernard William, **V.C.**, ✠✠ 8/Notts & Derby		,, Ramicourt
,, ,,	WHEATLEY, 2/Lt. John Charles,* 3(5)Notts & Derby		,, ,,
,, 4.	BANNESTER, 2/Lt. John, 16/London		
,, ,,	FELL, Pte. Kenneth George,* 1/Artists		In France
,, ,,	O'CONNOR, Lieut. Bernard Joseph, 3/R. Fusiliers		
,, 5.	CANNING, 2/Lt. Ernest Harold, 1/Gloucester (R.A.F.)		Accident
,, ,,	LLOYD, 2/Lt. Evan Christian,* 3(1)S. Wales Borderers		Near St. Quentin
,, ,,	QUINN, 2/Lt. James Ewart, 8/King's Liverpool		,, Cambrai
,, ,,	ROBERTSON, 2/Lt. James,* 19(7)London		

* Died of Wounds.

ROLL OF HONOUR

1918.

Oct.	6.	GRIMSLEY, 2/Lt. William Henry, 9/Yorks	
,,	7.	BAKER, Pte. Vernon Stanley, Artists	*Died*
,,	8.	ARCHER, 2/Lt. Henry Charles, 1/Monmouth ...	*Near Sequehart*
,,	,,	CRANE, 2/Lt. Lucius Francis, 14/Worcester ...	,, *Cambrai*
,,	,,	DUCKWORTH, 2/Lt. Walter Clarence, 13/Welch (1/Shrop. L.I.)	,, *St. Quentin*
,,	,,	HARRY, Sub-Lt. Francis Clifford, Hawke Bn., R. Naval Div.	,, *Cambrai*
,,	,,	JAMES, 2/Lt. Harry Garfield, R.F.A.	,, ,,
,,	,,	LOOKER, 2/Lt. Arthur Donald, 1(G/B)Suffolk (15/Essex)	*Near Bois Grenier*
,,	9.	HARTLEY, Lieut. Alfred,* R.G.A.	
,,	,,	WINCH, 2/Lt. Edward Nightingale,* 8/R. West Kent...	
,,	10.	CASSON, Pte. Henry Gent,* 1/Artists	*Niergnies*
,,	,,	GOTELEE, L/Cpl. Frederick, 1/Artists	*Died in France*
,,	11.	CRADDOCK, 2/Lt. Victor,* 5/South Stafford	*Near Bohain*
,,	12.	HALLIWELL, Capt. Frederick, 17/Manchester ...	,, *Neuvilly*
,,	13.	DELANDRE-GROGAN, Lieut. Leon Victor St. Patrick,✠ 13/York & Lanc.	*In France*
,,	,,	SINCLAIR, Lieut. Eric Russell,✠ 7/Argyle & Suth'd H'drs	,, ,,
,,	14.	FISHER, 2/Lt. Charles Heath,✠ 12/East Surrey ...	
,,	16.	GODDARD, 2/Lt. Gordon Cecil, 9/East Surrey ...	*Near Haussy*
,,	,,	SMITH, Capt. Geoffrey Hubert,✠ 1/Coldstream Guards	*Missing, believed killed*
,,	,,	VINCENT, 2/Lt. Charles Issom Francis, 1/Coldstream Gds.	
,,	17.	BROMHAM, Lieut. Charles Adolphus Row, 5/Devon ...	
,,	,,	JACQUES, 2/Lt. William Gladstone, 5/Notts & Derby	*Near Fresnoy-le-Grand*
,,	18.	TURNBULL, Capt. Maxwell.✠ 8/Border	*Died*
,,	19.	DE BURIATTE, Lieut. Warwick Huxley, R.G.A. ...	*Accident at Enfield*
,,	21.	PURVIS, Lieut. John Easton, R.N.V.R.	*Mine-sweeping near Ostend*
,,	22.	BEVAN, Capt. Thomas William, R. Engineers ...	*Died at Dunkirk*
,,	,,	ROBINSON, Pte. George Milner, Artists	*Died*
,,	23.	HARVEY, 2/Lt. William Henry, R.F.A. (S/R) ...	
,,	,,	RIPPERGER, Lieut. Harold Theodore Alvin,✠ 4/Gloucester	
,,	,,	SPINK, Lieut. Edward Wodehouse, 7/Lancashire Fusiliers	*Near Beaurain*
,,	,,	STEPHENS, Lieut. Cecil Hubert, R.F.A.	
,,	,,	SUTTON, Lieut. William Henry, 2/Welch	
,,	,,	WELBY, 2/Lt. Davis, R.G.A. (S/R)	*Died*
,,	24.	MARKS, 2/Lt. John, 3/Durham L.I.	
,,	,,	MITCHELL, Pte. David Dalrymple, Artists	*Died*
,,	,,	MORRIS, 2/Lt. Alfred Arthur Thomas,✠ 6/Middlesex ...	*Near Inchy*
,,	,,	THOMAS, Lieut. William Barton, 7/Worcester ...	*Near Varchain*
,,	25.	HARDMAN, Capt. Kenrie, 3/Highland L.I.	
,,	,,	STICKLAND, Sgt. Charles Stuart, Artists	*Died*
,,	26.	DICKSON, 2/Lt. Geo. Hubert Murray, 6/Black Watch...	
,,	,,	EMERY, Lieut. Walter Herbert Vernon, 7/East Lancashire	*Died*
,,	,,	NIXON, 2/Lt. Thomas William,* 7/York & Lancaster ...	
,,	27.	BURMANN, Capt. Robert Moyle, D.S.O.,✠ 2/Border ...	*Near Fontaine-au-Bois*
,,	28.	CULLING, Pte. Victor James, Artists	*Died*
,,	29.	HOWARD, Lieut. Gilbert Gordon,* 6/Gloucester ...	
,,	,,	NICHOLSON, Lieut. Bernard Geo. Maurice, 13/Northumb. Fus.	*Died*
,,	30.	DODD, Lieut. Albert, R.A.F.	*Near Le Cateau*

* *Died of Wounds.*

ARTISTS' RIFLES, 1918.

1918.			
Oct. 30.	Fish, Lieut. Benjamin Leslie, 12(18)Middlesex	...	Near Le Cateau
,,	,, Grey, Pte. William Cecil, Artists	... ...	Died
,,	,, Prosser, Capt. Arthur Edward,* 1/Worcester	...	P.O.W. (23rd)
,,	,, Wells, Pte. Jack, Artists	... ...	Died
,,	31. Golding, Capt. Harold William, A.S.C. (8/Somerset L.I.)		
,,	,, Murray, Pte. Robert McNab, Artists	... ...	Died
Nov.	1. Barrett, Lieut. Jack Harper Phillips. 1/Lincoln (R.A.F.)		,,
,,	,, Wicks, Pte. Francis Heywood, Artists	... ...	,,
,,	2. Hulse, Pte. Charles William, Artists	... ...	,,
,,	,, Ingleton, Lieut. Herbert John,* 4(8)Lancashire Fus.		Near St. Quentin
,,	3. Llewellyn, 2/Lt. Vivian, 14/R. Welch Fusiliers	...	
,,	4. Brock, Lieut. Cecil Howard,* 8/Devon	... ...	Near Pommereuil
,,	,, Hunter, Capt. Charles James, 2/Bedford (Labour Corps)		Died
,,	,, Lechertier, Lieut. Jacques Alfred R.F.A.	...	Near Le Quesnoy
,,	,, Owen, Capt. Malcolm de Brissac, ✠ 1/Hertford	...	Near Johinetz
,,	,, Owen, Lieut. Wilfred Edward Salter, ✠ 5/Manchester ...		Near Sambre Canal
,,	,, Roch-Austin, Lieut. Sidney Leslie,* 4/West Riding	...	Near Maubeuge
,,	,, Cannon, Pte. Ernest Edward, 2/Artists	... ...	Died
,,	,, Fletcher, Pte. Cecil Brasher, 2/Artists	... ...	,,
,,	,, Pearman, Pte. Carl Herbert, 2/Artists	... ...	,,
,,	,, Rheam, Pte. Herbert Leopold, 2/Artists	... ...	,,
,,	,, Wehrle, Sgt. Alfred, 2/Artists	... .	,,
,,	5. Adair, Pte. Edward Samuel Baker, 2/Artists	...	,,
,,	,, Marshall, 2/Lt. Harry,* Labour Corps	... ...	Estaires (Oct. 29)
,,	6. Pepper, Capt. Alwyn Tayton, R. Engineers	...	Died at Salonika
,,	8. Bregazzi, 2/Lt. Edward, 5/Notts & Derby ...	...	Died
,,	,, Shaw, Lieut. Walter Douglas,* ✠ R. Fusiliers (10/Manchester)		
,,	,, Thomas, Sgt. Reginald, Artists	... ...	Died
,,	9. Alington, Cpl. Gervase Winford, 1/Artists (17/London)		Near Harvengt
,,	,, Davis, 2/Lt. Philip Henry Halton, 3/Manchester	...	
,,	,, Pegram, Capt. Charles Ernest, ✠ 17/Rifle Brigade	...	Died
,,	,, Williams, Lieut. William Harold, R.G.A. ...	...	Near Valenciennes
,,	10. Hobson, Capt. Robert Carl, ✠ ✠ 12/Northumb. Fusiliers		Died
,,	,, Garbutt, Sgt. Joseph Herbert, 1/Artists	... ...	Near Harvengt
,,	,, Croft, Major Benjamin, 1/Artists	... ...	,, ,,

ARMISTICE.

,,	11. Bevington, Pte. Thomas Pincombe, Artists	...	Died
,,	,, Elliott, Pte. Horace J., Artists ...	... ...	,,
,,	,, Halls, Pte. William James, Artists	... ...	,,
,,	,, Power, Pte. Bryan, Artists	... ...	,,
,,	,, Roberts, Lieut. John, ✠ R.F.A	... ...	,,
,,	,, Woodforde, Pte. George Augustus,* 1/Artists		Wounded in France (Sept. 27)
,,	12. Shea, Lieut. Richard Thomas, R.G.A.	... ...	Died
,,	13. Yewdall, Pte. Mark, 1/Artists ...	... ...	Died at Etaples
,,	17. Davies, 2/Lt. David Harold,* 1/Wilts	... ...	Cambrai (Aug. 30)

* *Died of Wounds.*

ROLL OF HONOUR

1918.
Nov. 17.	DOBSON, Lieut. Nathaniel George,* 2/Border (1/Cam.)		
,, 20.	THOMSON, Pte. Bothwell, Artists ...		Died
,, 22.	EVANS, Lieut. Percy Lewis, R.A.F.		
,, 25.	STAINTON, Lieut. Ernest,* 7/Worcester		
,, 26.	BIGGS, 2/Lt. Seward, A.S.C.		Died near Cambrai
,, ,,	POOLE, 2/Lt. Leslie Stanley Richard, R.A.F.		
Dec. 6.	THORPE, 2/Lt. Albert Edward, 3/Yorks (11/East Yorks)		Died
,, 12.	PLUMPTON, 2/Lt. Robert, 6/Yorks		,,
,, 18.	COOPER, Lieut. Frederick Edmund,* 26/R. Fusiliers ...		
,, 19.	ASHWIN, Pte. Mauley Frederic, Artists		Died
,, 20.	BRIGGS, Lieut. Ernest Frederick, R.N.R. ...		Died on Service
,, ,,	IMROTH, 2/Lt. Leslie, 8/Hampshire		Died
,, ,,	MACARTHY, Pte. Jeremiah James, Artists ...		,,
,, 27.	WETHERALL, 2/Lt. Eric Francis Cecil, Labour Corps...		Died at Lille
,, ,,	ANSON-JONES, 2/Lt. John Samuel, R.G.A. ...		Died

1919.

1919.
Jan. 9.	SLATTERY, Capt. Francis James, R. Engineers		Died
,, 24.	WHITE, 2/Lt. Thomas Herbert, ✠ 7/East Lancs. (R.A.F.)		,,
,, 30.	BERKELEY, Lieut. Christopher, Coldstream Guards (R.A.F.)		Accident
,, ,,	RAWLINS, Capt. Guy Vernon Champion, R.E. (Tank Corps)		Died
Feb. 4.	ROUGHT, Lieut. Charles Gardiner, 2/R. West Surrey ..	Died after repatriation	
,, 13.	GUNN, 2/Lt. Edmond Alan, R.G.A. ...		Died
,, 15.	BURLEY, 2/Lt. Ernest Sidney, Labour Corps		,,
,, 17.	WHITEHEAD, Lieut. Edgar Joseph William, R.G.A. (R.E.)		,,
,, 22.	GRATWICK, Lieut. Harold Duncan, 4/Devon		,,
,, 28.	MILLS, 2/Lt. Robert Cecil Lloyd, 6/Northampton		Died after repatriation
Mar. 7.	STUART, 2/Lt. Herbert Gordon,* 3/London ...		Mariecourt (27/8/18)
,, 13.	TRATMAN, Lieut. Leslie William Draycott, R.A.F.		Died after repatriation
,, 23.	ARCHER, Pte. Percy John, Artists		Died
,, 26.	NORDEN, Pte. William Alfred, Artists		,,
,, 27.	MINORS, Lieut. Roland Towers, 7/Worcester (R.A.F.)	Accident at Namur (26th)	
Apr. 20.	GERHARDI, Lieut. Charles, R.A.F.		Accident in Esthonia
,, 22.	HUNT, Lieut. Cyril Frank, R.A.F.		Accident
May 10.	NORTON, Lieut. George, R.A.F. ...		
July 15.	GOOLDEN, Capt. Alexander Wood, 134/Baluchistan Infantry (late 1/E. Surrey) Near Fort Sandeman, Afghan Frontier		
Sept. 23.	BOOTH, 2/Lt. Edward Arthur, General Staff		At Kolvetski, N. Russia

* Died of Wounds.

SECTION II.

LIST OF
DECORATIONS, HONOURS
AND
REWARDS FOR SERVICES IN THE FIELD

OBTAINED BY MEMBERS OF THE CORPS

SINCE AUGUST 4TH, 1914.

V.C.

The Victoria Cross Decoration was instituted January 29th, 1856, for the purpose of signalising special individual acts of bravery. It may be conferred on any rank. The Badge consists of a Bronze Cross patée with the Royal Crown in the centre and underneath a scroll bearing the inscription "For Valour." The colour of the ribbon is red.

HALLOWES, 2/Lt. Rupert Price, *M.C.* 4/Middlesex
    HOOGE, BELGIUM, between 25th September and 1st October, 1915. For most conspicuous bravery and devotion to duty.
    2/Lt. Hallowes displayed throughout these days the greatest bravery and untiring energy, and set a magnificent example to his men during four heavy and prolonged bombardments. On more than one occasion he climbed up on the parapet, utterly regardless of danger, in order to put fresh heart into his men. He made daring reconnaissances of the German positions in our lines. When the supply of bombs was running short he went back under heavy shell fire and brought up a fresh supply. Even after he was mortally wounded he continued to cheer those around him, and to inspire them with fresh courage.
[Reg. No. 1422.   Gazetted 5th April, 1915.   Killed in action 30th Sept., 1915]

FLEMING-SANDES, 2/Lt. Arthur James Terence ... ... 2/East Surrey
    HOHENZOLLERN REDOUBT, FRANCE, September 29th, 1915. For most conspicuous bravery.
    2/Lt. Fleming-Sandes was sent to command a company which at the time was in a very critical position. The troops on his right were retiring, and his own men, who were much shaken by continual bombing and machine-gun fire, were also beginning to retire, owing to shortage of bombs. Taking in the situation at a glance, he collected a few bombs, jumped on to the parapet in full view of the Germans, who were only twenty yards away, and threw them.
    Although very severely wounded almost at once by a bomb, he struggled to his feet and continued to advance and throw bombs till he was again severely wounded. This most gallant act put new heart into his men, rallied them, and saved the situation.
[Reg. No. 1482.   Gazetted 9th May, 1915]

MELLISH, Capt. the Rev. Edward Noel ... Chaplain to the Forces (R.A.C.D.)
    ST. ELOI, FRANCE, 27th to 29th March, 1916. For most conspicuous bravery.
    During heavy fighting on three consecutive days he repeatedly went backwards and forwards under continuous and heavy shell and machine-gun fire, between our original trenches and those captured from the enemy, in order to tend and rescue wounded men. He brought in ten badly wounded men on the first day from ground swept by machine-gun fire and three were actually killed while he was dressing their wounds. The battalion to which he was attached was relieved on the second day, but he went back and brought in twelve more wounded men. On the night of the third day he took charge of a party of volunteers, and once more returned to the trenches to rescue the remaining wounded. This splendid work was quite voluntary on his part, and outside the scope of his ordinary duties.
[Gazetted 5th May, 1915

CATHER, Lieut. Geoffrey St. George Shillington ... Adjutant 9/Royal Irish Fusiliers
    Near HAMEL, FRANCE, 1st July, 1916. For most conspicuous bravery.
    From 7 p.m. till midnight he searched "No Man's Land," and brought in three wounded men. Next morning at 8 a.m. he continued his search, brought in another wounded man, and gave water to others, arranging for their rescue later. Finally, at 10.30 a.m., he took out water to another man and was proceeding further on when he was himself killed. All this was carried out in full view of the enemy, and under direct machine-gun fire and intermittent artillery fire. He set a splendid example of courage and self-sacrifice.
[Reg. No. 685.   Gazetted 22nd May, 1915.   Killed 2nd July, 1916]

BENNETT, Lieut. Eugené Paul, *M.C.* 2/Worcester
    Near LE TRANSLOY, FRANCE, 5th November, 1916. For most conspicuous bravery in action when in command of the second wave of the attack. Finding that the first wave had suffered heavy casualties, its commander killed and the line wavering, Lieut. Bennett advanced at the head of the second wave, and by his personal example of valour and resolution reached his objective with but sixty men. Isolated with his small party, he at once took steps to consolidate his position under heavy rifle and machine-gun fire from both flanks, and, although wounded, he remained in command directing and controlling. He set an example of cheerfulness and resolution beyond all praise, and there is little doubt that but for his personal example of courage the attack would have been checked at the outset.
[Reg. No. 1253.]   Gazetted 1st January, 1915]

CATES, 2/Lt. George Edward ... ... 2/Rifle Brigade
    E. of BOUCHAVESNES, FRANCE, 8th March, 1917. For most conspicuous bravery and self-sacrifice. When engaged with some other men in deepening a captured trench, this officer struck with his spade a buried bomb, which immediately started to burn. 2/Lt. Cates, in order to save the lives of his comrades, placed his foot on the bomb, which immediately exploded. He showed the most conspicuous gallantry and devotion to duty in performing the act which cost him his life, but saved the lives of others.
[Reg. No. 3035.]   Gazetted 27th February, killed 9th March, 1917]

DEAN, Lieut. Donald John ... ... 8/Royal West Kent (T.F.)
    N.W. of LENS, FRANCE, 24th to 26th September, 1918. For most conspicuous bravery, skilful command, and devotion to duty when holding, with his platoon, an advanced post established in a newly-captured enemy trench north-west of Lens. The left flank of the position was insecure, and the post, when taken over on the night of September 24th, was ill-prepared for defence. Shortly after the post was occupied the enemy attempted, without success, to recapture it. Under heavy machine-gun fire consolidation was continued, and shortly after midnight another determined enemy attack was driven off. Throughout the night Lieut. Dean worked unceasingly with his men, and about 6 a.m. on September 25th a resolute enemy attack, supported by heavy shell and trench mortar fire, developed. Again, owing to the masterly handling of his command, Lieut. Dean repulsed the attack, causing heavy enemy casualties. Throughout the 25th and the night of September 25th-26th consolidation was continued under heavy fire, which culminated in intense artillery fire on the morning of the 26th, when the enemy again attacked and was finally repulsed with loss. Five times in all (thrice heavily) was this post attacked, and on each occasion the attack was driven back. Throughout the period, Lieut. Dean inspired his command with his own contempt of danger, and all fought with the greatest bravery. He set an example of valour, leadership and devotion to duty of the very highest order.
[Reg. No. 3692.]   Gazetted 4th October, 1916]

VANN, Lieut.-Col. Bernard William, *M.C. & Bar; Croix-de-G.* 8(6)Notts & Derby (T.F.)
    BELLENGLISE, FRANCE, 29th September, 1918. For most conspicuous bravery, devotion to duty and fine leadership during the attack at Bellenglise and Lehaucourt. He led his battalion with great skill across the Canal du Nord through a very thick fog and under heavy fire from field and machine guns. On reaching the high ground above Bellenglise the whole attack was held up by fire of all descriptions from the front and right flank. Realising that everything depended on the advance going forward with the barrage, Lt.-Col. Vann rushed up to the firing line and with the greatest gallantry led the line forward. By his prompt action and absolute contempt for danger the whole situation was changed, the men were encouraged and the line swept forward. Later he rushed a field gun single-handed and knocked out three of the detachment. The success of the day was in no small degree due to the splendid gallantry and fine leadership displayed by this officer. Lt.-Col. Vann, who had on all occasions set the highest example of valour, was killed near Ramicourt four days later, when leading his battalion in attack.
[Reg. No. 1800.]   Gazetted 2nd Sept., 1914.   Killed in action, 3rd Oct., 1918]
                                                              (11 times a casualty. ED.)

D.S.O.

The Distinguished Service Order was instituted by Queen Victoria, September 6th, 1886. May be conferred on Commissioned Officers who have been specially mentioned in despatches for meritorious or distinguished service in the field or before the enemy. Bars may be added for additional acts of gallantry. Since August 1st, 1918, this Order has been awarded in respect of active service for "services in action" only, i.e., for service under fire or for distinguished individual service in connection with air-raids, bombardments or other enemy action. The Badge of the Order is a gold cross, enamelled white, edged gold, having on one side the Imperial Crown in gold on a red enamelled ground, on the reverse side the Imperial and Royal Cypher (both sides being surrounded by a wreath of laurels enamelled green). The ribbon is red, edged blue. Bars are indicated (in undress uniform) by silver rosettes on the ribbon.

ANDREWS, Capt. Stephen Arthur ... ... 7/Royal Sussex
  Near EPEHY, 18th September, 1918. For conspicuous gallantry and good work. His company was allotted the task of clearing the railway embankment of the enemy. Although enfiladed by machine-gun nests from the village, and having sustained heavy casualties, he personally led forward the remainder of his company, and was one of very few to reach the objective. He then organised under very heavy fire and held the position until the situation was cleared up. [Reg. No. 1915

AUSTEN, Major Ernest Edward 1/Artists
  In EGYPT, awarded 1st January, 1919.

BARE, Capt. Alfred Raymond, *M.C.* ... ... 1/2 Loyal North Lancashire
  GIVENCHY, 18th April, 1918. For conspicuous gallantry and devotion to duty. Under cover of a heavy barrage the enemy attacked, very quickly surrounding a strong point, where this officer had his company headquarters and one platoon. In face of superior numbers he put up a stout resistance until forced to retire on to another strong point, where the position was very critical, the officer in charge having been killed. He took command, and after a stiff fight, drove back the enemy. He was twice wounded during the fight. [1296

BLACKWOOD, Lt.-Col. Albemarle Price ... ... 2/Border Regt. (Adjt. 1/Artists)
  BUTKOVA DZUNA, 20th December, 1917. For conspicuous gallantry and devotion to duty. He conducted a most successful raid on a village in the enemy's lines, which resulted in the capture of 55 prisoners and heavy casualties to the enemy. The success of the enterprise was due to his forethought and skilful handling of his command.

BURMANN, Capt. Robert Moyle, *M.C.* 2/Border & East Lancs. (Brigade-Major 20/Inf. Brig.)
  Awarded 3rd June, 1918.

CARRINGTON, 2/Lt. Charles Worrell ... ... Grenadier Guards
  FONTAINE-NOTRE-DAME, 27th November, 1917. For conspicuous gallantry and devotion to duty. When part of the advance was held up by two enemy machine guns firing from a house he at once organised and led a bayonet charge and captured the house and its occupants. He then led a successful attack on the second objective, and having captured it, beat off a counter-attack. Later, when his flank became exposed, and the enemy attacked him from the rear, he fought his way back, and brought his men out in good order. He set a magnificent example of courage and initiative. [7781

DISTINGUISHED SERVICE ORDER.

CUMBERLEGE, Capt. Geoffrey Fenwick Jocelyn ... ... 11/Royal Fusiliers
S. of MIREAUMONT TRENCH, 17th February, 1917. He dashed along the line rallying his own battalion and men of other units. He succeeded in restoring order and in reorganising the line at a most critical time. Throughout the day he inspired all ranks by his high example of courage and devotion to duty. [1889

CUTTING, Major Raymond Howarth, *M.C.* ... ... 1/Devonshire (att. M.G.C.)
Awarded 3rd June, 1918. [1142

EDLMANN, Major Francis Joseph Frederick ... ... 12/Northumberland Fusiliers
Awarded 1st January, 1917. [1634

EDWARDS, 2/Lt. Cyril George ... ... 7/West Yorkshire
REINCOURT, 27th July, 1917. For conspicuous gallantry and devotion to duty. Having gone out with a N.C.O. to reconnoitre the enemy's wire, they were attacked by bombs. The first one he seized before it exploded and threw it back, and, when the second fell, realising that they could not both escape unharmed, he threw his legs over it to smother the explosion, and thus protected the N.C.O. By this splendid act of gallantry and self-sacrifice he saved the life of his comrade at the risk of his own. The N.C.O. was able to drag him back to our lines, where he showed great pluck in reporting the information which he had gained by his daring reconnaissance. [4804

ELKINGTON, Capt. Christopher Garrett 8/Gloucestershire
GRANDCOURT, 18th November, 1916. With six men he attacked and silenced an enemy machine gun. Later he displayed great courage and ability in organising the defence of the position. He was twice wounded, but remained at duty directing operations until he was again severely wounded. [2501

FARRINGTON, Capt. Windham Brookes ... ... 3/Notts & Derby (R.F.C.)
In FRANCE, 24th December, 1917, to 11th March, 1918. On five occasions during a period of three months he has led formations on long-distance bombing raids, in which despite bad weather conditions, he has found and bombed his objectives with the most excellent results. All the operations in which he has taken part have proved highly successful, and his capabilities have stood out most prominently. He is a keen and most efficient pilot, and by his courage and determination has set a splendid example to his squadron. [2733

GELSTHORPE, Capt. Alfred Morris ... ... 8/Durham L.I. (att. M.G.C.)
S.E. of YPRES, 25th to 28th September, 1917. While he was completing most elaborate arrangements in an advanced position for a machine-gun barrage on the following morning, the enemy attacked during the night under a most intense barrage. He immediately got all his guns into action with great effect, and made a personal reconnaissance forward to see if he could use them to better advantage. His teams suffered heavy casualties during this attack, but he carried out his full barrage programme on the following morning under a heavy bombardment. He showed qualities of leadership and initiative of the highest order, and his example of courage and contempt of danger had the most inspiring influence on his men. [2640

GOLDING, Capt. John ... ... R.A.M.C.
Awarded 3rd June, 1917. [3231

GOLDTHORP, Lt.-Col. Robert Heward ... ... 4/West Riding (1/Artists)
BOURLON WOOD and MŒUVRES, on 27th September, 1918. For conspicuous gallantry and devotion to duty. When the leading companies were held up by machine-gun fire, suffering heavy casualties, he went forward collecting personnel and reorganising the attack, which resulted in the capture of the objective. He showed a fine offensive spirit, which encouraged his men at a critical period.

GREENWOOD, Lt.-Col. Charles Francis Hill 22/London
Awarded 1st January, 1918.

GRIERSON, Capt. Kenneth MacIver 22/Manchester
In ITALY, 27th October, 1918. He was in command of one of the leading companies in the attack. He led his men across the Piave in a magnificent manner. When the enemy bank had been reached he crawled forward and helped to cut a gap in the wire to within 15 yards of the enemy; all this time he was under observation and fire from the embankment, which was still held by the enemy. The splendid example he set to his men contributed in a large extent to the successful capture of the first objective. Later, in the taking of all objectives, he showed himself to be a fine leader both in skill and courage. All the houses and strong points were tackled under his direction in a systematic and dashing way. [3343

HARVEY, 2/Lt. Albert, *M.C.* 6/Liverpool
YPRES, 31st July, 1917. For conspicuous gallantry and devotion to duty. Having led his company to their objective, he noticed that a farm, some 500 yards ahead, was holding up the attack on the left. He at once organised a small party, with which he worked round the flank and rushed the farm, capturing three machine guns and killing and capturing a number of the enemy. By this prompt and plucky action he saved the brigade many casualties. His initiative and enterprise in action are at all times admirable. [4659

HENDERSON, 2/Lt. Charles Ernest 10/London
Near POELCAPPELLE, 7/8 October, 1917. For conspicuous gallantry and devotion to duty in leading a patrol through the enemy outposts to a position in the enemy's main line of resistance, which was over 900 yards from our line. His patrol of 20 captured 23 unwounded prisoners and killed or wounded another 25 of the enemy. Though the rifles and Lewis gun jammed owing to mud, he succeeded in covering the withdrawal of the patrol, every man returning safely. He showed magnificent courage and resource. [4676

HENDERSON, Capt. Ernest James, *M.C.*... ... ... 2/East Lancashire
W. of BETHENCOURT, 24th to 28th March, 1918. For conspicuous gallantry and devotion to duty. When his C.O. was wounded he took command of the battalion, and handled it with great judgment and success. He invariably displayed the utmost courage and disregard for personal danger, although frequently exposed to heavy machine-gun and rifle fire, and his fine example inspired all ranks with him. Ultimately he was wounded. [1828

HINGLEY, Lt.-Col. Alfred Norman, *M.C.* 13/Middlesex
Near RIEUX, 10th October, 1918. For great gallantry. When the advance met with heavy machine-gun and shell fire, and the leading companies had lost many officers, he personally led the battalion to its final objective. Again, on October 11th, near Avesnes-les-Aubert, under an intense enemy barrage, it was due to his personal courage and leadership that the ground gained by the battalion was maintained. He set a very fine example to all.
[2914

HOARE, Capt. Walter John Gerald ... ... 11/Royal Fusiliers
TRONES WOOD, 18th July, 1916. With two sergeants, one of whom was wounded by the intense shell fire, he dug out a buried sergeant and rescued him alive. He has done fine work throughout the operations. [3781

HOBSON, Major Harry Royd ... ... R.A.S.C.
Awarded 1st January, 1918. [2334

HUGHES, Capt. Hugh Llewellyn Glyn ... ... R.A.M.C.
LEIPZIG SALIENT, 6th July, 1916. For conspicuous gallantry and devotion to duty during operations. He went out in broad daylight, under heavy fire, and bandaged seven wounded men in the open, lying out in an exposed spot for one and a half hours. At nightfall he led a party through a heavy barrage and brought the seven men back. [890
BAR TO D.S.O.
LEIPZIG SALIENT, 21st, 25th & 27th August and 4th September, 1916. On four separate days he showed an utter contempt for danger when collecting and tending the wounded under heavy shell fire.

DISTINGUISHED SERVICE ORDER. 49

JONES, 2/Lt. Reginald Rees ... ... Welsh Guards
    YSER CANAL, 31st July, 1917. For conspicuous gallantry and devotion to duty during an advance. When the leading waves were temporarily held up by fire from a blockhouse he pushed up to the obstacle and fired his rifle through the slits, regardless of the danger which confronted him. He then entered the blockhouse himself, dealt with the occupants, and enabled the advance to be continued. He was later badly wounded in the head, having acted throughout the operation with great gallantry and initiative. [7655

KING, 2/Lt. Mark ... ... Coldstream Guards
    SAILLY, 15th March, 1917. He led his platoon through an intense hostile barrage, displaying the greatest bravery. Later, on reaching the first objective and finding his left flank exposed, he got his men out of the enemy's front line, formed front to the left, advanced 400 yards, and captured an enemy second line trench, thereby saving a critical situation. [3642

LEAKE, Capt. George Ernest Arthur 4/London
    BULLECOURT, 15th May, 1917. For conspicuous gallantry and devotion to duty when in command of his company. He showed a splendid example of coolness, disregard of danger, and cheerfulness, and, although wounded, he remained at duty. It was largely owing to his influence that all ranks showed such a splendid spirit under the most intense hostile barrage, which lasted for 14 hours. [3371

MICKLEM, Major Charles ... ... Royal Marine Artillery (No. 2 Howitzer)
    Awarded 1st January, 1919. [2409

MILES, Capt. Lancelot George ... ... 2/Royal Highlanders
    BERNAFAY WOOD, 10th July, 1916. He handled his company with great skill and coolness during a heavy bombardment. He also led his company with great dash in an assault, during which he captured four machine guns. During the attack he was severely wounded by a bomb. [1368

MOORE, Major Harold Edward ... ... No. 1 Signal Coy. (R. Monmouth) R.E.
    Awarded 3rd June, 1919. [734

MOORE, Lieut.-Colonel Robert Frank, *M.C.* ... ... 1/Notts & Derby
    Near ST. CHRIST, W. of the Somme, 22nd March to 2nd April, 1918. For conspicuous gallantry and devotion to duty during lengthy operations. After his C.O. had been killed, he took command of the battalion, which he handled with great skill and judgment, beating off several determined attacks, and when finally compelled to withdraw, doing so in a masterly manner, and with a minimum of casualties. His conduct throughout the operations set a fine example of courage and leadership, and was of great value in maintaining the high morale of the battalion. [2648

ROSHER, Lieut.-Col. John Brenchley, *M.C.* ... ... 10/Durham L.I.
    CANTAING, 21st November, 1917. For conspicuous gallantry and devotion to duty. On our cavalry being temporarily held up, and whilst the reinforcing infantry were still some way in the rear, he immediately despatched two companies to the assistance of the cavalry, and himself led up a third company as reinforcements. His prompt action immediately resulted in the capture of the objective with slight casualties. [1624

BAR TO D.S.O.
    E. of MARCOING, 3rd December, 1917. For conspicuous gallantry and devotion to duty. When the enemy attacked in great force positions held by his battalion he displayed the greatest courage and ability, inspiring his men to beat off three attacks. When finally pressed back by superior numbers he reorganised the remnants of the battalion, and advancing, re-occupied the trenches from which he had been temporarily ejected.

D

DISTINGUISHED SERVICE ORDER.

RUSSELL, 2/Lt. Robert Tor. ... ... Indian Army R/O
    In MESOPOTAMIA, 1917. For conspicuous gallantry and devotion to duty in charging the enemy's trench, which was strongly held. He then led a bombing attack and cleared 200 yards of the trench. Later, he maintained his position for four hours when reinforcements arrived.
    [260

SAGAR, Capt. Arnold Leslie ... ... 8/East Lancashire (13/K.R.R.C.)
    TRESCAULT, 12th September, 1918. For conspicuous gallantry and devotion to duty. This officer got his company into position for the attack despite heavy shelling, then leading the front wave, he gained his objective. When held up at a strong point, he crawled out with a Lewis gun and one man to a flank, enfilading it with such success that forty prisoners, two machine guns and one trench mortar were captured. During the ensuing thirty-six hours his company beat off three determined counter-attacks with heavy loss. He also led a bombing party, clearing a trench and killing or capturing the whole of the enemy. He showed exceptional qualities as a leader.
    [8072

SAVORY, Squadron-Commander Kenneth Stevens ... ... R.N.A.S.
    CONSTANTINOPLE, 14/15 April, 1916. In recognition of his services on the night of 14/15 April, when he carried out a flight to Constantinople and dropped bombs upon points of military importance, returning safely to his base after a long flight in rough and stormy weather.
    [2256
            BAR TO D.S.O.
    CONSTANTINOPLE, 9th July, 1917. In recognition of his services on the night of 9th July, when a successful attack was carried out against the Turkish-German fleet lying off Constantinople. When the Goeben, surrounded by warships (including submarines), had been located, the attack was made from a height of 800 feet. Direct hits were obtained on the Goeben and on the other enemy ships near her. Big explosions took place on board them, followed by a heavy conflagration. The War Office at Constantinople was also attacked, and a direct hit obtained.

STERNDALE-BENNETT, Commander Walter ... ... Royal Naval Division, R.N.V.R.
    BEAUCOURT, 13th November, 1916. He assumed command of and handled his battalion with marked courage and ability. He personally collected a party and bombed the enemy out of part of their second line, where they might have held up the attack.
    [2977

TAYLOR, Capt. Bruce Mitchell, *M.C.* ... ... 1/D.C.L.I.
    Awarded 1st January, 1918.
    [1932

THOMPSON, Capt. Arnold John, *M.C.* ... ... 1/Scots Guards
    Awarded 3rd June, 1918.
    [1225

THOMPSON, Capt. Claude Ernest, *M.C.* ... ... 2/South Lancashire
    Awarded 1st January, 1918.
    [1038

TRELOAR, Capt. George Devine ... ... Coldstream Guards
    PILKEM RIDGE, 31st July, 1917. For conspicuous gallantry and devotion to duty on two successive occasions. He led his company across a canal under very heavy barrage, and, finding the only available bridge was broken, he personally secured a mat from the original line, and laid it down for his company to cross, thereby saving great congestion and countless lives. Later, when the regiment on his left was held up by machine-gun fire, he immediately grasped the situation, and pressed forward with another company, finally capturing the position. By his great presence of mind and personal example of gallantry and cheerfulness he kept his company going under the most adverse circumstances.
    [4208

DISTINGUISHED SERVICE ORDER.

WALBY, Capt. Herbert Charles, *M.C.* ... 4/North Staffordshire (9/Yorkshire L.I.)
HENDECOURT, 9th September, 1918. For conspicuous gallantry during an attack. He led the support company and eventually came up with the leading waves and took the objective, where he reorganised his men under very heavy fire. In a second attack later in the day his fine example inspired those under him, and when the enemy counter-attacked he personally led forward two platoons to a position from which he could bring fire to bear on them. [7297

WENYON, Lieut.-Col. Herbert John ... ... 8/Royal West Kent
S.E. of YPRES, 9th September, 1917. He collected a party, and led them through heavy shell fire in a counter-attack upon one of our posts, which had been captured by the enemy, and although the position was exceptionally strong, it was retaken at the first attempt. This was entirely due to Captain Wenyon's prompt action and the determined energy which he displayed at a critical moment. [1945

BAR TO D.S.O.

VADENCOURT CHATEAU, 21st March to 5th April, 1918. For conspicuous gallantry and devotion to duty. He organised defences against heavy enemy attacks and held vastly superior numbers of the enemy at bay, inflicting heavy losses on them. He set a very fine example of courage and good leadership.

WILLANS, Capt. Harry, *M.C.* 2/Bedford
Awarded 3rd June, 1918. [1030

WRIGHTSON, Lieut. Edward ... ... 4/Northumberland Fusiliers
In ITALY, 27th October, 1918. On the Piave, in the initial attack, he was left in command of the company, all other officers being killed or wounded. This company had orders to form a defensive flank, but Lieut. Wrightson, seeing that the attack in front was held up by uncut wire, led his company forward, cut a belt of wire by hand under severe machine-gun fire and assisted in taking the first objective. He personally shot down an enemy machine gunner who was causing many casualties. Ultimately his company formed a defensive flank to the brigade, and though losing over 50 in casualties he maintained and even improved his position by enterprise and patrols. On 29th October, he led his company again in an attack over several kilometres, capturing many prisoners and machine guns. Throughout the entire operations he showed exceptional gallantry and marked powers of leadership. [6782

YUILL, Capt. Harry Hogg, *M.C.* ... ... R.E.
Awarded 3rd June, 1917. [3393

D.S.C.

The Distinguished Service Cross, a Naval Decoration, instituted in June 1901, and formerly known as the "Conspicuous Service Cross," has since October 1914 been awarded for services before the enemy to Officers below the rank of Lieut.-Commander, and to Warrant and subordinate Officers previously eligible. It consists of a Silver Cross with the reverse side plain, and having on the obverse side, in the centre, the Imperial and Royal Cypher, surmounted by the Imperial Crown. Bars may be added for additional acts of gallantry.

CUCKNEY, Flight-Lieut. Ernest John ... ... R.N.A.S.
    ZEEBRUGGE, 1917. For conspicuous gallantry and ability when taking part in a raid on the seaplane station.
                        BAR TO D.S.C.
    On the 3rd September, 1917, he bombed an enemy submarine, and probably severely damaged her.
                                                                                  [Reg. No. 4360

McGREGOR, Capt. (Acting Flight-Commr.) Norman Miers ... ... R.N.A.S.
    In FRANCE, 12th December, 1917. In recognition of his skill and courage in aerial combats. Whilst leading his flight on an offensive sweep he encountered a body of Albatross scouts. In the general fight which ensued he attacked a scout which was engaging one of our machines and drove it down out of control, and it was seen to crash. Act. Flt.-Cdr. McGregor has destroyed several enemy machines, and has led his flight with great dash and judgment.
                                                                                                        [2925

SIEVEKING, Flight-Lieut. Lancelot Giberne ... ... R.N.A.S.
    In recognition of services in dropping bombs on enemy railway lines and ammunition dumps on the night of 11/12 July, 1917.
                                                                                                              [1925

SIMPSON, Flight-Capt. George Goodman ... ... R.N.A.S.
    For gallantry and able leadership in aerial fighting, notably on the following occasions:—
    On 3rd May, 1917, he drove down a hostile aeroplane out of control.
    On 11th May, 1917, while on offensive patrol with five other machines, he attacked six hostile aircraft. One of these he brought down out of control, and a few minutes later he attacked another at close range and brought it down in flames.
    On 23rd May, 1917, he led a formation of five machines to attack at least twice that number of hostile aeroplanes. Both formations became split up, and a general fight ensued. Five times during the combat he drove off hostile aeroplanes from another of our machines, and one of those which he attacked was seen to go down in a spin.   [1090

M.C.

The Military Cross was instituted as a Decoration on December 28th, 1914, to reward Distinguished Services rendered by Officers of certain ranks in the army in time of war. Bars may be added for additional acts of gallantry. Since August 1st, 1918, it has, like the D.S.O., been awarded for "services in action" only. The Decoration consists of a Cross of Silver, having on each arm the Imperial Crown and bearing in the centre the Royal and Imperial Cypher. The ribbon is white with a purple stripe. Bars are indicated (in undress uniform) by small silver rosettes on the ribbon.

ABEL, 2/Lt. James Edgar ... ... 6/Royal West Kent
    LATEAU WOOD, 20th November, 1917. For conspicuous gallantry and devotion to duty. When his company commander became a casualty he assumed command at a critical period and worked his men forward to a strong point, whence the enemy were developing heavy machine-gun fire, and silenced them by concentrated rifle fire. His courage and fine leadership saved many casualties, and enabled the battalion to continue the advance.

ADAMS, 2/Lt. Arthur Marston 9/Liverpool
    E. of LE VERGIER, 4/5 May, 1917. For conspicuous gallantry and devotion when in charge of reconnoitring patrols and raiding parties, frequently under hazardous conditions. On one occasion he entered an enemy sap, capturing prisoners, and returning without a casualty.

ADAMS, Lieut. Berthold ... ... 25/Northumberland Fusiliers
    POELCAPPELLE, 13th to 16th October, 1917. For conspicuous gallantry and devotion to duty in reorganising his company, having frequently to go over the top from shell hole to shell hole exposed to the enemy's snipers. He went out and bandaged several wounded who were lying in the open, and remained with his company although wounded.

ADAMS, 2/Lt. Oliver Haynes ... ... R.G.A.
    WESTHOEK, 16/17 August, 1917. For conspicuous gallantry and devotion to duty as Forward Observing Officer. Having established an observation post, he went repeatedly through heavy barrages to get information. In addition to this he displayed the utmost gallantry and disregard of personal danger in rendering first aid to wounded infantry men and placing them in a trench for safety before sending up stretcher-bearers.

ADAMS, 2/Lt. Thomas James ... ... 12/Royal Inniskilling Fusiliers
    S. of ARDICHY, 26th March, 1918. For conspicuous gallantry and devotion to duty. When some of the enemy gained an entrance into the trench he rushed forward at the head of his men and drove them out, personally killing an officer and several men with the bayonet. He did splendid work.
                            BAR TO M.C.
    GULLEGHEM, October 15th, 1918. During the attack he showed great gallantry. He led his platoon in the face of the heaviest enemy fire and showed great coolness and daring throughout the attack. In the village of Heule, when his company was held up by heavy enemy fire, he personally led an assaulting party, capturing thirteen of the enemy and himself inflicted many casualties upon the enemy. He set a fine example of courage and endurance.

ADAMS, Lieut. Wilfred Carne ... ... 2/Royal Berks
    ARRAS, 17th March, 1917. During a raid on the enemy's trenches he handled his men in a most gallant manner, and was largely responsible for the success of the raid. Later he assisted in rescuing a wounded officer.

ADDISON, 2/Lt. Roger ... ... 10/East Lancashire
    Awarded 3rd June, 1918.

AINGE, 2/Lt. David Alfred Lloyd ... Att. 2/Royal Welch Fusiliers (S. Reserve)
    LES BŒUFS, SAILLY SAILLISEL, 1st September, 1918. For conspicuous gallantry and resource in controlling his company during a determined counter-attack after his company commander had been wounded. He personally held an advanced post with a few men and a Lewis gun, beating off several efforts of the enemy to force a way round his exposed flank. He stuck to his post until dark, and, having collected the rest of his company, established a good line of defence.

ALDOUS, Lieut. George James ... ... R.A.S.C.
    Awarded 1st January, 1919.

ALLBURY, 2/Lt. William ... ... 18/Durham L.I.
    W. of VIEUX-BERQUIN, 27th August, 1918. This officer showed great skill and determination in leading his men during an attack, over unknown ground, under heavy machine-gun fire, to an objective which was very oblique to the front of the assembly position, and was not defined by any particular feature. He accomplished his task with great success, capturing a machine gun and its whole detachment. While selecting the line for consolidation he moved about, under very heavy fire, encouraging and steadying the men by his resolute behaviour.

ALLEN, 2/Lt. Henry Cecil ... ... R.F.A.
    BEAUCOURT, 13th November, 1916. He displayed great courage and determination in laying and repairing a line under heavy fire.

ALLERTON, 2/Lt. Arthur Russell 8/Liverpool
    E. of YPRES, 20th September, 1917. He captured an enemy strong point with his platoon and held it in spite of continual artillery and machine-gun fire. He displayed coolness and self-possession throughout, which had the greatest influence on his men.

ANDERSON, 2/Lt. Eric Edwin ... ... Irish Guards
    BROOMBEKE, 9th October, 1917. For conspicuous gallantry and devotion to duty when in command of his platoon. He attacked a machine-gun position, capturing the two guns, and killed all the garrison. He was responsible for capturing two more machine guns at the first objective. He had previously carried out a very valuable reconnaissance.

ANDERSON, Capt. David Wilson 6/London
    Near YPRES, 20th September, 1917. For conspicuous gallantry and devotion to duty. By his skilful leadership his company captured all its objectives. When all the other officers became casualties he exposed himself fearlessly to the enemy's fire, and by his personal encouragement ensured the consolidation of the captured positions and repelled several counter-attacks, inflicting heavy casualties on the enemy.

BAR TO M.C.
    Near POELCAPPELLE, 3rd October, 1917. In spite of difficult natural conditions and the total absence of all landmarks, he led his company to within 100 yards of the barrage line before an attack. Although his men were being continually bogged, he inspired them by his personal example to push on, and succeeded in capturing a farm held by the enemy. In spite of heavy casualties he fought his way from one position to another until he had gained his objective, which he successfully consolidated and held.

ANDREW, Capt. Reginald Barrett William Goldsworthy 15/London
    SHAFAT, 27th December, 1917. During an enemy attack he led his platoon through an intense artillery and machine-gun barrage over very difficult country to render assistance to a battalion at a critical juncture, which, thanks to his timely aid, was able to repulse the enemy attack. His courageous determination and initiative were most praiseworthy.

BAR TO M.C.
    WULVERGHEM, 3/4 August, 1918. For conspicuous gallantry and good leadership during an advance. After his company had relieved another battalion he made a personal

reconnaissance of the front line, during which he was wounded but remained at duty, and the following night set up his patrols and took up a new line. Later, he made a daylight reconnaissance under enemy fire and obtained accurate information of the position. He showed marked courage and devotion to duty.

ANDREWS, 2/Lt. Lionel Raymond ... ... 5(4)Royal Lancaster
GIVENCHY, 9th April, 1918. For conspicuous gallantry and devotion to duty. Finding that a strong party of the enemy had occupied an artillery observation post in rear of the support line, this officer took two men and bombed them out, inflicting casualties and taking prisoners. Then, finding that his company headquarters were over-run by the enemy, he organised a party of bombers and cleared them out, too. His initiative and leadership were of great value.

ANDREWS, Lieut. Stephenson Arthur ... ... 7/Royal Sussex
YPRES, 31st July and 1st August, 1917. He led his company with great gallantry and dash in the attack, gaining all his objectives, consolidating his position, and holding it for two days. He set a splendid example to his men by his coolness under heavy fire.

BAR TO M.C.
Near CARNOY, 26th August, 1918. For conspicuous gallantry. He showed great courage in bombing a strong point from which the enemy were holding up the advance by heavy machine-gun fire. He led a few men forward, captured the gun, and killed five of the crew, enabling the remainder to advance and reach their objective. Throughout the operations from 22nd to 28th August his courage and leadership inspired all under his command.

APPLETON, 2/Lt. James ... ... 4/Yorkshire L.I.
GREENLAND HILL (north of Arras), 22/23 September, 1918. He was in charge of the leading wave of the company in a night attack. The enemy shelling was very heavy during the advance, but he rallied the men and was the first to enter the enemy post. He set a fine example of cool courage under fire, and proved himself a leader of great ability. During the consolidation he personally reconnoitred his platoon front and got in touch with troops on his flanks.

ARTHUR, 2/Lt. Frederick Parle 4/Liverpool
North of LE CATEAU, 10/11 October, 1918. In command of a platoon he displayed conspicuous gallantry in wading up to his neck in crossing the Selle River. Subsequently, under heavy fire, he made three journeys to and from battalion headquarters, bringing in reports and exact dispositions of all companies, which had been previously obscure.

ASHDOWNE, Lieut. Kenneth 3/Essex (5/Leicestershire)
BOIS DE RIQUERVAL, 11th October, 1918. For conspicuous gallantry during the operations. He rendered most valuable assistance to his commanding officer throughout some fourteen hours' continuous fighting. On several occasions he took charge of parties of his own and of another battalion, reorganising and disposing of them to the best advantage.

ATKIN-BERRY, Lieut. Henry Gordon ... ... 59/Field Coy., R.E.
PONT-SUR-SAMBRE, 7th November, 1918. He was in command of bridging operations over the river Sambre. In spite of enemy rifle fire from the opposite bank he succeeded in constructing a light pontoon bridge for the advancing infantry, showing great gallantry and determination.

ATKINSON, Lieut. Edward Arthur ... ... North Irish Horse (5th Cyclist Bn.)
LE BURGUE, 22nd August to 1st September, 1918; especially on 23rd August, 1918. For conspicuous gallantry and good leadership during the advance. When the left flank of a battalion was severely threatened, realising the situation, he, of his own initiative, led forward three Lewis gun teams under heavy fire and brought them into action, nullifying the attempts of the enemy, and enabling the battalion to hold its position.

BACON, Capt. Douglas Charles ... ... 2(20)London
E. of FLESQUIERES, 27th September, 1918. For most conspicuous gallantry and resource during the attack. He led his company with great dash in the attack, capturing a battery of field guns, fifteen machine guns, and ninety prisoners. Subsequently he organised and took charge of the line held by three companies of his battalion, and two platoons of another. He kept battalion headquarters fully informed throughout the day. Although both his flanks were exposed, he held the line under heavy enemy artillery and machine-gun fire for twenty-four hours, during which period he repulsed two counter-attacks. He did splendid work.

BAILEY, 2/Lt. Herbert Packer ... ... 3/East Surrey
Near ST. ELOI, 7th June, 1917. He displayed the greatest gallantry in handling a Stokes gun, following the first line infantry up to the final objective, where he consolidated later in the day. He showed great judgment, and was instrumental in repelling an enemy counter-attack by the skilful use of his gun.

BAILEY, Capt. John Vernon Moncas ... ... Royal Army Ordnance Corps
BLARGIES, 19th to 21st May, 1918. For conspicuous gallantry and devotion to duty. When the enemy aeroplanes bombed the ammunition depot, this officer voluntarily remained in the face of heavy fire to uncouple and save half an ammunition train, the remainder of which was already alight. With the aid of another officer and some men he got the salvaged portion of the train away to comparative safety. His gallantry and coolness were of great service.

BALL, Capt. Arthur Hugh ... ... R.G.A.
Awarded 1st January, 1918.

BALL, Capt. Frank Leslie ... ... 8/East Yorks
Awarded 1st January, 1917.

BALL, 2/Lt. Gerald Harman ... ... Machine Gun Corps
ARLEUX, 19th February, 1918. He was in command of a machine-gun post which the enemy attempted to raid under cover of an intense bombardment. His machine gun was put out of action by a shell, and the enemy succeeded in entering the trench. He at once engaged them, and after severe hand-to-hand fighting drove them out without any casualties among his own men. He handled a very awkward situation with the greatest coolness and courage.

BALL, Capt. Sidney Charles ... ... 5/Royal Lancaster
N.E. of POELCAPPELLE, 26th October, 1917. For conspicuous gallantry and devotion to duty when in command of his company in an attack. Under difficult conditions of ground and heavy fire from "pill-boxes" he pushed forward reinforcements to the gaps caused by casualties to the battalion. When the battalion had lost all its officers he rallied the men and reorganised the line.

BALL, Capt. Thomas Harold 5/Leicestershire
Near ETROEUGNT, 7th November, 1918. For conspicuous gallantry and good leadership during the advance. He led his company forward with such dash that he surprised an enemy field battery. The company captured over 20 prisoners, killed six of the enemy and captured or killed all the horses.

BALL, 2/Lt. William Arthur 5/Lincolnshire
Near ECOUST, 21st March, 1918. For conspicuous gallantry and devotion to duty when he was the senior company officer left. He was put in command of the remnants of four companies, about seventy men, and throughout the subsequent four days' fighting displayed the greatest skill, coolness and courage in organising successive defensive positions. His own personal example inspired the men to great efforts, and to a great extent contributed to their steadfastness.

MILITARY CROSS.

BANTING, Capt. Arthur Digby ... ... 250th Siege Battery, R.G.A.,
    Awarded 3rd June, 1919.

BARDSLEY, Lieut. Albert ... ... 12/Loyal North Lancashire
    GIVENCHY, 9th to 16th March, 1918. For conspicuous gallantry and devotion to duty. This officer handled his transport most efficiently throughout eight days' operations. Each night supplies had to be brought up under heavy shell fire, and when water pumps were broken by shelling he quickly organised another system of supply, which necessitated his constant supervision, having to keep water carts on the move to avoid shell fire. His coolness and cheerfulness were a great asset.

BARE, Capt. Alfred Raymond ... ... 1/Loyal North Lancashire
    Awarded 3rd June 1917.

BARKAS, 2/Lt. Geoffrey de Gruchy 1/London
    SPECTRUM TRENCH, 7/8 October, 1916. He showed marked courage and initiative during the consolidation of the position. He established a bombing post on his exposed flank and maintained his position for 32 hours until relieved.

BARKER, Capt. Rowland Francis 2/Worcestershire
    E. of YPRES, 25th September, 1917. He commanded his company with great skill and gallantry during an enemy attack. His tactical dispositions were sound, and he showed great determination and initiative. He had the most responsible position, and continued to hold it, though his right flank was enveloped. He set a splendid example to his men.

BARNES, 2/Lt. Alfred Douglas 23/London
    GRAINCOURT, 9th December, 1917. For conspicuous gallantry and devotion to duty in an advanced post, which was repeatedly attacked by large numbers of the enemy. Time after time they obtained a footing in it, only to be driven out. He went about calmly encouraging the men, and organising counter-attacks, and was fighting continuously for six hours. His conduct throughout was a splendid example to all ranks.

BARNES, Lieut. Reginald Charles ... ... 4/York & Lancaster
    BULLECOURT, 3rd May, 1917. He twice led his men against the enemy's trenches, and rallied men of his own and other units under very heavy fire.

BARNETT, Lieut. Raimond Austin 1/Artists
    S. of MARCOING, 30th December, 1917. For conspicuous gallantry and devotion to duty. He led a bombing party with great determination and drove back the enemy, who were occupying part of our lines. He inflicted heavy casualties on the enemy and re-established the position.

BARON, 2/Lt. Frank Oseland ... ... 4/South Lancashire (/London)
    NEUVILLE VITASSE, 7/8 April, 1917. When in command of a patrol he penetrated the enemy's front line and brought back valuable information, owing to which a serious obstacle to the advance was greatly diminished.

BARRETT, Capt. Wilfrid Morris 12/London
    NEUVILLE VITASSE, 9th April, 1917. Although wounded in the head, he continued to lead his company with the utmost gallantry until they reached their objective. He then organised the position and continued to superintend for some time.

BARROW, Lieut. Thomas Henry 22/London
    Near TOURNAI, 7th November, 1918. For conspicuous gallantry and devotion to duty. Whilst he was bringing his company up to the front line on a very dark night they came under very heavy shell fire, which inflicted several casualties to his company, he himself being wounded. He nevertheless carried on for two hours, and then after reporting that the relief was complete he reported to the aid-post.

BARTON, 2/Lt. Guy Stanley ... ... 1/Royal Welch Fusiliers
FESTUBERT, 16th May, 1915. For conspicuous gallantry and devotion to duty, when attacking with three bombers houses occupied by the enemy. On the morning of the 17th May he was wounded and sent down to the base, but, hearing on his way that the grenade company was without an officer, he refused to go any further and returned to take command.

BATE, Lieut. Herbert Roland ... ... 6/Manchester (19/Royal Sussex)
WARGNIES, 4th November, 1918. He took over command of his company on the 2nd November, 1918, and led it with great gallantry and judgment throughout the attack. It was due to his fine leadership through heavy enemy barrage that such great success was won.

BATE, Capt. Robert Edmund de Breteuil ... ... 5/York & Lancaster
GOMMECOURT, 27th March, 1918. For conspicuous gallantry and devotion to duty during an enemy attack. He led a bombing party composed of brigade headquarter details to a threatened point in the line, and held up the enemy by attacks for two days, showing a fine example of courage and coolness.

BATES, 2/Lt. Frederick Percy ... ... 4/Oxford & Bucks L.I.
S. of ASIAGO, ITALY, 26th August, 1918. For conspicuous gallantry and devotion to duty during a raid. He led his platoon with marked skill and determination, himself accounting for several of the enemy. Having cleared up the whole of the area allotted to him, he, although wounded in the shoulder, gave valuable assistance to the platoon on his flanks.

BATZER, 2/Lt. Robert John 10/London (1/Artists)
TILLOY, 27th August, 1918. For conspicuous gallantry and devotion to duty. This officer led his company with great dash in an attack on a village, pushed through it, and captured a machine gun, which he turned on the enemy. Throughout the operations he set a fine example and led his company successfully, owing to previous personal reconnaissances made under fire.

BAYLIS, 2/Lt. Roland Harry ... ... 7/Royal West Surrey
BRAY-CORBIE ROAD, 8th August, 1918. For conspicuous gallantry and initiative during an attack. He commanded the support platoon of the leading company, and on reaching his objective found his right flank open. On his own initiative he worked round, and in the face of heavy machine-gun fire twice led his men to the attack, knocking out four enemy machine guns and capturing about twenty-five prisoners. His splendid work enabled the troops on his right to continue their advance.

BAYZAND, 2/Lt. Geoffrey ... ... Coldstream Guards
Near HOUTHOULST FOREST, 9th October, 1917. For conspicuous gallantry and devotion to duty when in charge of the battalion forward party advancing in rear of the leading battalion. Later, he was in charge of all carrying parties, and successfully brought up material and water in spite of continuous shelling and the almost impassable condition of the ground. Fresh carrying parties were detailed each time, but he took charge of each one.

BAR TO M.C.
S. of GAVRELLE, 27/28 February, 1918. When in command of a party raiding the enemy trenches, he led his men close up under our barrage, which had the effect of avoiding casualties to his party and of surprising the enemy to a far greater degree than otherwise would have been the case. He showed fine judgment in deciding when the object of the raid had been attained and in ordering the withdrawal at the earliest possible moment, he himself being the last to return to our trenches. His courage, powers of leadership, and ability were beyond all praise, and contributed largely to the initial success of the raid.

BEAL, Capt. Leonard Frank 2/Bedford
POZIERES, 7th to 9th August, 1916. For conspicuous gallantry during operations. He consolidated his position under heavy shell and machine-gun fire, and got into touch with the troops on his right. In spite of shell-fire he rendered a most useful report with map. He had previously done fine work in consolidating and holding a position in a wood under very difficult circumstances.

MILITARY CROSS. 59

BEATON, 2/Lt. Grover Cleveland ... ... 143rd Siege Battery, R.G.A.
 Near VILLERS-FAUCON, 17th September, 1918. When a section of his battery, situated several hundred yards off, was subjected to a heavy mustard gas and high explosive bombardment, and the command post. in which two officers were hit, he at once went to their assistance, and although himself suffering from the effects of the gas, carried one officer, who had been mortally wounded, to a place of safety, and then returned and assisted the other officer, who had also been wounded, out of danger. He then returned a third time, rallied the men and ensured that every possible precaution was taken. He showed the greatest gallantry and pluck.

BEESLEY, Lieut. Herbert ... ... 5/Lancashire Fusiliers
 WIELTJE, 31st July, 1917. For conspicuous gallantry and devotion to duty during an attack. With great gallantry he pushed forward to the furthest objective of the Brigade, under heavy machine-gun and rifle fire. When the enemy counter-attacked, though twice wounded, he continued to hold his post on the flank until relieved. He showed a quick grasp of the situation and great courage and coolness.

BEETHAM, Lieut. George Clarence ... ... 5/York & Lancaster
 HAVRINCOURT, 20th November, 1917. For conspicuous gallantry and devotion to duty. He led his men with great determination in an attack under heavy machine-gun fire. He rushed an enemy machine gun and captured it, together with the whole team. He then reorganised his men and captured the final objective, taking over sixty prisoners.

BELCHER, Lieut. Arthur Edward Irving 2/Yorkshire
 Near RIDGE WOOD, 8th May, 1918. For conspicuous gallantry and devotion to duty while in command of the company in close support. Thanks to his coolness and good leadership his line was held intact, although the enemy had forced the front line. He also very gallantly led his company in a counter-attack later in the day.

BELL, Capt. David Cockburn ... ... 9/Middlesex (R.F.C.)
 In ITALY, 1917. For conspicuous gallantry and devotion to duty. When on observation duty, together with another officer, in a balloon, which was set on fire by an enemy machine, he remained in the burning balloon endeavouring at very great risk to himself to get his companion, who had been rendered insensible by a bullet wound in the head, overboard in his parachute. Being unable to do this, he was compelled to abandon his companion, whose death was subsequently found to have been due to the bullet wound, and to jump from the burning balloon.

BELL, 2/Lt. Henry Leonard 1/London
 Near FREMICOURT, 24th March, 1918. For conspicuous gallantry and devotion to duty. He went forward with a Lewis gun and two men when the enemy were about to attack. By carefully ranging his gun he succeeded in putting a number of the enemy out of action and in breaking up their attack. Later in the day, when his company commander became a casualty, he took command, and led his men with marked skill.

BENNETT, 2/Lt. Eugené Paul 2/Worcestershire
 Awarded 1st January, 1916.

BENSON, 2/Lt. Thomas Norman ... ... 5(4)Gloucester
 KNOLL, 24/25 April, 1917. He handled his company with great skill and courage under most critical conditions. He withdrew his men in the face of heavy fire with slight casualties. By his personal bravery and determination he set a fine example to those under him.

BENTLEY, 2/Lt. Alfred 4/Norfolk
 YPRES, 11th August, 1917. He led the assaulting platoons of his company in a most gallant manner to the recapture of a strong point which was affording the enemy an important advantage over our lines of communication. By his coolness and fine personal example

under most trying circumstances all subsequent attempts by the enemy to recapture the strong point were frustrated. During the afternoon he went out on patrol and captured two of the enemy from a concrete emplacement, which was afterwards of great tactical value, and the following night, although wounded and seriously gassed, he extricated a number of officers from a dug-out who had been gassed at the same time as himself.

BERLINER, Capt. Philip Barnett 7/London
    MALARD WOOD, 8th August, 1918. For conspicuous gallantry in action. He was leading his company with great determination through the enemy's front lines when he was severely wounded in the leg, but he struggled on for a thousand yards with the help of his runner, encouraging and directing his men. All the other officers had become casualties, and his courage and endurance were of particular value to the success of the attack.

BERNAYS, Capt. John Stewart Noall 6/Leicestershire
    EAUCOURT L'ABBAYE, 25th August, 1918. For conspicuous gallantry. When an enemy counter-attack was launched on his company, his swift appreciation of the situation and skilful handling of his men under heavy fire, saved a very doubtful situation. Later, he again displayed great ability during an attack, and throughout the whole operations his courage and cheerfulness set a fine example to all ranks (at BEAULENCOURT, 1st September, 1918).

BERTIE, Capt. Alberic Willoughby ... ... R.F.A.
    Awarded 3rd June, 1918.

BESCH, 2/Lt. Roy Cressy Frederick 1/Artists
    Awarded 1st January, 1919.

BESSANT, 2/Lt. John Archibald ... ... R.E.
    LEIPZIG SALIENT, 21st August, 1916. He laid out and superintended the construction of 250 yards of communication trench up to the captured enemy trenches. He got the work completed by daylight. The whole work was carried out under heavy shell fire.

BLACK, Lieut. James ... ... Irish Guards
    BROOMBEKE, 7th to 10th October, 1917. For conspicuous gallantry and devotion to duty as Adjutant during three days' operations. When the trenches of one of the support companies were being blown to pieces he went from battalion headquarters and led the company forward into a new position.

BLACKHURST, 2/Lt. Sydney 7/London
    S.E. of YPRES, 7th June, 1917. He led his company with the greatest gallantry and determination to their objective. Although wounded in three places, he disregarded his wounds until the objective had been consolidated three hours later, although they were sufficiently severe to justify him not remaining on duty. He set a splendid example of courage and determination, which had an immense moral effect on his men.

BLAKE, Major Charles Edwin Norman ... ... R.F.A.
    Awarded 1st January, 1918.

BLANCHARD, 2/Lt. Henry Claude Allan 1/Artists
    Near WESTROOSETEKE RIDGE, 30/31 October, 1917. When owing to casualties the command of the company devolved upon him he remained at his post for six hours after he was severely wounded, and although in great pain established communication with the company in support and refused to leave until reinforcements arrived.

BLUNDELL, Lieut. Douglas Roper 20/London
    Awarded 3rd June, 1919.

MILITARY CROSS.

BOND, 2/Lt. Gerald Aubrey ... ... 3/County of London Yeomanry
E. of YPRES, 2nd to 11th August, 1917. For conspicuous gallantry and devotion to duty on several occasions when bringing up rations and material to the front line on pack animals, over very difficult country and under almost continuous shell fire. In spite of casualties to animals and a stampede caused by shells, he never failed to deliver the whole of the stores. Throughout he set a very fine example to his men.

BONE, Capt. Frederick Howard 2/Wiltshire
MORCHIES, 22nd to 25th March, 1918. For conspicuous gallantry and devotion to duty. He formed a defensive flank with half his company, and with the remainder reinforced the front line, inflicting severe losses on the enemy and holding them in check for many hours. He subsequently withdrew, and, although in an exhausted state, helped with the reorganisation of the battalion. He showed untiring energy and great coolness in the face of overwhelming numbers.

BOON, 2/Lt. Ernest George Fred ... ... R.G.A.
Near YPRES, 22nd October, 1917. During a bombardment a shell hit a stack of shells, exploding some and setting fire to the cartridges. At great personal risk and under fire the whole time, he succeeded in extinguishing the fire before it spread to a pile of fused shells.

BORET, 2/Lt. John Auguste ... ... 4/Royal West Surrey (R.F.C.)
In FRANCE, August and September, 1917. For conspicuous gallantry and devotion to duty on many occasions. He has taken part in forty-one night bombing raids, many of which were carried out at a very low altitude and in bad weather. He has successfully inflicted considerable damage upon his objectives.

BOURDILLON, Lieut. Tom Lewis ... ... 8/K.R.R.C.
SWITCH TRENCH, 15th September, 1916. Although wounded, he led his company with great courage and initiative, and organised the consolidation of the position gained.

BOX, 2/Lt. Kenneth James ... ... 3/Yorkshire L.I.
Awarded 3rd June, 1918.

BOYTON, 2/Lt. Jack Lyons 5/Leicestershire
EPEHY, 21st March, 1918. For conspicuous gallantry and devotion to duty while employed as battalion intelligence officer during an enemy attack. He was continuously in the battalion observation post, whence he kept in touch with both front-line companies and sent back reports hourly to battalion headquarters. In the evening he made a reconnaissance and gained valuable information as to the enemy dispositions and the position of the battalion on the left. He performed his duties with much courage and ability.

BRACHI, Lieut. Maurice ... ... 3/London Field Co., R.E.
VIMY RIDGE, 21st May, 1916. For conspicuous ability and good personal example and care in organising a combined R.E. and Infantry party to occupy advanced trenches under very heavy fire.

BREALY, 2/Lt. Samuel George ... ... 6/Royal Fusiliers
E. of YPRES, 31st July, 1917. For conspicuous gallantry and devotion to duty whilst acting as Liaison Officer. He showed the greatest courage and initiative in obtaining valuable information under intense machine-gun and shell fire. It was owing to his gallantry and dash that the leading battalions were kept in touch with one another, and thus greatly contributed to the success of the operation.

BRENCHLEY, 2/Lt. John ... ... 4/Coldstream Guards
Near BOESINGHE, 27th to 31st July, 1917. For conspicuous gallantry and devotion to duty whilst putting out bridges across a canal. It was entirely due to his untiring and gallant efforts that the bridges were kept in repair, in spite of frequent breaks by hostile shell fire, and that they were in a serviceable condition by zero hour, in good time for our attack.

MILITARY CROSS.

BREWER, Capt. Charles Herbert ... ... 2/Bedfordshire (R.A.F.)
 In FRANCE, 10/11 March, 1918. He set out to make a special railway reconnaissance, and though the weather conditions became very bad he continued his task with the greatest determination. His engine began to fail when he was a long distance over the enemy's lines. By skilful piloting he succeeded in crossing the enemy's trenches, but the machine crashed in "No Man's Land," and turned completely over. Heavy machine-gun fire was opened by the enemy, and though his jaw was broken he extricated the observer, who was pinned under the machine and was unconscious, and dragged him to a shell-hole in the face of the enemy's fire. He showed splendid courage and resource.

BROADBRIDGE, Capt. Myles O'Brien 8/Devonshire
 Awarded 1st January, 1916.

BROATCH, 2/Lt. Percy ... ... 32/Northumberland Fusiliers
 E. of HARGICOURT, 26th August, 1917. He led his men to attack and got into action on the final objective in a very short time. Although half his men became casualties he kept his mortars in action and supplied with ammunition, until relieved three days later. It was only owing to his brilliant leadership and cheerful example that the mortars were kept in action.

BROMFIELD, 2/Lt. Frank Larden ... ... 1/East Lancashire
 Awarded 1st January, 1919.

BROOKE, 2/Lt. Cecil Bernard ... ... Machine Gun Corps
 CAMBRAI, 20th November, 1917. For conspicuous gallantry and devotion to duty. He took command of a party of infantry who had lost their officers and senior N.C.O.s and led them forward to the objective. He also brought his machine guns into action in spite of heavy casualties.

BROOKE, 2/Lt. Leonard ... ... 4/Loyal North Lancashire
 E. of YPRES, 20th to 25th September, 1917. For conspicuous gallantry and devotion to duty as intelligence officer during an action. He established an observation post in a commanding and conspicuous position, and worked under heavy shell fire throughout a critical period, having only one signaller left out of his party. Later, he found himself the only officer in the front line, and took command until the battalion was relieved, showing marked coolness and contempt of danger.

BROOKS, Capt. Douglas Cecil Jack ... ... 9/Welch Fusiliers
 Awarded 4th June, 1917.

BROWN, Capt. Alfred John ... ... 6/Royal Sussex (R.F.C.)
 In FRANCE, 2nd March, 1918. While on patrol work he and his patrol attacked two enemy two-seater machines, one of which was driven down out of control, the other being seriously damaged. On the following day he attacked a hostile reconnaissance machine, which he forced to land in our lines. On a later occasion he volunteered to attack a hostile aerodrome in foggy weather. He dropped four bombs from a height of 200 feet, which blew in the sides of one of the hangars, and then attacked horse and motor transport on the road, finally engaging enemy troops in the main street of a village with machine-gun fire. He has shown great skill and daring as a leader of offensive patrol.

BROWN, 2/Lt. Andrew Terras ... ... 3/West Yorkshire
 Awarded 1st January, 1918.

BROWN, 2/Lt. Ernest Bertram ... ... 5/South Staffordshire
 BUCQUOY, 13/14 March, 1917. For conspicuous gallantry and devotion to duty. He led two platoons into the enemy's lines, and maintained his position until ordered to retire. He assisted to bring in several wounded men under heavy fire, and throughout set a splendid example to his men.

BROWN, Capt. Harold Gladstone ... ... 8/York & Lancaster
   E. of YPRES, 18th September, 1917. For conspicuous gallantry and devotion to duty when in command of a raiding party. He led his party against an enemy strong point, and was the first to enter it, shooting two of the enemy with his revolver and bayoneting a third. Though under fire from another strong point he very coolly made a careful reconnaissance of both positions, and brought back valuable information. He set a magnificent example of coolness under fire to his men, and it was largely due to his initiative and energy that the operations were successful.

BROWN, Lieut. Sydney ... ... 6/Northumberland Fusiliers
   POEILLY, 21st to 23rd March, 1918. For conspicuous gallantry and devotion to duty. This officer handled his company with skill and resource for some ten days' fighting, until he was wounded. When in battalion reserve he made several counter-attacks, and closed a gap in the right flank. His company found the rearguard at the crossing of a river, and it was mainly due to his leading that the enemy was held off while the retirement was being effected.

BROWN, 2/Lt. Walter James ... ... 4/South Lancashire
   Awarded 1st January, 1918.

BROWNE, Lieut. Aubrey George 4/Norfolk (1/M.G.C.)
   N. of FRESNOY, 24th September, 1918. For conspicuous gallantry while in charge of a battery of eight machine guns, which he got into action under very heavy shell and machine-gun fire. He then pushed forward under intense machine-gun fire, and did splendid work in repelling a vigorous counter-attack launched by the enemy.

BRYSON, 2/Lt. George ... ... 1/Cameron Highlanders
   Near BERTHANCOURT, 18th September, 1918. For conspicuous gallantry in command of his platoon. Under heavy machine-gun fire he charged and knocked out a machine gun which was holding up the advance and captured the gun crew, thus enabling his men to reach the second objective.

BRYSON, Capt. Robert Edwards ... ... 12/Scottish Rifles (R.A.F.)
   ST. QUENTIN, 21st March, 1918. When on contact patrol work he was subjected to the most severe machine-gun and rifle fire from the ground, and received a serious wound. Despite this, and the most adverse weather conditions, he succeeded in locating the enemy positions, landing his machine safely behind our lines and bringing back most valuable information. By his disregard of personal danger and unfailing devotion to duty he has set a splendid example to all ranks.

BULLPITT, 2/Lt. James ... ... 1/Machine Gun Corps
   Awarded 1st January, 1919.

BURBURY, 2/Lt. Arthur Vivian ... ... 2/Yorkshire (R.F.C.)
   CAFTET WOOD, 15th September, 1916. When observing from a balloon at a height of 3,000 ft. the cable was cut by a shell. He destroyed his papers, ripped the balloon, a most difficult operation in the air, and then got down in his parachute.

BURDER, 2/Lt. Claud Vernon 8/Middlesex
   Near WESTHOEK, 16th August, 1917. He led his company through heavy shell fire to an exposed position with great gallantry and ability. Though short of ammunition and suffering many casualties, by his fine example he inspired his men, and held the position until relieved. He sent in most valuable information, and set a splendid example of courage and resolution.

BURMANN, Lieut. Robert Moyle .. .. Adjutant, 2/Border
   Awarded 1st January, 1916.

BURROUGHS, Capt. Percy William 24/London
  AVELUY WOOD, 6/7 April, 1918. For conspicuous gallantry and devotion to duty. He constantly displayed the utmost courage in visiting all his posts and looking after his men during heavy enemy machine-gun and shell fire. By his skilful dispositions he successfully maintained his line against repeated attacks, although for nearly six hours his left flank was unprotected. Finally he counter-attacked at a critical time, capturing two machine guns and many prisoners. He set a splendid example of courage and cheerfulness which greatly inspired all ranks with him.

BURTON, Lieut. Ralph Withers ... ... 1/East Surrey (M.G.C.)
  Awarded 1st January, 1918.

BUTTFIELD, 2/Lt. Leonard Frank ... ... Bucks Battn. Oxford & Bucks L.I.
  Near ST. JULIEN, 26th August, 1917. In an attack when his company officers had become casualties he took command, reorganised the men, and consolidated the positions won, and held the line until relieved. He showed complete disregard for personal safety, and his good leading contributed largely to the success of the attack.

CAHILL, Capt. John Archibald ... ... 2/Royal Berkshire
  MOISLAINS RIDGE, 4th March, 1917. He took command of his company and successfully repelled a strong enemy counter-attack He set a magnificent example to his men.

CAMPBELL, 2/Lt. Andrew ... ... R.F.A.
  BUCQUOY RUSIEUX, 25th March, 1918. For conspicuous gallantry and devotion to duty. This officer showed initiative and resource when in charge of an ammunition dump. Having no 18-pdr. ammunition, he went and found another dump, which had been deserted, under fire. He commandeered a train, loaded it up, and by this means kept the batteries of the division supplied.

CAMPBELL, Lieut. Guy ... ... Motor Machine Gun Corps
  Awarded 1st January, 1916.

CAMPBELL, 2/Lt. Stanley Victor 4/Border
  TEMPLEUX to DEMUIN, 21st to 31st March, 1918. For conspicuous gallantry and devotion to duty throughout ten days of severe fighting, and until finally wounded. He invariably displayed the utmost courage and a total disregard of personal danger. On one day he twice led a counter-attack, causing heavy casualties to the enemy and holding up their advance for a considerable time. Later, he fought a magnificent rearguard action, his fine example inspiring all with him to do their utmost.

CANNON, Major Herbert Cooper ... ... 6/Royal West Surrey
  Awarded 14th January, 1916.

CAPPER, 2/Lt. Ernest Raphael 3/Essex
  S.E. of MONCHY-LE-PREUX, 3rd August, 1917. For conspicuous gallantry and devotion to duty. After the enemy had secured a footing in a portion of our trench he organised a bombing attack with his platoon and cleared them out, and when his original bombers had sustained casualties and were too tired to throw bombs accurately he collected a fresh squad of men from another unit and attacked again. His excellent leading, clear orders, and great coolness under fire very largely contributed to the success of the attack.

CARD, 2/Lt. Arthur Henry 12/Middlesex
  TRONES WOOD, 14th July, 1916. He led the left half of the line which cleared a wood of the enemy, capturing a strong point and a machine gun. He retained control over his men under most difficult circumstances. He has also carried out most useful reconnaissances.

MILITARY CROSS.

CARNELLEY, Lieut. Herbert ... ... R.E.
 ESCAUT CANAL, 1/2 October, 1918. For conspicuous gallantry and devotion to duty. He was in charge of a party of sappers employed on reconstructing a partially destroyed footbridge across the canal. In spite of rifle fire from the opposite bank, he carried on the work with great determination until he was severely wounded.

CARR, Capt. Leslie George ... ... 4(1)London
 FREMICOURT AREA, 24th March, 1918. For conspicuous gallantry and devotion to duty. He remained behind with his Lewis gun till his company had taken up a new position, covering the withdrawal and inflicting heavy losses on the enemy at close range. On each occasion, when he rejoined his company, he immediately reorganised and gave battle. During the whole operations he showed great ability and coolness under very difficult conditions.

BAR TO M.C.
 GREY FARM, 10th April, 1918. For conspicuous gallantry and devotion to duty during a hostile attack, when, with two companies, he held on to a position and covered the retirement of the battalion until it was complete. With great skill he then withdrew his men through a gap in the enemy's lines, and succeeded in rejoining the battalion without the loss of a man.

CARR, Capt. Mathew ... ... 2/Royal Scots Fusiliers
 Awarded 1st January, 1917.

BAR TO M.C.
 Awarded 1st January, 1919.

CARTER, Lieut. Henry William ... ... 5/Royal West Surrey
 Awarded 3rd June, 1919.

CASSELS, 2/Lt. James Stuart ... ... 9/Royal Sussex
 BEAUMONT HAMEL, 3rd September, 1916. He was for many hours under very heavy shell fire, and when the second and third waves failed to reach their objectives, he greatly assisted his company commander in reorganising the men for another attack. He displayed great coolness and utter contempt for danger.

CATTELL, Capt. Alfred George 24/London
 LE FORREST and ST. PIERRE VAAST WOOD, 30th August and 2nd September, 1918. For marked gallantry and good work. On both occasions he led his company in the attack and gained the objectives, taking prisoners, capturing one 77 mm. gun and a number of machine guns. Although his right flank was exposed and dangerously threatened, he held on to and personally superintended the consolidation of the positions gained.

CAWLEY, Lieut. James Donald ... ... 80th Battery, 15th Brigade, R.F.A.
 FOREST OF MORMAL, 4th November, 1918. For conspicuous gallantry and devotion to duty, while the battery was firing a barrage in support of the attack under heavy fire. One gun received a direct hit, three gunners being wounded. He at once went and attended to the wounded, carrying them one by one to a safe place. He then returned to the battery, and by his coolness and determination kept the men's morale at a high level under trying conditions.

CHANDLER, Capt. Alfred Leonard ... ... R.A.S.C.
 Awarded 1st January, 1918.

CHANDLER, Capt. Cecil William ... ... 8/Royal Munster Fusiliers
 GUILLEMONT, 3rd September, 1916. Although wounded, he led his men and beat off repeated enemy attacks, displaying great courage and initiative throughout.

CHAPMAN, 2/Lt. Basil Edmund ... ... 5(8)Norfolk
 YPRES, 13/14 August, 1917. When an enemy gas shell penetrated the roof of a shelter in which seven officers were sleeping, he, although seriously affected by the gas, climbed through a hole in the roof and eventually managed to extricate these officers, who had been gassed at the same time as himself. He showed splendid gallantry and devotion to duty.

E

MILITARY CROSS.

CHATTERTON, Lieut. Richard ... ... R.G.A.
    BERKILI FORD, SALONICA, 17th to 19th September, 1918. For conspicuous gallantry and devotion to duty when the section was under heavy shell fire and gas. During the whole of the enemy bombardment he walked out in the open from gun to gun encouraging the detachment.

CHEEL, 2/Lt. Edgar Stacey ... ... 3/Royal West Kent
    SOMME, 22nd March to 2nd April, 1918. For conspicuous gallantry and devotion to duty during an enemy advance. When most of the officers in the battalion had become casualties, he collected all men near him and organised them for defence. Throughout his work was of a high order, and he was of great service to his acting battalion commander.

CHEVERTON, Major Thomas Bird ... ... R.F.A.
    Awarded 3rd June, 1918.

CHILD, Capt. Arthur James ... ... 1/Artists (R.F.C.)
    Awarded 1st January, 1918.

CHILVERS, 2/Lt. Joseph Ernest ... ... 3/East Kent (att. 7th)
    RONSSOY, 18th to 25th September, 1918. For conspicuous gallantry and ability during the operations. After his company commander had been wounded, he assumed command, and, during the advance, with a small party, crawled forward and dealt with an enemy machine gun which had been causing casualties. Throughout the whole of the operations, though twice wounded, he displayed great courage and initiative.

CHRISTIE, Capt. John Fairfax 1/Herts
    E. of AMIENS, 26th March, 1918. For conspicuous gallantry and devotion to duty. This officer's company covered the retirement of two brigades, and was then sent back by him as ordered. He himself remained with one man, and noticing that the division on the right was being heavily pressed, he took a Lewis gun up to a position where he could enfilade the enemy, and with the man to carry spare drums, inflicted severe casualties, bringing them to a halt. The following day he organised a delaying action and held up an attack. Throughout the ten days' operations until he was wounded he did much good work.

CLASS, Lieut. Herbert Rudolph ... ... 5/Royal Warwick
    MOATED GRANGE, 1st July, 1916. For conspicuous gallantry. Throughout an intense bombardment, which wrecked the defences, he moved about with utter contempt of danger, encouraging his men. He materially assisted in reorganising the defences and in repelling the enemy's infantry.

CLIVELY, Major Richard Constantine ... ... 16/Tank Corps
    QUENNEMONT COPSE, September 29th, 1918. For conspicuous gallantry and excellent leadership. When the situation was obscure, and it was obvious that the attack had miscarried, and the enemy was holding the line in strength only 500 yards in front, he held a conference with the infantry company commanders, and under heavy shell and machine-gun fire organised a fresh attack to endeavour to reach the start line. He distributed his tanks amongst the infantry, and by his coolness set a splendid example to all ranks.

COCK, 2/Lt. Geoffrey Hornblower ... ... General List and R.F.C.
    On the GAPAARD—OOSTAVERNE ROAD, 6th June, 1917. On many occasions he showed great courage and determination in attacking and destroying hostile aircraft, and in dispersing hostile troops from a low altitude. His skill as a formation leader has set a fine example to the other pilots of his squadron.

CODD, 2/Lt. Cyril Joseph Charles ... 14/Durham L.I. (Machine Gun Corps)
    REGHA TRENCH, 23rd to 31st October, 1916. He displayed great courage and determination during the consolidation of the position, and by skilful handling of his guns was instrumental in repelling two counter-attacks.

COKE, 2/Lt. Edward ... ... R.F.A.
  LOMBARTZYDE, 10th July, 1917. As artillery Liaison Officer, at a time when all communication with his artillery group was severed, he made repeated attempts to restore the connection, and personally crossed a river under heavy fire in his efforts to mend the cable and to lay fresh ones. He showed the greatest gallantry and disregard of danger throughout the operations, and only desisted from his efforts on receiving the direct order from his headquarters to do so.

COLE, Lieut. Gordon James ... ... 17/Rifle Brigade
  N. of FAMPOUX, 23rd March, 1918. When the enemy had forced an entrance into the front line trench and were bombing along it, and the situation appeared to be critical, he went forward from headquarters to reconnoitre. He collected all available men and formed a defensive flank and then organised and took part in a counter-attack which drove out the enemy and completely re-established the position. He showed splendid skill and resource in a most difficult situation.

COLE, 2/Lt. William Maurice 5/Leicester
  Near LE TOURET, 9/10 June, 1918. For conspicuous gallantry and devotion to duty. He led a patrol in daylight to the enemy's lines, crawled through three belts of wire, surrounded, with three of his men, an enemy organised shell-hole and tried to take the sentry prisoner. The man resisted, and the noise disturbed an enemy machine-gun post close by, so they shot him for identification. Next day he again led a daylight patrol and gained valuable knowledge of the enemy's movements, locating several posts and the time at which they were manned.

COLEMAN, 2/Lt. George Herbert 5/Liverpool
  Near RAILWAY WOOD, 4/5 March, 1917. In leading two separate bombing attacks against the enemy, he remained to the last superintending the withdrawal of his party, and then carried a wounded man back to safety under heavy fire.

COLES, Lieut. Edgar Lermitte ... ... 5/Royal West Surrey
  TARA HILL, 23rd August, 1918. For conspicuous gallantry and energy during the attack. On reaching his objective in command of a company, he was senior officer left in the battalion, and supervised the reorganisation practically single-handed, completing it in a very short time, though the men were tired and inexperienced. He showed fine determination under trying conditions.

COLLINS, 2/Lt. John Edmund 22/London
  METZ, 23rd March, 1918. For conspicuous gallantry and devotion when fighting a rearguard action. Although his platoon suffered many casualties, and was almost surrounded, by his disregard of danger and skilful leadership he held up the enemy for three hours, at a time when delay was of the greatest importance. His gallant conduct undoubtedly saved the battalion and enabled the withdrawal to be completed.

COLVIN, Capt. Alexander 5/Essex
  GAZA, 26th March, 1917. For conspicuous gallantry and devotion to duty. He led his company with great dash and gallantry in an attack upon a strongly fortified redoubt, which he successfully captured, and afterwards thoroughly reorganised and consolidated the position. On the following day he displayed great coolness when in command of a portion of our front line trench.

COMBER, 2/Lt. Turner 9/Essex
  W. of ALBERT, 27th March, 1918. When in command of a company he repulsed with heavy loss the numerous determined attacks launched by the enemy against his position, though the latter was enfiladed by machine-gun fire from both flanks. His gallantry and able leadership merited the highest praise.
  BAR TO M.C.
  Near MANANCOURT, on the night of 5th September, 1918. For conspicuous gallantry and determination. He went forward and took command of a company that had got separated from the battalion during the attack and lost all its officers except one. Having collected the company together in the pitch darkness he got it into position. Although much fatigued the men led by him gained their objective, killing many of the enemy and taking a number of prisoners and machine guns. He behaved splendidly.

MILITARY CROSS.

CONIBEER, 2/Lt. Ralph William ... ... 3/East Surrey
  BOURSIES, 23/24 October, 1918. For conspicuous gallantry and devotion to duty during the operations. He led his platoon forward with great skill and gained his objective in face of determined enemy opposition. After he was wounded he would not leave his platoon until he had handed over a thoroughly well organised defensive position. His conduct throughout was most praiseworthy.

CONRAN, Capt. Edward Dennis ... ... 2/Royal Munster Fusiliers
  Awarded 3rd June, 1916.
                              BAR TO M.C.
  LE CATELET, 4th October, 1918. For conspicuous gallantry, determination and resource when in command of a platoon in the attack. By his cheerfulness and complete disregard of danger he set a good example to all under his command. He materially assisted the attack on VILLERS FERME on 6th October, 1918, by outflanking the enemy and bombing down his trench.

COOKE, 2/Lt. Michael James 3/Norfolk
  Near LAGNICOURT, 21st March, 1918. For conspicuous gallantry and devotion to duty during a hostile attack, when the expeditious manner in which he moved the Lewis guns of his company to its threatened flank was largely reponsible for holding up the enemy's advance. Throughout the action he commanded his men, under extremely heavy fire, with the greatest courage and skill until severely wounded.

COOKE, 2/Lt. Philip Andrew ... ... 8/K.R.R.C.
  ROCLINCOURT, 1/2 July, 1916. For conspicuous gallantry when the enemy exploded a large mine, destroying part of our defences. He at once organised bombers, drove off the enemy, and greatly assisted in the consolidation of the position under heavy fire.

COOP, 2/Lt. Richard Wallace ... ... R.F.A.
  YPRES, 16th August, 1917. For conspicuous gallantry and devotion to duty as F.O.O. He sent back valuable information under very great difficulties. He had to fall back under the enemy counter-attack, but was one of the last to return, and narrowly escaped capture.

COOPER, 2/Lt. Edward Priestly ... ... 1/East Yorks
  Awarded 1st January, 1917.

COOPER, 2/Lt. Thomas Charles ... ... 11/Royal Lancaster
  BOURLON WOOD, 25th November, 1917. For conspicuous gallantry and devotion to duty. He assisted greatly in the capture of the final objective, and continually rallied men of various units and held his position against counter-attacks. He set a splendid example of courage to his men.

CORMACK, 2/Lt. Arthur Richard ... ... Machine Gun Corps
  HERMIES, VILLERS-AU-FLOS, 1918. For conspicuous gallantry and devotion to duty, when he commanded his section so well that his guns wiped out the personnel of three machine guns and silenced two others; and when he retired his section without loss, after waiting until the enemy was within 100 yards of him, enabled the garrison of a village to get clear. Again, when his battery made a fine stand, his calm forethought and determination were prominent.

CORNISH, 2/Lt. George Mervin ... ...Grenadier Guards
  LES BŒUFS, 15th September, 1916. Though twice wounded and streaming with blood, he continued to lead in the advance. Not till after the trench was firmly in our hands did he allow himself to be taken to the dressing station.

CORRELL, 2/Lt. Charles Edward 5/Yorks
  Awarded 1st January, 1917.

MILITARY CROSS.

CORRY, 2/Lt. John Edgar .... 3/Royal West Surrey
S. of METEREN, 12th to 14th April, 1918. For conspicuous gallantry and devotion to duty. He twice led counter-attacks with great dash against the enemy to restore the situation. Owing to his courage and cheerfulness, many attacks by the enemy were completely repulsed. He has previously done fine work.

COTTAM, Capt. Algernon Edward .... 2/East Surrey
W. of BAPAUME, 21st to 23rd August, 1918. For conspicuous gallantry in action. He made frequent reconnaissances to the front over ground swept by artillery, machine-gun and rifle fire, and in spite of thick mist and other difficulties, he obtained important information of the positions occupied by the enemy. Throughout two days' operations he showed a splendid example of courage and initiative and untiring energy.

COURTAULD, Capt. Stephen Lewis .... 1/Worcester (M.G.C.)
Awarded 1st January, 1918.

COXHEAD, 2/Lt. Henry Jessop .... 13/Royal Sussex
Awarded 3rd June, 1917.

CRAMPTON, 2/Lt. Hubert 5/Manchester
Awarded 3rd June, 1917.

CRAN, Capt. Robert Charles .... 2/York & Lancaster
Near GRICOURT, 24/25 September, 1918. For conspicuous gallantry and fine leadership in action. He personally led the assault on the final objective on the 24th. He assumed control of the entire front line of the battalion and displayed high powers of leadership and organisation. He set a very fine example of coolness and courage to all ranks.

CREED, 2/Lt. Thomas Percival 5/Leicester
ANDOVER PLACE, December, 1916. With a small party of men he attacked and drove off an enemy patrol. He displayed great courage and determination throughout.

CRISP, Lieut. George William 23/London
Near HAPPY VALLEY, 22nd August, 1918. He exhibited unusual qualities of initiative and marked ability in dealing efficiently with unexpected and difficult situations when immediate action was essential and it was impossible to refer to his commanding officer. When the enemy successfully attacked part of the line he carried out the reorganisation of the survivors and the defence of the second line with great gallantry and complete success in spite of intense fire.

CROCKER, 2/Lt. William Charles 4/Dorset
ORS, 4th November, 1918. He led his platoon with great dash and determination during the attack, which involved crossing the canal under heavy machine-gun fire. In mopping up the village of Ors he took over 80 prisoners with his platoon, and later on captured a group of houses with further prisoners. Throughout he set a fine example to his men.

CROOK, 2/Lt. Leslie Arthur .... 2/Royal West Surrey
Near BAZENTIN, 15th to 21st July, 1916. For conspicuous gallantry in action. He set a fine example under heavy fire, and displayed great powers of leadership till he was wounded.

CRONEEN, 2/Lt. Seymour .... R.A.S.C.
HILL 60, 23rd September, 1917. For conspicuous gallantry and devotion to duty. He was in charge of a convoy of twelve wagons ordered to load at a supply dump which was under heavy shell fire. He first reconnoitred the road, and then brought the wagons up singly until they had all been loaded and safely despatched, the whole task being carried out under shell fire. It was entirely due to his devotion to duty and determination that the task was carried out without loss or confusion.

MILITARY CROSS.

CROSLAND, 2/Lt. Leonard ... ... R.G.A.
    GAZA, 15/16 October, 1917. Though himself severely wounded he remained under heavy shell fire with a badly wounded man, rendering him assistance, and finally got him under cover.

CROUCH, Capt. Francis Harris ... ... 5/Lancashire Fusiliers
    Awarded 1st January, 1918.

CROWTHER, Lieut. John Edward Marmaduke ... ... 11/East Surrey
    SENSEE VALLEY, 23rd March, 1918. For conspicuous gallantry and devotion to duty. This officer in command of a company was ordered to reconnoitre a village, and subsequently his company led the attack. During the whole time he was fearlessly exposing himself under intense shell and machine-gun fire, and he fell wounded when directing and encouraging his platoons which were held up by enemy strong points. Although badly wounded, he gave full directions to the nearest officer before allowing himself to be taken to the dressing station.

CUDDON, Capt. Philip Basil 2/Hampshire
    MONCHY, 14th April, 1917. For conspicuous gallantry and devotion to duty. He displayed great ability in placing a part of the village in a good state of defence at a most critical stage. On a later date he led his company into action, captured a trench containing a large number of the enemy, and defended the right flank of the Division when the advance was held up.

                        FIRST BAR TO M.C.
    BOESINGHE, 9th October, 1917. For conspicuous gallantry and devotion to duty. He commanded his company with marked ability throughout the operations, and when a further advance was ordered at short notice, he conducted it with the greatest skill and determination, and carried it out with complete success. He displayed great judgment in difficult situations, and set a high example of courage to his men.

                        SECOND BAR TO M.C.
    Near VIEUX BERQUIN, 3rd April, 1918. For conspicuous gallantry and devotion to duty. When the line on the left suddenly broke under an enemy attack, this officer galloped up and took the men forward, re-establishing the original firing line. His energy and drive saved a very critical situation.

CULLERNE, 2/Lt. Alan Baird ... ... 7/Royal West Kent
    BERNAFAY WOOD, 27/28 August, 1918. For conspicuous gallantry and enterprise during the operations. Keeping close up with the barrage he reached the objective with his company, and, pressing on, he gave the enemy no time to reorganise. Later, when the troops on both flanks were driven back, he superintended the defence of the flanks under heavy fire and ultimately enabled the line to be re-established.

CUMBERLEGE, Capt. Geoffrey Fenwick Jocelyn ... ... 2/Oxford & Bucks L.I.
    Awarded 1st January, 1919.

CUNDALL, Capt. Herbert Ayres ... ... 1/South Stafford
    BULLECOURT, 12th May, 1917. For conspicuous gallantry and devotion during an attack, when, although severely wounded, he continued to lead his men on with great bravery until wounded a second time. He has on previous occasions done fine work.

CUNNINGHAM, 2/Lt. James Joseph Ignatius 12/London
    NEUVILLE VITASSE, 9th April, 1917. His company being held up by thick wire and fired on by an enemy machine gun, he led his platoon and broke through the wire into the enemy trench, where he attacked and dispersed the machine-gun team. His prompt action saved many casualties.

MILITARY CROSS. 71

CURTIS, 2/Lt. Frank ... ... Machine Gun Corps
    LAGNICOURT, 21/22 March, 1918. For conspicuous gallantry and devotion to duty during a hostile attack, when in command of four forward guns, which he controlled with great courage and skill. After all his guns had been destroyed by shell fire he took command of another battery whose officer had been wounded, and when the infantry in this sector had been ordered to retire he covered the withdrawal with his guns. Throughout the day he set a splendid example of courage and cheerfulness.

CUTLER, 2/Lt. Edward Cecil ... ... 7/Royal Sussex
    AVELUY WOOD, 26th March, 1918. For conspicuous gallantry and devotion to duty when his platoon was attacked by strong enemy forces and almost completely surrounded. He showed great skill and coolness in rallying his men and beat off the attack. Next day, during a heavy enemy attack, he was severely wounded, but refused to allow himself to be taken away until the situation was restored and he had handed over the command to a N.C.O.

CUTTING, Major Raymond Howarth 1/Devon
    Awarded 1st January, 1917.

DALTON, 2/Lt. John 1/Bedford
    N. of YPRES, 5th to 10th October, 1917. For conspicuous gallantry and devotion to duty when in command of the left platoon of the battalion. On the first night in he crossed very boggy ground to the right company headquarters of the battalion on our left, laid a tape from there a distance of about 300 yards to our left post, and got one of their companies to dig in and join up with our left. It was due to his action that our left flank was made secure.

DALY, 2/Lt. Augustus Joseph ... ... R.F.A.
    N. of ZILLEBEKE LAKE, 6/7 September, 1917. For conspicuous gallantry and devotion to duty. While he was helping to drag two guns out the gun position a shell burst, killing and wounding fourteen men. Though himself wounded, he managed to carry all the wounded off the track into shell holes. He later collected two teams and got his guns into the new position.

DANGERFIELD, 2/Lt. Paul ... ... 1/East Kent
    Awarded 1st January, 1916.

DANIELL, Lt.-Col. Thomas Edward St. Clare ... ... R.F.C.
    Awarded 1st January, 1917.

DAVIDSON, 2/Lt. Kenneth Chisholm ... ... 11/Gordon Highlanders
    YPRES, 31st July, 1917. For conspicuous gallantry and devotion to duty. When commanding his platoon during an advance, an enemy strong point manned by machine guns threatened to hold up the right flank of his battalion. With great courage and initiative, he organised a bombing party, personally led it against the position, and after a fierce encounter, killed the garrison and put the guns out of action. On reaching the first objective, he took command and reorganised half of the battalion, and throughout the advance he displayed the greatest personal courage and gallantry in the forefront of the fighting.

DAVIES, 2/Lt. Arthur Charles 11/Essex
    N. of ST. QUENTIN, 19th September to 17th October, 1918. For conspicuous gallantry and devotion to duty as Intelligence Officer during the operations. On the 17th October especially, when the position was very obscure owing to the heavy mist, he made his way to the assaulting troops, put some who had lost direction on their right way, and cleared up the situation generally. All this was done under heavy machine-gun fire.

DAVIES, 2/Lt. Derek Ben ... ... Welsh Guards
    FLESQUIERES, 27th September, 1918. For conspicuous gallantry and devotion to duty. He volunteered to take out a party to deal with the enemy machine guns in ORIVAL WOOD, which were enfilading his company. He succeeded under intense fire in killing six of the enemy and capturing the guns. His example was inspiring to all ranks.

MILITARY CROSS.

DAVIES, 2/Lt. Frederick Harry ... ... R.A.F.
In FRANCE, 8th and 11th March, 1918. Whilst on artillery observation duty he engaged a hostile scout, which he succeeded in sending down out of control. He then continued to observe for the shoot, and successfully accomplished his task. Later, whilst again on artillery patrol, though attacked by five hostile aeroplanes, he, by successful manœuvring, enabled his observer to fire several bursts into the leader of the formation, whose machine was seen to go down in a vertical nose-dive and crash to earth. Continuing the fight against the remaining four hostile machines, he eventually forced them away, and succeeded in ranging on and neutralizing three hostile batteries. He set a magnificent example of skill and determination.

DAVIES, 2/Lt. Gwylon ... ... 4/Northumberland Fusiliers
CAULINCOURT, 21st to 27th March, 1918. For conspicuous gallantry and devotion to duty. During a withdrawal this officer volunteered to go forward and locate the enemy position, returning with valuable information. Some days later he showed great coolness under heavy fire, encouraging his men and leading a counter-attack with great dash. He held on till forced to withdraw for want of ammunition.

DAVIES, Lieut. Henry ... ... 6/Royal Welch Fusiliers
SAPIGNIES—BITHUCOURT, 21st to 26th March, 1918. For conspicuous gallantry and devotion to duty in action. In every phase of the fighting he led his men in a most splendid manner. His tireless energy and courage under heavy fire and in critical circumstances were most praiseworthy.

DAVIES, 2/Lt. Thomas Talvin 4/Welch
BOURLON WOOD, 23rd November, 1917. For conspicuous gallantry and devotion to duty. When his company had reached their objective he heard that men of another battalion on his left were in difficulties. Collecting a few men he went to their assistance, and by pushing forward enabled them to continue their advance. Returning to his company he repeatedly led his men forward and did much to bring the heavy enemy counter-attacks to a standstill. He showed splendid coolness and initiative,

DAVIES, Lieut. Tudor Huab ... ... R.E.
Awarded 3rd June, 1918.

DAVIS, 2/Lt. Melville Allen Duff ... ... 9/K.R.R.C.
YPRES-MENIN ROAD, 21st to 25th August 1917. For conspicuous gallantry and devotion to duty. He was in charge of all the carrying and ration parties up to the front line, and carried out his task under very heavy shell fire with great success. During an enemy counter-attack, when bombs were urgently needed in the front line, he led a carrying party with bombs up a road under an intense barrage. He also took command of his company, reorganised them and brought them out successfully.

DAVIS, 2/Lt. Ralph ... ... Leicester
GUEUDECOURT, 25th September, 1916. He led his men in the attack with great courage and initiative. Later he ran along the parapet under heavy fire to give instructions for the consolidation, and set a splendid example.

DAVIS, Capt. Richard Nevill 2/Leicester
MONTNOIR, 17th April, 1918. For conspicuous gallantry and devotion to duty during an enemy attack. He kept the situation well in hand during the temporary absence of his commanding officer, and ensured the right flank of his battalion being thrown back so as to enable the front positions to be maintained. He continually sent back information as to the situation. His work has been splendid, and his coolness under fire most noticeable.

MILITARY CROSS. 73

DAVIS, 2/Lt. Thomas Henry Clifford ... ... R.F.A.
SAVERNAKE WOOD, 18th September, 1916. When his O.P. was blown in and himself wounded he remained and dressed a severely-wounded telephonist and brought him in. On another occasion he sent back valuable information and carried out a daring reconnaissance.

BAR TO M.C.
DEMICOURT, 22nd November, 1917. For conspicuous gallantry and devotion to duty. Whilst reconnoitring a position for a forward observation post, accompanied only by an orderly, he encountered a party of sixteen of the enemy, all of whom he brought into our lines as prisoners. He continually showed the greatest gallantry and enterprise.

DAWE, 2/Lt. Sidney Charles 5/Lincoln
CROISILLES-HENIN ROAD, 31st March, 1917. He led his platoon in the most gallant manner, and inflicted heavy casualties on the enemy. Later, although wounded, he remained at his post until the position was consolidated.

DAWSON, 2/Lt. Frederick Albert ... ... 8/East Surrey
POELCAPPELLE, 12th October, 1917. Shortly after the attack was launched the leading platoons of his company were held up by intense machine-gun fire. He pushed on and, in conjunction with his company commander, made great efforts to carry forward the attack. After his company commander became a casualty, he took command of the company and some men of another division, and again attempted to renew the attack.

DAY, Lieut. John Percival ... ... 9/Rifle Brigade
DELVILLE WOOD, 19th to 30th August, 1916. He twice carried out difficult and dangerous reconnaissances, and on one occasion led a successful bombing attack with great skill and courage.

DEATON, 2/Lt. Albert Joseph 6/Gloucester
ST. JULIEN, 16th August, 1917. In an attack he led his platoon with great dash and judgment. When held up by machine-gun fire he got his Lewis gun into action at once, silenced the hostile gun and charged the position. He inflicted considerable losses on the enemy by his prompt action.

DEBONO, Lieut. George Peter ... ... 5/Royal Berks
E. of ARRAS, 9th April, 1917. He showed great courage and ability when commanding his company. He led them against an enemy battery, capturing it and many prisoners. He set a fine example throughout.

DEER, Lieut. John Hartley ... ... K.R.R.C.
N. of KEMMEL, 11th August, 1918. For conspicuous gallantry and determination. He held on to the post of which he was in command, though entirely surrounded by the enemy, who were eventually repelled with heavy casualties. It was chiefly owing to his courage and tenacity that the flank of the battalion was maintained intact.

DE LANDRE-GROGAN, Lieut. Leon Victor St. Patrick ... 1(5)York & Lancaster
Near GAVRELLE (N. of ARRAS) on the night of September 22/23, 1918. For conspicuous gallantry and good leadership during a successful minor operation. He led his platoon against an enemy trench and successfully cleared it and carried out consolidation. The following night the enemy counter-attacked in force but were driven off with loss. The success of the operation was greatly due to his able leadership and fine example to his men.

DEVEREUX, 2/Lt. Richard Harding Frank ... ... 10/Rifle Brigade
    Awarded 1st January, 1917.

DICKMAN, 2/Lt. Henry Alderman ... ... 167th A. T. Coy., R.E.
    Awarded 1st January, 1919.

DIXON, Lieut. Alfred Chessington ... ... 11/Tank Corps
    Awarded 3rd June, 1919.

MILITARY CROSS.

DONALDSON, 2/Lt. Alfred James ... ... 9/Royal West Kent
    Near KLEIN ZILLEBEKE, 31st July and 1st August, 1917. For conspicuous gallantry and devotion to duty. During two days of severe fighting he made journeys under heavy fire to maintain touch with the battalions on the flanks and with the front line. He also reconnoitred and laid out the assembly area under fire and guided the companies to their tapes.

DORE, 2/Lt. William Charles Henry ... ... Labour Corps
    CAESTRE, 2nd December, 1917. For conspicuous gallantry and devotion to duty. He showed the greatest coolness and determination in his handling of his men in a most difficult situation.

DORRINGTON, 2/Lt. Stanley Flowers 3/Northampton
    GAZA, 2nd November, 1917. For conspicuous gallantry and devotion to duty. He displayed conspicuous courage and skill in the capture of a post, and, when compelled to withdraw, he successfully extricated his platoon across a shell-swept area. His dashing example was beyond all praise.

DOUGLAS, 2/Lt. George Frederick ... ... R.E.
    S. of ST. JULIEN, 8th September, 1917. For conspicuous gallantry and devotion to duty when in charge of gas projectors emplaced in a very exposed position. A hostile barrage being put down on and behind the projector emplacements he distributed his men in shell holes, and, without calling for any assistance from them, himself completed the final connections. Witholding his fire until the appointed time he fired four out of the five batteries, only returning to cover after having assured himself that all the projectors had fired. This involved careful and cool-headed work in a very exposed position and under exceptionally heavy fire.

DOWDEN, 2/Lt. Henry James ... ... 312th Brigade, R.F.A.
    HAVRINCOURT, 18th September, 1918. For conspicuous gallantry and devotion to duty. In reponse to a S.O.S., this officer at once got all the guns into action, and maintained a quick rate of fire in spite of heavy barrage. He fired one gun himself until the detachment was collected, and then assisted to bind up a wounded officer.

DOWSON, Lieut. Sydney Houghton ... ... 1/Royal Warwick
    Awarded 1st January, 1919.

DOYLE, Lieut. Algernon Gordon ... ... 123rd Field Coy., R.E.
    Near MONTAY, 15/16 October, 1918. For conspicuous gallantry and determination in connection with bridging the RIVER SELLE. On the night of 15/16 he took measurements of the river to enable a tank bridge to be made. On the 16th he prepared the necessary materials for the bridge, and that night worked for nine hours breast-deep in the water under heavy shell and machine-gun fire and sniping. When approaching daylight forced him to stop work, he had, by twenty-three hours' continuous work under most trying conditions, ensured the success of the scheme. He continued the work during the next two nights, and the bridge was satisfactorily completed twenty-four hours before zero. His bridging work proved of great value in the attack on the 20th.

DRAKEFORD, Capt. Herbert 7/Liverpool
    HOUPLINES, 15/16 July, 1917. For conspicuous gallantry and devotion to duty during a determined hostile raid upon our front line. He organised a post for defence, and succeeded in beating off a strong party of the enemy from both front and rear. He then visited all the front line positions in his sector under an intense barrage, during which he killed one of the enemy and obtained identifications.

DUCKWORTH, 2/Lt. John Edwin Hardie 7/Worcester (16/Devon)
    Near RONSSOY, 18th September, 1918. For conspicuous gallantry and initiative when he led the attack splendidly and was the first man on the objective between TOINE WOOD and ORCHARD POST. At one period he got considerably in advance of the main force but still pushed on. Without the courageous example set by this officer it is doubtful whether this position would have been taken at the time. One hundred prisoners and a machine gun

were captured in this sector alone. During consolidation, with a Welsh officer he crawled round a machine gun which was still firing and rounded it up. He and his party were also responsible for the capture of an enemy field gun.

DUDLEY, 2/Lt. Arnold Tiffany 3/Yorks
 HILL 60, 7th June, 1917. For conspicuous gallantry and devotion to duty in leading his company successfully when all the other officers had become casualties. He showed great judgment in his selection of strong points for the defence, and set a fine example to his men of coolness under heavy shell fire. Although wounded, he remained in command for 36 hours.

DUNBAR, Capt. Sir Archibald Edward, Bart. ... ... 12/West Yorks
 BAZENTIN-LE-GRAND, 14th July, and LONGUEVAL, 23rd July, 1916. He led his company in the attack with great dash, and skilfully consolidated his position. During a later attack he handled his company with great skill under heavy shell fire. He has set a fine example.

DUNKERTON, Lieut. Edmund Lloyd Hain ... ... 5/York & Lancaster
 BOURLON WOOD, 27th November, 1917. For conspicuous gallantry and devotion to duty. He led his platoon against a village under heavy fire. After his company commander had been wounded, he took command of the company, and three times went through a heavy barrage to reorganise his men. When the line had given way, he led his men forward again and saved a critical situation. He set a splendid example of determination and resource.

         BAR TO M.C.
 STEENWERCK, 11th April, 1918. For conspicuous gallantry and devotion to duty. He led his company in a successful attack on houses filled with enemy snipers and machine guns. Having gained his objective, he took charge of and successfully led another company who had lost all their officers. By his fine example of courage and good leadership he contributed largely to the success of the attack.

DURRANT, Major Reginald Tom ... ... 223rd Brigade, R.F.A.
 Awarded 1st January, 1919.

DURUTY, 2/Lt. Charles Eric ... ... 10/Royal Warwick
 S. of BOIS DE BEIZ, 21st September, 1918. For conspicuous gallantry and devotion to duty. After two companies detailed for an attack had reached their objective, communication with them except by runner was impossible for some time. During this period this officer, as Battalion Intelligence Officer, despite artillery barrage, very heavy machine-gun fire and numerous snipers, on two separate occasions carried out personal reconnaissances as far as the forward occupied posts, bringing back much valuable information to his commanding officer. He has on very many occasions carried out exceptionally valuable patrol work both by day and night.

DUTHIE, 2/Lt. Donald James ... ... 6/Royal Warwick
 Awarded 1st January, 1918.

DUTTON, Lieut. Wilfred Joseph 4/Gloucester
 AVE, on the ASIAGO PLATEAU, 23/24 October, 1918. In a night raid he led his company with conspicuous gallantry, quickly overcoming all enemy resistance and capturing fifty prisoners and three machine guns. By his personal example of courage and determination he contributed very largely to the success gained by his company.

DUXBURY, 2/Lt. Andrew Marshall ... ... 6/Oxford & Bucks L.I.
 Awarded 1st January, 1918.

DYKES, 2/Lt. Oswald ... ... R.F.A.
 BERTHANCOURT, 18th September, and FRESNOY, 24th September, 1918. For conspicuous gallantry and resource while in command of his battery, which was subjected to very heavy hostile fire and gas shelling, severe casualties being caused to personnel and equipment, in spite of which operations were successfully carried out.

EDE, 2/Lt. Edwin William ... ... 5/Royal Fusiliers
 E. of HANGARD, 2nd April, 1918. For conspicuous gallantry and devotion to duty while commanding a company in attack. He showed great coolness and determination under very heavy fire, and got his Lewis gun into action to counter the enemy machine guns.

EDGHILL, 2/Lt. Ashley Gay ... ... 4/Lancashire Fusiliers
    AYETTE, 3rd to 5th April, 1918. For conspicuous gallantry and devotion to duty while in command of his T.M. Battery during raids on hostile trenches. The attacks were carried out under a Stokes mortar barrage, as artillery could not be used, and were completely successful, resulting in the capture of three machine guns and several prisoners, and causing heavy enemy casualties. He carried out his programme in spite of heavy artillery and machine-gun fire, displaying a fearless devotion to duty which greatly inspired his men.

EDMINSON, Lieut. Leonard Oswald 12/Manchester
    Awarded 1st January, 1919.

EDMUNDS, Lieut. John 21/London
    BOURLON WOOD, 4/5 December, 1917. For conspicuous gallantry and devotion to duty. He remained with another officer and a few men in the front line for four hours after the position had been evacuated. He carried out his task with marked ability, and at the appointed time withdrew without a casualty and without the enemy suspecting that the line had been evacuated.

EDWARDS, 2/Lt. Griffith Oliver ... ... 3/Northumberland Fusiliers
    HILL 60 Sector, 7/8 June, 1917. For conspicuous gallantry and devotion to duty in commanding two platoons during an attack. His coolness and cheerfulness under heavy shell fire steadied his men, and later, when sent up to reinforce, he did so with great promptness and exactitude.

EDWARDS, Capt. William Howell ... ... 11/Royal Welch Fusiliers
    Near MONTAY, 20th October, 1918. In the attack he showed conspicuous gallantry as adjutant. Under constant machine-gun fire he made the preliminary arrangements for the assembly of the battalion east of the RIVER SELLE. It was largely due to his skill that the battalion was able to assemble so close to the first objective without enemy knowledge.

EGLINGTON, Lieut. Dudley Charles ... ... 2/Royal Highlanders (R.F.C.)
    LILLE, 20th May, 1917. For conspicuous gallantry and devotion when acting as an observer. In the course of a fight with several Albatross scouts, in which he shot down one, the pilot was wounded and fell over the control lever insensible, causing the machine to dive with the engine full on. He climbed out, standing outside the fuselage on the lower plane, dragged the pilot back, and, switching off the engine, pulled the machine out of its dive. Not being a trained pilot, his act exhibited great fearlessness and skill.

EILOART, 2/Lt. Ferdinand Robert ... ... R.G.A.
    Awarded 3rd June, 1918.

ELKINGTON, Lieut. Howard George 21/London
    DESSART RIDGE—BAZENTIN WOOD, 21st March, 1918. For conspicuous gallantry and devotion to duty in command of a company, especially during difficult withdrawals, when his coolness and courage were pre-eminent. At one critical moment he hastily reorganised and established a defensive flank, which gave time for a new position to be taken up in rear.

ELLEN, Lieut. Walter ... ... 8/Royal Sussex
    Awarded 3rd June, 1919.

ELLIOTT, Lieut. Alfred Ernest Thomas 10/London (1/Artists)
    MOEUVRES, 27th September, 1918. By conspicuous gallantry and determination he led his company to their objective, when he pushed forward and allowed companies in rear to consolidate. By his determination and fine example he held a most important point during a very critical period in the fight in spite of fierce opposition, and later rendered invaluable assistance to troops on his flanks by giving them information and enabling them to continue the attack.

MILITARY CROSS.

ELLIOTT, 2/Lt. Arthur Godfrey ... ... Grenadier Guards
    BOURSIES, 3rd September, 1918. For conspicuous gallantry during an attack. Having obtained his objective with his company, he at once pushed forward patrols to the next tactical feature, thereby enabling the advance of the battalion to be expedited. Later, during consolidation of a position, he displayed the greatest coolness and devotion to duty under heavy gas shelling, and, though gassed himself, remained at duty until three out of his four platoons had established themselves.

ELLIOTT, Lieut. Ernest Edward ... ... 9/Royal West Surrey
    HAMEL, 26th to 28th March, 1918. During three days' operations, he carried out a valuable reconnaissance under direct machine-gun fire. Though twice wounded he refused to withdraw, but remained with his men and continued to render valuable service until the battalion was relieved. His coolness under fire was a splendid example to his men.

ELLIS, 2/Lt. Joe ... ... 13/East Yorks
    Near ALEXANDROVO, 8/9 June, 1919. For marked gallantry and devotion to duty. Although the Russian flanking party had withdrawn, he attempted to rush a hostile post with eight men. On 15th June, with a patrol of 12 other ranks, he kept up a running fight for three hours with an enemy patrol about 100 strong. A splendid leader, who can always get the best out of his men.

ELLIS, 2/Lt. Reginald Donald ... ... Durham L.I.
    Awarded 4th June, 1917.

ELLIS, Lieut. Robert ... ... R.A.M.C.
    Awarded 4th June, 1917.

ELLIS, 2/Lt. Shirley Duncan ... ... 173rd Tunnelling Co., R.E.
    DOUBLE CRASSIER, 12th March, 1916. For conspicuous gallantry when rescuing, under very heavy shell-fire, some men who had become imprisoned in an old mine. At the first three attempts to reach them he was driven back by heavy fire.

ELTON, Capt. Herbert Sauzier 2/London
    In FRANCE, 21st to 27th March, 1918. For conspicuous gallantry and devotion to duty as battalion reconnaissance officer. On many occasions he was ordered to lead Tanks to their starting-points over very difficult ground, and always succeeded. He also displayed wonderful courage and initiative on the battlefield in obtaining information from neighbouring infantry and carrying orders to isolated Tanks. His services were invaluable throughout the operations.

ELVY, Major Leslie Thomas 13/London
    Awarded 1st January, 1919.

EVANS, 2/Lt. Bernard Scott ... ... 4/Royal West Surrey
    FONTAINE, 23rd April, 1917. He led his platoon with great courage and coolness. By his splendid leading he was mainly responsible for the success of the advance, during which 500 prisoners were taken. Though wounded in the head, he stuck to his work.

EVANS, 2/Lt. Douglas William 10/London
    ST. QUENTIN, 21/22 March, 1918. For conspicuous gallantry and devotion to duty. When his four guns were early put out of action, he took charge of two guns of another section and repelled many enemy assaults and assisted the infantry to hold the line. He showed great coolness and skill in the use of his guns.

EVANS, Lieut. Hugh Elwyn 5/Yorks
    Awarded 3rd June, 1918.

EVANS, 2/Lt. Thomas Evander ... ... 11/Royal Welch Fusiliers
SALONIKA, 27/23 March, 1917. When in command of a patrol he encountered a much stronger hostile party, which attempted to ambush and surround him. He at once attacked, and inflicted severe loss on the enemy. He handled his patrol with great ability and coolness throughout, setting a very fine example of courage and resource.

BAR TO M.C.
MORTHO WOOD, near VILLERS OUTREAUX, 8th October, 1918. He showed great gallantry and devotion to duty during the attack. On reaching the enemy wire he went forward to try and find gaps, and though badly wounded while doing so, remained at duty till daylight, when he organised his platoon and continued the advance until obliged by his wound to go back. He set a fine example of courage and determination.

EVANS, 2/Lt. Thomas Kelvin ... ... 3/Northumberland Fusiliers
VIEUX BERQUIN, 7th August, 1918. He made a reconnaissance in advance of a patrol which was held up by machine-gun fire from two points. By working close up he was able to locate the exact position of these guns. He further located two machine-gun posts further behind, from which our men were being sniped, and again two more posts from which a machine gun was captured. He was out for nearly four hours, most of the time behind the enemy's posts. He displayed conspicuous gallantry and skill.

EWEN, 2/Lt. Henry Spencer 23/London
W. of GRAINCOURT, 8th December, 1917. For conspicuous gallantry and devotion to duty. He organised and supervised the construction of a communication trench under heavy shell fire. Though he was twice badly shaken by bursting shells, he showed great courage and disregard of danger, and encouraged his men, when casualties were caused among them, by his splendid example.

FAGAN, 2/Lt. Herbert Archer 5/Yorks
W. of WANCOURT, 23rd April, 1917. He took a party and, working down a trench, cleared the enemy machine guns which were holding up the attack. The same night, under heavy barrage, he went down to headquarters and reported on the situation.

BAR TO M.C.
Near FONTAINE-LES-CROISILLES, 26th June, 1917. When in command of supports he crawled 300 yards on two occasions across the open at great personal risk to gain touch with the attacking company, which was completely isolated. He brought back information of the greatest value to battalion headquarters by this energetic and gallant action.

FAIRBAIRN, Capt. George Henry ... ... 9/Rifle Brigade
FLAVY-LE-MARTEL, 23rd March, 1918. For conspicuous gallantry and devotion to duty. When his commanding officer had become a casualty he took charge of the battalion, and proved himself a capable leader under the most trying circumstances. He held on to positions to the last moment, retiring last himself and rallying the remains of his battalion.

FAIRBAIRN, 2/Lt. William Frank ... ... 5/York & Lancaster
Near PASSCHENDAELE, 9th October, 1917. For conspicuous gallantry and devotion to duty when in command of his company, after all the other officers had been killed or wounded. He made a defensive flank to join up with troops on our left, and showed great powers of command under trying circumstances.

FAIRBAIRNS, Lieut. Reginald Holland ... ... R.A.S.C. (M.G.C.)
GUEUDECOURT, 25th September, 1916. Although wounded he led the first wave of the attack with great courage and determination. Later, when again wounded, he tried to continue, but his wounds prevented him.

FAIRTLOUGH, Capt. Gerard Howard ... ... R.E.
DEMUIN, 30th March, 1918. For conspicuous gallantry and devotion to duty. During recent operations, when the enemy pressed back the troops on the right, he collected a party of runners, orderlies and stragglers under heavy machine-gun fire and checked the enemy advance.

FALK, Capt. Cecil Joseph ...   3/Wilts
E. of NOYELLES, 4th November, 1918. For conspicuous gallantry and initiative during an attack. The officers commanding the two leading companies early became casualties, and the companies became somewhat disorganised. He immediately moved forward his support company, reorganised the line, and reached and consolidated the final objective, commanding all three companies until relieved by the arrival of the C.O. He has done consistent good work.

FARRIMOND, 2/Lt. William ...   15/Royal Warwick
W. of MERVILLE, 19/20 July, 1918. He brilliantly executed a raid on the enemy's trenches, his party killing every one of the enemy they met, and he himself accounting for some. He showed great determination and skill, and his daring inspired his party with the utmost confidence.

FEARN, Capt. Cecil Augustus ...   4/K.O.Y.L.I.
Near AVESNES-LE-SEC, 13th October, 1918. For conspicuous gallantry and devotion to duty. He displayed the greatest courage in consolidating, under heavy fire, a position just gained, and, when one of his posts was attacked and casualties occurred, he collected men from a neighbouring post, and re-established the position. His cheerful courage and energy inspired all ranks with confidence.

FERGUSON, 2/Lt. David Gordon ...   1/East Kent
Awarded 1st January, 1916.

FERGUSON, 2/Lt. James Scott ...   5/Seaforth Highlanders
Near LE HAMEL, 10th April, 1918. For conspicuous gallantry and devotion to duty during a hostile attack, when, in spite of their flank being exposed, his company maintained the position. Again, when he was the only officer left in the company, he managed to protect the left flank of the battalion when the troops on the left had retired, and so saved a critical situation.

FIGG, Capt. Sydney Vavasseur ...   1/Royal Warwick
Awarded 3rd June, 1918.

FISHER, 2/Lt. Henry Cecil ...   16/Middlesex
Awarded 1st January, 1918.

FISHER, 2/Lt. William Eric ...   R.A.S.C.
Awarded 1st January, 1917.

FLEMING, 2/Lt. Herbert Sidney ...   5/Northumberland Fusiliers
Near LAVENTIE, 1918. This officer, who was commanding a platoon, had orders to advance. An hour after receiving the orders he led his platoon forward, and, although he had never seen the country before him during daylight, kept direction accurately, quickly taking each objective as he came to it. Although met by hostile machine-gun fire, he pushed on through two hostile strong points, capturing a machine gun and the gunners, and establishing himself well in advance of his final objective. By his coolness under fire not only did he set a good example to his platoon but inflicted many losses on the enemy, whom he encountered in greatly superior numbers.

FLINT, Capt. Hugh ...   1/Hampshire
Awarded 1st January, 1918.

FOORD, 2/Lt. Basil Arthur ...   7/London
Near ARRAS, 28/29 May, 1918. For conspicuous gallantry and devotion to duty while in charge of the right attacking platoon in a raid on the hostile lines. He displayed a fine fighting spirit and powers of leadership, personally accounting for many of the enemy. When the time for withdrawal came, he remained behind to assure himself that all his casualties were brought back, assisting to carry some of them himself. He was the only surviving officer, and his gallant behaviour throughout was a fine example to all ranks.

MILITARY CROSS.

FORBES, Lieut. George Freeman Murray 1/Gloucester
    N. of GRICOURT, 29th September, 1918, when a frontal attack was held up, this officer on his own initiative worked round on a flank and entered the enemy's trenches. By this action he was enabled to organise a bombing attack party which worked up to the trench and took the enemy by surprise and caused him to retire. This enabled the frontal attack to gain their objective. He showed the greatest gallantry, initiative and resourcefulness.

FOULKES, 2/Lt. Edward ... ... South Lancashire
    PLOEGSTEERT, 11th April, 1918. For conspicuous gallantry and devotion to duty during an enemy attack. This officer displayed exceptional coolness and good leadership under very difficult circumstances. He rallied and reorganised men with marked success, and when compelled to withdraw did so by successive rushes, under covering fire, checking the enemy advances.

FRANKLIN, Lieut. Leslie ... ... 9/Yorkshire L.I.
    PROSPECT HILL, near LE CATELET, 3rd October, 1918. For gallantry and ability in commanding his company during the attack. His skill and initiative were most marked. Again, on the night 7/8 October, when his company took part in the attack on VILLERS FERME, near VILLERS OUTREAUX, he displayed the same gallantry and coolness and captured his objective under very heavy rifle and machine-gun fire.

FRASER, 2/Lt. Alan Cumming 7/London
    MALARD WOOD, 8th August, 1918. For conspicuous gallantry and good leadership. When the advance on his flank was held up by heavy machine-gun fire he worked his Lewis gun forward with great courage and disregard of danger, and silenced the machine guns. Our advance was then pushed on. Throughout the operations his fine example inspired confidence in all ranks.

FRASER, 2/Lt. Alexander ... ... 6/Royal Highlanders
    LONGAVESNES, 21st to 30th March, 1918. For conspicuous gallantry and devotion to duty. As battalion signalling officer he kept up communications under most difficult circumstances. When practically all the officers had become casualties he organised the men of all units around him and by his coolness and good leadership covered the withdrawal of other troops. By his cheerfulness and utmost disregard of danger he set a magnificent example.

FRIEND, 2/Lt. Charles Percy 3/Wilts
    Near MORCHIES, 22/23 March, 1918. For conspicuous gallantry and devotion to duty. As company commander he kept his men under a fine state of control in the face of great odds. He organised his line of defence with the greatest skill, and by his fine example kept up the spirit of his company, which inflicted heavy casualties and held the enemy in check at a critical moment.

FRIGHT, 2/Lt. Harold William ... ... 5/South Lancashire
    Near TOURNAI, 8th November, 1918. For conspicuous gallantry and devotion to duty in action. He led his platoon with great determination in the face of heavy machine-gun fire, in endeavouring to force a passage across the ESCAUT RIVER, and was wounded in the leg by a machine-gun bullet. His company, despite heavy casualties, hustled the enemy to the river bank, and almost prevented the last bridge being blown up.

FRYER, 2/Lt. Thomas James Harold ... ... K.R.R.C.
    PLOEGSTEERT WOOD, 12/13 July, 1916. For conspicuous gallantry during a raid on the enemy's trenches. He dragged a wounded man from the enemy's wire to safety, and assisted others to get under cover. He crossed "No Man's Land" three times under heavy fire while carrying out his gallant work.

FURZE, Capt. Gordon ... ... Coldstream Guards
    Awarded 3rd June, 1919.

MILITARY CROSS.

GARBUTT, 2/Lt. John Restarick ... ... Royal West Kent
    S. of HEBUTERNE, 17th July, 1918. He led his platoon forward from the reserve company through heavy shell fire with great gallantry and ability, reaching the forward companies with ammunition and entrenching tools, immediately after the objective had been gained, thereby greatly assisting the consolidation. When he found that one of the forward companies had lost nearly all its officers, he sent his platoon back, remaining himself to assist in the organisation and consolidation of the position, which was successfully carried out in spite of heavy shell and machine-gun fire. He displayed throughout great coolness and complete disregard of danger.

GARDNER, Capt. Henry ... ... R.A.
    Awarded 3rd June, 1919.

GARRARD, 2/Lt. Cyril Proctor ... ... R.E.
    LOCRE, 21st August, 1918. For conspicuous gallantry and devotion to duty when in charge of a section working on tracks immediately behind the assaulting infantry. In spite of heavy fire he kept in touch with the situation by constant personal reconnaissance, and thus enabled the work to be pushed forward rapidly with small loss. His party was instrumental in capturing seven prisoners.

GASCOIGNE, Lieut. Hugh ... ... R.T.O. (14/Worcester)
    Awarded 3rd June, 1919.

GAWLER, Capt. Harry Stephen ... ... 9/York & Lancaster
    Awarded 1st January, 1919.

GAULDER, 2/Lt. Charles William Edward ... ... 5/Yorkshire L.I.
    Near ORSINVAL, 4th November, 1918. For conspicuous gallantry and devotion to duty when in command of Stokes mortar section. When the leading wave was held up by machine-gun fire, he brought up a mortar, and, despite casualties caused by the heavy fire directed on him, silenced the machine guns. The promptness with which he grasped the situation enabled the infantry to advance and gain their objective with small loss.

GAYWOOD, 2/Lt. Frederick James ... ... 8/East Surrey (T.M.B.)
    S. of MIRAUMONT, 15th February, 1917. He established his two guns within 100 yards of the enemy and bombarded an enemy post, thereby enabling the infantry to capture the post.
                             BAR TO M.C.
    CHERISY, 3rd May, 1917. He accompanied and supported the assaulting battalion with his trench mortar, knocking out two enemy machine guns and accounting for a number of the enemy. When retirement became necessary he rendered his gun useless and assisted in reorganising the infantry.
                             SECOND BAR TO M.C.
    Near PRIEZ FARM, 1st September, 1918. For conspicuous gallantry and devotion to duty. He kept his company close behind the barrage, and took the farm in the first rush, the garrison of about 100 retiring. By the time the enemy counter-attacked he had organised a strong defence, and easily beat them off. With the assistance of two other officers he gradually rounded up the enemy in the vicinity, and after seven hours' fighting they surrendered. His initiative and leadership gained this very formidable strong point.

GEORGE, Major Walter Hope ... ... 16/M.G.C.
    Awarded 3rd June, 1919.

GIBBONS, Capt. James FitzGeorge ... ... 2/Notts & Derby
    GINCHY, 13th September, 1916. He reconnoitred the position under very heavy fire. Later he organised and most gallantly led his company in an attack. He was severely wounded.

GIBBS, 2/Lt. Eric Noel 10/London (1/Artists)
   THILLOY, 27th August, 1918. For conspicuous gallantry and able leadership. After his company commander had become a casualty this officer took command and materially assisted the advance by working his men round to a flank and engaging enemy machine guns which were holding up the company in front. Throughout the day he set a fine example to those around him.

GIBBS, Capt. Lawrence Henry ... ... 10/Lancashire Fusiliers
   GOUZEAUCOURT, 9th September, 1918. For conspicuous gallantry and devotion to duty. This officer led his men through a heavy gas bombardment and reached the objective, driving the enemy out, killing two with his revolver. His company was then counter-attacked from the flank, but the attack was repulsed, with the loss of twenty-two prisoners. He set a splendid example throughout the day's fighting, constantly exposing himself and encouraging his men.

GIBBS, Capt. Thomas Raleigh ... ... 2/Highland L.I.
   N. of VERTAIN, 23rd October, 1918. For most conspicuous gallantry and initiative during the operations. On reaching his objective he discovered a pocket of the enemy holding a sunken road. He rushed forward with one N.C.O. and killed two of the enemy and captured thirty. Six machine guns were found in the road, and but for his dash and courage a dangerous situation would have arisen.
                    BAR TO M.C.
         Awarded 1st January, 1919.

GIBSON, Lieut. Archibald ... ... 2/Royal Scots Fusiliers
   LEDEGHEM, 14th October, 1918. During the advance he was conspicuous for his initiative and contempt of danger. His company was in support, and on seeing the front company held up by heavy machine-gun fire he personally reconnoitred the ground and then pushed a platoon round the flank which captured the position and thus allowed the flank to advance. After taking the final objective he went forward under machine-gun fire and sniping, got in touch with his flanks, and selected the best positions for his men.

GIBSON, 2/Lt. Dudley Robert ... ... 4/Royal Berks
   FAUQUISSART, 19th July, 1916. He led his platoon with great dash up to the enemy wire. Finding they could not get through, he patrolled till he found a gap, through which he led them on under heavy fire.

GIFFORD, 2/Lt. William Douglas Gowthorp ... . 4/York & Lancaster
   Near RANSART, 17/18 February, 1917. He personally conducted the raiding parties back to the supporting troops, and, on hearing that one group had not returned, he went back, found it, and let it back through the gap. He previously carried out several daring reconnaissances of the enemy's position.
                    BAR TO M.C.
   NEUVE EGLISE, 13th April, 1918. For conspicuous gallantry and devotion to duty during a counter-attack which repulsed the enemy from a village. He personally killed seven and wounded four of the enemy, and with his small party he captured four enemy machine guns and fifty-one prisoners. He did very fine service.

GILCHRIST, 2/Lt. James ... ... 3/Royal Scots Fusiliers
   Near YPRES, 31st July, 1917. For conspicuous gallantry and devotion to duty. Having led his company to its objective, he held on throughout the day under a very heavy bombardment, although twice buried during the afternoon by enemy shells. He showed a splendid example of devotion to duty and courage under the heaviest fire.

GILKS, Capt. Humfrey Livingstone 1/Artists
         Awarded 1st January, 1917.

MILITARY CROSS. 83

GILL, Lieut. Hugh Stanley ... ... R.F.A.
    FONTAINE-LES-CROISILLES, 28th May, 1917. At great personal risk he extinguished a burning ammunition dump. His promptitude and fearlessness saved several hundred rounds of ammunition, and probably many lives as well.

GILLESPIE, Lieut. Thomas Leslie 4/Worcester
    E. of BAILLEUL, 1st September, 1918. For conspicuous gallantry and good leadership. When his company, which had been ordered to move up and fill a gap between two corps, was held up by machine-gun fire, he went forward and by personal reconnaissance located the enemy machine guns, and turned his Lewis guns on to them with great effect, thus clearing the way for his company. The success of the advance was largely due to his fine courage and personal example.

GILLOTT, Lieut. Cecil ... ... 14/Durham L.I.
    Near MORCHAIN, 25th March, 1918. For conspicuous gallantry and devotion to duty. When defending part of a line with his platoon, although wounded early in the attack, he remained with his men until hit for the third time. By his fine example of coolness and absolute disregard for personal safety, his platoon was able to inflict heavy losses on the enemy, and to hold them up until they had worked round the flanks.

GJERTSEN, Capt. Rudolf 4/Essex
    Awarded 1st January, 1918.

GLOVER, 2/Lt. Montague Charles ... ... 6/Royal Warwick
    AVE, ITALY, 4th October, 1918. For conspicuous gallantry and determined leadership in a raid. He led his platoon with courage and ability, and set a very fine example to those under him.

GOACHER, Capt. Frederick 1/Artists
    MOEUVRES, 27th September, 1918. He displayed most gallant leadership, capturing more than 200 prisoners in the Canal. He then reorganised and, pushing on, led his company to their objective. He inspired his men by his utter disregard of danger, and continued to set a splendid example until wounded a short while afterwards.

GODDARD, 2/Lt. Wilfred John ... ... 7/Royal West Kent
    In FRANCE, 24/25 April, 1918. For conspicuous gallantry and devotion to duty. He led his company in a successful counter-attack under heavy machine gun and shell fire, kept his men well in hand, and maintained his position under extremely heavy fire during the next day.

GODFREY, Capt. Ernest Gordon 6/London
    Awarded 1st January, 1918.

GODFREY, 2/Lt. Stanley Charles ... ... 2/Royal Scots Fusiliers
    GUN TRENCH, 30th September, 1915. For conspicuous gallantry when the Germans had succeeded in entering Gun Trench and were bombing down it. It was largely owing to the personal bravery and initiative of 2/Lt. Godfrey that their advance was stopped. He organised bombers, collected bombs and attacked the enemy, gaining some ground. He was continuously fighting from 6.30 p.m. till 5 a.m. next day.

GOLDIE, Capt. Bernard Charles Mary 10/London
    Near SIVRI TEPE, EGYPT, 19th September, 1918, For conspicuous gallantry and dash during the operations. He, in conjunction with another officer, each in command of a platoon of the advanced guard, though taken on both flanks by machine-gun fire, pushed on, captured their objective and several prisoners. This manœuvre turned Sivri Tepe, and was instrumental in causing the enemy to retire, thus materially assisting the advance.

MILITARY CROSS.

GOLDSBURY, 2/Lt. Charles Melville 7/London
    Near HOLLEBEKE, 9/10 July, 1917. When in command of a raid, he was the first to reach the farm which was the objective, and in spite of enemy barrage and heavy rifle fire dashed on ahead and bombed the place, setting it on fire and capturing 10 prisoners. He was severely wounded whilst returning, having remained behind in the burning building to search for a trench mortar. The success of the enterprise was entirely due to his splendid example of fearlessness and personal leading.

GOSLETT, Capt. Raymond Gwynne ... ... R.A.S.C.
    Awarded 1st January, 1918.

GOSNEY, Lieut. Harold William ... . 13/Rifle Brigade
    Near LOUVIGNIES, 4th November, 1918. For conspicuous gallantry and cool ability. His company commander and others being wounded, he reorganised the company, and on reaching the first objective he personally went along his line, adjusting liaison on both flanks. On reaching the final objective, and finding himself the senior officer present, he superintended consolidation on the battalion front.

GOTCH, 2/Lt. Davis Ingle 6/Northampton
    REGINA TRENCH, 25th to 29th October, 1916. For conspicuous gallantry in action. Although several times buried himself, he was constantly helping to dig out others, and by his cheerfulness and courage afforded a fine example to all ranks.

GOULD, 2/Lt. Arthur Nutcombe 1/Gloucester
    E. of POELCAPPELLE, 31st March and 1st April, 1918. He was in command of a patrol which was fired on by an enemy machine gun at a range of 30 yards. and three of his men were wounded. He succeeded in dragging two of them back with the help of the third man a distance of 200 yards to a point where he could return to our lines and bring back help. His courageous and determined action prevented the men from falling into the enemy's hands.

GOULD, Lieut. Cyril Edward ... ... 280th (London) Brigade, R.F.A.
    SEBOURG, 5th November, 1918. Whilst coming into action in a new position, his battery came under heavy fire, which caused a block in the traffic and the ditching of one of the guns. He displayed great presence of mind and coolness, quickly found another route of advance, and eventually got the battery forward into action. He thereby enabled not only his battery but many others in the rear to get forward and into action.

GRAHAM, Lieut. Keith 15/Hampshire
    MENIN, 2nd October, 1918. For conspicuous gallantry and devotion to duty. Although nearly surrounded by enemy machine guns he held his position and succeeded in capturing a strong concrete dug-out in a farm. He showed coolness and resource in the face of determined resistance.

GRAHAM, 2/Lt. Thomas Eric ... ... 2/Scottish Rifles
    Near FRELINGHEM, 1st October, 1917. For conspicuous gallantry and devotion to duty. When sent out on a patrol with three men to examine a river, he found a footbridge, crossed it, and made a thorough reconnaissance. On returning, the enemy made an unsuccessful attempt to cut him off, and he withdrew his patrol under fire without a casualty. On the following night when on patrol he was instrumental in the discovery of a second footbridge, and owing to his good leadership his patrol gained most valuable information. On both occasions he showed great determination and sound judgment.

GRAY, Capt. Harold Vernon 6/Gloucester
    HOLNON WOOD, 22nd March, 1918. For conspicuous gallantry and devotion to duty. The enemy were believed to have penetrated into a position held by an advanced right company, and he was sent to report on the situation. He displayed great courage and resource both in going and returning under heavy shell fire, organised the position, and successfully returned with a very clear report.

MILITARY CROSS.

GRAY, 2/Lt. Harry Albert ... . Royal West Kent
N. of YPRES-MENIN ROAD, 3rd October, 1917. For conspicuous gallantry and devotion to duty in maintaining direction as leader of an assaulting wave. When his company commander became a casualty he reorganised the company, which had lost over 60 per cent., and beat off several minor attacks. He remained with his men in a shallow trench when they were being heavily shelled, when he might have gone to his headquarters. The good work done by the company was mainly due to his splendid example.

GRAY, Lieut. James ... ... 5/Royal West Surrey
Near GRAND ROZOY, 29th July, 1918. He repeatedly distinguished himself in action, especially when he led his company, with a total disregard for personal safety, under intense and accurate machine-gun fire. He inspired his men with great confidence, and successfully dealt with some difficult situations.

GRAY, Lieut. Samuel Alexander 23/London
HAPPY VALLEY, 22nd August, 1918. He carried out several important reconnaissances under heavy fire, bringing back information of essential value on each occasion. Later, when the enemy attacked with some success, he fought a determined rearguard action, holding successive positions to the last moment. Throughout the operations his gallantry and devotion to duty were conspicuous examples to his men.

GREEN, 2/Lt. Arthur ... ... 3/D.C.L.I.
Near MERVILLE, 12th April, 1918. For conspicuous gallantry and devotion to duty. He acted as adjutant until he was wounded, and rendered the utmost assistance in re-forming and reorgansing a defensive line at a time when great pressure was being brought against the battalion and the position was obscure. His personal example under trying conditions and heavy fire at close range was altogether admirable.

GREEN, Lieut. George Richard ... ... Grenadier Guards
Awarded 3rd June, 1918.

GREEN, Capt. William Charles ... ... 1/South Stafford
Awarded 1st January, 1918.
BAR TO M.C.
Near BOIS DE LUXEMBOURG, 27/28 May, 1918. For conspicuous gallantry and devotion to duty during an enemy attack. When the enemy had broken through on his left and his company had suffered severe losses, he rallied the remainder of his men and held on for a considerable time. Having lost touch with troops on his right, he withdrew to a trench in rear and again maintained touch with them. His numbers being greatly depleted, he attached himself to the troops on the right until wounded the following day.

GREENWOOD, Lieut. James Hurst ... ... 11/Royal West Kent
YPRES-COMINES CANAL, 14th June, 1917. For conspicuous gallantry and devotion to duty. Although wounded in the jaw, he continued to lead his company with great dash and fearlessness, rushing and capturing a machine gun which was holding up his advance. This was the second occasion on which he had captured an enemy machine gun.

GRIERSON, Lieut. Kenneth McIvor 22/Manchester
Awarded 3rd June, 1918.

GRICE, 2/Lt. William Stanley ... ... R.G.A.
Awarded 1st January, 1918.

GRIFFIN, Capt. Arthur Ethelbert ... ... R.E.
Awarded 1st January, 1919.

GRIFFITH-JONES, Lieut. William Lionel Phillips ... ... 3/Durham L.I.
POTYZE, 14/15 March, 1916. For conspicuous gallantry. He took part in a raid on the enemy's trenches, and was the first man to enter them. He shot the sentry and set a fine example of coolness.

MILITARY CROSS.

GRIFFITHS, 2/Lt. William Henry ... ... 16/Royal Warwick
ACHIET-LE-GRAND, 21st to 23rd August, 1918. For conspicuous gallantry and good leadership. He led his platoon in an attack with great skill to the final objective in spite of heavy machine-gun fire. When the flanks were exposed and a withdrawal became necessary, he maintained his position for two hours over a thousand yards in advance of the new line covering the withdrawal, and then brought back his men in perfect order. In a later attack he captured all his objectives and took command of a large number of troops who had lost their leaders. The success achieved was largely due to his courage and coolness.

GUTTRIDGE, 2/Lt. John Frederick 9/Yorks
Awarded 1st January, 1919.

HACK, 2/Lt. Walter Pank 10/Lincoln
Near POELCAPPELLE, 22nd to 24th October, 1917. Seeing two of the enemy about 200 yards from our trenches trying to get away he covered them with a Lewis gun and went out himself and brought both back prisoners.

HADRILL, 2/Lt. Cedric Ivor ... ... 10/East Yorks
FORET DE NIEPPE, 28th June, 1918. Soon after the commencement of an important attack this officer went well forward and established a signal station, from which he kept up communication between battalion headquarters and the companies, notwithstanding the heavy enemy shell fire, which constantly broke the wires. His personal courage and coolness under trying circumstances were a fine example to his men, and he sent back valuable information from his position in the front line.

HALL, Capt. Alner Wilson 1/Artists
Awarded 3rd June, 1919.

HALL, 2/Lt. Lionel Everard ... ... 1/K.R.R.C.
Near VERMELLES, 28th September, 1915. For conspicuous gallantry at the quarries. He led his bombers and threw bombs himself against the Germans for nearly three hours until completely exhausted. By his courage and example he eventually worked his way up the trench and cleared it of the enemy.

HALLIDAY, 2/Lt. Clarence Peter ... ... 2/Yorkshire L.I.
FAYET, 14th April, 1917. He led his platoon with great skill in the face of heavy fire, and placed his machine guns to such advantage that he was able to materially check the enemy counter-attack, thereby rendering valuable assistance at a critical period.

HALLIDAY, Lieut. Howard Edwin. 7/Worcester
ASIAGO PLATEAU, ITALY, 10/11 October, 1918. For conspicuous courage and determination during a night raid on enemy trenches at SEC. In spite of the darkness and a heavy enemy barrage, he led his men straight to the final objective, where he engaged the enemy with great gallantry. An enemy machine gun opened fire on his party at close range; he at once, with only a few men, rushed the gun, putting the team out of action, and brought the gun back to his lines.

HALLOWES, 2/Lt. Rupert Price 4/Middlesex
HOOGE, 19th July, 1915. For conspicuous gallantry on the night of 19th July, when owing to shortage of bombs the enemy was advancing down the communication trench. He got out of his trench, exposing himself fearlessly, and fired at the enemy in the open, hitting several. He also assisted in making a block, dug out a communication trench under heavy shell fire, and rebuilt a parapet that had been blown in. Throughout the night he assisted in keeping touch and supplying bombs.

HAMILTON, Capt. Herbert James ... ... 1/D.C L.I. (R.A.F.)
Over COMINES, 12th October, 1917, to 26th March, 1918. For conspicuous gallantry and devotion to duty. He has on many occasions displayed the utmost dash and fearlessness in

engaging enemy aircraft at close range, and has succeeded in destroying a considerable number. He also attacked with machine-gun fire, and from low altitudes, enemy formations on the ground, and dropped bombs on points of importance behind the hostile lines. He has invariably shown great determination and a fine offensive spirit.

HANCOCK, Capt. Ernest ... ... R.G.A.
BEUVRY, 18th April, 1918. For conspicuous gallantry and devotion to duty. The section in which this officer was in command was being heavily shelled, during the course of which a 15-in. shell destroyed the drainage system in the vicinity and flooded one gun position, while in the other the gun platform was smashed by a shell. He managed to get them both into action again and kept them firing. He was several times knocked over by shell explosions.

HARDING, 2/Lt. Geoffrey Philip 6/Northampton
CHERISY, 3rd May, 1917. For conspicuous gallantry and devotion to duty, in outflanking and bombing an enemy machine gun, putting it out of action. His courage and determination were a splendid example to his men.

HARDMAN, 2/Lt. William Frederick Kerr ... ... R.E.
MESSINES, 7th June, 1917. He showed complete disregard of danger in assisting to search deep dug-outs and cellars of a village for traps and mine charges. His coolness under constant heavy shell fire kept up the spirits of his men and set a fine example of courage. He extricated two men who had been buried by a shell although exposed to fire himself. His work was most efficient.

HARPER, Lieut. Edward Russell ... ... R.A.S.C.
GIBERCOURT, 21st March, 1918. For conspicuous gallantry and devotion to duty. He brought up the battery transport and got away two guns under intense machine-gun fire, afterwards returning with a corporal, started up and got safely away with the two remaining F.W.D.'s in spite of machine-gun fire which riddled the lorries.

HARRISON, Capt. Frank ... ... 9/Royal Munster Fusiliers
Awarded 3rd June, 1917.

HARRISON, 2/Lt. John George 3/Lincoln
N. of POELCAPPELLE, 4th October, 1917. He took command of his company in an attack when he was the only officer left. He reorganised his men, sited his posts with great judgment, and sent in a very clear and useful report on the situation. He was largely responsible for repulsing an enemy counter-attack. He showed great courage and initiative, and his contempt of danger had a great effect on his men.

HARRISON, 2/Lt. Edward Harrison ... ... R.E.
E. of NIEUPORT, 10th July, 1917. For conspicuous gallantry and devotion to duty when in charge of the maintenance of canal bridges. By his untiring energy and disregard of personal safety he succeeded in repairing these bridges, although they were frequently cut by hostile fire, thereby maintaining communication under very trying and critical conditions.

HART, 2/Lt. Joseph Aubrey ... ... 2/East Surrey
Awarded 1st January, 1918.

HARVEY, Capt. Albert, *D.S.O.* 6/Liverpool
DON, 15/16 October, 1918. For conspicuous gallantry on the night of 15/16 October, when in face of considerable difficulties and hostile fire, he got his company over the HAUTE DEULE CANAL. For this purpose he made a rough raft himself, was the first man across, and established a bridgehead at this point, thus enabling the brigade to cross and clear the enemy out of DON, a strong position. Throughout the advance, he commanded his company with skill.

MILITARY CROSS.

HARVEY, 2/Lt. Eric Howard 5/Gloucester
  N. of OVILLERS, 27th August, 1916. For conspicuous gallantry during operations. After a senior officer had been wounded he led a bombing attack against a trench held by 40 of the enemy. He drove them out and consolidated the captured trench.

BAR TO M.C.
  DOULIEU, 12th September, 1918. He led his company with gallantry and ability in an attack, and drove the enemy, with many casualties, from the position where he was holding up our advance. At one time his men were practically surrounded and under heavy fire, through which he rushed without hesitation to warn an advancing battalion of the position of his company. He averted what might have been a most unfortunate accident by his promptitude and disregard of danger.

HASSLACHER, 2/Lt. Alfred John Emil ... ... 7/London (169th T.M.B.)
  Near CROISILLES, 27th August, 1918. He brought his section of mortars into action behind the first wave of infantry, and successfully engaged several machine guns of the enemy which were causing casualties. He was severely wounded, but continued to direct and control his teams until all the ammunition had been expended. His courage and endurance were a splendid example to his men.

HAWKSWORTH, 2/Lt. Henry Charles Harold 10/Essex
  YPRES, 31st July, 1917. For conspicuous gallantry and devotion to duty. When the two assaulting battalions of an attack were short of ammunition and it was of the utmost importance that a fresh supply should reach them as soon as possible, he led an ammunition party forward about two-and-a-half miles over the most difficult country, exposed the whole time to the heaviest shell fire and without a guide. One third of his party were knocked out, but he safely delivered the ammunition, and hearing on his return journey that a hostile counter-attack was probable, he turned his party about and again reported to the battalion headquarters in case his aid should be required. His determination and devotion to duty set a splendid example to his party.

HAYNES, Lieut. Charles Graham ... ... 4/K.R.R.C.
  SCHWABEN REDOUBT, 21st October, 1916. For conspicuous gallantry in action. He led bombing attacks with great courage and determination, and finally, after bombing for one and a half hours, was able to capture two officers and fifty men.

BAR TO M.C.
  S.E. of YPRES, 20th September, 1917. For conspicuous gallantry and devotion to duty. He successfully led attacks on three strong points, and, later, aided by one man, he captured a dug-out and took two officers and four other ranks prisoners.

HEDGES, Lieut. Norman Hammett ... ... 5/York & Lancaster
  GOMMECOURT, 27th March, 1918. For conspicuous gallantry and devotion to duty while commanding a company. He repulsed a severe enemy counter-attack. Next day, under heavy machine-gun fire, he captured his objective, and though wounded maintained his position for four days. He set a fine example of courage and leadership.

HEMPHILL, Capt. Howard Hislop 2/Leicester
  YPRES, 1st October, 1917. For conspicuous gallantry and devotion to duty. He led his company with great coolness through an intense barrage to counter-attack the enemy; he reorganised after heavy losses, and held on to a portion of the front line for thirty-six hours.

HENDERSON, Capt. Ernest James ... ... 2/East Lancashire
  E. of YPRES, 31st July, 1917. For conspicuous gallantry and devotion to duty in leading his company throughout important operations under most difficult circumstances. Although exposed to heavy hostile fire on the right flank, he successfully consolidated his objective, and by this means ensured the safety of the right flank of his division. Later in the day, he successfully repelled two counter-attacks, setting a personal example throughout that greatly inspired and encouraged his men.

HENDERSON, Capt. Kenneth Robert ... ... 2(6)Yorkshire
 ARCHANGEL. He has carried out the duties of company commander and adjutant of mixed force at BOLSHE-OZERKI, and has worked in a very efficient way. He has had continuous service on this front since November, 1918, and in the four engagements which his company has taken part he has proved to be a fearless and good leader of men.

HENEY, 2/Lt. John Henry Waldo ... ... 1/Coldstream Guards
 Near VILLERS POL, 4th November, 1918. For conspicuous gallantry and devotion to duty. He took charge of two sections at the commencement of the attack and cleared the whole right flank of some half dozen machine guns which were enfilading it. He killed several himself, and with his handful of men collected over a hundred prisoners. After the attack he and a few others beat off a counter-attack on the right flank.

HEWITT, 2/Lt. Arthur Edgar ... ... 22/London (T.M.B.)
 YPRES, 10th June, 1917. On several occasions he has rendered most invaluable assistance to the attacking infantry, personally reconnoitring forward positions and establishing his guns where they could co-operate with the greatest effect. His pluck and energy under fire have always been most marked.

HIBBARD, 2/Lt. Hamilton Edgar, *D.C.M.* 9/London (1/Artists)
 RUMILLY, 8th October, 1918. For conspicuous gallantry and initiative. During the advance he came suddenly on a strong point in which were eight enemy machine guns. By prompt action and fearless leadership he rushed the post, overcoming the garrison and taking the crews prisoners.

HIBBERT, Capt. John Geoffrey ... ... A.O.D.
 Awarded 1st January, 1917.

HICKSON, Capt. Reginald Davies 9/Essex
 ARRAS, 23rd March, 1917. With great coolness and a total disregard for danger he went forward under very heavy fire, and personally superintended the withdrawal of his advanced parties at a most critical time.

HIDE, Lieut. James Burchell ... ... 305th Siege Battery, R.G.A.
 Awarded 3rd June, 1919.

HIGGINSON, Capt. John Victor ... ... 2/Royal Welch Fusiliers
 GIVENCHY, 5/6 July, 1916. For conspicuous gallantry during a raid. Owing to his brilliant organisation and fine leading of his company the raid was a complete success.

HIGLETT, Lieut. George Willibert ... ... Bucks Bn./Oxford & Bucks L.I.
 ASIAGO PLATEAU, 16th June, 1918. For conspicuous gallantry and devotion to duty while commanding a company in the second line during an enemy attack. Throughout the fighting he maintained excellent liaison with the forward battalion, sending back valuable information. When the front line was broken he held up the enemy with Lewis gun fire, and by constant patrolling kept touch with the division on his right, closing up a very wide gap in the second line. He showed great fearlessness, and by reinforcing his threatened flank undoubtedly prevented the enemy's further advance.

HILL, 2/Lt. Arthur Dudley 1/Middlesex
 Awarded 1st January, 1916.

HILL, 2/Lt. Charles Vincent ... ... Oxford & Bucks L.I.
 Near ST. JULIEN, 22nd August, 1917. He led his platoon with the utmost gallantry on a concrete machine-gun emplacement, which he captured, killing three of the enemy. Being wounded, he directed the fire of his platoon from the top of the gun emplacement on to another enemy machine gun, which he captured. His cheerfulness and courage under heavy fire had a splendid effect on his men.

HILL, 2/Lt. Joseph Shirley ... ... R.F.A.
Near MONCHY-LE-PREUX, 17th June, 1917. For conspicuous gallantry and devotion to duty under very heavy shell fire. A shell burst at the mouth of his telephone pit, killing a major and wounding him and another officer. He extricated himself, and although wounded in five places, succeeded in digging the officer out. He then carried him on a stretcher, with the aid of a bombardier, to the dressing station, through a very heavily shelled area, before having his own wounds dressed.

HILLYER, Lieut. William Harold ... 3rd London Field Coy. (171st Mining Coy.) R.E.
HILL 60, near YPRES, between 2nd and 17th April, 1915. In mining operations the task of completing and charging one of our mines was one of great difficulty and strain. Lieut. Hillyer worked and watched long hours at the end of a gallery 165ft. long and 3ft. by 2ft. 3in. in size, knowing that the enemy was counter-mining close by. His pluck and endurance were remarkable and resulted in the successful explosion of the mine and consequent capture of the hill.

HINDMARSH, 2/Lt. Clifford ... ... 7/Loyal North Lancashire
S.W. of BERMERAIN, 23rd October, 1918. He led forward his platoon with the greatest gallantry. He attacked in turn a succession of hostile machine-gun nests, and by his initiative, coolness and determination succeeded in establishing the left front of the battalion on its final objective and taking some fifty prisoners, including two officers.

HINGLEY, Capt. Alfred Norman 13/Middlesex
CARENCY SECTOR, 1st to 11th April, 1917. For over 10 days this officer showed most conspicuous bravery and was a splendid example to all, carrying out his duties under very heavy bombardment. Though wounded he carried on until his battalion was relieved five days later.

HOAL, 2/Lt. Edward Garner 8/Manchester
ABRAHAM HEIGHTS, 6th to 11th October, 1917. For conspicuous gallantry and devotion to duty when in command of his company after the company commander had been wounded. He acted as guide to another company which had to take up a new position under heavy shell fire.

HOBBS, Capt. Wilfred 2/Bedford
Awarded 3rd June, 1918.

HOBSON, Lieut. Robert Carl ... ... 12/Northumberland Fusiliers
WYTSCHAETE, 16th April, 1918. For conspicuous gallantry and devotion to duty. Throughout a week's fighting this officer's energy and enthusiasm remained undiminished. At the end of that period, when acting as liaison officer, he voluntarily remained in the forward area until late in the evening, keeping brigade headquarters fully supplied with first-hand information.

BAR TO M.C.

Awarded 3rd June, 1918.

HOCKEY, 2/Lt. Alfred Lennon 21/London
JERUSALEM, 9th December, 1917. For conspicuous gallantry and devotion to duty. On a heavy enfilade fire being opened from a house on the flank, he, with great dash and initiative, attacked and drove out a much superior force of the enemy, and held the position under a heavy cross fire from machine guns, displaying the most courageous determination and energy.

HODGKINS, 2/Lt. Albert Edward ... ... R.F.A
Near WESTHOEK, 10th August, 1917. For conspicuous gallantry and devotion to duty when Forward Observing Officer. He remained with the most advanced infantry practically all day during an attack, and, although his wire was constantly cut, he personally renewed it

under heavy fire, and got most valuable information through of impending counter-attacks. The night before he had succeeded, under great difficulties, in establishing visual communication by lamp from battalion to group headquarters. His courage and ability were most marked.

HOGARTH-SWANN, 2/Lt. Arthur Lionel 7/Norfolk
E. of GONNELIEU, 20th November, 1917. For conspicuous gallantry and devotion to duty in an attack. When his company commander was killed early in the advance he took command, and, though wounded, led the company to the capture of the objective. He showed courage and leadership of a high order.

HOLDAWAY, Lieut. Neville Aldridge 8/Manchester
ABLAINZEVILLE, 27th March, 1918. For conspicuous gallantry and devotion to duty. When this officer observed that the officer in charge of an important advanced post had become a casualty, he immediately went up through a heavy barrage and took command. He organised and controlled the fire of the garrison with such effect that the enemy began to waver, so he promptly advanced, inflicting severe casualties; but, finding them too numerous, he withdrew, after ascertaining their dispositions. His courage and coolness throughout the whole operations were very marked.

HOLDSWORTH, 2/Lt. Harry ... ... 4/East Lancashire
Near BRIASTRE, 19/20 October, 1918. He led his platoon on the night with great gallantry in face of heavy fire against a strong enemy position. On the final objective he located an enemy machine-gun post on the front of the battalion that was enfilading our line. He led a party of six men against the post, and by his determined assault captured one officer and four other ranks of the enemy, together with three machine guns. He did fine work.

HOLGATE, 2/Lt. Leonard George ... ... 10/Lancashire Fusiliers
MARTINPUICH, 25th August, 1918. For conspicuous gallantry during an attack. He led his platoon with the greatest determination, and drove the enemy back, and it was due to his courage and leadership that the objective was gained. He was seriously wounded, but refused to be moved to the rear until three more seriously wounded men were first taken to the aid post.

HOLLAND, 2/Lt. Arthur Leslie 1/Artists
S. of MARCOING, 30/31 December, 1917. For conspicuous gallantry and devotion to duty. He took command of a company when his company commander became a casualty and successfully led it to a new position which he consolidated. He brought in several wounded men from the front of the lines under heavy fire, and set a splendid example of coolness and courage to his men.

HOPLEY, Lieut. William Arnold ... ... 3/Royal Warwick
MESSINES, 10th to 19th April, 1918. For conspicuous gallantry and devotion to duty. During ten days' operations, when in command of two light trench mortars, he was frequently under the heaviest fire of all descriptions. On all occasions he set a fine example of courage and devotion to duty to his men, and his dispositions were marked by skill and ability. On one occasion, when both his mortars were buried and his detachment had been reduced to a quarter of their effective strength, he nevertheless managed to bring the mortars into action again and inflicted severe casualties on the enemy.

HOPWOOD, 2/Lt. John ... ... R.F.A.
KEMMEL, 20th July, 1916. For conspicuous gallantry. When his battery was heavily bombarded and a direct hit ignited an ammunition store, he at once went in and got the fire under at great personal risk before anyone else arrived on the scene. Some of the ammunition exploded, and the position was being shelled while he was working.

HORLEY, Lieut. Cyril Rupert ... ... 2/Oxford & Bucks L.I.
Awarded 3rd June, 1919.

HORNE, Capt. Owen Walters 2/Essex
 FAMPOUX, 9th April, 1917. When commanding the right company it was largely due to his leading that direction was kept over a three mile advance. When held up at the fourth objective by uncut wire he went to the front and personally supervised the cutting in front of a strongly held trench.

HORSLEY, Capt. Oswald ... ... 2/Gordon Highlanders (R.F.C.)
 ANGLE WOOD, 18th August, 1916. He led the first line of the advance, capturing and consolidating his objective. Though wounded and put into a shell-hole he continued to direct operations and refused to be moved back till the position was safe.

BAR TO M.C.
 In FRANCE, March, 1918. He has brought down completely out of control three hostile machines, and of two others which he engaged one he fought to within a distance of 200ft. from the ground, forcing it to land, the second spinning down to the ground out of control, he being unable to observe it crash owing to the presence of other hostile machines. He has carried out accurate and valuable reconnaissances, and has set a magnificent example of determined gallantry and skill whilst leading low-flying and bombing patrols.

HOSKING, 2/Lt. James Cecil ... ... 10/D.C.L.I.
 MŒUVRES, 30th November, 1917. For conspicuous gallantry and devotion to duty when employed in carrying ammunition to the front line. During three days' operations he went backwards and forwards, without rest, through heavy barrages, and enabled the line to be maintained. He assisted on one occasion in repelling an enemy attack, and set a splendid example of energy and resource to his men under difficult conditions.

HOWARD, Major Hugh Lloyd ... ... 3rd Corps Signal Coy., R.E.
 Awarded 3rd June, 1917.

HOWCROFT, 2/Lt. Stewart Martin ... ... 1/Royal West Surrey
 Near VELDHUEK, 25th September, 1917. When the company commanders of two companies who had made a counter-attack were wounded, he took command, and showed great ability and coolness in controlling the situation for two days under continuous fire.

HOWE, 2/Lt. Vernon Arthur 3/Norfolk
 S.E. of FORET DE NIEPPE, 10/11 May, 1918. For conspicuous gallantry and devotion to duty when in command of a platoon carrying out a raid on an enemy post. He bombed an enemy trench, sent a Lewis gun round to enfilade it, and then, seeing that it was being successfully dealt with, he pushed on with only two men, and searched the houses which were his final objective.

HUDSON, 2/Lt. Edward Palmer ... ... R.F.A.
 BAILLEUL, 28th March, 1918. When the battery was heavily shelled in a forward position he set a splendid example of coolness and courage to his men. Later in the day, he took command of the battery in a most difficult situation and conducted a withdrawal under heavy fire. It was largely owing to his determined efforts that the operation was successfully carried out.

HUGHESDON, Capt. Reginald Howard ... ... 1/D.C.L.I.
 E. of YPRES, 4th October, 1917. Though wounded early in the assault he continued to lead his men until the objective was gained.

HUGHES, Capt. Hugh Llewellyn Glyn, *D.S.O.* ... ... R.A.M.C.
 Near FREMICOURT, 21st to 23rd March, 1918. For conspicuous gallantry and devotion to duty. He worked day and night in the open, in spite of the heaviest shell and machine-gun fire, tending the wounded and helping them back to safety, with a spirit of cheerfulness and self-sacrifice rarely seen. After being wounded he still continued to perform his duties, until the wound necessitated his evacuation.

MILITARY CROSS.

HUNT, Capt. Archibald Henry 20/London
 N.E. of SOLESMES, 20th October, 1918. For conspicuous gallantry in the operation. Though his right flank was exposed, he led his company on to its objective through a heavy enemy barrage and captured a field gun. He then consolidated the position gained and held on to it for three days under trying conditions.

HURNDALL, Lieut. Charles Frederic ... ... R.F.A.
 Awarded 3rd June, 1918.

HYAMS, 2/Lt. Henry David 23/London
 Awarded 1st January, 1918.

IMRIE, 2/Lt. David Patrick Cuthbert 1/London
 WARNETON, 9th April, 1918. For conspicuous gallantry and devotion to duty. He was in charge of a platoon occupying a strong point, and after both flanks had been forced back he held on and inflicted very heavy casualties on the enemy at close range, thus delaying the enemy's advance and allowing the troops, which had withdrawn, to take up a new position. His tireless energy and cheerfulness deserve the highest praise.

IRELAND, 2/Lt. Ernest Pinnock ... ... Tank Corps
 Near ST. JULIEN, 22nd August, 1917. When acting in support of another officer, the tank commanded by the latter became ditched, whereupon 2/Lt. Ireland attempted to tow it out with his own, but got ditched in the attempt. He unditched his own tank and brought all the wounded and the guns of both tanks safely out of action, although while doing so his tank was put out of action by shell fire. During the whole of this time he was under heavy shell and machine-gun fire. He showed great gallantry and fearlessness.

IRVING, Capt. George Gray Hammond ... ... 9/Rifle Brigade
 ACHIET-LE-GRAND, 21st to 25th August, 1918. For conspicuous gallantry and devotion to duty. He made a personal reconnaissance of the outpost line under heavy machine-gun fire, and returned with information of great importance. During five days' operations he was untiring in his efforts to arrange food, water and ammunition supplies, and by his masterly grip of the situation rendered invaluable service.

JACKSON, Capt. Mark Keith 6/Warwick
 E. of VILLERS PLOUICH, 3rd to 5th December, 1917. For conspicuous gallantry and devotion to duty in action. Although in a very exposed position with his company, he maintained it for many hours under a very heavy shell fire. Later, seeing a company of another unit on his left being hard pressed, he gallantly led a party of men across the open to attack the enemy on the flank, and was wounded while so doing.

         BAR TO M.C.
 BAC ST. MAUR, 6th September, 1917. He organised the final attack which drove the enemy out of his positions with great skill, and carried it out with courage and determination, capturing many prisoners and four machine guns. His conspicuous courage and devotion to duty inspired all the men of the company under his command.

JACKSON, 2/Lt. Stewart Spiers 6/Worcester
 LA VACQUERIE, 3rd December, 1917. For conspicuous gallantry and devotion to duty. When sent up with reinforcements to a post which was almost surrounded by the enemy he led his men through heavy rifle and machine-gun fire. He went forward alone to reconnoitre the best means of approach, and by his coolness and courage succeeded in bringing timely assistance to the garrison of the post.

JAGGER, Lieut. Charles Sargeant 13/Worcester
 NEUVE EGLISE, 11th to 14th April, 1918. For conspicuous gallantry and devotion to duty while commanding a company. He beat off several attacks by superior forces, and when his right flank was exposed and communication cut he still held on to his position. He made a valiant fight, and not until he was compelled to do so did he order a retirement.

MILITARY CROSS.

JAMES, 2/Lt. Lawrence Edward 7/London
    S.E. of YPRES, 20th September, 1917. When the advance of his company was held up by enfilade fire from a dug-out he quickly made up a party, and after hard fighting captured the position, accounting for eight of the enemy. His prompt action was invaluable to the battalion.

JAMES, 2/Lt. William Thomas 1/London
    N.W. of BULLECOURT, 16th June, 1917. He took command of his company when his other officers had become casualties, and consolidated and held a position for 24 hours, although subjected to repeated bombing attacks and sniping from all sides. His conduct and bearing throughout were most creditable, and set a splendid example to his men.

JARVIS, Captain Arthur 1/Gloucester
    Awarded 3rd June, 1919.

JEFFERYS, Capt. Arthur Harold ... ... 7/Middlesex (Loyal North Lancs.)
    GIVENCHY, 18th April, 1918. For conspicuous gallantry and devotion to duty. As soon as the enemy barrage lifted he ordered his company to stand to, and when he found that the enemy had penetrated the trenches he led an immediate counter-attack and drove them back some distance. He then organised and led bombing parties to clear the enemy out, and join up with a company on the left. He succeeded in this, and, although wounded, insisted on reorganising the sector, and did not leave till the next day.

JERWOOD, Capt. Edward Longsden ... ... 1/Royal Berks
    S. of RICHEBOURG L'AVOUE, May 15th, 1915. For conspicuous gallantry and devotion to duty during a night attack on the enemy's trenches, when in charge of machine guns, He established a machine gun in position in the second captured German trench under rifle and machine-gun fire, and also recovered a machine gun that had been lost between the first and second German trenches. On 17th May he gallantly led a section which established two machine guns in the firing line under shell fire, and set a fine example to the men under his command.

FIRST BAR TO M.C.
    Near OPPY, 29th April, 1917. For conspicuous gallantry and devotion to duty in leading his company during an attack. By his dispositions and personal example he was able to repulse several heavy counter-attacks until himself wounded. The reports he sent back were invaluable.

SECOND BAR TO M.C.
    Near BERMERAIN, 24th October, 1918. For marked gallantry and devotion to duty. When in command of the support company he noticed that the left front company and the battalion on his left were held up by heavy enfilade machine-gun fire. He promptly advanced his company and captured the final objective.

JERWOOD, Capt. John Hugh ... ... 10/Durham L.I.
    S.E of HOOGE, 21/22 and 24/25 August, 1917. He maintained his position regardless of withdrawals on his right and left and of the fact that the enemy had penetrated the line on both his flanks. He displayed a coolness and fearlessness which inspired all ranks with confidence.

JOHNSON, Capt Alfred Forbes ... ... R.G.A.
    Awarded 1st January, 1919.

JOHNSON, Capt. Charles Beckett 5/Border (9/Liverpool)
    Awarded 3rd June, 1919.

JOHNSTON, 2/Lt. John Darrell 5/Gloucester
    E. of YPRES, 22nd August, 1917. During the attack he led his company through the barrage and took up and consolidated a position. He took command of the forward line and

organised the defence of four different units. He displayed exceptional qualities of leadership, and by his cheerfulness and disregard of danger inspired all ranks to consolidate and hold on at a critical time. His organisation of the line helped the troops on his flanks to hold on to the objectives.

JOHNSTONE, Lieut. Robert ... ... 4/London (R.F.C.)
Near LE TRANSLOY, 17th October, 1916. For conspicuous gallantry in action. He has shown marked courage and initiative in turning our artillery on to columns of enemy infantry. On one occasion he carried out counter battery work in cloud and mist at 800 feet under heavy fire from the ground.

JONES, Lieut. Percy Hudson ... ... R.E.
FESTUBERT, 18th April, 1918. For conspicuous gallantry and devotion to duty. As brigade signalling officer he displayed untiring energy in his efforts to establish communication with battalions which had become dislocated owing to heavy bombardment and mist. Throughout the day he was up and down seeing what could be done to improve matters, regardless of personal risk.

JONES, 2/Lt. Reginald Lucas 9/London
Near WESTHOEK, 16th August, 1917. For conspicuous gallantry and devotion to duty on several occasions in hand-to-hand fighting. On one occasion he cleared a tunnel dug-out with a Lewis gun, inflicting heavy casualties on the enemy.

JOSEPHS, 2/Lt. Edward Albert Robert 5/Gloucester
S. of POELCAPPELLE, 4th October, 1917. For conspicuous gallantry and devotion to duty. He took command of his company in an attack and led it forward under heavy fire. He showed great initiative and energy in organising and consolidating the captured ground.

JUPP, Lieut. John Morton Scott 10/Manchester
BRIASTRE, 20th October, 1918. For marked gallantry and determined leadership. He was in command of a company, and under heavy machine-gun fire, dashed forward with a few men, shooting several of the enemy with his rifle and capturing the guns. Later, finding that the company on his flank had not reached its objective, he led a platoon and attacked the enemy on his flank.

JULL, 2/Lt. Robert Charles ... ... R.G.A.
Awarded 1st January, 1918.

JUNGIUS, Lieut. Ernest James Theodore ... ... 1/Bedford (M.G.C.)
Awarded 3rd June, 1918.

KEEP, 2/Lt. Alan Ralph ... ... 3/Royal West Surrey
OVILLERS, 27th July and 13th August, 1916. For conspicuous gallantry during operations. He kept his battery continually in action day and night under heavy shell fire, thereby materially assisting the infantry to capture enemy trenches.

KEEY, Lieut. Cecil Walter 7/London
SAULCOURT and EPEHY, 7th September, 1918. For conspicuous courage and devotion to duty during the operations. He was in charge of two mobile trench mortars, and had both guns put out of action, and the majority of the teams wounded. Despite the fact that he was wounded in the face he took over the remnants of two companies of infantry who were left without an officer and reorganised them, and consolidated on a line just west of CAPRON COPSE. His initiative and courage in the face of great danger were a splendid example to all ranks concerned.

KEKEWICH, 2/Lt. Stanley Buck ... ... R.F.A.
LA VACQUERIE, 30th November, 1917. For conspicuous gallantry and devotion to duty. He assisted his battery commander in man-handling the guns back when the ammunition was exhausted during an enemy attack. He set a splendid example of coolness and courage under heavy fire.

MILITARY CROSS.

KELTY, Lieut. Stanley William 9/Liverpool (30/M.G.C.)
WERVICQ, 14th October, 1918. For conspicuous gallantry and initiative. During the attack he twice went forward to reconnoitre the ground prior to the advance of his guns. When an enemy post was holding up our advance he crept forward to ascertain the strength with which it was held. He obtained most useful information concerning the enemy's position, although persistently fired at by snipers and machine guns. Later, he took his guns boldly forward and had them in their consolidated positions within half an hour of the capture of the locality.

KENNEDY, Lieut. Cyril Arthur Reginald ... ... R.F.A. (Y/9/T.M.B.)
Near STEENBEEK, 15th October, 1918. For conspicuous gallantry and devotion to duty. He was in charge of mobile 6-in. mortar in close support of the infantry. When the attack began heavy enemy machine-gun fire was immediately opened on the mortar and its detachment. With great coolness and gallantry he continued to keep his mortar firing and render very material assistance in diminishing the enemy's fire, and thus enabling the infantry to continue their advance.

KERCKHOVE, 2/Lt. Herbert Vincent ... ... 4/East Surrey
HAUSSY, 16th October, 1918. For gallantry and resourceful leading during the attack. After several attempts had failed to rescue a wounded man who was lying in front of our posts he crept out under heavy maching-gun fire and got the man in. Later, he organised a party of 10 men and surrounded an enemy post in a sunken road, which was inflicting great damage and casualties upon the attacking force, and succeeded in capturing the whole garrison of 60, with two trench mortars and two anti-tank rifles. His courage and coolness were admirable.

KERR, 2/Lt. John Vass 7/London
Near HANGARD, 24th April, 1918. This officer's platoon was subjected to very heavy fire during an enemy attack, which drove back the troops on either flank. His determination encouraged his platoon to stand fast and pour a steady fire into the advancing enemy, causing them to bring up a large number of troops, supported by two tanks, against him. Although his men began to waver, he went round the platoon, regardless of personal danger, and rallied them at the critical moment by his example, so that not one of the enemy reached his post. But for his gallant stand a considerable amount of ground would have been lost.

KIDD, Lieut. Claude Bernard 15/Cheshire
Near EPEHY, 24th August, 1917. He did remarkably fine work when his company was holding a position for many hours from early morning till late at night, while heavily shelled. It was entirely due to his efforts that the men were kept together. He encouraged his men throughout the day, continually going up and down the trench. His conduct was splendid, and he set a fine example.

KING, 2/Lt. Bernand Ellis 10/Norfolk
Awarded 1st January, 1918.

KING, 2/Lt. Harry Norman ... ... 4/Loyal North Lancashire
Near CORDONNERIE, 29th July, 1917. For conspicuous gallantry and devotion to duty when leading his platoon in a raid on the enemy trenches. After fierce hand-to-hand fighting, in which his platoon sergeant and four section leaders were all wounded, an enemy party superior in numbers appeared on his right. He at once collected his men, charged this party, and in a second hand-to-hand fight put them to flight. Although half his platoon had become casualties he remained out in "No Man's Land" until ordered to retire, when he collected wounded and brought them in. His absolute contempt of danger and fine leadership so inspired his men that they completely routed a force of twice their strength.

KINGDON, 2/Lt. Frank Denys ... ... 29th Battery R.F.A.
SAPIGNIES, 25th August, 1918. For conspicuous gallantry. When heavy enemy fire killed two men and wounded several others of his battery he organised a stretcher party and got them to a place of safety under heavy shelling. By his example of coolness he kept the battery in action and saved several lives. Later, while observing under heavy enfilade fire, he showed marked devotion to duty, and kept up communication with his battery by visual, and got back valuable information.

B. W. VANN, V.C. [pp. 45, 336.

Copyright.]

DEFEAT OF THE PRUSSIAN GUARD AT NONNE BOSCHEN WOOD BY THE 2ND OXF. AND BUCKS L.I.

(From the picture by Capt. W. B. WOLLEN, in the possession of the Officers of the Battalion. By permission.)

KNIGHT, 2/Lt. Alfred Ovenden ... ... 12/Loyal North Lancashire
    GOUZEAUCOURT, 30th November, 1917. For conspicuous gallantry and devotion to duty. During the preliminary portion of the attack he showed great courage and exercised complete control over his company. On the enemy opening a heavy barrage, and while they were seen to be advancing, he ordered all the sections with which he could get into touch to retire, only leaving the position himself when the enemy were not more than 300 yards away. It was very largely due to his courage and skill that the whole company were extricated from a very awkward situation with very few casualties.

KNOWLES, 2/Lt. Roland Ernest ... ... R.G.A.
    N.W. of HEBUTERNE, 5th April, 1918. Whilst on duty at the guns under heavy enemy bombardment he helped to rescue the wounded from a blown-in dug-out. He kept all the guns in action, moved from pit to pit with the greatest coolness, and personally assisted in serving the guns when short of men. He displayed fine courage, and set a high example by his behaviour.

LAING, 2/Lt. Ivan ... ... Coldstream Guards
    Near GINCHY, 15/16 September, 1916. When he was the only officer left in his company, he reorganised his men, rushed forward through a heavy barrage, and remained out securing the front till ordered to withdraw.

LAMBERT, 2/Lt. Philip Felix ... ... 2/West Riding
    FAMPOUX, 9th to 11th April, 1917. He displayed great courage and resource in taking command of his company in the advance. When the party was withdrawn at night he did good work in organising the defence of a captured trench; he set a fine example throughout.

LAMBDIN, Lieut. John Reginald ... ... 7/West Yorks (2/Durham L.I.)
    Near ST. QUENTIN WOOD. For marked gallantry and devotion to duty on the night of 17/18 September, 1918. He was sent to show the battalion guides the route to the assembly position. He took the party up and got shelled. Out of sixteen guides six came back, the remainder being killed. Although himself badly shaken, he returned to the battalion and, ractically unaided, guided the companies into position. He then volunteered to take a message over ground swept by shell fire.

LAST, Capt. Ernest Reginald 1/Liverpool
    VIMY RIDGE, 1/2 June, 1916. For conspicuous gallantry. He organised an assault on the enemy's trenches, and displayed great coolness and an utter disregard of personal danger during the operation, which was carried out under a heavy hostile bombardment.

LAWLESS, Capt. Philip Henry 18/Middlesex
    Awarded 1st January, 1919.

LEE, Capt. Reginald William 4/Essex
    ALI-EL-MUNTAR, EGYPT, 26th March, 1917. For conspicuous gallantry and devotion to duty. During an attack he went back under heavy machine gun and rifle fire at close range, collected and brought up reinforcements regardless of his own safety. He then organised and skilfully led the final assault from his part of the line.

LEECH, Lieut. Arthur William ... ... 6/Northumberland Fusiliers
    Near HARBONNIERES, 27th March, 1918. For conspicuous gallantry and devotion to duty. During a counter-attack, when his commanding officer had become a casualty, he took command of the battalion and successfully led the attack to its objective, capturing two machine-guns and several prisoners. This successful counter-attack was instrumental in holding up the enemy at a critical moment, and great praise was due to this officer.

MILITARY CROSS.

LE FEVRE, 2/Lt. Frank Ewart Bayliss 3/Lincoln
    S.W. of LENS, 1st July, 1917. For conspicuous gallantry and devotion to duty during an assault upon the enemy's position. When the leading company was temporarily checked he pressed forward, killing many of the enemy, and personally taking a prisoner. When he could go no further he dug in. He afterwards made it his special mission to keep touch between the right and left companies, repeatedly passing over ground which was under fire, and showing a complete contempt for danger. His consistent coolness under fire has always set a magnificent example to his men.

LEITH, Lieut. George Hector ... ... 18/Machine Gun Corps
    FORET DE MORMAL, 4th November, 1918. During the attack he handled his section of machine guns with great courage and skill under heavy machine-gun fire, enabling them to select positions of great value, from whence they were able to inflict heavy casualties on the enemy, as well as to neutralise the enemy's fire, and materially assisted the advance of the infantry. He has consistently done good work.

LEWIS, Capt. Francis Attwater 5/Welch
    Awarded 11th April, 1918.

LEYBOURNE, Capt. Philip Edwin 8/Hampshire
    Awarded 3rd June, 1918.
BAR TO M.C.
    S.E. of La CLYTTE, 8/9 August, 1918. For conspicuous gallantry and good leadership. He was the first to reach the objective on the front of the company of which he was in command. When the position had been gained he consolidated with skill and promptitude, in spite of many casualties, sending back valuable information to battalion headquarters. Throughout the operation his fine example had a great effect on his men.

LINDSAY, Lieut. Gordon Parmiter 2/Border
    Near BAPAUME, January, 1917. For conspicuous gallantry and devotion to duty. He displayed great courage and initiative during a raid, and was the last to leave the enemy's front line trench. Later he made a gallant attempt to rescue a wounded man.

LISTER, 2/Lt. Alfred Walton ... ... R.F.A.
    FLEURBAIX, 9th April, 1918. For conspicuous gallantry and devotion to duty. When the battery position was being heavily shelled he helped to keep up the fire of his battery by running from one gun to another, passing orders. When the order was given to limber up he helped with the teams so that the guns were got away under shell and machine-gun fire. He worked day and night when he and another officer were the only two left with the battery, inspiring all ranks to do their utmost.

LLOYD-JONES, Lieut. John 2/Yorkshire
    Awarded 1st January, 1916.

LOCKWOOD, Lieut. Eric Jardine 5/Essex
    EGYPT, 19th September, 1918. For conspicuous gallantry and devotion to duty. In the attack on KEFR KASIN, he led his platoon with great dash, taking all his objectives on three successive positions in very difficult country. He set a very fine example to his men.

LONGBOTHAM, Lieut. Currer Benjamin ... ... 32/Northumberland Fusiliers
    S.W. of ASIAGO, 15th June, 1918. For conspicuous gallantry and devotion to duty during an enemy attack. When his company commander had been killed he, though wounded in the head, commanded the company throughout the day, and only went to the Aid Post when ordered to do so by the commanding officer in the evening. He set a very fine example of grit and perseverance to his men.

MILITARY CROSS.

LONGSTAFF, Capt. Ralph ... 8/East Yorks
    Awarded 1st January, 1917.

LORD, 2/Lt. Gilbert Henry ... 5/Royal Lancaster
    Near WIELTJE, 31st July to 2nd August, 1917. For conspicuous gallantry and devotion to duty when all his officers and N.C.O.'s had become casualties and he himself was wounded in the hand. He took command of his company, and carried on under heavy shell fire and very adverse weather conditions, until he was again wounded in two places, displaying admirable courage and devotion to duty.

LORIMER, Capt. John Scott ... 1/Norfolk
    Awarded 1st January, 1917.

LORT, 2/Lt. William Vincent ... 7/London
    ALBERT SECTOR and "NO MAN'S LAND," July, 1918. For conspicuous gallantry and ability in action. He and a N.C.O. went out to the help of a fighting patrol who had suffered severe casualties. He promptly organised stretcher parties, and made many journeys to and from the front line under heavy machine-gun fire, himself unaided carrying one man 100 yards. When all casualties were clear he twice attempted to rescue the Lewis gun, and was wounded when nearly succeeding.

LOTT, Capt. Francis Albert ... 1/Welch (32/M.G.C.)
    Near ORS, 4th November, 1918. For conspicuous courage and devotion to duty at the crossing of the OISE-SAMBRE CANAL. He carried out personal reconnaissance, and pushed his guns boldly forward before the attack. During the attack he opened an intense fire on enemy machine guns, and swept the points from which the bridging parties could be fired on. This made it possible for the canal to be bridged very quickly.

LOVELL, 2/Lt. Bertram ... Tank Corps
    YPRES, 31st July, 1917. For conspicuous gallantry and devotion to duty. He rendered most valuable assistance to the infantry, and when his tank had become badly ditched under heavy shell fire he formed two strong points with his crew, and kept them supplied with ammunition until he was wounded. He remained with his men in one of these strong points for over an hour, until he became so weak from loss of blood that the crew persuaded him to go back to the dressing station. He set a splendid example of pluck and devotion to duty.

LOVERIDGE, Capt. John Leonard ... 4/Royal Berks
    HANGARD WOOD, 27/28 April, 1918. For conspicuous gallantry and devotion to duty. He made a reconnaissance under heavy enemy barrage, and next day led his section to the starting point, in spite of the fact that his tanks had been observed by the enemy and were submitted to heavy fire. Throughout he showed great coolness and initiative.

BAR TO M.C.
    Awarded 3rd June, 1918.

LUCAS, 2/Lt. Clifford James ... 7(17)London
    E. of WULVERGHEM, 28th September, 1918. For conspicuous gallantry and devotion to duty. Previous to the assault he had led daring reconnaissances of two craters, and in the assault, with the knowledge gained, he led his platoon round the first, killing the garrison, and then rushed the second. The same night he drove out nest after nest of machine-guns with his platoon, his energetic leadership inspiring his men with great confidence.

LYNE, Capt. Howard William ... 1/Yorkshire L.I.
    S. of LE CATEAU, 17th October, 1918. For conspicuous gallantry during the operations. He led his company to the objective with energy and skill. Subsequently he found that the enemy threatened his left. He immediately formed a defensive flank, and under heavy fire held his ground throughout the day.

LYONS, Capt. Ernest Frederick 10/Devon
    Awarded 1st January, 1919.

MCBAIN, 2/Lt. Hubert ... ... 2/Durham L.I.
    MORCHIES, 21st March, 1918. For conspicuous gallantry and devotion to duty. He led a counter-attack and established a block in a trench at a very critical time. He held this position for four hours, and greatly assisted his battalion to maintain its position. He showed great fearlessness and devotion to duty. In the afternoon he was wounded.

MCCALL, 2/Lt. Archibald ... ... 4/K.O.S.B.
    YPRES, 31st July and 1st August, 1917. For conspicuous gallantry and devotion to duty. When all the other officers of his company had become casualties he took command, and led them with the greatest gallantry and skill during the severe fighting which ensued, returning after the capture of each strong point and collecting more men, whom he led forward. While doing this gallant work he fell severely wounded in the head, having very materially assisted in the capture of the position.

MCCARTHY, 2/Lt. Thaddeus Francis ... ... 4/Loyal North Lancashire
    WESTHOEK RIDGE, 10th August, 1917. For conspicuous gallantry and devotion to duty. When in charge of the battalion carrying and ration parties he carried out his work with the greatest coolness and ability, and although by reason of the heavy shell fire it was of a most arduous and dangerous nature it was due to his exertions and personal supervision that rations arrived regularly. On another occasion during an attack he led his men forward with great coolness, setting a fine example to those around him. He afterwards took over and reorganised another company whose officers had all become casualties.

MACDONALD, Lieut. Kenneth ... ... 7/Seaforth Highlanders
    N.E. of YPRES, 28th September to 3rd October, 1918. For most conspicuous gallantry and determined leadership during the operations. He led his company with great skill against the enemy positions on the BRODSEINDE RIDGE, and on more than one occasion captured parties of the enemy practically single-handed. His fearlessness inspired all ranks under him.

MCDOUGALL, Peter Aitken ... ... R.A.F.
    In FRANCE, 19th February to 12th March, 1918. For conspicuous gallantry and devotion to duty. He always showed great initiative and skill in attacking enemy aircraft, and drove down or destroyed several enemy machines. On one occasion while on patrol he encountered three enemy two-seater machines, and though his engine was giving trouble he attacked them single-handed and drove one of them down out of control, having shot the observer. On another occasion, after driving down an enemy machine, he attacked and silenced a battery of six guns which were firing on our machines. His example of pluck and determination was of the utmost value to the squadron.

MACFARLANE, 2/Lt. Donald Murray ... ... 19/Lancashire Fusiliers
    Near ZONNEBEKE, 23rd October, 1917. On a wireless station being blown in by hostile shell fire he organised a rescue party from his platoon, which was quartered in adjacent dug-outs. In spite of heavy shell fire he succeeded in digging out six wounded men and had them carried back to a dressing station. By his prompt action and fine example of courage the lives of these men were saved.

MACINNES, 2/Lt. William Alexander ... ... 4/Highland L.I.
    Near SERRE, 10/11 February, 1917. For conspicuous gallantry and devotion to duty. He led his platoon in a most gallant manner, and inflicted many casualties on the enemy. Later, he reorganised his men and materially assisted in repulsing a hostile counter-attack.

BAR TO M.C.

    NIEUPORT, 10th July, 1917. For conspicuous gallantry and devotion to duty during an intense hostile bombardment of the town. He occupied the brigade observation post, which was unprotected, and at the top of a conspicuously high building, for twelve hours under intense shell fire. His work enabled the brigade commander to keep in touch with the situation, as all other means of doing so were being continually interrupted, and in spite of the shells bursting all round his post and passing through the building he declined to vacate it, except to repair his telephone wires. He set a magnificent example of fearlessness and devotion to duty.

MACKAY, 2/Lt. Donald John Everall ... ... R.E.
LA BASSEE CANAL, 18th April, 1918. For conspicuous gallantry and devotion to duty. When the enemy was seen massing in force at the head of a pontoon bridge, in spite of the shelling and machine-gun fire, he and his men swung and sank the bridge, and then assisted the garrison to man the trenches and repulse the enemy. Undoubtedly his coolness and resource under most difficult conditions saved what might have been a serious situation.

McKEOWN, 2/Lt. Felix Quinn ... ... R.G.A.
CHAUNY, 21st March, 1918. For conspicuous gallantry and devotion to duty. His section was under intense shell fire, and he found it impossible to keep the communication line working, so he established a post in the open, and from there maintained connection all day with the brigade, and got messages through to the section by runners. He was wounded in the evening.

MACKIE, Lieut. William Gordon ... ... 5/West Riding
KEMMEL, 27th April, 1918. For conspicuous gallantry and devotion to duty. This officer personally reconnoitred under heavy machine-gun fire the whole front of the battalion, which had been ordered to advance at short notice, without having had an opportunity of examining the ground beforehand. When the flank was threatened the reserve company of which he was in command was pushed into the gap, and he made able dispositions of his platoons and Stokes and Vickers guns. Under heavy fire he crawled forward and secured maps and papers from wounded and dead enemy in front of our lines. Later, when fifty of the enemy endeavoured to rush one of his posts, he turned a Lewis gun on them and accounted for them all. He was severely wounded—losing an eye while doing this—but he did not desist until the enemy was completely repulsed. His gallantry and initiative were conspicuous throughout the day, during the whole of which he was under close machine-gun fire.

McKINLEY, 2/Lt. Charles 16/London (1/Artists)
At NIERGNISS, 8th October, 1918. For conspicuous gallantry and initiative. When the situation was very obscure, he carried out two exceedingly comprehensive reconnaissances, although subjected to heavy machine-gun and artillery fire, thereby clearing up the situation on the Divisional front and obtaining information of the utmost value.

McKINTY, 2/Lt. Henry Bernard ... ... R.F.A.
BERTINCOURT, 23rd March, 1918. For conspicuous gallantry and devotion to duty while in charge of the guns of a battery who were covering the withdrawal of a division. The battery was under heavy machine-gun fire at a range of about 900 yards. He continued to shoot his guns till the last possible moment, and then withdrew them successfully. On this occasion he behaved with the greatest coolness, and all through the operations showed great courage and energy.

McMILLAN, 2/Lt. Ernest Albert ... ... 1/Cameron Highlanders
17th October, 1918. For very gallant and skilful leading of a platoon sent out to do a flanking movement. He successfully accomplished his task, enfilading the enemy's position and clearing a ridge. By so doing, this platoon virtually captured the whole of the battalion's objective, with forty-two prisoners and ten machine-guns, without a single casualty being incurred.

McWALTER, Lieut. Thomas Brown ... ... 12/East Surrey
In front of WYTSCHAETE, 3/4 September, 1918. For conspicuous gallantry while commanding a fighting patrol. He was ordered to drive out enemy posts, and so enable other troops to advance. In spite of extreme darkness and swampy ground he overcame determined resistance and gained his objective. Throughout the whole operation he set a fine example of courage and good leadership.

MACE, Capt. Edgar Robert ... ... 3(1)Liverpool
AVETTE, 14/15 July, 1918. For conspicuous gallantry in leading his company in a raid against the enemy outpost system, when nine prisoners were captured and as many more killed. The success was due to his very thorough all-night reconnaissances. He showed the calmest determination, and his personal example inspired a fine offensive spirit in the men he took over the parapet.

BAR TO M.C.

ERVILLERS and MORY COPSE, 23rd August, 1918. For conspicuous gallantry and fine leadership during an attack. He led his company splendidly, captured his objective, and then made himself secure against an enemy counter-attack. Next day he led his company forward from reserve successfully and consolidated a position. Throughout the operations his fine example of courage and determination inspired his men.

MACHIN, 2/Lt. Norman Frederick ... ... Coldstream Guards
GINCHY, 15th September, 1916. He led his men with great dash, rallied them under heavy machine-gun fire, and brought them on through a heavy barrage till he fell wounded.

MADDEN, 2/Lt. Clarence Rowland 4/Lincoln
S.W. of LENS, 19th June, 1917. For conspicuous gallantry and devotion to duty. Throughout an attack upon enemy trenches he displayed exceptional coolness and cheerfulness, and when the position was won he promptly brought rapid fire to bear upon the retreating enemy, causing very heavy casualties. He also showed great initiative in personally attending to all the details in connection with blocking, bombing and mopping-up parties, setting a fine example to his men of courage and self-possession under fire.

MADDOCK, Capt. Richard Henry ... ... 2/Royal West Surrey
Awarded 1st January, 1916.

MADDOX, 2/Lt. Leonard George 22/London
W. of ALBERT, 3rd August, 1918. For conspicuous gallantry and devotion to duty. He led a daylight patrol, and brought back valuable information which enabled the battalion to move forward and establish posts in the old lines. Later, he did fine work in getting rations and ammunition through to the forward outpost company under heavy shelling of gas and high explosives.

BAR TO M.C.

S. of ALBERT, 22/23 August, 1918. He displayed great courage and coolness during an advance under heavy fire of all descriptions, and captured a chalk pit strongly held by the enemy with machine-guns. When his platoon was counter-attacked in force he repulsed the enemy with loss, controlling his men with judgment and ability.

MAINGOT, 2/Lt. Joseph Henry ... 2nd Service Bn. British West Indies Regt. (R.F.C.)
Awarded 11th April, 1918.

MAINGOT, Capt. Patrick Sherlock ... ... 9/East Surrey
S.E. of CAMBRAI, 9th October, 1918. For conspicuous good leadership and gallantry when in command of a company. Again, on 16th October, during the attack on HAUSSY, he manœuvred his men splendidly, and took his objective in spite of heavy opposition, with very few casualties. When the enemy counter-attacked and practically surrounded him he extricated his men in a most masterly manner. He showed marked courage throughout.

MALE, Capt. Sidney John ... ... 23/K.R.R.C.
Awarded 1st January, 1918.

MALPASS, Capt. Charles Edward ... ... 11/Royal West Kent (1/Artists)
THILLOY, 27th August, 1918. For conspicuous gallantry and devotion to duty. Whilst in command of a company this officer rendered great service in clearing up the situation by personal reconnaissance under heavy fire. Throughout the day his coolness and determination inspired the men in the attack.

MANN, Capt. Deane ... ... Royal West Surrey
Awarded 1st January, 1917.
BAR to M.C.
Near HAMEL, 26th and 28th March, 1918. When the enemy attacked he at once organised a counter-attack and drove the enemy back. On the following day, hearing that the enemy had broken through on the flank, he made a reconnaissance under intense machine-gun fire and in full view of the enemy, and brought back valuable information. He set a splendid example of courage and coolness to his men.

MANN, Capt. Douglas Bruce Upfield ... ... 4/Somerset L.I.
Awarded 3rd June, 1919.

MANN, 2/Lt. Frederick Randall 2/Hampshire
Awarded 1st January, 1916.

MANSFIELD, Lieut. Francis Turquand ... ... 171st Tunnelling Co., R.E.
WULVERGHEM—MESSINES ROAD, 28th September, 1918. On the evening of 28th September, he closely followed the infantry patrols and removed 16 tank mines in face of the enemy under heavy rifle and machine-gun fire. The next morning he removed 44 additional tank mines on the same road. In the subsequent operations he showed great courage in pushing forward with the infantry patrols, inspecting bridges and roads and removing unfired demolition charges.

MARGETSON, Lieut. Edward 1/Artists
S. of MARCOING, 30th December, 1917. For conspicuous gallantry and devotion to duty. He kept up communication during an enemy attack under the most difficult conditions, laying telephone lines and personally carrying messages under heavy fire. He showed great initiative and skill.

MARSDEN, 2/Lt. Walter ... ... 4/Loyal North Lancashire
WIELTJE, 31st July, 1917. For conspicuous gallantry and devotion to duty during and after an attack. He led his platoon with splendid dash and gallantry, capturing two enemy trench mortars at the head of his men and killing many of the teams. Later, he supervised the construction of a strong point under heavy machine-gun and shell fire, showing the utmost disregard of personal danger.
BAR TO M.C.
E. of YPRES, 20th September, 1917. With a party of twelve men, seeing troops ahead held up, he at once pushed forward through them and established himself in the trench beyond. This position became untenable owing to an enemy strong point 150 yards ahead. He therefore attacked it with his party and drove the enemy out.

MARSHALL, 2/Lt. Francis ... ... R.F.A.
E. of YPRES, 20th September, 1917. For conspicuous gallantry and devotion to duty. In an attack he showed great energy and courage when acting as forward liaison officer. Throughout his tour of duty he exposed himself to heavy fire, while he spotted guns, made sketches of the whole position, and identified strong enemy points.

MARTIN, 2/Lt. Arthur William Dight ... ... 3/Royal Highlanders
S.W. of RHEIMS, 28th July, 1918. He climbed the heights overlooking an enemy position, and established communication with the division on the left under heavy machine-gun and shell fire. He then brought a valuable report to battalion headquarters. Next he proceeded under intense barrage to rejoin his company, and finding that they had lost all their officers he assumed command, and commanded them with conspicuous gallantry, showing the greatest coolness and determination.

MARTIN, Capt. Ernest Wilfred Leigh ... ... R.A.S.C.
    Awarded 1st January, 1918.

MARTIN, Capt. Granville Basnett 10/London
    CONTALMAISON WOOD, 22nd March, 1918. For conspicuous gallantry and devotion to duty on two occasions. First, on seeing the greater part of two battalions retiring, he rushed forward in the open under machine-gun fire and rallied and reformed them. Secondly, when the enemy made three attacks, penetrating a portion of the line each time, he organised and led a counter-attack on each occasion, which drove out the enemy, largely owing to his brilliant leading and example.

MARTIN, Lieut. Reginald Dean 8/Northampton
    ETREILLERS, 21st March, 1918. For conspicuous gallantry and devotion to duty when battalion intelligence officer. He advanced through a heavy barrage to find out the situation. He led forward a party that had gone astray in time to prevent the enemy from reoccupying a trench. He brought back information of the greatest value throughout the day, and has at all times shown great ability and courage.

MASKELL, 2/Lt. Henry Percy 3/Wilts
    Near GOUY, 4th to 6th October, 1918. For conspicuous gallantry during the operations. He worked with endless energy throughout. During the attack on the 4th, when the left flank of his company was detached from the battalion, he showed great initiative in regaining touch and consolidating his position. The fact that his company captured eight machine guns and over 50 prisoners was largely due to his fine courage and leadership in mopping-up dug-outs and enemy snipers.

MASON, 2/Lt. Henry James 3/Essex
    S. of MORLANCOURT, 8th August, 1918. For conspicuous gallantry and devotion to duty during an attack. He led his platoon splendidly, attacking and destroying three enemy machine-gun positions and killing the crews. He rendered most valuable assistance during consolidation of the final objective, and his conduct throughout was marked by courage and cheerfulness.

MASON, Capt. Kenneth Sydney ... ... 10/Bedford (M.G.C.)
    Awarded 3rd June, 1917.

MATTHEW, Capt. David ... ... R.A.M.C. (1/Artists)
    Near WESTROOSEBEKE RIDGE, 30/31 October, 1917. During two days' heavy fighting he established a dressing station in an advanced position, whence he continually went forward to dress wounded and organise carrying parties under heavy fire. He inspired his men to continue their work by his splendid example.

MATTHEWS, Capt. Gwyn Hobson ... ... 3/Machine Gun Corps
    COURCELLES, 21st August, 1918. For conspicuous gallantry and initiative in command of two sections of machine guns during an attack. He successfully brought his guns into action against enemy pockets which the infantry had overlooked in the fog, and captured many prisoners. Throughout the action he handled his guns with great skill, and set a fine example to all under his command.

MATTHEWS, 2/Lt. William Henry ... ... 1/East Surrey
    LONGUEVAL WOOD, 23rd July, 1916. He organised and led with great dash an attack on a strongly defended enemy post, capturing and putting out of action several machine guns, and killing many of the enemy.

MAXTED, 2/Lt. Claude Bretherton 6/London
S. of YPRES-COMINES CANAL, 7th June, 1917. He led his company during an assault with great dash and determination, inspiring those round him by his coolness and indifference to danger.

MAY, Capt. Herbert Richard Dudfield 5/Warwick
E. of VILLERS PLOUICH, 3rd December, 1917. For conspicuous gallantry and devotion to duty. He stood his ground in an isolated advanced trench for over 20 hours against a strong enemy attack, and was successful in holding it until ordered to withdraw. He afterwards took his company into another part of the line and led three charges against the enemy. He showed great gallantry, coolness and untiring energy, inspiring all ranks under him.

MAYO, 2/Lt. Alfred Harrison ... ... 3/East Yorks (Tank Corps)
Near HAMEL, 4th July, 1918. For conspicuous gallantry and devotion to duty as a tank commander. Perceiving a tank broken down within 300 yards of the enemy, he left his own tank and, in spite of heavy shell fire and being under direct observation of the enemy, he arranged a tow rope himself and took the disabled tank in tow. He was heavily shelled for some distance, but brought the broken-down tank back to its rallying point, a distance of about 7,000 yards.

MAXWELL, 2/Lt. George Barton ... ... 32/Machine Gun Corps
Near SEQUEHART, 1st October, 1918. For great courage and initiative in the fighting on this date. When the enemy counter-attacked and our infantry were driven back, he kept his guns going till he was practically surrounded and our barrage had fallen behind him. He then fought his way out, and with his revolver put out of action five of the enemy who attacked him. During a second counter-attack he stayed in action till the last, and then helped to form a new line and held it with his guns assisted by infantry he had helped to collect. Later, he beat off a further local counter-attack with his guns. By his personal courage and example to his men he rendered the greatest service.

MEACHEM, 2/Lt. Frank Reginald ... ... 1st London Heavy Battery, R.G.A.
Near SEBOURG, 5th November, 1918. On the night of 5th November he was in charge of a gun and six ammunition and store wagons, and was proceeding to join two guns in position on the eastern outskirts of SEBOURG. When nearing the gun position he came under enemy shell fire, which killed three of his men and wounded six, besides killing five horses. Though badly shaken he organised a party and cleared the road, and brought his gun and wagons to the position with the least possible delay. He showed great pluck and determination.

MEADOWS, Lieut. Charles Stanley ... ... 292nd Brigade, R.F.A.
Awarded 3rd June, 1919.

MEREDITH, 2/Lt. Alexander Charles ... ... 8/Rifle Brigade (M.G.C.)
LONGUEVAL, 18th August, 1916. For conspicuous gallantry in action. Owing to his coolness and pluck he was able to hold his position for six hours under heavy artillery fire, and to bring his four guns into action in the captured trench in excellent fire positions.

[MESSOM, 2/Lt. Harold ... ... 2/Royal West Surrey]
In the London Gazette of 23rd June, 1915, an award of M.C., intended for 2/Lt. Messom, who had been mentioned in Despatches, for gallant conduct in February 1915, was by a clerical error published in the name of another officer in his Regiment of very similar name. On the mistake being discovered, that notification was cancelled. But in the meantime 2/Lt. Messom had been killed in action, and it is understood that the error could not be further rectified as at that date posthumous awards (except of V.C.) were inadmissible. ED.

MIDGLEY, Lieut. Thomas Herbert ... ... 466th (N. Midland) Field Co., R.E.
Awarded 3rd June, 1919.

MIEVILLE, Capt. Walter Stokes 1/Artists
    S. of MARCOING, 30th December, 1917. For conspicuous gallantry and devotion to duty. When ordered to support a counter-attack he walked forward across the open to one of the advanced companies under machine-gun fire and obtained information of the utmost value. His coolness and gallantry were a splendid example to all those under him.

MILLIGAN, Capt. Andrew ... ... 8/West Yorks
    N.E. of SOLESMES, 20th October, 1918. During the attack, when the situation was obscure, he went forward to the outpost line under very heavy fire, reorganised the dispositions of the right flank of the battalion which was in the air, and brought back most valuable information. He has shown consistent courage.

MITCHELL, Lieut. Allan ... ... 4/York & Lancaster
    GRAINCOURT, 22nd November, 1917. For conspicuous gallantry and devotion to duty. When sent with his company to reinforce the forward troops he found the situation very critical. He continually moved about in the open organising his position. When the troops on the left were heavily counter-attacked, he crossed about 200 yards of open ground under heavy fire, rallied and reorganised them, and led them to a new position, thereby undoubtedly saving the flank from being turned.

MOIR, Capt. Kenneth Macrae ... ... 5/East Surrey
    Awarded 1st January, 1919.

MOLLER, Lieut. Arthur Appleby ... ... Grenadier Guards
    HOUTHULST FOREST, 12th October, 1917. For conspicuous gallantry and devotion to duty when in command of a company. After reaching his objective, finding he was much harassed by fire from a post on his front, he at once organised a raid on it. Keeping it under a steady fire, he worked up an assaulting party on flank and rear, who dealt effectively with all who remained in the post. One machine gun was captured.

MONEY, Capt. David Frederick 1/Artists
    Awarded 3rd June, 1919.

MOODY, Capt. Percy ... . 2/Royal Welch Fusiliers
    Awarded 1st January, 1916.
                            BAR TO M.C.
    GIVENCHY, 5/6 July, 1916. For conspicuous gallantry during a raid. He organised and led his company with great dash, the result being that the raid was completely successful.

MOORE, 2/Lt. Charles Christopher ... ... 8/Lancashire Fusiliers
    E. of HARGICOURT, 18th March, 1918. When in command of a patrol he came into contact with 50 of the enemy who were advancing to raid our trenches. Owing to the skilful manner in which he handled his patrol he succeeded in cutting his way out and in returning to our lines. On his arrival he at once organised another party, returned with these men to the scene of the fight, and brought in the three wounded men whom he had been forced to abandon temporarily. His gallantry was most praiseworthy.

MOORE, Capt. Francis William 10/Devon
    Awarded 3rd June, 1917.

MOORE, Lieut. Frank Leonard 1/Monmouth
    RAMIECOURT, 3/4 October, 1918. For great gallantry and devotion to duty. During operations he went out from battalion headquarters under heavy fire to locate position of "C" Company, who were somewhere in front of RAMIECOURT. He remained out for over two hours. Later on same day he, with the assistance of stretcher-bearers, brought in a wounded officer under shell fire.

MOORE, Capt. Harold Edward ... ... Royal Monmouth R.E.
    Awarded 3rd June, 1916.

MOORE, Capt. John Leslie Mackenzie ... ... R.E.
    ARRAS BOISIEUX, 21st March, 1918. For conspicuous gallantry and devotion to duty in maintaining the railway service under heavy shell fire. By his action the withdrawal of railway artillery was carried out, and all supplies evacuated.

MOORE, 2/Lt. Leslie Thomas ... ... R.E.
    MONTELIMONT FARM, near VILLE-SELVE VILLAGE, 24th March, 1918. For conspicuous gallantry and devotion to duty while his company were engaged in covering a retirement under heavy artillery and trench-mortar fire. With great stubbornness he held on to an extremely bad position, finally withdrawing his troops skilfully in good order. His fine conduct contributed greatly to the success of the retirement, and caused the saving of several wounded.

MOORE, Capt. Robert Frank ... ... 1/Notts & Derby
    Awarded 3rd June, 1917.

MOORE, 2/Lt. William Robert ... ... 1/East Yorks
    E. of MEAULTE, 3/4 June, 1916. During an intense bombardment 2/Lt. Moore showed himself to be a fearless and inspiriting leader. He led a bombing party with great gallantry and dash. His personal example had a most inspiring effect on his men.

MORGAN, Lieut. Ernest Leslie ... ... R.F.A.
    E. of YPRES, 15th October, 1917. For conspicuous gallantry and devotion to duty in continuing to assist in laying out new lines to the batteries, after having been himself half buried by a shell. During many days' operations it was entirely due to his fine example that communications from brigade headquarters to the batteries were kept intact.

MORRIS, 2/Lt. Alfred Arthur Thomas 6/Middlesex
    MORY, 24th March, 1918. For conspicuous gallantry and devotion to duty. This officer took command of the company when its commander had been killed, and when the enemy broke through the line he rallied his men and recovered the trench from which they had been driven. The following day, in a rear guard action, he showed skill and coolness in extricating his men in an orderly manner.

MORROW, 2/Lt. Frederick ... ... R.E.
    BIHECOURT, 21st March, 1918. For conspicuous gallantry and devotion to duty in charge of a cable burying party, when he helped to man a most important redoubt. Although gassed early in the morning he remained in charge of a mixed party of R.E. and infantry throughout the day, fighting until relieved. Returning from hospital as early as possible he continued doing most valuable work in laying cable lines.

MORTIMER, 2/Lt. Arthur Broadbent ... ... 7/West Yorks
    S.E. of AULNOY, 1st November, 1918. During the counter-attack by the enemy on our positions he showed great gallantry. He seized a Lewis gun and ran forward under very heavy machine-gun fire and brought fire to bear on the enemy's flank, causing many casualties and capturing one unwounded prisoner. This action threw the right flank of the enemy into confusion.

MORTON, Lieut. William Cattell ... ... 3rd London Brigade R.F.A.
    Near LINDENHOEK, 1st June, 1917. Assisted by two of his men, he showed the greatest promptness and courage under heavy shell fire in extinguishing serious fires amongst the ammunition of his battery. He also displayed great gallantry and resource in attending to a wounded man under fire, getting him to a place of safety.

MILITARY CROSS.

MORTON, Capt. William Chamberlin ... 1/London
CACHY, 24/25 April, 1918. For conspicuous gallantry and devotion to duty. In command of a company forced to fall back he more than once rallied and reorganised his men, taking up successive defensive lines and holding up the enemy attack, although he had lost all his officers and most of his non-commissioned officers.

MOSS, Capt. Vincent Newton ... 1/East Kent
Near HULLUCK, 24/25 June, 1917. During a raid he led his party into the enemy support line, where he remained three hours reorganising them after heavy casualties. Although wounded he personally supervised the repulse of a bombing attack, and remained to the last, finally withdrawing his party without further loss.

BAR TO M.C.
NOYELLES, 21st November, 1917. For conspicuous gallantry and devotion to duty. Finding during a relief that strong parties of the enemy with machine guns were still in possession of a large part of the village, he immediately led his company forward, and with the help of two tanks cleared the enemy from the position, capturing about 20 prisoners and a large quantity of stores and war material.

MOSSMAN, 2/Lt. Harold Alexander ... 3/Royal Berks
POELCAPPELLE, 12th October, 1917. He kept the direction of the right flank of the battalion in an advance over heavily shelled ground. When his company reached its forward position he walked over the open, reorganising it and rallying some wavering troops, and keeping them under his command.

MUNRO, 2/Lt. Donald George ... 18/London
Near VERMELLES, 16th December, 1915. For conspicuous gallantry and ability at the Quarries. He was in command of a party of grenadiers in a very exposed position in the front line, and repulsed a succession of violent bomb attacks made by the enemy.

MUNT, Major Edsal ... R.F.A.
LANNOY, 4th May, 1918. For conspicuous gallantry and devotion to duty. At dawn the enemy commenced a heavy bombardment on the battery position. As the battery was not firing, this officer decided to withdraw the detachments to a place of safety. While telephoning these instructions a shell burst in the roof over his head, bringing the brickwork on the top of him and burying him. He crawled out, trying to get to the guns, when another shell burst close by, again burying him. He managed to crawl out, and though much shaken, got to the guns and superintended their withdrawal. The bombardment continued for an hour, and it was due to his action that only one man was wounded.

MURCH, 2/Lt. Alfred Henry ... 11/Royal Warwick
DACAUT WOOD, 15th April, 1918. For conspicuous gallantry and devotion to duty during an attack. He was in charge of an advanced post. Seeing that the advancing troops would be held up by the wire in front he went out with one man under heavy machine-gun fire and commenced to cut it. He continued this work until badly wounded.

MURRANE, Capt. Hugh Dudley ... 6/Royal Lancaster
Awarded 3rd March, 1919.

MURRAY, 2/Lt. George ... R.F.C.
Awarded 18th December, 1917.

NEEDHAM, Lieut. Leslie William ... 20/London
EAUCOURT L'ABBAYE, 1st & 4th October, 1916. He led his men with great courage and initiative, capturing the objective. Later, he consolidated and maintained his position. He set a splendid example throughout.

NELSON, 2/Lt. Lewis Archibald 2/Leicester
S. of NEUVILLE VITASSE, 9th April, 1917. He rendered valuable assistance to the infantry, making gaps in the wire and clearing the enemy trench, thus saving many casualties. Later, he reached his objective entirely unsupported, and remained in action for four hours.

NETHERCOT, 2/Lt. Robert Pinkerton ... ... 8/West Yorks
ECOUST, 3rd May, 1917. Although wounded in three places, he rallied his men and led them forward in the face of very heavy hostile fire.

NEWBERRY, 2/Lt. Thomas Frederick ... ... Machine Gun Corps
Awarded 30th January, 1920.

NEWLAND, Lieut. Arthur Mansfield ... ... Coldstream Guards
PILCKEN RIDGE, 31st July, 1917. For conspicuous gallantry and devotion to duty. When his company commander was killed he took command and led his men to their objective with the greatest gallantry and skill, afterwards organising his defence under heavy machine-gun fire, with complete disregard of his own personal safety, setting a splendid example to all ranks.

NEWMAN, 2/Lt. Arthur James ... ... R.G.A.
Near HOLLEBEKE, 15th September, 1917. When it was reported that one of the dug-outs near the gun had been blown in, he dashed out under heavy fire, organised a party, extricated the occupants, two of whom were killed, and got away a wounded man.

NEWTON, 2/Lt. Clement Vaughan ... ... 9/Royal Sussex
VERHAEST FARM, 7th June, 1917. After leading his company with great determination and courage to its objective, he showed skill and fearlessness in consolidating, personally leading out his covering parties and fearlessly exposing himself to machine-gun and rifle fire, in order to supervise and encourage the work. He held his line for four days, setting a fine example to his men.

NEWTON, Capt. William Godfrey 1/Artists (23/London)
Near FLERS, 18th September, 1916. For conspicuous gallantry in action. He placed a lamp in the open to guide a night assault. Later, although wounded, he rallied the men round him and bombed the enemy with great courage and determination. He set a fine example.

NICOL, 2/Lt. Ian Sinclair ... ... R.F.A.
CHAULNES, 25th March, 1918. For conspicuous gallantry and devotion to duty. This officer was forward observation officer on a critical occasion. He got most valuable information throughout the day, and when the infantry was retiring he rallied stragglers and sent them back into the firing line, restoring a threatening situation.

NICHOLLS, 2/Lt. Edward John ... ... 7/Royal Warwick
S.E. of POELCAPPELLE, 4th October, 1917. When the right flank of his company was held up by heavy machine-gun fire during an advance, and the company commander was killed, he took command and led an attack on the machine gun, which he captured, putting the entire team out of action. He then led his men forward and captured his objective, setting a splendid example of courage and determination.

NICKSON, 2/Lt. George Bernard ... ... R.G.A.
Near YPRES, 18th September, 1917. When a truck containing ten tons of H.E. shells and cartridges was set on fire, with the help of four men he uncoupled the burning truck, pushed it clear, and then succeeded in extinguishing the fire.

NIMMO, Capt. William Wilson ... ... R.F.A.
 Near VLAMERTINGHE CHATEAU, 19th August, 1917. A bomb was dropped by an enemy aeroplane on an ammunition dump, and set fire to some boxes and camouflage. He, accompanied by the battery sergeant-major, at once ran to the place and separated the burning boxes and camouflage, which was burning on the top of boxes containing live rounds. There is no doubt that by his prompt action he saved a large number of rounds from being destroyed, and also prevented many casualties.

NORMAN, 2/Lt. Sigurd Oswald ... ... 19/Notts & Derby (M.G.C.)
 FEUCHY CHAPEL, 10th April, 1917. He fought his tank with the greatest skill and energy, locating and silencing several enemy machine guns, and later, unsupported, he passed through the enemy lines and dealt with many targets.

NYE, Lieut. Frederick 18/Middlesex
 Awarded 3rd June, 1919.

OAKEY, 2/Lt. John Martin ... ... 7th Rifle Brigade (R.E.)
 BULLICOURT, April, 1917. When in command of four trench mortar batteries he carried out a most successful piece of work. Two thousand rounds of ammunition had to be carried a distance of 2,500 yards. This was successfully accomplished, in spite of enemy fire and the difficulty of working over open ground at night.

O'BRIEN, Lieut. James ... ... 2/D.C.L.I.
 SALONIKA. He carried a message under very heavy fire. He later displayed great courage and coolness in going back to organise and direct bearer parties.

O'DONOVAN, Capt. Robert Anthony 1/Worcester
 MOISLAINS RIDGE, 4/5 March, 1917. He performed consistent good work throughout the day, and was largely responsible for the success of the operations. He set a splendid example of courage and determination.

BAR TO M.C.

 S. of OPPY, 6th October, 1819. For most conspicuous gallantry and good work. He carried out a daring and highly successful raid with his company, capturing an enemy's strong point, with four machine guns and 38 prisoners. He himself was first into the position. It was entirely due to his able leadership that the position was captured and the way cleared for a further successful advance during the day by other companies on his left.

OGDEN, Lieut. William Edward 5/Manchester
 E. of YPRES, 31st July, 1917. For conspicuous gallantry and devotion to duty during an attack in leading forward a platoon that had lost its commander and its direction. It was due to his fine leadership and disregard of personal danger that the final objective was captured.

OLDFIELD, Capt. Reginald Theodore 2/Bedford
 S. of BRAY CORBIE ROAD, 6th August, 1918. For conspicuous gallantry and devotion to duty during an enemy attack. Finding that the enemy were occupying the trench immediately on his flank, he made an effective bomb block, and at the same time moved a section of his platoon to prevent the enemy moving round his flank. He effectively beat off the attack, and finally forced the enemy completely out of the support system. His gallant and able leadership prevented a serious penetration of the line at this point.

BAR TO M.C.

 E. of RONSSOY, 21st September, 1918. He was in command of an assaulting company, which had both flanks exposed. After making a thorough reconnaissance of the country round QUENCHETTES WOOD, locating the enemy's positions accurately, he, with the co-operation of four machine guns, then led two successful bombing attacks up DUNCAN AVENUE and POT LANE, which enabled him to get in touch with units on both flanks and clean up a large body of the enemy.

MILITARY CROSS.

OLVER, Lieut. John Dennis Circuit ... ... R.A. (T.M.B.)
    Awarded 1st January, 1917.

ORMISTON, 2/Lt. Walter Hugh 13/London
    Near MOEUVRES, 21st November, 1917. For conspicuous gallantry and devotion to duty. When his platoon was held up by hostile machine-gun fire he rushed forward to a gap in the wire, but, being left with only five men, he withdrew and brought them safely back. Though slightly wounded and badly shaken by a bomb in an enemy bombing attack he remained at his post until the battalion was relieved two days later.

OSTLE, Capt. Henry Knight Eaton 1/Artists (2/Border)
    Awarded 1st January, 1916.

OSWALD, Lieut. Harold Robert ... ... 4(13)Welch
    N. of LE CATEAU, 19th to 21st October, 1918. For great gallantry and initiative before and during the attack. He was indefatigable on the 19/20 October in carrying out reconnaissances across the RIVER SELLE in face of the enemy, who was holding positions on the east bank in great strength. During the attack he rushed an enemy machine gun with a few men whom he collected, killing the crew and capturing the gun.

OVERTON-JONES, Lieut. Edward ... ... Coldstream Guards
    Awarded 3rd June, 1918.

OWEN, Lieut. Malcolm de Brissac 1/Hertford
    S.E. of HAVRINCOURT, 18/19 September, 1918. For conspicuous gallantry and devotion to duty. This officer was in command of the right front company when the enemy broke in at two points, but, by skilful handling of the supporting platoons, he stopped them from advancing further than the front line. He then made a daring reconnaissance under heavy machine-gun fire, and, organising a counter-attack, drove the enemy out again from one of the points. The next day he counter-attacked the other point, and succeeded in completely restoring the line.

OWEN, 2/Lt. Wilfred Edward Salter 5/Manchester
    FONSOMME LINE, 1/2 October, 1918. For conspicuous gallantry and devotion to duty in the attack. On the company commander becoming a casualty he assumed command and showed fine leadership, and resisted a heavy counter-attack. He personally manipulated a captured enemy machine gun from an isolated position, and inflicted considerable losses on the enemy. Throughout he behaved most gallantly.

OWERS, 2/Lt. Frederick Thomas 13/London
    BOURLON WOOD, 2nd to 4th December, 1917. GRAINCOURT, 11th December, 1917. For conspicuous gallantry and devotion to duty when in command of advanced posts during lengthy operations. On one occasion he was bombed and fired on the whole day, but maintained his position. Later, when surrounded on three sides, he withdrew his platoon under orders, but after dark he reoccupied the post, and handed it over intact to the relieving unit.

PADDLE, 2/Lt. Kenneth Cecil Lawrence ... ... R.G.A.
    Near GIVENCHY, 2nd November, 1917. For conspicuous gallantry and devotion to duty as forward observation officer in a very exposed position in the front trenches. Owing to the enemy's heavy fire one officer was wounded and two men were killed close to him, and although the enemy sent over a large number of trench mortar bombs whenever he ordered his battery to open fire, he persisted with his duties until his task had been completed.

PAINE, 2/Lt. George Gordon ... ... 2/Royal Berks
    Awarded 1st January, 1916.

PALMER, 2/Lt. Percy Reginald ... ... 12/Royal Welch Fusiliers (Leicester)
    Near HULLUCH, 12/13 February, 1917. He displayed great courage and determination in firing a torpedo under most difficult conditions. Later, he rescued two wounded men.

MILITARY CROSS.

PARK, 2/Lt. Ronald Hubert Mungo ... ... Irish Guards
    Near LANGEMARCKE, 9th October, 1917. For conspicuous gallantry and devotion to duty when in charge of a section of machine guns which he established in a well-chosen position from which to bring in direct fire upon the enemy's approaches. He worked untiringly to establish a large reserve of ammunition, and when the enemy counter-attacked they were twice subjected to a heavy fire from his guns.

PARKER, Major John Amplett ... ... R.E.
    Near MERVILLE, 11th April, 1918. For conspicuous gallantry and devotion to duty. His field company was digging a system of posts when the enemy attacked. He manned the posts with his men and a few other troops, and held the position for some time against determined attacks, showing great coolness under heavy machine-gun fire. He was severely wounded.

PARKIN, 2/Lt. John ... ... R.G.A.
    Awarded 1st January, 1918.

PARKES, Lieut. George Henry ... .. 3rd Reserve Cavalry (13/Hussars)
    Near HADRANIYAH, MESOPOTAMIA, 29th October, 1918. For conspicuous gallantry and devotion to duty. In an assault on a strongly entrenched plateau he was in command of the Hotchkiss guns, and by his marked personal courage and skilful handling of them under fire, cleared the right flank of the enemy and undoubtedly saved the regiment many casualties.

PASSINGHAM, 2/Lt. Edward George ... ... 1/Northumberland Fusiliers
    Near ARRAS, 20th March, 1917. He led a raiding party with great courage and determination through uncut wire, and succeeded in entering the enemy's front-line trenches, where he personally shot three of the enemy.

PATERSON, 2/Lt. Frank James 4/London
    PEIZIERE, 10th September, 1918. For conspicuous gallantry and dashing leadership. This officer was detailed to mop-up part of the village. Although badly held up by enemy machine-gun fire he led his platoon on and showed great initiative, and set a splendid example by rushing two enemy machine guns, which he captured, killing the crews of both. In the attempt he was wounded, but carried on until his platoon had completed its task, and were definitely established on the objective.

PAYTON, 2/Lt. Sidney ... ... 15/Tank Corps
    VRAU-VRAUCOURT, 31st August, 1918. For conspicuous gallantry and determination while in command of a tank. Ahead of other tanks and without infantry support he attacked and cleared machine-gun nests, killing several of the crews, and then, with his corporal, he entered dug-outs and took more prisoners. Later, while still ahead, he silenced another machine gun and took the crew prisoners. He was in action for seven hours and set a splendid example of courage and devotion to duty.

PEAL, Lieut. Arthur Francis Henry ... 5/York & Lancaster (148th T.M.B.)
    YPRES, 28/29 June, 1918. For conspicuous gallantry and devotion to duty while in charge of two mortars which were taken out into "No Man's Land" during a raid on the enemy's trenches. Immediately the operation started enemy shelling became heavy, together with rifle and machine-gun fire; and soon afterwards one mortar became useless owing to a damaged striker. He personally remedied the defect and brought the mortar into action again immediately. By his fine example of coolness and determination he kept his mortars firing exactly to time, each of which expended 80 rounds.

BAR TO M.C.
    HASPRES, 13th October, 1918. For conspicuous gallantry in action whilst in command of the trench mortar section. He worked his gun forward with the greatest courage and determination, covering the advance of the leading companies, and later, when the enemy counter-attacked, although portions of the gun mountings were missing through casualties, he continued to fire the mortars until forced to withdraw.

[pp. 44, 357.
A. J. T. FLEMING-SANDES, V.C.

Recapture of British Tank from the enemy at Seranvillers. Oct. 8th 1918

Sketch by Capt. Paget who was attached to Tank Corps & was on the spot the same day.

PEARSON, 2/Lt. William George Frederick ... ... 8/Royal Sussex
    PREUX, 4th November, 1918. He showed conspicuous gallantry and devotion to duty whilst employed on the repair of forward roads. In the face of heavy machine-gun fire he made the necessary reconnaissance of the road, and the road was pushed forward, and finally completed, under very difficult conditions.

PEGRAM, Capt. Charles Ernest ... ... 17/Rifle Brigade
    PASSCHENDAELE, 1/2 December, 1917. For conspicuous gallantry and devotion to duty. He formed up his company at the assembly position although the enemy were sniping from an advanced post fifty yards away, and led them to the attack under intense machine-gun fire. When most of his men had become casualties and his left flank was in the air, he formed a defensive flank and established touch with the unit on his left.

PERL, Capt. Bernard Huson ... ... Artists : 5/Royal Lancaster
    Awarded 3rd June, 1918.

PERROTT, 2/Lt. Eustace Stroud 8/London (1/Artists)
    THILLOY, 27th August, 1917. For conspicuous gallantry and devotion to duty. When the situation in front of a village was obscure this officer went forward through heavy machine-gun fire and obtained information of the greatest value to his company commander, and remained out well in advance, sending in information till he was wounded.

PETHERBRIDGE, Capt. Charles Arthur ... ... 2(17)Royal Scots
    ZILLEBEKE, to E. of COURTRAI, 28th September to 20th October, 1918. For continuous gallantry and devotion to duty during a month's fighting. He was acting as adjutant, and was at all times in the fighting zone. He carried out his work at all times with zeal and energy. He was invaluable to his battalion commander, and by his actions and courage inspired all ranks.

PHEYSEY, 2/Lt. John Edward ... ... R.F.A.
    YPRES, 14th July, 1917. When getting ammunition forward to the guns, in spite of his having already made three journeys in 48 hours under heavy shell fire, a distance of eight miles each time, he volunteered to make a fourth, in the course of which he was severely wounded. He displayed the finest devotion and very great coolness whilst carrying out this duty, and set a splendid example to officers and men.

PHILLIPS, 2/Lt. Fenton Ellis Stanley ... ... R.F.C.
    GINCHY, 3rd September, 1916. For conspicuous gallantry and skill. He has done fine contact patrol work. On one occasion he came down to a low altitude while making a report, and his machine was much damaged by rifle and machine-gun fire, but he carried on and successfully put our artillery on to the enemy, who were massing for a counter-attack.

PIERCE, Lieut. Alfred ... ... 283rd Siege Battery R.G.A.
    Awarded 3rd June, 1919.

PILE, 2/Lt. Samuel John Haughton 13/Middlesex
    Near Loos, January, 1917. During a raid on the enemy's trenches he completely overcame the resistance of the enemy by shooting their leaders. He led his party beyond their objective, and later effected a skilful withdrawal.

PITCHER, Lieut. Walter Henry Blythe ... ... Coldstream Guards
    BROEMBEKE, 9th October, 1917. For conspicuous gallantry and devotion to duty in leading his company and maintaining direction under most difficult circumstances. During a counter-attack he displayed great initiative, altering his positions to make a defensive flank, which proved of the utmost value.

MILITARY CROSS.

PITTS, 2/Lt. Arthur Walter ... ... R.A.S.C.
  Awarded 3rd June, 1917.

PLATT, 2/Lt. Oswald Gordon ... ... 5/Yorkshire L.I.
  HINDENBURG LINE, 3rd May, 1917. For conspicuous gallantry and devotion during an attack. His seniors becoming casualties very early he assumed command, rallying wavering troops of various units, establishing a position and holding it under intense fire until it became untenable. He was the last to retire. Twice before he has been recommended for great gallantry.

POCOCK, 2/Lt. Reginald William ... ... R.F.A.
  Near BOESINGHE, 12th October, 1917. When in command of a party of trench mortars under heavy shell fire he constructed a track and succeeded in bringing into action three guns which were badly bogged in shell-holes, and then assisted in bringing up ammunition.

PODD, Capt. Jack Kenneth ... ... 2/West Yorks
  Near ETTERPIGNY, 25th March, 1918. For conspicuous gallantry and devotion to duty. After the battalion had launched a counter-attack he pushed forward to a very advanced position and sent back excellent reports containing most valuable information, which he could only get at considerable risk. Later he displayed great courage and resource in reforming troops who had been driven back, and re-establishing a line. In these operations he was wounded.

POGUE, 2/Lt. Reginald Thomas ... ... 6/Dorset (Tank Corps)
  WARVILLERS, 3rd to 9th August, 1918. For conspicuous gallantry with his tank in clearing the way, and thus enabling the infantry to advance practically without loss. He inflicted severe casualties on enemy machine-gunners, and was largely responsible for the capture of prisoners. In action, four times within the week, he set a splendid example, and always kept his tank tuned up for emergency.

POLL, Lieut. Dudley Erskine 24/London
  ST. PIERRE VAAST WOOD, September 2nd, 1918. For most conspicuous gallantry and initiative. Whilst on the ridge in front of VAUX WOOD he crawled over the open to the rear to bring up reinforcements, although absolutely exposed to intense rifle and machine-gun fire. He personally posted the reinforcements on the exposed flank and thus relieved the danger of a flank attack against the position on the ridge. Throughout the operations he set a fine example to all ranks.

POTHECARY, Lieut. Herbert Martin Rixson ... ... 8/West Yorks
  DICKEBUSCH LAKE, 14th July, 1918. For conspicuous gallantry during an attack. When all the officers of his company had become casualties he assumed command, and, though wounded, he led them on and captured his final objective. He remained with the front line company until the battalion was relieved. He displayed great courage, ability, and devotion to duty.

POTTS, Capt. Joseph Harold 23/London
  Awarded 3rd June, 1919.

POWELL, 2/Lt. Laurence ... ... R.F.A.
  Awarded 1st January, 1919.

POWER, Capt. Charles Montague ... ... 2/Scottish Rifles
  Awarded 1st January, 1918.

MILITARY CROSS.

PRATT, Capt. Harold Douglas 2/London
Near CROISILLES, 27th August, 1918. He carried out a reconnaissance on the flank of the battalion with great skill, and obtained such successful results that, owing to his information, the artillery were able to concentrate on a large body of enemy who were assembling for a counter-attack, and dispersed them with very heavy loss. He was later on wounded in three places by the explosion of a shell as he was attacking a machine gun that was causing casualties. His gallantry and ability were conspicuous and he rendered most valuable service.

PRESTON, 2/Lt. John Frank 7/London
Near YPRES, 7th June, 1917. He led his platoon twice to the attack of a position, which was finally captured, together with 80 prisoners. His resolute leading and courageous behaviour were of the highest assistance in bringing about a successful result.

PROSSER, Capt. Arthur Edward 1/Worcester
S. of OPPY, 7th October, 1918. During the afternoon he brought forward two of his platoons into the ROUVROY-FRESNES line, and led them through advanced troops which were hung up and captured a further 1,000 yards of the line. He himself rushed two machine guns which were enfilading our troops, and captured seventeen prisoners. His splendid example, courage and leadership enabled touch to be gained all along the line. Later in the evening he himself pushed forward into NEUVIREUL and captured two heavy trench mortars which had been causing many casualties to the battalion on his left.

PULLINGER, 2/Lt. Charles Edward ... ... 7/K.R.R.C.
WANCOURT, 10th April, 1917. He took command of the company at a very critical time, although he himself was wounded. In the face of heavy fire of all kinds he collected and reorganised the company, and successfully consolidated his position.

PULLMAN, Capt. Harold John ... ... Bucks Bn./Oxford & Bucks L.I.
ST. JULIEN, 16th August, 1917. He led his company with great skill and determination in an attack. When two preceeding waves were held up, he sent up flanking parties and rushed the enemy blockhouses. He re-formed his company and proceeded towards his objective.

PURVES, 2/Lt. John Murdow ... ... R.F.A.
Near LANGEMARCKE, 16th August, 1917. When laying forward cables this officer and his party were confronted with a very heavy hostile barrage and intense machine-gun fire. With great determination he pushed on with four men and succeeded in getting his telephone lines across a river. His personal courage and perseverance set a splendid example to his party, and it was entirely due to his disregard of his own safety that the work was successfully carried out, the party being under heavy fire all the time. He was severely wounded whilst engaged on this duty.

PYKETT, Lieut. George Frederick ... ... 16/Royal Warwick
Awarded 1st January, 1919.

QUARE, Capt. Herbert Alfred Brame ... ... 9/Munster Fusiliers
Awarded 3rd June, 1917.

RABINO, 2/Lt. Francis Aloysius ... ... 3(1)Dorset
SAMBRE CANAL, 4th November, 1918. For gallant and able leadership in the attack. He commanded the platoon which first effected a crossing over the canal, and it was chiefly owing to his energy and initiative that a crossing was effected at a very critical time of the attack. In the subsequent advance he again showed great ability.

MILITARY CROSS.

RACTIVAND, 2/Lt. Dometrius ... ... 3(1)Shropshire
    Awarded 3rd June, 1919.

RADCLIFFE, Lieut. Charles Netten 19/London
    Near NEUVILLE-ST.-VAAST, 30th August, 1916. For conspicuous gallantry during a raid on the enemy's trenches. He carried out the previous reconnaissances, and showed great determination during the raid, bringing back several enemy prisoners.

BAR TO M.C.

    DEIR-YESIN, 8th December, 1917. For conspicuous gallantry and devotion to duty. Throughout the advance he displayed unremittingly the greatest skill and energy in leading his men. In the culminating assault he led the first wave, and afforded an example of dash and determination which contributed largely to the success of the charge.

RADFORD, Lieut. John Arundel ... ... 8(1)Somerset L.I.
    Near VERCHAIN, 24th October, 1918. He led his company with great courage and determination to the furthest objective. He gained the final objective with only a few men, consolidated the position, and, although his right flank was completely exposed throughout the day he held on, and successfully repulsed a counter-attack after dark.

RALPH, 2/Lt. John Leslie ... ... 16/Royal Welch Fusiliers
    ENGLEFONTAINE, 4th November, 1918. He showed great gallantry under difficult conditions. During the advance he handled his platoon with such prompt initiative that parties of the enemy encountered were dispersed at once; and also by skilful use of Lewis-gun fire he drove the enemy from a road which threatened the left of the final objective.

RANDALL, Capt. Joseph Edward 5/Border
    LYS and LAWE, 13th March, 1918. For conspicuous gallantry and devotion to duty. He carried out his work as Brigade Intelligence Officer with great energy. For four days he worked unceasingly, practically without sleep and always under fire. His information was of great value, and he successfully guided counter-attack troops into their positions by day and night.

REAH, Lieut. Herbert William ... ... 517th (London) Field Co., R.E.
    Awarded 3rd June, 1919.

REDLER, 2/Lt. Harold Bolton ... ... R.A.F.
    HAM, 23rd March, 1918. He encountered four enemy two-seater machines, and attacking the lowest drove it to the ground with its engine damaged. Later, he attacked one of five enemy two-seater machines, and drove it down out of control. He has destroyed in all three enemy machines and driven three others down out of control. He continually attacked enemy troops and transport from a low altitude during operations, and showed splendid qualities of courage and determination throughout.

REED, Lieut. John Philip 14/Liverpool (14/Yorkshire)
    Near ZILLEBEKE, 7th June, 1917. He led his company in the attack with exceptional skill and courage, consolidating under heavy machine-gun fire and maintaining cheerfulness under trying circumstances, which greatly inspired the morale of his men.

MILITARY CROSS.

REED, Lieut. William ... ... R.E.
    ARQUES, 19th April, 1918. For conspicuous gallantry and devotion to duty. During a night air raid this officer was in charge of the workshops and technical stores dump, next to a large ammunition dump and kite-balloon depot. At 10 p.m. two fires were started by bombs in the ammunition dump. With the exception of the anti-aircraft machine-gun crew, all men were sent to safety. Violent explosions on the dump filled the air with shells and fragments, and the camp was continually bombed by the light of the fire. He sent all the machine-gun crew away, and fired the two machine guns himself until they both jammed. Later a fire broke out in the balloon shed, which he helped to extinguish, saving a great deal of valuable material. He worked continuously for five hours under continuous bombing and explosives.

RERRIE, 2/Lt. Henry Godden ... ... 2/York & Lancaster
    LOOS-CRASSIER, 22nd April, 1917. When in command of his platoon he was subjected to severe artillery and machine-gun fire, and in a very isolated position. Throughout the day, although himself wounded, he set a splendid example to his men under most trying conditions.

BAR TO M.C.

    COUILLET WOOD, 20th November, 1917. For conspicuous gallantry and devotion to duty. When his platoon was held up by machine-gun fire and bombers, though wounded he overcame the enemy's resistance and captured two machine guns and 28 prisoners. He remained with his platoon throughout the action.

REYNOLDS, Capt. Harry Norman ... ... 7/Royal Warwick
    ST. JULIEN, 27th August, 1917. He led his company in an attack, and assisted in taking an enemy stronghold. Later he reorganised the remnants of his company and rushed a block-house, capturing the garrison. He showed great personal courage, and by his example encouraged his men.

BAR TO M.C.

    ASIAGO PLATEAU, ITALY, 15/16 June, 1918. For conspicuous gallantry and devotion to duty when the enemy had broken through. He pushed forward, stopping their advance, and, driving them back, capturing a machine gun and holding positions all night under intense machine-gun fire. Next day he again drove them back, capturing three machine guns and many prisoners, following them as far as their own lines. He did splendid work.

RHODES, Capt. Dunstan ... ... R.G.A.
    VERMELLES, 23/24 April, 1917. PONT DU HEM, 1st May, 1917. He showed a fine example of courage when the battery was heavily shelled by gas shells. He continually exposed himself, moving about to ensure the men's safety, and personally seeing to the clearing of loaded ammunition wagons.

RICH, Capt. Cecil Olvar 1/Wilts
    NEAR PLOEGSTEERT, 17th February, 1917. He continually carried out daring patrols of the enemy's wire, and the success of a raiding party was largely due to his information.

BAR TO M.C.

    MARCOING, 20th November, 1917. For conspicuous gallantry and devotion to duty. He led his tanks into action with great skill and coolness. After he had advanced some distance a masked field battery opened fire at about 100 yards range. Though one tank was put out of action, and he was severely wounded, he effectively silenced the battery, and enabled the infantry to continue the advance. He set a splendid example to all ranks.

RICHARDS, Lieut. Lincoln Winfield 5/Lincoln (12/Norfolk)
    VIEUX BERQUIN, 19th August, 1918. For conspicuous gallantry and devotion to duty during an attack. He rushed an enemy post, shooting the officer and putting the remainder to flight. He was the first to reach the final objective, cheering on and encouraging his men. His courage and leadership inspired his men at critical stages of the attack.

RICKATSON, 2/Lt. Hugh Cecil ... ... 1/Artists : Coldstream Guards
GOUZEAUCOURT, 30th November, 1917. For conspicuous gallantry and devotion to duty. When his company had to remain under fire in the open during an attack while a flanking movement was being carried out his example of coolness and courage was an inspiration to his men. On arriving at the objective, though wounded, he superintended the consolidation of the position under intense fire.

RICKWOOD, 2/Lt. John Edgell ... ... 5/Royal Berks
Near DOURGES, 15th October, 1918. For conspicuous gallantry and initiative. He volunteered to cross the HAUTE DEULE CANAL and make a reconnaissance. After crossing the canal at PONT-A-SAULT his presence was discovered by the enemy, who kept him covered with their machine guns. In spite of this he worked his way along the eastern bank of the canal and brought back most valuable information, which enabled his company to form a bridgehead.

RIDLINGTON, Lieut. Alfred Charles ... ... 17th Armoured Car Bn. (Tank Corps)
LE CATEAU-MARETZ ROAD, 9th October, 1918. He displayed marked gallantry and skill when in charge of a section of armoured cars. He first attacked a machine-gun post which was holding up our advance, and, in conjunction with the infantry, successfully cleared it and captured the guns. In proceeding forward with two cars a bridge was blown up behind him by the enemy, separating him from the second car and from our troops. With one car, however, he went forward through MAUROIS and HONNECHY, which were both strongly held by the enemy, of whom he killed five in one spot in the latter village. His prompt action prevented the railway bridge from being blown up by the enemy.

RIGOLD, 2/Lt. Ernest Edward ... ... 82nd Siege Battery R.G.A.
NUPPE HALTE, 20th April, 1916. For conspicuous gallantry. When the cartridge store became ignited during a bombardment he went out under fire with two gunners and put the fire out. They were in great danger from an explosion.

RIPPERGER, Lieut. Harold Theodore Alvin ... 4/Gloucester (7/Lancashire Fusiliers)
E. of HEBUTERNE and BEAUREGARD DOVECOTE, 21st to 23rd August, 1918. For conspicuous gallantry during an attack. He led the attack on a position and successfully checked the enemy's counter-attack. Finding his right flank in the air he attacked the enemy in a trench on his right flank, and in conjunction with another company captured an officer and about 90 other ranks. He showed great courage and ability to command.

ROBERTS, Lieut. Frederick Arthur Donkin ... ... 18/Lancashire Fusiliers
VIJEWEGEN, 14th October, 1918. During the operations south-west of LEDEGHEM and subsequent operations south of GULLEGHEM he was conspicuous for his gallant and skilful leadership. In the attack south of MOORSEELE, when hostile machine guns were holding up the advance, he led his men forward and secured valuable positions and inflicted heavy losses on the enemy.

ROBERTS, 2/Lt. Henry ... ... 7/West Yorks (1/East Yorks)
Near LIMONT FONTAINE, 7th November, 1918. During the operations he showed fine and determined leadership. When the advance of his battalion was held up by machine-gun fire he took command of two platoons, and led them forward, working round the enemy's flanks, and causing him to retire and abandon his machine guns. Later he led another attack on a machine gun.

ROBERTS, 2/Lt. John ... ... R.F.A.
Near YPRES, 25th November, 1917. For conspicuous gallantry and devotion to duty. He was in charge of a party building a gun position, and when they were heavily shelled he ordered the men to take cover. When one of the party was severely wounded he and one man went back, and though twice knocked down by shells succeeded in carrying him to cover.

MILITARY CROSS.

ROBERTSON, 2/Lt. Albert 7/Shropshire
Near HEKIN and HENINEL, 21st to 28th March, 1918. For conspicuous gallantry and devotion to duty in leading his platoon. On several occasions he withstood determined enemy attacks under intense bombardment, successfully directing his platoon when compelled to withdraw.

ROBERTSON, 2/Lt. Frank Bruce 1/Leicester
QUADRILATERAL, 15/16 September, 1916. He performed most valuable work requiring great courage, twice passing through a very heavy barrage to obtain information. Previously he had done fine work.

ROBINSON, Lieut. Harry ... ... 4(9)Northumberland Fusiliers
MARESCHES, 1st November, 1918. For great gallantry and good work. He advanced with his platoon to the RIVER RHONELLE, placed a bridge across, and then successfully helped to mop-up the village of MARESCHES. Later, after the enemy had counter-attacked, he advanced with two platoons, collecting men of other regiments, and eventually established our position north-east of the mill, which he held until relieved. In the operation he took 40 prisoners.

ROBINSON, 2/Lt. Norgrove Stewart ... ... R.G.A.
ST. QUENTIN, 21st March, 1918. For conspicuous gallantry and devotion to duty. This officer, commanding the left-half battery, was engaged in pulling into position when the enemy opened a heavy and concentrated fire, inflicting a number of casualties on the men, who had been up all night. Only one gun was in position, but he got the second gun into action, only to be destroyed by a direct hit, which killed or wounded the whole detachment. Meantime, with great exertions he got the third gun into action, and kept the two guns firing till midday, when the ammunition was expended. His conduct throughout the day was admirable.

ROCHFORD, 2/Lt. John Robert ... ... 10/Royal Warwick
Near LOUPART WOOD, 25th March, 1918. For conspicuous gallantry and devotion to duty in directing the fire of his company with the greatest coolness when the troops on both flanks had withdrawn. His splendid example inspired his men to hold on until the last possible moment, and in the final withdrawal he was again conspicuous in handling his men to provide the necessary covering fire.

ROE, Lieut. Alfred ... ... 7/Lancashire Fusiliers
Near ARMENTIERES, 1st February, 1918. For conspicuous gallantry and devotion to duty. He led his party to their final objective, obtained valuable identifications, and brought his party back without a casualty. He set his men a splendid example.

ROLLES, 2/Lt. Nathaniel ... ... 14/Royal Warwick
Near GOUZEAUCOURT, 27th September, 1918. He led his platoon in the attack with conspicuous gallantry under heavy fire to the further objective, during which his company lost 60 per cent., including all the officers. His consistent courage and determination in the face of heavy odds in keeping his men together, and rallying leaderless men of other units, was worthy of the highest praise.

ROSCOE, Major William ... ... 2/South Lancashire (25/M.G.C.)
BEAUREVOIR. For gallantry, initiative and devotion to duty throughout the period 8th to 18th October, 1918. On the night 7/8 he was in charge of the machine-gun barrage in front of BEAUREVOIR. He moved his company into positions under heavy shell fire, personally reconnoitring each position and sighting all guns. Later, on 17th October, at LE CATEAU, he was again in charge of the machine-gun barrages, which he contrived to fire repeatedly on various targets at the request of the infantry.

ROSE, 2/Lt. Eric William ... ... Lancashire Fusiliers
SAPIGNIES, 25th March, 1918. For conspicuous gallantry and devotion to duty in action. Although a very junior officer he commanded his company with great courage and ability, and his resolution in the leading of a counter-attack was worthy of the utmost praise.

Rose, Lieut. Matthew Howard 22/Manchester
    Guillemont, 21st August, 1916. For conspicuous gallantry and determination on reconnaissance. Having discovered some of the enemy in a dug-out at the bottom of a steep bank, and being accompanied by only one man, he returned to our lines, and the same night organised a successful bombing party against the dug-out, capturing a machine gun. The success of this raid was entirely due to the coolness and ability displayed by Lieut. Rose.

Rosher, Capt. John Brenchley .... 10/Durham L.I.
    Awarded 1st January, 1917.

Rought, Lieut. Philip .... R.E.
    Awarded 1st January, 1918.

Rowland, Capt. Frank Skinner .... 6/Notts & Derby
    Near Lievin, 9th May, 1917. For conspicuous gallantry and devotion to duty in making his way on two occasions to advanced posts which were under heavy hostile shell fire. He rallied and reorganised the men, who were considerably shaken, remaining with them until the enemy's fire slackened, and restoring their confidence. He showed great initiative and disregard of danger.

Bar to M.C.

    Richebourg St. Vaast, 3rd September, 1918. He handled his company with remarkable skill and gallantry in an attack. Being in support when the company in front was held up, he displayed commendable initiative and great disregard of danger in reconnoitring close to the enemy's position, whereby he was able to attack them in flank, killing or taking prisoners many of them, and capturing a machine gun.

Rundell, Capt. Leslie Eric 7/London
    Loos, 14th February, 1916. For conspicuous gallantry. When the enemy exploded a mine, destroying a portion of our trench, his prompt initiative and disregard of personal danger under heavy fire enabled the near edge of the crater to be seized and consolidated.

Bar to M.C.

    Vimy Ridge, 21st May, 1916. For conspicuous gallantry and ability during an enemy attack. He dealt most resolutely with a situation which for a while was very precarious.

Rutherford, 2/Lt. Stanley .... 3/East Surrey
    Awarded 3rd June, 1918.

Salter, Lieut. Carl Russell Colley 20/London
    Shab Sallah, 29th December, 1917. During the attack, after his company commander had become a casualty, he took charge of the company, which he reorganised under heavy machine-gun and rifle fire, repulsed an attack on his flank, and personally led a charge against the enemy on his front. His leadership, coolness and initiative largely contributed to the success of the operations.

Saunders, Capt. Cornelius James 24/London
    Awarded 3rd June, 1917.

Savage, 2/Lt. James Percival 13/London
    Jerusalem, December, 1917. For conspicuous gallantry and devotion to duty. On the enemy gaining a temporary footing on the right flank of the line he immediately collected a few men and charged into the midst of the enemy, whom he succeeded in holding in check until that section of the line was reorganised, after which the enemy were completely repulsed. His gallantry and presence of mind undoubtedly averted the possibility of critical developments.

MILITARY CROSS.

SAVOURS, 2/Lt. Herbert Jay ... ... 3/Royal Fusiliers
    FONTAINE-AU-BOIS, LEVAL and MONT DOURLERS, 3rd to 8th November, 1918. For conspicuous skill and gallantry in leading his company during the operations. In spite of a dense fog he made good each stage of the advance until the final objective was reached, where his company captured an enemy field battery near LES ETOQUIES. He set a very fine example to his men.

SAWNEY, 2/Lt. Leslie Thomas ... ... 7/West Yorkshire
    BUCQUOY, 23/24 May, 1918. For conspicuous gallantry and devotion to duty in charge of a raiding party against a suspected hostile post, which he had previously located by a daring reconnaissance under heavy fire. When the raiding party approached the post the enemy were found to be on the alert and in great force, and his party came under heavy rifle fire. He nevertheless rushed forward in advance of his men and engaged the enemy in hand-to-hand fighting. Having inflicted severe casualties on them, he gave the signal for the raiding party to retire, and was himself the last man to leave the trench. His fine courage and leadership throughout set a fine example to all ranks with him.

SCOONES, 2/Lt. Thomas Collins ... ... 2/Gordon Highlanders
    Awarded 1st January, 1916.

SCOTT, Capt. Charles Edell ... ... 12/K.R.R.C.
    Awarded 3rd June, 1919.

SCOTT, 2/Lt. Frank Munro 10/Liverpool
    PASSCHENDAELE, 4th to 12th October, 1917. For conspicuous gallantry and devotion to duty in directing traffic during eight days' operations with very little rest. His fine example, great coolness and judgment had a marked influence on the troops crowded on the road, when excitement would have added to the dangers and difficulties caused by heavy congestion.

SCOTT, Capt. Robert Francis Cloete 1/Lincoln
    Awarded 3rd June, 1919.

SCOTT, Lieut. Theodore Gilbert 4/Norfolk
    VIRY NOREUIL, 24th March, 1918. For conspicuous gallantry and devotion to duty when at a critical stage of a heavy enemy attack he collected a party of 50 men at a bridgehead and directed a deadly fire upon the advancing enemy masses, delaying their advance. He continued to walk about under heavy machine-gun fire, encouraging his men until ordered to retire to a new line of defence. He set a magnificent example of courage and leadership.

SCOTT-JAMES, 2/Lt. Rolfe Arnold ... ... R.G.A.
    Near BEAURAIN, 28th March, 1918. Whilst the battery was in action, and also on the occasion when the guns had to be quickly withdrawn, he at all times, by his example and disregard of danger, kept the detachments working coolly and efficiently, despite the most intense hostile shelling.

SCUDAMORE, 2/Lt. Charles Greenwich 7/London
    HENINEL, 13th April, 1917. Although wounded he continued to lead his men, and gave directions for the holding of the captured positions, and returned to hand in his report before having his wound attended. He set a fine example throughout.

SCURLOCK, Lieut. Stephen John ... ... 8/Lancashire Fusiliers
　　Near MERRIES and CELERY COPSE, 13th August, 1918. For conspicuous gallantry and devotion to duty. After his company commander had been killed he ably reorganised his company, which had suffered heavy casualties, under heavy fire. He also made a personal reconnaissance and brought back very valuable information. He did fine work.

SCRUTTON, Major Alan Edward ... ... 1/Artists (2nd & 15th Tank Corps)
　　BAYONVILLERS, 8th August, 1918. This officer showed conspicuous ability and gallantry. In order to make certain that his tanks reached their starting-points in good time, and went into action ahead of the infantry, he went with them to the starting-point and went into action on foot with the infantry. He afterwards rallied his tanks at the first objective, reorganised them there, and detailed sections for tasks in the second phase of the operations. In this phase his tanks encountered heavy resistance from heavy field guns firing over open sights, but he nevertheless kept in close touch with them throughout, and went on with them to their final objective, which they reached after overcoming very formidable resistance at many points on the way. He has at all times shown remarkable initiative, powers of leadership, and contempt of danger.

SCRUTTON, Lieut. John Austin ... ... R.E.
　　Awarded 3rd June, 1916.

SELFE, Capt. Arthur Edward Ferrour ... ... 1/Artists: Coldstream Guards
　　PILKEM RIDGE, 31st July, 1917. For conspicuous gallantry and devotion to duty. During an attack he displayed remarkable initiative and grasp of a difficult situation in capturing his own objective as well as a strong point outside his area which would have considerably held up the attack. On obtaining his objective he quickly reorganised under heavy machine-gun fire, and throughout this day and the following one kept his company going under the most adverse circumstances by his splendid personal example.

SELIGSOHN, 2/Lt. Heinrich Leon 3/London
　　NOREUIL, 22nd March, 1918. For conspicuous gallantry and devotion to duty. Having brought up a party of men from the transport lines he took up a line in front of a village, where he was attacked in great force. He held out for many hours, but was finally driven back. He rallied his men on the other side of the village, and with the greatest dash and determination led a charge through the village and recaptured the line, thereby undoubtedly saving a very serious situation.
　　　　　　　　　　　　BAR TO M.C.
　　Near CHIPILLY, 8th August, 1918. For conspicuous gallantry in action. With a small party of headquarter details he attacked the enemy in a wood, killing and making prisoners of several, and capturing many machine guns. His splendid example, until he was seriously wounded and unable to carry on, had a most inspiring effect on all ranks.

SESSIONS, 2/Lt. Donald Humphrey ... ... R.F.C.
　　In FRANCE, 2nd May to 10th November, 1917. During two months he did 111 hours flying on artillery work, often under heavy anti-aircraft fire. He constantly observed most successfully for the artillery, causing direct hits on gun pits, fires and explosions.

SHANKS, Lieut. Martin Hollis 1/Suffolk
　　Awarded 3rd June, 1918.

SHARP, 2/Lt. Matthew 7/London
　　Awarded 1st January, 1918.

SHAW, Lieut. Walter Douglas ... ... Royal Fusiliers (10/Manchester)
RIENCOURT, 30th August, 1918. For conspicuous gallantry and devotion during an attack, when his company was exposed to a very hostile barrage. His coolness and leadership took the company successfully through. Later, being exposed to heavy machine-gun fire, he halted his company, taking up a position in shell holes. He then led forward a platoon, outflanking the hostile machine guns, compelling them to withdraw, and successfully led the company to its objective. His courage and resource were worthy of the highest praise.

SHEPHERD, Lieut. Walter Scott 2/Wilts
Awarded 1st January, 1917.

SHERLOCK, Lieut. Cecil Claris 7/Middlesex
Near YPRES, 20/21 September, 1917. For conspicuous gallantry and devotion to duty. He rallied his men, who had been scattered by shell fire, and led them forward to their work. He showed splendid courage and leadership, and rendered valuable service in his preparations for the attack.

SHERLOCK, 2/Lt. Frederick 8/Norfolk
IRLES, 10th March, 1917. He displayed marked courage and determination in carrying out the work of clearing a village. He set a fine example to his men throughout, and succeeded in capturing 27 prisoners.

SHILCOCK, 2/Lt. Harold Gordon 7/London (7/Middlesex)
BULLECOURT, 31st August, 1918. When his company commander was wounded shortly after the attack commenced he took command, and led his men with gallantry and resolution to their objective, where he held his position under difficult conditions and against determined efforts of the enemy to outflank and penetrate our line. His example of courage and able leadership largely contributed to the success achieved.

SHORT, Capt. John Rodwell 13/Yorkshire
Near VILLERS GUISLAIN, 14th March, 1917. Prior to the raid on the enemy trenches he made several personal reconnaissances of the enemy's wire and positions, and it was largely owing to his gallantry and fine leadership that the attack was pressed home. The hostile trenches were entered, several of the enemy killed and two prisoners captured, at a time when identifications were of incalculable value. He had previously shown the greatest skill and judgment in organising, equipping and training his men for the raid, for the undoubted success of which he was largely responsible.

SHORT, 2/Lt. Harold ... ... 1/Loyal North Lancashire
N. of BAPAUME-CAMBRAI ROAD, 22nd March, 1918. For conspicuous gallantry and devotion to duty in leading his platoon through a heavy barrage to reinforce a corps line. On the succeeding days, and until he was wounded, he was a model of coolness and courage to his men, and his cheerfulness throughout the operations was of invaluable assistance to all ranks with him.

SIBREE, Capt. Herbert John Hyde 1/Norfolk
LONGUEVAL, 27th July, 1916, and FALFEMONT FARM, 4th September, 1916. When his company was held up by machine-gun fire, and he himself was wounded, he continued to move about under heavy fire reorganising his company until he was again wounded. On another occasion he led an attack which resulted in the capture of 100 prisoners.

SIMMONS, Capt. Frank Keith, *M.V.O.* ... ... 1/Artists : 2/Highland L.I.
Awarded 3rd June, 1919.

SIMPSON, 2/Lt. James Gordon ... ... 12/Royal Sussex
    WYTSCHAETE, 16th April, 1918. For conspicuous gallantry and devotion to duty. Under very heavy fire he successfully led his company in a counter-attack to their objective. He was twice wounded, but continued to encourage his men to advance. He set a fine example of devotion to duty and contempt for personal safety.

SINCLAIR, 2/Lt. Eric Russell ... ... Argyll & Sutherland Highlanders
    Near YPRES, 20th September, 1917. For conspicuous gallantry and devotion to duty in an attack. Though wounded at the beginning of the attack he went forward and established his platoon in a good position on their objective. When heavily counter-attacked, he showed a fine example of courage and initiative which contributed largely to the repulse of the enemy.

SIZEN, 2/Lt. Reginald ... ... 6/Royal Fusiliers
    BOURLON WOOD, 27th November to 3rd December, 1917. For conspicuous gallantry and devotion to duty when in command of a platoon. His company commander having become a casualty during an attack, he took command, displaying great courage and skill in consolidating the posts at the objective, and suffering few casualties although the area was swept by heavy fire. He set a fine example of keenness and cheerfulness and was ever ready to grasp the situation, and act on it with rapidity and discretion.

BAR TO M.C.

    E. of AUCHONVILLERS-AVELUY WOOD, 26th to 29th March, 1918. For conspicuous gallantry and devotion to duty. He was in command of a platoon, and by his own personal gallantry and powers of leadership was instrumental in keeping his part of the line intact and breaking up enemy attacks. On another occasion, owing to casualties, he was placed in command of a company, with which he held the right of the line and carried out a most successful and difficult relief. He showed splendid powers of command, and set a very high example during a most trying period.

SKEVINGTON, Capt. Alan Percival ... ... 2/West Yorks (M.G.C.)
    BOURLON WOOD and MOEUVRES, 29th November to 5th December, 1917. For conspicuous gallantry and devotion to duty. He performed most efficient and gallant service in the handling of his machine guns, and assisted materially in repelling an enemy attack. His guns were subjected to intense shell fire, and four of them were put out of action, but he held his position for eight days, setting his men a splendid example of determination and resource.

SKIPPON, 2/Lt. David Leslie ... ... 14/Tank Corps
    Near VILLERS-LES-CAGNICOURT, September 2nd, 1918. His tank proceeded well ahead of the infantry, and in face of direct and accurate enemy field-gun fire he showed great determination in overcoming enemy resistance. He continued fighting his tank until it received several direct hits, himself and all his crew being badly wounded. The action of this officer's tank was particularly gallant and useful.

SLANEY, 2/Lt. Arnold John Robinson 17/London
    JERUSALEM, 8th November, 1917. For conspicuous gallantry and devotion to duty. Leading his platoon on the directing flank of the assault, his courage and fine leadership enabled his men to carry the objective and advance beyond it on the heels of the retreating enemy, who suffered heavy casualties. Taking up a line with marked rapidity, he organised his defence with great skill, and from it inflicted further heavy casualties on the enemy, whose whole line gave way.

SLATER, Lieut. George Edward Herbert 1/Border
    Near HOOGEMOLEN, 22nd October, 1918. For great gallantry and devotion to duty. He held his company together in the assembly position when subjected to heavy shell fire. Later, he led them to the assault and penetrated the enemy's lines to a depth of 1,500 yards. With his strength reduced to 19 rifles, he held on for some time and then withdrew to a fresh position and consolidated.

SMART, 2/Lt. James Lamont ... ... 8/West Yorks (M.G.C.)
Near GAVRELLE, 23rd April, 1917 For conspicuous gallantry and skill in an attack, when he succeeded in getting all his guns into position under heavy fire. and inflicting very severe casualties on the enemy. He set a fine example of courage and initiative.

SMART, 2/Lt. William Pechey 5/Liverpool
Near ARMENTIERES, 7/8 February, 1918. For conspicuous gallantry and devotion to duty during a raid on the enemy's trenches. He commanded a party which searched the enemy's trenches and captured eight of the enemy and one machine gun. By his personal example of determination and courage he was responsible for the success achieved by his party. Before the raid he had reconnoitred " No Man's Land " under enemy machine-gun fire, and obtained valuable information.

SMIRKE, Capt. Edward Alexander ... ... 7/Lancashire Fusiliers
TEMPLEUX QUARRIES, 21st March, 1918. For conspicuous gallantry and devotion to duty during a retirement, when he took command of the battalion, which he retained until wounded. By his cool leadership and personal disregard of all danger he held his men together in the most difficult circumstances, organising and leading counter-attacks continuously.

SMITH, Lieut. Arthur Wedgwood Gifford ... ... 7(2)Bedford
PREUX AU BOIS, 4th November, 1918. During the attack, while acting as battalion intelligence officer he showed great skill in marking out the route for the approach march and getting the battalion into position on a very dark night. Subsequently, when the situation was obscure, he went forward under heavy fire, and got in touch with all the companies, and established a report centre practically in the front line, sending back information which was invaluable in dealing with enemy strong points.

SMITH, 2/Lt. Ernest Rees .... Motor Machine Gun Corps
Near LA VACQUERIE, 1st December, 1917. For conspicuous gallantry and devotion to duty. During the defence of our position, by his splendid example of courage and coolness, he undoubtedly saved some of the guns of a neighbouring brigade and effectively checked the enemy's advance in that sector. After the guns had been got away he remained in defence of the positions. He sent in valuable information to the generals of two brigades, carried out machine-gun defence work, and greatly assisted in organising the infantry defence.

SMITH, 2/Lt. Frank Edward Corbitt Douglas ... ... 3/Durham L.I.
Near YPRES, 20th to 22nd September, 1917. For conspicuous gallantry and devotion to duty. During a counter-attack by the enemy he led his platoon forward out of the trenches, the better to meet the attack, and brought his left flank up so that the enemy were enfiladed and driven back in disorder. He set a fine example to his men throughout the operations.

SMITH, 2/Lt. George Ernest ... ... R.G.A.
Near MORCHIES, 15th April, 1917. He got his battery into action in spite of the most difficult conditions, and rendered invaluable assistance to the infantry at a critical time.

SMITH, Capt. Geoffery Hubert ... ... 1/Coldstream Guards
Near MOYENVILLE, 21st to 23rd August, 1918. For conspicuous gallantry and fine leadership in an attack through an impenetrable fog. On reaching the objective his company commander was killed. He at once took charge and reorganised the company, which was being heavily bombarded. Later he captured the final objective, and although his right flank was in the air he so disposed his command as to give very good security.

SMITH, 2/Lt. Gordon Richard ... ... 3/West Riding
Near ROBECQ, 18th July, 1918. For most gallant service in connection with a raid. Though severely wounded shortly after his Stokes mortars opened he urged his teams to continue firing. Four men were killed and one wounded besides himself, but owing to his indomitable spirit the survivors stuck it out and completed the firing. The barrage was most accurate, many enemy dead being found by the raiding party.

SMITH, Lieut. Morrison Churchill ... ... R.M.L.I.
  Awarded 3rd June, 1919.

SMITH, Capt. Harold Rees ... ... M.G. Corps
  Near GUEMAPPE, 23rd April, 1917. He commanded his tank in a most successful manner. He destroyed a machine-gun emplacement and several snipers' posts, and later materially assisted in stemming the enemy advances.

SMITH, Lieut. Leslie Horace ... ... M.G. Corps
  JONCOURT, 1st October, 1918. For great gallantry and good work. When two of his guns and teams were partly buried by enemy barrage prior to a counter-attack he extricated such of the men as had not become casualties. He then under very heavy fire pushed forward four guns to the advanced posts, and defended the exposed left flank of the brigade. engaging enemy parties at close range and effectively breaking them up.

SMITH, 2/Lt. Percy Landon ... ... 11/Royal Warwick
  RIEZ DU VINAGE, 30th June, 1918. For conspicuous gallantry and devotion to duty in commanding a wave of a raiding party which successfully penetrated the enemy's lines in daylight. Heavy casualties were inflicted on the enemy, about 50 being killed and five taken prisoners. He was almost entirely responsible for the preliminary reconnaissance. He did splendid service.

SMITH, 2/Lt. Sydney Bernard ... ... Loyal North Lancashire
  RICHEBOURG L'AVOUE, January, 1917. He carried out a dangerous reconnaissance of the enemy's wire. Accompanied by another officer and N.C.O. he forced his way to the enemy's trench. Later, although himself wounded, he assisted to carry a wounded man a distance of 250 yards.

SMITH, Capt. Walter Campbell 1/Artists
  Awarded 1st January, 1917.

SMITH, Capt. William Leslie 2/Worcester
  Awarded 3rd June, 1918.

SMITHER, Capt. Samuel Thomas ... ... 10(17)London
  S. of YPRES-COMINES CANAL, 7th June, 1917. For conspicuous gallantry and devotion to duty in command of a bombing party which was to co-operate with the tanks in the capture of a position. The tanks having failed to arrive at the right moment, he successfully took the position with a bombing party, and established communication with the battalion on his left, displaying great coolness and resource at a critical moment.

BAR TO M.C.
  CONTALMAISON, 25th March, 1918. For conspicuous gallantry and devotion to duty. When the enemy were pressing their attacks down a communication trench this officer, moving along the top of the parapet and using his revolver, himself led two counter-attacks which drove the enemy back. His courage and the determination with which he led his men undoubtedly produced this successful result.

SECOND BAR TO M.C.
  Near MOISLAINS, 5/6 September, 1918. During the operations he displayed great gallantry and initiative in leading his company to the attack, and also in assisting the other company commanders, who were junior subalterns, in the reorganisation and consolidation. His contempt of danger set a fine example to those under him, and his clear reports of the situation were of the greatest assistance to his commanding officer.

MILITARY CROSS.

SOLOMON, Staff-Capt. Jerrold Bernard ... 2/Oxford & Bucks L.I. (R.F.C.)
In FRANCE, 20th and 24th November, 1917. He carried out a patrol lasting nearly three hours in a very high wind and low clouds, flying at an average height of 500 ft., and brought back a valuable report. During the flight he attacked and drove down an enemy two-seater machine under heavy rifle and machine-gun fire from the ground. He also made a valuable reconnaissance in very bad weather, flying at an average height of 100 ft. under heavy rifle and machine-gun fire, in the course of which he engaged a hostile battery with his machine gun. He set a splendid example of courage and determination.

SOUTTEN, Major Arthur Camille 11/London
Near YPRES, 23rd September, 1917. For conspicuous gallantry and devotion to duty. He was on his way to a forward post alone when he saw a party of six of the enemy approaching. He covered them with his revolver and took them all prisoners.

BAR TO M.C.
CROZAT CANAL, 21/22 March, 1918. For conspicuous gallantry and devotion in action when he went forward with four scouts to locate the position of the enemy. During the reconnaissance his four scouts were wounded, and it was only by crawling under heavy fire that he was able to take back information of the highest importance. His courage and determination were very marked.

SOWARD, 2/Lt. Frank ... ... 5/D.C.L.I.
Awarded 1st January, 1918.

SPAFFORD, 2/Lt. Arnold Victor ... ... 3/West Riding
HAVRINCOURT, 15th to 18th September, 1918. When the company commander became a casualty this officer took charge, and led on with great skill and gallantry, securing the objective, which was strongly held by the enemy. For a time his advance was held up by machine guns, but after a personal reconnaissance he worked up a trench with bombing squads and Lewis gunners, and drove the enemy out with great loss.

SPENCER, 2/Lt. Joseph Thomas ... ... 8(2)London
E. of POZIERES, 19th September, 1918. For most conspicuous gallantry during the operations. This officer gallantly rallied his men under very heavy hostile machine-gun fire, rushed the machine-gun post, and succeeded in taking the crew prisoner. During this period he displayed an utter disregard of danger and inspired his men. He was subsequently wounded.

SPICER, 2/Lt. Edward Masters ... ... 4/East Lancashire
Near PASSCHENDAELE, 9th October, 1917. When in command of his platoon he was largely instrumental in repelling counter-attacks, and regained control over his men in very trying circumstances.

SPRAWSON, Capt. Evelyn Charles ... ... R.A.M.C.
Awarded 1st January, 1918.

SPURRELL, Lieut. Richard Kenilworth ... ... 9/D.C.L.I.
Near ARRAS, 14th October, 1917. When he was in command of a section of a raiding party his section encountered severe opposition, but effected an entry by hand-to-hand fighting, during which he personally killed two of the enemy, his party taking eight prisoners. He had previously carried out two reconnaissances.

SQUIRE, 2/Lt. Edwin Ross 5/Lincoln
Near LENS, 1st July, 1917. For conspicuous gallantry and devotion to duty when commanding a flank company of an assault. Finding the enemy in a strong position and offering considerable resistance he at once organised his company for defence, and repulsed two counter-attacks. Throughout the day he held on to the positions he had taken, organising them in a very able manner under heavy fire of all kinds, and doing work which was extremely valuable, as well as being of an exceptionally difficult nature.

MILITARY CROSS

STAHL, Capt. Arthur ... R.F.A.
Awarded 3rd June, 1919.

STALMAN, Lieut. Alfred Claude ... 6/West Riding
Near BAILLEUL, 13th April, 1918. For conspicuous gallantry and devotion to duty. During an attack by the enemy this officer noticed a dangerous gap in our line on the flank of the brigade. He immediately counter-attacked with much gallantry under heavy fire, and although shot through the arm he succeeded in retaking and holding our original posts.

STANCLIFF, 2/Lt. Robert ... 2/London
BEAURAINS, 18/19 March, 1917. He led his platoon in a most gallant manner, and personally reconnoitred an enemy trench. Later he single-handed attacked and captured two of the enemy. He was subsequently wounded.

STATON, 2/Lt. William Ernest ... R.A.F.
IN FRANCE, March, 1918. On one occasion, when on offensive patrol, he, by the skilful handling of his machine and accurate shooting, destroyed two enemy aeroplanes and brought down a third out of control. In addition, during the nine days previous to this, he had destroyed five other enemy machines, two of these being triplanes. The services which he has rendered have been exceptionally brilliant, and his skill and determination are deserving of the highest praise.

STEEL, 2/Lt. Edward Gerald ... 20/London
EAUCOURT L'ABBAYE, 1/4 October, 1916. He led his platoon with great courage and determination to their final objective. Later he consolidated and maintained his position for four days until relieved. He set a splendid example to his men.

STENTIFORD, Lieut. Ronald Hastings ... 5/Leicester (M.G.C.)
Near LENS, 8/9 June, 1917. He led his sub-section forward under heavy fire with great initiative and determination, and by his supporting fire at point blank range enabled the storming party to get forward. Later in the attack he covered the retirement with great skill, successfully accounting for 50 of the enemy, who were approaching over the open. He did not withdraw his guns until the last possible moment.

BAR TO M.C.
Near DICKEBUSCH, 7/9 May, 1918. For conspicuous gallantry and devotion to duty. This officer was in charge of a section of guns for three days' fighting. After enduring a heavy bombardment, when both he and his men were suffering from the effects of gas, he accomplished a counter-attack in the evening. When the bulk of the infantry was checked he pressed on by using concealed approaches with a thin wave of infantry, and came into action just behind, filling a gap which might at any moment have been penetrated by the enemy. He showed the greatest coolness and judgment in getting his guns into position and checking the enemy.

STEPHENS, 2/Lt. George ... /Gloucester
Near BIACHES, 4th February, 1917. He handled his platoon with great gallantry, and materially assisted in repelling a strong enemy raiding party.

STEPHENS, 2/Lt. Kenneth Thomas ... 3/Worcester
MONT DE LILLE, 13th April, 1918. For conspicuous gallantry and devotion to duty. During a hostile attack he showed the greatest courage and initiative. With another officer he organised a counter-attack and drove the enemy back, inflicting heavy casualties.

STEPHENS, Capt. Warren Trestrail ... ... 6/Notts & Derby
    Awarded 3rd June, 1919.

STEVENS, 2/Lt. Cyril Parker ... ... 3/D.C.L.I.
    Awarded 3rd June, 1919.

STEVENS, Capt. William Cecil 1/Worcester
    Near YPRES, 31st July, 1917. For conspicuous gallantry and devotion to duty. During important operations he showed very quick grasp of the situation, and was of the greatest assistance to his commanding officer. On one occasion, when no orderlies were available, he himself carried an important message under very heavy shell fire with the utmost fearlessness and disregard of personal danger.

                      BAR TO M.C.

    Near ST. CHRIST, N. of SOMME, from 22nd March to 2nd April, 1918. For conspicuous gallantry and devotion to duty during 11 days of very severe fighting. Throughout the whole of this period, acting as adjutant, his untiring efforts were constantly directed to the handling of the battalion, and his fine example set a standard for all ranks, which enabled them to carry out the duties assigned to them. After his commanding officer had been wounded he assumed increased responsibilities with the greatest courage and resource, and the ability of the battalion to respond to the calls made on it at critical moments was largely due to his fine work.

                      SECOND BAR TO M.C.

    TRESLON and SOULEUSE RIDGES, 27th May, 1918. For conspicuous gallantry and devotion to duty during an enemy attack. He did invaluable work in keeping men of his battalion together during severe fighting under heavy fire, when any lack of resolution would have been fatal to prospects of success. Two days later he was conspicuous by the way in which he helped to control the fight and reorganise defences during a long and hard-fought fight.

STEWART, Lieut. Oliver ... ... 9/Middlesex (R.F.C.)
    Between BRUGES and OSTEND, 13th July, 1917. For conspicuous gallantry and devotion to duty. He has done consistent good work for six months, both on escorts and offensive patrols, and has displayed great fearlessness and skill during severe fighting at close range with enemy machines, successfully holding his own, although on several occasions outnumbered by them.

STEWART, 2/Lt. William Hinton ... ... 211th Siege Battery (R.G.A.)
    Awarded 3rd June, 1919.

STONE, Capt. William Herbert ... ... 1/Royal Warwick
    Near MERVILLE, 28th June, 1918. During an attack he led his company with conspicuous gallantry and great dash to the capture of their objective. He then took a party with a Lewis gun in pursuit of the retreating enemy, on whom he inflicted severe losses. Having destroyed a bridge over the river he consolidated a selected position well in advance of the objective, and though badly wounded he continued to direct operations for some time. During all this time he was under heavy enemy machine-gun and sniping fire at short range.

STOREY, 2/Lt. Kenneth ... ... 2/Durham L.I.
    HOOGE, 9th August, 1915. For conspicuous gallantry and skill when in command of bombing parties. He was seriously wounded while directing his men. The success of our attack and the subsequent holding of the position were largely due to the coolness and dash of the bomb throwers under 2/Lt. Storey.

STORM, 2/Lt. William George ... ... 5/York & Lancaster
    THIEPVAL, 16/17 September, 1916. He led a party of volunteers in an attempt to surprise an enemy post. Though unsuccessful, owing to heavy machine-gun fire, he succeeded by fine leadership in bringing back the whole of his party, including the wounded. He himself was the last to return.

STOUT, Lieut. Frank Moxon 20/Hussars
  HAIRPIN, 25/26 January, 1916. For conspicuous gallantry and resource. When he heard of an enemy working-party in the vicinity he took a corporal and light machine gun down a sap, mounted the corporal on his back to enable the latter to fire over the parapet, and opened fire. Later, mounted on the corporal's back, Lieut. Stout opened fire, although by this time they had been discovered. Next morning 14 dead enemy were counted, and more must have been wounded.

STRATTON, 2/Lt. Gilbert Leonard ... ... R.F.A.
  RAMADI, 11th July, 1917. When his section was subjected to intense and accurate fire from six hostile guns he worked with great courage and coolness, and succeeded in silencing two of them. Though exposed to the fiercest heat he displayed extraordinary energy throughout the day, and set a fine example of courage and determination to his section.

STRODE, Capt. Maurice ... ... 2/West Surrey
  GHELUVELT, 26th October, 1917. When several battalions were held up by machine-gun fire, and many men of different units were without leaders owing to casualties, although he was on duty at battalion headquarters, he voluntarily went forward, and in spite of heavy fire got 100 men into a suitable defensive position.

BAR TO M.C.

  Awarded 1st January, 1918.

SULLIVAN, 2/Lt. Stanley Frederick ... ... /Gloucester
  Near POELCAPPELLE, 9th October, 1917. When in command of his platoon during an attack he captured a concrete emplacement held by two enemy machine guns, and later assisted in capturing a strong point by working round its flank. He took out a patrol of six men to gain touch with the company on his right, and though three were killed he continued until he had gained touch.

SUTCLIFFE, Lieut. Fred 8/Hants
  Awarded 3rd June, 1919.

TAMBLYN, Capt. Horace William ... ... 181st Tunnelling Co. R.E.
  Awarded 3rd June, 1919.

TAPPER, Capt. Michael John ... ... 1/Artists (Tank Corps)
  This officer has acted as Staff Captain to the brigade since its formation on 1st February, 1917. Throughout the ARRAS battle, the operations in the YPRES SALIENT from 31st July to 20th October, and the CAMBRAI battle, he has shown the utmost untiring energy and capacity for organisation. The task of providing supplies, etc., has often been one of very great difficulty, but on no occasion has there been any failure in the arrangements he has made.

TAPLIN, Capt. George Aubrey ... ... 65th Siege Battalion (R.G.A.)
  Awarded 3rd June, 1919.

TAPPLY, Capt. Mark 10/Norfolk
  Near ALBERT, 26/27 March, 1918. During the enemy attack he rushed forward, and by his coolness and courage inspired such confidence in his men whose officers were casualties that a new line was established. On the following day, when the enemy were about to attack a detached post, he collected reinforcements and led them to the post, which he found to be surrounded by the enemy. Cutting his way through the enemy he succeeded in establishing a fresh position from which the enemy could be checked. His courage, skill and initiative were most conspicuous.

TARRANT, 2/Lt. Henry Geoffrey Nelson ... ... 6/Royal Berks
  Near MIRAUMONT TRENCH, 17th February, 1917. He pushed home the attack with such determination that, in spite of weak numbers, he succeeded in capturing 70 prisoners. He finally got in touch with the unit on his left, and consolidated the position he had gained.

MILITARY CROSS.

TAUTZ, 2/Lt. Reginald Hugh ... ... 10/Manchester (Loyal N. Lancs)
   Near NIELTZE, 19/20 May, 1917. For conspicuous gallantry and devotion to duty when in command of a raiding party. Finding the gap, previously cut, had been repaired, he cut his way through under fire and cleared 70 yards of enemy trench, displaying the greatest determination and courage.

TAYLOR, Capt. Bruce Mitchell ... ... 1/D.C.L.I.
   Awarded 14th January, 1916.
                           BAR to M.C.
   GIVENCHY SECTOR, 6/7 February, 1917. During a raid on the enemy's trenches he directed the operations with marked skill, and set a splendid example to all ranks.

TAYLOR, Lieut. Ernest Reginald 7/Essex
   Near HOLLEBEKE, 26th July, 1917. For conspicuous gallantry and devotion to duty when battalion signalling officer. When his headquarters were heavily shelled and set on fire he remained behind at great personal risk to collect his instruments and disconnect the telephone, although he well knew that the ammunition stored there might explode at any moment. The dug-out blew up very shortly afterwards, and he then went to another station under very heavy shell fire and sent back valuable information to the brigade.

TAYLOR, 2/Lt. George Arthur 4/Lancaster
   Near YPRES, 20th September, 1917. He led his company with the greatest gallantry and resource, personally initiating and carrying out a successful assault upon an enemy strong point. He reached his objective and carried out consolidation in spite of heavy fire. He was a constant example of courage and determination to his company.

TAYLOR, Lieut. Leslie Francis ... ... 1/K.R.R.C.
   VILLERS-BRETONNEUX, 26th April, 1918. For conspicuous gallantry and devotion to duty. He brought a machine gun and team into a position which enfiladed the enemy's attack, and, driving them back, caused their capture by another party. His section then remained in position on a railway embankment, preventing any penetration by the enemy.

TERRY, Capt. Sidney Frederick 1/Wilts
   Awarded 3rd June, 1918.

THOMAS, 2/Lt. Lewis John ... ... 4(15)Welch
   MORVAL, 1st September, 1918. For conspicuous gallantry and initiative in an assault. He led his company with the greatest dash, and accounted for nine machine guns and their teams. Single-handed, when on one occasion separated from his company, he effected the capture of 15 of the enemy, whom he forced to surrender while he covered the entrance of the dug-out. He showed splendid courage and determination.

THOMAS, Lieut. Robert William 7/London
   Near BOURLON WOOD, 2/3 December, 1917. For conspicuous gallantry and devotion to duty during a night attack. All the other officers of the company were wounded, and owing to darkness and heavy hostile fire entrenching became a matter of great difficulty. He displayed great skill and coolness in establishing communication with the troops on either flank and getting his men well dug in before daylight.

THOMAS, 2/Lt. Thomas ... ... R.G.A.
   ASIAGO PLATEAU, 15th June, 1918. For conspicuous gallantry and devotion to duty. He took two linesmen over two miles along heavily-shelled roads and re-established communication after the telephone lines had been cut. Throughout the day he showed complete disregard of danger.

THOMPSON, Capt. Arnold John ... ... Adjutant 1/Scots Guards
   Awarded 3rd June, 1917.

THOMPSON, Capt. Claude Ernest ... ... 2/South Lancashire
    Awarded 3rd June, 1916.
BAR TO M.C.

    WIELTZE, 31st July, 1917. For conspicuous gallantry and devotion to duty. Having gone forward to clear up the situation he found it was critical owing to the enemy envelopment of our left flank. He promptly organised a defensive flank, which held out long enough to save a arge portion of the brigade from being cut off. It was due to his ability and promptness that a disaster was averted, and his good staff work contributed very largely to the success of the whole operation.

THOMPSON, Capt. George Kenneth ... ... 5/East Lancashire (9/Yorks)
    RUE DU BOIS, on night of 31st December, 1915, and 1st January, 1916. :For conspicuous gallantry and ability. Although hampered by searchlights and Verey lights, he led, with great dash and determination, a successful attack on the enemy trenches.
BAR TO M.C.

    CONTALMAISON, 10th July, 1916. For conspicuous gallantry in action. He led the first line in the attack with great dash, and though wounded stuck to his duty and continued to do fine work until midnight, when he was ordered back with a message. He was then sent to hospital.

THOMSON, Lieut. George Gordon 3/Gloucester
    Near MORLANCOURT, 8th August, 1918. For conspicuous gallantry and devotion to duty during an attack. As battalion signalling officer he kept up communication with companies, on one occasion repairing the wire under intense shell fire. When the adjutant became a casualty he assumed his duties, and it was largely due to his energy and fine example that the troops were quickly reorganised and the line firmly established.

THORNE, Lieut. Alfred John Parker ... ... West Lancashire Div. Eng. (R.E.)
    Near YPRES, 20th September, 1917. For conspicuous gallantry and devotion to duty in constantly going backwards and forwards under heavy shell and snipers' fire to ensure the consolidation of two points. It was largely due to his fine example and contempt for danger that the work was so rapidly and successfully completed. He has shown a fine example of coolness and courage on many occasions.
BAR TO M.C.

    Near MESPLAUX FARM, 9th April, 1918. For conspicuous gallantry and devotion to duty when detailed to reconnoitre a bridge which had been unsatisfactorily demolished. Despite an enemy machine gun directed on the bridge he made his reconnaissance, returning for explosives, and then assisted in placing and firing the charges. His coolness was largely responsible for the satisfactory demolition of this bridge, which the enemy were known to be within 30 yards of.

THORNE, Capt. Philip Howard ... ... R.E.
    Awarded 1st January, 1918.

TIDDY, 2/Lt. Eric William Lacey ... ... /Gloucester
    KNOLL, 24/25 April, 1917. The two companies on his left overshot their objective, and were cut off. He displayed great bravery and judgment in moving his company to such a position as to be able to finally hand over a continuous line. He set a fine example throughout.

TIDY, Capt. Warwick Edward 9/Manchester
    Awarded 1st January, 1917.

TILLEY, Capt. John Ernest 12/Hampshire
    HAMEL, 28th March, 1918. For conspicuous gallantry and devotion to duty, both in command of his company and also temporarily in command of the battalion, when he led a successful counter-attack after a day and night of intense bombardment, during which the battalion suffered heavy losses. He set a fine example to officers and men by his courage and initiative.

TOMLING, Flying-Officer George Gibson ... ... R.A.F.
    Awarded 12th February, 1919.

MILITARY CROSS.

TOTTON, Capt. Arthur Knyvett ... 1/D.C.L.I.
GUILLEMONT, 3rd September, 1916. Though wounded early in the day he led on to the first objective, where he bombed the enemy dug-outs, and was again hit by a bomb. He then went on to the second objective, being wounded a third time on the way.

TOWER, 2/Lt. Herbert George Eric ... 3/Norfolk
AVION, 23/24 April, 1917. He carried out a dangerous reconnaissance in order to report on the enemy's wire, and later attacked with his company, and although severely wounded he continued to direct and encourage all ranks with him.

TREACHER, 2/Lt. Henry ... 9/Royal Surrey
Awarded 1st January, 1917.

BAR TO M.C.

MARBAUT, 20th July, 1918. For conspicuous gallantry and initiative. He went with his runner to the flank of the company that was being enfiladed by machine-gun fire, and, working forward under heavy fire, killed the gunner with a bomb and captured the gun. His skill and dash were worthy of great praise and saved many casualties.

TRELOAR, Capt. George Devine, *D.S.O.* ... Coldstream Guards
FONTAINE NOTRE DAME, 27th November, 1917. For conspicuous gallantry and devotion to duty. He led his company in an attack with great skill and daring to the furthest objective under intense fire, consolidated his position, and repulsed three counter-attacks. When the enemy got round his flank, which had become exposed, he carried out a masterly withdrawal, inflicting heavy casualties on the advancing enemy. He established a defensive position, and collected troops of all units to join in the defence. He showed magnificent energy, leadership and courage.

TRERY, Lieut. Norman Horace ... 504th (Wessex) Field Coy., R.E.
RIVER ESCAUT, near ESPAIN. For conspicuous gallantry and devotion to duty on the night of 26/27 October, 1918, whilst charged with making and launching rafts across the river. The work throughout was subjected to heavy fire, and his party was driven off it several times. At length he called for volunteers and succeeded in launching the raft, crossing to the enemy bank and making fast the tow rope.

TRIMM, 2/Lt. Charles Algernon ... R.F.A.
POTYZE, 19th August, 1917. For conspicuous gallantry and devotion to duty when the battery position was being heavily shelled. The camouflage of two guns caught fire, and this officer at once ran out and, filling buckets from adjacent shell-holes, succeeded in extinguishing the fire, although the sandbags around the guns had caught alight. After he had got under cover he saw that an ammunition dump had been hit and was alight, and he, accompanied by a gunner, again went out to extinguish the fire.

TROHEAR, 2/Lt. Thomas ... 3/Notts & Derby
Near RIBECOURT, 20th November, 1917. For conspicuous gallantry and devotion to duty. He crossed difficult country six times under heavy fire to keep touch with the company on his left. On arrival at the objective he led the way down an enemy dug-out and captured two officers and 15 other ranks.

TUNSTALL, Capt. the Rev. James Thomas ... Royal Army Chaplain's Dept. (1/Lincoln)
Near YPRES, 4/5 October, 1917. For conspicuous gallantry and devotion to duty in dressing the wounded, succouring the dying, and burying the dead under fire. On two occasions when the aid post in which he was working was blown in he succeeded in extricating all the wounded, although under heavy fire.

BAR TO M.C.

OVILLERS, 23/24 October, 1918. For conspicuous gallantry and devotion to duty tending and evacuating wounded during the attacks. He followed close behind the leading troops throughout the attack, and by collecting and locating wounded under heavy shell fire, and by bringing ambulances forward, was personally responsible for the evacuation of large numbers of casualties.

TURNBULL, Capt. Maxwell 3/Border
    Awarded 3rd June, 1918.

TURNER, 2/Lt. Alfred Hartin ... ... 9(8) E. Surrey (55th T.M.B.)
    ALBERT, 22nd August, 1918. For conspicuous gallantry and good leadership during the attack when in charge of a section of light trench mortars. He kept his guns in action for an hour at zero under heavy shelling, and then took them forward, bringing them to bear on an enemy machine-gun post, which he destroyed. Later he again moved them up and assisted the front line troops, his initiative being of great assistance.

TURNER, Lieut. Harold Keynes ... ... 2/Shropshire L.I.
    Awarded 1st January, 1916.

UMBERS, Lieut. John Ludford ... ... 4/Northumberland Fusiliers
    Near ASIAGO, 15th June, 1918. For conspicuous gallantry and devotion to duty during an enemy attack. He was responsible for obtaining much valuable information concerning the enemy's movements throughout the day under heavy shell fire, and thus enabled the various situations to be dealt with rapidly and successfully. He did valuable service.

VANN, Capt. Bernard William ... ... 8/Notts & Derby
    For conspicuous gallantry on several occasions:—
    KEMMEL, 24th April, 1915. When a small advanced trench which he occupied was blown in, and he himself wounded and half buried, he showed the greatest determination in organising the defence and rescuing buried men under heavy fire. Although wounded and severely bruised, he refused to leave his post till directly ordered to do so.
    YPRES, 31st July and subsequent days, he ably assisted another officer to hold the left trench of the line, setting a fine example to those around him. He was slightly wounded. On various occasions he has led patrols up to the enemy's trenches and obtained valuable information.

                        BAR TO M.C.
    BLAIRVILLE, 21/22 September, 1916. He led a daring raid against the enemy's trenches, himself taking five prisoners and displaying great courage and determination. He has on many previous occasions done fine work.

VAUGHAN, Lieut. Edwin Stephen C. ... ... 8/Royal Warwick
    LANDRECIES, 4th November, 1918. During the attack he displayed great courage and determination. In face of strong opposition he led his men forward to their objective, resulting in the capture of the bridge across the canal before the enemy could destroy it. Later, during the advance towards MAROILLES, 5/6 November, he again did good work.

VERGETTE, 2/Lt. George ... ... R.F.A.
    HEUDECOURT, 21st March, 1918. For conspicuous gallantry and devotion to duty in action. When the battery wagon lines came under heavy shell and gas shell fire, he superintended their clearing under great difficulties owing to the casualties inflicted. He then went through a very heavy gas shell barrage and informed the battery of the new position of the wagon lines. Throughout the operations he set a fine example of grit and courage.

VERNON, 2/Lt. Cyril Harker 4/Welch
    RAILWAY WOOD, 10th May, 1917. In spite of being subjected to very heavy fire he succeeded in destroying an enemy barricade. He was very severely wounded.

VINCENT, 2/Lt. Cecil Richard Causabon 18/London
    Near BOURLON, 30th November, 1917. For conspicuous gallantry and devotion to duty. He was in command of a company holding the line against an enemy attack, and showed the greatest courage and resource under heavy shell fire. He organised his command with great ability in critical circumstances, and set a fine example to his men.

MILITARY CROSS.

Voss, 2/Lt. Gordon Philips ... ... Tank Corps
Awarded 1st January, 1917.
Bar to M.C.
Ypres, 31st July, 1917. He went forward with the attacking infantry to act as guide to the tanks. He rendered valuable service under heavy machine-gun fire to a tank which was put out of action. Though slightly wounded he continued his work, and under heavy fire helped three tanks back to their positions after the attack. His coolness and example under firehad a great effect on his men.

Wadsworth, Lieut. Arthur 13/Middlesex
Awarded 3rd June, 1919.

Wagner, Lieut. Dixon Park ... ... 11/Dublin Fusiliers
Near Boesinghe, 9th August, 1917. For conspicuous gallantry and devotion to duty. Having taken over and established two advanced posts close to a farm which was strongly held by the enemy, he displayed the greatest gallantry and determination during the difficult work of consolidation under close rifle fire and heavy shelling.
Bar to M.C.
St. Louis, in the Courtrai sector, 20/21 October, 1918. For conspicuous gallantry and initiative. When both Lewis guns of his platoon were put out of action, and he was unable to advance owing to machine-gun fire, he, by a daring reconnaissance, located the enemy machine gun, which he engaged and silenced with rifle fire, thus enabling his platoon to get forward. His fine action greatly facilitated the general advance of his company to its objective.

Wakely, 2/Lt. Arthur Day ... ... 2/South Lancashire
Wytschaete Ridge, 7th June, 1917. For conspicuous gallantry and devotion to duty in commanding his company after his company commander was wounded, and enveloping and capturing two enemy machine guns which were holding up our advance. He afterwards went forward through a barrage and captured seven prisoners in a dug-out. He then reorganised his company, which was mixed up with other troops, and pushed forward, showing fine judgment and leadership throughout.

Walby, Capt. Herbert Charles ... ... 4/North Stafford (10/Yorkshire L.I.)
Near Wytschaete, 25/26 April, 1918. For conspicuous gallantry and devotion to duty. When the battalion camp was being shelled and gassed he supervised the movement of the battalion; and when the battalion had counter-attacked and penetrated the enemy's line he went out, and under heavy fire got into touch with isolated detachments. His coolness and disregard of danger were a fine example to all.
Bar to M.C.
Rabassa Rairne, 28th May, 1918. For conspicuous gallantry and devotion to duty throughout operations. When the commanding officer was wounded he took command of the battalion and held on to the position until almost surrounded. He then led his men through a narrow gap in the enemy's lines and took up another position about 500 yards in rear, from which he withdrew later in the day, in conformity with the troops on his flanks, and occupied some heights with 400 men collected from various units. He held this position until the withdrawal, when he led the last party across a river before the bridges were blown up. Throughout a trying period he showed unfailing courage and good leadership.

Walford, Capt. John Osborn 1/Worcester
Bazuel, 18th October, 1918. In the attack he commanded a company in the leading wave with conspicuous courage and skill. When the advance was held up by heavy machine-gun fire he made a personal reconnaissance, and, gaining touch with a company on the left, he gave orders to the remainder of the line to advance, gaining the objective with few casualties. His company captured a complete battery of 4·2-inch howitzers.

WALKER, 2/Lt. Henry Edward ... ... R.A.F.
    KEFR SABA DIER BALLUT, 19th March to 10th April, 1918. For conspicuous gallantry and devotion to duty during many flights and encounters in the air, when often single-handed he was most successful in bringing down enemy machines, and invariably displayed the utmost skill and resolution. He has been engaged in 14 combats, which have either been decisive or have resulted in enemy aircraft being driven down to a low height, and he has on occasions gone up as many as five times in one day.

WALLWORK, Lieut. John Wilson ... ... R.A.F.
    LENS, PONT D.—VENDIN, 6th March, 1918. For conspicuous gallantry and devotion to duty. During recent operations he participated in many offensive low-flying and bombing attacks, and carried them out with great courage and determination. From very low altitudes he bombed enemy troops and transport, inflicting heavy casualties. He caused while on offensive patrol more than one enemy machine to crash, and brought down others out of control. He set a magnificent example of courage and skill.

WALTON, 2/Lt. Sydney ... ... 3/Durham L.I.
    Near HEUDECOURT, 21st March, 1918. For conspicuous gallantry and devotion during a counter-attack when acting as adjutant to the battalion. On the objective being gained he organised bombing parties, cleared the trench of the enemy, and reorganised the line. Later, after the battalion had been driven out of a position, he rallied the men in his vicinity, and led them in a successful counter-attack on the lost ground.

WALTERS, 2/Lt. Sydney Evelyn ... ... 9/Tank Corps
    Near MORMAL FOREST, 4th November, 1918. During the action he reconnoitred and taped routes through most difficult country prior to the attack. In the attack he led his tanks with great coolness and judgment through heavy shelling up to their jumping-off place, and ensured their starting at zero in complete touch with their infantry. Throughout he displayed complete disregard of personal danger and devotion to duty.

WARD, Capt. Harold Frederick ... ... 2/East Surrey
    MONCHY-LE-PREUX, 8/9 and 9/10 August, 1917. For conspicuous gallantry and devotion to duty when in command of his battalion raiding party. The night before the raid he accompanied patrols to ascertain if the enemy's wire was sufficiently cut. This was done under machine-gun and rifle fire, and he brought back most valuable information. On the night of the raid itself he led the centre of the attack, and showed the greatest gallantry and coolness in visiting the other sub-sections and ascertaining that all objectives had been gained. His fine example largely contributed to the success of the operation.

                        BAR TO M.C.
    GONNELIEU, 20th November, 1917. For conspicuous gallantry and devotion to duty. He led his company with great courage and initiative in an attack, capturing his objective, together with two field guns and 100 prisoners. He set a splendid example of determination and contempt of danger.

WATKINS, 2/Lt. William Henry Ernest ... ... 1/East Yorks
    Near MEAULTE, 3/4 June, 1916. For conspicuous ability in controlling and disposing of his men. He showed great courage and disregard of danger, and even after being partially buried he inspired his men and kept up their morale.

WATSON, 2/Lt. Arthur Vivian Cradock ... ... Machine Gun Corps
    Near MASNIERES, 20th November, 1917. For conspicuous gallantry and devotion to duty during an engagement. He brought up pack animals loaded with ammunition close to the front line, and then led them forward under heavy fire to the captured position. His daring and skilful work enabled the guns to be got into action and maintain their fire for a much greater length of time than would otherwise have been possible. Though he suffered casualties amongst his men and animals, he delivered ammunition to all the guns and then returned and brought up a second load.

WATSON, Major Thomas William ... ... R.F.A.
    Awarded 1st January, 1918.

MILITARY CROSS.

WATT, 2/Lt. Hugo Burr Craig … … … … 8/Durham L.I.
   Awarded 1st January, 1918.

WEAVER, Capt. Frederick … … … … … 22/London
   BOURLON WOOD, 30th November to 2nd December, 1917. When his company was heavily shelled and gassed during a period of four days, by his personal example and disregard of danger he constantly rallied his men. His determined efforts helped materially in maintaining the position.

WEBB, Lieut. Clarence Harold … … … … 3/Norfolk
   Near ALBERT, 30th June to 1st July, 1918. For conspicuous gallantry and devotion to duty. Finding the right battalion was out of communication he at once proceeded to the front line, having to crawl most of the way, being continually subjected to machine-gun fire. He established communication successfully, and later the same day he managed to restore the line at a point within 30 yards of the enemy. By his unbounded energy and perseverance he maintained forward communications during a period of great importance.

WEEKS, Capt. William Edward … … … … 17/Royal Sussex
   FORET DE LILLE, 18th October, 1918. When in command he showed initiative and skill in leading his company. He pushed forward and captured the village, setting a fine example of dash and determination to his men. Again, on 20th October, he made a reconnaissance of the bank of the RIVER SCHELDT under heavy fire, and sent back very valuable information.

WEIR, 2/Lt. James … … … … … 5/Scottish Borderers
   Near YPRES, 19th August, 1917. For conspicuous gallantry and devotion to duty in taking charge when a shell had killed or wounded all the officers and several men at a company headquarters, evacuating the wounded, and reorganising the company, though the position was exposed to direct observation and under heavy fire.

BAR TO M.C.

   Near POZIERES, 22/23 July, 1918. For conspicuous gallantry and ability. He assembled the battalion for attack under extremely difficult conditions and on ground which was entirely unfamiliar to him. When the enemy replied to our preliminary barrage he showed great courage, and by his able bearing steadied the men. It was entirely due to him that the battalion effected the relief and formed up in time to assume the offensive.

WELCH, 2/Lt. Stanley Thomas … … … … Tank Corps
   Awarded 3rd February, 1920.

WELLBORNE, 2/Lt. Harry Harold Gordon … … … R.A.S.C.
   HAVRINCOURT, 21st to 24th March, 1918. For conspicuous gallantry and devotion to duty when in charge of a convoy delivering supplies to two brigades. He conducted each wagon to the battery lines, and afterwards brought back the wagons under heavy shell fire to the company lines. By his coolness and control of his convoy he ensured the delivery of rations under very trying circumstances. Three days later, without guides and under heavy shell fire, he managed to find each battery and the headquarters of each brigade, and gave them information to enable them to draw rations. It was entirely owing to his persistent efforts that the artillery were able to obtain rations on that day.

WELSH, 2/Lt. Robert … … … … 5/Gordon Highlanders
   Near LANGEMARCKE, 31st July, 1917. For conspicuous gallantry and devotion to duty. He led his platoon against an enemy strong point with the utmost coolness and determination under machine-gun and rifle fire, and captured the position after fierce hand-to-hand fighting. Later he took his platoon through a heavy barrage and established an outpost line, which he held under very trying circumstances until relieved 36 hours later.

WELTE, 2/Lt. Ernest James … … 505th Battery, 65th Brigade (R.F.A.)
   S. of ENGLEFONTAINE, 4th November, 1918. For marked gallantry while in charge of an 18 pdr. in taking it to a very forward position. The gun was man-handled down the bad road and placed within 150 yards of a house known to be a strong enemy machine-gun post. Under heavy machine-gun and shell fire he destroyed this post and cover around it by his fire, and it was due to his courage and initiative that the infantry were able to take this point without opposition.

WENGER, 2/Lt. Theodore Lanternier ... ... Machine Gun Corps
    MESSINES, 12th June, 1917. For conspicuous gallantry and devotion to duty in repairing a badly damaged tank under heavy shell fire and in full view of the enemy, and driving it back to safety. He has consistently displayed a very high standard of determined courage and ability when engaged in salvage work, and has set a very fine example to all.

WEST, Capt. Frank 1/Devon
    Awarded 3rd June, 1919.

WEST, Lieut. Richard Goy ... ... 3/Grenadier Guards
    HAMELINCOURT, 22nd August, 1918. For conspicuous gallantry with a patrol, when he made persistent attempts to penetrate the enemy defences. He located five machine guns and brought back valuable information. The next morning he led his platoon with great determination and captured the position. He was then wounded.

WHEATE, Lieut. Thomas Ernest ... ... 190th Brigade R.F.A.
    HEESTERT, 25/26 October, 1918. For conspicuous gallantry and devotion to duty during operations when attached with half a section to an infantry battalion. The initiative he displayed was of the highest order, and his courage in handling his guns, and the superb way in which he brought them into action, with utter disregard to his own personal safety, was most praiseworthy.

WHEELER, Capt. William Robert 22/London
    N. of PERONNE, 30th August to 6th September, 1918. For conspicuous gallantry and ability during the advance. He skilfully led his company through heavy artillery and machine-gun fire to the final objective. Later, during a further attack, when temporarily held up, he took hold of two companies and led them with the utmost determination, in spite of strong opposition.

WHINNEY, Charles Toller 11/Middlesex
    N. of MEDVYEJA-GORA. For marked gallantry and good leadership. On the night 15/16 May, 1919, during operations which led up to the capture of a position, he was in charge of the advanced guard of two platoons sent out to exploit the success already obtained. Encountering an enemy armoured train he so manœuvred his men that they got within rifle-bombing range of it and forced it to withdraw. On the 12th June, S. of MEDVYEJA-GORA, he secured the left flank of the attack, and handled his platoon with the skill he invariably displayed.

WHITAKER, Capt. Donald Nicoll ... ... 12/Hampshire (6/Royal Lancaster)
    Near MONCHY, 18th June, 1917. For conspicuous gallantry and devotion to duty. Although knocked down and buried by a shell, which rendered him unconscious, during an intense enemy bombardment, he insisted on returning to his company, as soon as he regained consciousness, in order to conduct the defence of the advanced posts and trenches which they were occupying. He was a second time buried by a shell, but remained in command until the attack had been beaten off, setting a magnificent example of pluck and devotion to duty.

WHITE, 2/Lt. John Broadwood 7/London
    During the advance from BRAY to LICRAMONT, 22nd August to 6th September, 1918. For conspicuous gallantry as intelligence officer. On many occasions he was called upon to make difficult and dangerous reconnaissances, which he invariably carried out with extreme capability.

WHITE, 2/Lt. Thomas Herbert ... ... 7/East Lancashire
    E. of KLEIN ZILLEBEKE, 24/25 September, 1917. While on patrol he encountered an enemy machine-gun post. With one man he immediately rushed the post, capturing the gun and its crew.

WHITEAWAY, Major Edward George Lang ... ... 5/Yorkshire L.I.
    Awarded 1st January, 1918.
BAR TO M.C.
    VAUL, 29/30 August, 1918. He taped out a position for assembly in advance of our positions under heavy machine-gun and shell fire, and though wounded did not desist from his work until it was completed. His gallant devotion to duty ensured the success of the start of next day's operations.

MILITARY CROSS.

WHITEHEAD, 2/Lt. Frederick William ... ... R.F.A.
    Near MONCHY-LE-PREUX, 10th May, 1917. When orderly officer his promptness and energy in directing the supply of ammunition to his battery and in getting the wagons and teams away under heavy shell fire averted many casualties. Although somewhat badly disabled, he carried on till all was clear.

WHYTE, Capt. Angus McIntosh ... ... 2/Tank Corps
    Awarded 1st January, 1919.

WIGHT, 2/Lt. Lauder Lylestone ... ... 1/East Surrey
    MORVAL, 25th September, 1916. He handled his company with great courage and determination. Later, although very severely wounded, he remained at his post.

WILES, Lieut. Osborne David ... ... 7/Shropshire L.I.
    23rd October, 1918. For conspicuous gallantry and devotion to duty. During the operations which resulted in the capture of VERTAIN and ESCARMAIN, he carried out a reconnaissance under heavy machine-gun and shell fire, obtaining very valuable information. Although wounded, he remained at duty and continued to render valuable service during the night, 23/24 October, and on subsequent days.

WILKES, Lieut. George Thomas ... ... 7/East Surrey
    Awarded 1st January, 1917.

WILKIE, Lieut. James ... ... 7/Loyal North Lancashire (11/East Lancashire)
    Awarded 3rd June, 1919.

WILKINSON, 2/Lt. Arthur Buttle ... ... R.F.A.
    VILLERS BRETTONNEUX, 31st April, 1918. For conspicuous gallantry and devotion to duty. He volunteered to go round the front line to obtain information which was urgently required. He had to crawl most of the way under heavy rifle and machine-gun fire, and succeeded in sending back most valuable information.

WILLANS, Capt. Harry 2/Bedford
    Awarded 1st January, 1917.

WILLETT, 2/Lt. Francis William 4/Leicester
    FONTAINE-LE-CROISELLES, 3rd May, 1917. For conspicuous gallantry in an attack, when, although wounded, he maintained a forward position with a Lewis gun team all day, and until all the team had become casualties. Before withdrawing he buried the gun,

WILLIAMS, 2/Lt. Harold 3/Manchester
    BULLECOURT, 12th May, 1917. For conspicuous gallantry and initiative in pushing forward his posts, and making and consolidating two strong points under heavy artillery and machine-gun fire. He set a fine example of courage and skill.

WILLIAMS, Capt. Noel Victor ... ... 62/Machine Gun Corps
    VAULX VRAUCOURT, 24th to 31st August, 1918. When temporarily in command of his company he was called upon, at short notice, to draw up a plan of action for launching his company to an attack. He carried out his task with conspicuous ability, and after the objective had been gained, he made a personal reconnaissance of the guns, under heavy shell and machine-gun fire, co-ordinating their dispositions so as to meet the tactical requirements of the situation. His courage and energy set a splendid example to all ranks.

WILLIAMS, 2/Lt. William James ... ... 3/Royal Welch Fusiliers
    PILCKEM, 31st July, 1917. For conspicuous gallantry and devotion to duty. When his company officer was wounded he took command, rallied his men, and kept them well in hand under very heavy fire, and showed a splendid example of steadiness throughout.

WILLIAMS, 2/Lt. William Theophilus ... ... 2/East Kent
    Near "Fosse 8," BETHUNE. 28/29 September, 1915. For conspicuous gallantry and devotion to duty. He took charge of a small party of bombers, and during 17½ hours he and his bombers threw close on 2,000 bombs, while the enemy responded with about five times that number. It was raining nearly all the time, and the damp fuses had to be lit from cigarettes, yet the enemy were held up. 2/Lt. Williams, though wounded, refused to leave his post, and it was mainly due to his bravery and that of his party that the trench was finally held.

WILLIAMSON, Lieut. William Henry Rowe ... ... R.A.S.C.
    Awarded 1st January, 1917.

WILLS, 2/Lt. Arthur Reynolds ... ... 10/Royal West Surrey
    Near ZILLEBEKE, 6th August, 1917. For conspicuous gallantry and devotion to duty. Although wounded during heavy fighting and told by the Medical Officer to leave the line, he returned to the trenches and carried on with his duty, setting a splendid example to all ranks by his pluck and coolness.

WILLIS, Lieut. Cyril Reginald ... ... Indian Mountain Battery, R.A.
    Awarded 3rd June, 1919.

WILLIS, Lieut. Dan Hugh ... ... 7/Royal Warwick
    Awarded 3rd June, 1917.

WILSON, Lieut. John Baxenden ... ... 5/Northumberland Fusiliers
    Near PASSCHENDAELE, 18th December, 1917. For conspicuous gallantry and devotion to duty. On hearing his posts being engaged by the enemy he immediately proceeded to the scene of action, and found that his men had captured an officer, thirteen other ranks and a machine gun. Hearing that there was apparently another machine gun out in "No Man's Land," he organised a patrol, and succeeded in finding and bringing back three other machine guns. On the following night he again patrolled "No Man's Land" to try and find other machine guns, which were said to be there. Throughout this period he performed continual acts of courage and coolness under fire.

WILTON, 2/Lt. Ralph Antrobus ... ... 15/Royal Warwick
    ROCLINCOURT, 22nd May, 1916. For conspicuous gallantry when in charge of a raiding party. He led his men, under heavy fire, to within twelve yards of the enemy parapet, and though struck down he continued to urge his men forward.

WINTLE, 2/Lt. George Howard 4/Gloucester
    LA VACQUERIE, 2nd December, 1917. For conspicuous gallantry and devotion to duty. When he had been wounded, knowing that only a few officers survived, he returned, after having his wound dressed, with a number of men who had lost their way. With these men he reinforced the battalion, got into touch with the battalion on his left, and helped to take up a new position under the most difficult conditions.

WINSHIP, Lieut. Ernest Roland 8/Middlesex
    Near CROISILLES, 24th to 30th August, 1918. For conspicuous gallantry and devotion to duty. During several day's operations he carried out valuable reconnaissances and obtained information which contributed materially to the success of the advance, and enabled dispositions to be made to meet an enemy counter-attack. He showed great skill and resource.

WITCOMBE, Capt. Charles Edward 2/Gloucester
    Awarded 1st January, 1917.

BAR TO M.C.

    Awarded 1st January, 1919.

MILITARY CROSS.

WOMACK, 2/Lt. Bertie ... ... 6/Royal West Surrey
E. of MORLANCOURT, 22/23 August, 1918. For conspicuous gallantry and devotion to duty. This officer, under heavy machine-gun and artillery fire, laid a tape within 100 yards of the front line to enable battalion to get direction in moving off for the attack. On several occasions during the operation he operated in front of our advanced posts, and enabled the infantry to destroy the machine-gun posts before casualties could be inflicted on us. At MAUREPAS, 29th August, he pushed out in front of the leading wave, and by careful observation directed the men safely through a barrage.

WOOD, 2/Lt. Sydney George ... ... 7/Northumberland Fusiliers (R.E.)
LANGEMARCKE, 24th October and 4th November, 1917. For conspicuous gallantry and devotion to duty when in charge of all visual stations and power buzzer and wireless stations between brigade headquarters and battalions. Though several times affected by gas, he set a splendid example under heavy shelling, and maintained communication in the forward area.

WOOD, 2/Lt. Walter Bertram ... ... 8/Hampshire (R.F.C.)
Near DOUAI and LAMBRES, 24/25 June, 1917. For conspicuous gallantry and devotion to duty on many occasions, when engaged with hostile aircraft, during which he has shown a fine offensive spirit and the utmost fearlessness. He has had no less than 23 combats, in the course of which he has destroyed and driven down numerous enemy machines, frequently attacking several single-handed, and on one occasion fighting with his revolver when he had run short of gun ammunition.

BAR TO M.C.

Near POLYGONE WOOD, 31st July, 1917. For conspicuous gallantry and devotion to duty in attacking enemy aircraft. On several occasions he has shown admirable dash and determination in attacking hostile machines single-handed, destroying some and driving others down out of control. He has also displayed great daring in attacking enemy infantry and transport with machine-gun fire at very low altitudes, in spite of attacks by hostile aircraft whilst so engaged.

WOODCOCK, Lieut. Humphrey Neville Hodson ... ... 6/Royal West Kent
Near EPEHY, 22nd September, 1918. During operations he showed great gallantry in an attack upon an entrenched enemy machine gun. He led his platoon across the open with great dash and shot two of the enemy. The enemy counter-attacked with superior numbers, and drove him out; but he reorganised and led his men to a second attack which was completely successful. Though wounded he waited to see the post consolidated before going down.

WOODROW, 2/Lt. Arthur Blackford ... ... 11/Royal Sussex
Near YPRES, 25th to 27th October, 1917. He led his men in the attack on a strong point, which he captured with seven prisoners. Though severely wounded, he remained at duty for several hours, and sent excellent reports back to battalion headquarters.

WOODYEAR, 2/Lt. Reginald Percy ... ... 7/Royal West Kent
Near HEINGARD, 12th April, 1918. For conspicuous gallantry and devotion to duty in leading his company in an attack on an enemy position under heavy machine-gun and shell fire. He led his men with great dash, and never wavered until the objective was reached. He consolidated his position and maintained it until relieved. By his determination he succeeded in restoring a critical situation.

WOOTTON, Lieut. Kenneth Edwin ... ... 10/London (Tank Corps)
MARCOING, 20th November, 1917. For conspicuous gallantry and devotion to duty in attack. He went forward in the leading tank of his section and put several enemy machine guns out of action. It was due to his splendid initiative and determination that the infantry reached their objective with very few casualties.

WORDEN, 2/Lt. Ernest Harold Glover ... ... 3/Royal Berks
   SANCTUARY WOOD, 31st July, 1917. Though badly wounded he led his men with great gallantry under heavy shell and machine-gun fire to their objective. He set an excellent example of courage and endurance throughout.

WORNUM, 2/Lt. William Esmond ... ... R.G.A.
   WESTOURTRE, 28th July, 1918. For conspicuous gallantry and devotion to duty. This officer's battery came under heavy shell fire while he was on duty as section commander, but by his coolness and determination he kept the guns in action all night and the next day. On one occasion, one of his detachments having suffered heavily, he personally acted as layer to one of the guns.

WORRALL, Lieut. Samuel ... ... R.G.A.
   Awarded 1st January, 1919.

WRIGHT, 2/Lt. George Edward ... ... R.A.S.C.
   ERVILLERS, 23rd March, 1918. For conspicuous gallantry and devotion to duty in maintaining his guns in action and in keeping up the supply of ammunition under very trying conditions. On two occasions he returned to old evacuated positions and salved ammunition in order to keep the battery supplied. Later, it was due to his great energy and cheerful example that six guns and stores were saved, and that his men, though worn out with fatigue, so ably performed their duties.

WRIGHT, 2/Lt. Herbert Alexander ... ... R.G.A.
   CORBIE, 19th July, 1918. For conspicuous gallantry when ordered to move a gun from a position which was under heavy shell fire, shells dropping among the guns and causing several casualties. He cleared the wounded with the help of two non-commissioned officers, and then with great coolness and determined energy he caused the gun to be dismounted and moved before it sustained serious damage from the heavy shelling.

WRIXON, Lieut. Maurice Percival Bentley ... ... Grenadier Guards
   ARLEUX, 19th February, 1918. During a hostile raid he was in charge of all the front posts, and on hearing rifle fire walked through a most intense barrage to the left flank post, where the raid was taking place. Immediately grasping the situation, and on seeing that two strong enemy parties had penetrated between our posts, he organised bombing parties, and opened fire with a machine gun on one of the enemy parties, which retired, leaving one of their wounded. Seeing the other party coming up behind him he ran down the trench to meet them, killed the leading man, and, supported by a few men, drove back this party, killing and wounding several. His great personal courage, coolness, and the fine military qualities which he displayed were a magnificent example to all ranks.

YATES, Major Henry George ... ... R.F.A.
   Awarded 1st January, 1918.

YATES, Capt. William 3/Cheshire
   GUYENCOURT, 27/28 May, 1918. For conspicuous gallantry and devotion to duty during a retirement. He showed great skill and determination in maintaining his position with very few men in the face of heavy enemy attacks. In particular one night he reorganised his men and parties of stragglers and dug in a line, and in spite of heavy shelling and machine-gun fire, repelled all enemy attacks for 12 hours until ordered to retire. He showed excellent leadership throughout.

YOUNG, Lieut. Oliver ... ... 4/Northumberland Fusiliers
   Near CONCAVREU, 27th May, 1918. For conspicuous gallantry and devotion to duty. He took charge of a small party and successfully held up the enemy for a considerable period

while the engineers destroyed a bridge. He organised a skilful defence in spite of heavy rifle and machine-gun fire. His consistent gallantry while fighting a rearguard action set a fine example to all men serving under him, and caused heavy losses to the enemy.

YUILL, Lieut. Harry Hogg ... ... 170th Mining Coy., R.E.
For conspicuous gallantry and devotion to duty on several occasions :—

CUINCHY, 29th May, 1915. When one of the leads to a charge in a mine broke close to the charge, he at once untamped the top of the charge and crawled into the mine to find and mend the break, although the Germans were working so close he could hear them talking.

CAMBRIN, 24th and 29th June. At great personal risk, he charged mines, well knowing the Germans to be charging against him, and managed to fire his charges before they succeeded in doing so.

CUINCHY, on the night of 21/22 August. Again 2/Lt. Yuill exhibited great skill and bravery in directing mining operations. The enemy were working within a few feet of our galleries, opposite No. 5 and 7 mines, and it became a race which mines would be first exploded. The situation was critical, but owing to his splendid example and energy two shafts were sunk in time, charged and tamped. The resulting explosions must have blown in the German galleries and the miners in them.

FISHER, 2/Lt. Charles Heath ... ... 12/East Surrey
Near WYTSCHAETE, 3/4 September, 1918. For conspicuous gallantry on reconnaissance. In spite of the fact that his runner was wounded, he returned himself and gave a valuable report as to the position of one of our posts in front of the line. He afterwards conducted three men with rations and water back to this post, in spite of the country through which they had to pass being under continuous machine-gun and snipers' fire.

NELSON, Lieut. William Percival ... ... R.A.M.C. (1/Artists)
RUMILLY, 8th October, 1918. For gallantry and devotion to duty. During a very severe bombardment of artillery and machine guns he constantly went out to the help of the wounded, attending them with utter disregard for danger, and was the means of saving several lives and alleviating a great deal of suffering. He has at all times set a striking example by his fearlessness and devotion to duty.

SMITH, Capt. Walter Campbell ... 1/Artists (4th Bn., Special Brigade, R.E.)
(Particulars omitted from page 126)

This officer was in command of a double company ("P" and "Q") operating on the 55th Divisional front. Throughout the enormous work involved in the preparations, he handled the difficult situations that arose with insight and resource, and by his careful attention to detail and indefatigable energy enabled the complicated operations to be carried through without a hitch.

The services referred to were rendered on the BLAIREVILLE-FICHEUX front between 13th and 28th June, 1916, culminating in the gas attack launched from that front on the latter date.

D.F.C.

The Distinguished Flying Cross is awarded to Officers and Warrant Officers for acts of gallantry when flying in active operations against the enemy. The Decoration has a ribbon of violet and white alternative diagonal stripes, running at an angle of 45°, showing violet triangles in the top left-hand and bottom right-hand corners. Bars may be added for additional acts of gallantry.

BEENEY, Lieut. James Alexander ... ... 24/London (R.A.F.)
   Awarded 1st January, 1919, for continuous good service for ten months. [5362

CANNING, Lieut. Ernest Harold ... ... 1/Gloucester (R.A.F.)
   FRANCE, 28th August, 1918: also many other dates. This officer has displayed marked courage and skill in bombing enemy transport, etc., at low altitudes. He took a conspicuous part in the attack on bridges over a river between ARRAS and CAMBRAI: subjected to very heavy machine-gun fire he descended to 150 feet to exactly locate their position, and bombed them from a low altitude. [4824

COULSON, Lieut. Charles Stanley Lomas ... ... 80th Squadron, R.A.F.
   N. of MORLANCOURT, 9th August, 1918, and many other places and dates. During the late operations this officer has set a brilliant example of courage and skill, notably on one occasion when, observing a party of the enemy in a trench firing at some of our infantry, he repeatedly dived on the trench, firing at the occupants and distracting their attention from our troops. Eventually he was wounded twice in the leg, but succeeded in reaching his aerodrome. [762695

DEW, 2/Lt. Edward Alphonse ... ... 205th Squadron, R.A.F.
   Near BAILLEUL, 19th May, 1918, and many other places and dates. A keen and dashing officer, who has taken part in numerous bombing raids and photographic reconnaissances. Whilst on a bombing raid his machine, flying in rear of the formation, was attacked by five enemy scouts. Two of these he engaged at close range; at the outset he was dangerously wounded in the thigh. Despite this he continued firing his guns until he fainted from loss of blood. He succeeded in bringing down one of the scouts in flames. [766687

FAIRBAIRN, Flying-Officer Arthur Reginald ... ... 4th Balloon Section, R.A.F.
   W. of FRIODMONT, 23rd October, 1918, and many other occasions. During recent operations this officer's balloon was singled out for attack three times in two days. On the third day he was again attacked by six scouts when at a height of 1,500 feet. He behaved with the utmost coolness and gallantry in helping his fellow observer, who was inexperienced, out of the basket before parachuting himself. His determination in pushing his balloon forward during the recent advance has been most praiseworthy. [6284

FRANK, Lieut. Charles Frederick ... ... 19th Balloon Section, R.A.F.
   Near GUOY, FRANCE, 8th October, 1918: also numerous other dates and places. Lieut. Frank has co-operated with our artillery in 184 successful shoots, proving himself an exceptionally capable and efficient officer, with keen powers of observation. On 8th October, under most difficult conditions, he succeeded in giving observations for three shoots. During this flight, owing to his proximity to actual operations, he was enabled to transmit valuable information as to hostile infantry movements. [5492

GOUDIE, Capt. Norman ... ... 5th Squadron, R.A.F.
   AMIENS—ROYE, 8th August, 1918, with 2/Lt. Robert McKinley Jamison, R. Irish Rifles. Thrice on one date these officers carried out at extremely low altitudes, and in face of intense rifle and machine-gun fire, reconnaissances of an important road. During one of these reconnaissances, observing a party of the enemy holding our infantry, they dived on them and forced them to retire, and on another occasion they bombed a large party of the enemy, causing them to surrender to our infantry. [7287

DISTINGUISHED FLYING CROSS.

GROOM, Lieut. Victor Emanuel ... ... 20th Squadron, R.A.F.
N.W. of WERVICQ, 8th May, 1918: also numerous other dates and places. An officer of great courage and dash, who never hesitates to attack the enemy regardless of the superiority in numbers. While on a recent patrol this officer was one of a formation of eight that engaged twenty-five hostile scouts. Lieut. Groom shot down one, and his observer (Lieut. Hardcastle) a few minutes later destroyed another. On a later date, accompanied by the same observer, they were attacked by twelve scouts; two of these they shot down. [762330

HAWORTH, Lieut. Peter ... Lancashire Fusiliers; 15th Balloon Section, R.A.F.
Awarded 1st January, 1919, for general service as a Balloon Commander in the Ypres salient. [7800

HEPBURN, Capt. Allan ... ... 88th Squadron, R.A.F.
TOURNAI, 12th October, 1918, and several other dates and places. This officer made a very fine flight, calling for courage and determination of a high order. Thick clouds were within 200 feet of the ground and the visibility was so bad that practically no flying was attempted. Despite these adverse conditions this officer volunteered to cross the lines. Climbing through the clouds, which were several thousand feet in depth, he flew above them, guided by compass, with no view of the ground. Continuing his flight until he estimated that he was in the vicinity of a certain objective, he descended, and found himself 150 feet over an enemy railway station. Dropping his bombs, he destroyed a passenger train, and afterwards engaged enemy troops and transport with machine-gun fire. Having caused considerable damage, Capt. Hepburn climbed through the clouds and found his way home. [8179

HICKS, Lieut. George Rensbury ... ... 74th Squadron, R.A.F.
Awarded 3rd June, 1919, for good service and very gallant conduct on various occasions.
[760635

HOWARD, Capt. George Vivian ... ... 7th Squadron, R.A.F.
Awarded 3rd June, 1919, for good service on reconnaissance, photographic service, and also in counter-battery work. [4528

JONES, Lieut. William Ernest Frank ... ... 101st Squadron, R.A.F.
Between ALBERT and PROYART, 14th June, 1918. This officer carried out a comprehensive reconnaissance by night in heavy rain at a height of only 400 feet. He returned to his aerodrome in the face of a blinding storm, after a flight of three hours. He has carried out sixty-four night bombing raids. His courage and perseverance are exceptional. [7645558

LAGESSE, Capt. Camille Henri Raoul ... ... 29th Squadron, R.A.F.
Near NEUF-BERQUIN, 28th May, 1918. When on wireless interception duty Capt. Lagesse, in company with another officer, was attacked by seven scouts. Engaging one, he followed it down from 11,000 feet to 2,000 feet, when it crashed. Bold in attack, skilful in execution, he has proved himself on many occasions to be a fine airman.

BAR TO D.F.C.
E. of BAILLEUL, August, 1918, and numerous other dates and places. A scout leader of marked ability and daring who, since 28th August, has destroyed thirteen enemy aeroplanes, displaying at all times brilliant leadership and courage. On 2nd October, when leading a patrol of four machines, he dived on eight Fokkers; four of these were destroyed, Capt. Lagesse accounting for one. [766025

MACDONALD, Lieut. Eric Norman ... ... Independent Air Force, R.A.F.
Awarded 3rd June, 1919, for 13 successful night bombing raids.

NICHOLAS, 2/Lt. Gerald Basil ... ... 102nd Squadron, R.A.F.
LANDRECIES, 14/15 October, 1918, and many other dates and places. This officer has carried out 95 night bombing raids, and has displayed marked skill and initiative. He has been extremely successful in low reconnaissances and attacks on ground targets, having twice obtained direct hits on trains at a height of about 800 feet. [766565

K

POGSON, 2/Lt. Desmond Philip ... 104th Squadron, Independent Air Force, R.A.F.
MANNHEIM, 22nd August, 1918, and many other occasions. In a recent long-distance bombing raid his petrol tank received a shot immediately after crossing the line, but he continued on his journey and bombed the distant objective. On the return journey very fierce fighting occurred, during which both leaders and deputy-leaders of our formations were shot down, and the remaining machines lost touch with each other. At this critical moment 2/Lt. Pogson ordered his observer to tie his handkerchief to the gun-mounting to indicate that his was the leader's machine. He then circled over the area three times and picked up five of our machines, and in face of very hostile opposition got them into formation and brought them all safely home. The prompt action of this officer was highly meritorious, and undoubtedly saved the remaining machines, which could not have coped with the greatly superior formations of the enemy. [766417

RANDALL, Flying-Officer George Ebbon ... ... 20th Squadron, R.A.F.
W. of LOVERALL, FRANCE, 10th November, 1918, and many other dates and places. A brave and resourceful flight commander who has, within the last four months previous to November 11th, led 71 offensive patrols. On 10th November, engaging a superior number of enemy aircraft, he himself shot down two and the remainder were driven off by his flight. In addition to the foregoing he has four other enemy machines to his credit. [762307
BAR TO D.F.C.
WAZIRISTAN (No details yet published).

ROSS, Capt. Charles ... ... 25th Squadron, R.A.F.
On the DOUAI—CAMBRAI Road, 13th August, 1918. Since October last this officer has carried out 240 hours' service flying, mainly on long solo photographic reconnaissances at very low altitudes. In this arduous and trying service he has shown exceptional skill, perseverance and courage, notably on one very important reconnaissance, when he was attacked by ten enemy aeroplanes. Engaging one at close range, this officer shot it down in flames, and in face of the hostile attack he completed the reconnaissance. [765422

SARGANT, Capt. Frederick Herbert St. Clair ... ... 38th Squadron, R.A.F.
Awarded 1st January, 1919. GHISTELLES, 3/4 October, 1918, and 26 night raids.
[7691

STATON, Capt. William Ernest, *M.C.* ... ... 62nd Squadron, R.A.F.
S. of ARMENTIERES, 3rd May, 1918, and many other dates and places. This officer has already been awarded the Military Cross for gallantry and devotion to duty. Since this award he has accounted for eleven enemy aeroplanes—nine destroyed and two shot down out of control. He has proved himself a most efficient flight commander and an enterprising leader, setting a very fine example to his squadron. [765057
BAR TO D.F.C.
E. of DURY, 15th September, 1918, and many other dates and places. This officer has already been awarded the Military Cross and the Distinguished Flying Cross for conspicuous gallantry and devotion to duty. Since his last award he has destroyed five enemy machines and driven down one out of control. His example of courage and resource is a fine incentive to the other pilots of his squadron.

WALKER, Capt. Henry Edward, *M.C.* ... ... 111th Squadron, R.A.F.
EGYPT, 16th September, 1918. A gallant and courageous officer who has served continuously on the front for twelve months, during which period he has shot down several enemy machines. Throughout recent operations his bombing has been exceptionally accurate, a large percentage of direct hits on transport, etc., being obtained. [762920

WILLIAMSON-JONES, Capt. Clarence Edward ... 1/Manchester ; 59th Squadron, R.A.F.
Over BOURSIES, 22nd March, 1918 ; Near BEAUMETZ, 23rd March, 1918, and many other occasions elsewhere. This officer has completed over fifty successful G.B. shoots, frequently under adverse weather conditions, and in face of severe opposition from aeroplanes and antiaircraft fire. The success of these operations was in many cases mainly due to his courage and perseverence. On one occasion, flying at 2,000 feet, he held up for a time the advance of hostile infantry. [1410

A.F.C.

The Air Force Cross is awarded to Officers and Warrant Officers for acts of courage or devotion to duty when flying, although not in active operations against the enemy. This Decoration has a ribbon of red and white alternate diagonal stripes, ⅛" wide, showing red triangles in the top left-hand and bottom right-hand corners. There are no "Deeds" published for the Air Force Cross.

BORET, Capt. John Auguste ... 4/R. West Surrey (36th Squadron, R.A.F.)
    Sea Patrol, N.E. Coast of England. [Reg. No. 3586

CHICK, Lieut. Arthur Leslie ... ... 4/Essex (22nd T.D., R.A.F.)
    Gormanstown, Ireland. [764087

CLARKE, Capt. George Malcolm ... ... 2/Leinster (153rd Squadron, R.A.F.)
    Home Defence, North Weald. [1533

DIMMOCK, Capt. Norman Herford ... ... 141st Squadron, R.A.F.
    Biggin Hill, Kent. [3624

DOWN, Lieut. Harold Hewter ... ... Artists (28th T.D., R.A.F.)
    Weston-on-the-Green. [3442

DUPONT, Lieut. Alfred Norman ... ... 5/Leicester (68th Wing, R.A.F.)
    Seaton Carew. [4084

HOPPS, Lieut. Frank Linden ... ... 5/Yorkshire L.I.
    Flight, Marseilles to Egypt, 28th September, 1918. [7730

MESSENGER, Capt. Alfred Lewis ... ... No. 2 Obs. School, R.A.F.
    Manston, Kent. [5706

PARK, Lieut. Ralph Stuart ... ... R.A.F.
    Awarded 3rd June, 1919. [762379

PEEBLES, Lieut. Arthur John Douglas ... ... R.A.F.
    Awarded 3rd June, 1919. [763956

PERN, Lieut. Claude ... ... R.A.F.
    Awarded 4th November, 1918. [7898

RILEY, Capt. Alan Incell ... ... Artists (R.A.F.)
    Awarded 3rd June, 1919. [6122

STEWART, Major Oliver, M.C. 9/Middlesex
    Awarded 4th November, 1918. [2289

TURNER, Lieut. Cyril Charles Teesdale ... ... R.A.F.
    Test Pilot, Hendon. [4856

YOUNG, Lieut. William Arnold Gemmell ... ... R.A.F.
    Turnberry, Ayrshire. [4432

THE MOST HONOURABLE ORDER OF THE BATH.

To be Companion:—MAY, Colonel Henry Allan Roughton, V.D. ... Artists' Rifles

THE MOST DISTINGUISHED ORDER OF ST. MICHAEL AND ST. GEORGE.

To be Companion:—SHIRLEY, Lt.-Colonel William ... ... Artists' Rifles

THE ROYAL VICTORIAN ORDER.

To be Members:—BARE, Capt. Arnold E.; SIMMONS, Capt. Frank K. (*4th Class*) ,,
TYER, Lieut. Austin Arnold ... ... (*5th Class*) ,,

THE MOST EXCELLENT ORDER OF THE BRITISH EMPIRE.

This Order, instituted in 1917, and extended in December, 1918, is conferred for important services rendered to the Empire, and is awarded to both men and women. It consists of 5 classes:—(i) Knights Grand Cross; (ii) Knights Commanders; (iii) Commanders; (iv) Officers; (v) Members. There are both Military and Civil Divisions of the Order: the Insignia for each is the same, but the ribbon of the Military Division is distinguished by a vertical red stripe in the centre.

To be Military Knight Commander (K.B.E.).

EDIS, Colonel Sir Robert William, C.B., V.D. ... Hon. Colonel Artists' Rifles

To be Military Commanders (C.B.E.).

BUNCE, Major W. Leslie ... 3/Liverpool   NEIGHBOUR, Capt. Sydney W. 1/Artists
Operations in Archangel.

To be Military Officers (O.B.E.)

ALLEN, Capt. F. J.	... R.A.S.C.	HARRISON, Major F. ...	... Staff
BAKER, Major C. B.	2/Oxford & Bucks L.I.	HAWKSFORD, Major F. H.	R.F.C.
BARTON, Major B. C.	... R.A.S.C.	HODGKINSON, Capt. H. D.	R.A.S.C.
BONNER, Lieut. S. A.	... R.E. (Signals)	IVORY, Capt. H. F. ...	R.A.S.C.
BIRCH, Major W. K.	... /Devon	KLEIN, Capt. A. B. L. ...	1/Norfolk
BRUNTON, Capt. G.	... Labour Corps	LAWRENCE, Capt. J. H.	R.A.S.C.
BUSTARD, Capt. F.	... 5/R. Lancaster	MAKALUA, Major M. J. M.	13/R. Sussex
CAMERON, Capt. J.	... R.E. (Signals)	MANN, Capt. P. R. ...	4/London
CHILD, Lt.-Col. A. J.	... R.F.C.	MATTHEWS, Major H. E.	4/Sussex
COOKE, Capt. P. A.	... /K.R.R.C.	MITCHELL, Capt. J. M. ...	R.A.F.
CREMETTI, Major P. E.	8/R. Scots Fus.	MONTEATH, Sub-Lt. D. T.	R.N.V.R.
DADSON, Major R. T.	... 17/London	NEOBARD, Capt. H. J. C.	7/R. Berks
DANIELL, Lt.-Col. T. E. St. C.	R.F.C.	NEWTON-CLARE, Major H. J.	R.A.F.
DIBBEN, Major C. R.	... 9/Leicester	PADFIELD, Major F. H.	Artists (I.W.T.)
EDGE, Major P. G.	... 2/Artists	RAINSFORD, Capt. G. ...	/R. West Surrey
EDWARDS, Capt. R. O.	Tank Corps, R.E.	STEWART, Lieut. J. ...	2/R. Scots Fus.
FELKIN, Capt. S. D.	... R.N.A.S.	THOMPSON, Lieut. J. B.	5/Border
FIELDING, Capt. W. H.	... R.E.	THOMAS, Capt. P. E. ...	... R.E.
GEDDES, Capt. W. J.	... R.F.A.	WIDDERSON, Capt. A. J.	/Yorkshire L.I.
GIBBS, Capt. G. Y.	... R.A.S.C.	WILKINS, Capt. R. ...	R.A.O.D.
GOSS, Lieut. L. S.	... Surgeon, R.N.	WORSSAM, Major C. A.	R.A.O.D.
GREIG, Capt. D. McN. ...	R.A.F.		

To be Military Members (M.B.E.)

ABBOT-ANDERSON, Capt. L. G.   Artists
ANGELL, Lieut. B. O. ... R.A.F.
BARRACLOUGH, 2/Lt. J. G.   5/R. Fusiliers
BLAIR, 2/Lt. J. M.   5/East Surrey
BLAND, Lieut. A. ... General List
BOND, 2/Lt. C. H. C. ... R.A.S.C.
BROOK, Capt. L. T. ... 1/Lincoln
CAMPBELL, Lieut. G.   8/Northumb. Fus.
CHARNAUD, Capt. F. C.   Intelligence Dept.
CIRCUITT, 2/Lt. C. M. L. ... 16/London
DAND, Lieut. J. H. ... R.F.C.
DUNELL, Capt. A. G. ... R.A.S.C.
DE ST. CROIX, Capt. L. L.   R.A.S.C.
ELLIS, Lieut. H. C. ... R.A.S.C
EVANS, Lieut. B. S.   4/R.West Surrey
FRYER, Lieut. S. E. ... General List
GODFREY, Capt. S. C.   2/R. Scots Fus.
HANDLEY-READ, Capt. E. H.   M.G.C.
HOLLIDGE, Lieut. A.   R.A.S.C. (A.C.C.)

JANSON, Lt. F. E. Jersey Militia (R.A.O.D.)
KEEPING, Capt. H. B. ... R.A.S.C.
MATTHEWS, Lieut. E. F.   2/Shropshire L.I.
MATTHEWS, Capt. T. ... R.G.A.
PHILLIPS, Lieut. E. T. A.   R.G.A.
RUST, Capt. P. ... ... Artists
SMALL, Capt. V. ... 3/Scottish Rifles
STANSFIELD, Major H. ... R.F.C.
SMITH, Lieut. C. E. B. McF. 2/Notts & Derby
TOMSON, Lieut. H. G. ... 1/Suffolk
WALKER, Capt. H. F. ... R.F.C.
WALKER, Capt. R. H. ... R.E.
WEST, Capt. W. G. ... Artists
WESTERN, Lieut. J. G. ... R.A.F.
WHITE, Major B. G. ... R.E. (I.W.T.)
WILLIS, Capt. C. H. S. ... Artists
WITNEY, Capt. J. H. ... R.A.O.C.
WOLFF, Capt. J. D. ... R.G.A.

THE ROYAL VICTORIAN MEDAL.

3164 BALE, Sgt. Frank Stewart
 178 ENGLISH, Sgt. Alfred Cecil

2846 HILL, Sgt. Arthur Bernard
 799 WILLIAMS, Sgt. Gordon

THE DISTINGUISHED CONDUCT MEDAL.

     EMSLIE, Staff-Sergt.-Maj. Peter
 5566 BEDDOW, Cpl. Frank Meyrick
10311 COCKS, Cpl. Frederick Edward

6513 COVIELLO, Cpl. Ambrose
9291 CUTLER, Pte. Henry
6286 FOX, CSM Ernest

THE MILITARY MEDAL.

766852 ALINGTON, Pte. Gervase Winford S.
    "   "   "   " Bar to M.M.
766504 BOVINGTON, Pte. Thomas Pincombe
764631 BROWN, Pte. Robert
  8729 GREENING, Pte. Frank Vernon
 10095 HAWKINS, Cpl. Charles Frederick
766476 HIBBARD, Cpl. Clifford Joseph
  6925 HOPPER, Sgt. George

10099 LLOYD, Pte. Oswald Octavius
766487 ORTON, Cpl. William John
10259 RAYMOND, Cpl. Alfred James
 5963 RIMINGTON, Pte. William
 1916 RISDON, Sgt. Montague Tristram
 4937 ROUTH, Pte. Frank Reginald
765050 SLY, L/Cpl. Harold Frederick
 6684 WALMSLEY, Cpl. Harold

THE MERITORIOUS SERVICE MEDAL.

     PAYTON, RSM William Thomas
 1926 BAX, QMSI William Molyneux
 2903 BLAIKLEY, Sgt. Ernest
764631 BROWN, Pte. Robert
768951 DUNCAN, Sgt. William Gordon
768269 GERHARDI, Sgt. Thomas E.
  211 HACK, RQMS Matthew Starmer

 1521 HARPER, QMSI Hubert Harry
 5507 INGALL, Cpl. Edward Franklin
 2302 PULLEN, CQMS Colin Stuart
  516 SAMSON, CQMS Alfred Joseph
    5 STARTIN, CQMS Eric Charles
 1946 STRODE, Sgt. Julian
10209 THORNE, Col.-Sgt. George Conrad

FOREIGN ORDERS and MEDALS.

Name	Unit	Award	Country
ASHMORE, Lieut. Joseph W.,	R.A.	Croce di Guerra	Italy
BAKER, Capt. Cyril B.,	2/Oxford & Bucks L.I. (R.F.C.)	Croix de Guerre	Belgium
BARKER, Capt. Albert,	R.G.A.	Croix de Guerre	France
BEADLE, Lieut. Leslie A.,	/Warwick	Silver Medal for Valour	Italy
BELL, Capt. David Cockburn,	9/Middlesex	Bronze Medal for Valour	Italy
BIRD, Capt. Arthur Wheen,	R.F.C.	Silver Medal for Valour	Italy
BOBY, Capt. Robert S. P.,	6/Lancashire Fusiliers	Silver Medal for Valour	Italy
BRUCE, Capt. Reginald,	R.E.	Bronze Medal for Valour	Italy
BUXTON, Lieut. Oswald,	/Berks	Bronze Medal for Valour	Italy
CAITHNESS, Capt. Wilfred W.,	R.F.A.	Croce di Guerra	Italy
CANNON, Major Gordon Mewburn,	R.A.O.C.	Croce di Guerra	Italy
CARR, Capt. Matthew,	/R. Scots Fusiliers	Croix de Guerre	France
CARTER, Lieut. Alfred Cecil,	R.A.S.C.	Légion d'Honneur (Chevalier)	France
CHILD, Lt.-Col. A. J.,	R.A.F.	Order of St Maurice & St. Lazarus (Cavaliere)	Italy
CRUICKSHANK, Capt. Eric,	R.A.	Croix de Guerre	France
CUMBERLEGGE, Capt. G. F. G.,	2/Oxford & Bucks L.I.	Croce di Guerra	Italy
DANGERFIELD, Lieut. Paul,	1/East Kent	Legion d'Honneur (Knight)	France
DAVIS, Lieut. Dudley Frederick,	R.F.A.	Ordre du Merite Agricole	France
DUFF, 2/Lt. Gordon,	R.G.A.	Legion d'Honneur (Knight)	France
EDWARDS, Major Reginald O.,	Tank Corps	St. Anne, 2nd Class with Swords	Russia
EMSLIE, Staff-Sgt.-Major Peter,	1/Artists	Medaille Militaire	France
FALCK, 2/Lt. Lionel Louis,	R.F.C.	Croix de Guerre	Belgium
FARRINGTON, Capt. Windham B., D.S.O.,	3/Notts & Derby	Croix de Guerre	France
FELKIN, Capt. Samuel Denys,	R.N.A.S.	Ordre de Leopold (Chevalier)	Belgium
FELLOWS, Lieut. Frank Bennett		Order of Avis	Portugal
FORD, Lieut. Leslie Beaumont,	1/Artists	Order of the Crown (Chevalier)	Roumania
FORTUNE, Lieut. George Edgar	3/West Yorks	Croce di Guerra	Italy
GALLOP, Sgt. Percy Champness,	1/Artists	Croix de Guerre	Belgium
GJERTSEN, Capt. Rudolph,	4/Essex	Croix de Guerre	France
GOLDING, Capt. John, D.S.O.,	R.A.M.C.	Ordre du Merite Agricole (Chevalier)	France
GOODRICK, Capt. M. G.,	R.G.A.	Order of the Nile (4th Class)	Egypt
GOSLETT, Capt. Raymond Gwynne,	R.A.S.C.	Order of El Nahda	King of the Hedjaz
GOULD, Capt. Robert Macdonald,	7/Middlesex	Silver Medal for Valour	Italy
GRAY, Lieut. James,	5/Royal West Surrey	Croix de Guerre	France
GREEN, Capt. William Charles,	1/South Stafford	Croix de Guerre	France
GRIERSON, Capt. Kenneth M.,	22/Manchester	Bronze Medal for Valour	Italy
HARRAP, Lieut. Benjamin Clifford,	R.G.A.	Croix de Guerre	France
HIGHAM, 2/Lt. John Arthur,	R.F.C.	Croix de Guerre	Belgium
HORN, Lieut. Marmaduke Langdale,	R.F.C.	Croix de Guerre	Belgium
HUGHES, Capt. Hugh L. G.,	R.A.M.C.	Croix de Guerre avec Palmes	France
JERMYN, Capt. O. R.,	Forestry Directorate, R.E.	Ordre du Merite Agricole	France
KING, C-S-M Charles William W.,	1/Artists	Bronze Medal for Valour	Italy
KLEIN, Capt. Adrian B. L.,	/Norfolk	Order of St. Stanislaus (3rd Class)	Russia
KNIGHT, Lieut. H. F.,	Special List	Medaille Militaire	France
LAGESSE, Lieut. Camille Henri Raoul,	R.F.C.	Croix de Guerre	France
LEVER, 2/Lt. Ernest Harry,	R.G.A.	Legion d'Honneur (Knight)	France
MACDONALD, 2/Lt. James,	R.F.C.	Bronze Medal for Valour	Italy
MAKALUA, Capt. Matthew James Mannia,	13/Sussex	Croix de Guerre	France

FOREIGN ORDERS AND MEDALS.

MASTERS, Lieut. Ernest Harold, R.A.F.	Croix de Guerre avec Palmes	France
MIEVILLE, Lieut. Arthur Manclark, 2/East Yorks	Silver Medal for Valour	Italy
MITZAKIS, 2/Lt. Albert Victor Marcel, 13/London	Croix de Guerre	France
MURRAY, 2/Lt. George Vernon, /Loyal N. Lancs	Croix de Guerre avec Palmes	France
NATHAN, Lieut. C., 7/Wilts ...	Order of the Crown (Cavaliere)	Italy
NEIGHBOUR, Capt. S. W., 1/Artists	Order of St. Anne	Russia
NEOBARD, Capt. Harold John Cooke, 7/Berks	Legion d'Honneur (Knight)	France
NORRIS, Sgt. Samuel George, 1/Artists ...	Ordre de Leopold (Chevalier)	Belgium
PARKES, C-Q-M-S Norman Eric, 1/Artists ...	Croix de Guerre	France
PARTINGTON, Capt. Leigh, 1/Northumberland Fusiliers	Croix de Guerre	Belgium
PEARCE, Lieut. Cuthbert, R.F.A. ...	Silver Medal for Valour	Italy
PIKE, Lieut. George Brooke, R.A.F. ...	Croix de Guerre avec Etoile	France
POPHAM, Flight-Lt. Arthur Ernest, R.N.A.S. ...	Croix de Guerre	France
PORTERS, Lieut. R. H., Staff	Order of St. Stanislaus (Swords, 3rd Class)	Russia
POWELL, Capt. Walker Philip, /Oxford & Bucks L.I.	Silver Medal for Valour	Italy
REYNOLDS, Capt. Harry N., 7/R. Warwick	Silver Medal for Valour	Italy
ROSS, Lieut. Charles, R.F.C.	Croix de Guerre	France
SANDLAND, Major Kenneth, D.A.D.R.T.	Military Commr., Order of Avis	Portugal
SAUNDERS, Capt. Cornelius James, 24/London ...	Croix de Guerre	Belgium
” ” ” ” ” ...	Croix de Guerre	France
SHEPHERD, 2/Lt. Walter Scott, 2/Wilts ...	Silver Medal for Valour	Italy
SIMS, Capt. Nugent Woolcott, R.G.A. ...	Bronze Medal Al Valore	Italy
SIMMONS, Capt. Frank Keith, 1/Artists 2/Highland L.I.	Croix de Guerre	France
SMITH, 2/Lt. George Ernest, M.C., R.G.A. ...	Croix de Guerre	France
SOLOMON, Major Jerrold Bernard, R.A.F.	Croix de Guerre avec Palmes	France
” ” ” ” ”	Croix de Guerre	Belgium
STAHL, Lieut. Arthur, R.F.A.	Croix de Guerre	Belgium
STEPHENS, Col.-Sgt. W. J., 1/Artists	Medaille Militaire	France
STEVENS, Lieut. William Cecil, 1/Worcester ...	Croix de Guerre	France
STRODE, Capt. Maurice, 2/R. West Surrey	Silver Medal for Valour	Italy
TAYLOR, Lieut. Norman Samuel, R.A.F.	Croce di Guerra	Italy
TAYLOR, 2/Lt. Philip Salmon, Egyptian Labour Corps	Order of the Nile (4th Class)	Egypt
TAYLOR, Cpl. William Joseph, 1/Artists	Croix de Guerre	Belgium
TEMPLE, Lieut. Alfred, R.A.S.C.	Croix de Guerre	Belgium
THOMAS, 2/Lt. Thomas, R.G.A.	Bronze Medal for Military Valour	Italy
VANN, Lt.-Col. Bernard William, V.C., 8/Notts & Derby	Croix de Guerre	France
WEBB, Capt. Walter John, R.E.	Croix de Guerre	France
WHEELER, Capt. William Robert, 22/London ...	Croix de Guerre	Belgium
WILLIAMSON, Capt. William Henry R., R.G.A. ...	Croce di Guerra	Italy
WILSON, Major H. G., 23/London	Order of the Nile	Egypt
WILSON, Lieut. Philip, R.F.C.	Croix de Guerre	France
WOODYEAR, 2/Lt. Reginald Percy, 7/R. West Kent	Croix de Guerre	France
YUILL, Major H. H., R.E.	Croix de Guerre	France

MENTIONED IN DESPATCHES

RECEIVED FROM

ALLENBY, General Sir Edmund H. H.	EGYPT and PALESTINE, 1917/18
CAVAN, General F. R. Earl of	ITALY, 1918
FRENCH, Field-Marshal Sir John D. P.	FRANCE and FLANDERS, 1914/15
HAIG, Field-Marshal Sir Douglas	FRANCE and FLANDERS, 1916/19
HAMILTON, General Sir Ian S. M.	DARDANELLES, 1915/16
HOLMAN, Maj.-Gen. H. C. (with Gen. Denikin)	MURMANSK, ARCHANGEL, 1919
IRONSIDE, Major-General W. E.	NORTHERN RUSSIA, 1919
MARSHALL, Lieut.-General Sir W. R.	MESOPOTAMIA, 1918
MAUDE, Lieut.-General Sir Stanley	MESOPOTAMIA, 1917
MILNE, General Sir G. F.	SALONICA, 1917/18
MONRO, General Sir Charles	DARDANELLES, GALLIPOLI, 1916
MURRAY, General Sir Archibald	EGYPT, 1916/18
NIXON, General Sir John	MESOPOTAMIA, 1916
PLUMER, General Sir Herbert G. O.	ITALY, 1918
POOLE, Major-General F. C.	NORTHERN RUSSIA, 1918
RAWLINSON, General H. S. Lord	NORTHERN RUSSIA, 1919
TOWNSHEND, Major-General C. V. F.	MESOPOTAMIA, 1916
TRENCHARD, Major-General Sir H. M.	INDEPENDENT Air Force R.A.F., 1917/18
VAN DEVENTER, Lieut.-General Sir J. L.	EAST AFRICA, 1918
WINGATE, General Sir F. Reginald	EGYPT, 1916/19

In the following list the Theatre of War in which a Mention was gained is indicated, together with the approximate date, by the surname of the Commander submitting the Despatch. Figures in brackets show the number of times mentioned, if more than one. An asterisk against a number denotes that the Regimental prefix 76 is here omitted (to save space).

1347	Adams, Lieut. A. G.	Milne	1611	Barnett, Capt. H. A.	Haig
4686	Addison, 2/Lt. R., M.C.	,,	5464	Barrow, Lieut. J. H.	,,
2954	Aldous, Lieut. G. J., M.C.	Haig	1236	Barton, 2/Lt. G. S., M.C.	French, Haig
4007	Allen, Lieut. C. J.	,,	3708	Barry, Lieut. E.	Allenby
989	Allen, Capt. F. J.	,,	2328	Base, Major E. G. G.	Haig
3724	Allen, Lieut. H. C., M.C.	,,	4214	Base, Lieut. E. H.	Marshall
868	Ambler, Capt. C.	,,	3940	Baseley, 2/Lt. A. L.	Haig
4798	Andrew, 2/Lt. R. B.W. G., M.C.	Milne	1866	Bate, Capt. R. E. de B.	,,
1915	Andrew, Capt. S. A., D.S.O., M.C.	Haig	3894	Batstone, 2/Lt. R. K.	,,
6836	Archer, Lieut. J.	,,	1662	Baumgarten, Lt. J. M. V.	,,
6552	Ash, Major S. H.	,,	1926	Bax, QMS W. M.	French
9248	Ashford, 2/Lt. F. M.	,,	5333	Beach, 2/Lt. T. S.	Haig
7961	Ashleigh, 2/Lt. B. H. K.	,,	8158	Beadnell, 2/Lt. H. J. L	Allenby
7630	Atchison, 2/Lt. H. P. R.	,,	478	Beaumont, Lieut. E. E.	Haig
4170	Atkinson, Capt. W.	,,	5565	Beauvais, Capt. L.	Allenby
—	Austen, Major E. E., D.S.O.	French	*5494	Bell, 2/Lt. O.	Trenchard
65	Ball, Major S. C., M.C.	Haig	1253	Bennett, 2/Lt. E. P., V.C., M.C.	French
1254	Barber, Capt. B. K. B.	,,	5092	Bennett, 2/Lt. S. E.	Haig
1296	Bare, Capt. A. R., D.S.O., M.C.	Haig(2)	2243	Benson, 2/Lt. O.	,,
8057	Barker, Lieut. A.	Haig	2438	Benson, 2/Lt. R. E.	,,
6840	Barnes, Lieut. A. F.	,,	1558	Bertie, 2/Lt. A. W.	,,

MENTIONED IN DESPATCHES. 153

2980	Bevis, Lieut. L. C. ...	*Haig*
5831	Birch, Major W. K. ...	,,
1463	Birtles, Capt. R. P. ...	,,
1615	Blair, Lieut. J. M. ...	*Marshall*
6371	Blackmore, 2/Lt. O. W. ...	,,
1832	Blackwood, Capt. N. F., D.S.O.	*Haig*
1537	Bonner, Lieut. S. A. ...	,,
2126	Box, 2/Lt. E. H. ...	*Milne*
2635	Boxhall, Capt. F. S. ...	*Haig*
4630	Brasher, Lieut. W. ...	,,
676	Brindley, Capt. S. G. ...	,,
588	Broad, Capt. K. S. ...	,,
932	Broadbridge, Capt. M. O'B.	*French*
2274	Brodrick, Capt. P. ...	*Haig*
8011	Brown, Capt. A. T. ...	,,
3838	Browne, Lieut. A. G. ...	,,
8002	Browne, 2/Lt. W. S. ...	,,
6786	Brumwell, Lieut. B. H. ...	*Marshall*
1505	Bulpitt, 2/Lt. J. ...	*Haig*
6667	Bunce, Capt. W.L. *Ironside, Rawlinson*	
—	Burmann, Capt. R. M., D.S.O.	*French*
	,, ,, ,,	*Haig* (4)
	,, ,,	*Plumer*
3614	Bustard, Capt. F. *Allenby, Murray*	
2606	Butler, Capt. F. W. ...	*Haig*
2452	Buttemer, 2/Lt. E. D. A.	,,
2944	Buxton-Knight, Capt. O.	,,
167	Cahill, Capt. J. A., M.C. ...	*Haig*
2259	Caithness, Capt. W. W. ...	,,
*5681	Cameron, Capt. J. ...	,,
*4684	Campbell, Lieut. A. ...	,,
652	Campbell, Lieut. G. ...	*French*
1166	Cannon, Lieut. H. C.	*French, Haig*
3767	Cardell, Lieut. J. E. ...	*Allenby*
1591	Carr, Capt. M., M.C. ...	*Haig*
7781	Carrington, 2/Lt. C. W., D.S.O.	,,
2315	Carter, Lieut. H. W. ...	,,
2178	Causton, Major D. K. ...	,,
2934	Chase, 2/Lt. G. P. ...	,,
9356	Chadwick, 2/Lt. C. H. ...	,,
780	Chandler, 2/Lt. A. L. ...	,,
3573	Charnaud, Lieut. F. C. ...	*Milne*
—	Chatfeild-Clarke, Lt.-Col. S.	*Haig*
5239	Chatterton, 2/Lt. R. ...	*Milne*
1427	Cheriton, Capt. W. G. L. ...	*Haig*
505	Chetwood, Lieut. E. S. ...	,,
77	Child, Lt.-Col. A. J., M.C., O.B.E.	*Haig*(3)
1833	Circuitt, Capt. C. M. L. ...	*Haig*

9751	Clarke, 2/Lt. H. G. ...	*Haig*
3172	Clarke, Capt. P. L. D.S.O.	,,
7773	Clarke, Lieut. H. E. ...	,,
7589	Clarke, 2/Lt. J. W. ...	,,
3829	Class, Lieut. H. R. ...	,,
710	Clausen, CQMS G. F.	,,
4890	Clayton, Capt. A. O. ...	,,
5680	Clayton, 2/Lt. E. G.	*Allenby*
5113	Clegg, Lieut. W. ...	*Haig*
899	Cliveley, 2/Lt. R. C.	*Hamilton*
3713	Cole, Lieut. P. J. L. ...	*Haig*
1227	Colvin, Capt. A. ...	
1888	Cook, Lieut. C. A. B. ...	*Haig*
6136	Coppock, 2/Lt. H. S. ...	,,
*2363	Corfield, Lieut. F. J. A. ...	*Cavan*
1603	Cottam, 2/Lt. A. E. ...	*Haig*
8687	Coulson, Lieut. C. S. L., D.F.C.	
	Mentioned in French Despatches (2)	
2453	Cowley, Capt. J. N. ...	*Allenby*
3011	Cremetti, Capt. P. E., O.B.E.	*Milne*
5743	Culley, 2/Lt. W. W. B. ...	*Haig*
1889	Cumberlege, Capt. G. F. J., D.S.O.	
		Haig (2)
4925	Cundy, 2/Lt. C. W. ...	*Haig*
1142	Cutting, Major R. H., D.S.O.	*Plumer*
2104	Dadson, Capt. R. T. ...	*Haig*
2365	Dale, 2/Lt. F. J. ...	*French*
7585	Daly, 2/Lt. A. J. ...	*Haig*
1668	Dangerfield, 2/Lt. P. ...	*French*
3691	Deacon, Lieut. E. T. ...	*Haig*
8012	Dean, Capt. H. S. C.	*Rawlinson*
4713	Dean, Capt. W. T. *Ironside, Rawlinson*	
3495	Deedes, Lieut. R. ...	*Haig*
3395	Delafield, Lieut. F. H. ...	,,
3524	Depass, Lieut. R. D. ...	*Milne*
2236	De Ste. Croix, Capt. L. L.	
1715	Done, Lieut. J. P. C. ...	*Haig*
4891	Dowsing, Lieut. S. H.	*Van Deventer*
6733	Driver, Lieut. E. T. ...	*Haig*
7656	Duckworth, Capt. J. E. H.	
6792	Dudley, 2/Lt. H. E. ...	*Haig*
4625	Du Henume, Capt. F. H. ...	,,
1790	Dunbar, Major Sir A. E., M.C.	,,
2663	Dunell, Capt. A. G. ...	,,
964	Durand, Capt. E. D. ...	,,
*5116	Dyall, 2/Lt. A. ...	,,
3791	Edlmann, 2/Lt. E. ...	,,
1634	Edlmann, Major F. J. F., D.S.O.	
		Haig (2)

MENTIONED IN DESPATCHES.

—	Edlmann, Major H. E. ...	*Haig*
4804	Edwards, 2/Lt. C. G., D.S.O.	,,
9688	Edwards, 2/Lt. H. ...	,,
2326	Edwards, Major R. O. ...	*Holman*
6184	Edwards, 2/Lt. W. H. ...	*Haig*
1826	Egerton, Lieut. B. S. ...	,,
1954	Elder, Lieut. A. A. ...	*Milne*
2501	Elkington, Capt. C. G., D.S.O.	*Haig*
5338	Elkington, Lieut. G. L. ...	*Milne*
9382	Ellen, 2/Lt. W. P. ...	*Haig*
1078	Ellis, Capt. R. ...	,,
1931	Elton, Capt. H. S. ...	,,
7809	Fabling, Lieut. H. W. ...	*Marshall*
7462	Fairchild, 2/Lt. J. B. W.	*Haig*
1749	Fairholme, Major H. W.	,,
895	Fairtlough, Lieut. G. H.	,,
6201	Farrant, Lieut. V. T. ...	,,
6987	Farrimond, 2/Lt. W. ...	*Plumer*
2733	Farrington, Capt. W. B., D.S.O.	*Haig*
8093	Fawkes, Capt. F. H. ...	,,
7034	Fellows, Sgt. F. B. ...	,,
1428	Fergusson, 2/Lt. D. G. ...	*French*
*3848	Field, 2/Lt. Edward, D.S.O.	*Haig*
1787	Fielding, Capt. W. H. ...	*Allenby*
1488	Figg, Capt. S. V. ...	*Haig*
2478	Finnis, Capt. W. T. ...	*Marshall*
1810	Fisher, 2/Lt. A. W. ...	*French*
2599	Fischer, Capt. H. C., M.C.	*Haig*
4729	Fisk, Lieut. W. E. ...	,,
2196	Flint, 2/Lt. H. ...	,,
1424	Forbes, 2/Lt. A. ...	*French*
1057	Ford, 2/Lt. R. D. ...	,,
4035	Forrester, Capt. J. ...	*Haig*
3530	Foskett, Lieut. H. H. ...	*Plumer*
9119	Francis, Lieut. I. ...	*Haig*
2698	Franklin-Adams, Major B. J.	*Marshall*
5900	Fraser, Capt. E. A. ...	*Haig*
7561	Fraser, Lieut. G. T. ...	,,
3162	Frater, 2/Lt. A. H.	*Air Ministry*
5841	Freeman, Capt. G. H. ...	*Milne*
4927	Frost, Lieut. A. St. J.	*Earl of Cavan*
6216	Gardner, Capt. H. ...	*Haig*
7303	Gaulder, Lieut. C. W. E.	
2640	Gelsthorpe, 2/Lt. A. M, D.S.O.	
		Haig, Marshall
1549	George, 2/Lt. W. H. ...	*French*
8530	Gibbons, 2/Lt. W. E.	*Earl of Cavan*
383	Gibbs, Lt. G. Y.	*Maude, Marshall*
10062	Gibson, Lieut. J. A. ...	*Marshall*
2605	Gibson, Capt. R. B. ...	*French*
199	Gilks, 2/Lt. H. L. ...	,,
144	Gilks, Capt. H. L., M.C. ...	*Haig*
9727	Girvan, Capt. C. ...	,,
6140	Gjertson, Capt. R., M.C.	,,
5756	Glen, Sgt.-Inst. V. ...	,,
8549	Glenton, Lieut. F. ...	,,
5404	Glover, 2/Lt. C. W. ...	,,
7508	Gluckstein, Lieut. L. H. ...	*Cavan*
1457	Godfrey, Capt. S. C.	*French, Plumer*
1341	Godfrey, 2/Lt. V. ...	
1409	Goldie, Lieut. R. G. ...	*Haig*
1522	Golding, Capt. H. W. ...	,,
3231	Golding, Capt. J., D.S.O.	*French, Haig*
—	Goldthorpe, Lt.-Col. R. A., D.S.O.	*Haig*
1606	Goodman, 2/Lt. R. M. ...	*French*
5999	Goodway, Capt. H. W. ...	*Haig*
6256	Gordon, Lieut. S. R. ...	*Allenby*
*5975	Gordon, 2/Lt. A. H. ...	,,
2240	Goslett, Capt. R. G.	*Wingate*(2)
3508	Gotch, 2/Lt. D. I. ...	*Haig*
682	Gould, Sgt.-Inst. J. R. S.	,,
4158	Gould, 2/Lt. L. C. ...	*Plumer*
2173	Gould, Capt. W. S. ...	*Marshall*
1378	Granger, 2/Lt. E. E. W.	*Haig*
—	Greenwood, Lt.-Col. C. F. H., D.S.O.	
		Haig(3)
6000	Greenwood, Lieut. C. ...	*Marshall*
753	Grice, Sgt.-Inst. A. N. ...	*Haig*
3343	Grierson, Capt. K. McI. D.S.O.	*Cavan*
3275	Griffin, Lieut. A. E. ...	*Haig* (2)
1570	Griffin, Staff-Lt. S. W. ...	*Haig*
6278	Gunn, Lieut. H. J. ...	,,
8315	Guttridge, Lieut. J. F. ...	*Plumer*
211	Hack, RQMS M. S. ...	*Haig*
9059	Haddon, Capt. B. L.	*Anti-Aircraft*
2569	Haggis, Sgt. Bernard ...	*Cavan*
2796	Hale, Lieut. G. T. ...	*Haig*
5258	Hall, Capt. A. L. ...	,,
1398	Hall, 2/Lt. L. E. ...	*French*
1422	Hallowes, 2/Lt. R. P., V.C.	,,
1333	Halse, Lieut. E. A. ...	*Hamilton*
5121	Hanna, 2/Lt. W. H. ...	*Haig*
965	Hare, 2/Lt. B. U. ...	*French*
5442	Harris, Lieut. J. L. ...	*Haig*
1521	Harper, CQMSI H. H.	,,
2547	Harris, Lieut. C. R. ...	*Marshall*
2783	Harrison, Capt. W. R. E., D.S.O.	
		Haig, Marshall

MENTIONED IN DESPATCHES.

6802	Hart, 2/Lt. E. J.		*Haig*
454	Hart, 2/Lt. J. A.		*Milne*
1839	Hartopp, Capt. C. W. E. C.		*Haig*
4659	Harvey, 2/Lt. A., D.S.O.		*Haig*
2034	Harvey-James, Capt. A. K.		,,
2455	Harwood, Lieut. A. W.		*Plumer*
2620	Haskins, 2/Lt. L. J.	...	*Haig*
4640	Hayes, 2/Lt. A. P.	...	,,
4676	Henderson, 2/Lt. C. E., D.S.O.		,,
10365	Henderson, Cpl. C. R.	...	,,
1828	Henderson, Capt. E. J., D.S.O.		*Haig*
2770	Hendry, Lieut. H. D.	...	*Milne*
*5620	Herron, Capt. R. W. C.		*Haig*
2721	Hetherington, 2/Lt. E. C.		,,
1388	Hewitt, Capt. M. B.		,,
1552	Hibbert, Capt. J. G., M.C.		*Haig*
2459	Hichens, Lieut. B. S.	...	*Allenby*
8003	Hide, 2/Lt. J. B.	...	*Haig*
4827	Higham, 2/Lt. J. A.	...	,,
1987	Hill, 2/Lt. A. D.	...	*French*
6402	Hill, 2/Lt. T. G.	...	*Haig*
2046	Hillyer, Lieut. W. H.	...	*French*
2914	Hingley, Lt.-Col. A. N., D.S.O.		*Haig*
4562	Hitchcock, Lieut. L.	...	*Marshall*
3781	Hoare, Capt. W. J. G., D.S.O.		*Haig* (2)
2261	Hobbs, Lieut. W.	...	*Haig*
2334	Hobson, Major H. R., D.S.O.		*Milne*
4599	Holroyd, Capt. V. H.	...	*Haig*
*5882	Hope, Lieut. H. J.	...	,,
3835	Hopwood, Capt. J., M.C.	...	,,
1115	Horley Capt. C. R.	...	,,
1446	Horsfall, 2/Lt. A. M.	...	*French*
1437	Horsley, 2/Lt. O.	...	,,
8029	Howard, Lieut. A.	...	*Haig*
1721	Howard, 2/Lt. E. H.	...	,,
2318	Howard, Major H. L.	...	*Haig* (2)
1004	Hughes, Capt. H. A. M.		*Milne*
890	Hughes, Capt. H. L. G., D.S.O.		
1700	Hughes, 2/Lt. T. McK.		*Haig*
806	Hunter, Major A. P.	...	,,
1380	Hurt, Capt. W. G.		*West Africa*
1676	Hyams, Lieut. G.	...	*Haig*
5507	Ingall, Cpl. E. F.	...	,,
8132	Ivens, Lieut. F. B.	...	,,
1338	Ivory, Capt. H. F.		*Haig, Cavan*
1748	James, Capt. G.	...	*Haig*
3262	Jameson, Lieut. R. H.	...	,,
5127	Jefferys, Capt. A. H.	...	,,
584	Jerwood, Capt. E. L.	...	*French*
5206	Johnson, Capt. C. B.	...	*Haig*
295	Jones, 2/Lt. C. T.	...	*French*
5446	Jones, Lieut. H. N.	...	*Allenby*
3608	Jones, Lieut. P. H.	..	*Haig*
7655	Jones, 2/Lt. R. R., D.S.O.		,,
7451	Jones, 2/Lt. W. H.	...	,,
7116	Jull, 2/Lt. R. C.	...	*Milne*
3550	Jupp, 2/Lt. J. M. S.		*Haig*
6357	Justice, 2/Lt.. W. B.	...	,,
6011	Kendon, 2/Lt. G.	...	,,
173	Kibble, Lieut. A. W.	...	,,
2831	King, 2/Lt. B. E.		*Murray*
3642	King, 2/Lt. M., D.S.O.	...	*Haig*
5912	Ladell, 2/Lt. C. S.	...	,,
*6025	Lagesse, Capt. C. H. R., D.F.C.		,,
4441	Laithwaite, 2/Lt. A., D.S.O.		,,
3734	Lambert, 2/Lt. C. O.	...	,,
3643	Land, CSM L. F.	...	,,
953	Last, Capt. E. R.	...	,,
3039	La Touche, Capt. A. P. H.		,,
1447	Lawless, Capt. P. H.	...	,,
2241	Lawrence, Capt. J. H. (2)		,,
3371	Leake, Capt. G. E. A., D.S.O.		,,
—	Lefroy, Major T. E.	...	,,
2257	Leftwich, Capt. N. G.	..	,,
7874	Leith, 2/Lt. G. H.	...	,,
5958	Lever, Capt. E. H.		*Plumer*
4615	Liddell, Lieut. A. R.	...	*Haig*
893	Liddle, Capt. D., M.P.	...	,,
8115	Lloyd, 2/Lt. G. L.	...	,,
1847	Lloyd-Jones, Lieut. J.	...	*French*
4122	Long, Lieut. T. D.	...	*Haig*
5270	Loveless, Capt. R. B.	...	,,
5314	Lowe, Capt. J. L.	...	,,
2801	Lupton, Lieut. L.	...	,,
*5017	Lyon, 2/Lt. F. T. B.	...	,,
1744	Mackintosh, 2/Lt. H. L.		*French*
3363	McCann, Lieut. W. J.	..	*Allenby*
4785	McCorquodale, 2/Lt. G. M.		*Milne*
9336	McDowall, 2/Lt. R. A.	...	*Haig*
2690	McKeever, Lieut. G. N.		,,
8833	McKie, Lieut. R. D.	...	,,
1989	Maddock, Capt. R. H.	...	*French*
854	Maile, Capt. W. S.	...	*Haig*
5021	Maingot, Capt. P. S.	...	*Hamilton*
1396	Mann, 2/Lt. F. R.		*Hamilton*
2217	Mann, Capt. P. R.	...	*Haig*

MENTIONED IN DESPATCHES.

4882	Marrable, Lieut. C. G. ...	Haig		6548	O'Brien, Capt. J., M.C. ...	Allenby
1405	Marshall, Lieut. O. F. B.	Milne		1449	Oldfield, 2/Lt. R. T.	French, Haig
1848	Martin, Lieut. E. A.	Haig, Cavan		—	Ostle, Lt.-Col. H. K. E., M.C.	,, ,,
4392	Martin, Lieut. R. D. ...	Haig		9662	Ord, Capt. H. E. M. ...	Haig
6766	Mason, 2/Lt. F. ...	Cavan		2111	Page, Capt. W. I. P. G. ...	
2920	Massy-Burnside, Capt. G. E.	Haig		1154	Paine, 2/Lt. G. G. ...	French
9618	Mathias, 2/Lt. D. E.	Milne		1981	Palmer, Capt. W. W. ...	Haig
2040	Matthews, Lieut. E. F. ...	,,		5985	Parker, Lieut. A. A. F. ...	,,
—	May, Lt.-Col. H. A. R., C.B.	French		3620	Parker, Capt. F. G. ...	,,
2392	Merfield, Lieut. S. H. ...	Haig		608	Parkes, 2/Lt. H. F. ...	French
1390	Messom, 2/Lt. H. ...	French		1527	Partington, Capt. L. ...	Haig
2409	Micklem, Major C., D.S.O.	Haig		6653	Paterson, 2/Lt. R. F. ...	,,
1110	Mieville, Lieut. A. M. ...	Milne		3601	Pattison, Capt. R. ...	,,
745	Mieville, Capt. W. S. ...	Haig		7973	Pearson, 2/Lt. A. M. W. ...	,,
2697	Middleton, Capt. S. ...	,,		2249	Pearson, 2/Lt. R. O. ...	French
1368	Miles, Capt. L. G., D.S.O.	Haig		1052	Penrose, Capt. G. A. ...	Haig
4662	Miller, Lieut. J. A. ...	Cavan		8039	Pepper, Lieut. W. A. ...	,,
3081	Miller, Lieut. J. G. R. ...	Haig		3611	Perkins, 2/Lt. L. ...	,,
5707	Miller, Lieut. R. A. ...	,,		2466	Perry, Capt. G. M. ...	,,
*5561	Miller, 2/Lt. T. S. ...	Marshall		5213	Perry, 2/Lt. P. R. W. ...	,,
3579	Milligan, Capt. A. ...	Haig		1414	Petherbridge, Capt. C. A.	,,
1125	Minshull, Capt. J. L. ...	,,		1846	Phipps, Lieut. P. ...	,,
7455	Mitzakis, 2/Lt. A. V. M.	,,		6475	Piper, 2/Lt. N. ...	,,
1462	Molyneux, Capt. E. S. ...	,,		7660	Plant, 2/Lt. H. N. ...	Plumer
—	Money, Capt. D. F. ...	,,		2842	Pollard, Capt. J. L. ...	Haig
912	Moody, Capt. P., M.C.	French, Haig		2286	Popham, Capt. A. E.	Air Ministry
734	Moore, Capt. H. E., D.S O.	French, Haig		5073	Powell, 2/Lt. W. P. ...	Haig
2895	Moore, Capt. J. L. M. ...	,,		5705	Price, Capt. B. P. ...	Marshall
2648	Moore, Lt.-Col. R. F., D.S.O.	Haig		3935	Price, 2/Lt. F. M. ...	Haig
4063	Moore, Capt. W. J. ...	,,		8600	Priestley, Lieut. L. S. ...	,,
3910	Mordecai, 2/Lt. L. R. ...	,,		1468	Priday, 2/Lt. A. K. ...	,,
1451	Morris, 2/Lt. F. B. ...	,,		3008	Prosser, 2/Lt. A. E. ...	French
3956	Morris, 2/Lt. T. B. ...	,,		6120	Pykett, Lieut. G. F. ...	Plumer
2613	Morton, Lieut. W. C. ...	,,		1160	Quare, Capt. H. A. B. ...	,,
4173	Mouldey, 2/Lt. W. E. ...	,,		7617	Quick, Sgt. S. ...	Haig
81	Munt, Major E. ...	,,		6770	Radford, 2/Lt. J. A. ...	,,
2745	Myers, Capt. D. ...	,,		3789	Raikes, Lieut. A. F. M.	,,
823	Naylor, Capt. T. H. ...	,,		2018	Randall, Lieut. D. M. ...	,,
7135	Neal, Lieut. L. ...	Cavan		5537	Rayner, Capt. R. S. ...	,,
1112	Neale, Capt. G. B. ...	Haig		1244	Reed, 2/Lt. D. L. ...	,,
—	Neighbour, Capt. S. W.			5871	Reed, Lieut. W., M.C. ...	,,
		Haig (2), Rawlinson		2323	Rhodes, Lieut. D., M.C.	,,
2366	Neobard, Capt. H. J. C.	Milne		3360	Rhodes, Lieut. H. ...	,,
3177	Nettleton, 2/Lt. J. ...	Haig		6693	Richardson, Lieut. H. B.	,,
6115	Newman, 2/Lt. C. E. S.	,,		2578	Rix, Capt. L. G. ...	,,
3533	Newton, Capt. C. V., M.C.	Haig (3)		8678	Roberts, Capt. J. ...	,,
5862	Noble, Capt. J. M. ...	Haig		262	Robertson, Major C. B.	Marshall
1963	Oakey, Lieut. J. M. ...	,,		6123	Robertson, Lieut. R. J.	Haig

MENTIONED IN DESPATCHES. 157

1213	Robey, 2/Lt. A. E. L.	*Marshall*
3986	Robinson, Capt. E. A. K.	*Haig*
5030	Robinson, Capt. F. W. ...	*Haig*
1617	Robinson, Capt. W. P. ...	,,
165	Rogers, Capt. C. M. ...	,,
898	Roscoe, Lieut. W. ...	,,
1624	Rosher, Lt. Col. J. B., D.S.O.	*Haig* (4)
3151	Ross, 2/Lt. W. J. E.	*Haig*
6961	Roussiano, Lieut. T. ...	*Milne*
*6791	Roxburgh, 2/Lt. J. A. ...	*Haig*
1240	Rundell, Capt. L. E., M.C.	,,
8072	Sagar, Capt. A. L., D.S.O.	,,
3288	Salmon, 2/Lt. M. W.	*French, Haig*
1183	Sanderson, Lieut. H. F.	*Haig*
6339	Sands, 2/Lt. G. F. ...	,,
58	Saunders, Capt. C. J. (3)	,,
1455	Saunders, Capt. J. A. ...	*Milne*
2123	Saxon, Major V. D. J. ...	*Haig*
1732	Scoones, 2/Lt. T. C. ...	*French*
2116	Scott, Capt. C. E. ...	*Haig*
819	Scrutton, Major A. E. ...	,,
329	Scrutton, 2/Lt. J. A. ...	*French*
7761	Searle, 2/Lt. W. D. W. ...	*Plumer*
1612	Seeman, Major F. H. ...	*Haig*
2232	Selfe, 2/Lt. E. D. ...	,,
274	Seymour, Lieut. J. ...	,,
1163	Shanks, Capt. M. H. ...	
1536	Shepherd, Major W. S., M.C.	*Haig*
1018	Sherlock, 2/Lt. C. C.	,,
7706	Sherwin, 2/Lt. H. C. ...	,,
2805	Short, Capt. J. R., M.C. ...	
3612	Silcock, 2/Lt. B. B.	*Hamilton*
6730	Silk, 2/Lt. E. ...	*Haig*
2607	Simeon, Capt. C. B. ...	,,
—	Simmons, Cpt. F. K.	*French* (2) *Haig* (2)
2591	Simpson, 2/Lt. H. G.	*Hamilton*
*4911	Simson, Lieut. J. H. ...	*Haig*
724	Skevington, Lieut. A. P.	,,
6080	Slattery, Lieut. F. J. ...	,,
8534	Small, Capt. V.	*Rawlinson, Poole, Ironside*
9041	,, ,, ,, ,, Smith, 2/Lt. A. E. ...	*Haig*
8662	Smith, Major H. C. ...	,,
6320	Smith, 2/Lt. R. M. ...	,,
929	Smith, Lt.-Col. W. C. M.C.	*Haig* (2)
3252	Smith, Lieut. W. T. ...	*Haig*
*6664	Snowden, 2/Lt. W. C. ...	,,
375	Solomon, Capt. J. B. ...	,,
6944	Southam, Sub-Lt. A. W.	*Admiralty*
8807	Spafford, 2/Lt. A. V. ...	*Haig*
86	Sprawson, Capt. E. C. ...	*French*
2926	Stahl, Lieut. A. ...	*Haig*
6930	Stace, Capt. J. A. ...	,,
1997	Stanesby, Lieut. R. W. J. ...	,,
9991	Stark, Lieut. J. D. ...	,,
7162	Stansfield, Major H., M.B.E.	,,
2373	Stephens, L/Cpl. W. J. ...	,,
1608	Stephenson, 2/Lt. K. L.	*French*
2977	Sterndale-Bennett, Comdr. W., D.S.O. *Munro, Haig* (2)	
3340	Stevens, Capt. H. J. H.	*Van Deventer*
458	Stevenson, Lieut. A. F. ...	*Monro*
2785	Stewart, Sgt. J. D. ...	*Haig*
1717	Storey, 2/Lt. K. ...	*French*
5324	Strang, Lieut. W. ...	*Allenby*
6629	Stratton, Lieut. G. L., M.C.	*Marshall*
1946	Strode, Sgt. J. ...	*French, Haig*
1071	Suckling, Sgt. P. H. ...	*Haig*
3111	Suiter, Capt. C. R. ...	,,
7949	Summerfield, Capt. A. B.	*Marshall*
8069	Summersell, 2/Lt. J. G. ...	*Allenby*
4103	Sutcliffe, Lieut. F. ...	,,
6713	Symons, Capt. J. R. ...	*Haig*
2141	Taplin, Capt. G. A. ...	,,
1467	Tapper, Capt. M. T. ...	,,
1932	Taylor, Capt. B. M., D.S.O., M.C.	*French, Haig*
*4726	Taylor, Lieut. J. F. ...	*Haig*
*6235	Taylor, 2/Lt. P. S. ...	*Murray*
6367	Thomas, Lieut. P. E. ...	*Haig*
1225	Thompson, Capt. A. J., D.S.O., M.C.,	*French, Haig* (2), *Plumer*
1038	Thompson, 2/Lt. C. E., D.S.O., M.C.	*Haig* (3)
3783	Thompson, 2/Lt. C. V.	*Maude*
599	Thorne, Lieut. P. H. ...	*Haig*
*6292	Thrippleton, 2/Lt. H. ...	,,
6163	Tidy, Lieut. J. O. ...	,,
3126	Tilley, Capt. J. E. ...	,,
1956	Toller, Lieut. W. G. ...	,,
9010	Tooley, 2/Lt. R. F. ...	,,
1768	Treatt, Capt. C. C. ...	*Allenby*
4208	Treloar, Capt. G. D., D.S.O.	*Haig*
7334	Truman, Major E. D. ...	*Maude*
7988	Truscott, 2/Lt. M. J. ...	*Haig*
1177	Tucker, Capt. N. P. ...	*Milne*

MENTIONED IN DESPATCHES.

*4803	Turnbull, Lieut. M.	...	*Haig*
7361	Turnbull, 2/Lt. M.	...	,,
1190	Turner, Lieut. H. K.	...	*French*
1275	Tweedie-Smith, 2/Lt. A.		*Haig*
—	Tyer, Capt. A. A.	*French,*	*Haig* (2)
7794	Van-der-Noot, 2/Lt. H. E.		*Haig*
1800	Vann, Capt. B. W., V.C., M C.		*French*
,,	,, ,, ,, ,,		*Haig*
2823	Vaughan, Lieut. F. S.	...	*Allenby*
4293	Vernon, 2/Lt. H. R.	...	*Haig*
216	Vincent, 2/Lt. E. S.	...	*Maude*
*4804	Vincent, 2/Lt. J.	...	*Haig*
7828	Wailes, Capt. F. G.	...	,,
7297	Walby, 2/Lt. H. C., D.S.O.		,,
1865	Wakeley, 2/Lt. J. E. S. ..		.,
905	Walker, Lieut. R. H.	...	*Marshall*
1796	Wallis, Sgt. A. O. S.	...	*French*
3815	Ward, Capt. N. G.		*Haig*
2337	Warren, Capt. A. N.	...	,,
2614	Watson, Major T. W.	...	,,
5084	Watt, 2/Lt. J. M.	...	,,
2486	Watts, Lieut. H. L.	..	,,
3303	Weale, Lieut. W. W. C.	...	*Allenby*
5459	Weaver, Capt. F., M.C.	...	*Haig*
2902	Webb, 2/Lt. R. D. A.	...	,,
8278	Webb, Capt. H. F.	...	,,
2826	Webb, Capt. W. J.	*French,*	*Haig*
7676	Webber, 2/Lt. W. J.	...	*Haig*
1121	Weber-Brown, Capt. W. A.		,,
1945	Wenyon, Capt. H. J., D.S.O.		,,
1399	West, Capt. F.	...	*Plumer*
3373	Westlake, Sgt. A. M.	...	*Haig*
1241	Weston, Sgt. D. G.	..	*Haig* (2)
6505	Whitaker, 2/Lt. G. M.	...	*Haig*
2876	Whiteaway, Major E. G. L.		,,
2540	Wilkins, Capt. R.	...	,,
1030	Willans, Capt. H., D.S.O., M.C.		*French*
,,	,, ,, ,, ,,		*Plumer*
5302	Williams, Capt. L. E.	...	*Haig*
2059	Williams, 2/Lt. W. T.	...	*French*
1972	Williamson, Lieut. W. H. R.		*Plumer*
1155	Willis, Sgt. C. R.	...	*French*
1497	Wilson, Major H. G.	...	*Haig*
7932	Winkworth, Lieut. S.		*Air Ministry*
3242	Witcombe, Cpl. S. F.	...	*French*
2654	Wood, Major P. N.	...	*Monro*
4946	Woolveridge, 2/Lt. C. L.		*Haig*
6610	Worrall, 2/Lt. S.	...	,,
6782	Wrightson, Lieut. E., D.S.O.		*Cavan*
5763	Wynne, Lieut. R. B.	...	*Haig*
8165	Wyrall, 2/Lt. E.		..
3393	Yuill, Lieut. H. H., D.S.O., M.C.		
		French,	*Haig* (3)

ADDENDA :—

BROUGHT TO NOTICE.

(Secretary of State's Mentions.)

For Distinguished Services rendered in connection with the War.

Shirley, Lieut.-Col. William, C.M.G. ... ... Artists' Rifles

For Valuable Services rendered in connection with the War.

Horsley, Colonel Walter Charles, V.D.   Artists' Rifles ; Town Major, Englebelmer
Shaw, Lieut.-Col. Edward St. Lawrence (2) ... 1/E. Surrey : No. 15 (Artists' Rifles) O.C.B.
Shirley, Lieut.-Col. Herbert J., C.M.G. ... 1/Artists : 5/Lancashire Fusiliers : R.A.M.C.

Abbot-Anderson, Capt. L. G. ...	Artists	Homewood, Lieut. T. S. ...	R.G.A.
Alliston, Lieut. G.	10/E. Surrey (Staff)	Horsburgh, Capt. A. L. ...	8/London
Anns, Capt. H. F. ...	25/London	Hutchinson, Capt. N. W. ...	R.A S.C.
Armour, Lieut. W. N. McS. ✠	16/H.L.I.	Jennings, Capt. J. W. ...	R.A.F.
Balfour, 2/Lt. C. G. C.	Coldstream Gds.	Keene, 2/Lt. G. G. ...	R.A.O.D.
Barugh, Lieut. W. H. ...	4/Northumb. Fus.	Layborn, Lieut. T. A. E. ...	R.A.F.
Binder, Capt. A. E. L. ...	7/Worcester	Lee, 2/Lt. E. J.	1/Lancashire Fus.(M.G.C.)
Blomfield, Capt. C. J. ...	Artists	Lock, RSM H. (2)	Rifle Brigade (Artists)
Blundell, Major A. H. ...	Artists	Maynard, Capt. F. G. ...	8/Lincoln
Carter, 2/Lt. H. S. ...	5/R. West Kent	Meredith, Lieut. R. S. ...	R.A.O.D.
Chapman, 2/Lt. H. E. S. ...	R.A.O.D.	Mitchell, Capt. J. M. ...	R.A.F.
Chatham, Lt. R. F.	4/Oxford & Bucks L.I.	Moore, Lieut. L. P. ...	Artists
Coleman, Capt. R. ...	Artists	Mundy, Lieut. W. F.	Highland L.I.
Collett, Major F. G. ...	R.A.O.D.	Nathan, Sergt. J.	Artists
Collins, Capt. A. J. ...	30/Middlesex	Newton, Capt. A. R. ...	2/Devon
Cooper, Capt. D. J. ...	Artists	Newton, Capt. C. E. ...	Artists
Cory, CSM R.	Artists	Oram, Major R. G. ...	9/London
Cowling, Capt. J. A. ...	R.A.F.	Price, Capt. D.	R.A.F.
Drewry, Col.-Sergt. A. S. (2)	Artists	Roberts, Lieut. E. R. ...	10/London
Edwards, Capt. G. C. (2) ...	Artists	Sargant, Capt. F. H. St. C.	R.A.F.
Ellis, Lieut. C. V. ...	25/London	Smith, Sergt. A. V. ...	17/O.C.B.
Fairhurst, 2/Lt. W. E. ...	4/Essex	Stafford, Capt. L. H. G. ...	10/London
Farrier, 2/Lt. A. V.	5/D.C.L.I. (R.F.C.)	Tate, Lieut. A. F. ...	Labour Corps
Farrow, Lieut. J. W. ...	R.A.O.D.	Thompson, Capt. J. B. ...	Border
Garner, Lieut P. R. ...	R.F.C.	Turnbull, Capt. R. F. ...	Artists
Gemmell, Lieut. J. A. B.	1/L. North Lancs	Walker, Lieut. A. F. C. ...	Artists
Giles, Lieut. M. H. ...	3/South Lancs	Wallis, Lieut. L. P. ...	R.A.F.
Glibbery, CQMS H. E. ...	Artists	Watts, Capt. H. C. ...	24/London
Goss, Lieut. L. S. ...	Surgeon R.N.	Whinney, Capt. C. T. ✠ ...	11/Middlesex
Grant, Major J. ...	3/Highland L.I.	White, Major B. G. ...	R.E.
Hawkesford, RSM F. H. ...	Artists	Willis, Capt. C. H. S. ...	Artists
Hawkesford, Major F. H. ...	R.A.F.	Wood, Lieut. P. N. ...	R.F.A.
Heyes, Capt. L. ...	1/R. West Surrey	Wykes, Capt. R. A. ...	3/Devon

ADDENDA:—

SECTION III.

ROLL OF COMMISSIONS
GAZETTED SINCE 4TH AUGUST, 1914.

THE REGIMENTAL PLEDGE.	ITS FULFILMENT.
In Parliament: A.D. 1909.	In the Field: 1914—1918.

Commands and Staff	67
Royal Air Force	936
Regular Regiments	1,635
Special Reserve	608
Territorial Force	2,661
New Armies	3,090
Other Arms and Units	1,259
Total Officers	10,256

"THE ARTISTS."

Mr. W. F. D. SMITH (U.) asked the Secretary for War if the Artists Corps was to be reduced to 400 men; whether the corps at present had 700 men in the ranks; and when was the decision to effect the reduction arrived at?

Mr. HALDANE: After careful consideration it has been decided that if this unit can undertake that a percentage of its members will be prepared to join the Territorial Force as officers, if required, on mobilisation, the War Office will be justified in giving the corps in exchange for this undertaking a full establishment of eight companies. The strength of this unit on June 1 amounted to 25 officers and 637 non-commissioned officers and men.

Major ANSTRUTHER-GRAY: May I ask what percentage was asked for?

Mr. HALDANE: We have not stated that so far: we will settle it afterwards. I have reason to think that this arrangement will be agreeable to the Corps.

(including practically the whole of the Establishment of 8 companies serving at date of Mobilisation).

ROLL OF COMMISSIONS.

Abbreviations made use of :—

K/A—Killed in Action.   P/W—Prisoner of War.   ꟽ—Mentioned.
Acc/K—Accidentally Killed.   w—Wounded.   ✠—Military Cross.
D/W—Died of Wounds.   d—Died.   F/D—Foreign Decoration.

The name of a Regiment, or number of a Battalion, in brackets, indicates that the Officer was attached to such second unit.

The rank given in the right-hand column is the highest attained, whether Permanent, Temporary, Acting or otherwise.

COMMANDS AND STAFF.

	Lieut.	BURMANN, Robert Moyle, D.S.O. ✠	Staff-Capt., 20/Inf. Brigade, ꟽ(6)
3614	Pte.	BUSTARD, Frank, O.B.E.	Asst. Embarkation Staff-Officer, Major, ꟽ(2)
2072	,,	CHRISTMAS, Dudley Vyvyan	Staff-Capt.
3011	,,	CREMETTI, Paul Eugene, O.B.E.	Major D. A. A. G., ꟽ(2)
2034	,,	HARVEY-JAMES, Arthur Keedwill	Staff-Capt.
	Capt.	SIMMONS, Frank Keith ✠, M.V.O., F/D	Staff-Lt. G.H.Q., Brig.-Major, ꟽ
375	Sgt.	SOLOMON, Jerrold Bernard ✠, F/D	Brigade-Major, ꟽ
3100	Pte.	ALLISTON, Geoffrey	Staff-Capt., War Office, ꟽ
1832	,,	BLACKWOOD, Neville Foster	R.T.O. Capt., ꟽ
1537	,,	BONNER, Stanley Abbott, O.B.E.	R.T.O. Major, ꟽ
3128	,,	BOVET, Verner Charles Aloys	R.T.O. Capt.
2178	,,	CAUSTON, Dudley Knight	R.T.O. Major, ꟽ
3573	,,	CHARNAUD, Frederick Christian, M.B.E.	Interpreter (Intelligence) Capt., ꟽ
471	Sgt.	DE PURY, Charles Frederick	R.T.O. Staff-Lieut.
1016	Corpl.	ELLIOTT, Harold Ferox	R.T.O. Capt.
248	Sgt.	FRY, George Charles Lovell	R.T.O. Lieut.
1549	,,	GEORGE, Walter Hope ✠	Special Appointment. Major, ꟽ
1570	,,	GRIFFIN, Sydney William	Interpreter (Intelligence Dept.) ꟽ
1839	Corpl.	HARTOPP, Charles W. E. Cradock	R.T.O. Capt., ꟽ
2835	Pte.	HERVEY, George Arthur Kenneth	R.T.O. Capt.
806	Sgt.	HUNTER, Arthur Percival	R.T.O. Major, ꟽ
2644	Pte.	NOAD, Colin Kenneth	Staff-Lieut.
1183	,,	SANDERSON, Harold Francis	R.T.O. Lieut., ꟽ
3172	Pte.	SANDLAND, Kenneth	R.T.O. Major
1196	L/Cpl.	WOLSTENHOLME, John Bernard W.	R.T.O. Lieut.
2880	Pte.	ANNS, Harold Falkner	Staff-Lieut., ꟽ
1296	,,	BARK, Alfred Raymond, D.S.O. ✠	Staff-Capt., ꟽ
761110	Cpl.	BIRCH, Wm. Kenning, O.B.E.	Major, ꟽ
3569	Pte.	BOOTH, Edward Arthur	Staff-Lieut.
2126	,,	BOX, Ernest Hyatt	Staff-Capt., ꟽ
63610	,,	BROWN, Lionel, M.B.E.	Capt., Directorate of Labour
2345	,,	BURBURY, Arthur Vivian ✠	Staff-Lieut.
4410	,,	CAFFAREY, Bernard James	Staff-Capt.
1548	CQMS	CHETWOOD, Henry John	Staff-Lieut. 1stClass, D.G.T.R.T.E.
64950	Pte.	CLOUTTE, Herbert James	Specially Employed; 2/Lt.

COMMANDS AND STAFF. 163

4360	Pte.	CUCKNEY, Ernest John, D.S.C.	...	*Staff-Lieut.*
8168	Sgt.	DANIELL, Thos. Edw. St. Clare ✠, O.B.E.		*Lt.-Col., Dir. of Equipment*
768535	Sgt.	DICKS, Henry Victor ...	...	*Specially Employed; 2/Lt.*
8225	L/Cpl.	DIX, John Wellington ...	...	*Staff-Lieut., West African F.F.*
1097	Sgt.	EATON, John Edward Caldwell	...	*Staff-Lieut.*
1765	Pte.	FARMER, Horace Edwin	...	*Staff-Capt.*
2905	Sgt.	FORD, Leslie Beaumont	...	*Staff-Lieut.; A.D.C.*
7822	Pte.	FRYER, Sidney Ernest, M.B.E.	...	*Staff-Lieut.*
61	Sgt.	FURZE, Gordon ✠ ...	...	*Staff-Capt., 2/Guards' Brigade*
768317	Pte.	GARDNER, Oswald J. ...	...	*Education Officer; Lieut.*
2240	,,	GOLDSCHMIDT, Harold Henry Arthur	...	*Staff-Lieut.*
763298	,,	GRAHAM, James ...	*Staff-Lieut.; Employed War Office*
2334	,,	HOBSON, Harry Royd, D.S.O.	...	*Lieut.-Col., A.A.Q.M.G.,* 🎖
765902	Lieut.	HALKETT, Guy Wallace ...	...	*Brigade Major*
2255	Pte.	HOLLIS, Henry Lewis ...	...	*Major, D.A.Q.M.G.*
765577	,,	JERMYN, Oliver Reynolds	...	*Capt., Forestry Directorate*
761297	RSM	LOVELL, George Herbert	...	*Major, D.A.D.O.S.,* 🎖
5774	Pte.	LESLIE-SMITH, James ...	...	*Staff-Capt.*
14447	,,	LAWLESS, Philip Henry ✠	...	*Major, D.A.A.G.,* 🎖
2475	,,	MAKALUA, Matthew James, O.B.E., F/D	...	*Major, D.A.D.M.*
998	,,	MARTIN, Victor Callingham	...	*Staff-Capt.*
2895	,,	MOORE, John Leslie Mackenzie ✠, 🎖	...	*R.T.O., Capt.*
4394	,,	OUTLAW, William Henry	*Asst. Director Local Resources; Major*
231	Lieut.	PINDER-BROWN, Henry ...	...	*R.T.O., Capt.*
7266	Sgt.	PORTERS, Robert Halsted, M.B.E., F/D	...	*Staff-Lieut.*
7196	Pte.	POTTS, Francis Sidney ...	...	*Staff-Lieut.*
766286	Sgt.	SIDGWICK, Frank ...	*Major, Ministry of Labour*
767817	Pte.	SAUNDERS, William Lawrence	...	*Specially Employed; 2/Lieut.*
762032	,,	SKENE, George Alexander	*Employed under Dir. of Timber Supplies; Lieut.*
85	Sgt.	SMITH, Harold Rees ✠ ...	...	*Major, D.A.A.Q.M.G.*
4022	Pte.	THOMAS, Alban Musgrove	...	*Staff-Lieut.*
1225	,,	THOMPSON, Arnold John, D.S.O.✠ ...	...	*Brigade-Major,* 🎖(3)
1768	,,	TREATT, Chaplin Court	...	*Major, R.A.F.,* 🎖
5562	,,	WALKER, Harold Frederick, M.B.E.	...	*Flying Officer, R.A.F.*
6180	,,	WIDDERSON, Andrew James, O.B.E.	...	*Staff-Capt.*
10	CSM	WRENTMORE, John Harris	...	*Staff-Lieut. (Recruiting)*
761980	Pte.	WYNN-WERNICK, Frederick Corbet	*Lieut., Min. of National Service*

RAILWAY TRAFFIC OFFICERS (LIEUTENANTS).

3243	Cpl.	ALLBUTT, Herbert Stanley	805	CQMS	GOUGH, Herbert George	
2713	Pte.	BORRAJO, Sydney Alphonzo	2179	Pte.	JEWELL, Charles Francis	
3012	,,	BOUGHTON, Frederick Charles			Hawkins	
9632	,,	BRETHERTON, Francis	202	CQMS	KNIGHT, Henry Frampton	
1548	CQMS	CHETWOOD, Henry John	3551	Pte.	MARTIN, Richard Ivatt	
765499	Pte.	CHIGNELL, Alan Herbert	159	CSM	MARVIN, Douglas Ward	
7528	,,	COLEMAN, Frederick Charles	766580	Pte.	MASON, Landon Randolph	
2144	,,	FRANCIS, Charles William	2054	Pte.	SELWAY, Edgar John	
1936	,,	GASGOINE, Hugh ✠	3426	,,	VANDYKE, Percy Reginald	

ROYAL NAVAL AIR SERVICE.

			Flight Sub-Lieut.	
2082	Pte.	Brisley, Cuthbert Everard ...	16/11/14	*Major R.A.F. K/A* 30/7/18
3090	,,	Bush, Richard Eldon ...	11/ 7/15	*Injured* 24/3/16
4360	,,	Cuckney, Ernest John ...	17/11/15	*Flight-Lieut. (Staff),* D.S.C.
3261	,,	Edmonds, Wilfred Bell ...	16/12/15	*From 9/Somerset L.I.*
2657	,,	Felkin, Samuel Denys ...	25/ 5/15	*Flight-Capt. R.A.F.,* O.B.E., F/D
472	,,	Morrell, Charles M. ...	15/ 4/15	*Interned in Holland*
2286	,,	Popham, Arthur Ernest ...	30/10/15	*Capt.,* F/D, ❦
2256	,,	Savory, Kenneth Stevens ...	11/ 9/14	*Major,* D.S.O. AND BAR, ❦
1965	,,	Sieveking, Lancelot de Giharne	7/ 7/15	*Capt.,* D.S.C. *P/W* 10/12/17
1909	,,	Simpson, George Goodman ...	8/ 7/15	*Capt.,* D.S.C.
1061	,,	Tomlinson, Noel Bannister ...	8/ 9/14	*Flight-Capt. R.A.F.*
763757	Pte.	Atherley, Sydney H. ...	25/ 3/17	*Lieut.*
767199	,,	Bellamy, Kenneth John Gunning	12/12/17	
2433	,,	Gillespie, Leslie Herbert Gray ...	3/11/16	*Drowned* 10/12/17
4703	,,	Littleboy, Vernon Hatherton ...	21/12/16	*Acc/K* 22/12/17
2925	,,	McGregor, Norman Myers ...	5/ 2/16	*Fl.-Lieut. (Capt. R.A.F.)* D.S.C.
765005	,,	Podmore, John Donald ...	7/ 2/18	
3332	,,	Power, Ronald Victor	30/ 8/16	
2597	,,	Pownall, Charles Herbert ...	29/ 8/16	*Flight Sub-Lieut.*
766237	,,	Underhay, George Flaxman ...	7/ 1/18	*Lieut.*
760917	,,	Wilkinson, Ernest George ...	22/ 4/17	*Flight Sub-Lieut.*
2127	,,	Winter, Rupert Randolph ...	5/ 2/16	*Flight.-Commr. K/A* 9/2/18

ROYAL FLYING CORPS.*

			Gazetted to R.F.C.	
	Lieut.	Child, Arthur James ...	1/ 1/16	*Lt.-Col.,* ✠, O.B.E., F/D, ❦(3)
	2ndLt.	Harvey, Eric Blake ...	-/ 8/15	*Capt. P/W, repat.,* 22/11/18
	2ndLt.	O'Brien, Joseph Andrew ...	29/ 3/16	
	2ndLt.	Tallentire, Arthur Tom ...	-/ -/15	*Killed (in France)* 20/10/15
2383	Pte.	Adams, Ronald Blake ...	4/ 9/15	*From 4/Middlesex*
2345	,,	Burbury, Arthur Vivian ...	1/10/15	*Balloon Officer, Staff-Lieut.*
2617	,,	Clark, Walter Llewellyn ...	17/ 2/16	*(15/Middlesex), Capt. K/A* 23/5/17
1274	,,	Clifton, Edward Noel ...	17/11/15	*(Coldstream Gds.), Lt. w.* 25/1/15
1868	Sgt.	Daniell, Thos. Edward St. Clare	8/ 9/15	*Lt.-Col. (Staff),* ✠, O.B.E.
2572	Pte.	Green, James Henry ...	7/11/15	
3276	,,	Hakewill, Thomas George ...	-/ 2/16	*Killed in Egypt* 11/2/16
1700	,,	Hughes, Thomas McKenny ...	22/11/15	*(2/K.R.R.). K/A* 26/2/18. ❦
375	Sgt.	Solomon, Jerrold Bernard ...	15/10/15	*Major,* ✠, F/D, ❦(2)
1768	Pte.	Treatt, Chaplin Court ...	27/ 1/15	*From North Lancs.,* ❦
2320	,,	Trier, Henry Alwyn T. ...	-/ 8/15	*Lieut.*
3567	,,	Western, James George ...	31/ 7/15	*Lieut.* M.B.E.

[* It is possible that this List does not include all Officers gazetted originally to other Arms who were subsequently *attached* to the R.F.C. or R.A.F.—Ed.]

ROYAL FLYING CORPS.

			Gazetted to R.F.C.	
6677	Pte.	BARLOW, William Geoffrey	15/ 3/16	Lieut.
7525	,,	BLACKWOOD, John	13/ 3/16	Major
6099	,,	COCK, Geoffrey Hornblower	3/ 6/16	
6753	,,	COWLING, John Arnold	18/ 4/16	Capt., ℞
7287	,,	GOUDIE, Norman	22/ 4/16	Capt., D.F.C.
2158	,,	HORN, Marmaduke Langdale	-/ -/16	Lieut., F/D
6294	,,	MACKAIN, Henry Fergus	18/ 3/16	Killed in Action 27/2/17
2113	,,	NEAL, Harry	-/ -/16	
3961	,,	RADCLIFFE, Ernest John	20/ 1/16	Killed (Brooklands) 20/2/16
7015	,,	RUCK, John Arthur	17/ 3/16	Acc/K 25/5/16
6592	,,	SMITH, Arthur William	3/ 6/16	Lieut.
7586	Pte.	ABBOT, Thomas Walker	27/ 1/17	Lieut., ✠ K/A 18/8/17
760593	Sgt.	ACKERMANN, Gerald	27/10/17	A.E.O.
765428	Pte.	ADAMS, Philip Walter	12/10/17	
760621	,,	ADAMSON, Christopher Patrick	13/ 4/17	P/W 22/10/17
764006	,,	ALBERRY, William Charles	13/12/17	
7891	,,	ALBURY, Norman Howard	7/ 2/17	K/A 15/9/17
763144	,,	ALLEN, Cyrus	7/ 6/17	K/A 16/7/18
763017	,,	ALLEN, Geoffrey Walker	6/ 4/17	Capt. (Medical)
8000	,,	ANDERSON, Frederick St. Kervin	28/ 2/17	w. 21/11/17
766009	,,	ANDERSON, Patrick Alexander	26/ 8/17	K/A 19/10/17
7587	L/Cpl.	ANDERSON, Richard Wm. L.	27/ 1/17	K/A 11/6/17
763223	Pte.	ANDREWS, Alfred Edmund Claude	21/ 4/17	Lieut.
2884	Cpl.	ANGELL, Bruce Othniel	18/ 9/16	Lieut., M.B.E.
7502	Pte.	APPLEYARD, Victor Harold	7/ 2/17	
7629	,,	ARBERY, Ernest Edward	27/ 1/17	K/A 6/6/17
8151	,,	ARNOLD, Henry	27/ 1/17	Lieut. w. 28/8/17
7799	,,	ARNOLD, John Kenneth	7/ 2/17	Lieut.
7920	,,	ATCHLEY, Rowland Waldegrowe	10/ 9/16	A.E.O.
766239	,,	ATHERTON, Jack	22/10/17	
765491	,,	ATKINSON, John Frederick Victor	11/ 8/17	w. 26/6/18
763485	,,	AYTON, Robert Conrad	14/ 4/17	Lieut.
8079	,,	BABER, John Montague	7/ 2/17	Lieut.
5829	,,	BAILEY, Louis John	5/ 9/16	K/A 17/6/17
763773	,,	BAKER, Francis Brackstone	14/ 4/17	Lieut.
8149	,,	BAKER, George	20/ 2/17	
766959	,,	BALDWIN, Arthur Cyril	7/ 2/18	
5194	,,	BALLARD, Allan Leslie	5/ 9/16	
765154	,,	BALMFORD, Walter Crowther	17/ 5/17	Lieut.
762051	,,	BANKHART, Paul Geoffrey	5/ 4/17	
7102	,,	BANKS, Leonard Glover	26/10/16	Lieut.
4967	,,	BARKER, Leslie Ivan	7/ 7/16	
765492	,,	BARKER, Augustine William	11/ 8/17	
762572	,,	BARNETT, William Augustus	14/ 4/17	D/W 15/11/17
761691	,,	BARRATT, Frederic Henry	5/ 5/17	Lieut.
4245	,,	BARTLETT, Clarence Hubert	27/ 1/17	P/W 7/12/17

			Gazetted to R F.C.	
760961	Pte.	BARTON, Clarence Harry ...	5/ 4/17	K/A 26/10/17
6043	,,	BARTON, Sydney Frederick	10/ 9/16	Lieut. A.E.O.
764008	,,	BATEMAN, Arthur James	5/ 5/17	Lieut.
764009	,,	BAYLEY, Cyril Dunstan Wakefield	13/ 4/17	Lieut.
761642	,,	BEAUFORT, Percival Stanley	28/11/17	A.E.O.
4494	,,	BEAUMONT, Charles Leslie	27/ 1/17	K/A 20/5/17
478	L/Cpl.	BEAUMONT, Eugene Edward	5/11/16	Lieut., ℔
5362	Pte.	BEENEY, James Alexander	11/ 7/16	Lieut., D.F.C.
766775	,,	BELCHER, Frank ...	7 /2/18	
760728	,,	BELL, Charles William	13/ 4/17	Lieut.
765494	,,	BELL, Oliver	11/ 8/17	K/A 24/8/18. ℔
764413	,,	BENNETT, Wilfred	21/ 4/17	Lieut.
766374	,,	BERDINNER, Charles Richard	20/12/17	
1452	Sgt.	BERDOE, James Stanley ...	10/ 9/16	Lieut.
4172	Pte.	BERKELEY, Christopher ...	29/10/15	Lieut. Acc/K 1/2/19
7557	,,	BERNIE, Walter Gregor ...	27/ 1/17	
764224	,,	BERTRAND, Leon ...	7/ 6/17	Lieut.
763812	,,	BEVAN, Wilfred	7/ 6/17	K/A 3/12/17
4378	L/Cpl.	BINER, Frank Armsden ...	27/ 1/17	K/A 3/12/17
762887	Pte.	BIRCH, Reginald Allan ...	7/ 6/17	Lieut.
762613	,,	BIRKS, Herbert Arthur ...	13/ 2/17	Lieut.
6324	,,	BISHOP, Frank Ernest ...	5/ 9/16	K/A 12/7/17
765488	,,	BISPHAM, David Charles ...	23/ 9/17	Acc/K 4/11/17
761942	,,	BLOOMER, David William Howard	14/ 4/17	
1245	Sgt.	BOMFORD, Herbert James Powell	3/11/16	Lieut. w. 15/11/17
764872	Pte.	BOND, Frank Edgar	21/ 4/17	Lieut. w. & P/W 30/11/18
765859	,,	BOOSEY, Ralph ...	23/ 9/17	
763563	,,	BOOT, Maurice Wilson ...	7/ 6/17	
3586	,,	BORET, John Auguste ...	10/10/15	Lieut., ✠, A.F.C.
760374	,,	BOSWOOD, Leslie John ...	5/ 5/17	Lieut. K/A 3/9/18
7886	,,	BOUIE, Jean Augustine Andre	27/ 1/17	Acc/K 24/3/17
5939	,,	BOUSFIELD, Colin ...	25/ 5/16	Observer
762054	,,	BOWDEN, Gerald Joice ...	17/ 3/17	
762605	,,	BOXER, Edward Morris ...	24/ 5/17	
765905	,,	BOYD, Cecil Nicholas ...	23/ 9/17	Missing
5568	,,	BRAINES, Thomas Frederick	5/ 9/16	Lieut.
765342	,,	BRAITHWAITE, Basil Foster	30/ 5/17	P/W 22/11/17
765373	,,	BRAITHWAITE, Norman ...	7/ 6/17	Flying Officer. w. 10/6/18
766011	,,	BRAMLEY, Jack Alexander	18/ 1/18	Pilot Officer
1260	,,	BREWER, Charles Herbert	14/11/14	Capt., ✠. w. 17/6/15 & 23/3/18
5468	,,	BREWER, Eric ...	5/ 9/16	Lieut. w. 28/11/17
765217	,,	BRICKNELL, Daniel Francis H. ...	15/ 6/17	Lieut.
766680	,,	BRIDGE, Alfred James ...	18/ 1/18	w. 9/11/18
765108	,,	BRIDGE, Cyril ...	15/ 6/17	Missing 26/7/16
7733	,,	BRIGGS, Frederick ...	5/11/16	E.O.
8157	,,	BRISTOW, Frederick Lawrence	27/ 1/17	Capt.
763380	,,	BROADHURST, Thomas Clifford	7/ 6/17	Acc/K 28/9/17

			Gazetted to R.F.C.	
1621	Sgt.	BROCKMAN, Frank George	16/10/16	Lieut. w. 18/4/17
2706	Pte.	BROOK, Clifford Hardman	21/ 1/15	Capt.
765707	,,	BROWN, Ernest Ainsidee Jellicorse	3/11/17	
7482	,,	BROWN, Edward John	26/ 9/16	K/A 17/8/17
6844	,,	BROWN, John William	5/ 9/16	Lieut. P/W 11/10/18
6748	,,	BROWN, Frank Percival	5/ 9/16	Lieut. w. 18/6/17
762299	,,	BROWN, William John C.	14/ 4/17	Lieut.
765985	,,	BRUCE, Robert Francis	12/ 9/17	
767200	,,	BRUCE, Ronald Reid Hardcastle	7/ 3/18	
7824	,,	BRYSON, John	27/ 1/17	
765157	,,	BUCHANAN, Francis Stanley	6/ 9/17	
761370	,,	BUCKTON, Clifford	11/ 8/17	
765012	,,	BULL, William	26/ 8/17	
5893	,,	BULLOCK, Austin Bernard	5/ 9/16	Lieut.
765218	,,	BURGESS, George William	2/ 7/17	Lieut.
765912	,,	BURSLAM, Frank Grant	23/ 9/17	w.
5046	,,	BUTT, Alfred	25/ 5/16	(From 2/Bedford) K/A 4/1/18
5570	,,	CABLE, Leonard	5/ 9/16	(Administrative)
764416	,,	CAIN, Douglas Walter Thomas	13/ 4/17	Lieut. w. 3/10/17
2094	Cpl.	CANDY, Rupert George	13/ 3/16	Flight Lieut.
765581	Pte.	CAREY, Robert Benson	23/ 9/17	Lieut.
765266	,,	CARLAW, Hamish White	21/ 4/17	
764685	,,	CARSON, William Frank	15/ 6/17	Lieut.
767210	,,	CARTER, Alan	27/ 2/18	Acc/K 25/6/18
1189	Cpl.	CARTER, William Charles	26/ 4/17	Capt.
3588	Pte.	CASSELS, James Stuart	5/12/15	(From 9/Sussex) Lieut.
8080	,,	CASSIDY, Arthur James	27/ 1/17	Lieut.
764977	,,	CASTLEMAN, Frederick B. Goodwin	21/ 4/17	Lieut.
765986	,,	CATON, Edmund Percy	14/11/17	Kite Balloon Section
766331	,,	CAVE, Clement Fortes	7/ 2/18	℞
760873	,,	CAWSON, George Adrian	7/ 6/17	K/A 30/11/17
7588	,,	CAYFORD, George Everitt	27/ 1/17	Killed 16/7/17
763359	,,	CHADWICK, Cyril Henry	31/ 7/17	Lieut. A.E.O., ℞
761753	,,	CHAMPION, Alfred	7/ 2/17	(To Tank Corps) Lieut. w. 8/8/18
761446	,,	CHAPLIN, Frederick Perry	17/ 3/17	Lieut.
760678	,,	CHAPMAN, Alfred Arthur	17/ 3/17	
8209	,,	CHAPMAN, Edward Charles	27/ 1/17	
760522	,,	CHANCEY, Percy	20/12/17	
762446	,,	CHEERS, Donald Heriot Anson	27/ 6/17	Acc/K 17/4/18
6751	,,	CHESTER, George Stanley	27/ 1/17	Lieut.
764087	,,	CHICK, Arthur Leslie	27/ 6/17	A.F.C. w. 15/11/18.
765029	,,	CHISWELL, Robert Mervyn Frank	17/ 5/17	Lieut.
762746	,,	CHURCH, Ernest Henry	28/ 8/17	w. 18/1/18
765267	,,	CLARK, Frederick Sloan	7/ 6/17	Lieut. P/W 7/12/17
5733	,,	CLARK, Laurence Fraser	26/ 9/16	
1533	,,	CLARKE, George Malcolm	1/ 1/15	(From 2/Leinster) Capt., A.F.C.
762825	,,	CLEGG, George William	14/ 4/17	

			Gazetted to R.F.C.	
765311	Pte.	CLEMENTSON, Leslie Howell ...	17/ 5/17	*Administrative*
4842	,,	CLOWES, Richard	9/ 9/16	*Lieut.*
764962	,,	COATES, Frank Spencer ...	14/ 7/17	
8054	,,	COATES, Sydney	27/ 1/17	K/A 27/5/17
7935	,,	COBB, Reginald Lawrence ...	10/ 9/16	A.E.O.
6099	,,	COCK, Geoffrey Hornblower ...	2/ 6/16 ✠	P/W 10/9/17
76421	,,	COLEMAN, Francis Daniel ...	17/ 5/17	*Lieut.*
767137	,,	COLIN, Barthelmy Jules ...	15/ 2/19	
765500	,,	COLLANDER-BROWN, Wm. Hugh	11/ 8/17	*Lieut.*
3244	,,	COLLINS, Arthur Duppa ...	14/ 1/17	D/W 1/4/17
763361	,,	COLLISON, Frederick Laing ...	27/ 8/17	*Lieut.*
765419	,,	COLVILLE-JONES, Thomas ...	14/ 7/17	*Capt.* D/W while P/W 24/5/18
4215	,,	CONDER, Reginald Edward ...	27/ 1/17	*Lieut.* w. 18/6/17
766582	,,	CONYNGHAM, Dalton Parry ...	18/ 1/18	
763196	,,	COOMBE, Alfred Stanley Naylor ...	21/ 4/17	*Missing* 16/5/18
7818	,,	COOMBS, Vernon Courtenay ...	28/ 2/17	w. & P/W 4/10/17
762972	,,	COOPER, Gordon John ...	13/ 4/17	*Lieut.*
766190	,,	COOPER, Sidney	7/ 2/18	
1199	Sgt.	COOPER, Sidney	7/ 1/17	*Lieut.* w. 20/4/17
765113	Pte.	CORNFORD, Kenneth Melville A.	5/ 5/17	*Lieut.*
3980	,,	CORRY, Frank Moring ...	7/11/15	D/W 12/12/17
4772	,,	COSTON, James Alfred Carr ...	28/ 2/17	
762695	,,	COULSON, Charles Stanley Lomas	7/ 6/17	*Lieut.*, D.F.C. w. 9/8/18. ✠
7573	,,	COURTICE, John Clarence ...	10/ 9/16	A.E.O.
765759	,,	COURTNEY, William Edward L. ...	11/ 8/17	P/W 12/11/18
765927	,,	COUTTS, Frederick	26/ 8/17	
766807	,,	COVELL, Eric Herbert ...	7/ 2/18	
4340	L/Cpl.	COWLIN, Alfred Charles ...	27/ 1/17	
762716	Pte.	COWPER, Cecil Featherstone ...	17/ 5/17	*Lieut.*
766246	,,	COX, Leonard John ...	22/10/17	*Lieut.*
5837	,,	CRABB, John Bawden ...	7/10/16	*Lieut.*, O.E.O.
765114	,,	CRAWLEY, Douglas Vivian ...	11/ 8/17	
8236	,,	CRICKMORE, Edwin Bruce ...	28/ 2/17	P/W 29/10/18
760401	,,	CROCKETT, Wallace John ...	7/11/17	K/A 19/9/18
764883	,,	CRYER, Harold James ...	7/ 6/17	Acc/K 13/10/17
765454	,,	CULLEN, James Marsh ...	23/ 9/17	
762990	,,	CUMMING, James	21/ 4/17	
4751	,,	CURTIS, Hubert James ...	27/ 1/17	*Missing*
760648	,,	CURTIS, Henry Neville ...	6/ 4/17	K/A 22/10/17
765163	,,	DAFFORN, Ernest Edward ...	15/ 6/17	*Lieut.*
764820	,,	DALPIAZ, Germano ...	21/ 4/17	
765928	,,	DANGER, Eric Oscar ...	26/ 8/17	*Lieut.* w. 2/10/18
765531	,,	DANIEL, Frank Charles ...	26/ 8/17	*Lieut.*
7590	,,	DAND, James Huddart ...	27/ 1/17	M.B.E.
8168	,,	DANN, Henry Norman Groves ...	27/ 1/17	K/A 15/9/17
762606	,,	DARBY, Ernest Hubert Wynn ...	14/ 4/17	
760760	,,	DAVIES, Frederick Harry ...	28/ 2/17	*Capt.*, ✠

ROYAL FLYING CORPS.

			Gazetted to R.F.C.	
764981	Pte.	DAVIES, John David Griffith ...	21/ 4/17	*Observer*
766514	,,	DAVIES, Richard Lewis	4/11/17	
6845	,,	DAVIES, Richard Stanley ...	5/ 9/16	*Lieut.*
764059	,,	DAVIES, William Edgar	30/ 5/17	*Lieut.*
767150	,,	DAVIES, Wilfred Thomas	17/ 3/18	
765698	,,	DAVIS, Ronald Herbert	13/ 8/17	*Missing* 6/9/18
762614	,,	DAVIS, Roy K.	14/11/17	*Kite Balloon Observer*
766515	,,	DEARLOVE, Basil John	7/ 3/18	
8058	,,	DE FONTENAY, Phillippe Auguste	3/ 2/17	*Lieut.*
765824	,,	DE GERSIGNY, Noel	24/ 1/18	
4746	,,	DENNIS, Leonard Victor	27/ 1/17	
762020	,,	DE ST. FELIX, Phillipe ...	17/ 3/17	
766687	,,	DEW, Edward Alphonse ...	18/ 1/18	D.F.C. *w.* 22/7/18
763026	,,	DIAMOND, William Edward de B.	13/ 4/17	*w.* and *P/W* 21/9/17
763874	,,	DICKENS, Edward Charles ...	12/ 5/17	*Lieut.*
9640	Sgt.	DICKSEE, Harold John Hugh ...	27/ 9/16	*Lieut. w.* 27/12/17
765699	Pte.	DIDCOTT, Frederic Ernest ...	11/ 8/17	*Lieut.*
3624	L/Cpl.	DIMMOCK, Norman Hereford ...	5/ 9/16	*Capt.,* A.F.C.
7505	Pte.	DINGLE, William Warren ...	27/ 1/17	*Observer*
766016	,,	DODD, Albert	12/10/17	*K/A* 30/10/18
763615	,,	DONE, Richard	17/ 5/17	*Lieut.*
3442	,,	DOWN, Harold Hunter	4/ 1/17	*Lieut.,* A.F.C.
761312	,,	DOWSETT, Henry George ...	7/ 3/18	*Acc/K* 17/7/18
6212	,,	DRAPER, Marcus	27/ 1/17	*Acc/K* 7/2/17
6733	,,	DRIVER, Edgar Thomas	27/11/16	*Lieut.,* M
5994	,,	DRUMMOND, Joseph Rayson ...	27/ 1/17	*K/A* 22/9/18
763011	,,	DUDBRIDGE, Morton	5/ 4/17	
762697	,,	DUFFY, Frank	24/ 5/17	*Lieut.*
765438	,,	DUGGAN, Lewin Bowring ...	25/11/17	(*From /Hereford*)
764606	,,	DULIN, William Walter Motta ...	5/ 5/17	*Lieut. K/A* 29/7/18
4084	,,	DUPONT, Alfred Norman ...	11/11/15	*Lieut.,* A.F.C.
765439	,,	DUNCAN, James Athol Gordon ...	11/ 8/17	*Acc/K* 15/2/18
765763	,,	DUNFORD, Charles William ...	12/ 9/17	*w.* 10/12/17
765324	,,	EASON, Walter Stanley ...	11/ 8/17	*Lieut.*
4456	Cpl.	EASTCOTT, John Noel ...	27/ 1/17	
763266	Pte.	EDGE, James Dallas	15/ 8/17	*Lieut.*
765226	,,	EDINOW, Samuel	25/ 6/17	
7326	,,	EDMONDS, Edward Peregrine Pell	27/ 1/17	*D/W* /9/18
763384	,,	EDWARDS, Joshua Price ...	7/ 6/17	
764692	,,	ELLIS, Albert Edward ...	15/ 6/17	*Lieut.*
4632	L/Cpl.	ELLIS, Guy Stuart ...	27/ 1/17	*K/A* 12/7/17
2626	Sgt.	ENGUELL, George James ...	5/11/16	*Capt.,* A.E.O.
7483	Pte.	ETHERIDGE, Donald Harding ...	5/11/16	A.E.O.
760473	,,	EVANS, Francis Bernard ...	13/ 9/17	*K/A* 17/2/18
765615	,,	EVANS, Percy Lewis	23/ 9/17	*K/A* 22/11/18
762748	,,	EVANS, Richard Ralph	3/11/17	
764488	,,	EVERETT, Ernest	7/ 6/17	*Lieut.*

ROYAL FLYING CORPS.

				Gazetted to R.F.C.	
6496	Pte.	EWBANK, Charles Henry Preston		29/ 8/16	*Lieut.*
762401	,,	FACEY, Reginald Vaughan	...	7/ 6/17	*Lieut.*
6284	,,	FAIRBAIRN, Arthur Reginald	...	27/ 1/17	D.F.C.
3182	,,	FALCK, Lionel Louis ...	...	4/ 6/15	(*From* 9/*Middlesex*) F/D
764428	,,	FARRELL, Kenneth George	...	5/ 5/17	
4505	Cpl.	FARRIER, Archibald Victor	...	16/ 1/16	w. 24/11/17 ℞
763059	Pte.	FARTHING, Arthur ...	...	2/ 7/17	*Lieut.*
762829	,,	FATTORINI, Thomas ...	...	6/ 4/17	K/A 13/8/18
765700	,,	FAUCETT, Lawrence Wm.	...	7/ 2/18	
763496	,,	FAULKNER, Harold Frederick	...	5/ 5/17	*Lieut.*
763639	,,	FEAR, Robert Stanley ...	...	27/ 6/17	D/W 5/3/18
765587	,,	FELLS, Sidney Frederick John	...	11/ 8/17	
7439	,,	FELTON, Arthur Reginald	...	27/ 1/17	
7440	,,	FELTON, Clifford Twyford	...	27/ 1/17	*Lieut.*
765091	,,	FENN-SMITH, Warren Kemp	...	26/ 8/17	K/A 18/1/18
764091	,,	FERGUSON, John Cecil ...	...	28/ 8/17	*Lieut.* w. 27/8/18
767123	,,	FEWKES, Leslie	...	7/ 2/18	
765538	,,	FFOULKES-JONES, Edwin Jocelyn		26/ 8/17	*Lieut.*
764554	,,	FIELD, Stanley	...	18/ 4/17	*Hon. Lieut.*
763821	,,	FINKE, Rudolph Frederick G. B.		3/11/17	
761936	,,	FOOT, David Victor ...	...	17/ 3/17	Acc/K 4/5/17
762557	,,	FOSTER, Frank Hawley ...	...	5/ 4/17	K/A 3/6/17
8354	,,	FOSTER, Franklin James ...	...	28/ 2/17	K/A 23/8/17
765325	,,	FRANCIS, William George	...	15/ 6/17	K/A 10/3/18
763739	,,	FRANCIS-HAWKINS, Fitzroy H. M.		15/ 6/17	
5492	,,	FRANK, Charles Frederick	...	5/ 9/16	*Lieut.*, D.F.C.
3387	,,	FRASER, Cecil Garnet ...		7/11/15	(*From* 2/*Leicester*), Lt. w. 6/1/16
3162	,,	FRATER, Alexander Hay	...	24/10/15	(*From* 2/*D.C.L.I.*), ℞
767138	,,	FRENCH, Robert Harold	...	7/ 3/18	
6380	,,	FREW, John Glover Hugo	...	26/ 9/16	Capt. w. & P/W 6/7/17
7311	,,	FRISBY, Ernest Chalinder	...	5/11/16	*Lieut.*, A.E.O.
766811	,,	FULLER, Roland Usher ...		24/ 1/18	
4118	,,	GALE-HASLEHAM, Dudley Alfred		27/ 1/17	
765680	,,	GALLARD, Wm. Jack Herbert	...	11/ 8/17	
7939	,,	GANE, Arthur	...	5/11/16	*Lieut.*, A.E.O.
3617	Sgt.	GARNER, Percy Rowlands	...	5/11/16	*Lieut.*, A.E.O.
8355	Pte.	GARDINER, Herbert Michael	...	28/ 2/17	*Lieut.*
766110	,,	GARNETT, Arthur Wormwell	...	7/ 2/18	
766837	,,	GARROD, John Douglas Loveless		24/ 1/18	
7895	,,	GEDGE, Lathom Sidney Victor	...	27/ 1/17	*Lieut.*
764491	,,	GIBBON, Harold Merlyn ...	...	7/ 6/17	
764063	,,	GIBSON, James Alexander	...	21/ 6/17	
764768	,,	GILES, Albert	...	5/ 7/17	
763125	,,	GILLBARD, Gurdon ...	...	5/ 7/17	
764985	,,	GILLINGS, George Arthur	...	17/ 5/17	*Lieut.* w. 12/10/17
764595	,,	GITTINGS, Howard Stanley	...	21/ 4/17	
3747	L/Cpl	GLAZER, David Philip ...	...	26/ 9/16	

ROYAL FLYING CORPS.

			Gazetted to R.F.C.	
6761	Pte.	GODING, Rupert Ross	27/ 1/17	
8023	,,	GOLDBY, Frederick Lyster	27/ 1/17	
763785	,,	GOLDS, Ronald Leslie	7/ 6/17	*Lieut.*
764987	,,	GOODEARLE, Francis Roy	21/ 4/17	
761407	,,	GOODMAN, Keeley Ian	12/11/16	*Lieut.*
7287	,,	GOUDIE, Norman	19/ 4/16	*Capt.*, D.F.C.
8182	,,	GRACE, Alfred Alexander George	28/ 2/17	K/A 26/6/17
760908	,,	GRAMMONT, Reginald Thomas	25/10/17	
762451	,,	GRANT, Frank Douglas	14/ 4/17	w. 27/10/17 & 30/1/18
763691	,,	GRAY, Charles Gilbert Dunbar	17/ 5/17	*Lieut.* P/W 17/11/17
765991	,,	GRAYSON, Edward	14/11/17	*Flying Officer*
765939	,,	GREAVES, Herbert Francis Kenneth	26/ 8/17	
3572	,,	GREEN, James Henry	7/11/15	*Capt.*
765446	,,	GREEN, Wilfred Barratt	11/ 8/17	*Flight-Lieut.*, D.F.C., F/D(2)
764578	,,	GREENAWAY, Bramwell Victor	5/ 7/17	
765332	,,	GREENE, Richard Ernest	15/ 6/17	
764829	,,	GREENHILL, Herbert Percy	21/ 4/17	
765269	,,	GRIFFITH, Frederick	5/ 5/17	
764432	,,	GRIFFITHS, D. R.	13/ 4/17	*Lieut.*
762330	,,	GROOM, Victor Emmanuel	26/ 4/17	(*From West Yorks*). *Lt.*, D.F.C.
763390	,,	GROVES, John	16/ 4/17	
763332	,,	GUNNING, William George	18/ 4/17	
6885	,,	HADDON, Henry	10/ 9/16	*Lieut.* A.E.O.
762405	,,	HAGGART, Edmund Charles	7/ 6/17	*Lieut.*
761204	,,	HAIGH, Guy Rhodes	25/10/17	*Lieut.*
765702	,,	HALL, Edward Thomas	23/ 9/17	
3829	,,	HALL, William Eric	5/12/15	(*From 22/London*). *Lieut.* w. & P/W 24/11/17
764319	,,	HAMILTON, Cyril William	14/ 4/17	*Lieut.* w. 22/10/17
1238	,,	HAMILTON, Herbert James	29/ 8/15	*Capt.*, ✠ Acc/K 13/6/18
762102	,,	HAMILTON, Morris McNeil	13/10/17	
762975	,,	HAMMERSLEY, Cyril	6/ 4/17	
764143	,,	HANAFY, Sydney Reginald	13/ 6/17	D/W 24/11/17
766519	,,	HANSON, Harry	14/11/17	*Lieut.* w. 21/3/18
762519	,,	HARDMAN, Donald	10/ 5/17	
763158	,,	HARDY, Lawrence Cecil	5/ 7/17	
7982	,,	HAREL, Louis Octave	27/ 1/17	*Lieut.* K/A 18/8/17
1384	,,	HARGREAVES, Cyril Augustus	27/ 1/17	D/W 15/8/17
765457	,,	HARGREAVES, Willoughby F.	26/ 8/17	Acc/K 21/2/18
7858	,,	HARRIS, Arthur Stuart	27/ 1/17	*Lieut.*
765171	,,	HARRIS, Percy Edmund	21/ 4/17	*Hon. Lieut.*
765037	,,	HARRISON, Edward Cyril	7/ 6/17	w. 25 5/18
765270	,,	HARRISON, Frank	8/ 9/17	
764026	,,	HARRISON, Fred Norman	5/ 5/17	*Lieut.*
6342	,,	HARTLEY, Allan	26/ 9/16	*Lieut.*
765122	,,	HARTLEY, Arthur Samuel	21/ 4/17	
8009	,,	HASLEDEN, Eric Frank	27/ 1/17	*Lieut.*

			Gazetted to R.F.C.	
763583	Pte.	HASSALL, James Edwin Guy	13/ 4/17	*Lieut.*
5851	,,	HASTINGS, Norman William	27/ 1/17	
3132	RSM	HAWKSFORD, Francis Henry	10/ 9/16	*Major*, O.B.E., ✠
7800	Pte.	HAWORTH, Peter ...	19/12/16	(*From Lancs Fus.*) *Obs.*, D.F.C.
762955	,,	HAWTHORNE, Frank Maudsley ...	3/ 1/18	
760570	,,	HAYNES, Frederick Henry	27/ 8/17	
3170	,,	HEATHCOTE, Niels Hugh de V. ...	4/ 1/17	*Lieut.*
763034	,,	HEDGES, Robert Bernard Taylor	23/ 5/17	*Lieut. w.* 3/5/18
2921	Sgt.	HENDERSON, Edward Murray	21/ 8/16	*Lieut.*
8179	Pte.	HEPBURN, Allan ...	27/ 1/17	*Lieut.*, D.F.C. *w.* 1/10/17
765906	,,	HERRERA, Joseph Ascension	23/ 9/17	
765313	,,	HEWAT, Richard Alexander	21/ 4/17	K/A /8/18
760635	,,	HICKS, George Rensbury	3/11/17	*Lieut.*, D.F.C.
765305	,,	HICKS, Harry Ronald ...	21/ 4/17	K/A 12/10/17
4827	,,	HIGHAM, John Arthur ...	27/ 1/17	*Lieut.*, F/D. *w.* 24/11/17. ✠
763065	,,	HILLS, Edward Algernon Ray	13/ 4/17	*w.* 22/10/17
763553	,,	HIND, Ivan Frank	10/ 5/17	
764945	,,	HITCHING, Arthur Stanley	21/ 4/17	
4683	L/Cpl.	HODGKINS, Alfred	5/11/16	*Lieut.*, A.E.O.
764990	Pte.	HOLBECHE, Colin George	21/ 5/17	
766796	,,	HOLMAN, Herbert Guy ...	12/ 2/18	*w. & P/W* 9/7/18
762900	,,	HOOD, Ronald ...	24/ 5/17	*Lieut.*
4534	,,	HOOD, Ronald Paton ...	27/ 1/17	K/A 28/9/17
764894	,,	HOPGOOD, Francis John ...	7/ 6/17	*Lieut. P/W* 14/5/18
7730	,,	HOPPS, Frank Linden ...	6/ 8/16	(*From Yorkshire L.I.*). *Lt.*, A.F.C.
1437	,,	HORSLEY, Oswald	15/12/14	(*From* 2/*Gordons*). *Capt.*, ✠✠, *w.* 9/1/15 & 20/7/15. *Acc/K* 9/8/18. ✠
8029	,,	HOWARD, Alan ...	5/11/16	*Capt.*, A.E.O. ✠
4528	,,	HOWARD, George Vivian ...	27/ 1/17	*Lieut.*, D.F.C.
764497	,,	HOWELLS, George James	7/ 6/17	K/A 23/11/17
766305	,,	HUBBARD, Norman Frederick S. ...	2/12/17	
764068	,,	HUCKLEBRIDGE, Edward Cecil ...	13/ 4/17	*Lieut.*
766955	,,	HUDSON, Harry James ...	24/ 1/18	
762453	,,	HUGHES, Gilbert Cyril ...	14/ 4/17	*Lieut.*
765174	,,	HUGHES, Ronald Baskerville ...	21/ 4/17	K/A 31/5/17
764146	,,	HULL, Herbert Cranley ...	11/ 5/17	E.O.
762617	,,	HUMPHRIES, Leslie Glendower ...	21/ 4/17	K/A 16/9/17
4449	L/Cpl.	HUNSTONE, George Neil	27/ 1/17	K/A 28/6/17
762618	Pte.	HUNT, Cyril Frank	21/ 4/17	K/A 22/4/19
6567	,,	HUNTER, George Frederick	5/ 9/16	
7897	,,	HUNTER, George Thomas F.	27/ 1/17	*Lieut.*
764246	,,	HUNTER, Harry ...	13/ 4/17	D/W 5/11/17
4091	,,	HURLEY, Alfred Vincent	5/ 9/16	*Lieut.*
8210	,,	HURLEY, William Michael Mary	27/ 1/17	*Lieut.*
762608	,,	HURST, William M.	14/ 4/17	
765040	,,	IKIN, Alfred Edward	6/ 5/17	K/A 11/3/18
762304	,,	IVES, Edgar Donald Kirk	5/ 5/17	

			Gazetted to R.F.C.	
764030	Pte.	Ivison, Thomas	21/ 4/17	Lieut.
8134	,,	Jackson, Arthur	27/ 1/17	K/A 7/2/17
762618	,,	Jackson, Henry Gilbert	14/ 4/17	Lieut. w. 5/6/18
764704	,,	Jackson, Wm. Arthur Frederick	15/ 6/17	
766556	,,	James, Arthur Colin	13/12/17	
5445	,,	James, Edwin Archibald	5/ 9/16	
5345	,,	Jarvis, Archibald Henry	28/ 2/17	Lieut.
760700	,,	Jarvis, Patrick Wm. Lemnel	13/ 4/17	Lieut.
762857	,,	Jeff, Robert Nemmo Williamson	5/ 4/17	Lieut. P/W 11/8/17
7450	,,	Jennings, Edward Dudley	27/ 1/17	P/W 16/6/17
2638	CQMS	Jennings, John Wilfred	10/ 9/16	Capt., A.E.O. ⌘
584	Pte.	Jerwood, Edward Longsden	27/ 1/15	(From 1/Berks). Capt., ✠✠✠ w.9/11/18 ⌘
762880	,,	Johnson, Frank Hollawell	14/ 4/17	
6764	,,	Johnson, Stanley Morrel	27/ 1/17	Died from Injuries 25/5/17
3136	,,	Johnstone, Robert	2/ 7/15	(From 4/London). Lieut., ✠
2287	,,	Jones, Alfred Gordon Newton	27/ 1/17	Lieut.
762273	,,	Jones, Arthur Idwal Morris	5/ 7/17	
764995	,,	Jones, Douglas Hemming	5/ 5/17	Lieut. w. 10/4/18
764499	,,	Jones, Eric Kyffin	7/ 6/17	
3752	,,	Jones, Frank Bernard	27/ 1/17	Lieut.
7806	,,	Jones, Henry Victorian	27/ 1/17	Lieut.
764650	,,	Jones, William Basil	5/ 5/17	Lieut. w. 9/10/17
764558	,,	Jones, William Ernest Frank	21/ 4/17	Lieut., D.F.C.
764579	,,	Joseph, John Rhys	21/ 4/17	d. 23/4/17
763427	,,	Joseph, Michael Baron	6/ 5/17	Observer. w. 5/6/18
765239	,,	Kearton, Richard	16/ 6/17	
765421	,,	Keen, Frederick Francis	14/ 7/17	Lieut.
760822	,,	Keenahan, Joseph Eric Anthony	11/ 8/17	Lieut. w. 22/3/18
5911	,,	Kelsly, Philip George	5/ 9/16	Lieut.
6804	,,	Kemp, Allan Frederick	5/ 9/16	Lieut.
762436	,,	Kendall, Sidney	14/ 4/17	Lieut. P/W 18/12/17
761431	,,	Kibble, Harold James	28/ 8/17	Lieut.
765504	,,	Kidd, Arthur Lindsay	11/ 8/17	Lieut. P/W 14/1/18
765274	,,	King, Kenneth Vivian	1/ 6/17	K/A 30/7/18
8211	,,	Knight, Alan Gwyer	27/ 1/17	
765685	,,	Knight, Robert	13/ 8/17	
7578	,,	Knock, Norman Herbert	10/ 9/16	A.E.O.
766481	,,	Knowles, Arthur Richard	13/12/17	Lieut.
766309	,,	Knowles, Cecil George	7/ 2/18	
766413	,,	Knox, Percy Joseph	3/11/17	Lieut.
7452	,,	Labrow, Leonard	7/ 2/17	Lieut.
764653	,,	Lacy, Arthur Ord	5/ 5/17	Lieut.
766025	,,	Lagesse, Camille Henri Raoul	26/ 8/17	Lieut., D.F.C. AND BAR, F/D, ⌘
764151	,,	Lamb, James Ernest	18/ 4/17	Lieut.
6172	,,	Lambert, Frank Percival	15/10/16	
766055	,,	Landless, Maurice	13/12/17	

				Gazetted to R.F.C.	
764966	Pte.	LANE, Ronald Basil	...	15/ 6/17	*Lieut. w.* 4/7/18
765842	,,	LANGFORD, James Ches.	...	26/ 8/17	*Lieut.*
765635	,,	LASKER, Robert Sidney	...	11/ 8/17	*Missing* 13/6/18
764439	,,	LATHAM, Leslie Sawyer	...	18/ 4/17	*Lieut.*
763464	,,	LATHAM, William Gladstone	...	13/ 4/17	*Lieut. w.* 19/8/18
5264	,,	LAW, Edgar Rowland	...	5/ 9/16	*w. & P/W* 13/4/17
762667	Cpl.	LAWSON, Vincent Wade	...	25/ 9/17	*Assist. Gunnery Inst.*
762456	Pte.	LAYBORN, Thomas A. E.	...	5/ 5/17	*Lieut.*, ⚔
765907	,,	LAZZARI, Reoul	...	1/ 9/17	
8287	,,	LEAKE, Robert	...	5/11/16	*Lieut., E.O.*
762621	,,	LEDGER, Raymond	...	21/ 4/17	
760681	,,	LEECH, Norman Henry	...	24/ 1/18	
762649	,,	LEETE, Bernard Moore T. S	...	17/ 5/17	*Lieut.*
8047	L/Cpl.	LEGGE, Lawrence	...	11/10/16	*Major, E.O.*
760583	Pte.	LEIGHTON, Kenneth Alfred Wm.		17/ 3/17	*Lieut. P/W*
766056	,,	LEVICK, Cyril	...	27/ 2/18	*K/A* 16/6/18
765000	,,	LEWIS, Arthur Gordon	...	15/ 6/17	*Lieut.*
4548	,,	LEWIS, Charles Ambrose	...	27/ 1/17	*Capt.*
6874	,,	LEWIS, Cyril William	...	26/ 9/16	*Lieut.*
762881	,,	LEWIS, Leslie Allin	...	3/ 5/17	*Lieut.*
764658	,,	LEWIS, Thomas Hugh Lloyd	...	14/ 4/17	*Lieut.*
765773	,,	LINFORD, Bernard Owen M.	...	26/ 8/17	*Lieut.*
765212	,,	LITTLE, Harold Ross	...	5/ 5/17	*Lieut. w.* 23/8/18
763183	,,	LITTLER, Tom	...	13/ 4/17	*K/A* 3/7/17
765348	,,	LIVINGSTONE, Frederick Maurice		15/ 6/17	*Lieut.*
2319	,,	LIVOCK, Eric Stuart	...	29/ 9/15	*K/A* 8/11/17
762837	,,	LOMAS, Lionel Frank	...	13/ 4/17	
3680	,,	LONG, Arthur William	...	27/ 1/17	
7093	,,	LONG, John Thomas	...	5/ 8/16	*w.* 22/8/17. *Killed* 8/10/17
762859	,,	LONGDEN, George	...	14/ 4/17	
765133	,,	LOUDON, Robert Monteith Watson		21/ 4/17	*Lieut.*
762412	,,	Low, Henry Vales	...	17/ 4/17	*Lieut. E.O.* 3
761979	,,	LUDSKI, Jessel Charles	...	17/ 3/17	
767178	,,	LUKE, Arthur William George		27/ 2/18	
8212	,,	LYNN, Dennis Leonard	...	27/ 1/17	
765409	,,	MACAULAY, John	...	14/ 7/17	
761637	,,	MACDONALD, Eric Norman	...	13/ 9/17	D.F.C. *w.* 5/11/18
766870	,,	MACDONALD, James	...	7/ 3/18	D.F.C., F/D
765043	,,	MACDOUGALL, Peter Arthur		21/ 6/17	*Lieut.*, ✠
4881	,,	MACGREGOR, Charles Stuart		27/ 1/17	*Lieut. Obs. Officer*
764610	,,	MACLAREN, Duncan	...	5/ 5/17	*Lieut.*
765490	,,	MACLENNAN, John Carnock		14/ 7/17	
765098	,,	MACNAUGHTON, Robert	...	5/ 5/17	
5019	,,	MAINGOT, Joseph Henry	...	7/ 7/16	*(From Brit. W. Ind. R.) Lieut.*, ✠
6421	,,	MALABAR, Robert Frederick		5/ 9/16	*Lieut.*
764373	,,	MANN, William George	...	7/ 6/17	*K/A* 28/11/17
765425	,,	MANTEGAZZA, Rinaldo	...	13/ 8/17	

ROYAL FLYING CORPS.

			Gazetted to R.F.C.	
763535	Pte.	MARGETSON, Emil Alexander ...	15/ 6/17	Acc./K 16/6/17
3514	,,	MARGOLIOUTH, Alfred Henry ...	11/ 7/16	K/A 2/4/17
7428	,,	MARKS, Albert Edward ...	7/ 2/17	Lieut.
763131	,,	MARRIOTT, Dennis Wynn ...	2/ 7/17	Lieut.
762839	,,	MARSDEN, Geoffrey Rutland ...	7/ 6/17	
763110	,,	MARTIN, Alan David ...	21/ 4/17	Lieut.
3515	,,	MARTYN, August Noor ...	11/ 9/16	Lieut.
765044	,,	MARTYR, Harry Arthur Charles ...	21/ 4/17	Lieut.
2426	,,	MARVIN, Henry Leslie ...	16/ 4/17	K/A 26/10/17
766482	,,	MASKALL, Robert George ...	3/ 1/18	
760644	,,	MASON, Cyril Arthur ...	14/ 4/17	Lieut. w. 13/5/18
763073	,,	MASON, George ...	21/ 4/17	Killed 4/5/17
7815	,,	MASSEY, Raymond ...	27/ 1/17	
765846	,,	MASTERS, Ernest Harold ...	26/ 8/17	F/D.
7171	,,	MATTHEW, Charles Frederick ...	7/ 7/16	Lieut.
762522	,,	MATTHEWS, Cyrille Charles ...	17/ 5/17	
765724	,,	MATTHEWS, James Archibald ...	21/10/17	Missing 3/10/18
762275	,,	MATTHEWS, John Christopher ...	25/ 6/17	Lieut.
8083	,,	MAURITZEN, Roy Walter ...	28/ 2/17	
762998	,,	MAY, Geoffrey Theodore Cornelius	30/ 5/17	Flying Officer. w. 7/11/18
766797	,,	MAYNE, William Ernest ...	18/ 1/18	
763070	,,	MCCUBBIN, Brian Arthur ...	13/ 4/17	
765936	,,	MCDONALD, Duncan Colin ...	11/ 8/17	Missing
909	,,	MCGORRERY, Cedric Marston ...	24/ 2/15	(From R.A.S.C.) Lieut.
762530	,,	MCILWRAITH, Wilfred Lawry ...	17/ 5/17	Lieut.
8288	,,	MCLAREN, Robert Angus ...	28/ 2/17	Lieut. w. 18/1/18
762597	,,	MERCHANT, Arthur Douglas ...	21/ 4/17	
5706	,,	MESSENGER, Alfred Lewis ...	5/ 9/16	Capt., A.F.C.
763856	,,	MESSULAM, Robert ...	14/ 7/17	Lieut.
766914	,,	MIDDLETON, Alexander Gordon...	17/ 3/18	
6114	,,	MILLAR, Maximillian Attila ...	27/ 1/17	Lieut.
4755	,,	MILLS, Kenneth Le Gaye ...	28/ 2/17	D/W 11/11/17
765796	,,	MIMMACK, Stanley Cresswell ...	1/ 9/17	Lieut. w. 7/6/18
765865	,,	MINTER, Lawrence John ...	26/ 8/17	Lieut.
762788	,,	MITCHELL, Eric Theodore ...	14/ 4/17	Lieut.
6878	,,	MITCHELL, John Mitchell ...	21/ 8/16	Capt.M.B.E.,A.E.O. w.4/6/17.
762239	,,	MONTGOMERIE, Hugh Seton ...	26/ 4/17	Lieut. w. 25/5/18
4716	,,	MOORE, Jack Greville ...	28/ 2/17	K/A 2/4/18
760839	,,	MORETON, Norman Houghton ...	6/ 4/17	K/A 30/5/18
764037	,,	MORRIS, Ernest Graham ...	7/ 6/17	
3956	,,	MORRIS, Tom Bernard ...	30/11/15	Lieut., D/W 23/7/17.
5069	,,	MORSE, Gerald Ernest ...	5/ 9/16	Acc/K 31/10/17
765509	,,	MORTIMER, Leonard ...	11/ 8/17	
4576	,,	Moss, Wm. Thomas Gregory ...	27/ 1/17	Acc/K 5/7/17
8167	,,	MULL, Edgar ...	27/ 1/17	Lieut.
762761	,,	MULLEN, John Wilfred ...	5/ 4/17	Lieut. w. 21/8/17
6188	,,	MULLINS, Reginald Mark	26/ 9/16	

ROYAL FLYING CORPS.

			Gazetted to R.F.C.	
4680	L/Cpl.	MUNCEY, Frank Thomas	27/ 1/17	*Lieut. Kite Balloon Officer*
6014	,,	MUNRO, Douglas Alfred James	27/ 1/17	*Lieut.*
765726	Pte.	MURDOCK, Harry Samuel	12/ 8/17	*Lieut.*
7442	,,	MURRAY, George	26/ 1/17	*Lieut.*, ✠ (O). *w.* 6/4/18
4934	,,	MUSSARED, William John	27/ 1/17	*Lieut.*
2222	,,	MUSSLEWHITE, Felix James	28/12/15	(*From A.O.D.*). *Capt.*
765640	,,	NAILER, Raoul Cedric Fitzroy	11/ 8/17	*Lieut.*
766901	,,	NASH, Henry Alfred	12/ 2/18	*K/A* 14/5/18
764203	,,	NASH, William Hollick	7/ 6/17	*Lieut.*
6348	,,	NATHAN, Cyril Herbert	15/ 5/16	(*From A.O.D.*). *Capt.*
1112	CSMI	NEALE, Geoffrey Brockman	15/10/16	*Capt.*, ℞
766078	Pte.	NEWMAN, Edward Michael	3/11/17	*Lieut.*
7484	,,	NEWMAN, Geoffrey Lewin	28/ 2/17	*Lieut.*
2808	L/Cpl.	NEWTON-CLARE, Herbert John	17/ 8/15	(*From A.O.D.*). *Major*, O.B.E.
766565	Pte.	NICHOLAS, Gerald Basil	12/ 2/18	D.F.C.
766486	,,	NICHOLAS, Thomas Uriah Jerald	7/ 2/18	
762488	,,	NICHOLSON, John Fairless Wm.	15/ 6/17	*Lieut.*
762939	,,	NIXON, Leslie Gordon	6/ 4/17	*Lieut. Missing* 18/12/17
765046	,,	NOAKES, Harold Thomas	5/ 5/17	*K/A* 23/7/17
763401	,,	NORBURY, Vernon	13/ 4/17	*Lieut.*
1584	,,	NORMAN, Roland Frank H.	29/ 9/14	(*From 6/Leicester*). *Lt. w.* 1/7/16
760712	,,	NORRISH, George	27/ 2/17	
765692	,,	NORTON, George	23/ 9/17	*Acc/K* 10/5/19
4492	,,	NUDING, Eric Gordon	27/ 1/17	*Lieut.*
765138	,,	OLIVER, Hubert William	17/ 5/17	*Lieut.*
764001	,,	O'NEILL, Gordon Leonard	25/ 4/17	*Lieut.*
6388	,,	ORD, Bernard	5/ 9/16	*Lieut. w.* 6/6/17, 10/10/17
1664	,,	ORDISH, Bernard Wm. Arthur	15/10/16	*P/W. Repatriated* 17/9/16
763590	,,	ORRELL, John Turton	14/ 4/17	*K/A* 2/12/17
5866	,,	O'SHEA, Francis Joseph	27/ 1/17	*Lieut.*
763591	,,	OWEN, Herbert Ernest Malcolm	30/ 5/17	*Acc/K* 18/7/17
765776	,,	OXLEY-BOYLE, Eric Hardy	11/ 8/17	*Lieut.*
8145	,,	PADDLE, Leslie Harold	27/ 1/17	*Lieut.*
763012	,,	PAIN, Charles Heathcote S.	10/ 5/17	*w.* 15/8/18
760737	,,	PALMER, Wm. Samuel Hudson	15/ 8/17	*Acc/K* 15/9/17
762379	,,	PARK, Ralph Stuart	14/ 4/17	*Lieut.*, A.F.C.
765188	,,	PARKINSON, Norman	17/ 5/17	*Lieut.*
7485	,,	PAUL, Arthur Reginald	27/ 1/17	*K/A* 22/1/18
766118	,,	PAULTON, Harold F.	4/11/17	
328	CSM	PAYNE, James Alfred	10/ 9/16	*Capt.*
761448	Pte.	PEARCE, George Harry	8/11/17	
763956	,,	PEEBLES, Arthur Zenda	17/ 5/17	*Lieut.*, A.F.C.
765372	,,	PEMBERTON, Alfred Louis	7/ 6/17	*Lieut. w. & P/W* 26/6/18
760323	,,	PENNICK, Henry William Fredk.	24/ 1/18	
762276	,,	PENTECOST, Charles Gordon	6/ 5/17	*K/A* 27/3/18
7986	,,	PERCY, Archibald Felix	27/ 1/17	*Lieut.*
7898	,,	PERN, Claude	7/ 2/17	*Lieut.*, A.F.C.

E. N. MELLISH, V.C. [pp. 44, 49].

CAVALRY OF THE AIR (Bombing German Artillery).

[Capt. W. B. Wollen.

ROYAL FLYING CORPS.

				Gazetted to R.F.C.	
7914	Pte.	PERRING, Charles Richard	...	27/ 1/17	K/A 27/3/18
762012	,,	PERRING, Robert Brett	...	14/11/16	
765955	,,	PHILCOX, Alfred Reginald		15/ 1/18	
765468	,,	PIKE, George Brooke	...	14/ 3/18	F/D
7594	,,	PILLING, Sydney Hargreaves	...	27/ 1/17	Lieut.
763133	,,	PIPER, Edward Hoerule	...	7/ 6/17	Missing 6/6/18
764663	,,	PITCHFORD, Ashley Norman	...	7/ 6/17	Lieut.
5026	,,	PLATT, Alfred Guy	...	26/ 9/16	Lieut.
766417	,,	POGSON, Desmond Philip	...	3/11/17	D.F.C.
5868	,,	POOLE, Leslie Stanley Richard	...	5/ 9/16	Died 22/11/18
764612	,,	POPPLEWELL, Harry Molyneux S.		5/ 7/17	
765285	,,	POTTER, Henry Albert	...	14/ 7/17	Lieut.
764120	,,	POWELL, Ernest Arthur	...	21/ 6/17	
762911	,,	PRENTICE, Courtney Napier		26/ 8/17	
763309	,,	PRESTON, Harold	...	7/ 6/17	
762599	,,	PRICE, Dudley	...	21/ 4/17	Capt., M
762866	,,	PRYCE, Hugh Erfyl	...	14/ 4/17	Lieut. w. 22/7/18
766659	,,	PRYCE-JONES, John		13/12/17	
763596	,,	PRYKE, Edgar	...	13/ 4/17	D/W 30/11/17
2262	,,	PULLEN, Frank John	...	26/ 5/15	Lieut. w. 24/8/15, 6/4/18
764340	,,	PUMFREY, Montague Albert V. K.		22/ 7/17	
765628	,,	PURSER, Norman Frederick	...	26/ 8/17	K/A 28/2/18
4607	,,	PYNE, Percy	...	11/ 7/16	Hon. Lieut. w. 21/4/17
7899	,,	QUELCH, Leslie Melville	...	27/ 1/17	Lieut.
4053	Sgt.	RAINFORD, Ralph	...	5/11/16	Capt. A.E.O.
762307	Pte.	RANDALL, George Ebbon	...	5/ 4/17	Lieut. D.F.C. AND BAR
764165	,,	RANKIN, Cavin Robert		21/ 4/17	
765880	,,	RATCLIFFE, Joseph Henry		26/ 8/17	
766143	,,	RATCLIFFE, Joseph William		23/ 9/17	
4911	,,	RAWBONE, Charles Robert	...	28/ 2/17	Died 18/12/17
765190	,,	RAWNSLEY, Percy	...	21/ 4/17	w. 5/4/18
765506	,,	RAYNER, Albert Henry	...	14/ 4/17	Lieut.
765191	,,	READ, Arnold Holcombe	...	26/ 6/17	Lieut. A.E.O.
766261	,,	READER, William	...	7/ 2/18	
765956	,,	READING, Vernon Jack	...	26/ 8/17	K/A 26/3/18
6426	,,	REASON, David Jordan	...	26/ 9/16	Lieut. w. 15/10/17
5418	,,	REDDING, Ronald William	...	5/ 9/16	Lieut.
7596	,,	REDLER, Harold Bolton	...	27/ 1/17	✠ Acc/K 21/6/18
8380	,,	REEKIE, John	...	28/ 2/17	Lieut.
762883	,,	REEVES, Harry Cosford		13/ 4/17	
763626	,,	REILLY, Michael Leeds Paine	...	26/ 6/17	Lieut.
761926	,,	REYNOLDS, Francis	...	28/ 8/17	
765192	,,	RICKARDS, Cecil George	...	17/ 5/17	
6122	,,	RILEY, Alan Incell	...	5/ 9/16	Capt. A.F.C.
6655	,,	ROBERTS, Edward Griffiths	...	26/ 9/16	Lieut.
763279	,,	ROBERTS, Gavern Brooke	...	14/ 4/17	K/A 26/9/17
7014	,,	ROBERTS, Lawrie Paterson	...	7/ 2/17	K/A 23/2/18

M

763042	Pte.	ROBINS, Percy Donald ...	14/ 4/17	*Lieut.*
760594	,,	ROBINSON, Cyril Charles Edward	7/11/17	*K/A* 28/4/18
7256	,,	ROBINSON, Donald Greenwood ...	10/ 9/16	*A.E.O.*
766570	,,	ROBINSON, Leslie Thos. Albert ...	24/ 1/18	
5286	,,	ROBINSON, Richard Arthur ...	27/ 1/17	
763797	,,	ROBINSON, William Stanley ...	14/ 4/17	*Lieut.*
765515	,,	ROBSON, Eric Stuart ...	26/ 8/17	
764797	,,	ROBSON, Leonard D. H. ...	13/ 4/17	
6771	,,	ROBSON, William ...	27/ 1/17	
761074	,,	ROCHELLE, William Aubrey ...	6/ 5/17	*Lieut.*
762416	,,	ROGERS, Arthur Forbes ...	7/ 6/17	*K/A* 16/7/18
765602	,,	ROGERS, Charles Edward ...	4/11/17	
762353	,,	ROGERS, James Walter ...	21/ 4/17	
766818	,,	ROGERS, Oliver Leonard	14/11/17	*Observer*
8094	,,	ROGERS, William Roland ...	27/ 1/17	*Lieut.*
766660	,,	ROLINSON, Frank ...	24/ 1/19	*Hon. 2/Lt.*
766208	,,	ROLPH, John Gladwyn ...	8/11/17	*Lieut. w.* 2/9/18
765422	,,	Ross, Charles ...	14/ 7/17	*Lieut.* D.F.C. F/D
7746	,,	Ross, Geoffrey Arthur ...	27/ 1/17	
5001	,,	Ross, James Kenneth ...	5/ 9/16	*D/W* 9/4/17
7690	,,	Ross, Peter Cunningham ...	27/ 1/17	*D/W* 26/6/17
2940	,,	ROSSELLI, John Edgar ...	5/ 6/15	*Lieut.*
764206	,,	ROWE, Stanley Thomas ...	6/ 7/17	*Lieut.*
7015	,,	RUCK, John Arthur ...	17/ 3/16	*Acc/K* 25/5/16
765731	,,	RUDGE, Arthur Edgar ...	13/ 8/17	*Lieut. K/A* 22/6/18
6477	,,	RUNNELS-MOSS, Cyril Gower V. ...	27/ 1/17	*Lieut. d.* 5/12/17
763666	,,	RUSHWORTH, Norman ...	5/ 5/17	
760340	,,	RYLANDS, Eric Claude ...	13/ 4/17	
760607	,,	SADLER, Philip Herbert ...	14/ 4/17	
765826	,,	SAGE, Douglas Michael ...	26/ 8/17	*Lieut. w.* 4/1/18, *K/A* 18/12/17
6656	,,	SALMON, Sidney Arthur ...	5/ 9/16	*Lieut.*
4256	,,	SAWDY, Bertram Francis ...	26/ 9/16	*Lieut. w.* 27/8/17
7691	,,	SARGANT, Frederick Herbert St. C.	27/ 1/17	*Capt.* D.F.C. ✠
763370	,,	SAVAGE, William Leslie ...	14/ 4/17	*Acc/K* 16/6/17
765802	,,	SAWBRIDGE, Robert John Wanley	26/ 8/17	*Lieut.*
8259	,,	SAWYER, Robert Henry ...	28/ 2/17	*d.* 28/9/18
764615	,,	SCARLETT, Lewis Stacey ...	5/ 5/17	
765020	,,	SCHOFIELD, James William ...	5/ 5/17	*Lieut.*
766622	,,	SCHOLES, John ...	7/ 2/18	
5382	,,	SCHOOLEY, Norman Vincent ...	7/ 2/17	
760297	,,	SCOTT, Eric Douglas ...	15/ 6/17	
765705	,,	SCULTHORPE, Arthur ...	3/11/17	
764364	,,	SEDGWICK, Douglas Webb ...	11/ 4/17	
760628	,,	SEFI, Cedric Richard Randolph	6/ 4/17	*Lieut.*
7517	,,	SESSIONS, Donald Humphrey ...	27/ 1/17	✠ *K/A* 20/6/18
765142	,,	SESSIONS, Reginald Victor ...	17/ 5/17	
762843	,,	SEWARD, Walter John ...	14/ 4/17	*Lieut. w.* 26/9/17
5965	,,	SHARPE, Henry Norman ...	8/ 7/16	(*From* 3/*Leicester*). *Acc/K* 26/1/17

ROYAL FLYING CORPS.

766819	Pte.	SHELDRICK, Reginald Holford	... 13/12/17	
765290	,,	SHEPHERD, Percival Tennyson	... 14/ 7/17	
1349	L/Cpl.	SHEPPERD, Harold Easton	... 27/ 1/17	
6026	Pte.	SHILSTONE, Arthur Bernard	... 27/ 1/17	*Lieut.*
8034	,,	SHORT, Herbert Clifford	... 7/ 9/16	*(From A.O.D.). Lieut.*
6390	,,	SIMKIN, Rowland Ive	... 27/ 1/17	
7997	,,	SIMMONS, William Albert	... 7/ 2/17	
8017	,,	SIMPSON, Cecil Hamilton	... 10/ 9/16	*Lieut., A.E.O.*
6559	,,	SIMPSON, Samuel Ephraim Moss	26/ 9/16	*Lieut.*
764584	,,	SLATER, Sidney Arthur	... 13/12/17	
765144	,,	SMALLWOOD, William Spencer	... 10/ 5/17	*K/A* 25/1/18
6275	,,	SMELLIE, Blair	... 27/ 1/17	
7946	,,	SMITH, Colin	... 27/ 1/17	*Acc/K* 11/3/17. *(C.C.)*
7915	,,	SMITH, Carl Anastasia	... 10/ 9/16	*Capt., A.E.O.*
7725	,,	SMITH, Charles Littler	... 28/ 2/17	
7259	,,	SMITH, Frank Leslie	... 5/ 9/16	*Lieut. Interned, Holland* 15/11/17
6203	,,	SMITH, Henry Cooke	... 5/ 9/16	*w.* 4/11/18
766121	,,	SMITH, John Palmer	... 13/12/17	*Lieut.*
7707	,,	SMITH, Thomas Edmund	... 27/ 1/17	*K/A* 14/7/17
8184	,,	SMYTHE, Leslie Lionel William	... 10/ 9/16	*Lieut.*
766664	,,	SNOWDEN, William Craven	... 14/ 3/18	⌖
765054	,,	SPALDING, Frederick	... 17/ 5/17	*Lieut.*
4736	,,	SPEARING, Joseph Reginald	... 27/ 1/17	*Lieut.*
765478	,,	SPEIGHT, Richard Hayton	... 14/ 7/17	*Lieut.*
765571	,,	STANILAND, William Francis	... 24/ 1/18	
763980	,,	STANLEY, Sidney Edgar	... 14/ 4/17	*d.* 19/10/17
7162	,,	STANSFIELD, Harold	... 10/ 9/16	*Major E.O.* M.B.E. ⌖
765057	,,	STATON, William Ernest	... 5/ 5/17	*Lieut.* ✠ D.F.C. *w.* 9/10/18
763849	,,	ST. CLAIR-FOWLES, Marcus F.	... 24/ 6/17	*Lieut.*
1249	Sgt.	STEER, Wilfred	... 27/ 9/16	*Lieut.*
7621	Pte.	STENNETT, Jesse Norman	... 7/ 2/17	*Lieut.*
760852	,,	STEPHENS, Llewellyn	... 17/ 3/17	*Acc/K* 10/6/17
766033	,,	STEPHENSON, Arthur Charles P.	23/ 9/17	*Lieut.*
761993	Sgt.	STERNDALE-BENNETT, Thomas C.	27/ 8/17	*E.O.* 3
760939	Pte.	STEVENS, Leslie Herbert	... 6/ 5/17	*Lieut., Indian Army*
762104	,,	STEVENSON, Ralph Tapley	... 17/ 3/17	*K/A* 31/8/18
2289	,,	STEWART, Oliver	... 27/10/14	*(From* 9/*Middlesex) Capt.* ✠ A.F.C.
762626	,,	STOKES, Walter Ronald Forster	... 17/ 5/17	*Lieut.*
764075	,,	STOREY, Herbert Ellis	... 21/ 4/17	
7908	,,	STRADLING, Frank Bedford	... 20/ 2/17	*Lieut. (Dental)*
764272	,,	SURFLEET, John	... 17/ 5/17	*Lieut.*
766289	,,	SUTCLIFFE, Arnold Clough	... 26/ 1/18	
6560	,,	SUTCLIFFE, Arthur Leslie	... 26/ 9/16	*Lieut. P/W* 27/10/17
7950	,,	SUTHERLAND, Donald Charles	... 5/11/16	*Lieut.*
764510	,,	SWABY, Jeffrey William	... 15/ 6/17	
766147	,,	SWALES, John Simpson	... 7/ 2/18	
765323	,,	SWEETING, Alan Ernest	... 11/ 8/17	*Acc/K* 2/8/18
764914	,,	SYMONDS, Spencer Leslie Hatten	7/ 6/17	*K/A* 12/11/17

4436	Pte.	TAYLOR, Edgar Richard ...	27/ 1/17	Lieut.
760432	,,	TAYLOR, Gordon William	26/ 8/17	
8293	,,	TAYLOR, Neil Joseph	28/ 2/17	Lieut. P/W 1/10/17
765199	,,	TAYLOR, Norman Samuel	21/ 5/17	Lieut. F/D
765740	,,	TAYLOR, William Ralph ...	11/ 8/17	
5553	,,	TEBBS, Charles Edward ...	10/ 9/16	Lieut., A.E.O.
2641	,,	THIERRY, Frederick George	25/ 8/16	K/A 12/1/17
765252	,,	THEAK, William Edward	21/ 4/17	
764550	,,	THOMAS, Emrys ...	21/ 6/17	Lieut.
765146	,,	THOMPSON, Frederick Harry	15/ 6/17	Lieut.
764352	,,	THOMPSON, Harold Victor	13/ 4/17	K/A 26/9/17
765742	,,	THOMPSON, Leonard	11/ 8/17	K/A 23/8/18
762918	,,	THOMSON, John Mounsey	24/ 5/17	
767020	,,	THORP, Charles Evans ...	10/ 1/18	K/A 30/8/18
3916	,,	THORPE, James Henry ...	14/11/16	Lieut.
4720	,,	THUELL, William Johnson	7/ 7/16	K/A 1/6/17
8019	,,	TIGAR, Anthony Augustine	27/ 1/17	Lieut.
762946	,,	TILBURY, Robert William	17/ 3/17	d. 18/3/18
764392	,,	TODD, James William	7/ 6/17	
8056	,,	TOMLING, George Gibson	27/ 1/17	Lieut. ✠
765294	,,	TONKS, Horace Henry ...	17/ 5/17	
765254	,,	TRATMAN, Leslie William Draycott	15/ 6/17	P/W. d. 13/4/19
764616	,,	TRAVISS, Arthur ...	15/ 6/17	
764393	,,	TRELEASE, Reginald Henry	7/ 6/17	Lieut.
7434	,,	TRUSSELL, Harry Percival	27/ 1/17	
1605	,,	TRUBSHAWE, Walston Vyvyan	3/ 3/15	Lieut. w. 26/3/15, -/5/16
766794	,,	TUNNICLIFFE, Walter	7/ 2/18	
4856	,,	TURNER, Cyril Charles Teesdale	27/ 1/17	Lieut. A.F.C.
7889	,,	TYACK, Raymond	3/ 2/17	
765100	,,	UNDERWOOD, Joseph Harold	25/ 4/17	Lieut.
766401	,,	UNDERWOOD, Roy Garon	3/11/17	Acc/K 25/9/18
7275	,,	USHER, Cecil William	27/ 1/17	Lieut.
765065	,,	VALE, Reginald Ewart	21/ 4/17	Lieut. w. 18/6/18
763803	,,	VINCENT, Reginald Denis C.	7/ 6/17	
765083	,,	VIRGO, Cyril Percy	15/ 6/17	Lieut. w. 18/3/18
764215	,,	VIZARD, Harold Charles ...	15/ 6/17	Lieut.
765201	,,	WAKEHAM, Richard Dean	14/ 6/17	Lieut., A.E.O.
2525	,,	WAKEMAN, Frank Trevor	17/10/17	Lieut. K/A 30/10/17
762920	,,	WALKER, Henry Edward	18/ 4/17	Lieut. ✠ D.F.C.
7566	,,	WALLACE, James Henry	27/ 1/17	Lieut.
762242	,,	WALLER, Hardess de Warrenne ...	14/ 4/17	Lieut.
6776	,,	WALLIS, Leonard Powers	28/ 2/17	Lieut., M
765096	,,	WALLWORK, John Wilson	21/ 4/17	Lieut. ✠
7675	,,	WALTHO, Stanton	28/ 2/17	Lieut.
764521	,,	WARBURTON, Henry	28/ 8/17	w. 18/6/18
8169	,,	WARD, Frederick	10/ 9/16	Lieut. A.E.O.
765068	,,	WARD, Sidney Lester	25/ 4/17	
762442	,,	WARDEN, Walter Norman Hastings	10/ 5/17	

ROYAL FLYING CORPS.

764589	Pte.	Warton, Adams Henry	...	7/ 6/17	Lieut.
763607	,,	Warwick, William Geoffrey	...	4/ 6/17	
5429	,,	Waters, Harry Ernest	...	5/ 9/16	Lieut.
8514	,,	Watson, Frederick Arthur	...	28/ 2/17	Lieut.
762817	,,	Watson, John Douglas	...	10/ 5/17	Lieut.
5882	,,	Watts, Wilfred Edward	...	28/ 2/17	Lieut. P/W 1/12/17
764919	,,	Wattson, Cyril Beavon	...	7/ 6/17	K/A 8/10/17
765070	,,	Weaver, Clifford Francis	...	7/ 6/17	Lieut.
760590	,,	Webb, Derek Errol	...	27/ 8/17	Missing 29/10/18
8278	,,	Webb, Harry Frederick	...	21/ 9/17	Capt. w. 22/3/18 ℳ
764519	,,	Webberley, John William	...	7/ 6/17	
7879	,,	Webster, Thomas Milligan	...	27/ 1/17	Lieut. P/W 18/9/17
766668	,,	Weeks, William Stanley	...	13/12/17	
765296	,,	Welldon, John Cedric	...	24/ 7/17	
764467	,,	West, Arthur	...	4/ 6/17	
5976	,,	West, Mortimer Sackville	...	7/ 2/17	Acc/K 11/11/17
760971	,,	Wheeler, Edward Victor	...	17/ 3/17	
765574	,,	Wheeler, Willoughby Shaw	...	26/ 8/17	Lieut.
762071	,,	Whitaker, Harry Vivian	...	26/ 8/17	Lieut.
764619	,,	White, Francis Edward	...	7/ 6/17	Lieut.
762441	,,	White, Reginald Stuart	...	10/ 5/17	Lieut. w. 8/6/18
760664	,,	White, Willoughby Lindley C.	...	18/ 3/17	Lieut. w. 20/11/17
760305	,,	Whitehead, Eric Wilfred	...	3/11/17	Acc/K 18/2/18
765021	,,	Whyte, George Henry	...	30/ 5/17	K/A 4/12/17
763649	,,	Wightman, John Francis	...	7/ 6/17	K/A 4/9/17
765297	,,	Wilcox, Basil Syers	...	2/ 7/17	
762988	,,	Wild, William	...	21/ 4/17	Lieut. w. 12/6/18
765073	,,	Wilkins, Frank Bertram	...	21/ 4/17	Lieut.
766371	,,	Williams, George	...	14/ 3/18	
3523	,,	Williams, George Gordon	...	14/10/16	Lieut.
767074	,,	Williams, Hemdrick Desmond	...	17/ 3/18	
4555	,,	Williams, Roland Vaughan	...	27/ 1/17	K/A 5/6/17
762382	,,	Williamson, Gerald Douglas	...	3/ 3/17	D/W 1/1/18
7919	,,	Williamson, James Colney	...	27/ 1/17	Lieut. P/W 30/8/18
765320	,,	Wilson, Alan Forsyth	...	7/ 6/17	Lieut.
2873	,,	Wilson, Cecil Eustace	...	7/ 9/16	K/A 16/4/17
765369	,,	Wilson, Humphrey Hamilton	...	30/ 5/17	K/A 19/2/18
6852	,,	Wilson, Philip	...	26/ 9/16	Lieut. F/D
766201	,,	Wilson-Haffenden, James R.	...	10/ 1/18	
763672	,,	Wimpenny, Ronald Stenning	...	13/ 4/17	Lieut.
7932	,,	Winkworth, Stevenson Richard	...	7/10/16	Lieut. A.E.O. ℳ
763375	,,	Winser, Frank Edwards	...	13/ 4/17	K/A 20/8/17
765205	,,	Winsor, Arthur William	...	2/ 7/17	Lieut.
765076	,,	Winter, Douglas William	...	21/ 4/17	Lieut.
763995	,,	Wood, Geoffrey Arnold	...	13/ 4/17	Lieut.
6243	,,	Wood, Herbert McGregor	...	5/11/16	Lieut. A.E.O.
764954	,,	Wood, John	...	7/ 6/17	Lieut.
5193	,,	Wood, John Edward	...	27/ 1/17	Lieut.

6781	Pte.	Wood, John Saville	27/ 2/17	Lieut.
4567	,,	Wood, Walter Bertram	2/ 6/16	Lieut. ✠✠ K/A 11/11/17
765301	,,	Woodhouse, Percy Wilfred	14/ 7/17	K/A 28/3/18
766730	,,	Woodman, Cyril Graeme	7/ 2/18	
762861	,,	Woodman, William Lawson	13/ 4/17	Lieut.
4705	,,	Woolliams, Frank Hawker	27/ 1/17	Lieut.
764552	,,	Worstenholm, John	7/ 6/17	K/A 25/9/17
6728	,,	Worthington, Charles Edward	5/ 9/16	Lieut.
7797	,,	Wright, Dederick Roe Murray	27/ 1/17	Lieut.
765152	,,	Wynn, John	30/ 5/17	
765974	,,	Yates, Sidney	11/ 8/17	Lieut. w. 4/9/18
764944	,,	Yates, Victor John	17/ 5/17	
8062	,,	Young, John Edward Rostrom	27/ 1/17	K/A 7/7/17
4432	,,	Young, William Arnold Gemmell	7/ 7/16	Lieut. A.F.C.

ROYAL AIR FORCE
(Formed April 1st, 1918).

The Regimental Prefix (76) should be added to all the following numbers except Davies, G. R.

			Gazetted to R.A.F.	
5829	Pte.	Abbott, William Frank	1/ 4/18	
7735	,,	Arnold, Edward	17/10/18	
7460	,,	Bacon, Percy	27/ 2/19	
7050	,,	Bailey, Thomas	17/ 5/18	
6677	,,	Baker, Albert George	1/ 4/18	
7737	,,	Baker, Vernon E.	4/ 4/19	
6633	,,	Berkeley, Comyns John A.	23/ 9/18	
7491	,,	Booth, Albert Allen	24/ 2/19	Hon. 2/Lt.
6962	,,	Bradley, Frank	24/ 1/19	Hon. Pilot Officer
3610	,,	Brown, Lionel	11/ 2/19	
7742	,,	Brown, Thomas	22/ 3/19	Hon. 2/Lt.
7447	,,	Browning, Alfred James	29/ 1/19	Hon. 2/Lt.
7148	,,	Burns, Walter John	27/ 3/19	
6709	,,	Chadwick, John Hampton	8/ 4/19	Hon. 2/Lt.
6592	,,	Clarke, Henry William	1/ 4/18	
7137	,,	Colin, Barthelmy Jules	15/ 2/19	
8913	,,	Cook, Ernest John	7/ 8/18	
1201	L/Cpl.	Curtis, William Arthur	1/ 4/18	Capt. D.F.C.
6382	Pte.	Dade, Harry Dennison	1/ 4/18	
2189	CSM	Davies, Glynder Rhys	8/ 5/18	
7676	Pte.	Deltiel, Edmund Lewis Roger	19/10/18	
7282	,,	Denny, Reginald Leigh	5/ 2/19	
5533	,,	Dick, George Ronald Archbutt	1/ 4/18	
6345	,,	Dickson, Lamont Thomson	1/ 1/19	
0199	Sgt.	Eastaugh, Charles James	21/10/18	
6712	Pte.	Ellis, Arthur George	21/10/18	
5701	,,	Field, Vyvyan Mervyn	27/ 4/18	

5117	Pte.	FINCH, Eric Lewis Walter Joseph	1/ 4/18	*Lieut.*
6596	,,	FLEMING, Donald Malcolm	1/ 4/18	
0124	,,	FLINN, Charles Henry	1/ 4/18	
6334	,,	FOSTER, Sydney Imbert	26/ 4/18	
7277	,,	GALLOP, Arthur James	10/ 3/19	*Hon.* 2/*Lt.*
5576	,,	GARDEN, William Eilam	3/ 7/18	
4362	,,	GIBLETT, Harold Daird	15/ 4/18	
7309	L/Cpl.	GLOVER, William A. L. Dinwiddie	7/11/18	
7560	Pte.	GODDARD, Frederick Charles	17/ 7/18	
7444	,,	GOODWIN, Benjamin Ernest	11/ 2/19	*Hon.* 2/*Lt.*
7587	,,	GREEN, Frederick Douglas Harvey	20/ 3/19	*Hon.* 2/*Lt.*
4532	,,	HARRIS, James Albert Leslie	1/ 4/18	
6346	,,	HILL, Arthur Gerald	1/ 4/18	
6893	,,	HODGES, Henry Price	9/ 7/18	
7400	,,	HOLTON, William Henry	1/11/18	
7205	,,	HOPKINS, Cecil Alfred	7/11/18	
7058	,,	IRELAND, Douglas Wallace Stanton	3/11/18	
7191	,,	KNOWLES-BROWN, Arthur William	18/ 9/18	
7386	,,	LONG, Sidney Henry	24/ 1/19	*Hon.* 2/*Lt.*
5638	,,	MACQUEEN, Alexander John	1/ 4/18	
5847	,,	MATTHEWS, George John James	1/ 4/18	
7436	,,	McTURK, Edward	15/ 2/19	*Hon.* 2/*Lt.*
6392	,,	MORRIS, Francis Leo	26/ 2/19	*Hon.* 2/*Lt.*
7062	,,	NADIN, William Edge Fields	24/ 1/19	*Hon.* 2/*Lt.*
6485	,,	NAPIER, Richard William	1/ 4/18	
7510	,,	NAYLER, Edwin Bennett	24/ 2/19	*Hon.* 2/*Lt.*
7424	,,	OXLEY, Gilbert Leonard	26/ 2/19	*Hon.* 2/*Lt.*
1756	,,	PHILLIPS, John Fredk. Montague	18/ 8/18	*Airship*
6616	,,	PHILLIPS, Thomas Martin	1/ 4/18	
7417	,,	POWELL, George Roberts	22/ 2/19	*Hon.* 2/*Lt.*
7111	,,	PRATT, Percy Dymond	10/ 1/19	*Hon.* 2/*Lt.*
1359	,,	ROLSTON, Jack Lewis	24/ 8/18	
6085	,,	ROTHERA, Joseph	1/ 4/18	*Hon.* 2/*Lt.*
7161	,,	SCRIVEN, Sidney Albert	2/10/18	
7819	,,	SCRUBY, Roy King Fordham	20/ 1/19	*Hon.* 2/*Lt.*
7379	,,	SELL, Arthur Edward	12/ 9/18	
2791	,,	SEWELL, John	1/ 4/18	
7457	,,	SHARP, Francis Greenwich	15/ 2/19	*Hon.* 2/*Lt.*
7517	,,	SHELDON, George Hebberton	27/ 2/19	*Hon.* 2/*Lt.*
7792	,,	SHERRY, John	26/ 2/19	*Hon.* 2/*Lt.*
6453	,,	SMITH, Richard Nathan	29/ 6/18	*Obs. Officer*
7184	,,	SOUCHON, Henry Gay	22/ 8/18	
7648	,,	STRICKLAND, John Arthur	25/ 2/19	*Hon.* 2/*Lt.*
6908	,,	TAYLOR, Frank Victor	10/ 2/19	*Hon,* 2/*Lt.*
6293	,,	TIBBLES, James Charles	11/ 2/19	*Hon.* 2/*Lt.*
6576	,,	VALENTINE, Henry	18/ 2/19	*Hon.* 2/*Lt.*
6099	,,	WALKER, Walter Leslie	23/ 8/18	
4035	,,	WHITEHEAD, Clarence	15/ 6/18	
6496	,,	WILLCOX, Charles John	1/ 4/18	

CAVALRY REGIMENTS.

HOUSEHOLD BATTALION.

2nd Lieut.

7992	BARNARD, Arthur George	... ...	27/12/16 *Capt. w. —/10/17*
764182	BIRD, John Woodall	... ...	26/ 6/17 *Killed in action* 21/12/17
8222	BOLITHO, Victor Ayling	... ...	28/11/16 *Lieut. D/W 9/4/17*
5835	BROOKE, Henry ...	... ...	26/ 9/16 *Lieut.*
7453	LOWRIE, John Edward	... ...	29/11/16 *Lieut.*
7470	WILLIAMSON, Harry	... ...	26/ 9/16 *Capt. w.* 26/12/16

20TH HUSSARS.

1645	STOUT, Frank Moxon	... ...	1/ 9/14 *Lieut.* ✠ *M-G Corps Cav.*

RESERVE HUSSARS.

763608	ADAMS, Thomas William	...	... 23/ 2/18
766242	BARLEY, Walter Herbert	...	... 28/ 2/18
764083	BEAUVAIS, Charles James Cawood	...	23/ 3/18
764315	CROSS, Robert John	...	... 23/ 2/18
764772	HINE, Frederick Learoyd	...	... 23/ 2/18
765179	KEMP-GEE, Percival Norman	...	23/ 2/18
762836	MOSS, Herbert Stanley	...	... 1/ 5/17 *Died* 4/8/18
8627	PARKES, George Henry	...	... 18/ 2/17 *Lieut.* ✠
7846	PITMAN, Robert Octavin	...	... 16/ 9/16 *Lieut.*
763670	TIZARD, Ernest Ralph Charles	...	23/ 2/18

RESERVE DRAGOONS.

760647	COLLINGS, John Stanley	...	... 1/ 5/17 *Lieut.*
762478	ELTON, Clarence Bailey	...	... 1/ 5/17 *Lieut.*
762435	HOTCHKISS, Archibald	...	... 14/12/17
764385	SIMEONS, William Raymond	...	21/12/17 *w.* 23/10/18
762943	SMITH, George Geoffrey	...	... 1/ 5/17 *Lieut.*

RESERVE LANCERS.

765976	KING, William Cyril Campbell	...	14/12/17
765980	SHERINGHAM, Anthony Ilex...	...	14/12/17
6033	THORLEY, Horace William ...	...	22/12/16 *Killed in action* 8/8/18

From this page onwards, rank at date of Commission is omitted in the case of Privates or Cadets. ED.

RESERVE CAVALRY REGIMENTS.

762774	BARBER, William	... 24/ 8/17	2	
761680	BROCKLISS, William J. ...	... 23/ 2/18	6	
7443	COOK, Herbert Henry ...	... 15/ 2/19	4	
767383	DAVIES, Llewellyn Ladd ...	... 14/ 2/19	2	
2292	DAWKINS, Cpl. John Raymond	... 22/12/16	3	Lieut.
7678	FILMER, Vivian Reginald Royal	... 24/ 7/16	3	Killed in action 25/11/17
767384	GORING, Leonard John ...	... 14/ 2/19	2	
765902	HALKETT, Guy Wallace ...	... 23/ 5/18	1	Brigade Major
763066	HINDE, George Norman ...	... 8/ 7/17	5	
6618	HOLDERNESS, L/Cpl. Leslie Cyril	... 22/12/16	3	Lieut
8089	HOPKINS, John Leslie ...	... 23/11/16	13	Lieut. w. 9/4/18
762434	HORWOOD, Ernest Bentall ...	... 8/ 7/17	4	
763068	KENNEY, Douglas George ...	... 13/ 3/19	3	
6577	LOYNES, John Harvey ...	... 22/12/16	4	Lieut.
7679	MACKINNON. Neil Livingstone	... 24/ 7/16	5	Lieut. w. 17/10/18
763109	MACKRELL, Herbert Reginald	... 24/ 9/17	5	
762650	MASSEY, Albert Ewart ...	... 8/ 7/17	5	
765374	NORDEN, Richard Watts ...	... 24/ 9/17	2	
760544	PURVIS, John Leighton Fortescue	... 14/ 2/19	4	
767837	RAEBURN, Francis Colin ...	... 14/ 2/19	4	
7661	RANDALL, Edward Joseph John	... 22/12/16	5	Lieut.
768078	SHEPHARD, Edward Frank ...	... 13/ 3/19	5	
7827	SPARROW, Arthur Christopher G.	... 22/12/16	4	Lieut.
8323	STROTHER, Frederick Webb	... 11/ 1/17	6	Lieut.
764050	WHITE, Edward Edwin John	... 23/ 5/18	4	
767209	WYATT, Ralph	... 18/10/18	6	

YEOMANRY REGIMENTS.

		2nd Lieut.	
2906	AGAR, Thomas Forrester ...	... 2/ 4/15	*Royal Glasgow. Lieut. (R.E.)*
3786	BOND, Gerald Aubrey ...	... 19/10/15	*3/London. Lieut. ✠ (12/Middx.)*
2159	DELMEGE, Hugh Barry Evans	... 9/ 7/15	*Bedfordshire*
2889	GOODBODY, John Barrington	... 5/ 2/15	*West Kent. Capt. (10/E. Kent)*
4972	HETHERINGTON, Howard Walklett	... 28/ 6/16	*S. Notts Hussars. Lieut. (R.A.F.)*
2285	METCALFE, Percy Hubert Geldart	... 23/ 2/15	*Dorset*
6071	MONCKTON, Iven Parry ...	... 4/ 1/16	*South Notts Hussars. Lieut.*
5867	PERCIVAL, Eric James ...	... 4/ 7/16	*Lovat's Scouts*
4345	QUARTERMAINE, Charles George	... 26/11/15	*R. Bucks Hussars. Capt. P/WCamp*

YEOMANRY REGIMENTS.

762947	Armsden, Reginald	... ...	26/ 4/17	1/*Montgomery. w. –/9/18*
6922	Barron, L/Cpl. George Herbert A.		28/11/16	1/*Scottish Horse. Lieut.*
764542	Beckett, Cecil John Robert	...	30/10/17	1/*D. of Lancaster*
6695	Blankley, Cecil Hubert	... ...	26/ 9/16	1/*Leicester. Lieut. w. 4/6/17*
765155	Brown, Charles Kenneth	... ...	24/ 9/17	1/*West Kent*
764879	Burrows, Harold Norman	...	24/ 8/17	1/*Derby*
7526	Butterfield, James		29/ 7/16	*Essex. Lieut.*
765265	Campbell, William Robert Caldwell		28/11/17	1/*D. of Lancaster*
764755	Coombe, Reginald George Bradford		23/ 4/18	1/*Surrey*
5990	De la Cour, Herbert Hedges Hyde		26/ 9/16	1/*N. Devon. Lieut. w. 1/11/18*
763028	Drake, Stuart Edmund	...	24/11/17	1/*S. Notts Hussars*
765935	Gilbert, Sydney Paul	..	27/ 2/18	1/*Suffolk*
764141	Gould, William John Edward	...	28/11/17	*D. of Lancaster*
6264	Harris, Harold Maltby	...	26/ 9/16	3/*London. Lieut. K/A 16/6/17*
763102	Hanbury, Harold Greville	...	28/ 6/17	1/*Warwickshire*
765945	Hopkinson, Cyril Oswald John	...	27/ 2/18	1/*Surrey*
4879	Houghton, Alan Lutman	...	26/ 9/16	1/*Devon. Lieut. w. 9/10/18*
763067	Hunter, John Ernest	...	24/11/17	1/*Dorset*
764778	Kirkbridge, Herbert James	...	13/ 1/18	1/*Derby*
764370	Larken, John Savage	...	2/10/17	1/*West Kent. K/A 21/9/18*
762560	Laverton, Walter King	...	7/ 7/17	1/*Derby*
762218	Leader, Colledge	... ...	24/ 8/17	1/*Leicester*
764152	Leverett, John Ivison	...	30/ 5/17	1/*Lovat's Scouts. w. 8/5/18*
765399	Macdonald, Eric Pond	...	24/11/17	1/*Dorset*
764545	McNeil, Arthur Anderson	...	24/11/17	1/*Lothian & Border Horse*
761185	Musgrave, Joseph	... ...	29/ 3/17	1/*Westmorel'd & Cumberl'd. Lieut.*
764942	Phillips, Malcolm McGregor	...	5/12/17	1/*D. of Lancaster*
765875	Robertson, Thomas Struan	...	14/12/17	1/*Res. King Edward's Horse*
765960	Rose, Charles	... ...	23/ 4/18	1/*London*
764361	Sanderson, Arthur Buchanan	...	26/ 4/17	1/*Lovat's Scouts. Lieut.*
6297	Smith, Gilbert Kirke	...	8/ 1/17	*Yorks Dragoons. Lieut.*
767683	Stokes, Geoffrey Calcott	...	4/ 3/19	*Bucks*
764726	Taylor, John Fielding	...	18/12/17	1/*Derby. Lieut.* ⚔
765293	Taylor, Reginald	... ...	5/12/17	1/*D. of Lancaster*
768106	Thomson, Ivor Thearle		17/ 3/19	*Surrey*
766746	Wells, Arthur John	...	18/ 3/18	1/*D. of Lancaster*
6779	Westendarp, Hermann Emil Alfred		30/ 9/16	1/*West Kent. w. 27/8/18*
762042	White, William Geoffrey Beauchamp		18/ 4/17	1/*Wilts*
8298	Whitworth, Frank	... ...	22/12/16	*Essex. Lieut.*
3989	Wiles, L/Cpl. Ernest Edward	...	19/ 8/16	*Surrey*

ROYAL ARTILLERY.

R.H.A. and R.F.A.

(A/L: 514)

2nd Lieut.

4349	BEAK, Frank Leslie ...	...	30/ 9/15	*Attached R.E. K/A 9/4/18*
1558	BERTIE, Alberic Willoughby	...	25/ 2/15	*Capt.* ✠
1393	BLAKE, Cpl. Charles Edwin Norman	20/ 8/15	*Major.* ✠ *K/A 30/7/18*
1770	BLISS, Francis Kennard	...	9/ 7/15	*Killed in action 28/9/16*
1684	CHANTREY, Leslie Hewer	...	30/10/15	*(From 9/Royal Sussex)*
1747	COLE, Arthur Philips	...	30/10/14	*w. (Dardanelles) 21/5/15*
2305	CRUICKSHANK, Eric ...	...	6/10/14	*Lieut.* F/D. *D/W 26/9/18*
1418	DAVIS, Dudley Frederick	...	27/ 2/15	*Capt. w. 1/7/16*
2748	DODD, Ernest John ...	...	26/ 6/15	*w. –/5/16 K/A 17/7/17*
580	GILL, Hugh Stanley ...	...	27/ 2/15	*Lieut.* ✠ *8/12/15*
2620	HASKINS, Leonard Jesse	...	5/ 8/15	*Lieut.* ⚜
2490	LADEFOGED, Cpl. Niels Nielson	...	30/ 8/15	*(To R.G.A.)*
1324	LAVER, Basil Leslie ...	...	27/ 2/15	*Lieut.*
949	LAVER, L/Cpl. Charles Hardiman	...	27/ 2/15	*Lieut.*
2726	LISTER, John Curtis	...	22/ 9/15	*Killed in action 20/5/17*
1361	LUMB, Herbert	...	12/ 9/14	*d. 28/10/15*
1124	MORGAN, Ernest Leslie	...	27/ 2/15	*Lieut.* ✠ *w. –/9/17*
81	MUNT, L/Cpl. Edsall	...	27/ 2/15	*Major.* ✠ ⚜
1617	ROBINSON, Wyndham Percy	...	27/ 2/15	*Lieut. w. –/11/16* ⚜
3535	SHEPHERD, Thomas Duncan	...	3/ 5/15	*Capt.*
2351	THORESBY-JONES, Mervyn ...	...	20/ 1/15	*Lieut. (Inspection Staff)*
1518	TROWBRIDGE, Bernard Bromley	...	28/ 7/15	*Lieut.*
2654	WOOD, Percy Neville	...	28/12/14	*Major. w. at Ypres –/12/15* ⚜
1155	WILLIS, Sgt. Cyril Reginald ...	...	11/ 2/16	*Lieut.* ✠ *Indian Mtd. Battery.* ⚜
768310	ALLEN, William Alfred	...	8/ 4/19	
766825	ALLDRED, Stanley Douglas ...		5/ 9/18	
4966	ANDERSON, William Wallace	...	16/ 9/16	*Killed in action 10/11/16*
7458	ARNALL, Harry	...	12/ 1/17	
767580	BARBER, Albert Edwin	...	8/ 5/18	
766340	BARBOUR, George Brown	...	5/ 8/18	
767829	BARCKLEY, Arthur Edward Whitehead	10/ 2/19	
5724	BAX, Frank Leonard	...	12/ 1/17	
7718	BEARN, Arthur Frederick	...	12/ 1/17	
5891	BERRY, John William	...	12/ 1/17	
765697	BINNS, Henry Innes	...	19/ 9/18	
765341	BOLTON, Arthur	...	28/ 8/17	*w. 19/10/18*
6971	BRITTAIN, Samuel Taylor	...	6/12/17	
767245	BROADBENT, Conrad Fletcher B.	...	5/ 2/19	
766681	BROADBENT, Edward Warwick	...	8/ 2/19	
767981	BROADBRIDGE, Montague Cecil	...	5/ 4/19	
766505	BROADLEY, Albert	...	12/ 2/19	
7884	BROWN, Malcolm Frederick	...	12/ 1/17	*w. 1/5/17*
767295	BRYANT, Stanley Grant	...	8/ 8/18	
8233	BURWASH, Herbert Arthur	...	30/ 1/17	

ROYAL ARTILLERY.

2542	BUTTEMER, Eric Douglas Archibald	27/10/15	*Lieut. (From R.M.A.)* ⚔
764684	CAMPBELL, Andrew ...	2/ 9/17 ✠ ⚔ (2)	
764287	CANTY, Frederick Joseph ...	14/10/17	*Lieut.*
765434	CAREY, Charles McLeod ...	1/ 4/18	
766154	CAROLL, John Art ...	27/11/17	
765383	CARSON, Wilfred John ...	6/10/17	
7460	CARTWRIGHT, Sidney Herbert	17/11/16	*w.* 17/4/18
766102	CAVENAGH, Francis Alexander	26/ 8/18	*Education Officer*
761631	CAWLEY, James Donald ...	21/ 2/17 ✠	
765384	CHALLIS, John Alexander McDonald	16/ 7/17	
764633	CHANDLEY, Reginald Thos. Francis	1/ 9/18	
4657	CHATFEILD-CLARKE, L/Cpl. Howard C.	21/ 2/17	
763022	COATES, George Thomas ...	28/ 5/17	
8085	COKE, Edward ...	12/ 1/17 ✠	*w.* 5/11/17
766188	COLEMAN, Charles Henry ...	1/ 9/18	
766300	COLEMAN, Guy William Jordan	1/ 8/18	
760487	COLLEY, L/Cpl. Reginald Harding ...	15/ 1/18	
7529	COLLINS, Walter Leslie Fenn	12/ 1/17	*Lieut. w.* 16/8/17
574	COOPER, Sidney Walter ...	28/12/14	
766512	CORBETT, Harold Stevenson	2/ 8/18	
7530	CORSER, Frederick George ...	12/ 1/17	*Lieut. w.* —/5/17
767053	COWAN, Alexander ...	1/ 8/18	
763924	CROOKES, Noel Richard Dillon	2/ 9/17	
766381	CUMMING, Bernard Douglas	26/ 9/18	
762800	DALY, Oliver R. ...	6/ 6/17	*w.* 9/11/17
766594	DANIEL, Arthur Freer ...	2/ 8/18	
7533	DAVIES, Thomas Lewis ...	18/ 1/17	*w.* 7/11/18
764553	DICKINSON, Sydney ...	4/ 2/18	
7653	DIX, John Arnold ...	12/ 1/17	
765534	DRYSDALE, Alexander Monteith	15/ 8/18	
5440	DUNSTON, George Hubert ...	18/12/16	*Lieut.*
760733	EARNSHAW, CSM Percy Harold	19/ 8/18	
1826	EGERTON, Cpl. Bryan Selwyn	18/ 8/15	*Lieut.* ⚔
768066	EVANS, Thomas Watkin ...	7/ 4/19	
767261	FAHY, Dermot Francis ...	15/ 2/19	
762781	FLETCHER, Charles Harrington	17/ 5/17	*w.* 3/9/17
765540	FOSS, William ...	5/ 8/18	
766922	GARMONSWAY, George Norman	28/ 8/18	
9760	GEDDES, William John ...	22/ 6/17	*Capt.* O.B.E. (*R.E.*)
8126	GILMORE, Arthur Norris ...	12/ 1/17	*Lieut.*
767994	GRADDON, William Douglas ...	7/ 4/19	
765881	GRASSICK, William Henderson	17/ 6/18	*d.* 9/2/19
767106	GRAY, Harold Leonard ...	10/ 2/19	
767211	GUBBINS, Alfred Blakeney Gough ...	5/ 9/18	
7475	HALFORD, Robert C. ...	23/12/16	*Lieut. w.* 24/8/17
762576	HALL, L/Cpl. Maxwell ...	29/12/17	
765887	HARVEY, William Henry ...	10/ 6/18	*Killed in action* 23/10/18
760405	HEALD, Sgt. Henry Claypole	10/ 2/19	

7881	HEMPSON, Oswald Arthur	12/ 1/17	w. 18/10/17
766164	HENDERSON, Rex Eugene	23/11/17	
6763	HILL, Cornelius John Keeting	27/ 1/17	
7805	HODGE, Francis Edwin	4/ 1/17	w. 23/8/17
7731	HODGKINS, Albert Edward	12/ 1/17 ✠	w. 22/10/17
763335	HORN, Frederick William	5/ 8/17	w. 23/11/18
764702	HUDSON, Robert Coates	14/ 1/18	
7929	HUMPHERSON, Sidney Frederick	4/ 1/17	*Lieut.*
767289	JOHNSON, Alexander Rayner	2/ 9/18	
7670	JONES, William Samuel	12/ 1/17	*Lieut.*
766435	JOSLING, Harold William	26/ 8/18	
767143	KEITES, William Lawrence	2/ 8/18	
5767	KEKEWICH, Stanley Buck	2/ 9/16	*Lieut.* ✠
767996	KIPPING, Stanley Percival	7/ 4/19	
7539	KNIGHT, Harry	12/ 1/17	
762249	LARDELLI, Maurice Strachan	1/ 6/17	
762540	LEDGER, Gilbert	11/ 3/17	*Lieut.*
767909	LEWIS, Francis	8/ 3/19	
762140	LEWIS, Ralph Pollard	17/ 5/17	
766438	LIDDINGTON, Harold Vere	3/ 8/18	
766389	LINDARS, Louis Henry	26/ 8/18	
764659	LOCK, James Palmer	13/10/17	*Died of wounds* 2/2/18
767325	LOGAN, William Wright	21/10/18	
767594	LOVELL, Percy Trangott	13/ 3/19	
8156	LYONS-CAMPBELL, Archibald	30/ 1/17	
767798	MACGREGOR, George Gordon	20/ 2/19	
7727	MACKAY, Robert Lindsay	9/ 2/17	*Lieut.*
767595	MARTYN, Redvers Noel	10/ 2/19	
767597	MAY, Stuart	15/ 2/19	
765416	MAYBIN, John Alexander	15/ 7/18	
7320	McFADYON, John Craig	12/ 1/17	11*th Divl. Amm./C. K/A* 6/6/17
1581	MICHELSEN, Arthur Conrad	21/ 2/17	*Lt.* w.-/1/16,-/7/17. *K/A* 18/10/17
766257	MILLER, Frederick	26/ 8/18	
765688	MOCHRIE, David Russell	7/ 2/19	
6405	MOFFAT, George Ross	2/ 9/16	*Lieut.* w. 18/10/17
762959	MORGAN, Eric Ronald	17/ 5/17	
768014	MORGAN, Sidney Conrad	7/ 4/19	
6337	MOULDING, Edgar Percy	12/ 1/17	*Lieut.*
765691	NEALE, Bertie Philip	18/ 8/18	
761356	NICHOLS, Hedley William	9/ 2/18	
768087	NICHOLSON-LAILEY, John Raymond	7/ 4/19	
7465	NICOL, Ian Sinclair	12/ 1/17 ✠	*P/W* 26/7/18
767368	NORRIS, Charles Albert	15/ 2/19	
4095	NORRIS, Frank Charles	12/ 9/16	*Lieut.*
768045	PAGE, George Frederick	7/ 4/19	
8005	PAGE, Stanley Clarence Martel	11/ 2/17	w. 19/9/18
7546	PAICE, Eric Bertie	12/ 1/17	w. 30/4/18
761236	PARK, Arthur	15/ 2/19	

ROYAL ARTILLERY.

766841	PATON, Allen John W. ...	... 4/ 2/19	
760937	PAUL, CSM Vivian Charles	... 7/ 4/19	
762308	PEIRCE, Arthur Russell ...	... 24/ 6/17	w. 10/6/18
766567	PETER, Gerald	... 15/ 2/18	
762727	PHEYSEY, John Edward ...	... 17/ 4/17 ✠	
766196	PHIPPS, John Degory Baron	... 23/ 9/18	
760451	PICK, Nelson	... 12/ 8/18	
762185	POCOCK, Reginald William ...	... 28/ 2/17 ✠	
762702	PREEN, Arthur Frank ...	... 3/ 6/17	w. 11/7/18
767706	PULFORD, Robert George ...	... 10/ 2/19	
5870	PURVES, John Murdow ...	... 12/ 1/17	Lieut. ✠ w. 16/8/17
7785	RATCLIFF, Sidney Arthur ...	... 12/ 1/17	Killed in action 31/3/17
762183	RAWE, Charles Henry ...	... 26/ 3/17	Killed in action 24/4/18
2268	RAWES, Alexander Newling ...	... 21/ 2/17	P/W 26/4/18
765801	READ, Horace Cleveland ...	... 15/ 7/18	
766197	REID, Clive Ronald ...	... 5/ 8/18	
765958	REMNANT, Eustace Archibald	... 15/ 7/18	
766765	REECE, Frederick William ...	... 26/ 2/19	
7550	REYNOLDS, Leonard Arthur	... 21/ 1/17	Lieut. w. 18/4/18
762686	ROBERTS, John	... 28/ 4/17	Capt. ✠ w. 24/8/17, 4/6/18
767269	ROBINSON, Douglas Hepworth	... 13/ 3/19	[d. 11/11/18 ℞
7762	ROSE, Frederick Charles ...	... 12/ 1/17	
6235	RUMFORD, William Archibald	... 12/ 1/17	w. 17/11/17
767647	SCOUGALL, John Muir ...	... 20/ 2/19	
3144	SENDALL, Claude Hume ...	... 14/ 6/15	w. 11/4/18
761927	SHERWIN, Harry Collumbell	... 5/ 4/17 ℞	
762263	SIMMONDS, Austin Gundry ...	... 17/ 5/17	Acc/drowned 2/6/17
768103	SIMPSON, Charles ...	... 7/ 4/19	
7551	SIMPSON, James Sieder Muir	... 12/ 1/17	Lieut.
768128	SMITH, Charles Horne Cecil	... 7/ 4/19	
7645	SMITH, John Poole ...	... 13/ 1/17	Lieut.
764508	SMITH, Sidney Charles ...	... 1/ 9/18	
1669	SPARLING, Philip Sidney ...	... 4/12/16	Lieut.
767649	SWANTON, Ernest Frederick William	5/ 4/19	
760959	TAAFFE, Leonard Charles ..	... 7/ 4/19	
6913	THOMAS, Walter Stanley ...	... 12/ 1/17	
767731	TILL, William Plumer ...	... 10/ 2/19	
7692	TOBUTT, Ronald Leslie William	... 11/ 2/17	
8088	VILE, Thomas Henry ...	... 12/ 1/17	Lieut.
762136	WAITE, Frederick John ...	... 30/ 3/17	
760638	WALLACE, Sgt. William ...	... 14/10/18	
764733	WARD, Charles Richard Francis	... 12/ 8/18	
760866	WARREN, Harvey	... 17/ 4/17	
7521	WATSON, William Findlay ...	... 11/ 2/17	w. 17/11/17
760284	WEISS, L/Cpl. Robert Alfred	... 27/ 1/17	Lieut.
760489	WHITE, Herbert Raymond ...	... 12/ 1/18	
7677	WHITEHOUSE, Stuart Wellesley	... 12/ 1/17	Lieut.
766879	WHITMORE, Edward Walter	... 13/ 2/19	

768356	WHYTEHEAD, Henry Layard	...	7/ 4/19	
766669	WILKINSON, Walter	...	7/ 4/19	
7717	WOODWARD, Gerald de Maine	...	19/ 2/17	
7657	WOOLF, Emanuel	...	12/ 1/17	*Lieut.*

Royal Field Artillery : Special Reserve.

(A/L: 575)

2259	CAITHNESS, Wilfred W. ...	...	28/ 4/15	*Capt.* F/D *w.* –/2/17 ⚔
2188	DAVIS, Thomas Henry Clifford	...	8/10/15	*Lieut.* ✠ ✠ *w.* –/9/16, –/12/17
1880	HAEFFNER, Frederick Wilfred	...	1/ 7/15	
4510	MARSDEN, Douglas Herbert	...	22/ 1/16	*Lieut. w.* 28/5/17
2738	NIMMO, William Wilson ...	...	8/10/15	*Major* ✠
2634	NOWELL, Wilfrid James ...	...	1/ 7/15	*Killed in action* 9/4/17
2218	OLVER, John Dennis Circuit	...	8/ 4/15	*Lieut.* ✠ *Killed in action* 29/4/17
2945	POWELL, Lawrence	...	8/10/15	*Lieut.* ✠
4022	THOMAS, Alban Musgrove ...	...	18/10/15	*Lieut. (Staff)*
7628	ALLEN, Greville John Buxton	...	2/ 2/17	*Lieut. w.* 22/10/17
765378	ANDERSON, Horace Ince ...	...	30/ 8/17	*Lieut.*
5106	ANDREW, William Blair Spencer	...	1/ 2/17	*Lieut.*
5107	ARNOLD, Ralph Francis ...	...	16/ 6/19	*Lieut. w.* 27/9/17
764178	BAILEY, Edgar Samuel ...	...	11/ 1/18	*w.* 13/6/18
6432	BALFOUR, Alan Scot	...	3/ 8/16	*(R.F.C.) Killed in action* 13/1/18
764222	BARTER, Henry Edward ...	...	11/ 8/17	*Lieut.*
762231	BELLHOUSE, David James ...	...	17/ 4/17	*Lieut.*
764180	BENTLEY, Cyril Jack	...	8/ 9/17	*Lieut. w.* 5/4/18
762692	BERNARD, Herbert Antoine	...	7/ 9/17	*w.* 31/10/18
5043	BISCOE, Charles Henry ...	...	1/ 2/17	*Lieut. w.* 5/6/18
761861	BISHOP, Thomas Charles ..	...	19/ 4/17	*Lieut.*
7962	BOLTON, Harold Stanley ...	...	9/ 1/17	*Lieut.*
7741	BRAY, Cecil Francis	...	15/12/16	*Lieut.*
2616	BRIDSON, Eric	...	4/ 2/17	*Lieut.*
5434	BROWNING, Frederick ...	...	10/12/16	*w.* 15/12/17
7684	CARR, Ralph Sampson ...	...	5/ 2/17	*Lieut.*
764570	CHURCH, Clarence Thomas ...	...	11/ 8/17	
7368	COOP, Richard Wallace ...	...	9/ 1/17	*Lieut.* ✠ *w.* 29/8/17
762774	CORK, John Frederick ...	...	15/ 9/17	
7227	CORKILL, Lawrence Lancey ..	...	9/ 1/17	*Lieut.*
764314	CORNELIUS, Joshua Charles ...	...	28/ 9/17	*w.* 15/10/18
6200	COUNSELL, Henry Cecil ...	...	16/12/16	*Killed in action* 27/5/18
7902	COX, Ernest Henry George ...	...	5/ 3/17	*Lieut.*
7531	CRUTTENDEN, Robert Frost ..	...	4/ 2/17	*Lieut.*
7585	DAY, Augustine Joseph ...	...	11/ 2/17	*Lieut.* ✠ *w.* 19/11/17, 31/7/18 ⚔
7740	DAVIDSON, L/Cpl. Theodore	...	9/ 1/17	*Lieut. w.* 3/11/17
7150	DAWSON, George Gardiner ...	...	1/ 2/17	*Lieut.*
760430	DENNISON, Charles Haddon	...	9/12/17	*w.* 11/5/18
764193	DOWDEN, Henry James ...	...	11/ 8/17	*Lieut.* ✠
765386	DYER, William Spafford ...	...	7/ 9/17	*Lieut. w.* 13/6/18

ROYAL ARTILLERY.

8146	Dykes, Oswald	5/ 3/17	Lieut.	✠
763735	Eager, Waldo McGillycuddy	11/ 8/17		
764021	Ellis, Howard	7/ 9/17		
8096	Fahy, Conor Patrick J.	11/ 2/17	Lieut.	w. 27/10/17
1643	Fairbairns, Joseph Maurice	24/ 4/17	Killed in action 20/8/17	
7667	Forster, Harold	9/ 1/17	Lieut.	
765388	French, William Henry	7/ 9/17		
7421	Gent, George Edward	9/ 1/17	Killed in action 14/9/17	
762591	Gilvray, George Frederick	11/ 8/17		
7993	Gourlay, Clifford White	25/ 1/17	Lieut.	w. 8/9/17
7584	Gray, James Henry	11/ 2/17	P/W 18/4/18	
4877	Greenwall, Emile Boris	4/ 2/17	Lieut.	w. 1/10/17
761971	Gunn, Henry Somerville	3/ 6/17	Lieut.	
7463	Hacker, Thomas Hindle Stanford	15/12/16	Lieut.	
762405	Hadley, John Aubrey	24/ 6/17	Lieut.	w. 15/11/18
6574	Hall, Sydney Francis	9/ 1/17	Lieut.	
764066	Heady, Harold	11/ 8/17		
6452	Heavans-Trewman, Reginald F. P.	11/ 1/17	Lieut.	
8032	Haynes, Dudley Hugo	9/ 1/17	Lieut. w. 12/9/17	K/A 16/5/18
6349	Hibbert, Arthur James	28/11/16	Drowned 14/8/17	
6617	Higgins, Donald Akin	21/ 9/16	Lieut.	
5952	Hill, Joseph Shirley	12/ 1/17	Lieut. ✠	w. –/6/17
5015	Hooper, George William Ewart	4/ 2/17	Lieut.	
8082	Houlston, Francis Henry	9/ 1/17	Lieut.	
6221	Hudson, Edward Palmer	2/ 9/16	Lieut. ✠	w. 16/10/18
3184	Hughesdon, Arthur Hamilton	2/12/16	Lieut.	Killed in action 27/9/18
8111	Hulbert, Bernard William	11/ 2/17	Lieut.	w. 15/6/18
763952	Jepson, Leslie Robert	14/ 9/17		
763911	Jones, Sydney George	14/ 9/17		
7790	Kennedy, Cyril Arthur Reginald	4/ 2/17	Lieut. ✠	w. 1/11/19
763304	Kingdon, Frank Denys	30/ 8/17	Lieut. ✠	w. 27/9/18
2958	Kingswell, L/Cpl. Charles William	17/ 4/17	Lieut.	
2486	Ladefoged, Esper Louborg Nielso	28/11/16	Lieut.	
7957	Lawrence, Stanley Goldbraith	11/ 2/17	Lieut.	
764655	Lechertier, Jacques Alfred	14/ 9/17	Killed in Action 4/11/18	
5108	Leggett, L/Cpl. Sydney James	15/12/16	Lieut.	w. 29/6/17
7579	Lewis, George Powell	1/ 2/17	Lieut.	
765398	Lightbourn, Francis Gwynne	7/ 9/17		
7268	Lipschitz, Joshua Maurice	9/ 1/17	Lieut.	w. 29/11/18
764153	Lister, Alfred Walter	14/ 9/17	Lieut. ✠	w. 2/11/18
8115	Lloyd, George Llewellyn	9/ 1/17	Lieut. ⚑	
5314	Lowe, John Lawrence	16/ 9/16	Lieut. ⚑	
7664	Mackinnon, L/Cpl. George Wilson	15/12/16	Lieut.	Educ. Officer. w. 18/5/17
766170	Mahon, John Fleming	23/11/17		
762549	Manners, Christopher	25/ 3/18		
763855	Mark, Jeffrey	14/ 9/17	Lieut.	w. 29/4/18
7541	Marshall, Francis	3/ 3/17	Lieut. ✠	w. 25/10/18
7047	McKinty, Henry Bernard	1/ 2/17	Lieut. ✠	w. 1/7/17

Copyright.] [Capt. E. HANDLEY-READ.

ARRAS (Little Square).

A TIGHT CORNER: GETTING THE GUNS AWAY. [Capt. W. B. Wollen.

762759	MEADOWS, Charles Stanley ...	11/ 8/17	*Lieut.*	✠
7767	MIDDLETON, Robert E. ...	25/ 1/17	*Lieut.*	w. 10/11/17
7377	MOOLENAAR, L/Cpl. Frank Anthony	10/ 1/17	*Lieut.*	w. 24/10/17
766172	MORDEN, Clifford Sefton ...	29/ 6/17		
7658	MUNRO, William Pearce ...	4/ 2/17	*Died of wounds* 5/9/18	
8196	NAPIER, William Florence ...	12/ 2/17	*Lieut.*	
4367	NEWMAN, Arthur James ...	27/11/16	*Lieut.* ✠	w. 3/5/18
8038	NICHOLSON, Francis Hamilton	12/ 2/17	*Lieut.*	
763859	NICHOLSON, Richard Lavoisier	15/ 9/17		
7659	NICOLL, George Stalker ...	15/12/16	*Lieut.*	
7333	NOBLE, George Alfred ...	9/ 1/17	*Lieut.*	w. 16/10/17
761695	PANTLIN, Louis Alfred ...	19/ 4/17	*Lieut.*	
6653	PATERSON, Robert Frank ...	6/12/16	*Lieut.*	w. 15/11/18 ℞
7548	PAUL, Reginald Walter ...	1/ 2/17	*Lieut.*	
760058	PEARCE, Cuthbert ...	11/ 8/17	*Lieut.* F/D	
7479	PLATT, Claud Lucian Francis	9/ 1/17	*Killed in action* 27/5/18	
7004	POPE, Frank William ...	9/ 1/17	*Lieut.*	
764794	POWELL, Martin ...	15/ 9/17		
7722	PRESTON, William Forbes Amyas	12/ 2/17	*Lieut.*	w. 22/10/17, 2/10/18
8139	PRICE, George Herbert ...	4/ 2/17	*Lieut.*	
7516	RANDALL, Edgar Langley ...	4/ 2/17	*Lieut.*	
6654	RANKEN, John Sanderson ...	15/12/16	*Lieut.*	w. 5/11/17
6338	RICHARDS, Ferdinand Arthur	1/ 2/17	*Lieut.*	w. 17/1/18
762728	ROBERTS, William Charles Lee	15/ 9/17		
6625	SALISBURY, William Leslie ...	18/12/16	*Lieut.*	
761335	SAMSON, Ivan Anthony Cuthbert	18/ 2/17		
760298	SCOTCHER, Harry Goodleft ...	5/ 4/17	*Lieut.*	w. 11/10/17, 19/6/18
5033	SCOTT, Ivan Joseph ...	5/ 3/17	*Lieut.*	w. 10/10/17
764262	SHEEHAN, John Joseph ...	14/ 9/17		
7466	SMITH, Bertram Kingsley ...	9/ 1/17	*Lieut.*	w. 16/10/17
6029	SMITH, Lawrence Godfrey ...	16/ 9/16	*Lieut.*	w. 16/10/17
7947	SMITH, Walter Douglas ...	9/ 1/17	*Lieut.*	
7948	SMITHER, Bernard ...	9/ 1/17	*Lieut.*	
7260	SNALLAM, Frederick Randolph	26/ 2/17	*Lieut.*	
7306	STAINES, L/Cpl. John Samuel	15/12/16	*Lieut.*	
766032	STANDRING, John Samuel Harold	1/ 3/18		[K/A 23/10/18
5222	STEPHENS, Cecil Hubert ...	1/ 2/17	*Lieut.*	w. 17/9/17, 18/10/17
6629	STRATTON, Gilbert Leonard...	2/ 9/16	*Capt. (Staff)* ✠ ℞	
3253	STREATHER, Cecil Turner ...	4/ 2/17	*Lieut.*	w. 12/12/17
763448	STUART, Edmund Cuthbert ...	24/ 8/17	*Lieut.*	
4738	STUART, L/Cpl. Henry Lonjan	5/10/16	*Lieut.*	
760929	TAIT, Norman ...	23/ 2/18		
7916	THOMAS, Arthur Hornby ...	4/ 2/17	*Lieut.*	
765407	THOMPSON, John Waldo ...	7/ 9/17	*Lieut.*	
766179	THOMSON, Robert F. ...	23/11/17		
6963	TIDDY, John Lewis ...	1/ 2/17	*Lieut.*	w. 29/11/18
5225	TRIMM, Charles Algernon ...	10/ 1/17	*Lieut. & Adjt.* ✠	
766179	URQUHART, Aeneas McKay	23/11/17		

ROYAL ARTILLERY.

5559	VERGETTE, George	...	...	...	16/12/16	Lieut.	✠	w. 17/4/18
7556	WARE, Vivian	...	...	...	4/ 1/17	Lieut.		w. 24/4/18
7276	WATT, Charles Frederick	...	...	9/ 1/17	Lieut.		
762966	WELLS, Maurice Godfrey	...	...	4/11/17	Killed in action 28/3/18			
761508	WELTE, Ernest James	...	...	14/ 1/18	✠			
2391	WHEATE, Thomas Ernest	...	...	4/ 2/17	Capt.	✠		
8160	WHEELER, Thomas Benjamin	...	4/ 2/17	Lieut.				
764173	WHIBLEY, Stuart Napier	...	...	15/ 9/17	Capt.			
7834	WHITEHEAD, Frederick William	...	4/ 2/17	Lieut.	✠			
761876	WILKINSON, Arthur Buttle	...	...	2/ 2/17	Lieut.	✠	w. 21/9/17	
6271	WILLIAMS, Vincent Givilym	...	15/ 2/17	Lieut.				
761491	WRIGHT, Albert	...	...	...	8/12/17	Lieut.		
2942	BUXTON-KNIGHT, Albert	...	...	23/ 2/18				

(A/L: 659)

Royal Horse Artillery: Territorial Force.

Berkshire.

| 3105 | CARDELL-OLIVER, John Edward | ... | 21/ 3/15 | Capt. | R.H.A. |

Nottinghamshire.

| 2087 | ARMSTRONG, Geoffrey Donisthorpe | ... | 21/ 4/15 | Capt. | R.H.A. |
| 4652 | TREIFUS, Albert | ... | ... | ... | 28/12/15 | Lieut. | R.H.A. |

Royal Field Artillery: Territorial Force.

Cheshire Brigade.

| 1251 | STARLING, John Edward | ... | ... | 1/12/15 | Lieut. | w. 27/9/17 |

East Anglian Brigades.

3467	BLACKALLER, Charles Drummond	...	8/ 5/15	2/Bde.	Lieut.	(Labour Corps)
1729	CATLING, Wallis Robert	...	...	22/10/15	1/Bde.	Lieut.	w. 5/9/17
2453	COWLEY, John Norman	...	...	16/ 2/15	4/Bde.	Lieut.	ℳ
2055	DAVY, Leslie Brereton	...	...	22/ 8/15	1/Bde.	Lieut.
1951	GRICE, Leslie Clark	...	...	17/12/15	1/Bde.	Died of wounds 20/4/17
2163	HURNDALL, Charles Frederic	...	25/ 7/15	1/Bde.	Lieut.	✠

London Brigades.

1529	DAWSON, William Charles Palliser	...	6/ 2/15	5/Bde.	Lieut.	(Min. of Labour)
3879	DREYFUS, Trevor Henry	...	...	15/11/15	1/Bde.	Lieut.
2702	GOULD, Cyril Edward	...	...	27/ 8/15	1/Bde.	Lieut.	✠
2459	HICHENS, Basil Sneath	...	...	27/ 2/15	5/Bde.	Lieut.	ℳ
1905	LOWTHER, Walter Joseph J.	...	11/ 8/15	5/Bde.	(From 12/London)
2613	MORTON, William Cattell	...	...	15/12/14	3/Bde.	Lieut. ✠ D/W 22/7/17 ℳ
1129	POWELL, Charles Sydney	...	...	24/11/15	2/Bde.
2681	SONDHEIM, Albert	...	...	5/ 5/15	1/Bde.	Lieut.
2574	WALLICH, Cyril Collings Norton	...	12/ 8/15	7/Amm. Column

R.F.A. (T.F.)

North Midland Brigades.
1202	Pope, L/Cpl. William John Crickmay	2/11/15	3/Bde. Lieut.
1738	Saint, Sgt. Harry	5/ 6/15	3/Bde. Lt. (M. of Lab.) w. 16/4/16

Northumbrian Brigades.
3724	Allen, Henry Cecil	8/ 7/15	2/Bde. Capt. ✠ w. 1/9/17, 17/4/18 ℳ
1356	Cheverton, Sgt. Thomas Bird	23/ 4/15	2/Bde. Lieut. ✠ K/A 24/3/18
2146	Durrant, L/Cpl. Reginald Tom	9/ 4/15	2/Amm. Column Capt. ✠
3824	Gall, William Sydney	8/10/15	2/Bde. Lieut. w. & P/W 4/9/18
3690	Griffiths, Alexander	7/ 8/15	2/Bde. Lieut.
3835	Hopwood, John	8/10/15	2/Bde. Capt. ✠ w. 18/6/18 ℳ
3814	Lancaster, L/Cpl. John W. Cyril	8/10/15	2/Bde. Lieut.
2117	Miller, Cecil	9/ 4/15	2/Bde. Lieut.
3218	Searson, Alexander Moore	28/ 3/15	4/(Howitzer) Bde. Lieut.
2926	Stahl, Arthur	15/ 4/15	2/Bde. Capt. ✠ F/D ℳ
3815	Ward, Noël Groom	8/10/15	2/Bde. Capt. ℳ
1825	Walker, L/Cpl. Gilbert Wilson	23/ 4/15	2/Bde. Lieut. w. 11/11/18
2614	Watson, Thomas Wilson	9/ 3/15	2/Bde. Capt. ✠ ℳ
2596	Yates, Sgt. Henry George	18/ 3/15	2/Bde. Major ✠

West Riding Brigades.
2784	Gibbs, Harry Beckett Swift	12/ 3/15	3/Bde. Lieut.
1612	Seeman, Cpl. Frank Harold	27/ 4/15	1/Bde. Lieut. ℳ

Welch Brigades.
4108	Roberts, Walter Henry	1/12/15	2/Bde. Lieut.

Wessex Brigades.
3129	Browne, Bernard Meredith	4/11/15	Lieut.
3774	Stone, Oliver John	4/11/15	P/W 22/9/16
3520	Treadgold, L/Cpl. John Reginald W.	11/ 7/15	(1/Amm. Column) Lieut.
2273	Allen, Sgt. Edward	7/ 8/16	
6309	Darley, Charles Francis	1/ 9/16	Lieut. West Riding R.H.A.
7752	Goodsall, Robert Harold	6/12/16	Lieut.
763658	Greenbank, Jonathan Richard	1/ 9/17	
2495	Harris, L/Cpl. Dudley Ryde	28/ 8/16	Lieut.
765397	Klingner, Frederick Victor	1/ 9/17	
2991	Liell, L/Cpl. Kingsley	26/ 7/15	w. 23/8/18, 21/9/18
765558	McManus, Alexander	17/ 6/18	
765288	Pyke, Edward Joseph	25/ 2/18	
2996	Wood, Basil Drew	8/ 8/16	

ROYAL GARRISON ARTILLERY.

(A/L: 547)

			2nd Lieut.	
2746	BALLARD, Frank Charles	...	10/ 3/15 *Lieut.*	*w.* 25/8/17
2135	DAVIES, Frederick Bryan	...	10/ 2/15 *Lieut.*	
2836	FIELDEN, Lionel	...	4/12/14 *Lieut.*	
2933	HODGINS, Arthur Wilfred M.	...	26/ 1/15 *Lieut.*	
2454	MACKENZIE, Frederick Boyce	...	26/ 3/15 *Capt.*	*Acc/Killed* 4/7/18
1969	RIGOLD, Ernest Edward	...	23/ 9/14 *Lieut.* ✠	
2141	TAPLIN, George Aubrey	...	20/10/14 *Lieut.* ✠ 𝕸	
762072	ACKERNLEY, Ronald Clifford	...	19/ 2/17 *Lieut.*	
763807	ADAMS, Robert Charles	...	20/ 4/17 *Lieut.*	*w.* 16/10/17
764282	ADAMSON, John Wilfred Edward	...	20/ 7/17	
763756	ASHMORE, Joseph William	...	9/ 4/17 *Lieut.*	F/D
763090	ASHTON, Charles Henry	...	20/ 4/17 *Lieut.*	
762603	ATKINS, Harold Emmanuel	...	28/ 4/17 *Lieut.*	
8057	BARKER, Albert	...	5/ 1/17 *Lieut.*	F/D 𝕸
9186	BARRACLOUGH, Thomas Herbert	...	13/ 1/17 *Lieut.*	
767522	BEAN, Howard Leslie	...	29/ 7/18	
766153	BEATON, Grover Cleveland	...	2/12/17 ✠	*Died of wounds* 30/9/18
763054	BEEBY, Maurice Owen	...	28/ 4/17 *Lieut.*	
763811	BEESON, Leonard Alfred	...	20/ 4/17 *Lieut.*	*w.* 7/9/17
762852	BELFIELD, James Henry	...	1/ 7/18	
764127	BELL, William George Albert	...	27/ 4/17 *Lieut.*	
764412	BENEDICTUS, Joel Henry	...	20/ 7/17 P/W 9/4/18	
7860	BENN, Anthony Norar Munro	...	8/ 1/17 *Lieut.*	
764179	BENTHALL, Gilbert	...	6/ 1/18	
8001	BERRY, Thomas Alfred	...	11/ 2/17 *Lieut.*	
764956	BILLINGTON, George	...	8/ 4/19	
2299	BISHOP, Keith Ford	...	27/10/15 *Killed in action* 8/8/16	
765648	BLANE, Thomas Herbert	...	4/ 2/18	
763487	BOOTH, John	...	20/ 4/17 *Lieut.*	
765884	BOUGHTON, George	...	25/ 3/18	
761242	BOWER, George Richard	...	1/ 9/17	
7570	BOWER, George Stanley	...	17/11/16 *Lieut.*	
763488	BOWIE, Allan Stuart Hunter	...	9/ 4/17 *Lieut.* P/W 8/5/18	
764184	BOWLING, Arthur Henry	..	20/ 7/17 *Killed in action* 29/9/18	
763056	BOYLE, James Alexander	...	27/ 4/17 *Lieut.*	
764185	BRETT, Cyril Charles	...	20/ 7/17 *w.* 15/10/17	
764187	BRISTOL, Leonard	...	1/ 9/17	
4916	BROCKLEBANK, Sydney John	...	13/10/16 *Lieut.*	
764226	BROWN, Ernest	...	20/ 7/17	
763446	BRYCE, Adam Whiteford	...	20/ 7/17	
8884	BUDGE, William Symons	...	13/ 1/17 *Lieut.*	
6097	BUDGEN, William Harold	...	27/ 1/17 *Lieut.*	
8208	BUNDLE, Henry Wilfred	...	13/ 1/17 *Lieut.*	
762445	BURTON, Albert Alfred Charles	...	20/ 4/17 *Lieut.*	*w.* 15/8/17
766342	CANDY, Walter Edward	...	1/ 7/18	
761493	CARTER, Albert Horace	...	18/ 9/18	
763289	CHAMBERLAIN, Benjamin	...	20/ 7/17	

7471	CHAMBERS, Samuel ...	17/11/16	*Lieut.*
5239	CHATTERTON, Richard	12/ 9/16	*Lieut.* ✠ 𝕄
763636	CLAPHAM, Thomas ...	20/ 4/17	*Lieut.*
766157	CLARKE, Harold F. ...	2/12/17	
763360	CLAYTON, Edgar Charles Darwin	20/ 7/17	
765925	COCKRELL, Philip	25/ 2/18	
8636	COOK, George Rope ...	13/ 1/17	*Lieut.*
7443	COOKE, Herbert Henry	10/ 1/17	*Lieut.*
762876	COOPER, Francis Arbuthnot Lambe	20/ 4/17	*Lieut.*
7835	CORNISH, Henry Dauncey ...	10/ 1/17	*Lieut.*
760163	CORY, CSM Ralph	8/ 2/19	𝕄
8770	CRICHTON, Alexander Cansh	13/ 1/17	*Lieut.*
764636	CUDD, Wilfred Alfred	30/ 7/17	
764017	CULL, Anders Eric Knos	27/ 4/17	*Lieut.*
766159	DALY, Roland Oliver	2/12/17	𝕄
8711	DANGER, Henry George	13/ 1/17	*Lieut.*
763460	DAVIDSON, Henry Herbert ...	20/ 4/17	*Lieut.*
763613	DAVIES, John Llewellyn	20/ 4/17	*Lieut.*
764823	DAY, Reginald Harry	14/10/18	
766158	DALES, John Frank ...	17/12/17	
7322	DE LA BERE, L/Cpl. Stephen Baghot	25/ 2/17	*Lieut.* w. 11/10/17
8637	DENCHAR, Vivian Henderson	13/ 1/17	*Lieut.*
763946	DEW, Percival Roderick	10/ 6/17	
5748	DOBB, Bertram Forster	12/ 9/16	*Lieut.*
762300	DOBB, William Charles Noel Foster	4/ 5/17	
762431	DONAGHY, Robert Andrews...	11/ 4/17	*Killed in action* 28/5/18
762366	DONALD, Thomas Hunter ...	27/ 5/17	
763265	DOWNEY, Thomas Philip ...	20/ 7/17	
7784	DUFF, Gordon	17/11/16	F/D(2) w. 2/5/17
767523	DYER, Albert Edwin	29/ 7/18	
764639	EATON, George Ernest	20/ 7/17	
765440	EBDON, Reginald Arthur	4/ 2/18	
763230	EDWARDS, Harold Thomas ...	20/ 4/17	*Lieut.* w. 29/12/17
765653	ELLERKER, William Tindall	4/ 2/18	
6472	EVANS, Thomas Cwmanne ...	30/11/16	*Lieut.*
5752	EVETTS, Raymond Cecil Thomas	28/ 8/16	*Lieut.*
8093	FAWKES, Francis Hanley ...	17/11/16	*Lieut.* 𝕄
762779	FENTON, David	26/ 3/17	*Lieut.*
8929	FOALE, William Ernest	13/ 1/17	*Lieut.*
765885	FORSTER, Joseph Makepeace	13/ 5/18	
766689	FORSTER-KNIGHT, George ...	1/ 7/18	
763123	FRANCIS, Ivor	27/ 4/17	*Lieu.* 𝕄
767433	FRANKLAND, Charles Hayes	12/ 2/19	
5841	FREEMAN, George Herbert ...	12/ 9/16	*Lieut.* 𝕄
765655	FROST, William Frank	10/ 6/18	
760649	GALLAGHER, James ...	20/ 5/18	w. 11/8/17
761257	GALLOWAY, Leslie Douglas ...	4/ 3/18	
761542	GAMMON, Keith	18/ 3/18	

ROYAL ARTILLERY.

764429	GATES, Charles Edward	... 20/ 7/17	P/W 23/5/18
761698	GILDING, Edmund Bushnell	... 11/ 3/17	*Lieut.* w. 4/9/18
765936	GILLETT, Percy Thomas Robert	... 25/ 2/18	
7111	GLADWIN, Duncan Ray Morley	... 11/ 2/17	*Lieut.*
765886	GOERING, Ernest Frederick	... 25/ 2/18	
8439	GOLDING, Oliver	... 13/ 1/17	*Lieut.*
8420	GOODRICK, Maurice George	... 13/ 1/17	*Lieut.*
763822	GRANT, Ronald	... 13/ 7/18	
769246	GRAY, Charles Giles	... 10/12/16	*Lieut.*
763747	GREEN, Frederick James	... 20/ 4/17	*Lieut.*
763234	GREGORY, John Stephen	... 21/12/17	
762974	GROOCOCK, Arthur David	... 20/ 4/17	*Lieut.*
760589	GRUNDY, CSM George Francis	... 8/ 2/19	
763423	HADEN, Victor William	... 20/ 4/17	*Lieut.*
761882	HAINES, Leonard Winston	... 28/ 4/17	*Lieut.*
763660	HALES, William Claude	... 18/ 6/17	
9097	HALSEY, Ernest	... 13/ 1/17	*Capt. & Adjt.*
766162	HAMILTON, James Grey	... 2/12/17	
766163	HARE, Harold Richard	... 2/12/17	
765993	HARLAND, Richard	... 18/ 2/18	*Killed in action* 16/6/18
5096	HARRAP, L/Cpl. Benjamin Clifford	... 17/11/16	*Lieut.* F/D w.
7245	HAYWARD, Arthur Lawrence	... 10/ 1/17	*Lieut.*
3025	HAYWARD, L/Cpl. Alfred Robert	... 1/ 9/16	*Lieut.*
765448	HEY, Percy	... 4/ 2/18	✠
764027	HICKS, Athelstan Maud	... 27/ 4/17	*Lieut.*
765413	HINDE, Walter Butterfield	... 4/ 3/18	
765862	HISCOCKS, Charles Edward	... 25/ 3/18	
767427	HODGES, Alban Ernest Hill	... 1/ 7/18	
766165	HOGARTH, Gordon William	... 4/ 1/18	
764244	HOLMES, Kenneth England Maxwell	25/ 6/17	
2867	HOME, Geoffrey Wyville	... 21/ 1/17	*Lieut.*
8894	HOOD, John Edmund	... 13/ 1/17	*Lieut.*
975	HOWE, George Hubert	... 10/ 4/15	*Lieut.* w. 31/8/17
763458	HOWE, Percival Presland	... 20/ 7/17	
760251	HOWELLS, Sgt. Frank William	... 8/ 2/19	
7157	JACOBS, Thomas Windsor	... 10/ 1/17	*Lieut.*
761461	JAMES, Edward William Harold	... 13/12/17	
9102	JAMES, Percy Stuart	... 13/ 1/17	*Lieut.*
5371	JEFFERY, George James	... 30/11/16	*Lieut.*
763764	JOHNSON, John Francis Fielder	... 1/ 9/17	
767984	JOHNSTON, William	... 7/ 4/19	
766073	JONES, Aubrey Tarran	... 18/ 2/18	
763617	JONES, David	... 20/ 7/17	
7116	JULL, Robert Charles	... 17/11/16	*Lieut.* ✠ 🎖
763828	KEMBLE, John Albert Edgar	... 8/ 3/19	w. 30/10/17
766074	KENT, John	... 11/ 2/18	
7072	KIMBER, Dudley Vernon	... 14/10/17	
765997	KING, Guy Standish	... 11/ 2/18	

R.G.A.

Number	Name	Date	Rank	Notes
762454	KNOWLES, Peter	20/ 4/17	Lieut.	
762208	KRUSE, Hubert Sydney	28/ 4/17	Lieut.	
763305	LANEY, Ernest Charles	25/ 5/17		
6336	LEAHY, Eugene	17/ 9/16	Lieut.	
761292	LEVY, Oliver Charles	14/10/18		
764033	LEWIS, James	5/ 7/17		
7640	LIGHTLEY, Edmund	17/11/16	Lieut.	
766204	LLOYD, Guy Yuyn Llewelyn	8/ 4/18		
767239	LOADER, George Sidney	8/ 2/19		
8613	LOCKETT, Cecil Charles	13/ 1/17	Lieut.	
766972	LOOSELEY, Charles Abraham	3/ 4/19		
763913	LORD, Cecil Grundy	27/ 5/17		
764035	LUCAS, Thomas Mackworth	28/ 4/17	Lieut.	
761000	LUSCOMBE, Sgt. Valentine Courtenay	12/ 9/18		
765775	LYFORD, Ernest	4/ 3/19		
763341	MARTIN, Cyril Frederick	20/ 4/17	Lieut.	
5918	MASSEY, Cpl. Hugh	13/ 1/17	Lieut.	
767596	MAY, Reginald Reuben	5/ 2/19		
8833	McKIE, Robert Denholm Mackroy	13/ 1/17	Lieut.	ℳ
8522	MELLES, Robert Ernest	13/ 1/17	Lieut.	
2697	MIDDLETON, Stephen	22/ 4/15	Capt.	w. 15/4/18 ℳ
7542	MILLS, Ernest Thomas	27/ 1/17	Lieut.	w. 7/11/17
5919	MILLS, Frank Osgood	17/12/16	Lieut.	
7376	MOFFETT, Thomas Henry	10/ 1/17	Lieut.	
6072	MORGAN, Harold	9/ 7/16	Lieut.	
760755	MOSSE, CQMS Sidney Hugh	5/ 2/19		d. —/2/20
764038	MOULE, Arthur James Coram	28/ 4/17	Lieut.	
763765	MOXON, George Henry	28/ 4/17	Lieut.	
762487	NEIGHBOUR, Gerald	1/ 7/17		
764249	NELSON, Roger	1/ 7/18		
764250	NEWBERRY, George Herbert	20/ 7/17		
5864	ODDY, Douglas Cooke	13/ 1/17	Lieut.	
760102	OLDHAM, CQMS Edward Harold	3/ 2/19		
767110	OLIVER, Thomas Stuart	1/ 7/18		
7543	OLLEY, John Francis	17/11/16	Lieut.	
765850	PACE, Arthur	17/ 3/18		
7958	PADDLE, Kenneth Cecil Lawrence	21/ 1/17	Lieut.	✠
5277	PARSLOE, Jack Alphonso Eugene	13/ 1/17	Lieut.	
3717	PATTISON, Sgt. Edgar Edwin L.	13/ 1/17	Lieut.	
8756	PENNY, Frank	13/ 1/17	Lieut.	
763623	PERCIVAL, Frederick George	20/ 7/17		w. 31/10/17
7254	PETRIE, Percy Canterbury	17/11/16	Lieut.	
7728	PIERSON, Victor Majolier	27/ 1/17	Lieut.	
7660	PLANT, Harry Neal	17/11/16	Lieut.	ℳ
762580	PRESTON, Ivor Kerrison	24/12/17		
765512	PROVIS, Eric John	29/ 4/18		
7944	PURCHASE, Walter Henry	10/ 1/17	Capt. & Adjt.	
763654	PUTT, Jarvis	20/ 4/17	Lieut.	

764102	QUARMBY, Rupert Llewellyn	27/ 5/17	Lieut.	
764655	RAMSAY, William McAllister	22/ 7/17	Lieut.	w. 17/10/18
764382	RIPPENGAL, Arthur Henry	20/ 7/17	Lieut.	
764583	RIVERS, Frank Wilfred	20/ 7/17		
766946	ROBINSON, William Arthur Boker	1/ 7/18		
4749	ROWE, L/Cpl. Claude Bernard	20/12/16	Lieut.	
769393	ROWE, Harold Charles	7/ 3/19		
763732	SEWELL, Edward John	1/ 9/17	Died of wounds 10/4/18	
764263	SHARP, Colin Stanley	20/ 7/17		
764345	SHARP, John Frederick	30/ 7/17		
762844	SHAUL, Percy John	27/ 4/17	Lieut.	
761316	SHEA, Richard Thomas	28/ 4/17	Lieut.	d. 12/11/18
767527	SHERIDAN, Charles Wesley	29/ 7/18		
763958	SIDEY, William Hepburn	20/ 4/17	Lieut.	Died of wounds 13/10/17
764171	SKEATS, Leonard Frank	28/ 4/17	Lieut.	
5548	SMITH, Frederick Herbert Corbitt D.	26/ 9/16	Killed in action 10/12/17	
6888	SMITH, George Ernest	17/11/16	Lieut. ✠ F/D	
761826	SMITH, Seymour	27/ 4/17	Lieut.	w. 1/9/17
6628	SMITH, Sidney	30/11/16	Lieut.	w. 2/10/17
4580	SMITH, Victor Charles Compton	6/ 7/16	Lieut.	w. 21/9/17
763046	SOUTHERN, Alfred John	23/ 4/17	Lieut.	w. -/7/18
8808	SPENCE, William Brown	13/ 1/17	Lieut.	w. 9/3/18
760692	SPENCER, Sgt.-Inst. Spencer	1/ 7/18		
764269	STAVELEY, William	20/ 7/17		
763439	STEVENS, Francis Anthony	1/ 7/18		
3159	STREET, Sgt. Hugh Wren	31/ 1/17	Lieut.	
764306	STRICKLAND, Robert Bateman	20/ 7/17	w. 30/4/18	
766124	SUMMERTON, Frederick George	1/ 7/18		
762584	TAYLOR, Arthur Henry Spencer	-/12/17		
8042	TEE, Clifford Vernon	1/ 9/17	Died of wounds 11/8/18	
763994	THOMPSON, Fred Robert Thoresby	20/ 7/17	Lieut.	
764273	THOMPSON, Richard Sydney	20/ 7/17		
762282	THOMPSON, William	17/ 5/17	Lieut.	
761875	TILLY, Edgar Horace	5/ 3/17	Lieut.	w. 31/10/18
764107	TIPPETTS, Richard Alexander Ferguson	3/ 8/17		
763960	TOLERTON, William	28/ 4/17	Lieut.	
761232	TOWELL, Harold West	15/ 6/18		
764276	TRAVERS, Edgar William	1/ 9/17		
762770	TURNER, Cecil Percy	27/ 5/17	Lieut.	
762610	TURNER, Walter James	28/ 4/17	Lieut.	
763314	TUTTE, Alfred Ernest Victor	20/ 7/17		
764214	TYLER, Arthur Thomas	20/ 7/17	w. 8/11/17	
767602	VEALE, Lionel Percy Valery	12/ 2/19		
763480	WALKER, Henry	20/ 4/17	Lieut.	
9082	WALLER, Leon John	13/ 1/17	Lieut.	
9046	WALLER, Trueman Augustus Riviere	13/ 1/17	Lieut.	
9135	WALTER, Charles	13/ 1/17	Lieut.	
763769	WAND, Samuel James George	28/ 4/17	Lieut.	

767285	WARREN, Hugh St. John Percy	...	8/ 2/19		
762096	WAYDELIN, Frederick John ...	...	28/ 4/17	Lieut.	
763631	WEBB, Geoffrey Fuller	...	28/ 4/17	Lieut.	
762818	WEIGHT, Allen Fremantle	...	27/ 4/17	Lieut.	
762819	WEIGHT, Sidney Lewis	...	20/ 4/17	Lieut.	
6340	WEST, George Malcolm Watson	...	20/ 8/16	Lieut.	
763982	WEST, Sydney Hague	...	20/ 4/17	Lieut.	
764590	WHICHER, Cecil Thomas	...	20/ 7/17		
766933	WHITE, Norton Summers	...	1/ 7/18		
764051	WHITE, Sidney William	...	28/ 4/17	Lieut.	
763805	WHITTAKER, Charles Joseph	...	28/ 4/17	Lieut.	
763087	WHITTAKER, Gilbert Whalley	...	4/11/18	Lieut.	
767075	WILLIAMS, Reginald Seidler...	...	5/ 2/19		
766006	WILLIAMS, Thomas	...	24/ 6/18		
1972	WILLIAMSON, William Henry Rowe...	25/11/14	Capt.	✠ F/D ᛙ	
766404	WILLSON, Albert	...	1/17/18		
763902	WILSON, Percy Macdonald ...	...	20/ 7/17	w. –/4/18	
6549	WINDER, L/Cpl. Walter	...	8/ 1/17	Lieut.	
763142	WRIGHT, Albert Alexander ...	...	20/ 4/17	Lieut. ✠	
7263	YATES, William Fletcher	...	31/ 1/17	Lieut. w. 13/9/18	

Royal Garrison Artillery: Special Reserve.

2636	DE BURIATTE, Warwick Huxley	...	9/ 7/15	Lieut.	Acc/Killed 19/10/18
2696	DINHAM, George Albert	...	16/12/15	Capt.	
2982	GOLDSMITH, George Lawrence	...	16/12/15	Lieut.	
2323	RHODES, Dunstan	...	27/ 8/15		
7626	ABSON, Percy	...	23/11/16	Lieut.	
7627	ACTON, Richard	...	23/11/16	Lieut.	
7354	ADAMS, Oliver Haynes	...	1/12/16	Lieut. ✠	
4139	ADAMS, Stanley Alfred	...	10/ 1/17	Lieut.	
8110	ADDERLEY, Charles Joseph Henry ...	13/12/16			
6501	AITKEN, Robert	...	20/11/16	Lieut.	
6675	AKEHURST, Charles Henry	...	8/ 1/17		
5934	AMERY, Thomas Ford	...	10/ 1/17	Lieut.	
7862	ANSON-JONES, John Samuel...	...	1/12/16	d. –/12/18	
7788	ASCHE, Harold Carstin John	...	1/12/16	Lieut.	
765414	ASHBOURNE, Thomas Gordon William	19/ 8/17			
7630	ATCHISON, Harold Percy Reynolds...	1/12/16	Lieut. ᛙ		
762772	ATHOE, George Benfield Jones	...	1/ 9/17		
5039	BAILEY, Cpl. William Edward	...	1/12/16	Lieut.	
4334	BALL, Sgt. Arthur Hugh	...	19/ 7/16	Capt. ✠	Died of wounds 13/10/17
8231	BANTING, Arthur Digby	...	18/12/16	Lieut. ✠	
8104	BARCLAY, Maurice George Henry F.	25/ 1/17	Lieut.		
6840	BARNES, Sgt. Albert Frederick	...	25/ 1/17	ᛙ	

4977	BARTLETT, Harold Frederick Walter	30/ 8/16	*Lieut.* *w.* 30/10/17
7436	BEACHAM, Oliver Harry	13/12/16	*Lieut.*
6148	BEACHELL, Reginald Peel	5/10/16	*Lieut.*
762660	BEBINGTON, John Arthur	11/ 3/17	
4950	BENNETT, Edward Henry	13/12/16	
761920	BENNETT, John Nichol	11/ 3/17	*Killed in action* 19/5/17
7748	BENTLEY, L/Cpl. Harold Crompton	23/11/16	*Lieut.*
760398	BIGGS, James Henry Cedric	23/ 8/17	*Lieut.*
6599	BINNS, Alfred	1/12/16	*w.* 7/4/17
8070	BLANCO-WHITE, George Rivers	23/11/16	*Lieut.*
5394	BOOKLESS, Thomas	18/12/16	*Lieut.* *w.* 13/7/17
6454	BOON, Ernest George Fred	27/11/16	*Lieut.* ✠
7603	BOURCHIER, Leonard Grove Gabbett	5/10/16	
761831	BRACEWELL, James Rawston	27/11/16	*w.* 11/8/17
762133	BREARCY, Archibald Duncan	2/ 5/17	
7840	BRERETON, John Lancelot	8/ 1/17	
5237	BREWER, Leonard George Tye	8/ 1/17	
6443	BRINE, George Edward	23/11/16	*Capt.* *w.* 16/4/18
7631	BROMLEY, Ernest James	23/11/16	*Lieut.*
762233	BROWN, Arthur William	2/ 5/17	
6786	BRUMWELL, Bernard Henry	23/11/16	ℳ
6198	BRUNT, Stanley Herbert	1/12/16	
7632	CABLE, James Sydney	23/11/16	*Lieut.* *d.* 5/9/18
765381	CALDER, Roy Croaker	19/ 8/17	
7934	CAMPBELL, Christopher James	23/11/16	
761808	CARLTON, John	10/ 3/17	
760584	CARLTON, Cpl. John	11/ 3/17	
5615	CARTER, Sidney Victor	8/ 1/17	
6210	CHARLES, David Sibbering	23/11/16	
766156	CHILD, Philip Albert	2/12/17	
5984	CLARK, Alec Gordon	1/ 9/16	
7773	CLARK, Harold Everitt	10/12/16	ℳ
5735	CLEMONS, Cuthbert John Savigny	30/ 8/16	*Lieut.*
77777	COCKELL, Frederick Harold	18/12/16	
7108	COLE, Cecil Clarke	1/12/16	*Died of wounds* 13/10/17
764419	COLE, Francis William	8/ 9/17	
7605	COMBER, Henry Cantley	24/12/16	
8025	COMFORT, Harry William	18/12/16	
7922	COMYN, Charles Heaton Fitzwilliam	23/11/16	
8063	COOPER, Reginald Brodie	8/12/16	
7870	COWELL, Percy Septimus	13/ 2/16	
2630	COWNIE, Ivor Thomas William	7/ 7/16	*w.* 30/10/17
7369	CRANE, Lancelot	18/12/16	*d.* 15/3/18
7293	CROOK, Donovan	18/12/16	*Capt.*
763023	CROSLAND, Leonard	12/ 3/17	✠ *w.* 11/10/17
6669	CROUCH, William Ballard	23/11/16	*Killed in action* 13/4/17
761112	CROW, Basil Edward	13/ 3/17	
5743	CULLEY, Sgt. Walter Willoughby Basil	20/12/16	ℳ

7738	CURTIES, L/Cpl. Thomas Steven P.	18/12/16	
8113	CUTTING, L/Cpl. Cecil George	1/12/16	
7936	CUTTLE, Elliott	23/11/16	
7560	DAVENPORT, Salusbury Fynes	18/12/16	
7937	DAY, Francis Henry Coryton	13/12/16	
8052	DE MATTOS, George William	2/ 2/17	
2303	DENNIS, Arthur Scotney	23/11/16	*Lieut. w.* 14/8/17
7802	DEVEREUX, L/Cpl. Thomas	11/ 1/17	
763450	DILLON, Thomas James	30/11/17	
761962	DIXON, William Scarth	13/ 3/17	
7979	DRIVER-HOLLOWAY, Thomas H.	8/ 1/17	*Lieut. w.* 6/11/17
8170	DUNN, Andrew Landale	11/ 2/17	
7445	EARP, L/Cpl. George Norman	18/12/16	*w.* 4/2/18
6254	EDMOND, Alexander Duncan	1/12/16	
4060	EDWARDS, L/Cpl. Frederick Stanley	10/ 1/17	✠
7841	EILOART, Ferdinand Robert	8/ 1/17	✠
7980	ELLERY, Henry William Oswald	8/ 1/17	
6214	ELLIOTT, Frederick Thomas	18/12/16	
6715	EVANS, William Emnys	8/ 7/16	℞
7462	FAIRCHILD, Joseph Bryant Wilson	25/ 1/17	℞
6137	FAUNCH, L/Cpl. Ernest Alfred	5/10/16	*Killed in action* 4/5/17
762369	FENNING, Wilson George	13/ 3/17	
7938	FERGUSON, Maurice Gurney	18/12/16	
762101	FERGUSON, Thomas	2/ 4/17	
8087	FLAWN, Neville George	23/11/16	
761283	FLUX, Henry John	21/ 2/18	
2661	FOULSHAM, Frank Chester	2/ 8/16	*Capt. w.* 9/4/17
7534	FOWLER, Francis Archibald	18/12/16	*Capt. Killed in action* 28/7/17
6458	FOX, John Harper Graham	13/12/16	
6979	FRANCE, Barry Edwin	18/12/16	
7782	FREEMAN, Percy	10/ 1/17	
8014	FROST, Walter	13/12/16	*w.* 15/8/17
6153	FULBECK, Charles Edward	23/11/16	
7294	GABBOTT, Edgar Parr	23/11/16	*Capt.* ✠ *w.* 6/11/17 ℞
6216	GARDNER, L/Cpl. Henry	23/11/16	
5687	GASSON, Stanley	11/ 2/17	
7535	GATTY, David Ivor Vaughan	23/11/16	
5903	GIBBS, Thomas Harry	5/10/16	
7218	GIBSON, Stanley Rutherford	13/12/16	
4089	GILLON, Cpl. Geoffrey Symonds	5/ 8/17	
765389	GLENNIE, George Henry	22/ 7/16	*Staff-Capt.* ℞
5404	GLOVER, Charles William	18/12/16	
6170	GOOD, Richard Whittall	1/12/16	
6449	GOTHARD, Clifford Frederick	18/12/16	
6837	GRAY, Charles Reginald	5/ 8/17	
765391	GRAY, Joseph Everard	2/ 5/17	
761991	GRENSIDE, Harold Cutliffe	10/12/16	*Capt.* ✠
923	GRICE, William Stanley		

ROYAL ARTILLERY.

7757	GRUNDY, Charles Victor	... ...	8/12/16
5692	GUERRIER, Arthur Philip	... ...	13/12/16
765392	GUNN, Edmond Alan	... ...	30/ 8/17 *d.* 13/2/19
7329	GURNEY, Percival Sydney	... ...	18/12/16 *P/W* 16/1/18 ⚔
7668	HALLPIKE, Christopher George	...	8/12/16 *Killed in action* 6/4/18
6334	HAMILL, John	... ...	23/10/16 *Lieut.*
762191	HAMMOND, Richard Fisher	...	5/ 2/17 *w.* 22/8/17
762879	HANCOCK, Ernest	... ...	13/ 3/17 *Capt.* ✠ *w.* 4/9/18
762122	HARTLEY, Alfred	... ...	2/ 4/17 *Died of wounds* 9/10/18
8178	HARTREE, Cyril	... ...	18/12/16 *Killed in action* 28/5/18
763584	HAYDON, Robert Alexander	...	6/ 7/17
764699	HENDERSON, Colin Keith	...	31/ 1/18
7063	HEYWOOD, Frank	... ...	8/12/16 *Lieut. w.* 18/11/18
8003	HIDE, James Birchell	...	13/12/16 *Lieut.* ✠ ⚔
7905	HIGHAM, Reginald Lachlan	...	8/ 1/17 *Lieut. w.* 3/10/18
6402	HILL, Thomas Gaundey	...	5/10/16 *Lieut.* ⚔
763887	HOLLOWAY, Herbert John	...	13/10/17
5124	HOLMAN, Walter Manley	...	8/ 1/17 *Lieut. w.* 6/4/18
6382	HOLMES, George Robert	...	24/12/16 *Lieut.*
4068	HOMEWOOD, Talbot Stephenson	...	23/ 9/16 *Lieut.* ⚔
765394	HOOPER, Victor Albert	...	30/ 8/17
764433	HUDSON, Eli Bennison	...	1/ 9/17
6222	HUGHES, Francis Allen	...	8/ 1/17 *Lieut.*
6372	HUNTER, James Douglas	...	23/11/16 *Lieut. w.* 1/9/17, 24/4/18
7449	HUNTER, Robert Younger	...	18/12/16 *Lieut.*
8510	HUSKINSON, Arthur William	...	13/ 3/17 *Lieut.*
762485	INGLIS, Thomas Graham	...	27/ 2/17 *Lieut.*
484	JOHNSON, Alfred Forbes	...	18/12/16 ✠
7593	JOHNSON, Arthur Haynes	...	18/12/16 *w.* 16/5/18
762592	JOHNSON, William Spencer	...	11/ 3/17
8046	JONES, George Arthur	...	23/ 9/16 *Lieut.*
7451	JONES, William Henry	...	23/11/16 ⚔
6357	JUSTICE, Walter Burgess	...	1/12/16 ⚔
4899	KASSELL, Lewen Cawood	...	23/11/16 *Lieut.*
7940	KEAY, William Howard	...	18/12/16
5511	KELLY, L/Cpl. Bernard Ronald	...	13/12/16
761047	KELLY, L/Cpl. William	...	13/ 3/17 *Lieut.*
6011	KENDON, L/Cpl. David Geldersleve		18/12/16 ⚔
7538	KENYON, Samuel	... ...	18/12/16
7509	KING, Dennis Hoare	...	8/ 1/17 *w.* 24/5/18
6012	KING, William	... ...	18/12/16
6224	KIRKPATRICK, Kenneth John	...	8/ 1/17
8120	KIRKUS, Cuthbert Hayward	...	23/11/16 *Capt. Killed in action* 31/7/17
7564	KNOWLES, Roland Ernest	...	18/12/16 ✠
2458	LAMB, L/Cpl. Thomas Slater	...	23/11/16
7832	LANGHORNE, Arthur J.	...	18/12/16
762904	LAUGHLAND, David Stuart	...	13/ 3/17
6265	LAWSON, Philip Hugh	...	8/ 1/17

7389	LAZARUS, George Maitland ...	23/11/16	
7763	LEDWARD, Charles Harold ...	1/12/16	
5958	LEVER, Ernest Harry	15/ 9/16 F/D ℟	
4184	LEVETT, Sydney Cornelius Blair	23/11/16	
765556	LEWIS, William Augustus Howe	18/ 3/18	
6701	LUMSDEN, Frederick	23/11/16	
7833	LUCAS, Archibald William Tindall ...	10/ 1/17	
761462	LYE, Percival W.	8/ 4/18	
7941	LYNN, Sydney	11/ 1/17	w. 28/8/17
766169	MACBETH, Benjamin James George	23/11/17	
761930	MACGREGOR, Herbert James	2/ 4/17	
5779	MALLETT, Norman ...	18/12/16	
766171	MARTIN, Angers	2/12/17	
5415	MATTHEWS, Thomas	9/ 7/16	*Capt.* M.B.E. *Died of wounds* 27/6/18
7861	MAYCOCK, Sydney Herbert ...	12/ 2/17	
7984	MAYOR, Bertram Robert	13/11/16	
765660	MCDONALD, John	29/ 4/18	
763430	MCHAILE, John Edgar	30/ 6/17	
765400	MCKELVEY, George Frickleton	30/ 8/17	
762938	MCKEOWN, Felix Quinn	11/ 3/17 ✠	w. 24/4/18
765401	MCLELLAN, Charles David ...	5/ 8/17	
6387	MEACHAM, Frank Reginald	28/11/16 ✠	
763731	MILLER, John Anderson	23/ 4/17	
765402	MILLIAN, John Currey	19/ 8/17	
2576	MOLLIAR-SMITH, Herbert	23/11/16	
765690	MORGAN, Lascelles Daniel ...	18/ 2/18	
7643	MORRISON, Robert Archer ...	1/12/16	
8004	MORRISON, Thomas Henry ...	8/ 1/17	w. 21/11/18
5860	MORRISON, William ...	18/12/16	
3284	MOSES, Frank Samuel	28/11/16	*Died of wounds* 31/8/18
761002	NASH, Herbert Mason	18/12/16	
3348	NETHERY, Wallace Claude Elison ...	18/12/16	
762532	NICKSON, George Bernard ...	13/ 3/17 ✠	w. 18/10/17
7964	NISBETT, Edgar Charley	10/ 1/17	
6813	NIXON, Walter	1/12/16	
5525	NORCOMBE, L/Cpl. Thomas Percy ...	13/12/16	
766079	NUTHALL, Stuart	25/ 2/18	
6960	O'SULLIVAN, Horace Alexander	23/10/16	*Killed in action* 22/4/17
7873	PAINE, Reginald Stuart	18/12/16	
7429	PALFREYMAN, Frederick James	11/ 1/17	
761315	PARK, John Lawrence	28/ 6/16	*Lieut.*
7959	PARKIN, John	10/12/16 ✠	
7854	PEIRCE, Alfred	13/12/16 ✠	
761706	PERRY, Arthur Ernest Cecil	21/ 2/18	*Died of wounds* 20/6/18
764453	PHILLIPS, Edgar Lewis	1/ 9/17	
7855	PHILLIPS, Ernest Thomas Adams ...	13/12/16	*Lieut.* M.B.E.
762209	PODMORE, George Conrad ...	2/ 5/17	
7549	PORT, L/Cpl. Frederick John	8/ 1/17	

7160	PORTER, Bernard Arthur	18/12/16	
765469	PORTER, James	18/ 2/18	
7704	PORTER, Oliver John	20/12/16	
762609	PRIESTLEY, Leslie Stuart	20/ 3/17	Lieut. M
763434	PRING, Arnold Lydden	1/ 8/18	
6260	READ, Selwyn	5/10/16	Lieut. w. 29/9/17
764582	READING, Arthur Alfred	2/ 9/17	
7965	REDPATH, William Henry	24/12/16	w. 26/9/18
763507	REEVE, James	9/ 8/17	w. 15/4/18
2323	RHODES, Dunstan	27/ 8/15	✠ M
6233	RIDDETT, Basil Perry	20/12/16	
764042	RIGBY, Alfred	2/ 9/17	
6466	ROBERTSON, David	13/12/16	w. 23/6/17
737	ROBINSON, Cpl. Norgrove Stuart	4/12/16	Lieut. ✠ w. 21/5/18
5139	ROGERS, L/Cpl. Cecil Ernest	5/10/16	w. 10/10/17
7865	ROSMALLCOCQ, Gerald Augustine	13/12/16	
6467	ROUGHTON, Harold	1/12/16	
7890	SALUSBURY, John Thelwall	13/12/16	
763600	SARGENT, Leslie Harold	20/ 4/17	Lieut. w. 5/1/17
765665	SCHELL, Frederick Stanley	4/ 3/18	Killed in action 22/8/18
761985	SCHOTT, William	2/12/17	
6125	SCOTT, William David	20/ 8/16	
8102	SCOTT-JAMES, Rolfe Arnold	13/12/16	✠
763114	SCRIMGEOUR, John Murray	23/12/17	
765363	SERGEANT, John Prosper	18/ 2/18	
766087	SETTLE, Richard Hardcastle	4/ 2/18	
762419	SHARPE, Percy Barlow	2/ 5/17	
7515	SILLERY, William	13/12/16	w. 11/8/17
761127	SIMS, Nugent Woolcott	18/12/16	Capt. F/D w. –/7/18
6428	SLATTER, Arthur Wittard	13/12/16	
7581	SMALLPAGE, Frederic Hartley	8/12/16	
765008	SMITH, Frank Glennie	16/ 9/17	Lieut. w. 21/4/18
766040	SMITH, Norman Ralph	25/ 2/18	
761209	SPANTON, William Burke	4/12/16	
762769	STAMMERS, Francis Alan Roland	11/ 3/17	w. 11/5/18
762944	STEPHENS, Beryl Louis	11/ 3/17	
762520	STEWART, Francis John	13/ 3/17	
760865	STEWART, Sgt. William Hinton	13/ 3/17	✠
762656	STIRLING, Archibald Colin	19/ 8/17	
764587	STOKES, Christopher William	8/ 9/17	w. 19/6/18
4663	STONE, Reginald Holmes	4/ 8/16	
764172	STONE, William Barnes	1/10/17	
6415	STONEHAM, Edward William	20/ 8/16	Lieut.
4737	STRICK, L/Cpl. Richard Boase K.	20/ 8/16	Lieut.
762309	SUGDEN, Frank Edward	1/ 7/17	
7949	SUMMERFIELD, Alfred Bernard	23/11/16	Capt. M
8069	SUMMERSELL, James Gleed	13/12/16	
7968	SUTHERLAND, George Kenneth	23/11/16	

764209	Swift, Albert Dean	1/11/17	
765520	Tait, Duncan Christie	18/2/18	
762281	Tebbutt, Herbert Charles	20/3/17	
766089	Tennant, George Montague Colvin	4/3/18	
4229	Thomas, Cpl. Philip Edward	23/11/16	*Killed in action* 9/4/17
7007	Thomas, Thomas	1/12/16 ✠	F/D
5293	Thompson, Arthur Edward	20/8/16	
5878	Thorburn. John McCavey	23/11/16	
762688	Thorne, Frederick Charles	13/3/17	
5294	Topping, Samuel	18/12/16	*Capt. w.* 1/5/18
5426	Tomkins, Samuel Edward	23/11/16	*w.* 17/6/18
763216	Toop, Alexander George	11/3/17	*w.* 12/11/17
8007	Tracey, Bernard David	8/1/17	
8036	Trench, Frederick Charles	13/12/16	
7988	Truscott, Maurice John	13/12/16	𝔐(2)
760513	Tweedle, L/Cpl. Ralph	26/1/18	
5818	Van Essen, Everard Cecil	20/8/16	*Lieut.*
4293	Vernon, Cpl. Henry Robert	5/10/16	*w.* 6/10/17 𝔐(2)
7828	Wailes, Francis George	18/12/16	𝔐
766180	Wailes, Herbert G.	2/12/17	
5560	Wakeford, Arthur James	29/11/16	*Lieut.*
6549	Walker, Arnold Learoyd	5/10/16	*Lieut. w.* 18/10/18
6861	Walker, William Harrington	1/12/16	*w.* 17/5/18
7166	Warburton, Charles Marsden	8/1/17	*w.* 22/4/18
5820	Warren, Harvey Stanley	30/12/16	*Lieut. w.* 3/6/18
760683	Welby, Davis	1/7/17	*d.* 23/10/18
6505	Whitaker, Geoffrey Maurice	20/8/16	𝔐
3106	Whitehead, Edgar Joseph William	1/12/16	*d.* 17/2/19
6862	Wilders, Charles Alban	8/1/17	*w.* 15/8/17
762343	Wilde, William Hornsby	11/3/17	
8095	Wilkinson, Ernest Percival	23/11/16	
764079	Willcox, George Harold	28/5/17	
6550	Williams, Robert Pryce	1/12/16	
8031	Williams, William Harold	18/12/16	*Killed in action* 9/11/18
6241	Wilson, Henry Armstrong	8/11/16	
764863	Wilson, William Laurie	29/9/17	
7867	Wolff, James Daniel	13/12/16	*Capt.* m.b.e.
5307	Wornum, William Esmond	1/12/16 ✠	
6610	Worrall, Samuel	1/12/16 ✠	𝔐
761361	Worseldine, Stanley Chas. Harwood	8/4/18	
763770	Wray, William John Osterfield	30/11/17	
7320	Wright, Cecil Lawrence	13/12/16	*Killed in action* 7/7/17
7583	Wright, Walter Whitmore	20/12/16	*Killed in action* 23/8/17

(A/L: 750b) ## Royal Garrison Artillery: Territorial Force.

Cornwall (Duke of Cornwall's).
1501 SIMPSON, Maurice Barrow ... ... 30/ 3/15 *Lieut.*

Devon.
2182 HONOUR, Frank Leslie 30/ 7/15
1583 HOPE, W. Edward C. ... ... 22/ 6/15 *Lieut.*

Dorsetshire.
3142 PENNY, William Nevill ... ... 9/ 4/15 *Lieut.*

Glamorgan.
3778 LEWIS, Clifford Michael ... ... 24/ 3/16 *Lieut.*

Hampshire.
2853 AMAN, John Godfrey ... ... 11/ 8/15 *Lieut.*

Kent.
2284 EASTMAN, Cpl. Archibald Garey ... 16/12/15 *Lieut.*
900 GRAY, Eric Balfour ... ... 7/10/15 *d.* 20/12/17

Lancashire (Heavy Battery).
3560 MONROE, Robert ... ... 6/12/15 *Lieut. w.* 11/6/18

2nd London (Heavy Battery).
4410 CAFFAREY, Bernard James ... ... 1/12/15 *Staff-Capt.*
2355 DAVIS, Arthur Felix ... ... 29/12/15 *Lieut.*

Sussex.
2531 WOLTON, Ronald Arthur Guy ... 27/ 3/15 *Lieut.*

Wessex (Heavy Battery).
1376 OELRICHS, Cpl. Richard Vaughan ... 18/ 7/15 *Capt. Amm. Col. w.* –/6/17
2586 WARD, Francis Norris ... ... 27/12/15 *Lieut.*

6715 HAYCOCK, Harry ... ... 4/ 9/16 *Lieut.*
760580 OWEN, Geoffrey Leyland ... ... 20/12/16 *Lieut.*
7467 SMITH, Matthew Purdon ... ... 1/12/16 *Lieut.*
765479 STEPHENSON, William Stanley ... 13/ 5/18 *Lieut.*
761231 STONEHOUSE, Arthur Dudley ... 20/12/16 *Lieut.*

ROYAL ENGINEERS.

2nd Lieut.

1450	BIRNIE, Reginald	19/ 1/16	(*From 2/Gordon Highlanders*)
1483	BULL, Joseph William	23/12/15	(*From 2/E. Lancs.*) *D/W* 1/10/16
3325	ELLIS, Shirley Duncan	11/ 9/15	✠ *Died* 19/3/16
3414	FRYER, Robert Eliot	7/ 7/15	*Major. Wounded*
3275	GRIFFIN, Arthur Ethelbert	3/ 2/15	*Capt.* ✠ 🎖
2076	GUY, John Keble	9/12/14	*Lieut.* 🎖
3388	HEYWOOD, Edward Percival	19/ 5/15	*Lieut.*
2707	HILL, Edwin Vivian	10/ 8/15	*Lieut.*
2318	HOWARD, Hugh Lloyd	1/10/14	*Major* ✠ 🎖 (2)
3096	HUSBAND, Charles Thomas Main	15/10/15	*Lieut.* 250*th Tunnelling Co.*
1858	PARKER, John Amphlett	24/10/14	*Major* ✠
3188	RAWLINS, CQMS Guy Vernon C.	26/ 2/15	*Capt.*
735	ROBINSON, Alfred Douglas	16/ 6/15	*Lieut.*
2129	ROBINSON, John Charles	29/ 8/15	(*From 10/S. Stafford*) *Lieut.*
1853	ROBERTS, Charles Henry	12/ 9/15	(*From 1/York & Lancs.*) *w.* –/6/16
1496	ROUGHT, Philip	31/ 3/15	*Lieut.* ✠
1203	ROWLAND, Douglas Mayhew	9/ 1/16	*Signal Service*
3288	SALMON, Maurice William	13/ 3/15	*Lieut. Wounded* –/10/15 🎖
3340	STEVENS, Henry John Henley	23/ 4/15	*Lieut.* 🎖
905	WALKER, Sgt. Reginald Henry	27/ 2/15	*Lieut.* M.B.E. 🎖
3050	WALLS, Cpl. Francis Hugh	16/ 6/15	*Lieut.*
2826	WEBB, Walter John	24/10/14	*Lieut.* F/D 🎖
3393	YUILL, Harry Hogg	23/ 4/15	*Major* D.S.O. ✠ F/D 🎖 (2)
4007	ALLEN, Cecil John	24/12/15	*Lieut.* 🎖
6348	BISPHAM, Charles	28/ 5/16	*Lieut. Wounded* 3/5/18
959	CORNISH, Sgt. Alfred Charles	17/11/15	*Lieut.*
1484	DAWSON, Sgt. Alan Delwaide	17/11/15	*Lieut.*
5682	DONALDSON-SELBY, T. Tyssen Grey	14/ 1/16	*Lieut.*
4789	DOWDESWELL, Frank	14/ 1/16	*Capt.*
6399	DOUGLAS, George Frederick	3/ 6/16	*Lieut.* ✠
4005	FAVELL, Walter Rupert Aldridge	17/11/15	*Lieut.*
5177	HANCOCK, Wesley	25/ 6/16	*Lieut.*
3344	HARPER, Ernest Edward	17/10/15	*Major*
7230	HARRIS, Emanuel Vincent	19/ 5/16	*Lieut.*
6061	HARRISON, Edward Harrison	7/ 5/16	*Lieut.* ✠ *Wounded* 13/8/17
3851	HOLM, Frank Diederick	2/ 2/16	*Lieut. Killed in action* 14/5/17
3608	JONES, Percy Hudson	2/ 1/16	*Lieut.* ✠ 🎖
2708	LOMAX, Cpl. Gordon Charles	28/ 4/16	*Lieut.*
6623	MALLOCH, David	3/ 6/16	*Lieut. Killed in action* 14/9/16
2852	MATTHEW, Cpl. John Richard	14/12/15	*Capt.*
2895	MOORE, Cpl. John Leslie Mackenzie	12/ 5/15	*Capt.* ✠ 🎖
7282	PARRY, Samuel	25/ 6/16	(*R.A.F.*) *Killed in action* 3/5/18
6409	RAWSTHORNE, Herbert Crompton	18/ 3/16	*Lieut.*
5871	REED, L/Cpl. William	5/ 6/16	*Lieut.* ✠ *Wounded* 2/5/17 🎖
6080	SLATTERY, Francis James	30/ 1/16	*Capt. w. & P/W* 5/8/18 *d.* 9/1/19

ROYAL ENGINEERS.

6089	STEVENS, L/Cpl. Roland Hongel	11/ 2/16	Lieut.
5550	SUGDEN, Wilfred Hart	15/ 5/16	Lieut.
7164	SYRETT, Reginald Moody	2/ 6/16	Lieut.
4741	TAMBLYN, Horace William	19/11/15	Lieut. ✠ Wounded 4/10/18
7334	TRUMAN, Egerton Danford	20/ 3/16	Major 🎖
5884	WILSHIRE, Harold Bradley	15/ 4/16	Lieut.
3861	YATES, Joseph	17/11/15	Lieut.
767794	ALEXANDER, Claud	18/ 1/19	
764602	ALLISON, George Henry	8/ 9/17	Lieut. T.F.
6552	ASH, Sidney	14/ 1/17	Major. 🎖
6453	BAKER, L/Cpl. Charles G.	12/ 2/17	Lieut.
760478	BALL, Harwood Thomas Stafford	4/ 9/18	
761410	BATZER, Albert Edward	30/ 3/18	
5333	BEACH, Thomas Stanley	13/11/16	Lieut. w. 8/10/17 🎖
765647	BELL, James Hunter	2/11/18	
767825	BERRY, Albert Edward	16/ 8/18	
761615	BESTOW, Sydney Francis	30/ 9/17	Lieut.
7481	BEVERIDGE, David Alston	11/ 2/17	Lieut.
763653	BLAIR, Alexander	17/ 3/17	Lieut.
767329	BONNYMAN, George Alexander	28/ 9/18	
767853	BRACE, Lewis	27/ 8/18	
1062	BRITTENDEN, James Edward	6/11/16	Lieut.
768011	BROWN, Frederick	14/ 2/19	
6305	BROWN, Philip	9/ 9/16	Lieut.
8002	BROWNE, Walter Stowell	27/ 1/17	Lieut. 🎖
768221	BROWNLIE, John	9/ 2/19	
6096	BRUCE, Reginald	6/11/16	Capt. F/D
7199	BRUGES, John Parsons	31/12/16	Lieut.
768192	BRYAN, Robert	18/ 1/19	
763148	BUCKNELL, Leonard Holcombe	14/ 7/17	Lieut.
764111	BUTCHER, Donald John	14/ 9/18	
765651	CAMERON, John	13/ 7/18	Capt. O.B.E.
5472	CARNELLEY, L/Cpl. Herbert	6/11/16	Lieut. ✠ Wounded 16/10/18
766426	CHARLES, Norman Henry	23/ 2/18	
3511	CHRISTLOW, Joseph Williams	28/ 5/15	(From W. Yorks) Major
5240	CHRISFIELD, Douglas Frederick	1/11/16	Lieut.
767359	CONOLLY, Frederick George	18/ 1/19	
766511	CONSTABLE, Alfred Bertie	29/10/18	
760363	COOK, L/Cpl. William Saunders	31/ 7/17	Lieut.
6277	COUSINS, Harold Francis	13/ 8/16	Lieut. London Elec. Engineers
3386	COX, William George	1/10/16	Died 22/9/18
761724	CRYAN, Robert	14/ 3/17	Lieut.
762400	DALE, Frank Alfred	18/ 1/19	
767826	DE LAPORTE, Antoine	16/ 8/18	
768229	DIAMOND, Ivan John Anelly	18/ 1/19	
5991	DICKMAN, Henry Alderman	25/12/16	Lieut. ✠
760585	DOLBEAR, Albert	27/ 8/18	Wounded –/8/17

R.E.   211

7109	DRYLAND, Leslie George	23/ 7/16	Lieut.	
5338	ELKINGTON, Sgt. George Leonard	4/10/16	Lieut.	᛭
5683	ELLIS, Theodore Moorhouse	1/11/16	Lieut.	
5250	FIELD, Joseph	3/12/16	Lieut.	
767923	FRANKLIN, L/Cpl. Curtis	1/ 2/19		
767924	FRANKLIN, Kellogg	1/ 2/19		
2698	FRANKLIN-ADAMS, CSM Bernard I.	10/ 1/17	Major.	᛭
765443	GERRANS, Harold Henry	18/12/17	Lieut.	
767362	GIGGINS, Reginald Charles	18/ 1/19		
2755	GILL, Sgt. Rowland Roy	15/ 7/16	Lieut.	
6988	GOODWIN, Cpl. Bernard Malcolm	12/ 2/18	Lieut.	
765975	GORDON, Andrew Howard	15/12/17	Lieut.	᛭
767467	GREEN, Angus Llewellyn	2/11/18		
6000	GREENWOOD, Charles	13/11/16	Lieut.	᛭
5313	GURTON, Sgt. William Henry	1/11/16	Lieut.	
5760	HARDIE, Norman	6/11/16	Lieut.	Wounded –/2/17
767895	HARDING, Percy Hugo	2/11/18		
6312	HARDMAN, L/Cpl. William F. Kerr	9/ 9/16	Lieut.	✠ Died of wounds 28/10/17
766186	HARGER, Edwin Oscar	22/12/17	Lieut.	Died of wounds 23/9/18
767711	HARRIS, Augustus Alfred	19/ 5/18		
2699	HANBURY, Sgt. Frederick Capel	24/ 9/16	Capt.	
763333	HAND, Ernest Francis	28/ 7/17	Lieut.	
764935	HANDFORD, Sydney	31/ 8/17	Lieut.	
7113	HANTON, Peter Kydd	23/ 7/16	Lieut.	
1839	HARTOPP, Cpl. Chas. Wm. Everard C.	27/ 4/15	Capt.	᛭
8081	HARVEY, William Sidney	14/ 1/17	Wounded 24/1/18	
5443	HATFIELD, Samuel	3/12/16	Lieut.	
3209	HAWTREY, Ralph	21/ 4/15	Killed in action 3/9/16	
765501	HICKS, Stanley Vyvian	15/12/17	Lieut.	
768230	HINSHALWOOD, Robert Kirkland	9/ 2/19		
763035	HOLDEN, William Clifford	28/ 7/17	Lieut.	
768196	HOUSTON, Thomas	18/ 1/19		
6979	HOWKINS, Francis	31/ 3/16	Lieut.	Wounded 22/5/18
6154	HUDSON, Thomas	1/11/16	Lieut.	
1534	HUGHES, Thomas Harold	18/ 3/15	Capt.	
766894	INGRAM, John Thornton	12/10/18		
766838	IRWIN, Reginald Wosley	27/ 8/18		
764991	JACK, James Frederick Semple	27/10/17	Lieut.	Wounded 15/8/18
901	JAQUES, Sgt. Thomas Arnold	3/12/16	Lieut.	
766306	JENKINS, Gilbert Ramsden	5/ 2/18	Lieut.	
762504	JENKINS, Harold John Blewitt	28/ 7/17	Lieut.	
765553	JENNINGS, James	23/ 2/18		
6450	JONES, Frank Cuthbert	19/ 8/16	Lieut.	
762486	KEMP, George	13/ 3/17	Lieut.	
761218	KENYON, Reginald	19/ 1/17	Lieut.	
6517	LANGFORD, L/Cpl. Thomas Henry	14/ 1/17	Lieut.	
2708	LOMAX, Cpl. Gordon Charles	28/ 4/16	Lieut.	
767828	MACDONALD, Charles Alex.	16/ 8/18		

767505	MACKENDRICK, Bruce	...	...	2/ 6/18 *Wounded* 20/11/18
6386	MACKAY, Cpl. Donald John Everall			22/ 9/17 *Capt.* ✠
767438	MALAN, James Garfield Montague	...		3/ 7/18
2757	MANSFIELD, Francis Turguand		...	14/11/14 (*From* 3/*R. W. Kent*) *Lieut.* ✠
7274	MAYER, Julius Joseph	...	...	21/ 8/16 *Lieut.*
6436	MCKIM, William Rowand	...	...	17/ 7/16 *Lieut.*
6113	MEDLAND, James Edward Percy		...	5/ 9/16 *Killed in action* 23/3/18
762760	MIDGLEY, Thomas Herbert	...	...	5/ 5/17 *Lieut.* ✠
5318	MILLS, Walter Vernon	...	...	11/ 9/16 *Lieut.*
767509	MIX, Archibald Eugene	...	...	2/ 6/18
760511	MOKLER, L/Cpl. Leonard Walter		...	19/ 5/17 *Lieut.*
6519	MOORE, Leslie Thomas	...	...	6/11/16 *Lieut.* ✠
6464	MORROW, Frederick	...	...	11/ 9/16 *Lieut.* ✠ *Wounded* 6/4/18
768098	MOTTERSHEAD, Robert Fallows		...	31/ 1/19
6175	MOZLEY, Frederick William	...	...	6/11/16 *Lieut.*
449	MULLENS, Geoffrey Thomas		...	26/ 5/17 *Capt.* (*Inspector of Works*)
8242	NEWCOMBE, John Carr	...	...	25/12/16 *Lieut. Killed in action* 21/3/18
767693	NICOL, Ray Thomas	...	...	27/ 8/18
5862	NOBLE, James Morton	...	...	6/11/16 *Capt.* 𝕸
767511	NOTT, Gordon E.	...	...	31/ 9/18
764906	OWEN, Basil Cowley	...	...	28/ 4/17 *Lieut.*
6020	OWENS, Jack	...	...	14/ 1/17 *Lieut. Wounded* 3/1/18
4399	PAPWORTH, Cpl. Alfred Wyatt		...	19/ 8/16 *Killed in action* 2/4/17
8180	PEACOCK, Charles Richard	...	...	1/11/16 *Lieut.*
761707	PENDEREL-BRODHURST, Sgt. B. R.		...	28/ 7/17 *Killed in action* 1/10/18
2724	PEPPER, Sgt. Alwyn Tayton	...		1/11/16 *Capt. Died* 6/11/18
767514	PETRY, Allan McNab	...	...	2/ 6/18
6272	POWELL, Wallace Gerald	...	...	13/11/16 *Lieut.*
766802	PURSEY, Herbert Stanley	...	..	8/ 9/17 *Lieut.*
765404	QUAIL, Henry Charles	...	...	30/ 6/17 *Killed in action* 18/2/18
2018	RANDELL, Donald Murray	...	...	22/12/18 *Lieut.* 𝕸
6742	REAH, Herbert William	...	...	11/ 2/17 *Lieut.* ✠
5925	REASIDE, L/Cpl. David	...	...	11/ 2/17 *Lieut.*
5635	RICCOMINI, James Arthur	...	...	13/11/16 *Lieut.*
767515	RICHARDSON, Charles Albert		...	2/ 6/18
768235	RICHARDSON, James Eugene		...	9/ 2/19
767450	RISSIK, Gerard Hendrick	...	...	13/ 7/18
7926	ROBERTSHAW, William Lancelot		...	11/ 2/17 *Lieut. Wounded* 9/4/18
761933	ROBIN, Sgt. Charles Collas	...	...	13/ 5/18 *Special List*
767389	SCHOFIELD, Harold	...	...	9/ 2/19
5602	SHINER, Lawrence Alexander David			4/10/16 *Lieut.*
767639	SILLEY, Henry Arthur John	...	...	5/10/18
764911	SIMSON, John Hedley	...	...	17/11/17 *Lieut.* w. -/4/18, 22/9/18 𝕸(2)
5874	SMITH, Eric Bertram	...	...	29/ 1/17 *Lieut.*
2023	SOMERSET, James Herbert	...	...	15/ 8/15 *Lieut.*
766398	SOUL, Charles Frederick	...	...	9/ 2/19
766454	STAMP, Laurence Dudley	..	...	27/ 4/18
765904	STEVENS, Alexander	...	...	4/ 9/17

8325	STEVENS, Paul Laval	25/12/16	Lieut.	
6031	STEWARD, Donald Henry	29/ 9/16	Lieut.	
5812	STILGOE, Nathaniel Gordon	16/ 4/17	Lieut.	
761288	STRONNOR, Randolph Cecil	25/ 2/17	Lieut.	Wounded 10/9/17
764802	SUMMERS, Albert Robinson	17/11/17		
765967	SWAN, Thomas Aikman	24/ 1/17	Lieut.	
765521	TALBOT, Leonard Henri	23/ 2/18		
764540	TAYLOR, Charles Allison	2/10/17		
767069	TEATHER, Reginald Herbert	2/ 6/18		
6367	THOMAS, Cpl. Percy E.	4/10/16	Capt.	O.B.E. 🎖
6321	THOMASSON, Wilfred Joseph Mate	14/ 1/17	Capt.	
768079	THOMSON, Alexander Ralph	2/11/18		
5557	TINNISWOOD, L/Cpl. Alfred	11/ 2/17	Killed in action 1/10/18	
768002	TOCQUE, Frederick Arthur Charles	18/ 1/19		
2767	TOOTHILL, John Cedric Penman	28/ 9/18		
766035	TRAFFORD, Francis Noel	23/ 2/18		
7901	TRERY, Norman Horace	14/ 1/17	Lieut.	✠
3462	VERNHAM, James Rene	1/10/16	Lieut.	
767520	WARD, Arthur Lanceley	31/ 8/18		
768006	WARDLOW-RAMSEY, Ernest	2/11/18		
763867	WARNER, Thomas Henry	28/ 7/17		
5607	WARREN, L/Cpl. Henry George	19/11/16	Lieut.	
760135	WATSON, Sgt. Douglas John	18/ 1/19	Wounded 30/10/17	
760436	WELCH, Herbert Archibald	17/11/17		
6777	WELCH, John Francis Warlow	22/10/16	Lieut.	
760235	WHITBY, Sgt. Charles	29/11/17		
6205	WHITE, George Frederick	6/11/16	Lieut.	
6506	WILLIAMS, Harold	13/ 8/16	Lieut.	
5302	WILLIAMS, Llewellyn Ebenezer	3/12/16	Major.	Wounded 29/1/18 🎖
767733	WILLIAMS, Rhys	18/ 1/19		
762873	WILLIAMS, Sgt. Thomas	19/ 5/18		
7031	WILLMOT, L/Cpl. Edmund Charles	13/11/16	Lieut.	
761664	YOUNG, Beverley	17/ 7/18		
6688	YOUNG, William Cecil	11/ 2/17	Lieut.	

Inland Water Transport.

764969	ABLITT, Cpl. Henry	1/ 8/17		
765984	ALLEN, John Gordon	31/10/17		
761742	ATKINSON, Clifford Garnett	26/ 3/17		
762443	AVELING, Norman Harford	1/ 6/18		
766297	BENNETT, Gordon Charles	15/10/17		
4688	BESSANT, Sgt. Hubert Walter	18/ 9/16	Capt.	
8309	BEVAN, Thomas William	1/ 2/17	Staff-Capt.	Died 22/10/18
765833	BURNS, David Brunel	14/10/17		
763772	CLARKE, Stanislaus Eustace	27/ 4/17		
765836	DAVIES, Henry	31/10/17		
766098	DEWEY, Leonard	15/10/17		

ROYAL ENGINEERS.

7809	FABLING, Harold William ...	... 18/ 9/16	Lieut.	🎖
8065	FARMBOROUGH, James Cooper	... 18/ 9/16	Lieut.	
761399	FORD, Leonard Charles ...	... 22/ 2/18		
678319	GLANEY, Sidney Archibald ...	... 6/11/18		
7903	GLINISTER, Albert Colenso ...	... 18/ 9/16	Lieut.	
764058	GLUCKSTEIN, Montague ...	... 19/ 3/17	Lieut.	
2214	HASLEHUST, CSM Guy Bartlett	... 18/ 9/16	Capt.	
9390	HERTSLET, Henry Reginald Edward	12/ 1/17	Lieut.	
763973	HORSBURGH, Leonard Gordon	... 26/ 3/17	Lieut.	
7882	JOHNSON, Charles ...	... 18/ 9/16	Lieut.	
766194	LE MAISTRE, Frederick Wyatt	... 15/ 8/17		
766026	LEWIS, Gerald ...	... 14/10/17		
7399	LIVOCK, Ralph Payne ...	... 18/ 9/16	Lieut.	
766720	LONG, Frederick William ...	... 15/ 1/18		
762336	MACINTOSH, John Macausland	... 23/ 4/17	Lieut.	
766700	MEAD, James Robins ...	... 15/ 1/18		
765561	MILLER, Thomas Sidney ...	... 14/10/17	🎖	
2267	MILLS, Henry Graham Hunt	... 12/11/16	Lieut.	
7868	MISICK, Frederick Clark ...	... 18/ 9/16	Lieut.	
762459	NEWBY, Frederick Wales ...	... 15/ 6/17	Lieut.	
765601	PITCHER, Horace Bedford ...	... 5/ 8/17		
5795	PRICE, Benjamin Percival ...	... 18/ 9/16	Lieut.	🎖
2602	SWINNEY, Sgt. Leslie Alfred Edward	10/10/16	Major.	
4871	WALKER, Sgt. Dunstan Massey Joseph	18/ 9/16	Lieut.	
3686	WATT, Sgt. Joseph James ...	... 18/12/16	Lieut.	
1363	WHITE, RSM Bruce Gordon ...	... 4/ 9/16	Major.	M.B.E. 🎖
7598	YOUNG, Charles Octavius ...	... 18/ 9/16	Lieut.	

Special Reserve.

Royal Monmouthshire.

734	MOORE, Harold Edward ...	... 5/ 8/14	Capt.	D.S.O. ✠ 🎖
2607	SIMEON, Cornwall Barrington	... 13/10/14	Capt.	🎖
1469	SMITH, Arthur Douglas Noel	... 3/ 2/15	Capt.	

Motor Cyclist Section.

329	SCRUTTON, Cpl. John Austin	... 12/ 1/15	Lieut.	✠ 🎖
766313	PALMER, Philip Somerset ...	... 30/ 3/18		

ATTACHED R.E. FOR ARMY SIGNAL SERVICE.

Lieut.	FAIRTLOUGH, Gerrard Howard	... ...	*Capt. 1/Artists (3/Cavalry Div.)*	
			✠ *Died of wounds* 13/6/18 🎖	
1997	STANESBY, Reginald William J.	... ...	*(From 9/York & Lancs.)*	

Territorial Force.

DIVISIONAL ENGINEERS.

East Anglian Division.

3767	CARDELL, Joseph Edmond ...	... 20/ 7/15	*Lieut.*	✠
1787	FIELDING, Walter Harrison ..	... 17/ 9/14	*Capt.* o.b.e.	✠

Highland Division.

3273	DOYLE, Algernon Gordon ...	... 21/ 3/15	*Lieut.*	✠

East Lancashire Division.

3695	LEES, Geoffrey	... 6/ 8/15	*Lieut.*

West Lancashire Division.

598	THORNE, Sgt. Alfred John P.	... 11/ 3/15	*Lieut.* ✠ ✠ *w.* 26/4/18	✠

First London Division.

4041	ADAMS, William Baddeley ...	... 20/12/15	*w.* 18/2/18
3950	FENNING, Robert William ...	... 15/ 1/16	*Lieut.*
599	THORNE, Sgt. Philip Howard	... 15/12/14	*Capt.* ✠ *w.* (*Dardanelles*) –/9/15, 30/11/17 ✠ (2)

Second London Division.

2559	BRACHI, Maurice	... 18/ 2/15	*Lieut.* ✠ ✠
2164	CURTIS, Harold Thomas ...	... 27/ 2/15	*Capt.*
1897	DUNNAGE, Gerald Eckett ...	... 9/ 6/15	*Lieut. w.* 19/10/17
2275	LEGG, L/Cpl. Will	... 6/ 6/15	*w. & P/W* 10/9/18
2046	HILLYER, William Harold ...	... 30/ 9/14	*Capt.* ✠ *w.* 15/5/15 *K/A* 22/5/16 ✠
3056	KNUTH, L/Cpl. Christopher H. L. ...	10/10/15	*Lieut.*

South Midland Division.

2298	BESSANT, John Archibald ...	... 10/ 9/15	*Lieut.* ✠
2092	WILSON, Denis Medland ...	... 10/ 9/15	*Lieut. Prisoner of war* –/12/15
765612	BRAMALL, Denys Henry ...	... 17/ 7/17	*Lieut.* (*North Midland*)
2485	CLAPTON, William Thomas ...	... 20/ 4/15	*Lieut.* (*1/London*)
763060	FOSTER, Henry Oswald ...	... 16/ 6/17	*Lieut.* (*Home Counties*)
761924	GARTH, Horace Richard ...	... 1/ 4/17	*Lieut.* (*Wessex*)
761143	HILL, George Finlay Burd ...	... 1/ 4/17	*Lieut.* (*Northumberland*)
761260	LANT, Arthur Edward ...	... 1/ 4/17	*Lieut.* (*Northumberland*)
763069	LAURIE, Alexander Mackray	... 17/ 7/17	*Lieut.* (*2/London*)
765357	MILLER, William Harold ...	... 1/ 4/17	*Lieut.* (*North Midland*)
764904	MUIR, Robert George ...	... 8/ 9/17	*Lieut.* (*East Lancs.*)
764253	PERKINS, Joseph	... 17/ 7/17	*Lieut.* (*2/London*)
7644	ROBERTS, Haydn Parke ...	... 6/ 7/16	*Lieut.* (*South Midland*)
764564	ROBINSON, Alfred Keon ...	... 17/ 7/17	*Lieut.* (*2/London*) *P/W* 15/6/18
764116	WRIGLEY, Percy Bernard ...	... 17/ 7/17	*Lieut.* (*2/London*) *K/A* 23/3/18

FORTRESS ENGINEERS.

Cinque Ports.
2024 ATKIN-BERRY, Henry Gordon ... 12/ 6/15 *Lieut.* ✠

Cornwall.
3423 GORDON, Ernest ... ... 25/ 6/15 *Lieut.*

Devon.
1715 DONE, John Paul Cussons ... ... 20/ 6/15 *Lieut.* ℞
6067 KINGDON, Roger ... ... 8/ 8/16 *Lieut.*

Hampshire.
2183 BEVIS, Douglas Arthur ... ... 9/12/14 *Lieut.*
2560 DAVIES, Tudor Yuab ... ... 27/ 6/15 *Lieut.* ✠
2770 HENDRY, Harry Duncan ... ... 27/ 6/15 *Wounded* –/6/16 ℞
2180 SMITH, Walter Austen Neumann ... 27/ 6/15 *Lieut.*

Kent.
4638 BLANC, L/Cpl. Louis David ... 6/11/15 *Lieut.*

East Riding.
6212 WEST, Kenneth ... ... 28/ 7/16 *Lieut.*

ELECTRICAL ENGINEERS.

London.
876 BLACKIE, Alfred ... ... 28/ 4/15 4/Co. *Lieut.*
5942 BURTON, Robert Griffiths ... 27/ 3/16 *Lieut.*
1487 ENGELBACH, Reginald ... 23/ 1/15 *Capt.*

Tyne.
5275 MURRAY, John Bernard ... ... 28/ 1/16 *Lieut.*

Staff for R.E. Services.

Temporary Inspectors of Works.
2552 MURRELL, Harold Franklin ... 10/ 2/15 *Hon. Capt.*
3093 NICHOLLS, William ... ... 25/ 2/15 *Capt.*

FOOT GUARDS.
GRENADIER GUARDS.

			2nd Lieut.	
1076	Crisp, Cpl. Francis Edward Fitzjohn		15/12/14	Killed in action 5/1/15
1186	Moller, Arthur Appleby ...	...	15/12/14	Lieut. ✠
3604	Arbuthnott, John ...	...	16/ 1/16	Lieut. Died of wounds 15/9/16
1413	Cornish, George Mervyn ...	...	16/ 1/16	✠ Wounded –/9/16
6167	Cottle, Walter Edward Worsdale ...		16/ 1/16	(To M/G Gds.) K/A 31/7/17
4522	Flower, Cpl. Alfred Chegwin	...	4/ 1/16	Lieut. Killed in action 25/9/16
2339	Harvey, Douglas ...	...	16/ 1/16	Wounded –/9/16 K/A 27/3/18
4732	McNiell, L/Cpl. John Douglas	...	13/ 1/16	Lieut.
6179	Sim, Lancelot George Earle ...		22/ 1/16	Killed in action 14/9/16
3192	Thrupp, Cpl. Maurice	...	13/ 1/16	Killed in action 31/7/17
3583	West, L/Cpl. Richard Goy ...	...	22/ 2/16	Lieut. w. 18/9/17, 10/9/18
764624	Allen, Dudley Attwood Kingdon ...		30/10/17	
767280	Anderson, Cyril Alfred	...	28/ 8/18	
7141	Ayles, Francis Powell	...	22/ 1/17	Lieut. (R.A.F.) Acc/K 1/6/18
760775	Ball, Sgt. William Bruce	...	30/ 5/17	Lieut.
764475	Batchelor, Luke Harold ...		30/ 5/17	Lieut.
762264	Bidwell, Thomas Edward Palmer ...		31/ 7/17	Lieut.
7780	Borthwick, Hon. Algernon Malcolm		24/ 8/16	Lieut. Wounded 25/9/17
6919	Burt, George Crickmay	...	24/ 8/16	Lieut. Wounded & P/W 2/5/18
7781	Carrington, Charles Worrell	...	24/ 8/16	Capt. D.S.O. w. 15/4/18 ✠
7339	Elliott, Arthur Godfrey	...	13/ 7/16	Lieut. ✠ w. 11/8/17, 23/9/18
7755	Ennor, Frank Harvey	...	29/11/16	Lieut. Wounded 29/3/18
765539	Fitch, Conrad Arthur	...	31/10/17	Wounded 14/5/18
8566	Fleet, William Alexander ...		19/ 1/17	Killed in action 18/5/18
765715	Gillett, Hugh Vernon	...	30/ 1/18	
7592	Green, George Richard	...	24/ 8/16	Lieut. ✠ Wounded 2/5/18
7201	Greenhill, Frederick William Ridge		26/ 8/16	Killed in action 10/10/17
768165	Hawksley, Thomas Edwin ...		16/ 3/19	
7776	Hollins, Cecil Braithwaite ...		6/ 9/16	Lieut. Wounded 13/12/17
6588	Jacks, Roderick Newton	...	6/ 9/16	Lieut.
4829	King, Eric George Lauder ...		9/ 1/16	Killed in action 22/7/17
2701	Knight, Sgt. Donald John ...		16/11/16	Lieut.
762364	Langley, Francis Jasper	...	1/ 5/17	Killed in action 27/8/18
766441	Mortimore, Eustace Alick ...		27/ 3/18	
7456	Ogle, L/Cpl. Henry Robert	...	6/ 9/16	Lieut. Wounded 11/8/17
2276	Paget-Cooke, L/Cpl. Oliver Daynell		15/ 4/15	Lieut. Wounded 11/5/18
8257	Pembroke, William Alfred ...		19/ 1/17	
6673	Rolfe, Raymond Harold	...	6/ 9/16	Killed in action 23/4/18
7778	Roper, William Horace Stanley	...	6/ 9/16	Died of wounds 11/10/17
7786	Smith, Thomas ...	...	24/ 8/16	Lieut.
7403	Sutton, Kenneth Herbert Mackay...		18/ 8/16	Lieut. Wounded 13/8/17
2156	Tate, Eric Dean ...	...	16/11/16	Lieut. Wounded 13/4/18
768796	Taylor, Harold St. George...		10/ 3/19	
Capt.	Tetley, John Charles Dodsworth ...		11/10/16	Capt. Killed in action 9/10/17
7075	Wall, Richard Bernard St. Quinton		6/ 9/16	Lieut.
6507	Wrixon, Maurice Percival Bentley...		24/ 8/16	Lieut. ✠ Wounded 6/4/18

COLDSTREAM GUARDS.

			2nd Lieut.	
2nd Lt.	Furze, Gordon	... ...	23/ 4/15	4 Capt. ✠ *To Staff*
,,	Kelsey, Leigh Bentall	...	22/ 5/15	*Lieut. (To M/G Gds.)*
,,	Perry, Gordon MacKintosh		29/ 4/15	*Lieut.(To M/G Gds.)w. 11/9/18* ⚔
3756	Bulteel, Walter Gordon	...	30/ 6/15	1 *Capt. (Commdg. T.M.B.)*
1274	Clifton, Edward Noel	...	1/ 1/15	1 *Capt. (To R.A.F.) w. 25/1/15*
1265	Clifton, Harold Norton	...	1/ 1/15	1 *Died of wounds 1/2/15*
2740	Fildes, Geoffrey Philip	...	29/ 3/15	5 *Lieut.*
3087	Hoblyn, Sgt. Walter Frederick		30/ 6/15	4 *Died of wounds 1/10/15*
3619	Kirk, Cpl. Arthur Wilson	...	30/ 6/15	5 *Lieut. w. (Hulluck) 9/10/15*
1627	Spencer, Thomas Dever	...	13/ 3/15	5 *Capt.*
3581	Spinney, Cpl. Ronald Henry		30/ 6/15	2 *Lieut. Died of wounds 2/7/16*
Capt.	Selfe, Arthur E. Ferrour	...	20/ 4/16	*Capt.* ✠ *w. 31/7/17, 27/11/17*
4170	Atkinson, L/Cpl. William	...	29/10/15	5 *Capt. Wounded 10/4/18* ⚔
4172	Berkeley, Christopher	...	29/10/15	5 *(R.A.F.) Acc/Killed 30/1/19*
4035	Forrester, L/Cpl. Joseph	...	22/10/15	*Capt.* ⚔
4182	Grissell, Francis	... ...	29/10/15	5 *Killed in action 15/9/16*
4203	Kimberley, Harold Crane	...	22/10/15	*Lieut.*
3642	King, Mark	... ...	31/ 5/16	*Lieut.* D.S.O. *w. 20/4/18* ⚔
4061	Laing, L/Cpl. Ivan	... ...	22/10/15	✠ *Killed in action 30/11/17*
5770	Laing, L/Cpl. Walter	...	2/ 6/16	*Lieut.*
4094	Machin, Norman Frederick		22/10/15	*Capt.* ✠
3909	Maitland-Edwards, R. Sheridan	...	16/11/15	*Lieut.*
4062	Montgomery, Norman Stevenson	...	22/10/15	*Killed in action 17/6/16*
2462	Newland, Cpl. Arthur Mansfield	...	19/11/15	*Lieut.* ✠ *Wounded 11/12/17*
5212	Orr, Charles Wilfred Leslie	...	29/ 2/16	
1678	Overton-Jones, Edward	...	6/12/15	*Lieut.* ✠ *Wounded 6/9/17*
3397	Pitcher, Sgt. Walter H. Blythe	...	1/11/15	*Capt.* ✠ *Wounded 15/12/17*
4208	Treloar, L/Cpl. George Devine	...	20/10/15	*Major* D.S.O. ✠ ⚔
4050	Warmington, Stanley James	...	20/10/15	*Lieut.*
5645	Ball, Samuel Harper	...	31/ 5/16	*Lieut. (To M/G Gds.)*
5051	Colman, Charles Wyndham Tawell		31/ 5/16	*(To R.A.F.) Pilot Officer*
4774	Jacks, Walter George Cyril	...	31/ 5/16	*Lieut. (To R.A.S.C.)*
4998	Nichols, William Alfred	...	31/ 5/16	*Lieut. (To M/G Gds.)*
6237	Smith, Geoffrey Hubert	...	31/ 5/16	*Capt.* ✠ *Missing, believed killed, 16/10/18*
7747	Balfour, Cramond George Clarke	...	29/11/16	*Lieut.* ⚔
5647	Barlow, Hyla Mortimer Durant	...	14/ 8/16	*Wounded 21/5/18, 11/9/18*
7779	Bayzand, Geoffrey	...	14/ 8/16	*Capt.* ✠ ✠ *Wounded 12/4/18*
7857	Boycott, Harold Charlton	...	14/ 8/16	4 *Lieut. Died of wounds 21/3/18*
8127	Brenchley, John	... ...	10/ 8/16	✠ *Killed in action 12/10/17*
761424	Burn, Sgt. Thomas Christopher	...	27/ 2/18	*Capt.*
7842	Cordingley, Thomas Rushton	...	20/12/16	*Lieut.*
7848	Cresswell, George James Richard		14/12/16	*Lieut. Wounded 12/5/18*
8159	Evans, William	... ...	29/11/16	*Lieut. w. 11/8/17, 14/3/18*
767220	Harrison, Cpl. Alban Christopher	..	3/ 2/19	
7760	Hanson, James	... ...	14/ 8/16	*Lieut.*

COLDSTREAM GUARDS.

763885	HEATH, Gerard Bower	1/ 5/17	2	*Died of Wounds* 22/5/18
765708	HENEY, John Henry Waldo...	28/11/17	✠	
762958	INMAN, John James Thomas	31/ 7/17		
764324	JACKSON, William	26/ 6/17		*Wounded* 26/8/18
9128	MERRIMAN, Edward Claude B.	19/ 1/17		*Wounded* 2/5/18
767822	MILLAR, Laurence Peel ...	5/ 2/19		
762999	MILLER, Stanley Joseph Hopkins	26/ 6/17		
764504	MOSLEY, Eric Bond	31/ 7/17		*Wounded* 3/4/18, 24/10/18
7837	NORTON, Robert Holland ...	14/ 8/16		*Lieut.*
7595	PINDER, Arthur Gladstone ...	14/ 8/16		*Lieut.*
767144	SMITH, William Henry ...	26/ 6/18		
7856	STOPS, John Faulkner ...	14/ 8/16		*Lieut.*
765869	TALBOT, Joseph Herbert George	27/ 3/18		
763896	TASKER, Edward Clough ...	26/ 6/17		*Lieut.*
8148	TYLER, Leith	20/12/16		*Lieut.*
764047	VINCENT, Charles Issam Francis	1/ 5/17	1	*Killed in action* 16/10/18
1137	WILLMER, Sgt. Charles Henry	14/ 8/16		*Lieut.*
762358	WILSON, Frederick William ...	1/ 5/17		
8217	WOODBURY, Edward Berkley Cherlton	18/ 9/16		*Wounded* 11/10/18

SCOTS GUARDS.

		2nd Lieut.		
1270	METHUEN, Hon. Anthony Paul	15/ 8/14	1	*Major* D.S.O. ✠ *Bde.-Major A.D.C. w.* 11/5/15 ₩(3)
1225	THOMPSON, Arnold John ...	1/ 1/15	1	*Lieut. & Adjt.* ₩
1406	THOMPSON, John Cecil Caster	1/ 1/15	1	*Lieut. Killed in action* 25/1/15
1419	WELD, Hugh Edward ...	1/ 1/15	1	*Killed in action* 25/1/15
6431	ADAMS-ACTON, Gladstone Murray	24/ 8/16		*Lieut.*
760871	ANDREWS, Robert Collingwood	30/ 5/17		*Wounded* 13/12/17
765882	HOPE, Henry John	31/10/17		*Wounded* 10/9/18 ₩
8132	IVENS, Francis Burdett ...	29/11/16		*Lieut.* ₩
765683	KAY, Tom Kilbourne ...	28/11/17		
768028	LODGE, Douglas Rimington ...	3/ 3/19		
7721	MILNE, L/Cpl. John Archibald Dickie	24/ 8/16	1	*Killed in action* 12/10/17
768184	PAGE, Philip Price	10/ 3/19		
6437	POCOCK, George Clifford ...	5/10/16		*Capt. Wounded* 14/6/18
762811	ROBINSON, Donald Lorraine	29/ 4/17		*Lieut.*
765870	WALLIS, George Peter Dudley	28/11/17		*Wounded* 19/6/18

IRISH GUARDS.

		2nd Lieut.	
3629	MUNRO, Ronald George	21/ 7/15	(*From London Irish*) ✠ *w.* 8/1/16 *D/W* 19/9/16
5393	BLACK, James	30/ 5/16	*Capt.* ✠
4422	HAMILTON, Charles Robert	30/ 5/16	*Lieut.*
8223	ANDERSON, Eric Edwin	28/11/16	*Lieut.* ✠
765883	BAGGALLAY, Frank Christopher	24/ 4/18	
766508	BURKE, Frederick William	29/ 4/18	
8044	DOWLER, Edgar Hastings	29/11/16	*Lieut.* Wounded 24/10/17
8283	FANSHAWE, Harvey Vernon	28/11/16 I	*Died of wounds* 9/10/17
766252	HEDGECOCK, Arthur Thomas	29/ 5/18	
7350	KANE, Justin John	18/ 8/16	Wounded 20/9/17
767660	LAWLESS, Arthur Percy	31/ 2/19	
8271	LOFTING, Hugh John	25/ 1/17	
7540	MACGRATH, Michael Reginald	18/ 8/16	*Lieut.*
2437	NICHOLSON, Cecil Alfred John	9/12/14	*Lieut.* *w.* 28/4/17, 11/5/18
7547	PARK, Ronald Hubert Mungo	18/ 8/16	*Lieut.* ✠
763310	PULLEYN, James	28/11/17	
767090	SYMINGTON, Percy Kinnear	29/ 5/18	
766501	TAYLOR, Arthur Edward	27/ 3/18	
762363	TOOLEY, Francis William	30/10/17	
7794	VAN DER NOOT, L/Cpl. Harold Edward	29/11/16	Wounded 15/8/17, 15/12/17 ₥
7758	WELLS, Alfred Langton	29/11/16 I	*Killed in action* 9/10/17
767036	WOODBRIDGE, Douglas Sydney	28/ 8/18	

WELSH GUARDS.

		2nd Lieut.	
8346	BANESS, Horace Edward	30/12/16	
761668	BOWYER, Cpl. Claude Tadman	30/ 5/17	Wounded 20/12/17
7893	BYRNE, Thomas Edmund	29/11/16 I	*Killed in action* 9/3/18
762556	DAVIES, Charles Ernest	31/10/17	Wounded 31/5/18
762364	DAVIES, Daniel Alexander	17/10/16	
764425	DAVIES, Derek Ben	31/ 7/17	✠
763818	DAVIES, Evan Jones	26/ 6/17 I	*Killed in action* 28/3/18
766598	GREENACRE, Walter Douglas Campbell	26/ 6/18	
766072	HAWKSLEY, Ernest Bourchier	30/ 1/18	
766253	HOFFGARD, Gustav Adolph	31/ 7/18	
8098	JENKINS, John Charles	20/12/16	
7655	JONES, Reginald Rees	20/12/16	D.S.O. *D/W* 25/8/17 ₥
7942	MANLEY, Gerald David	20/12/16	
761169	WALTERS, Sgt. Ivor Gwynne	29/ 5/18	
761210	WALTERS, Sgt. Thomas Glyn	29/ 5/18	
765375	WATSON, Thomas Browning	30/ 1/18	
765610	WHARTON, Arthur	29/ 5/18	

INFANTRY.

In alphabetical order.

THE ARGYLL & SUTHERLAND HIGHLANDERS.*

{ 91st Foot.
{ 93rd Foot.

Regular Battalions (Nos. 1 & 2).

2nd Lieut.
2541	GUNN, Malcolm Roy	... ...	9/ 5/15	*1 Lieut.*
5191	SCOTT, John Lennox	... ...	9/10/16	*1*

Special Reserve Battalions (Nos. 3 & 4).

763128	KIDD, Robert John	... ...	26/ 4/17	*4*	
765709	WATSON, Guy Fraser Tennant	...	18/12/17	*3*	*Wounded* 23/9/18

Territorial Battalions (Nos. 5 to 9).

5763	HUGHES, Andrew	... ...	1/ 6/16	*8*	
766503	ADAM, William	... ...	10/ 9/18	*5*	
765444	GORDON, James Edgar	... ...	28/11/17	*7*	
5656	HISLOP, David Hall	... ...	6/ 9/16	*5*	*Wounded* 29/9/16
763729	HURRELL, Lionel Hubert Murray	...	26/ 4/17	*6*	
5447	KINNEAR, George Alexander	...	20/12/16	*8*	
4550	McCALL, Ernest Bryson	...	6/ 1/16	*8 Lieut.*	
7816	SINCLAIR, Eric Russell	...	25/10/16	*7* ✠	*w.* 3/10/17 *K/A* 13/10/18
765048	SINCLAIR, John	... ...	28/11/17	*8*	
6562	WHITAKER, Foster	... ...	26/ 9/16	*5*	*Died of wounds* 3/5/17
765749	WILSON, James Blackburn	...	24/ 5/18	*7*	

Service Battalions (New Armies).

2943	PEGG, Harvey George	... ...	2/ 1/15	*13 Capt.*	*Adjutant*
768010	BOYLE, David Henry	... ...	4/ 3/19		
6211	DIXON, John George	... ...	5/ 9/16	*Lieut.*	
767028	HAMILTON, James Alexander	...	4/ 2/19		
767833	HARWOOD, George William	...	28/ 3/19		
763160	KINNEAR, Alexander	... ...	26/ 4/17	*14*	*Wounded* 13/4/18
766800	KIRKPATRICK, John	... ...	5/ 3/19		
768174	MILLER, Joseph	... ...	18/ 3/19		
767165	WILSON, Charles Clunie	...	5/ 2/19		

* *Title changed (1st January, 1921) to " The Argyll & Sutherland Highlanders (Princess Louise's)."*

THE BEDFORDSHIRE & HERTFORDSHIRE REGIMENT.

Regular Battalions (Nos. 1 & 2).   16th Foot.

		2nd Lieut.		
1394	BALLARD, Robert Francis Cooper ...	28/11/15	2 Lieut.	Killed in action 30/7/16
1033	DE BURIATTE, L/Cpl. Harold	... 15/12/14	2 Capt.	Wounded 15/8/18
1841	BEAL, Leonard Frank ...	... 20/ 3/15	2 Major ✠	Wounded 16/5/16
1842	BOYS, Richard Harvey ...	... 17/ 3/15	2	Wounded 16/5/15 K/A 13/11/16
1260	BREWER, Charles Herbert ...	... 15/12/14	2 Lieut.	Wounded 17/6/15
1929	DABELL, Norman Victor ...	... 15/12/14	2 Lieut.	Staff
1599	D'AVIGDOR, Gerald Henry ...	... 10/ 7/15	2 Lieut.	
1549	GEORGE, Walter Hope ...	... 3/ 3/15	2 Major	Wounded 3/7/15 ⎇ (2)
2605	GIBSON, Robert Bowness ...	... 1/11/14	2 (From 3/S. Staffs.) ⎇	
2261	HOBBS, Wilfred ...	... 10/ 7/15	2 Capt. ✠	Wounded ⎇
1949	HUNTER, Charles James ...	... 10/ 7/15	2 Capt.	w. 25/9/15 d. 4/11/18
1415	JUNGUIS, Ernest James Theodore ...	30/ 4/16	1 (M.G.C.) Lieut.	
1434	KELLIE, Esmond Lawrence ...	... 1/ 1/15	1 Killed in action 19/4/15	
1604	KIRCH, Charles Sidney ...	... 1/ 1/15	1 Killed in action 19/4/15	
1322	LARDNER, Reginald Seymour ...	... 20/ 3/15	2 (R.A.F.) Lt.	w. 16/5/15 [⎇ (2)
1449	OLDFIELD, Reginald Theodore ...	... 15/ 8/15	2 Capt. ✠✠	w. 25/9/15, 9/10/18
1036	RAMSAY, Weston	... 20/ 3/15	2 Capt. & Adjt.	w. 20/4/15
1608	STEPHENSON, Kenneth Langton ...	15/ 8/15	2 Killed in action 26/9/15 ⎇	
1431	STONIER, William John ...	... 3/ 3/15	2 Lieut.	w. 18/5/15, 25/9/15
				K/A 27/4/17
1030	WILLANS, Harry ...	... 15/12/14	1 Capt. & Adjt. D.S.O. ✠	
				Wounded 7/7/16, –/6/18 ⎇ (2)
764291	CORNELIUS, Herbert Walter ...	... 1/ 8/17	1 Killed in action 20/7/18	
760071	DALTON, John	... 23/ 3/17	1 Capt. ✠	
6007	HUNTER, Robert Moore ...	... 18/ 3/17	1	
763456	LAUGHTON, Joseph Thornton	... 26/ 4/17	1 w. 23/10/17 D/W 29/9/18	

Special Reserve Battalions (Nos. 3 & 4).

1158	ROEBER, Sgt. Oscar ...	...	... 7/ 5/15	From 10 Lieut. w. –/7/16
3287	ROEBER, David Arnold	...	... 7/ 5/15	,, 10 Killed in action 14/8/16
768328	TAYLOR, Roy Frederick	...	... 17/ 3/19 3	

Territorial Battalion (No. 5).

Capt.	RICKATSON, Hugh Cecil ...	... 3/11/15	5 Capt. ✠	Wounded 15/12/17
,,	SELFE, Arthur Edward Ferrour	... 17/12/15	5 Capt. ✠	w. 17/8/17, 11/12/17
36	CUBITT, CQMS Charles Nutting	... 3/11/15	5 Lieut.	Wounded 13/9/18
3905	HAWKEN, L/Cpl. Gerald Humphrey	1/11/15	5 (Sikhs) Lieut.	

763518	CALDERBANK, Percy	11/ 5/17	5	
762270	FOSTER, Frank Mortimer	29/ 3/17	5	
762679	HOWARTH, Richard	28/ 3/17	5	
763365	LAMIGEON, Richard Oswald	29/ 3/17	5	
766560	LEWIS, John	24/ 4/18	5	
762787	MACKLIN, David Harold	29/ 3/17	5	*Killed in action* 27/3/18
6962	RUDOLPH, Geo. Rupert	5/ 9/16	5	
764073	SHOTT, Percival	3/ 7/17	5	*Lieut. Wounded* 12/3/18
6504	WATSON, Henry James Arthur	26/ 9/16	5	*Lieut. Killed in action* 23/8/18
6687	WILKINS, Claude Glibbery	5/ 9/16	5	*Wounded* 28/6/18

Territorial Battalion (No. 11)

(formerly the Hertfordshire Regiment, T.F.)

1930	BAKER, Herbert Norman	2/ 9/15	1	2/*Nigerian Regt. Died* 30/8/17
2212	BROAD, John Eric	29/11/15	1	*Lieut. Killed in action* 23/3/18
3812	BRUNSDON, Arthur Frederick Ernest	15/10/15	1	*Labour Corps. Lieut.*
3776	BULL, Lawrance	15/10/15	1	*Lieut. Wounded* 24/3/17
1421	CHRISTIE, John Fairfax	26/ 9/14	2	*Capt. & Adjt.* ✠ *w.* 18/5/15, 24/4/18
3857	FRITH, Reginald William	15/10/15	1	*Lieut. Wounded* –/12/16
4029	O'SHANE, Cpl. Cormac	17/11/15	1	*Lieut.*
4096	OWEN, L/Cpl. Malcolm de B.	5/10/15	1	*Lieut.* ✠ *K/A* 4/11/18
4100	RAVENSCROFT, Richard Birkbeck	24/12/15	1	*Lieut. Killed in action* 16/8/17
3426	VANDYKE, Cpl. Percy Reginald	15/10/15	1	*Lieut. R.T.O.*
3816	WEEKS, Charles Henry	15/10/15	1	*Lieut. (Tank Corps)*
3848	WHITE, Frank Edmund	15/10/15	1	*Lieut.*
6886	HAMMOND, Arthur Edwards	11/ 7/16		*Lieut. Wounded* 13/7/18
767544	ABBOTT-GREENWOOD, Wilfred Eric W.	4/ 3/19	1	
763942	ALLEN, Frederick Ernest	27/ 6/17	1	(5/*Bedford*)
3493	BOGGEN, John Hickey	26/ 9/16	1	*Lieut. Wounded* 27/5/18
3221	DOVE, William Watkins	26/ 1/17	1	*Lieut. w.* 11/12/17, 27/5/18
763463	KNEE, Harold James	29/ 3/17	1	*Lieut. w.* 24/4/18, 5/10/18
4143	PRIEST, William Henry	26/ 1/17	1	*Wounded* 26/4/17
7480	TENNANT, Bernard Victor Ashlin	20/12/16		*Lieut.*

Service Battalions (New Armies).

3166	CALDWELL-COOK, Cpl. Edward A.	6/ 4/15	10	*Lieut.*
2418	MASON, Kenneth Sydney	23/11/14	10	(*M.G.C.*) *Major* ✠
5046	BUTT, Alfred	25/ 5/16	10	(*R.F.C.*) *K/A* 4/1/18
767421	BARRETT, Frederick Fox	4/ 3/19		
764308	BLAKE, Francis Joseph	31/ 7/17		
767556	DINSDALE, Cyril Albert Metcalfe	5/ 3/19		

THE BEDFORD & HERTS (S/B)

761116	HUGHES, William	...	2/ 8/17 8 ✠	w. 17/7/18	D/W 14/9/18
2918	KAYE, Cpl. Hugh Gordon	...	19/ 9/16 6		
769316	PATRICK, Frederick Augustus Page	...	19/ 2/19		
4939	SMITH, Arthur Wedgwood Giffard	...	24/ 1/17 8 ✠		
767669	SPOONER, Harold George	...	3/ 3/19		
763027	DONOVAN, Terence Norbert	...	29/ 3/17 (7)		
763179	FRANKLIN, Arthur Thomas	...	29/ 3/17 (1)		
762120	GALLICHAN, Henry Nicholas	...	11/ 2/17 3	Garrison Battalion	
763362	GREENWOOD, Arthur Donald	...	1/ 3/17 (2)	Killed in action 30/8/18	
7312	HUNT, Frank	...	20/12/16 (4)		
764147	JACKSON, William Arthur	...	20/ 5/17 (1)		
6959	OAKLEY, William George	...	26/ 9/16 8	Lieut.	
763412	SOWDEN, Percy John	...	29/ 3/17 (5)		
765981	STAPLETON, William Howell	...	27/ 2/18	(5/R. Berks)	K/A 26/8/18
7469	WELLER, Henry John	...	19/12/16 8	Lieut. w. —/6/17, 17/4/18	

THE ROYAL BERKSHIRE REGIMENT.*

Regular Battalions (Nos. 1 & 2).

{49th Foot / 66th Foot}

2nd Lieut.

2676	ADAMS, Wilfred Carne	...	26/ 5/15 2	Capt. Wounded 13/9/15, 7/7/16
2874	BLACKBURN, Harry Dudley	...	29/ 8/15 1	(R.F.C.) Killed in action 5/4/17
1769	BRIDGE, Donald Gerald Clive	...	20/ 3/15 2	Died of wounds 23/5/16
168	CAHILL, Cpl. John Archibald	...	14/ 2/15 2	Capt. Wounded 10/3/15, 1/7/16 Killed in action 16/8/17 ▩
2934	CHACE, George Purves	...	29/ 8/15 1	Capt. & Adjt. ▩
419	COOK, Charles Stark	...	24/10/15 1	Lieut.
1719	DAY, Morris	...	20/ 3/15 2	Killed in action 9/5/15
584	JERWOOD, Ed. Longsden	...	27/ 1/15 1	Capt. ✠✠✠ w. (2) ▩
1786	LINDLEY, George William	...	20/ 3/15 2	Lieut. Wounded 29/9/15
1154	PAINE, George Gordon	...	26/ 5/15 2	Capt. ✠ Wounded 29/7/15 Died of wounds 27/3/18 ▩

Special Reserve Battalion (No. 3).

761212	ADAMS, Bernard Randall Cole	...	28/11/17 3
763224	AYRES, Frank Ernest	...	28/ 3/17 3 (2) Wounded 23/10/18
762292	MANNING, James Walter Geoffrey	...	26/ 4/17 3 (1) Wounded 6/10/17
8241	MOSSMAN, Harold Alex.	...	25/ 1/17 3 (6) ✠ w. 16/5/17 K/A 25/4/18
767535	PRICE, Herbert Leo	...	4/ 3/19 3
766002	SHORT, Sydney Charles Terry	...	1/ 5/18 3
8329	WORDEN, Ernest Harold Glover	...	25/ 1/17 3 (6) ✠ Wounded 13/8/17

* Title changed (1st January, 1921) to "The Royal Berkshire Regiment (Princess Charlotte of Wales's)."

ROYAL BERKSHIRE REGIMENT (T/F & S/B). 225

Territorial Battalion (No. 4).

5233	BARTMAN, Wilfred Arthur ...	... 16/ 6/16 4 Lieut.	(A.P.D.)
6279	BUXTON, Oswald	... 16/ 6/16 4 Lieut.	F/D w. 26/8/18
3856	GIBSON, Dudley Robert ...	... 11/11/15 4 Ind. Army.	Lieut. ✠ w. 19/7/16
5260	HEPPELL, Harry Denby ...	... 16/ 6/16 4 Killed in action 5/4/17	
5128	LENNARD, Walter Daniel ...	... 16/ 6/16 4 Lieut.	Wounded 7/9/17
4973	LEPPARD, Percy Henry ...	... 16/ 6/16 4 Lieut.	Wounded
4689	LOVERIDGE, John L. ...	... 12/ 6/16 4 Lieut. ✠ ✠	Wounded 24/8/18
4302	MARSH, Charles James Macauley	... 18/ 6/16 4 Lieut.	Wounded 10/9/18
4272	WOOD, Douglas	... 16/ 6/16 4 Lieut.	Wounded 29/8/17
766506	BROOKS, Alfred George ...	... 25/ 9/18 4	
760286	CLARK, Leslie Edward Cyril	... 30/ 5/17 4	
767449	HINE, Hubert Joseph Kels ...	... 4/ 2/19 4	
5929	THORNTON, Charles William	... 11/ 7/16 4 Lieut.	
761409	WOOLFE, William Swift ...	... 26/ 3/18 4	

Service Battalions (New Armies).

2211	BIRD, Arthur Wheen ...	... 13/11/14 9 Capt.	Wounded 4/6/15 ✠
5049	COBB, Reginald	... 25/ 5/16 9 Killed in action 13/10/16	
2796	HALE, Geoffrey Thomas ...	... 24/11/14 9 Lieut. M.G.C. ✠	
2754	HOWE, Charles Kingsley ...	... 19/ 9/15 6 Killed in action 1/7/16	
2366	NEOBARD, Harold John Cooke	... 24/11/14 7 Capt. O.B.E. F/D w. 18/1/15 ✠	
761254	ADCOCK, Charles Willamot ...	... 26/ 6/17 5 Wounded 2/1/18	
1133	BIRCH, Sgt. Arthur	... 12/11/16 Died of wounds 17/2/17	
7571	BRAZIER, Anthony David Cecil	.. 19/12/16(2) Killed in action 10/3/17	
766780	COLES, Albert John	... 28/ 8/18 8 (1/Bedford)	
3494	DEBONO, Geo. Peter ...	... 1/ 8/16 5 Lieut. ✠	
763326	FARMER, Albert Edward ...	... 1/ 3/17 6 Prisoner of war 27/4/18	
8129	GIBBS, Horace Austin ...	... 19/12/16 Killed in action 29/4/17	
762452	GUINEE, James	... 29/ 3/17 Lieut.	
7012	GUY, Reginald Churchill ...	... 3/ 4/17 8 Killed in action 24/8/18	
5014	HAMEL-SMITH, Arnold Harcourt	... 18/ 3/17 5 Lieut.	
8027	HENLEY, Arthur Edward ...	... 19/12/16(1) Wounded & Prisoner of war	
7411	HOOPER, Henry Raby ...	... 23/11/16 Lieut. Wounded 13/8/17	
5017	LAUGHLIN, George Elliot ...	... 24/ 3/17 5 Lieut.	
5589	MATTHEWS, Joseph Henry ...	... 8/ 5/17 5 Lieut. Killed in action 27/3/18	
6847	MAYO, Sidney Harold ...	... 5/ 9/16 Lieut.	
760476	MCCLELLAN, John Frank Maxwell ...	25/ 9/17 Lieut. Wounded 16/10/18	
7013	MCMULLEN, Cpl. John Robert	... 3/ 4/17 Prisoner of War 13/5/18	
767497	MORDEN, Hardy Wilson ...	... 14/ 8/18 51st Grad. Bn.	
7325	MURRAY, Peter	... 12/11/16 6 Lieut.	
763699	NOTT, Christopher Arthur ...	... 30/10/17 Wounded 4/5/18	
7766	PALMER, Henry William S. ...	.. 19/12/16 Lieut. Wounded 14/12/17	
763039	PEARCE, George William ...	... 29/ 3/17 Lieut.	

P

ROYAL BERKSHIRE REGIMENT (S/B).

762491	RICKWOOD, John Edgell	...	...	24/ 9/17	✠	*Wounded* 2/4/18
764850	ROWE, Gilbert James Burberry		...	24/ 9/17		*Died of wounds* 17/4/18
767999	SCRIVENER, Winston Edwin Redvers			5/ 3/19		
763410	SMITH, Leonard Pitman	...	...	1/ 3/17	5 *Lieut.*	*Wounded* 10/12/17
4596	SMITH, Neville	...	...	26/ 9/16		
762671	SWAFFIELD, Frederick	...	...	1/ 3/17	8	
2951	TARRANT, Sgt. Henry Geoffrey Nelson			12/11/16	✠	*Killed in action* 31/7/17
3480	TIGAR, Geoffrey Herbert	...		14/ 8/16	6	*Killed in action* 13/10/17
764518	URRY, Alex. Claude ...	...	...	30/10/17		*Prisoner of war* 7/6/18
764933	WALLACE, Duncan Crichton		...	30/10/17		
7261	WESTON, Alex. Thomas	...	...	21/12/16	5 *Lieut.*	
6419	WHITE, L/Cpl. Lionel Ellenthorpe		...	5/ 9/16	5 *Capt.*	
4373	WICKETT, Thomas Penberthy		...	8/ 5/17	5	*Died of wounds* 20/11/17
763008	WINSTANLEY, William Lidiard		...	24/ 9/17		*Lieut. Wounded* 3/4/18
761784	WYKES, Ernest Arthur Innes		...	26/ 6/17	5	*Killed in action* 30/11/17

THE BORDER REGIMENT.

Regular Battalions (Nos. 1 & 2).

{34th Foot
{55th Foot

Capt.	OSTLE, Henry Knight Eaton	...	28/ 5/15	2	2nd-in-C. [*To 10/York & Lancs., Lt.-Col.* ✠ *w.* 25/9/15 ₥(2)
Lieut.	BURMANN, Robert Moyle	...	8/ 4/15	2	*Capt. Bde.-Maj.* D.S.O. ✠ ₥(6)
				2nd Lieut.	[*Killed in action* 27/10/18 ₥(6)
1537	BALES, Keith...	... ...	20/ 3/15	2	*Killed in action* 16/5/15
1693	BEAUMONT, Wilfred Newton		12/ 6/15	2	*Killed in action* 25/9/15
1547	BYNG, Harry ...	... ...	20/ 3/15	2	*Died of wounds* 16/5/15
1614	CUTHBERTSON, Frank Tebbet		15/12/14	2	*Lieut.*
2494	DAY, L/Cpl. William Leonard		15/ 8/15	2	(*R.F.C.*) *w.* 25/9/15 K/A 6/4/17
1606	GOODMAN, Reginald Moon ...		20/ 3/15	2	*Killed in action* 17/5/15 ₥
2673	GRINTER, Trayton Golding ...		15/ 8/15	2	*Lieut. Wounded* 25/9/15
3641	JOHNSON, Wilfred Lloyd	...	28/11/15	2	*Killed in action* 19/4/16
1598	KROHN, Nicholas Adolf	...	20/ 3/15	2	*Killed in action* 16/5/15
1327	LINDSAY, Gordon Parmiter ...		20/ 3/15	2	*Lt.* ✠ *w.* 16/5/15, -/4/16, -/2/17
1594	PRYNNE, George Michael Fellows		20/ 3/15	2	*Lieut. Wounded* 8/7/16
1551	SAMPSON, Harold Fehrsen	...	15/12/14	2	*Lieut. w.* 11/3/15, -/11/15, -/7/16
1817	SHEPPARD, Horace James Gurney		20/ 3/15	2	*Lieut.*
1489	SIMPSON, William Ronald Carde		20/ 3/15	2	*Killed in action* 16/5/15
1600	SLATER, George Edward Herbert		20/ 3/15	2	*Lieut.* ✠ *w.* 16/5/15, 8/11/18
2957	TODHUNTER, Arthur Jackson		10/ 7/15	2	*Lieut. Wounded* 15/9/15
3631	THOMPSON, Hugh Thomas ...		19/ 7/16	1	*Lieut. w.* 27/1/17, 14/8/17 P/W (*From Sandhurst*)

765268	Dobson, Nathaniel George	...	11/ 6/17	2 Lieut. (1/Camb.)	D/W 17/11/18
7688	Gianella, Cecil Leonard	...	19/12/16		
4928	Greenwood, John Shaw	...	13/ 4/17	2	
764889	Haw, Eustace Arthur	...	27/11/17		
761372	Hislop, William Archer	.	25/ 6/17	2	
761626	Shepherd, Geoffrey Wm. Boutflower		25/ 6/17	2	
761395	Watson, Roger Alan	...	24/ 6/17	2 Lieut.	Wounded 4/12/17
761076	Wynne, Eric Stuart ...	...	24/ 6/17	1 Lieut.	Wounded 27/8/18

Special Reserve Battalion (No. 3).

2343	Mackenzie, Roderick Sandford	...	9/12/14	(From 10/Norfolk)
7510	Law, Kenneth Knight	...	6/ 8/16	Lieut.
766278	Luscombe, Victor ...	...	26/ 5/18	(4/Suffolk)

Territorial Battalions (Nos. 4 & 5).

2943	Bruckman, Richard Theodore	...	3/ 1/15	4 Capt.	
2730	Thompson, John Berwick	...	6/ 3/15	5 Capt. Adj. o.b.e. ℟	
4148	Ball, Wallace Maurice	...	19/12/15	4 Lieut.	
4511	Baxter, Rowland Percival	..	27/10/15	5 Wounded –/7/16	K/A 16/9/16
5334	Bickley, Claude Harry	...	2/ 6/16	5 Lieut.	
4379	Cain, Charles William	...	19/12/15	4 Lieut.	
3925	Dobson, Frank Owen	...	27/12/15	5 Lieut.	
4803	Ebbles, John Kenneth	...	15/ 6/16	5 Lieut.	
3937	Feltham, Alan	...	18/11/15	5 Killed in action 18/9/16	
4828	Jupp, Edwin Percy ...		15/ 6/16	5 Lieut.	
4161	Lewis, Norman Cecil	...	19/12/15	4 Lieut.	
4902	Randall, Sydney Herbert	...	20/ 6/16	5 ✠ Wounded 13/8/17, 13/9/18	
4869	Robinson, Charles Frederick		15/ 6/16	5 Lieut.	
2440	Shaw, Lionel Gillyatt	...	16/ 9/15	5 Lieut. Wounded 4/7/18	
3111	Suiter, Charles Richards	...	18/ 8/15	5 Lieut. ℟	
6094	Borwick, Robert Hartley	...	11/ 7/16	5 Lieut.	
7712	Campbell, Stanley Victor	...	19/12/16	4 Wounded 9/5/17, 23/4/18	
7069	Childs, Clarence Lancelot	...	11/ 7/16	5 Wounded 13/8/17	
7073	Gibson, Alex. William	...	11/ 7/16	5 Lieut.	
6917	Gowan, George Henry	...	11/ 7/16	5 Lieut.	
7246	James, Henry Stoddart	...	20/12/16	5 Killed in action 23/4/17	
5206	Johnson, Charles Beckett	...	11/ 7/16	5 Capt. ℟	
764070	McKenzie, Leonard...	...	27/ 6/17	4	
6232	Pickles, Harry	...	5/ 9/16	4 Killed in action 14/4/17	
766703	Pollard, James	...	26/ 6/18	4	
5188	Randall, Joseph Edward	...	11/ 7/16	5 ✠	
5190	Sadler, Alwyn Kenneth	...	11/ 7/16	5 Lieut.	
760928	Stout, John Mitchell	...	27/ 3/17	4 Wounded 14/5/18	
765339	Thompson, Alexander Chas. Graham		27/ 3/18	4 Lieut. (8/K.O.S.B.)	
763214	Thorburn, John ...	...	27/ 3/17	4	
5641	Truscott, Geoffrey Herbert Cardew		11/ 7/16	5	

Service Battalions (New Armies).

4400	ARMSTRONG, Leonard William	... 26/ 5/16	*1 Killed in action* 19/5/17	
3703	CLARK, Frank Longman ...	... 16/ 1/16	*8 Lieut. Wounded*	
3432	ELDER, Ian Nichol	... 16/ 1/16	*7 Lieut.*	
3615	EVERS, James McElroy Shortt	... 7/11/15	*7 Lieut. Wounded* –/12/15	
3447	JENKIN, Arthur Maxwell ...	... 16/ 1/16	*7 Lieut. Wounded* –/2/16	
3677	JOHNSON, James Herbert ...	... 16/ 1/15	*8 Lieut. Wounded* 7/6/17	
2008	ROMANES, James	... 9/ 9/14	*6 Capt.* 17/3/15 *Wounded* –/9/15	
5723	BARR, Cuthbert Beck ...	... 21/12/16	*(2) Lieut.*	
5565	BEAUVAIS, Lawrence... ...	... 7/ 7/16	*10 Capt.* ℞	
769204	BOUTFLOWER, Charles ...	... 15/ 2/19		
765452	BROWN, William Ian ...	... 28/11/17	*8 Wounded* 30/8/18	
761251	BURNETT, CSM Theodore Ridley	... 15/ 2/19		
769127	CARR, Frank Arnold... ...	... 14/ 2/19		
769227	CARR, Laurence	... 14/ 2/19		
768226	CAVAGHAN, Tom	... 17/ 3/19		
769367	FLEMING, Stanley Wilkinson	... 15/ 2/19		
767218	GILL, Henry Stuart	... 6/ 2/19		
765456	GILLIAT, Alan	... 28/11/17	*8*	
765616	GRAHAM, Hugh Jamieson ...	... 28/11/17	*8*	
1557	HENDERSON, Angus	... 18/ 3/17	*6*	
769075	HOGGARTH, Arthur Henry Graham...	15/ 2/19		
763456	HOPE, Oscar William ...	... 1/ 3/17	*8 Lieut.*	
7129	ISAACS, Maurice Seymour ...	... 26/ 1/17	*8 Lieut.*	
4251	KEENAN, L/Cpl. Felix William	... 7/ 7/16	*12*	
767475	LAMBLE, Alfred Henry ...	... 6/ 2/19		
768700	LEWIS, Frank Thomas ...	... 13/ 2/19		
768152	LONG, Oswald Ambrose ...	... 17/ 6/19		
761306	LOWE, George Michael ...	... 26/ 6/17	*6*	
768736	MACDONALD, Richard ...	... 17/ 3/19		
765278	MACKIE, James Herd ...	... 28/11/17	*8 Wounded* 16/5/18	
765598	MATHESON, Dugold Welsh MacLeod	28/11/17	*11*	
767367	NELSON, Ernest Martindale...	... 3/ 3/19		
763403	PARK, Herbert Sidney ...	... 1/ 3/17	*(1) Killed in action* 26/10/17	
766031	ROUVRAY, Frederick George	... 24/ 5/18	*(1)*	
768047	SCOTT, Edward Robert ...	... 6/ 3/19		
769374	SCOTT-NICHOLSON, Edwin ...	... 15/ 2/19		
768557	SLY, William	... 14/ 2/19		
762816	TROTTER, John Baxter ...	... 1/ 3/17	*Lieut. Wounded* 30/8/18	
7361	TURNBULL, Maxwell... ...	... 5/ 9/16	*8 Capt.* ✠*w.*3/6/18. *d.*18/10/18 ℞	
6276	TWEEDY, Gerald Vincent ...	... 26/ 9/16	*Killed in action* 13/4/17	
8330	WRIGHT, John	... 15/ 2/19	*Wounded* 30/12/17	

THE CAMBRIDGESHIRE REGIMENT (T.F.)

			2nd Lieut.	
764135	DIGBY, Fredk. Newton Dale Drake...		30/ 5/17	*Lieut. Wounded* 14/11/17
765792	HUCKLE, Henry William ...	...	27/ 2/18	*Killed in action* 5/9/18
6901	TOWNSEND, Cecil Alfred ...	...	5/ 9/16	*Lieut.*

THE CAMERON HIGHLANDERS.

Regular Battalions (Nos. 1 & 2). 79th Foot

			2nd Lieut.	
1177	TUCKER, Norman Poulter ...	...	9/ 5/15	2 *Capt.* ℍ
761069	GORDON, Arthur Forbes ...	...	26/ 6/17	1 *Died of wounds* 18/4/18
760877	HORABIN, Thomas Lewis ...	...	26/ 6/17	1
2863	MCINTYRE, Edgar ...	...	1/ 3/15	1 *(From R.A.S.C.) Capt.*

Special Reserve Battalion (No. 3).

4331	CAMERON, Stuart Stillingfleet	... 28/12/15 *Lieut. Wounded* 11/4/17

Territorial Battalion (No. 4).

2752	BARTHOLOMEW, Benjamin James	...	2/ 7/15	4 *Wounded* –/6/16 *K/A* 18/11/16
1767	COURTNEY, Claude ...	...	16/ 6/15	4 *Lieut. Wounded* 6/9/17
1129	POWELL, Charles Sydney ...	..	14/ 4/15	4 *(To R.F.A.) Wounded* 22/8/15
3654	SARGEANT, Wyndham ...	...	17/10/15	4 *Lieut.*

Service Battalions (New Armies).

5832	BLACK, Finlay Keir ...	...	5/ 9/16	5 *Lieut.*
766422	BRYSON, George ...	...	26/ 6/18	1 ✠ *Wounded* 4/10/18
766057	MCMILLAN, Ernest Albert ...	...	26/ 6/18	2 ✠

CHANNEL ISLANDS MILITIA.

THE ROYAL MILITIA OF THE ISLAND OF JERSEY.
3rd or South Battalion.

		2nd Lieut.		
2236	DE STE. CROIX, Leslie Lawson	... 24/12/14	*(To R.A.S.C.) Capt.*	M.B.E.
2283	COX, Alfred Reginald Somers	... 24/12/14	*(To R.A.S.C.) Capt.*	*w.* 25/6/18
2332	HUTCHINSON, Noel Wilfred...	... 9/ 2/15	*Capt.* ℍ	
2353	JANSON, Frederick Ernest ...	... 9/ 2/15	*Lieut.* M.B.E.	*(R.A.O.D.)*
768163	FARRELL, Robert Hamilton...	... 17/ 3/19		

THE CHESHIRE REGIMENT.

22nd Foot

Regular Battalions (Nos. 1 & 2).

971	HARTLEY, William Edwin ...	2nd Lieut. 11/ 6/15	2	Killed in action 2/10/15
2257	LEFTWICH, Nigel George ...	24/10/15	2(10)	Lt. Wounded. K/A 15/4/18
3327	KING, Robert ...	24/10/15	2(10)	Lieut.
761230	LEICESTER, James ...	25/ 6/17	1	

Special Reserve Battalion (No. 3).

762778	DARLINGTON, Herbert Leonard	29/ 3/17	3	Wounded 13/11/17
763835	RALSTON, Kenneth Bowman	31/ 7/17	3	Lieut. P/W & w. 26/4/18
765295	TOWNSEND, Edgar ...	28/11/17	3	

Territorial Battalions (Nos. 4 to 7).

2149	DAVIES, William Edward ...	6/ 3/15	5	Died of wounds 29/1/16
2743	HUGGILL, Henry Percy ...	26/ 3/15	5	Lieut. Wounded 20/11/18
3097	PYM-MANNOCK, Francis Louis A. ...	26/ 3/15	6	(To 6/R. Welch Fusiliers) Lieut.
2403	SEALE, Barney ...	6/ 3/15	5	Lieut.
3991	BEARD, Cecil Angus...	30/11/15	7	Lieut. Prisoner of war
3460	FREETH, L/Cpl. Charles Edward	2/ 9/15	5	Lieut. (1/5 Welch)
4258	SWINDELL, John Frederick ...	1/ 1/16	7	Lieut.
3990	YORKE, Reginald Charles ...	30/11/15	7	Lieut.
764415	BROOKES, Percy ...	28/ 8/17	6	Killed in action 22/11/17
764423	DAVIDSON, William Henry ...	28/ 8/17	6	Wounded 3/12/17
764020	DISLEY, Harold Rostron ...	30/ 5/17	4	
765681	HAGGART, James Gordon F. G. T....	18/12/17	5	Wounded 17/6/18
764025	HAMMOND, Frederick ...	30/ 5/17	4	Wounded & P/W -/7/18
762978	HARDMAN, Lawrence ...	26/ 4/17	5	
765944	HOLLAMBY, Henry John ...	27/ 2/18	4	Wounded & P/W -/10/18
4776	NEWTON, Henry Monck ...	3/ 7/16	4	Lieut.
6767	NEWPORT-GWILT, Richard John	5/ 9/16	4	Lieut.
766268	ORRETT, Cpl. Harry Eyre ...	24/ 5/18	5	
763602	SCOTT, Arthur ...	26/ 4/17	4	Wounded 22/8/17
766991	SHEPHEARD, Stanley Joseph	29/10/18	4	

Service Battalions (New Armies).

2687	ALLEN, Ernest Vivian ...	23/12/14	15	(To 17) Capt.
2603	BURTON, Clifford Earp ...	27/ 5/15	14	Lieut.
1812	DICKINSON, Cpl. Colin James Henry	14/ 6/15	15	Killed in action 28/7/16
3316	FARROW, Ronald James Richard	12/12/15	13	Lieut.
3317	GOULD, Arthur ...	12/12/15	13	Killed in action 13/5/16
2029	KIDD, Claude Bernard ...	29/ 5/15	15	Lieut. ✠ K/A 24/3/18

CHESHIRE REGIMENT (S/B).

2184	SMALL, L/Cpl. Dudley Francis	... 8/ 6/15	*15 Capt.*	*Wounded, 22/4/18*
4128	SWANN, Pelham Barton ...	... 8/12/15	*15 Lieut.*	
2253	WRAY, Leslie Hugh ...	... 16/12/14	*16 Lieut.*	
2938	YOUNG, Leonard George Birmingham	2/12/14	*10 Lieut.*	
765433	BYTHEWAY, Arthur William...	... 28/11/17	*13 Wounded & P/W 23/7/18*	
768418	DOODY, Frank Stapledon ...	... 12/ 2/19		
769074	EDMINSON, Harold Clark ...	... 14/ 2/19		
762802	ELFORD, Percy William Tapson	... 28/ 8/17		
767558	ELLIS, Frank Peter	... 4/ 3/19		
766552	ENGLISH, Frank Goodhand ...	... 28/ 5/18 *3*		
764696	FOWDEN, Bernard Lowther ...	... 17/ 3/19		
766135	GROVE, Albert George ...	... 26/ 3/18 *52*		
6062	HENRI, Arthur William ...	... 7/ 7/16 *17*		
764028	HILDER, Ernest Cecil Lake ...	... 28/ 8/17	*Wounded 6/5/18*	
7080	HODSON, Philip	.. 21/12/16 *3*		
769521	HOPE, Brian	... 15/ 2/19		
7064	HUDSON, Joseph Wright ...	... 19/12/16	*Lieut.*	
760703	HUTSON, Arthur Baron ...	... 31/ 7/17	*Lieut.*	
766434	IRWIN, Harlow	... 25/ 6/18 *52*		
766075	LANG, Reginald Samuel ...	... 26/ 3/18 *(51)*		
764502	McDONALD, John	... 28/ 8/17	*Lieut.*	
763893	MADGE, Herbert Ernest ...	... 29/ 8/17		
767598	OAKLEY, Edgar Robinson ...	... 6/ 3/19		
768234	OLDHAM, Maurice Anderson ...	... 17/ 3/19		
5534	POTTER, Charles Vernon ...	... 7/ 7/16 *17 Lieut.*		
6818	RATCLIFFE, Herbert Charles ...	... 5/ 9/16	*Capt.*	
764539	REARDON, William Richard ...	... 28/ 8/17	*Wounded 15/11/18*	
767885	RHODES, Frederick Maurice ...	... 3/ 3/19		
5449	ROBINSON, Arthur Victor ...	... 7/ 7/16 *17 Wounded 24/4/18*		
766062	ROYCROFT, John Hedley ...	... 26/ 3/18 *51*		
768105	TAYLOR, Allan Roy	... 17/ 3/19		
766092	TROTMAN, Lionel William ...	... 26/ 3/18 *51*		
766670	WILLIAMS, William George ...	... 3/ 2/19		
764280	WOOD, Nevil Pressal ...	... 31/ 7/17		
7139	WORTHINGTON, Geoffrey ...	.. 21/12/16 *3 Lieut.*		
762659	YATES, William	... 29/ 3/17 *3* ✠		
764520	YOUNG, Thomas	... 28/ 8/17 *3 Prisoner of war 16/5/18*		

THE CONNAUGHT RANGERS.

Regular Battalions (Nos. 1 & 2). {88th Foot / 94th Foot}

2nd Lieut.
3708	BARRY, Edward	... ...	7/11/15	*1 Wounded –/4/16* 🎖
3553	OKEY, William Ewart	... ...	7/11/15	*1 Killed in action 21/1/16*
1475	REEVE, Frank	... ...	10/ 7/15	*1 Lieut.*
1213	ROBEY, Arthur Eric Linton	...	7/11/15	*1 Lieut. Wounded –/1/16* 🎖

Special Reserve Battalions (Nos. 3 & 4).

766096 LEONARD, John James ... ... 28/ 5/18 *3 (R.F.C.)*

Service Battalions (New Armies).

763327	FLINN, Herbert Ernest	... ...	29/ 3/17
768495	TICHBORNE, William	... ...	5/ 2/19

THE DUKE OF CORNWALL'S LIGHT INFANTRY.

Regular Battalions (Nos. 1 & 2). {32nd Foot / 46th Foot}

2828	CARNE, Maxwell Halford	...	10/ 7/15	*2 Died of wounds 23/12/16*
1774	CATTLE, Alfred Philip	...	10/ 7/15	*1 Lieut. Wounded 16/11/15*
814	COLLEY, Sgt. Archibald	...	14/ 2/15	*2 Killed in action 15/3/15*
3162	FRATER, Alexander Hay	...	24/10/15	*2 Lieut.*
1238	HAMILTON, Herbert James	...	29/ 8/15	*1 Lieut.*
1460	HUGHESDON, Cpl. Reginald Harold		10/ 7/15	*1 Capt.* ✠ *w. –/8/16, 21/10/17*
1576	MARTIN, Richard Donald	...	9/ 5/15	*2 Lieut.*
1523	O'BRIEN, James	...	9/ 5/15	*2 Capt.* ✠
1509	O'BRIEN, John	...	9/ 5/15	*2 Lieut. Wounded 12/6/15*
2170	SCOTT, Donald Norman	...	10/ 7/15	*2 Lieut.*
1753	STEVENS, John Longbourne	...	23/ 4/15	*1 Lieut. Wounded*
1283	TOTTON, Arthur Knyvett	...	23/ 4/15	*1 Capt.* ✠
1932	TAYLOR, Bruce Mitchell	...	5/ 4/15	*1 Major* D.S.O. ✠✠ *K/A 6/11/17* 🎖
1048	WOOD, Bernard Gregory	...	23/ 4/15	*2 Lieut.*
3540	STEPHENSON, Hubert Victor	...	2/10/16	*1 Killed in action 8/5/17*

Special Reserve Battalion (No. 3).

8274	OSBORNE, John	...	25/ 1/17	*3(6) Wounded 11/9/17*
765328	STEVENS, Cyril Parker	...	28/11/17	*3* ✠
765253	TIDMARSH, Frank Egerton Vaughan		28/11/17	*3*
762919	TUCKER, John Morgan	...	29/ 3/17	*3*

DUKE OF CORNWALL'S L.I. (T/F & S/B).   233

Territorial Battalions (Nos. 4 & 5).

1447	D'Ambrumenil, Wilfred ...	... 5/ 6/15	4	Lieut.	
4129	Blanc, L/Cpl. Louis Gerald	... 22/11/15	4	Lieut.	
4505	Farrier, Archibald Victor ...	... 16/ 1/16	5	Lieut.	
4183	Harris, Leonard	... 22/11/15	4	Lieut.	
4174	Nivet, Eugene Lionel Anthony	... 22/11/15	4	Lieut.	
4500	Soward, Frank	... 15/ 1/16	5	Capt. ✠	
6904	Doughty, John	... 5/ 9/16	4	Lieut.	
6063	Hodge, William Eric ...	... 31/ 7/16	5	Lieut.	
762272	Hughes, Claude Edward Cecil	... 3/ 8/17	5	Wounded 4/5/18	
761167	Luscombe, Reginald Anson...	... 3/ 8/17	5	Wounded 2/11/17	
7454	McAllister, Alexander ...	... 20/12/16	4	Lieut.	
765953	Page, John Oswald ...	... 24/ 4/18	4		
5922	Palmer, Henry John ...	... 26/ 9/16	5	Lieut.	Killed in action 29/3/18
5966	Smith, Leon Walter ...	... 26/ 9/16	4	Lieut.	Killed in action 12/4/18

Service Battalions (New Armies).

2003	Andrews, Thomas Edward ...	5/11/14	9	Lieut.	(M.G.C.)
1530	Gillett, Sydney Eric ...	28/11/14	9	Lieut.	Wounded 22/9/15, –/9/16
2202	Girling, Stephen Eastaugh ...	5/11/14	9	Lieut.	Killed in action 29/9/18
2700	Lailey, Eric Lilliwhite ...	11/11/14	7	Lieut.	Killed in action 28/2/16
2637	Lailey, Guy Patrick Barnard ...	18/10/14	7	Capt.	Wounded 30/9/16
3224	Morris, William Francis ...	2/ 4/15	9	Lieut.	
2591	Simpson, Henry Gordon ...	5/11/14	9		Killed in action 16/6/15
1844	Spurrell, Richard Kenilworth ...	5/11/14	9	Capt.✠	w. 27/10/17, 20/12/17
1991	Thornton, Hugh Cholmondeley ...	17/ 6/15	10	(From 11/Middlesex) Major Private Sec. to S. of S.	
762537	Agnew, Rudolph John ...	3/ 8/17	6		
768243	Barham, Geoffrey Cornelius Arthur	17/ 3/19			
762526	Beckingsale, John Edgar ...	2/ 8/17	6		Killed in action 23/8/17
7300	Beringer, Bernard	5/ 9/16			
767493	Bray, John	5/ 2/19			
7385	Boothroyd, Norman ...	21/12/16	7	Lt.-Col.	Wounded 30/4/18
767217	Bodilly, Ralph William Talbot ...	5/ 2/19			
766466	Dawe, Edward Merideth ...	25/ 6/18			
766496	Derry, Charles	26/ 6/18			
763783	Dunn, James Henry... ...	27/ 6/17	6		
767616	Free, Stanley Clark Hazell ...	6/ 2/19			
7374	Glencross, Douglas George ...	21/12/16	6	Lieut.	
767777	Goodwin, John	4/ 3/19			
5057	Goss, William Arthur ...	16/ 4/17	6		
7349	Grahame, Kenneth Moir ...	19/12/16	6		
5495	Green, Arthur	26/ 9/16	6	Lieut. ✠	Wounded 12/4/18
7044	Hearn, Leonard Webb ...	21/12/16	6		Killed in action 18/10/17
7837	Hobbs, William Charles ...	19/12/16	10		

DUKE OF CORNWALL'S L.I. (S/B).

5506	HOLLIS, Arthur Reginald	... ...	26/ 9/16	*10 Killed in action* 12/9/18
7448	HOSKING, James Cecil	... ...	19/12/16	*10 Capt.* ✠
765238	KING, William Francis	... ...	22/12/17	
761504	MARTIN, Thomas George	... ...	3/ 8/17	*7 w.* 9/5/18, *w. & missing* 15/7/18
3390	MILES, Harold Gordon	... ...	1/ 8/16	*10 Lieut. Killed in action* 4/8/16
7400	MILLMAN, Francis William ...		23/11/16	*7 (To Labour Corps) Lieut.*
765625	MORGAN, Harold John	... ...	18/12/17	
765600	PARRY-JONES, Richard John Samuel		18/12/17	
765704	PARSLOW, Jack Wilmshurst ...		18/12/17	
764406	PENALUNA, William ...	... ...	26/ 6/17	
4959	POTTER, Arthur Leslie	... ...	26/ 4/17	*6*
761009	RAISIN, Francis Stephen	... ...	3/ 7/17	*6 Lieut. Wounded* 22/8/17
767208	ROSSITER, Robert John	... ...	5/ 2/19	
764565	ROWE, Humphrey Arthur	... ...	18/12/17	
766771	TERRY, Arthur Frederick	... ...	26/ 6/18	*10*
767228	TILBROOK, Russell Harman...		5/ 2/19	
768051	TREGENZA, Norman Kelly	... ...	18/ 3/19	
767785	TURNER, L/Cpl. Charles Eric		4/ 3/19	*(7/Devon)*
763084	TURNER, Henry Mornington		30/ 5/17	*7 Wounded* 26/9/17
763685	WILLIAMS, Campbell Pugh ...		26/ 4/17	*Wounded* 20/11/17, *Wounded & missing* 3/10/18

THE DEVONSHIRE REGIMENT.

Regular Battalions (Nos. 1 & 2).

11th Foot

2nd Lieut.

1347	ADAMS, Arthur Gwyther	...	14/ 2/15	*2 Lieut. Indian Army* ᛗ
1086	COLE, John Trevor ...		1/ 1/15	*1 Lieut. (2/Dorset)*
1142	CUTTING, Raymond Howarth		27/ 1/15	*1 Lt.-Col.* D.S.O. ✠ ᛗ
1810	FISCHER, Alexander William		1/ 1/15	*1 Died of wounds* 12/5/16 ᛗ
1648	JACOB, Cecil Otway Reed	...	27/ 1/15	*2 Capt. w.* –/7/16 *K/A* 29/11/17
1566	LLOYD, Francis Burrows	...	29/ 8/15	*2 Wounded* –/2/16 *K/A* 3/10/16
1045	LORD, Frank Samuel	...	27/ 1/15	*2 Died of wounds* 12/3/15
1590	NEWTON, Alfred Reginald ...		7/11/15	*2 Wounded* 3/7/16 ᛗ(2)
1399	WEST, Frank		27/ 1/15	*1 Capt.* ✠
1144	WILSON, Herbert Christopher		7/11/15	*2 Lieut. Wounded* –/2/16, 30/10/18
1159	WINDSOR, Mark Gillham	...	14/ 2/15	*2 Died of wounds* 10/3/15
1404	WYKES, Ronald Arthur	...	29/ 8/15	*2 Lieut.* ᛗ
763231	BATEMAN, Edw. Frank	...	10/ 3/17	*2 Lieut.*
3741	BROOMAN, Frank Robert	...	7/11/16	*2 Wounded* 14/5/17
2172	BROOMAN, Hubert Benjamin		7/11/16	*2*
2804	BUCKLEY, Charles Hector Simeon	...	31/ 7/16	*2 Wounded* –/7/18
764753	COLES, Robert Victor	...	31/10/17	*1*
765120	GIBBONS, Henry Vincent	...	31/10/17	*1 (10/D.C.L.I.)*
1495	PERTWEE, Lionel		7/11/16	*Lieut.*

Special Reserve Battalion (No. 3).

992	ELKINGTON, Guy Waterman	... 7/10/14	3 *Lieut.* (1/*Suffolk*)
2976	GETHIN, Percy Francis ...	... 30/ 3/15	3 *Killed in action* 28/6/16
3574	MUNRO, Samuel Hector ...	... 22/ 6/15	3 *Lieut. Wounded* –/9/16
2678	PHILLIPS, Fenton Ellis Stanley	... 13/ 1/15	3 ✠ (*R.F.C.*) *K/A* 13/10/16
7394	BOWDEN, Joseph Llewellyn	... 22/11/16	3(2) *Lieut.*
765934	EVANS, John Ewart	... 27/ 2/18	3 *Killed in action* 27/9/18
4896	HASWELL, Reginald Merryweather...	22/11/16	3(9) *w.* 13/8/17, 30/10/18
765772	KNIGHT, Albert Edward ...	... 21/ 2/18	*Wounded* 16/10/18
762173	NAPIER, Charles William Skipwith ...	26/ 4/17	(8) *Lieut.*
765308	PELLS, Cyril Elmore ...	... 28/11/17	*Killed in action* 27/5/18
765957	REED, Cyril	... 27/ 2/18	
765962	SCHRADER, Frederick Justin	... 27/ 2/18	
765477	SNOW, Godfrey Mackenzie ...	... 28/11/17	*Wounded* 11/7/18

Territorial Battalions (Nos. 4 to 7).

2130	ADDINGTON, Gerald ...	... 5/ 8/14	6 *Lieut.*
1647	BEER, Cpl. George Tidbury	... 20/ 4/15	5 *Lieut.*
1694	HEMPHILL, Robert Douglas	. 18/ 6/15	6 *Lieut. Wounded* 13/8/17
1207	STRONG, Harold Vesey ...	... 22/ 4/15	6 *Lieut.*
2574	WALLICH, Cyril Collings Norton ...	9/12/14	5 (*To R.F.A.* (*T.F.*) *Lieut.*
4313	BROMHAM, Charles Adolphus Row ...	29/12/15	5 *Lieut. Killed in action* 17/10/18
5076	SAMUELS, Louis	... 2/ 6/16	6 *Lieut.*
766629	AITKEN-DAVIES, Edward ...	... 24/ 5/18	6
766243	BARLOW, Ian Alexander ...	... 25/ 9/18	5
4979	BOURNE, Philip Reginald ...	... 11/ 7/16	4
6604	BOWDEN, Rothwell Cazaly ...	... 26/ 9/16	4 *Lieut. Wounded* 27/6/17
2538	CABESPINE, Eric Walter Hamilton...	11/ 7/16	4 *Wounded* 23/8/17
4953	CHADWELL, Arthur Ernest ..	... 11/ 7/16	4
6908	GRATWICK, Harold Duncan ...	... 26/ 9/16	4 *Died* 22/2/19
7159	KRUSE, Eric Cuthbert ...	... 26/ 1/17	4
767662	PADDON, Cyril Evens ...	... 12/11/18	6
766039	PAGE, Percival Stevens ...	... 23/ 5/18	4
760209	PARKER, Sgt. Frederick Prosper	... 30/ 4/18	5
763725	PATTERSON, Henry Marden ...	... 27/ 6/17	4 *Wounded* 5/12/17, 5/8/18
7789	RICHARDSON, Frederick Samuel	... 20/12/16	4
763681	SHEARMAN, Harold Heffer ...	... 13/ 5/17	4
5697	SHORT, Frederick Percival ...	... 11/ 7/16	5 *Lieut.*
761873	STARTIN, Geoffrey	... 17/ 6/17	4
762672	TALL, John Jeffrey	... 27/ 3/17	4 *Killed in action* 15/2/18
764725	TAPPER, George Henry ...	... 30/10/17	6
7359	TARBET, Victor	... 26/ 1/17	4 *Killed in action* 4/10/17
765082	TUCKETT, David John ...	... 31/10/17	4

Service Battalions (New Armies).

989	ALLEN, Frederick John	... ...	18/12/14	9 *Died of wounds* 27/9/15
974	BALDERSON, L/Cpl. Henry Leslie P.		15/ 9/14	8 *Wounded* –/9/15 *K/A* 23/7/16
932	BROADBRIDGE, Myles O'Bryen	...	17/ 9/14	8 *Capt.* ✠ *Wounded* 26/9/15 ℳ
1397	HULM, Wynne Odyerne	...	17/ 9/14	8 *Lieut. Died of wounds* 25/9/15
723	LYONS, L/Cpl. Ernest Frederick		17/ 9/14	10 *Major* ✠ *Wounded* 24/4/17
448	MOORE, Francis William	...	17/ 9/14	10 *Lieut. & Adjt.* ✠ *D/W* 26/4/17
2763	SANDOE, Montague William A.	...	20/11/14	11 *Lieut. Killed in action* 8/5/17
3303	WEALE, William Wells Charles	...	2/ 9/15	11 *Lieut. Interpreter* ℳ
765752	ALLDEN, Wilfred Lewis	...	27/ 8/18	15
762884	ASHPLANT, William Raymond	...	29/ 3/17	8 *Wounded* 14/11/17, –/10/18
768949	BRADSHAW, William	...	5/ 2/19	
3587	BROCK, Algernon Bertram	...	7/11/16	9 *Died of wounds* 26/10/17
3024	BROCK, Cecil Howard	...	15/ 8/16	8 *Died of wounds* 4/11/18
760572	BROWN, Douglas Frederick	...	5/ 2/19	
765435	CLARKE, Francis Vernon	...	19/ 5/18	15
766245	COLLIER, Edward Albert	...	24/ 5/18	51 *Wounded* 14/10/18
764819	CRAWFORD, Percy	...	10/ 3/17	
7151	DAWSON, John Stewart	...	21/12/16	*Lieut.* (7/*D.C.L.I.*)
7152	DENCH, Bertram	...	21/12/16	*Lieut.* (10/*D.C.L.I.*) *w.* 5/5/18
766225	DUNN, Harold Black	...	24/ 5/18	51 *Killed in action* 30/8/18
763689	EDWARDS, Harold	...	26/ 4/17	ℳ
763847	ELLIOTT, Harry Peterson	...	26/ 4/17	
763231	EXLEY, Frederick Horace	...	10/ 3/17	
768026	GLENDINING, William Cecil	...	6/ 3/19	
764198	HARDWICK, Clifford	...	10/ 3/17	
764893	HOOLE, Douglas Robert	...	10/ 3/17	*Capt.*
767236	JOINT, Philip John	...	6/ 2/19	
7351	KARSLAKE, Harry Howard	...	21/12/16	(1/*D.C.L.I.*) *K/A* 23/4/17
763462	KING, Edward George	...	10/ 3/17	*Lieut.*
7250	MARKS, Eric Gordon	...	21/12/16	*Lieut.* (10/*D.C.L.I.*)
762623	MARTIN, Leslie Norman	...	29/ 3/17	*Lieut.*
765431	MURDO, George	...	10/ 3/17	*Lieut.* (*Labour Corps*)
768402	NICKALLS, Benjamin Arthur	...	17/ 3/19	
768484	NICKS, Albert Edward	...	13/ 2/19	
7342	NORMANDALE, Lancelot	...	21/12/16	(6/*D.C.L.I.*)
7281	PALMER, Leonard	...	21/12/16	(1/*D.C.L.I.*) *Wounded* 12/4/17
760561	PARKYN, Harold Septimus	...	12/11/18	
768076	PRIDEAUX, John Britton Laurence C.		17/ 3/19	
9537	READ, Vernon Sidney	...	10/ 3/17	
764256	ROWLEY, Sidney Smith	...	10/ 3/17	
5541	RUSSELL, James Drummond	...	5/ 9/16	(*10*) *Lieut.*
7432	SHELTON, Frederick Norman	...	21/12/16	(7/*D.C.L.I.*)
7257	SHOVELL, Ernest George	...	21/12/16	(10/*D.C.L.I.*)
767420	SLEE, William Alfred	...	15/ 2/19	

7402	SMITH, Gordon Hamilton ...	... 23/11/16	*(8) Killed in action 9/5/17*
765970	TUCKER, James David ...	... 27/ 2/18	*52 Grad. Bn.*
8845	WAGGETT, Arthur Calvert ...	... 10/ 3/17	
761847	WARD, Charles Harold ...	... 27/ 6/17	
764278	WEST, Cecil John De la Warr	... 10/ 3/17	
4467	WHITEHOUSE, Tom Henry Innes ...	10/ 3/17	
7009	WONNACOTT, James Palmer	... 23/11/16	
765259	WOODWARD, Egbert Gordon	... 2/ 4/17	

THE DORSETSHIRE REGIMENT.

Regular Battalions (Nos. 1 & 2). {39th Foot / 54th Foot}

2nd Lieut.

1086	COLE, John Trevor ...	... 1/ 1/15	*(2) (From 1/Devon)*
4189	GRIFFITH, John Ellerthorpe	... 20/11/15 *1*	*(From 3/Bn.) Lieut.*
1127	GREEN, Harold John	... 9/ 5/15 *1 Capt.*	
1116	MACEY, Clifford James	... 9/ 5/15 *1 Killed in action 25/5/15*	
5439	DIGBY, Laurence ...	... 19/12/16 *1 Lieut. Wounded 1/5/18*	

Special Reserve Battalion (No. 3).

3444	HARTNETT, Daniel Patrick ...	... 9/10/15 *3 Lieut.*	
762246	BALL, Harold Charles James	... 26/ 4/17 *3 Wounded 29/10/17*	
6545	BATEMAN, Kennedy Steer Delamain	26/ 9/16 *3 (5)*	
762266	BRYANT, Geoffrey Ernest ...	... 29/ 5/17 *3*	
764378	PARSONS, Albert Frank ...	... 1/ 8/17 *(21/K.R.R.C.) P/W 14/5/18*	
6720	ROBINSON, Vincent Owen ...	... 8/ 7/16 *Lieut. (6/Somerset L.I.) w. 11/6/17*	
6478	STOCK, John Lancelot Walmsley ...	8/ 7/16 *(6/Somerset L.I.) D/W 3/5/17*	

Territorial Battalion (No. 4).

4214	BASE, Edward Harold	... 2/ 6/16 *4 Lieut.*	
4394	OUTLAW, William Henry	... 2/ 6/16 *4 Major*	
4284	POOL, Marcus Lionel	... 2/ 6/16 *4 Lieut.*	
4854	ROPER, Ernest William	... 12/ 6/16 *4 Lieut.*	
5159	SLOOT, John Nicholas Charles	... 31/ 5/16 *4 Lieut.*	
765784	BUTTERWORTH, Herbert Bertram ...	27/ 2/18 *4*	
765673	CHAMBERLAIN, George Frederick ...	27/ 2/18 *4*	
766247	CROCKER, William Charles ...	... 26/ 6/18 *4* ✠	
765676	DANIEL, Walter Lawrence ...	... 27/ 2/18 *4*	
5947	GARLAND, Arthur Sherrington Talbot	26/ 9/16 *4 Lieut.*	

765621	Hodgson, Cpl. Sidney George	...	27/ 2/18	4
765879	Mason, William Talbot	...	26/ 6/18	4
766001	Ratcliffe, Claude ...	...	27/ 2/18	4
765778	Snelling, Walter John	...	22/ 3/18	4

Service Battalions (New Armies).

3165	Challis, Charles Lewis	...	12/ 7/15	7 Lieut. Wounded –/1/17
3704	Moore, Kenneth Hartley	...	12/12/15	6 Killed in action 7/7/16
4299	Rowe, George Laver	...	14/ 8/15	7 [(6/Somerset)
4563	Hobbs, Geoffrey Harold Chapman	...	25/ 5/16	7 Lieut. Killed in action 16/9/16
6635	Woolnough, Frederick Ullathorne	...	26/ 5/16	Capt. Died of wounds 22/3/18
6046	Brown, Walter James	...	26/ 9/16	5
764012	Burfoot, William Martin	...	27/ 6/17	–/Dorset & R.A.F. K/A 22/5/18
5745	Curtis, Wilfred Harry	...	2/ 5/17	6 Wounded –/6/18
767219	Graham, Andrew George Norman	...	5/ 2/19	
766348	Hurnell, Horace Frederick	...	26/ 6/18	
7158	Kellaway, George Lionel	...	21/12/16	Lieut. (12/Hants)
763912	Lambert, Stanley Ashley	...	27/ 6/17	
4407	Lemon, Lionel Theodore	...	19/12/16	Killed in action 12/4/17
768583	Mason, David Harold	...	7/ 3/19	
761601	McEwan, Herbert Hugh	...	20/10/17	Lieut.
5861	Pogue, Reginald Thomas	...	2/ 5/17	6 ✠
765892	Rabino, Francis Aloysius	...	29/ 5/18	✠ Wounded 16/10/18
5636	Ryan, Cyril Hammond	...	7/ 7/16	7 Lieut. Wounded –/12/16
4552	Shave, Leslie Harrie	...	21/ 2/17	6 Killed in action 12/4/17
766980	Stott, Frederick	...	20/11/18	
767944	Symes, Bryant Gustavus	...	17/ 3/19	
5819	Warr, Thomas Edward	...	2/ 5/17	6 Died of wounds 14/10/17

THE ROYAL DUBLIN FUSILIERS.

Regular Battalions (Nos. 1 & 2).

{102nd Foot
{103rd Foot

				2nd Lieut.	
1691	Collyer, Wilfred Thomas	...	...	1/ 1/15	2 Capt.
615	Elphick, Sgt. Richard	...	...	1/ 1/15	2 Capt. Wounded 9/5/15, 1/7/16
1555	Judd, Frederick George	...	...	9/ 5/15	2 Capt. Killed in action 24/5/15
761503	Johnstone, John Balfour	...	...	19/ 9/17	1
760891	Spiess, William Frederick	...	...	8/ 8/17	1 Wounded 29/9/18

ROYAL DUBLIN FUSILIERS (S/B).

Service Battalions (New Armies).

8299	BLAKE, Harry Moore	...	25/ 1/17	*11*
761767	CAHILL, Michael	...	20/12/16	*11 Lieut.*
769092	DUNN, William Waggott	...	14/ 2/19	
765536	FAIR, James	...	27/11/17	*11*
3714	FLYNN, Cpl. Edward Henry	...	—/ 1/17	*8 Wounded* 20/9/17
764940	GORMAN, Arthur	...	28/ 8/17	*11 Wounded* 17/9/18
3644	MARLOW, Charles Dwyer	...	19/ 9/16	*8 Wounded* 7/8/17 *K/A* 17/8/17
761506	McALESTER, Cpl. Charles James	...	4/ 2/19	
8277	WAGNER, Dixon Park	...	25/ 1/17	*11* ✠✠ *Wounded* 14/10/18

THE DURHAM LIGHT INFANTRY.

Regular Battalions (Nos. 1 & 2).   { 68th Foot
                                                       { 106th Foot

2nd Lieut.

1423	ELLIS, Reginald Donald	...	15/ 8/15	*2 Lieut.*
1717	STOREY, Kenneth	...	1/ 1/15	*2 Capt.* ✠ *w.* 11/8/15 ⌬
1058	THOMPSON, Charles Henry	...	15/ 8/15	*2 Killed in action* 3/6/16
2371	WILLIAMS, Noel Victor	...	15/ 8/15	*2 Lieut.*
3421	BARKER, Thomas Baxter	...	12/ 7/15	*1 (From 17) Lieut. w.* —/12/15
763379	BOWE, Eric Arthur	...	25/ 9/17	*1 Killed in action* 27/5/18
5582	JAMES, Hugh William	...	6/ 9/16	*2 Capt.*
2728	PALMER, John Stanley	...	15/ 9/15	*(From R.M.C.) D/W* 18/10/16
3237	THURGOOD, William James	...	7/11/16	*2 Lieut.*

Special Reserve Battalions (Nos. 3 & 4).

2775	WORNUM, George Gray	...	16/ 1/15	*3 Lieut.*
2528	WRIGHT, Cyril Carne Glenton	...	21/10/14	*4 Adjt. D.L I. (2/Northumb. Fus.)*
5582	JAMES, Hugh William	...	6/ 9/16	*2 Capt.*
7513	McGIBBON, William Patrick	...	20/12/16	*4 (7/D.C.L.I.) K/A* 23 9/17
766027	METCALFE, Charles Pulfrey	...	1/ 5/18	*4(15) Wounded* 26/10/18
7825	UPTON, Roger Maitland	...	20/12/16	*4(20) Killed in action* 7/6/17

Territorial Battalions (Nos. 5 to 9).

2640	GELSTHORPE, Alfred Morris	...	5/11/14	*8 (To M.G.C.) Capt.* D.S.O. ⌬(2)
2105	WADHAM, Cpl. Samuel Macmahon	...	26/ 2/15	*8 Capt.*
3849	FROUD, Harold William	...	30/10/15	*5 Lieut. w.* —/9/16 *D/W* 27/7/17

240 DURHAM L.I. (T/F & S/B).

3502	GREEN, Archibald George Noble	... 22/10/15	8 Lieut.	Prisoner of war 23/5/18
3893	TOZER, Matthew Charles ...	... 30/10/15	5 Lieut.	
4179	VOS-UTERLIMMEGE, George H.	... 21/12/15	8 Lieut.	
6393	ADAMSON, Cecil	... 26/ 9/16	5 Lieut.	
766272	ALLEN, Desmond	... 24/ 4/18	5	
763611	CALLENDER, Ernest ...	... 30/ 5/17	5	
4154	CUDWORTH, Reginald	... 27/ 7/16	8 Lieut.	Wounded –/2/17
5398	DAVEY, Sydney	... 5/ 9/16	5 Lieut.	w. 28/6/18, 11/9/18
762932	DENHOLM, William Harold ...	... 28/ 3/17	8	Wounded 11/9/18
764094	GREEN, Ernest Albert	... 16/ 6/17	6	
763422	HARRISON, Frederick Claude Smith	28/ 3/17	8	Prisoner of war 12/8/18
761401	HESLOP, John Charles	... 3/ 8/17	1(6) Lieut.	Wounded 27/3/18
5953	HIND, William Martin	... 26/ 9/16	5	Wounded –/1/17
765948	JOHNSTONE, Andrew Aitchison	... 27/ 2/18	5	
763533	MACDONALD, Eric Angus Gordon ...	1/ 3/17	5	Wounded 17/5/17
766282	PECKSTON, John Grant	... 1/ 5/18	7	
3251	SHEPHERD, Leslie Graham ...	... 19/12/16	5	
6392	WATT, Hugo Burr Craig	... 7/ 1/17	8 Lieut. ✠	w. 4/10/17 K/A 24/8/18

Service Battalions (New Armies).

3805	BAINBRIDGE, Joseph	... 5/10/15	19 Lieut.	
3102	BUTLAND, William Henry ...	... 7/11/15	10	Died of wounds 31/1/16
3075	CLARKE, Vincent Charles ...	... 7/11/15	10	w. –/3/16 D/W 12/10/16
2035	CODD, Cyril Joseph Clarke ...	3/10/15	14 Lieut. ✠	(M.G.C.) w. 12/4/18
3032	DAWS, Harold	... 28/11/15	10	Killed in action 26/12/16
1623	FAIRBAIRN, George Eric	... 24/10/14	10	Died of wounds 20/6/15
2425	GILLOTT, Cecil	... 3/10/15	14 Lieut. ✠	w. –/11/16, 19/4/18
3658	HINES, Austin	... 28/11/15	10	Died of wounds 15/12/15
1962	JERWOOD, John Hugh	... 3/12/14	10 Major ✠	w. –/11/15, 9/10/17
1126	MASSINGHAM, Godfrey	... 8/10/14	15 Lieut.	[K/A 21/3/18
4226	MEACOCK, Robert Hugh	... 25/ 5/16	21	Killed in action 19/10/16
4332	MELLOR, Arnold	... 10/ 1/16	21	Wounded –/11/16
3475	MOORE, Percival	... 15/ 4/15	19 Lieut.	
3330	TAYLOR, Robert Clark	... 1/ 3/15	19 Capt.	
1624	ROSHER, John Brenchly	... 23/ 9/14	10 Lt.-Col.	D.S.O.(2) ✠ w. –/8/15,
1928	WILSON, Harold George	... 26/ 1/15	16 Lieut.	[–/11/15, –/8/16 ℳ(2)
761539	ALLBEURY, William ...	... 2/ 4/17	18 ✠	F/D
763814	BREWER, Alexander George	... 30/ 5/17	14	Wounded 20/12/17, 25/6/18
2960	BROMLEY, L/Cpl. Cyril John Herbert	16/12/16		Lieut.
763287	BORROWDALE, William Graydon	... 29/ 3/17		
763173	CARNEY, John Joseph	... 29/ 3/17	19	
764821	DAVISON, Thomas ...	... 24/ 9/17	14	
766461	HALFORD-ADCOCK, Herbert Harfield	10/ 9/18		
769150	JACKSON, Francis Henry	... 14/ 2/19		
763338	KEMP, George Hubert	... 1/ 3/17	(R.F.C.)	Killed in action 1/6/18

E. P. BENNETT, V.C. [pp. 45, 381.

Crown Copyright.] [By permission of the Imperial War Museum.
JOINT ROAD-CONTROL POST (French Troops and Artists).

Crown Copyright.] [By permission of the Imperial War Museum.
M/G INSTRUCTION AT G.H.Q., FRANCE.

DURHAM L.I. (S/B). 241

763250	MARKS, John	1/ 3/17	Lieut. Killed in action 24/10/18	
763832	MATTHEWS, Beyton Frazer Stanwix	15/ 2/19		
7511	McBAIN, Hubert	19/12/16	✠ Wounded 19/5/17	
5787	NEWCOMBE, Percy Charles	17/12/16	Capt. (-/N. Stafford) w. 12/9/18	
6568	PHILLIPS, George Hale	19/12/16		
763804	PRIESTMAN, Charles Cyril ...	30/ 5/17	18	
766315	REID, Alexander Tennant ...	29/ 5/18		
766262	ROBERTSON, Frederick Kearton ...	3/ 2/19		
765734	SHARP, Ernest Goulding	26/ 6/18		
5547	SMITH, Frank Edward Corbitt Douglas	26/ 9/16	13 Lieut. ✠ (R.G.A.)	
767730	TAYLOR, Robert	3/ 3/19		
763510	WALTON, Sydney	1/ 3/17	✠ Wounded 4/12/17	
2225	WHITE, Cpl. Clarence Alfred Burker	12/11/16	22	
767842	WOOD, John	27/12/18		

Attached to Labour Corps.

764812	BIRCH, Cpl. Harold	10/ 3/17	Capt.
761309	COLLINGS, Lionel Lapidge ...	10/ 3/17	(R.A.F.) Died at Netley 3/10/18
763986	COOK, William Tucker ...	10/ 3/17	Lieut.
763097	CORY, Douglas Howard Crawford ...	10/ 3/17	Lieut.
760416	COWL, Clifford Horace Henry	10/ 3/17	Lieut.
762186	FARNES, Herbert Edgar ...	10/ 3/17	Lieut.
762221	PATON, Thomas Howard Moore	10/ 3/17	Lieut. Wounded 11/6/17
761394	PRESTWICH, Herbert Webb ...	10/ 3/17	Lieut.
762064	ROBERTS, Oswald Dale ...	10/ 3/17	Lieut.
761011	ROFFEY, L/Cpl. Norman Laurence ...	10/ 3/17	Lieut.
762155	ROUTH, Reginald Paul ...	10/ 3/17	Lieut.
760805	SMITH, Cpl. Frederick Allan	10/ 3/17	Lieut.
4962	STAINES, L/Cpl. Tom Fenn	10/ 3/17	Lieut.
761477	THOMPSON, Richard Taylor	10/ 3/17	Lieut.
762793	WEBB, Philip Henry	10/ 3/17	Lieut.
761904	WEBBER, Walter James ...	10/ 3/17	Lieut. ℳ
761357	WYNN, George William Limerick ...	10/ 3/17	Lieut.

THE ESSEX REGIMENT.

Regular Battalions (Nos. 1 & 2). {44th Foot / 58th Foot}

2nd Lieut.

2449	ALLEN, Geoffrey Austin ...	24/ 7/15	2 Killed in action 1/7/16
845	GLENCROSS, Sgt. Leslie Harold	26/ 5/15	2 Lieut. Wounded -/7/16
1476	GOODCHILD, Stanley Cecil ...	15/ 8/15	2 Killed in action 1/7/16
1070	HORNE, Owen Walters ...	9/ 5/15	2 Lieut. ✠ w. & P/W 22/10/17
2556	JASPER, Reginald Frederick T.	24/ 7/15	2 Wounded -/7/16

Q

1773	MIDDLEDITCH, Archibald Milne	...	3/12/14	2 Lieut.	Killed in action 1/7/16
1876	PURKISS-GINN, Stewart	...	10/ 7/15	2 Lieut.	
1872	ROBINS, Arthur Howis	...	10/ 7/15	2 Lieut.	Acc/wounded 7/8/15
2263	STRAIGHT, Robert Malcolm	...	15/ 8/15	2 Lieut.	
996	WARD, Laurence James	...	15/ 8/15	2 Capt.	
765110	BRYANT, Alexander Lawrence	...	31/10/17	1	
760565	DAVIES, Arthur Charles	...	4/ 8/17	1 ✠	Wounded 5/12/17
6791	DAVIS, James Martineau	...	26/ 9/16	2 Lieut.	
762517	EDEY, William John...	...	8/11/16	1 Killed in action 1/2/18	
762287	GARVIN, William Miles	...	6/10/17	1 Killed in action 23/9/17	
765175	HUNT, Arthur Warner	...	31/10/17	1(11) Died of wounds 28/4/18	

Special Reserve Battalion (No. 3).

2581	GIBSON, Geoffrey Currey	...	15/ 8/14	3(1) Capt.	Wounded –/9/15
1385	WARNER, L/Cpl. Bernard Oldershaw	25/ 4/15	3(1) Lieut. w. 1/7/16 K/A 19/5/17		
5332	ASHDOWNE, Kenneth	...	26/ 9/16	3 Lieut. ✠	Wounded 1/6/18
766151	HIGHAM, Leonard ...	...	1/ 5/18		
763111	MOORE, Kenneth William James	...	1/ 3/17	(11) Killed in action 15/9/17	
763245	SPRATT, Noel Newton	...	28/ 3/17	Wounded 3/10/18	

Territorial Battalions (Nos. 4 to 8).

573	BARBER, Sgt. John ...	...	16/ 4/15	4 Lieut.	(R.E.) K/A 27/9/17
1227	COLVIN, Sgt. Alexander	...	15/ 4/15	5 Capt.	✠ 🏵
4698	COPE, Sgt. Howard Septimus	...	13/ 6/16	7 Lieut.	Prisoner of war 16/5/18
1626	DEACON, Sgt. Roderick Scripps	...	3/ 4/15	4 Lieut.	(6/Suffolk)
4713	DEAN, Sgt. William Thomas	...	13/ 6/16	7 Lieut.	🏵
1015	ELLIOTT, L/Cpl. Hedley E. Denys ...	15/12/14	5 Lieut.	Prisoner of war 8/5/18	
3819	GAGE, Thomas William	...	20/ 8/15	4 Lieut.	
1208	LEE, Reginald William	...	7/ 3/15	4 Capt.	✠ 🏵
1917	MAVOR, Hilary Raphael	...	23/ 9/14	5 Capt.	R.T.O.
2545	PINNEY, Frank Stanley	...	11/ 3/15	6 Lieut.	Wounded 12/10/18
2206	SCUDAMORE, Stephen	...	2/ 3/15	6 Lieut.	
2470	SEALE, Cedric Stephen St. Brelade...	23/ 3/15	7 Lieut.	Wounded 26/8/15	
2522	TURNER, L/Cpl. Ronald	...	15/ 4/15	5 Killed in action 15/8/16	
4008	AULAGNIER, Frank Charles ...	...	13/ 1/16	7 Lieut.	
1659	BRYANT, Edgar Humphrey ...		19/12/15	5 Lieut.	
2932	DODD, Harry Ernest .	...	29/10/15	6 Capt.	w. 13/11/17, 26/10/18
3974	DURLACHER, Neville Godfrey	...	10/11/15	6 Lieut.	Wounded 14/9/18
2416	GOODRICH, Eustance Edmund	..	3/10/15	4 Lieut.	
3822	JOAD, Sidney Frank ...	...	25/11/15	4 Lieut.	
1824	JOHNSTON, Edgar John Circuit	...	26/11/15	5 (From 12/Warwick) Lieut.	
3593	MACAULAY, Sgt. William Henry	...	18/11/15	5 Capt.	Wounded 10/9/18
1211	ORDISH, Fairman John	...	3/10/15	4 Lieut.	
4512	PALMER, L/Cpl. Francis Noel	...	20/ 1/16	5 Lieut.	

ESSEX REGIMENT (T/F). 243

3855	PETHER, Wilfred Guy ...	... 25/11/15 4	Lieut. (–/Oxford & Bucks)
4030	PINE, L/Cpl. Alfred Walter	... 18/11/15 5	Lieut.
4487	REW, L/Cpl. Douglas Jolland	... 31/ 5/16 5	Killed in action 28/6/17
2995	THEAK, Horace Leonard ...	... 10/10/15 4	Lieut. Died of wounds 4/5/17
4671	WILKINSON, William Donald	... 2/ 6/16 5	Killed in action 14/11/16
1259	WILLIAMSON, Gerald Coutts	... 10/10/15 4	Lieut. Killed in action 9/10/17
4408	BIRD, Charles Edwin ...	... 23/ 6/16 5	Killed in action 17/2/17
6251	CLARK, Gilbert Stuart ...	... 11/ 7/16 7	Lieut.
6101	CUNNINGHAM, Leslie Charles	... 5/ 9/16 4	Lieut.
763721	DENNY, Stanley Edward ...	... 27/ 6/17 4	
765837	EVANS, Reginald Buckingham	... 29/ 5/18 5	Wounded 26/10/18
763968	FAIRHURST, William Ewart ...	... 11/ 5/16 4 ℞	
6140	GJERTSEN, Rudolf	... 5/ 9/16 4	Capt. ✠ F/D ℞
764242	HICKS, George Albert ...	... 17/ 6/17 4	
5126	HUGHES, Alfred Vernon ...	... 5/ 9/16 4	Wounded 31/8/17
762937	LOCKWOOD, Eric Jardine ...	... 27/ 3/17 4 ✠	
6162	PARFITT, Alfred John ...	... 5/ 9/16 4	
764845	RABBAGE, Percy	... 17/ 6/17 4	
764849	RIPPER, Frank Sterley ...	... 17/ 6/17 4	
763436	SCAIFE, Arthur John	... 27/ 3/17 4	
5032	SCOTT, Cecil	... 11/ 7/16 7	Killed in action 31/7/17
6142	SERVANTE, Stewart Quartermain	... 6/ 8/16 6	Lieut.
6301	TAYLOR, Ernest Reginald ...	... 11/ 7/16 7	Capt. ✠ Killed in action 11/8/18
5554	THOMAS, George Henry ...	... 11/ 7/16 7	Wounded 15/8/17
766065	THOMSON, Basil Wilfred ...	... 19/11/17 6	
6144	TWEDDLE, William John ...	... 5/ 9/16 4(7)	Killed in action 16/4/17
765525	WATSON, Francis George ...	... 18/12/17 7	
6133	YOUNG, Vivian Cecil Hardinge	... 19/12/16 4	

Service Battalions (New Armies).

3468	FARRAR, Francis Joseph ...	... 25/ 3/15 10	Lieut.
4448	FINN, William	... 25/ 5/16 12	Lieut.
2629	GARDNER, George Herbert ...	... 14/ 8/15 12	To O.D.
3526	GRAY, Hugh Richard ...	... 20/ 7/15 12	Lieut. Wounded 1/7/16
3086	HICKSON, Reginald Davies ...	... 10/ 3/15 9	Capt. ✠ Died of wounds 30/4/17
3110	NESLING, Robert Edward ...	... 28/11/15 8	
1998	PRICE, Kenneth Dodds ...	... 12/12/15 11	
2447	RANALOW, Arthur Vivian ...	... 28/11/15 10	
4255	RIDGWAY, William	... 9/ 3/16 18	
4444	RUTHERFORD, William Francis	... 8/ 3/16 18	
5084	WATT, John Millar	... 2/ 6/16 12	Lieut. ℞
1683	WITHER, Alexander MacCraig	... 26/ 2/15 12	Lieut.
767293	ALEXANDER, Nathaniel ...	... 17/ 3/19	
765216	BILLING, Arthur William ...	... 28/11/17	Lieut. Wounded 22/8/18
768146	BLAXILL, Alan Donald ...	... 17/ 3/19	

ESSEX REGIMENT (S/B).

768895	BOWMAN, John Herbert	... ...	17/ 3/19	
767768	BRAMWELL, John Cameron ...	...	3/ 3/19	
762554	BRAY, William	...	30/ 5/17	*Lieut.*
768335	BRIDGE, William Arthur ...	...	17/ 3/19	
760147	BROWN, Sgt. William John ...	...	5/ 2/19	
760973	BROWNE, Sidney Noel ...	...	26/ 6/17	*9*
769226	BUNFORD, John Henry ...	...	5/ 2/19	
768096	BURCHELL, Cecil Malcolm ...	...	18/ 3/19	
767869	BUTT, Douglas Morton ...	...	4/ 3/19	
7366	CAPPER, Ernest Raphael ...	...	21/12/16	*9 Capt.* ✠ *D/W as P/W* 24/12/17
762779	CARPENTER, Archibald H. Downes		26/ 4/17	
5474	CHAPLYN, Cyril Edward ...	...	25/ 2/17	*Wounded* 13/8/17, *K/A* 26/4/18
760155	COMBER, Turner	...	8/ 8/17	*9 Capt.* ✠ ✠ *K/A* 19/9/18
768083	CRICK, William Ernest ...	...	17/ 3/19	
8249	CRUSE, George Albert ...	...	25/ 1/17	*To M.G.C. Wounded* 25/5/17
767441	DAWE, Walter William Frederick	...	6/ 2/19	
762589	DEE, James	...	29/ 3/17	*Lieut.*
4845	EAST, William	...	24/ 1/17	*11 Wounded* 2/5/17
767983	EMBERSON, William Stanley...	...	18/ 3/19	
765412	EVENETT, Percy Martin ...	...	18/12/17	*Wounded* 17/9/18
765678	FINDLAY, Lawrence Hewgill ...		18/12/17	*Wounded* 21/8/18
760856	GILMOUR, L/Cpl. Robert ...	...	8/ 8/17	*9*
3358	GOODYEAR, Frederick ...	...	25/ 1/17	*(2) Died of wounds* 23/5/17
767936	GOULD, Alec	...	13/ 2/19	
768344	HAWES, John William ...	...	12/ 2/19	
4187	HAWKSWORTH, Henry Chas. Harold		14/ 8/16	*10 Lieut.* ✠ *K/A* 21/3/18
761286	HEWKLEY, Norman Thomas ...		8/ 8/17	*9*
763104	HODSON, Frederick Charles Moxey		29/ 3/17	
767943	KING, Gerald	...	-/ -/19	
765131	KING, Harry Garfield ...	...	31/10/17	*10 Killed in action* 26/4/18
768071	LAING, Wilfred Davie ...	...	17/ 3/19	
769184	LICHFIELD, George Frederick ...		5/ 2/19	
767807	MARSHALL, Leo Gregory ...	...	5/ 3/19	
765597	MASON, Henry James ...	...	18/12/17	*Lieut.* ✠
767880	McAVOY, Denis George ...	...	5/ 3/19	
768279	MEARS, Stephen Samuel ...	...	19/ 3/19	
768153	MERCER, Geoffrey Hamish ...	...	17/ 3/19	
765241	MOIR, Edwin William Cecil...	...	28/11/17	
768281	MORLEY, Bernard John ...	...	17/ 3/19	
768031	PENWILL, Leslie Charles Bingham	...	17/ 3/19	
767130	PRICE, William Leonard ...	...	4/ 3/19	
3598	READ, Leonard St. Clair ...	...	6/11/16	*Died while PW* 20/12/16
762985	ROCHFORD, Clement... ...	...	29/ 3/17	*(6) Lieut.*
764121	SADLER, William Robert ...	...	15/ 2/19	*Wounded* 23/3/18
768304	SHAW, Cedric Norman ...	...	17/ 3/19	
767458	SHEPPEE, Harold Vaughan ...	...	5/ 2/19	
766287	SIMS, Arthur James Frederick ...		1/ 5/18	*Lieut. Wounded* 8/10/18
768217	SMITH, Esmond Louis ...	...	17/ 3/19	

ESSEX REGIMENT (S/B).

768261	SMITH, Percy Dugmore ...	... 17/ 3/19	
765779	SOUSTER, Stanley Richard ...	... 18/12/17	
766288	STRIDE, Harold John ...	... 26/ 6/18	
763313	TAYLOR, George Thomas ...	... 29/ 3/17	*Killed in action* 2/11/17
768019	THIELÉ, William Charles ...	... 19/ 3/19	
762424	TUBBS, Cyril Lawrence ...	... 28/11/17	*Wounded* 24/5/18
767091	WALLACE, Arthur Cyril ...	... 12/ 2/19	
768308	WORTH, Harry Ivie Stanley John ...	... 17/ 3/19	

THE ROYAL FUSILIERS

(CITY OF LONDON REGIMENT).

Regular Battalions (Nos. 1, 2, 3 & 4). 7th Foot

2nd Lieut.

2367	GUINNESS, Robert Celestin ...	... 17/ 2/15	4 *Capt. Bde. M/G.O. w.* —/3/16
1408	MADAN, Arthur Gressley ...	... 23/ 8/14	*1 Capt. Bde. M/G.O. w.* —/1/17
910	MEAD, Bernard Wallace ...	... 5/ 4/15	4 *Died of wounds* 2/6/15
292	PRICE, L/Cpl. Harold Strachan	... 23/ 4/15	3 *Killed in action* 24/5/15
1178	STEARNS, Eric Gordon ...	... 5/ 4/15	4 *Died of wounds* 6/8/15
1651	YOUNG, Henry Harman ...	... 9/ 5/15	3 *Lieut. Killed in action* 24/5/15
762327	DYER, Francis Everton ...	... 30/ 5/17	4 *Wounded* 6/9/18
763534	MACLACHLAN, Robert ...	... 1/ 3/17	4 *Lieut. Wounded* 7/11/18
5022	MAINGOT, Ronald Joseph ...	... 19/12/16	2 *Lieut. Wounded* 17/12/17
5960	O'CONNOR, Bernard Joseph ...	... 26/ 9/16	3 *Lieut. Killed in action* 4/10/18
5530	PENNY, Bernard Willoughby	... 18/ 3/17	2 *Died of wounds* 18/8/17

Special Reserve Battalions (Nos. 5 to 7).

3422	DUNT, Leslie Ambrose ...	... 12/ 6/15	6 *Lieut.*
7999	ADAMS, Alfred Edward St. John	... 26/ 1/17	6 *Lieut. Wounded* 10/10/17
763285	BARTHOLOMEW, Sydney Arthur	... 28/ 3/17	5 *Employed at W.O.*
4915	BOLLAND, Frederick William Henry	8/ 7/16	7(26) *Killed in action* 7/6/17
761715	BYERS, Arthur Paulet ...	... 29/ 3/17	6(4)
766045	COOK, Raymond Arthur ...	... 23/ 4/18	5
762750	GJEMS, Albert Ole Moller ...	... 29/ 3/17	5(2) *Killed in action* 8/8/17
762785	MASTERS, Charles William ...	... 30/ 5/17	5(8) *Killed in action* 30/8/17
762350	NOKES, William	... 30/ 5/17	6(1)
767632	WILLIAMS, John Alfred Arkill	... 5/ 3/19	6

Service Battalions (New Armies).

2347	ARTHUR, James Ferguson	5/ 1/15	14 Lieut.		
2587	BASTABLE, L/Cpl. Francis J. Norman	29/ 6/15	14 Lieut.	Wounded	
1958	BULGIN, Reginald	22/12/14	15 Lieut.	Wounded –/8/16	
1992	CHUTER, Henry Athelstan	22/12/14	16 (R.F.C.)	K/A 25/3/17	
1490	COLLEY, Ernest Vincent	9/ 2/15	16 (Tank Corps)	D/W 23/8/17	
2889	CUMBERLEGGE, Geoffrey F. J.	6/10/14	11 Bde. Major D.S.O.	✠ F/D
2583	DAVIES, Victor Kenneth Neville	15/ 6/15	15 Lieut.	[w. –/9/16 ℞(2)
4317	DEER, John Hartley	8/ 1/16	14 Lieut.	✠ 18/K.R.R. ℞
1589	GILLBEE, Sidney John	24/10/15	10 Lieut.	Wounded –/3/16
3781	HOARE, Walter John Gerald	7/10/14	11 Capt. D.S.O.	K/A 25/10/16 ℞
3256	JONES, William Riels	7/ 4/15	12 Lieut.	
2471	LARLHAM, Percival Edward	12/ 3/15	12 Capt.	
2482	PEACOCK, Edward Gordon	7/11/15	9 Killed in action 7/7/16	
4816	SHAW, Cpl. Walter Douglas	5/ 2/16	27 ✠ Died of wounds 8/11/18	
2342	SKEET, Challon Hasler Lufkin	13/11/14	12 Lieut. Prisoner of war 29/10/15	
2647	THORN, Arthur Percy	9/ 1/15	15 Lieut.	
2646	THORN, Frederick Charles	9/ 1/15	15 Lieut.	
7078	ADDIS, David Malcolm	21/12/16	26 Lieut. Died of wounds 9/6/17	
768264	ALEXANDER, Robert Guy	17/ 3/19		
767294	BALDWIN, Arthur Edward	5/ 2/19		
763840	BANCKS, Henry Arthur	26/ 4/17	Lieut. Wounded 2/1/18	
763943	BARKER, Ronald Alfred	30/ 5/17	20 Lieut. Wounded 26/4/18	
5830	BARRACLOUGH, Jackson Garth	5/ 9/16	17 Lieut. M.B.E.	
767147	BELL, Stanley John	5/ 3/19		
763358	BOUND, Rowland Beavis	28/ 3/17	Lieut. Emp. Min. of Shipping	
763983	BRAIN, Percy George	27/ 6/17 (2)	Wounded 20/12/17	
763020	BREALY, Samuel George	28/ 3/17	12 Lieut. ✠ (M.G.C.)	
767671	BRUCE, Sydney Frank	–/ 3/19		
763843	BUCKINGHAM, Lawrence Frederick	30/ 5/17	24 Capt. (R.A.F.)	
768688	BURNETT, Cyril Frederick Parry	13/ 2/19		
763288	BURROWS, Walter Frank	1/ 8/17	13 Wounded 21/9/18	
767982	CAPP, Edward Henry	13/ 2/19		
767552	CHEESMAN, Gordon Byron	6/ 3/19		
767902	CHURCHMAN, Stanley	6/ 3/19		
768120	COCKMAN, Reginald Talfourd	10/ 3/19		
764191	COCKELL, Dudley Hugh	31/ 7/17	32 Wounded 24/5/18	
767710	COLEMAN, Allan John Peddie	4/ 3/19		
769364	COOKE, Stanley Charles Frank	5/ 2/19		
6151	COOPER, Frederick Edmund	19/12/16	26 Lieut. Died of wounds 18/12/18	
764192	COWAN, Alfred	1/ 8/17	Employed Ministry of Munitions	
768950	DAY, George Harold	17/ 3/19		
761406	DEVEREUX, Wilfred	30/ 5/17		
768142	DYNE, Francis Leigh Bradley	12/ 2/19		
763177	EDE, Edwin William	28/ 3/17	11 Capt. ✠ K/A 30/8/18	
763030	EVANS, George Emlyn Thomas Hulse	28/ 3/17	11	

761442	FISHER, George Richard Samuel	2/ 8/17	22	Wounded 18/4/18
767461	FOLKES, Cpl. Percy Leonard	5/ 2/19		
764196	FRANCIS, William Joseph	27/ 6/17	12	Killed in action 23/3/18
6104	FROST, Edgar Allen ...	19/12/16	13	Lieut.
768320	GREEN, Albert Victor	18/ 3/19		
765716	GREENFIELD, Ernest Flamank	1/ 5/18	51	Grad. Bn.
760651	HANKIN, Frederick ...	26/ 4/17	11	Lieut.
4895	HARRIS, L/Cpl. Francis	4/ 1/17	11	Wounded 12/9/18
762834	HAWKER, Sgt. Stanley Wm. Adrian	3/ 2/19		
7304	HAYES, Frederick Charles ...	22/11/16	32	Lieut.
763181	HENDRY, Charles Arthur	26/ 4/17	9	Killed in action 27/3/18
768167	HILDERSLEY, Stanley H. Hamilton	18/ 3/19		
761536	HOPPER, Sgt. George	4/ 3/19		Wounded 30/10/17 ⚑(2)
763529	HUGGINS, Robert Henry	1/ 3/17	9	Capt. (K.A.R.)
1676	HYAMS, Geoffrey	9/ 6/15	38	Capt. (Late R.L.R.) ⚑
762835	IRELAND, John Watson	28/ 3/17	22	Prisoner of war 10/5/18
765946	ISAACS, Vincent Harcourt	27/ 2/18	9	Killed in action 21/9/18
762505	JENKINS, John Lewis	3/ 2/19		
5508	JONES, L/Cpl. Albert Ashton	5/ 9/16		
6516	JONES, Robert Holford	5/ 9/16	13	Lieut.
766866	JORDON, Leslie Clifford Ellismere	6/ 2/19		
767680	KESSELS, Stanley Harold	4/ 3/19		
765555	KILHAM, Frank Lawton	28/11/17	13	Wounded 8/3/18
763890	LANE, Herbert Alexander	30/ 5/17	22	Wounded 9/1/18
765370	LANGDON, Edgar Mortimer ...	28/11/17		Lieut. w. Commdt. P/W Camp
760690	LARCOMBE, Harry Reginald Reader	26/ 4/17		Killed in action 2/9/17
765951	MANN, Percival John	27/ 2/18		
763468	MARTIN, Alban Stotesbury ...	26/ 4/17	17	Lieut.
766763	MELLOR, Bernard Francis	3/ 2/19		
767912	MOODY, John Clive ...	3/ 3/19		
765186	MORRIS, Walter Brabazon	28/11/17	11	Wounded 4/9/18
762864	MULLANE, Bernard Patrick ...	24/ 4/17	9	Died of wounds 1/4/18
7252	MUMFORD, Thomas John Curtis	21/12/16	13	Lieut.
7332	NICHOLSON, Humphrey Arthur	5/ 8/16	31	Prisoner of war 14/5/18
765464	NORMAN, Martyn	27/11/17		
765599	NORRIS, Arthur	18/12/17	52	Grad. Bn. w. 12/10/18
763432	O'DONOHUE, Mortimer William	30/ 5/17	26	Lieut. Wounded 31/8/17
766656	OWEN, Albert Edward	26/ 6/18		
5352	PEARSON, William Donovan	27/ 2/17	13	Lieut. Wounded 24/4/17
768074	PEPPIATT, Cyril Frederick	17/ 3/19		
760714	PHILLIPS, Clifford Solomon...	26/ 4/17		Wounded 9/5/18
768201	POLLEY, Norman George Frederick	17/ 3/19		
765513	PROVIS, Harold	18/12/17		
767823	PURVER, Thomas Gabriel	5/ 3/19		
765470	PYE, Harry Arnold ...	28/11/17	26	Wounded 26/4/18
764177	REID, Algernon Frederick	25/ 4/17		From R.A.F.
767526	ROBINSON, Alexander Guyot	6/ 2/19		
762471	SAVOURS, Herbert Jay	29/ 3/17	11	Lieut. ⚑ Wounded 13/8/17

763603	SEABROOKE, Joseph ..	...	30/ 5/17 23	Wounded 12/12/17
762914	SIZEN, Reginald	...	29/ 3/17 23	✠ ✠
5421	SMYTH, Leonard Charles	...	5/ 9/16	Lieut. (Labour Corps)
765604	SPEAKMAN, Alan Edwards	...	18/12/17	Killed in action 5/9/18
769029	STEAVENSON, Harold Vernon	...	5/ 2/19	
767628	STIFF, Cecil Robert ...	...	17/ 3/19	
6451	STREDDER, Cecil Alfred Edward	...	26/ 9/16 24	Lieut.
766796	SUTHERIN, Vivian Oscar	...	3/ 2/19	
763171	TAYLOR, Cecil Henry	...	29/ 3/17 8	Lieut.
761374	TIERNEY, Thomas Joseph	...	26/ 4/17 24	
763014	TOOLEY, Ronald Frank	...	29/ 3/17 9	Lieut. ℳ
764277	TREVELYAN, Dennis John	...	1/ 8/17 32	
5357	TUBB, Stanley William Adam	...	18/ 3/17 13	Lieut.
767888	TUBBS, Edwin Homewood	...	12/ 2/19	
767466	WADIE, Victor Hubert	...	6/ 2/19	
767273	WALWIN, Reginald Edgar	...	6/ 2/19	
766945	WARD, George Morton	...	6/ 2/19	
768597	WATTS, James Neil ...	...	5/ 2/19	
767761	WHITAKER, Bernard Theodore	...	5/ 3/19	
763006	WHYTE, Mark Gilchrist	...	29/ 3/17 20	Killed in action 19/8/18
763143	YOUNG, James Cecil	...	26/ 4/17 32	Killed in action 6/4/18
767762	YOUNGMAN, Reginald	...	4/ 3/19	

THE GLOUCESTERSHIRE REGIMENT.

Regular Battalions (Nos. 1 & 2). {28th Foot / 61st Foot}

2nd Lieut.

1865	WAKELEY, John Eric Stanley	...	11/ 6/15 1	Died of wounds 9/9/16 ℳ
2053	WITCOMB, Charles Edward ...	...	29/ 8/15 2	Lieut. ✠ Wounded
6047	BROWNE, William Robert	...	20/12/16	Wounded 18/10/17
4824	CANNING, Ernest Harold	...	14/ 4/17 1	(R.A.F.) D.F.C. Acc/K 5/10/18
4801	COX, Lupton James ..	...	6/ 1/17 1	Killed in action 18/4/18
4793	DENTON, Leslie Albert	...	6/ 1/17 1	Lieut.
6643	DOHERTY, Fred	...	26/ 9/16 1	
3469	FORBES, George Freeman Murray	...	7/11/16 1	Lieut. ✠
2051	GOULD, Arthur Nutcombe	...	7/11/16 1	Lieut. ✠ Wounded 7/5/18
765591	HENLEY, Walter George	...	27/11/17	(2/4 Leicester) w. 3/10/18
761575	LAMBERT, William Henry	...	5/ 8/17 1	Wounded 28/9/18
7931	PULLEN, Godfrey Frank	...	22/11/16 1	Lieut. Wounded 9/10/18

GLOUCESTERSHIRE REGIMENT.

Special Reserve Battalion (No. 3).

766982	ADAMS, Anstey George Curtis	...	30/10/18	
763752	CLARKE, Howard Gilbert ...	...	27/ 6/17 (*1*)	*T.M.B.* ✠
6376	FOSKETT, L/Cpl. Robert F. J.	...	8/ 7/16 (*8*)	*Lieut.*
764207	ROWDEN, Edgar John	...	1/ 8/17	*Lieut.*
8265	WARREN, Ivan John	...	25/ 1/17 (*1*)	*Died of wounds* 8/3/18

Territorial Battalions (Nos. 4 to 6).

3562	CHUTTER, George Philip ...	...	1/11/15 5	*Lieut. Killed in action* 15/6/18
4153	CRUICKSHANK, Herbert William	...	1/11/15 5	*Lieut. Wounded* 11/10/17
4739	HARVEY, Eric Howard	...	16/10/15 5	*Capt.* ✠ ✠ *w.* 13/5/18 *K/A*
4185	HOLMES, Edward John	...	1/11/15 5	*Lieut.* (6/*Devon*) [30/9/18]
3906	HOUGHTON, Noel Dudley ...	...	1/11/15 5	*Lieut. Wounded* –/7/16
4190	LINTERN, Leslie Edwin	...	1/11/15 5	*Lieut.*
4227	PAGE, Harry Albert ...	...	17/12/15 6	*Lieut.*
4127	RUBINSTEIN, Ronald Francis	...	1/11/15 5	*Capt. P/W (released* 20/11/18)
6470	BIRCH, Alfred Victor	...	15/ 6/16 6	*Lieut.*
4723	BORRIE, Percy John ...	...	15/ 6/16 6	*Lieut.*
4262	DEATON, L/Cpl. Albert Joseph	...	16/ 6/16 6	*Lieut.* ✠
4561	GRAY, Cpl. Harold Vernon ...	...	15/ 6/16 6	*Lieut.* ✠
4344	HOWARD, Gilbert Gordon ...	...	15/ 6/16 6	*Lieut. Died of wounds* 29/10/18
4812	JOHNSTON, John Darrell	...	2/ 6/16 5	*Capt.* ✠ *Wounded* 18/4/18
3975	LYLE, Cpl. Alfred Houston ...	...	2/ 6/16 5	*Lieut.*
5064	MALLETT, Archibald Walter	...	16/ 6/16 6	*Lieut. Wounded* 20/12/17
4661	MAY, Richard Hermon	...	15/ 6/16 6	*Lieut. Wounded* 20/10/18
5075	ROSE, William Henry Smith	...	15/ 6/16 6	*Lieut. Wounded* –/4/17
5805	SKEY, Leonard George	...	15/ 6/16 6	*Lieut.*
4796	STONE, Max Thomas Burgoyne	...	2/ 6/16 5	*Lieut.*
5103	WOODROFFE, Alfred Graham	...	15/ 6/16 6	*Lieut.*
6092	ASTON, Alfred John George...	...	5/ 9/16 4	*Lieut. Wounded* 7/4/17
6745	BAILEY, Gilbert	...	29/ 9/16 4	*Lieut. Wounded* 26/3/17
6182	BAND, George Eliot ...	...	26/ 9/16 4	*Wounded* 27/8/17, 3/12/17
5463	BARRETT, Henry	...	23/11/16 4	*Wounded* 8/11/16
6785	BEADELL, Alfred George	...	5/ 9/16 4	*Killed in action* 13/4/17
764084	BEAVON, Donald James	...	30/ 5/17 4	*Killed in action* 27/8/17
4646	BEAVON, Cpl. John Alfred ...	...	5/ 9/16 4	*Lieut.*
763919	BEESON, Alfred Charles	...	17/ 6/17 4	
4296	BENSON, L/Cpl. Thomas Norman	...	5/ 9/16 4	*Lieut.*
6249	BEST, Gordon	...	26/ 9/16 4	*Wounded* 7/9/17
5041	BICKLEY, L/Cpl. Alec	...	11/ 7/16 6	*Lieut. Wounded* 17/9/16
5042	BICKLEY, L/Cpl. Cecil Wallace	...	11/ 7/16 6	*Lieut.*
5729	BUNN, Robert William Edwin	...	5/ 9/16 4	*Capt.*
5614	BURDETT, Basil	...	5/ 9/16 4	*Lieut.* (*M.G.C.*) *Missing* 13/6/18
5648	CAYLEY, Percy John..	...	5/ 9/16 4	*Lieut. Wounded* 1/2/17

GLOUCESTERSHIRE REGIMENT (T/F)

6098	CLEAVER, Percival Arthur ...	...	5/ 9/16	4	*Lieut. Wounded* 10/9/17
5573	COATES, Richard Reginald ...	...	5/ 9/16	4	*Lieut.*
765530	COOPER, William Charles ...	...	27/11/17	6	*Wounded* 17/6/18
908	CROWE, L/Cpl. Arthur Alex. Roberts		5/ 9/16	4	*Lieut.*
6102	DUTTON, Wilfred Joseph	...	5/ 9/16	4	*Lieut.* ✠
4155	ELLIOTT, Wilby Charles	...	26/ 9/16	4	*Lieut.* ⚔
4893	ELLIS, L/Cpl. Hubert French	...	4/ 9/16	4(8)	*Lieut.*
6758	FERRIS, Henry Norman	...	29/ 9/16	4	*Killed in action* 9/10/17
6055	FLEMING, Sidney Herbert	...	29/ 9/16	4	*Lieut.*
6056	FOX, Edwin Clement	...	26/ 9/16	4	*Lieut.*
7154	GALLOP, Harold Henry	...	21/12/16	3	*Lieut.* ⌊K/A 16/9/18 ⌉
5255	GRIFFIN, Edward William ...	...	4/ 8/16	6	*Lieut. (R.A.F.) w.* 10/9/17 ⌋
6001	GROSE, Henry Hicks	...	19/ 9/16	4(5)	*Lieut.*
7853	GURNEY, Kenneth Gerrard ...		19/12/16	5	*Died of wounds P/W* 17/12/17 ⚔
5013	HADLEY, Ernest Sidney	...	26/ 9/16	4	*Killed in action* 27/8/17
6106	HARRIS, Cornelius Arthur ...	...	23/11/16	4	*Lieut.*
6220	HOLLINGSWORTH, Christopher R.	...	26/ 9/16	4	*Lieut.*
764098	JOSEPHS, Edward Albert Warwick	...	27/ 6/17	5	✠
763829	KETHRO, George Gordon	...	30/ 5/17	4	
6708	KOWIN, James	...	5/ 9/16	4	*Lieut.*
6609	LEE-SMITH, Kenneth	...	23/11/16	5	*Lieut.*
5773	LEMON, L/Cpl. Martin Mark Stanley		5/ 9/16	4	*Lieut. (M.G.C.)*
762374	LINDREA, Wilfred George ...	...	29/ 3/17	4	*Killed in action* 30/3/18
6228	LOOMS, Alfred	...	5/ 9/16	4	*Lieut.*
6122	MACE, Alfred	...	5/ 9/16	4	*Lieut. Wounded* 1/9/17
5781	MATTOCKS, Charles Frederick	...	26/ 9/16	4	*Lieut.*
5347	MEADE, Cyril	...	5/ 9/16	5	*Killed in action* 5/4/17
5274	MILLER, Frederick Charles ...	...	4/ 8/16	6	*Lieut. Killed in action* 24/4/18
5375	MURCH, Leslie Charles	...	26/ 9/16	4	*Lieut.*
5961	OSBORNE, Frank John	...	5/ 9/16	4	*Lieut. Wounded* 16/4/17
5865	OSBORNE, Percy Arthur	...	11/ 7/16	6	*Wounded* 11/7/16
6717	PAINTER, Herbert Thomas Harold...		5/ 9/16	4	*Lieut.*
5790	PEARS, Norman	...	26/ 9/16	4	*Killed in action* 24/4/17
763624	PHILLIPS, Ernest	...	30/10/17	4	
5074	PRICE, Frederick Norman ...	...	5/ 9/16	4	*Lieut.*
6817	PUTTICK, Hubert Claude ...	...	26/ 9/16	4	*Lieut.*
5281	RAGGETT, Edward Leonard...	...	11/ 7/16	6	
6692	RAWLINGS, Frank Richard ...	...	26/ 9/16	4	*Prisoner of war* 4/1/18
5214	RIPPERGER, L/Cpl. Harold T. Alvin		26/ 9/16	4	*Lieut.* ✠ *K/A* 23/10/18
762581	ROBERTS, Daniel John	...	26/ 4/17	4	*Wounded* 10/9/17
765193	SANKEY, Humphrey ...	...	28/11/17	5	*Lieut.*
5803	SHINER, Frederick Walter ...	...	26/ 9/16	4	*Lieut. (R.E.)*
6932	SHUTE, George Francis	...	5/ 9/16	4	*Died while P/W* 13/10/17
760843	SILES, Sidney Herbert	...	13/ 5/17	4	
5807	SLEAP, Josiah Weldon	...	5/ 9/16	4	*Wounded* 8/10/17
7238	STEEL, Norman	...	11/ 7/16	5	*Killed in action* 16/8/17
4940	STEPHENS, George ...	...	26/ 9/16	4	*Lieut. Wounded* 25/8/17
5713	STREETS, Alfred William	...	26/ 9/16	4	*Lieut.*

GLOUCESTERSHIRE REGIMENT (T/F).   251

6429	SULLIVAN, Stanley Frederick	... 26/ 9/16	4 Lieut.	✠
6659	TEBB, James Bertram ...	... 26/ 9/16	4 Lieut.	
1311	TIDDY, L/Cpl. Eric William Lacey ...	26/ 9/16	4 Lieut.	✠
6541	TUSSAUD, Bernard Augustin	... 26/ 9/16	4 Lieut	
4934	VAUGHAN, L/Cpl. Matthew Francis	26/ 9/16	4 Lieut.	
5971	WALTER, Arthur Kitchener...	... 29/ 9/16	4 Lieut.	
7008	WARREN, Edwin Dorey ...	... 26/ 9/16	4 Lieut.	Wounded 22/10/17
6347	WATTS, Arthur Henry ...	... 26/ 9/16	4 Lieut.	
5085	WHITE, Charles Dare ...	... 11/ 7/16	6 Capt.	
6725	WILSON, Ian MacLellan Turner	... 26/ 9/16	4 Lieut.	
6665	WINTLE, Howard George ...	... 5/ 9/16	4 ✠ ✠	Wounded 7/9/17, 20/12/17
768094	WIX, Ernest Henry	... 17/ 3/19	4	

Service Battalions (New Armies).

2504	CORNWALL, Reginald Edwin	... 8/ 1/15	13 Capt.	(4/Yorks)
2732	EGERTON, Frederick Clement C.	... 8/ 1/15	9 Capt. & Adjt.	Inst. Duties
2501	ELKINGTON, Christopher Garrett	... 23/11/14	8 Capt. D.S.O.	Wounded ✠
2311	GARDINER, Philip Edwin ...	... 7/ 5/15	13 Lieut.	
2122	HAMMOND, Hugh Jerold ...	.. 29/10/14	Capt.	Died of wounds 23/3/18
2479	KIRKBY, Noel Walter ...	... 12/ 3/15	13 Lieut.	(4/Yorks)
2042	WHITWORTH, Arthur Stuart ...	... 2/11/14	10 Capt.	
7148	CARNON, John Stanley Murray	... 21/12/16	10 Lieut.	Wounded 9/10/18
761493	CARTER, Albert Harry ...	... 17/ 3/19		
768508	CHEETHAM, John Crompton	... 13/ 2/19		
769633	COLLYER, Charles Alexander Stewart	15/ 2/19		
767904	DAW, Eustace Ernest William	... 17/ 3/19		
7635	DRUCE, Clifford John ...	... 25/ 1/17	Lieut.	Wounded 21/12/17
763150	DURRANT, Jack Riley Garton	... 26/ 4/17		
5652	EATON, Harold	... 26/ 9/16	13 Killed in action 31/7/17	
768646	ELWORTHY, Sidney George ...	... 13/ 2/19		
768822	ESSEX, Alexander Clinch ...	... 5/ 2/19		
767874	FLEMING, Robert Bruce ...	... 6/ 3/19		
7328	FRAMPTON, John Reginald ...	.. 7/ 7/16	13 Killed in action 3/7/17	
765321	GEDYE, Alfred John	... 18/12/17	(1/Dorset)	Wounded 11/8/18
768825	GIBB, Roger	... 20/ 3/19		
7155	GILLARD, Sidney Herbert ...	... 21/12/16	12 Lieut.	
765589	GURNEY, Ronald Wilfred ...	... 3/ 2/19		
767125	HALL, Robert Clive	... 4/ 3/19		
7410	HERRING, David Duncan ...	... 23/11/16	12 Prisoner of war 14/6/18	
761673	HUGHES, John Basil William	... 23/ 5/18	Prisoner of war 2/11/18	
3570	JAMES, Samuel Forest ...	... 19/ 9/16	8 Lieut. Killed in action 18/11/16	
7424	JARVIS, Arthur	... 19/12/16	(1) ✠	
768545	KENSETT, Percy Frank ...	... 13/ 2/19		
6293	LEMON, Kenneth Charles ...	... 7/ 7/16	15 Lieut.	
767939	LOVETT, Francis James ...	... 5/ 3/19		
768172	LYON, William Walter ...	... 12/ 2/19		

765507	MASON, George Bowler	...	... 27/11/17	
768030	MORAN, Patrick Francis	...	... 6/ 3/19	
768946	POPE, Frederick John	...	... 13/ 2/19	
762642	PURTON, Thomas Downes	...	... 3/ 8/17	8 Wounded 10/4/18
764846	REED, William Arthur	...	... 28/11/17	
7188	SYKES, Isaac ...	...	... 21/12/16	14 Wounded (P/W) 17/9/18
768092	TAIT, Alfred Andrew Donald		... 17/ 3/19	
7404	THOMSON, George Gordon	...	... 23/11/16	14 ✠
5428	TROTMAN, Ewart Washington		... 26/ 2/17	8 Lieut.
4818	TROUNCE, William Robert	...	... 24/ 1/17	10 Lieut.
768306	VENMORE, James Archer	...	... 17/ 3/19	
3525	VINCENT, Basil Brittten	...	... 20/ 6/16	8 Killed in action 23/7/16
768597	WATTS, James Harold	...	... 17/ 3/19	
767042	WEST, Harry ...	...	... 17/ 3/19	
4780	WILSON, Robert Travis	...	... 24/ 1/17	10 Lieut.
3568	WOOD, David Cardale	...	... 20/ 6/16	8 Lieut. Killed in action 23/7/16
768864	YIEND, Denis Andrew	...	... 17/ 3/19	

THE GORDON HIGHLANDERS.

Regular Battalions (Nos. 1 & 2).   {75th Foot / 92nd Foot}

			2nd Lieut.	
1369	BERRY, John Anthony	...	... 20/ 3/15	1 Killed in action 25/9/15
1450	BIRNIE, Reginald	... ...	... 3/ 3/15	2 Capt. R.E. Wounded 18/4/15
691	CHATER, Cpl. Alfred Dougan		... 15/12/14	2 Capt. Wounded 11/3/15
1766	DUFF, John Crerar	...	... 5/ 4/15	2 Wounded 12/5/15 K/A 10/6/15
1215	DUFF, Keith Mitchell	...	... 5/ 4/15	2 Lieut.
1373	GILES, Geoffrey	... ...	... 20/ 3/15	2 w. 17/5/15, –/4/16 K/A –/7/16
1437	HORSLEY, Oswald	... ...	... 15/12/14	2 Capt. ✠ ✠ (R.F.C.) w.9/1/15, 20/7/15 Acc/Killed 19/8/18 ⌘
1436	HORSLEY, L/Cpl. Siward Myles		... 15/12/14	2 Wounded 12/3/15 d. 25/12/20
997	MULOCK, Edward Ross	...	... 15/12/14	2 Killed in action 11/3/15
1468	PRIDAY, Arthur Kenneth	...	... 20/ 3/15	2 Wounded 25/9/15
1732	SCOONES, Thomas Collins	...	... 3/ 3/15	2 Lieut. ✠ ⌘
2411	WATES, Sidney Benjamin	...	... 20/ 3/15	2 Capt. Wounded 18/6/15
1367	WILLIAMSON, John Maurice		... 20/ 3/15	2 Killed in action 16/5/15
8107	CRANNA, Alexander Park	...	... 29/12/16	1(5) Lieut.
763875	DOUGLAS, Frederick ...	...	... 26/ 4/17	1 Lieut. Wounded 26/9/17

Special Reserve Battalion (No. 3).

763715	MARTIN, Alfred Ernest	... ...	28/ 8/17	3 (*M.G.C.*) Wounded 2/10/18

Territorial Battalions (Nos. 4 to 7).

4375	LILLEY, L/Cpl. Eric Seddon	... 10/12/15	*4 Lieut.*
765938	GRANT, John	... 26/ 6/18	*7*
764556	GUNN, William Hamish ...	... 28/ 8/17	*4* Wounded 3/6/18
5388	WELSH, Robert	... 13/12/16	*5 Lieut.* ✠

Service Battalions (New Armies).

3744	DAVIDSON, Sgt. Kenneth Chisholm...	16/12/15	*11* Wounded –/11/6, 17/8/17
766599	HENSON, Arthur Edw.	4/ 2/19	
768255	MACAULAY, Donald Ian ...	17/ 3/19	
768323	MACKENZIE, Edward Cyril ...	17/ 3/19	
766352	MCPHERSON, MacGill ...	6/ 2/19	
767975	ROBERTSON, Lawrence George ...	5/ 3/19	
768260	RUSSELL, Hector Gordon ...	17/ 3/19	
767500	WALKER, Denzill Robert Augustus ...	14/ 8/18	*51 Grad. Bn.*

THE HAMPSHIRE REGIMENT.

Regular Battalions (Nos. 1 & 2).

{37th Foot
{67th Foot

2nd Lieut.

1655	D'ARCY, Norman Carden ...	... 23/ 4/15	*1 Lieut.* Wounded 8/7/15
2203	BURDGE, Conrad Chawner .	... 9/ 5/15	*1 Lieut.* Wounded 12/6/15
2365	DALE, Felix John	... 26/ 5/15	*1 Lieut.* Wounded 3/9/15 ⚔
2196	FLINT, Hugh...	... 9/ 5/15	*1 Capt.* ✠ Wounded 4/6/18 ⚔
1880	MUDGE, James	... 26/ 5/15	*1 Lieut.* Wounded –/10/17
2352	MCNAIR, William Lennox ...	7/12/14	*2 Lt.* w. 9/6/15 (*Fr.* 12/*Warwick*)
5232	ANDERSON, Reginald Thomas	26/ 9/16	*2 Lieut.*
3433	BEAZELEY, George Edward Armitage	7/11/16	*1 Lieut.*
1282	CUDDON, Philip Basil.. ...	15/ 9/14	*1 Capt. Bde.-Maj.* ✠✠✠ F/D ⚔
809	CUTMORE, Sgt. Horace Edison Vernon	1/ 1/17	*2* Wounded 9/10/17
3735	HOBSON, Geoffrey Hamilton	... 7/11/16	*1* Died of wounds 14/4/17
762321	MEEK, Gerald Arthur ...	... 26/ 4/17	*1*
8324	SNYDER, Lorne	... 25/ 1/17	*(2)* Killed in action 23/4/17
7096	SWAN, Percy Walter	... 19/12/16	*(2)*
765202	WEST, Stanley Ewart ...	... 27/11/17	*1*
4568	YATES, Frederick	... 19/12/16	*(2)* Died of wounds 30/11/17

Special Reserve Battalion (No. 3).

469	HALCROW, Cpl. Arthur Palmer	...	30/ 9/14	(2) Lieut. Killed in action 23/4/17
3446	HONE, Cpl. Reginald Arbery	...	31/ 7/15	Lieut.
8846	MARTIN, Richard	...	19/12/16	Lieut.

Territorial Battalions (Nos. 4 to 9).

3168	CAPES, Gerard Alphonsus ...	...	16/ 4/15	4 Lieut. Wounded 8/3/17
2304	HOWE, Eric Graham ...	...	27/ 2/15	9 Cyclist Bn. Lieut. Inst. Duties
1875	HOWGRAVE-GRAHAM, H. M.	...	31/10/14	9 Cyclist Bn. Capt.
2061	NAPIER, Macvey	...	3/10/14	5 Lieut. O.C.B.
4542	BROADBRIDGE, Frank Lionel	...	16/ 3/16	9 Lieut.
4112	COOMBS, Adrian Roy ...	...	19/12/15	8 Lieut. Wounded 5/5/17, 5/9/17
4010	CROSS, L/Cpl. James Ralph	...	19/12/15	8 Lieut. (To Min. of Labour)
4012	DARRACOTT, Joseph Stuart ...	...	16/ 1/16	9 Lieut. Wounded –/11/16, 8/5/17
4248	GOSSLING, Frank Foley ...	...	14/ 1/16	9 Lieut.
4305	IMROTH, Leslie	...	25/12/15	8 Wounded 30/11/17 Died 20/12/18
3801	JARRY, Martin	...	30/ 9/15	8 Lieut.
1114	PRICE, L/Cpl. Herbert ...	...	19/ 8/15	4 Lieut.
1313	STEBBING, Percy Edward ..	...	20/ 8/15	8 Lieut. Wounded 7/10/18
4103	SUTCLIFFE, Fred	...	19/12/15	8 Capt. & Adjt. ✠ ℞
3161	VAWDREY, Ralph Hastings ...	...	23/10/15	4 Lieut.
4524	WILSON, William Cronin ...	...	7/12/15	8 Lieut.
4567	WOOD, Walter Bertram ...	...	2/ 6/16	8 Lieut.(R.F.C.) ✠✠ K/A 11/11/17
4654	BACON, Sidney Frederick William	...	11/ 7/16	8 Lieut.
4573	CARTER, Alfred Bertram ...	...	11/ 7/16	8 Lieut.
4982	CARTER, Henry John ...	...	11/ 7/16	8 Lieut.
5943	COLSON, Herbert John Corbett	...	11/ 7/16	9 Lieut.
3777	DUNWOODY, John Orr ...	...	26/ 9/16	5 Lieut. Wounded 29/8/17
763032	GAMMON, Albert Kenneth ...	...	26/ 4/17	5 Lieut.
4626	GREER, Alexander	...	11/ 7/16	8 Lieut.
4647	HARDIE, William Johnstone	...	11/ 7/16	8 Lieut.
4526	HITCHCOCK, Leonard ...	...	11/ 7/16	8 Lieut. (4/Dorset) ℞
4627	LEYBOURNE, Philip Edwin ...	...	11/ 7/16	8 Capt. ✠✠ K/A 4/9/18
5776	LOVELESS, Ralph Edgar ...	...	28/ 9/16	6 Lieut. Wounded 14/5/17
762595	MASON, Harold George ...	...	29/ 3/17	4 Lieut.
760701	MEATYARD, George Waite ...	...	27/ 3/17	4 Lieut. Wounded 26/10/17
4577	PARISH, William Everett ...	...	11/ 7/16	8 Lieut.
4556	REYNOLDS, Cyril Walter ...	...	11/ 7/16	8 Lieut.
762845	STEDMAN, Arthur Herbert Dunlop		27/ 3/17	4 Lieut.
765964	STOCKEN, Carl August ...	...	27/ 2/18	5
4620	TACKLEY, Reginald Charles	...	11/ 7/16	9 Lieut.
5551	TAYLOR, Harold Sydney ...	...	26/ 9/16	5 Lieut.
4585	WILLCOX, Maurice William	...	11/ 7/16	8 Lieut.
763007	WINCER, Allen	...	26/ 4/17	5 Wounded 10/5/18

Service Battalions (New Armies).

2779	FRENCH, Archibald Charles...	... 13/11/14	*11 Capt.*	
1396	MANN, Frederick Randall ...	... 1/ 1/15	*13*(2) ✠	Wounded 16/8/15 ℳ
2580	NEWMAN, William Alfred ...	... 28/ 1/15	*12 Lieut.*	
5062	STADDEN-LEA, Cecil James	... 25/ 5/16	*13 Lieut.*	
3126	TILLEY, L/Sgt. John Ernest	... 3/ 5/15	*12 Lieut.* ✠	ℳ(2)
1999	TITLEY, Richard Kenneth ...	... 29/10/14	*14 Lieut.*	Wounded 30/6/16
2537	TRESS, Gerald Courtney ...	... 5/12/14	*13 Capt.*	
2165	WHITAKER, Donald Nicholl W.	... 12/ 9/15	*12 Capt.*	(*O.C.B.*) ✠ ℳ
766804	BENNETT, Thomas Harper ...	... 28/ 5/18	(2)	
767188	BRADLEY, Archibald John ...	... 31/10/18		
768292	CAWTE, Edward Vivian ...	... 17/ 3/19		
769228	CLARKE, William Percival ...	... 5/ 2/19		
4447	COLEMAN, L/Cpl. Cuthbert Thomas	19/12/16	*15 Lieut.*	
7176	COLLIER, Philip Frederick ...	... 19/12/16	*15 Lieut.*	Wounded 16/6/17
7177	COOPE, Thomas Edwin ...	... 19/12/16	*15 Lieut.*	
768609	CURTIS, Ronald Hamilton ...	... 17/ 3/19		
765930	DAVIES, Henry Spry...	... 13/ 3/18		
766915	EALES, Christopher ...	... 27/ 3/18	*17*	
7321	ELKINGTON, Walter Henry ...	... 21/12/16	*11 Lieut.*	Killed in action 22/3/18
765033	ENGLAND, Harry Frank ...	... 31/10/17	*11 Capt.*	(7/*R. Irish*)
767615	FLEMING, Leonard Patrick ...	... 6/ 2/19		
768067	FLIGHT, Brian Patrick	... 17/ 3/19		
6325	GAY, Frederick George	... 26/ 9/16	*Lieut.*	
763451	GLOVER, Harold ...	... 29/ 3/17	*11*	
7126	GRAHAM, Keith ...	... 19/12/16	*15* ✠	Wounded 19/10/18
767561	HARRIS, George Leslie ...	... 4/ 3/19		
769339	HUNT, Arthur ...	... 17/ 3/19		
7313	HUSSEY, Thomas Archibald	... 19/12/16	*14 Capt.*	Wounded 13/4/18
765995	JARVIS, Frank Jordan ...	... 15/ 4/18	*51 Grad. Bn.*	
765275	KNIGHT, Henry de Boyne ...	... 28/11/17	*11*	
765897	LAVERS, Francis George ...	... 13/ 3/18		Wounded 5/10/18
768903	LEAL, James Henry ...	... 5/ 2/19		
765998	LEE, Cecil Frank ...	... 1/ 5/18		
768957	MASON, Cecil Julian Marsh	... 14/ 2/19		
5520	MERRETT, Arthur Edwin ...	... 5/ 9/16	*15*	Killed in action 18/12/16
767883	MULES, John Charles Gordon	... 6/ 3/19		
2655	NASH, L/Cpl. Paul ...	... 19/12/16	*15*	
769154	ONSLOW, Offley Laban ...	... 5/ 2/19		
6327	OWEN, Leonard Arthur ...	... 26/ 9/16	(*R.F.C.*)	
765797	PAFFORD, Harry John ...	... 21/ 2/18		
4046	PAGE, Howard ...	... 23/11/16	*15*	
765959	ROBINSON, Herbert ..	... 27/ 2/18		
762624	ROPER, Frederick Herbert ...	... 29/ 3/17		Wounded 23/11/17
765007	SANDELL, Cyril Maurice ...	... 20/10/17	*Lieut.*	Wounded 27/5/18
765668	TAYLOR, Claude ..	... 18/12/17	*51 Grad. Bn.*	
7416	TYLER, Norman Fielder ...	... 19/12/16	*14*	Wounded 16/8/17
763981	WADE, Joseph Barnard	... 27/ 6/17		

THE HIGHLAND LIGHT INFANTRY.

Regular Battalions (Nos. 1 & 2).

{71st Foot / 74th Foot}

2nd Lieut.

1959	ANNAND, Allan Young	...	11/ 6/15 *1 Wounded* –/3/16 *K/A* 10/1/17
2980	BEVIS, Leslie Cubitt	...	24/10/15 *2 Lieut. w.* –/3/16, 18/4/18 ✠
392	CLOSE, Cpl. Max Arthur	...	1/ 1/15 *1 Killed in action* 12/3/15
1444	GIBBS, Thomas Raleigh	...	1/ 1/15 *1 Capt.* ✠ ✠ *Wounded* 12/3/15
1301	MUMMERY, Harry Norman S.	...	20/ 3/15 *1 Capt. w.* 22/5/15, 17/4/16, 19/4/18
1724	PAYNE, Charles Geraint C.	...	27/ 1/15 *1 K/A* 12/3/15 [*d.* (*P/W*) 6/8/18
2812	WHITESIDE, Miles Bruce Dalziel	...	9/12/14 *1 Lieut.* (*R.A.F.*) *w.* 20/8/15,
1613	WORNUM, Thornton Hilton	...	1/ 1/15 *1 Capt.* [2/1/17 *Acc/K* 13/6/18
764939	DARK, Stanley George	...	12/ 5/17 *1*
766921	GARDEN, James Alexander	...	23/ 6/18 *1*
764115	HALL, William Towler	...	13/ 5/17 *1*
764116	HEWETT, Frederick Stanley	...	13/ 5/17 *1*
763585	IM THURN, Archibald McKenzie	...	12/ 5/17 *1*
760643	LONGLEY, Philip Robert Hamer	...	1/ 6/17 *1 Wounded* 2/5/18
765187	MUNDAY, William Frank	...	13/ 5/17 *1* ✠
764391	THOMAS, Stanley Stratton Lloyd St. G.		12/ 5/17 *1*
764279	WILKINS, Edward Munro	...	5/ 2/17 *1*

Special Reserve Battalions (Nos. 3 & 4).

1454	HARDMAN, Kenric	...	5/11/14 *3(1) Lieut. w.* 22/5/15 *Killed*
7226	BROOKS, Cyril Bernard	...	23/11/16 *4 Lieut.* [*in action* 26/10/18
765303	BRUCE, Robert Cathcart	...	23/11/17 *3(2)*
5578	GARVIE, Hamilton Alexander	...	6/ 9/16 *3 Lieut.*
6869	GRANT, John	...	5/ 9/16 *3 Lieut.* ✠
5659	MACINNES, William Alexander	...	5/ 9/16 *4 Lieut.* (*11/Border*) ✠ ✠
762544	THOMAS, Hector Welford Munro	...	27/ 6/17 *3(14) Lieut.*

Service Battalions (New Armies).

2822	COLQUHOUN, James Clifton	...	12/12/14 *13 Capt. Wounded* –/10/15
2375	HUGO, Reginald Graeff	...	5/12/15 *11 Lieut. Died of wounds* 28/3/18
3566	PRIESTMAN, Alan	...	5/12/15 *11 Lieut.*
7198	SCOTT, Alexander	...	18/ 2/16 *13 Lieut. Killed in action* 24/4/17
7100	ARMOUR, Wm. Nicol McSkimming	...	2/ 5/17 *16* ✠
768570	BUCHANAN, William	...	15/ 2/19
767140	CRAWFORD, Joseph Ernest	...	6/ 2/19
5201	FERGUSON, Douglas Chalmers	...	21/ 9/16 *Died of wounds* 26/1/17
6924	GILLIES, Kenneth	...	13/12/16 *Wounded* –/5/17
7719	HAMILTON, Arthur Donald	...	13/12/16
8892	HILLIS, John	...	1/ 3/17 *6 Wounded* 5/10/18
768058	KELLY, John Donald	...	17/ 3/19
768546	KIDD, Norman	...	13/ 2/19
6320	SMITH, Rose McKenzie	...	6/ 9/16 *17 Wounded* 12/10/18 ✠
769486	WHITELAW, William	...	19/ 2/19

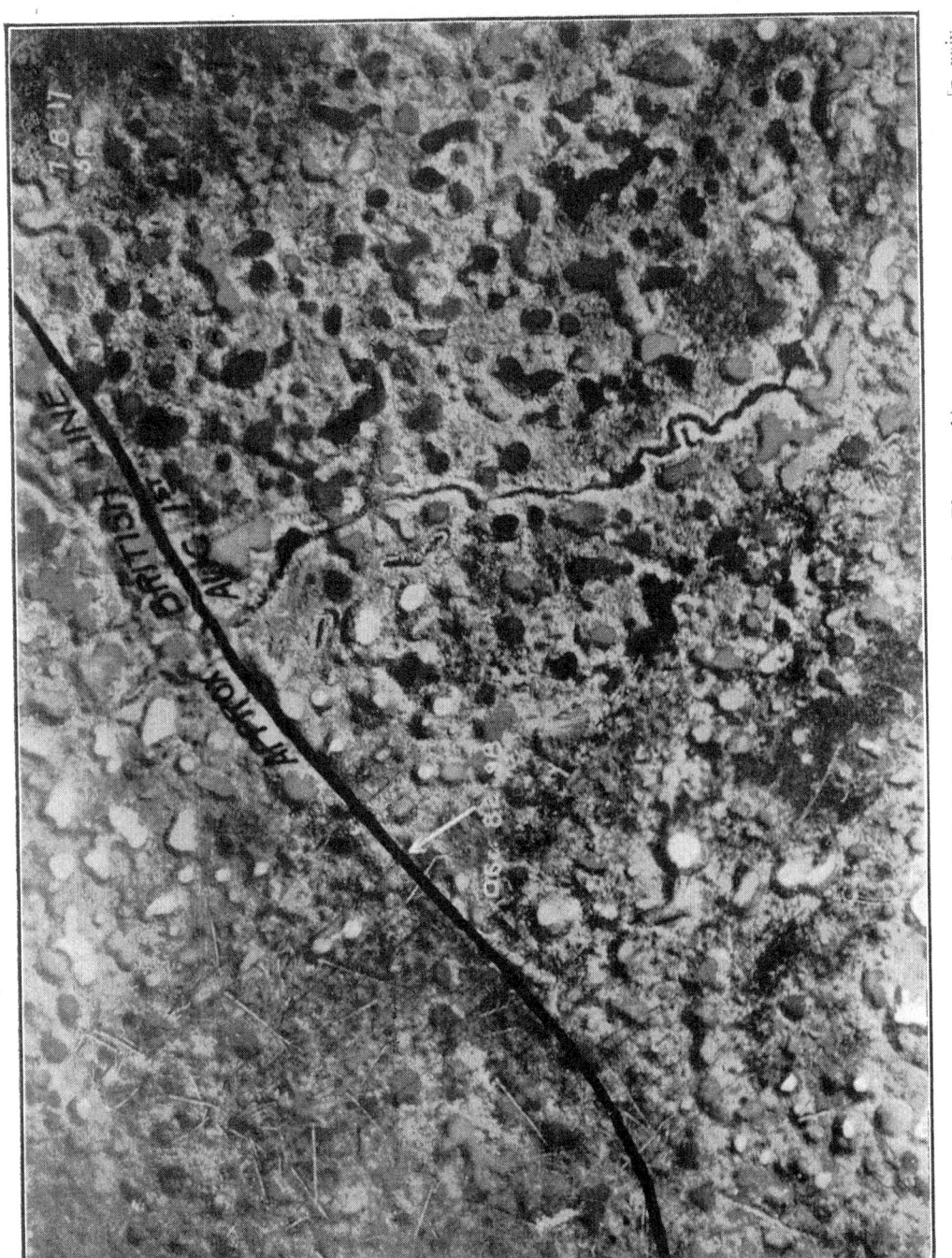

A SHELL-PITTED AREA (Aeroplane Photograph).

RE-CAPTURE OF SANCTUARY WOOD BY THE BLACK WATCH, 1916.

[Capt. W. B. Wollen.

Copyright.]

THE ROYAL HIGHLANDERS
(THE BLACK WATCH).

{ 42nd Foot
{ 73rd Foot

Regular Battalions (Nos. 1 & 2).

		2nd Lieut.	
1187	EGLINGTON, Dudley Charles	... 20/ 3/15 2 *Lieut.* ✠ *w.* 8/10/15, –/8/16
1294	HOLLAND, Basil Thomas ...	... 31/12/14 2 *Killed in action* 10/3/15
1682	HUTCHISON-INNES, Owen ...	... 1/ 1/15 2 *Killed in action* 6/1/16
1368	MILES, Lancelot G. ...	... 1/ 1/15 2 *Major* D.S.O. *w.* 26/5/15, –/10/15 } ✠(2)
1079	MOORE, Gerald Grantley	... 1/ 1/15 1 *Lieut. w.* 10/5/15

Territorial Battalions (Nos. 4 to 7).

766037	DICKSON, George Hubert Murray	... 1/ 5/18 6 *Killed in action* 26/10/18
761352	FRASER, Alexander ...	... 2/ 3/17 6 ✠
762066	GRANT, Jack Lawton	... –/ 3/17 4
765550	HERD, George Grosvenor ...	... 27/11/17 7 *Wounded* 1/8/18
767566	HUTCHESON, Charles Roger	... 4/ 3/19 4
6982	LAIDLAW, George Howard ...	... 20/12/16 4 *Lieut.*
768075	PHILIP, Thomas Vincent Rorison	... 17/ 3/19 5
768077	REID, David Drummond	... 17/ 3/19 5
765088	WHAMOND, John ...	... 27/ 2/18 5 *Wounded* 3/9/18

Service Battalions (New Armies).

2448	LUNN, Bryan Holdsworth ...	... 14/11/14 11
2417	MURRAY, Edward Douglas ...	... 28/ 1/15 11 To 8 *Died of wounds* 20/7/16
1321	SCOTT, Ronald Joycelyn Leslie	... 21/10/14 10 *Capt. To Indian Army*
768359	BOTT, Dudley Allan Lockhart	... 19/ 3/19
769207	GIBSON, David ...	... 5/ 2/19
769241	HORNE, John Campbell ...	... 5/ 2/19
768911	ANDERSON, John Lennox ...	... 5/ 2/19
769209	KERR, Thomas Howard ...	... 5/ 2/19
5269	LOUDOUN, Thomas ...	... 5/ 9/16 (2) *Lieut. Killed in action* 8/6/18
7813	MARTIN, Arthur William Dight	... 25/ 1/17 ✠ *Wounded* 21/8/18
768050	SWABEY, Kenneth ...	... 17/ 3/19
7708	YOUNG, George Ernest Robertson	... 22/11/16 9 *Lieut. Wounded* 5/9/17

THE ROYAL INNISKILLING FUSILIERS.

Regular Battalions (Nos. 1 & 2).

27th Foot
108th Foot

2nd Lieut.

2516	COMPSTON, Paul	... ...	27/10/14	*1 Lieut. To Indian Army*
2591	SIMPSON, Henry Gordon	... ...	5/11/14	*1 Killed in action 14/6/15* ᛭

Special Reserve Battalions (Nos. 3 & 4).

762993 HARLEY, Mervyn Ruthven 26/ 9/17 *4*

Service Battalions (New Armies).

3652	PETTITT, Leonard Cecil ...	... 12/12/15	*9 Lieut.*
4217	SHANKEY, Eugene William ...	... 22/ 1/16	*6 Lieut.*
764177	ADAMS, Thomas James ...	... 31/ 7/17	*12* ✠ ✠ *w. 13/4/18, 15/11/18*
762496	ANDERSON, Ernest James ...	... 18/ 3/19	
768388	BAIRD, Robert	.. 17/ 3/19	
765498	BURY, William Gladstone ...	... 27/11/17	*12*
6494	CARMICHAEL, Evory William	... 7/ 7/16	*12*
761371	FINNIGAN, Francis ...	... 3/ 8/17	*7*
762754	HUGHES, Alfred Patrick ...	.. 28/ 8/17	*12 Wounded 20/9/18*
762634	LINDOP, Reginald Alexander Erskine	3/ 8/17	*7 Wounded 26/9/17*
765627	PURNELL, Augustine James ...	28/11/17	*12*
5419	ROBBINS, L/Cpl. Arthur Hodder ...	17/ 1/17	*8 Capt. & Adjt. K/A 22/3/18*
767089	STEWART, William	.. 17/ 3/19	
768627	STRAWBRIDGE, Robert	19/ 3/19	
762494	UNIACKE, Richard Haygate Fitzgerald	24/ 9/17	*12*
765748	WILSON, Alexander Gordon ...	21/ 2/18	*12(13) Killed in action 27/8/18*

THE ROYAL IRISH FUSILIERS
(PRINCESS VICTORIA'S).

Regular Battalions (Nos. 1 & 2).

87th Foot
89th Foot

2nd Lieut.

2000	LE MARE, Ralph ...	... ...	23/ 4/15	*1 Sp. emp. King's African Rifles*
2001	LE MARE, Reginald	... ...	11/ 6/15	*1 Lieut. Acc/wounded 10/7/15*

Special Reserve Battalions (Nos. 3 & 4).

1898	BIRD, Eric Stephen	... 9/10/15	*3(8) Killed in action 12/8/17*
7609	McGIBNEY, Francis George	... 10/11/16	*4(1) Killed in action 3/5/17*
1209	SUTTON, Geoffrey Alfred ...	... 7/ 7/16	*3 Wounded 14/8/15 K/A 27/11/17*

Service Battalions (New Armies).

765089	BENNETT, James	...	...	13/ 5/17	3/Garrison Battalion
764181	BEWSEY, John Charles	...	...	12/ 5/17	3/Garrison Battalion
762896	HESLOP, Gerald Edward	...	...	31/10/17	3/Garrison Battalion
764536	JONES, Cecil ...	...	...	12/ 5/17	3/Garrison Battalion

THE ROYAL IRISH REGIMENT.

Regular Battalions (Nos. 1 & 2.)   18th Foot

2nd Lieut.

1057	FORD, Royston Dearmer	...	14/ 2/15	1 *Killed in action* 15/3/15 ℳ
1280	O'FLYNN, Gerald ...	...	14/ 2/15	1 *Capt. M/G Officer*
2169	LYNAM, Edward W. O'Flaherty		26/ 5/15	1 *(1/R. Irish Rifles)*
3429	BARRY, Austin Cyril	...	7/11/16	2 *Lieut.*

Special Reserve Battalions (Nos. 3 & 4).

2354	BLANCKENZEE, Geoffrey E. S.	...	8/ 2/15	4' *Lieut.*
4323	HENNA, John Ramsay	...	1/ 1/16	3(6) *Killed in action* 9/9/16
7412	JONES, Herbert Joaquin	...	26/11/17	4(6) *D/W in Germany* 29/3/18

Service Battalions (New Armies).

768923	LETT, William Thomas Congley	...	15/ 2/19

*THE ROYAL IRISH RIFLES.

Regular Battalions (Nos. 1 & 2).   {83rd Foot / 86th Foot}

2nd Lieut.

1182	HELLMERS, Alfred ...	...	20/ 3/15	1 *Died of wounds* 11/5/15
1585	MEW, Gordon Morrison	...	3/ 3/15	1 *Wounded* 9/5/15
1006	PARKES, Herbert Percy	...	3/ 3/15	1 *w.* 9/5/15 *(Tank Corps) Capt.*
1519	SOULBY, Alfred Christopher...		3/ 3/15	1 *Lieut. Wounded* 26/4/15, 9/5/15
1663	WINDUS, Charles Eric	...	3/ 3/15	1 *Killed in action* 9/5/15
7132	DOHERTY, Patrick ...	...	3/ 4/17	1 *Died of wounds* 1/8/17
6797	ENNIS, Reginald Joseph	...	3/ 4/17	1 *Killed in action* 16/8/17
762261	STROHM, Edward Charles	...	30/ 5/17	*Prisoner of war* 15/5/18

* *Title changed (1st January, 1921) to " The Royal Ulster Rifles."*

Service Battalions (New Armies).

2233	MONAGHAN, Denis Lawrence	... 22/ 9/14	*15 (To Tank Corps) Lieut.* Bde. M/G O. K/A 24/11/17
764623	ADDY, Leonard	... 28/ 8/17	*17*
764604	BEVERIDGE, Reginald Frank	... 28/ 8/17	*18 Wounded 5/4/18*
764628	BRANFORD, John George	... 28/ 8/17	*19 Wounded 30/10/18*
764876	BROWN, William Charles	... 28/ 8/17	*20*
764831	HADDOCK, Joseph Henry	... 28/ 8/17	*14 Killed in action 24/3/18*
761565	HALLINAN, Charles	... 19/12/16	*17*
764651	KEMPSON, Horace Leopold	... 28/ 8/17	*20 Prisoner of war 16/5/18*
764654	LANE, Frank Stewart	... 28/ 8/17	*17*
768399	LONG, William Henry	... 17/ 3/19	
1209	SUTTON, Geoffrey Alfred	... 10/ 7/16	*Killed in action 27/11/17*

THE EAST KENT REGIMENT
(THE BUFFS).

Regular Battalions (Nos. 1 & 2). 3rd Foot

2nd Lieut.

1980	BOOTH, Frederick Atkins	... 12/ 6/15	*2 Killed in action 27/9/15*
2078	CAPPER, Athol Henry	... 15/ 8/15	*1 Lieut. Wounded 16/10/15*
1668	DANGERFIELD, Paul	... 23/ 4/15	*1 Lieut.* ✠ F/D (*M.G.C.*) *w. 27/6/15, —/5/16* 🎖
1428	FERGUSON, David Gordon	... 24/ 7/15	*1 Capt.* ✠ *w. 11/8/15, —/4/18* 🎖
1984	FORD, H. F. Paul	... 29/ 8/15	*1 Lieut.* 🎖
1863	FOX, Harry Gerald	... 4/11/14	*2 Capt. & Adjt. (4/Warwick)*
1901	GREIFFENHAGEN, Norman	... 15/ 8/15	*1 Died of wounds 22/12/15*
985	HILLS, Malcolm Arthur	... 29/ 8/15	*1 Killed in action 15/9/16*
1670	MOSS, Vincent Newton	... 23/ 4/15	*1 Lieut.* ✠✠ *w. 18/9/15, 26/10/18*
1990	SMITH, Ernest Kennedy	... 24/ 7/15	*1 Died of wounds 22/12/15*
2059	WILLIAMS, William Theophilus	... 11/ 6/15	*2 Lieut.* ✠ *Wounded 21/10/15* 🎖
5246	DAVIS, Percy Warren Theo.	... —/ 1/17	*1 Killed in action 30/3/17*
3660	GROOM, Charles Robin Napier	... 12/11/16	*1 (7/N. Staffs.)*
7878	OWEN, Philip Richard Tudor	... 9/11/16	*1 Wounded 15/12/17*

Special Reserve Battalion (No. 3).

764978	CHILVERS, Cpl. Joseph Ernest	... 1/ 5/18	*3* ✠ 🎖
7863	DIPLOCK, Ronald Marcus	... 26/ 1/17	*3(1)*
766606	LILLEY, John Leslie	... 29/ 5/18	*3(10)*
4395	PHILLIPS, Reginald Gurwen	... 7/ 7/16	*3(8) Killed in action 26/1/17*

Territorial Battalions (Nos. 4 & 5).

2536	D'OMBRAIN, Rowland Maund	...	25/ 9/14	5 (53rd Sikhs) K/A 8/3/16
2099	SANGSTER, Alfred William ...	...	17/11/14	4 Capt.
3211	SEALE, John Hector	...	2/ 4/15	4 Lieut.
2474	SWAINSON, Charles Grein D'Oye	...	22/ 9/15	4 Lieut.
7355	BANWELL, Frank Edward	...	19/12/16	4 Lieut.
5727	BREWER, Cyril Edward Stanislaus ...		11/ 7/16	5 Lieut. (R.E.)
767495	BUNN, Robert Frederick Ives	...	4/ 3/19	4
5757	GREENWOOD, L/Cpl. Frederick Wm.		11/ 7/16	5
765606	STEVENS, Douglas Harcourt	...	18/12/17	4 Killed in action 7/8/18
7990	WIDDOP, Arthur Norman	...	20/12/16	4 Lieut. Killed in action 30/9/18

Service Battalions (New Armies).

2155	CAESAR, Leslie Vernon	...	3/ 5/15	9 Lieut. Wounded 13/10/17
2725	HANDS, Joseph Garrett	...	7/12/14	9 Lieut.
2783	HARRISON, William Robert Eric	...	25/ 1/15	8 Capt. (R.A.F.) w.5/3/17 P/W
2034	HARVEY-JAMES, Arthur Keedwill	...	16/10/14	9 Capt. A.P.M. K/A 15/4/17
1902	HOBBES, Herbert Halliwell	...	20/10/14	7 Capt. (Labour Corps)
3651	Moss, Reginald Barnes Newton	...	3/ 5/15	8 Killed in action 7/10/16
2588	QUARTERMAINE, Harold Luxford	...	30/12/14	7 Lieut. (–/Manchester)
3374	SACKETT, Alexander Allen ...		3/ 5/15	8 Capt. A.M.F.O.
2593	SPENCER, Jenner Gray	...	30/12/14	7 Staff-Lieut. (R.A.F.)
4239	SMYTH, Cleveland St. John		20/ 9/15	9 Lieut.
3238	VARGO, Edward Henry	...	28/11/15	6 Lieut. Wounded –/3/16
768387	ALLEN, John Gwyn	...	30/ 3/19	
768037	BRENNAND, Eric William ...		6/ 3/19	
762384	BREWER, Francis Henry James	...	29/ 3/17	
767893	BRUDENELL, Clement Shenstone	...	4/ 3/19	
765159	Cox, Horace Rupert Burghall	...	24/ 5/18	Wounded 5/10/18
769593	CURWEN, Robert ...	...	5/ 2/19	
767557	DIXON, Sydney Fielding	...	4/ 3/19	
3155	GOOD, Christopher Frank	...	3/10/16	8 Lieut. Wounded 25/4/17
5584	JONES, Reginald Thomas	...	5/ 9/16	Wounded 1/10/18
768277	LEECH, Sydney Fuller	...	18/ 3/19	
767752	LUCK, Donald Henley	...	4/ 3/19	
766810	MCKENZIE-FOWLER, F. Learmouth		28/ 5/18	
767910	MARCHANT, Stephen George	...	5/ 3/19	
764338	PARRY, John Walter Granville		20/ 3/19	
767954	PLUNKETT, Donald William		6/ 3/19	
769049	PUNNETT, Arthur Hugh ...		5/ 2/19	
764041	READ, Edward Chapman ...		5/ 2/19	Wounded 31/10/17
768285	SANDYS, Albert Fedarb	...	17/ 3/19	
766979	SIMINSON, Bertram Donald Newton		12/11/18	
767117	TAYLOR, Ivan Maxwell	...	5/ 2/19	
763606	WARNER, Francis Edwin	...	26/ 4/17	6 Lieut.

THE ROYAL WEST KENT REGIMENT
(QUEEN'S OWN).

Regular Battalions (Nos. 1 & 2).

{50th Foot
97th Foot

2nd Lieut.

1977	BULLEN, Geoffrey	...	9/ 5/15	*I Lieut. Wounded*
1081	CARPENTER, Cpl. Alec Edward		9/ 5/15	*I Lieut. (M.G.C.) w. 27/6/15*
2570	FLEMING, Atholl Douglas	...	15/ 8/15	*I Lieut. Wounded –/8/17*
3094	FLEMING, John Alister	...	15/ 8/15	*I Died of wounds 22/7/16*
706	FROST, Cpl. Kenneth	...	27/ 1/15	*I Killed in action 22/2/15*
1298	LEATHERDALE, Donald Ryan	...	11/ 6/15	*I Lieut. Killed in action 22/7/16*
1771	PEACHEY, George Frederick	...	9/ 5/15	*I Lieut.*
1713	WALTERS, Robert S.	...	11/ 6/15	*I Lieut.*
1573	WHITE, Leslie Spencer	...	27/ 1/15	*I Acc/K (bomb throwing) 15/3/15*
763565	BROWN, Arthur George	...	31/ 7/17	*I Prisoner of war 17/9/18*
760933	DANIEL, Archibald Morris	...	28/ 6/17	*I Killed in action 4/10/17*
7447	GRAY, Harry Albert	...	19/12/16	✠ *Died of wounds 15/7/18*
760779	HILL, Percival Joseph	...	27/ 6/17	*I Wounded 26/10/18*
762068	LEISHMAN, William Green	...	27/ 6/17	*I*
5065	MANSFIELD, Frank Alfred	...	12/12/16	*I Lieut.*
8243	NURSE, William Ivan	...	25/ 1/17	*I Wounded 21/5/17, 11/10/17*
765147	WATTS, Percy Edward	...	31/10/17	*I*
765075	WINCH, Edward Nightingale	...	31/10/17	*I Died of wounds 9/10/18*

Special Reserve Battalion (No. 3).

1891	CRASTON, John	...	27/10/14	*3(I) Died of wounds 18/4/15*
2487	HALL, Wilfred B. Compton		13/ 1/15	*3 (To Norfolk Regt.) Lieut.*
2757	MANSFIELD, Francis Turquand		14/11/14	*3 (To R.E.) Lieut.* ✠ *(–/Middlesex)*
3329	STUART, William Esmé Montague	...	26/ 6/15	*3(6) Killed in action 7/10/16*
764625	ATTWOOLL, Frederick John	...	24/ 9/17	*3 Wounded 11/7/18*
4409	BULLMAN, Haddon Robert Horsley		7/ 7/16	*3 (M.G.C.) K/A 30/11/17*
763261	DANIEL, Kenneth Henry	...	1/ 8/17	*3(II) Wounded 27/9/18*
765682	HARRIS, Donald Charles Ainscombe		18/12/17	*3*
765306	JENKINS, William Victor	...	28/11/17	*3 Wounded 18/9/18*

Territorial Battalions (Nos. 4 & 5).

3380	LAZENBY, Bernard Walter	...	16/ 4/15	*5 Lieut. Wounded 4/10/18*
1896	HARTMAN, Carl Herbert	...	24/ 8/15	*5 Lieut.*
4163	MOORCROFT, William	...	20/11/15	*5 Lieut. Killed in action 2/7/18*
4147	NAUGHTON, John Joseph	...	20/11/15	*5 Lieut. Wounded 20/11/17*
1513	STEPHENS, Robert Miller	...	11/ 8/15	*5 Killed in action 27/9/18*
3823	VAUGHAN, Francis Seymour		1/10/15	*5 Lieut. (R.F.C.) K/A 7/3/18* 🎖
763809	ALLNUTT, Ernest Francis	...	30/ 5/17	*4*

767664	BRACKETT, Frederick J. Newbegin	5/ 3/19	4	
5731	CARTMELL, Robert Joseph Gregory	11/ 7/16	4	
763985	CLOQUET, John Sharpe Neale	31/ 7/17	4	
764431	GIBSON, Arthur John	31/ 7/17	4	*Wounded* 19/9/18
762049	LONG, Bertram Ernest	25/ 9/17	4	*Prisoner of war* 17/5/18
762757	MABEY, Cyril Doublet	1/ 5/18	5	
762684	MAXEY, Percy	26/ 6/17	4	*Wounded* 7/1/18
760240	MEATES, Gerald Mayo	26/ 4/17	4	
765952	NOTT, Percy James	27/ 2/18	4	*Wounded* 15/10/18
763734	TERRY, Thomas Edward Reynolds	30/ 5/17	4	

Service Battalions (New Armies).

3114	BROWNLEE, Frank	5/12/15	6	*Lieut. Wounded* –/11/16
2266	COOKSEY, Philip Thomas	3/10/15	8	*Lieut. w.* –/9/16, 19/9/17
3206	COOMBS, Claude Stuart	24/10/15	6	*Wounded* –/3/16 D/W 6/7/16
4885	DONALDSON, Alfred James	25/ 5/16	9	*Lieut.* ✠ ℞
1944	DOVE, Sydney Ernest	3/10/15	8	*Killed in action*, 16/8/16
2026	FLEMING, James Scott	13/ 5/15	9	*Capt. & Adj. w.* 17/10/18
4599	HOLROYD, Vivian Hutchence	25/ 5/16	9	*Capt.* ℞
2821	MARSH, Clifford Henry	14/11/14	9	*Lieut.*
2674	PURVER, Bernard Arthur	16/10/14	11	*Lieut.*
2329	SMITH, Stanley Bayliss	3/10/15	8	*Lieut.*
2281	STONEHAM, Gerald Towell	2/12/14	8	*Lieut.*
3372	VAUGHAN, Richard Creswell	17/ 6/15	9	*Killed in action* 16/4/17
2296	WADE, Ralph	14/10/14	9	*Lieut.* ℞
1945	WENYON, Herbert J.	3/10/15	8	*Lt.-Col.* D.S.O. AND BAR F/D(2) }
4330	WOODCOCK, Humphrey Neville H.	25/ 5/16	9	*Lieut.* ✠ *w.* 18/9/18 [℞(2) }
761375	ABEL, James Edgar	14/ 9/17	6	✠ *Died of wounds* 22/12/17
7224	ALLCHIN, Sydney Milton	21/12/16	3	*Killed in action* 13/12/17
762637	ADDISON, Charles Rattray	1/ 7/17		*Lieut.*
760753	BERNARD, Henry Fitzgerald Wilson	12/ 4/17	11	*Wounded* 14/10/18
767481	BOLES, Ralph Podmore	13/ 3/18	52	
7709	BROCK, Reginald Lewis	5/ 9/16		(9/L.N. Lancs.)
769107	BROWNE, Owen Henry Gill	15/ 2/19		
769420	BULL, William George	17/ 3/19		
4982	CARTER, Henry Seaman	12/ 4/17	11	*Lieut.* ℞
4992	CHEEL, Edgar Stacey	19/12/16		✠ *To Labour Corps*
761683	CHURCHWARD, Leonard	4/ 8/17	10	*Wounded* 21/8/17
764288	CLARIDGE, William Stanley	1/ 8/17	11	*Wounded* 13/9/18
7213	CLELAND-HOLLAMBY, D. Macdonel	19/12/16		
7214	CLELAND-HOLLAMBY, Reginald C.	19/12/16		
761321	COOPER, Thomas Frederick	4/ 8/17	10	
763570	COWPER, Reginald Hugh	29/ 3/17		
763383	CRIGHTON, John Stafford	1/ 8/17	8	*Wounded & P/W* 6/4/18
4970	CROWE, Francis Michael	12/ 4/17	8	
763550	DADD, Thomas Ewart	27/ 6/17	11	
5746	DAVISON, Herbert William	7/ 7/16	9	

ROYAL WEST KENT (S/B)

3692	DEAN, Donald John	... ...	4/10/16	*11* **V.C.** *w.* 12/3/17, 10/10/17, 25/10/18
767483	FITCH, Isaac Foster	...	13/ 8/18	*52*
3674	FRICKER, Edwin ...	...	31/ 7/16	*7 Killed in action,* 29/9/16
4971	FULLER, Thomas ...	...	24/ 1/17	*6 Wounded* 25/4/17
762664	GAINS, Alfred Thomas	...	28/ 3/17	
764984	GARBUTT, John Restarick	...	30/10/17	*(1)* ✠ *Wounded* 28/6/18
768056	GARRETT, Arthur William	...	18/ 3/19	
762607	GODDARD, Wilfred John	...	31/ 7/17	*7* ✠ *Wounded* 4/2/18
768181	GOODE, Geoffrey Hamilton	...	17/ 3/19	
761648	GREEN, Henry James	...	27/ 6/17	*10 Lieut. Wounded* 31/7/17
5496	GREENWOOD, James Hurst	...	24/ 1/17	*11* ✠ *Died of wounds* 24/7/18
769345	GROUT, Maurice Henry .	...	5/ 2/19	
763199	HARDING, Victor Robert	...	26/ 9/17	*Wounded* 20/5/18
765769	HAYNE, Robert Luscombe	...	19/ 7/18	*(1)*
760943	HODGE, Lionel Clifford	...	3/ 8/17	*6 Killed in action* 30/11/17 ℞
5088	HOLMES, Markwell ...	...	12/ 4/17	*8*
768345	HUNT, Edward Gowers	...	3/ 2/19	
761182	JOHNSON, Holland Sydney Vincent		26/ 6/17	*10*
6622	JONES, Thomas Philip	...	26/ 9/16	*7*
4794	KEATES, Bertie ...	...	24/ 1/17	*6*
767719	KENTSBEER, Harry Robert	...	3/ 3/19	
767463	LANE, Gerald Bernard	...	5/ 2/19	
763163	LEDGER, Arthur Percy	...	26/ 4/17	*(10) Wounded* 13/8/17
762337	MICHELL, Arthur Charles	...	3/ 8/17	*7 Killed in action* 12/10/17
764789	OWEN, Gerald Albert	...	24/ 5/18	
7499	PARKER, Thomas Cecil	...	5/ 9/16	*(7/L.N. Lancs.)*
761034	PHILLIPS, John Robert	...	26/ 4/17	*Wounded & P/W* 18/9/18
768016	PILCHER, Walter ...	...	12/ 2/19	
761277	RICHARDSON, Arthur Balfour	...	25/ 6/17	*8 Killed in action* 21/3/18
3199	ROBERTS, Thomas William	...	31/ 7/16	*7 Killed in action* 30/9/16
3350	ROCHAT, Roy Richard	...	2/ 8/16	*8 Wounded* 15/10/16
4832	RODNEY, Burnett William	...	12/ 4/17	*11 Killed in action* 20/4/17
3720	SMITH, Kingsley Thompson	...	4/10/16	*11*
762729	STANLEY, Tom Harold	...	27/ 6/17	*(8)*
769030	STREETER, Sidney Augustus	...	14/ 2/19	
767195	TAYLOR, John ...	...	5/ 2/19	
768494	THOMPSON, Edward Robert	...	3/ 2/19	
761311	TRURAN, William Frank James	...	26/ 6/17	*10*
7165	VICKER, Reginald Charles Godwin		19/12/16	*(M.G.C.)*
766538	VINNICOMBE, Thomas Hurst	...	26/ 6/18	*(R.A.F.)*
5228	WATERHOUSE, Gilbert Wilmot	...	24/ 1/17	*6 Died of wounds* 10/4/17
7189	WESTCOTT, Edmund Joseph	...	21/12/16	
767292	WHARTON, Thomas Rowland L. J.		6/ 3/19	
768523	WILLIAMS, Gilbert ...	...	15/ 2/19	
767274	WILD, Frederick Newbury	...	5/ 2/19	
768358	WILKS, Thomas Neate Barford	...	18/ 3/19	
4863	WOODYEAR, Reginald Percy	...	25/ 2/17	*7 Lieut.* ✠ F/D
767119	YORK, William Alfred	...	5/ 2/19	

*THE KING'S ROYAL RIFLE CORPS.

Regular Battalions (Nos. 1, 2, 3 & 4).

60th Foot

		2nd Lieut.	
1132	Addy, Kenneth James Balguy	3/ 3/15	1 Killed in action 3/10/15
1122	Cassidy, Cyril Martin	23/ 4/15	1 Died of wounds 17/5/15
1024	Croft-Smith, Edwin Spencer	5/ 4/15	4 Killed in action 8/5/15
1134	Crook, Francis William	23/ 4/15	2 Lieut. Wounded 9/5/15
1398	Hall, Lionel Everard	3/ 3/15	1 Lieut. ✠ w. 28/9/15, –/2/16 ᴍ
1708	Hardy, Cyril Ernest	3/ 3/15	1 Lieut. Wounded 18/5/15
1827	Haynes, Charles Graham	5/ 4/15	4 Lieut. ✠✠ (R.A.F.) w. 8/5/15
1287	Hodgkinson, Robert John	5/ 4/15	4 Lieut. Wounded 10/5/15
1700	Hughes, Thomas McKenny	11/ 6/15	2 Lieut. (R.F.C.) K/A 5/2/18 ᴍ
1336	James, John Stephen Harvey	3/ 3/15	1 Killed in action 16/5/15
1709	Morris, Clive Wilson	23/ 4/15	2 Killed in action 9/5/15
1633	Parker, Frederick Neville	3/ 3/15	1 Acc/Killed 28/4/15
1562	Taylor, Leslie Francis	3/ 3/15	1 Lieut. ✠ (M.G.C.) w. 25/5/15 Killed in action 27/5/18
6647	Hamilton, Reginald Beaumont	12/11/16	1
7137	Taylor, David Henry	19/12/16	2 Prisoner of war 3/9/17

Special Reserve Battalions (Nos. 5 & 6).

3326	Bulkeley-Hughes, George M. W.	16/ 6/15	6 Capt. w. 3/9/16 K/A 27/2/17
3058	Paul, Edgar Newton	16/ 6/15	6 Capt. Killed in action 27/12/17
1400	d'Argenton, Hugh	16/ 5/15	5(4) Lieut.
765756	Biggs, John Heron Egerton	27/ 2/18	6 (R.F.C.)
762736	Cross, Leonard William Alan	27/ 2/18	6
767803	Culver, Norman John	5/ 3/19	5
765537	Farey, Philip Noel Meredith	27/ 2/18	6(18) Wounded 18/9/18
762551	Slingsby, Henry Victor	26/ 4/17	5(1) Wounded 2/4/18
6627	Smerdon, Harold Escott	22/11/16	6 Lieut. (I.A.) Wounded 14/6/17

Service Battalions (New Armies).

2060	Arnold, L/Cpl. Bernard Marcus	19/ 9/15	7 Died of wounds 6/2/16
2561	Bird, Stanley Treadgold	19/ 9/15	7 Died of wounds 20/8/16
222	Bourdillon, Thomas Lous	6/ 3/15	8 Major ✠ w. 30/7/15, –/8/16 } Killed in action 24/8/17
2516	Compston, Paul	27/10/14	15 Lieut. (1/Inniskg.) w. 9/6/15
2410	Cooke, Philip Andrew	28/11/15	8 Staff-Capt. ✠ O.B.E.
2712	Deedes, Herbert Phillip	24/ 9/15	16 Capt. & Adjt. K/A 16/7/16
2326	Edwards, Reginald Owen	24/10/14	16 Major O.B.E. Wounded ᴍ
2359	Evans, Rhys David	12/12/15	10 Lieut. Interned in Holland
3485	Farran, Charles	28/11/15	9 Killed in action 24/8/16
2265	Findlay, John Wilfred	22/12/14	14 Capt.

*Title changed (1st January, 1921) to "The King's Royal Rifles."

2340	HAMILTON, Claude William	...	28/11/15	10 (R.G.A.) Wounded –/6/16 Killed in action 6/11/16
1464	HILLAS-DRAKE, Robert Fitz-Hill		23/ 2/15	10 Lieut. Acc/wounded 19/10/15
2074	HOWELL, John	...	11/12/14	15 Killed in action 25/9/15
3560	HAYHURST, Christopher	...	12/12/15	11 Lieut.
2197	MACKINLEY, David Murray		19/ 9/15	8 Capt. Wounded –/12/15
3110	NESLING, Robert Edward	...	28/11/15	8 Lieut.
1998	PRICE, Kenneth Dodds		12/12/15	11 Lieut. Wounded –/9/16
2447	RANALOW, Arthur Vivian	...	28/11/15	10 Lieut.
2759	ROGERS, Robert Murray	...	19/ 9/15	8 Lieut. Killed in action 2/7/16
2116	SCOTT, Charles Edell	...	19/ 9/15	8 Lieut. ✠ Wounded 3/7/16 ☒
4316	COOK, Percy Mellows	...	8/ 3/16	18 Capt. Killed in action 4/10/16
4150	CHRISTMAS, Edwin Cecil Russell	...	8/ 3/16	18 Capt. Killed in action 7/10/16
4216	CRICK, Thomas Henry	...	8/ 3/16	18 Lieut. Wounded –/9/16
4382	EELES, George Nixon	...	11/ 3/16	18 Lieut.
4319	FRYER, Thomas James Harold	...	8/ 3/16	18 Lieut. Wounded
4224	LANGFORD, John Joseph	...	8/ 3/16	18 Killed in action 15/9/19
4231	LANGFORD, Wallace George		8/ 3/16	18 Died of wounds 27/6/16
4280	LAYCOCK, Joseph Harris	...	8/ 3/16	18 Killed in action 17/10/16
4298	MALE, Sidney John	...	8/ 3/16	23 Capt ✠ w. 3/9/16, 21/11/17,
4617	NIVISON, L/Cpl. Robert Butler	...	25/ 5/16	15 Lieut. K/A 5/9/16 [5/9/18
4255	RIDGWAY, William	...	9/ 3/16	18 Killed in action 7/10/16
4444	RUTHERFORD, William Francis	...	8/ 3/16	18 Lieut.
4778	TURNER, Alfred James	...	2/ 6/16	22 Lieut.
4643	WALLIS, William Mayne	...	25/ 5/16	22 Lieut. Wounded 13/9/18
4623	YATEMAN, L/Cpl. Frederick William		25/ 5/16	15 Lieut.
768203	ARMITAGE, Lindley Robertson	...	17/ 3/19	
762885	BAKER, Frank Vincent	...	28/ 3/17	21 Killed in action 22/3/18
762948	BARRETT, Arthur Edmund		28/ 3/17	8 Lieut. Killed in action 23/8/17
763019	BEIGHTON, John Durrant Kennedy		28/ 3/17	21 Wounded 15/8/17 P/W 6/5/18
762950	BRENNAN, Francis King	...	28/ 3/17	8
4981	CALDER, William Paul		12/11/16	18 Killed in action 14/6/17
8199	CARR, Cedric Errol	...	19/12/16	13 Wounded 13/8/17, 10/9/18
764817	CHART, Eric	...	30/ 5/17	21 Wounded 3/10/17
762057	CLARKE, Alfred Stanley	...	29/ 3/17	
4530	COOK, Herbert Henry Marston	...	7/ 7/16	22 (M.G.C.)
762717	CRABTREE, Mannhew Boulton	...	28/ 3/17	21 Wounded 23/8/17
764689	DAVIS, Melville Allen Duff	...	30/ 5/17	9 ✠ Died 29/5/18
4317	DEER, John Hartley	...	8/ 1/16	14 ✠ ☒
768439	DIXON, Geoffrey Lloyd	...	17/ 3/19	
5899	FARNAN, Alfred Walter	...	7/ 7/16	22 Wounded –/9/16
7011	FORD, Frank Beeton	...	1/ 5/17	12
4485	GAWTHROP, William Oliver		24/ 1/17	12 Lieut. Wounded 5/12/17
2979	GRAY, George Sidney	...	7/ 7/16	24 (M.G.C.)
769310	HAWES, Edward Montague	...	19/ 2/19	
767971	HAWKINS, Donald M. Culworth		6/ 3/19	

KING'S ROYAL RIFLES (S/B).

768182	HILTON, Richard Byron	... 17/ 3/19			
767835	JAMES, Ernest Livingstone	... 3/ 3/19			
766387	KENDALL, Frederick John	... 5/ 2/19			
4389	KING, Jack Terence	... 5/ 9/16		w. 8/10/17 P/W –/1/18 🎖	
5513	KNOWLES-BROWN, Frank Henry	... 24/ 1/17	12	Lieut. Wounded 15/3/17	
6488	LAMBERT, Robert	... 24/ 1/17	12		
762858	LANGSTON, Herbert Pembridge	... 29/ 3/17	18	(R.E.) Wounded 21/11/17	
5267	LEIGH, Herbert Gordon	... 7/ 7/16	22	Lieut. To R.E. w. –/8/16,⎱	
768372	LOCKIE, Leslie Powell Deverill	... 18/ 3/19		[17/5/18]⎰	
763695	LOWRIE, William Arthur	... 30/ 5/17	20	Wounded 30/10/17	
6229	MARRIOTT, Hugh Bowyer	... 13/ 4/17	17	Wounded 5/10/18	
763204	MATHER, Harold George	... 28/ 3/17	16		
767672	McCONACHY, John Lawrence	... 6/ 3/19			
763306	McKING, Eric	... 25/ 9/17	11	Killed in action 24/3/18	
7117	MOLYNEUX, James Herbert	... 18/ 3/17	12	Killed in action 16/8/17	
763589	MORANT, John Gambier	... 30/ 5/17			
6810	MUNSEY, William Frederick	... 18/ 3/17	12	Killed in action 16/8/17	
6116	NICOL, George Galway	... 26/ 9/16			
7253	PAGE, Frederick James	... 19/12/16	16	Lieut. Wounded 4/5/17	
1981	PALMER, Walter William	... 19/ 9/15		Capt. Wounded –/9/16 🎖	
767369	PENDRED, Wilfred Allen	... 5/ 2/19			
6578	PENTY, Norman	... 26/ 9/16	8	Lieut.	
763938	PRIOR, Edwin George	... 16/ 6/17	10	Prisoner of war 15/1/18 🎖	
3157	PULLINGER, Charles Edward	... 2/10/16	✠	Wounded 23/4/17, 13/9/17	
764506	ROGERS, Geo. Thomas Henry	... 28/ 8/17			
766145	RUSSELL, Luther Maurice	... 26/ 3/18	51	(R.B.)	
768215	SCANTLEBURY, John Ernest	... 17/ 3/19			
767001	SHARP, Thomas Hicks	... 3/ 3/19			
1107	SIMPSON, Rolf	... 26/ 9/16	18	Killed in action 26/5/17	
6487	SMITH, Herbert Leslie	... 12/11/16	10	Lieut. Wounded 18/10/18	
762768	SPARKE, Lionel Frank	... 28/ 3/17	21	Lieut. Wounded 11/8/17	
761420	SUGDEN, John Reginald	... 27/ 2/18			
5552	TAYLOR, William Henry	... 18/ 3/17	12		
762847	THACKERAY-TURNER, Ernest	... 28/ 3/17	8		
762512	VILLIERS, Arthur Henry	... 29/ 5/18			
768130	WALKER, Charles Valentine	... 17/ 3/19			
1825	WALLIS, Douglas McGregor	... 24/11/16		Wounded 17/2/17	
767840	WARD, William Harry	... 5/ 3/19			
7803	WARHAM, Joseph	... 26/ 1/17	8	Died of Wounds 7/5/17	
762495	WELLS, Sydney Archibald	... 21/10/17	12		
5299	WELTER, Leslie Dingman	... 13/ 4/17	17	Killed in action 18/6/17	
766540	WEST, Leslie Challoner	... 26/ 6/18	12	Emp. Min. of Labour	
761107	WILDING, Leonard Scrivener	... 27/ 3/18			
7099	WILLIAMSON, Kenneth Harper	... 4/ 1/17	7	Died of wounds 19/4/17	
762397	WILLIS, George Henry	... 26/ 4/17	11	Prisoner of war 17/1/18 🎖	
762464	WOODHOUSE, William Joseph	... 26/ 4/17			
6937	WORTHY, Sydney	... 5/ 9/16	9		

THE LANCASHIRE FUSILIERS.

Regular Battalions (Nos. 1 & 2).
20th Foot
2nd Lieut.
1378	GRANGER, Ernest Everys Wyatt	...	3/ 3/15	2 Capt. w. 9/7/15, –/5/16 K/A
1335	STANWELL, William Alexander	...	26/ 5/15	2 D/W 9/7/15 [16/8/17 ⚔]
1935	PARKER, Edward Thompson	...	18/12/14	(1) Killed in action 16/11/15
763317	BATHURST, Alan		29/ 3/17	
764884	DOYLE, William Francis	...	29/ 8/17	Wounded 22/4/18
4130	GLASS, Leonard George	...	19/12/16	2 Killed in action 9/10/17
763182	HUCKLEBRIDGE, Percy Alwyne	...	1/ 3/17	1 Wounded 3/5/18

Special Reserve Battalions (Nos. 3 & 4).

2703	EDWARDS, Eric David	...	10/ 3/15	3 Lieut. Wounded –/7/16
2798	LUCAS, John Kenneth	...	29/10/15	4 Lieut.
765379	ARMSTRONG, Richard Walder	...	1/ 8/17	4 (M.G.C.)
764289	CLARKE, Alfred Lord	...	1/ 8/17	3 Killed in action, 27/3/18
6757	EDGHILL, Ashley Gay	...	26/ 9/16	4 Capt. ✠ (T.M.B.) D/W 15/4/18
5621	GLASON, John Apollonious	...	4/ 9/16	4(16) Wounded 28/6/18
6005	HARDIE, William		19/12/16	4(13) Died of wounds 18/4/17
6202	INGLETON, Herbert John	...	26/ 9/16	4(8) Died of wounds 2/11/18
8075	JONES, Clifford Ernest	...	7/ 7/16	4 Wounded 18/11/17
762334	KIRCHNER, Leo George	...	26/ 4/17	3(1) Lieut. Wounded 9/10/17
6475	PIPER, Norman		4/ 9/16	4 Wounded 9/9/18 ⚔
766210	ROBSON, Leslie H. ...		26/ 3/18	3 Wounded 10/9/18
6236	RUSHMORE, Ernest Reginald	...	4/ 9/16	4(11) Killed in action 6/9/17
764568	WALKER, Arthur Stanley	...	28/ 8/17	4

Territorial Battalions (No. 5 to 8).

Major	SHIRLEY, Herbert J., C.M.G., T.D.	...	9/ 6/15	5 Lt.-Col. Commdg. ⚔
2801	LUPTON, Leonard		3/10/14	8 (To 3/R. Lancaster) Lieut.
4758	ANDREWS, Reginald	...	2/ 6/16	7 Lieut. Killed in action 31/7/17
3484	ANONI, Arthur Frank	...	17/11/15	5 Lieut.
3743	BAINBRIDGE, Thomas	...	6/ 8/15	6 Lieut.
4717	BARTON, Edwin William	...	2/ 6/16	5 Lieut. Died 27/4/17
3940	BASELEY, Albert Lawrence	...	6/12/15	6 Lieut. Killed in action 11/8/17 ⚔
4002	BATTOCK, Thomas William	...	22/12/15	5 Lieut.
4771	BEESLEY, L/Cpl. Herbert ...		2/ 6/16	5 Lieut. ✠ Wounded 13/8/17 ⚔
3668	BELL, Guy Bayford	...	17/11/15	5 Lieut. M.G.C. K/A 28/4/17
3798	BEST, George Hubert Thomas	...	6/ 8/15	(5) Lieut.
3943	BOBY, Robert Sydney Pearce	...	10/12/15	6 Lieut. F/D
4335	BRAENDLE, Henry August ...		21/ 1/16	8 Lieut. Wounded –/8/16
3799	CRAN, Charles Robert	...	6/ 8/15	5 Capt. (14/York & Lancs.)
3901	CROKER, Frederick Reginald	...	6/12/15	6 R.F.C. Killed in action 27/4/17
3413	CROUCH, Cpl. Frank Harris	...	3/12/15	5 Capt. ✠ K/A 21/3/18

LANCASHIRE FUSILIERS (T/F).

4695	EWING, Cpl. John Hawkins	2/ 6/16	7 Capt.	Wounded 21/1/17
4747	GODFREY, L/Cpl. Henry	2/ 6/16	5 Lieut.	Killed in action 9/9/16
4235	GRIFFITHS, Herbert Plowman J.	1/ 1/16	8 Lieut.	
3897	HOWARD, Horace Herbert Walters	6/12/15	8 Lieut.	
4003	JACOB, Claude Goddard	22/12/15	8 Lieut.	
2244	KIRK, Cpl. Kenworth Linton	11/ 9/15	7 Lieut.	Prisoner of war 25/4/18
4719	KNIGHT, Edward James	16/ 6/16	7 Lieut.	Killed in action 12/5/17
2521	LAMBERT, L/Cpl. Cecil Osmond	30/ 7/15	(5) Lieut.	4/London 𝕄
4762	LAWRIE, Thomas	2/ 6/16	5 Lieut.	
3921	LEE, L/Cpl. Edwin James	6/12/15	8 Lieut.	Wounded –/12/16 𝕄
3910	MORDECAI, Cpl. Leslie Roy	29/11/15	5 Capt.	Wounded 13/7/17 𝕄
4173	MOULDEY, Walter Edwin	6/12/15	6 Lieut.	Wounded 25/6/16 𝕄
3496	PETTIT, L/Cpl. Leonard Henry	15/12/15	8 Lieut.	
3960	PROCTER, George Henry Vincent	6/12/15	8 Lieut.	Killed in action 6/9/17
4369	ROE, Alfred	27/11/15	7 Lieut.	✠ 𝕄
3498	ROWLANDS, L/Cpl. John Walter	17/12/15	7 Lieut.	
3964	SCURLOCK, Stephen John	6/12/15	8 Lieut. ✠	Wounded 24/10/17 𝕄
2521	SMIRKE, Cpl. Edwin Alexander	11/ 9/15	7 Capt. ✠	Wounded 18/4/18 𝕄
4289	SPINK, Edward Wodehouse	20/12/15	7 Lieut.	Killed in action 23/10/18
3968	SPRINGBETT, Sydney Arthur	22/12/15	8 Lieut.	
4228	STURT, Humphrey Morriston	22/12/15	8 Lieut.	Died 17/1/18
4269	SWEENEY, Ronan Linley	17/12/15	8 Lieut.	
3748	TWEEDY, Charles Francis	17/11/15	5 Lieut.	Killed in action 9/10/17
3632	UNGER, Frederick Audley	17/11/15	5 Lieut.	
4405	WELDON, Henry Arthur C. Bowers	22/12/15	7 Lieut.	𝕄
3929	YOUNG, Harold Francis	7/12/15	6 Lieut.	
763941	ADDIE, Robert Leathem	31/ 7/17	5	Killed in action 20/11/17
764482	CHADWICK, Wilfred	31/ 7/17	6	Wounded 11/5/18
1170	ESSEX, Percy Clifford	9/ 7/16	5	Killed in action 9/9/16
5370	JACKSON, John Henry	11/ 7/16	5	Killed in action 9/9/16
764621	LOVELL, Edward Caton	28/ 8/17	5	Killed in action 12/11/17
762685	MOORE, Charles Christopher	28/ 8/17	(6) ✠	Prisoner of war 25/4/18
6474	MUCKLOW, Stuart Leslie	26/ 9/16	5 Lieut.	
765737	STABLER, Athol William Edward	27/ 2/18	8	Wounded 12/10/18
3645	THOROGOOD, Edward Linford	2/12/15	8 Lieut.	Killed in action 3/9/18
763630	TRUESDALE, Reginald	26/ 4/17	6	Wounded 18/4/18
288	WALKER, Richard	20/ 6/16	5	Killed in action 9/8/16
764860	WATKIN, Ernest Walter	29/ 8/17	7	
766738	WHITWORTH, Walter Haworth	24/ 5/18	7	Died of wounds 14/9/18
4872	WILLIAMS, Claude S. Maur	4/ 8/16	5 Lieut.	
763221	WORTHINGTON, James	31/ 7/17	7	

Service Battalions (New Armies).

1232	BARNS, Howard Martin	24/ 3/15	18 Lieut.	Wounded –/5/16
761627	BELL, Cecil Charles	5/ 8/17	16	Killed in action 28/11/17
762347	BURNS, David Graham	26/ 4/17	16 Lieut.	

768414	CHADWICK, James Blackwell	5/ 2/19	
762361	CHALLIS, Ivor James	26/ 4/17	11 Killed in action 14/4/18
766218	CHARLTON, George James	26/ 3/18	52
767358	COAKLEY, John	5/ 2/19	
763258	COLLINGE, James	28/ 3/17	10 Lieut. Wounded 19/8/17
767905	EATOUGH, John Oliver	5/ 3/19	
763152	EILBECK, William Arthur	26/ 4/17	Wounded 26/7/17
767041	ELLAMS, George Ernest	3/ 2/19	
763180	GRELLIER, Arthur Berteau	28/ 8/17	Killed in action 26/3/18
763453	HALL, Philip Henry	28/ 3/17	10
763300	HARRIS, Hubert Alfred	29/ 3/17	20 Lieut.
768832	HENNESSY, John James	17/ 3/19	
764891	HEYWOOD, Harry	28/ 8/17	
765827	HOLGATE, Leonard George	13/ 3/18	Wounded 11/9/18
763931	JAMIESON, John	31/ 7/17	9(16) Killed in action 3/4/18
761547	MACFARLANE, Donald Murray	23/ 6/17	19 ✠
760860	MARRVAT, Hugh Palliser	23/ 6/17	19
766977	MAUDSLEY, Hugh Pearson	5/ 3/19	
765795	MICKLETHWAITE, Tom Dudley Aspey	21/ 2/18	(2)
768374	MILLER, James	3/ 2/19	
764374	MILLER, John Bernard	24/ 9/17	
769300	MORRELL, Patrick Frank Arthur	14/ 3/19	
760861	MOSS, Gordon Owen	23/ 6/17	19
763433	O'GARR, John William	28/ 3/17	19 Emp. Min. of Munitions
7611	OGDEN, George Sidney	19/12/16	Lieut. Wounded 19/4/18
769242	PARKER, Alexander Henderson	2/ 2/19	
5529	PARRY, Samuel Hindley Ascroft	18/ 3/17	18 Capt. Wounded 28/10/18
1925	PRESCOTT, Reginald Julius	18/ 3/17	18 Killed in action 15/4/17
764719	RIGBY, Daniel Francis	28/ 8/17	
766619	RILEY, Leonard	17/ 3/19	
7974	RILEY, Paul	19/12/16	(8) Killed in action 10/10/17
7264	ROBERTS, Frederick Arthur Donkin	19/12/16	18 Lieut. ✠ ℳ
763798	ROSE, Eric William	28/ 8/17	2 ✠ Killed in action 5/4/18
5218	SKELTON, Henry	18/ 3/17	11 Wounded 1/5/18 K/A 2/10/18
5666	SMEARDON, Ernest Noel	19/12/16	Lieut.
764912	SMITH, Herbert Dudley	28/ 8/17	Killed in action 17/3/18
762915	SMITH, James Reginald	24/ 9/17	Lieut.
7296	STEAD, Horace Stuart	19/12/16	9 Killed in action 23/3/18
764211	TIMSON, Frank Arthur	1/ 8/17	Wounded 10/5/18
760832	TRESTRAIL, Lawrie	23/ 6/17	
767732	WALKER, Frank Benjamin	19/ 3/19	
765819	WILLIAMS, Bertram Allen	13/ 3/18	
8084	WINGROVE, William Edward	25/ 1/17	Emp. Min. of Munitions
7285	WRIGHT, George St. John	19/12/16	(2)

THE EAST LANCASHIRE REGIMENT.

Regular Battalions (Nos. 1 & 2). {30th Foot. 59th Foot.}

No.	Name	Date	Bn.	Notes
Lieut.	Byrne, Alan Walter	2/6/15 2nd lieut.	1	Capt. Wounded 18/6/15
1483	Bull, Joseph William	10/7/15	2	(To R.E.) D/W 1/10/16
2205	Clarke, John Moulding	11/6/15	1	Lieut. (10/Som.L.I.) Min. of Lab.
1667	Ellen, Eric Adrian	10/7/15	2	Capt. Killed in action 30/1/17
2069	Hatfield, Frederick Edmund	26/5/15	1	Capt. Wounded –/12/15, –/7/16
1828	Henderson, Ernest J.	20/3/15	2	Capt. D.S.O. ✠ w. 9/5/15, 25/3/18
1109	Howell, Herbert Edgar	20/3/15	2	Killed in action 9/5/15 [M]
2011	Jones, Kenneth Champion	10/7/15	1	Wounded 8/1/16 K/A 1/7/16
2038	Keable, Benjamin	10/7/15	2	Lieut. Wounded 26/7/15
1904	Mallett, Eric Sydney	10/7/15	1	Killed in action 1/7/16
1073	Marshall, Sgt. Augustus de la Poer	20/3/15	2	Killed in action 9/5/15
1914	Marshall, John Hamilton	24/7/15	2	Wounded –/3/16 K/A 23/10/16
1113	Nevill, Eric	20/3/15	2	Lieut. Wounded 26/7/15
1873	Newcombe, Richard	26/5/15	1	Capt. M.G.O. K/A 1/7/16
1520	Norton, Alfred George	20/3/15	2	Killed in action 9/5/15
1994	Reynolds, David	10/7/15	1	Lieut.
1217	Thomas, Heinrich W. M.	11/6/15	1	Capt. Killed in action 1/7/16
1219	Wheate, Arthur	11/6/15	1	Wounded –/5/15 D/W 5/4/16
762514	Bromfield, Frank Larden	26/4/17	1	✠
763120	Bramwell, James	30/5/17	1	
764275	Taylor, Stephen	28/8/17	1	
6774	Thompson, Jacob Cyril	26/9/16	2	

Special Reserve Battalion (No. 3).

No.	Name	Date	Bn.	Notes
6814	O'Meara, Leon Alfred	6/8/16	3(6)	Killed in action 6/2/17

Territorial Battalions (Nos. 4 & 5).

No.	Name	Date	Bn.	Notes
3992	Boswell, L/Cpl. Claude Oliver	17/12/15	5	Killed in action 9/10/17
4042	Foster, Reginald Frank	17/12/15	5	Lieut. w. 26/5/17 Ind. Army
3994	Farrow, L/Cpl. Alfred	22/12/15	4	Lieut. (2/5 L Fus.) w. 12/8/18,
4079	Gray, George Sinclair	22/12/15	4	Lieut (M.G.C.) [30/8/18]
4159	Hampshire, Stanley	22/12/15	4	Killed in action 9/10/17
4122	Long, Thomas Drildord	22/12/15	4	Lieut. [M]
4028	McCormick, L/Cpl. Harry	17/12/15	5	Died of wounds as P/W 8/5/17
4099	Phillips, Percy Alfred	27/12/15	4	Lieut. w. 15/8/17 P/W 23/4/18
4207	Spicer, Edward Masters	22/12/15	4	Lieut. ✠ P/W 3/5/18
3915	Thompson, George Kenneth	17/12/15	5	Capt. ✠ ✠
3193	Wernham, Herbert Fuller	25/11/15	5	
6883	Bamber, Donald William Bewsher	11/7/16	4	Wounded 13/8/17
762734	Bartlett, Frederick Harold	28/8/17	4	
4002	Battock, Thomas William	22/12/15	5	Lieut. Killed in action 21/3/18
763876	Dutton, Vincent Joseph	28/8/17	(4)	
765943	Holdsworth, Harry	24/5/18	4	✠

764967	Morgan, William Llewellyn	...	31/10/17	5
6590	Morris, William Alexander	...	26/ 9/16	4 Wounded 29/8/17
760407	Seymour, Bernard Gilbert ...	...	26/ 3/18	4
5873	Slater, John Elwyn	...	11/ 7/16	5 Lieut. Killed in action 3/5/17
6082	Stephenson, Allan	...	5/ 9/16	4 Lieut.
761454	Taylor, John Birley	...	15/ 9/17	4 Killed in action 24/12/17
764077	Tomlinson, John Ernest	...	25/ 9/17	4

Service Battalions (New Armies).

2114	Chowne, Gerald Henry Tilson	...	8/ 1/15	9 Capt. Died of Wounds 2/5/17
2052	Freeman, Clifford John Austin	...	10/ 6/15	10 Lieut.
3293	Gibbs, Lawrence Henry	...	3/10/15	7 Lieut. ✠ [23/3/18]
2201	Smith, Cyril Baynes	...	7/11/15	8 Capt. w. –/5/16, 24/4/17,
3783	Thompson, Cecil Victor	...	7/11/15	8 Capt. w. 19/1/16 K/A 6/2/17 ⌬
4686	Addison, Roger	...	6/ 9/16	10 ✠ Wounded 5/6/17 ⌬
763816	Broadbent, Eric Gladstone	...	30/ 5/17	Wounded 15/6/18
763516	Burr, Everett Harold	...	26/ 4/17	Wounded 29/8/17 P/W 14/6/18
762385	Carruthers, Alexander Robert	...	26/ 4/17	Wounded 12/4/18
762587	Corlett, Richard Lovell	...	28/ 3/17	
767775	Cotton, Rex	...	17/ 3/19	
761044	Emery, Walter Herbert Vernon	...	3/ 8/17	7 Died 26/10/18
760904	Faulkner, Roscoe	...	24/ 6/17	7 Lieut. Wounded 28/9/18
764197	Gittings, Charles	...	28/ 8/17	(5) Killed in action 21/3/18
767935	Gornall, Leslie Ashworth	...	5/ 3/19	
763581	Grimshaw, James Edward	...	26/ 4/17	
1237	Gurner, Eric Davidson	...	1/ 5/17	8
5848	Heath, William Frederick	...	1/ 5/17	8
764597	Holmes, Frederick William	...	28/ 8/17	Wounded 22/4/18
760706	James, Stuart Tom	...	26/ 4/17	
761416	Jeffreys, James Robert	...	24/ 6/17	7
762457	Leach, John	...	28/ 3/17	
761048	Lowe, Edgar	...	3/ 8/17	7
5914	Lowick, James Shirley	...	1/ 5/17	8 Wounded 13/8/17
763240	Lyons, Edward Thomas	...	26/ 4/17	Killed in action 4/10/17
763698	Marriott, James Sefton	...	25/ 9/17	
764072	Moses, L/Cpl. Lewis Frederick Chas.		28/ 8/17	(5) Wounded 28/3/18
763242	Nutcombe, Thomas Arthur	...	26/ 4/17	(R.F.C.) K/A 2/8/18
764252	Osborne, Edward Bertram	...	25/ 9/17	(5) D/W while P/W 1/4/18
764339	Pinder, Leonard	...	28/ 8/17	(5) Prisoner of war 29/4/18
7028	Pocock, Raglan Lionel Alfred	...	1/ 5/17	8 Killed in action 25/8/17
5027	Prada, Luis Enrique	...	25/ 3/17	8 Wounded 28/8/17
8072	Sagar, Arnold Leslie	...	26/ 1/17	8 Capt. D.S.O. ⌬
764853	Saunders, Harry Augustus	...	24/ 9/17	
764858	Turner, Arthur	...	24/ 9/17	
1164	Tyer, Eric	...	1/ 5/17	w. 12/4/18 P/W 13/8/18
4819	Walker, Vernon Lee	...	1/ 5/17	8 Killed in action 29/5/17
761053	White, Thomas Herbert	...	3/ 8/17	7 ✠ (R.A.F.) w. 23/4/18 d. 24/1/19

THE LOYAL NORTH LANCASHIRE REGIMENT. 273

{ 47th Foot
{ 81st Foot

Regular Battalions (Nos. 1 & 2).

2nd Lieut.

1630	GEMMEL, James Allison B. S.	... 26/ 5/15	*1 Lieut. Wounded* –/9/16 ⚑
1098	GOLDIE, Cpl. Paul	... 11/ 6/15	*1 Killed in action* 25/9/15
1409	GOLDIE, Robert	... 11/ 6/15	*1 Lieut. (M.G.C.)*
1768	TREATT, Chaplin Court ...	... 27/ 1/15	*1 Lieut. (R.F.C.)*
766020	GORRELL, John Norman ...	... 27/ 3/18 *1*	

Special Reserve Battalion (No. 3).

| 1653 | GARDINER, John H. ... ... | 9/11/14 *3(1) Wounded* 23/10/15 |

Territorial Battalions (Nos. 4, 5, 12 & 14).

2009	CROW, Arthur Arnold ...	... 26/11/14	*5 Capt. Comm^n·resign^d·(Med.unfit)*
			K/A as Pte. (–/Essex) 10/10/17
303	MOREWOOD, Sgt. Thomas Christmas	1/12/14	*5 Major (R.A.S.C.)*
3148	ATKINS, Charles Arthur ...	... 5/ 8/15	*(4) Lieut.*
4024	BRETT, Jasper	... 6/12/15	*5 Lieut. (R.E.)*
4072	BRYANS, John	... 6/12/15	*5 Died of wounds* 28/10/17
4056	CANTY, Cpl. Harold ...	... 6/12/15	*5 Capt. Wounded* 8/6/17
3983	HART, L/Cpl. Thomas Elliott	... 3/12/15	*5 Lieut. (To Labour Corps)* ⚑
3076	KING, Harry Norman ...	... 5/ 8/15	*(4) Lieut.* ✠ *Wounded* 5/10/17 ⚑
4092	LAWRENCE, Henry Wilfred ...	... 6/12/15	*5 Lieut. Wounded* 9/11/17
4074	MURRAY, George Vernon ...	... 6/12/15	*5 Lieut. Wounded* 23/5/17 F/D(2)
3488	NEWTON, Walter Claude ...	... 30/ 7/15	*(4) Killed in action* 4/7/17
3611	PERKINS, Leonard	... 30/ 7/15	*(4) (To 4/Northampton) Lieut.*
3696	SMITH, Malcolm Guy ...	... 30/ 7/15	*4 Lieut.*
4350	THOMSON, Hugh Dalrymple ...	... 6/ 1/16	*5 Lieut.*
3988	WEST, Frederick John ...	... 6/12/15	*5 Capt. (To Labour Corps)*
4722	BAILEY, Samuel Herbert ...	... 27/12/15	*12 Lieut.*
4111	BUTTERS, Philip Percy ...	... 27/12/15	*12 Lieut.*
4043	HEDGES, Walter Frederick ...	... 27/12/15	*12*
4785	McCORQUODALE, George Melville ...	27/ 1/16	*12 Lieut.* ⚑
4710	PAWSEY, Alfred Maxwell ..	... 6/ 1/16	*12 Lieut.*
4164	PIVETEAU, Gabriel Joseph Lewis	... 27/ 1/16	*12 Lieut.*
4113	POWELL, Rees Thornton ...	... 12/11/15	*12 Capt.*
4039	WARD, Harry Ernest ...	... 12/12/15	*12 Lieut.*
4186	YOUNG, Clement Arthur ...	... 27/12/15	*12 Lieut.*

* *Title changed (1st January, 1921) to "The Loyal Regiment (North Lancashire)."*

5887	Ashton, Arthur	11/ 7/16	12	*Lieut.*
765262	Bannister, John Bernard	28/11/17	4	
6303	Bardsley, Albert	11/ 7/16	12	*Capt.* ✠ *Wounded* 10/6/17
6377	Bellis, Alan Waddington	26/ 9/16	4	*Prisoner of war* 27/4/18
6679	Bigger, Ivan Walter Edward Lennox	11/ 7/16	4	*Lieut.*
763564	Brooke, Leonard	26/ 4/17	4	✠ *Killed in action* 9/4/18
764310	Brown, David Leadman	28/ 8/17	5	
6397	Brown, Felix Cuthbert	11/ 7/16	4	*Lieut.*
763319	Brown, Edward William Walter	28/ 8/17		*Wounded* 7/1/18, 15/8/18
6398	Bury, Wilfred Hope	11/ 7/16	4	*Lieut. Wounded* 1/11/18
760899	Crabb, Harry Leslie	11/ 5/17	4	
5368	Faber, Edward Greg	11/ 7/16	12	*Lieut.*
4728	Falby, Edward Frederick	11/ 7/16	4	*Killed in action* 9/9/16
762803	Fright, Harold William	28/ 8/17	5	(*To* 5/*S. Lancs.*) *Lieut.* ✠
766022	Hargreaves, Walter John	24/ 4/18	4	[*w.* 1/7/18, 23/11/18]
6802	Hart, Edmund John	2/ 6/16	12	*Lieut.* 𝕄
6006	Haworth, Leonard	17/ 7/16	5	*Lieut.*
5907	Holden, Herbert Seymour	26/ 9/16	4	*Wounded & P/W* 18/10/17
6217	Howard, Stanley Boothby	26/ 9/16	4	*Lieut.*
6649	Jackson, Wilfred Lind	11/ 7/16	12	*Lieut.*
6315	Jenkinson, Francis Crofts	4/ 6/16	12	*Wounded* 13/3/17
6223	Kennedy, John	5/ 9/16	4	*Lieut.*
5699	Knight, Alfred Ovenden	2/ 6/16	12	*Lieut.* ✠
6679	Lennox-Bigge, Ivan Wm. Edward	11/ 7/16	4	*Lieut.*
6807	Lewis, Henry Stephen	2/ 6/16	12	*Lieut.*
6227	Lloyd, Stanley Clement	26/ 9/16	4	*Lieut.*
5917	Marsden, Walter	5/ 9/16	4	*Lieut.* ✠ ✠ *P/W* 14/1/18
763831	Mascall, Vallance Cook	28/ 8/17	4	*Wounded* 19/1/18
4733	Mather, Volney	2/ 6/16	12	*Killed in action* 31/7/17
5702	McCarthy, Thaddeus Francis	5/ 9/16	4	✠ *w.* 25/8/17 *K/A* 14/4/18
765687	Mitton, Paul Dury	18/12/17	4	
5349	Muckleston, Henry Paul	2/ 6/16	12	*Lieut.*
6425	Parker, Geoffrey	26/ 9/16	4	*Killed in action* 9/4/17
5634	Pulpher, Herbert Hamilton	2/ 6/16	12	*Lieut.*
5537	Rayner, Robert Stanley	5/ 9/16	4	*Capt.* 𝕄
5353	Riding, George Edward	11/ 7/16	5	*Lieut.*
6821	Selby, Edgar Wynne	26/ 9/16	4	*Lieut.*
5806	Skingley, Thomas George	5/ 9/16	4	*Wounded* 25/8/17
6468	Stonehouse, Robert Alfred	26/ 9/16	4	*Killed in action* 28/4/17
6831	Varah, George Liddon	26/ 9/16	4	*Prisoner of war* 23/5/18
5454	Vernon, Frank Lawson	11/ 7/16	12	*Lieut. Acc/killed* 8/11/16
5932	Vipond, Frank Rowley	27/ 6/17	4	
762312	Walsh, Cpl. Alan Dudley	30/10/18	4	
4621	Walton, Leon Maitland	11/ 7/16	4	*Lieut. Killed in action* 17/11/16
6528	Watt, Alexander Lindsay Ivan W.	2/ 6/16	12	*Lieut.*
6934	Waye, William Basil	26/ 9/16	4	*Lieut. Wounded* 11/4/17

LOYAL NORTH LANCASHIRE REGIMENT.

Service Battalions (New Armies).

3113	BENNETT, Harry Dare	... 22/ 1/15	8 Capt.	Wounded -/7/16
4682	COOKE, Leonard Austin	... 27/12/15	12 Lieut.	
3174	HARRISON, W. S. B.	... 9/ 1/15	9 Killed in action 7/7/16	
1960	TINDAL-ATKINSON, Claro Paschal	... 31/ 8/14	10 Capt. (R.A.F.) w. 13/8/17	
2551	WILLIS, Norman Steward	... 23/ 2/15	10 Lieut.	Wounded -/4/16
3341	WOOLEY, Eric Christensen	... 12/12/15	10 Lieut.	Wounded -/7/16
762641	BIGGER, Trevor Henry Lennox	... 30/ 5/17	8	
2429	CLARIDGE, Charles Gordon	... 12/11/16	7 w. 31/8/17 P/W 6/6/18	
7054	CREASE, Sydney Herbert	... 18/ 3/17	7	
762256	CULLERNE, Alan Baird	... 1/ 7/17	7 ✠ Wounded 15/8/17	
763260	CULLUM, Henry Westhorpe	... 28/ 8/17	Wounded 19/1/18	
761782	EDWARDS, Cecil Guy	... 3/ 3/19		
5898	ELTOFT, William Crinan	... 5/ 9/16	Lieut. (To R.E. Signals)	
8055	FERGUSON, Alan Cort Wright	... 19/12/16	Wounded 21/8/17	
7323	GRANT, James Arden	... 19/12/16	8 Wounded 18/6/17	
6460	GRIFFITHS, Frederick Victor	... 5/ 9/16	(21/K.R.R.)	
764144	HARRIS, Sydney Ernest	... 28/ 8/17	(4) Died of wounds 15/5/18	
5695	HAY, Robert	... 24/ 1/17	9	
7231	HIELD, Hugh	... 19/12/16	8 Wounded 18/8/17	
6997	HINDMARSH, Clifford	... 18/ 3/17	7 ✠	
766926	HODGSON, Ronald	... 28/12/18		
7232	HOWARD, Albert Leonard	... 19/12/16	10 Killed in action 18/9/18	
763749	JACKSON, John Arthur	... 31/ 7/17	Prisoner of war 26/7/18	
3571	JAMES, Charles Holloway	... 27/ 6/16	7 Lieut.	
2279	JONES, Harold Newton	... 22/11/16	7 Lieut.	
5956	KELLY, Charles Leonard	... 1/ 5/17	10 Wounded 26/9/17	
764544	LAMBERT, Walter	... 28/ 8/17		
764271	LARKIN, Joseph	... 31/ 7/17		
5021	MAINGOT, Patrick Sherlock	... 1/ 5/17	10 ✠ ℳ	
7657	MATTHEWS, Stanley Ernest	... 19/12/16	Prisoner of war 2/11/17	
3120	MILLAR, Hugh Frederick	... 12/11/16	10	
768280	MOLYNEUX, George Wynne	... 10/ 3/19		
7316	MOSS, Edgar Nuttall	... 19/12/16	Lieut. Wounded 15/10/18	
764446	MOTTRAM, Charles Edmund	... 28/ 8/17	Wounded 8/6/18	
7876	PARRY, Gerald Owen	... 19/12/16	Lieut.	
5028	QUESNEL, Robert Emmanuel	... 24/ 1/17	10 Wounded 24/4/17	
764164	RAGG, Claroll Watkins	... 29/ 8/17	Lieut. (5/S. Lancs.)	
764104	REED, Arthur Edwin	... 31/ 7/17		
764261	SHORT, Harold	... 31/ 7/17	✠ Wounded 15/4/18	
1359	SMITH, Sidney Bernard	... 12/11/16	10 Major ✠ Wounded 17/4/1	
768129	SMITH, William	... 17/ 3/19		
6773	SPURGEON, Victor Fairfax	... 19/12/16	Lieut.	
7900	STANDEN, Leslie Richard	... 12/12/16	Lieut.	
5458	WAY, Robert Edmond Allen	... 1/ 5/17	10 Died of wounds 29/5/17	
767786	WHITESIDE, William	... 3/ 3/19		
761614	WILKIE, James	... 24/ 6/17	7 ✠	
766911	WOODRUFF, Frank George	... 25/ 6/18		

THE SOUTH LANCASHIRE REGIMENT
(THE PRINCE OF WALES' VOLUNTEERS).

Regular Battalions (Nos. 1 & 2).
{ 40th Foot
{ 82nd Foot

2nd Lieut.

2548	CASE, Geoffrey	... ...	29/ 8/15	2 *Lieut.* w. 25/9/15 K/A 22/3/18
898	ROSCOE, William	... ...	27/ 1/15	2 *M.G.C. Lieut.* ✠ w. 23/6/15 ℞
1038	THOMPSON, C/Sgt. Claude Ernest		27/ 1/15	2 *Lt.-Col.* (5/*S. Lancs.*) D.S.O. ✠ ✠
				Wounded –/3/15, 9/8/15 ℞(2).
7811	SMITH, Sidney Paxton	...	26/ 1/17 (5)	
8010	ST. GEORGE, Acheson Reginald	...	26/ 1/17 (5)	

Special Reserve Battalion (No. 3).

3038	GILES, Mark Harold	...	7/ 5/15	3(2) *Lieut.* ℞
3010	HILLIAR, Gordon Edward	...	5/ 3/15	3(2) (2/*E. Lancs.*) K/A 25/9/15
3043	LINDEN, Garnett Harold	...	25/ 4/15	3(4) *Lieut.* *Wounded* 2/10/17
3312	McLEAN, Archibald John	...	12/ 5/15	3 *Lieut.* (*M.G.C.*) w. –/11/16
3055	McWILLIAM, Sgt. Edgar Cumbo		7/ 5/15	3
3966	SIMPSON, John Ray	...	29/10/15	3 *Lieut.*
1174	WALKER, Edmund A. Hornsey	...	17/ 9/14	3(4) *Capt.* *Wounded* 6/11/16
762317	CHARLTON, Frank Tysoe	...	26/ 4/17	3 *Died of wounds* 3/10/18

Territorial Battalions (Nos. 4 & 5).

3669	BROWN, Sgt. Walter James	...	11/ 1/16	4 *Lieut.* ✠ ℞
4361	DALBY, Frederick Binnie	...	7/ 1/16	4 *Lieut.* *Wounded* –/12/16
4729	FISK, William Edgar	...	31/ 5/16	4 *Lieut.* ℞
4784	JOHNSON, Frank Lawrence	...	2/ 6/16	4 *Lieut.* *To King's African Rifles.*
5182	LAMBERT, Eric Clifford	...	19/ 6/16	4 *Lieut.*
5921	NIMMO, Adam Arthur	...	22/ 1/16	5 *Lieut.*
5923	PAUL, Robert Buchanan	...	22/ 1/16	5 *Lieut.*
4464	TODD, Charles Leslie Morgan	...	7/ 1/16	4 *Died of wounds* 4/8/16
4196	TUCKER, Duncan George Samuel	...	28/ 1/16	4 *Lieut.*
4482	TURNER, George Herbert	...	7/ 1/16	4 *Lieut.*
4586	WOODS, Cpl. Clement Alfred	...	7/ 1/16	4 *Lieut.*
5099	WELLS, Robert	... ...	19/ 6/16	4 *Lieut.*
6146	AISTON, William	... ...	26/ 9/16	4 *Lieut.*
6535	ATHERTON, Arthur William	...	23/11/16	4 *Lieut.*
7568	BARKER, Frederick	... ...	20/12/16	4 *Lieut.*
6571	BARON, Frank Oseland	...	5/ 9/16	4 *Lieut.* *Wounded* 21/4/17
6095	BROCKHURST, Arthur Harold	...	5/ 9/16	4 *Lieut.*
6135	CAREY, Richard Mein	...	5/ 9/16	4 *Lieut.* *Wounded* 21/4/17
764418	CLEVELAND, John Thomas Ernest	...	28/ 8/17	4
763197	DOUGLAS, Reginald March	...	31/ 7/17	4 *Wounded* 9/5/18
4014	FALLOW, Henry Fife	...	6/ 8/16	4 *Wounded* 13/8/17
6201	FARRANT, Victor Thomas	...	11/ 7/16	4 *Lieut.* ℞

6909	HARRISON, Norman	...	5/ 9/16	4	Lieut. Wounded –/–/17
7669	HEATON, Frank	...	26/ 1/17	4	Wounded 21/9/17
762529	HILTON, John Henry	...	17/ 6/17	4	
764243	HOLLINGSWORTH, Edward	...	31/ 7/17	5	Wounded 6/2/18
763930	HUBBLE, William George	...	31/ 7/17	4	
766697	LEE, Donald Melville	...	23/ 6/18	4	
6385	LINES, Arthur James	...	5/ 9/16	4	Lieut. Wounded –/7/17
6602	PEACOCK, George	...	20/12/16	4	
762840	PERTWEE, John Whittaker	...	25/ 9/17	4	
6269	ROTHWELL, Stanley	...	26/ 9/16	4	Wounded 13/8/17, 21/6/18
762135	SMEDLEY, William Herbert	...	28/ 8/17	4	
6529	WARD, David Harold	...	5/ 9/16	4	
762005	WHITE, Herbert Blanchford	...	25/ 9/17	5	Wounded 7/5/18
764468	WILD, Harold	...	28/ 8/17	4	
5826	WORMALD, Henry	...	26/ 9/16	4	

Service Battalions (New Armies).

2056	CATFORD, Walter Arundel	...	3/ 4/15	11	To 10/E. Surrey
899	CLIVELY, Richard C.	...	17/ 9/14	6	To Tank Corps Major ✠ ℳ
1740	FRY, David Chamberlain	...	19/10/14	11	Major (M.G.C.)
1318	HORSEY, Cyril James	...	17/ 9/14	6(7)	Died of wounds 22/11/16
281	JARVIS, Sgt. Ernest Cory	...	17/ 9/14	6	Capt. w. –/8/15 K/A 28/8/16
3312	McLEAN, Archibald John	...	12/ 5/15	10	To 3
2970	MANNING, Archibald R. Oswald	...	14/ 1/15	11(13)	Capt. Wounded 18/6/18
823	NAYLOR, L/Cpl. Thomas Henry	...	17/ 9/14	10	Capt. w. 19/8/15, 10/6/18 ℳ(2)
2031	SHANKS, Edward Buxton	...	3/12/14	8	
553	SHUFFREY, Gilbert	...	17/ 9/14	6	Lieut. Wounded –/8/15
2468	THEVENARD, Charles Wirgeman	...	13/10/14	9	Capt.
234	VANDERVELL, Sgt. Frank	...	17/ 9/14	6	Major Bde. M/G Off. w. 6/9/18
1174	WALKER, Edmund A. Hornsey	...	17/ 9/14	6	To 3
6838	ARCHER, John	...	26/ 9/16	7	Lieut. ℳ
7363	BAYNES, John Ernest	...	19/12/16	11	Lieut.
6136	COPPOCK, Hugh Searle	...	5/ 9/16	(2)	Lieut. w. 22/1/17, 9/6/17 [K/A 10/4/18 ℳ]
768642	CURRAN, Cyril Robert Philpot	...	17/ 3/19		
7327	FARNSWORTH, Sydney Richard	...	19/12/16	7	Wounded 7/10/16
763820	FOULKES, Edward	...	26/ 4/17	8	✠ Wounded 1/5/18
8033	GOLDING, Harold Gordon Lancelot	...	19/12/16		Lieut.
7353	LIDGETT, John Cuthbert	...	19/12/16	11	Lieut. Killed in action 23/3/18
6808	LITTLER, Frank	...	5/ 9/16	8	Lieut. Killed in action 23/7/17
763834	PRICE, Richard Halstead	...	26/ 4/17		
6880	SMITH, John Carrington	...	26/ 9/16	7	Lieut.
763648	STILWELL, Clifford Francis	...	27/ 6/17	7	Lieut. Wounded 17/1/18
7324	TICEHURST, Arthur George	...	19/12/16	8	Lieut.
7989	WAKELEY, Arthur Day	...	19/12/16	7	Lieut. ✠ Wounded 13/6/17
767242	WARD, Arthur	...	5/ 2/19		
762820	WILLIAMS, Edward	...	29/ 3/17		
767940	WILLIAMS, John	...	5/ 3/19		
7624	WILKINSON, David Havelock	...	19/12/16		Wounded 1/10/18

*THE ROYAL LANCASTER REGIMENT
(THE KING'S OWN).

4th Foot

Regular Battalions (Nos. 1 & 2).

2nd Lieut.

197	ELLIS, L/Cpl. Francis Henry	...	14/ 2/15	2 *Wounded P/W* 11/5/15
1511	JEWERS, Stuart Frank	...	14/ 2/15	2 *Lieut. Wounded* 25/4/15
1119	WIMBUSH, Nelson Norman		14/ 2/15	2 *Lieut. Wounded* 8/5/15
6250	BROWN, Richard Leslie	...	-/ 1/17	1 *Wounded* 17/9/18
761520	FOX, Joseph ...	...	2/ 8/17	1 *Wounded* 24/10/17
764048	WALL, Alan Mansfield	...	29/ 8/17	1 *Prisoner of war* 6/6/18

Special Reserve Battalion (No. 3).

2801	LUPTON, Lionel	...	3/10/14	3 *Lieut.* ₩(2)
766333	FARMER, Charles Arthur	...	29/ 5/18	3
762731	WHITE, Stanley Clarke	...	26/ 4/17	3

Territorial Battalions (Nos. 4 & 5).

Lieut.	PERL, Bernard Huson	...	18/ 3/16	5 *Capt. & Adjt.* ✠ ₩
65	BALL, C/Sgt. Sidney Charles	...	24/12/14	5 *Major* (9/*Liverpool*) O.B.E.
3614	BUSTARD, Frank	...	11/ 6/15	5 *Major* ₩(2)
3259	BUSTARD, Ralph	...	2/ 4/15	5 *Capt. Wounded* 5/5/15
3828	CADDY, William Lynass	...	30/ 7/15	5 *Capt.*
3395	DELAFIELD, Frederick Herman	...	30/ 7/15	5 *Lieut.* ₩
3882	GILLESPIE, Isidore	...	3/12/15	5 *Wounded* 16/4/17
3066	HUTCHINSON, George Herbert	...	5/ 8/15(5)	*Capt.*
3073	KIRTON, Henry Harold	...	5/ 8/15(5)	*Capt.*
3866	SLEIGH, Wallace Robert	...	30/ 7/15(5)	*Lieut.*
3555	THOMSON, Norman	...	30/ 7/15	5 *Lieut.*
761173	ABRAHAMSON, Harold	...	28/ 8/17	4 *Wounded* 22/6/18
763632	ANDREWS, Lionel Raymond		28/ 8/17	5 *Lieut.* ✠
5162	APPLEYARD, Charles Herbert	...	11/ 7/16	5 *Lieut. w.* 23/4/17, 10/5/18
5888	AVISON, Frank	...	11/ 7/16	5 *Lieut.* (*R.A.F*)
5309	BEAZLEY, Tom Forest	...	11/ 7/16	5 *Lieut. Wounded* -/11/16
6045	BROOKE, Frank	...	11/ 7/16	5 *Lieut. Wounded* -/11/16
762555	CONROY, Edmund Peter	...	24/ 9/17	4
5441	FORD, Clement William	...	5/ 9/16	5 *Wounded* 30/5/17 *K/A* 31/7/17
6671	FOXON, Sidney William	...	5/ 9/16	4 *Lieut. Wounded* 19/3/17
5354	GOODMAN, Joseph	...	11/ 7/16	5 *Killed in action* 11/4/17
6171	HONEY, William James	...	26/ 9/16	4 *Lieut.*
5509	KEIGHLEY, Lindon Rayner	...	5/ 9/16	4 *Lieut. Died of wounds* 3/12/17
3265	LEWIS, Davis Robert Thomas		11/ 7/16	5 *Lieut.*

*Title changed (1st January, 1921) to "The King's Own Royal Regiment (Lancaster)."

5775	Lord, Gilbert Henry	... ...	11/ 7/16 5	Lieut. ✠ Wounded 15/8/17 🎖
2760	Notley, Albert Carr	...	29/ 8/17 5	(5/S. Lancs.) K/A 30/5/18
5377	Park, Albert Barton	... ...	11/ 7/16 5	Lieut.
7729	Paterson, James Stuart	... ...	5/ 9/16 4	Lieut. Wounded 1/12/17
764562	Pickbourne, Maurice	...	28/ 8/17 5	Lieut. Wounded 30/6/18
766531	Sams, Rueben Alfred	...	24/ 5/18 5	
5216	Sciama, Abraham ...	...	26/ 9/16 4	Lieut.
764267	Smith, Herbert Alexander ...		31/ 7/17 5	Wounded 12/10/18
6525	Stephenson, John Charles		26/ 9/16 4	Lieut. Wounded 22/5/18
6204	Taylor, George Arthur	...	5/ 9/16 4	Lieut. ✠ Wounded 20/9/17
7522	White, Harold Damant	...	26/ 9/16 4	Lieut.
4976	Whitworth, Edward Charles	...	5/ 9/16 4	Lieut. Wounded 18/9/18
766319	Wilkinson, Charles Norman	...	1/ 5/18 5	Wounded 2/9/18

Service Battalions (New Armies).

647	Buckle, Francis Danno	... ...	6/ 9/14 6	Lieut. 🎖
1427	Cheriton, William George L.		17/ 9/14 6	Capt. (19/Hants)
3245	Conway, Joseph Michael	...	12/12/15 7	Killed in action 7/7/16
1653	Gardiner, John H.	... ...	9/11/14 10	To 3/Loyal North Lancs.
63	Higgins, L/Cpl. Herbert Edward P.		17/ 9/14 6	Capt. Killed in action 10/8/15
1676	Hyams, Geoffrey ...	...	10/ 6/15 10	Lieut.
766	Jurgens, Sydney George	...	17/ 9/14 6	Lieut. Died of wounds 7/8/15
1754	Madan, Nigell Cornwallis ...		19/ 9/14 8	Lieut. Killed in action 3/3/16
550	Manlove, Cpl. John Edward Davis		17/ 9/14 6	Capt. (Ind. Army) w. 29/5/17
551	Murrane, L/Cpl. Hugh Dudley	...	17/ 9/14 6	Capt. ✠ Wounded 8/11/15
216	Vincent, Sgt. Edward Sydney		17/ 9/14 6	Major 🎖
2165	Whitaker, Donald Nicoll W.		12/ 9/15 6	Lieut.
764007	Bailey, Arnold ...	...	29/ 8/17 8	Killed in action 24/3/18
764744	Barber, Edward Hanson	...	29/ 8/17	Wounded 17/9/18
6353	Beswick, John Charles	...	15/ 4/17 11	Prisoner of war D/W 22/4/17
764749	Brickell, Arthur Mervyn ...		29/ 8/17	
6884	Briggs, William Lonsdale ...		23/11/16	Died of wounds 14/9/17
764975	Brown, John Aisbett	...	19/ 8/17	
6565	Cook, Henry Walter	...	5/ 9/16 8	Wounded 25/4/17
761567	Cooper, Thomas Charles	...	5/ 8/17 11	✠ Wounded 4/6/18
6994	Fairbairn, Maurice	...	2/ 4/17 11	Killed in action 7/7/17
5755	Gitsham, Arthur Herman ...		18/ 3/17 8	
767907	Gledhill, Arnold Crosland		5/ 3/19	
5768	King, Llewelyn John Rowland		5/ 9/16	
4390	Leslie, Allan Dunbar	...	26/ 1/17 8	Wounded 4/4/18, 8/11/18
766785	Levy, George ...	...	3/ 3/19	
7280	Lindsay, James Gray	...	19/12/16	
762862	Maywood, Reginald Alfred Josephson		1/ 3/17	Wounded 17/9/18
764900	McNulty, Michael Stuart ...		28/ 8/17	
764505	Niven, Alan Scott ...	...	28/ 8/17	Killed in action 4/11/17
762740	Pearce, Norman ...	...	30/ 5/17	(1) Killed in action 12/10/17

ROYAL LANCASTER REGIMENT (S/B)

7613	PHILLIPS, Percival John	19/12/16	Wounded 4/9/17
764573	PRESTON, Benjamin Fred	28/8/17	
762415	PRICE, Frederick	30/5/17	
7616	PYE, Fred Eric Eustace	19/12/16	Lieut. Wounded 1/5/17
763042	ROCHE, John Arthur Edgar	29/3/17	
765045	SHUTT, Donald Bethune	1/8/17	Wounded 20/7/18
764387	SMITH, George William	29/8/17 *II*	Killed in action 28/3/18
764509	STEER, John Stanley	28/8/17	Wounded 15/5/18
769631	THOMPSON, Frank	15/2/19	
764358	WHITMORE, Allen	29/8/17 *II*	Wounded 11/5/18, 15/6/18

THE LEICESTERSHIRE REGIMENT.

Regular Battalions (Nos. 1 & 2).

17th Foot

2nd Lieut.

1009	BROWN, L/Cpl. Harold Atherton	3/3/15 2	Killed in action 15/5/15
1401	DAVIS, Richard Nevill	3/3/15 2(1)	Capt. ✠ Wounded 17/5/15
3387	FRASER, Cecil Garnet	7/11/15 2	Wounded 6/1/16
1694	HEMPHILL, L/Cpl. Howard Hislop	20/3/15 2	Capt. ✠ w. 25/9/15 P/W 𝔐
2509	KENNEDY, John Gilbert	28/11/15 1	Killed in action 14/9/16
2234	ROBERTSON, Frank Bruce	28/11/15 1	Lieut. (1/K.A.R.) ✠ Wounded
1577	WILKINSON, Ernest Alexander	3/3/15 2	K/A 25/9/15 [30/8/18 𝔐]
763939	ROBERTS, Trevor Lane	30/10/17	

Special Reserve Battalion (No. 3).

5987	COLLINS, Frederick George	8/7/16 3	Lieut. (Garr. Bn. York L.I.)
5344	HYDE, Henry Cameron	8/7/16 3(6)	Lieut. Wounded 3/5/18
5707	MILLER, Ronald Alexander	8/7/16 3(6)	Lieut. 𝔐
6019	OTTEY, Raymond Gascoyne	8/7/16 3	(R.F.C.) Killed in action 28/7/17
766030	REEVES, Roland Stuart	27/2/18 3	
4855	SHARPE, John Stanley	8/7/16 3(7)	Prisoner of war 26/7/18
5451	SMITH, Charles William	8/7/16 3(9)	Lieut.

Territorial Battalions (Nos. 4 & 5).

4493	ALLEN, Charles Stanley	14/12/15 5	Capt.
4948	BALL, Thomas Harold	2/6/16 5	Lieut. ✠
4980	BOYTON, Jack Lyons	18/6/16 5	Lieut. ✠ Wounded 23/4/18
4027	CREED, Thomas Percival	11/11/15 5	Capt. ✠ Wounded —/7/16
4084	DUPONT, Alfred Norman	11/11/15 5	Lieut.
2514	JOHNSON, Reginald Cyril Bigmore	14/10/15 4	Lieut.
4073	MEASURES, Percy	11/11/15 5	Lieut. Killed in action 31/12/17
5025	NELSON, L/Cpl. Lewis Archibald	18/6/16 5	Lieut. ✠ Wounded

LEICESTERSHIRE REGIMENT (T/F). 281

4082	PIERREPONT, Arthur Downey	...	11/11/15 5	*Lieut.*
3923	REYNOLDS, William Henry	...	11/11/15 5	*Lieut.*
3928	STENTIFORD, Ronald Hastings	...	11/11/15 5	*Capt.* ✠ ✠
4903	WALLEY, John Clifford ...	...	18/ 6/16 5	*Lieut.* w. 5/6/17 K/A 23/3/18
765418	BRYNING, Frank Alfred ...	...	28/11/17 5	
5734	CLARKE, Francis William Harry	...	15/ 7/16 4	*Wounded & P/W* 17/9/17
761414	COLE, William Maurice ...	...	2/ 8/17 5	✠ w. 2/7/17 K/A 20/6/18
764484	COLQUHOUN, Robert Walter Stuart		31/ 7/17 4	
763674	GREASLEY, Joseph Ernest ...	...	1/ 5/18 4	
761699	HARRISON, Francis Samuel ...		31/ 7/17 5	
6206	WILLETT, Francis William ...	...	5/ 9/16 4	*Capt.* ✠ w. 3/5/17, 8/10/17, 27/10/17

Service Battalions (New Armies).

1703	BERNAYS, John Stewart Noad	...	7/11/15 6	*Capt.* ✠ *Wounded* 17/5/17
2096	DIBBEN, Cecil Reginald ...	...	2/12/14 9	*Major* O.B.E.
1584	NORMAN, Roland Frank H.	...	29/ 9/14 6	*Lieut.*
5097	JUDGE, Leopold James ...	...	25/ 5/16 10	*Lieut.*
5319	PHILLIPS, Sidney Vernon ...	...	25/ 5/16 10	*Killed in action* 14/8/16
4858	UNDERWOOD, John ...	...	25/ 5/16 10	*Died of wounds* 16/4/17
6244	WATSON, Charles Herbert ...	...	2/ 6/16 12	*Lieut.* w. 13/4/18 P/W 22/5/18
763417	BRANCH, Charles Stanley ...	...	28/ 3/17 9	
764311	CHRISTY, John George ...	...	31/ 7/17	*1(5) Killed in action* 3/10/18
766332	CULPEPER, Bernard Armel ...	...	23/ 6/18	
763925	CURSLEY, Norman Sharpe ...	...	27/ 6/17	*(Tank Corps)* w. 17/10/18
7370	DADLEY, Eric Arthur ...	...	19/12/16	*Lieut.*
763155	GADD, Clement Arthur ...	...	6/ 3/19	
766471	GARNER, Albert Edward ...	...	26/ 6/18	
767542	GOADBY, Albert Willson ...	...	4/ 3/19	
6855	GROOCOCK, George Hughes ...	...	7/11/16 9	
5761	HEBDEN, George Spencer ...	...	7/ 7/16 12	*Killed in action* 22/4/17
763394	HOLLAND, Douglas Henry ...	...	29/ 3/17	
763586	ISBELL, Herbert ...	..	30/ 5/17	
768577	KEAY, Cecil Francis McLaren	...	17/ 3/19	
5913	LEE, Albert Henry	...	3/ 5/17 6	*Wounded* 16/4/18
761030	MARTIN, Charles Stanley ...	...	3/ 5/17 6	*Killed in action* 4/10/17
5632	MOUNTFORD, Frederick Godfrey	...	3/ 5/17 6	*Wounded* 18/10/18
763665	ROGERS, Harry Burdett ...	...	30/ 5/17	*Wounded* 11/9/18
766285	SALTER, John Frederick ...		26/ 6/18	
6772	SAVAGE, Wilfred Albert ...	...	5/ 9/16	*(1) Wounded* –/–/17
4602	SENNETT, Raymond Langharne	...	2/ 6/16	*8 Lieut.* w. 3/5/17, 2/11/17, 22/3/18
763800	SMITH, Edward Langham ...	...	1/ 8/17	
5224	STRANG, William	...	7/ 7/16 12	*Lieut.*
761653	THIRLBY, Stuart Longston ...	...	2/ 8/17 6	*Killed in action* 23/3/18
6126	THOMAS, William Hope ...	...	5/ 9/16	*(1) Killed in action* 11/4/18
767499	TILLEY, Percy Frederick ...	...	4/ 3/19	
767556	WESTON, Roland Edgar ...	...	5/ 3/19	

THE LEINSTER REGIMENT.
THE PRINCE OF WALES' (ROYAL CANADIANS).

Regular Battalions (Nos. 1 & 2).   {100th Foot / 109th Foot}

2nd Lieut.

1780	BARNETT, Denis Oliver	...	1/ 1/15	2	Wounded 6/5/15 D/W 16/8/15
588	BROAD, Kenneth Stephen	...	1/ 1/15	2	Capt. w. 24/4/15, 29/4/16 ✠
1533	CLARKE, George Malcolm	...	1/ 1/15	2	Lieut. Wounded
760528	GIRARD, Geoffrey Marcus Erskine		20/ 4/17	2	Acc/killed 16/11/17
764792	PARKS, George Cecil	...	28/ 8/17	2	Prisoner of war 11/5/18

Service Battalions (New Armies).

764844	PEARSON, Leonard Morgan Jones	...	28/ 8/17	7	
764946	TRICKS, Denis Norman Frederick	...	28/ 8/17	7	Wounded 20/9/18

THE LINCOLNSHIRE REGIMENT.

Regular Battalions (Nos. 1 & 2).   10th Foot

2nd Lieut.

1777	BARRET, Jack Harper Phillips	...	23/ 4/15	1	Lt. (R.A.F.) w. 16/6/15 d. 1/11/18
1008	BROOK, Leonard Thornicraft		27/ 1/15	1	Lieut. M.B.E. Wounded 28/4/15
2656	BUDIBENT, Cecil	...	24/ 7/15	2	Killed in action 25/9/15
2372	FRAZIER, Francis Wearne	...	23/ 4/15	1	Lieut. Wounded 2/6/15, 25/9/16
1010	GILBY, Alexander John		27/ 1/15	1	Lieut. (M.G.C.) w. 18/4/15
2452	GREEN, Frank Clifford	...	23/ 4/15	1	Killed in action 16/6/15
1625	JACQUES, William Harold		26/ 5/15	1	Lieut. Wounded -/7/16
2249	PEARSON, Reginald Oswald		26/ 5/15	1	Killed in action 16/6/15
791	ROWLAND, Grafton Maurice	...	10/ 7/15	1	Lieut. Wounded -/7/16
2246	SCOTT, Robert Francis Cloete		11/ 6/15	1	Lieut. ✠
2260	TAYLOR, William Allen	...	24/ 7/15	2	Lieut. Wounded 14/9/15, -/8/16
764304	BALL, William Arthur	...	29/ 8/17	(5) ✠	
764438	JONES, William Claude	...	29/ 8/17		
764445	LUNN, Alick Robinson	...	29/ 8/17	(5)	
763668	SHARPE, Percy	...	29/ 8/17	(4)	
760968	SOWERBY, Victor Holgate	...	5/ 7/17	2	Died of wounds 31/7/17

Special Reserve Battalion (No. 3).

3782	SPENCER, L/Cpl. John Charles A. ...	20/10/15 *3 Lieut.*	*Wounded* 1/7/16
5089	MURRAY, Alfred Seymour	2/ 6/16 *3 Lieut.*	
7978	ASKEY, Cecil Harry Leonard	20/12/16 *3(8) Lieut.*	*Died of wounds* 5/4/18
763582	HARRISON, John George ...	26/ 4/17 *3* ✠	*w.* 19/4/18, 9/9/18, 5/11/18
766192	HARVEY, Ralph	1/ 5/18 *3*	
7671	KNOTT, Claude Douglas ...	26/ 1/17 *3(7)*	
764039	NAINBY, William	27/ 6/17 *3(2)*	

Territorial Battalions (Nos. 4 & 5).

3806	BOON, Sydney John Lewis	13/10/15 *5 Lieut.*	
3843	BURR, Bert	30/11/15 *5 (R.A.F.) Wounded* 23/6/17	[13/2/18]
5166	CHAMBERS, Morris Tonge	31/ 5/16 *4 Lieut.*	
4116	DAWE, Sydney Charles ...	30/11/15 *5 Capt.* ✠ *w.* 11/7/17 *Acc/killed*	
3791	EDLMANN, Edmund ...	13/10/15 *5 (Intel. Corps) Capt. w.*28/6/17 ℞	
5178	HARVEY, Robert Geo. Bosworth ...	2/ 6/16 *5 w.* 27/10/17 *K/A* 25/12/17	
4281	LeFEVRE, Frank Ewart ...	30/11/15 *5 Lieut.* ✠ *P/W* 9/3/18	
3788	LEPINE, Robert Dawson ...	13/10/15 *5 Lieut.*	
3935	PRICE, Frank Maurice ...	21/11/15 *5 Died of wounds* 4/6/17 ℞	
4021	RUDALL, William Lockhart	30/11/15 *5 Lieut.*	
4290	SQUIRE, Edwin Ross ...	30/11/15 *5 Lieut.* ✠	
4777	STEVENS, Gorham Venton	31/ 5/16 *5 Wounded* 24/12/17 *Died* 18/1/18	
6281	BARKER, Edward Watson ...	11/ 7/16 *4 Wounded* 10/10/17	
763225	BARKER, Henry Watson ...	28/ 8/17 *4 Killed in action* 17/4/18	
765031	DIXON, William Swansea ...	31/10/17 *4 Killed in action* 30/4/18	
4956	EVISON, Francis Charles ...	5/ 9/16 *4 Wounded* 13/8/17	
763908	GIBBONS, Frederick Ralph ...	31/ 7/17 *4 Prisoner of war* 13/6/18	
764535	HOPKINSON, Harold ...	28/ 8/17 *5*	
4997	MADDEN, Clarence Rowland	5/ 9/16 *4* ✠ *Wounded* 17/12/18	
767529	NICHOLLS, Norman Cathcart	15/10/18 *4*	
764381	REED, Percival Sydney Victor	31/ 7/17 *4 Wounded* 1/11/18	
762533	REVILL, Leslie Edward Howard	31/ 7/17 *5*	
5284	RICHARDS, Lincoln Winfield	5/ 9/16 *4 Lieut. Wounded* 2/9/18	
5927	RUDD, Reginald George ...	26/ 9/16 *4 Wounded* 5/5/17	
5425	TOLHURST, Gerald	26/ 9/16 *4 Lieut.*	
5431	WILLCOCK, Charles Leonard	5/ 9/16 *4 Lieut.*	

Service Battalions (New Armies).

2829	CARRE, Edward Mervyn ...	3/10/15 *8 Lieut. K/A* 16/10/16 *(R.F.C.)*	
2497	DICKINSON, George Sidney	19/ 9/15 *7 Capt. Killed in action* 2/7/16	
1802	HODGSON, David Crowe ...	3/10/15 *8 Lieut. Wounded* –/3/16	
2988	LANE-CLAYPON, Joseph Charlton ...	5/12/15 *7 Lieut. Wounded* –/2/16	

LINCOLNSHIRE REGIMENT (S/B).

3119	MAYNARD, Frank George	...	31/ 3/15	8 *To* 10/*Bn. Capt.* ℳ
5156	KISSANE, Richard		25/ 5/16	9
2900	RHODES, Cecil William ...		3/10/15	8
3026	ROSKILLY, Sydney Theo. H.		12/10/15	*1 Garr. Bn.*
2066	TREDINNICK, George Harold		19/ 9/15	7 *Lieut. w.* –/3/16, 29/10/17
768244	BARKER, John William ...		17/ 3/19	
7310	DICKINSON, Walter Stanley ...		19/12/16	*(8) Killed in action* 23/4/17
5486	ELSOM, Harold		19/12/16	*Lieut. Killed in action* 28/4/17
761322	HACK, Walter Park		4/ 8/17	10 ✠ *Wounded* 9/4/18
7330	HARRISON, William Trevor		19/12/16	*(2) Wounded* 24/12/17
6186	HARVEY, Mortimer		5/ 9/16	8 *Lieut.*
764365	HEALEY, Arthur John ...		29/ 8/17	*Wounded* 12/2/18
5068	HOWELL, Christopher Robert		14/ 4/17	8
6462	JERONS, Bernard ...		26/ 9/16	8 *Lieut. Wounded* 20/5/18
761676	KING, James Measure ...		26/ 6/17	*Wounded* 7/6/18
763502	NABE, Harold Pembroke ...		30/ 5/17	
764715	OLIVER, Thomas Frederick		29/ 8/17	6
763188	ORCHARD, Cyril Henry ...		1/ 3/17	*Wounded* 13/9/17
765511	PERCIVAL, George		1/ 5/18	
767534	POTTER, Leslie Cartwright ...		6/ 2/19	
767726	ROBERTS, Frank Alan ...		4/ 3/19	
767183	SOUCHON, Adrian Marcel ...		4/ 2/19	
765605	STANSBURY, Gordon ...		19/12/17	*Wounded* 7/10/18
6593	TAYLOR, Leslie Reginald ...		7/ 7/16	*11 Lieut.*
5928	TEDDER, Oswald Stanley ...		26/ 9/16	8 *Killed in action* 27/4/18
767629	THOMPSON, John Edmund ...		20/ 3/19	
767684	TOMLINSON, Felix Cecil ...		4/ 3/19	
764514	TUPHOLME, Geoffrey ...		28/ 8/17	
764804	VINCENT, John		28/ 8/17	*Wounded* 11/9/18 ℳ
764551	WATTS, John George ...		19/12/17	
764523	WHARTON, Leslie Eric ...		28/ 8/17	*Wounded* 2/9/18

*THE LIVERPOOL REGIMENT
(THE KING'S).

Regular Battalions (Nos. 1 & 2). 8th Foot

			2nd Lieut.	
1756	CARLTON, George Frederick	...	3/ 3/15	*1 Lieut. M.G.C. w. 18/5/15*
1818	HARRIS, Eric Roser	...	3/ 3/15	*1 Lieut. Wounded 3/5/15*
852	HUDSON, Charles Herbert	...	3/ 3/15	*1 Killed in action 15/6/15*
953	LAST, Cpl. Ernest Reginald	...	3/ 3/15	*1 Capt.* ✠ ✠ *w. 16/5/15 K/A*
1644	MORTEN, Galbraith	...	3/ 3/15	*1 K/A 16/5/15 [24/3/18* ₪*)*
1605	TRUBSHAWE, Walston Vivian	...	3/ 3/15	*1 Lieut. R.F.C. w. 26/3/15, –/5/16*
7745	HENRY, George Adam	...	25/ 1/17	*(9) Lieut. Wounded 3/7/17*
1512	WHITE, Percy Frederick	...	20/ 6/16	*1 Lieut.*

Special Reserve Battalions (Nos. 3 & 4).

766296	ARTHUR, Frederick Paris	...	1/ 5/18	*3* ✠ *Wounded 12/11/18*
6667	BUNCE, William Leslie	...	5/ 9/16	*3(12) Major* O.B.E. ₪*(2)*
6069	MACE, Edgar Robert	...	7/ 7/16	*3(1) Major* ✠ ✠
763416	ZARADI, David	...	1/ 8/17	*3(1)*

Territorial Battalions (Nos. 5 to 10).

3700	ABBOTT, William	...	30/ 7/15	*9 Lieut.*
4834	ADAMS, Arthur Marston	...	18/ 6/16	*9* ✠ *Died of wounds 20/9/17*
3306	BOAK, Charles Brightman	...	30/ 7/15	*9 Lieut. Wounded 4/6/17*
4838	BRACE, Joseph	...	2/ 6/16	*9 Lieut. Wounded –/9/16*
3670	CANDLER, Arthur Percy	...	30/ 7/15	*9*
3384	CAPON, Stanley Robert	...	8/11/15	*7 Lieut. Wounded –/8/16*
3501	COWPER, L/Cpl. Archibald Leonard	...	14/ 1/16	*7 Lieut. Wounded 24/7/17*
2882	DRAKEFORD, Herbert	...	16/ 6/15	*7 Capt.* ✠ ₪
4341	DUNN, Ernest George	...	20/ 1/16	*10 K/A 10/6/17 (M.G.C.)*
4401	GULICK, John Davies	...	22/ 1/16	*10 Lieut. Prisoner of war 12/1/18*
4825	GUMMER, Basil Austin	...	31/ 5/16	*9 Killed in action 12/8/16*
3576	HANSFORD, John Scriven	...	27/10/15	*8 Lieut.*
3577	HORTH, Frederick John	...	28/10/15	*5 Lieut. Wounded 22/11/18*
3665	JAMES, William Ewart	...	30/ 7/15	*7 Lieut.*
5414	MALLINSON, Bertrand	...	2/ 6/16	*9 Lieut.*
4830	MAURICE, Frank Julian	...	31/ 5/16	*9 (Min. of Labour)*
4795	POOLEY, Robert Mark	...	31/ 5/16	*9 Lieut.*
3773	PYBUS, James William	...	30/ 7/15	*7(13) Capt. Wounded 11/9/17*
5539	RICHARDS, Charles Walker	...	19/ 6/16	*8 Killed in action 27/9/16*

*Title changed (1st January, 1921) to "The King's Regiment (Liverpool)."

3965	Shield, L/Cpl. William James	26/ 1/16	6	Killed in action 2/3/17
4499	Sisson, L/Cpl. John Akitt ...	7/ 1/16	8	Interned in Holland
4833	Smith, George Nelson ...	31/ 5/16	9	(R.A.F.) Pilot Off.
3521	Udall, Christopher Herbert	30/ 7/15	9	Lieut. Emp. Com. Depot
3613	Voysey, Fred Waller ...	30/ 7/15	9	Lieut.
3634	Whitehouse, Horace H. ...	30/ 7/15	5	Lieut.
3728	Wigzell, Howard Elphick	30/ 7/15	9	Lieut.
3687	Yeoman, L/Cpl. Edwin William	3/11/15	7	Lieut.
760758	Allerton, Arthur Russell ...	26/ 6/17	8 ✠	Wounded 14/3/18
764126	Anderson, Robert William	31/ 7/17	6	
5195	Beck, Thomas William ...	5/ 9/16	5	Lieut.
765670	Beresford, Jack	28/11/17	10	
5363	Bowers, Charles Stanley ...	11/ 7/16	7	Lieut. Wounded 19/6/17
6843	Brown, Alfred Williamson	11/ 7/16	9	Lieut.
763192	Brown, Norris Maltby	11/ 5/17	5	
4884	Buchanan, Lawrence Gordon	11/ 7/16	10	Lieut.
765650	Bushby, Edmund Fleming	23/ 5/18	6	
6749	Cackett, Clarence William	26/ 9/16	7	Lieut. Wounded 25/4/18
765304	Cartman, James Victor ...	28/11/17	5	Killed in action 19/6/18
763290	Chilton, Albert Edwin	31/ 7/17	5	Wounded 1/5/18
5050	Coleman, George Herbert	26/ 9/16	5 ✠	Wounded 2/10/17, 14/10/18
4674	Colley, Douglas James ...	11/ 7/16	6	Killed in action 29/11/16
765453	Cooke, Aubrey	28/11/17	6	
3200	Dudley, Noel Montague Charles ...	11/ 7/16	5	Lieut. Died of wounds 11/10/16
761794	Dunn, William Henry ...	11/ 2/17	7	Capt.
765838	Fitzpatrick, John Terence	23/ 5/18	7	Wounded 14/10/18
5900	Fraser, Eric Alston ...	11/ 7/16	9	Capt. Wounded 3/5/18 ℳ(2)
761697	Frost, Niels Pelis Austin ..	3/ 8/17	7	Lieut. Wounded 9/10/17
4769	German, Arthur George ...	11/ 7/16	10	Lieut.
763728	Girvan, Charles	26/ 4/17	7	ℳ
763270	Griffith, John Richard ...	26/ 4/17	7	
764557	Harris, William Carey	24/ 9/17	8	
4659	Harvey, Albert ...	11/ 7/16	5	Major D.S.O. ✠ ℳ
760886	Holloway, Robert John ...	25/ 9/17	5	
763722	Hooper, Frederick	25/ 9/17	5	
762648	Hutton, William Stanley ...	25/ 9/17	6	Wounded 29/4/18
764325	Jones, Glan	31/ 7/17	7	
764327	Kelty, Stanley William ...	25/ 9/17	9 ✠	Wounded 28/3/18, 18/9/18
764149	Kershaw, Hulbert	25/ 9/17	6	Wounded 16/5/18
762681	Knox, Thomas Cowe	24/ 9/17	7	Killed in action 19/8/18
763397	Lacey, Everitt Arthur ...	25/ 9/17	7	
761287	Leaning, Reginald William	25/ 9/17	9	Killed 31/5/18
6373	Littler, Albert Edward ...	11/ 7/16	9(13)	Wounded 9/4/17
765017	Lyon, Cpl. Francis Thomas Balmain	31/10/17	10	Lieut. ℳ
764332	Maylin, Bertram Henry ...	31/ 7/17	8	Missing 7/5/18
765461	McKechnie, William ...	28/11/17	6	
6482	McLellan, Robert Belsher	11/ 7/16	9	Lieut. (M.G.C.)

LIVERPOOL REGIMENT (T/F).

6812	NICHOLLS, Joseph Ernest ...	... 11/ 7/16	9	*Lieut.*
764335	NICHOLSON, John Alexander	... 25/ 9/17	8	*Prisoner of War* 2/5/18
766526	NOBLE, Leslie Reginald ...	... 17/ 4/19	9	*Wounded* 22/8/18
5526	OATES, Herbert Prudent ...	... 12/11/16	5	*Killed in action* 20/9/17
765851	QUINN, James Edward ...	... 23/ 5/18	8	*Killed in action* 5/10/18
766835	RIDGWAY, Ivor	... 26/ 6/18	10	
3657	SCOTT, Frank Munro ...	... 11/ 7/16	10	*Lieut.* ✠ (*Military Police*) ℟
764266	SMART, William Pechy ...	... 31/ 7/17	5	✠ *Prisoner of war* 24/7/18
764349	SPRIGINGS, Reginald Henry	... 30/10/17	5	
762986	STEPHENS, Reginald Chester	... 27/ 6/17	7	
765965	STOREY, John	... 10/ 9/18	6	
763083	TODD, Leslie Winstanley Carter	... 30/ 5/17	5	*Wounded* 10/11/17
6778	WELDON, Edward Jack ...	... 23/11/16	7	
3290	WHITE, George Fenwick ...	... 26/ 9/16	10	*Lieut.*
5670	WHITTON, William Edward	... 11/ 7/16	10	*Lieut.*
762571	WILSON, John Cameron ...	... 31/ 7/17	7	

Service Battalions (New Armies).

3376	BROWNE, Henry Needham ...	15/ 5/15	16	*Lieut.*
3375	WALKER, L/Cpl. Charles ...	15/ 5/15	16	*Capt.* ℟
767343	ABRAHAM, Ernest Edward Unwin ...	6/ 2/19		
7909	ARLISS, Edward William Hugh ...	19/12/16		*Lieut.* w. 18/4/17, 7/12/17
5935	ASHTON, Percy	26/ 9/16	12	*Wounded* –/2/17, 12/10/17
767766	BANNER, David Redvers ...	5/ 3/19		
762497	BARRATT, John Leslie ...	26/ 4/17	(13)	*Lieut. Killed in action* 27/9/17
766585	BARRINGTON, Walter Oscar ...	6/ 2/19		
764745	BARTON, Mortlock Mackenzie ...	24/ 9/17		*Wounded* 30/4/18
763191	BASSETT, Henry William ...	10/ 3/17		
768144	BAXENDALE, Thomas James ...	17/ 3/19		
764681	BAXTER, Hugh	24/ 9/17		
764398	BIGGS, Francis Guy ...	10/ 3/17		
763634	BROOKE, Arthur	10/ 3/17		
6710	CAREFULL, John Holt ...	5/ 9/16	12	*Capt. Killed in action* 21/3/18
766299	CHRISTIAN, Albert Millais Crossley	24/ 5/18		
767331	COUPLAND, Arthur John ...	6/ 2/19		
767097	COWEY, Thomas William ...	6/ 2/19		
767612	DAINTY, Sydney	6/ 2/19		
763612	DAVIES, Edward James ...	10/ 3/17		
763153	EDWARDS, George Henry ...	10/ 3/17		*Prisoner of war* 24/3/18
760140	ESCH, Ray Edward ...	25/ 6/17	19	
763268	EYRE, Frank Thomas ...	10/ 3/17		*Capt.*
763641	FLETCHER, Henry ...	10/ 3/17		*Lieut.*
6139	GATHERAL, George Morton ...	16/ 4/17	12	*Prisoner of war* 16/5/18
47856	GIBSON, Keith Gooden ...	3/ 3/19		
764287	GILL, Charles Lovett ...	10/ 3/17		
7473	GLOVER, Norman ...	19/12/16	12	

LIVERPOOL REGIMENT (S/B).

764577	GRAVES, Edwin	10/ 3/17	
766133	GRAY, Frederick Wavell	26/ 3/18	
764239	GREIG, Harold Graham	29/ 8/17 12	Lieut. Wounded 20/11/17
764318	GREY, Hugh Kinghorn	29/ 8/17 12	Wounded 24/12/17
3758	GRICE, Stephen	14/ 8/16 17	
765231	GWYNN, Eric John Crowther	10/ 3/17	
769520	HARRISON, George	19/ 2/19	
764644	HARVEY, Frederick Ernest Edwin	10/ 3/17	
761883	HASTIE, Peter Duncanson	11/ 4/17	
4388	JONES, Maurice Broadbridge	19/12/17	Prisoner of war 22/5/18
768398	JONES, Robert Martin	26/ 6/18	
763184	LOWE, William Cottrell	10/ 3/17	
763641	NEWCOMBE, Frank Viner	10/ 3/17	
766443	OLDBURY, Howard Edward	26/ 6/18	To Army Cyclist Corps
767913	OWEN, Arthur James	5/ 3/19	
764716	PAWSON, Francis George	10/ 3/17	
4901	PHILLIPS, Gilbert Arthur	28/ 3/17 12	Wounded 28/8/17
763079	RADCLIFFE, Edward Allen	26/ 4/17	
762810	RICH, Charles Allen	10/ 3/17	
765516	ROSTRON, Stanley Rumney	21/ 2/18	
763723	SALWEY, David Ernest Lilford	10/ 3/17	
763311	SAULL, Harold Truscott	10/ 3/17	(Labour Corps) Died 21/10/18
767887	SHAW, Arthur Edward	12/ 2/19	
763684	SMITH, Arthur Henry	27/ 6/17	(36/Northumb. Fusiliers)
763281	SQUIBBS, Charles Frederick	10/ 3/17	
763185	STEPHENS, John Hall	10/ 3/17	
764671	SWATMAN, Cecil Maitland	24/ 9/17	
767708	THOMPSON, Harry	3/ 3/19	
768020	WALLACE, John McGilp	17/ 3/19	
762801	WARD, Frederick Victor Childerson	10/ 3/17	
764673	WHARTON, Arthur Clifford	24/ 9/17	Wounded 30/4/18
764053	WILLIAMS, Kenneth Homfray	27/ 3/18	
764302	WOODS, Eric Evelyn	29/ 8/17 12	Died of wounds 18/5/18

THE LONDON REGIMENT (T.F.)

FIRST BRIGADE— 1st (City of London) Battalion: Royal Fusiliers.

		2nd Lieut.	
2827	ATKINSON, Edward Arthur ...	12/ 2/15	*Lieut.* { Resigned Re-enlisted in 4/London K/A 4/11/18 }
2424	BARKAS, Geoffrey de Gouchy	22/ 7/15	*Capt.* ✠ *Wounded* 28/8/18
2854	BOOTH, Ronald George Jackson	21/ 3/15	*Lieut.*
2485	CLAPTON, William Thomas	20/ 4/15	*Lieut.* (R.E.)
1308	COOKE, L/Cpl. Bernard Campbell	20/ 6/15	*Lieut.* R.T.O. *w.* –/12/15, –/9/16
2389	DICKINSON, Lionel St. Clair	22/ 7/15	*Killed in action* 15/9/16
2469	HORSBURGH, Arthur Lindsay	20/ 4/15	(8) *Capt.* ✠
2394	HUGGINS, Douglas Frank	22/ 7/15	*Capt. Killed in action* 29/8/18
1772	MORTON, William Chamberlain	5/ 5/15	*Lieut.* ✠
2861	PAPWORTH, Reginald	22/ 7/15	*Lieut.*
3171	PATRICK, Cecil Warren	6/ 7/15	*Capt. Wounded* 22/1/16
1334	PETLEY, Sgt. Hugh	24/ 4/15	*Capt. Killed in action* 16/9/16
4181	AITKENS, John Butler	20/12/15	*Lieut.*
4822	CARR, Leslie George	3/12/15	*Capt.* ✠✠ *w.* –/9/16 K/A 27/4/18
4151	CLARK, Joseph Arthur	3/12/15	*Lieut. Wounded* –/7/16
5698	JAMES, William Thomas	31/ 5/16	*Lieut.* ✠
4220	JOHNSON, Robert William Stanley	26/11/15	*Lieut.*
3298	PATTEN, Herbert Thomas	5/ 8/15	*Lieut.*
4288	SMALLMAN, Charles Stanley	26/11/15	*Lieut. Wounded* 10/9/18
1218	THOMAS, Rudolph	24/ 8/15	*Lieut.*
4337	VILLENOWETH, Alexander Ch. A.	26/11/15	*Lieut.*
4396	WILLIAMS, Harold Edward	26/11/15	*Wounded* –/7/16 K/A 7/10/16
764220	ABEL, Frederick William Perowne	30/10/17	*To Ministry of Labour*
762553	BELL, Henry Leonard	26/ 4/17	*Lieut.* ✠ *w.* 12/4/18 *To Lab. Corps*
762712	BIRD, Leonard Grafton	29/ 3/17	*Lieut.*
762643	BROWN, Charles Edward George	27/ 3/17	*Lieut. Wounded* 10/11/17
762644	BROWN, Richard John Holdsworth	30/ 5/17	*Lieut. Wounded & P/W* 21/3/18
761272	CROMPTON, Abraham Alexander	16/ 6/17	
763491	CROWDY, Herbert Percy	29/ 3/17	*Lieut. Wounded* 1/9/17
765223	CUMNER, Cyril William	28/11/17	*Killed in action* 24/4/18
763157	GRETTON, Ernest William	27/ 3/17	*Lieut.*
762373	IMRIE, David Patrick Cuthbert	26/ 4/17	*Lieut.* ✠ (4/*South Stafford*)
763989	LAWRENCE, Stanley Borcham	16/ 6/17	*Lieut.*
766256	LINE, John Paul	26/ 6/18	
765793	MARTIN, Edwin John	27/ 2/18	*Killed in action* 4/9/18
764168	SADLER, Norman Gerald	24/ 5/18	

2nd (City) Battalion: Royal Fusiliers.

4144	BOUSTRED, Richard Warren W.	3/12/15	*Lieut. w.* 29/6/17 *To Min. of Lab.*
1931	ELTON, Herbert S.	25/ 9/14	*Capt.* ✠ *w.* 11/9/16 (*Tank Corps*) ✠
1350	MANSON, Sgt. Alexander Murray	29/ 9/15	*Lieut. Wounded* 3/7/16
3723	WIDDECOMBE, Cpl. Arthur James	29/ 9/15	*Capt.*
4033	WILLIAMS, Cpl. Henry Evan Vincent	3/12/15	*Died of wounds* 22/5/17

2/LONDON REGIMENT (T/F).

766104	COATES, William Henry Everest	... 23/ 6/18	
765823	FROST, Francis Arnold ...	... 23/ 6/18	
4619	STANCLIFF, Robert	... 4/ 8/16	*Lieut.* ✠ *Wounded* 19/3/17
766209	STECKLEY, Harold Brodie ...	... 31/10/17	

3rd (City) Battalion: Royal Fusiliers.

2899	AINSWORTH, Sidney Joseph	... 24/ 1/15	*Wounded* 19/5/17
2689	BURN, Harry Frederick James	... 16/ 1/15	*Lieut.*
1885	CHRISTMAS, Bernard Lovell	... 3/12/14	*Capt. w.* 27/10/15 *Died of wounds*
2498	DE PINNA, Charles David ...	... 24/ 4/15	*(R.A.F.)* [18/5/16]
546	HAY, Henry Jupp	... 24/ 1/15	*Capt.*
1168	JAGO, Edward Gordon ...	... 4/ 6/15	*Lieut.*
3734	LAMBERT, L/Cpl. Cecil Osmond	... 24/ 9/15	*Hon. Lt. in Army To Lancs. Fus.*
1125	MINSHULL, John Lewis . .	. . 23/ 1/15	*Capt. Killed in action* 2/4/17 ✠
2585	PUGH, Thomas Pugh ...	... 28/ 1/15	
1152	REDDALL, Cpl. Horace Cecil	... 12/ 6/15	*Lieut.*
547	RODGERS, John	... 24/ 1/15	*Capt.*
3098	SIMON, Harold James Behrens	... 12/ 6/15	*(2) Lieut.*
762892	DOTTRIDGE, Henry Roland...	... 31/ 7/17	*Wounded* 2/3/18
5151	EVELYN, Albert Finlayson ...	... 5/ 9/16	*Lieut.*
765541	FRASER, Charles Douglas ...	... 28/11/17	*Killed in action* 22/3/18
5576	FROY, William Alan	... 26/ 9/16	*Lieut.*
766354	PATERSON, Frank James ...	... 26/ 6/18	✠ *Wounded* 27/9/18 [8/8/18]
763347	SELIGSOHN, Henry Leon ...	... 26/ 4/17	*Capt. & Adjt.* ✠ ✠ *w.* 13/11/17,
765811	STUART, Herbert Gordon ...	... 27/ 2/18	*Died of wounds* 11/3/19

4th (City) Battalion: Royal Fusiliers.

1616	COTTON, Edward Norman ...	... 9/ 4/15	*Capt. Wounded* 29/6/17
471	DE PURY, Sgt. Charles Frederick P.	15/11/15	*Lieut. R.T.O.*
3308	HEWLETT, Harold Alcester Tom	... 15/ 8/15	*Capt. Killed in action* 23/8/18
1364	HORNE, Sgt. Geoffrey Scott ...	... 30/ 7/15	*Capt. Wounded* 12/4/18
3137	JONES, Harry	... 2/ 7/15	*Lieut. w.* –/7/16 *K/A* 15/5/18
3136	JOHNSTONE, L/Cpl. Robert	... 2/ 7/15	*Lieut. (R.A.F.)* ✠
3371	LEAKE, George Ernest Arthur	... 2/ 7/15	*Capt. D.S.O. D/W* 2/6/17
3074	MONKMAN, Sgt. Eric Arthur	... 2/ 7/15	*Lieut.*
1560	TOWSE, William Norman ...	... 8/10/14	*Capt. Killed in action* 15/9/16
1617	WALMISLEY, Shaftesbury Edgar	... 2/ 7/15	*Lieut.*
1595	WILLIAMS, Henry Jameson M.	... 16/ 1/15	*Lieut.*
5175	GRIMSDELL, Reginald Edward	... 21/ 6/16	*Killed in action* 25/9/16
4607	PYNE, Percy	... 11/ 7/16	*Hon. Lt. (R.A.F.) w.* 21/4/17
765220	CAMPKIN, Reginald Ernest ...	... 28/11/17	*Killed in action* 28/3/18
764779	LEWIN, Wilfred Eusebius ...	... 30/10/18	
2578	RIX, Leslie Gordon	... 4/ 2/15	*Capt. Killed in action* 11/2/17 ✠

LONDON REGIMENT (T/F). 291

SECOND BRIGADE— 5th (City) Battalion: London Rifle Brigade.

1918	COLLINS, Arthur Jefferies	...	16/ 1/15	*Capt.* ℳ
3529	FORBES, L/Cpl. Lawrence	...	5/ 8/15	*From 9/Middlesex D/W 9/7/17*
2210	HIGHAM, Eric Edward	...	16/ 1/15	*Wounded 21/9/17*
975	HOWE, George Herbert	...	11/ 4/15	*To R.G.A.*
2667	KEDDIE, George Douglas F.		16/ 1/15	*Capt.*
3997	WARNER, Archibald	..	28/10/15	*Killed in action 1/7/16*
1943	WHEATLEY, Fletcher Mortimer	...	4/ 5/15	*Lieut. Wounded 23/1/16*
5145	WILLS, William Anthony	...	21/ 6/16	*Lieut.*
2483	WOOD, Trevor Ley Conduer		16/ 1/15	*Lieut. 29/5/15*
3013	FURRELL, L/Cpl. Bernard	...	20/12/16	*Lieut.*
2624	LINTOTT, Sgt. Harry Chamen		20/12/16	*Died of wounds 22/3/18*
764721	RUXTON, James	... ...	30/ 5/17	
761225	THOMPSON, Roderick Charles	...	3/ 8/17	*Prisoner of war 14/5/18*
7555	WARD, Dudley Theophilus	...	26/ 1/17	*Killed in action 20/9/17*

6th (City) Battalion: Rifles.

3899	AMOS, Ernest Albert	...	2/11/15	*Lieut. Wounded 10/8/18*
3840	ANDERSON, David Wilson	...	11/ 7/16	*Capt.* ✠ ✠ *Killed in action 8/8/18*
3797	BELTON, Frank Hubert	...	2/11/15	*Lieut.*
2274	BRODRICK, Percival	... ...	30/ 9/14	*Capt. (Staff)* ℳ
3130	COTTON, Gilbert	... ...	3/ 6/15	*Lieut. (R.E.)*
2534	FARADAY, Roy	... ...	26/ 2/15	*Lieut. (M.G.C.) K/A 7/6/17*
3618	GODFREY, L/Cpl. Ernest Gordon	...	2/11/15	*Capt.* ✠ *Wounded 11/11/18*
2526	KELLER, Francis Frederick	...	6/11/14	*Lieut. Died of wounds 22/5/17*
2278	LAKE, Harold Charles Evan	...	23/ 4/15	*Lieut.*
2413	LATHBURY, Robert James	...	6/11/14	*Capt. Wounded —/4/18, —/5/18*
5855	LLOYD, Thomas Rice	...	11/ 7/16	*Lieut.*
5783	MAXTED, Claud Brotherton	...	10/ 7/16	*Capt.* ✠ *Wounded 4/6/17, 2/5/18*
2174	MONKTON, Arthur Reginald	...	22/ 4/15	*Lieut.*
3707	SMART, Edgar Herbert	...	2/11/15	*Lieut. Killed in action 30/11/17*
6083	TAYLOR, Ernest Charles	...	11/ 7/16	*Lieut.*
3125	TERRY, John Norman	...	25/ 6/15	*Capt. Died of wounds 20/9/16*
1698	TEW, Arthur Healey	...	29/ 4/15	*Lieut.*
1043	TUCKER, Cyril	... ...	6/11/14	*Lieut.*
2062	WEBB, John Timms	...	21/10/14	*Killed in action 9/5/15*
3173	WESTCOMBE, Albert Bernard		25/ 6/15	*Lieut.*
6670	BELL, Frank William	...	5/ 9/16	*Lieut.*
4875	COWNLEY, Arthur Lucien	...	5/ 9/16	*Lieut.*

7th (City) Battalion.

3080	BERLINER, L/Cpl. Philip Barnett	...	4/ 7/15	*Lieut.* ✠ *Wounded 28/8/18*
1458	KIRBY, Wilfred Howard	...	24/ 4/15	*Capt. (To Min. of Labour)*
1942	LUDBROOK, Percy	... ...	22/ 9/15	*Lieut. [D/W 10/12/17* ℳ }
1240	RUNDELL, Leslie Eric	...	15/10/14	*Capt.* ✠ ✠ *w. 5/6/15, —/5/16* }

7/LONDON REGIMENT (T/F).

5339	Evershed, Philip Douglas	10/7/16	Capt.	Killed in action 22/8/18
4242	Halsey, Eric Charles	20/12/15	Lieut.	Killed in action 19/6/17
3983	James, Lawrence Edward	29/10/15	Capt. ✠	w. 27/8/17 P/W 25/4/18
3084	McConnel, John Edward Gordon	12/8/15	Lieut.	
3962	Ridgway, Henry Collinson	29/10/15	Killed in action 7/10/16	
6411	Scothorne, John Parr	11/7/16	Lieut.	
6273	Scudamore, Charles Greenwich	10/7/16	Capt. ✠	Wounded 18/5/18
6274	Scudamore, Stanley	10/7/16	Lieut.	(To Min. of Labour)
5638	Smith, Alexander Thomas Speir	10/7/16	Lieut.	
3967	Smith, L/Cpl. Harold Benjamin	29/10/15	(K.R.R.)	D/W 20/5/17
3979	Thomas, Robert William	29/10/15	Lieut. ✠	Wounded –/4/18
6596	Watson, Clifford Thomas	11/7/16	Lieut.	Died of wounds 3/12/17
763737	Bailey, Arthur	30/5/17	Lieut.	
7753	Ball, Arthur Chatterton	20/12/16	Missing 18/4/18	
765493	Barnes, Reginald Charles	28/11/17	Lieut.	Wounded 22/3/18
8161	Benstead, Harry Edwin	19/12/16	Killed in action 14/4/17	
7408	Blackhurst, Sydney	20/12/16	Lieut. ✠	Wounded 19/6/17
8162	Boyer, Ernest Alexander	26/1/17	Killed in action 5/4/18	
766298	Brett, Bertram Lynton Wooldridge	23/5/18	Wounded 12/10/18	
763318	Brewer, Cecil Ernest	30/5/17	Lieut.	Wounded 11/9/18
766735	Butler, Stephen James	24/5/18		
6049	Chamberlain, Herbert Roy Malcolm	29/7/16	Lieut.	(To Ministry of Labour)
763228	Chiazzari, Henry William	27/3/17	Lieut.	
7911	Clarke, Donald Bruce	19/12/16	Lieut.	Wounded 20/4/17, 22/12/17
7955	Clayton, Seymour Lewis	26/1/17	Lieut.	
762826	Cleland-Hollamby, Leslie Knowles	29/3/17	Lieut.	
766853	Clow, John Percy	4/2/19		
766732	Cocke, Philip Merteus	26/6/18	Wounded 29/11/18	
765222	Constance, William Ernest	28/11/17	Killed in action 9/8/18	
763637	Cook, Arthur Smalley	30/5/17		
763781	Cook, Horace Montague	30/5/17	Killed in action 21/3/18	
767189	Cope, Ernest Harold	5/2/19		
762877	Cox, Geo. Beckett	26/4/17	Killed in action 16/8/17	
765675	Craven, Ernest Blaumont	27/2/18		
766499	Craven, Cecil Edward Philpott	10/9/18		
8163	Crosier, Vernon Swann	26/1/17	Died of wounds 6/4/18	
8155	Cuff, Joseph	20/12/16	Lieut.	Wounded 19/5/17
765455	Dansey, Felix Ramon Arthur	18/12/17	Killed in action 25/7/18	
765929	Davidson, William Henry Boyle	24/5/18	Wounded 18/9/18	
765871	Doe, Charles Vernon	26/6/18	(1/London)	
764137	Earee, Robert Clarence Westall	30/5/17		
765355	Edwards-Trollip, John	25/9/17	Killed in action 27/8/18	
762630	Fairney, Leonard	26/4/17	Wounded 17/12/17, 19/9/18	
767361	Ferguson, Robert Michael Joseph	5/2/19		
7772	Foord, Basil Arthur	20/12/16	Lieut. ✠	
765645	Fraser, Alan Cumming	30/10/17 ✠	Wounded 9/8/18 K/A 31/8/18	
766406	Fraser, Ian Mackintosh	24/5/18	Wounded 27/9/18	

767056	GARDNER, Wilfred Owen	29/10/18	
763683	GIBB, Howard Robertson	26/ 4/17	
766751	GILL, Graham Gordon	3/ 2/19	
768114	GILLETT, Francis Charles Bernard	3/ 2/19	
762558	GLENTON, Frederick	26/ 4/17	*Lieut.* ✠
765424	HALLS, James Lawrence	28/11/17	
766842	HARTLEY, George Clissold	24/ 5/18	*Wounded* 18/9/18
762784	HASSLACHER, Alfred John	27/ 3/17	✠ *Wounded* 21/9/18
8193	HAYNES, Reginald Joseph	25/ 1/17	*Lieut.*
766232	HEARNSHAW, Herbert	26/ 6/18	
765234	HEWETT, William Geoffrey	28/11/17	*Prisoner of war* 20/5/18
7500	HOOKER, Malcolm Ward	19/12/16	*Lieut.*
762722	HOPKINS, Charles Edwards	28/ 8/17	*Wounded* 18/12/17
766254	HOWSE, Henry Arthur Greenway	4/ 2/19	
764703	IRWIN, William George	25/ 9/17	
766182	JOLLEY, James	26/ 6/18	
767246	JONES, Edgar Dutton	3/ 2/19	
8188	KEEY, Cecil Walter	20/12/16	*Lieut.* ✠ *Wounded*
764776	KEMP, William James	25/ 9/17	*Prisoner of war* 17/5/18
765568	KERR, John Vass	28/11/17	✠
765828	KIMBER, Eric Dixon	24/ 4/18	
766815	KING, Ernest Coleby	4/ 2/19	
762153	KNOX, Horace Henry	28/ 8/17	
7639	LANGLEY, Reginald Knight	19/12/16	*Prisoner of war* 10/5/18
765983	LAVOIPIERRE, Marie-Joseph M. Louis	27/ 2/18	
7672	LAZENBY, Horace	20/12/16	*Lieut.* *Wounded* 1/6/18
8186	LEE, James Robertson Leonard	25/ 1/17	
763891	LIDDIARD, Thomas Gilbert	26/ 6/17	
760591	LISSER, Henry Charles Joseph	3/ 2/19	
765721	LORT, William Vincent	18/12/17	✠ *Wounded* 2/8/18
766310	LUCAS, Clifford James	26/ 3/18	*Capt.* ✠
765240	MATCHAM, John Noel Lancaster	28/11/17	
765978	MAULE-FFINCH, Eric Herbert Justus	24/ 5/18	*Killed in action* 27/8/18
765979	MAULE-FFINCH, Knightly Harry O'D.	24/ 5/18	
763340	McHARDY, Stewart John	30/10/17	*Killed in action* 30/4/18
763537	MENZIES, Clifford Douglas	27/ 3/17	*Prisoner of war* 12/10/17 ✠
765644	MILLER, Albert Henderson	31/10/17	*Prisoner of war* 31/5/18
766562	MILLER, George William	26/ 6/18	
7695	MITCHELL, Robert Greig	26/ 1/17	*Lieut.*
768352	MORTON, Clifford Fielding	5/ 2/19	
765903	MURRAY, Marischal	23/ 5/18	
766183	NORTON, Elliott	26/ 3/18	
767253	NORTON, Howard Stead Marston	18/ 3/19	
767254	NORTON, Kenneth Stacey Marston	18/ 3/19	
765338	PARKER, Herbert Hambley	25/ 9/17	*Wounded* 15/4/18
765466	PERRY, Reginald Walter	27/11/17	*Lieut.* *Wounded* 9/8/18
763755	PETERS, Theodore	30/ 5/17	
762726	PHILLIPS, Alexander	26/ 4/17	*Prisoner of war* 12/10/17

7/LONDON REGIMENT (T/F).

767416	PLUMMER, Albert Alexander	5/ 2/19	
765727	POLLEY, William Stanley	27/ 2/18	
764852	PORTEOUS, Robert Alexander	25/ 9/17	
762882	POTTER, Anthony Francis	25/ 9/17	*Wounded* 9/9/18
763595	PRATT, Harold Douglas	26/ 4/17 ✠	*Wounded* 19/9/18
5187	PRESTON, John Frank	29/ 7/16	*Lieut.* ✠
763209	PULFORD, Jack Falconer	27/ 6/17	
763077	PULLEY, Evelyn	28/ 8/17	*Wounded* 18/12/17
763741	PURKISS, Sydney Herbert	25/ 9/17	
765245	PURVIS, Tom	28/11/17	
765874	QUIGLEY, Frank	23/ 5/18	
763990	REID, Raymond Edgar	30/ 5/17	
763508	RICHARDSON, Samuel Jonas	30/ 5/17	
765486	RITCHIE, Douglas Ransford	28/11/17 *Lieut.*	*Wounded* 22/5/18
763597	ROAD-KNIGHT, Charles	26/ 4/17	
763210	ROBERTS, Francklin Allender	27/ 3/17	*Killed in action* 8/8/18
765473	ROBINSON, Alfred Chasey	28/11/17	*Prisoner of war* 3/6/18
765570	ROBINSON, Victor Lloyd	28/11/17	*Wounded* 28/8/18
766360	ROLFE, Claude Hamilton	27/ 8/18	
6579	ROOTS, Percy William	29/ 7/16	*Lieut.* w. 17/3/17 K/A 11/6/17
762841	ROSE, Alexander St. John	29/ 3/17	*Lieut.*
765247	ROSS, Harold	28/11/17	
765730	ROSS, Hunt	24/ 4/18	
764306	ROSS, Rupert John	27/ 3/17	*Prisoner of war* 12/10/17
765248	ROUGHTON, Willie	28/11/17	*Wounded* 13/12/18
767429	ROUSE, Redvers Percival Yates	4/ 2/19	
766572	ROW, George Kingsley	8/10/18	
765517	RUSSELL, John Francis Rbt. Vaughan	18/12/17	
762536	SCOTT, John Johnstone	24/ 4/18	
765518	SEATON, John William	27/11/17	
8193	SHARP, Matthew	19/12/16 ✠	*Died of wounds* 11/2/18
766584	SHAW, Frank Routledge	2/10/18	
763542	SHILCOCK, Harold Gordon	28/ 8/17 ✠	
763408	SIEMS, Frederick Walter Montgomery	26/ 4/17	*Prisoner of war* 26/12/17
8117	SIMMONS, Stanley Jack Raven Burton	26/ 1/17	*Lieut.*
766407	SIMMONS, Robert Dewdney	26/ 6/18	*Killed in action* 23/9/18
766820	SIMPSON, George Montague Fayers	24/ 5/18	*Wounded* 4/10/18
765805	SLATER, Harold Edgar	27/ 2/18	
765736	SMITH, Edward	27/ 2/18	
767116	SMITH, Edgar Hardwick	5/ 2/19	
765807	SMITH, Joseph Clarence	27/ 2/18	*Wounded* 19/9/18
762195	SOLOMON, Cecil Stuart	27/ 3/17	*Lieut.*
766581	STANISTREET, Charles Raymond	26/ 6/18	
763628	STOCKEN, Harry Charles Vernon	30/ 5/17	
766064	TAPLEY, Charles Mark	24/ 5/18	
766944	THORN, Frederick John William	29/10/18	
765609	TYLER, William Alfred	27/ 2/18	*Killed in action* 27/8/18
765524	VERNON, Richard Denis	18/12/17	*Wounded* 6/9/18

7/LONDON REGIMENT (T/F).

766266	WADE, John Talbot	...	24/ 5/18	*Capt.*
763551	WALLIS, William Robert	...	30/ 5/17	*Wounded* 24/4/18
763249	WHITE, Frank Reginald	...	26/ 4/17	
762707	WHITE, John Broadwood	...	30/ 5/17	✠
766408	WILHELM, Primus Maximillian	...	24/ 5/18	*Wounded* 18/9/18
765526	WILKES, Benjamin Cookman	...	19/12/17	
765527	WILKES, George Lionel	...	30/10/17	*Killed in action* 20/4/18
7857	WILLIAMS, Harold Willie	...	19/12/16	*Lieut.*
762570	WILLIAMSON, Arthur Faure	...	26/ 4/17	*Lieut.*
766671	WOOD, Christopher	...	3/ 2/19	
764081	WOOLNER, Herbert Chester	...	30/ 5/17	
765821	ZEYLMANS, Peter Cornelius	...	24/ 5/17	

8th (City) Battalion: Post Office Rifles.

2nd Lieut.	LEVERSON, Darrell Louis F.	...	6/11/15	
1970	BLACKING, William Henry Randoll	...	12/ 6/15	*Capt. & Adjt.*
2125	HAYES, Noel	...	5/ 5/15	*Lieut.*
2335	KENNEDY, L/Cpl. Launcelot R. A. E.		30/ 7/15	*Killed in action* 15/9/16
2406	MILLER, John Lockhart	...	22/ 4/15	*Lieut. Killed in action* 21/5/16
2441	SKULL, Arthur	...	17/ 4/15	(5/*Middlesex*)
2185	WRIGHT, Thomas	...	25/ 7/15	*Capt.*
1622	WEBB, Cpl. Christopher Rahere	...	12/ 6/15	*Lieut.*
4672	BROWN, John McIntyre	...	11/ 6/16	*Lieut.*
4209	HENDERSON, Eric	...	4/ 1/16	*Lieut. Killed in action* 7/6/17
257	KEENE, Sgt. Richard Francis	...	5/10/15	*Lieut.*
4570	PETERS, Maurice Wilmot	...	1/ 6/16	*Lieut. Wounded* –/11/16, –/6/17
2396	POTTER, Frederick John	...	5/10/15	*Killed in action* 21/5/16
4651	SCOTT, Robert	...	11/ 6/16	*Lieut.* (*To Ministry of Labour*)
3351	STARLING, Marwood Cooper	...	15/10/15	*From* 5/*R. West Surrey Lieut.*
3046	WALLACE, Cranstoun l'Estrange	...	15/ 8/15	*Lieut. Prisoner of war* –/5/16
2554	WILKINSON, Sgt. Cyril T. Anstruther		1/12/15	*Capt.*
4781	WOOLLEY, Arthur	...	11/ 7/16	*Lieut.* (4/*N. Stafford*)
765023	ARTHUR, John Charles Frederick	...	30/10/17	*To Ministry of Labour*
767547	BACON, Ronald Hotson	...	3/ 3/19	
760708	BAINES, Kenneth Charles	...	30/10/17	*Wounded* 2/5/18
767548	BARBER, Walter Russell	...	4/ 3/19	
766068	BUCKLAND, Frank William	...	10/ 9/18	
764228	CAMPBELL, Frank	...	10/ 9/18	
767003	CARTER, Maurice James	...	29/ 3/19	
763121	CAVILL, Percy Rundle	...	12/11/18	
763721	DUNCAN, Philip Courtney	...	27/ 6/17	*Killed in action* 30/10/17
764763	EASTON, Phillip	...	30/10/17	*To Ministry of Labour*
760705	EDGE, Edward Holden	...	27/ 3/17	*Killed in action* 22/3/18
765097	HAWLEY, Leslie Harvey	...	30/10/17	*Wounded* 7/5/18
765458	JOHNSON, Rowland Nicholas	...	28/11/17	*Wounded* 8/8/18

763396	KNIGHT, Frederick William	30/10/17	
765181	LEES, John Henry	13/11/18	
763618	LEE-SMITH, Sgt. Greville	24/ 5/18	
761001	MITCHELL, Sgt. Frank Crown	5/11/18	
766119	PLUMMER, William Graham	34/ 5/18	
765450	POWELL, Sgt. John Hirst	24/ 4/18	*Wounded* 1/9/18
766083	POWL, Stanley Robert	26/ 6/18	
766326	READING, William	24/ 5/18	*Wounded* 26/9/18
765872	REEVES-MOORE, Robert	24/ 5/18	
766450	ROBINSON, Archibald Robert Thomas	26/ 6/18	*Wounded* 26/10/18
766327	SPENCER, Joseph Thomas	29/ 5/18 ✠	*Wounded* 7/10/18
762689	VENABLES, Alexander	25/ 9/18	
765633	WEISS, Hubert Foveaux	27/ 2/18	*Died of wounds* 3/9/18
761436	WILKINSON, Dudley Frank	25/ 9/17	
765972	WILLS, George	27/ 2/18	*Wounded* 14/10/18
763996	WOOD, Norman	26/ 6/17	

THIRD BRIGADE— 9th (County) Battalion: Queen Victoria's Rifles.

2664	FARMILOE, Thomas Howard	1/ 6/15	*Lieut.* ⚔
2740	FILDES, Geoffrey Philip	12/ 1/15	*To Coldstream Guards Lieut.*
214	ORAM, Sgt. Richard Goodhart	4/ 2/15	*Major* ⚔
5231	AMOR, Ernest Hamilton	11/ 7/16	*Lieut. Wounded* 2/11/17
5087	BARTMAN, Cyril	11/ 7/16	*Lieut. Wounded* 28/4/17
5242	COLES, Frank Ernest	11/ 7/16	*Lieut. Wounded* –/11/16
2115	CUSHING, Ernest Charles	12/ 9/15	*Lieut. (To Labour Corps)*
5400	EASTERBROOK, Henry George	11/ 7/16	*Lieut. Died of wounds* 25/4/18
7674	GOLDSBURY, Charles Melville	11/ 7/16	*Lieut.* ✠ *Wounded* 18/9/17
2722	GUTTERIDGE, Richard Howard	12/ 9/15	*Killed in action* 2/10/16
5409	JONES, Reginald Lucas	11/ 7/16	*Lieut.* ✠ *Wounded* 30/8/17
5271	LUDLOW, Lionel	11/ 7/16	*Killed in action* 8/10/16
5272	MADDOCK, Owen Loftus	11/ 7/16	*Killed in action* 7/10/16
4306	MELHADO, Sgt. Clifford	4/ 1/16	*Lieut.*
5278	PARSLOW, Albert Jack	11/ 7/16	*Died of wounds* 10/10/16
5133	PLUNKETT, Joseph Robert	11/ 7/16	*Capt. & Adjt. Wounded* 16/10/18
5134	POOLEY, John Edmund Noel	11/ 7/16	*Lieut.*
5288	SEDGLEY, Henry Frederick	11/ 7/16	*Killed in action* 22/9/18
5810	SPAUL, Eric Arthur	11/ 7/16	*Lieut. (To Ministry of Labour)*
5192	THEAR, Archibald White	11/ 7/16	*Lieut. Wounded*
5424	THORNTON, Herbert Boucher	11/ 7/16	*(M.G.C.) Killed in action* 9/7/17
4988	WARREN, Alan Rowland	11/ 7/16	*Killed in action* 8/10/16
765710	BROADHURST, Herbert	18/12/17	
7574	CUNNINGHAM, Joseph Francis	20/12/16	*Lieut.*
6600	CUNNINGHAM, Philip Joseph	5/ 9/16	*Lieut.*

10th (County) Battalion: Hackney.

942	BETBEDER, Garton Louis ...	29/ 7/14	*Lieut.*
3039	LA TOUCHE, Arthur P. H. ...	5/ 5/15	*Capt.* 🎖
2751	PULLEN, Eric Whitford ...	20/ 4/15	*Lieut.* (*Min. of Labour*) *w.* 18/6/17
1922	STAFFORD, Lancelot Henry G.	25/11/14	*Capt.* 🎖
4377	ALLAN, William ...	9/ 1/16	*Lieut. R.A.F.*
4066	APERGIS, Tasso Scott ...	18/11/15	*Killed in action* 9/9/16
4143	BAKER, Felix Edward ...	8/11/15	*Lieut.*
4359	BALL, Eber John ...	9/ 1/16	*Lieut.* (*Tank Corps*)
5890	BATH, Cpl. Reginald Fred ...	11/ 7/16	*Killed in action* 7/10/16
4353	BENJAFIELD, Harry Wilfred ...	4/11/16	*Lieut.* (*Staff*)
5047	CANTER, L/Cpl. Francis ...	12/ 6/16	*Lieut.* 22/*R. Fusiliers*
4453	CROOM, William Charles ...	11/ 7/16	*Killed in action* 7/6/17
4381	CURRIE, James Alexander ...	4/ 1/16	*Killed in action* 13/3/17
4455	DAVIS, Uriah Philip ...	1/ 6/16	*Killed in action* 16/4/17
4414	DEAN, Reginald Evan ...	9 /1/16	*Killed in action* 7/6/17
5612	EVANS, Douglas William ...	11/ 7/16	*Lieut.* ✠
4417	FRANSHAM, William Henry Elwin ...	9 /1/16	*Lieut.*
4457	GLOVER, Cyril John ...	11/ 7/16	*Died of wounds* 8/10/16
1913	GOLDIE, Barnard Chas. ...	20/10/15	*Capt.* ✠
4523	GRANT, Edward H. Stuart ...	21/ 6/16	*Lieut.*
4557	GRUNDY, Frederick ...	2/ 6/16	*Lieut.* (*Staff*)
4676	HENDERSON, Charles Ernest ...	1/ 6/16	*Capt.* D.S.O. *w.* −/5/17, −/11/17 🎖
4180	MARGOLIOUTH, John Frederick ...	16/11/15	*Lieut. Wounded* −/8/16
5705	MARTIN, L/Cpl. Granville Basnett ...	12/ 6/16	*Capt. & Adjt.* ✠
4191	MARTIN, Hugh Alan ...	8/11/15	*Capt.*
4120	MARTIN, Reginald James ...	18/11/15	(2) *Capt.& Adjt. w.*−/5/17, 13/9/17
4553	MOODY, Beverley Charles ...	2/ 6/16	*Lieut.* (*R.A.F.*)
4554	MORGAN, Jacob ...	2/ 6/16	*Lieut.*
4442	MORGAN, William Lawrence ...	4/ 1/16	*Lieut. Wounded* −/9/16
4145	MOSS, L/Cpl. Reginald Ernest ...	18/11/15	*Lieut.*
6176	OAKENFULL, Herbert Joseph ...	11/ 7/16	*Killed in action* 9/10/16
3601	PATTISON, Robert ...	29/10/15	*Capt. Killed in action* 27/12/17 🎖
3831	PETTIT, L/Cpl. Hector Browning ...	20/10/15	*Lieut.*
4986	SIEVEY, Victor Cecil ...	11/ 7/16	(*Ministry of Munitions*)
5384	SMITHER, Samuel Thomas ...	1/ 6/16	*Capt.* ✠ ✠ ✠ 🎖
4975	STRAWSON, Percival Chatterton ...	1/ 6/16	*Lieut.*
3970	STURTON, Henry Chatfield ...	29/10/15	*Capt. Wounded* −/9/18
4178	WHITE, Frederick Charles ...	18/11/15	*Lieut.*
4374	WOOTTON, Kenneth Edwin ...	9/ 1/16	*Lieut. To Tank Corps* ✠
765614	CONWAY, Francis Henry ...	18/12/17	*Wounded* 28/11/18
761298	GRIFFITHS, Sydney Archibald ...	5/ 7/17	(*R.A.F.*)
763303	KING, Herbert John ...	28/ 3/17	✠ *Wounded* 17/9/18
6779	LAWRENCE, Henry Percy ...	26/ 9/16	*Lieut. w.* 17/2/17, 27/8/18, 1/9/18
7273	MARTINEZ, Harry Elias Nunez	26/ 1/17	

11th (County) Battalion: Finsbury Rifles.

1803	AKERMAN, Ralph Portland ...	... 19/ 1/15	*Wounded* 13/9/15 *D/W* 3/10/15
2706	BROOK, Clifford Hardman ...	... 21/ 1/15	*Lieut.* (*R.A.F.*)
479	BROWN, Humphrey Gilmour	... 31/ 8/14	*Capt. Wounded* –/6/16
2240	GOLDSCHMIDT, Harold Henry A. ...	10/ 4/15	*Capt.*
2215	JONES, Lloyd Owen	... 10/ 4/15	*Lieut.*
2224	JORGENSON, Ernest Stuart Lyon	... 31/ 8/14	*Capt.*
1103	LAWRENCE, Francis Charlton	... 8/ 6/15	*Lieut.*
2217	MANN, Percival Ramsay ...	... 31/ 8/14	*Capt.* O.B.E. ᛭
1859	OWEN, Frank Denys ...	... 9/ 1/15	*Lieut. Wounded* –/12/17
1808	SOUTTEN, Cpl. Arthur Camillo ...	13/ 6/15	*Lt.-Col.* (8/*Bn.*) ✠✠ *w.* 7/5/18
2486	WATTS, Cpl. Henry Lionel ...	18/ 3/15	*Lieut.* ᛭
4724	BRADSHAW, Herbert Leo ...	8/ 1/16	*Lieut.*
4270	CALLCOTT, Henry Norman H. ...	12/ 1/16	*Lieut.*
4124	HANNAH, Thomas Roe ...	8/ 1/16	*Capt. Wounded* 19/10/18
4343	HODGSHON, Frederick William ...	30/12/15	*Lieut.*
4063	MOORE, William Joseph ...	8/ 1/16	*Lieut. Wounded* –/10/17, –/5/18 ᛭
4821	SANDERSON, Gerald Stanley ...	8/ 1/16	*Killed in action* 22/7/16
4085	WARD, Frederick William ...	10/ 1/16	*Lieut.*
764003	CHARD, Harry Athelstan ...	... 26/ 4/17	*Lieut.*
761430	GARDEN, John Bruce ...	9/10/18	*Wounded* 17/8/17

12th (County) Battalion: The Rangers.

2420	How, Francis Radcliffe ...	.. 18/ 3/15	*Lieut.* (*O.C.B.*) *Wounded*
1905	LOWTHER, Walter Joseph ...	... 30/ 3/15	(*To R.F.A.*)
3630	OSBORNE, Francis William ...	... 22/ 9/15	
1706	REINECKE, Cpl. Arthur Julius ...	25/ 8/15	*Lieut. Wounded* 4/7/16
672	WELLSMAN, L/Cpl. Edgar Stanley ...	21/ 3/15	*Lieut.*
5040	BARRETT, Wilfred Morris ...	... 12/ 6/16	*Lieut.* ✠
4951	BROWN, Malcolm Beck ...	... 11/ 7/16	*Lieut.* (*R.A.F.*)
5738	COWELL, Harry Cyril Hall ...	10/ 7/16	*Capt. & Adjt.*
5052	CUNNINGHAM, James J. Ignatious ...	12/ 6/16	*Lieut. Wounded* 2/6/17
4593	DURSTON, Charles Giles ...	11/ 7/16	*Lieut. Killed in action* 7/10/16
5366	DAY, John William	11/ 7/16	*Lieut. Wounded* –/4/17, –/12/17
5764	JAMES, Percy Leonard Samuel ...	11/ 7/16	
6087	LANGTON, L/Cpl. Edwin Simmons W.	11/ 7/16	*Lieut. Wounded* 7/5/17
5270	LOVELESS, Rupert Bramble ...	12/ 6/16	*Capt. w.* 11/12/17, 12/10/18 ᛭
5777	LYAL, David Hume ...	10/ 7/16	*Lieut. Wounded* –/11/16
5412	MACE, Howard Kimberley ...	12/ 6/16	*Lieut.*
5778	MAIDMENT, Cyril Vaughan ...	10/ 7/16	*Lieut. Wounded* 21/4/17
5789	PEACOCK, Stanley Claude ...	11/ 7/16	*Lieut. Wounded* 2/4/17
5378	PEEBLES, Percy Norman ...	.. 11/ 7/16	*Killed in action* 9/4/17
5422	SPENLE, Henry Emile ...	... 12/ 6/16	*Lieut.* (*Staff*)
5078	SMITH, Herbert Charles ...	... 12/ 6/16	*Lieut.*
4941	STONE, Edward James ...	... 1/ 6/16	*Lieut.*

5813	STONES, Douglas Henry	...	11/ 7/16	*Lieut. Wounded* 16/5/18
5815	TARRANT, Reginald Walter		11/ 7/16	*Lieut. Wounded* 28/8/18
5609	TUCKER, Stanley Walter	...	11/ 7/16	*Lieut. Wounded* –/11/16
5303	WILLIS, Cyril Louis	...	12/ 6/16	*Lieut. Killed in action* 7/10/16
764952	SEED, Charles William Stanley		31/10/17	
765971	TWINE, Charles Ernest	...	27/ 2/18	*Wounded* 30/9/18

FOURTH BRIGADE— 13th (County) Battalion: Princess Louise's (Kensington).

2nd Lt.	HANKINS, Harold William	...	7/11/15	*Capt. & Adjt. Wounded* 4/7/16
755	ELVY, Leslie Thomas	...	7/ 3/15	*Capt.* ✠
4380	CARROLL, Leo Grattan	...	7/ 1/16	*Lieut.* w. 10/11/17 (*N.A C.B.*)
4476	CLARK, Robert	...	7/ 1/16	*Lieut. Wounded* –/9/16
2173	GOULD, William Stanley	...	28/ 9/15	*Lieut.*
4658	GAYNOR, Harold Francis	...	12/ 1/16	*Prisoner of war* 27/3/18 ⚑
4470	GRAINGER, John Chambers	...	28/ 1/16	*Lieut.*
5346	LISSACK, Maurice Solomon	...	10/ 7/16	*Lieut. Wounded* 10/11/17
4210	LOCKHART, Reginald Frank	...	7/ 1/16	(*M.G.C.*) *D/W.* 10/7/17
3594	NIGHTINGALE, Cpl. Charles Thrupp	...	15/10/15	*Lieut.*
4253	PILGRIM, Henry Bastick	...	7/ 1/16	*Killed in action* 1/7/16
3762	RIVINGTON, Kenneth A. Stewart	...	15/10/15	
1171	STOCKMAN, Sgt. George Donovan	...	15/10/15	*Lieut.*
3585	TAYLOR, Basil Franklin	...	15/10/15	*Lieut.* (*Staff*)
4483	WILLIAMS, Hopkin	...	7/ 1/16	*Lieut.*
4569	YOUNG, Albert Louis Gwynne	...	7/ 1/16	*Lieut.*
7383	ACKERMAN, Edgar Charles	...	26/ 9/16	*Lieut.*
7067	BARNETT, L/Cpl. Reginald Oliver	...	1/ 7/16	*Lieut.*
2118	BENBOW, Sgt. Louis Julian	...	15/10/16	*Lieut.*
6613	BLOXHAM, Leonard Albert	...	5/ 9/16	*Lieut.* (*Staff*) *Wounded* 4/3/18
766302	DEWSON, Leslie Jackson	...	26/ 6/18	
764487	ELLIS, Frederick William	...	28/ 8/17	*Killed in action* 3/3/18
7234	LEGGETT, George William	...	21/12/16	*Lieut.*
762562	MATHESON, Herbert	...	30/ 5/17	(*15*) *Lieut. Killed in action* 24/3/18
7455	MITZAKIS, Albert Victor Marcel	...	26/ 1/17	*Capt.* F/D *Wounded* 21/3/18 ⚑
760732	ORMISTON, Walter Hugh	...	30/ 5/17	✠ *Wounded* 8/12/17
763002	OWERS, Frederick Thomas	...	30/ 5/17	✠ *Wounded* 27/4/17
2084	SAVAGE, James Percival	...	15/10/16	*Capt.* ✠
7433	TONNOCHY, Alec Bain	...	19/12/16	*Lieut.*

15th (County) Battalion: Civil Service Rifles.

2975	PHELPS, Francis William	...	28/ 9/15	*Lieut.* (*M.G.C.*)
4798	ANDREW, Reg. B. W. Goldsworthy		2/ 6/16	*Capt.* ✠✠ *Wounded* 20/9/18 ⚑
6280	ARUNDELL, Thomas Henry	...	10/ 7/16	*Lieut.*
4630	BRASHER, Walter	...	12/ 6/16	(*6*) *Lieut.* ⚑
5796	BROAD, Walter Victor Mantach	...	12/ 6/16	*Lieut. Killed in action* 22/3/18
5336	CRIBBETT, Wilfred Charles Geo.	...	12/ 6/16	*Lieut.*

15/LONDON REGIMENT (T/F).

5094	DENNY, Ernest	12/ 6/16	(*K.R.R.*) *Died of wounds* 4/8/17
4625	DU HEAUME, Francis Herbert	1/ 6/16	*Capt. Wounded* 15/10/18 🎖
4574	HOOLE, Geoffrey	12/ 6/16	*Killed in action* 15/9/16
5408	HOUNSELL, Frank William	10/ 7/16	*Lieut. (Staff) Wounded* 29/8/18
4423	HUTTON, Percy Granville	11/ 6/16	(*R.A.F.*)
4460	JARVIS, Maurice Frank	10/ 7/16	*Lieut.*
4634	MARCHANT, Charles Victor	12/ 6/16	*Wounded* 7/6/17 *K/A* 30/11/17
5112	MARGRETT, George Montague	10/ 7/16	*Lieut. Wounded* 22/12/17
7441	MITCHELL, George Rowe	10/ 7/16	*Lieut.*
5131	MORROW, Alexander	12/ 6/16	*Lieut. Wounded* 4/10/17 🎖
5861	MORTON, L/Cpl. George Charlton	12/ 6/16	*Lieut. Wounded* 20/11/17
4558	NEWTON, Cyril Frank	2/ 6/16	*Lieut.*
5135	POTTS, James Phillips	12/ 6/16	*Lieut. Prisoner of war* 10/1/18 🎖
4664	THOMPSON, Frank Dickinson	1/ 6/16	(*K.R.R.*) *Killed in action* 13/1/17
5402	ETHERIDGE, Alfred Hollis	12/ 7/16	*Lieut.*
765588	GARRETT, Maurice Humphries	27/11/17	*Killed in action* 2/9/18
4742	GLYNN, Alfred Henley	10/ 8/16	(*Yorkshire L.I.*) *D/W* 12/2/17
763954	MARKHAM, Leslie Albert	27/ 6/17	*Wounded* 17/4/18
766607	MIALL, Eric John	25/ 9/18	
762230	SMART, Claud Augustus	30/ 5/17	
766319	THROWER, Sydney Walter	23/ 5/18	
765149	WHEELER, Edward Nelson	31/10/17	

16th (County) Battalion: Queen's Westminster Rifles.

538	BULL, Sgt. Ronald J. H.	26/ 8/14	*Capt. Killed* 13/7/17
1833	CIRCUITT, Clifford Marmaduke	11/ 4/15	*Capt.* (*R.A.S.C.*) M.B.E. 🎖
2435	COLLIER, Eric Cecil Frederick	6/11/14	*Lieut.* 24/12/14
4471	FARMER, Geoffrey John	22/ 2/16	*Lieut.*
2535	HORNE, James Anthony	14/ 2/25	*Killed in action* 11/7/16
3952	IVESON, Cyril Charles	14/12/15	*Lieut. Wounded* 7/7/16
2162	YEATES, Arthur Gerald Vavasour	22/ 7/15	*Killed in action* 1/7/16
4637	BAKER, Thomas Sidney	10/ 7/16	*Killed in action* 14/4/17
5105	BATES, Reginald Naunton	14/ 6/16	*Lieut.*
5680	CLAYTON, Eric George	14/ 6/16	*Lieut.* (*Min. of Labour*) 🎖
3693	DENT, Horace Benjamin	10/ 7/16	(*R.A.F.*)
5754	FRASER, Kenneth	14/ 6/16	*Lieut.*
5183	LEETE, Francis Bertram	14/ 6/16	*Lieut. Wounded* 15/10/18
4851	MASON, Henry	14/ 6/16	*Lieut.*
6302	TROTTER, Stuart Ernest	10/ 7/16	*Lieut.*
5142	WALL, Cyril Charles	15/ 6/16	*Capt.* (21/*K.R.R.C.*)
4685	WRENN, Cecil	14/ 6/16	*Lieut.* (4/*Norfolk*)
5330	WRIGHT, Alfred Kyrle Terrett	14/ 6/16	*Died of wounds* 10/12/17
4446	YEATES, L/Cpl. Stanley Charles	8/ 7/15	*Lieut. Killed in action* 14/4/17
766545	BANNESTER, John	24/ 4/18	*Killed in action* 4/10/18
762773	BASSHAM, Robert Anthony	30/ 5/17	*Wounded* 13/3/18

16/LONDON REGIMENT (T/F).

5465	BAWTREE, Edward	... 5/ 9/16	Lieut.	Wounded –/1/17
765671	BOTHAMLEY, Basil Parkinson	... 18/12/17		
762797	BROOKE, Alfred Charles ...	... 27/ 3/17	Lieut.	
763071	MANN, John Godfrey ...	... 27/ 2/18		
762763	PALLETT, Leslie Clarkson ...	... 25/ 9/17		
766873	PUCKLE, Owen Standidge	... 3/ 2/19		
765735	SIMONDS, Sydney Francis ...	... 27/ 2/18		
762921	WARNER, Francis Banks ...	... 26/ 4/17		
5827	YOUNG, John Herbert ...	... 11/ 7/16	(R.F.C.)	

FIFTH BRIGADE— 17th (County) Battalion: Poplar & Stepney Rifles.

2104	DADSON, Reginald Thornton	... 14/10/14	Adjt.	Major O.B.E. 🎖
2686	NEWTON, Murray Edell ...	... 7/ 5/15	Lieut. (R.A.F.)	K/A 18/6/17
2402	UNDERWOOD, Cyril Henry ...	... 8/ 6/15	Capt.	Killed in action 2/5/18
5571	CARO, Jacob Pisa	... 10/ 7/16	Killed in action 2/5/18	
3307	CLEAVE, Stanley William ...	... 26/ 1/16	Lieut.	Wounded 15/5/18
5836	COOKE, Archibald Barton ...	... 10/ 7/16		
5402	ETHERIDGE, Alfred Hollis ...	... 12/ 7/16		
4363	FOSTER, Edgar Henry ...	... 10/ 7/16	Lieut.	
4318	FOX, Arthur Wells	... 7/ 6/16	Lieut.	
5999	GOODWAY, Harold William ...	... 11/ 7/16	Capt.	Wounded 2/1/18 🎖
4384	GREENIDGE, Samuel Clyde Clarke ...	9/ 1/16	Lieut.	🎖
5504	HILL, Claude Harold ...	... 10/ 7/16	Lieut.	Wounded 30/9/18
4252	LEE, Cpl. Esmond Christin ...	... 13/ 1/16	Lieut.	
4212	OSBORN, Malcolm	... 7/ 1/16	Lieut.	🎖
6178	ROWLAND, William Roland ...	... 10/ 7/16	Killed in action –/6/17	
4961	SLANEY, Arnold John Robinson	... 10/ 7/16	Lieut.	✠
5827	YOUNG, John Herbert ...	... 10/ 7/16	Lieut.	
763025	DAY, Edward Thomas ...	... 24/ 4/18		
762895	FRASER, Roderick Donald ...	... 28/11/17		
760656	LAITHWAITE, Alan	... 26/ 4/17	Lieut. D.S.O.	w. 10/11/17 🎖
6546	LAZARUS, Joseph Philip ...	... 5/ 9/16	Lieut.	Wounded 16/4/17
765506	MARTIN, Austin Gardiner ...	... 27/11/17		
7335	VANDERPLANK, Hubert Cecil	... 29/ 8/16	Lieut.	Wounded 24/5/18
7917	WALMSLEY, Allan Armstrong	... 26/ 1/17	Lieut.	Wounded 24/9/17
760599	WILLIAMS, Maxwell Henry ..	... 26/ 4/17	Killed in action 19/9/17	

18th (County) Battalion: London Irish Rifles.

818	CONCANNON, Cpl. James Blake	... 7/ 3/15	Capt. & Adjt.	
3138	JUDD, Charles Edward ...	... 12/ 6/15	Lieut. (Labour Corps)	
3629	MUNRO, Ronald George ...	... 21/ 7/15	(Irish Gds.) Lieut. ✠	D/W 19/9/16
3418	POWER, Henry Teevan ...	... 9/ 7/15	Lieut.	

18/LONDON REGIMENT (T/F).

2247	ROBERTS, Edward Richards	... 27/ 2/15	(10) Lieut. ☫
1757	TOPHAM, Geoffrey Ronald G.	... 27/ 2/15	Wounded –/5/16 (R.A.F.)
5361	ASHBRIDGE, John Prentice ...	... 10/ 7/16	Lieut. Wounded 20/11/17
3931	BARTLETT, John Duncan ...	... 29/10/15	Lieut. (R.E.)
3941	BATTERSBY, Reginald Hugh	... 6/11/15	Lieut. Wounded 20/4/18, –/5/18
5044	BRAYDON, Kevin ...	... 14/ 6/16	Killed in action 23/12/17
4598	CANNAN, L/Cpl. Vincent Cooper	... 21/ 1/16	Lieut. Wounded –/7/16, 4/1/18
3919	COCUP, Charles Herbert ...	... 6/11/15	Lieut.
3920	CURLING, Frank Trevor ...	... 6/11/15	Capt. w. -/11/16, -/2/18 K/A 31/8/18
5203	GARDNER, Reginald David C.	... 10/ 7/16	Lieut.
6057	GLENDENING, Alfred George	... 10/ 7/16	Lieut.
5118	GRAY, Cyrus Keswick ...	... 10/ 7/16	Killed in action 14/4/17
4826	HAYLOCK, Stanley William ...	... 10/ 7/16	Capt. To Indian Army
5856	McCORMICK, Arthur Eric ...	... 10/ 7/16	Lieut.
5701	MACNAMARA, George Edward	... 10/ 7/16	Lieut.
4831	MITCHELL, John Leishman ...	... 10/ 7/16	Wounded 24/5/17 D/W 6/6/17
6017	NEWTON, Geoffrey Broughton	... 10/ 7/16	Prisoner of war 18/4/18
4075	O'BYRNE, Michael ...	... 6/11/15	Lieut.
3977	OLIVER, Arthur Allen ...	... 6/11/15	Lieut.
5379	PERRY, Albert Francis ...	... 10/ 7/16	Lieut. (Ministry of Munitions)
5285	RICHARDSON, Robert Harold	.. 10/ 7/16	(R.F.C.) Killed in action 6/11/17
4642	RICHENS, Richard Ivor ...	... 10/ 7/16	Died of wounds 14/4/17
3888	SANDERSON, Sidney Charles	... 6/11/15	Killed in action 11/10/16
3889	SHAW, Ernest Benjamin ...	... 6/11/15	Lieut.
3936	SHERIDAN, Robert ...	... 6/11/15	Lieut. Wounded 21/9/18
5667	STEDMAN, William Walter Thomas	10/ 7/16	Killed in action 13/11/16
3898	TOMS, Stanley Muir ...	... 27/10/15	Died of wounds 8/12/17
3971	TYSON, Howard Cecil ...	... 6/11/15	Lieut. Wounded 16/2/18
4860	VINCENT, Cecil Richard Causdlon ..	10/ 7/16	Lieut. ✠ w. 29/6/18, 6/9/18
6038	WILSON, Harold Benjamin ...	... 10/ 7/16	Killed in action 7/4/17
7649	ACTON, John Wade Douglas ...	... 19/12/16	Lieut. Wounded 23/4/17, 4/10/18
8118	CHAPMAN, Robert William Tydd	... 26/ 1/17	Lieut. Wounded 28/8/18
5167	CONRAD, Alfred George ...	... 4/ 9/16	Lieut.
765376	PARKES, Percy Reginald ...	... 28/11/17	Died of wounds (P/W) 4/4/18
6660	THOMPSON, Richard Seward ...	... 26/ 1/17	Killed in action 16/6/17
767658	WILSON, Harry Cecil ...	... 4/ 3/19	
8068	WRIGHT, Reginald George Stuart	... 25/ 1/17	

19th (County) Battalion: St. Pancras.

4836	ANGAS, Reginald	... 14/ 6/16	Lieut. Wounded 18/3/17, 8/12/17
4416	FIXTER, Tom	... 9/ 1/16	Lieut.
4223	JOHNSON, Francis Hugh ...	... 9/ 1/16	Killed in action 15/9/16
4307	PALMER, Frederick Sidney ...	... 9/ 1/16	Lieut.
4165	RADCLIFFE, Charles Netton ...	... 12/11/15	Lieut. ✠✠ Wounded 22/12/17
4426	ROWSON, Tom Hollingworth	... 9/ 1/16	Killed in action 15/9/16
3463	SHILLITO, George	... 29/ 5/15	Lieut.

19/LONDON REGIMENT (T/F). 303

4257	STEVENS, Charles	9/ 1/16	*Lieut.*	
4328	TYNDALL, James	9/ 1/16	*Died of wounds* 4/6/17	
765441	ELEY, Ralph Corban	28/11/17	*Killed in action* 24/3/18	
4443	MUFF-FORD, John Waldemere Daniel	29/ 9/16	*Lieut.*	
765693	ROBERTSON, James	18/12/17	(7) *Died of wounds* 5/10/18	
2385	SCANTLEBURY, Charles Warren Oliver	18/12/17	*Lieut. Wounded* 8/7/16	
765249	SMITH, Ivor Clifford	28/11/17	*Prisoner of war* 10/5/18	
4792	WILSON, William Wyatt	14/ 7/16	*Lieut.*	

20th (County) Battalion: Blackheath and Woolwich.

4759	ANDREWS, L/Cpl. Walter Thornton...	14/ 6/16	*Lieut. (To Ministry of Labour)*
4188	BACON, Douglas Charles	15/10/15	*Lieut.* ✠ *Wounded* 22/5/17
3649	BISHOP, Percy Bartram	30/ 7/15	*Lieut. Wounded* –/9/16
4468	BLUNDELL, Douglas Roper	14/ 6/16	*Lieut.* ✠ *Wounded* 7/12/18
4859	CLARKE, Edwin Alfred	14/ 6/16	*Died of wounds* 1/10/16
4362	DUCE, William	5/ 1/16	*Lieut. w.* –/9/16 *P/W* 26/6/18
3082	GILBERT, Cpl. Montague	2/11/15	*Lieut. Wounded* –/1/17
3884	HELLICAR, Geoffrey Theodore ...	15/10/15	*Killed in action* 27/7/16
3807	HUNT, Archibald Henry	2/11/15	*Lieut.* ✠
5018	LONG, Francis Charles	11/ 7/16	*Lieut. Wounded* 10/12/17
3896	MALCOLM, Kennith James	15/10/15	*Lieut. Killed in action* 19/2/18
3955	MAXWELL, Wellwood	2/11/15	*Died of wounds* 16/9/16
2460	NEEDHAM, Leslie William	16/ 6/15	*Lieut.* ✠ *To War Office*
4356	NELSON, Harry	7/ 1/16	*Lieut. Killed in action* 15/9/16
4984	PATTISON, Stuart Percy	11/ 7/16	*Lieut. (R.A.F.)*
4370	SALTER, Carl Russell Colley... ...	11/ 7/16	*Lieut.* ✠
5665	SILVESTER, Reginald	11/ 7/16	*Killed in action* 7/6/17
4371	SMITH, Norman Havelock	7/ 1/16	*Killed in action* 23/3/18
4508	SPURGEON, L/Cpl. Donald F. Parker	14/ 6/16	*Lieut. w.* 20/11/17, 15/5/18
4450	STEEL, Edward George	7/ 1/16	*Lieut.* ✠ *[K/A* 10/9/18
5385	STONE, Alan	14/ 6/16	*Lieut.*
4168	WEATHERLY, Laurence Edwin M. ...	15/10/15	*Lieut. w.* 20/11/17 *K/A* 19/2/18
763808	AILLES, Harold Charles	26/ 4/17	*Lieut.*
4237	GRAY, James	11/ 8/16	*Lieut. Wounded* 21/12/17
765549	HEPBURN, Dudley Frankland ...	28/11/17	

SIXTH BRIGADE— 21st (County) Battalion: First Surrey Rifles.

4469	CLISBY, Hartley E.	21/ 1/16	*Lieut. Wounded* –/8/16
3948	EDMUNDS, John	5/12/15	*Lieut. Wounded* 13/9/18 ✠
5995	ELKINGTON, Howard George ...	11/ 7/16	*Capt.* ✠
4273	FRENCH, Sydney	5/12/15	*Lieut.*
2693	GEARY, Ronald Fitzmaurice ...	23/ 9/14	*Killed in action* 15/1/16
3639	GIBSON, John Rowland	13/ 1/16	*Lieut.*
4929	HOCKEY, Alfred Lennox	14/ 6/16	*Lieut.* ✠ *Wounded* 11/4/18
4930	HODGE, Frederick George	13/ 6/16	*Killed in action* 31/10/17
4342	HOMBROW, Victor Percival	4/ 1/16	*Lieut.*

4397	Hoskyns-Abrahall, Theo.	14/ 6/16	Capt.	Wounded
4160	Hunter, Alexander Forbes	5/12/15	Lieut.	Killed in action 23/5/16
4545	Jones, Cecil Greenstreet	2/ 1/16	Lieut.	
4753	Jones, Stanley Alfred Morgan	11/ 7/16	Capt.	(4/D.C.L.I.) w. 16/11/17
4547	LeChene, Henry Paul	21/ 1/16	Lieut.	(Colonial appointment)
4506	Lucas, Herbert Demmaire	21/ 1/16	Lieut.	
5704	Martin, Cyril Basnett	11/ 7/16	Lieut.	Killed in action 30/3/18
4254	Richmond, Hugh Bowten	6/ 1/16	Lieut.	Killed in action 9/12/17
5799	Robinson, Harold Shillito	1/ 6/16	Lieut.	(R.A.F.) w. –/9/16
4206	Smith, Edward	5/12/15	Lieut.	
4166	Snead, Harold Mortimer	5/12/15	Lieut.	(Staff)
4104	Trafford, William Charles S.	5/12/15	Lieut.	Wounded –/5/16, 12/9/17
4274	Watson, William Percy	5/12/15	Lieut.	
4428	Webster, John Henry	6/ 1/16	Lieut.	(Ministry of Labour)
765672	Broomfield, Harold Francis	27/ 2/18		
764199	Harvey, Herbert Atherton	16/ 8/17		
765173	Hitchings, Frederick Arthur	28/11/17		Wounded 14/5/18
1688	Holland, Frederick Ronald	4/ 6/18	Lieut.	
762680	Isaacs, Frank Henry	26/ 4/17		Wounded 26/9/17
5625	Justice, Herbert Maxwell	5/ 9/16		Wounded & P/W 5/6/18
765099	Ratcliffe, Cornwallis St. Aubyn	16/ 6/17		

22nd (County) Battalion: The Queen's.

1296	Bare, Alfred Raymund	25/ 9/14	Capt.	(Staff) D.S.O. ✠ w. 18/4/18)
3837	Hall, Thomas Nelson	14/12/15	Lieut.	[To 1/Loyal N.Lancs. ⋈(2))
3839	Hall, William Eric	5/12/15	Lieut.	R.A.F.
4853	Nowell, Charles	1/ 6/16	Lieut.	Wounded –/9/16
4584	Walker, Cpl. Thomas George	1/ 6/16	Lieut.	R.T.O.
140	Watts, George Hugh	12/10/14	Capt.	Wounded 22/3/15
5459	Weaver, Frederick	1/ 6/16	Capt.	✠ ⋈
5464	Barron, Thomas Henry	11/ 7/16	Lieut.	✠ w. 5/10/16, 7/11/18 ⋈
4918	Child, Frederick James	11/ 7/16	Lieut.	
4516	Hewitt, L/Cpl. Arthur Edgar	11/ 7/16	Lieut.	✠ (T.M.B.)
5801	Seddon, Arthur Leslie	11/ 7/16	Lieut.	(R.A.F.)
5816	Taylor, Pryce Christopher	11/ 7/16	Lieut.	(R.A.F.)
5736	Collins, John Edmund	19/12/16	Lieut.	✠
761597	Fellows, Frank Bennett	26/ 6/18	Lieut.	F/D ⋈
8147	Gray, Douglas	20/12/16		Wounded 18/4/18
766518	Green, Arthur John	10/ 9/18		
4640	Hayes, Alfred Paul	1/ 9/16	Lieut.	⋈
6291	Larkman, Raymond	5/ 9/16	Lieut.	
763467	Maddox, Leonard George	28/11/17		✠ ✠ Killed 30/8/18
767339	Myers, Morris Ferdinand	26/ 6/18		
5543	Scholfield, Christopher	11/ 7/16		
763766	Stockins, William James	26/ 4/17	Lieut.	Missing 21/6/18

G. E. CATES, V.C. [pp. 45, 341.

Copyright.] A GERMAN TANK. [Capt. E. HANDLEY-READ.

23rd (County) Battalion. [⚜(3)

Capt.	GREENWOOD, Charles Francis H.	... 23/ 1/10	*Lt.-Col. To* 22/*Lond.* (*O/C*)	D.S.O.
2nd Lt.	NEWTON, William Godfrey ...	... 17/10/14	*Lt.-Col. To* 21, 19, 22/*Lond.* (*O/C*)	
			[✠ *w.* 18/9/16, 24/3/18	
423	BALLARD, L/Cpl. Maurice Arnold ...	13/ 3/15	*Died of wounds* 29/5/15	
1375	HALCROW, L/Cpl. Malcolm E.	... 13/ 3/15	*Capt. Wounded* –/7/16	
1497	WILLSON, Sgt. Harold Grainger	... 19/ 3/15	*Major* F/D ⚜	
3434	BEN OLIEL, John Bernard ...	... 11/11/15	*Lieut.*	
1958	BULGIN, Reginald	... 22/12/14	(*Att. from R. Irish Fusiliers*)	
4799	CRISP, George Williams ...	... 15/ 6/16	*Lieut.* ✠	
4921	DAVIES, John Rhys	... 15/ 6/16	*Died of Wounds* 28/11/17	
6310	EWEN, Henry Spencer ...	... 11/ 7/16	*Lieut.* ✠ *w.* 12/1/18 *K/A* 5/4/18	
4420	GRAY, Samuel Alexander ...	... 11/ 1/16	*Lieut.* ✠	
4421	HALL, William Joseph ...	... 9/ 1/16	*Lieut.*	
5153	HENDY, George Francis ...	... 11/ 7/16	*Lieut. Wounded* 20/4/18	
4324	HERRATT, John	... 11/ 1/16	*Lieut.*	
3858	HOLMES, Frederick	... 30/ 7/15	*Lieut.*	
4406	HYAMS, Henry David ...	... 15/ 6/16	*Lieut.* ✠	
3216	JACOB, Augustus Fitzgerald ...	... 5/ 8/15		
4243	KENNETT, Alfred Claude ...	... 9/ 1/16	*Lieut. Wounded* 13/10/17	
4037	LEVIEN, L/Cpl. Charles Henry	... 11/11/15	*Lieut.*	
4932	LEWIS, Cecil J. Burghley ...	... 15/ 6/16	*Lieut.*	
3976	LYNES, L/Cpl John Algernon	... 11/11/15	*Lieut.*	
3764	MAEBY, L/Cpl. John Hume ...	30/ 7/15	*Capt. Died of wounds* 18/11/17	
5210	MANSEL-HOWE, Charles Torworth ...	11/ 7/16	*Lieut. Killed in action* 9/8/18	
4434	MATTHEWS, L/Cpl. Frank Nevill	... 23/12/15	*Lieut.* 16/*Rifle Brigade*	
3450	OPPENHEIMER, L/Cpl. Lehman James	5/ 8/15	*Died* 8/11/16	
5072	POTTS, Harold Joseph ...	... 12/ 7/16	*Lieut.* ✠	
5215	ROSSELLOTY, Gerald A. Crampern ...	11/ 7/16	*Lieut. To Indian Army*	
4368	QUARTERMAN, Percy Harold	... 11/ 1/16	*Lieut. Killed in action* 9/10/17	
4347	SAYERS, Horace George D.	... 11/ 1/16	*Lieut. Drowned at sea* 2/6/17	
3978	SEABROOK, Cpl. Albert Lionel	... 11/11/15	*Lieut.*	
3914	SELVEN, William Arthur ...	... 9/11/15	*Lieut.*	
3892	SNELLING, Leonard Maurice	... 11/11/15	*Lieut. R.A.F.*	
5875	STONE, Harold	... 5/ 9/16	*Killed in action* 8/6/17	
5082	SWIFT, Frederick	... 11/ 7/16	*Lieut.*	
5398	VINCENT, Walter John ...	... 11/ 7/16	*Lieut Wounded* 20/11/17	
4329	WEEDEN, Wilfrid Arthur ...	... 11/ 1/16	*Lieut.*	
2928	WHIDDINGTON, William Arthur	... 5/ 8/15	*Lieut.*	
763561	BARNES, Alfred Douglas ...	... 30/ 5/17	✠ *Wounded* 23/4/18	
762935	HARVEY, John William ...	... 25/ 9/18		
765467	PHILLIPS, Leslie Jack ...	... 28/11/17		

24th (County) Battalion: The Queen's.

165	ROGERS, Sgt. Charles Murray	... 2/ 9/14	*Major M.G.C.* ⚜	
58	SAUNDERS, Sgt. Cornelius James	... 1/ 9/14	*Bt.-Major G.S.O* ✠ F/D ⚜(3)	
5722	ASHMAN, Herbert William ...	... 11/ 7/16	*Lieut.*	
5362	BEENEY, James Alexander ...	... 11/ 7/16	*Lieut.* D.F.C. (*R.A.F.*)	
4978	BENWELL, Lionel Newton ...	... 11/ 7/16	*Lieut.*	
4673	BURROUGHS, Percy William ...	... 11/ 1/16	*Capt.* ✠ *Wounded* 29/8/18	

306   LONDON REGIMENT (T/F).

5730	CADMAN, Joseph Frederick ...	... 11/ 7/16	*Lieut. Wounded* –/4/17, 11/9/18
4246	CATTELL, Alfred George ...	... 6/ 1/16	*Lieut.* ✠
5744	CURTIS, Henry Thomas ...	... 11/ 7/16	(*K.O.Y.L.I.*) *D/W* 12/2/17
5367	DYKE, Cyril John ...	... 11/ 7/16	*Killed in action* 7/11/17
4667	JAMES, Charles Gordon ...	... 11/ 7/16	*Lieut.*
4546	KENWARD, Athol Horace White	... 13/ 1/16	*Lieut. M.G.C.*
3678	LEAR, Edward C. Rutherford	... 30/ 7/15	*Lieut.*
3769	LIVERMORE, Ernest Bernard	... 27/10/15	*Killed in action* 15/9/16
5374	MEAKINS, L/Cpl. John Burchell	... 11/ 7/16	*Lieut.*
4616	MOWER, Eric Elsdon ...	... 11/ 7/16	*Lieut.*
3542	MURPHY, Thomas Joseph ...	... 30/ 7/15	*Lieut.*
5213	PERRY, Percy Robert Wenman	... 11/ 7/16	*Lieut.* ₥
4431	POLL, Dudley Erskine ...	... 11/ 7/16	*Lieut.* ✠
3890	SLAUGHTER, Vivian ...	... 18/ 7/16	*Lieut.*
3178	SMART, Sgt. Robert Borlase	... 30/ 7/15	*Lieut.* (*M.G.C.*)
3739	STRAND, Alister Carmichael	... 30/ 7/15	*Lieut.*
5386	SUTHERLAND, John Alexander	... 11/ 7/16	*Killed in action* 8/12/17
3203	WARNER, Eric Terence Hugh	... 16/ 6/15	*Lieut.*
4404	WATTS, Harold Claude ...	... 11/ 1/16	*Capt.* ₥
5300	WESTCOTT, Albert ...	... 15/ 6/16	*Lieut.*
4509	WETTONE, Henry Frederick	.. 12/ 1/16	*Lieut. Wounded* 7/6/17
4665	WHEELER, William Rocert ...	... 11/ 7/16	*Lieut.* ✠ F/D(2)
5613	BATCHELOR, Edward ...	... 5/ 9/16	*Killed in action* 26/9/17
766420	BOLTON, Thomas Allen ...	... 7/10/18	

25th (County) Battalion: Cyclists.

2880	ANNS, Harold Falkner ...	... 28/ 3/15	*To R.A.F. Staff*
2769	GIFFEN, Lionel Edward ...	... 8/ 8/15	*Capt. To I.A.R.O. w.* –/5/17
2875	HAMBLEY, Richard Luskey ...	... 13/ 3/15	*Capt. To I.A.R.O.*
2442	JONES, Thos. Joseph William	... 23/ 6/15	*Lieut. To I.A.R.O.*
3875	CARPENTER, Hubert Granville	... 6/ 8/15	*Lieut. To Div. Cyclists.* (4)
4454	DANIELS, Hugh Arthur William	... 9/ 1/16	*Lieut.*
4560	DAVENPORT, Henry Stephen	... 9/ 1/16	*Lieut. Wounded* 22/12/17
4452	DE LA COZE, Francis Mare ...	... 2/ 1/16	*Lieut.*
4924	ELLIS, Clarence Victor ...	... 15/ 6/16	*Lieut.* (*10*) ₥
4925	EPPS, Ralph Septimus G. ...	... 15/ 6/16	*Lieut. Wounded* 3/10/17
5172	FAULKNER, Harold Edward	... 15/ 6/16	*Lieut. R.A.F.*
4847	FIELD, Reginald Thomas ...	... 15/ 6/16	*Lieut. Wounded* 28/4/17
4926	FULLER, George J. F. Franklin	... 15/ 6/16	*Lieut. Wounded* –/2/17
4440	GLUCKMAN, Philip ...	... 12/ 1/16	*Lieut. Killed in action* 8/10/16
4648	HAWKINS, Geoffrey ...	... 12/ 1/16	*Lieut.*
4591	RALEIGH, Roland Arthur ...	... 9/ 1/16	*Lieut.*
4463	SAMPSON, Charles Alexander	... 16/ 1/16	*Capt.* ✠ *w.* –/5/17, –/12/17 ⎫
4800	SHEPHERD, Ernest ...	... 15/ 6/16	(*15*) *Lieut.* [*K*]*A* 9/9/18 ⎭
4883	SIDDALL, Thomas Arthur ...	... 15/ 6/16	*Died of wounds* 17/4/17
5158	TERRY, Edward Fenton ...	... 15/ 6/16	*R.A.F.*
5037	WILLIAMS, Francis James ...	... 15/ 6/16	*Lieut.*
4810	HOLTHAM, L/Cpl. Edward James	... 11/ 7/16	*Lieut. Wounded* 26/10/17
765899	MARSH, William Eric ...	... 23/ 5/18	
766533	SMITH, Frederick Thomas ...	... 2/10/18	

[**28th (County) Battalion: Artists' Rifles.**

THE ARTISTS' RIFLES.

(Recognised as an Officers' Training Corps by Army Order No. 429 of 1915.)

ABBREVIATIONS.

2 or 2/28 = Original 2nd (Reserve) Bn.
3 or 3/28 = Original 3rd Bn. subsequently designated 2/28.
15/O.C.B. = No. 15 (Artists' Rifles) Officer Cadet Bn.
(Q) = Passed Regular Officers' Examinations for promotion to Major.
(q) = Passed Regular Officers' Examinations for promotion to Captain.
(H) = Qualified at School of Musketry (Hythe).

V.D. = Volunteer Officers' Decoration.
T.D. = Territorial ,, ,,
$p.$ = Certificate of Proficiency.
$p.s.$ = Passed School of Instruction (pre-war).
¶ = War Service previous to 1914.
† = Served overseas with 1/28, either as Officer or in other ranks.
O/C = Commanding Officer.
2 i/c = 2nd in Command.

(i.) Officers at date of Mobilization.

Honorary Colonel.
EDIS, Col. Sir Robert William, C.B., V.D. $p.$ 16/12/02 *Awarded* K.B.E.

Lt.-Colonel.
†MAY, Henry Allan Roughton, V.D. (T.) $p.s.$ 13/ 1/03 *Colonel.* C.B. O/C 1/28 (1914–15, 1920) *Comdt. Southern Commd. Offrs.' School of Inst.* 🎖

Majors.
†CHATFEILD-CLARKE, Stanley, V.D. (Q.)   1/ 4/08 *Lt.-Colonel.* O/C 1/28 (1916–17) 🎖

¶†EDLMANN, Herbert Elliot, T.D. (*H.*) (Q.)   9/12/12 *Major.* O/C 1/28 (1917) 🎖
    Hon. Lt. in Army, 11 Sept., 1901.

Captains (Hon. Majors).
HIGHAM, S. Stagoll, V.D. (Q.) $p.s.$ ...   4/11/02 *Major.* *A.P.M. 2/London Division* 2 i/c 3/28 & 15/O.C.B.
¶†SHIRLEY, Herbert J., C.M.G , T.D. (Q.) $p.s.$ 3/12/07 *Lt.-Col.* O/C 2/5 *Lancs. Fusiliers :* *Lt.-Col. R.A.M.C.* (Malta) : O/C 1/28 (1921). 🎖(2)

Captains.
†INNES, Charles Gordon D., T.D. (*H.*)(q.)$p.s.$ 27/ 5/09 *Major. Staff-Lt. : A.P.M. at G.H.Q.*

†EDWARDS, Harry Passmore (q.) T.D. $p.s.$ 31/ 5/09 *Major.* 2 i/c 2/28

WEST, William George, T.D. (*H.*) $p.s.$ 4/ 9/09 *Capt. Assist. Director of Munitions Contracts* M.B.E.

¶†GREENWOOD, Charles Francis H. (*H.*) 23/ 1/10 *Lt.-Col. To 23/Lond. :* O/C 22/Lond.
(Q.) $p.s.$ D.S.O. 🎖(3)

†KEENE, Alfred Valentine, T.D. $p.s.$ ...   7/ 1/11 *Major. Physical & Bayonet Training Supvsg. Officer*

¶†AUSTEN, Ernest Edward (q.) $p.s.$ ...   9/12/12 *Major. To H.Q. Staff of Dir.-Genl. R.A.M.C.* D.S.O. 🎖

Lieutenants.

†CROFT, Benjamin (q.) (H.) T.D. p.s. 28/ 5/06 Major. Instr. XV. Corps School Killed in action 10/11/18

†NEAME, Arthur John, T.D. p.s. 4/ 9/09 Major. Adjt. 2/28. Instr. First Army Infantry School

†ROYDS, Alan Francis, T.D. p.s. ... 4/ 9/09 Capt.

†NEIGHBOUR, Sydney W., T.D. (q.) 13/ 7/10 Capt. Adjt. 1/28 Bde.-Major, Dvina Force. O.B.E. F/D w. 28/4/17 ✠(3)

†BARE, Arnold Edwin (q.) ... 7/ 1/11 Capt. M.V.O. Killed in action 30/10/17

†OSTLE, Henry K. Eaton, T.D. ... 9/12/12 Lt.-Col. 2 i/c 2|Border: O/C 10/York & Lancs. O/C 8/Somerset L.I.: O/C 3/28. ✠ w. 25/9/15 ✠(2)

†SIMMONS, Frank Keith (q.) ... 18/12/12 Capt. Staff-Lt. G.H.Q. To 1/Highland L.I. Bde.-Major ✠ M.V.O. F/D ✠(3)

THOMPSON, Arthur Ralph ... 20/12/13 Capt.

Second Lieutenants.

2nd Lieut.

†HALL, Alner Wilson ... ... 4/ 3/11 Lt.-Col. ✠ O/C 1/28 Cadre (Feb.–May /19)

†GILKS, Humphrey Livingston ... 23/10/12 Capt. Adjt. 6/London ✠

✠BURMANN, Robert Moyle ... 23/10/12 Capt. Adjt. 2/Border: Bde.-Major, 20/Inf. Bde. D.S.O. ✠✠ Killed in action 27/10/18 ✠(6)

†TYER, Austin Arnold ... ... 5/ 3/13 Capt. (Special Bde. R.E., Loos) To 50/Bde. R.F.A. F/D. ✠

†MONEY, David Frederick ... 5/ 3/13 Capt. Adjt. 1/28 ✠ ✠

†FAIRTLOUGH, Gerard Howard ... 24/ 6/14 Capt. To R.E. Signals, 3rd Cav. Div. ✠ Died of wounds 13/6/18 ✠

RICKATSON, Hugh Cecil ... 24/ 6/14 Capt. To 5/Bedford. To Coldstream Guards ✠ w. 15/12/17

Adjutant.

¶†BLACKWOOD, A. P. (Capt. 2/Border) 20/10/12 Brig.-Genl. D.S.O. ✠(2)

Quartermaster.

†SMITH, John Ambrose ... ... 8/ 7/14 Lieut.

Medical Officers (R.A.M.C.).

†DE SEGUNDO, Major Charles Sempill, V.D. p. p.s. ... ... 2/ 7/09 Major. M.O. i/c Med. Div., 6/Genl. Hosp., [France. O.B.E.

JONES, Capt. Dudley Wm. Carmalt 16/ 4/13 Colonel. A.M.S. To 2/London R.F.A.

(ii.) Officers promoted from the ranks after Mobilization.

		2nd Lieut.	
1907	†Abbot-Anderson, Sgt. Louis G.	18/ 4/15	*Capt. Adjt.* 15/*O.C.B.* M.B.E. 🎖
499	†Adams, Cpl. Walter Alwyn Cole ...	17/10/14	*Major. To R.E. Adjt. w.* 7/6/17
2809	†Baillie-Hamilton, L/Cpl. George	12/ 5/16	*Lieut.*
398	†Barnett, CQMS Raimond Austin...	18/11/15	*Capt. Adjt.* 1/28. ✠ *w.* 5/4/18, 23/8/18 🎖
1472	†Bayne, Sgt. Henry Gerald ...	12/ 5/16	*Lieut.*
1480	Boswood, Sgt. Charles G. Gordon	10/12/15	*Lieut. To Food Ministry*
2782	Bowling, L/Cpl. Tom	29/ 4/15	*Capt. Adjt.* 3/28
35	†Byrne, L/Cpl. Alan Walter ...	17/10/14	*Capt. To* 1/*East Lancs.* (2 i/c) *Wounded* 18/6/15, –/8/15
505	†Chetwood, Cpl. Ernest Stanley ...	17/10/14	*Capt. Adjt. G.H.Q. Staff College. Killed in action* 30/10/17 🎖
77	†Child, Sgt. Arthur James... ...	17/10/14	*Lt.-Col. To R.F.C.* O.B.E. ✠ F.D. 🎖(2)
133	†Coleman, Sgt. Reginald	14/ 2/15	*Capt. Adjt. Southern Com. Off. School of Inst.* 🎖
2310	Cooper, Sgt. Douglas Jinkings ...	7/ 2/15	*Capt.* 15/*O.C.B.* 🎖(2)
536	Edge, Cpl. Percy Granville ...	17/10/14	*Major. Aajt.* 3/28. (*R.A.F.*) M.B.E.
118	†Edwards, Sgt. George Cyril ...	18/ 4/15	*Capt. Adjt.* 3/28. *Brev.-Maj.* 🎖(2)
2427	Elmslie, Sgt. Noel	18/ 3/15	*Capt.* 15/*O.C.B. Emp. Ministry of Munitions*
2905	†Ford, Sgt. Leslie Beaumont ...	12/ 5/16	*Capt. A.D.C.* F/D [*To Ind. Army*]
2684	Frankish, L/Cpl. William Martin...	29/ 4/15	*Capt. To* 11/*Rifle Bde. w.* 16/4/17
481	†Frost, Sgt. Alan	17/10/14	*Capt. To M.G.C.* K/A 17/10/17
1659	Girling, L/Cpl. Frederick John ...	17/10/14	*Capt. To R.A.S.C.*
948	†Godfrey, CQMS Stephen Mervyn	12/ 5/16	*Lieut. Killed in action* 30/12/17
1058	†Goulder, Sgt. Arthur Christopher	14/ 2/15	*Capt. Wounded* 6/4/18
2753	†Groom, Cyril	14/ 2/15	*Lieut.* 1/28 *M.G. Off. Killed in action* 30/12/17
2136	Hankins, Harold William ...	14/ 2/15	*To* 13/*London Wounded* 4/7/16
2290	Harvey, Eric Blake	18/ 3/15	*Capt.* (*R.F.C.*) P/W–/7/16
367	†Haslam, QMS James	12/ 3/16	*Lieut. Killed in action* 30/10/17
1388	†Hewitt, Sgt. Malcolm Brian ...	12/ 3/16	*Capt. Adjt.* 1/28 🎖
74	Howard, L/Cpl. Bernard F. ...	17/10/14	*Lieut.*
1534	Hughes, Thomas Harold... ...	18/ 3/15	*Capt.* 15/*O.C.B. Emp. R.E.*
1809	Job, Sgt. Ernest Dalzel ...	19/11/14	*Capt. To M.G.C. Killed in action* 11/7/16
1286	Kelsey, Cpl. Leigh Bentall ...	22/ 5/15	*Lieut. To Coldst. Gds. w.* 11/12/17
864	†Kyle, L/Cpl. James	17/10/14	*Lieut. T.M.B. To R.A.M.C.*
1695	Laing, Cpl. James Gordon ...	17/10/14	*Major. To M.G.C. Wounded* 27/6/16 *Killed in action* 3/10/18
2621	†Lee-Hankey, William	29/ 6/15	*Capt.* 15/*O.C.B.*
644	†Lepingwell, Sgt. George Bikerton	18/ 4/15	*Capt. Wounded* 30/12/17
2941	Leverson, Darrell Louis F. ...	6/ 5/15	*Lieut. To* 8/*London To Staff*
6	†Light, C/Sgt. Frederick Robert ...	21/10/14	*Capt. Q.M.* 2/28 *&* 1/28

1739 †Lubbock, Cpl. Humphrey Thornton 18/ 4/15 *Capt.* 15/*O.C.B.*
761 †Margetson, Sgt. Edward ... 12/ 3/16 *Lieut.* ✠ *Wounded* 25/3/18
263 Marshall, Sgt. John Warwick, T.D. 17/10/14 *Capt.*
745 †Mieville, Sgt. Walter Stokes ... 17/10/14 *Capt.* ✠ *w.* 10/11/17 15/*O.C.B.* ℞
347 Newton, Sgt. Charles Edward ... 7/10/14 *Capt. Brevet-Major* ℞
833 †Newton, L/Cpl. William Godfrey 17/10/14 *Lt.-Col. A.D.C. to C.G.S. To* 23, 21, 19, 22/*Lond.*: (*O.C.* 22/*Lond.*) ✠ *Wounded* –/9/16, –/4/18
2619 O'Brien, Sgt. Joseph Andrew ... 30/ 7/15 *Capt.* (*R.F.C.*)
¶64 †Padfield, CSM Frederick Henry ... 18/ 4/15 *Major. To R.E.*(*I.W.T.*) O.B.E
404 †Perl, CSM Bernard Huson ... 18/ 4/15 *Major To* 5/*R. Lancaster Adjt.* ✠
2466 Perry, Gordon Mackintosh ... 29/ 4/15 *Major. To Coldstream Guards Wounded* 15/9/16, 27/8/18
137 †Pike, Sgt. Charles William ... 26/12/14 *Capt. Wounded* 12/1/18
231 †Pinder-Brown, QMS Henry, T.D. 11/ 2/15 *Capt. To R.T.O.*
1822 †Porter, Cpl. Nigel Keith Farrar... 12/ 3/16 *Lieut. w.* 31/10/17 *To* 15/*O.C.B.*
51 †Prentis, Sgt. John Edward ... 17/10/14 *Capt.* ℞
746 †Robins, Robin Tillyard ... ... 19/11/14 *Capt. w.* 27/6/16 *To* 15/*O.C.B.*
3040 Rouse, Sgt. Guy Neville ... 11/ 7/15 *Lieut.*
84 †Royds, CSM John Iltid ... 18/11/15 *Lieut. Killed in action* 22/3/18
¶241 †Rust, CSM Percy, T.D. ... 18/ 4/15 *Capt.* M.B.E. ℞
819 †Scrutton, Alan Edward ... 17/10/14 *Major. A.D.C. to C.G.S. To Tank Corps* ✠ *Wounded* 31/7/17 ℞
274 †Seymour, CSM Joseph ... ... 12/ 3/16 *Capt.* ℞
2749 †Shinner, L/Sgt. W. Goodwin Blake 18/ 3/15 *Lieut. Died of wounds* 2/1/18
929 †Smith, L/Cpl. Walter Campbell ... 17/10/14 *Lt.-Col.* ✠ *Spec. appt.* ℞(2)
2080 †Spencer, Sgt. George ... ... 14/ 2/15 *Capt.* (11/*Rifle Bde.*) *Died of wounds* 4/12/17
1288 †Tallentire, Cpl. Arthur Tom ... 17/10/14 (*R.F.C.*) *Acc. killed* 20/10/15
1467 †Tapper, Michael John ... ... 17/10/14 *Capt. Asst. Camp Comdt. G.H.Q. To Tank Corps* ✠ ℞
2075 Tetley, Sgt. John C. Dodsworth ... 19/11/14 *Capt. To* 3/*Gren. Gds. Killed in action* –/10/17
2245 †Thompson, Cpl. Clarence Valentine 14/ 2/15 *Capt. To* 11/*Rifle Bde. Wounded*
359 Turnbull, CSM Richard Frank ... 11/ 2/15 *Capt. Q.M.* 3/28 ℞
1820 †Walker, CQMS Aubrey F. Cumnor 15/ 9/15 *Capt. Q.M.* 15/*O.C.B.* ℞
2744 Wheeler, Sgt. Ernest Bostock ... 10/12/15 *Capt.* 15/*O.C.B.*
799 †Williams, Sgt. Gordon ... ... 12/ 3/16 *Capt. Medal* R.V.O. *Killed in action* 30/10/17
315 †Willis, CSM Cecil Herbert S. ... 18/ 4/15 *Capt. Adjt.* 15/*O.C.B. Adjt.* 10/*York & Lancs. A.D.C. to G.O.C.* 37/*Div.* M.B.E. ℞(2)
534 †Willis, Sgt. Eric Fitzgeorge ... 10/12/15 *Capt.* 15/*O.C.B. Killed in action*
142 Winckworth, Sgt. Sidney Howard 27/ 2/15 *Capt. To R.T.O.* [27/3/18
2506 †Young, Fergus Ferguson ... ... 14/ 2/15 *Capt. Wounded* 27/9/18

2368 †Beausire, Sgt. Frederick Robert 5/10/16 *Capt.* 15/*O.C.B. To O/C Depot*
7850 Bell, Sgt. Reginald Otto ... 19/ 1/17 *Lieut.*
2428 †Besch, Roy Cressy Frederick ... 21/ 7/16 *Lieut.* ✠
766636 †Birkett, Frederick Seetree ... 24/ 9/18 *Lieut.*

3228	†Blight, Sgt. William	1/ 3/17	Lieut.
1245	†Bomford, Sgt. Herbert James P.	3/11/16	Lieut. (R.F.C.) Wounded 15/11/17
7829	Bradshaw, L/Cpl. John	11/ 2/17	Lieut.
2762	Coulson, Sgt. George	5/10/16	Capt. 15/O.C.B. 🎖
761377	†Coviello, Sgt. Ambrose	3/ 3/19	D.C.M.
761405	†Creasey, Sgt. Robert Douglas	24/ 5/18	Lieut.
763151	†Dancer, L/Cpl. Luke	28/11/17	Wounded –/5/18
764019	†Davenport, Cyril Robert	29/ 5/18	Wounded 9/10/18
764951	Day, Arthur Percival	15/ 7/17	Lieut.
7981	†Ellett, Sgt. Harold Picton	19/ 1/17	Lieut. Wounded 29/3/18
642	Ellis, CSM Austin Dennie	5/10/16	Lieut.
178	†English, CQMS Alfred Cecil	5/10/16	Medal R.V.O. Killed in action 30/12/17
2698	Franklin-Adams, CSM Bernard I.	26/ 9/16	Major. To R.E.(I.W.T.) 🎖
2788	Gamble, Sgt. David Bertram	5/10/16	Lieut.
761056	†Goacher, Sgt. Frederick	26/ 4/17	Capt. ✠
2699	Hanbury, Sgt. Frederick Capel	26/ 9/16	Capt. To R.E.(I.W.T.)
762333	†Heming, Cpl. Percy	12/11/18	
760011	Hoather, RSM William Henry	15/ 7/17	Lieut. 15/O.C.B.
4809	†Holland, L/Cpl. Arthur Leslie	27/ 6/17	Lieut. 15/O.C.B. ✠ w. 15/1/18
2950	†Howe, Cpl. Arnold Ewart	10/ 7/16	Killed in action 30/10/17
1221	†Jones, Sgt. Owen Edward	19/ 7/16	Lieut.
764372	†Laurent, Henry Fraser	29/ 5/18	Wounded 9/10/18
1730	†Lightfoot, Sgt. Francis Bertram	24/10/16	Killed in action 30/12/17
765847	Mainwaring, Ernest Charles	18/11/17	Lieut.
765562	Morison, Roderick Henry	28/11/17	Lieut. To Guards M/G Regt.
2140	†Nott, Sgt. Donald George	5/10/16	Lieut. 15/O.C.B.
766952	†Owen, L/Cpl. Phillip Henry A.	4/ 3/19	Wounded 30/12/17
1677	†Park, Sgt. Charles Allen Roberson	12/ 4/17	Prisoner of war 30/12/17 🎖
765189	†Paterson, George	28/11/17	
766358	†Read, Arthur Bellamy Holditch	12/11/18	
761073	†Reckin, Sgt. Gustav	30/10/17	Capt. To Indian Army R.O.
7049	Russ, Sgt. Oswald Harraway	25/ 1/17	Lieut. To Guards M/G Regt.
1515	†Salisbury, Sgt. Walter Frederick	5/10/16	Lieut. Died of wounds 30/12/17
760707	†Seabrook, Arthur Davenport	29/ 5/18	
765047	†Sharvell, George William Charles	17/ 3/19	
765355	†Silcock, Cpl. Francis Howard	28/11/17	w. & P/W 24/3/18 To O.C. Depot
765572	†Southwell, Cpl. Stedman Alec	28/11/17	Wounded 10/9/18
760269	†Stephenson, Sgt. Cyril	3/ 3/19	
1610	†Stephenson, Cpl. Geoffrey Langton	15/ 7/16	Lieut. Wounded 4/4/18
765813	Thomas, Anthony James	12/11/18	
765573	†Wanostrocht, L/Cpl. Dudley V.	28/11/17	Wounded 31/5/18
765482	Williams, Graeme Douglas	18/11/17	
2913	†Woodroffe, Cpl. Geoffrey Edward	10/ 7/16	Lieut. To Tank Corps w. 12/11/17
769376	†Wright, John	15/ 3/19	
768988	Allen, Geoffrey Norton	17/ 3/19	
766634	Biggart, Andrew Stevenson	4/ 2/19	
768246	Bruce, L/Cpl. Alastair Henry	17/ 4/19	

OFFICERS OF THE ARTISTS' RIFLES.

760303	†CHANDLER, William Frank	...	4/ 3/19
763495	†ELKINS, L/Cpl. Alfred James	...	3/ 2/19
764494	†HARRISON, Samuel Percival	...	17/ 3/19
762835	IRELAND, John Watson ...	...	3/ 2/19
763976	†KNOTT, Harold ...	...	17/ 3/19
768547	LEWIS, L/Cpl. Mervin ...	...	17/ 3/19
670064	†NEWBERRY, Cpl. Henry Sidney ...		5/ 3/19
4715	NOEL, L/Cpl. Gerald Hamlyn	...	4/ 2/19
767284	NORTH, William Leslie ...	...	6/ 2/19
760573	SMALL, Sgt. Ernest Victor	...	3/ 2/19
767019	STEEN, John Dunbar ...	...	5/ 2/19

M/2 955342	†ANDREW, Lionel Ensor	...	27/ 2/18	*From R.A.S.C. Wounded* 9/10/18
M/2 152263	†BECKE, Harry Reginald	...	27/ 2/18	,, ,,
S/ 34378	†GOSNELL, Cpl. Vernon Clifford	25/ 9/18		*From R.F.C.*
34283	WALTON, Cpl. Thos. Eric Leslie	3/ 2/19		,, ,,

(iii.) Retired members rejoined as Officers after Mobilization.

HORSLEY, Lt.-Col. (Hon. Col.) Walter Charles V.D. *p.s.*	6/ 9/14	2	*Lt.-Col.: O/C* 2/28 *&* 104/*P.B. Town-Major, Englebelmer.* ✠
BLOMFIELD, Capt. Charles J., T.D. *p.s.*	... 9/11/14		*Major. O/C A.C.: O/C Depot* ✠
BLUNDELL, Lieut. Alfred Herbert *p.s.*	... 7/ 9/14	2,3	*Major. 2 i/c* 15/*O.C.B.* ✠
¶FOSTER, Lieut. Edward Charles *p.s.*	... 19/10/14	2	*Capt. Employed Commd. Depot*
FURZE, Sgt. Gordon	... 23/ 4/15	3	*Capt. To Coldst. Gds. Staff-Capt. 2/Guards Bde.* ✠
¶LEFROY, Sgt. Tracy Edward ...	... 26/11/14	2,3	*Major 2 i/c* 8/*R. Warwick Killed in action* 5/12/17 ✠(2)
LEIGH-BENNETT, Pte. E. P. ...	... 31/10/14		*Capt. Seconded* M.B.E. ✠(2)
MOORE, Pte. Leonard P.	... 21/12/15	3	*Lieut.* ✠
SELFE, Lieut. Arthur Edward Ferrour *p.s.*	7/ 9/14	1,2	*Capt. To* 5/*Bedfd. To Coldst. Gds.* ✠ *w.* 31/7/17, 27/11/17
SPENS, Archibald Hope	... 19/12/16	3	*Lieut.*
TURNER, Charles William ...	... 15/ 7/17	3	*Lieut.*
VESEY, Sgt. Harold Guillaume ...	... 25/ 1/16	3	*Capt. Employed Min. of Mun.*

(iv.) Retired Officers of other Regiments gazetted after Mobilization.

¶SHIRLEY, Lt.-Col. William (Indian Army)	28/ 9/14	2,3	*Lt.-Col. C/O* 3/28 *&* 15/*O.C.B.* [C.M.G.] ✠
¶RYCROFT, Major Sir Richard N., Bart. (*Hon. Lt. in Army*) *p.s.*	12/ 2/15	3	*Major*

(v.) Officers transferred or attached after Mobilization. To 1/28.

HARINGTON, Lt.-Col. John, 3/Rifle Brigade, D.S.O. ... (O/C Nov./17–Jan./18) Brig-Genl. [C.M.G.
JOHNSON, Lt.-Col. Francis Shand Byam, 1/R. Lancaster ... ... (O/C Jan.–May/18) D.S.O. w.–/5/18
WILKINSON, Lt.-Col. Herbert Gordon, 5/London ... (O/C May–Aug./18) w. 23/8/18
LEGG, Major John Francis, 5/London ... ... (OC/ Aug.–Sept./18) 2 i/c Sept./18–
GOLDTHORP, Lt.-Col. Robert Heward, 4/W. Riding (O/C Sept./18–Feb./19) D.S.O.
BRACEY, Major Geoffrey John, 5/Norfolk ... ... 2 i/c 1918
CLUTTERBUCK, Major Noel S., R.M.L.I., D.S.O. ...
LATHOM, Major Forbes Wm. Farquhar, 2/Bedford, M.C. Wounded 23/3/18

From 5/London.
ADDISON, 2/Lt. Vivian ... ...
BRODIE, 2/Lt. Cyril Frederick Clements ... ... Wounded 20/4/18
FURZE, Capt. Claude ... ... Killed in action 5/4/18
GORE, 2/Lt. Walter ... ...
HELM, 2/Lt. Cecil ... ...
HIGGS, 2/Lt. Harry Leonard ... ... Killed in action 27/3/18
HUMMERSTONE, 2/Lt. Laurance George ... ... To R.A.F. –/1/18
KITCHING, Capt. Geoffrey Charles ... ... Prisoner of war 24/3/18
LINTOTT, 2/Lt. Henry Chamen ... ... Killed in action 21/3/18
MOORE, Capt. Ernest George ... ... Wounded 21/8/18
MORRIS, 2/Lt. John Harold ... ... Wounded 27/9/18
NEWELL, 2/Lt. Francis Alister ... ... Killed in action 24/3/18
PETLEY, Lieut. Reginald Edmund, M.C. ... ... Prisoner of war 24/3/18
PIGGOTT, 2/Lt. John ... ... Wounded 22/3/18
REEVE, 2/Lt. George Robey, M.C. ... ...
SAMPSON, 2/Lt. Horace William ... ... Killed in action –/5/18
WILLIAMSON, Lieut. Frank ... ... Killed in action 24/3/18
YOUNG, 2/Lt. Alan Catchpool ... ... Killed in action 24/3/18

From 6/London
JONES, 2/Lt. Stanley Goring ... ...

From 7/London
BEAVAN, Lieut. Robert William ... ...
CHANDLER, 2/Lt. George Hammond ... ...
HEWSON, 2/Lt. Stanley Barton ... ... To T.M.B.
SMITH, 2/Lt. Claude Douglas ... ...
TAYLOR, 2/Lt. E. G. L. ... ... Wounded 27/9/18
VAN COLLER, Lieut. Louis ... ...

From 8/London.
CARMALT, 2/Lt. Herbert Edward ... ...
RICHARDSON, 2/Lt. Arthur George ... ... Wounded
VENABLES, 2/Lt. Alexander Lones ... ...

From 9/London.
HIBBARD, 2/Lt. Hamilton Edgar, D.C.M. ... ... ✠ To R.A.F.
PRIEST, 2/Lt. Clements Edward ... ...

From 10/London.

BATZER, 2/Lt. Roland John	Wounded 27/8/18 ✠
CONWAY, 2/Lt. Francis Henry	
COOPER, 2/Lt. John Frederick	
DAVIS, 2/Lt. George	
ELLIOTT, 2/Lt. Alfred Ernest Thomas	✠
GARDNER, 2/Lt. E. M.	Killed in action 27/9/18
GARDNER, 2/Lt. James William	To T.M.B.
GIBBS, 2/Lt. Eric Noel	✠
JACKSON, 2/Lt. Arthur Frederick	
KING, 2/Lt. Hubert Weston	Killed in action 10/11/18
MACNAUGHTON, 2/Lt. Algernon	Killed in action –/10/18
PAVEY, 2/Lt. Phillip Robert Vernon	
PERROTT, 2/Lt. Eustace Stroud	Wounded ✠
REID, 2/Lt. Algernon Frederick	

From 16/London.

CHESTER, 2/Lt. Harold Stuart	
CONNOLLY, 2/Lt. Francis John	Wounded 27/9/18
ELPHICK, 2/Lt. Harold George Thorp	
FARRINGTON, 2/Lt. Frederick Victor	
LEIGHTON, 2/Lt. William James Cuthbert	
MCKINLEY, Lieut. Charles	✠
MITCHELL, 2/Lt. T. P.	
NORFOLK, 2/Lt. William John Alfred	
NORMAN, 2/Lt. Reginald Cecil	

From 17/London.

DRIVER, 2/Lt. Horace Owen	Wounded
JOHNSON, 2/Lt. George	

From 21/London.

BLANCHARD, 2/Lt. Henry Claude Allan	Wounded 30/10/17, 27/9/18 ✠

From Royal Air Force.

YEABSLEY, 2/Lt. Gilbert Valentine	

From R.M.L.I.

STOCKS, 2/Lt. A. F.	Transport Officer

From 6/Royal West Kent

CLARIDGE, 2/Lt. William Stanley	
MALPASS, Capt. Charles Edward	✠ Killed in action 10/10/18

From 10/South Wales Borderers.

ASHFORD, 2/Lt. Stanley Rust	Wounded 27/8/18
EAMES, 2/Lt. Frank	To R.A.F. ✠
EVE, 2/Lt. Victor Leonard	Wounded 22/8/18
HERMELIN, Capt. Alec	
MORGAN, 2/Lt. Reginald Samuel Leigh	To T.M.B.
PITTEN, 2/Lt. William Howell	

Attached to 3/28.

SHAW, Lt.-Col. Edward St. Lawrence,	1/East Surrey	O/C 15/O.C.B. ⌘(3)
BEETON, Major E. C. ...	1/R. Sussex	*To Brigade-Major*
CASSERLY, Major J. H. G. ...	Indian Army	*To Brigade-Major*

AYTON, Lieut. M. C., M.C.	... ...	... 3/Suffolk
CLAY, Capt. R. R., M.C.	... ...	... Hants Yeomanry
CHAPLIN, Lieut. L. F. C.	... ...	... 1/Gloucester
COOPER, Capt. A. E.	... ...	... From T.F. Reserve
EVANS, Lieut. H. K.	... ...	... 4/Wilts.
FRANKLIN, Lieut. H., M.C.	... ...	... 1/Manchester
GATES, Capt. P. H.	... ...	... 2/Lincoln Regt.
GUTHRIE, Lieut. L. R.	... ...	... From T.F. Reserve
MALTBY, Lieut. R. A. L.	... ...	... 1/Durham L.I.
MYERS, Capt. W. ...	... ...	... 19/Manchester
PEACH, Capt. C. S. ...	... ...	... From T.F. Reserve
TUCK, Capt. N. J. ...	... ...	... 1/Norfolk
UNDERWOOD, Lieut. C. H. ...	...	... 17/London
WHITE, Capt. J. D., D.S.O., M.C. ...	...	... 8/Middlesex

Royal Army Medical Corps: attached.

DAVIS, Capt. Haldin	... 3
FINLAY, Capt. Gilbert Laurig Kerr ...	... 1
GOODBODY, Capt. Francis Woodcock ...	... 2, 3
GREEN, Capt. H. Melvill	... 3
LAWSON, Major George Langrigg Leathes	... 3
MATTHEW, Capt. David	... 1 ✠
NELSON, Capt. William Percival ...	... 1 ✠
NIX, Capt. Sydney	... 3
¶RICKETTS, Capt. Arthur, C.M.G. (*Hon. Captain in Army* 7/2/03)	... 3
Dow, Lieut.	... 1 *M.O. Reserve Corps (U.S. Army)*
GOOS, Lieut.	... 1 ,, ,, ,,
VINEYARD, Lieut.	... 1 ,, ,, ,,

Royal Army Chaplains' Department: attached.

CURTIS, Capt. Rev. H.	... 3
DAVEY, Capt. Rev. George L.	... 3
DICKINSON, Capt. Rev. Harry ...	... 1 Assist. Chaplain G.H.Q. *Killed in action* 30/10/17
NEWPORT, Capt. Rev. H.	... 1
ROBINSON, Capt. Rev. Basil Cautley ...	... 1

G.H.Q. MACHINE-GUN SCHOOL
(IN FRANCE).

Artists' N.C.O.'s and Men appointed Sergeant-Instructors.

1041	BAGGALLAY, Geoffrey Thomas	28/12/14	To 2/Lt. 1/Welch Regt.
1417	BATH, Frederick Nathaniel	14/12/14	To 2/Lt. M.G.C.
2328	BAX, Edwin George Goodson	14/12/14	To 2/Lt. M.G.C.
1926	BAX, William Molyneux	17/ 3/15	I.S. M.S.M.
2028	BELCHAMBER, Douglas Foster	14/12/14	To 2/Lt. M.G.C.
1621	BROCKMAN, Frank George	4/ 4/15	To 2/Lt. R.A.F.
1081	CARPENTER, Cpl. Alec Edward	28/12/14	To 2/Lt. 1/West Kent Regt.
2071	CLARK, Ronald Boyd	14/12/14	To 2/Lt. R.A.S.C.
710	CLAUSEN, George Frederick	28/12/14	To 2/Lt. M.G.C.
574	COOPER, Sidney Walter	28/12/14	To 2/Lt. R.F.A.
2189	DAVIES, Glyndn Rhys	27/ 7/15	To 2/Lt. R.A.F.
940	DICKSEE, Harold John Hugh	14/12/14	To 2/Lt. R.A.F.
1837	DOLL, Peter John	22/ 7/15	
1479	DOUGLAS, Arthur Herbert	14/12/14	To 2/Lt. M.G.C.
631	FELLOWS, Lancelot Dermond	17/ 3/15	
676	FICKLIN, Alfred Hildyard	17/ 3/15	
2632	FLETCHER, L/Cpl. Ralph Belward	27/ 4/15	To 2/Lt. M.G.C.
434	FLETCHER, Robert Combe	27/ 4/15	To 2/Lt. R.A.S.C.
777	FOSKETT, Arthur Sefton	14/12/14	To 2/Lt. 2/Middlesex
2755	GILL, Rowland Roy	27/ 4/15	To 2/Lt. R.E.
682	GOULD, James Robertson S.	28/12/14	To 2/Lt. M.G.C.
753	GRICE, Algar Norman	17/ 3/15	
773	GRIFFITH, Frank Stanley	14/12/14	To 2/Lt. M.G.C.
1521	HARPER, Hubert Harry	17/ 3/15	
1974	HOPKINS, George Henry Stanton	17/ 3/15	
1555	JUDD, Frederick George	14/12/14	To 2/Lt. 2/Dublin Fusiliers
1092	JUPPA, Cecil Lewis William	11/ 1/15	
1415	JUNGUIS, Ernest James Theodore	4/ 4/15	To 2/Lt. 1/Bedford
490	LEE, L/Cpl. Joseph	14/12/14	
629	LEIGHTON, William	14/12/14	
1405	MARSHALL, Oscar Fuller Ben	14/12/14	To 2/Lt. 1/Yorkshire L.I.
2810	MILLEN, Alfred Dyson	27/ 4/15	To Army Chaplain
1051	MILLS, Henry Jackson	14/12/14	To 2/Lt. 2/Middlesex
1112	NEALE, Geoffrey Brockman	17/ 3/15	To 2/Lt. R.A.F.
2378	OAKESHOTT, Harold Alan	27/ 4/15	To 2/Lt. M.G.C.
2527	ORTON, Ernest Henry	14/12/14	To 2/Lt. Scottish Rifles
177	PAGE, L/Cpl. Harold Thomas	4/ 4/15	
2778	PALMER, William	27/ 4/15	To 2/Lt. M.G.C.
2192	ROGERS, George Robert	30/ 8/15	To 2/Lt. /Suffolk & M.G.C.

G-H-Q. MACHINE-GUN SCHOOL.

1649	Roper, Bevil William	28/12/14	
516	Samson, Cpl. Alfred Joseph	11/ 1/15	
4136	Samson, Thomas Frederick	10/ 8/15	
763	Sheehan, L/Cpl. Frank George Edw.	14/12/14	*To 2/Lt. Motor M/G Service*
1019	Sherlock, Gerald	4/ 4/15	
2972	Sloan, James William Jeffreys	27/ 4/15	*To 2/Lt. M.G.C.*
1249	Steer, Wilfred	11/ 1/15	*To 2/Lt. R.A.F.*
1093	Suggate, William Allen	28/12/14	*To 2/Lt. M.G.C.*
1177	Tucker, Norman Poulter	28/12/14	*To 2/Lt. 2/Cameron Highlanders*
1377	Voss, Gordon Phillips	11/ 1/15	*To 2/Lt. Motor M/G Service*
1345	Whitaker, Bernard Joseph G.	28/12/14	*To 2/Lt. 2/West Riding Regt.*
1438	Witt, Cyril Tansley	22/ 4/15	
1651	Young, Henry Harman	14/12/14	*To 2/Lt. 3/Royal Fusiliers*
1975	Athol, Charles Colborn	24/ 8/15	*To 2/Lt. M.G.C.*
1762	Bagley, Ernest Gordon	7/ 8/15	
887	Barker, Reginald Jack	24/ 8/15	
1611	Barnett, Harold Andrew	25/ 8/15	*To 2/Lt. R.A.S.C.*
2269	Bolter, Charles Albert	7/ 8/15	*To 2/Lt. M.G.C.*
1505	Bulpitt, L/Cpl. James	8/10/15	*To 2/Lt. M.G.C.*
2313	Burrow, L/Cpl. Archibald Charles	24/ 8/15	
1850	Butterick, Frank	24/ 8/15	
349	Dangerfield, Richard James	7/ 8/15	
2251	Day, George Hague John	24/ 8/15	*To 2/Lt. Royal Fusiliers*
2532	Dew, Archibald Henry Everrett	24/ 8/15	
1940	Easthaugh, Charles James	7/ 8/15	*To 2/Lt. R.A.F.*
2177	Farrow, George Harold	24/ 8/15	*To 2/Lt. M.G.C.*
200	Groom, William Owen	24/ 8/15	
2004	Howard, Frederick Charles	7/ 8/15	*To 2/Lt. M.G.C.*
420	Ingall, Harold Elfric	7/ 8/15	
2331	Jackson, Arthur Stanley	8/10/15	
2959	Jukes, L/Cpl. Sidney Clapham	24/ 8/15	
1923	Kilner, Sidney Arthur	24/ 8/15	
1173	Lance, Frederick Percival	24/ 8/15	
2650	Lewington, Charles	24/ 8/15	*To 2/Lt. M.G.C.*
1395	Parsons, Cpl. George Mernard	24/ 8/15	
2981	Selfe, Cpl. Leonard Pelham	24/ 8/15	
2776	Sloan, Charles Hannington	19/ 6/15	*To 2/Lt. M.G.C*
1811	Smyly, Cecil Ferguson	24/ 8/15	
1920	Stanway, Eric Adrian	7/ 8/15	
2021	Staples, Hugh Whittaker	8/10/15	
2785	Stewart, James Douglas	24/ 8/15	
1957	Stock, Ernest Thomas	24/ 8/15	
2767	Toothill, John Cedric Penman	7/ 8/15	
1391	Williamson, James Alexander	24/ 8/15	
1425	Willis, Ambrose Baldwin	24/ 8/15	
1157	Woods, Cpl. Arthur Vere Roleston	11/10/15	

G-H-Q. MACHINE-GUN SCHOOL.

760485	ADAMS, Arthur Cyril	*Killed in action* -/3/18
760328	AUSTIN, Maurice Gerald	
2737	BACK, Albert Frederick	
2382	BATHURST, Charles John	
768558	BUTLER, Edward Lindived	
873	CAMP, Alfred Fisher	*To 2/Lt. Unattached List T.F.* [18/6/18]
1685	CLAYTON, Alfred Hughes	
4358	DEW, Wallace Browning	
5171	EGERTON, Roland Harding	
3530	FOSKETT, Henry Horan	*To 2/Lt. M.G.C.* 26/7/17
1894	FRANGHAIDI, Geo. Paul	
5620	GIBBONS, James	
5689	GILLEY, James	
6760	GILLGRASS, Alfred	
5756	GLEN, Vuran	
3154	GIBBONS, James Francis	
6381	GRIERSON, Richard Henry Frederick	
3338	HOLMES, John Maurice	*To 2/Lt. Tank Corps* 27/7/17
6110	LEEDING, William Joseph	
1865	MOULD, Ronald	*To 2/Lt. Tank Corps* 26/4/17
2386	MOYLAN-JONES, Reginald Arthur Withers	
3476	O'REGAN, Alphonsus John	*To 2/Lt. M.G.C.* 26/8/17
6021	PARKES, Norman Eric	
7186	PARKIN, John Austin	
763978	POWELL, John Henry	
6718	PROUDFOOT, Alexander	
3019	PRYKE, Alfred William	
2870	RYLANDS, Eric Cland	*To 2/Lt. R.F.C.* 19/4/17
5712	SCOTT, Reginald P.	
7495	SMITH, James Percy	
7645	SMITH, John Poole	
2901	STONE, Percy Ray	
2953	TUBBS, Sgt. William Edward	*To 2/Lt. Tank Corps* 19/12/17
1699	WEBB, Edgar Oliver	*To 2/Lt. M.G.C.* 26/4/17
761788	WEBSTER, William John	
1939	WHEELER, Arthur Gilbert	

CHELSEA SCHOOL OF INSTRUCTION.

557	IRWIN, CSM Hugh Gourlay	26/11/15	*M/G Instructor*
995	HOLGATE, Sgt. Basil	-/3/16	,, ,,
2338	NICHOLLS, Sgt. William Ewart	-/3/16	,, ,,

THE MANCHESTER REGIMENT. 315

Regular Battalions (Nos. 1 & 2). {63rd Foot / 96th Foot}

		2nd Lieut.	
1602	ROBINSON, Arthur Hine	20/ 3/15	*1 Lieut. Killed in action* 26/4/15
1410	WILLIAMSON-JONES, Clarence E.	20/ 3/15	*1 Lieut. (R.A.F.)* D.F.C. *w.* 27/4/15
763881	GALLAGHER, Charles Francis	27/ 6/17	*(7)*
2927	GOODING, Hector Ernest	12/11/16	*2*
764052	WILCOCK, Harold	27/ 6/17	*(9)*

Special Reserve Battalions (Nos. 3 & 4).

3902	DUNCAN, Alexander	21/10/15	*4 Lieut. To M.G.C. w.* 1/9/16
3557	HOWARD, William Edward	24/ 7/15	*4 To M.G.C.*
3121	MOORE, Francis Skinner	24/ 7/15	*4 Lieut. To M.G.C.*
3775	TOWERS, Wilfrid Goodwin	21/10/15	*4 Killed in action* 2/4/17
761853	CLARKE, John William	20/12/17	*4(22) Wounded* 14/4/17 ✠
7532	DALE, Austin Frederick	26/ 1/17	*4*
766185	DAVIS, Philip Henry Hatton	1/ 5/18	*3 Died of wounds* 9/11/18
2841	FARADAY, Lawrence Baumer	26/ 1/17	*4(10)*
762995	KENT, Percy Edward Albert	29/ 3/17	*3(2)*
762668	MOORE, Robert Clarke	26/ 4/17	*4*
765403	PARKHURST, George Henry	1/ 8/17	*3 (8/Worc.) Killed in action* 3/6/18
764563	PRIME, Arnold	29/ 8/17	*4 Killed in action* 21/3/18
7390	RATHBONE, Leonard	22/11/16	*4(17) Prisoner of war* 14/6/18
7987	SANT, Ronald	19/12/16	*4 Lieut. Wounded* 31/7/17
765406	SMITH, Donovan Richardson McC.	1/ 8/17	*4 (1/Worc.) D/W* 27/5/18
7392	SPENCER, Richard Austin	22/11/16	*4 Lieut. (R.F.C.)*
764106	SPENCER, William	27/ 6/17	*3*
6859	STOTT, Walter Goodwin	26/ 9/16	*4 (15/Cheshire) K/A* 19/9/18

Territorial Battalions (No. 5 to 10).

3817	ATKIN, L/Cpl. Heriot Duckworth	2/12/15	*5 Prisoner of war* 25/4/18
1278	BAIRD, Stuart	4/ 8/15	*10(11) Lieut.*
4114	BATE, Herbert Rowland	16/12/15	*6 Lieut.* ✠
3875	BATEMAN, John William	2/12/15	*5 Lieut. Wounded* 24/4/17
4760	BRIGGS, Herbert Bradley	1/ 6/16	*5 Lieut. Wounded* 17/9/18
3790	CHAPLIN, Sydney Stranger	20/11/15	*5 Lieut. Killed in action* 21/3/18
3149	COLLINS, Stanley Thomas	2/12/15	*8 Lieut.*
4152	COPE, Gerald Quin	16/12/15	*9 Died of wounds* 24/5/17
4718	CRAMPTON, L/Cpl. Hubert	2/ 6/16	*5 Lieut. To 6/Gloucester* ✠
1656	DALE, Robert Jacomb Norris	18/ 6/15	*9 (R.F.C.) Killed in action* 31/1/18
3757	DEIGHTON, L/Cpl. Ralph Hugh	7/ 2/15	*5 Lieut. (Tank Corps)*
4752	DORAN, Thomas Arthur	2/ 6/16	*5 (R.A.F.) Pilot Officer*
4078	DOWNER, Frederick	11/12/15	*5 Lieut.*

3800	FEARNE, Sidney		2/12/15	10 Lieut.
4701	FOSTER, William Arthur		1/ 6/16	5 Lieut.
3904	GREGG, Reginald Arthur		19/12/15	5 Lieut. Wounded 7/10/17
3537	HALLETT, Lawrence		2/12/15	8 Lieut.
3933	HAWKINS, L/Cpl. Bertram Lewis		2/12/15	5(1) Lieut.
3715	HAYDOCK-WILSON, Hugh		2/12/15	9 Lieut. Wounded 26/10/17
3844	HENSON, Eric Dwight		21/12/15	5 Lieut. (M.G.C.)
4198	HOAL, Edward Gormer		6/12/15	8 Capt. ✠
4297	HOBROUGH, Francis Richard		16/12/15	8 Lieut. (Tank Corps)
3863	HOLDAWAY, Neville Aldridge		6/12/15	8 Lieut. ✠
2797	HORNABROOK, Alan Wiseman		4/ 3/15	5 Lieut.
3821	JACKMAN, Reginald James		11/12/15	5 Lieut.
4731	JUBB, Norris		31/ 5/16	5 Lieut.
3550	JUPP, John Morton Scott		2/12/15	10 Capt. ✠ w. 27/4/18 ℳ
3726	LAUDER, Douglas Munro		2/ 1/16	8 Lieut.
3793	MACDONALD, Alan Leslie		20/11/15	8 Killed in action 19/5/17
3650	MILNE-ROBERTSON, W. Mercet		2/11/15	5 Lieut. (M.G.C.)
4479	NEWTH, Robert Charles		2/ 6/16	10 Lieut.
3836	NEWTON, Cuthbert Raymond		6/12/15	8 To Min. of Labour
4721	OGDEN, Frederick William		3/ 6/16	5
3911	OGDEN, William Edward		11/12/15	5(18) Capt. ✠ Wounded 13/5/18
4193	OLIVER, Herbert William		11/12/15	5 (R.A.F.) Pilot Officer
4080	O'SHAUGHNESSY-LEVY, R. Percy		19/12/15	5
4756	OWEN, Wilfred Edward Salter		2/ 6/16	5 Capt. ✠ K/A 4/11/18
539	PEARCE, Geoffrey Owens		29/ 4/15	5 Lieut.
4132	PHILLIPOWSKY, Ivan Ritchie		7/12/15	7
3771	PITT, Benno Ormangardo		2/12/15	9 Lieut. (Ind. Army)
4144	PRIESTLY, Henry		7/12/15	7 Lieut.
4076	REEVE, Garnet Norman Bray		16/12/15	9 w.24/10/17, 3/8/18 K/A 1/9/18
4304	SALTER, Leonard E.		10/ 1/16	8 Lieut. (M.G.C.) w. 26/10/17
5321	SHAW, Eric William		22/ 6/16	7 Lieut.
3867	SMITH, Rowland Arthur		2/12/15	10 Lt. (3/Lancs. Fus.) w. 11/8/17,)
4032	SOULSBY, Edward Dodds		11/12/15	5 Lieut. [12/7/18, 28/11/18)
3697	SPINK, L/Cpl. Leonard Robert		7/12/15	9 Lieut. (M.G.C.)
3868	STRAFFORD, Clement Arnold S.		2/12/15	5 Lieut.
4133	THORNTON, Reginald Arthur		18/ 1/16	6 Lieut. Prisoner of war
3645	THOROGOOD, Edward Linford		2/12/15	8
4520	TOLLETT, George William		2/ 6/16	10 Lieut. Prisoner of war
3795	URIE, William Alexander Elliott		2/ 2/15	5 Lieut. Wounded 28/6/18 P/W
4169	WILSON, L/Cpl. Leonard Archibald		16/12/15	6 Lieut.
6611	ALLMEY, Reginald Frederick		26/ 9/16	5 Wounded 7/2/17
761196	AINSWORTH, Herbert Green		24/ 6/17	9 Killed in action 9/10/17
764410	ANDREW, Frank Douglas		22/ 8/17	7 D/W while P/W 4/4/18
763904	AVINS, William Wyatt		27/ 6/17	9
6536	BARTRAM, George Alfred		16/ 9/17	9 (M.G.C.)
762949	BAXTER, Gerald William		28/ 3/17	10 Wounded 4/6/17 K/A 9/10/17
764131	CARMICHAEL, Gilbert		31/ 7/17	10 Capt. Killed in action 21/3/18

MANCHESTER REGIMENT (T/F).

762824	CHAPMAN, Henry Randal ...	... 28/ 3/17	10	Killed in action 9/10/17
6197	CHAPMAN, Walter ...	... 11/ 7/16	10	
5461	CHURCH, Thomas Edgar ...	... 11/ 7/16	10	
6864	COKE, Henry Manners	... 11/ 7/16	10	
763727	DAWSON, Gilbert James Cameron ...	25/ 9/17	9	
763878	ELLISON, Harold	... 30/ 5/17	5	Prisoner of war 3/5/18
6699	GILLIATT, Robert Vincent ...	... 11/ 7/16	10	Lieut. w. 18/8/17 P/W &
762721	GOUGH, James Alexander ...	... 25/ 9/17	10	[Died of wounds 25/5/18}
763578	GRAY, John Alan	... 25/ 9/17	10	
6762	HARGREAVES, Rowland ...	... 26/ 9/16	5	Lieut.
4533	HIGGINS, L/Cpl. Edward ...	... 5/ 9/16	5	Lieut.
5407	HORNABROOK, Edward Mersham ...	11/ 7/16	5	Lieut.
762577	HUDSON, Horace Sayer ...	... 2/ 8/17	9	
762372	HULL, Gerald Victor ...	... 31/ 7/17	9	Capt. Wounded 10/10/18
765177	JONES, Robert Edward ...	... 30/ 1/18	6	Wounded 12/8/18
4670	LEWIS, David Ilid	... 11/ 7/16	10	Lieut.
6068	LOFTHOUSE, Charles Thornton ...	11/ 7/16	7	Lieut.
5411	LOWE, Samuel Thomason ...	... 11/ 7/16	10	Lieut.
4709	NICHOLSON, Thomas ...	... 11/ 7/16	5	Prisoner of war 8/7/18
4268	REEDER, Robert	... 11/ 7/16	10	Killed in action 6/1/18
763404	ROBSON, Frederick Josiah ...	... 26/ 4/17	8	Wounded & P/W 13/8/18
763411	SMITH, Walter Bernard ...	... 26/ 4/17	7	
6912	SMITH, William Proctor ...	... 26/ 9/16	5	Lieut.
764348	SPREADBURY, Harold Vernon ...	31/ 7/17	10	Wounded 6/6/18
763413	STONE, Hugh William ...	... 13/ 5/17	5	
4597	TAUTZ, Reginald Hugh ...	... 8/ 7/16	10	Capt. ✠ w. 2/10/17, 21/6/18
763213	TAYLOR, Charles William Brooke ...	16/ 6/17	5	
764512	TIMMS, Archibald	... 16/ 6/17	5	
763547	WALKER, Norman Horme Esher ...	27/ 3/17	5	
762396	WHEATLEY, Ernest Herod ...	... 26/ 4/17	8	Wounded 30/8/17
763482	WHEELER, Percy Victor ...	... 25/ 9/17	5	
763839	WHITTAKER, Basil Keoth ...	... 31/ 7/17	10	Prisoner of war 10/5/18
765072	WILCOCK, William Croft ...	... 13/ 5/17	5	
764080	WILLIAMS, Albert	... 30/ 5/17	5	Wounded 18/8/17
8187	YOUNG, Leslie Duncan ...	... 19/12/16	7	Killed in action 7/10/17

Service Battalions (New Armies).

1220	BARR, Guy	... 16/ 1/16	16	Wounded 24/5/16, –/7/16
4687	BAYLEY, John Roy ...	... 2/ 6/16	25	Lieut.
3267	BOLTON, Thomas Tertius ...	... 21/ 7/15	25	Wounded
3031	BOWLY, Reginald Walter ...	... 1/ 4/15	22	Lieut. w. 13/11/17 K/A 29/5/18
2635	BOXALL, Frank Stuart ...	... 19/ 1/15	19	Capt. (Staff) ℞
4240	CAIGER, Francis Everett ...	... 4/ 2/16	25	From 9/E. Yorks
2968	EDMINSON, Leonard Oswald ...	3/ 3/15	12	Lieut. ✠ w. –/10/18 ℞
3214	GRIMWOOD, Herbert ...	... 1/ 4/15	22	Capt. P/W (Austria)
4458	HARLEY, Norman Francis ...	... 2/ 6/16	27	Prisoner of war –/10/16
3406	ILETT, John James ...	... 19/ 7/15	25	Lieut.

MANCHESTER REGIMENT (S/B).

3448	JENSEN, Cyril Thornton ...	... 19/ 7/15	25(*17*) (*T.M.B.*) *K/A* 10/5/16
4241	OWEN, Cpl. Stanley John ...	... 15/ 1/16	25 *Lieut. To Min. of Labour*
4283	PLESTED, Horace George ...	... 26/ 5/16	(*4*) *Killed in action* 30/7/16
3070	ROSE, L/Cpl. Howard M. ..	... 3/ 4/15	22 *Lieut.* ✠ *Wounded* –/4/16
3200	STREET, l./Cpl. Edmund Alger	... 5/ 4/15	22 *Killed in action* 2/6/16
1559	TIDY, Sgt. Warwick Edward	... 13/ 5/15	*19 Capt.* ✠
3218	WOOD, John Patrick Henry	... 3/ 4/15	22 *Capt. w.* –/7/16 *K/A* 11/1/17
767344	BAMPTON, Harold Richard ...	... 6/ 2/19	
5008	BARKER, Theodore ...	... 10/ 4/17	22 *Killed in action* 13/5/17
6969	BELL, Frederick Alexander ...	... 19/12/16	*12 Lieut. Wounded* 24/5/17
768390	BERRY, Walter Richard	... 17/ 3/19	
768054	BROADY, George Sheard ...	... 6/ 3/19	
766590	BURGESS, Harold ...	... 3/ 2/19	
763871	CALVERT, William Henry ...	... 29/ 8/17	22
768313	CATHCART, William Clements	... 17/ 3/19	
767743	CATTERALL, George ...	... 5/ 3/19	
763872	CHAPMAN, Donald James ...	... 27/ 6/17	(*9*)
763175	CROFTS, Guy Prescott Shipley	... 1/ 3/17	*19*
768113	CURRIE, Claude ...	... 18/ 3/19	
767832	DOWELL, Alfred Edwin ...	... 3/ 3/19	
765032	DREY, Robert Fornand ...	... 27/ 2/18	*11*
6854	FARRINGTON, Roy Leech ...	... 26/ 9/16	(*1*) *Lieut.*
761758	FLINT, Reginald Perdue ...	... 25/ 9/17	(*9*)
767169	GEE, Arthur Smith	... 5/ 2/19	
3343	GRIERSON, Kenneth McIvor	... 2/ 8/16	22 D.S.O. ✠ *F/D w.* 17/10/17 ⓅⓌ
6801	GROS, Henri Samuel ...	... 5/ 9/16	20 *Lieut.*
764887	HALL, Harry William ...	... 29/ 8/17	(*9*)
764065	HALLIWELL, Fred ...	... 29/ 8/17	*19 Killed in action* 22/4/18
764241	HALLIWELL, Frederick ...	... 29/ 8/17	*11 Capt. Killed in action* 12/10/18
7422	HASTINGS, Vincent Patrick ...	... 19/12/16	22
767299	HERBERT, Lawrence Augustus	... 6/ 2/19	
7464	HESLOP, Eric Charles ...	... 25/ 1/17	*12*
766864	HOOSON, Donovan John Stewart	... 3/ 2/19	
4761	HUSTON, Arthur Richard ...	... 1/ 5/17	22
763554	HYDE, Samuel ...	... 26/ 4/17	
767470	JELKS, William Murray ...	... 6/ 2/19	
1899	JONES, Horace Frank Nielson	... 20/ 6/16	22 *Lieut.*
3565	KLUGMAN, Julius Victor ...	... 2/ 8/16	22 *Lieut. Wounded* 27/9/18
762980	KNOWLES, Stanislaus Alfred	... 28/ 3/17	*17*
767474	LAMB, Arnold Lewis ...	... 15/ 3/19	
764783	MAWSON, Stanley ...	... 29/ 8/17	*19*
762907	MOSS, Gerald Alec ...	... 31/ 7/17	*19*(*2*) *Killed in action* 10/8/18
764117	MOTTERSHALL, Herbert Stanley	... 27/ 6/17	*Died of wounds* 9/10/17
762414	NASH, Phillip Geoffrey ...	... 26/ 4/17	*21 Killed in action* 5/10/17
7135	NEAL, Leslie	... 21/12/16	*24 Lieut.* ⓅⓌ
766902	O'CONNOR, John Louis ...	... 4/ 3/19	
768886	OWRID, Thomas ...	... 14/ 2/19	

MANCHESTER REGIMENT (S/B).

767624	PANTER, Gerald	... 4/ 3/19		
764661	PARKES, Alfred	... 29/ 8/17	21	
762111	PAULSEN, Percy Henry .	... 3/ 2/19		
764793	PENTY, Walter Smith ...	... 1/ 8/17	11	
3597	PLUMMER, Alfred James ...	... 2/ 8/16	21	Wounded 4/9/16, 11/5/17
767112	RAWLINSON, Harry	... 6/ 2/19		
5137	RICHARDS, Ernest Harry ...	... 19/12/16	21	Killed in action 2/4/17
762567	ROOCROFT, Edgar Talbot ...	... 28/ 3/17		
764208	SMART, Herbert William ...	... 31/ 7/17	(9)	
763669	SUTER, Eric James	... 26/ 4/17		Wounded 23/11/17
761194	WALLACE, George Douglas ...	... 25/ 6/17	21	Killed in action 26/10/17
763605	WALSH, Alfred	... 28/ 3/17		Wounded 14/11/17
764569	WALTON, George Kelmore ...	... 28/ 8/17		Lieut. Wounded 30/8/18
764920	WHITTLES, Thomas	... 28/ 8/17		
7345	WHITWORTH, John Cyril ...	... 19/12/16	21	Lieut.
761106	WHITWORTH, L/Cpl. Sidney...	... 1/ 5/18		Capt.
7053	WILLIAMS, Harold	... 19/12/16	22	Lieut. ✠ P/W 22/11/17
5825	WOOLLAM, Harry Morgan ...	... 26/ 9/16		Lieut.

THE MIDDLESEX REGIMENT
(THE DUKE OF CAMBRIDGE'S OWN).

Regular Battalions (Nos. 1, 2, 3 & 4).   {57th Foot / 77th Foot

		2nd Lieut.	
2383	ADAMS, Ronald George H. ...	... 2/12/14	To 16/London
1884	AUSTIN, Herbert Eric ...	.. 5/12/15 4	(R.A.F.) Pilot Officer
2128	CHAPMAN, Bruce Oswald ...	... 26/ 5/15 3	Lieut.
3272	CHURCHFIELD, Sidney Percival	... 16/ 1/16 4	Killed in action -/7/16
1888	COOK, Charles Alfred Barton ...	... 29/ 8/15 4	Lieut. ⓜ
1440	DEWES, Bryan Osmond ...	... 14/ 2/15 1	Killed in action 30/7/15
1420	ELLIOTT, Philip Maurice ...	... 14/ 2/15 3(2)	Wounded 9/5/15 K/A 1/7/16
777	FOSKETT, Arthur Sefton ...	... 23/ 4/16 2	Lieut. M.G.C.
199	GILKS, Harold Langton ...	... 5/ 4/15 4	Capt. ✠ (1/Artists) ⓜ
1422	HALLOWES, Sgt. Rupert Price ...	... 5/ 4/15 4	V.C. ✠ Killed in action 30/9/15 ⓜ
965	HARE, L/Cpl. Bernard Urmston	... 23/11/14 1	Killed in action 25/9/15 ⓜ
2615	HARE, Evan Amyas Alfred ...	... 27/ 1/15 2	Killed in action 10/3/15
1987	HILL, Arthur Dudley ...	... 23/ 4/15 1	Lieut. ✠ ⓜ
1988	HILL, Arthur Lionel ...	... 23/ 4/15 1	Killed in action 25/9/15
3296	HORNE, John Gibson ...	... 7/11/15 4	(R.A.F.) Flying Officer
3197	KING, Thomas Charles ...	.. 3/10/15 1	Lieut. M.G.C. w. -/3/16
3322	LOFTS, Frank	... 16/ 1/16 4	Lieut. Wounded -/11/16
2757	MANSFIELD, Francis Turquand	... 14/11/14 (4)	3/R. West Kent

MIDDLESEX REGIMENT (R/B).

2742	MELLISH, Richard Coppin	...	12/ 6/15	*1 Killed in action 25/9/15*
1051	MILLS, Henry Jackson	...	23/ 4/16	*2 Lieut. M.G.C. K/A 30/5/18*
1637	OWEN, Vaughan Edward O'Neill	...	23/ 4/15	*3 Capt.*
3620	PARKER, Francis Gordon	...	28/11/15	*1 Capt.* ✠
2847	RAYMENT, L/Cpl. Christopher Graham		11/ 6/15	*1 Lieut. Wounded –/7/16*
1498	ROBERTS, Arthur Harold	...	26/ 5/15	*3 Lieut. Wounded 17/9/15*
1130	SHARPE, Charles Lancelot Arnot	...	14/ 2/15	*3 Died of wounds 25/4/15*
1546	SPATZ, Walter	...	23/ 4/15	*2 Killed in action 1/7/16*
994	TIGAR, Harold Walter	...	23/ 4/15	*3 Killed in action 9/5/15*
1011	WHITFELD, Frederick Ashburnham H.		14/ 2/15	*3 Killed in action 23/4/15*
1881	WILLIAMS, Ernest Alfred M.	...	23/ 4/15	*4 Lieut. Wounded 7/5/15, 18/9/15*
2793	WILLIAMS, Hugh Meredith	...	16/ 1/16	*4 Lieut. Wounded 26/2/16*
3784	WILSON, John	...	5/12/15	*2 Killed in action –/7/16*
4233	BACKHOUSE, Herbert Franklin	...	1/ 5/17	*4 Killed in action 25/8/18*
5462	BARBER, Percival Henry	...	3/ 4/17	*1 Lieut. Wounded 23/4/17*
5981	BARTLETT, Leonard	...	22/11/16	*4 Lieut. Wounded 24/4/17*
6866	COOMBS, Arthur Conrad	...	2/ 5/17	*4*
760977	CRAY, Harold Frederick	...	7/ 7/17	*1 Wounded 5/12/17*
761085	DUFFY, William Arthur	...	26/ 6/17	*1*
760536	GODWIN, Charles Robert	...	26/ 6/17	*1* ✠
762407	JOHNSON, Arthur Dunphy	...	25/ 9/17	*3*
765485	MUNRO, James Garrett	...	21/10/17	*1*
6521	NEDEN, Harold George	...	26/ 9/16	*4(19) Wounded 30/1/17, 2/10/17*
761010	RAPLEY, William Godfrey	...	7/ 7/17	*1 Killed in action 25/9/17*

Special Reserve Battalions (Nos. 5 & 6).

3547	FENWICK, Cecil James	...	1/10/15	*5 (–/Oxford & Bucks) w. –/7/16*
1545	GRIFFITHS, Hubert Percy	...	14/12/14	*5 Lieut. To West African F.F.*
2644	NOAD, Colin Kenneth	...	29/12/14	*6 Lieut. To Staff-Lieut. I.A.*
2668	NOAD, Frederick Mitchell	...	29/12/14	*6 Lieut. To West African F.F.*
2441	SKULL, Arthur	...	17/ 4/15	*5 (8/London) Capt.*
4690	WILKINSON, Ambrose Joseph	...	2/ 6/16	*6(12) Killed in action 26/9/16*
763277	REID, Archibald David	...	28/ 3/17	*5(4) Died of wounds 8/8/17*

Territorial Battalions (Nos. 7 to 10).

2484	ALLEN, William Samuel Barnett	...	2/ 4/15	*9*
2086	ARMSTRONG, Martin Donisthorpe	..	17/ 6/15	*8 Lieut.*
1504	BAILEY-CHURCHILL, John L. A.	...	21/ 5/15	*9 Lieut. Wounded 12/10/17*
2766	BALL, Leslie Alfred	...	10/11/14	*10 Capt. Killed in action 4/10/17*
2510	BELL, David Cockburn	...	21/ 5/15	*9*
2333	BROUGH, Wilfrid James	...	2/ 4/15	*9 Lieut.*
3336	BURDER, Claud Vernon	...	25/ 6/15	*8 Capt. R.T.O.* ✠ *w. 16/8/17,* [*30/11/17*]
947	CARR, Cpl. Frederick Bernard	...	9/10/14	*7 Lieut.*
3204	CARR, James Benjamin	...	18/ 5/15	*10 Lieut.*

Copyright.] [Capt. W. B. Wollen.

TERRITORIALS AT POZIERES.

CADETS SELECTING AND CUTTING BRUSHWOOD, France, 1915.

[By permission of the Imperial War Museum.]

Crown Copyright.

MIDDLESEX REGIMENT (T/F).

2601	COLLINS, Horace Alexander	3/10/14	9	*Capt.*
3524	DE PASS, Ronald David	2/ 5/15	10	*Lieut. R.A.F. w.* 2/5/17 ✠
3182	FALCK, Lionel Louis	4/ 6/15	9	
3529	FORBES, L/Cpl. Lawrence	5/ 8/15	(9)	*To* 5/*London*
2330	Fox, Graham Laidler	21/ 5/15	9	*Lieut.*
2431	GILLESPIE, L/Cpl. Gordon Wood	2/ 3/15	9	*Lieut. R.A.F. Presumed K/A*
2432	GINGER, Leonard Stanbridge	14/ 3/15	8	*Lieut. M.G.C.* [13/4/17]
1049	GOULD, Robert Macdonald	9/10/14	7	*Major* F/D *w.* –/9/16
2768	GREGORY, Wallace James I. D.	11/ 6/15	9	*Cap. & Adjt. R.E.*
1477	HARE, John Thornton	18/ 9/14	10	*Capt. Wounded* 27/9/15
2547	HARRIS, Cyril Raymond	21/ 5/15	9	*Lieut.* ✠
3802	JOHNSTON, John Alexander	3/ 9/15	7	*Lieut. To M.G.C.*
977	KAY, Walter Glassford	14/10/14	7	*Lieut.*
2198	KEEPING, Claude Jeffery	10/12/14	8	*Lieut. Killed in action* 24/8/18
2690	MCKEEVER, Gerald Neal	22/ 5/15	9	*Lt. To M.G.C. w.* 18/10/17 ✠
2392	MERFIELD, Sidney Henry	3/ 7/15	8	*Lieut. To M.G.C.* ✠
2186	MUMMERY, Harold Halton	2/ 3/15	7	*Lieut. Wounded* 10/9/18
1788	PERKS, Harold	9/10/14	7	*Capt. Prisoner of war*
3158	ROBIN, Norman Ollivier	26/ 5/15	10	*Lieut.*
4815	SANDFORD, Charles J. Vavasour	16/ 6/16	8	*Died of wounds* 6/5/17
2195	SHARP, Raymond	19/ 6/15	9	
1018	SHERLOCK, Cecil Claris	21/ 5/15	7	*Lieut.* ✠ *w.* –/7/16, 14/5/18 ✠
2289	STEWART, Oliver	27/10/14	9	*Lieut.*
2750	WINSHIP, Ernest Roland	3/ 7/15	8	*Lieut.* ✠
2832	WOOD, Hubert	5/ 3/15	9	*Adjt. (M.G.C.)*
2510	BELL, David Cockburn	21/ 5/15	9	*Capt.* ✠ F/D *(R.F.C.)*
4662	BOND, Sidney Albert	31/ 7/16	7	✠
764976	BRITTAN, Norman Frank	24/ 9/17	7	
7869	BROOKS, Wilfred Johnson	26/ 1/17	7	
766682	CAMPBELL, James Taite	29/10/18	10	
6755	DAVIS, Edw. Maximilian	5/ 9/16	7	*Lieut. Wounded* 22/9/18
760673	DAYTON, Sgt. William Robert	27/ 2/18	8	
765766	FLINT, George Herbert	27/ 2/18	10	
762830	FRENCH, Douglas Hutley	25/ 9/17	10	
764771	HEWITT, Frank Malcolm	30/10/17	7	(11/*R. Fus.*) *w.* –/8/18, 18/9/18
5127	JEFFERYS, Arthur Harold	25/ 7/16	7	*Lieut.* ✠ *Wounded* 9/5/18 ✠
762756	KIMBER, John Arnold	26/ 4/17	9	*Wounded* 1/9/17, 5/12/17
763753	LANGLEY, Walter Robert	30/ 5/17	10	*Wounded* 22/12/17
765460	LEESE, James Francis Favell	21/ 1/18	8	
5220	SMITH, Robert Alfred	5/ 9/16	7	*Lieut.*
760716	TURNER, Reginald Alfred	5/11/18	9	
763442	WOODS, Cyril	24/ 9/17	8	

x

Service Battalions (New Armies).

2405	BERRY, Berry Oscar ...	...	26/ 3/15	*14*
2618	BUTT, Charles Frederick	...	10/ 3/15	*13 Capt. & Adjt. (R.E.)*
2317	CARD, Arthur Henry	...	9/ 1/15	*12* ✠ *Killed in action 26/9/16*
952	CHAPMAN, John Frank	...	4/ 6/15	*18 Lieut. Wounded –/6/16*
2617	CLARK, Walter Llewelyn	...	22/12/14	*15 Capt, (R.F.C.) K/A 23/5/17*
978	CROSS-SHEEN, CQMS Ronald		10/ 3/15	*11 Capt. & Adjt.*
2599	FISHER, Henry Cecil	...	12/12/15	*16 Capt.* ✠ *w. 10/10/17* ℞
1545	GRIFFITHS, Hubert Percy	...	20/10/14	*14 To 5*
2914	HINGLEY, Alfred Norman	...	3/10/15	*13 Lt.-Col.* D S.O. ✠ *w. 25/10/18* ℞
1380	HURT, William George	...	16/11/14	*13 Capt. To W. African Regt.*
3845	IBBOTSON, Cecil Clayton	...	7/ 8/15	*14 Lieut.* [*w. –/–/18* ℞]
4614	JENKINS, Arnold Collier	...	26/ 5/16	*Lieut. To R.A.F. w. –/8/16*
2166	LATHAM, Harold ...	...	12/12/15	*16 Lieut. Wounded –/6/16*
1447	LAWLESS, Philip Henry	...	7/ 5/15	*18 Capt. & Adjt.*
2881	PALMER, Arthur Baillie Bentinck	...	4/ 2/15	*17 Lieut. (R.A.F.) Acc/K 23/8/18*
3451	PRESCOTT, William ...	...	10/ 3/15	*13*
2844	REID, Douglas ...	...	18/12/14	*15 Lieut.*
1941	SKERRY, James Bradwell	...	11/ 5/15	*17 Killed in action –/6/16*
284	STUART-COOK, Sgt. Henry ...		4/ 2/15	*11*
1991	THORNTON, Hugh Cholmondeley	...	4/ 1/15	*11 Lieut. To 10/D.C.L.I.*
2792	THISTLETON, John Francis ...		11/ 2/15	*14 To 7/W.Yorks*
1553	WHINNEY, Charles Toller	...	22/ 8/14	*11 Lieut.* ✠ *Wounded 10/12/17* ℞
2609	WILLIAMS, Llewelyn David ...		23/ 1/15	*15 Lieut.*
4295	ABBOT, William ...	...	5/ 9/16	*22 Wounded 6/11/18*
3510	ASHENDEN, Edward James ...		4/10/16	*23 Wounded 7/6/17, 6/9/18*
1660	ASHFORD, Cpl. Aubrey Charles		19/12/16	*15*
766958	BADDELEY, Austin Wright	...	4/ 2/19	
6041	BAKER, Percy Richards ...		7/ 7/16	*24 Wounded –/11/16*
768389	BALDWIN, William James Fleetwood		5/ 2/19	
766067	BARRATT, Arthur John	...	23/ 5/18	*32*
768111	BELL, Harold Benjamin	...	12/ 2/19	
4949	BEER, John Tidbury	...	7/ 7/17	*25 Wounded –/11/16*
7364	BILBY, Eustace John	...	19/12/16	*(2) Killed in action 16/8/17*
762642	BLAKE, Arthur Edward	...	5/ 8/17	*20 Wounded 12/12/17, 15/6/18*
769205	BRIGGENSHAW, Robert John	...	4/ 3/19	
767740	BRIGGS, Harold Thomas	...	3/ 3/19	
765109	BROWN, Horace Gilbert	...	31/10/17	
765156	BROWN, Reginald Herbert ...		31/10/17	
767276	BUNKER, Herbert Edwin	...	5/ 2/19	
7348	BUTT, Herbert ...	...	19/12/16	*Lieut.*
762675	CHANTRILL, Charles Hubert	...	30/ 5/17	*26*
7168	CHAPLIN, Thos. Haliburton Goodwill		7/ 7/16	*Lieut.*

MIDDLESEX REGIMENT (S/B).

766640	CHRISTIE, Herbert James	3/ 2/19	
764055	CLARKE, Francis	26/ 9/17	*16* Wounded 29/12/17
769277	CLERY, Lumley Lawrence	5/ 3/19	
764112	COLE, Cecil Charles Edward	3/ 3/19	
1918	COLLINS, Arthur Jefferies	15/ 1/15	*30* Capt.
6615	COPELAND, Ernest Frederick	7/ 7/16	*25* Lieut.
769091	CUTLER, William Herbert	3/ 3/19	
768295	DAVENPORT-HANDLEY, Humphries J.	12/ 2/19	
768084	DAVIS, Cyril Lance	18/ 3/19	
767555	DELL, Cecil James	3/ 3/19	
761672	DUDDY, James Frederick Ernest	14/ 4/17	
768249	DUNMORE, Cyril William	17/ 3/19	
764885	ELLIOTT, Frederick William	26/ 9/16	*(4)*
767573	EVANS, Henry Rex Gillatt	3/ 3/19	
3592	FAULKNER, John Bradfield	25/ 2/17	*13* Wounded 18/8/17
3705	FISH, Benjamin Leslie	21/ 6/16	*12(18)* Died of wounds 30/10/18
765168	FRECKER, Sgt. Albert Charles	5/ 2/19	
764769	GILES, James	29/ 8/17	*20*
5948	GOLDBURG, Philip	7/ 7/16	*15* Lieut.
768218	GOUDA, Willie Walter Finlayson	17/ 3/19	
7142	GUY, Robert	19/12/16	*20* Lieut.
768041	HALL, Cyril Ruxton	3/ 4/19	
7663	HARE, Lionel Harold Eustace	24/ 8/16	Lieut.
768541	HARRISON, Edward Lewis	13/ 2/19	
766553	HOLLAND, Richard Henry	24/ 5/18	Wounded 12/9/18
760479	HOLT, Granville Grindroe	25/ 6/17	*13* Wounded 21/8/17
760553	HOOKE, Arthur Holman	27/ 6/17	*20* Wounded 12/12/17
763888	HOWELL, Hubert David	30/ 5/17	*11*
761313	IREDALE, John Taylor	4/ 2/19	
768232	JOHNSON, Douglas Dunphy	19/ 3/19	
763461	JONES, Ernest Owen	30/ 5/17	*12* Wounded 4/6/18
4994	JONES, William Henry Lake	7/ 7/16	*25* Lieut.
765180	KILLICK, Stephen George	31/10/17	
7352	LEAROYD, L/Cpl. Ernest Smith	19/12/16	*20* Killed in action 23/11/17
762507	LEAVER, Stanley Horace	26/ 4/17	*17* Killed in action 9/4/18
763108	LEONARD, George Conrad	30/10/17	
6589	LESTER, Reginald Mountstephens	7/ 7/16	*25* Lieut.
3609	LEVESON, Adolphus Henry	7/11/16	*16* Lieut.
767637	LINTER, Frank Cyril	3/ 3/19	
768477	LOCK, Percy	5/ 2/19	
760018	MANVELL, Francis George	17/ 3/19	
762458	McMILLAN, Roland John	2/ 8/17	*17*
768480	McWILLIAM, William Rea	5/ 2/19	
767366	MIEVILLE, Louis Charles	5/ 2/19	
767622	MODLEN, Sidney Edwin	3/ 3/19	

MIDDLESEX REGIMENT (S/B).

6809	MORRIS, Alfred Arthur Thomas	... 26/ 9/16	*21* Lieut. ✠ w. 12/12/17	D/W
769153	NEECH, Walter Punshon ...	... 14/ 2/19		[24/10/18]
767808	NELSON, John Peel	... 3/ 3/19		
761529	NEWMAN, CSM Charles Stanley	... 14/ 2/19	ℳ	
5853	NORRIS, Victor Lawrence ...	... 26/ 9/16	*23*	
762960	OSMOND, Wilfred Hamilton ...	... 26/ 4/17		
764377	PAGE, Frederick William Robert	... 24/ 9/17		
764040	PARRISH, Edwin Percy ...	... 27/ 6/17	*23*	
768706	PATON, Edward Curphey ...	... 13/ 2/19		
5794	POYNTON, Allen	... 4/ 5/17	*18*	
3718	PILE, Samuel John Houghton	. 21/ 9/16	*13* ✠ Wounded	
767694	RICHARDS, Charles Alexander Frank	3/ 3/19		
763135	RICHARDSON, Thomas Havelock	... 26/ 4/17		
766618	RIEDINGER, Stanley Lewis John	... 17/ 3/19		
767702	ROBINSON, Claude Cecil ...	... 17/ 3/19		
767782	ROBINSON, Leslie	... 3/ 3/19		
3621	ROGERSON, Harold	... 21/ 2/17	*13*	
763044	ROSS, Roderick O'Connor ...	... 26/ 9/17	*17*	
761155	ROWLAND, Harold Evans ...	... 7/ 3/19		
7187	ROWNTREE, Douglas Woodville	... 19/12/16	(*1*) Wounded 12/3/17, 19/4/18	
767783	SADLER, Harold Abraham ...	... 17/ 3/19		
6900	SARGOOD, Hugh Frank ...	... 1/ 4/17	*16*	
767824	SCHOFIELD, Charles Eric ...	... 17/ 3/19		
6580	SEARCY, John Henry ...	... 26/ 9/16	*21*	
767695	SHEPHERD, Maurice William	... 3/ 3/19		
5289	SHERRARD, Leslie Herbert ...	... 7/ 7/16	*25* Lieut.	
764801	SORRELL, Frederick George	... 26/ 9/17		
767162	STACEY, Maurice Robert ...	... 5/ 2/19		
767307	SUTTON, Walter Dudley ...	... 6/ 2/19		
760777	SWAN, Kenneth Thomas ...	... 26/ 9/17	Wounded 11/5/18	
767446	TOWNSEND, Phillip Paulson	... 6/ 2/19		
767698	TRANGMAR, Harold Edgar ...	... 3/ 3/19		
6542	TYE, Frederick	... 4/ 5/17	*18* ✠	
760477	WADSWORTH, Arthur ...	... 25/ 6/17	*13* ✠	
761496	WEBB, Bernard Hugh ...	... 12/ 2/19		
767845	WELLMAN, Gordon Menzies...	... 17/ 3/19		
767846	WHADCOAT, Charles John ...	... 5/ 3/19		
1882	WILLIAMS, Harold Oswald ...	... 21/ 9/16	*13* Killed in action 21/1/17	
766728	WILLOUGHBY-DAVIS, Vernon	... 3/ 2/19		
767373	WURR, Alexander Hewitt ...	... 12/ 2/19		

THE MONMOUTHSHIRE REGIMENT (T.F.)

			2nd Lieut.	
3229	EVANS, Frank Taynton	...	21/ 5/15	*Capt.*
2414	HARPER, Edward Russell	...	19/ 3/15	*Capt. Adjt.* ✠ *(R.A.S.C.)*
3122	MOORE, Reginald Elsenham M.	...	21/11/15	*Lieut.* [*Officer*]
3655	SHARPE, Horace Edmund	...	21/11/15	*Capt.* w. 26/4/18, 2/10/18 *Educ.*]
5674	ARTHUR, Walter Headley	...	17/ 6/16	*Lieut.*
4873	BARR, Robert Allan	...	17/ 6/16	*Lieut.*
4991	BROWNE, Herbert William	...	11/ 7/16	*Lieut.*
4841	CLERY, Gerald John	...	17/ 6/16	*Lieut.*
4983	COOPER, William Reginald Donne	...	17/ 6/16	*Lieut.*
4639	DUNCAN, Charles Percy Hochee	...	17/ 6/16	*Lieut.* Wounded 20/12/17
5208	KIRBY, Norman Francis	...	31/ 5/16	*Lieut.*
4775	LLOYD, David Howard	...	8/ 7/16	*Lieut.*
4882	MARRABLE, Christopher George	...	17/ 6/16	*Capt.* Wounded 23/5/17 ℞
4497	MOLLETT, Frederick Norman	...	18/ 6/16	
4933	MOORE, Frank Leonard	...	17/ 6/16	*Lieut.* ✠ Wounded 12/12/18
4814	RICHARDS, Arthur	...	3/ 7/16	Died of wounds 27/6/17
763609	ARCHER, Henry Charles	...	25/ 9/17	Killed in action 8/10/18
5691	GOWER, Frederick William	...	5/ 8/16	*Lieut.* Wounded 2/7/17
6059	HAGGIS, Ernest Victor	...	5/ 8/16	*Lieut.* Wounded 25/8/17
4897	HILL, Walter Percy	...	5/ 8/16	*Lieut.* Wounded 22/12/17
6620	HOWELLS, George Davey	...	5/ 9/16	*Lieut.* (15/*Cheshire*) K/A 28/2/18
763038	LIBBY, William Norman	...	16/ 6/17	*Lieut.* (*Labour Corps*)
5130	MASDING, Stanley Henry Percy	...	5/ 8/16	*Lieut.* (*R.A.F.*)
765799	PROSSER, David Russell	...	24/ 4/18	
5356	REMINGTON, William	...	5/ 8/16	*Lieut.*
5354	SECCOMBE, James Horace	...	5/ 8/16	*Lieut.*
7646	SOUPER, Charles Alexander	...	11/ 2/17	*Lieut.*
764724	SWASH, Frederick Clifford	...	29/ 8/17	
763349	THOMPSON, Ronald William	...	26/ 4/17	Killed in action 11/4/18
5356	TODD, Cyril Kerridge	...	5/ 8/16	*Lieut.*
766458	WILLIAMS, Arthur Thomas	...	26/ 6/18	
764740	WILLIAMS, Thomas Brinsmead	...	28/ 8/17	*Lieut.*
8078	YENDALL, Raymond B.	...	24/ 8/16	*Lieut.* (*Tank Corps*) P/W 29/10/18

THE ROYAL MUNSTER FUSILIERS.

Regular Battalions (Nos. 1 & 2). {101st Foot / 104th Foot}

			2nd Lieut.	
447	CONRAN, Edward Denis	...	23/ 4/15 2	Capt. ✠ ✠ w. 8/10/15, 22/5/16, [14/10/18 ⌘
1723	DENNYS, Kenneth Rose	...	1/ 1/15 2	Killed in action 9/5/15
1446	HORSFALL, Arthur Mendelssohn	...	1/ 1/15 2	Killed in action 9/5/15 ⌘
3363	McKANN, William John	...	24/10/15 2	Lieut. ⌘
819	PAGE, Francis Trafford	...	1/ 1/15 2	Killed in action 9/5/15
1442	PARKER, Wilfred Horsley	...	1/ 1/15 2	Killed in action 9/5/15
1540	RABONE, Maxwell	...	1/ 1/15 2	Died of wounds 21/8/15
4917	CALLANAN, Michael	...	26/ 9/16 2	Killed in action 20/12/16
5797	GROVE-PRICE, William F.	...	26/ 9/16 2	Lieut.
5512	KELLY, Edward Heald F.	...	12/11/16 2	

Special Reserve Battalions (Nos. 3, 4 & 5).

2910	FRASER, Claude Tancred	...	10/ 3/15 5 Lieut.
7124	CLANCY, Jeremiah	...	25/10/16 5 Prisoner of war 21/9/17
6548	O'BRIEN, James	...	25/10/16 5 (1/R. Innis. Fus.) w. 5/12/17

Service Battalions (New Armies).

218	CHANDLER, Cpl. Cecil W.	...	28/ 9/14 8 Capt. ✠ w. –/8/16 K/A 30/3/18
537	HARRISON, Frank	...	28/ 9/14 9 Major O.B.E. ✠
472	MORRELL, Charles	...	28/ 9/14 9 Lieut. To R.F.C.
1160	QUARE, Herbert Alfred Brame	...	26/ 9/14 9 Capt. ✠ w. 25/5/17 ⌘
1628	UZIELLI, Edward Noel	...	5/10/14 9 Lieut.
1370	WATTS-RUSSELL, Cpl. John Charles		5/ 1/15 9 Capt. Wounded –/1/16
767503	BULGAR, Arthur Gerard	...	6/ 2/19
762714	CAROLIN, Horace George	...	29/ 3/17 Wounded 6/11/18
766485	COSGROVE, Hubert Gregory	...	26/ 9/17 (2) Lieut. Wounded 25/3/18
762718	CRONIN, William Francis	...	3/ 3/19
768882	MEANY, William	...	14/ 2/19
766613	O'CONNOR, Charles Anthony		24/ 3/19
3401	WALSH, John Edward	...	1/10/16 8 Wounded

THE NORFOLK REGIMENT.

Regular Battalions (Nos. 1 & 2).
9th Foot

		2nd Lieut.
1031	CHATER, Guy Leathley ...	... 27/ 1/15 *1*
1541	FARQUHARSON, Hugh Joseph	... 1/ 1/15 *1 Died* 27/8/16
2393	KLEIN, Adrian B. L. ...	... 11/ 6/15 *1 Capt.* O.B.E. F/D *w.* 30/9/15
1300	LORIMER, John Scott ...	... 11/ 6/15 *1 Lieut. (T.M.B.)*
2058	MARTIN, Ernest William ...	... 11/ 6/15 *1 Killed in action* 27/7/16
1727	SIBREE, Herbert John Hyde	... 1/ 1/15 *1 Capt.* ✠ 🎖
1538	TYLER, Guy Cromwell ...	... 1/ 1/15 *1 Capt. w.* 3/5/15 *D/W* 22/8/18
2515	BURNETT, Fossett Sidney ...	... 20/10/15

Special Reserve Battalion (No. 3).

4351	TOWER, Herbert George Eric	... 19/ 6/16 *3 Lieut. To Indian Army* ✠
763092	BRADLEY, William Charles ...	... 29/ 3/17 *3 Lieut.*
768186	PRICE, Edwin Henry ...	... 17/ 3/19 *3*
766336	RAMSEY, Henry Oswald ...	... 28/ 5/18 *3*
766337	REDMAN, Everett Dorton ...	... 29/ 5/18 *3*

Territorial Battalions (Nos. 4 to 6).

3107	ADAMS, Robert ...	... 23/ 5/15 *5 Killed in action* 12/8/15
3156	HEMSWORTH, Noel Edward C.	... 9/ 7/15 *5 From* 7/*Worcester*
3104	OLIPHANT, L/Cpl. Marcus Francis ...	28/ 3/15 *5 Killed in action* 12/8/15
3796	ALLWOOD, Charles ...	... 30/ 7/15 *(4) To* 6/*West Riding*
3623	BENTLEY, Alfred ...	... 30/ 7/15 *(4) Lieut.* ✠ 🎖
3838	BROWNE, Aubrey George ...	... 30/ 7/15 *(4) Lieut.* ✠ 🎖
3768	CASLON, Eric William ...	... 23/ 9/15 *6 Lieut.*
3438	CHEESEWRIGHT, Cpl. Frederick Cecil	30/ 7/15 *(4) Lieut.*
3576	HOOD, Fred Watson ...	... 30/ 7/15 *(4) Capt. Base Remt. Dep., Lahore*
2851	NORRIS, William Forbes ...	... 16/ 8/14 *5 Lieut. (A.C.C.) K/A* 25/8/15
3683	SHARPE, William Dalton Colombo ...	30/ 7/15 *(4) Killed in action* 9/10/17
3870	TICE, Stanley Arthur ...	... 30/ 7/15 *(4) Lieut. Wounded* 10/2/18
6147	AMES, Hugh Elgar	... 26/ 9/16 *6 Lieut.*
6544	ARMES, Thomas William ...	... 23/11/16 *4 Lieut.*
7681	BEGG, Arthur ...	... 21/ 1/17 *4 Capt. Died* 21/3/18
764414	BLAKE, Leonard Garson ...	... 28/ 8/17 *5 Wounded* 4/2/18
6972	CHAPMAN, Basil Edmund ...	... 5/ 9/16 *4 Lieut.* ✠ *w.* 28/8/17 🎖
762946	CHAPMAN, Thomas Stanbrooke	... 27/ 3/17 *4 Wounded* 8/6/17
761259	HODGES, Charles William Rowlatt ...	29/ 5/18 *5*
6914	LANE, John Rupert Chandos ...	... 23/11/16 *4 Wounded* 15/4/18 *P/W*
6295	MORTEN, Hamish Macpherson	... 5/ 9/16 *6 Lieut.*
7689	PALMER, Harold Garwood ...	... 26/ 1/17 *4 Wounded* 12/11/18
763644	PAYNE, Charles Curtis ...	... 30/ 5/17 *4*
766081	PINK, Percy	... 24/ 5/18 *4*

762065	Scolding, George Henry	25/ 4/17	5	Killed in action 26/3/18
6438	Scott, Theodore Gilbert	26/ 9/16	4 ✠	Wounded 8/5/18
5548	Stubington, Richard Edwin	5/ 9/16	6 Lieut.	Wounded 24/10/17
764864	Woodcock, Cecil Wilfred	25/ 9/18	5	

Service Battalions (New Armies).

3483	Allen, Mervyn Richard William	28/11/15	7 w. –/7/16	Killed in action 2/8/17
2376	Blackborn, Clifford Thomas	12/12/15	8 Lieut.	w. –/7/16, 23/8/17
2729	Daniell, Charles Henry P.	7/12/14	10 Lieut.	
2487	Hall, Wilfred B. Compton	10/10/15	1/G.B.	
2831	King, Bernard Ellis	13/11/14	10 Lieut. ✠ 🎖	
2343	Mackenzie, Roderick Sandford	9/12/14	9 Lieut.	To 3/Border
2446	Read, Odden Hewlett	3/10/15	9 Lieut.	Wounded –/7/16
3190	Saqui, Leslie Vernon Harcourt	24/10/15	7 Lieut.	To M.G.C.
2232	Selfe, Edgar Donald	12/12/15	9 Capt.	w. 4/2/18, 10/6/18 } [Killed in action 7/8/18 {
5083	Tapply, Mark	25/ 5/16	10 Capt. & Adjt. ✠	w. 11/10/16
4603	White, Douglas Cyril	25/ 5/16	10 Prisoner of war 1/12/17 Repatd.	
764411	Baker, Percy Albert	29/ 8/17	7	
6263	Barton, George Frank	26/ 9/16	7	Killed in action 9/4/17
768036	Barwood, Frederick John	17/ 3/19		
763562	Benton, Sydney	30/ 5/17	(1) K/A 27/10/17	
761404	Bird, Philip Arthur	29/ 5/18	Wounded 1/11/18	
768813	Blake, Sidney George	17/ 3/19		
7750	Brown, Allan Robert	26/ 9/16	7 Lieut.	Wounded 2/1/18
1147	Case, Frederick Marcus Beck	1/ 8/16	7 Lieut.	
763094	Catton, Eric Draycott	29/ 3/17	Lieut.	
767004	Cook, Arthur Hugh	6/ 2/19		
4727	Cooke, Michael James	19/12/16	9 Lieut. ✠	Wounded 10/5/18
3018	Dawkins, Charles Cyril	7/11/16	7 Lieut.	Wounded 2/8/17, 24/8/18
764761	Dutton, Clarence Eldred	29/ 8/17		
765982	Gilliat, Leofric	1/ 5/18		
3392	Goossens, Adolphe Antony	1/ 8/16	7 Lieut.	
762518	Gordon, William Pasley London	29/ 8/17	Wounded 18/12/17	
4909	Harrison, Charles Edward	5/ 9/16	Lieut.	
765093	Harvey, Albert Frederick	31/10/17	7	
768043	Haylett, Frank Ernest	18/ 3/19		
761341	Hogarth-Swann, Arthur Lionel	26/ 6/17	7 Lieut. ✠	w. 10/12/17, 11/9/18
767716	Horrax, Charles Benson	17/ 3/19		
764322	Howe, Vernon Arthur	29/ 8/17	Lieut. ✠ 🎖	
5059	Jones, Cyril Gordon	12/11/16	9	Killed in action 20/11/17
765277	Mack, Edmund Hytton	18/12/17		
769250	Moore, Arthur Montague	15/ 2/19		
763168	Norwak, Charles Fred.	26/ 4/17	Lieut.	Wounded 7/9/17
7026	Oldfield, Claud Courtney	19/12/16	9 Capt.	
7544	Orchard, Oliver	26/ 1/17	8 Lieut.	Wounded 7/4/18
3417	Page, John Canler	5/10/16	9	Killed in action 18/10/16

NORFOLK REGIMENT (S/B).

3408	PAGE, Thomas Spencer ...	... 5/10/16	9	*Killed in action* 19/10/16
5663	RHODES, William Frederick ...	... 12/11/16	9	*Capt.*
763599	ROLLINSON, Edward Howard	... 29/ 8/17	(4)	
7048	ROSS, Francis William ...	... 19/12/16	8	*Lieut.*
767516	ROYDEN, Thomas William Eardley ...	5/ 3/19		
766998	RUDDERAM, Joseph Edward	... 17/ 3/19		
1535	SHERLOCK, Arthur Frederick	... 24/ 1/17	8 ✠	*Wounded* 27/8/17
768218	STACEY, Henry Charles ...	... 17/ 3/19		
764723	SUMMERS, George Douglas ...	... 29/ 8/17		*Lieut. w. & P/W* 30/11/17
768061	THEOBALD, Geoffrey St. John	... 17/ 3/19		
768062	THEOBALD, Ivan St. John ...	... 17/ 3/19		
768158	TIBBENHAM, Donald Claude	... 17/ 3/19		
6368	WEBB, Clarence Harold ...	... 5/ 9/16	8 *Lieut.* ✠ 🎖

THE NORTHAMPTONSHIRE REGIMENT.

Regular Battalions (Nos. 1 & 2).

{48th Foot
{58th Foot

2nd Lieut.

3352	BARNETT, Harold Frank William	... 24/10/15	1	*Prisoner of War*
2879	COCKERILL, Frederick Charles	... 24/10/15	1	*Lieut. Wounded* 12/8/16. 11/6/18
1575	HALCROW, Oscar Henry ...	... 7/11/15	1	*Lieut.*
1755	PEAKE, John Thelwal ...	... 20/ 3/15	2	*Died of wounds* 11/5/15
1631	RANDALL, Reginald Wigmore S.	... 20/ 3/15	2	*Killed in action* 9/5/15
5574	ELLIOT, Nichol ...	... 14/ 4/17	1	*(T.M.B.) K/A* 10/7/17
1815	GROWSE, John Hartley ...	... 16/ 8/16	2	*Capt. Died of wounds* 28/3/18

Special Reserve Battalion (No. 3).

761468	COOK, William Tebbutt ...	... 30/ 1/18	3(7)	*Wounded* 24/10/18
765532	DAWSON, Roger Graham ...	... 27/11/17	3(6)	*Killed in action* 18/9/18
765314	JONES, Harry ...	... 28/11/17	3(2)	*Prisoner of war* 8/7/18
764807	THOMAS, Arthur Lewis ...	... 31/ 7/17	3(2)	*Killed in action* 24/4/18

Territorial Battalion (No. 4).

1679	BLACKWELL, Philip William	... 8/ 9/15	4	*Lieut. (To Min. of Shipping)*
5310	CHICK, Albert Eric ...	... 14/ 6/16	4	*Lieut.*
2890	GOSSE, Reginald Wilkes ...	... 24/ 3/15	4	*Lieut.*
3611	PERKINS, Leonard ...	... 8/ 9/15	4	*Lieut.* 🎖
6283	BURT, Arthur Herbert ...	... 26/ 9/16	4	*Lieut.*
766510	CAPP, Richard Whiteman ...	... 10/ 9/18	4	
766437	KILSBY, George Alfred ..	... 26/ 6/18	4	*Killed in action* 18/9/18
764843	PARKER, Thomas Ryder ...	... 16/ 6/17		

Service Battalions (New Armies).

4040	CAINE, Cyril Victor	...	20/ 9/15	8 *Lieut.*
2965	FLETCHER, Malcolm Reginald	...	24/10/15	5 *Lieut.*
2800	HAMILTON, Noel Crawford	...	13/11/14	6 *Killed in action* 14/7/16
3209	HAWTREY, Ralph	...	22/ 4/15	8
1150	HUNTER, James Whitaker	...	19/ 9/15	5 *Killed in action* 9/7/16
2068	LAYMAN, Arnold Thomas	...	19/ 9/15	5 *Lieut.*
4392	MARTIN, Reginald Dean	...	25/ 5/16	8 *Wounded* 11/10/18 ✠ 𝕸
1451	MORRIS, Dennis Wells	...	9/ 1/15	*Lieut.*
2264	POWNALL, Noel Lee	...	16/ 1/15	8 *Wounded* 19/8/18 *M.G.C.*
1950	SAINSBURY, Peter Crush	...	24/10/15	5 *Lieut. Wounded* –/3/16, 16/10/18
2294	WEEDON, Victor Campbell	...	5/ 5/15	8 *Lieut. Wounded* –/8/16
763286	BELL, Robert James	...	28/ 3/17	(4) *Killed in action* 2/11/17
768222	BRYAN, Leonard John	...	17/ 3/19	
768604	CAVE, Robert Newman	...	17/ 4/19	
762891	CLEAVER, George Leslie	...	28/ 3/17	
763174	COOKE, Alfred Molyneux	...	28/ 3/17	
6788	COOPER, George Spencer	...	5/ 9/16	6 *Killed in action* 17/2/17
765834	CROFT, Harold Dan.	...	13/ 3/18	(*M.G.C.*)
768533	CURRALL, William Joseph Rowden	...	13/ 2/19	
767949	DICKENS, Frank	...	5/ 3/19	
762130	DORRINGTON, Stanley Flowers	...	28/ 3/17	*Lieut.* ✠
762059	GIFFARD, Denbow Godfrey Cecil	...	28/ 3/17	*Wounded* 15/11/17
3508	GOTCH, Davis Ingle	...	14/ 8/16	6 *Lieut.* ✠ *P/W* 23/3/18
6105	GRAHAM, Edmund Alexander	...	18/ 3/17	6 *Wounded* 14/5/18
761590	GREEN, Charles William Sydney	...	17/ 3/19	
7091	HARDING, Geoffrey Philip	...	3/ 4/17	6 *Lieut.* ✠
7271	HEATH, Philip Stanley	...	19/12/16	*12 Lieut.*
762390	HILL, Bertram Alan	...	20/ 4/17	*Wounded* 8/5/18
7247	JONES, Albert Edward	...	19/12/16	*13 Lieut.*
5766	JONES, John James	...	18/ 3/17	6 *Wounded* 20/4/18
7038	KEW, Ernest	...	2/ 5/17	7
763398	MARCHANT, Howard Holt	...	26/ 4/17	
767818	MAYES, Richard Berkeley	...	3/ 3/19	
762696	McNALLY, Irwin	...	26/ 4/17	*Prisoner of war* 15/6/18
763697	McNALLY, Reginald James Colvin	...	26/ 4/17	*Wounded* 29/8/17
5317	MILLS, Robert Cecil Lloyd	...	3/ 4/17	6 *Wounded* 29/4/18 *Died* 28/2/19
768124	MITTON, George Croft	...	17/ 3/19	
766610	MUMFORD, George	...	3/ 3/19	
762909	PICKERING, Geo. Anthony Raymond	...	28/ 3/17	(4) *Killed in action* 2/11/17
764344	PITTS, Stanley Edward	...	28/ 3/17	
4636	ROSS, Austin Felton	...	13/ 4/17	*Lieut. Wounded* 28/4/18
7960	SMITH, Geoffrey Harold	...	19/12/16	(2) *Died of wounds* 10/7/17
763048	TAYTON, Wilfred Edward	...	26/ 4/17	*Wounded* 30/8/17
766456	TOMPKINS, Reginald William	...	3/ 2/19	
4862	WALKER, Gordon Henry	...	18/ 3/17	6 *Killed in action* 10/11/17
5561	WARNER, Henry James	...	3/ 4/17	6 *Killed in action* 3/6/17
765747	WHITE, Arthur James	...	27/ 2/18	
7239	YOUNG, William	...	19/12/16	*13 Wounded* 11/10/18

THE NORTHUMBERLAND FUSILIERS. 331

Regular Battalions (Nos. 1 & 2.) 5th Foot

		2nd Lieut.	
1254	BARBER, Bradley King Bell ...	... 12/ 6/15	*1 Capt. (R.F.C.) K/A 4/9/17*
2395	Fox, Douglas Charles ...	... 15/ 8/15	*1 Killed in action 23/7/16*
1441	GARDNER, Henry Edgar ...	... 29/ 8/15	*2 Lieut. Wounded 28/10/18*
3183	GREEN, Harry ...	... 24/10/15	*1 Lieut.*
3215	HOWGILL, Richard John Frederick ...	24/10/15	*1 Capt. R.T.O.*
1527	PARTINGTON, L/Cpl. Leigh ...	... 12/ 6/15	*1 Capt.* F/D *K/A 28/3/18*
1886	PASSINGHAM, Edward George	... 10/ 7/15	*1 Lieut.* ✠ *w. –/7/16 K/A 3/5/17*
1242	PROBERT, Arthur James ..	... 10/ 7/15	*1 Killed in action 9/4/17*
831	ROSE, Stewart Alan ...	... 24/ 7/15	*2 Lieut. w. 1/10/15, –/3/16 K/A [28/3/18*
2023	SOMERSET, James Herbert ...	... 15/ 8/15	*1*
3202	WARE, Albert Francis ...	... 24/10/15	*1*
2022	WATSON, Bryan ...	... 15/ 8/15	*1*
1924	WILKINS, Geoffrey ...	... 26/ 5/15	*2 Died of wounds 3/10/15*
2369	WOODROFFE, Bernard Charles	... 24/ 7/15	*2*
2374	WOODROFFE, Kenneth Drury	... 24/ 7/15	*2 Lieut.*
2528	WRIGHT, Cyril Carne Glenton	... 21/10/14	*(2) From 4/Durham L.I.*
763089	APPS, Jack Harry Mason ...	... 1/ 3/17	*1 Killed in action 20/11/17*
3667	BATEMAN, James ...	... 19/ 6/16	*1 Lieut.*
3181	DODD, Thomas Courtnay ...	... 19/ 6/16	*1 Lieut.*
763372	SMITH, Henry ...	... 1/ 3/17	*1*
763350	TRAVELL, Norman Eric ...	... 1/ 3/17	*Wounded 12/10/17*

Special Reserve Battalion (No. 3).

| 765910 | SCOTT, Alfred Aelred ... | ... 25/ 9/18 | *3* |
| 764515 | WALKER, William Francis ... | ... 28/ 8/17 | *3(9) Killed in action 9/4/18* |

Territorial Battalions (Nos. 4 to 7).

2145	BURNETT, Charles Guy Arbouin	... 22/ 2/15	*7 Lieut. Killed in action 30/6/16*
3663	COLLING, George Cecil ...	... 11/ 5/15	*6 Lieut.*
3486	GROVES, Cpl. Henry Fisher ...	... 11/ 5/15	*6 Capt. (R.A.F.)*
3552	LEECH, Arthur William ...	... 11/ 5/15	*6 Lieut.* ✠ *Died of wounds 2/4/18*
3679	LLEWELLYN, John Trevor ...	... 10/ 6/15	*6 Lieut.*
3223	LOVELL, Percy Wells ...	... 11/ 5/15	*6 Capt. Wounded 22/6/18, 14/9/18*
3339	RUSSELL, Arthur Vere ...	... 11/ 5/15	*6 Capt.*
3478	SHAW, Philip	... 11/ 5/15	*6 Capt. Killed in action 26/10/17*
3491	STANTON, Stephen James Bridges	... 11/ 5/15	*6 Lieut. Wounded 10/4/18*
2110	TRINDER, Arnold James ...	... 22/ 2/15	*7 Killed in action 16/6/15*
3481	WHITE, Esmonde Ricarde Burke	... 11/ 5/15	*6 Killed in action 5/1/16*
3852	BEATON, Percy Frederick ...	... 21/10/15	*5 Lieut. Wounded –/8/16, 18/6/17*
3412	BROWN, Sgt. Sydney ...	... 17/ 8/15	*6 Capt.* ✠ *Wounded 27/4/18*
3713	COLE, Philip James Linten ...	... 1/11/15	*7 Lieut.*

NORTHUMBERLAND FUSILIERS (T/F).

3926	HAWKEN, Bernard Roger Philip	1/11/15	7 Lieut. To 113th Infantry I.A.
3854	LETTS, Arthur Pender	21/10/15	5 Wounded –/9/16, 21/9/17
4743	LINGARD, Horace	1/11/15	7 Lieut.
3803	SARGENT, Ernest Vernon	21/10/15	5 Lieut. Killed in action 27/5/18
4540	SOMAN, Claude David	1/10/15	4 Lieut.
3479	THOMAS, Lancelot Arthur Smith	21/10/15	5 Lieut.
2989	WESTLAKE, Max Edward K.	5/10/15	7 Lieut.
3402	WILSON, Cpl. Jack Baxenden	21/10/15	5 ✠ Wounded 27/4/18
2550	WOOD, Sydney George	3/12/15	7 Lieut. ✠ Wounded 17/6/18
4744	WOODWARD, William James	1/11/15	7 Lieut.
5936	BANKS, John William	11/ 7/16	4 Lieut.
6678	BARUGH, William Henry	26/ 9/16	4 Lieut. ℳ
765674	CHAPMAN, Alastair Hugh	23/ 6/18	5
5437	DAVIES, Geraint	11/ 7/16	4(9) Capt. Died of wounds 14/4/18
8153	DAVIES, Gwylon	26/ 1/17	4 ✠
5054	EMERY, Maurice Frederick	11/ 7/16	4 Lieut.
764194	EMMERSON, Ernest Newton	17/ 6/17	5
763154	FLEMING, Herbert Sidney	17/ 6/17	5 ✠
6683	GRAHAM, Peter	26/ 9/16	4 Prisoner of war 23/5/18
5905	HEATON, Charles Stanley	11/ 7/16	4
6313	HERDMAN, Thomas Adam	26/ 9/16	4 Lieut.
6064	HOME, Albert Edmund	11/ 7/16	7 Lieut.
6010	JOHNSON, Thomas Archibald	11/ 7/16	5 Lieut.
4931	JONES, Trevor	11/ 7/16	4 Lieut.
6928	MORTIMER, Oscar William	26/ 9/16	4 Lieut.
765463	MUCKLE, Robert	28/11/18	4
4764	MURPHY, John	27/ 6/16	6 Wounded 1/11/17 K/A 25/8/18
6407	PICKERSGILL, Edgar	26/ 9/16	5 Wounded 7/5/18
6693	RICHARDSON, Hugh Booth	26/ 9/16	4 Lieut. Wounded 23/1/18 ℳ
4346	ROBINSON, Harry	11/ 7/16	4 Lieut. ✠ Wounded 11/4/18
5545	SENIOR, William Edward	11/ 7/16	4 Lieut.
5642	UMBERS, John Ludford	11/ 7/16	4 Lieut. ✠
5933	WRIGHT, Edward Frank Macer	11/ 7/16	4 Killed in action 2/4/17
6782	WRIGHTON, Edward J.	11/ 7/16	4 Lieut. D.S.O. ℳ
4864	YOUNG, Oliver	26/ 9/16	4 Lieut. ✠ Wounded 27/4/18

Service Battalions (New Armies).

652	CAMPBELL, Guy	23/12/14	8 Lieut. (I.W.T.) M.B E. ✠ ℳ
2722	COWELL, Philip Barnham	3/10/15	12 Wounded 3/7/16
2727	DAVIES, Robert William M.	3/ 4/15	16 (R.F.C.) K/A 6/4/17
3993	DICKINSON, Henry Waite	3/10/15	12 Lieut. D/W P/W 9/8/18
1634	EDLMANN, Francis Joseph F.	23/12/14	12 Major D.S.O. w. 21/10/15,
4354	FLINT, L/Cpl. Charles William	6/ 1/16	32 K/A 2/7/16 [7/11/17 ℳ]
4364	GAMBLE, Percy Alexander	6/ 1/16	32 Lieut. Prisoner of War 1/5/18
4321	GODWARD, Graham	6/ 1/16	32 Capt. (Labour Corps)
2936	HOBSON, Robert Carl	3/10/15	12 Lieut. ✠ ✠ Died 10/11/18

NORTHUMBERLAND FUSILIERS (S/B). 333

3538	Horsley, Vivian	... .	5/12/15	*12 Lieut. Wounded 25/8/16*
3531	Kirby, George Thomas	... ...	6/ 5/15	*15 Capt. (To 6/Bn.)*
1906	Malcolm, Eric Aitken	...	22/ 9/14	*12 Lieut. Wounded –/7/16*
2030	Nicholson, Bernard George M.	...	3/10/15	*13 Lieut. w. –/7/16 Died 29/10/18*
1973	Reynolds, Leslie	...	3/10/15	*12*
3653	Roper-Nunn, Cyril Douglas E.	...	21/10/15	*10 Lieut. w. 5/10/18, 12/11/18*
1316	Shaw, Leonard Herbert	...	17/ 9/14	*8 Lieut. (To 1/G.B. E. Yorks)*
4427	Smith, John Richard Gutteridge	...	22/ 1/16	*15(8) Died of wounds 30/12/16*
4644	Ablett, Leslie Wallace	...	25/ 5/16	*31 Wounded 13/6/17 K/A 15/10/17*
4655	Blenkin, Frederick	...	25/ 5/16	*31 Lieut.*
4541	Broatch, Percy	...	2/ 6/16	*32 Lieut.* ✠
4604	Browne, Langford Kjffin	...	25/ 5/16	*32(25) Killed in action 9/4/17*
4504	Calkin, John Ernest	...	25/ 5/16	*32 Killed in action 9/4/17*
4339	Carter, Arthur Ernest	...	25/ 5/16	*31 Prisoner of war 8/6/18*
4543	Cooper, Charles Richard	...	25/ 5/16	*31 Lieut. Wounded 3/12/17*
4668	Cowper, Leonard Harris	...	2/ 6/16	*32 Died of wounds 7/11/16*
4624	Dawson-Scott, Cecil Edward	...	25/ 5/16	*32 Lieut. Wounded 19/4/17*
6196	Eve, Roy Montague	...	25/ 5/16	*31 Lieut.*
4700	Fentum, Clarence George	...	25/ 5/16	*32 Lieut. Wounded 19/4/17*
5753	Forsyth, John Dalton	...	2/ 6/16	*32 Lieut. Wounded 19/4/17*
6261	Hacklett, Leslie Arnold	...	25/ 5/16	*31 Lieut. (R.A.F.) P/W 25/9/18*
5610	Holloway, L/Cpl. Leonard	...	25/ 5/16	*28 Lieut. Killed in action 9/4/17*
4459	Holmes, Frederick Charles Victor	...	25/ 5/16	*32 Lieut. Wounded 25/9/17*
4615	Liddell, Arthur Richard	...	25/ 5/16	*32 Capt. P/W 3/5/18* ✠
4549	Longbotham, Currer Benjamin	...	2/ 6/16	*32 Lieut.* ✠ *Wounded 1/7/18*
4517	McKie, Douglas Hanlin	...	25/ 5/16	*32 Lieut. Died of wounds 11/4/17*
4740	Ridley, Bevis Hy. Winspear	...	25/ 5/16	*32 Lieut. Wounded 9/4/17*
3840	Schofield, Roland Stanley	...	26/ 5/16	*31 Lieut.*
4519	Smith, Eric Waldon	...	25/ 5/16	*32 Lieut. Wounded 21/11/17*
4230	Willmott, Stanley John	...	25/ 5/16	*32 Lieut. Prisoner of war 7/6/18*
763377	Adams, Barthold	... ...	1/ 3/17	*25 Lieut.* ✠ *w. 31/10/17, 9/4/18*
763633	Baker, John Charles	...	30/ 5/17	
3709	Baynes, Vernon	... ...	21/ 6/16	*21 Lieut. w. –/8/16, 14/6/18*
6891	Boggon, Nicholas Gordon	...	1/ 4/17	*24*
764186	Brigham, William	... ...	31/ 7/17	*Prisoner of war 25/5/18*
2384	Burbridge, Donald George	...	16/ 9/17	*24(19) Wounded 20/5/18*
7387	Butler, Ernest James	...	19/12/16	*(9) Lieut.*
767440	Cain, Robert Henry	...	24/ 3/19	
763093	Carr, Robert	... ...	27/ 6/17	*Wounded 28/10/17, 1/12/17*
765757	Cater, Cuthbert Dwight	...	18/12/17	*52*
6553	Clark, Stephen Hanley	...	26/ 9/16	*Lieut. To R.E.*
767713	Copeland, William Thomas Copeland		3/ 3/19	
7337	Coxon, William Basil	...	19/12/16	*26 Capt. Killed in action 11/4/18*
3439	Cross, Lester Bloomfield	...	10/ 9/16	*13 Lieut.*
763926	Darling, Norman	... ...	30/ 5/17	
763521	Davies, Joshua Howell Rees	...	18/12/17	*Wounded 16/10/18*
763551	Dear, Gerald James	...	26/ 4/17	

NORTHUMBERLAND FUSILIERS (S/B).

763521	DRYSDALE, Matthew Watt		28/ 3/17	9
5485	EDWARDS, Griffith Oliver		5/ 9/16	*11 Lieut.* ✠
5104	ELIAS, Hywell James		24/ 1/17	*31 Killed in action 5/6/17*
5360	ESKDALE, James Aloysius		18/ 3/19	*12 Wounded 15/6/17*
765535	EVANS, Thomas Kelvin		18/12/17	✠
6995	FAIRCLOUGH, Dennis Frank Colman	1/ 4/17	24	
6797	FENWICK, Horace Edgar		5/ 9/16	*8 Lieut.*
5252	FORSYTH, Thomas Taylor		18/ 3/17	*12*
765208	FOSTER, Arnold		28/11/17	
765542	GIBBON, Frederick William		18/12/17	*52(1) Killed in action 25/8/18*
760935	GREGORY, Percy John		25/ 6/17	*12 Killed in action 4/10/17*
765489	GRIFFITH, John		18/12/17	*51*
768042	HALLAM, Frederick Vissian		17/ 3/19	
762977	HAMMOND, Kenneth Lawton C.		29/ 3/17	*23 w. 11/9/17 K/A 22/3/18*
767659	HEAP, Norman Redvers		4/ 3/19	
762994	HENRY, Norman Charles		26/ 4/17	*Prisoner of war 8/6/18*
3759	HERBERT, Sydney Montague		1/ 8/16	*13 Capt. Wounded 17/10/17*
762632	HEWITSON, John		26/ 4/17	*23 Killed in action 11/11/17*
4677	HODGSON, George		7/ 7/16	*32 Lieut.*
762678	HOPKINS, Henry George		29/ 3/17	*25*
765395	HOWSON, John Howard		1/ 8/17	*Wounded 10/9/18*
762147	HURN, Francis Lewis		13/ 4/17	
765496	JACKES, Albert Eric		1/ 8/17	
763530	JOHNSON, Arthur Dineen		28/11/17	
762903	KIRKBRIDGE, George Henry		25/ 6/17	
762633	LAUGHTON, Geoffrey		26/ 4/17	*26 w. 9/6/17 K/A 5/12/17*
762561	LEWIS, Harold Lockwood		29/ 3/17	*24 w. 22/9/17 K/A 22/10/17*
6404	LOCK, James Alexander		7/ 7/16	*31(10) Killed in action 25/9/16*
5517	LOFTING, Charles Edgar		—/ 1/17	*8 Died of wounds 10/1/17*
3716	McCLARENCE, Stanley		7/11/16	*27 Killed in action 10/4/17*
764905	OLDFIELD, Alfred Edward		18/12/17	*51 Wounded 28/11/18*
3534	PARSLOW, Archibald Joseph		3/10/16	*21 Lieut.*
765564	PORTER, Frank Septimus		27/11/17	
762565	PRINGLE, George Cother William		30/ 5/17	*Wounded 23/4/18*
6121	QUARRELL, Charles Hubert		3/ 5/17	*13 Killed in action 16/6/17*
8105	Ross, Charles Grant		25/ 1/17	
3156	SCATTERGOOD, Tom Victor		—/ 1/17	*21 Died of wounds 6/6/17*
764462	STEEL, John		28/11/17	*Wounded 6/9/18*
765209	TAYLOR, Stafford Gray		22/12/17	
761336	THOMAS, George		25/ 6/17	*12 Wounded 22/10/17*
762703	TOLKIEN, Charles		26/ 4/17	*Prisoner of war 6/7/18*
763479	WAGER, Wilson Stanley		29/ 3/17	*16 Killed in action 12/7/17*
6633	WHITWORTH, Arthur George Richard	19/12/16	*24 Died of wounds 30/3/18*	
763754	WILSON, Andrew		27/ 6/17	*9*

*THE NOTTS & DERBY REGIMENT   335
(THE SHERWOOD FORESTERS).

Regular Battalions (Nos. 1 & 2).   {45th Foot / 95th Foot}

2nd Lieut.

2887	ALLEN, Maurice Reginald	...	... 24/10/15	2 *Killed in action* 13/9/16
868	AMBLER, Christopher	...	... 29/ 8/15	1 *Capt.* w. 31/7/17, 29/5/18 ▥
1323	COPLAND, Dudley Charles James	...	3/ 3/15	1 *Killed in action* 9/5/15
1711	DIAMOND, Arthur Graham Hubert	...	3/ 3/15	1 *Lieut. Wounded* –/3/15, 13/8/17
2503	DICK, George Frederic Graeme		3/ 3/15	1 *Killed in action* 9/5/15
2020	FLETCHER, Percy	... ...	... 10/ 7/15	1 *Lieut.*
1657	GIBBONS, James FitzGeorge		.. 23/ 4/15	2 *Capt.* ✠ *Wounded* –/9/16
2897	KAY, George Alexander	...	... 10/ 7/15	2 *Killed in action* 9/8/15
2774	KAY, James du Percy		... 10/ 7/15	2 *Lieut.*
2134	MARTIN, Frederick Arthur	...	... 15/ 8/15	2 *Died of wounds* 7/9/15
1675	MILLAR, Eric Fortune	...	... 23/ 4/15	1 *Lieut.* w.9/5/15 [K]A29/5/18 ▥
2648	MOORE, Robert Frank	...	... 29/ 8/15	1 *Lt.-Col.* D.S.O. ✠ w. 11/5/18
1244	REED, L/Cpl. Douglas Lancelot		... 24/10/15	2 *Lt.* (R.A.F.) w. –/9/16, 1/6/18 ▥
2878	REYNOLDS, Frank	... ...	.. 24/10/15	2 *Killed in action* 13/9/15
1862	SMITH, Cecil E. B. McFarlane		... 23/ 4/15	2 *Lieut.* M.B.E.
1565	SPINNEY, William Sidney	...	3/ 3/15	1 *Lieut. Wounded* –/10/15
498	STABLES, Walter Williams Godfrey	...	26/ 5/15	1 *Lieut.*
1461	STRIBLING, Fred George	...	26/ 5/15	1 *Lieut. Died of wounds* 8/7/16
1890	THRUPP, Raymond Melville		... 7/11/15	1 *Lieut. Wounded* –/2/16, –/7/16
2033	WATSON, Clifford T.	...	3/ 3/15	1 *Lieut. Wounded* 9/5/15
6238	SUFFOLK, Francis Frederick	...	... 5/ 9/16	1 *Capt. Wounded* 18/11/18
5295	TROHEAR, Thomas ...	...	... 5/ 9/16	2 *Lieut.* ✠ *Wounded* 15/12/17

Special Reserve Battalions (Nos. 3 & 4).

3042	BYLES, Arthur Benzeveille	...	... 2/ 4/15	2 *From* 13/Bn. D/W 11/12/17
2733	FARRINGTON, Windham Brookes	...	19/12/14	3 *Capt.* D.S.O. ✠ F/D
3041	HUGHES, Bernard Victor	...	... 8/ 7/16	4 *Lieut. Wounded* 15/8/17
3108	LOUP, Louis Anthony		... 25/ 6/15	3 *Lieut.*
762325	ADAMS, Percy Horace	...	... 29/ 5/17	4(1) *Killed in action* 3/10/18
767876	HARGREAVE, Edwin Brooks		... 3/ 3/19	3
766480	KEEBLE, George Hedley	...	... 28/ 5/18	3
762294	RICHARDSON, Cecil ...	...	... 30/ 5/17	3 (M.G.C.)
762338	RUSSELL, John Freeman	...	... 6/ 4/17	3(11)
762355	SCHULER, William Edward Durant	...	26/ 4/17	4(15) *Wounded* 3/9/17
766493	SPENCER, Eric Dale ...	...	... 28/ 5/18	4 *Wounded* 28/10/18
762510	STONE, Percival Martin	...	... 26/ 4/17	3(9) *Wounded* 29/12/17

* *Title changed (1st January, 1921) to " The Sherwood Foresters (Nottinghamshire & Derbyshire Regiment)."*

Territorial Battalions (Nos. 5 to 8).

3549	JONES, Ernest	... ...	8/ 5/15	6 *Lieut.*
1800	VANN, Bernard William	...	2/ 9/14	8 *Lt.-Col.* **V.C.** ✠✠✠ *w.*24/4/15, [—/10/15 *K/A* 3/10/18 ☧(2)
3853	BENNETT, William Barney	...	30/ 7/15	(8) *Killed in action* 11/4/17
3787	BURTON, Cyril Henry	...	30/ 7/15	7 *Killed in action* 1/7/16
3980	CORRY, Frank Moring	...	7/11/15	8 *R.F.C. Died of wounds* 13/12/17
4631	COWLEY, Alexander	...	11/ 1/16	8 *Killed in action* 1/7/17
3311	DAY, Thomas George	...	7/ 11/15	8 *Lieut.*
4310	ESAM, Edward Smith	...	26/11/15	8 *Lieut.*
3639	GIBSON, John Rowland	...	30/ 7/15	(8) *Lieut. To* 21/*London*
3820	HEATH, Clement Ralph	...	19/11/15	6 *Wounded* 12/10/17
4087	HICKS, L/Cpl. Charles Hubert	...	11/ 1/16	8 *Lieut. Killed in action* 21/7/18
4387	HUTCHINS, Alan Thomas Good	...	17/ 1/16	8 *Lieut.*
4480	KING-STEPHENS, Lionel Eustace	...	11/ 1/16	8 *Died of wounds* 20/12/16
4279	KNIGHT, Herbert William	...	19/11/15	8 *Lieut.*
3394	KIRBY, Harold Gabriel	...	15/10/15	8 *Lieut.*
4119	LIPSCOMBE, Denys de Bohume	...	7/11/15	8 *Lieut. Wounded* 11/10/17
6074	MULLAN, Denis Richard	...	21/ 6/16	6 *Lieut.*
4097	PARKER, Douglas Harold	...	7/11/15	8 *Lieut.*
4107	RANSON, L/Cpl. Denys Francis	...	7/11/15	8 *Lieut.*
4285	ROBINSON, John Lees	...	19/11/15	6 *Lieut. Wounded* 16/4/17
4142	ROWLAND, Frank Skinner	...	19/11/15	6 *Capt.* ✠✠
4167	STEPHENS, Warren T.	...	19/11/15	6 *Lieut.* ✠
4200	TUFT, Gerald Hugh	...	19/11/15	6 *Killed in action* 27/4/17
4105	VISSER, Gilbert Frederick	...	7/11/15	8 *Wounded* 4/12/17
3633	WARRY, John Lucas	...	11/ 9/15	8 *Capt. Died of wounds* 27/4/17
3826	WILLIAMS, Francis Stanley	...	5/ 8/15	(8) *Lieut. Killed in action* 20/9/17
762874	ATKINS, George Lewis	...	28/11/17	5
6149	BENNETT, Albert Henry	...	5/ 9/16	5 *Died of wounds* 6/11/16
764874	BREGAZZI, Edward	...	16/ 6/17	5 *Died* 9/11/18
765264	BREWER, Horace Henry	...	28/11/17	7
764481	BUSWELL, Horace Bertram	...	31/ 7/17	7 *Prisoner of war* 17/5/18
764013	CAMP, Herbert Mortimer	...	31/ 7/17	5
5679	CATTERALL, Albert	...	2/ 2/16	7 *Lieut. Killed in action* 21/3/18
765408	CONNOLLY, Sydney Moorcroft	...	17/ 6/17	5
6152	COX, Reginald John	...	26/ 9/16	5 *Wounded* 3/5/18
764925	CUNDY, Claude William	...	24/ 9/17	7 *Lieut.* ☧
762832	GRANGE, Frank	...	28/ 8/17	6
766070	GRIFFITHS, Thomas Vernon	...	23/ 5/18	6
763299	HARE, Phillips Vere	...	31/ 7/17	8
763929	HARRISON, Ernest Hildyard	...	11/ 5/17	5
765502	HUNTER, Arthur	...	28/11/17	5
764097	JACQUES, William Gladstone	...	26/ 6/17	5 *Killed in action* 17/10/18
761573	JARCHOW, Christopher John Frederick	11/ 5/17	5 *Lieut.*
6231	OFFILER, Harry Cecil	...	26/ 9/16	5 *Lieut.*
761363	PARKINSON, Leonard	...	2/ 8/17	6

NOTTS & DERBY REGIMENT (T/F).

764162	Powe, George Hector	...	28/ 8/17	7
766318	Smith, Hubert Lionel	...	26/ 3/18	7
763170	Staley, Harold	...	27/ 3/17	5 *Wounded* 11/9/18
764271	Stevens, James Montague ...		31/ 7/17	5 *Wounded* 18/9/18
763414	Tatlow, William Basil	...	31/ 7/17	8 *Wounded* 7/5/18
765292	Taylor, Percy Silverton	...	28/11/17	7
762849	Tomlinson, George Cliftin ...		30/ 5/17	5 *Wounded* 15/12/17
765200	Turner, Joseph	...	25/ 9/17	8
764808	Williams, William Jones	...	29/ 8/17	6
4691	Woods, James Albert	...	2/10/16	5 *Lieut.*

Service Battalions (New Armies).

2939	Brown, Frederick Charles ...		14/11/14	9 *Killed in action* 7/8/15
4531	Davis, Ralph	...	19/ 6/16	19 ✠
4526	Drapes, George Russell	...	25/ 5/16	19 *Wounded* 17/10/17
3301	Harle, Norman Hector	...	3/ 4/15	14 *To* -/ *Yorks. Lieut.* (*R.A.F.*)
4660	James, Reginald William	...	25/ 5/16	13 *Wounded* 19/8/16
4477	Jurjans, Arend	...	25/ 5/16	19
2070	Longstaff, Reginald Frederick C....		19/ 9/15	10 *Wounded* 19/9/15, -/7/16
4650	Neal, John Edward ...		25/ 5/16	19 *Lieut. Wounded* -/8/16
4518	Norman, Sigurd Oswald	...	25/ 5/16	19 *Lieut.* ✠
4498	Prentice, John Frederick ...		2/ 6/16	19 (8/*Leicester*) *Wounded* -/9/16
4602	Sennett, Raymond Langharne	...	2/ 6/16	19
5292	Stockwin, George Henry	...	7/ 7/16	13
1996	Swanston, Charles Brian R.	...	29/12/14	11 *To* 13 *Lieut.* (*R.A.F.*)
4474	Vos, L/Cpl. John	...	2/ 6/16	19
4473	Vine, Christian Courtney	...	2/ 6/16	19 *Wounded*
3201	Warburton, Ernest	...	9/ 3/15	13 *Wounded & P/W* 6/10/16
4622	Warland, Leslie Guy	...	25/ 5/16	19 *Wounded*
767022	Adams, Kenneth	...	4/ 2/19	
767688	Beattie, John Alexander Norris	...	3/ 3/19	
6853	Betts, Thomas Walter	...	3/ 4/17	17 *Killed in action* 31/7/17
4783	Bracewell, Harry ...		3/ 4/17	17 *Lieut. Killed in action* 20/9/17
763817	Calverley, Edwin Victor ...		15/ 7/17	
768293	Clarke, Herbert Lovell	...	13/ 2/19	
763654	Coates, Arnold	...	26/ 4/17	
763747	Ellis, Frederick Gordon	...	28/ 3/17	*Prisoner of war* 4/6/18
762387	Elphick, Edw. Rutherford ...		26/ 4/17	
765654	Fell, Edward	...	18/12/17	51
764986	Goodbrook, Percy Henry ...		31/10/17	
768576	Greenshields, Lockhart Wilson		5/ 2/19	
766644	Hart, Walter	...	19/ 3/19	
767057	Henderson, Roy Galbraith...		13/11/18	
7272	Hill, Alexander Augustus ...		19/12/16	9 *Lieut.*
767484	Legg, Arnold Henry	...	6/ 2/19	
765180	Livesey, John William	...	31/10/17	

767691	LOWLES, Harry	...	3/ 3/19	
762377	MACBEAN, Cecil Aubrey	...	29/ 3/17	*Wounded* 11/10/17
765725	MAYO, Bernard Alfred James	...	18/12/17 *51*	*Wounded* 20/9/18
762468	MERRETT, Harold Edmund...	...	30/ 5/17 *10*	*Died of wounds* 17/8/18
768585	NELSON, Jesse	...	15/ 2/19	
768154	PROWSE, Chas. Henry	...	21/ 3/19	
768791	ROBERTS, Oswald Price	...	15/ 2/19	
767638	SCREATON, Edwin	...	4/ 3/19	
763667	SHARP, Fred Bernard	...	26/ 4/17	
764507	SMITH, Leslie Cunningham ...	...	25/ 9/17	
762916	SMITH, Stephen Austin	...	26/ 4/17	
765009	SUTTON, Reginald Bennett ...	...	31/10/17 *9*	
769190	SWANWICK, Eric Drayton	...	5/ 2/19	
4987	TATE, William Edward	...	11/ 6/16	*Lieut.*
768717	TAYLOR, Joseph	...	17/ 3/19	
768328	TAYLOR, Percy	...	17/ 3/19	
763842	THOMPSON, Wilfred Leslie ...	...	30/ 5/17	*Lieut.*
766724	TOPHAM, Paul James Robert	...	3/ 2/19	
7019	WATERSON, Frederick Paris	...	3/ 4/17 *17*	*Killed in action* 31/7/17
766494	WHEATLEY, Cpl. John Charles	...	26/ 6/18 *(5)*	*Died of wounds* 3/10/18
768383	WOODIFIELD, Frank ...	...	17/ 3/19	
766008	YOUNG, Lionel George	...	26/ 3/18	

THE OXFORD & BUCKS LIGHT INFANTRY.

Regular Battalions (Nos. 1 & 2).

{ 43rd Foot
{ 52nd Foot

			2nd Lieut.	
886	BAKER, Cyril Bennett	...	1/ 1/15 2 *Major* O.B.E.	[*Wounded* 11/5/15 *(R.A.F.)* F/D }
3671	ELLAM, Herbert John	...	12/12/15 2 *Lieut.*	*Wounded* 18/4/18
1115	HORLEY, Cyril Rupert	...	27/ 1/15 2 *Capt.* ✠	*Wounded* 23/3/15
998	MARTIN, Victor Callingham...	...	1/ 1/15 2 *Capt.*	(2/*Rifle Bde.*) *Staff*
375	SOLOMON, Sgt. Jerrold Bernard	...	27/ 1/15 2 *Major*	(*R.A.F.*) ✠ F/D(2) ℞
4968	BARTLETT, Leonard ...	...	19/12/16 2 *Lieut.*	*Killed in action* 1/10/18
762430	COLEMAN, Charles Blake	...	2/ 8/17 2 *Missing* 27/4/18	

Special Reserve Battalion (No. 3).

764811	BARNES, Leslie Frederick	...	24/ 9/17 *3*	
762466	COLLINGE, Frederick John ...	...	26/ 4/17 *3*	
763762	CREAK, William Arthur	...	1/ 8/17 *3(2)*	*Wounded* 2/7/18
766250	FREETH, Harold Francis	...	27/ 3/18 *3*	
764360	WINDROSS, Herbert Leslie	...	1/ 8/17 *3(2)*	

Territorial Battalions (No. 4 & "Bucks Bn.")

3081	MILLER, Cpl. John Guy Raymond ...	19/ 6/15	4 Lieut.	℞
3855	PULLMAN, Harold John ...	23/ 3/15	B. Lieut.	✠
5725	BORE, Thomas Edgar ...	30/ 6/16	„ Lieut.	
5798	BUTTFIELD, Leonard Frank ...	30/ 6/16	„ Capt. ✠	w. 12/4/18
4888	CHATHAM, Robert Feltham ...	30/ 6/16	„ Wounded 8/5/17 ℞	
5894	DUXBURY, Andrew Marshall ...	18/ 6/16	„ Capt. ✠ Killed in action 30/3/18	
5179	HIGLETT, George Willibert ...	30/ 6/16	„ Lieut. ✠	
4385	HILL, Charles Vincent ...	18/ 6/16	„ Lieut. ✠ w. 6/9/17	
5097	HUGHES, Reginald George ...	18/ 6/16	„ Lieut.	
5073	POWELL, Walter Philip ...	30/ 6/16	„ Lieut. F/D ℞	
4912	REEVE, Louis St. John ...	30/ 6/16	„ Lieut.	
7068	TAYLOR, Herbert Samuel ...	18/ 6/16	„ Lieut. Killed in action 28/4/17	
6784	BACON, William George ...	26/ 9/16	4 Lieut.	
6248	BATES, Frederick Percy ...	15/ 9/17	4 ✠	
6564	BIRD, Cyril Leslie ...	26/ 9/16	4 Lieut. To Min. of Pensions	
5466	BOWLER, William James Bertram ...	26/ 9/16	4 Lieut.	
8176	BOWMAN, Claude Herbert ...	20/12/16	4 Killed in action 16/8/17	
5236	BRETTELLE, Leonard Maurice Clifford	5/ 9/16	4	
766012	BROWN, John Henry ...	23/ 5/18	4	
4840	CARLOSS, George Edward ...	5/ 9/16	4 Lieut.	
763779	CLAYTON, Sidney William ...	27/ 2/18	4 Lieut.	
7650	COFFIN, Thomas Ambrose ...	26/ 9/16	4 Lieut.	
762363	CORFIELD, Frederick John Arthur ...	15/ 9/17	Bucks Bn. Lieut.	
6867	DAVIES, Conrad Hughes ...	26/ 9/16	4 Lieut. ℞	
6495	DUNAND, Alfred Maurice ...	26/ 9/16	4 Lieut. Prisoner of war 7/10/18	
6054	ELLIS, John Eric ...	4/ 9/16	4 Wounded 5/9/18	
6645	ELLISON, Arthur Maylor ...	26/ 9/16	4 Lieut.	
766017	FARNES, Thomas Harris ...	23/ 5/18	4	
5489	FAWCETT, Edwin Haney ...	5/ 9/16	4 Lieut.	
6799	FLEEMING, William Henry ...	26/ 9/16	4 Capt. Wounded 10/9/17	
5491	FOLD, Edward Stanley ...	26/ 9/16	4 Wounded 5/2/18	
7110	GILL, William Rey ...	5/ 9/16	4(5) Killed in action 21/8/17	
5847	HAWKES, Thomas William Potter ...	11/ 7/16	4 Wounded 5/9/17	
5501	HERBERT, Sydney Herbert ...	26/ 9/16	4	
768197	HUDGELL, Ernest William George ...	4/ 3/19	4	
6887	KINDELL, Albert Oswald William ...	26/ 9/16	4 Lieut.	
5155	KING, Ebenezer Frederick ...	5/ 9/16	4 Lieut.	
6226	LEDGER, Harold George ...	26/ 9/16	4 Lieut. Prisoner of war 22/5/18	
5780	MASSING, Gilbert Cheston ...	5/ 9/16	4 Lieut.	
5786	MORBS, George Wentock ...	26/ 9/16	4 Lieut.	
4303	NORMAN, Raymond Elder ...	5/ 9/16	4 Lieut. Wounded 16/8/17	
6118	OLIVIER, Basil Coutts Carr ...	5/ 9/16	4 Lieut. Wounded 28/4/17	
6296	PIPERNO, Joseph Henry ...	5/ 9/16	4 Lieut.	
7737	RAMAGE, Leslie George Edgar ...	26/ 9/16	4 Lieut. Wounded 28/8/18	
5542	RYDINGS, Douglas Gerald ...	5/ 9/16	4 Lieut. Wounded 18/10/17	

6858	STOCKEN, Herbert ...	26/ 9/16	4 Lieut.	Wounded 22/9/17
6084	TAYLOR, Frank Percival ...	5/ 9/16	4 Lieut.	
5556	THOMAS, Reginald ...	5/ 9/16	4 Lieut.	Wounded 23/8/18
7406	TUTHILL, Frederick Villiers	5/ 9/16	4 Lieut.	
6915	TYSON, Claude Richmond ...	26/ 9/16	4(5) Killed in action 22/8/17	
4861	VOKES, Basil ...	5/ 9/16	4(5) Killed in action 15/2/17	
5823	WILKINS, Alfred Thomas Adams ...	5/ 9/16	4 Wounded 24/12/17, 24/4/18	
4757	WILLIS, George Ward ...	26/ 9/16	4 Wounded 12/10/18	

Service Battalions (New Armies).

1843	LONG, Walter Brian ...	7/11/15	6 Lieut.	(R.A.F.)
3118	MCMILLAN, William ...	5/12/15	5 Lieut.	
3240	WALKER, Harold Saxon ...	12/ 7/15	9 Lieut.	
3241	WILMOT, L/Cpl. Douglas Alfred T....	12/ 5/15	9 Lieut.	
768080	ALEXANDER, Hugh Reeve ...	17/ 3/19		
1339	BASSETT, L/Cpl. Geoffrey Edward ...	5/11/15	Lieut. From R.A.S.C. Killed	
768245	BEDFORD, Ernest Reginald ...	17/ 3/19	[in action 21/3/18]	
768602	BENSON, Harold Weeden ...	17/ 3/19		
763711	BRADEN, William Eric ...	17/ 3/19		
7241	BUTTERY, Robert Arthur ...	19/12/16	5(4) Killed in action 15/6/18.	
766221	COVINGTON, Ronald Leslie ...	1/ 5/18		
3664	CRAIG, John Henry ...	31/ 7/16	5	
766130	DYE, John Edward ...	1/ 5/18		
762432	FAWCETT, Woodford ...	1/ 8/17	5 Killed in action 21/3/18	
764062	GATES, Walter Cecil ...	31/ 7/17		
762177	HARRIS, Geoffrey George Hubert W.	4/ 2/19	Wounded 7/8/17	
760237	HESSE, L/Cpl. Ethelbert Thomas ...	17/ 3/19		
763501	LEWIS, Alexander Hastings ...	29/ 3/17	Wounded 15/4/18	
764929	MASH, John Leonard ...	22/ 1/18		
760704	MASTERS, Frederick Jas. ...	3/ 2/19		
761344	MEAKINS, Sgt. Arthur Thos. ...	5/11/18		
765281	NICHOL, William Alexander ...	28/11/17		
765086	NOBLE, Robert ...	28/11/17		
4286	RODGER, Frederick Claude Graham	3/ 3/19		
765806	SMITH, Harry Neville ...	21/ 2/18		
761191	STACE, John Alfred ...	25/ 6/17	5 Wounded 25/9/18 M	
767653	TYLER, Gerald Leslie ...	4/ 3/19		
764394	VICCARS. Arthur Edward ...	31/ 7/17		
7347	WELLS, Henry Eustace ...	19/12/16	Lieut.	
765818	WENN, Robert Anderson ...	13/ 3/18		
769009	WESTBURY, James ...	14/ 2/19		

THE RIFLE BRIGADE
(THE PRINCE CONSORT'S OWN).

Regular Battalions (Nos. 1, 2, 3 & 4).
{ Rifle Brigade

2nd Lieut.

998	MARTIN, Victor Callingham	...	27/ 1/15	2	*From 2/Oxford & Bucks*
174	RAVEN, L/Cpl. Frank Percy	...	11/ 6/15	*3*	*Capt. Wounded* 10/1/16, –/8/16
3180	BROWN, William	...	27/ 2/17	2	*Wounded* 13/8/17
3035	CATES, George Edward	...	27/ 2/17	2	**V.C.** *Killed in action* 9/3/17
5945	DENNIS, Bernard Waymark ...	...	12/11/16	*1*	*Lieut. Missing*
3177	NETTLETON, John	...	12/11/16	2	*Wounded* 30/10/18 ℳ
3178	SHORE, Bernard Alexander Royle	...	12/11/16	2	*Lieut.*
763767	SUTTON, Arthur Albert	...	30/ 5/17	2	*Wounded* 22/4/18
763899	TURNER, Henry Rede	...	30/ 5/17	*3*	
5328	WELLS, Eric Irwin ...	...	12/11/16	2	*Lieut.* ✠

Special Reserve Battalions (Nos. 5 & 6).

7761	CUNNINGHAM, Benedict Joseph	...	20/12/16	*5(1)*	*Lieut. Wounded* 14/5/17
765582	CUNNINGHAM, Francis Augustine J.		28/11/17	*5*	
8138	DAY, Edward Victor Grace ...	...	23/11/16	*6*	*Lieut. To I.A. w.* 17/4/17
762476	DENT, Reginald Teasdale ...	...	26/ 4/17	*6*	*Killed in action* 24/3/18
761219	LEE, Frederick Rupert Mark	...	28/11/17	*6*	*Wounded* 4/11/18
7793	TALBOT, John Angelo	...	26 /1/17	*5(10)*	*Lieut. Wounded* 14/8/17

Service Battalions (New Armies).

1961	BUCKLEY, Joseph Michael ...	...	19/ 9/15	*9*	*Capt. w.* –/8/16 *K/A* 23/12/17
1792	CHESTERTON, Hugh ...	...	13/10/14	*13*	*Capt.* ✠ *Wounded* 1/7/16
1365	DAY, John Percival ...	...	19/ 9/15	*9*	*Lieut.* ✠ *w.* –/9/16, 18/5/17
1140	DEVEREAUX, Richard Harding F.	...	7/11/15	*10*	*Lieut. Wounded* –/9/16
1764	FAIRBAIRN, George Henry ...	...	19/ 9/15	*9*	*Lieut.* ✠ *Wounded* –/9/16
2507	FARMILOE, Kenneth Meakin		19/ 9/15	*8*	*Lieut. Wounded* –/9/16
3600	FORTUNE, Stanley Welsh ...		7/11/15	*10*	*Wounded* –/2/16 *K/A* 13/3/16
2348	GOSNEY, Harold William ...		19/ 9/15	*7*	*Lieut.* ✠ *Wounded* –/12/15
1968	HIGGINS, Charles Alleyn ...		29/12/14	*11*	*Capt. (R.F.C.) w.* 28/10/15
1646	IRVING, George Guy Hammond		19/ 9/15	*9*	*Lieut.*
1148	JONES, Vaughan		11/ 8/15	*14*	*Lieut. w.* –/7/16, 30/10/17
2079	LAWSON, Arthur Cyril ...		9/11/14	*13*	*Wounded* –/4/16 *D/W* 6/7/17
3014	MATTHEWS, Edward Philip ...		19/ 9/15	*8*	*Lieut. w.* –/11/15 *D/W* 6/9/16
2720	MEREDITH, Alexander Charles		19/ 9/15	*8*	*Lieut. M.G.C.* ✠ *w.* –/8/16
1963	OAKEY, John Martin ...		19/ 9/15	*7*	*Major (R.E.)* ✠ ℳ
3141	PALMER, Charles Ward ...		28/11/15	*12*	*Lieut. Wounded* –/2/16
1276	POLGREEN, John Clifford Vesey		19/ 9/15	*9*	*Capt. w.* 27/11/14, 15/7/16,⎫
1760	RAYMOND-BARKER, Cecil L.		12/ 5/15	*12*	*K/A* 25/9/15 ⎭ [5/8/18]
2572	REACHER, Stanley William ...		10/ 2/15	*16*	*Capt. Died of wounds* 4/7/16
2952	RUSSELL, Sidney Herbert ...		19/ 9/15	*9*	*Lieut. w.* 18/5/17, 17/4/18

RIFLE BRIGADE (S/B).

1877	Seward, Jack Ravenscroft	19/ 9/15	8	Lieut. Wounded –/11/15
3007	Singleton, John Henry	12/12/15	10	
2337	Warren, Alfred Norman	19/ 9/15	7	Prisoner of war 18/6/18 ☩
4960	Benton, Albert Samuel	25/ 5/16	9	Lieut. Wounded –/8/16
4411	Cole, Sgt. Gordon James	7/ 7/16	17	Lieut. ✠
4904	Goodrich, Hugh B. V.	7/ 7/16	17	
6002	Hale, Cecil Freemaux Winsbury	7/ 7/16	17	
6065	Hugh-Jones, Kenneth Herbert	8/ 7/16	5(12)	Capt. K/A 20/9/17
6013	Lee, Frank Stanley	7/ 7/16	17	Lieut. w. 4/5/17 K/A 22/3/18
4435	Moors, Sgt. Bertie Reginald	7/ 7/16	17	Lieut.
5350	Osman, Cpl. Leslie William	7/ 7/16	17	Lieut.
4098	Pegram, Cpl. Charles Ernest	7/ 7/16	17	Capt. ✠ w. 23/4/18 Died 9/11/18
6414	Stephany, L/Cpl. Myers	7/ 7/16	17	Lieut.
6300	Swales, Edward	7/ 7/16	17	Lieut.
4048	Urry, L/Cpl. Reginald Thorpe	7/ 7/16	17	Lieut. Wounded 11/6/17 P/W
4376	Wade, L/Cpl. George Edward Ahern	7/ 7/16	17	Lieut. Killed in action 3/5/17
6418	Ware, Cpl. Douglas Hugh Sankey	7/ 7/16	17	Lieut.
762552	Ackroyd, John Cyril	3/ 8/17	16	
6839	Baggs, Ernest Erasmus	26/ 9/16		Lieut. To Labour Corps
6570	Baker, Bentley George	5/ 9/16		Capt. w. 1/6/17, 20/9/17, [20/8/18, 4/9/18]
767738	Ballard, John Cooper	3/ 3/19		
762427	Betts, Arthur John	30/ 5/17	12	Wounded 29/4/18
767532	Bradshaw, Percy Scarr	14/ 8/18	52	
4969	Brand, Percy Alfred Easterling	26/ 9/16	12	Lieut. Killed in action 28/9/17
5150	Carson, Murray Alexander	12/11/16	10	Wounded 12/3/17
3205	Chapman, Cpl. Montague Gerald H.	6/10/16	10	Killed in action 14/8/17
766684	Cheshire, Laurence Scadeng	3/ 2/19		
3169	Clark, Norman Ralph	6/ 1/17	12	Lieut. Wounded –/5/17, 16/8/17
764979	Clark, Roland Hope	31/10/17	16	Died of wounds 24/3/18
763195	Coles, Herbert	29/ 8/17		Killed in action 18/11/17
766189	Conoley, Theodore Stanley	1/ 5/18	52	
464	Cossar, Cpl. Norman Thomson	12/11/16	7	Killed in action 15/5/17
761571	Fallon, John Reginald	17/ 9/17		Wounded 23/3/18
7035	Fowle, Arthur Charles	20/ 4/17	12	
760958	Garnett, John	17/ 9/17		
762481	Gwatkin, Vernon Charles Henry	26/ 4/17		
766644	Hart, Walter	25/ 9/18		
767469	Hind, Herbert Charles Otter	5/ 3/19		
6008	Johnson, Frederick Blacktire	20/ 5/17	13	Killed in action 31/5/17
766717	Jones, Peter Lewis	3/ 2/19		
768072	King, John Bethell	17/ 3/19		
762683	Maggs, Lawrence Eric	29/ 3/17	9	
762274	Mallett, Edgar Anthony	26/ 4/17		
3187	Martin, Duncan Roderic	6/10/16	10	Lieut. Wounded 9/4/18
766440	Martin-Smith, Frederick Alexander	29/ 5/18		
764840	Melvin, John Wilson	26/ 9/17		

7673	MEMBREY, Robert Henry	...	... 19/12/16	16	Wounded 15/6/17, 6/10/17
762635	MODLEN, Charles Leslie	...	... 24/ 4/17		
763751	MUNDAY, John	... ...	... 26/ 4/17		Wounded & P/W ℳ
5596	NEWELL, Arthur Francis	...	... 5/ 9/16	8	Capt. Died of wounds 4/4/18
768183	O'FLAHERTY, Herbert Fdk. R. Legrand		17/ 3/19		
763308	OWENS, Harold Hedworth	...	... 29/ 8/17		
5661	RANDALL, Edward	... ...	... 5/ 9/16	9	
764457	SAUNDERS, Gordon William		... 29/ 8/17		
762472	SHANNAW, Charles James Francis	...	14/ 4/17		From R.F.C.
763312	SIMON, John Malcolm	...	... 26/ 9/17		
762422	STOBBS, Horace Leopold	...	... 30/ 5/17	12	
764672	TAYLOR, Sidney Alexander	...	... 26/ 9/17		Wounded 25/4/18
8152	WALLINGFORD, Sidney	...	... 19/12/16		To R.A.F.
763917	WOOD, Norman Chapman	...	... 26/ 9/17		
762359	YORK, Thomas John Pinches		... 26/ 4/17		
764593	YOUNG, Hugh	... ...	... 29/ 8/17		Prisoner of war 14/6/18

*THE ROYAL SCOTS
(LOTHIAN REGIMENT).

Regular Battalions (Nos. 1 & 2).   1st Foot

2nd Lieut.

2360	CUXSON, Basil Pryce	...	... 12/ 6/15	2	Killed in action 14/7/15
1256	MAYO, Charles Douglas	...	... 11/ 6/15	2	Lieut. w. & prisoner 25/9/15
1169	PEASE, Donovan	... ...	... 11/ 6/15	2	Lieut. P/W (Hanover) -/10/15
1414	PETHERBRIDGE, Charles Arthur		... 11/ 6/15	2	Capt. ✠
3023	SPINNEY, Frank	... ...	... 11/ 6/15	2	Died of wounds 2/10/16
7739	BIDDULPH, Percival Vincent		... 5/ 8/16	1	Lieut.
7726	COWIE, Harold Albert	...	... 13/12/16		Lieut. Wounded 9/2/18
6169	GIBSON, Archibald	... ...	... 13/12/16		Lieut. ✠ Wounded 30/10/18
6850	WEIR, Charles Hooker	...	... 9/ 9/16		Lieut.

Special Reserve Battalion (No. 3).

762586	CALLENDER, Arthur Herbert		... 1/ 8/17	3(8)	Wounded 11/4/18
762254	COOMBS, William Kitchen	...	... 25/ 1/17	3	(8/R. Welch Fusiliers)
6820	SCOTT, James Francis	...	... 9/ 9/16	3(13)	Killed in action 23/4/17

*Title changed (1st January, 1921) to "The Royal Scots (The Royal Regiment)."

ROYAL SCOTS.

Territorial Battalions (Nos. 4 to 10).

765106	BOYD, George	...	31/10/17	8
763382	COSSAR, Claude Thomson ...	...	26/ 4/17	4 Lieut.
7808	HARVEY, Frederick Bright ...	...	26/ 1/17	10 Lieut.
8191	METCALFE, George ...	...	26/ 1/17	10 Lieut. Died of wounds 12/4/18
768237	SMITH, Arthur Brown	...	17/ 3/19	4
6828	THOMSON, George Vallance Bruce ...		19/12/16	10 Killed in action 22/3/18
768560	WATT, James Macdonald	...	5/ 2/19	

Service Battalions (New Armies).

2773	DAVIES, G. Vere Faithful	...	2/12/14	13 Wounded 29/9/15
6709	AREND, Ronald Sydney	...	1/ 5/17	12 Killed in action 23/3/18
5726	BORTHWICK, William Taylor	...	5/ 9/16	17 Lieut. Wounded 19/5/17
5476	COATS, William Evans	...	4/ 1/17	17 Died of wounds 4/11/17
6644	DONALDSON, William	...	1/ 5/17	12 Killed in action 5/6/17
7373	DUFF, Francis McKenzie	...	19/12/16	Lieut. ✠ P/W
769245	FERGUSON, William Archibald	...	5/ 2/19	
676350	FINNIGAN, Edward Aloysius	...	5/ 2/19	
764022	FORBES, Duncan	...	30/ 5/17	13 Killed in action 28/3/18
769048	MACGREGOR, James Stewart ...	...	14/ 2/19	
6533	MACOUAT, John	...	5/ 9/16	12 Killed in action 12/4/17
769212	MORT, Frederick	...	5/ 2/19	
768355	SMITH, John Malcolm	...	14/ 2/19	
762964	TODD, James	...	28/ 3/17	(2) Wounded & P/W 22/5/18

THE ROYAL SCOTS FUSILIERS.

Regular Battalions (Nos. 1 & 2).

21st Foot

2nd Lieut.

1591	CARR, Mathews	...	3/ 3/15	2 Lieut. ✠ ✠ F/D ℞
1457	GODFREY, Stanley Charles ...		20/ 3/15	2 Capt. M.B.E. ✠ ℞(2)
1341	GODFREY, Victor	...	20/ 3/15	2 Killed in action 1/7/16 ℞
1267	SIEVEKING, Geoffrey Edward	...	20/ 3/15	2 Lieut.
1758	STEWART, Jack	...	15/12/14	2 Lieut. O.B.E. Wounded –/5/16
1578	WALLACE, John Roger	...	15/12/14	2 Killed in action 22/4/15
6800	GILCHRIST, James	...	5/ 9/16	2 Lieut. ✠ Wounded 10/9/18

Special Reserve.

762521	KEIZER, Maximilian ..	...	... 26/ 4/17	3 Lieut. Wounded 9/4/18
762280	SLEEP, Charles Frederick	...	... 26/ 4/17	3 Lieut.
762732	WOOD, Edwin Leonard		... 26/ 4/17	3(1) Killed in action 26/9/17

Territorial Battalions (Nos. 4 & 5).

3945	CROALL, John James	...	... 2/11/15	5 Capt. Killed in action 4/10/17
766036	WOOD, John William	...	... 24/ 5/18	4

Service Battalions (New Armies).

3410	BANNATINE, John Douglas	...	... 6/ 5/15	9 Lieut.
3011	CREMETTI, Paul Eugene	...	... 9/12/14	8 Major O.B.E. ℞
5063	MACKENKIE, Kenneth	...	... 25/ 5/16	9 Lieut.
2666	MCKERROW, Hugh Douglas		... 26/ 9/16	(7) Lieut.
769856	REID, Wallace	... ...	.. 17/ 3/19	
5223	STIVEN, Albert	... ...	... 5/ 9/16	(2) Killed in action 24/1/17

THE KING'S OWN SCOTTISH BORDERERS.

Regular Battalions (Nos. 1 & 2).   25th Foot

2nd Lieut.

1829	MILES, Herbert Francis	...	... 9/ 5/15	2 Capt. w. 4/6/15 Killed in action 3/9/16
5575	ELWELL, Bernard Livingstone		... 5/ 9/16	Lieut. (2/Border)

Territorial Battalions (Nos. 4 & 5).

4678	LAING, L/Cpl. Donald McLeod		... 25/ 6/16	4
4260	WEIR, James	... ...	... 1/ 1/16	5 Lieut. ✠ ✠ Wounded 5/8/18
762178	FARQUHARSON, Alan George		... 30/10/17	5 Missing 11/5/18
4679	MCCALL, Archibald ...	...	... 24/ 6/16	4 ✠ Died ot wounds 23/8/17

Service Battalions (New Armies).

762954	DEARDEN, John Robert Biffin		... 26/ 4/17	Wounded 17/4/18
763524	GILLESPIE, Alexander Hamilton		... 29/ 3/17	Lieut.
768040	GRIERSON, James Tordoff	...	... 17/ 3/19	
6735	HOWARD, William Aloysius ...		... 24/ 2/17	7 Killed in action 24/4/17
762905	LINDSAY, John	... ...	... 26/ 4/17	
767485	MCILLWRAITH, Thomas Forsyth		... 14/ 8/18	
767955	SIME, William Elliot Boyd ...		... 17/ 3/19	
763992	STARK, James Duncan	...	... 27/ 6/17	6 Lieut. Died of wounds while P/W 3/9/18 ℞

THE SCOTTISH RIFLES
(THE CAMERONIANS).

Regular Battalions (Nos. 1 & 2). {26th Foot / 90th Foot}

41	HOOD, Sgt. Bernard ...	... 20/ 3/15	2nd Lieut. 2 *Lieut. (R.A.F.)*
2527	ORTON, Ernest Henry	... 20/ 3/15	2 *Killed in action* 9/5/15
1153	POWER, Charles Montague ...	... 20/ 3/15	2 *Capt.* ✠
1389	SEATH, Douglas Ambrose ...	... 20/ 3/15	2 *Wounded* 9/5/15 *K/A* 24/4/17
1640	STEVENS, Cyril Walter	... 20/ 3/15	2 *Capt. To Indian Army*
6290	LAIDLAW, James Clelland ...	... 22/11/16	(5/*Border*) *Capt. Killed in action* 6/11/17

Special Reserve Battalions (Nos. 3 & 4).

5479	CROOKSTON, William John ...	... 22/11/16	4 (8/*Border*) *Lieut. K/A* 12/4/18
763555	MONTGOMERY, Llewellyn Hughes ...	1/ 3/17	4 *Lieut.*

Territorial Battalions (Nos. 5 to 8, 15).

762640	BARRADELL-SMITH, Walter ...	... 29/ 3/17	5
766107	COWAN, John Arnold	... 4/ 2/19	5
763736	HUMPHRIES, John Charles ...	... 25/ 9/16	5
7642	LOUDON, William Forgie ...	... 22/11/16	

Service Battalions (New Armies).

3458	BRYSON, Robert Edwards ...	... 5/ 4/15	12 *Capt.* ✠ *Wounded* 21/3/18
3452	WILSON, Charles Geo. Gordon ...	... 7/ 4/15	11(9) *Killed in action* 9/4/17
767586	DUNLOP, Garvin Alexander	... 6/ 2/19	
5406	GRAHAM, Thomas Eric ...	... 19/12/16	(2) ✠ *Killed in action* 24/3/18
6278	GUNN, Herbert James ...	... 1/ 3/17	10 *Lieut.* ⚔
761166	KINNIBURGH, Thomas Frame ...	... 13/11/18	
762543	SMALL, Victor	... 29/ 3/17	*Capt.* ⚔
768093	THOMSON, Alexander Martin ...	... 10/ 3/19	
761278	WATSON, William Harper ...	... 25/ 6/17	10

THE SEAFORTH HIGHLANDERS

(ROSS-SHIRE BUFFS, THE DUKE OF ALBANY'S).

{ 72nd Foot
{ 78th Foot

Regular Battalions (Nos. 1 & 2).

2nd Lieut.
727 KIRKALDY, Charles Henry ... ... 13/ 2/15 *1 Killed in action* 10/3/15
417 MARVIN, Sgt. Donald ... ... 20/ 3/15 *1 Killed in action* 9/5/15

Special Reserve Battalion (No. 3).

7512 MACDONALD, Kenneth ... ... 22/11/16 *3(2) Lieut.* ✠ *Wounded* 21/4/17
8136 MACKENZIE, Aeneas ... ... 19/12/16 *3(8) Missing* 3/9/17
764566 SANDERSON, Alastair Fletcher ... 29/ 8/17 *3(2)*

Territorial Battalions (Nos. 4, 5 & 6).

765034 FERGUSON, James Scott ... ... 31/10/17 *5(4)* ✠

Service Battalions (New Armies).

2837 FORBES, Alexander Stuart ... ... 9/11/14 *10 Lieut. (To M.G.C.) D/W* }
2048 HAYNES, Frederick C. Gamble ... 28/11/15 *8 Capt.* [17/8/16 }
3602 KIRK, Leslie Douglas ... ... 5/12/15 *7 Capt.*
3603 WHYTE, Richard ... ... 5/12/15 *7 Lieut. (R.A.F.) w. –/7/16*
766500 FIELD, Arthur John 26/ 5/18
762833 HAMILTON, James Russell ... ... 26/ 4/17 *8 Lieut.*
767215 MAXWELL, John Crawford 27/ 3/18 *7*
764372 RAE, James ... ... 29/ 3/17 *(2) Killed in action* 4/10/17
768189 STISTED, Joseph Lawrence Heathcote 17/ 3/19

*THE SHROPSHIRE LIGHT INFANTRY
(THE KING'S).

Regular Battalions (Nos. 1 & 2).

{ 53rd Foot
{ 88th Foot

2nd Lieut.

2168	BOOTH, Henri Robert	...	11/ 6/15 2 *Wounded* 2/7/15
1954	ELDER, Alexander Austin	...	11/ 6/15 2 *Lieut.* ⌘(2)
796	FOULGER, L/Cpl. Maurice	...	23/ 4/15 *1 Killed in action* 9/8/15
2336	GOODALE, L/Cpl. Arthur William	...	10/ 7/15 *1 Killed in action* 9/8/15
1993	GRUGEON, Harold	...	26/ 5/15 2 *Lieut. Wounded* 7/12/16
3548	HITCHCOCK, Cyril Augustus	...	16/ 1/16 *1 Killed in action* 21/4/16
1059	ISAAC, Frank Philip	...	10/ 7/15 *1 Killed in action* 9/8/15
1638	JOHNSTON, Alec	...	14/ 2/15 *1 Lieut. w.* 9/8/15 *K/A* 22/4/16
1304	KOCH, L/Cpl. Marcus Addison	...	11/ 6/15 2 *Killed in action* 22/9/15
1745	MAIDLOW, Geoffrey	...	23/ 4/15 2 *Lieut. Wounded* 25/5/15
2040	MATTHEWS, Ernest Francis	...	24/10/15 2 *Staff-Lieut.* M.B.E. ⌘
1895	PAYNE, John Gibson	...	11/ 6/15 2 *Capt.* (*R.E.*)
1966	RUSHBRIDGE, William Gibbert	...	10/ 7/15 *1 Lieut.*
3400	SIMNER, Stanley Albert	...	16/ 1/16 *1 Lieut.*
2242	THORNE-WAITE, Arnold	...	12/ 6/15 2 *Lieut.*
1834	TIPPER, Alexander Arnold	...	26/ 5/15 2 *Died of wounds* 19/8/15
1190	TURNER, Harold Keynes	...	23/ 4/15 2 *Capt.* ✠ ⌘
1665	WILSON, Harold Algar	...	23/ 4/15 *1 Capt. w.* 19/6/15 *K/A* 6/1/16
765143	SHEPPARD, Reginald John	...	31/10/17 *1*

Special Reserve Battalion (No. 3).

764574	BANCROFT, Reginald	...	1/ 8/17 3
6732	BUCKLEY, Frank	...	26/ 9/16 3(5) *Wounded* 21/4/17
762467	GOODCHILD, Stewart John	...	25/ 9/17 3 *Killed in action* 28/3/18
763078	RACTIVAND, Demetrius	...	26/ 4/17 3(*1*) ✠

Territorial Battalions (Nos. 4 & 10).

2291	CLEGG, James Arthur	...	24/10/14 4 *Lieut.*
7953	BYGOTT, Edward	...	25/ 1/17 4 *Lieut. Wounded* 20/9/17
5587	KIRBY, Ralph William	...	26/ 9/16 4 *Lieut.*
4211	MASON, Arnold Henry	...	25/ 1/17 4
762438	TANSER, Harry Ambrose	...	27/ 3/18 4

*Title changed (1st January, 1921) to " The King's Shropshire Light Infantry."

Service Battalions (New Armies).

3361	COE, Ernest Wilfred	...	5/12/15	7 *Lieut.*
3495	DEEDES, Richard ...	...	12/12/15	7 *Capt. Wounded* 17/10/18 ⚔
395	ELLIOTT, Richard Derrick ...		9/ 1/15	9 *To 5 Missing P/W* 9/8/15
3305	GREENING, Cyril Benjamin ...		26/ 2/15	8 *Lieut.*
1953	GUYER, Aubrey King	...	3/10/15	5 *Lieut.*
3969	STARK, Mark Arnold Napier		23/11/15	9 *Lieut.*
767047	ACHESON, John Francis	...	30/ 7/18	
768289	BARTLETT, Kenneth Rogers		17/ 3/19	
768504	BLOWER, Arthur Benjamin ...		13/ 2/19	
765760	CREESE, Sydney Herbert	...	18/12/17	*Wounded* 19/11/18
7474	GRIFFEN, Harold Samuel	...	19/12/16	9 *Died of wounds* 9/4/17
765547	HARTY, William ...	...	27/11/17	(4) *Killed in action* 30/9/18
762346	HATFIELD-WRIGHT, Morden		26/ 4/17	
766475	HAWKES, Percival Joseph	...	29/ 5/18	
761305	HUGHES, Harry Osborne	...	3/ 8/17	5 *Wounded* 25/6/18
766023	JAMES, William Thomas Basil	...	1/ 5/18	*Wounded* 19/9/18
7426	LEE, Percy William ...	...	19/12/16	5 *Killed in action* 9/4/17
765276	LEECH, Robert Edward Holt		27/11/17	(4) *Killed in action* 30/9/18
765094	LYLE, Acheson Mervyn Acheson		31/10/17	6
765003	MORTISHEAD, James William		31/10/17	
765095	OLDHAM, Ernest Holloway		31/10/17	5
6556	PRESHOUS, William Reginald		26/ 9/16	*Lieut. (M.G.C.)*
765729	RAYBOULD, Clarence	...	21/ 2/18	
5601	ROBERTSON, Albert	...	25/ 2/17	7 ✠ *Wounded* 21/4/17
768331	WAKEFIELD, Cpl. Arthur John		17/ 3/19	
6543	WEBB, Arthur Pelham	...	5/ 9/16	5 *Killed in action* 9/4/17
5563	WILES, Osborn David	...	25/ 2/17	7 *Lieut.* ✠
6724	WILLIAMS, David Watkin	...	25/ 2/17	7 *Lieut.*

THE SOMERSET LIGHT INFANTRY
(PRINCE ALBERT'S).

Regular Battalions (Nos. 1 & 2).

13th Foot

2nd Lieut.

1666	MARTIN, Owen Sidney	...	14/ 2/15	*1 Wounded* 24/6/15
46	WILLIAMS, Theodore Edward		8/ 5/15	*1 Killed in action* 1/7/15
5592	MASSIE, Sidney Edward	...	30/ 4/17	*1 Killed in action* 8/5/17
5869	PRATT, Henry Edward	...	30/ 4/17	*1*

Special Reserve Battalion (No. 3).

762733	BARNES, Arthur Randall	...	... 20/ 4/17	3 *Killed in action* 4/10/17
765920	BUDDLE, Edward George	...	... 13/ 3/18	3
3700	LLEWELLYN, Arthur Henry	...	... 26/ 5/16	3(8) *Lieut.*
767128	MEAD, John Thorn	...	... 30/10/18	3
762437	MOGG, Lionel Hedley	...	... 30/ 5/17	3 *Wounded* 18/10/17

Territorial Battalions (Nos. 4, 5, 11 & 12).

5741	CRISP, Cyril Bright	... ...	... 11/ 7/16	5 *Died of wounds* 16/8/17
1470	MANN, Douglas Bruce Upfield		... 11/ 2/15	4 *Lieut.* ✠ ℳ
6040	BAIRD, Charles Alexander	...	... 26/ 9/16	4 *Lieut.*
5998	GOODMAN, Stuart	... ...	... 26/ 9/16	4 *Lieut. Wounded* 20/9/17
6003	HALLEWELL, Arthur Vincent		... 23/11/16	4 *Lieut.*
766554	JOHNSTONE, Frederick	...	... 28/11/17	4
766314	PARMINTER, Percy Douglas	...	... 26/ 6/18	4
6823	SPACKMAN, Reginald	...	... 26/ 9/16	4 *Lieut.*
765329	TETT, Harry	...	... 25/11/17	4

Service Battalions (New Armies).

2399	BOWERMAN, Arthur James	...	9/12/14	8 *Lieut.* (*R.F.C.*) K/A 9/9/16
6792	DUDLEY, Herbert Edward	...	7/ 7/16	9(6) *Killed in action* 23/8/17 ℳ
3261	EDMONDS, Wilfred Bell	...	10/ 6/15	9 *Lieut.* (*To R.F.C.*)
3208	FIELDING, Edward Fleming		... 30/ 1/15	9 *Lieut.*
2695	GRAVES, Arthur Glendower		... 17/12/14	9 *Lieut.*
1789	HOLMES, Richard ...	...	... 27/10/14	9 *Capt.* ℳ
1892	JOLIVET, Alfred Eugene	...	... 19/ 9/14	8 *Capt. w.* 26/10/15, -/5/16
2608	MAXWELL, Herbert A.	...	... 5/ 1/15	9 *Lieut. To Army Cyclist Corps*
5608	WHITE, Cpl. Royman Hansford		... 7/ 7/16	*Lieut.*
7145	ABERCASIS, Arthur ...	...	... 19/12/16	6 *Killed in action* 9/4/17
768937	ARNOLD, Douglas Herbert	...	... 13/ 2/19	
765782	BENTON, Sydney John	...	... 27/-. 2/18	
5567	BLEATHMAN, William Edward Percy		26/ 9/16	*Lieut.*
6787	BYWATER, William Edward	..	... 27/ 1/17	8 *Capt.*
3732	GOSSLING, Rupert Emerson	...	... 16/12/16	10 *Lieut.*
763063	HADDON, Baldwin Loney	...	... 28/ 3/17	12 *Capt. w.* 10/1/18, 8/8/18 ℳ
762747	HANNAFORD, William Allan		... 28/ 3/17	5 *Killed in action* 23/11/17
7575	HARGEST, Harry Lewis	...	... 19/12/16	*Lieut. Wounded* 12/9/17
768695	HORNE, Albert William	...	... 13/ 2/19	
768116	HORSMAN, Eric William	...	... 18/ 3/19	
7723	JEFFERYS, Denys Edell	...	... 5/ 9/16	*Capt.* (*M.G.C.*)
7183	LEIVERS, Frank Alex.	...	... 19/12/16	6 *Lieut. Missing* 18/4/18
767974	LINTON, William Evan	...	... 12/ 2/19	
767388	OLIVER, Eric Anthony Creswick		... 6/ 2/19	

SOMERSET L.I. (S/B). 351

6770	Radford, John Arundel	... ...	26/ 9/16	Capt. ✠ Wounded 21/9/18 ⚔
768188	Rowe, Henry Metford	... ...	17/ 3/19	
767727	Smith, Curil Vincent	... ...	3/ 3/19	
7907	Smith, John Henry ...	... ...	22/11/16	7 Missing 11/9/18
1550	Thatcher, William Arthur Norman		7/11/15	6 Lieut. Missing 13/5/18
765365	Tyler, Herbert Spencer	... ...	14/ 2/19	
762159	Unwin, Arthur Colclough	... ...	28/ 3/17	
7175	Walker, George Harold	... ...	19/12/16	6 Lieut. w. 2/11/17, 17/4/18
765487	Walter, Vivian Lucas	... ...	27/ 2/18	
766498	Woodward, Alec William Hutton ...		26/ 6/18	

THE NORTH STAFFORDSHIRE REGIMENT
(THE PRINCE OF WALES'S).

Regular Battalions (Nos. 1 & 2). {64th Foot / 98th Foot}

2nd Lieut.

1439	Mann, Frederick Christmas	... 27/ 1/15	1 Killed in action 12/3/15
1539	Paget, Leslie Robert ...	... 14/ 2/15	1 Lieut. Wounded 13/3/15, 5/8/15
2610	Thornewill, Allan Stafford	... 24/11/14	2 From 10 Capt.

Special Reserve Battalions (Nos. 3 & 4).

4920	Cotterill, Reginald Thomas	... 26/ 9/16	3(8)
6714	Gibson, George William ...	... 4/ 9/16	3(1) Lieut.
7297	Walby, Herbert Charles ...	... 14/ 7/16	4 (10/Yorks L.I.) Capt. D.S.O. {✠ ✠ Wounded 21/5/18 ⚔}

Territorial Battalions (Nos. 5 & 6).

4175	Bolton, Ralph Peter ...	... 15/11/15	5 Lieut. Wounded 1/7/17
3954	Johnson, Roland Finnis ...	... 15/11/15	5 Lieut. Wounded 17/8/17 ⚔
4140	O'Dell, Edward Seymour ...	... 14/11/15	Major F/D
4004	Snelling, Leslie Colin ...	... 15/11/15	5 Lieut. Wounded 14/12/17
4086	Williams, George Elford ...	... 15/11/15	5 Lieut.
4571	Pendleton, William ...	... 12/ 6/16	5 Lieut.
767967	Butler, Harry Colin ...	... 6/ 3/19	5
765529	Codling, Bernard Plumpton	... 27/11/17	5
762370	Gillespie, James William Morrison...	3/10/17	6
4322	Gossling, Tom Banks ...	... 11/ 7/16	6 Lieut. Wounded 16/2/17, 30/11/17
8370	Green, Arthur Fairbrother ...	... 16/ 9/17	6 Killed in action 21/3/18
6514	Heaton, Richard	... 26/ 9/16	5 Lieut. w. 26/9/17 P/W 5/6/18

763788	Hill, Alfred ...	30/ 5/17 5	Killed in action 13/9/17
7843	Humphrey, Godfrey Murray	20/12/16 5	Lieut.
5962	Rathbone, Thomas Ford ...	26/ 9/16 5	Killed in action 26/9/17
765475	Shelley, Percy Norman ...	27/11/17 5	
761629	Simon, Arthur Frederick Sewell	2/ 8/17 5	
767978	Stirzaker, Ronald ...	6/ 3/19 5	

Service Battalions (New Armies).

3035	Bolton, Gilbert Benson ...	12/12/15 8	Killed in action 18/11/16
4308	Clews, Lionel Charles ...	25/ 5/16 10	Lieut.
3276	Hakewill, Thomas George ...	2/ 3/15 11	To Royal Flying Corps
1554	Lawrence, Brian Lyndon ...	14/10/14 9	Lieut. Wounded 11/8/17
6868	Davis, Francis ...	26/ 9/16	Lieut. (9/R. Lancaster)
767347	Dimmock, Ernest Lawrence	5/ 2/19	
767541	Evans, Cyril Frank ...	4/ 3/19	
762590	Fellows, Cyril Walter ...	28/ 3/17	Killed in action 21/3/18
762574	Fenner, Alan Thomas ...	28/ 3/17 (6)	Died of wounds 8/12/17
6605	Greeves, Arthur Frederick William	26/ 9/16 8	Died of wounds 20/9/17
762753	Howe, Sidney George ...	28/ 3/17	Wounded –/10/17 P/W 21/3/18
765720	King, Charles Bertie Ernest	27/ 3/18	
764004	Mason, George ...	26/ 6/17 (1) ✠	Killed in action 15/4/18
766317	Sennett, Richard Herbert ...	26/ 3/18 (6)	Lieut. Wounded 3/10/18
762311	Thorley, William B. ...	26/ 4/17	
764049	Webberley, Reginald Selwyn	27/ 6/17	Died of wounds 30/9/17
766093	Whittet, Reginald Murray...	27/ 3/18 3(12)	Lieut. Wounded 30/8/18
766295	Wrightson, Laurence ...	27/ 3/18	Wounded 21/10/18
762709	Yates, Howard Rudge ...	28/ 3/17	

THE SOUTH STAFFORDSHIRE REGIMENT.

Regular Battalions (Nos. 1 & 2).

{ 38th Foot
{ 80th Foot

2nd Lieut.

1179	Christopherson, Harold Cecil	3/ 3/15	2 Capt.	Wounded 22/4/15
1105	Cundall, Herbert Ayres ...	26/ 5/15	1 Capt.	Wounded 25/9/15
2517	Green, William Charles ...	11/ 6/15	Lieut. ✠ ✠	F/D w. –/6/16
1029	Henderson, Lionel Edward	23/ 4/15	1 Capt.	Wounded 25/9/15
1508	Kirchner, Bernard Joseph	26/ 5/15	1 Lieut.	Wounded 25/9/15
1798	Lee, Walton Noel Olliff ...	23/ 4/15	1 Killed in action 25/9/15	
1744	Mackintosh, Cpl. Harry Leith	15/12/14	1 Died of wounds 5/3/15 ✠	
1816	Parkes, Theodore David ...	26/ 5/15	1 Capt. w. –/5/16	K/A 5/10/17
368	Reynard, Henry Corner ...	15/ 8/15	1 Killed in action 25/9/15	
1087	Silcock, L/Cpl. Arnold ...	15/12/14	2 Lieut.	Wounded 25/9/15

SOUTH STAFFORDSHIRE REGIMENT (R/B). 353

763539	GIBBONS, William Ernest ...	... 30/ 5/17	*1*	*Wounded* 28/3/18 🪖
7174	TEASDALE, Edward Grosvenor	... 13/ 4/17	*1 Lieut.*	*Wounded* 12/5/17
765148	WESTGARTH, George Walton	... 31/10/17	*1*	
5305	WOOD, George	... 19/12/16	*1 Lieut.*	*Wounded* 15/7/17

Special Reserve Battalions (Nos. 3 & 4).

2605	GIBSON, Robert Bowness ...	... 1/11/14	*3 Capt.*	*(1/Bedford)* 🪖
762469	OLIVER, Ian Maurice Lomas	... 26/ 4/17	*4*	*Wounded* 13/5/18
7840	PHILLIPS, Mark Hibbert ...	... 20/12/16	*4(1) Lieut.*	*Killed in action* 4/10/17
766823	WICKHAM-LEGG, George Patrick	... 25/ 9/18	*3*	

Territorial Battalions (Nos. 5 & 6).

5728	BROWN, Ernest Bertram ...	... 11/ 7/16	*5 Lieut.*	✠ 🪖
4320	GODFREY, William Edgar ...	... 27/11/15	*5 Lieut.*	*Wounded* 7/11/17
5152	HENDERSON, Robert Leslie Sinclair	11/ 7/16	*6 Lieut.*	
2908	JEFFCOCK, Robert Salisbury	.. 30/ 5/15	*6 Capt.*	*Killed in action* 1/7/16
2443	MONTAGUE-SMITH, Vernon M.	... 3/ 3/15	*5 Capt.*	
6500	SLATER, Harry	... 11/ 7/16	*6*	*Died of wounds* 28/5/18
4357	STEVENS, John Julian Church	... 27/11/15	*5 Lieut.*	*Wounded* –/9/16
6240	TAYLOR, Leonard Frank ...	... 11/ 7/16	*5*	*Killed in action* 14/3/17
763944	BUCKLEY, Sidney James ...	... 31/ 7/17	*5(2) Lieut.*	*Killed in action* 24/3/18
6100	COLLINS, Edward Douglas ...	... 19/12/16	*6 Lieut.*	
764015	CRADDOCK, Victor ...	... 27/ 6/17	*5*	*Wounded* 22/6/18 *D/W* 11/10/18
761301	HOARE, John Henry ...	... 25/ 6/17	*5*	*Wounded* 9/11/17
765798	PARTRIDGE, Gilbert Wright ...	... 22/ 3/18	*5 Lieut.*	
5964	ROBERTS, William Stephen Hill	... 26/ 9/16	*5 Lieut.*	
5639	TEW, William	... 26/ 9/16	*5 Lieut.*	
766005	WILLIAMS, Sydney Howard ...	... 27/ 3/18	*5*	
5306	WOOD, Cpl. Thomas ...	... 14/ 8/18	*6*	

Service Battalions (New Armies).

1451	MORRIS, Frank Basil ...	... 17/11/14	*11 Capt.*	*Adjt.* 🪖
2129	ROBINSON, John Charles ...	... 10/ 4/15	*10 Lieut.*	*To R.E.*
3026	ROSKILLY, Sydney Theo. H.	... 11/ 3/15	*11 Lieut.*	*To 1 G.B/Lincoln*
2520	SNOWDEN, Reginald Wallis	... 23/11/14	*8 Lieut.*	*Killed in action* 10/7/16
2858	WAUD, Louis Reginald ...	... 23/11/14	*10 Capt.*	*(8/Manchester) w.* 1/8/15
5147	BACON, William Samuel ...	... 24/ 1/17	*8*	*Wounded* 4/4/17
6439	DEFFEE, Charles Frederick ...	... 5/ 9/16	*9 Lieut.*	*Wounded* –/1/17
7686	DOWNES, Arthur	... 19/12/16		
768164	GARRATT, Herbert William ...	... 17/ 3/19		
767617	GREGORY, Ernest George ...	... 6/ 2/19		
765447	GREVILLE, William	... 27/11/17		

z

767877	Harness, John	... ...	4/ 3/19	
7666	Mason, Frederick ...	...	5/ 9/16	9 Staff-Lieut. 🎖
5802	Shaw, Edward Leslie	...	26/ 9/16	7 Lieut. Wounded 13/12/17
765694	Smart, Arthur Reginald	...	18/12/17	
768558	Taylor, James Douglas	...	13/ 2/19	
766400	Triggs, Harold La Riviere ...	...	1/ 5/18	
765611	Woollcombe, Louis Arthur William		18/12/17	(2) Wounded 27/6/18
765366	Wright, James Wilson	...	18/12/17	(2) Prisoner of War

THE SUFFOLK REGIMENT.

Regular Battalions (Nos. 1 & 2).

12th Foot

2nd Lieut.

2015	Allanson, Henry Peter ...	... 26/ 5/15	1 Wounded 23/10/15 K/A 20/7/16
1662	Baumgartner, L/Cpl. Julian M. Vane	19/ 9/15	2 Lieut. Wounded, Somme, 1916, Cambrai, 1918 🎖
2126	Box, Ernest Hyatt	... 26/ 5/15	1 Lieut. To Staff w. 4/7/15 🎖
992	Elkington, Guy Waterman	... 7/10/14	1 Lieut. To 3/Devon (M.G.C.)
2407	Foulsham, Ernest Chester ...	... 11/ 6/15	1
748	Gates, Douglas Leslie ...	... 26/ 5/15	1 Killed in action 1/10/15
1652	Greig, Donald McNeil ...	... 23/ 4/15	2 Lieut. (R.F.C.) o.b.e. Wounded 31/8/15, 18/10/15
1741	Hall, Norman de Haviland	... 24/10/15	2 Died of wounds 7/10/16
955	Hollinrake, John Charles	... 26/ 5/15	1 Lieut. (R.T.O.) w. 1/10/15
1004	Hughes, Herbert Alec Martin	... 14/ 2/15	1 Lieut. Wounded 6/5/15
1407	Kilner, Charles Ussher ...	... 15/ 8/15	1 Died of wounds 8/10/16
1416	Llarena, Eustace Fernando	... 27/ 1/15	2 Killed in action 18/6/15
1569	Law, Charles Lindsay G. ...	... 23/ 4/15	2 Killed in action 30/9/15
2457	Pulverman, Oscar Percy ...	... 12/ 6/15	1 Died of wounds 1/9/15
1163	Shanks, Martin Hollis ...	... 10/ 7/15	1 Capt. ✠ 🎖
2045	Tomson, Henry Gordon ...	... 24/10/15	1 Lieut. m.b.e
951	Windsor, Leslie St. Lawrence	... 27/ 1/15	2 Killed in action 10/6/15
761095	Perkins, Sydney	... 13/ 5/17	1
765006	Rawlins, Hubert William Burford...	13/ 5/17	1

Special Reserve Battalion (No. 3).

5113	Balls, Frank William ...	... 8/ 7/16	3 Lieut. (R.A.F.) Died 1/7/18
5985	Clark, Alexander ...	... 8/ 7/16	3 Lieut.
4278	King, Thomas Clifford ...	... 8/ 7/16	3 Lieut.
1587	Neely, Hugh Bertram ...	... 15/ 8/14	3(1) Died of wounds 25/4/15
2961	Willes, Edward Justice ...	... 5/ 5/15	3

7795	AIRD, George Morland ...	... 19/12/16 *3(2)*	*Wounded* 15/6/18
764473	ANNES, William Philip ...	... 1/ 8/17 *3(11)*	*Wounded* 4/5/18
7002	LEWIN, Harold John ...	... 6/12/16 *3*	*Wounded* 25/3/17
765472	RIBBANS, Erling	... 23/11/17 *3(7)*	*Wounded* 5/9/18
767654	WAINWRIGHT, John Noel ...	... 3/ 3/19 *3*	

Territorial Battalions (Nos. 4 to 6).

4071	ADENEY, Eric	... 14/11/15 *6*	*Lieut.*
4989	ALDOUS, Alfred James ...	... 15/ 6/16 *6*	*Lieut.*
4110	BRANDON, Harold	... 4/12/15 *6*	*Lieut. Wounded* 30/11/17
2327	CALDWELL-COOK, Francis ...	... 22/12/14 *5*	*Lieut.*
2072	CHRISTMAS, Dudley Vyvyan	... 22/12/14 *5*	*Staff-Capt. Killed in action* ⎫
4157	GOLDING, Clement Taylor ...	... 14/11/15 *6*	[23/10/15 ⎭
2083	HEALD, Sgt. Walter Marsden	.. 6/ 5/15 *5*	*Lieut. To A.O.D.*
2079	HERVEY, Eric George ...	... 23/12/14 *5*	*Capt. Indian Army R.O.*
6990	HOLT, Henry Frederick Gisborne	... 24/ 3/16 *4*	*Capt. (Remount Serv.)*
4325	LING, Gerard Alston ...	... 27/ 6/16 *4*	*Wounded* 14/5/17
2436	SHARLAND, Charles Norman A.	... 4/11/14 *6*	*Lieut.*
4001	STOCK, L/Cpl. Ralph ...	... 26/11/15 *6*	
6091	ADAMS, Francis	... 23/11/16 *4*	*Lieut.*
5937	BARBROOK, John Oliver ...	... 26/ 9/16 *4*	*Capt.*
6044	BOULTING, Stanley Ernest ...	... 26/ 9/16 *4*	*Lieut. Acc/killed* 4/4/17
4088	COCKBURN, George Percival	... 19/10/15 *6*	*Lieut. Killed in action* 23/3/18
6795	ELVIN, Arthur George ...	... 26/ 9/16 *4*	*Lieut. Died* 13/10/17
5577	GARNER, Arthur Leonard Charles	... 26/ 9/16 *4*	*Lieut.*
7508	GLUCKSTEIN, Louis Halle ...	... 20/12/16 *5*	*Lieut.* ✠
5622	HARE, Archie Winter ...	... 26/ 9/16 *4*	*Wounded* 2/9/18
5954	ISAACS, Henry Roland ...	... 26/ 9/16 *4*	*Killed in action* 9/4/17
5020	MAINGOT, Joseph Philip Leo	... 26/ 9/16 *4*	*Lieut.*
766525	MANLY, Haughton Crawford	... 26/ 6/18 *4*	
6857	RIGBY, Bertrand Ceslas ...	... 26/ 9/16 *4*	*Lieut. Wounded* 7/5/17
5811	STANFORD, George Wilfred ...	... 26/ 9/16 *4*	*Lieut.*
6239	SWINNOCK, William Eaves ...	... 26/ 9/16 *4*	*Lieut.*

Service Battalions (New Armies).

384	BOX, Charles Henry	... 28/11/15 *9*	*Wounded* –/8/16
3895	CHRISTOPHERS, Roland Banks	... 5/11/15 *12*	*Capt. Wounded* 22/12/17
3877	CURTIS, William	... 5/11/15 *12*	*Wounded* –/8/17
3949	EVANS, Thomas Henry ...	... 5/11/15 *12*	
3310	HORSNELL, Alick George ...	... 24/10/15 *7*	*Wounded* 24/11/15 *Killed in* ⎫
2631	HOWES, Elliott	... 1/ 4/15 *10(1)*	*Lieut.* [*action* 1/7/16 ⎭
3984	NOBLE, Arthur Valentine ...	... 5/11/15 *12*	*Wounded* –/11/16
3753	PALMER, Charles B. Ward ...	... 6/12/15 *7*	*Wounded* –/2/16, 23/8/17 ✠
3913	RAWES, Victor Newling ...	... 5/11/15 *12*	*Lieut. Wounded* 14/3/17
3986	ROBINSON, Edgar Arthur Knott	... 5/11/15 *12*	(*13/Welch*) *Lieut. w.* –/9/16, ⎫
4064	SHEEN, Cyril	... 29/11/15 *12*	*D/W* 3/5/17 [9/4/18 ✠ ⎭

3314	WRIGHT, Edwin Stanley	24/10/15 7	Wounded –/7/16 K/A 3/7/16
1927	ZINK, Edmund	7/10/15 10	Lieut. (R.A.F.)
7101	ARNOLD, Ralph Thomas	2/ 5/17	To 2/119 Infantry Ind. Army
1661	BAGENAL, Nicholas Beauchamp	28/10/14 11	Wounded –/8/16
766240	BALDWIN, Austin Provost	1/ 5/18 (2)	Killed in action 27/9/18
764678	BANKS, David Calder	15/ 7/17	
767489	BARLEY, Edward James	4/ 3/19	
764930	BEESLEY, Cyril James	16/ 6/17	1 G.Bn. Lieut. Wounded 3/9/17
765027	BROWN, Allan Ferguson	12/ 5/17	
763759	CHIPPINGTON, Horace Leonard	30/ 5/17	(16/R. Warwick) Died of
763517	CLARK, Ernest Charles	16/ 6/17	[wounds 23/8/18
761271	COXWELL, Leslie Lorith	26/ 6/17	Lieut. Wounded 8/9/17, 8/7/18
768392	CUBITT, Gerald Baker	5/ 2/19	
763294	CULLEN, Charles Geoffrey	16/ 6/17	
765030	DAVIS, Edward Norrey	16/ 6/17	
767346	DAY, Albert	5/ 2/19	
764824	DEAR, Thomas	16/ 6/17	
764638	DICKS, Arthur James	13/ 5/17	
764825	DUDDY, George Lionel Alfred	31/10/17 11	Killed in action 10/4/18
765427	DUVAL, Clement Arthur	15/11/17	
761273	ENGLISH, Frank	14/ 4/17	
5487	EYRE, Alfred Bernard Bucknall	2/ 5/17	
760776	FARMER, Alfred Victor	26/ 4/17	
7023	FREEMAN, Frederick John Capon	19/12/16	
2651	FOULSHAM, Charles Sidney	20/ 6/16	
767857	FOULSHAM, Robert	4/ 3/19	
765169	FUNNELL, Thomas Henry	13/ 5/17	
764238	GANDY, Frank	16/ 6/17	
761931	GILKES, Charles Arthur	11/ 2/17	
760934	GREEN, Arthur	2/ 5/17	Wounded 21/8/17
762738	HARVEY, George William	26/ 4/17	Wounded 2/5/18
765235	HINDMARSH, Frederick	18/ 8/17	
764892	HOLLICK, George	12/ 5/17	1 G.B. Lieut.
764498	JAMES, Gresham Paske Liddiard	21/ 5/17	
766971	JAY, Charles Gerald	12/11/18	
764649	JENNINGS, Charles Brownlees	16/ 6/17	
764993	JOHNSON, Arthur	31/10/17	
764897	KNIGHT, Henry James	12/ 5/17	
762335	LOOKER, Arthur Donald	14/ 4/17	(15/Essex) Killed in action
765134	LUCAS, Leonard Wells	16/ 6/17	[8/10/18
761151	MARCUS, Leslie John	11/ 2/17	
762809	MOORE, Ernest Abraham	14/ 4/17	Wounded 10/7/18
5595	NEWELL, Alan	5/ 9/16 (1)	Lieut.
764561	NEWMAN, Harold James	16/ 6/17	
764157	NOBBS, George Frederick Perkins	16/ 6/17	Wounded 13/5/18
768665	OWLES, Stanley Garrould	13/ 2/19	
4282	PALMER, Laurence William	2/ 5/17	Lieut. (M.G.C.)

SUFFOLK REGIMENT (S/B). 357

768046	PEDDAR, Herbert Spencer	17/ 3/19	
762079	PERCIVAL, Horace Arnott Birch ...	16/ 6/17	
767754	PLACE, Harry Mayne	4/ 3/19	
764664	POTTER, John Edward	16/ 6/17	
760841	QUAINTON, Arthur John	26/ 6/17	
763862	RAE, Lindsay Marsham	17/ 6/17	
763278	ROBBINS, Kenneth Arthur	29/ 3/17	
764851	RUSSELL, Herman	17/ 6/17	
763957	SHEPHERD, Thomas Joseph Nunn ...	21/ 5/17	
5219	SMITH, Charles Frederick	25/ 3/17	*12 (T.M.B.) Killed in action* [9/4/18]
768490	SMITH, Dawson Crisp	13/ 2/19	
5079	SMITH, Sydney Newman	2/ 5/17	*7 Killed in action 9/8/17*
762655	SOLSBURY, George Henry	17/ 6/17	
762095	STEWART, James	14/ 4/17	
6824	TAMLYN, John Reginald	2/ 5/17	*7 Wounded 23/8/17*
763546	TAYLOR, Arthur Cecil John ...	29/ 8/17	*9 Wounded 30/11/17*
761060	THACKER, Gilbert Doe Dwyer Way...	26/ 4/17	*Wounded 5/4/18*
769286	THOMPSON, Frank Wilfred	15/ 2/19	
6347	TRICKER, Russell	26/ 9/16	*7 Wounded 5/9/17, 16/4/18*
3722	WARREN, Samuel Timothy	16/ 1/16	*7 Lieut.*
762674	WHEELER, Percy Harriskine ...	29/ 3/17	
761172	WHITE, Richard Pratt	14/ 4/17	
763283	WILLIS, Walter Edward	28/ 3/17	
767437	WILSON, Alfred George	6/ 7/19	
767686	WOOD, John Ireland	4/ 3/19	
762285	YOUNGMAN, Cyril Fisher	26/ 4/17	*Wounded 26/9/18*

THE EAST SURREY REGIMENT.

Regular Battalions (Nos. 1 & 2).   {31st Foot / 70th Foot}

2nd Lieut.

1472	BAYNE, Edward Gordon	14/ 2/15	*2 Lieut. Wounded 30/3/15*
1983	BURTON, Ralph Withers	23/ 4/15	*1 Lieut.* ✠ *Wounded 4/11/15*
1040	DE BURIATTE, Sgt. John Philip ...	14/ 2/15	*2 Killed in action 12/3/15*
1403	CARTER, Rodney Thomas	10/ 7/15	*2 Lieut. M.G.C.*
1674	CHANDLER, Charles Robert ...	26/ 5/15	*2 Killed in action 29/9/15*
1063	COTTAM, Algernon Edward ...	26/ 5/15	*2 Capt.* ✠ ℞
3730	DARRELL, Albert	5/12/15	*1 Killed in action 25/12/15*
1482	FLEMING-SANDES, Arthur J. Terence	9/ 5/15	*2 Lieut.* **V.C.** *Wounded 29/9/15*
1759	GOOLDEN, Alexander Wood ...	9/ 5/15	*1 Capt. w.21/8/15 To Ind. Army* [*Killed in action 16/7/19*]

EAST SURREY REGIMENT (R/B).

454	HART, L/Cpl. Joseph Aubrey	...	9/ 5/15	2 Lieut. R.E. ✠ w. 1/8/15 🎖
1726	JONES, Lawrence	...	9/ 5/15	2 Capt. w. 1/6/15 K/A 4/10/17
1735	MATTHEWS, William Henry	...	9/ 5/15	1 Lieut. ✠ Wounded –/7/16
2412	TOPLEY, Alec Frederick	...	23/ 4/15	1 Lieut. Wounded 19/5/15
1596	UNWIN, Roland Buckley	...	23/ 4/15	1 Lieut. R.E. Wounded 7/10/17
1271	WARD, Harold Frederick	...	14/ 2/15	2 Capt. ✠ ✠ K/A 30/11/17
2041	WATT, John D.	...	23/ 4/15	2 Capt. (–/R. Sussex) w. 15/11/17
1192	WOODYEAR, Sydney John David	...	26/ 5/15	2 Capt. (Labour Corps)
1831	WIGHT, Lauder Lyleston	...	9/ 5/15	1 Lieut. ✠ Wounded
765024	BABER, Walter Horace	...	31/10/17	1 Died of wounds –/11/17
765052	SMITHER, Albert William	...	31/10/17	1
764953	TURNER, Alfred Hartin	...	31/10/17	1 ✠
765151	WOOD, EDGAR, John	...	31/10/17	1

Special Reserve Battalions (Nos. 3 & 4).

3362	AUSTIN, Cyril Bruce	...	...	–/ 7/15	4 Lieut.
4276	BRAY, Frank ...	...	...	16/11/15	3 Lieut. Wounded –/9/16
5444	HATTON, David Leslie	...	...	8/ 7/16	4 Lieut.
554	WHITEHEAD, L/Cpl. Henry Montague		15/ 8/14	4(2) Killed in action 14/4/15
760715	BAILEY, Hugh Maurice Samuel	...	26/ 4/17	4 Wounded 9/4/18
7309	BELL, Alfred Ernest	..	...	22/11/16	4(8) Wounded 17/4/18, 20/9/18
765585	ELLS, Frank Charles	...	...	28/11/17	3 Wounded 29/5/18
764138	FISHER, Charles Heath	...	...	30/ 5/17	4(12) Killed in action 14/10/18
764700	HOGG, Gordon Andrew	...	...	24/ 9/17	4 Wounded 19/4/18
762288	JOHNS, Reginald Cumming	...		29/ 5/17	3(12) Prisoner of war 18/4/18
764500	KERCKHOVE, Herbert Vincent	...	30/10/17	4 ✠
767453	MOIR, Leslie John Angus	...		6/ 2/19	3
764251	NICHOLLS, Harold	...	...	1/ 8/17	3(8) Died of wounds 7/8/18
764960	TUCKER, Henry Riseley	...	...	30/10/17	3

Territorial Battalions (Nos. 5 & 6).

2590	BARKER, Eric ...	...	...	25/ 3/15	6 Lieut.
1615	BLAIR, John Milligan	...	...	24/10/14	5 Major M.B.E. 🎖
1108	EVANS, Ulrick Richardson	...	...	28/ 8/14	5 Lieut. To Div. Signal Co.
2324	GILLETT, Edward Bailey	...	...	2/12/14	5 Capt.
2081	GREENWOOD, Sgt. John Eric	...		2/12/14	5 Capt.
2106	MOIR, Kenneth Macrae	...	...	24/10/14	5 Lieut. ✠
229	NICHOLLS, C/Sgt. Henry King	...		7/12/14	5 Major Killed in action 4/4/18
3900	ARNOLD, Reginald William	...		19/11/15	5 Capt. [To Labour Corps]
3440	DEMPSTER, Alfred Eric	...	...	11/ 8/15	6 Lieut. Wounded 13/3/18, 1/6/18
3441	DEMPSTER, L/Cpl. Edwin Nowell	...	11/ 8/15	6 Lieut. (M.G.C.) w. 26/3/17
2316	LOWRY, Vyvian Charles	...	...	18/10/15	5 (M.G.C.) Killed in action 9/4/18
3963	SALMON, Frederick Arthur	...		23/11/15	5 Lieut.
7921	BARLOW, Noel Fawckner	...	...	26/ 1/17	5 Wounded 7/5/18
5473	CARTWRIGHT, Spencer	...	...	11/ 7/16	5 Lieut.

EAST SURREY REGIMENT (T/F). 359

763758	CAVE, Russell George	...	30/ 5/17	5
766044	CLEMENT, George Percy	...	23/ 5/17	6 Wounded 7/11/18
760386	CREEGAN, L/Cpl. Edgar Wilson	...	11/ 9/18	5(9)
767397	HARKER, Charles Portas	...	5/ 2/19	6
763975	KEYES, Frank	...	27/ 6/17	5 Wounded 24/4/18
763273	LEA, George Henri	...	27/ 6/17	5
765364	TREGENZA, Edward Leslie	...	28/11/17	5
765330	TRUSCOTT, Christopher Marsden	...	28/11/17	5

Service Battalions (New Armies).

3100	ALLISTON, Geoffrey	...	10/ 3/15	10 Capt. (Staff) 🎖
2400	ARKWRIGHT, Alan Joseph	...	22/ 2/15	10 Lieut. To Labour Corps
2056	CATFORD, Walter Arundel	...	3/ 4/15	10 Lieut.
3069	CROWTHER, John E. Marmaduke	...	9/ 3/15	11 Lieut. ✠ w. -/9/16, 9/4/18
1957	DESLANDES, Denis George	...	24/10/15	7 Lieut. w. -/3/16 K/A 27/11/16
1494	FENWICK, Basil Arbuthnot	...	28/ 9/14	9 Capt. Wounded -/9/15 P/W
1492	GOLDS, Ingram Thomas	...	7/11/15	7 Capt. w. -/7/16 Killed in
1921	GREEN, Arthur Sidney	...	-/ 6/15	11 Lieut. [action 30/11/17 🎖]
4675	HART, Albert Henry	...	16/11/15	10 Lieut.
2721	HETHERINGTON, Ernest Cooper	...	5/ 1/15	8 Lieut. Wounded -/7/16 🎖
2931	LEAHY, James Michael	...	16/10/14	7 Lieut. Wounded -/3/16
2726	LISTER, Jack Curtis	...	18/12/14	9 Lieut. (R.F.A.)
4649	MORRIS, Walter Andrew	...	7/10/15	11 Lieut. Wounded 7/5/17 P/W
2434	MUSGROVE, G. H. Stuart	...	3/12/14	8 Lieut. Killed in action 1/7/16
2674	PURVER, Bernard Arthur	...	16/10/14	7 Capt. (11/R. W. Kent) K/A
1465	SCOFIELD, Eric William	...	19/ 9/14	10 Major (Tank Corps) [7/10/16]
1775	WAIGHT, George	...	5/ 9/14	8 Lieut. (Div. Cyclists)
1471	WILKES, George Thomas	...	7/11/15	7 Lieut. ✠ Wounded -/3/16
5720	ARDING, Leslie Hawkins	...	7/ 7/16	11 Lieut.
5475	CLARKE, Frank Leonard	...	7/ 7/16	10 Wounded 16/8/16
5579	GOLDING, L/Cpl. John Arthur	...	2/ 6/16	14 Wounded 17/4/18
5341	GOLDS, L/Cpl. Frank	...	25/ 5/16	11 Killed in action 5/10/16
4808	HART, Bernard Leslie	...	25/ 5/16	11 Lieut.
5590	McWALTER, L/Cpl. Thomas Brown		2/ 6/16	14 Lieut. ✠ Wounded
4867	MORRISON, Ronald Wm. Goldie	...	25/ 5/16	11 Lieut.
5381	ROSS, L/Cpl. James Alexander		25/ 5/16	14 w. -/9/16 Interned in Holland
5329	WHEELER, Sidney Armstrong	...	2/ 6/16	11 Lieut.
6920	ANDREW, Benjamin Sydney	...	22/11/16	8 Lieut.
7812	ARNOLD, Thomas Sorrell Dight	...	26/ 1/17	(7/Lancs. Fus.) D/W 11/10/17
7346	ASTINGTON, Thomas Jeffery	...	19/12/16	8 Killed in action 28/2/17
6746	BAILEY, Herbert Packer	...	5/ 9/16	12 ✠ Killed in action 31/7/17
767663	BALE, Henry Mapleston	...	4/ 3/19	
765645	BARBER, Harry Mason	...	18/12/17	8 Killed in action 8/8/18
643	BARTRUM, Arthur Allan	...	28/ 6/16	8 Killed in action 30/9/16
7418	BELHAM, Alan Stewart	...	19/12/16	9 Lieut.

EAST SURREY REGIMENT (S/B).

Number	Name	Date	Notes
5092	BENNETT, Stephen Edward	19/12/16	*12 Lieut.*
6842	BOWEN, Edgar Ernest Wedgewood	26/ 9/16	*7 Prisoner of war* 18/1/18
767932	CHANCE, George Percy	6/ 3/19	
766425	CHAPPELL, William	3/ 2/19	
762715	CLARKE, Arnold Ralfe	5/ 2/19	
766102	CONIBEER, Ralph William	1/ 5/18	✠ *Wounded* 8/11/18
768774	CORBIN, Gerald	13/ 2/19	
765761	CRUMPTON, George Reginald	18/12/17	
768360	CUMMINGS, Sidney Robert	17/ 3/19	
765713	DAVIS, Charles Herbert	18/12/17	*Wounded* 6/9/18
760549	DAWSON, Frederick Albert	1/ 7/17	*8 Killed in action* 6/8/18
760962	DIX, Cyril Bernard	1/ 7/17	*8 Killed in action* 10/8/17
5747	DIXON, D'Arcy Boulton	5/ 9/16	*Lieut.*
760983	FEARN, Herbert	1/ 7/17	*8 Killed in action* 12/10/17
762856	FITZ-GIBBON, Frederick Charles	12/ 2/19	
768538	FLINT, Alfred William	5/ 2/19	
3116	GAYWOOD, Frederick James	28/ 6/16	*8 Lieut.* ✠✠✠ *w.* 26/4/18
765170	GODDARD, Gordon Cecil	30/10/17	*9 Killed in action* 16/10/18
766692	GOODFELLOW, Arnold William	4/ 2/19	
767778	HAGGIS, Kenneth Charles	21/ 4/19	
5258	HALL, Albert Loader	26/ 9/16	*8 Capt. Killed in action* 4/4/18 ✠
768250	HARVEY, Walter Raymond	17/ 3/19	
767575	ITTER, Arthur	26/ 3/19	
765630	JOHNS, Gilbert Godwin	18/12/17	
7341	JOHNSON, William Stanley	19/12/16	*7 Died of wounds* 17/3/17
766524	LOYE, Robert Norman	26/ 6/18	
7185	MILLARD, Alfred George	19/12/16	*9 Died of wounds* 7/8/17
768073	NICOLL, William John	18/ 3/19	
766566	PARROTT, Lawrence Kingston	3/ 2/19	
769266	POWER, Percy	15/ 2/19	
768520	ROBERTS, Daniel Monteith	13/ 2/19	
7317	RUTHERFORD, Stanley	22/11/16	*13* ✠ *Wounded* 29/12/17
761380	SANDERSON, Reginald Woolley	2/ 8/17	*7 Wounded* 10/12/17
762279	SEATON, James William Sharpley	26/ 4/17	*Prisoner of war* 15/5/18
5217	SHERRIFF, Roderick Cedric	5/ 9/16	*9 Lieut. Wounded* 15/8/17
7414	SHILLINGLAW, Eric Charles	19/12/16	*8 Lieut.*
769188	SOLLEY, Stephen Wallace	5/ 2/19	
760404	STEPHENS, Adolphus	26/ 6/18	
768305	SUMNER, John Alexander	13/ 2/19	
767764	TAYLOR, James John	5/ 3/19	
760657	TAYLOR, Leslie Malcolm	5/ 2/19	
7344	TURNER, Stanley Borrington	19/12/16	*7 Lieut.*
7362	VANNER, William Alfred	19/12/16	*12 Lieut.*
765706	WALLER, John Claude	18/12/16	
767991	WALLIS, Francis Powers	17/ 3/19	
762381	WATTS, Alan Kingsford	26/ 4/17	
768863	WOOLLARD, Frank Griffiths	17/ 3/19	

*THE ROYAL WEST SURREY REGIMENT
(THE QUEEN'S).

Regular Battalions (Nos. 1 & 2). 2nd Foot

		2nd Lieut.	
693	AUSTIN, Sgt. Cyril Frederic	15/12/14 2	*Killed in action* 10/3/15 ⚔
1985	BATTISCOMBE, Humphrey	12/ 6/15 1	*Lieut. Wounded* 30/5/17
1821	BROCKLEHURST, Cpl. Thos. Pownall	26/ 5/15 2	*Capt. w.* 25/9/15 *Killed in action* –/7/16
1430	BROWN, Arthur Lyster	26/ 5/15 2	*Killed in action* 25/9/15
1387	BURRELL, John	1/ 1/15 1	*Capt. Wounded* 7/7/17, 10/10/17
1277	CROOK, Leslie Arthur	1/ 1/15 2	*Capt.* ✠ *w.* 10/2/15, 28/9/15, –/7/16 [*Killed in action* 25/9/17]
399	DE ROUGEMONT, Maurice Henry ...	27/ 1/15 2	*Killed in action* 16/5/15
2639	ELTHAM, Charles William ...	1/ 1/15 1	*Capt. w.* 9/9/15 *Killed in action* [3/11/16]
1658	FAIRTLOUGH, Launcelot Walter ...	14/ 2/15 2	*Lieut. w.* 18/5/15
1710	HEYES, Leicester	1/ 1/15 1	*Capt.* ⚔
1372	HUMPHREYS, Dudley Francis ...	15/12/14 2	*Died of wounds* 16/5/15
295	JONES, Charles Taylor ...	27/ 1/15 2	*Killed in action* 25/9/15 ⚔
1989	MADDOCK, Richard Henry ...	26/ 5/15 2	*Capt.* ✠ ⚔
1390	MESSOM, Cpl. Harold ...	15/12/14 2	(✠) *Killed in action* 16/5/15 ⚔
2180	MOORE, Francis Hallam ...	26/ 5/15 2	*Lieut.*
1402	PLANT, Fred George ...	23/ 4/15 1	*Killed in action* 25/9/15
1371	ROUGHT, Charles Gardner ...	15/12/14 2	*Prisoner of war Died* 4/2/19
1807	STRODE, Maurice	26/ 5/15 2	*Capt.* ✠ ✠ F/D *w.* 25/9/15 ⚔
1275	TWEEDIE-SMITH, Alan ...	1/ 1/15 1	*Killed in action* 13/10/15 ⚔
1986	WALCH, James Bernard Millard	26/ 5/15 2	*Killed in action* 25/9/15
761524	ATKINSON, William Laurence	23/ 6/17 1	*Wounded* 25/9/17, 8/8/18
7487	BARLEY, George Wellesley ...	22/11/16 2	*Lieut.*
764923	BULLOCK, William Henry ...	10/ 3/17 1	
761289	CHARLES, Cecil William Castle ...	23/16/17 1	*Wounded* 10/10/17
761376	CHURCHWARD, Harold Marcus ...	2/ 8/19 2	
763687	CORRY, John Edgar	27/ 6/17 1	✠ *Wounded* 18/12/17
760909	HASTINGS, Alfred Ronald ...	4/ 8/17 1	
760990	HIGGS, Reginald Frank ...	23/ 6/17 1	*Killed in action* 22/9/18
4898	HOWCROFT, Stewart Martin ...	1/ 5/17 1	✠
5532	PLOWMAN-BROWN, Charles Harold ...	26/ 9/16 1	*Lieut.*
760670	ROBINSON, Cecil Henry Melville ...	26/ 6/17 1	*Wounded* 20/9/17
1305	SHIPTON, John Edgar	1/ 5/17	
7319	SMITH, Charles Reginald	7/11/16 2	*Lieut. Wounded P/W*
4481	SWAINSON, W. Christopher Graindage	25/ 1/17 2	

Special Reserve Battalion (No. 3).

3196	KEEP, L/Cpl. Alan Ralph	21/ 4/15 3	*Lieut.* ✠ *To Min. of Mun.*
3210	MANN, L/Cpl. Deane	24/ 4/15 3	*Capt. Adjt.* 6/Bn. ✠ ✠
3160	THORNEYCROFT, Sgt. Edward Charles	20/ 3/15 3(2)	*Capt. Wounded* –/7/16

* *Title changed (1st January, 1921) to "The Queen's Royal Regiment (West Surrey)."*

765580	BULL, Walter	28/11/17	3	
765932	DONNE-SMITH, Leslie	27/ 2/18	3	Wounded 26/8/18
761994	MITCHELL, Alfred	29/ 3/17	3	
761846	OSMOND, Frank Edward	28/ 3/17	3	

Territorial Battalions (Nos. 4 & 5).

3430	BROWN, L/Cpl. Henry Colborne	6/ 6/15	5 Lieut.	Missing –/12/16
2315	CARTER, Harry William	23/ 6/15	4 Lieut.	✠ 🎖
2716	GUNNELL, Dudley Arthur	9/ 2/15	4 Capt.	R.T.O.
2430	GRAY, James	28/11/14	5 Capt.	Adjt. ✠ F/D
2539	MARZETTI, L/Cpl. Claude	9/ 2/15	4	
2529	MARZETTI, Leonard	9/ 2/15	4 Lieut.	
2077	McIVER, Colin Donald	9/ 2/15	4 Capt.	Wounded –/8/15
2682	McNAUGHT, L/Cpl. James McGach	9/ 2/15	4 Capt.	
2325	PRESTON, L/Cpl. Eric Watson	9/ 2/15	4 Capt.	
1046	SPICER, Robert William	13/11/14	4 Capt.	Killed in action 26/3/17
3586	BORET, John Auguste	10/10/15	4 Capt.	✠ A.F.C. To R.F.C.
2248	BROWN, Cyril George	2/10/15	4 Lieut.	Prisoner of war
2250	BROWN, L/Cpl. Frederick Proctor	5/10/15	4 Lieut.	Tank Corps
2672	COLES, Edgar Lermitte	19/ 9/15	5 Lieut.	✠ Wounded
2036	DAKIN, Edward Henry	10/10/15	4 Lieut.	Wounded 16/10/17
2065	DYNE, Hugh Edward Lubbock	29/10/15	5 Lieut.	
2728	EVANS, L/Cpl. Bernard Scott	3/11/15	4 Lieut.	M.B.E. ✠ w. 23/4/17
2489	GILLOTT, Arthur	5/12/15	5 Lieut.	
3825	HERKOMER, Seigfried Hubert	10/10/15	5 Lieut.	To T.F.R.
3886	HUGHES, L/Cpl. George Evan	10/10/15	4 Lieut.	
2133	JEPHSON, Charles Mitchell W.	3/11/15	5	Killed in action 27/12/17
3150	JOHN, Arthur Henry	10/10/15	4 Lieut.	
3578	LEMON, Reginald Henry	10/10/15	4 Lieut.	(R.A.F.)
2319	LIVOCK, Eric Stuart	29/ 9/15	4 Lieut.	(R.F.C.) K/A 8/11/17
1805	LOVELL, Anthony Henry	10/10/15	4 Lieut.	(R.A.O.C.)
3780	MACARTHUR, Roy	10/10/15	4 Lieut.	To T.F.R.
4192	MENHINICK, John Stanley	22/11/15	4 Lieut.	(1/Bn.)
3761	O'CONNOR, Denis Roderick	10/10/15	4 Lieut.	Wounded 24/10/17
3770	OLNEY, John Kilvington	17/10/15	4 Lieut.	M.G.C. w. 19/10/17
2985	PEMBERTON, Warwick Geoffrey T.	29/ 9/15	5 Lieut.	Wounded 26/8/18
2734	RIDPATH, L/Cpl. Fredk. Cecil Lacey	3/11/15	4 Lieut.	Killed in action 27/12/17
3832	RUDLING, Ernest Richard	10/10/15	4	Wounded 7/5/17
3351	STARLING, Marwood Cooper	5/ 8/15	5 Lieut.	To 8/London
2935	STONE, Hubert Clive	6/ 8/15	4 Lieut.	
3869	SWAIN, Tom Evelyn	10/10/15	5 Lieut.	w. 14/2/18, 30/10/18
8137	ASHFOLD, George Alfred	26/ 9/17	4	
766155	CHARLTON, Robert	1/11/17	4	Wounded 3/5/18
767248	DYSART, George Augustus Harrison	27/ 3/18	4	Wounded 8/11/18
762501	FRANKLAND, Thomas Leonard	31/ 7/17	4	
5946	FULLER, Ernest Paget	11/ 7/16	4	Killed in action 20/9/17
765229	GADD, Leonard Charles	18/12/17	4	

ROYAL WEST SURREY REGIMENT (T/F). 363

1017	Gossling, Hugh Foley ...	... 11/ 7/16	4	Lieut.
765232	Harris, William	... 28/11/17	4	Wounded 21/6/18, 26/8/18
767950	Houlder, Alfred Claude ...	... 5/ 3/19	4	
761093	Lord, Harold	... 26/ 6/18	5	
765018	Mercer, Reginald Ross ...	... 30/10/17	4	Wounded 19/1/18
8144	Montague, Jas. Chevin ...	... 26/ 1/17	4	
765728	Ramsay, David	... 27/ 2/18	4	
765471	Rayward, Clifford Charles ...	... 27/11/17	4	Wounded 19/9/18
6339	Sands, George Frederick ...	... 28/ 3/17	5	⚔
765820	Wilson, Edward William ...	... 13/ 3/18	4	

Service Battalions (New Armies).

1806	Brooks, Joseph Clifton ...	... 22/ 9/14	8	Capt. Wounded 9/10/15
1162	Butler, Herveius Alexander R.	... 15/ 9/14	6	Capt. Wounded -/7/16
1166	Cannon, Herbert Cooper ...	... 15/ 9/14	6	Major (D.L.I.) ✠ ⚔(2)
3207	Coppin, Richard Alfred ...	... 28/11/15	6	Capt. w. 14/3/16 K/A 11/4/17
1282	Cuddon, Philip B.	... 15/ 9/14	6	Capt. Bde. Maj. ✠✠✠ F/D ⚔
4923	Elliott, L/Cpl. Ernest Edward	... 25/ 5/16	9	Lieut. ✠ Wounded 18/4/18
4036	Hay, Robert	... 7/10/15	9	
3054	Lodge, Alfred Percy Derriman	... 22/12/14	9	To Nigeria Regt. Wounded
2419	Mahony, James	... 10/ 3/15	9	Lieut. w. 14/3/16 D/W 4/3/17
3513	McNair, Frederick Ronald ...	... 12/12/15	6	Capt. Wounded 18/4/18
1383	Ormerod, Thomas Laurence	... 17/ 9/14	6	Lieut. Wounded -/7/16
2705	Passmore, Arthur William ...	... 23/11/14	9	Killed in action 4/4/16
1052	Penrose, L/Cpl. George Alwyn	... 28/10/14	8	Capt. Killed in action 9/4/17 ⚔
1257	Read, Maurice Rix	... 15/ 9/14	6	Lieut. (M.G.C.) w. 11/4/18
1091	Semple, Wilfrid John ...	... 13/ 9/14	6	Lieut. (5/Lancs. Fus.)
1146	Simmons, Frederick Lionel ...	... 15/ 9/14	6	Lieut. (R.A.F.) w. 29/10/15
2666	Smith, Harry Edgar ...	... 28/11/15	6	Wounded -/4/16
4465	Waters, Edwin George Ross	... 2/ 6/16		Lieut.
7223	Adams, Arthur James ...	... 19/12/16	10	Lieut.
761383	Adams, Caleb Henry ...	... 26/ 8/17	10	Killed in action 20/9/17
766773	Baker, Leonard Walter ...	... 29/10/18		
7308	Batchelor, Robert Thomas ...	... 22/11/16	7	w. 16/5/17 K/A 23/3/18
764474	Batchelor, Sidney Crowhurst	... 17/ 3/19		
7569	Baylis, Roland Harry ...	... 27/ 1/17	7	Lieut. ✠
768601	Beale, Miles Complin ...	... 13/ 2/19		
767581	Bell, Philip Michael ...	... 3/ 3/19		
3005	Bird, Reginald Thomas ...	... 2/ 5/17	8	Wounded 3/12/17
1145	Bliss, Archibald	... 5/ 9/16	7	Lieut. Wounded 12/2/18
7301	Boden, John Posnett ...	... 22/11/16	6	Wounded 25/4/17
760527	Bolus, Lester	... 28/ 6/17	10	Wounded 12/10/17
764483	Cole, Thomas Alfred ...	... 31/ 7/17		
7149	Conquest, George	... 19/12/16	8	Lieut.
768148	Coombes, Cecil Harold James	... 10/ 3/19		
768180	Crickmay, George Hayter ...	... 18/ 3/19		
5481	Davey, Harold William ...	... 5/ 9/16		Lieut.

ROYAL WEST SURREY REGIMENT (S/B)

765115	Dodds, William Fenwick	31/10/17	
760655	Donkin, Cecil David George	10/ 3/17	
768316	Dunn, Daniel William	17/ 3/19	
761558	Eddison, Henry	10/ 3/17	
768340	Field, Humphrey Frank	17/ 3/19	
769094	Ford, Edward Vyvyan	5/ 3/19	
3675	Gaywood, Cyril Henry	31/ 7/16	7 *Lieut.*
763329	Gladman, Cyril William	25/ 6/17	*Wounded* 3/9/18
1291	Goldie, Maurice Francis	2/ 5/17	8
768231	Hocking, William Stanley	17/ 3/19	
767590	Houghton, Arthur Sereld	5/ 3/19	
768618	Howse, Thomas Frederick	3/ 2/19	
764323	Hudson, Edgar Hugh	31/ 7/17	*Wounded* 30/11/17
7181	Hullcoop, Ernest Frank	19/12/16	(2) *Lieut.*
766347	Humphrey, Reginald William	28/ 5/18	51/Grad. Bn.
766830	Hyatt, John Buchan	17/ 3/19	*Wounded* 13/5/18
6257	Jonas, Louis Nathaniel	2/ 5/17	8 *Wounded* 17/8/17
3407	Lake, Maurice Barthram Cassop	19/12/16	8 *Wounded* 15/8/17, 21/11/17
766524	Love, Robert Norman	26/ 6/18	
769023	Metcalf, Adrian	14/ 2/19	
767862	Newitt, Nigel Joseph	5/ 3/19	
763955	Parker, Walter Bernard	17/ 3/19	*Wounded* 30/10/17
6424	Parkes, James William	19/12/16	10 *Lieut.*
766490	Pollard, Cecil Leslie	26/ 6/18	
9272	Rainsford, George	10/ 3/17	Capt. O.B.E. (*Lab. Corps*) ☧(2)
767455	Randall, Leslie John Alfred	5/ 2/19	
769318	Rist, William King	5/ 2/19	
2502	Rogers, Cecil Walter	31/ 7/16	7 *Died of wounds* 28/12/17
767667	Round, Frank Harold	5/ 2/19	
762962	Saville, Arthur Henry	10 /3/17	
3409	Scrivener, Eric Robert	19/12/16	8 *Wounded* 15/8/17
762240	Sharp, Clifford Graham	4/ 8/17	11
767861	Simmonds, Donald George Henry	3/ 3/19	
767459	Slade, Kenneth Ray	5/ 2/19	
768262	Standring, George Lancelot	18/ 3/19	
1233	Steger, Basil Maurice	7/11/16	*Lieut.*
767133	Stillwell, Sidney	3/ 2/19	
768406	Taylor, Robert George	17/ 3/19	
3051	Thorn, Philip Edward	7/11/16	7 *Prisoner of war* 7/6/17
768947	Twyman, Charles Everard	3/ 2/19	
767699	Uwins, Cecil Charles George	4/ 3/19	
763718	Viall, John	26/ 4/17	
761381	Watson, Cpl. William Montague	15/ 9/17	*Lieut. w.* –/10/17, *Killed* –/8/18
7299	Watt, Charles Hallett	19/12/16	(1) *Lieut.*
764968	Weaver, Hughs Loftus	10/ 3/17	
767787	Wilkins, Norman John	5/ 3/19	
760919	Wills, Arthur Reynolds	28/ 6/17	10 ✠ *Wounded* 23/8/17
6242	Womack, Bertie	8/ 5/17	6 ✠
767788	Yeatman, Malcolm Bardsley	5/ 3/19	

THE ROYAL SUSSEX REGIMENT. {35th Foot / 107th Foot}

Regular Battalions (Nos. 1 & 2).

			2nd Lieut.	
2380	BROMLEY, Hugh Frederic ...	...	29/ 8/15	2 *Killed in action* 25/6/16
1491	HUTT, Harold Vernon	...	1/ 1/15	2 *Killed in action* 26/1/15
1680	TAYLOR, Lawrence Evered ...	...	1/ 1/15	2 *Lieut. Wounded* 9/5/15

Special Reserve Battalion (No. 3).

764784	BRAY, Frank Hugh ...	...	24/ 9/17	3(9) *Killed in action* 28/5/18
764948	BULLETT, Robert Ernest	...	24/ 9/17	3 *Wounded* 19/4/18
765462	MILBANK, Henry Richard ...	...	28/11/17	3(8)
8092	SHARP, Edward Ronald	...	25/ 1/17	3 *Wounded* 8/4/18
5007	WEST, Frederick Alexander ...	...	7/ 7/16	3 *Lieut. Wounded* 21/9/18
764809	WINN, Ernest Godfrey Cole	...	28/11/17	3(8) [*D/W* 6/10/20]

Territorial Battalions (Nos. 4 to 6).

4201	BULL, Geoffrey Howard	...	21/12/15	4 *Lieut.*
4117	DEANE, Arthur Reginald	...	28/10/15	5 *Died of wounds* 14/11/17
1035	FAZAN, Roy ...	...	14/ 5/14	5 *Killed in action* 9/5/15
23	PERRY, John Lutley	...	29/ 8/14	5 *Capt. Wounded* 9/5/15
7734	ATKINSON, George Hutton ...	...	11/ 7/16	6 *Lieut. Wounded* 17/4/18
6282	BERRY, Arthur Gilbert	...	5/ 9/16	4 *Lieut. Wounded* –/2/17
4766	BROWN, Alfred John	...	11/ 7/16	6 *Lieut.* ✠
4301	BURCH, James Cyril ...	...	11/ 7/16	6 *Lieut.*
7735	CAMPBELL, Alan	...	11/ 7/16	6 *Lieut.*
763778	CHARMAN, John Ewart	...	27/ 6/17	4 *Died of wounds* 25/9/17
4790	FINCH, L/Cpl. Arthur William Bernard		5/ 9/16	4 *Wounded & Prisoner of war*
2781	GARRARD, Sgt. Cyril Proctor	...	11/ 7/16	5 *Lieut.* ✠
764064	GLENISTER, Reginald Thomas	...	30/ 5/17	4 *Lieut.*
8201	GRICE, Stanley William	...	26/ 1/17	4 *Lieut.*
763740	JACKSON, Arthur Reginald Frederick		28/ 8/17	4 *Lieut.*
4900	MARKS, Leslie	...	11/ 7/16	6 *Lieut. Wounded* 12/6/17
1690	McGREGOR, Sgt. John Eric Miers ...		5/ 9/16	4 *Lieut.*
5430	WHITTLE, William George Alfred ...		29/ 7/16	6 *Lieut.*
4788	WIGGINS, Sidney	...	11/ 7/16	6 *Lieut.*
6037	WILSON, George Andrew Glanville ...		11/ 7/16	6 *Capt. Killed in action* 31/7/17

Service Battalions (New Armies).

230	BOWERS, Sgt. Cyril Robert Arbuthnot	11/ 3/15	10 *Capt.*
1684	CHANTREY, Leslie Hewer ...	...	9/ 1/15	9 *To R.F.A.*
2102	COX, Norman John ...	...	13/11/14	7 *Lieut. Killed in action* 23/8/15
2050	COXHEAD, Henry Jessop	...	15/11/14	13 *Capt. & Adjt. w.* –/1/17
1871	ELBOROUGH, Alfred Charles E.	...	7/12/14	8 *To* 6/*Yorks L.I. Capt. D/W*
2478	FINNIS, William Trevor	...	9/ 1/15	9 *To A.S.C.* [30/7/15]
2229	HERVEY, Alex Francis	...	9/ 1/15	8 *Lieut. w.* 17/9/15 (*W.O.*)

ROYAL SUSSEX REGIMENT (S/B).

2791	KEMP, Edward Adair	7/12/14	8 Lieut.	
2475	MAKALUA, Mathew James M.	15/11/14	13 Capt.	Wounded –/7/16
3588	CASSELS, James Stuart	5/12/15	9	
2869	D'IVERNOIS, Victor Hally Barton	3/10/15	9 Lieut.	Wounded –/11/16
2896	HILL, Charles Douglas Lucas	3/10/15	9 Killed in action 14/2/16	
3834	HOOD, Oswald	1/11/15	10 Killed in action 1/9/16	
3725	HURST, Victor de la Motte	5/12/15	9 Lieut.	
3533	NEWTON, Clement Vaughan	5/12/15	9 Capt. ✠ ℳ(2)	
3489	PEPPER, Edward George	10/1/16	7 Lieut.	Wounded –/8/16
3674	TREACHER, Harry	5/12/15	9 Capt. ✠ ✠ Wounded 7/11/18	
768332	ABBEY, Henry Robert Burrows	5/2/19		
762286	ACKROYD, James Anthony	4/3/19		
766917	ADOLPH, William Edgar Leonard	27/10/18		
765022	ALLEN, Thomas William	27/11/17	[15/11/17 ℳ]	
1915	ANDREWS, Stephen Arthur	7/11/16	12 Capt. D.S.O. ✠ ✠ Wounded	
765495	BLAGROVE, Henry Cyril	27/11/17	Lieut. Wounded 18/9/18	
765432	BRADLEY, Alfred Thomas	28/11/17		
763381	BULLOCK, Alan Durtnall	1/3/17	7 Prisoner of war 10/9/17	
767407	CHRISTIAN, William Aubrey	3/3/19		
5983	CLAPHAM, Alfred William	5/9/16	12 Lieut. [16/10/17 ℳ]	
3712	CLARK, Philip Lindsay	1/10/16	11 Capt. D.S.O. w. 9/3/17,	
761365	COWARD, Sgt. Duncan Cecil	4/3/19	Wounded –/4/15	
760689	CUTLER, Edward Cecil	26/4/17	Lieut. ✠ Wounded 18/4/18	
760874	DAVIS, Gerald	2/5/17	9 Lieut.	
761366	DENNETT, George Albert	4/3/19	Wounded –/5/15	
763385	ELLEN, Walter Parker	28/3/17	✠ ℳ	
5202	FINNEMORE, Henry Jas.	18/3/17	7 (R.F.C.) D/W 27/3/18	
3731	FISH, Barrow Edmondson	19/6/16	11 Killed in action 3/9/16	
4927	FROST, Alan St. John	4/1/17	(5) Lieut. ℳ	
767641	GLASSBOROW, Jn. Edwd. Redvers Lee	5/3/19		
768942	GOLDRING, Walter George	7/2/19		
766132	GRANT, George Duncan	24/5/18		
768115	GREAVES, Ronald George	17/3/19		
768421	HALL, Frederick John	5/2/19		
761925	HALL, Stanley Ernest	14/2/19		
765703	HALL, Valentine Octavius	18/12/17	51/Grad. Bn.	
765590	HEDLEY, Harold Thomas	27/11/17		
3627	HILL, Philip Hawker	7/11/16	Lieut. Wounded 28/11/17	
765595	JONES, Evan Walter	18/12/17	Wounded 9/11/18	
764150	KEYS, Frank Sydney	27/6/17	13	
4754	LUSTY, Reginald Arthur	20/9/17	13 Lieut. Prisoner of war 26/3/18	
3628	MEO, Innes Luigi	29/9/16	11 Prisoner of war 15/5/18	
768060	MILLS, Harold	18/3/19		
3465	MORRIS, Alwyn Jas.	7/11/16	7 Lieut. Wounded 18/9/18	
763556	MURRAY, Arthur	1/3/17	7 Killed in action 8/8/18	
5708	NEALE, Arthur Woodis	26/9/16	12 Prisoner of war 22/5/18	
767303	PALMER, Leslie Charles Guy	3/3/19		

ROYAL SUSSEX REGIMENT (S/B).

7081	PEARSON, William George Frederick	16/ 9/17		8 *Lieut.* ✠
767512	PERRIS, Leslie Robert	5/ 2/19		
6441	PERRY, Kenneth George	5/ 9/16	*11*	*Died of wounds* 1/11/16
767456	ROGERS, Leonard	5/ 2/19		
768555	SCOTCHER, Arthur Edwin	19/ 3/19		
765667	SHILSTON, Arthur Charles	18/12/17	*51*	
2893	SIMPSON, Jas. Gordon	7/11/16	*12*	✠ *Wounded* 10/8/17, 9/5/18
7391	SMITH, Clifford Henry Kingsley ...	22/11/16		8 *Lieut.*
762420	SMITH, Victor St. George	26/ 4/17		
763373	THORP, Percy Parkinson	28/ 3/17		*Wounded* 31/10/17
761803	TREW, Stanley Turner	28/ 3/17		
766981	WALKER, Henry Gratton	30/ 7/18	*52*	
8278	WEBB, Harry Frederick	21/ 9/17	*13*	*(To R.A.F.) Capt. Wounded* [22/3/18 ✠]
765716	WEEKS, William Edward	13/ 3/18		✠
8022	WOODHAMS, James Percy	25/ 1/17		*Wounded* 26/4/18
4913	WOODROW, Arthur Blachford ...	13/ 4/17	*11*	✠ *Wounded* 16/10/17

THE SOUTH WALES BORDERERS.

Regular Battalions (Nos. 1 & 2). 24th Foot

2nd Lieut.

3691	DEACON, Edwin Thomas	16/ 1/16	*1*	✠ [18/9/18]
1516	GOTELEE, L/Cpl. Geoffrey Harris ...	10/ 7/15	*1*	*w.* 2/9/16 *Capt. Killed in action*
897	SAUNDERS, Louis Desormeaux ...	12/ 6/15	*1*	*Killed in action* 26/9/15
2555	CHATFEILD-CLARKE, Horace Yelverton	24/11/15	*2*	*Killed in action* 23/4/17
5594	MORGAN, Dewi Rhys	26/ 9/16	*2*	*Lieut.*

Special Reserve Battalion (No. 3).

4433	BLORE, Eric	22/ 1/16	*3*	*Lieut.*
3415	GRESHAM, Hubert Trafford ...	7/ 6/15	*3*	*To* 12 *Capt.*
4250	HORDLE, Stanley Latour ...	20/11/15	*3*	*Lieut.*
763363	GWYNNE, Thomas Haydn ...	30/10/17	*3*	
765639	JAMES, Laurence	1/ 5/18	*3*	*R.A.F.*
763272	JONES, David Russell ...	31/10/17	*3*	
595	KENT, Sgt. Harold	5/ 9/16	*3(8)*	*Killed in action* 4/8/17
538	KENT, Sgt. Lionel Victor ...	5/ 9/16	*3*	*Lieut. Died of wounds* 31/7/17
6954	LEWIS, Arthur Thomas ...	26/ 9/16	*3(2)*	*Lieut. Wounded* 9/5/17
762087	LLOYD, Evan Christian ...	31/10/17	*3(1)*	*Died of wounds* 5/10/18
4327	MEREFIELD, L/Cpl. Bernard ...	26/ 5/16	*3(1)*	
763716	PATON, John Alfred	27/ 6/17	*3*	
763005	THOMAS, Reginald Ivor Victor Clifford	29/ 8/17	*3*	*Killed in action* 24/11/17

Service Battalions (New Armies).

2845	HITCHINGS, Douglas Brystock	10/ 6/15	10
763869	ARNOLD, Hedley Graham	29/ 8/17	(2) Killed in action 11/4/18
767146	BEAMAN, George Bernard	4/ 2/19	
7700	BROWN, Hiram Idris	19/12/16	(2) Lieut.
767540	DAVIES, Douglas Kimberley	5/ 2/19	
764758	DAVIES, Ernest Benjamin	29/ 8/17	
8026	DAVIES, Harry Harding	19/12/16	(2) Killed in action 10/11/17
764296	EVANS, David Thomas	29/ 8/17	
764298	GALLIENNE, John William Horrabine	29/ 8/17	
764300	GIBBS, Joseph Ernest Aynge	29/ 8/17	
753033	GRANT, Alexander Charles	29/ 8/17	
763382	HALL, Alfred Reginald Conrad	29/ 8/17	Lieut.
5121	HANNA, William Henry	5/ 9/16	Lieut. w. 21/8/17, 15/4/18 ⚑
765888	HEDLEY, Robert Richard	13/ 3/18	
761072	HILLIER, L/Cpl. Sidney Napier	3/ 8/17	6 Killed in action 25/3/18
7075	JOSLIN, Harold Alfred	3/ 5/17	5
763620	MATHIAS, David Emrys	30/ 5/17	
764546	MILLS, David Handel	28/ 8/17	
764785	MORGAN, Henry Gwyn	27/11/17	
764611	MORGAN, Reginald Samuel.Leigh	24/ 9/17	[11/4/18
765047	MORGAN, William Hugh	31/10/17	12 (Welch Regt.) Killed in action
764447	MURRAY, Hubert Reginald	29/ 8/17	Prisoner of war 3/10/18
764448	NICHOLAS, Edward Oswell	29/ 8/17	Wounded 22/10/17
765891	OLDHAM, Thomas John Frederick	13/ 3/18	
763622	PARKER, Leslie Roland	27/ 6/17	11 Killed in action 29/9/18
763977	PARRY, William Stanley	29/ 8/17	Wounded 8/5/18
6448	PHILLIPS, Reginald	26/ 9/16	(2) Killed in action 23/4/17
3425	POWELL, Howell John	14/ 4/15	Wounded -/-/16, 25/11/18
766283	POWELL, William	26/ 6/18	[Lieut. R. of O.
767725	ROBERTS, David Richard	3/ 3/19	
765603	ROWLANDS, Edw.	27/11/17	
5714	TAYLOR, George Henry	7/ 7/16	13 Lieut. Wounded 1/5/18
764463	THOMAS, Cyril Raymond	28/ 8/17	11(2) Killed in action 18/8/18
5883	WILLIAMS, Henry William Miles	3/ 5/17	5
764053	WILLIAMS, Kenneth Homfray	26/ 3/18	
765299	WILLIAMS, Thomas John	28/11/17	11
763483	WINDSOR, David Reginald	31/ 7/17	4 Prisoner of war 18/1/18 ⚑

THE ROYAL WARWICKSHIRE REGIMENT. 369

Regular Battalions (Nos. 1 & 2). 6th Foot

		2nd Lieut.	
2007	ALLEN, Norman	26/ 5/15	2(*14*) *Capt. w.* 25/9/15 K/A|
2523	CANNON, Stanley William Wood	11/ 6/15	2 *Lieut. w.* 25/9/15 [14/4/18|
2363	DIEMER, Philip Hilton	11/ 6/15	2 *Lieut. Wounded* 25/9/15
2717	DOWSON, Sydney Houghton	24/ 7/15	1 *Lieut.* ✠ *Wounded* –/7/16
1488	FIGG, Sydney Vavasour	24/ 7/15	1 *Lieut.* ✠ ▨ [3/9/16 ▨|
1424	FORBES, Alec	14/ 2/15	2 *Capt. w.* 18/7/15 *Killed in action*|
1101	HERBAGE, Percy Frederick William	10/12/14	2 *Lieut. Prisoner of war* 25/9/15
1285	MONK, George Bertram	15/12/14	2 *Killed in action* 19/12/14
1080	PEARCE, L/Cpl. Geoffrey Vincent	15/12/14	2 *Died of wounds* 19/12/14
787	STANDRING, Sgt. Benjamin Arthur	15/12/14	2 *Died of wounds* 19/12/14
1722	RAYNER, George Hugh	10/ 7/15	1 *Lieut.*
1836	SHARPE, Charles Barraud	24/ 7/15	1 *Wounded* 23/1/16
1692	WILLIS, Dan Hugh	24/ 7/15	1 *Lieut. Adjt.* 2/Bn. ✠
763118	BENNETT, George Arthur	25/ 6/17	1(6) *Killed in action* 3/12/17
763514	BOWLES, John Hobbs	26/ 4/17	1
765593	HOLLOWAY, Norman Eric	28/ 5/18	(1)
5908	HUDSON, Robert George	24/ 3/17	2
4763	LOWDER, Noel Reginald	27/ 2/17	1 *Killed in action* 3/5/17
5796	PRICE, Cyril Arnold	18/ 3/17	1
764605	SANDERS, Joseph Newbould	27/ 6/17	1(7)
7761	SEARLE, Walter David Westgate	25/ 1/17	2 ▨

Special Reserve Battalions (Nos. 3 & 4).

192	BLACK, 2/Lt. Francis Henry	15/ 8/14	4(*1*) *Capt. Killed in action* 25/4/15
2226	BENNETT, John Hadfield	24/11/14	4 *Lt. w.* 8/7/15 *To Min. of Mun.*
1863	FOX, Harry Gerald	4/11/14	4 *Capt. Adjt.* (2|E.Kent) *w.* 4/6/15
2455	HARWOOD, Arnold William	11/ 6/15	4 *Capt. w.* 18/6/18, 19/8/18 ▨
3320	INCH, Thomas Alfred de Lacy	22/ 5/15	4 *Lieut.* (*M.G.C. Cavalry*)
1864	PAYNE, John Oswald	1/11/14	4(*1*) *Killed in action* 25/4/15
3252	SMITH, William Travers	4/ 5/15	4(2) *Lt.* (*R.E.*) *w.* 21/8/16 *Killed*|
3656	TAVERNER, Eric Sherwood	28/12/15	4 *Lieut.* [*in action* 20/11/17 ▨|
762473	BANCROFT, Philip Lawrence	27/ 6/17	4
6841	BLAIBERG, Harold Ephraim	4/ 9/16	4(*16*) *Wounded* 25/5/17, 1/7/18
765380	BROWN, William Edgar	30/ 1/18	4(*14*)
763149	CLARK, Thomas John Chown	26/ 4/17	4 *Wounded* 24/10/17
766550	COLLINS, George Thomas W.	30/ 5/18	3
6489	EMERSON, George Cuthbert	26/ 9/16	4 *w.* 24/5/17 *To Min. of Labour*
764645	HARWOOD, Alfred Cecil	30/ 5/18	3 *Lieut.*
763951	HARWOOD, Eric Hardy	1/ 8/17	4
760911	KILBORN, William George	30/ 5/17	3

AA

762542	Newsom, Robert Augustus ...	...	26/ 9/17	3 Lieut. Wounded 25/4/18
764380	Preedy, Lawrence Jack ...	...	1/ 8/17	4(1) Killed in action 31/3/18
6120	Pykett, George Frederick ...	...	4/ 9/16	4(6) ✠ 🎗

Territorial Battalions (Nos. 5 to 8).

[🎗(2)]
2/Lt.	Lefroy, Tracy Edward	...	29/10/15	8 Major Killed in action 5/12/17
3829	Class, Herbert Rudolph	...	16/10/15	5 Lieut. (Army Signals) ✠ 🎗
2627	Jackson, Mark Keith	...	31/12/14	6 Lieut. ✠✠ Wounded 21/12/17,
2575	Jermyn, Clyford Henry	...	25/ 2/15	5 Lieut. [13/11/18]
3088	May, Herbert Richard Dudfield	...	21/ 8/15	5 Capt. & Adjt. ✠ w. 10/6/16
3766	Simpkin, Reginald John Henry	...	17/10/15	5 Killed in action 16/7/16
3191	Thorn, Robert Nelson	...	17/10/15	5 Lieut. [action 30/10/17]
3754	Wakeman, Frank Trevor	...	17/10/15	5 (R.F.C.) w –/4/16 Killed in
2525	Walsh, William Edward	...	25/ 2/15	5 Lieut. (R.A.F.)
5234	Benjamin, Horace Sydney ...	...	19/ 6/16	5 Lieut.
5235	Bird, Arthur Leonard	...	19/ 6/16	5 Killed in action 6/9/17
5678	Burr, Percival Bryan	...	19/ 6/16	5 Lieut. Wounded –/9/16
5133	Clegg, William	...	19/ 6/16	5 Capt.
4844	Dawson, Wilfred Leedham ...	...	11/ 7/16	6 Killed in action 3/12/17
4907	Duthie, Donald James	...	26/ 6/16	6 Lieut. ✠ 🎗
5251	Forsyth, James	...	26/ 6/16	6 Lieut. Wounded 26/3/17, 15/9/17
5070	Nicholls, Edward John	...	25/ 6/16	7 Lieut. ✠ 🎗
5265	Lear, Frederick Howard	...	26/ 6/16	6 Lieut.
5136	Reynolds, Harry Norman ...	...	3/ 7/16	7 Capt. ✠✠ F/D
5080	Stephens, Frederick Joseph	...	13/ 6/16	8 Lieut. Wounded 20/12/17
5324	Strang, William	...	25/ 6/16	7 Lieut. (N Lancs.) w. 26/9/18 🎗
5427	Tonks, Albert Edwin	...	13/ 6/16	8 Lieut. Wounded 10/4/18
4292	Vaughan, Edwin Stephen ...	...	19/ 6/16	8 Lieut. ✠ 🎗
5005	Walker, Sidney	...	13/ 6/16	8 Lieut. Wounded 10/4/18
4684	Whiteley, Charles Taylor ...	...	13/ 6/16	8 Lieut. Died of wounds 1/7/18
762796	Beadle, Leslie Arthur	...	21/ 4/17	6 Lieut. F/D
764478	Boullen, Charles Ernest	...	31/ 7/17	6
764286	Brown, Harold Vincent	...	31/ 7/17	8
764924	Carter, Percy	...	24/ 9/17	5
4954	Craig, Alexander George	...	11/ 7/16	6 Lieut. Wounded 17/3/17
765387	Ewels, Charles	...	31/ 7/17	7
765166	Frank, Harold Edwin	...	17/ 6/17	5
766249	Frank, Donald Arthur	...	23/ 5/18	7
4806	Gibbins, Roland Bevington	...	8/ 7/16	8 Capt. Killed in action 4/12/17
763525	Glover, Montague Charles ...	...	24/ 9/17	6 ✠
762413	Martindale, Donald Pugh	...	13/ 5/17	5
764213	Tregaskis, George ...	...	31/ 7/17	8
7098	Walker, Alfred	...	21/12/16	7 Lieut.

Service Battalions (New Armies).

3528	BALL, Frederick Cecil	...	... 12/12/15	*15 Lieut. Wounded* –/7/16
2677	COOPER, Stanley	... ...	... 5/12/15	*11 Wounded* –/8/16
1947	GIVAN, Harry Cook	... ...	... 24/11/14	*12(1) Lieut.*
2151	HARDING, Geoff. Harold	...	... 7/12/14	*13 (E. Lancs.) Wounded* –/4/16
3369	HUGHES, Herbert	... ...	... 5/ 4/15	*12 Lieut.*
1824	JOHNSTON, Edgar John Circuit		... 13/ 7/15	*12 To 5/Essex*
1531	MADDOCKS, John Anslow	...	... 3/10/14	*15 Lieut. Killed in action* 4/6/16
2352	McNAIR, William Lennox	...	... 7/12/14	*12 Capt. (2/Hants) w.* 9/6/15
1360	MOSSE, Phillip Godfrey	...	... 6/12/14	*13 (E. Lancs.) Killed in action*⎱
				[18/4/16⎰
2111	PAGE, William Ivan Gregory		... 7/12/14	*13 Capt. Rifle Brigade* ⚔
2572	REACHER, Stanley William	...	... 10/ 2/15	*11 Capt. To* 16/R.Bde. *Died of*⎱
2445	ROGERS, Clive Woods	...	... 25/ 3/15	*12 w.* –/4/16 [*wounds* 4/7/16⎰
1878	SUMMERFIELD, Gerald	...	... 15/ 2/15	*12 Lieut. Wounded* 6/6/18
2571	VOKINS, Kean Esse ...	...	... 5/12/15	*11 Killed in action* 10/7/16
5143	WARD, Norman John	...	... 25/ 5/16	*11 Killed in action* 11/8/16
2731	WATTS, Lawrence David	...	... 22/ 6/15	*12 Lieut. (Inniskgs.) w.* –/7/16
2444	WILLIAMS, Donald Mathew	...	... 20/ 3/15	*12(9) Killed in action* 9/4/16
3527	WILTON, Ralph Antrobus	...	... 12/12/15	*15* ✠ ✠
766628	ABBOTT, Norman	... ...	... 18/ 6/18	(2)
767739	BARKER, Bertram John	...	... 5/ 3/19	
5009	BERNARD, Andrew Joseph	...	... 12/11/16	*10 Lieut.*
764128	BOLWELL, Harold Cecil	...	... 30/ 5/17	(2)
766421	BRASSINGTON, Basil Edward		... 13/11/18	
7105	BUSHNELL, Charles Francis	...	... 22/11/16	*(8) Lieut.*
768294	CLEMMINGS, John Robert	...	... 18/ 3/19	
6566	CLINCKETT, Joseph Edwin	...	... 5/ 9/16	*14(2) Wounded* 22/10/17
763844	CULLEN, Percival Harold	...	... 28/11/17	(2)
760818	DURUTY, Charles Eric	...	... 18/ 3/19	*10* ✠
760729	EDINGER, Valentine ...	...	... 12/ 1/18	*(4) Killed in action* 23/8/18
5839	ELTHAM, Gordon	... ...	... 26/ 9/16	*(2) Lieut. w. & P/W* 26/2/17
761563	FARRIMOND, William	...	... 26/ 6/17	*15* ✠ ⚔
764195	FORRER, Leonard	... ...	... 27/ 6/17	*(2) Lieut. Wounded* 30/3/18
3626	FOWLE, Henry Albert	...	... 18/ 3/17	*15*
5902	FROST, William Edgar	...	... 24/ 3/16	*7*
766597	GATHERCOLE, Edgar Harry	...	... 3/ 2/19	
762615	GEORGE, Alan Lee ...	...	... 2/ 8/17	*15 Died of wounds* 14/4/18
5405	GOODCHILD, Samuel Thomas		... 19/12/16	*(2) Lieut.*
763615	GREW, Walter Ernest	...	... 26/ 4/17	*16 Killed in action* 7/10/17
763330	GRIFFITHS, William Henry	...	... 1/ 3/17	*16* ✠
5758	GULLY, Sydney	... ...	... 18/ 3/17	*15*
765393	HARCOURT, George Edwin	...	... 1/ 8/17	
7562	HARPER, Herbert	... ...	... 19/12/16	
6361	HOPLEY, William Arnold	...	... 26/ 9/16	(2) ✠
769208	JACKSON, Charles Edward	...	... 15/ 2/19	

767701	JONES, John Dudley Winston	...	3/ 3/19	
1176	LONG, Edward Bradfield ...	...	18/ 3/17	15 Wounded 9/4/17
3424	MANN, Cyril Charles	...	7/11/16	10 Lieut.
761576	MOORE, George Alexander ...	...	18/ 8/17	11 Killed in action 2/5/18
761553	MORRALL, John Bernard	...	3/ 8/17	10
767987	MOUSLEY, Norman Leslie	...	17/ 3/19	
6159	MURCH, Alfred Henry	...	1/ 5/17	11 ✠ Wounded 3/5/18, 5/11/18
3140	O'NEILL, Douglas Quirk	...	7/11/16	10 Killed in action 26/4/18
766259	OSBORNE, Harold William Shardlow		28/ 5/18	
6815	PEERS, Victor Albert	...	5/ 9/16	16 Lieut.
767645	RICHARDS, William Henry	...	3/ 3/19	
5031	ROCHFORD, John Robert	...	18/ 3/17	10 Capt. ✠
760515	ROLLES, Nathaniel ...	...	18/ 8/17	11 Wounded 7/6/18 ✠
5140	ROOKS, Frank Odey ...	...	18/ 3/17	10
764170	SEARLE, Robert Spencer	...	1/ 8/17	Wounded 16/4/18
6569	SMITH, Percy Landon	...	1/ 5/17	11 Lieut. ✠
3082	STONE, William Herbert	...	1/ 8/16	16 Capt. ✠ Wounded 12/7/18
760247	STREATER, John Wenlan	...	26/ 6/17	15 Died of wounds 22/7/18
7051	STUBBS, George Percival	...	1/ 5/17	11 Wounded 8/4/18
768079	THOMPSON, Alexander Ralph	...	17/ 3/19	
3060	TREADWAY, Harold Ligonier	...	7/11/16	15 Killed in action 9/5/17
761489	TRICKETT, John Madford	...	26/ 6/17	15 Wounded 8/11/17
5358	WHITTLES, Edward Derrick	...	5/ 9/16	From R.A.F.
6664	WILLIAMS, Thomas Stanley ...	...	26/ 9/16	16 Lieut.
767670	WILLIS, Alfred Elliott	...	4/ 3/19	
5763	WYNNE, Robert Bagshaw	...	1/ 5/17	11 Wounded 27/5/18 ℞

THE ROYAL WELCH FUSILIERS.

Regular Battalions (Nos. 1 & 2).

23rd Foot

			2nd Lieut.	[of wounds 27/2/17
3000	ADAMS, John Bernard Pye ...	...	16/12/14	1 Capt. Wounded -/6/16 Died }
1236	BARTON, Guy Stanley	...	1/ 1/15	1 Lieut. ✠ Wounded 17/5/15 ℞
1765	FARMER, Horace Edwin	...	11/ 6/15	1 Lieut. Wounded 25/9/15
1255	HIGGINSON, John Victor	...	1/ 1/15	2 Capt. ✠ w. 26/6/15, -/7/16 ℞
954	JONES, Cpl. Leonard	...	15/12/14	1 Killed in action 16/5/15
912	MOODY, Percy	...	1/ 1/15	2 Capt. ✠✠ w. 20/7/16 ℞(2)
885	OWEN, John Morris ...	...	1/ 1/15	2 Capt. w. -/2/16 K/A 23/4/17
608	PARKES, L/Cpl. Horace Frederick ...		15/12/14	1 Killed in action 12/3/15 ℞
1429	REES, L/Cpl. John Trevor ...	...	14/11/14	1 Killed in action 22/1/15
1855	RICHARDS, L/Cpl. Wilfred Arthur	...	11/ 6/15	1 Lieut. (York & Lancs.)
1934	WINTERS, L/Cpl. Jesse Williams	...	15/12/14	1 Major (Tank Corps)

Special Reserve Battalion (No. 3).

762822	AINGE, David Alfred Lloyd...	26/ 9/17	3 ✠
762823	ALLEN, George William Leslie	26/ 9/17	3
5038	ALLISON, Harry	8/ 7/16	3(1) *Killed in action* 27/8/18
6234	ROWLAND, Theodore ...	5/ 9/16	3(11) *Lieut.*
5975	WEBB, Hugh Victor Corthorn	8/ 7/16	3(2/G.B.) *Lieut.*
764054	WOOD, Norman John ...	27/ 6/17	3(13) *Wounded* 27/11/17

Territorial Battalions (Nos. 4 to 7).

3612	SILCOCK, Bertram Baber ...	11/ 6/15	7 *Killed in action* 10/8/15 ✠
3871	BLAIBERG, Alfred M. ...	26/10/15	7 *Lieut. Wounded* 22/11/17
3755	BROWN, Herbert James ...	26/10/15	7 *Lieut. Killed in action* 6/11/17
3862	CRAPPER, Charles	5/10/15	4 *Lieut. Empld. Recruiting Duties*
3416	GUTTERIDGE, Cpl. George William ...	5/10/15	4 *Lieut. Empld. P/W Company*
3956	MORRIS, Tom Bernard ...	30/11/15	5
3934	NICHOLLS, Eric Harry R. ...	30/11/15	5 *Lieut.*
3072	PECKOVER, Joseph Edmund	30/11/15	5 *Lieut.*
3411	PITTARD, Robert Sampson R. ...	5/10/15	4 *Lieut. Prisoner of war* 19/6/18
3097	PYM-MANNOCK, Francis Louis A. ...	12/10/15	6
3737	RICHARDSON, L/Cpl. Alan ...	5/10/15	4 *Lieut.*
3794	SARTIN, George Edward ...	26/10/15	7 *Lieut.*
2711	TASKER, Richard	5/10/15	4 *Lieut.* (*M.G.C.*)
3457	VALIANT, James	26/10/15	7 *Lieut. Died of wounds* 28/10/17
3917	WEBB, L/Cpl. Edward Charles Henry	30/11/15	5 *Lieut.*
3785	WYATT, Charles Percival ...	30/ 7/15	(4) *Capt.* (*Norfolk Yeomanry*)
4527	BILLHAM, Frank Denis ...	15/ 6/16	6(14) *Lieut.*
5611	CLARK, Albert Norman ...	19/ 6/16	4 *Lieut. Wounded* 25/6/15
5169	DAVIES, Harry	17/ 6/16	6 (*S.W.B.*) *P/W* 27/6/18 ✠
5684	EVANS, Robert Rowlands ...	14/ 6/16	6 *Lieut.*
4876	EVANS, William Henry ...	17/ 6/16	6 *Lieut. Wounded* 13/8/17
5694	HAWKINS, James	19/ 6/16	4 *Lieut.*
5123	HOLLAND, Henry ...	19/ 6/16	6 *Lieut. Wounded* 15/10/18
5657	JONES, Alan	19/ 6/16	4 *Lieut.*
4995	JURY, Reginald Allen ...	22/ 6/16	4 *Lieut. w.* 13/8/17 (*S.W.B.*)
4996	LANCASTER, John Hubert Leonard...	19/ 6/16	4 *Lieut.* [*Min. of Labour*]
4880	LEWIS, Cpl. Oliver Burns ...	19/ 6/16	4 *Lieut.* ✠
4852	NEVILLE, Hubert Morgan ...	19/ 6/16	4 *Lieut.*
5709	OWEN, Charles Herbert ...	17/ 6/16	4 *Lieut. Wounded* 10/3/17
4538	TIPPETTS, James Berriman	19/ 6/16	4(9)
5387	WELSH, Alexander Thorburn	14/ 6/16	4 *Killed in action* 3/5/17
4946	WOOLVERIDGE, Charles Lionel	17/ 6/16	4 *Lieut.* (*Min. of Lab.*) *w.* 4/12/17 ✠
767492	BOWEN, Henry Trevor ...	6/ 2/19	7
761618	EDWARDS, Arthur Edward ...	19/ 4/17	4
766277	EDWARDS, William Thomas	24/ 5/18	4 *Wounded* 7/10/18

6976	EMLYN, Oswald Ambrose	...	... 11/ 7/16	5 Lieut.
5751	EVANS, Cerdyn	... ...	... 11/ 7/16	4 Lieut.
763659	GRIFFITH, Gwilyn Wynne	...	... 26/ 4/17	6 Wounded 10/5/18
6383	HOWE, Claude Arthur	...	... 11/ 7/16	4 Capt. Killed in action 20/11/17
6871	HUGHES, Walter Owen	...	... 11/ 7/16	6 Wounded 13/8/17
5446	JONES, Herbert Newton	...	... 5/ 9/16	4 Lieut. 🎖
766717	JONES, Peter Lewis ...	...	... 4/ 3/19	4
6408	POZZI, Frederick William	...	... 11/ 7/16	6 Wounded 5/1/18, 10/5/18
6412	SHAW, Bernard Lynton	...	... 11/ 7/16	4 Lieut. (S.W.B.) Killed in action ⎱
766291	THOMAS, Rowland ...	...	... 24/ 4/18	4 [23/4/17] ⎰
5558	TURNER, Henry James	...	... 25/ 7/16	4 Lieut.
763284	WILSON, Reuben John	...	... 26/ 4/17	6
763743	WRIGHT, Arthur Aubrey	...	... 30/ 5/17	5

Service Battalions (New Armies).

1618	BROOKS, Douglas Cecil Jack		... 20/ 3/15	12 To 9 ✠ 🎖
1721	HOWARD, Esmé Hume	...	... 1/ 1/15	12 Capt. Adjt. [25/10/18]
2202	EVANS, Thomas Evandes	...	... 28/ 1/15	11 Lieut. ✠ ✠ w.–/11/16, 5/6/17,⎦
1642	JONES, Sgt. George Legh	...	... 4/11/14	11 Lieut. To M.M.G.S.
5276	PALMER, Percy Reginald	...	... 25/ 5/16	12 Lieut. ✠ Wounded –/1/17
764922	BELL, Thomas William	...	15/ 7/17	3/Garrison Bn.
761587	BOWEN, Ivan Gwilyn Jones ...		3/ 8/17	14 Lieut.
761588	BUCK, Norman Anwye	...	24/ 6/17	9 Wounded 5/10/17
763321	CASSELL, Herbert Ernest	...	12/ 5/17	3/Garrison Bn.
765437	COOMBES, Philip John	...	18/12/17	1/ ,, ,,
763490	COOP, Herbert Haigh	...	16/ 6/17	3/ ,, ,,
761055	DAVIES, Henry Rees	...	27/ 6/17	9
5650	DAVIES, William Lloyd	...	7/ 7/16	13 Killed in action 31/7/17
767665	DODD, Kenneth Hugh	...	4/ 3/19	
6184	EDWARDS, William Howell ...		7/ 7/16	18 Lieut. ✠ w. 23/4/18 🎖
762449	EDWARDS, Wilfred Bythell ...		30/ 5/17	
766943	EVANS, Hugh Richmond	...	4/• 2/19	
6905	EVANS, Vincent Howard	...	20/12/16	9 Wounded 21/6/17
5997	FOULKES-JONES, George Gwylyn		5/ 9/16	Lieut.
764826	FOUNTAINE, Arthur Clifford	...	13/ 5/17	3/Garrison Bn.
765211	GIBSON, Wilfred Wymers	...	16/ 6/17	3/ ,, ,,
763928	GRANT, Alexander ...		13/ 5/17	3/ ,, ,,
763616	HARPER, John Raymond	...	29/ 5/18	
3345	HARPER, Stanley William	...	19/12/16	Lieut.
763748	HARTNUP, Frank Valentine ...		16/ 6/17	3/Garrison Bn.
768297	HARVEY, Wilfred Roy		3/ 2/19	
767298	HAZELDEN, William Alfred ...		6/ 2/19	
7288	HEATLEY, Charles Frederick		19/12/16	16 Died of wounds 17/4/18
762898	HINE, Arthur John ...	...	12/ 5/17	3/Garrison Bn.
762484	HUGHES-DAVIES, Hugh Evan		29/ 5/17	3/ ,, ,,

767952	HUMPHRIES, George Rayner	5/ 3/19		
5853	JOHN, Arthur Stanley	7/ 7/16	18 Lieut.	Wounded 14/9/18
766758	JONES, James Powell	29/10/18		
7388	JONES, Clifford	22/11/16	15 Killed in action 1/8/17	
763587	KEARTON, Arthur Stanley	24/12/17	3/Garrison Bn.	
6805	KILVERT, Harry	26/ 9/16	9 Died of wounds 1/8/17	
764247	LAWRENCE, John Narbeth	1/ 8/17	Wounded 17/9/18	
7290	LEEK, Philip Arthur	19/12/16	Lieut.	
760997	LEWIS, John Philip	3/ 8/17		
762997	LEWIS, Thomas William	29/ 3/17	(1) Died of wounds 27/10/17	
767972	LEWIS, Eric Fuller	6/ 3/19		
767973	LEWIS, Tudor Fuller	6/ 3/19		
764034	LLEWELLYN, Vivian	27/ 6/17	14 Killed in action 3/11/18	
5516	LLOYD, Charles Trevor J.	7/ 7/16	18 Lieut.	
6422	MARTIN, William Howard	5/ 9/16	13 Killed in action 31/7/17	
764709	McDONOGH, Bertram Morgan	26/ 9/17	3/Garrison Bn.	
763205	MILLS, Basil Rupert	13/ 5/17	3/ ,, ,,	
5784	MILLS, Joseph Evan	7/ 7/16	18 Lieut. Wounded 2/7/17	
763679	MOORE, Malcolm Brockholes Harvey	19/ 8/17	3/Garrison Bn. w. 24/9/18	
763206	NATHAN, Maurice	17/ 6/17	3/ ,, ,,	
765280	NAYLOR, Thomas	17/ 7/17	3/ ,, ,,	
5523	NEAL, Charles Thomas David	5/ 1/17	16 Wounded 13/8/17	
764547	NIELD, Harold Mercer	16/ 6/17		
765282	OWEN, Henry James	28/11/17	16 Killed in action 24/8/18	
765243	OWEN, Hugh Wynn	3/ 2/19		
764538	PEARSON, Benjamin James	17/ 6/17	3/Garrison Bn.	
763075	PHILLIPS, Harry Croxford	15/ 4/17	3/ ,, ,,	
763368	PHILLIPS, John Reginald	1/ 3/17	Wounded 7/9/18	
762910	PIETERSON, Eric Sydney	16/12/17	3/Garrison Bn.	
763717	RALPH, John Leslie	1/ 8/17	✠	
764342	RAVENSCROFT, George Eaton	3/ 5/17	3/Garrison Bn.	
6330	REES, David Wyan	5/ 9/16	Lieut.	
4681	SAVOURS, Edgar Walter	27/ 1/17	Lieut. From R.F.C.	
7161	SCOURFIELD, David Perry	19/12/16	16 Lieut.	
768033	SIMS, Bertram Worman	17/ 3/19		
768034	SMITH, Alfred Wilkins	17/ 3/19		
763705	SMITH, Campbell	16/ 6/17	3/Garrison Bn.	
760730	SNEDDON, James	29/ 3/17	(2) Wounded 25/7/18	
7307	SYRETT, Alfred Montague	22/11/16	(1) Killed in action 4/5/17	
768932	TALBOT, Sidney Garson	13/ 2/19		
7018	TARDUGNO, L/Cpl. Roy	7/11/16	17 (R.F.C.) Killed in action 7/7/17	
761061	THOMAS, L/Cpl. Edward Trevor	27/ 6/17	10 Lieut. Wounded 28/6/18	
767651	THOMAS, Idris George	3/ 3/19		
6085	THOMAS, Tudor	5/ 9/16	19 Killed in action 25/11/17	
763478	THOMAS, Walter	17/ 6/17	3/Garrison Bn.	
767040	TOUT, Harold Stanley	23/ 6/17	3/ ,, ,,	
764588	WAINWRIGHT, Newbold Scott	17/ 6/18	3/ ,, ,,	

ROYAL WELCH FUSILIERS (S/B).

765257	WALTER, Rowland Kitchener	17/ 6/17	3/Garrison Bn.
761917	WATSON, Harry Townsend ...	17/ 6/17	3/ ,, ,,
764735	WEBB, Robert	17/ 6/17	3/ ,, ,,
767073	WILLIAMS, Basil Mewburn ...	4/ 2/19	
767700	WILLIAMS, Meyrick Richard	3/ 3/19	
763016	WILLIAMS, Robert Samuel ...	17/ 6/17	3/Garrison Bn.
6332	WILLIAMS, William James ...	19/12/16	16 ✠ *Killed in action* 19/9/17
765204	WING, Edgar Bruce ...	17/ 6/17	3/Garrison Bn.

THE WELCH REGIMENT.

Regular Battalions (Nos. 1 & 2).   {41st Foot / 69th Foot}

		2nd Lieut.	
1041	BAGGALLAY, Geoffrey Thomas	9/ 5/15	*1(2) Capt. To M.M.G.S. w.* 24/5/15, 25/9/15 *Assassinated in Dublin* 22/11/20 *A.P.M.*
1778	LOTT, Francis Albert	26/ 5/15	*1 Capt.* ✠
945	LUNN, Percy Reginald	9/ 5/15	*1 Capt. w.* 24/5/15 *Missing—*/7/16
1804	MILES, Alfred Crosfield Vernon	23/ 4/15	*2 Killed in action* 24/8/15
1386	MONRO, Harry	9/ 5/15	*1 Lieut. w. (Missing)* 24/5/15
2262	PULLEN, Frank John	26/ 5/15	*1 Lieut. Wounded* 24/8/15
765013	DAVIES, Haydn Prosser	31/10/17	*1*
764928	JONES, George Miller	31/10/17	*1*
7163	SUTTON, William Henry	19/12/16	*2 Lieut. Killed in action* 23/10/18

Special Reserve Battalion (No. 3.)

64058	DAVIES, Thomas John McLeod	27/ 6/17	*3(15)*
764822	DAVIES, William	24/ 9/17	*3 Wounded* 4/4/18
766071	HARRIES, William Thomas ...	27/ 3/18	*3 Wounded* 15/11/18

Territorial Battalions (Nos. 4 to 7).

1704	BROWN, Ulick	2/ 9/14	*6 Capt.*
1502	CARTER, Sgt. Arthur Charles	24/12/14	*6 Lieut. Officer Cadet Bn.*
3109	FOSTER, Arthur Edward	14/ 5/15	*5 Lieut.*
1000	MORRIS, John Ernest	1/12/14	*5 Capt. Adjt.*
3078	ST. QUINTIN, Richard Guy	23/ 6/15	*5 Lieut.*
3575	BENNETT, John Henry	2/12/15	*5 Lieut.*
2974	FILSELL, Gordon Vincent P.	2/12/15	*5 Lieut.*

3838	Frankenstein, Oscar Reginald	...	2/12/15	5 *Killed in action* 26/3/17
3779	Lewis, Francis Attwater	...	21/11/15	5 *Lieut.* ✠ ℳ
3061	Moore, Arthur James	...	2/12/15	5 *Capt.*
5376	Oswald, Harold Robert	...	28/ 6/16	4 *Lieut.* ✠
5030	Robinson, Francis Walter	...	28/ 6/16	4 *Lieut.* ℳ [*action* 20/9/17]
4070	Thomas, Lionel G. Theophilus	...	17/ 1/16	4 *Lieut.* (*M.G.C.*) *Killed in*
4859	Vernon, Cyril Harker	...	27/ 6/16	4 *Lieut.* ✠ ℳ
3077	Woods, Walter Antrobus	...	2/12/15	5 *Lieut.*
6531	Davies, Thomas Talvin	...	26/ 9/16	4 ✠ *Wounded* 8/12/17 ℳ
763655	Dodd, William	...	30/ 5/17	4
5651	Earl, Cyril Courtney	...	11/ 7/16	5 *Lieut. Wounded* 18/3/18
8035	Evans, David Morgan	...	20/12/16	4 *Lieut*
5056	Furmston, Charles William	...	26/ 9/16	4 *Wounded* 13/8/17
5653	Gibson, Reginald J. Campbell	...	23/11/16	4 *Wounded* 1/9/17
5951	Hallam, Henry James Brunsdon	...	5/ 9/16	4 *Lieut.*
6648	Harrington, Walter	...	5/ 9/16	5 *Killed in action* 21/6/17
5765	Jones, Edward Miles	...	26/ 9/16	4 *Wounded* 8/3/18
5273	Mathias, Ernest Jones	...	11/ 7/16	6 *Lieut.*
6174	Morris, Wain Gwyn	...	11/ 7/16	6 *Wounded* 21/3/18
763169	Raynes, Harold Bertram	...	27/ 3/17	4
5800	Robinson, William	...	26/ 9/16	4 *Wounded* 4/10/17
6730	Silk, Evan	...	26/ 9/16	4 ℳ
763682	Thomas, Lewis John	...	27/ 6/17	4 *Wounded* 20/9/18 ✠
6890	Twomey, George William	...	23/11/16	4 *Lieut.* (*M.G.C.*)
5606	Walters, John David	...	26/ 9/16	4 *Lieut.*
766094	Williams, Charles Harold	...	24/ 5/18	4 *Wounded* 12/10/18
5672	Wright, Sidney Matthew	...	5/ 9/16	4 *Lieut.*

Service Battalions (New Armies).

1352	Hedgcock, Stuart Edwin	...	9/10/14	8 *Capt. Staff*
1782	Hedgcock, Sydney Douglas	...	29/ 9/15	12 *Lieut.*
3234	Lloyd, Hamilton Samuel John	...	4/ 4/15	15 *Lieut. To M.M.G.S.*
2476	Meggitt, Arthur	...	12/ 1/15	16 *Capt.*
2477	Thomas, David Edwardes Jones	...	8/12/14	16 *Capt. To* 18/*Bn.*
7599	Augustus, Walter	...	19/12/16	*Lieut.*
7600	Bailey, Hubert Percy Andrew	...	19/12/16	17 *Killed in action* 24/11/17
765926	Cook, George Audrey	...	13/ 3/18	
762879	Davies, Herbert Claude	...	30/ 5/17	
762117	Davies, Trevor	...	28/ 3/17	*Wounded* 8/12/17
765584	Duckworth, Walter Clarence	...	28/11/17	(1/*Shrops. L.I.*) *K/A* 8/10/18
764640	Evans, Hugh Robert	...	24/ 9/17	18(9) *Killed in action* 19/9/18
767319	Evans, Jenkin Evan	...	4/ 3/19	
766473	Griffiths, Herbert Owen	...	26/ 6/18	

WELCH REGIMENT (S/B).

7994	HORN, Cyril Rowland	...	19/12/16	Lieut.
766138	JONES, Arthur Reginald	...	26/ 6/18	
763789	JONES, Llewellyn Price	...	26/ 4/17	3(9) Died of wounds 20/9/17
7983	LAUDERDALE, Thomas Maitland	...	19/12/16	Lieut.
8100	LORT, Roland Gilbert	...	19/12/16	Wounded –/5/17
764782	MARSHALL, Charles May	...	31/10/17	14
766929	MARTIN, Ernest Lambert	...	3/ 2/19	
763621	MORGAN, George Ernest	...	26/ 4/17	15 Wounded 13/12/17
764842	OWEN, Rees Osborn	...	24/ 9/17	Lieut. Prisoner of war 9/4/18
5531	PICTON, Clement John	...	5/ 9/16	Lieut.
768090	PROTHEROE, Percy Edward	...	17/ 3/19	
5283	REES, L/Cpl. R. Francesque Watkins		7/ 7/16	Lieut.
768259	ROBERTS, Robert Owen	...	14/ 2/19	
767846	SHADDICK, Hector Ernest	...	3/ 3/19	
768493	THOMAS, Thomas Price	...	12/ 2/19	
767839	TOWERS, Gilbert Leslie	...	3/ 3/19	
7849	WESSELL, William Master	...	19/12/16	Lieut.
763251	WILLIAMS, Arthur Jones	...	1/ 3/17	(4) Killed in action 3/11/17
763355	WOODHOUSE Christopher	...	26/ 9/17	18

*THE WEST RIDING REGIMENT
(THE DUKE OF WELLINGTON'S).

Regular Battalions (Nos. 1 & 2).   {33rd Foot / 76th Foot}

			2nd Lieut.	
3827	BROOKE, Jos. Aspinall Linton	...	7/11/15	2 Lieut. Wounded 1/7/16
1284	LAMBERT, Philip Felix	...	15/ 8/15	2 Lieut. ✠ w. –/11/16 Killed in
1345	WHITAKER, Bernard Joseph G.	...	9/ 5/15	2 Lieut. [action 5/5/17
6894	CROWTHER, Colin Campbell		1/ 4/17	2
763064	HATTERSLEY, George	...	29/ 3/17	(7)
763339	McDOWALL, Robert Allister	...	1/ 3/17	2 Lieut. Wounded 13/4/18 ℳ

Special Reserve Battalion (No. 3).

7461	COATES, Percy Harold	...	19/12/16	Lieut. Wounded 18/4/17
763393	HESKETT, John	...	29/ 3/17	(2) Killed in action 15/4/18
763081	SMITH, Gordon Richard	...	29/ 3/17	(2) Lieut. ✠ Wounded 1/8/18

* Title changed (1st January, 1921) to "The Duke of Wellington's Regiment (West Riding)."

Territorial Battalions (Nos. 4 to 7).

3796	ALLWOOD, Charles	...	2/ 1/16	6 *From* 4/*Norfolk*
1194	HAZEL, Dudley David Fraser	...	7/ 2/15	6 *Lieut. Died of wounds* 25/4/17
1100	STALMAN, Cpl. Alfred Claude	...	2/10/15	6 *Lieut.* ✠ *Wounded* 13/4/18
763447	BUCKLEY, Jock	...	30/ 5/17	6 *Wounded* 27/9/17
5168	CROCKER, Joseph ...	...	14/ 7/16	5 *Lieut. Killed in action* 19/9/17
764543	FITCH, Sidney Albert	...	28/ 8/17	6
762996	KENYON, Robert ...	...	24/ 9/17	4
5266	LEES, Harold Wilfred	...	11/ 7/16	5 *Lieut.*
5413	MACKIE, William Gordon	..	11/ 7/16	5 *Lieut.* ✠
6158	MALLALIEU, Joseph ...	...	5/ 9/16	6(7) *Died of wounds* 6/11/17
6187	MARLOR, Eric ...	...	26/ 9/16	6 *Lieut. Killed in action* 3/5/17
766060	READING, Sydney John	...	23/ 5/18	4 *Wounded* 5/11/18
763799	SIEMSSEN, Gordon Hermann	...	28/ 8/17	4 *Wounded* 15/5/18
763629	THORNTON, Harry ...	...	26/ 4/17	7
764734	WARD, Raymond ...	...	24/ 9/17	5
5974	WATKINSON, James Guy Blakeley	...	26/ 9/16	4 *Lieut.*
764357	WAY, George Charles	...	31/ 7/17	7 *Wounded* 18/5/18

Service Battalions (New Armies).

3115	CULLING, Harold William ...	...	28/11/15	9 *Killed in action* 7/7/16
2204	DANIELS, Douglas William Leslie	...	29/ 9/14	11 *Capt.* (*Lab.Corps*) *w.* 27/10/15
1793	MATTHEW, Archibald James	...	14/10/14	11 *Major Egyptian Army*
6350	MILFORD, Charles Archibald	...	12/ 6/16	*Lieut.*
7240	AINLEY, Wm. Henry Sykes ...	...	19/12/16	8 *Lieut. Wounded* 21/8/17
769090	CRABTREE, Jabez ...	...	5/ 2/19	
763187	DALBY, Bernard Cyril	...	1/ 3/17	8 *Lieut.*
763947	EDEN, Walter George	...	26/ 9/17	
763950	HARDWICK, Duncan ...	...	25/ 9/17	*Wounded* 24/4/18
6576	HICKS, John Sykes ...	...	19/12/16	8 *Lieut.*
6583	HOBSON, James Edward	.	19/12/16	8 *Lieut.*
764404	MORRISON, James ...	...	1/ 8/17	
768354	PLANT, Harold Mitchell	...	17/ 3/19	
6719	RHODES, William ...	...	26/ 9/16	9 *Lieut.*
6124	ROCH-AUSTIN, Sidney Leslie	...	5/ 9/16	(4) *Died of wounds* 4/11/18
766397	ROGERS, Leonard Edwin	...	26/ 6/18	(M.G.C.)
768326	SEARLE, Francis Herbert	...	17/ 3/19	
766088	SKINNER, Walter Willis	...	14/ 2/19	
762813	SPAFFORD, Arnold Victor	...	29/ 3/17	(7) *Lieut.* ✠ *Wounded* -/12/17 ℞
763801	STANSBURY, William Burghard	...	24/ 9/17	
764123	THOMAS, Percival Victor	...	31/ 7/17	
766667	WEBB, George Herbert	...	4/ 2/19	
762942	WHITE, Frederick Seymour ...	...	29/ 3/17	*Wounded* 22/10/17

THE WILTSHIRE REGIMENT
(THE DUKE OF EDINBURGH'S).

Regular Battalions (Nos. 1 & 2).   {62nd Foot / 99th Foot}

2nd Lieut.

502	BONE, Frederick Howard	...	...	3/ 3/15	2 *Capt.* ✠ *Wounded* 16/4/18
1823	CARDEN, Ronald Hugh	...	...	15/12/14	2 *Killed in action* 11/3/15
1120	CROWDY, Ronald St. John	...	...	27/ 1/15	1 *Capt. To M.G.C. A.P.M.*
1317	FRIEND, Frank Howard	...	...	3/ 3/15	2 *Lieut. Died of wounds* 29/5/15 ℍ
1138	KITCAT, Alfred James	...	...	15/12/14	2 *Lieut. Wounded* 12/3/15, 10/5/15
2543	MAVBROOK, Walter Richard	...	...	24/ 7/15	1 *Killed in action* 24/4/16
3151	ROSS, William John Edward	...	...	24/10/15	1 *Lieut. Wounded* –/5/16, –/7/16
1536	SHEPHERD, Walter Scott	...	...	15/12/14	2 *Major* ✠ F/D ℍ [12/11/18 ℍ]
2665	STOODLEY, Percy Ballard	...	...	12/12/14	*Died* 9/11/16
1725	STRAWSON, Frank M.	...	...	15/12/14	2 *Lieut. Wounded* 1/9/16
2579	TERRY, Sidney Frederic	...	...	24/ 7/15	1 *Capt. & Adjt.* ✠ *w.* –/7/16
6378	BOLDERO, Laurence John Gale	...	...	1/ 5/17	2 [*Killed in action* 24/3/18]
5834	BOWEN, Vivian Alexander Percy	...	...	1/ 5/17	3 *Wounded* 20/9/17
761179	CHANDLER, Archibald Henry	...	...	1/ 5/17	2 *Prisoner of war* 14/6/18
3584	ILLINGWORTH, John Richardson	...	...	19/ 9/16	1 *Lieut.*

Special Reserve Battalion (No. 3).

4890	CLAYTON, Arthur Oliver	...	...	2/ 6/16	3(2) *Capt. Killed in action* 21/3/18
6906	FALK, Cecil Joseph	...	...	5/ 9/16	3 *Capt.* ✠ [ℍ]
762291	MACQUEEN, John Frederick Frank	...	26/ 4/17	3	
6025	RANDALL, William Hubert	...	...	8/ 7/16	3 *Lieut. Wounded* 9/4/17

Service Battalions (New Armies).

3128	BOVET, Verner Charles Aloys	...	12/ 7/15	8 *To Staff*	
3391	RUSHTON, Frank Gregson	...	12/ 5/15	8 (*T.M.B.*) *Killed in action* 1/7/16	
3147	WHITE, Cresswell FitzHerbert T.	...	22/ 3/15	6 *Lieut.*	
763088	ANWYL, Richard John	...	...	26/ 4/17	*Lieut.*
7892	BAKER, Wm. John Winfield	...	...	19/12/16	*Wounded* 17/6/18
769125	BRIDELL, Leonard Thomas	...	...	15/ 2/19	
766588	BROWN, Louis Sydney	.	...	10/ 9/18	
7572	CAMPKIN, Dudley Jas.	...	...	19/12/16	*Lieut. Wounded* 6/4/17, 6/11/18
766223	DAVIES, David Harold	..	...	27/ 3/18	(1) *D/W while P/W* 17/11/18
8190	DEHN, Thomas George Rudolph	...	19/12/16	(2/*Berks*) *D/W* 19/4/17	
766224	DOWSON, Stanlet Thompson	...	...	26/ 3/18	*Prisoner of war* 29/8/18
7228	FRIEND, Charles Percy	...	...	19/12/16	6 *Wounded* 8/4/18 ✠
767636	JONES, Alfred Gwyn	...	...	3/ 3/19	
762982	MASKELL, Henry Percy	...	...	29/ 3/17	✠
767621	MILTON, Stanley Farrier	...	...	3/ 3/19	
5920	NATHAN, Charles	...	...	5/ 9/16	*Lieut.*
7715	PORTER, Sydney	...	...	19/12/16	*Lieut.*
5969	TUCKER, William Leighton	...	...	26/ 9/16	*Lieut.*
6830	TYLDESLEY, Frank	...	...	5/ 9/16	*Lieut.*

THE WORCESTERSHIRE REGIMENT. 381

Regular Battalions (Nos. 1, 2, 3 & 4). {29th Foot / 36th Foot}

			2nd Lieut.	
769	BARFOOT, Sgt. George Allan	...	3/ 3/15	3 *Killed in action* 20/6/15
1239	BARKER, Roland Francis	...	1/ 1/15	2 Capt. ✠ *w.* 26/9/15, 10/5/18
1253	BENNETT, Eugené Paul	...	1/ 1/15	2 Capt. **V.C.** ✠ *Wounded* –|11/16, [30/10/18 ⚔]
1481	BENINGFIELD, Maurice Victor	...	14/ 2/15	1 *Killed in action* 10/3/15
1463	BIRTLES, Roland Powell	...	3/ 3/15	1 Capt. *Killed in action* 4/3/17 ⚔
1478	COURTAULD, Stephen Lewis	...	3/ 3/15	1 Capt. ✠
2886	DORMAN, Richard Brooke	...	15/ 8/15	1 Capt.
2473	FALKNER-LEE, L/Cpl. Frank	...	26/ 5/15	1 Lieut. *Wounded* 13/6/15
1293	GOTCH, Duncan Hepburn	...	1/ 1/15	1 *Killed in action* 11/3/15
896	HALLWARD, Kenneth Leslie	...	3/ 3/15	3 Lieut. *w.* 3/4/15 *Killed in* [*action* 28/5/16}
1312	JAMES, Meredith Charles Clifton	...	24/ 7/15	1 *Died of wounds* 27/10/16
1462	MOLYNEUX, Eric Seymour	...	3/ 3/15	1 Capt. *Killed in action* 30/11/17 ⚔
3009	NEALE, Charles Douglas	...	24/ 7/15	2 Lieut. *Wounded* 26/9/15
1506	NOTT, L/Cpl. Leslie Hugh	...	26/ 5/15	1 Lieut.
1734	O'DONOVAN, Robert Anthony	...	9/ 5/15	1 Capt. ✠ ✠ *Wounded* 20/3/17
729	PALMER, Morris Cobb	...	1/ 1/15	1 Lieut. *Wounded* 11/3/15
3008	PROSSER, Arthur Edward	...	24/ 7/15	2 Capt. ✠ *w.* 15/7/16, 3/4/17} [& 7/11/17 *Died* (P/W) 30/10/18 ⚔(2)}
1222	SMITH, William Leslie	...	1/ 1/15	2 Capt. ✠ D/W 15/4/18 ⚔
1903	STEVENS, William Cecil	...	15/ 8/15	1 Lt.-Col. ✠✠✠ F/D ⚔
1432	WHITTLE, Walter Victor P. C.	...	14/ 2/15	1 *Killed in action* 13/4/15
1702	WIGHTWICK, Charles Frederick	...	9/ 5/15	1 Lieut. *Wounded* –/7/16
1026	WILSON, William Clement	...	3/ 3/15	1 Lieut. *Killed in action* 25/9/15
7286	ALLEN, Daniel George	...	19/12/16	3 Lieut.
765429	ASTIL, Frederick Harry	...	28/11/17	1 *Wounded* 30/10/18
762886	BARR, Leonard	...	16/ 3/17	1
762212	BAUGH, John	...	11/ 2/17	1
1737	BIRD, Eric James	...	7/11/16	4 *Died of wounds* 25/4/17
763945	CAPPER, William	...	31/10/17	1
5395	CARNOCHAN, Thomas Middlemass	...	26/ 9/16	1 Lieut. *Wounded* 17/4/18
761616	COWLEY, Robert Harvey	...	5/ 7/17	3
3616	FORSYTH, James Carson	...	6/ 1/17	1 *Killed in action* 31/8/17
763746	GALE, George Alexander	...	30/ 5/17	(8) Lieut. *Wounded* 16/7/18
7024	GILLESPIE, Thomas Leslie	...	5/ 1/17	2 ✠ *Wounded* 26/5/17
761258	HAGGERJUDD, William	...	27/ 2/17	1 [*in action* 21/3/18}
763643	JACKSON, Stewart Spiers	...	30/ 5/17	1(8) ✠ *Wounded* 9/3/18 *Killed*}
7134	KEAR, Basil Maurice	...	19/12/16	1 Lieut. *Wounded* 19/4/18
6957	MORGAN, Daniel Phillips	...	19/12/16	2 *Killed in action* 26/9/17
765244	PHILLIPS, Malcolm Henry	...	13/ 5/17	1
7615	PING, Alan Roy	...	26/ 1/17	3 *Killed in action* 3/8/17
765056	SPENCELAYH, Vernon Charles Henry	...	31/10/17	1

762295	STEPHENS, Kenneth Thomas	...	26/ 6/17 3 ✠
761509	SUTCLIFFE, James Henry ...	...	11/ 2/17 1
764917	WALFORD, John Osborne ...	...	17/ 6/17 1 ✠
765084	WITHAN, John Wilkinson	...	17/ 6/17 1
763357	YARROW, Duncan	...	17/ 6/17 1

Special Reserve Battalions (Nos. 5 & 6).

7172	NEWCOME, Clarke C. Upham	...	18/ 2/16 5 Lieut. Killed in action 17/8/17
764223	BENNETT, James Harry Robert	...	25/ 9/17 5
766947	BRYSON, John	...	30/ 1/18 5
762119	DE LEMOS, Charles	...	29/ 3/17 5 Prisoner of war 9/4/18
762277	PUDDEPHATT, Noel H. G. O.	...	30/ 5/17 6(1) Wounded 15/6/18

Territorial Battalions (Nos. 7 & 8).

3942	BINDER, Cpl. Augustus Ed. Louis	...	21/ 9/15 7 Wounded –/7/16 ℞
3818	BRITTON, Wilfred	...	21/ 9/15 7 Lieut.
3506	BROWN, Francis Arthur Noel	...	21/ 9/15 7 Lieut. Killed in action 21/7/16
2358	DRAKE, L/Cpl. Douglas Bell	...	9/ 3/15 7 Capt. Wounded 21/5/15
3563	DURKIN, Frank Vivian ...	...	21/ 9/15 7 Lieut.
3156	HEMSWORTH, Noel Edward C.	...	9/ 3/15 7 To 5/Norfolk Lieut.
4204	MINORS, Reginald Towers ...	...	20/ 8/15 7 To R.A.F. Capt. Acc/K 27/3/19
3706	READING, John Francis ...	...	21/ 9/15 7 Killed in action 29/4/16
3420	SOUTHAN, Reginald	...	15/ 4/15 7 Lieut. Employed M.G.C.
3464	THOMPSON, John Gordon ...	...	21/ 9/15 7 Lieut. Wounded –/7/16
4109	TURNER, Cpl. William Ernest	...	2/ 6/16 7 Killed in action 27/8/17
761632	BEACHAM, Cecil James ...	...	25/ 6/17 8 Killed in action 9/10/17
764477	BLACKLER, Edwin Francis ...	...	31/ 7/17 8
761909	COWLEY, Thomas Purcer ...	...	27/ 3/17 7
5480	DAVIES, Arthur Watkin ...	...	5/ 9/16 7 Wounded
7656	DUCKWORTH, John Edwin Hardie	...	26/ 9/16 7 Wounded 2/9/18 ✠ ℞
4263	HALLIDAY, Howard Edwin ...	...	11/ 7/16 7 ✠
6608	HANGER, Arthur Claud ...	...	26/ 9/16 7 Lieut.
761090	HEMMING, Jesse Clifford ...	...	3/ 8/17 8 Killed in action 27/8/17
6369	HITCHEN, David	...	23/11/16 8 Lieut.
5154	JOHNSON, Arthur William ...	...	11/ 7/16 7 (6/R.Warwick) w. 17/9/17
5782	MATTOCKS, William Thomas Ernest		23/11/16 7 Lieut.
5631	MILNES, William Alfred ...	...	5/ 9/16 7 Lieut.
761621	PENNINGTON, Henry Edward	...	3/ 8/17 8
5280	PULSFORD, Bernard Frank ...	...	26/ 9/16 7 Lieut. [28/6/17]
5664	RUMILLY, Alfred Henry Robinson	...	11/ 7/16 7 (R.Warwick) Died of wounds
5077	SHELDON, Harold Percival ...	...	11/ 7/16 7 Lieut. Wounded 22/12/17
6523	SHERLOCK, Thomas Paxton	...	26/ 9/16 7 Lieut.
5101	STAINTON, Ernest	...	11/ 7/16 7 Died of wounds 25/11/18
6827	THOMAS, William Burton ...	...	26/ 9/16 7 Killed in action 24/10/18
5970	TWIST, Walter Norman ...	...	26/ 9/16 7 Lieut.

5297	UNDERWOOD, Cyril Charles ...	... 5/ 9/16	7 (R. Warwick)	Killed in action
6662	WATKINS, Harold John ...	... 5/ 9/16	7 Lieut.	[4/2/17]
767685	WEAVER, William Arthur ...	... 4/ 3/19		

Service Battalions (New Armies).

2301	CALLENDER, George Wilfred	.. 22/12/14	13 Capt.	Killed in action 25/1/17
1184	CARTER, Sydney Noel ...	... 23/ 2/15	13 Capt.	(-/Lincoln) w. 1/7/16
2098	CLARKE, Robert Conningsby L.	... 8/ 1/15	13 Lieut.	[To Ind. Army
2093	HARLEY, John	... 8/ 2/15	13 Lieut.	Killed in action 4/6/15
2097	JAGGER, Charles Sargent ...	... 10/ 5/15	13(4) Lieut.	Wounded 13/11/15 ✠
2095	MARGETSON, Arthur Charles	... 26/ 8/15	13 Lieut.	
2157	STURT, Geoffrey Charles Napier	... 13/11/14	13 Capt.	Wounded
764961	ADAMS, Arthur Charles Henry	... 31/10/17	8	Killed in action 21/3/18
763918	ALDRICH, Arnold	... 30/ 5/17	8	Died 1/5/18
5160	ALLAN, Robert Imrie ...	... 26/ 9/16	11 Lieut.	
763810	ASHCROFT, Henry Harold ...	... 12/ 5/17		
764972	BEAMISH, Arthur Stanley ...	... 26/ 9/17	14 Capt.	Wounded 13/8/18
762545	BEVAN, Alexander Polhill ...	... 12/ 5/17		
765090	BOLTON, John Harding ...	... 28/11/17	(2)	
764129	BOTTERILL, Percy William ...	... 16/ 6/17		
762251	BOWIE, William Morland ...	.. 8/ 8/17		Wounded 11/4/18
5148	BRETT, Frederick Arnold ...	... 25/ 3/17	10 Lieut.	Wounded 20/9/17
765172	BROOKS-HILL, Reginald ...	... 17/ 6/17	1 G.B.	
4707	BRUNSKILL, John Jesmond ...	... 7/ 7/16	12(4)	Killed in action 23/4/17
762527	BRYANT, Stanley Clare ...	... 30/ 5/17		
767482	BURD, Walter ..	... 13/ 8/18		
765575	BUSS, Francis Buckley ...	... 16/ 6/17		
763255	CARDER, Sidney Marshall ...	... 16/ 6/17		
764014	CARR, John Duncan ...	... 12/ 5/17		
763419	CLEMENTS, Harold Montague	... 16/ 6/17		
765221	COTTERILL, Thomas Henry ...	... 12/ 5/17		
762318	CRANE, Lucius Francis ...	... 2/ 8/17	14	Killed in action 8/10/18
763845	DAVIES, Henry Thomas Walter	... 16/ 6/17		
761175	DAVIS, Robert Augustus ...	... 11/ 2/17		
766749	DAVISON, John Armitage ...	... 30/10/17		
6356	EWEN, Arthur John Clifford	... 7/ 7/16	12 Lieut.	
763948	FALKNER, William Barrat ...	... 13/ 5/17		Capt. Adjt. (1/G.B. Liverpool)
7088	FINDON, Richard Harold ...	... 19/12/16	9 Lieut.	Wounded 1/10/18
763296	FISHER, Thomas William ...	... 16/ 6/17		
765442	GANTLETT, Reginald Albert Reynolds	28/11/17		
763577	GIGG, William George ...	... 30/ 5/17	Lieut.	
763297	GINGER, Ashley Herbert ...	... 29/ 3/17		
7147	GLIBBERY, Alexander Betteridge	... 19/12/16	9 Lieut.	
763061	GRANT, Thomas Henry ...	.. 28/ 3/17	Lieut.	
761089	HALE, Henry Major ...	... 3/ 8/17	10	Wounded 12/9/17
761237	HYDE-PARKER, Arthur Charles	... 8/ 8/17	14	
760467	JAMES, William Henry ...	... 2/ 8/17	14	

WORCESTERSHIRE REGIMENT (S/B).

767014	KING, Geoffrey Burton	...	31/ 7/18	
760954	KINGSLEY, Harry Timothy	...	16/ 3/17	
765659	LANE, Henry Cecil John	...	1/ 5/18	
760996	LANG, Andrew Howill	...	2/ 8/17	*14 Wounded* 1/5/18
762410	LATOUR, Albert Ferdinand	...	26/ 4/17	*Lieut. Wounded* 11/4/18
762375	LUARD, Sydney D'Albie	...	14/ 4/17	
5211	MACLEOD, Eric Louis Hay	...	18/ 3/17	*10 Wounded* 25/5/18
768300	MASON, Denis Clifford	...	17/ 3/19	
765185	MAY, Frank	...	12/ 5/17	
7251	MILLER, Russell Alexander	...	19/ 5/16	*Lieut.*
767508	MINORS, William Jasper	...	6/ 2/19	
760682	MOLLETT, William Bastin	...	12/ 5/17	
6520	MOOHOUSE, Harry	...	5/ 9/16	*10 Lieut. Wounded* 27/9/17
764119	POWELL, Charles Albert	...	16/ 6/17	
763112	POWER, Francis William	...	14/ 7/17	
762306	QUIN-HARKIN, Arthur	...	26/ 5/17	
763598	ROBINSON, Marshall Field	...	17/ 6/17	
762961	ROBSON, Norman George Fenwick	...	14/ 4/17	
762687	RODEN, Harry John	...	26/ 4/17	*Lieut. Wounded* 15/12/17
764720	ROULSTON, Reginald Percy	...	17/ 6/17	
763979	SMITH, Frank Ingram	...	29/ 8/17	*Prisoner of war* 15/6/18
761953	STOGDON, Reginald Hugh Astley	...	12/ 2/17	
765810	STOOKE, Herbert Neville	...	18/12/17	
764856	STRATTON, George Kellow	...	17/ 6/17	*Staff Lieut.* (1/*Northampton*)
761594	STRONGITHARM, Arthur Drewery	...	8/ 8/17	
6932	THOMPSON, Herbert	...	7/ 7/16	*12 Lieut. Wounded* 4/10/17
765063	TRELIVING, Herbert	...	18/ 8/17	
764618	WEBB, Noel Duckworth	...	26/ 9/17	
764525	WHITING, Percy Edward	...	12/ 5/17	
765340	WILLIAMS, Stanley Fred	...	12/ 5/17	
766497	WINKLE, William Matthew	...	3/ 2/19	
763356	WRIGHT, Frank Stanley	...	26/ 5/17	

D. J. DEAN, V.C.

[pp. 45, 264.

THE RUNNER: OUR DUG-OUT IN THE LINE.

Copyright.] [Lieut. J. M. WATT.

THE YORK & LANCASTER REGIMENT. 385

Regular Battalions (Nos. 1 & 2).   65th Foot / 84th Foot

			2nd Lieut.	
3101	BUTLAND, George	... ...	7/11/15	2 [Killed in action 21/5/18] Wounded 4/6/15, 29/7/16
1853	ROBERTS, Charles Henry	...	23/ 4/15	1 Lieut. To R.E. w. 4/6/15, 8/9/18
1507	WREN, Leslie Randall	...	23/ 4/15	2 Lieut. Wounded 23/5/15
763760	FAIRBAIRN, William Frank	...	27/ 6/17	(5) ✠
7207	MALEHAM, Edgar Hubert	...	22/11/16	2(9) Lieut. Died of wounds 29/3/18
6088	RERRIE, Henry Gordon	...	3/ 1/17	2 ✠ ✠ Wounded 2/5/17, 5/12/17, [17/12/17, 20/6/18 🅼]

Special Reserve Battalion (No. 3.)

| 6985 | YOUNG, Edwin Victor | ... | ... | 8/ 7/16 | 3 Lieut. |

Territorial Battalion : No. 4 (Hallamshire) & 5.

3383	BARNES, Reginald Charles	...	8/ 7/15	4 Capt. (T.M.B.) ✠ w. 11/4/18 🅼
1866	BATE, L/Cpl. Robert Edmund de B.	28/ 1/15	5 Lieut. ✠ 🅼
3167	BOWEN, Charles Reginald	...	2/ 7/15	4 Capt.
2963	CLIVELY, John Harold	...	8/ 7/15	4 Killed in action 3/5/17
3131	DUNKERTON, Edmund Lloyd H.	...	12/ 7/15	5 Capt. ✠ ✠ w. 14/12/17, 9/5/18
3813	HARRISON, Charles Geoffrey	...	24/ 9/15	4 Lieut. Killed in action 27/11/17
1785	HEDGES, Norman Hammett	...	17/ 7/15	5 Capt. ✠ Wounded -/7/16 🅼
3176	HIGHAM, William Percy	...	5/ 7/15	4 Lieut. [action 7/7/16
2553	LONGSTAFF, Jack Campbell	...	3/ 7/15	5 Wounded -/7/16 Killed in
3279	LONSDALE, Percy Hayward	...	2/ 7/15	4 Lieut. Wounded 15/5/17
2850	MATTHEWS, Roland Paget	...	12/ 7/15	5 Lieut.
3792	McCARRAHER, Colin	...	24/ 9/15	4 Lieut. Wounded -/7/16
3681	MITCHELL, Alan	...	24/ 9/15	4 Lieut. ✠ 🅼
3399	NORMAN, Arthur Spencer	...	2/ 7/15	4 Lieut. Wounded 12/10/18
3657	PERRY, William	...	2/ 7/15	4 Lieut.
3789	RAIKES, Arthur Francis M.	...	24/ 9/15	4 Lieut. 🅼
3020	SHARPE, Gerald Norman	...	8/ 7/15	4 Killed in action 31/7/16
2499	SNOW, Richard Aslin	...	2/ 7/15	4 Killed in action 4/12/15
3930	ALLENGAME, Arthur Kenneth	...	26/11/15	5 Lieut.
4835	ANDERSON, Reginald	...	12/ 6/16	5 Lieut. Wounded 1/9/18
4077	BEETHAM, Christopher William	...	28/10/15	4 Lieut. Wounded -/9/16
4034	BEETHAM, George Clarence	...	14/11/15	5 Capt. Wounded 10/10/17
4656	CARSON, Robert Thomas	...	16/ 6/16	4 Lieut. w. 27/4/17, 30/11/18
4484	CLEGG, Charles Herbert	...	5/12/15	5 Lieut. Wounded -/9/16
4013	DODDS, Herbert Alexander	...	14/11/15	5 Lieut. Died 13/6/16
3973	FITZGERALD, Gerald	...	20/12/15	5 Lieut. Staff
4015	GORE, Ernest Collet	...	5/12/15	5 Lieut.

4016	HIGGINS, George Jeffries	... ...	28/10/15 4	*Lieut.*
4850	KIRK, John	...	16/ 6/16 4	*Lieut. Wounded* 23/10/17
4093	LUCAS, Ernest Henry Austin	...	14/11/15 5	*Lieut. Wounded* –/7/16
6173	McLAREN, Eustace	...	9/ 6/16 4	*Lieut.*
4019	O'DONNELL, Anthony Patrick	...	28/10/15 4	*Killed in action* 12/6/17
4121	PATTISON, John Edgar ...	...	5/12/15 5	*Lieut.*
4134	PEAL, Francis Arthur Henry	...	14/11/15 5	*Lieut.* ✠ ✠
4038	PYKE, Arthur Charles ...	...	28/10/16 4	*Lieut.*
4138	SONE, Thomas Eric	...	14/11/15 5	*Lieut. Wounded* –/7/16
4291	STORM, William George ...	...	5/12/15 5	*Capt.* ✠ *Killed in action* 9/10/17
5931	TYAS, Manuel	...	9/ 6/16 4	*Lieut.*
4055	WARING, Frank	...	5/12/15 5	*Died of wounds* 24/8/16
6492	BOWER, Basil Cedric ...	...	11/ 7/16 5	*Lieut.*
765919	BROOKS, Victor	...	23/ 5/18 5	*Wounded* 1/11/18
4612	BROWN, Harry	...	11/ 7/16 4	*Lieut.*
4613	CHRISTOPHER, Edgar Owen	...	11/ 7/16 4	*Lieut.*
4725	COLE, Alfred Ernest ...	...	17/ 7/16 4	*Lieut.*
6794	DUPLOCK, Frank William Morrison .		11/ 7/16 4	*Lieut.*
4846	ELMS, Ernest Charles ...	...	4/ 8/16 4	*Lieut.*
4633	GIBSON, Cecil Mervyn ...	...	21/ 7/16 5	*Killed in action* 5/5/17
4730	GIFFORD, William Douglas Gawthorp		11/ 7/16 4	*Capt.* ✠ ✠ *w.* 13/5/18 ⚔
766049	GROVES, Frederick	...	24/ 4/18 4	
765658	JENKINSON, John Mansell ...	...	18/12/17 4	
5758	KERR, Robert Thomas ...	...	13/ 7/16 4	*Killed in action* 23/11/16
762579	MULLIGAN, Arthur William Patrick..		28/ 8/17 4	*Wounded* 25/4/18
765853	SMITH, Arthur James ...	...	24/ 4/18 4	
4887	VEATS, Sydney Haydn ...	...	23/ 6/16 4	*Lieut.*
764866	YULE, James Gilbert ...	...	29/ 8/17 4	

Service Battalions (New Armies).

2044	BURT, Walter G.	...	8/ 9/15 15	*Lieut. Wounded* –/6/16
1001	CLARKE, L/Cpl. Thomas Purcell	...	17/ 9/14 6	*Lieut. Killed in action* 30/9/16
3799	CRAN, Charles Robert ...	...	6/10/15 14	*Capt. Wounded* 1/10/17 ✠
2107	ELLEN, Robin Basil	...	23/ 4/15 9	*Lieut.*
1525	HUMPHREYS, Brian	...	19/11/14 10	*Lieut.*
2437	NICHOLSON, Cecil Alfred John	...	9/12/14 9	*To 11*
1002	OXENFORD, Alfred Hempry	...	17/ 9/14 6	*Lieut.* [3/5/18 ✠ ⚔]
2805	SHORT, John Rodwell ...	...	23/ 4/15 9	*Capt. To* 13/*Yorks P*/*W* {
1997	STANESBY, Reginald William J.	...	9/12/14 9	*Lieut. To Sig. Serv. R.E.* ⚔
2787	WARD, Thomas Leonard ...	...	1/11/14 12	*Lieut. Staff-Capt.*
1027	WESTON, Wilfred James ...	...	17/ 9/14 6	*Lieut. Killed in action* 22/8/15
768143	ASKWITH, John Edwin ...	...	17/ 3/19	
764955	BARNETT, Alfred	...	12/ 5/17	
764284	BATTY, Charles	...	6/ 3/19	

6986	BLAKE, Arthur Thomas ...	... 26/ 9/16	*13* Lieut.	
763963	BROWN, Harold Gladstone ...	... 30/ 5/17	*8* Capt. ✠	
762662	BULL, Ernest Reuben ...	... 29/ 3/17	*13*	
763322	CAYLESS, Francis	... 1/ 3/17	*9*	
768024	CHAPMAN, George Willis ...	3/ 3/19		
762573	DE LANDRE-GROGAN, L. Victor St. P.	29/ 3/17	*12* Lieut. ✠	*Killed in action* [13/10/18]
3477	DURR-ROSS, Francis	... 27/ 6/17	*9*	
764982	ELMS, Walter George ...	... 25/ 9/17		
3295	ELSTON, James	... 12/11/16	*14*	
763031	FIDDAMAN, William Alfred Master ...	26/ 4/17		
764297	GALE, Harold Frederick ...	... 29/ 8/17		
6341	GAUNT, Benjamin William ...	... 26/ 9/16	*10* (*T.M.B.*)	*Killed in action* 7/9/18
762403	GAWLER, Harry Stephen ...	... 26/ 4/17	✠	
764024	GREEN, Oswald Henry ...	... 30/ 5/17		
763126	HALL, John Eric	... 26/ 4/17	*Wounded 12/10/18*	
763100	HALLMARK, Percy Harold ...	... 29/ 3/17	*Killed in action 2/9/18*	
767588	HASLAM, Harry Talbot ...	... 6/ 2/19		
766231	HAWORTH, Sydney	... 27/ 6/18		
7295	HEAP, Harold Schofield ...	... 19/12/16		
765273	HOLMES, Walter	... 5/ 3/19	*Wounded 30/10/17*	
763159	HUNT, Alfred Thomas ...	... 30/ 5/17	*8* *Wounded 10/9/17*	
4393	MOORE, Cuthbert Alec ...	... 12/11/16	*14* Lieut.	
764449	NIXON, Thomas William ...	... 29/ 8/17	*7* *Died of wounds 26/10/18*	
6931	PLATT, Howard Chappell ...	... 18/ 3/17	*13* *Wounded 12/11/17*	
762582	ROBERTS, Edward Lamplough	.. 28/ 3/17	*12*	
764567	SCHOFIELD, Colin Gladstone	... 28/ 8/17		
762615	STAPLETON, Reginald Walker	... 29/ 3/17		
5877	TAYLOR, James Burton ...	... 7/ 7/16	*15*	
4770	THOMPSON, Leonard ...	... 5/ 8/16	Lieut.	
763137	TUDOR, Charles Edward Harry	... 26/ 4/17		
6984	TUE, George Albert	... 7/ 7/16	*15*	
2161	VINER, Clement	... 12/11/16	*14* Lieut.	
762440	WATERWORTH, George William	... 26/ 4/17		

*THE YORKSHIRE LIGHT INFANTRY
(THE KING'S OWN).

Regular Battalions (Nos. 1 & 2).   {51st Foot / 105th Foot}

			2nd Lieut.	
2544	LYNE, Howard William	...	24/ 7/15 *1 Lieut.*	*Wounded* 27/11/18
1405	MARSHALL, Oscar Fuller Ben		9/ 5/15 *1 Lieut.*	(M.G.C.) ☒
1574	PEARN, Charles Lukey	...	26/ 5/15 *1 Lieut.*	*Wounded* 25/10/15, 8/9/16
2306	WELCH, Lawrence Arthur	...	24/ 7/15 *1 Capt.*	*w.* 3/7/16 (*To W. Yorks*)
761897	ARTHRELL, Henry James	...	11/ 2/17 *1*	
7303	GAULDER, Charles William Edward	22/11/16 *1 Lieut.*	(T.M.B.) ✠ *w.* -/4/18
763700	PARSONS, George Edward	...	27/ 6/17 (4)	*Wounded* 28/11/17
763003	PORRITT, Charles Herbert	...	13/ 5/17 *1*	
764175	TOWARD, Gilbert Wilson	...	17/ 6/17 *1*	
764353	TROLLOPE, Thomas Charles Stapleton	17/ 6/17 *1*	
762742	TYLER, Bartholomew	...	17/ 6/17 *1*	
764108	VERMONT, John	...	17/ 6/17 *1*	
765302	WOLSEY, Frank	...	17/ 6/17 *1*	

Special Reserve Battalion (No. 3).

| 762474 | BOX, Kenneth James | ... | 26/ 4/17 3 ✠ |
| 6547 | NICHOLSON, Charles Henry | ... | 26/ 9/16 3(6) *Lieut.* |

Territorial Battalions (Nos. 4 & 5).

3880	FEHR, Frederick Charles	...	11/11/15 4 *Lieut.*	
2860	HALL, L/Cpl. Thomas Francis Burton	29/ 9/15 5 *Lieut.*	*Wounded* 13/5/18
4081	HILL, John Ernest Victor	...	22/11/15 4 *Lieut.*	
4702	HOLTON, Joseph Rhodes	...	12/ 6/16 4 *Lieut.*	*Wounded* 21/1/18
3864	PLATT, Oswald Gordon	...	29/ 9/15 5 *Lieut.* ✠	
2876	WHITEAWAY, Edward Geo. Lang	20/ 3/15 5 *Major* ✠✠ *Wounded* -/8/18 ☒
6209	BINGHAM, Montague Hearfield	26/ 9/16 5 *Lieut.*	*Killed in action* 13/4/18
6603	BUTCHER, Thomas Robert Peel	26/ 9/16 4 *Lieut.*	*Wounded* 14/5/17
763095	CLOUGH, Stanley Beecroft	...	28/11/17 4	
761291	CRANMER, Guy Patterson	...	4/ 8/17 5	*Killed in action* 9/10/17
761427	DAVIS, Bernard Orlando		4/ 8/17 5	*Wounded* 24/10/17
761428	DAVIS, Rupert L. Horace	...	4/ 8/17 5	*Wounded* 24/10/17 P/W 17/8/17
764090	FEARN, Cecil Augustus	...	31/ 7/17 4 *Capt.* ✠	*Wounded* 11/10/18
766446	PITMAN, Alan Theodore	...	26/ 6/18 4	*Wounded* 1/10/18
766292	THRIPPLETON, Herbert	...	24/ 5/18 4 ☒	
761531	TIBBOTTS, Alexander Hugh	...	4/ 8/17 4	*Wounded & P/W* 17/5/18
766265	VAUX, Edwin Ernest	...	26/ 6/18 5	

Service Battalions (New Armies).

2683	BARNETT, Walter Durac	...	13/ 3/15 10	
2670	BYERLEY, Arthur James Allan	...	7/11/15 10 *Lieut.*	*Wounded* 23/4/17
1871	ELBOROUGH, Alfred Charles E.	...	7/12/14 6 *Capt.*	*Died of wounds* 30/7/15
1131	FRANKLIN, Leslie	...	24/10/15 9 *Lieut.* ✠	*Wounded* 5/11/18

* *Title changed (1st January, 1921) to "The King's Own Yorkshire Light Infantry."*

YORKSHIRE LIGHT INFANTRY (S/B.

Number	Name	Date	Notes
2193	GILL, Jack Woodward	19/ 9/15	6 Lieut. Killed in action 19/11/15
2659	JOHNSON, L/Cpl. Leonard Oswald	25/ 1/15	9 Lieut. To 11 Wounded 18/8/17
2147	KINGSTON, Henry Francis	29/12/14	9 Wounded –/6/16
3750	MAIDEN, Albert Augustus	16/ 1/16	6 Killed in action 16/9/16
1848	MARTIN, Edmund Archibald	22/ 9/14	8 Capt. Wounded 18/9/18 ℳ(2)
3760	MORRISH, Donald Bernard	16/ 1/16	6 (T.M.B.) Killed in action
2604	VINE, Eric	3/10/15	8 Lieut. [18/8/16]
761328	APPLETON, James	18/12/17	(4) ✠
764283	ASHDOWN, Percival Joyce	12/ 5/17	6 Lieut.
6612	AYKROYD, Thomas	5/ 9/16	Wounded 21/12/17
763486	BENNETT, William Garner	1/ 3/17	(5)
762875	BINDER, Eric Southan	28/ 3/17	(5)
5569	BROUGHTON, Thomas Dugdale	19/12/16	7 Died of wounds 11/4/17
760346	BUSH, Montague Herbert	12/ 5/17	1/Garr. Bn.
762515	BUTLER, Sidney Arthur Victor	26/ 4/17	Wounded 8/12/17
763549	CLARKE, John Fowe	29/ 3/17	Lieut. w. 27/11/17, 12/9/18
763568	CORKE, Ralph Taierry	26/ 4/17	
762528	COX, Reginald Walter	26/ 4/17	
763492	DILLON, Derrick Trollip	11/ 2/17	
764766	FACEY, William Henry	13/ 5/17	
765344	FOX, John	27/11/17	
764576	GLOVER, James	26/ 4/17	
762992	GOOD, Thomas Spellman	30/ 5/17	Wounded 18/12/17
762303	GREENWOOD, D'Arcy Stanfield	26/ 4/17	
8239	HALLIDAY, Clarence Peter	25/ 1/17	✠ Wounded 15/12/17
765657	HEATON, Lewis Hartley	18/12/17	
765312	HEWAT, Frederick Armitage	28/11/17	
762957	HEYWOOD, Albert Bertine	28/ 3/17	10 Killed in action 4/10/17
768441	HINDLE, Edward Victor	17/ 3/19	
762666	HUGHES, George William Victor	26/ 4/17	(5) Killed in action 27/11/17
762113	INNES, Frank Innes	11/ 2/17	
762408	KEEFE, Francis James Murray	26/ 4/17	Wounded 28/9/18
8240	KENNEDY, John Gordon	25/ 1/17	Wounded 11/10/17, 30/5/18
764657	LLOYD, Reginald James	14/ 5/17	
764781	LYNCH, George Anthony	16/ 6/17	
764537	NICHOLSON, Paul Chessum	28/ 8/17	9 Killed in action 26/4/18
5792	PERRIN, Alfred John	26/ 9/16	10 Killed in action 4/10/17
760581	POLLOCK, Horace	16/ 6/17	
764664	POPE, Daniel Harold	16/ 6/17	
762412	ROWLAND, Maurice	26/ 4/17	10 Acc/killed 4/10/17
765255	TRYER, Charles Kirby	28/11/17	
764803	TURNBULL, Matthew	12/ 5/17	Lieut. ℳ
763218	WATKINS, Leslie Foster	29/ 3/17	
764522	WELLSMAN, Francis	12/ 5/17	
6851	WILKINSON, William Reginald	5/ 9/16	10 Lieut.
761781	WILLIAMS, Robert Thomas	11/ 2/17	
764109	WILSON, Arthur	17/11/17	
765300	WOODS, Frederick Henry	15/11/17	

*THE YORKSHIRE REGIMENT
(ALEXANDRA, PRINCESS OF WALES'S OWN). THE GREEN HOWARDS.

Regular Battalions (Nos. 1 & 2). 19th Foot

			2nd Lieut.	
950	BELCHER, Cpl. Arthur Edward Irving	20/ 3/15	2 Lieut. ✠	Wounded 15/6/15
2345	BURBURY, Cpl. Arthur Vivian	... 14/ 7/15	2 To R.F.C.	
2220	CROSSE, Marlborough Evelyn B.	... 15/12/14	2 Killed in action 12/3/15	
1167	CUTTLE, Geoffrey	... 15/12/14	2 Killed in action 11/3/15	
1681	EAMES, Arthur Horwood ...	... 5/ 4/15	2 To 1/East Yorks	
1952	FISHER, Edward Humbert ...	... 20/ 3/15	2 Killed in action 19/5/15	
3301	HARLE, Norman Hector ...	... 3/ 4/15	[1/9/15, 7/7/16	
1830	HENDERSON, Kenneth Robert	... 20/ 3/15	2 Capt. ✠ w. 18/5/15, 15/6/15,	
2255	HOLLIS, Henry Lewis ...	... 15/12/14	2 Major D.A.A.Q.M.G. w.12/3/15	
1847	LLOYD-JONES, John	... 20/ 3/15	2 Capt. ✠ w.15/6/15 d. 11/3/18)	
			[⚘(2)	
1794	PICKUP, Alfred James ...	... 15/12/14	2 Lieut. w. 18/12/14, 14/3/15,	
			[Killed in action 26/9/15	
970	WEBB, Sgt. Cyril Francis ...	... 12/ 6/15	2 Lieut. Killed in action 25/9/15	

Special Reserve Battalion (No. 3).

764095	HADWICK, William	... 30/ 5/17	3(13) Prisoner of war 12/12/17
767631	WILEY, William	... 3/ 3/19	3

Territorial Battalions (Nos. 4 & 5).

3874	BELL, Victor Allan	... 17/10/15	4 Lieut.	
2471	CORRELL, Charles Edward ...	... 13/10/15	5 Lieut. ✠	
5397	CROSS, John George ...	... 18/ 6/16	5 Lieut.	Prisoner of war 6/5/18
3672	EVANS, Hugh Elwyn ...	... 13/10/15	5 Lieut. ✠	Killed in action 26/3/18
3635	FAGAN, L/Cpl. Herbert Archer	... 13/10/15	5 Lieut. ✠ ✠	w. -/7/16, -/7/17
3881	GARTLEY, L/Cpl. Wm. Harold Alex.	20/10/15	4 Lieut.	(18/Lancs. Fusiliers)
3883	GOLLAN, Alexander L. D. ...	... 20/10/15	4 Lieut.	
4017	JACQUES, Harry Whittaker ...	... 20/11/15	4(7)	
2479	KIRKBY, Noel Walter ...	... 29/ 5/15	4 Capt.	
1340	LEIGH-BREESE, Percival Lawrence ...	2/ 4/15	4 Lieut.	Wounded -/8/17, 31/5/18
4199	LUCKHURST, William Heartfield	... 16/11/15	4 Lieut.	Killed in action 24/4/17
4031	ROBSON, Joseph	... 16/11/15	4 Lieut.	Wounded 3/5/17
3998	WIGGINS, Thomas ...	...* 2/10/15	4 Lieut.	
2047	WINTERBOTTOM, Arthur Guy	... 13/10/15	5 Lieut.	Wounded -/7/16

*Title changed (1st January, 1921) to "The Green Howards (Alexandra, Princess of Wales's Own Yorkshire Regiment)."

YORKSHIRE REGIMENT (T/F).

765863	KENDRICK, Max Theodore ...	... 23/ 5/18	5
763865	SYKES, Harold Vincent ...	... 28/ 8/17	4 *Lieut.*
765069	WATSON, Charles	... 26/ 6/18	5

Service Battalions (New Armies).

782	CURREY, George Grafton ...	... 17/ 9/14	6 *Capt.*	*Killed in action* 21/8/15
961	DOVE, Hugh Vernon Bennett	... 3/10/15	*10 Lieut.*	
4249	GRIMSLEY, William Henry ...	... 12/ 1/16	9 *Lieut.*	*Killed in action* 6/10/18
4386	HOLDEN, Albert	... 14/ 1/16	*14 Lieut.*	
3321	LAMPSHIRE, Leslie Frank ...	... 12/12/15	9 *Lieut.*	
4326	McCULLOCH, Alfred Garey ...	... 12/ 1/16	*14 Lieut.*	*Wounded* 7/6/17, 1/9/18
4244	REED, John Philip	... 17/ 1/16	*14 Lieut.* ✠	
4219	WAUD, Frederick Croysdale ...	... 12/ 1/16	*14 Lieut.*	
6304	BARROWCLIFF, Frank ...	... 7/ 7/16	*14 Prisoner of war* 12/8/18	
3466	BIRD, Herbert Whitmore ...	... 7/11/16	*10 Capt.*	*w.* 3/10/17, 11/10/18
762465	BROWN, Wilfred	.. 26/ 4/17	9	
768529	COORE, Alban	... 13/ 2/19		
764635	CORNTHWAITE, John William	... 12/ 2/19		
7178	CROSS, Charles Harold ...	... 19/12/16	6 *Wounded* 17/8/17, 12/12/17	
767903	CROWTHER, David	... 5/ 3/19		
5993	DUDLEY, Arnold Tiffany ...	... 26/ 9/16	✠ *Wounded* 23/6/18	
762831	GOODLASS, Charles William ...	... 31/ 7/17	✠ *Wounded* 23/10/18 ⚔	
762331	GUTTERIDGE, John Frederick	... 26/ 4/17		
763883	HANSON, John Stead ...	... 25/ 9/17	*Wounded* 14/9/18	
7563	HEWITT, Harold James ...	... 19/12/16	*Lieut.*	
8116	JENNINGS, Phillip Hanson ...	... 19/12/16	*Lieut.*	
1340	LEIGH-BREESE, Percival Laurence ...	31/ 3/15	*11 Lieut.*	
763107	LAWRENCE, Frederick Charles	... 14/ 4/17	*Lieut.*	
763469	MARTIN, Leslie	... 1/ 3/17	*(10) Wounded* 20/11/17	
762906	MATTHEWS, Richard Malcolm	... 26/ 4/17	9 *Killed in action* 20/9/17	
765954	PEARSON, Robert	... 27/ 2/18	*(–/ W. Yorks) D/ W as P/ W* 7/8/18	
766082	PLUMPTON, Robert	... 28/ 5/18	*(6) Died* 25/12/18	
8112	RADLEY, Hamilton Cleighton	... 19/12/16	*Wounded* 5/5/17	
8105	RELPH, George Walton ...	... 19/12/16	*Wounded* 20/4/17	
766263	ROBINSON, Harold Douglas ...	... 28/ 5/18		
4195	SHAW, Leonard Bilton ...	... 5/ 9/16	*Lieut.*	
766264	THORPE, Albert Edward ...	... 1/ 5/18	*(–/E. Yorks) Died* 6/12/18	

THE EAST YORKSHIRE REGIMENT.

Regular Battalions (Nos. 1 & 2). 15th Foot

2nd Lieut.

2622	BAIN, James Charles	...	24/ 7/15	*1 Lieut.*	Wounded 11/8/15
1200	CAREW, Cyril Joseph Theodore	...	14/ 2/15	*2*	*Died of wounds* 29/4/15
2063	COMPER, George Quintyn	...	24/ 7/15	*1 Lieut.*	
1971	COOPER, Edward Priestly	...	23/ 4/15	*1 Lieut.* ✠✠	*w.* 5/7/15,–/7/16 P/W
2314	CORRIE, William Ronald	...	10/ 7/15	*1 w.*–/11/15	*Died of wounds* 23/4/17
2005	CRACKNELL, John Sidney	...	15/ 8/15	*1 Lieut.*	Wounded –/7/16
1681	EAMES, Arthur Horwood	...	5/ 4/15	*1 Lieut. (From 2/Yorks) w.*	
			[15/6/15	*Killed in action* 2/7/16)	
1609	GOULD, Vivian Frank	...	15/ 8/15	*1 Capt. & Adjt.* [–/6/16, 17/6/18]	
2517	GREEN, William Charles	...	11/ 6/15	*1 Lieut.*	*To S. Staffs* ✠✠ *w.)*
2567	HANNAFORD, Leonard Gordon	...	11/ 6/15	*1 Lieut.*	Wounded 8/8/15
1840	JENKINS, L/Cpl. Frederick Arthur	...	26/ 5/15	*2 Capt.*	Wounded –/10/15, –/7/16
1110	MIEVILLE, Sgt. Arthur Manclark	...	26/ 5/15	*2 Lieut.*	℞
2010	MOORE, William Robert	...	15/ 8/15	*1 Lieut.* ✠	*w.* 25/4/16, –/7/16
1362	RECKITT, Charles Edward Hay	...	9/ 5/15	*2 Lieut.*	Wounded 4/7/15
1003	SIMNETT, Robert Faulkner	...	5/ 4/15	*2 Capt.*	Wounded 3/5/15
1544	TOWNSEND, L/Cpl. Thomas	...	15/ 8/15	*1 Killed in action* 4/6/16	
2450	TRIER, Basil Maurice	...	10/ 7/15	*1 Lieut.*	Wounded 13/6/16
1705	TRIER, Norman Ernest	...	9/ 5/15	*2 Died of wounds* 6/10/15	
1874	WATKINS, William Henry Ernest	...	15/ 8/15	*1 Lieut.* ✠	Wounded 4/6/16
1712	WYATT, William Herbert	...	23/ 4/15	*1 Killed in action* 4/5/16	
3492	BENSON, Lyde	...	13/ 6/16	*1 Lieut.*	

Special Reserve Battalion (No. 3).

3262	JAMESON, Ralph Harold	...	8/ 4/15	*3 Capt.*
765011	BOYES, Bryan	...	31/10/17	*3*

Territorial Battalions (Nos. 4 & 5).

6134	BOOTHROYD, Frank	...	5/ 9/16	*5 Lieut.*
763775	BUTTERY, Walter	...	30/ 5/17	*5 Killed in action* 20/8/18
6168	COX, George Bernard	...	5/ 9/16	*5 Lieut.*
6445	FERRABY, David	...	5/ 9/16	*5 Lieut.*
763676	HEY, Robert	...	30/10/17	*5*
763426	HUTCHINSON, Stewart	...	27/ 3/17	*5*
763200	INGHAM, Charles Russell	...	26/ 4/17	*4 Prisoner of war* 29/5/18
767471	JOHNSON, Richard	...	6/ 2/19	*4*
763677	LOCKWOOD, George Kenneth	...	30/10/17	*5*
4483	MACKAY, James Waite	...	29/ 7/16	*5*
764036	MONKMAN, Frank Hastings	...	30/ 5/17	*5 Wounded* 10/9/18
6768	OAKDEN, George Frederic	...	26/ 9/16	*4 Wounded* 27/4/18, 30/9/18

EAST YORKSHIRE REGIMENT (T/F). 393

6351	PEER, Edmund Faithful	... ... 5/ 9/16	4 Killed in action 23/4/17
7136	SAXELBYE, Charles Hugh	... ... 21/12/16	5 Lieut.
765092	THOMPSON, Ralph	... 24/ 9/17	4 Prisoner of war 23/5/18

Service Battalions (New Armies).

2190	BALL, Frank Leslie	... 3/10/15	8 Lieut. ✠ Prisoner of war 4/6/18
4240	CAIGER, Francis Everett ...	... 1/ 1/16	9 Lieut. To 25/Manchester w.
1333	HALSE, Eric Arthur	.. 17/ 9/14	6 Capt. ℞ [8/5/17]
1860	HAYES, Mortimer Frederick	... 3/10/15	8 Capt. Killed in action 29/4/17
1381	HICKEY, Humphrey Gilbert	... 17/ 9/14	6 Lieut. Wounded 1/11/15
2221	LONGSTAFF, Ralph	... 3/10/15	8 Capt. ✠ w.-/11/16, 11/9/18
1297	MATTHEWS, Gwynn Hobson	... 17/ 9/14	8 Capt. w.-|3|16,-|5|16 (M.G.C.)
1976	SAMUEL, Gerard Stewart ...	... 3/10/15	8 Killed in action 14/7/16 [✠]
1316	SHAW, Leonard Herbert ...	... 17/ 9/14	1 G.B. Lieut.
1104	SPENCER, Arthur Farre ...	... 17/ 9/14	6 Staff-Capt.
1212	WILSON, Robert Philip ...	... 17/ 9/14	6 Lieut. Killed in action 7/8/15
762929	BOLTON, Percy	... 28/ 3/17	8 Wounded 10/6/18
5469	BROOKES, Arthur Walter ...	... 26/ 9/16	13 Lieut.
767078	CHAMBERLAIN, Spire Dent ...	... 6/ 2/19	
766344	CHIVERALL, Leslie Charles Henry ...	26/ 6/18	
3388	COTTRELL, Lennox Wallace ,	... 26/ 9/16	7 Lieut.
6973	CRANE, Reginald Hooper ...	... 19/12/16	(1) Killed in action 4/10/17
4892	EDWARDS, Arthur Ernest ...	... 19/ 4/17	8(7) Killed in action -/9/18
761619	ELLIS, Joe	... 2/ 8/17	10(13) ✠ Wounded 18/4/18
6838	FEILDEN, Guy St. Clair ...	... 12/11/16	12 Wounded 23/10/17
763387	FIELD, Henry Cecil Pinnock	.. 1/ 3/17	8 Lieut.
6948	GALLOWAY, Vincent	... 19/12/16	(5) Lieut. Wounded 17/5/17
765230	GAUNT, Harold Newman ...	... 28/11/17	Wounded 13/5/18
767858	GIBSON, James William ...	... 4/ 3/19	
762329	GITS, Edward Jerome ...	... 26/ 4/17	
762482	HADRILL, Cedric Ivon ...	.. 26/ 4/17	✠
5845	HALL, Joseph Stanley ...	... 26/ 9/16	12 Killed in action 5/5/17
767486	HERMAN, Richard	... 6/ 2/19	
5858	JAMES, Reginald Stanislaus ...	... 5/ 1/17	8 Lieut.
763889	KING, Maurice	... 26/ 4/17	Wounded 25/10/18
763531	LEGG, William George ...	... 30/ 5/17	
763241	MAYO, Alfred Harrison ...	... 26/ 4/17	✠
763538	PARKER, Thomas Cornwall ...	... 29/ 3/17	
767479	PENROSE, Leonard	... 5/ 2/19	
2176	RICKARDS, Leonard John ...	... 19/12/16	6 Wounded 12/6/17
5287	ROSCOW, Richard Eaton ...	.. 19/12/16	7 Lieut.
762568	SANGER, Henry Keith ...	... 26/ 4/17	10 Killed in action 13/4/18
762812	SMITH, Hubert Henry ...	... 28/ 3/17	Lieut.
5229	WILBY, John Frank	.. 6/ 1/17	7 Wounded 6/11/17
765210	WILKINSON, Frederick ...	... 27/11/17	
762794	WRIGHT, Arthur Samuel ...	... 28/ 3/17	8 Wounded 12/10/17 K/A 15/8/18

THE WEST YORKSHIRE REGIMENT
(THE PRINCE OF WALES'S OWN)

Regular Battalions (Nos. 1 & 2).

14th Foot

2nd Lieut.

2611	Podd, Jack Kenneth	29/ 8/15 2 Capt. ✠ w. 3/7/16, 19/4/18
724	Skevington, Alan Percival	3/ 3/15 2 Lieut. ✠ w. 10/5/18 ℞(2)
765026	Brazier, Jonathan Phillip	30/ 1/18 *1*
5742	Crosland, William Philip	18/ 3/17 2 Killed in action 16/8/17
765016	Labatt, Wilfred Henry Ernest	31/10/17 *1*

Special Reserve Battalions (Nos. 3 & 4).

5432	Rackett, Harold Walter	19/ 6/16 3 Lieut.
6558	Rowe, Sydney	26/ 9/16 4 Lieut.
6705	Symons, John Reginald	5/ 9/16 4 Capt. ℞

Territorial Battalions (Nos. 5 to 8).

3841	Bodimeade, Edward John	27/ 9/15 8 Lieut.
4312	Boxall, Ernest Mark	28/11/15 8 Lieut. Wounded 14/12/17
4026	Coy, Alfred Reginald	14/11/15 7 Killed in action 2/7/16
4011	Darby, Arthur Randle	14/11/15 7 Lieut. Wounded
5681	Dedman, William Albert	10/ 6/16 8 Lieut. Died 4/2/18
4805	Edwards, Harry Charles	11/ 6/16 7 Lieut.
3522	Fraser, W. Arnold	27/ 9/15 8 Lieut.
4807	Gilbert, George Howard	11/ 6/16 7 Lieut. Wounded 17/1/17
3885	Hodgson, Allan Thornbery	16/11/15 8 Lieut. Wounded 14/12/17
4811	Jeffery, John Ernest	11/ 6/16 7 Lieut.
4018	Johnson, William Frederick Leer	14/11/15 7 Lieut. Wounded 13/8/17
4051	Kitcat, Eustace Noyent	14/11/15 7 Lieut. Wounded 3/10/17
4052	Liffen, G. Theophile Tideswell	14/11/15 7 Lieut.
3579	Milligan, Andrew	27/ 9/15 8 Lieut. ✠ ℞
4177	Moore, Albert Reginald	28/11/15 8 Killed in action 12/4/17
4311	Nethercot, Robert Pinkerton	28/11/15 8 Lieut. ✠ Wounded 15/5/17
4734	Newton, Harold Eric	9/ 6/16 7 Lieut.
3958	Pearce, Harold Edgar	14/11/15 7 Lieut. Wounded –/7/16
4044	Penny, George	16/11/15 8 Killed in action 3/9/16
925	Pothecary, Sgt. Herbt. Martin Rixen	27/10/15 8 Lieut. ✠ Wounded 27/7/18
4221	Silmon, William Osmande Weld	28/11/15 8 Killed in action 28/2/17
4047	Smart, James Lamont	16/11/15 8 Lieut. ✠
4581	Speight, James Leslie	11/ 1/16 6 Died of wounds 9/10/17
2792	Thistleton, John Francis	21/ 1/16 7 Capt. From 14/Middlesex
3938	Thorn, Sackville Alexander	14/11/15 7 Lieut. Wounded –/1/18
3558	Thornhill, Basil William	27/ 9/15 8 Lieut. Wounded 3/5/17

4857	Tyrrell, Leonard Collin ...	... 22/ 6/16	5	Killed in action 9/10/17
3636	Weaver, Sidney Mackett ...	... 27/ 9/15	8	Lieut.
5978	Baggallay, William Ryder	... 11/ 7/16		Lieut.
5364	Burnard, Roderick Athelstan	... 11/ 7/16	7	Lieut. (T.M.B.) w. 5/5/17
5739	Cubitt, Stanley Wilson ...	... 11/ 7/16	7	Lieut. To R.A.F.
4804	Edwards, Cyril George	... 11/ 7/16	7	Capt. D.S.O. w. 11/8/17 ✠
4383	Fell, Alfred Lakeland ...	... 11/ 7/16	8	Lieut.
5095	Gibson, Alewyn Morland ...	... 11/ 7/16	6	Died of wounds 27/9/16
5655	Haydon, Percy Montague ...	... 11/ 7/16	8	Lieut.
5771	Lambdin, John Reginald ...	... 11/ 7/16	7	Lieut. ✠ Died of wounds 24/9/18
5380	Roberts, Harry	... 11/ 7/16	7	Lieut. ✠ Wounded –/12/16
5383	Searle, Gerald Douglas ...	... 11/ 7/16	7	Lieut.
760710	Allen, Sydney William ..	... 4/ 8/17	8	Wounded 3/4/18
764957	Bray, Sydney Herbert ...	... 31/10/17	8	Killed in action 20/7/18
761633	Dorn, James Stanley Gould ...	... 4/ 8/17	8	
764294	Elkington, Reginald Lawrence	... 31/ 7/17	7	
764490	Finnis, Henry John ...	... 31/ 7/17	8	
764140	Gibson, Walter Owens ...	... 31/ 7/17	6	
766233	Hetherton, John	... 26/ 3/18	5	
4017	Jacques, Henry Whittaker ...	... 20/11/15	7	Lieut.
5262	Jones, Godfrey Lemon ...	... 21/ 9/16	5	Wounded 14/5/18
762564	Mortimer, Arthur Broadbent	... 31/ 7/17	7	✠
765663	Porteous, James Douglas ...	... 18/12/17	7	Wounded 17/6/18 P/W 6/7/18
761352	Rhys, Griffith	... 4/ 8/17	8	Wounded 4/12/17
765514	Rigby, Harold Joseph ...	... 27/11/17	8	Prisoner of war 6/8/18
762313	Watkin, Frederick Thomas Huband	4/ 8/17	8	Wounded 23/10/17

Service Battalions (New Armies).

930	Browne, Arthur William ...	... 17/ 9/14	9	Capt. Wounded 7/8/15
5939	Bousfield, Colin	... 25/ 5/16	21	
3511	Christelow, Joseph William	... 28/ 5/15	13	
1067	Day-Lewis, Alfred Kay ...	... 15/ 9/14	9	Lieut. (M.G.C.)
1790	Dunbar, Sir Archibald E., Bart.	... 4/10/14	12	Major ✠ ✠
1328	Girling, Richard Oswald ...	... 17/ 9/14	9	Capt. Wounded –/8/15
3472	Leek, Major Frederick William	... 30/ 7/15	14	Lieut. Wounded 3/7/16
1793	Matthew, Archibald James ...	... 14/10/14	12	Major
1456	Miles, Martin Haddon ...	... 15/ 9/14	9	Wounded –/8/15
2930	Morland, Leonard Mark ...	... 25/ 1/15	12	Died of wounds 3/5/16
1346	Morris, Sgt. Charles Leigh ...	... 29/ 5/15	14	Lieut. Wounded –/11/16
1935	Parker, Edward Thompson ...	... 18/12/14	13	(1/Lancs. Fusiliers) Killed in action 4/6/15
931	Pearkes, André Mellard ...	... 17/ 9/14	9	Capt. Killed in action 7/8/15
5002	Sherman, Roland Keith ...	... 22/ 1/16	14	Lieut
4333	Summerskill, John Hedley	... 21/ 9/15	13	(–/Rifle Brigade)

WEST YORKSHIRE REGIMENT (S/B)

1799	Vann, Arthur Harrison Allard	... 1/10/14	12	Capt. Adjt. Killed in action [25/9/15
5282	Rawson, Ernest Stanley	... 7/7/16	20	Lieut.
5086	White, Harry	... 7/7/16	20	Lieut. Wounded 10/11/17
7977	Agar, Sidney William	... 25/1/17	10	Lieut.
763252	Ashford, Frederick Murray	... 28/3/17		ℳ
762628	Barker, Frederick Ernest	... 28/3/17	10	Killed in action 13/10/17
5841	Bottomley, Wilfred Aubrey	... 19/3/19		
6455	Broadbent, Thomas Edward	... 26/9/16		Lieut.
762232	Brook, William Stafford	... 29/3/17		
8011	Brown, Andrew Terras	... 25/1/17		Lieut. ✠ ℳ
7604	Carmichael, Herbert Michael	... 25/1/17	10	Lieut. Wounded 5/5/17
763907	Cave, Joseph	... 27/6/17	11	Died of wounds 21/9/17
762735	Clegg, James Heber	... 28/3/17	15	Prisoner of war 13/6/18
763292	Commin, Robert George	... 30/5/17		Lieut.
762991	Davies, Edward John	... 28/3/17	15	Lieut.
763656	Dawson, John Reginald	... 26/4/17		
7371	Dixon, Arthur	... 19/12/16	12	Wounded 5/12/17
763386	Emmett, Joseph Henry	... 1/3/17		Lieut.
762631	Featherstone, John Edward	... 28/3/17		Wounded 28/11/17
7278	Fortune, George Edgar	... 19/12/16	15	F/D
764142	Gratton, Donald Arthur	... 27/6/17	9	Lieut. Wounded 1/5/18
761203	Green, Allen	... 18/3/17	21	Killed in action 19/8/17
768211	Green, Harold	... 5/3/19		
762503	Hardwick, George Harold James	... 26/4/17		
763457	Houghton, George	... 28/3/17		Capt. Killed in action 27/8/18
762808	Howe, Robert Ernest	... 29/3/17		
764145	Hudson, John Wilkie	... 30/5/17		Wounded 24/4/18
762700	Lawson, John Philip	... 28/3/17	16	Lieut.
764999	Lees, Albert Alan	... 4/3/19		
765336	Lowe, Albert Ernest	... 28/11/17		
763399	Massy, William Geoffrey	... 1/3/17		Lieut.
765137	Mayoh, Thomas	... 31/10/17		
763503	Morley, Frank Stone	... 27/6/17		
763307	Mitchell, Edgar	... 28/3/17		
7378	Naylor, George Edgar	... 19/12/16	21	Lieut.
766872	Osborn, Leonard	... 29/10/18		
763113	Price, Arthur Percy	... 30/5/17		
763894	Rawnsley, Cephas	... 30/5/17	21	Lieut.
762535	Sawney, Leslie Thomas	... 24/9/17		✠ Wounded 8/8/18
6027	Simpson, Charles Harding	... 22/11/16	21	Lieut.
766767	Smith, Frank	... 17/3/19		
763212	Targett, Alfred Edward	... 28/3/17		Wounded 29/4/18
7381	Taylor, Edgar Austin	... 19/12/16	12	Wounded 29/8/18
765067	Ward, Harry	... 31/10/17		
765071	Weighall, Mark Henry	... 31/10/17		
762820	Yates, Gordon Albert	... 28/3/17		

OTHER UNITS AND SERVICES

(*In alphabetical order*).

ROYAL ARMY CHAPLAINS' DEPARTMENT.

3335	LAWRENCE, Rev. George ...	2/ 2/16	Capt.
2810	MILLEN, Sgt. Rev. Alfred Dyson ...	11/ 4/16	,,
1453	PADFIELD, Rev. Francis Joseph	26/ 6/15	,,
8183	PROCTOR, Rev. Thomas Hayes ...	19/ 9/16	,,
8763	THOMPSON, Rev. William ...	9/12/16	,,
8050	TUNSTALL, Rev. James Thomas ...	29/ 8/16	,, ✠ ✠

ARMY CYCLIST CORPS.

Divisional Cyclist Companies.

			2nd Lieut.
3505	BADEN-POWELL, Charles Leslie	... 23/ 5/15	20 [25/2/16]
3875	CARPENTER, Hubert Granville	... 23/ 8/15	To Mun. Fus. Died of wounds
2326	EDWARDS, Reginald Owen ...	... 9/10/15	From 6/K.R.R. [M.B.E.]
2481	HOLLIDGE, Alec	... 25/ 8/15	2/Lon. Div. To R.A.S.C.
2608	MAXWELL, Herbert A. ...	... 31/10/15	From 9/Somerset L.I.
2851	NORRIS, William Forbes ...	... 28/ 4/15	54 Lieut. (5/Norfolk) Killed in
3456	ST. NOBLE, George	... 22/ 5/15	20 [action 25/8/15
3517	STONE, Harold Mulready ...	... 10/ 5/15	Lieut. N. Midland Div.
1775	WAIGHT, George	... 8/12/14	From 8/E. Surrey
3453	WINKS, Arthur	... 1/11/15	Lieut. N. Midland Divn.

Huntingdonshire Cyclist Battalion.

5679	CATTERALL, Albert	2/ 2/16	Seconded for duty with Notts. &
			[Derby Regt. 10/6/16

Kent Cyclist Battalion.

1034	HODGE, William Robert Courtenay...	18/11/14	Capt. Wounded 21/9/17
2123	SAXON, Victor Duncan John ...	28/ 1/15	Capt. To W. L'ncs. Div. Cyc. Co. ᛯ
3918	WIDGERY, Frederick William ...	26/10/15	Lieut. 1/Wessex Division
5624	JONES, Llewellyn	26/ 9/16	Lieut. Wounded 8/11/18
4839	BURTON, Frederick James ...	10/ 7/16	W. Lancs. Divl. Cyclists
6712	CUMMINGS, Reginald Charles Alfred	5/ 9/16	Wessex Divl. Cyc. Staff Capt.
4813	KILBURN, John Edward ...	10/ 7/16	,, ,,
765559	MARTYR, Allan George ...	18/12/17	Devon Cyclist Battalion
7945	SMITH, Cecil Victor	25/ 1/17	Kent ,, ,,
6828	TAYLOR, Ernest Meins ...	26/ 9/16	Northern Cyclists

762600	WALSH, Victor Michael	28/ 3/17	*Sussex Cyclist Battalion*
763374	WARD, Aubrey Ernest	26/ 4/17	
762923	WATTS, Joseph Horace	13/ 4/17	

For other Cyclist Units see

9th (Cyclist) Battalion, Hampshire Regiment
25th (Cyclist) Battalion, London Regiment (T.F.)
6th (Cyclist) Battalion, Suffolk Regiment.
7th (Cyclist) Battalion, Welch Regiment.

ROYAL ARMY MEDICAL CORPS.

1078	ELLIS, Robert	5/ 8/14	*Capt.*	⌘
3231	GOLDING, John	8/ 4/15	*Capt.*	1/*Lon. San. Co.* ⌘
3134	HEDLEY, Wallace Tynemouth	12/ 4/15	*Capt.*	
1351	MATSON, Robert Charles	20/ 2/15	*Capt.*	
¶ 86	SPRAWSON, Sgt. Evelyn Charles	2/10/14	*Capt.*	1/*Lon. San. Co.* ✠ ⌘
883	TREWBY, Joseph Frederic	5/ 9/14	*Capt.*	1/*London General Hospital*
770	ADAMS, Sidney	9/ 6/16	*Capt.*	
760029	MEDLOCK, Charles Harold	28/ 2/17	*Lieut.*	

ROYAL ARMY ORDNANCE CORPS.

1426	ALLEN, Eric Richard	25/ 3/15	*Capt.*	
11	BAINES, CQMS Ellis Eyton	17/ 6/15	*Died of wounds 13/8/18*	
2736	COLLETT, Frederick George	28/12/14	*Major*	⌘
2833	DOUGLAS, William Stoddart	15/12/14	*Major*	
3052	DROWER, CQMS Edmund Gilbert	29/ 3/15	*Capt.*	
964	DURAND, Sgt. Ernest Durand	5/ 7/15	*Capt.*	⌘
¶1749	FAIRHOLME, Sgt. Henry William	20/ 3/15	*Lt.-Col.*	⌘
2973	FIRTH, Francis George	16/ 6/16	*Lieut.*	
2771	FITZGERALD, Kenneth Gordon	13/ 4/15	*Capt.*	
2633	FITZGERALD, Reginald Edward	23/11/14	*Lt.-Col.*	
2213	FURZE, Charles Gerald	8/ 2/15	*Major D.A.D.O.S.*	
318	HARTUNG, Charles Frederick Adolf	4/ 1/15	*Capt.*	
2907	HOBLYN, Cpl. Reginald Armstrong	16/ 7/15	*Lieut.*	
2222	MUSSELWHITE, Felix James	28/12/14	*Capt.* (R.A.F.)	
2073	PAGE, L/Cpl. Charles Carew	29/ 6/15	*Capt.*	
1689	PONTING, Phillip William	4/ 6/15	*Lieut.*	

ROYAL ARMY ORDNANCE CORPS.

6731	BAILEY, John Vernon	10/ 4/16	*Capt.*	✠ 🎖
2660	BEAUMONT-EDMONDS, Charles W. F.	13/ 3/16	*Lieut.*	
2094	CANDY, Cpl. Rupert George ...	13/ 3/16	*Lieut.*	
1854	CANNON, Gordon Mewburn ...	27/11/15	*Lieut.*	
1733	DENIS-BROWNE, Sgt. Ambrose George	12/10/15	*Lieut.*	
2	HAMMOND, Sgt. William	17/ 8/15	*Capt.*	
2083	HEALD, Sgt. Walter Marsden ...	2/ 7/15	*From 5/Suffolk*	
1552	HIBBERT, L/Cpl. John Geoffrey ...	1/11/15	*Major D.A.D.O.S.*	✠ 🎖
¶1748	JAMES, Sgt. Gilbert	2/ 9/15	*Capt.* 🎖	
6156	JONES, Harold Mount	16/ 6/16	*Lieut.*	
2307	LOVE, Geoffrey Robert Stuart ...	8/11/15	*Lieut. (Staff)*	
6348	NATHAN, Cyril Herbert	15/ 5/16	*Major*	
3859	ROSS, Cpl. Norman Herbert ...	6/ 5/16	*Lieut.*	
2808	NEWTON-CLARE, L/C. Herbert John	17/ 8/15	*Major (R.A.F.)* O.B.E.	
319	VALENTINE, Sgt. Walter Maynard ...	5/ 3/16	*Lieut.*	
1588	VIRET, Arthur William	2/ 9/15	*Capt.*	
6503	WALKER, Eric Hunstone	12/ 6/16	*Lieut.*	
2540	WILKINS, Raymond	15/11/15	*Capt.* O.B.E. 🎖	
2356	WORSNAM, L/Cpl. Charles Ardine ...	18/ 9/15	*Major* O.B.E.	
763962	ABBOTT, Kenneth Donald	24/ 8/18	*Lieut.*	
767502	ABERDEIN, Alexander	30/ 3/18	,,	
768095	ALLEN, Alfred Hylton	4/ 7/18	,,	
765260	ALSTON, William	22/ 9/17	,,	
766010	ANGEL, Richard	8/ 7/18	,,	
5719	ARDEN, Cpl. William Herbert ...	20/ 1/17	.,	
767049	ATKINSON, Hugh	28/ 3/18	,,	
766957	ATTFIELD, Arthur James	5/ 7/18	,,	
766463	BAKER, Henry Charles	24/ 8/18	,,	
766960	BALL, Ralph Thompson	2/ 4/18	,,	
766212	BALLANCE, Harold Edward William	28/12/17	,,	
761860	BARBER, CQMS John Howard ...	4/ 6/18	,,	
768334	BARHAM, Hugh	28/ 8/18	,,	
6938	BARKER, George Herbert	1/ 2/17	,,	
2916	BARNARD, L/Cpl. Sidney Stanley ...	13/ 7/16	,, *(R.A.S.C.)*	
765916	BARNES, John Ernest	25/ 9/17	,,	
762513	BATTERSBY, John Reginald	7/ 8/18	,,	
768463	BEECROFT, Arthur	26/ 8/18	,,	
764626	BEER, John Ashton	23/ 9/17	,,	
766042	BIGG, David	27/12/17	,,	
6970	BLUE, Archibald John	12/ 9/16	*Capt.*	
501	BLUNDEN, Sgt. Bernard Osmond ...	17/ 6/16	*Capt.*	
764975	BORRER, Arthur Cary Hampton ...	23/ 9/17	*Lieut.*	
765318	BOTT, Hubert Dudley	1/ 6/18	,,	
767357	BOULTON, Ernest Edward	8/ 4/18	,,	
767947	BOVET, Frederick Francis	8/ 7/18	,,	
767704	BOYS, Julius Claude	28/ 5/18	,,	
768132	BRADLEY-COOKE, Harold Jephson ...	4/ 7/18	,,	

7559	BRETHERTON, Cyril Herbert	17/ 1/17	Lieut.	
1733	BROWNE, Ambrose George Davis	12/10/15	Capt.	
9922	CAPE, Herbert Jonathan	2/ 3/17	Lieut.	
761501	CHAMPION, John Butler	12/ 2/17	Capt.	
760169	CHAPMAN, CSM Harold Edwin Sands	11/ 3/18	Lieut.	℞
764751	CHARTRES, Ernest Edward	24/ 8/18	,,	
768912	CLARKE, Frederick James	6/11/18	,,	
768606	CLAYTON, John Soutter	15/10/18	,,	
8435	CLEMENTS, John Edwin	2/ 2/17	,,	
768773	CLOWES, Dawson	2/11/18	,,	
760377	COOK, Francis Edward	2/ 6/18	,,	
766851	COOPER, John Eolos	3/ 4/18	,,	
768531	COYLE, L/Cpl. Edgar	6/11/18	,,	
761512	COZENS, Frederick George	27/ 9/18	,,	Wounded 27/12/17
768818	CROWE, William Henry	6/11/18	,,	
7754	CUFF, Arthur Samuel	21/10/16	,,	
7814	DALTON, Thomas Fitzgerald	1/11/16	,,	
760410	DAVIS, BQMS Edgar Frederick	27/ 9/18	,,	
762100	DEAN, Herbert Stewart Caswell	8/ 7/18	Capt.	℞
7338	DELL, Reginald Vincent John	4/10/16	Capt.	
763552	DOBSON, Richard	3/ 4/18	Lieut.	
6939	DOWNEY, Francis Nathaniel	3/ 8/16	,,	
4891	DOWSING, Sgt. Samuel Harold	1/11/16	,,	℞
6691	DREW, William	12/12/16	,,	
762007	DULLEY, Sgt. Harry Albert	11/ 4/18	Capt.	
768693	ELLIS, Philip Davenport	17/10/18	Lieut.	
5055	FAITH, Sgt. Aubrey	9/11/16	,,	
760982	FARROW, Sgt. James Walthew	23/ 9/17	,,	℞
7817	FENTON-JONES, Douglas William	25/11/16	Lieut.	
768990	FERRABY, Frank	6/11/18	,,	
8312	FOSTER, Thomas Sutcliffe	18/11/16	,,	
767993	FOX, Denman	8/ 7/18	,,	
768649	FRANCIS, Edw. Latham	28/ 8/18	,,	
768396	GEDNEY, Cyril Frederick William	28/ 8/18	,,	
7736	GODEFROI, Jocelyn	21/11/16	,,	
760034	GOLDIE, CQMS Joseph	3/ 6/18	Capt.	
762783	GOLDSMITH, William Leonard	23/ 1/17	Lieut.	
762319	GOLDSTEIN, Robert Moore	14/ 5/17	,,	
762371	GREENMAN, Sgt. Jas. Ernest	25/ 9/17	,,	
8657	GREENWOOD, Charles Hammerton	5/ 2/17	Capt.	
760294	GREGORY, Sgt. George	9/ 4/18	Capt.	Wounded 17/9/17
767533	HALLETT, Clements John Southcott	1/ 5/18		
760299	HENHAM, CSM Reginald James	11/ 6/18	Lieut.	℞
762031	HENRY, Charles	20/ 9/17	,,	
2907	HOBLYN, Reginald Armstrong	16/ 7/15	,,	
768996	HODGSON, James Vaughan	16/10/18	,,	
767717	HOWDEN, Joseph Bradley	4/ 6/18	,,	

THE ORIGINAL REGIMENTAL BADGE OF THE ARTISTS.

Motto contributed by Pte. GEORGE CAYLEY.
Badge designed by Pte. J. W. WYON, 1860.
(Engraver to the Signet.)

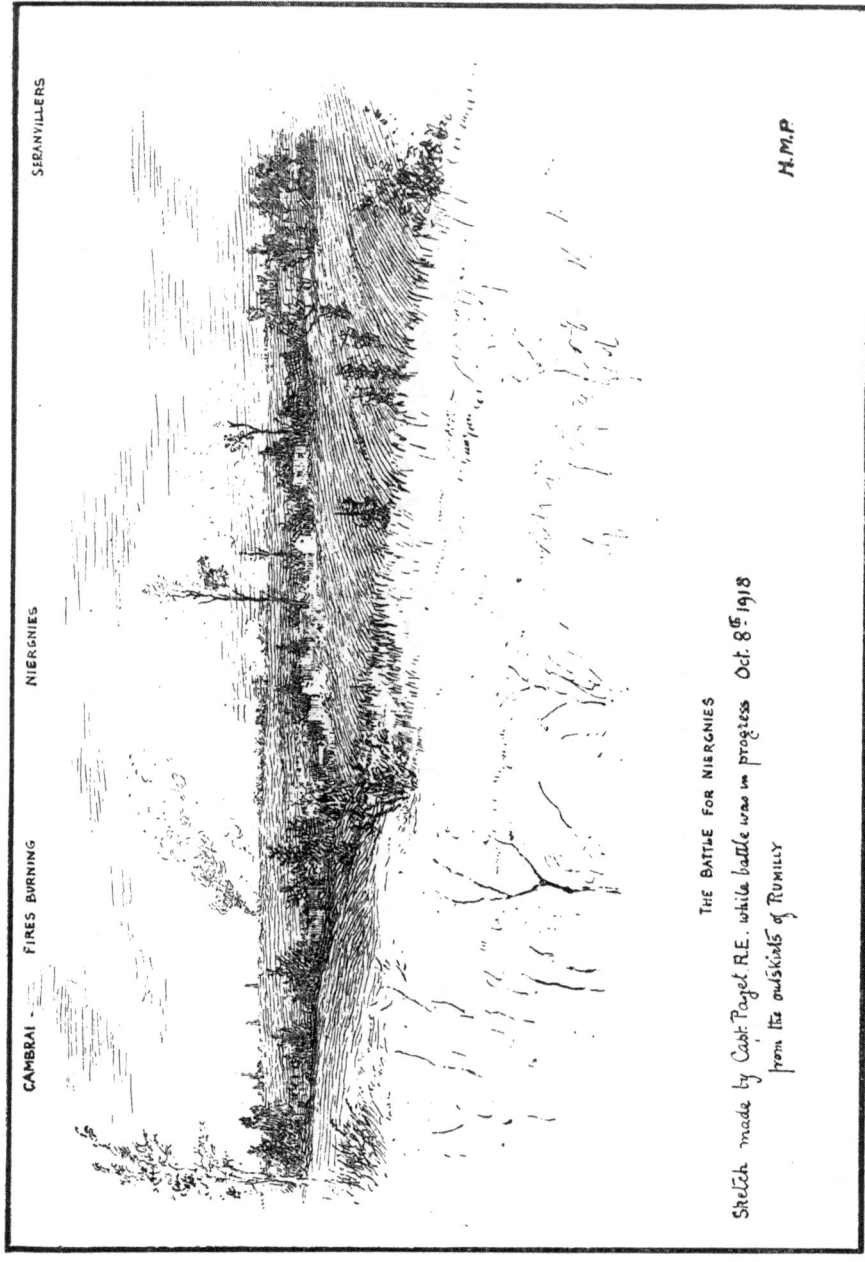

THE BATTLE FOR NIERGNIES

Sketch made by Capt. Paget R.E. while battle was in progress Oct. 8th 1918 from the outskirts of Rumilly

766554	Howe, L/Cpl. Walter Leonard	4/ 6/18	Lieut.	
764245	Hughes, L/Cpl. Frank	2/ 9/18	,,	Wounded 30/12/17
766521	Hunt, Harry Frederick	8/ 7/18	,,	
760270	Hutchinson, Sgt. Norman W. Hunter	18/ 4/17	,,	
764343	Ingrey, Sydney Arthur	27/ 5/18	,,	
761865	Inwood, Cpl. Charles	10/ 7/18	,,	Wounded 12/4/18
762014	Jones, Cecil Edmund	10/ 7/18	,,	
768298	Jose, Edward Salisbury	8/ 8/18	,,	
4486	Keene, L/Cpl. Geo. Gulliver	18/ 1/17	,,	ℳ
8584	Kennedy, Frederick Cuthbert de-B.	20/ 1/17	,,	
765362	Kirk, Sgt. Herbert William	10/ 7/18	,,	
760349	Kirton, Sgt. Smart	19/ 9/17	,,	
768955	Knapman, Theophilus Bearne	16/10/18	,,	
766053	La Hive, Bernard	26/ 3/18	,,	
6926	Laker, L/Cpl. John Charles	10/11/16	Major	D.A.D.O.S.
768443	Laming, Harold Edgar	28/ 8/18	Lieut.	
8691	Larcombe, Matthew Alfred	25/ 1/17	,,	
764835	Lee-Smith, Dennis Lee	23/ 9/17	,,	
7641	Lima, Walter	21/11/16	Capt.	
763532	Linder, Henry	27/ 2/17	Lieut.	
761297	Lovell, RSM Geo. Herbert	1/ 4/18	Major	(Staff) w. —/12/14 ℳ(2)
767618	Lucke, Frank Webster	8/ 1/18	Lieut.	
767661	Matthyssens, Frank Alexander	21/10/18	,,	
768460	McSweeney, Edward Archibald	16/10/17	,,	
7832	Meredith, Rowland Styant	15/11/16	Major	ℳ
767224	Michael, Cyril Aaron	9/ 7/18	Lieut.	
7943	Miller, John Maurice	15/11/16	,,	
8130	Morley, John Alfred	12/ 1/17	,,	
768482	Morse, William Ewart	9/ 9/18	Lieut.	
7749	Mullins, Claude William	3/ 8/16	,,	
763857	Murray, James Crossley	23/ 9/17	,,	
768375	Napier, John Struther	27/ 8/18	,,	
766912	Nicholson, Ernest Donald	8/ 4/18	,,	
764450	North, Edwin Bennett	16/ 4/18	,,	
766280	O'Callaghan, Jasper Pyne	28/12/17		
6879	Oldbury, Albert Edward	7/11/16	Lieut.	D.A.D.O.S.
760218	Oram, Herbert	4/ 6/18	Wounded 30/10/17	
762669	Palmer, Clement John	23/ 9/17		
766445	Pentreath, Henry Leslie	29/ 3/18		
760525	Percival, John Beaumont	18/ 9/17	Lieut.	
763680	Perry, James	7/ 8/18	Capt.	
764717	Petter, Cecil Herbert	7/11/18	Lieut.	
762598	Petts, George Albert	6/ 2/17		
6540	Pickard, Frank Reginald	5/ 2/17		
767370	Pile, George Houghton	3/ 6/18		
3044	Pollard, Arthur Howard	21/ 5/16	Lieut.	
4083	Poulston, Sidney	10/11/16	Lieut.	

769174	Ramsay, Andrew Cunningham	... 6/11/18	
763345	Ramsay, Arthur Ferdinand ...	... 24/ 9/17	
764166	Rattigan, Gerald Ernley ...	... 30/ 5/18	
761651	Ray, Phillip Clement ...	... 16/10/18	*Wounded* 16/3/18
763540	Reynolds, Alfred William ...	... 27/ 2/17	
767644	Reynolds, Harry Churchill	... 6/ 4/18	
767425	Riggs, Henry Seymour ...	... 30/ 3/18	
7343	Roberts, Herbert Leonard ...	... 9/ 8/16	*Major*
764343	Robothan, George Percy ...	... 27/ 5/18	
762380	Rudkin, Henry Cecil ...	... 10/ 4/18	
7006	Salt, Charles Henry ...	... 2/12/16	*Lieut.*
769176	Shann, Charles Eustace ...	... 23/10/18	
4352	Sheldon, Herbert John ...	... 4/ 8/16	*Capt.*
760516	Shread, cqms Arthur Charles	... 23/ 9/17	*Lieut.*
768000	Smiles, Alfred Ralph ...	... 12/ 7/18	
761101	Smith, Frederick Harold ...	... 1/ 6/18	*Lieut.*
8109	Smith, Herbert George ...	... 14/12/16	*Major*
760114	Spencer, Douglas	... 24/ 5/18	*Lieut.*
767916	Squire, Alfred Morgan ...	... 30/ 5/18	,,
764270	Steel, Joseph William ...	... 23/ 4/17	,,
765809	Stewart, James	... 5/11/17	,,
763348	Stillwell, William Martin Francis...	24/ 5/17	,,
760830	Stokoe, cqms Edward ...	... 5/ 7/18	*Capt.*
4502	Sutherland, Sgt. Alexander	... 2/ 2/17	*Lieut.*
763477	Swindell, John	... 14/ 2/17	,,
769051	Tautz, Percival Herbert ...	... 6/11/18	,,
766271	Taylor, Edgar Raymond ...	... 24/ 8/18	,, *Wounded* 6/4/18
768593	Teede, John Ernest ...	... 28/ 8/18	,,
765969	Thomas, Alroy Marguand ...	... 28/ 5/18	,,
767579	Thompson, John Edward Bendall ...	7/ 4/18	,,
7468	Tierney, John Patrick ...	... 2/12/16	,,
764212	Towerzey, Alec Reginald ...	... 12/ 4/18	,, *Wounded* 30/10/17
768857	Vickers, Vincent Rawson Scott	... 6/11/18	,,
761435	Wall, Tom	... 1/ 6/18	,, *Wounded* 30/10/17
8649	Watson, Alexander Silver Foord	... 5/ 2/17	,,
8175	Watson, Sydney Campbell ...	... 2/12/16	,,
6685	Wells, Bernard Norman ...	... 5/ 8/16	*Capt.*
765817	Wheeldon, Arthur Leonard	... 21/ 3/18	*Lieut.*
5716	Wild, George	... 10/11/16	,,
3219	With, Alexander Wolseley ...	... 27/12/16	,,
761382	Witney, Sgt. John Humphrey	... 11/ 6/18	*Capt.* m.b.e.
761663	Wood, John	... 10/ 4/18	*Lieut. Wounded* 26/10/17
761108	Wood, Robert Howard ...	... 9/ 4/18	,,

ROYAL ARMY SERVICE CORPS.

		2nd Lieut.		
3226	ACKROYD, George Francis	4/ 2/15	*Lieut.*	M.T.
2954	ALDOUS, George James	27/ 6/15	*Capt.*	✠ Wounded 20/4/18 ⌘
2612	BARTON, Cpl. Bertram Claude	22/ 2/15	*Major*	O.B.E.
2438	BENSON, Rupert Eric	16/ 5/15	*Lieut.*	⌘
3036	BERKELEY, Cpl. Geoffrey Stafford	22/ 3/15	*Capt.*	
2564	BOSTOCK-WILSON, Cpl. Eustace Leslie	12/ 4/15	*Lieut.*	To Indian Army
2606	BUTLER, Cpl. Frederick William	20/ 1/15	*Capt.*	(Canadian Siege Park) ⌘
2840	CARR, Cpl. Alwyn Charles Ellison	13/ 3/15	*Capt.*	
2971	CLARK, Sgt. Ronald Boyd	13/ 7/15	*Lieut.*	
1567	DITCHAM, Vivian Ashley	16/ 8/15	*Lieut.*	
2271	DOWNIE, Cpl. George Ansell	14/ 6/15	*Lieut.*	
60	FAIRBAIRNS, Sgt. Charles Percival	6/ 2/15	*Capt.*	
2772	FITZGERALD, Cyril Theobald	14/ 6/15	*Lieut.*	
1582	GAHAN, John	26/ 9/14	*Capt.*	To Indian Army
2628	GEORGE, Eric Beardsworth	5/ 7/15	*Capt.*	
2295	GIBB, Morrison William	18/ 5/15	*Major.*	To Tank Corps
1893	GILLIARD, Lionel Phillip	16/12/14	*Major*	
3357	GLENFIELD, Francis	12/ 4/15		
1522	GOLDING, Harold William	11/11/14	*Capt.*	Killed in action 31/10/18 ⌘
2240	GOSLETT, Raymond Gwynne	8/ 5/15	*Capt.*	✠
1603	GWYN, Aubrey George	14/ 6/15	*Lieut.*	
2139	HARRISON, Frank Orvin Percy	4/ 5/15	*Lieut.*	
2563	HARROWER, Alexander Bede	10/11/14	*Capt.*	
2334	HOBSON, Harry Roy	21/12/14	*Lt-Col.*	To Staff A.Q.M.G. D.S.O.
2207	HODGKINSON, Harry Drake	4/11/14	*Capt*	O.B.E.
3004	HORNSBY, Percy Reginald	5/ 6/15	*Capt.*	
1861	HUGGINS, Neville Llewellyn	31/ 3/15	*Lieut.*	To R.G.A. w. 13/10/17
631	HUTTON, L/Cpl. Arthur Miles	16/ 8/15	*Capt.*	
3455	KENT, John Charles	25/ 3/15	*Capt.*	
2016	KING, Thomas Claude	24/10/14	*Lieut.*	
2241	LAWRENCE, John Henry	25/ 5/15	*Capt.*	O.B.E. ⌘
893	LIDDLE, Sgt. Dudley Mark Percy	4/ 5/15	*Capt.*	O.B.E. ⌘
2991	LIELL, L/Cpl. Kingsley	26/ 7/15	*Lieut.*	
909	McGORRERY, Cedric Marston	24/ 2/15	*Lieut.*	
2863	McINTYRE, Edgar	1/ 3/15	*Capt.*	
2865	McINTYRE, Norman	1/ 3/15	*Lieut.*	Wounded 10/5/17 ⌘
854	MAILE, Sgt. William Stanley	14/ 6/15	*Capt.*	
2039	MARCH, Bernard Dunstan	2/ 3/15	*Capt.*	
2100	MILNE, Oswald P.	4/11/14	*Major*	⌘
1697	MOORE, John Henry	22/10/14	*Lieut.*	Wounded 9/6/17
2745	MYERS, Dudley	28/12/14	*Capt.*	⌘
3021	NOEL, Gambier Baptist Edward	24/ 5/15	*Lieut.*	Wounded 17/6/18
2276	PAGET-COOKE, L/C. Oliver Daynell P.	15/ 4/15	*Lieut.*	

2362	PITTS, Leonard Arthur Walter	...	5/ 6/15	Capt. ✠
2842	POLLARD, John Leslie ...	...	18/ 4/15	Capt. 🎖
2621	ROBERTSON, Charles Bruce ...	...	18/ 6/15	Major 🎖
2940	ROSSELLI, John Edgar	...	5/ 6/15	Lieut. To R.A.F.
1455	SAUNDERS, John Augustus ...	...	22/ 4/15	Capt. 🎖
2472	SELBY-BIGGE, John Amherst	...	21/ 1/15	Lieut.
3144	SENDELL, Claude Hume	...	14/ 6/15	Lieut. To R.F.A. w. 21/3/18
2108	SEWILL, Roger Waterloo	...	24/10/14	Capt.
2652	SHADWELL, Lancelot Cayley	...	20/ 2/15	
2557	SMITH, Arthur Douglas	...	22/ 3/15	Capt.
2398	SMITH, Norman Lang	...	14/ 6/15	Lieut.
2577	SPEIRS, John...	...	22/ 3/15	Lieut.
2508	STEVENSON, John Stanley	...	12/12/14	Lieut. Wounded 28/8/17
1542	SUTTON, Gilbert Francis	...	3/ 4/15	Lieut. To Indian Army
2866	TAFFT, John Raymond	...	22/ 3/15	Major
2152	TANNER, Arthur Ralph	...	28/11/14	Capt.
2027	TANNER, Edwin John	...	25/11/14	Capt.
1870	THORN, William Marchant Warner...		13/ 7/15	Lieut.
3099	THOMSON, L/Cpl. Gordon Duncan ...		24/ 5/15	Lieut.
2236	WALTON, Leslie Robert	...	25/ 5/15	Capt.
2902	WEBB, Rupert Dudley Clarkson	...	24/ 6/15	Lieut. 🎖
1121	WEBER-BROWN, Alven William	..	23/10/14	Capt.
3324	WHITTOME, John Eric	...	17/ 2/15	Lieut.
2812	WHITESIDE, Miles Bruce Dalzel	...	9/12/14	To Highland L.I. Acc/killed [13/6/18]
1972	WILLIAMSON, William Henry Rowe...		25/11/14	Lieut. ✠
1309	WRIGHT, Graham Edmund ...	...	8/ 2/15	Lieut. ✠ 🎖
3164	BALE, Sgt. Frank Stewart	...	6/11/15	Lieut.
1611	BARNETT, Harold Andrew ...	...	25/ 8/15	Capt. 🎖
2623	BARTON, Cecil George	...	18/ 9/15	Lieut. [action 21/3/18]
1339	BASSETT, L/Cpl. Geoffrey Edward ...		5/11/15	To Oxford & Bucks Killed in
1243	BRADFIELD, Godfrey Edward	...	14/10/15	Lieut. M.T. Wounded 17/9/18
2364	BEALE, Cpl. William Pierse	...	7/ 9/15	Lieut.
2375	BEST, Cpl. Charles Edward	...	28/ 8/15	Capt.
7699	BROCKLEHURST, Edward Howard	...	28/ 5/16	Lieut.
676	BRINDLEY, Samuel Gordon ...	...	25/ 8/15	Capt. 🎖
2944	BUXTON-KNIGHT, Oliver	...	8/ 8/15	Capt. 🎖
780	CHANDLER, Alfred Leonard	...	12/10/15	Capt. M.T. ✠ 🎖
1838	CIRCUITT, George Francis Langdale...		20/11/15	Capt. M.B.E. 🎖
1493	CLOSE, Sgt. Ralph Lea	...	29/10/15	Lieut
1910	COTTON, Gerald Vincent	...	2/11/15	Lieut.
78	COWELL, Sgt. Frank Howlett	...	26/ 9/15	Lieut. To 5/Oxfd. & Bucks L.I. [w. 21/3/18]
4247	CURRAN, Ernest Charles	...	25/10/15	Capt.
2663	DUNELL, Alan Gordon	...	27/ 9/15	Capt. M.B.E. 🎖
1938	DYBALL, John Francis	...	20/11/15	Capt.
2765	EDWARDS, Christopher	...	15/ 1/16	Lieut.
1290	EDWARDS, Sgt. William	...	26/ 9/15	Capt. Died of wounds 28/3/18

ROYAL ARMY SERVICE CORPS.

2103	EDWARDS, Harold Francis ...	13/12/15		
1826	EGERTON, Cpl. Bryan Selwyn	18/ 8/15	*Lieut.*	ℳ
2014	ELLERBY, H. Frank St. George	13/ 8/15	*Capt.*	
1887	FAIRBAIRNS, Reginald Holland	18/ 8/15	*Lieut.*	*To M.G.C.* ✠ *Wounded*
5840	FEHRMAN, Austin Albert Francis	28/ 5/16	,,	
434	FLETCHER, Sgt. Robert Combe	15/ 8/15	,,	
6616	FINN-KELCEY, Walter John ...	7/ 5/16	,,	
400	FISHER, CQMS William Eric ...	10/ 8/15	*Capt.*	✠
1564	FRISLEY, Herbert Rowell	24/10/15	*Capt.*	ℳ
1358	HAND, Henry George	8/ 8/15	*Capt.*	
181	HANKINS, L/Cpl. Thomas Pelham ...	25/ 8/15	*Major*	
1210	HOPSON, L/Cpl. Montagu Guy S. ...	5/ 9/15	*Lieut.*	
1338	IVORY, Harold Frank	24/10/15	*Capt.*	O.B.E. ℳ(2)
3195	KEATES, Bransby Cooper	30/ 9/15	*Lieut.*	
2138	KEEPING, Harold Balfour	1/ 1/15	*Capt.*	M.B.E.
173	KIBBLE, Sgt. Alfred William	21/ 9/15	*Lieut.*	ℳ
5627	LAXTON, Edward William Henry ...	—	*Lieut.*	
3186	LEONARD, Terence James ...	24/ 9/15	*Lieut.*	
3381	LEESE, Leonard Ernest Selwyn	2/11/15	*Capt.*	
6167	LIEBERT, Alfred John	19/ 6/16	*Lieut.*	
1435	MARTIN, Sgt. Ernest Wilfrid Leigh...	6/10/15	*Capt. & Adjutant*	✠
3139	MAWSON, Philip Sefton de Maine ...	2/11/15		
6848	MIDWINTER, Walter Hugh ...	14/ 5/16	*Lieut.*	ℳ
3985	PARKER, Aubrey Arthur Frederick ..	24/ 9/15	*Lieut.*	
1846	PHIPPS, Sgt. Percy ...	4/ 8/15	*Capt.*	ℳ
3044	POLLARD, Arthur Howard ...	21/ 5/16	*Lieut.*	
750	PURSER, Philip Warburton ...	25/ 5/15		
3360	RHODES, Horace	7/ 9/15	*Lieut.*	ℳ
2807	SETH-SMITH, Sgt. Gordon ...	6/ 9/15	*Lieut.*	
6631	TEMPLE, Alfred	14/ 5/16	*Capt.*	F/D
1411	THEAK, Leslie Frederick ...	29/10/15	*Lieut.*	
5389	WENGER, Theodore Lauternier ...	14/ 5/16	*Lt.-Colonel*	✠
765750	AGNEW, Reginald Colville ...	29/ 9/17		
7961	ASHLEIGH-BODDINGTON, H. Kennedy	26/10/16	*Capt.*	ℳ
3545	AUSTIN, John Leslie	26/ 7/16	*Lieut.*	
765102	BACON, Francis Charles	27/10/17		
764870	BARBER, Frederick ...	2/ 7/17	*Lieut.*	
765917	BARNES, Oliver Edward	29/ 9/17		
766341	BARTON, Arthur Lewis	29/ 9/17		
1339	BASSETT, Ralph Lea	5/11/15	*Lieut.*	
8158	BEADNELL, Hugh John Llewellyn ...	26/10/16	*Capt.*	ℳ
6195	BEAN, Douglas McGregor ...	26/ 3/17	*Lieut.*	
766774	BEAVAN, John	7/ 1/18		
8347	BELLAMY, Somers ...	21/12/16	*Lieut.*	
765236	BIGGS, Seward ...	27/10/17	*Died* 26/11/18	

ROYAL ARMY SERVICE CORPS.

1967	Bishop, Eric G. C.	24/ 7/16	Lieut.	To Indian Army
6371	Blackmore, Oscar Wilkie	26/10/16	Capt.	⚔
5833	Blindell, Charles William	26/10/16	Lieut.	
6471	Bonar, Hew Hunter	26/10/16	Lieut.	
765496	Bond, Cyril Harry Charles	29/ 9/17	M.B.E.	
7969	Bridges, Charles	21/12/16	Lieut.	
765497	Bridgett, Harry	29/ 9/17		
764309	Brookes, Arthur	9/ 5/17	Lieut.	
3436	Brophy, Cyril Joseph	21/12/16	Lieut.	
765755	Brown, Henry Davis	29/ 9/17	Lieut.	
760834	Burrows, Charles Alban Ellis	29/ 9/17		
769126	Burton, Frank	18/ 2/19		
4025	Byles, Sgt. William Hounsom	26/10/16	Lieut.	
761351	Calvert, Ralph Dutton	13/ 8/17	Lieut.	
7666	Carr, William Frederick	5/12/16	Lieut.	
7356	Carter, Alfred Cecil	16/ 8/16	Lieut.	F/D
6333	Chapman, James Taylor	7/ 8/16	Lieut.	
760747	Chaston, Walter Alan	2/ 3/18		
766779	Chesterton, Sidney James	7/ 1/18		
765411	Colquhoun, Wm. Harry Campbell	25/ 8/17		
766014	Cowie, Kenneth Vere	18/12/16		
8122	Craig, Robert Gray	21/12/16	Lieut.	
8064	Craven, Stanley Clifford	21/12/16	Lieut.	
5477	Crawford, Hugh	10/ 2/17	Wounded 16/10/17	
765385	Creer, Frederick Norman	29/ 6/17		
761469	Croneen, Seymour	29/ 6/17	Lieut.	✠
1784	Curtis, Sgt. Bertram Ernest	26/10/17	Lieut.	
765989	Davy, Edward Humphrey	29/ 9/17		
3307	Dawbarn, Arthur Leslie	12/ 6/16	Lieut.	
7633	Day, Ernest Stanley	21/12/16	Lieut.	
764819	Denny, Owen Lindsey	9/ 9/17		
2239	De St. Croix, Leslie Lawson	24/12/14	Capt.	Q.M.G. Dept. M.B.E. ⚔
765583	Dixon, William Ewart	29/ 9/17		
766097	Dovey, Arthur George	27/ 7/18		
4309	Downton, Sgt. Lionel Arthur	21/12/16	Lieut.	
1314	Driskell, Cpl. John Anthony	10/11/16	Lieut.	
6440	Dupas, Cpl. Felix Maximilian	12/ 2/17	Lieut.	
2669	Durrant, QMS Norman	26/10/16	Lieut.	
764113	Ellis, Harry Charles	9/ 5/17	Lieut.	M.B.E.
766191	Farnham, John Adrian George	27/ 5/18		
764767	Fawcett, Richard Metcalfe	1/12/17		
766809	Featherston, Harry	27/ 5/18		
8045	Field, John	26/10/16	Lieut.	
2478	Finnis, William Trevor	9/ 1/15	Major	⚔
5843	Goldby, Frank Lyster	21/12/16	Lieut.	
766048	Goode, Henry Percival	29/ 9/17		

ROYAL ARMY SERVICE CORPS. 407

764642	GRAVE, Frederick John	29/ 6/17	
763391	GREEN, Norman John	29/ 9/17	
632	GREENWOOD, Sgt. Frank Thomas	21/10/16	Lieut.
761780	GRIST, Sgt. Arthur Percy	29/ 9/17	
762257	GRUSKIN, Charles	12/ 5/17	
7768	GURDON, Frank	21/12/16	Lieut.
765617	GURNEY, Reginald Brodie	29/ 9/17	
8492	HAIGH, George Dick Duncan	21/12/16	Lieut.
765941	HALSALL, Herbert	29/ 9/17	
7279	HAMER, William	26/10/16	Lieut. Wounded 14/10/18
2414	HARPER, Edward Russell	19/ 3/15	Lieut. ✠
1521	HARPER, Hubert Harry	17/ 3/15	Capt.
763526	HARRIS, Albert	27/10/17	
5442	HARRIS, John Lindsay	26/10/16	Capt. Wounded M
765618	HARRIS, William Henry	29/ 9/17	
765620	HERRON, Robert Walter Cowell	29/ 9/17	Capt.
763425	HILL, Sheldon	9/ 5/17	Lieut.
2481	HOLLIDGE, Alec	25/ 8/17	Lieut. M.B.E.
766673	HOLLINGDALE, Gerald Francis	21/ 1/18	
765877	HONEY, George	27/10/17	
8226	HOOLE, Walter	6/11/16	Lieut.
766478	HORNBY, John Albert	18/12/17	
763498	INMAN, Ronald Kesterton	12/ 4/17	Lieut.
765567	JONES, Herbert Richard	29/ 9/17	
766349	JUMP, Walter Bertram	1/12/17	
7804	KEECH, Frank Sprake	21/12/16	Lieut.
763826	KEEVIL, Reginald Henry	25/ 6/17	
762936	KEMBALL, Sydney James	1/ 4/18	
765684	KINSEY, Henry William	27/10/17	
6384	LAKEMAN, Harold Leslie	22/ 9/16	(7/Lancs. Fusiliers) Killed in [action 22/8/18]
765843	LEWIS, Grafton	29/ 9/17	
765236	LYNCH, James Frederick Aloysius	27/10/17	
8135	LYNN, Hastings	26/10/16	Lieut.
760666	MACE, Sgt. Arthur Cruttenden	27/ 2/17	Lieut.
765596	MARCHANT, Arthur Reginald	29/ 9/17	
760144	MARES, Sgt. Frank Gardus	24/ 5/18	
763342	MAY, RSM Samuel	4/ 7/18	
764331	McLEOD, Edward Donald	29/ 6/17	
763165	McNULTY, George Henry	29/ 9/17	
765185	MIDDLETON, John	29/ 6/17	
1456	MILES, Martin Hedden	15/ 9/14	Capt. From 9/W. Yorks w. —/8/16
8048	MOON, John	21/12/16	Lieut.
763000	MOTT, George	27/10/17	
763935	NELSON, Joe	29/ 9/17	
762701	NEWMAN, Sydney	23/ 5/17	
766655	NUNN, Ernest Robert	26/ 5/18	
9662	ORD, Eustace Moon	27/ 2/17	Capt. M

764791	PAINE, Gerald Arthur	27/10/17
761867	PALMER, Ethelred Loyal	22/ 5/17
2709	PARKER, Reginald	11/ 7/15 *Capt.*
765914	PELLS, Henry Herbert	29/ 9/17
8039	PEPPER, William Arnold	26/10/16 *Lieut.* ✠
768807	PIGNATEL, Ernest Charles	22/ 2/19
765284	PINEGER, George Frederick Ross	27/ 5/18
760601	RAY, Allan Guy	21/ 1/18
767278	RICHARDSON, Frank Albert	24/ 5/18
764930	RIDDALL, Gervase	15/ 7/17
762461	ROBERTS, Charles St. John Courtney	25/ 5/17
6123	ROBERTSON, Robert Jerome	6/ 9/18 *Lieut.* ✠
760696	ROBSON, Leonard	21/ 1/18
766817	ROCHESTER, William Kaye	4/ 2/18
764959	ROWLANDS, Ernest	26/ 6/17
766791	ROXBURGH, John Armour	7/ 1/18 ✠
2090	SCRIVEN, Denis Ambrose	5/ 4/17
766930	SMALL, Harry Lionel	21/ 1/18
7783	SMITH, Cecil Arthur	26/10/16 *Lieut.*
1766	SMITH, Charles Reginald	11/ 9/16 *Lieut*
8123	SMITH, Edward Stuart	21/11/16 *Lieut.*
8194	SOLLOM, Vincent Peter	21/12/16 *Lieut.*
765055	SPEARING, Charles Howard	1/12/17
7711	STANTON, Roy	4/ 9/16
6331	STOKES, James Hawkes	26/10/16 *Lieut.*
767068	STOTESBURY, Robert King	23/ 5/18
761995	TATHAM, Ralph Percival	29/ 6/17 *Lieut.*
763604	TAYLOR, Reginald Archer	27/10/17
6163	TIDY, John Oswald	21/12/16 *Lieut.* ✠
765062	TITCHMARCH, Charles Harold	27/10/17
1956	TOLLER, L/Cpl. William George	12/ 9/16 *Lieut.* ✠
765423	TREVISSICK, William James	1/12/17
762965	TYE, Frederick	20/ 2/18
5102	TYSON, Arnold William	14/ 8/16 *Lieut.*
766367	UNDERWOOD, John Edward	20/ 9/18
8021	URQUHART, John Kennedy	21/12/16 *Lieut.*
765745	VAN LESSEN, Derrick Michael	27/10/17
762987	WAKEFIELD, Alfred Bazzante	28/ 4/17
765696	WALTER, George Leonard	29/ 9/17
2562	WATKINS, Percy Manning Clifford	21/ 9/16 *Lieut.*
766403	WATSON, Hugh Bernard	27/ 7/18
8185	WELLBORNE, Harry Harold Goodson	21/12/16 *Lieut.* ✠
764674	WICKMAN, Frank Thomas	29/ 6/17
5717	WITT, George Benjamin	26/10/16 *Lieut.*
2857	WOOD, Charles Kenneth	14/ 8/16 *Lieut.*
763051	WOOLLEY, William John	25/ 5/17
8165	WYRALL, Everard	26/10/16 *Lieut.* ✠

Territorial Force.

2496	HOLDEN, Edward Charles ...	27/ 3/15	*Lieut.*		1/*South Western Mounted Bde.*	
3536	ADAMS, Alexander Hector ...	5/ 5/15	*Lieut.*			
383	GIBBS, Gerard Yardley ...	6/11/14	*Lieut.*	O.B.E. ℳ(2)	*East Anglian*	
2794	SEABROOKE, Geoffrey Stanford	16/11/14	*Lieut.*	(*R.A.F.*)	*Divl. Train*	
4102	REDWOOD, Eric	2/11/15	*Lieut.*		2/*London Divl. Train*	

GENERAL LIST.

2nd Lieut.

768720	ALANTHWAITE, Sydney Victor ...	8/ 3/19	
769446	ALEXANDER, Wilson Walter Watkin...	8/ 3/19	
768161	ALFORD, Arthur William	17/ 3/19	S.B. –/*E. Surrey*
769359	ALGER, Aubrey Sampson	8/ 3/19	
767736	ASHWORTH, Arthur Reginald Egerton	8/ 3/19	
769447	BINDON, Guillerms Strong	8/ 3/19	
768290	BLAND, Albert	4/ 8/19	M.B.E.
767791	BLANSHARD, Charles John	3/ 3/19	
768081	BLORE, John Hockley	8/ 3/19	
769448	BOOTHROYD, Benjamin Manoah ..	8/ 3/19	*Overseas Forces*
769449	BOURHILL, Noygo Everard	8/ 3/19	
769475	BOYES, Cecil Edward Cubitt ...	8/ 3/19	
768434	BRERETON, Victor Fortescue ...	8/ 3/19	
767992	BROUSE, William Henry Davenport...	8/ 3/19	
768568	BROWNE, Arthur Woodthorpe Crayfoot	8/ 3/19	
768223	BUCKLAND, Lancelot Liddle Rorke...	8/ 3/19	
769450	BURMAN, Harold Seymour	8/ 3/19	
769363	BYNOE, Edward Dunbar	8/ 3/19	
767136	CAWSE, Alfred Westcott	8/ 3/19	
769510	CHURCHMAN, John Elie Lofts ...	8/ 3/19	
769492	CLARK, John	8/ 3/19	*Overseas Forces*
769039	COBB, Philip Hawlyn	8/ 3/19	
767921	COHEN, Reuben Copley	8/ 3/19	
769452	COLEPEPPER, Francis Ellerton ...	8/ 3/19	
769480	COULSON, Frederick Brian	8/ 3/19	
768472	CROSBIE, William Gustave	8/ 3/19	
767103	CROWTHER, Percy Facey Hunter ...	11/ 3/19	
768122	CURRIE, Cyril Hugh	8/ 3/19	
768315	DANVERS, Charles Henry Danby ...	8/ 3/19	*Overseas Forces*
769380	DAVIS, James Walwyn	8/ 3/19	
769244	DE CHAZAL, Edmund Mare ...	8/ 3/19	

GENERAL LIST.

769365	DE FOREST, John Wright	8/ 3/19	
769482	DE GEX, Ruthven Gore	8/ 3/19	
769381	DE ST.-CROIX, Phillip Ernest	8/ 3/19	
768820	DEWAR, Duncan	8/ 3/19	
768133	DICKSON, Robert Grant	8/ 3/19	
768899	DYSON, L/Cpl. Dyson Herbert	8/ 3/19	
769494	FISHER, Isaac James	8/ 3/19	
769323	FRASER, Donald William	8/ 3/19	*Overseas Forces*
760699	FRAY, Harry	8/ 3/19	*Wounded* 16/7/18
769407	FULLER, Harold Norden	8/ 3/19	
769612	GAWLEY, Robert James	8/ 3/19	
768318	GIBSON, James Thomson	8/ 3/19	
769594	GODDARD, Frederick Douglas	8/ 3/19	*Overseas Forces*
767705	GORDON, Alexander	8/ 3/19	
768918	GRIGOR, L/Cpl. John Alexander	8/ 3/19	
769642	HART, Gerald Raymond	8/ 3/19	
768652	HARBOTTLE, John Russell	8/ 3/19	
768831	HAWKINS, Henry Alexander	8/ 3/19	
769596	HAYNES, Leonard	8/ 3/19	
769112	HAYWOOD, Harold William	8/ 3/19	*Overseas Forces*
769233	HUGHES, Edward	8/ 3/19	
768655	HITCHMAN, John William Cross	8/ 3/19	
765708	HENRY, John Henry Waldo	1/ 8/18	*Overseas Forces* M.B.E.
768459	HOOKER, Jacob Thomas	8/ 3/19	
769312	HOWE, Joseph Arthur	8/ 3/19	
767995	HUGGINS, Hale Hunter	11/ 3/19	
768921	HUME, William Dingwell	8/ 3/19	
769115	JENNINGS, Percival John	8/ 3/19	
769461	KEELING, Ewart Abinger	8/ 3/19	
768368	KENNARD, Gabriel Vernon	8/ 3/19	
768578	KNEVITT, Edmund Brittain	8/ 3/19	
767926	KNOX, John	8/ 3/19	
769483	LACEY, Norman	8/ 3/19	
766736	LEVY, Frederick Walter	8/ 3/19	
769463	LINDBERGH, William Harold	8/ 3/19	
768758	LOCKETT, Maynard Vernon	8/ 3/19	
767816	LOWE, L/Cpl. Thomas Henry	8/ 3/19	
768213	LYNCH, Maurice Gordon Lloyd	8/ 3/19	
768976	MACKINTOSH, Coleridge Stewart	8/ 3/19	
769643	MACNICOL, Donald	8/ 3/19	
766415	MAINGOT, Louis Farfan	8/ 3/19	
767928	MANN, Ernest H.	8/ 3/19	
767045	MANN, James Wallace	8/ 3/19	
767997	MCGREGOR, Evan	8/ 3/19	
761150	MCNAMARA, John Percival	8/ 3/19	
769524	MCNIEL, Ronald	8/ 3/19	
769314	MEAD, Charles Edward	8/ 3/19	

768622	MILLARD, Ronald Vanstone	8/ 3/19
768659	MILLER, George Lane	9/12/18
768840	MILLER, Herbert Charles	8/ 3/19
768927	MILLER, Harry Duke	8/ 3/19
768661	MOIR, George Taylor	8/ 3/19
762250	MOIR, Stedman Esdaile	8/ 3/19
769371	MOIR, Thomas Niven	8/ 3/19
768842	MORTON, Hugh Macfarlane	8/ 3/19
769529	MURLY, Cecil John	8/ 3/19
767179	MURRAY, Stuart McPherson	8/ 3/19
768928	O'BRIEN-MOORE, Ainsworth	8/ 3/19
769625	O'DOWD, Eugene Michael	8/ 3/19
769351	ORCHARD, Albert	8/ 3/19
768353	OWEN, Edward Thomas	8/ 3/19
768485	PAGE, Maximilian J. I.	8/ 3/19
768806	PAGET, Bertie Kenneth	8/ 3/19
769264	PHILIP, James Buxton	8/ 3/19
769330	PHILIP, William Yalden	8/ 3/19
769265	PICKETT, William FitzClaire	8/ 3/19
769332	PULLEN, Leslie Edward	8/ 3/19
769333	RABIE, Eric Lynton	8/ 3/19
769066	REES, Joseph Frederick	8/ 3/19
769081	REYNOLDS, Charles Montague William	8/ 3/19
769587	ROGERS, Harold Murly	8/ 3/19
768325	ROSE, Alfred Edward	8/ 3/19
769215	RYDER, Charles Thomas W.	8/ 3/19
768556	SINCLAIR, Patric James	8/ 3/19
768591	SKEETE, Charles de Courcy	8/ 3/19
768674	SMITH, Edward Edmonds	8/ 3/19
768712	SMITH, Frank Harold	8/ 3/19
769068	SMITH, John Leslie	8/ 3/19
769484	SMITH, Medland Stace Carruthers	8/ 3/19
769395	STRACHAN, Henry Kendle	8/ 3/19
768018	SWANN, A/Sgt. Frederick Thomas	3/ 8/19
769485	TAPSON, Anthony Guy Ewart	8/ 3/19
769396	TAYLOR, Ernest Vernon	8/ 3/19
766821	TOONJAN, John Gregory	8/ 3/19
768140	TREDGOLD, Robert Clarkson	8/ 3/19
768330	VAN-EEDEN, Frederick	8/ 3/19
768035	VIVIAN, Gerald Herbert Everarde	8/ 3/19
768934	WAKEFIELD, Cyril Horace	8/ 3/19
768003	WEBB, Dodd Davies	8/ 3/19
767486	WHITTINGTON-LOWE, A/Sgt. E. H. R.	5/ 8/19
768680	WICHT, John Ditton	8/ 3/19
769085	WILKS, Edward Craven	8/ 3/19
769473	WOOD, Ernest Marshall	8/ 3/19
769055	WRENCH, E. Leonard	8/ 3/19

THE INNS OF COURT O.T.C.

2119 TERRELL, Wallis Carnaby ... ... 18/ 7/15 *Capt.* (*Instnl. Duties*)

LABOUR CORPS.

2nd Lieut.
766913	ADKINS, George	26/ 7/18	*Chinese L.C.*
765356	ALEXANDER, Albert Victor	16/12/17	
764676	ANDREWS, Charles Neefield	14/ 7/17	
762360	ANDREWS, Percy Charles	15/ 7/17	
764677	ANGELL, Thomas Craveley	16/12/17	
765353	ANNESLEY, Philip de Vere	24/ 2/18	
764868	ARMITAGE, John Walter	16/ 6/17	*Lieut.*
764743	ASHTON, Wyndham Rees	16/12/17	*Lieut.*
763906	BEALL, Robert William	16/ 6/17	
760588	BELL, Thomas Frederick	18/ 8/17	*Lieut.* Wounded 1/11/17
763091	BEVAN, Victor Reginald	26/ 1/18	
767245	BIRSE, Arthur Herbert	8/11/18	
764813	BLUCK, Gilbert Eustace	14/ 7/17	
763057	BRUNTON, Guy	10/ 3/17	*Capt.* O.B.E. *From Durham L.I.*
767214	BURLEY, Ernest Sidney	4/12/17	*Died* 15/2/19
766423	BURTON, Edward George	19/ 5/18	
763256	CATHERALL, Cecil	13/ 4/17	*Capt.*
766343	CHAMBERLAIN, James Ernest	19/ 5/18	
765785	CHARLESWORTH, Martin	16/12/17	
760259	CLARK, Arnold Bertram	14/ 7/17	*Lieut.*
764926	DADE, James Frederic	16/12/17	
763420	DAVIS, Joel William	14/ 7/17	*Lieut.*
760787	DAY, Montague Irvine Reid	12/ 5/17	*Lieut.*
763264	DERRY, Everard Gover	16/12/17	
336	DORE, William Charles Henry	15/ 6/17	*Lt.-Col.* O/C 48/*Lab. Group* ✠
765116	DYALL, Alan	16/ 6/17	*Lieut.* 🎖
765566	DYOTT, Hugh Felton	16/ 8/17	*Chinese L.C.*
760571	EYLES, Sgt. William George	7/ 9/17	*Lieut.*
764694	FAIRWEATHER, Hugh Forsyth	18/ 8/17	*Lieut.*
763122	FLEMING, Charles Brandon R.	16/ 6/17	*Lieut.*
764236	FOLKARD, Henry Francis	16/ 6/17	
764555	FRASER, Donald	23/ 6/18	*Lieut.*
767151	FRASER, James Wyllie	20/ 4/18	*Chinese L.C.*
764401	FREEMAN, William Arthur	27/ 7/17	*Lieut.*
765119	FULCHER, William James	14/ 7/17	*Lieut.*
763949	GERSON, John Leslie	19/ 5/18	
766112	GILLETT, Stanley	23/ 6/18	

LABOUR CORPS.

762184	GODBER, Leslie	14/ 7/17	*Lieut.*
769613	GREGORY, Harry	11/ 1/19	
767124	GUTHRIE, William	19/ 5/18	
761815	HANNAM-CLARK, Sgt. George Fredk.	16/12/17	
763236	HANNAN, Terence George	13/ 5/17	*Wounded* 27/7/17
760989	HARRISON, Frank Cyril	14/ 7/17	*Lieut.*
762751	HAWKINS, Charles Newcombe	16/ 6/17	*Lieut.*
765942	HERRINGSHAW, Edwin Arthur	23/ 6/18	
763497	HIRST, Francis Eric	16/ 6/17	*Lieut.*
765272	HOLDEN, John Willie	16/ 6/17	*Lieut.*
763714	HOLMES, Arthur	12/ 5/17	*Lieut.*
764701	HOLMES, Willie Ernest	14/ 7/17	
762207	HOOPER, Leonard Arthur	14/ 7/17	
767013	HORROBIN, Sydney Leigh	4/12/17	
765551	HOY, James Norman Robertson	16/12/17	
763825	HUGGINS, Willie London	14/ 7/17	*Lieut.*
764648	INNES, Eric Rawstone d'A.	18/ 8/17	*Lieut.*
760910	JAMES, John Stewart	16/ 6/17	*Lieut.*
761025	JAMIESON, Robert Kirkland	27/ 8/18	
766307	JOHNSTONE, Charles Manning	19/ 5/18	
767338	KING, George Alastair	19/ 5/18	
761147	LADELL, Claude Suchneil	14/ 7/17	*Lieut.* ℳ
761701	LAMB, Henry	12/ 5/17	*Lieut.*
764707	LEADBEATER, Alfred James Osman	16/ 6/17	*Lieut.*
767016	LIDDLE, Adam Robson	26/ 7/18	
765686	LOCKWOOD, Reginald	16/12/17	
765660	LODDER, William Charles	12/ 5/17	*Lieut.*
763730	MACDONALD, Alexander	16/12/17	
766840	MALLEN, Alexander	23/ 6/18	
762156	MARRIOTT, Clive	1/ 8/17	
761605	MARSHALL, Harry	8/ 5/17	(5/*Liverp.*) *Died of wounds* 5/11/18
763166	MAUGHAN, Martin Leslie	18/12/17	
760946	MAWSON, Joseph Howson	14/ 7/17	*Lieut.*
764838	MCCLELLAN, Reuben James	14/ 7/17	*Lieut.*
766839	MCGREGOR, Reginald Thomas	19/ 5/18	
765569	MENNELL, Edward Darcy	15/ 8/19	
764444	MEREDITH, Harry Rouse	28/ 8/17	*Lieut.*
766764	MOORE, Arthur William	19/ 5/18	
766335	MURPHY, Cecil Everard	23/ 6/18	
6115	NEWMAN, Claude Edwin Sandys	12/ 7/16	*Lieut.* ℳ
765283	PARKER, Maurice George	16/ 6/17	*Lieut.*
764907	PARRY, Sydney Herbert	18/ 8/17	*Lieut.*
765410	PATTON, Ernest	23/ 5/18	*Chinese L.C.*
766721	PEARSON, Eric Leslie	19/ 5/18	
763471	PENROSE, John	14/ 7/17	*Lieut.*
764407	PERKES, Alfred Roland	14/ 7/17	*Lieut.*
761013	PICTON, Thomas	23/ 6/18	

LABOUR CORPS.

763275	POSTON, Leslie Ivor	14/ 7/17	*Lieut.*
763369	REED, Robert Gibbard	14/ 7/17	*Lieut.*
767088	RENDLE, Hugh Bainbridge	19/ 5/18	
761036	RHODES, Oswald Newton	9/ 6/17	*Lieut.*
763627	ROBSON, Leonard	14/ 7/17	*Lieut.*
764932	ROCK-WEST, Owen Gerald	12/12/17	
765079	ROSE, Algernon	17/ 6/17	*Lieut.*
762354	SALWAY, Jasper Philip	14/ 7/17	*Lieut.*
763115	SEMMENS, Joseph James	14/ 7/17	*Lieut.*
760226	SEXTON, Arthur Alexander	14/ 7/17	*Lieut.*
766623	SHAYLOR, Harold	19/ 5/18	
764265	SIMPKIN, John William	14/ 7/17	*Lieut.*
765804	SKINNER, Ernest Harry Dudley	18/12/17	
763045	SMITH, Alfred Ernest	10/ 3/17	*Lieut.* M
765327	SMITH, Brice de Berniere	18/12/17	
765051	SMITH, John Stanley	14/ 7/17	*Lieut.*
764854	SMITH, Percy	21/ 5/17	*Lieut.*
765250	SPARROW, Frederick Poole	18/ 8/17	*Lieut.*
760927	SPENCER, John Wallace	18/ 8/17	*Lieut.*
762421	STAMPER, Christopher	5/ 9/18	
765251	STOKER, Frank Reginald	14/ 7/17	*Lieut.*
764389	STOREY, Ralph	14/ 7/17	*Lieut.*
762868	SWALLOW, Hubert	24/ 2/18	
762342	SWINDLEY, Eric Ion	18/ 8/17	*Lieut.*
761827	TATE, Arthur Frank	12/ 5/17	*Lieut.* M
766235	TAYLOR, Philip Salmon	9/11/17	*Egyptian L.C.*
766328	THOMAS, Howard Gordon Rhys	3/ 9/17	*Chinese L.C.*
761013	THOMAS, Picton	23/ 6/18	
765523	THOMPSON, Walter Douglas Hebson	16/12/17	
762611	VAUSE, Frederick	12/ 5/17	*Lieut.*
765615	VICKERS, Arthur Noel	16/12/17	
764216	WALLER, John Gamble	14/ 7/17	*Lieut.*
760289	WELLS, Denys George	14/ 4/17	*Lieut.*
765911	WEST, Edwin George	16/12/17	
764301	WETHERALL, Eric Francis Cecil	17/ 6/17	*Died* 27/12/18
764736	WHITE, Cyril Vernon	12/ 5/17	*Lieut.*
761228	WHITE, Norman Emery	14/ 7/17	*Lieut.*
765480	WHITLOCK, Francis Walter	23/ 6/18	
766329	WINTER, Philip Arundel	20/11/17	
764937	WOOLVERIDGE, Charles Skelton	18/ 8/17	*Lieut.*
764921	YELD, George Grenville	14/ 7/17	*Lieut.*

MACHINE-GUN CORPS. 415

		2nd Lieut.		
Lieut.	Frost, Alan	... 17/10/14	Capt.	Killed in action 17/10/17
2nd Lt.	Job, Ernest Dalzel	... 5/ 2/16	Capt.	Killed in action 11/7/16
Lieut.	Laing, John Gordon ...	... 5/ 2/16	Major	w. 27/6/16 Killed in [action 3/10/18
2003	Andrews, Thomas Edward ...	... 1/ 2/16	Lieut.	From 9/D.C.L.I.
1041	Baggallay, Geoffrey Thomas*	... 21/10/15	Capt.	From 2/Welch w.–/5/15,
2171	Bending, Charles Oscar ...	... 16/ 9/15	Lieut.	[–/12/17 A.P.M.
652	Campbell, Guy	... 1/ 3/15	Capt.	From 8/N.F. M.B.E. ✠ [Acc/killed 26/5/17 ⌬
899	Cliveley, Richard C. ...	... –/ 6/16	Major	From 6/S. Lancs. ✠ ⌬
1120	Crowdy, Ronald St. John ...	... 23/ 2/16	Capt.	From 1/Wilts A.P.M.
2640	Gelsthorpe, Alfred Morris ...	... 6/ 2/16	Capt. D.S.O.	From 8/Dur. L.I. ⌬
3557	Howard, William Edward ...	... 7/12/15	Capt. & Adjt.	From 4/Manchester [w. 2/10/17, 18/12/17]
1642	Legh-Jones, Sgt. George ...	... 18/11/15	Lieut.	From 11/R. Welch Fusiliers
3234	Lloyd, Hamilton Samuel John	... 29/11/15	Lieut.	From 15/Welch To I. Army
2720	Meredith, Alexander Charles	... 1/ 2/16	Capt.	From 8/R.B. ✠ w. –/8/16.
2233	Monaghan, Denis Lawrence ...	... 18/12/15	Lieut.	Killed in action 24/11/17
3190	Saqui, Leslie Vernon Harcourt	... 1/ 2/16	Lieut.	From 11/Norfolk
763	Sheehan, Frank George Edward	... 30/10/15	Lieut.	No. 4 Battery
85	Smith, Sgt. Harold Rees ...	... 18/ 8/15	Major	No. 8 Battery (D.A.A. & [Q.M.G., Tank C.) ✠
3420	Southan, Reginald	... 23/ 1/16	Lieut.	From 1/Worcester
1377	Voss, Sgt. Gordon Phillips ...	... 30/10/15	Lieut.	✠ ✠
762612	Acton, Geo. Raymond ...	... 26/ 4/17		Wounded 13/11/17
763744	Allan, Kenneth Ethelbert ...	... 30/ 3/17		
765781	Ashbrooke, John Jacob ...	... 21/ 2/18		Wounded 6/11/18
1975	Athol, Sgt/Inst. Charles Colbourne	16/10/16	Lieut.	Killed in action 26/8/18.
8040	Atter, William George ...	... 26/10/16	Lieut.	Wounded & P/W
761308	Babbage, Charles Ernest ...	... 29/12/16	Lieut.	
7910	Ball, Gerald Harman ...	... 10/ 2/16	✠	Killed in action 12/4/18
1417	Bath, csm Frederick Nathaniel	... 28/ 8/16	Lieut.	
2328	Bax, rsm Edwin Geo. Goodson ...	4/ 7/16	Major	⌬
2028	Belchamber, Douglas Foster ...	... 14/12/14	Lieut.	M.B.E.
7523	Benbow, Oliver Barrington ...	... 10/ 2/17	Lieut.	
2243	Benson, Sgt. Oscar	... 6/ 8/16	Lieut.	⌬
761540	Berkeley, A. Fitzhardinge Murray...	29/12/16	Lieut.	
7524	Blacktin, Thomas Sidney ...	... 10/ 2/17	Lieut.	
763378	Blower, Arthur Lawrence ...	... 26/ 4/17	Lieut.	Wounded 1/11/18
2270	Bolter, Arthur Edward ...	... 10/ 2/17	Lieut.	Wounded 11/4/18
2269	Bolter, qms Charles Albert ...	... 26/ 4/17		Killed in action 12/4/18
760106	Bond, Vivian Pullen ..	... 28/ 6/18		
761921	Boxall, Tom Maxby ...	... 31/ 1/17	Lieut.	
6510	Brocklehurst, Sydney Thomas	... 29/10/16	Lieut.	
761728	Brooke, Alfred Walter ...	... 29/12/16	Lieut.	
761423	Brooke, Cecil Bernard ...	... 29/12/16	Lieut.	✠

* *Assassinated in Dublin, 22/11/20, A.P.M.*

MACHINE GUN CORPS.

1505	BULLPITT, CSMI James	... ...	12/11/16	Lieut. ✠ 🎖
763997	BURNS, Harry Christopher ...	...	9/10/18	
763098	CALVERT, Charles Cowper ...	...	30/ 3/17	(Tank Corps)
762023	CHAMBERS, Philip Carlisle ...	...	31/ 1/17	(Tank Corps) w. 12/12/17 Killed
710	CLAUSEN, QMSI George Frederick	...	12/11/16	Lieut. 🎖 [in action 22/3/18]
1203	CORMACK, Sgt. Arthur Richard	...	12/ 7/16	Capt. ✠
7651	CROCKER, John Frederick ...	...	10/ 2/17	Lieut.
7395	CROSS, Arthur Valentine ...	...	9/12/16	Lieut.
1636	CRUTTENDEN, Sgt. Reginald ...	...	7/ 7/16	Lieut.
7503	CUMMING, Gordon Douglas ...	...	4/ 8/16	Lieut.
3876	CURTIS, Frank	...	29/12/16	Lieut. ✠ Wounded –/5/18, –10/18
761557	DERRY, Cyril John ...	...	28/ 6/18	Lieut.
5992	DIXIE, William Leonard ...	...	9/12/16	Lieut.
763099	DOUCHE, William Howard ...	...	27/ 5/17	Lieut. (Tank Corps)
1479	DOUGLAS, QMSI Arthur Herbert	...	26/ 7/17	Lieut.
762828	DOWSON, Reginald Algar ...	...	27/ 5/17	Lieut. (Tank Corps)
760725	DUKE, William Alan ...	...	31/ 1/17	Lieut. Wounded 13/12/17
762629	EASTWOOD, Robert George ...	...	27/ 6/17	Lieut. Wounded 16/5/18
761911	EDGAR, Bernard Ray ...	...	25/ 3/17	Killed in action 31/7/17
762477	EDMONDS, L/Cpl. William Henry	...	27/ 2/18	
6433	EDWARDS, Cecil Howard ...	...	10/ 2/17	Lieut.
766846	ELLINGSTON, John Rosky ...	...	30/ 7/18	
762301	EVANS, Herbert W. Cresswell ...		26/ 4/17	Lieut. Wounded 17/10/17
760903	EVANS, Thomas Pendry ...	...	6/ 8/16	Lieut.
1887	FAIRBAIRNS, Reginald Holland	...	6/ 2/15	Capt. ✠ Wounded –/11/16
2534	FARADAY, Roy	...	26/ 2/15	Lieut. From 6/London Killed in [action 7/6/17]
2177	FARROW, George Harold ...	...	21/ 1/17	
763848	FIELD, L/Cpl. Edward ...	...	26/ 9/17	Wounded 21/3/18 D.S.O. 🎖
2632	FLETCHER, QMSI Ralph Belward	...	12/11/16	Lieut. 🎖
761855	FORD, Thomas Frank ...	...	26/ 1/17	Lieut.
3530	FOSKETT, Sgt. Henry Horace ...		26/ 7/17	Lieut. Wounded 16/6/18 🎖
763880	FOSKETT, Noël	...	26/ 9/17	Wounded 28/6/18, 23/10/18
7215	FRASER, Eldred Leslie ...	...	2/12/16	(Tank Corps) Killed in action [20/11/17]
7561	FRASER, George Theodore ...	...	10/ 2/17	Lieut. 🎖
761795	GIBSON, Thomas	...	31/ 1/17	Lieut.
8124	GOOD, John Whipp ...	...	10/ 2/17	Lieut.
763269	GOULD, Charles Frederick ...	...	8/10/18	
682	GOULD, QMSI Jas. Robertson Sabbitson		–/ 8/17	Lieut. D/W 15/4/18 🎖(2)
4158	GOULD, Lawrence Charles ...	...	10/ 2/17	Lieut. 🎖
7396	GREEN, Joseph George Airey ...		29/10/16	(Tank Corps) K/A 23/11/17
773	GRIFFITH, Frank Stanley ...	...	25/ 8/18	Lieut.
5257	HAGGART, Donald Duncan ...	...	6/ 9/16	Lieut.
2796	HALE, Geoffrey Thomas ...	...	24/11/14	Lieut. From 7/Berks 🎖
6434	HALL, Francis Walter Gare ...		10/ 2/17	Lieut.
4000	HANDLEY-READ, Edward Harry	...	5/11/16	Capt. M.B.E.
6490	HARRIS, Harold Victor ...		29/12/16	Lieut.
7576	HAWKES, Ernest	...	10/ 2/17	Lieut.
6803	HEALD, Frank	...	9/12/16	Lieut. (Tank Corps)
762559	HEALEY, Harry Augustus Hubbard	...	13/10/18	

MACHINE GUN CORPS. 417

768440	Hewitt, Alfred Roy	... ...	17/ 3/19	*Guards M/G Regt.*
7607	Highmore, Charles B.	... ...	10/ 2/17	*Lieut.*
7127	Hinckley, Gilbert Percy	...	29/12/16	*Lieut.*
5623	Holmes, John Kerr Whitelaw	...	10/ 2/17	*Lieut.*
762752	Holwill, William Bertram	...	25/ 6/17	*Died of wounds as P/W* 16/5/18
1974	Hopkins, George Henry Stanton	...	25/ 2/17	*Killed in action* 31/7/17
6107	Hosken, Henry Richard	... ...	5/ 9/16	*Killed in action* 11/8/17
2004	Howard, Sgt/Inst. Frederick Chas.		16/10/16	*Lieut.*
5181	Howell, Henry	... ...	29/12/16	*Lieut.*
7305	Huggill, Sydney Charles Cook	...	29/12/16	*Lieut. Wounded* 5/10/17
7233	Hughes, Kenneth Edwin Alfred	...	30/10/16	*Lieut.*
6155	Hutton, Lorne de Hutton	...	29/12/16	*Killed in action* 23/3/18
766784	Ireland, Alfred	... ...	2/ 2/18	
7577	Jackson, William Arthur Lyth	...	10/ 2/17	*Lieut. Wounded* 25/8/17
7219	Jones, Edw. Raymond	...	9/12/16	*Lieut.*
1415	Jungius, Ernest Jas. Theodore	...	30/ 4/16	*Lieut. From* 1/*Bedford* ✠
7792	Kidd, Rolph Coone ...	...	10/ 2/17	*Lieut.*
7791	Kidd, John Coone ...	...	10/ 2/16	*Lieut. Wounded* 17/10/17
6765	King, Guy Stuart	... ...	29/ 9/16	*Lieut.*
7425	Leach, Thomas Henry du Blois	...	30/10/16	*Lieut.*
7874	Leith, George Hector	...	10/ 2/17	*Lieut.* ✠ ⋈
3398	Levy, Benjamin Harold	...	10/ 2/17	*Lieut.*
2650	Lewington, Charles	...	21/ 1/17	*Lieut.* [16/8/17]
6070	Mackay, Gordon	... ...	7/ 7/16	*From* −/*Middlesex Killed in action*
7565	Masterman-Smith, Phillip Aloise	...	10/ 2/17	*Lieut. Wounded* 18/6/17
762596	Maxwell, Geo. Barton	...	27/ 4/17	*Lieut.* ✠
1051	Mills, Henry Jackson	...	23/ 4/16	*Capt. From* 2/*Middx. Killed in [action* 30/5/18]
761314	Moor, Frank Herbert	...	25/ 2/17	*Lieut.*
760161	Morgan, Hugh T. ...	...	25/ 6/17	*Prisoner of war* 15/5/18
1867	Mould, Sgt. Ronald	...	26/ 4/17	*Lieut. Wounded* 28/8/18
762789	Newberry, Thomas Frederick	...	26/ 5/17	*Lieut.* ✠ *w.* 21/3/18 *P/W* 18/5/18
763207	Oakden, Geoffrey Edward ...	...	23/ 7/17	*Lieut. Wounded* 30/11/17
2378	Oakeshott, Sgt/Inst. Harold Alan...		21/ 1/17	*Lieut.*
760499	O'Regan, Alphonsus John ...	...	25/ 8/17	*Lieut. Wounded* 4/1/18, 5/9/18
2778	Palmer, William	.. ...	26/ 9/17	*Lieut.*
7237	Paton, Edw. Kesson	...	10/ 2/16	*Died of wounds* 3/5/17
6539	Paton, James Hill ...	...	29/12/16	*Prisoner of war* 4/6/18
762069	Pearson, Alfred Marcus Worthington		26/ 1/17	*Lieut.* ⋈
6769	Phillips, Llewellyn Edwards	...	29/12/16	*Lieut. Wounded* 8/4/18
7027	Pitt, Geoffrey	... ...	10/12/16	*Lieut.*
7680	Raymond, Alfred Francis	...	10/ 2/17	*Prisoner of war* 12/5/18
4985	Rhind, Peter Johnston	...	10/ 2/17	*Lieut.*
6352	Richard, Stanley	... ...	26/ 1/17	✠
766568	Robertson, Andrew Glasgow	...	29/10/18	
2192	Rogers, George Robert	...	16/ 9/17	*From* −/*Suffolk*
4299	Rowe, George Laver	...	14/ 8/15	*Lieut. From* 7/*Dorset*
7838	Service, George Brown	...	10/ 2/17	*Killed in action* 30/3/18
1019	Sherlock, Gerald ...	...	26/ 7/17	*Died of wounds* 21/4/18
2972	Sloan, James William Jeffrys	...	21/ 1/17	*Prisoner of war* 14/5/18
2776	Sloan, QMSI Cuthbert Harrington	...	26/ 7/17	*Lieut.*

DD

MACHINE GUN CORPS.

3738	SLOANE, William Henry St. John	...	10/ 2/17	*Lieut.*	
1445	SMITH, Sgt. Ernest Rees	...	28/ 6/16	*Lieut.* ✠	*Wounded* 16/5/18
762013	SMITH, Leslie Horace	...	26/ 4/17	*Capt. & Adjt.* ✠	*Wounded* –/9/17
760404	STEPHENS, Adolphus	...	12/10/18		
7518	STRACHAN, Charles	...	25/11/16	*Lieut.*	
1071	SUCKLING, QMS Percy Herbert	...	26/ 7/16	*Lieut.*	*Wounded* 24/3/18
1093	SUGGATE, William Allen	...	14/ 9/17	*Lieut.*	
6391	TARVER, Aubrey Ashton	...	20/12/16	*From* 18/*London*	*Prisoner of war*
767020	THORP, Charles Evans	...	17/ 8/18		
760930	TRITTON, Frederick John	...	31/ 1/17	*Lieut.*	
764354	TURNER, William Percy	...	26/11/18		
762241	WALLACE, William Ernest	...	26/ 4/17	*Lieut.*	*Wounded* 29/8/17
761408	WARREN, Geoffrey Leicester	...	25/ 3/17	*Lieut.*	*Wounded* 13/8/17
8218	WATSON, Arthur Vivian Craddock	...	5/ 9/16	*Lieut.* ✠	
7662	WEBB, Joseph Richard	...	10/ 2/17	*Lieut.*	
762924	WESTON, Maxwell	...	27/ 4/17	*Lieut.*	
761739	WHYTE, Angus McIntosh	...	31/ 1/17	*Lieut.* ✠	
2371	WILLIAMS, Noel Victor	...	15/ 8/15	*Lieut.*	*From* 2/*Durham L.I.* ✠
761989	WILLIS, L/Cpl. Francis Knowles	...	31/ 1/17	*Lieut.*	(*Tank Corps*) *w.* 23/10/17
762690	WOOD, Wilfred Rene	...	26/ 5/17	*Lieut.*	
7789	YERBURY, L/Cpl. Edgar Olive	...	10/ 2/17	*Lieut.*	*Wounded* 2/5/18

ROYAL MARINES.

2nd Lieut.

2920	MASSY-BURNSIDE, Godfrey E.	...	24/12/14	Capt.	*Wounded* 23/5/17 ℞
2811	DONNE, Arthur Courtenay	...	20/ 6/15	Capt.	*Wounded* 5/3/17
1303	GROVER, George Walter Montague	...	29/ 9/14	Capt.	
2983	HODDING, William Marchant	...	12/ 8/15	Capt.	
2685	HILL, Kenneth Howard	...	30/ 5/15	Capt.	
1813	LEECH-PORTER, John Edmund	...	20/ 3/15	Capt.	[*at Gaba Tepé*)
1289	LONGUET-HIGGINS, Kenneth Aislabie	1/10/14	Lieut.	*Died* 5/5/15 (*of wounds*)
2409	MICKLEM, Charles	...	11/ 9/14	Major	D.S.O. ℞
3365	WELCH, Richard Hubbard	...	1/10/15	Major	
763444	BONNETT, Ernest Charles	...	26/ 4/17		*Killed in action* 26/10/17
766101	CALHAEM, Richard Lionel	...	27/ 3/18		
767922	COOPER, John Sherman	...	13/ 9/18		
765988	DAVIES, Norman Kennedy	...	23/ 5/18		
762893	DOWNER, Reginald St. Quentin	...	29/ 3/17		
766752	HARDY, William James Redford	...	19/10/18		
7896	HOLMES, Henry Clarence	...	22/11/16		
762376	McADAM, Arthur Charles	...	30/ 5/17		*Died of wounds* 4/9/18
767619	MEAD, Cecil John Haarlem	...	28/ 5/18		
766871	OLDFIELD, Alfred Anthony	...	23/ 5/18		
762670	SMITH, Harrison Churchill	...	29/ 3/17	Major ✠ ℞	
763138	TURTON, Horace Reginald	...	26/ 6/17		
760227	WATTS, Ernest Joseph	...	13/ 9/18		

MISCELLANEOUS ESTABLISHMENTS.

CENSORS.

		2nd Lieut.	
2704	MEDLICOTT, George Probart	10/ 1/16	Lieut.
2691	NASH, Arthur Brian	29/ 7/15	Lieut.
1751	OXENFORD, Dudley	26/ 7/15	
1272	RENDELL, Francis Godfrey	15/ 8/15	
763504	O'CONNOR, Daniel	2/ 5/18	Capt.

STATIONERY SERVICES.

2992	BOLTON, Frederick William George	5/ 6/15	Lieut.
2629	GARDNER, George Herbert	6/12/15	Major
6999	JENNINGS, Stanley Herbert	28 /2/17	
766534	SHEFFINGTON, Harold Ernest	14/12/17	

INTERPRETERS.

6256	GORDON, Stephen Rees	2/ 2/16	Lieut.
7928	WHITTALL, Vernon	20/ 6/16	Lieut. ℳ
763227	BLENKIN, John Arthur	19/11/17	
766638	BRODERICK, Martin Joseph Aloysius	20/ 2/18	
7756	DERBYSHIRE, Frederick Charles	5/12/16	Capt.
8855	LUCAS, Lucas Max	7/ 2/17	
764451	PATERSON, Roland Worsley	20/ 2/18	
5809	SOMERVILLE, Sgt. Thomas Townshend	15/ 9/16	
7520	TWEEDIE, Charles William	10/ 1/17	

ROYAL MILITARY COLLEGE AND ROYAL MILITARY ACADEMY.

Discharged to enter Sandhurst.

		Gent. Cadet.	
2515	BURNETT, F. Sidney	4/ 5/15	Gazetted 2/Lt. Norfolk Regt. 20/10/15
2555	CHATFEILD-CLARKE, Horace J.	14/ 4/15	2/Lt. S.W.B. Killed in action 23/4/17
2728	PALMER, John Stanley	12/ 4/15	2/Lt. Dur L.I. 15/9/15 D/W 18/10/16
3425	POWELL, Howell John	14/ 4/15	2/S.W.B Wounded –/4/16
3631	THOMPSON, Hugh Thomas	26/11/15	To 2/Border Regt.
766925	HILL, Stephen Ernest	–/ 2/18	

Discharged to enter Woolwich.

2542	BUTTEMER, Eric Douglas Archibald	4/ 5/15	Lieut.
3697	MIDDLETON, Stephen	22/ 4/15	2/Lt. R.A.
765164	EDE, Charles Woodroffe		2/Lt. R.G.A. 6/8/18
763161	LANG, Edward Giles	4/10/17	2/Lt. R.A. 10/9/18
765087	PITELL, Adrien Philip		2/Lt. R.W. Surrey 28/4/18

ROYAL NAVY.

767799 SMITH, Robert Stanley ... 14/ 3/18 *Midshipman*

SURGEONS. ROYAL NAVY.

 519 Goss, L/Cpl. Leslie Stuart ... ... 20/11/15 *Lieut.* O.B.E. ℳ
3612 SILCOCK, Bertram Baber ... ... —/ 8/14 *To 7/R. Welch Fus. Killed in action*
[10/8/15]

ROYAL NAVAL RESERVE.

Sub-Lieut.
2219 BRIGGS, Ernest Frederick ... ... 23/ 1/15 *A.P. Died 20/12/18*
2758 CARSON, James Hodden Burleigh ... 20/ 8/15 *A.P. (Idaho)*
2919 JAMES, John Vincent ... ... 11/ 4/15 *A.P.*
2688 MCKNIGHT, Clancy Horsfall A. ... 7/ 5/15 *P. Lieut.*
1593 MILLER, Sydney Harold ... ... 7/11/14 *P. H.M.S. "Fiona" Lieut.*
3349 NEWTON, Ernest Leonard ... ... 24/ 4/15 *P. Lieut.*
1266 PINCHING, Charles Lawley ... ... 20/ 8/15 *P. Lieut.*
2208 SUTTILL, Roy ... ... 7/ 5/15 *P. Lieut.*
3125 THOMSON, Roy H. Goodisson ... 25/ 6/15 *A.P.*
2461 WILMOT, Walter Lennox ... ... 11/ 6/15 *A.P.*
761334 NEYROUD, Reginald Charles Elburn 8/10/18
2319 STEEN, George Arthur 16/ 1/17

ROYAL NAVAL VOLUNTEER RESERVE.

Sub-Lieut. [*wounds* 7/11/17 ℳ]
2977 STERNDALE-BENNETT, Walter ... 11/ 2/15 *Commander* D.S.O. *Died of*
1330 BOILEAU, Ernest Francis ... 25/12/15 *Lieut.*
 673 BONNETT, L/Cp. Frederick Wm. Lovell 7/10/14 *Lieut. "Drake" Bn., R.N.D.*
1510 CALLINGHAM, Lawrence Frederick ... 29/ 5/15 *Lieut. To "President"* [*w.* 8/5/15]
3378 CURWEN, John Patrick ... ... 27/ 3/15 *To "President" for Air Service*
1654 INMAN, Sgt. Gordon Henry Nesbit ... 12/ 5/15 *R.N.D. Depot Adjt. w.* 4/4/18
2518 KENNARD, Hyde Henry Ashley (Lieut.) 15/ 9/14 *Lt.-Comm. H.M.S. "Egmont"*
3772 PRATT, Cpl. Hartley Blythe ... —/ 9/15 *Lieut.*
6741 PURVIS, John Easton ... ... —/ 5/16 *Dover Motor Boat Patrol Killed*
[*Mine Sweeping* 21/10/18]

ROYAL NAVAL VOLUNTEER RESERVE.

2519	REDDICK, George Adam	...	15/ 7/15	*Killed in action* 13/11/16
2998	REDDICK, Henry	...	9/ 5/15	*Lieut. R.N.D. Depot*
458	STEVENSON, Sgt. Archibald Frank	...	30/ 1/15	*Lieut. "Hawke" Bn. w.* 5/6/15
3427	WAGNER, Caspar Henry Granville	...	15/ 6/15	*Killed in action* 13/11/16
840	WALKER, Sgt. William Douglas	...	12/ 5/15	*R.N.D. Depot*
3582	WALLIS, Cpl. Barnes Neville	...	-/ 9/15	
3003	WALLIS, Sgt. Wm. Herbert St. John		11/ 2/15	*Lieut. R.N.D. Depot*
762108	BEAUMONT, Percival	...	29/ 3/17	*Wounded* 13/11/18
767201	CARD, Lewin Henry	...	23/ 5/18	
4471	COOPER, Cpl. Frank Seymour	...	29/11/16	
768121	CUMBERBATCH, Hugh Charles	...	8/11/18	
8822	DAVSON, Percival May	...	11/11/16	
1279	DAY, Ernest Frank	...	16/ 6/16	*King's Messenger*
763784	DUTTON, Arthur Bancroft	...	26/ 8/17	
766046	FRIEND, Reginald Alfred	...	30/ 4/18	
763786	GREENE, David Wilson	...	29/ 5/17	*Died of wounds* 6/2/18
763851	HARRY, Francis Clifford	...	26/ 8/17	*Killed in action* 8/10/18
764029	IVERS, William Ewart	...	26/ 8/17	
763790	KELLAND, Robert Sydney	...	26/ 8/17	*Died of wounds* 19/5/18
766308	KIRBY, Forester	...	30/ 4/18	
7071	MARES, Arthur Francis	...	3/10/16	
767692	MONTEATH, David Taylor	...	1/ 9/18	O.B.E.
763795	PEARSON, Lloyd Mawson	...	26/ 8/17	*Wounded* 5/4/18
766836	SMITH, Wilfred Montague	...	12/ 6/18	
760403	SMYTH, Sgt. Montague	...	9/11/17	
6944	SOUTHAM, Alexander William	...	12/10/16	*Lieut.*
763838	TULLY, William	...	26/ 8/17	
767918	WOOD, Frederick Charles	...	9/ 4/18	

RESERVE OF OFFICERS.

			2nd Lieut.	
767741	BROMLEY, Frederick Edward	...	3/ 3/19	
760147	BROWN, Sgt. William John	...	3/ 3/19	
767360	CRADDOCK, Percy	...	3/ 3/19	
764697	FRY, Arthur John	...	3/ 3/19	*Wounded* 29/10/17
6473	LOBB, Archibald Josland	...	6/ 9/16	*Lieut.*
767507	MEESON, Albert	...	3/ 3/19	
767856	PARSON, Herbert Angelo	...	3/ 3/19	
767570	SLEIGH, Ralph P.	...	3/ 3/19	
767729	TAYLOR, James	...	3/ 3/19	
767327	WEBB, Rowland Alfred	...	3/ 3/19	

INDIAN ARMY RESERVE OF OFFICERS.

		2nd Lieut.		
766502	BATES, Henry	10/ 9/18		
762888	BREWSTER, John Alexander	28/ 8/17		
5836	COOKE, Archibald Barton	10/ 7/16	*Lieut.*	
765503	JEFFREE, Hugh	10/ 9/18		
766522	KINNEL, Brian	10/ 9/18		
762682	LAWRENCE, Herbert Alfred	24/ 9/17		
766195	MEDLICOTT, Cpl. Samuel John Edwd.	10/ 7/18		
765350	POLLARD, Clive Alfred	27/11/17		
765417	RICHER, Roland Admiral	28/11/17		
762248	SEVENOAKS, Patrick Lutman	3/ 6/18		
765359	SMITH, Charles Arthur Bernard	30/10/17		
2272	SUTHERLAND-HAWES, Henry Victor	25/ 8/17	*Lieut.*	2/*Bengal Lancers*

TERRITORIAL FORCE RESERVE.

3546	COOPER, L/Cpl. Alfred Ernest	18/ 8/15	*Lieut.*	*Att. Artists*
2304	WORLOCK, Sgt. Harford Thornhill	4/ 7/15	*Capt.*	*To R.F.A. Inst. Duties*

SPECIAL LIST.

		2nd Lieut.	
8307	A'BROOK, Willie Richard Cecil	27/10/17	*Indian Army*
761267	ATWELL, James Hunter	14/ 1/17	
768865	BAKER, Reginald Charles Wm. Pullen	8/12/18	*Education Officer*
762426	BARKER, Robert Alexander	28/ 3/17	
761679	BROCKLISS, Arthur Albert	23/ 2/18	*Indian Army*
762635	BUNNING, Reginald James	19/ 9/17	
5048	CARLESS, William Edward	17/ 4/16	*Lieut.*
763777	CHAPPELL, Walter	15/ 4/17	
764880	CHILDS, Leonard	7/10/17	
765613	CONRAN, Hatton Charles Ronayne	21/10/17	
766855	COPEMAN, Leopold	9/ 2/18	
769143	CORLETT, William Henry	12/11/18	*Education Officer*

768532	CURRALL, Richard Thomas ...	8/12/18	Capt.	Education Officer
760221	DAVIS, Sgt. Cyril	20/ 6/18	Capt.	(Intelligence Corps)
1097	EATON, Sgt. John Edward Caldwell...	14/12/16		
766109	FRADGLEY, Arthur Davidson ...	4/ 9/16		
768540	GARSIDE, William	8/12/18		
765992	GREGORY, Robert John ...	7/10/17	Wounded & P/W 19/6/18	
769096	HARTEG, William Gustave ...	29/11/18		
769169	LEWIS, George Waldron ...	8/12/18		
763892	LOCKIER, Arthur Ewart ...	19/ 9/17		
768924	MACGREGOR, James	12/11/18		
5209	MAITLAND, Norman Eric ...	6/ 9/16		
769659	MILLER, John Stuart ...	8/12/18		
761799	PEARCE, William Loe ...	14/ 1/17		
8937	RICHMOND, Oliffe Legh ...	3/ 2/17	Capt.	
7769	ROTHFIELD, Jacob	30/12/16		
761549	ROUSSIANO, Theodore ...	14/ 1/17	M	
764722	SHIEL, Sylvester	28/ 8/17		
7951	WATSON, John Bertram ...	2/ 8/16	Lieut.	
765896	WRIGHT, Harold James Lean ...	1/10/17	Lieut.	Interpreter
762795	WYATT, Victor Wyndham ...	19/ 9/17		

Dental Surgeons.

7682	BERGH, Victor Emanuel Dawson ...	1/11/16		
4058	BOWEN, Cuswell Glynne ...	26/10/15		
766244	BURCH, Henry James ...	1/ 8/18	Lieut.	
1528	CAMP, Cpl. Alfred Fisher ...	21/ 6/18	Capt.	
6640	CURTIS, William John ...	7/12/16	Lieut.	
6607	DEVERALL, Edmund Percy ...	12/11/16		
7444	DOHERTY, John William ...	11/ 9/16		
767679	FLANDERS, Fredk. George Pritchard	27/ 5/18	Capt.	
765309	GRAHAM-WHITE, Robert ...	31/ 7/17		
765546	HALDEN, Richard John ...	7/11/17	Capt.	
764096	HAWKINS, Cpl. Charles Frederick ...	1/ 4/18		
767796	HINDLE, John William ...	5/ 4/18		
6953	HUDSON, Frank Edward ...	17/ 9/16		
6314	HUGHES, Walter Owen ...	1/ 9/16		
764200	KIDNER, Charles Henry ...	25/ 5/18	Wounded 30/10/17	
767030	MACKAY, Stanley Tyrrell ...	1/ 4/18		
767158	MORRIS, Cecil Graves ...	5/ 4/18		
765510	NEWTON, Sydney Bullen ...	9/12/17	Capt.	
7283	PERCY, Arthur John	13/ 9/16		
763004	SALSBURY, Archibald Frank	24/ 6/17		
764456	SALISBURY, Frederick Robert	30/ 9/17		
6181	WILLIAMS, James Herbert ...	10/11/16		
7625	WILLIAMS, Malcolm Lloyd ...	2/11/16		
7077	WREN, Bernard Francis ...	22/ 8/16		

TANK CORPS.

		2nd Lieut.	
767198	AITKEN, William John	23/10/18	
762710	AITKEN, William Lockie Ewing	28/ 5/17	
760578	BATSTONE, Rowland Kirk	26/ 7/17	*Lieut.* ℻
766586	BELL, Percy Henry	7/10/17	
4353	BENJAFIELD, Harry Wilfred	4/ 1/16	*Lieut. From* 9/*London w.* 4/12/17
761422	BENNETT, Charles Stanley	26/ 7/17	*Lieut.*
767213	BENTON, Philip Francis	9/10/18	
766267	BOURNE, Hugh	28/ 9/17	
768724	BULLARD, Samuel	23/ 3/19	
766216	BURGESS, Frederick Joseph	4/ 3/19	
767052	CARDER, Francis Charles	13/11/18	
766845	COLLENETTE, Cyril Leslie	28/ 5/18	
768393	DEWAR, John Gordon Baxter	23/ 3/19	
761792	DIXON, Alfred Chessington	26/ 1/17	*Lieut.* ✠ *Wounded* 27/9/18
767142	ESMOND-JACK, Jack	6/ 3/19	
767332	FERN, Percy	6/ 3/19	
766828	FORSHAW, Richard	3/ 2/18	
2295	GIBB, Morrison William	18/ 5/15	*Major*
767250	GIFFORD, Reginald Patrick	21/10/18	
766860	GRAHAM, Robert Ramage	23/ 5/18	
766447	GWATKIN, Frederick Pitt	23/10/18	
767398	HARRISON, Charles Lyon Riseman	13/11/18	
766924	HASWELL, Henry Lawrence	23/10/18	
767815	HAWKE, Harold	6/ 2/19	
767234	HAWKEN, Thomas Walter	4/ 3/19	
767288	HILL, Cedric William	8/10/18	
766477	HILL, Charles Edward	23/10/18	
767127	HOLDEN, George Marland	8/10/18	
768654	HOLDEN, George Henry	23/ 3/19	
766052	HOWARD, Henry Weston	6/ 3/19	
7314	IRELAND, Ernest Pinnock	9/12/16	*Lieut.* ✠ *Wounded* 5/9/17
763239	JONES, Valder Edward	26/ 7/17	*Prisoner of war* 6/5/18
760097	KEEVES, James Herbert Arthur	24/10/18	
766867	KELLY, Paul Herrick	23/ 5/18	
767364	KENT, Charles Wilmot Thomas	4/ 3/19	
3643	LAND, CSM Leo Frederick	6/ 3/19	℻
766987	LAW, Harrington Robley	30/ 7/18	
766234	LAWRENCE, Leslie	28/ 9/17	
766719	LEE, Alfred Fraser	23/ 5/18	
764154	LONGTHORPE, Fred	27/ 6/17	*Died of wounds* 20/9/18
7205	LOVELL, Bertram	9/12/16	*Lieut.* ✠ *Wounded* 13/8/17
768426	LUMBY, Reginald Evelyn Ashley	23/ 3/19	
768350	MACINTOSH, Phinehas Raeburn	23/ 3/19	
767086	MAKIN, Lawrence Spencer Lamb	23/10/18	
765368	MEADON, Edwin Edgar	22/ 3/19	*Wounded* 30/12/17

TANK CORPS.

767365	MEDDINGS, Eustace Sharpley	4/ 3/19		
764580	MILLER, William Dick Brown	26/ 7/17		
768481	MORGAN, John Gwynne	23/ 3/19		
768324	NEWMAN, Reginald Noble	23/ 3/19		
6075	NORTH, Percy	7/ 7/16	Capt.	From -/Essex w. 23/8/18
766788	OLIVER, Spencer Harold	3/ 2/18		
767352	PARRY, Samuel Austin	21/10/18		
766789	PATERSON, Charles Raff	3/ 2/18		
764452	PAYTON, Sydney	28/ 8/17 ✠		
766790	PHILLIPS, Cyril Leslie	4/ 3/19		
767225	POGUE, Cecil William	23/11/18		
767038	PONTET, Henry	23/ 5/18		
766617	RACKHAM, Arthur Cyrus	6/ 3/19		[7/12/17
3580	RICH, Cecil Olvar	19/ 9/16	Lieut.	From 1/Wilts ✠ ✠ w.
763435	RIDLINGTON, Alfred Charles	1/ 3/17	Lieut.	From 3/York & Lancs.
763664	RIDLEY, John William Bradley	4/ 3/19		[✠ w. 22/11/18
765852	ROBERTS, Ernest George	23/10/18		
6374	ROBINSON, Trevor	26/ 9/16	Capt.	From R.A.F.
761751	RYCROFT, George James	31/ 1/18		
767095	SCOTT-EAMES, Gilbert	7/10/18		
767419	SHARP, Richard Herbert	4/ 3/19		[w. 19/9/18
6319	SKIPPON, David Leslie	3/ 4/17	Lieut.	(From 1/Middlesex) ✠
763703	SMART, Norman Herbert	24/ 4/17	Lieut.	From R. Warwick w.
767033	SMITH, Clement	23/10/18		[28/8/18
766535	SMITH, Gilbert	7/10/18		
767342	SMITH, Ronald Ivan David	22/10/18		
766850	STODEL, Jack Henry	23/ 5/18		
767134	SUGARS, Adrian Mathew Stanley	7/10/18		
767255	THOMSON, Albert	7/10/18		
767118	THWAITES, George Laurence	23/10/18		
766793	TRIEBNER, Frederick Havard	4/ 3/19		
760356	TUBBS, Sgt. William Edward	19/12/17		
766537	VINCENT, Anthony Francis	17/11/17		
766402	WALKER, John Hilton	17/11/17		
762283	WALTERS, Sydney Evelyn	27/ 3/18 ✠		
766370	WEIR, Thomas Bowick	7/10/18		
764078	WELCH, Stanley Thomas	27/ 5/17		
762967	WETENHALL, James Percy	30/ 3/17	Wounded & P/W 22/2/18	
767354	WICKETT, Cyril William	6/ 3/19		
767335	WILKIN, Leslie Jarvis	21/10/18		
766727	WILKINSON, Joseph	23/10/18		[w. 6/12/17
4374	WOOTTON, Kenneth Edwin	9/ 1/16	Capt. ✠	From 10/London

THE WEST AFRICAN REGIMENT.

1380   HURT, William George   ... Lieut. 15/12/15 *From* 13/*Middlesex*

THE WEST AFRICAN FRONTIER FORCE
(NIGERIA REGIMENT).

1545	GRIFFITHS, Hubert Percy	...	Lieut.	29/ 4/15	*From* 5/*Middlesex*
3054	LODGE, Alfred Percy Derryman		Lieut.	25/ 8/15	Gambia Co. *From* 9/*R.W. Surrey*
2668	NOAD, Frederick Mitchell	..	Lieut.	30/ 6/15	*From* 6/*Middlesex*

THE BRITISH WEST INDIES REGIMENT.

			2nd Lieut.	
6668	COOKE, George Gratton	...	5/ 9/16	*Lieut.*
762979	HUDDLE, Lester William	...	28/ 3/17 5	
5019	MAINGOT, Joseph Henry	...	7/ 7/16	(2/*Service Bn.*) *To R.A.F.* ✠ ✠
5023	MAINGOT, Vivian Joseph	...	7/ 7/16	,, ,, *Lieut.*
762730	WEATHERHEAD, Henry Douglas	...	25/ 4/17 5	

SUPPLEMENTAL LIST OF
FURTHER COMMISSIONS
ASCERTAINED DURING PRINTING OF THE FOREGOING.

761906	ADAMS, Alfred Francis	26/ 1/17	*M.G.C.*
5828	ANDERSON, John William Fettes	14/ 9/17	1/*Argyll & Suth. Highlanders*
765207	ASTBURY, Alec	12/11/17	*R.F.A.* ✠
8432	BOTT, Herbert Edmund	19/ 4/17	*R.G.A.*
7301	BOWDEN, John Posnett	22/ 7/17	3/*R. West Surrey*
4115	BOYCE, Arthur Frederick	30/ 3/16	*R.A.S.C.*
765108	BRIGGS, Cyril	24/ 7/17	*R.F.C.*
6511	BROWN, Charles Adrian	7/ 7/16	*R.F.C.*
762745	BROWN, Harold John	25/ 4/17	*E. Lancs.* [*Shahraban* 13/8/20 ⎫
1013	BUCHANAN, Edward Laurie	20/ 7/15	*R.F.A. & R A.F. Killed at* ⎬
5471	BURTON, Edward Reginald	10/ 7/16	7/*Notts & Derby Capt.*
764190	CADMAN, Harold Edward Smelter	26/ 9/17	1/*Suffolk*
763193	CALLF, George Stuart	27/ 3/17	5/*Liverpool*
2533	CARR, Frederick Robert	10/12/17	*R.G.A.*
6750	CARTER, Basil Ernest	25/ 9/16	*R.F.C. Lieut.*
764980	COATES, Lewis James Moncrieff	28/ 9/17	*Special List*
764818	COLEMAN, Francis Austin	6/ 9/17	*Labour Corps*
763291	COLLINS, Albert Henry	26/ 7/17	*M.G.C.*
2227	COOMBS, Hubert Carlisle	3/ 3/17	*R.F.A.*
3268	CROSFIELD, Stephen	20/ 3/15	–/*Cheshire R.A.F. Lieut.*
761139	DUXFIELD, Sgt. George Clifford	9/12/17	*R.G.A.*
3673	FINDLAY, Robert Morton	19/10/15	3/*London Yeo.* (*R.F.C.*) *Capt.*
767377	GERHARDI, Charles	24/ 4/19	*R.A.F. Killed in action* 20/9/19
765390	GOODERHAM, George Hamilton	2/ 7/17	*R.H.A. Capt.*
763198	GORDON, Herbert	31/ 7/17	4/*S. Lancashire*
764960	HARDING, Denys Aubrey	26/ 9/17	*M.G.C.*
2388	HARDING, Hal Russell	27/10/15	*R.F.A.* (*From R.M.A.*)
768803	HARRISON, Harold	7/10/17	*R.F.A.*
5502	HEWITT, Leonard William	22/11/16	3/*D.C.L.I.*
765331	HILDITCH, Cpl. Charles Henry	10/ 6/18	27/*Bde., R.F.A. Killed in action* ⎫
765592	HODGES, Cyril Evelyn	1/ 4/18	*R.A.F. Capt.* [23/10/18] ⎬
765041	JEFFERIES, Stanley Saunders	3/11/17	*Tank Corps*
762725	JEFFERYS, Cecil G. Magnus	29/ 8/17	8/*Middlesex*
763271	JENKINS, Ivor Charles	30/11/18	*M.G.C.*
761146	JOHNSON, William	26/ 5/17	*M.G.C.*
760501	JONES, Hugh Cobham Borrell	8/ 5/16	*SB*/*Middlesex Lieut.*
763238	JONES, John Weyman	26/11/17	*M.G.C.*
6873	LARKINS, Geoffrey Ingham	22/11/16	3/*W. Yorks*
4238	LUND, Percival Arthur	31/12/15	3/*R. Welch Fusiliers R.F.C. Lieut.*
765557	LUSCOMBE, David Arthur	17/ 3/18	*R.G.A.*

765722	LYFORD, Joseph	17/ 3/18	R.G.A.
756878	MARKHAM, Reginald Cecil S.	26/ 9/17	SB/Middlesex
5448	MARRIOTT, John Richard	12/ 9/17	Indian Army
765001	MARRIOTT, Cecil Lee	29/ 9/17	R.F.A.
4472	McGHEE, George Dilworth	7/ 1/16	8/Notts & Derby Lieut.
5066	MEADOWS, Reginald Melville	22/11/16	3/E. Surrey
3389	MELHUISH, Paul	21/ 4/18	R.E.
4125	MORGAN, David Ewart	16/ 6/16	25/London Lieut.
1156	MORGAN, Farrar Robert Horton	3/ 6/15	1/Border Capt.
4852	MORGAN, Melville Herbert	18/ 6/16	4/R. Welch Fusiliers Lieut.
2277	MORRIS, John Turner	27/11/14	R.E.
2223	MUSSELWHITE, Donald Woodward	4/12/16	R.A.S.C. Lieut.
7963	NASH, Ernest Alexander	12/ 8/16	R.N.V.R. Lieut.
8532	NASH, John Northcote	3/ 5/18	New Armies
1205	NEW, Joseph William	1/ 7/17	8/Middlesex (R.F.C.)
1543	NIGHTINGALE, Frederick Bayliss	19/ 2/18	Special List Lieut.
2293	NORMAN, Charles Patrick	19/ 5/17	R.F.A.
2643	NORRIS, George Stanley	3/ 3/17	R.F.A. (12/Bedford)
8757	PHILLIPS, Robert Lionel	12/ 9/17	Indian Army Capt.
6077	PHINN, Charles Walter	23/ 9/17	8/Oxford & Bucks L.I.
760379	PICKERELL, Leslie John	25/ 2/17	R.F.A.
2649	PIGGOTT, Maurice Wallace	11/ 3/17	Labour Corps Lieut.
5432	PLACKETT, Harold Walter	22/ 6/16	3/W. Yorks. R.E. Lieut.
5533	PORTEOUS, Frederick James	22/11/16	1/Scottish Borderers Lieut.
1791	PRESTON, Keith	27/ 2/18	Staff-Capt. (War Office)
6816	PUDDICOMBE, Frank Cecil	22/11/16	3/Devon
2904	QUIN, Desmond Hilary	2/10/18	4/R. West Kent
5925	RAESIDE, David	1/ 3/17	R.E.
764255	RAM, Herbert	7/11/17	R.F.A.
2176	RICHARDS, Leonard John	20/12/16	3/E. Yorkshire
4618	ROBINSON, Alfred	22/11/16	3/E. Yorkshire
4608	ROBSON, Cecil Hodge	1/11/18	20th Hussars
7746	ROSE, Geoffrey Arthur	17/ 9/16	11th Hussars
1370	RUSSELL, John Charles W.	21/12/14	R.E. Lieut.
4592	SANDEMAN, Robert John	-/ -/17	1/Scottish Borderers Lieut.
765732	SAYER, Cyril Eustace	18/ 3/18	R.G.A.
765733	SCOTT, Arthur William	15/ 4/18	R.A.
765894	SHAW, Alec Telfer	19/ 8/18	Interpreter Lieut.
4960	SILVER, George James	14/ 2/17	Indian Army
3662	SKILLER, Frederick Henry	26/ 6/17	M.G.C.
7915	SMITH, Karl Anastasia	9/ 9/16	R.F.C. Lieut.
6375	SMITH, Sydney Frederick Colley	15/ 1/18	Labour Corps
3914	SOLVEN, William Arthur	11/11/15	22/London Lieut.
765808	SPENCER, Arthur	15/ 4/18	R.G.A.
2967	STARBUCK, John William Sandford	1/ 6/18	R.E. Lieut.
968	STARTIN, Harold	-/ 7/16	R.F.C. Lieut.
7016	STEIN, Herbert Katzen	15/ 9/17	R.E.

SUPPLEMENTAL LIST OF FURTHER COMMISSIONS.

763211	STEVENSON, Joseph Harold	...	9/ 4/17	7/*London Lieut.*
3860	STOCK, Cecil Arthur	...	21/10/15	*R. Marines Lieut.*
764045	STORRY, Ernest Richard	...	29/ 9/14	5/*W. Riding*
2381	SWINSTEAD, Norman Hillyard	...	18/ 3/16	*R.E. Lieut.*
765522	TAYLOR, Thomas Mountford	...	11/ 3/18	*R.G.A.*
6594	THORN-DRURY, John George	...	27/10/16	1/*E. Kent Lieut.*
3289	TOURLE, Austin Joseph	...	25/ 9/16	10/*Liverpool*
2789	TURNER, Edward Eric	...	3/ 5/17	*R.F.C.*
763015	TURNER, Martin Stuart	...	26/ 9/17	*M.G.C.*
763440	VAN BEEK, Theodore Herman	...	26/ 8/17	*R.F.A.* [31/5/18 *Lieut.*
761130	VINCENT, Vivian	...	15/ 9/17	22/*Durham L.I. Killed in action*
3239	VINER, Cecil Charles	...	3/11/15	*R.F.A. Lieut.* ✠
6502	WADLOW, Bernard Victor	...	22/11/16	13/*Middlesex Lieut.*
6164	WALTER, John Brittain	...	27/ 2/18	*M.G.C.* [27/2/18
5881	WARD, Eric	...	10/ 9/17	10/*R. Fusiliers Died of wounds*
4787	WARDALL, Henry	...	22/11/16	9/*Essex Lieut.*
1699	WEBB, Sgt. Edgar Oliver	...	26/ 4/17	*M.G.C.*
4338	WEBSTER, Wilfred Bartlett	...	14/ 1/15	6/*R. Welch Fusiliers Capt.*
1752	WHALL, Louis G.	...	27/ 4/17	*M.G.C. Lieut.*
1939	WHEELER, Cpl. Arthur Gilbert	...	1/ 4/18	*R.A.F. Lieut.*
6780	WHITE, Douglas Archibald	...	12/11/16	8/*E. Surrey*
2786	WHITE, Lawrence Arthur	...	8/ 4/17	*R.F.A.* ✠
6562	WHITTAKER, Foster	...	6/10/16	2/*Lancs. Fusiliers Lieut.*
763141	WILLCOCK, Arthur	...	4/11/17	*R.F.A.*
764675	WILLIAMS, Hywel Ernest Brynmore		20/10/17	*R.F.A.*
1718	WILLIAMS, John Heber	...	18/ 5/17	*R.F.A.*
1391	WILLIAMSON, James Alexander	...	6/ 5/18	*R.G.A.*
762926	WINCER, L/Cpl. George Leslie	...	27/ 8/17	*Tank Corps*
762357	WARD, Denis R.	...	10/12/17	24/*London*

ANALYSIS OF COMMISSIONS.

Showing total Officers gazetted to each unit from the ranks of the Artists.

THIS LIST INCLUDES ALL THE FOOT GUARDS AND EVERY LINE REGIMENT IN THE OLD REGULAR ARMY.

Page of Roll	NAME OF REGIMENT OR UNIT	INFANTRY, R.A. & R.E.				Other Arms or Units	TOTAL
		Regulars	Special Reserve	Territ. Army	New Armies		
164	Air Force & Flying Corps, Royal	—	—	—	—	936	936
221	Argyll and Sutherland Highlanders	2	2	10	10	—	24
397	Army Chaplains' Department, Royal	---	—	—	—	6	6
397	Army Cyclist Corps	—	—	—	—	23	23
398	Army Medical Corps, Royal	—	—	—	—	9	9
398	Army Ordnance Department, Royal	—	—	—	—	199	199
403	Army Service Corps, Royal	—	—	5	—	276	281
187	Artillery, Royal	451	164	20	318	—	953
307	Artists' Rifles (Officers)	—	—	146	—	—	146
222	Bedfordshire Regiment	24	13	14	11	—	62
224	Berkshire Regiment, Royal	17	—	14	43	—	74
226	Border Regiment	27	3	32	40	—	102
229	Cambridgeshire Regiment	3	—	—	—	—	3
229	Cameron Highlanders	4	4	4	—	—	12
184	Cavalry Reserve Regiment	—	—	—	—	26	26
229	Channel Islands Militia	—	5	—	—	—	5
230	Cheshire Regiment	4	3	20	45	—	72
218	Coldstream Guards	64	—	—	—	—	64
162	Commands and Staff	—	—	—	—	67	67
232	Connaught Rangers	4	1	—	2	—	7
184	Dragoons Reserve Regiment	—	—	—	—	5	5
232	Duke of Cornwall's Light Infantry	13	5	13	46	—	77
234	Devonshire Regiment	19	13	27	52	—	111
237	Dorsetshire Regiment	4	7	14	21	—	46
238	Dublin Fusiliers, Royal	5	—	—	9	—	14
239	Durham Light Infantry	8	16	21	39	—	84
209	Engineers, Royal	221	2	18	—	—	241
241	Essex Regiment	17	6	51	66	—	140
245	Fusiliers, Royal	10	10	—	113	—	133
409	General List	—	—	—	—	125	125
248	Gloucestershire Regiment	11	5	96	51	—	163
252	Gordon Highlanders	15	1	4	8	—	28
217	Grenadier Guards	46	—	—	—	—	46
253	Hampshire Regiment	15	3	37	48	—	103
223	Hertfordshire Regiment (T.F.)	—	—	20	—	—	20
256	Highland L.I.	17	7	—	16	—	40

Analysis of Commissions—continued.

Page of Roll	NAME OF REGIMENT OR UNIT	INFANTRY, R.A. & R.E.				Other Arms or Units	TOTAL
		Regulars	Special Reserve	Territ. Army	New Armies		
257	Highlanders, Royal	5	—	9	13	—	27
184	Household Battalion	—	—	—	—	6	6
184	Hussars (20th)	—	—	—	—	1	1
184	Hussars (Reserve)	—	—	—	—	10	10
213	Inland Water Transport	—	—	—	—	38	38
258	Inniskilling Fusiliers, Royal	—	1	—	16	—	17
412	Inns of Court O.T.C.	—	—	1	—	—	1
258	Irish Fusiliers, Royal	2	6	—	—	—	8
220	Irish Guards	22	—	—	—	—	22
259	Irish Regiment, Royal	4	3	—	1	—	8
259	Irish Rifles, Royal	8	—	—	11	—	19
260	Kent Regiment, East	17	—	10	32	—	59
262	Kent Regiment, Royal West	18	8	18	80	—	124
265	King's Royal Rifle Corps	14	8	—	101	—	123
412	Labour Corps	—	—	—	—	140	140
268	Lancashire Fusiliers	5	14	55	48	—	122
271	Lancashire Regiment, East	22	1	23	39	—	85
273	Lancashire Regiment, Loyal North	4	1	68	48	—	121
276	Lancashire Regiment, South	5	8	37	29	—	79
278	Lancaster Regiment, Royal	6	3	38	38	—	85
184	Lancers Reserve Regiment	—	—	—	—	3	3
280	Leicestershire Regiment	7	7	19	33	—	66
282	Leinster Regiment	4	—	—	2	—	6
282	Lincolnshire Regiment	16	7	26	34	—	83
285	Liverpool Regiment	9	3	82	61	—	155
289	London Regiment	—	—	783	—	—	783
415	Machine-Gun Corps	—	—	—	—	157	157
315	Manchester Regiment	5	16	95	77	—	193
418	Marines, Royal	—	—	—	—	21	21
319	Middlesex Regiment	39	7	50	125	—	221
419	Miscellaneous	—	—	2	—	102	104
325	Monmouthshire Regiment (T.F.)	—	—	33	—	—	33
326	Munster Fusiliers, Royal	9	3	—	13	—	25
420	Naval Reserve, Royal	—	—	—	—	12	12
420	Naval Volunteer Reserve, Royal	—	—	—	—	36	36
420	Navy, Royal	—	—	—	—	1	1
327	Norfolk Regiment	9	5	27	52	—	93
329	Northamptonshire Regiment	6	4	8	48	—	66
331	Northumberland Fusiliers	19	2	49	99	—	169
335	Notts and Derby Regiment	22	12	55	58	—	147
338	Oxford and Bucks Light Infantry	6	5	52	30	—	93
421	Reserve of Officers	—	—	—	—	10	10

432 ANALYSIS OF COMMISSIONS—continued.

Page of Roll	NAME OF REGIMENT OR UNIT	INFANTRY, R.A. & R.E.				Other Arms or Units	TOTAL
		Regulars	Special Reserve	Territ. Army	New Armies		
421	Reserve of Officers, Indian Army	—	—	—	—	11	11
341	Rifle Brigade	9	6	—	81	—	96
163	Railway Traffic Officers	—	—	—	—	18	18
104	Sandhurst Cadets	6	—	—	—	—	6
343	Scots, Royal	9	3	7	14	—	33
344	Scots Fusiliers, Royal	7	3	2	6	—	18
219	Scots Guards	15	—	—	—	—	15
345	Scottish Borderers	2	—	4	8	—	14
346	Scottish Rifles	6	2	4	9	—	21
347	Seaforth Highlanders	2	3	1	9	—	15
348	Shropshire Light Infantry	19	4	5	28	—	56
349	Somerset Light Infantry	4	5	9	34	—	52
422	Special List	—	—	—	—	28	28
351	Staffordshire Regiment, North	3	3	17	18	—	41
352	Staffordshire Regiment, South	14	4	15	16	—	49
354	Suffolk Regiment	19	10	29	82	—	140
420	Surgeons, R.N.	—	—	—	—	2	2
357	Surrey Regiment, East	22	14	21	81	—	138
361	Surrey Regiment, Royal West	34	7	50	83	—	174
365	Sussex Regiment, Royal	4	6	20	65	—	95
367	South Wales Borderers	5	11	—	38	—	54
424	Tank Corps	—	—	—	—	28	28
369	Warwickshire Regiment, Royal	21	20	39	69	—	149
372	Welch Fusiliers, Royal	10	8	46	86	—	150
220	Welsh Guards	17	—	—	—	—	17
376	Welch Regiment	9	3	34	33	—	79
426	West African & West Indies Regiments	—	—	—	—	9	9
378	West Riding Regiment	6	3	16	23	—	48
380	Wiltshire Regiment	15	4	—	19	—	38
419	Woolwich Cadets	5	—	—	—	—	5
381	Worcestershire Regiment	35	5	34	75	—	149
185	Yeomanry	—	—	49	—	—	49
385	York and Lancaster Regiment	6	1	55	46	—	108
388	Yorkshire Light Infantry	11	15	17	40	—	83
390	Yorkshire Regiment	8	12	15	22	—	57
392	Yorkshire Regiment, East	20	14	15	27	—	76
394	Yorkshire Regiment, West	5	29	51	31	—	116
	TOTALS	1635	608	2661	3090	2262	10256

SECTION IV.

LIST OF
OTHER RANKS.

NON-COMMISSIONED OFFICERS AND MEN WHO SO FAR AS IS KNOWN DID NOT TAKE COMMISSIONS (MAKING, WITH SECTION III A COMPLETE ROLL OF THE ARTISTS' RIFLES FROM 4TH AUGUST 1914 TO DEMOBILISATION).

[This list does not include men originally enlisted in other Units who were subsequently *transferred* or *attached* to the Artists. Vide Preface—ED.]

434 OTHER RANKS: ARTISTS' RIFLES.

EXPLANATION OF ABBREVIATIONS ETC. USED.

- indicates Prefix 76 (omitted to save space).
a = Served overseas in Artists.
o = ,, ,, ,, other Units.
d = Died (natural causes).
e = Sgt-Instructor in England (R-F-C: O-C-B, etc.).
f = M/G Sgt-Instructor in France (G-H-Q).
k = Killed in action or died of wounds.

p = Prisoner of war.
w = Wounded.
₥ = Mentioned.
M-M = Military Medal.
M-S-M = Meritorious Service Medal.
F/D = Foreign Decoration.
¶ = War Service previous to 1914.

R-S-M Emslie, P.   2/Scots Guards   D-C-M   F/D   a, k 23/8/18
¶R-S-M Lock, H.   Rifle Brigade   ₥(2)
R-S-M Payton, W. T.   Rifle Brigade   M-S-M   a   ₥

-8236	Abbott, C. C.		-5751	Aldrich, W. L.	e
-7166	Abbott, E.	o	-2691	Alexander, T. H.	a, k 31/10/17
-6764	Abbott, H.	a	-5101	Alexander, Cpl. W. B.	
6666	Abbott, T. D.	o	-6630	Alford, F. E. B.	a
-9399	Abbott, W. J. C.		-6852	Alington, Cpl. G. W.	a, M-M (BAR)
-2399	à Brassard, Cpl. H.	a	-7098	Allanson, Cpl. J. B.	[k 9/11/18]
-3376	Aburn, E. M.	a, k 31/10/17	-7545	Allen, A. E.	a, w 10/11/18
-6843	Ache, J. E.	a	-7256	Allen, A. F.	o
-3189	Ackerman, Sgt. A. E.		-8987	Allen, L/Cpl. C.	
4964	Acland, S. N.	a	-9159	Allen, L/Cpl. J. A.	
-9140	Adair, E. S. B.	-	4275	Allen, J. D.	o
-0485	Adams, Sgt. A. C.	a, f, k 28/3/18	-6372	Allen, L. E.	a, k 4/1/18
-7048	Adams, B.	a, w 18/5/18, 27/9/18	6262	Allen, R. W.	
-2968	Adams, E. L.	a, k 27/9/18	-8310	Allen, W. A.	a
867	Adams, H. F.		-3222	Allenspach, Cpl. A. E.	
7696	Adams, J. C. V.	a	-9178	Allers, R. W.	
-9242	Adams, L. M.		-4303	Allinson, W.	e
-0357	Adams, L. R.	a, k 31/10/17	-7487	Allison, J.	
2377	Adams, P. L.	o	-9553	Allison, R.	
-3053	Adams, P. W.	o	-8989	Allison, W.	
6694	Adams, R. G.		-7099	Allman, C. R.	
770	Adams, S.		-4970	Allum, J.	a, k 31/10/17
3394	Adams, T.	o	-3673	Allnutt, E. J.	
-9607	Addleshaw, H. L.		-8893	Allwork, L/Cpl. A. T.	
-0807	Affleck, Cpl. B. P.	a, k 21/8/17	1849	Alpe, E. F. R.	a
-6410	Agostini, L.	o	-7605	Alston, J. B. E.	a
-5010	Ainsworth, Cpl. E.	a	-7100	Alwood, E. H.	a, w 27/9/18
6689	Airey, T. A.	a	-5915	Aman, A.	o
2231	Alder, T. V.		-6544	Ambler, H. F.	a
-4408	Alderson, G.	a	-1135	Ambler, Cpl. G. O.	
-9195	Alderson, Cpl. W. R.		-8809	Ambrose, E. R.	
-3443	Aldous, H. E.	a, k 31/10/17	-3548	Amery, R. H.	o
6783	Aldous, W. R.	o	-6152	Ames, G. A.	o

OTHER RANKS. 435

-4409	Amoore, R. H.	a, k 4/1/18	-5830	Ashworth, J. E.	o	
-3868	Amos, A. R.	a, k 31/10/17	-7546	Askew, L/Cpl. A.		
1601	Ancell, H.	a, k 27/3/18	-3651	Askew, F. C.	a	
-7920	Anderson, L/Cpl. A.		-3652	Askew, G. F.	a	
-8810	Anderson, C. B.		-8204	Askew, H. L.		
-8004	Anderson, E. G.		-7606	Askey, E. N. B.		
-4472	Anderson, H. C.	a, k 31/10/17	-6803	Aspell, W. H. R.		
-2638	Anderson, L/Cpl. H. J.		-6238	Aspinall, E.		
-7980	Anderson, Cpl. J. R.		-3117	Aspland, W. B.		
6966	Anderson, W. J.	a	-6066	Astles, W.		
-0948	Andrews, F. E.	a, w 22/3/18	-6128	Aston, L.		
-8177	Andrews, L. F.		-9690	Aston, S.		
5392	Andrews, R. G.	a	3029	Astor, W. K.		
-8682	Andrews, L/Cpl. S. T.		-0105	Atkins, A. H.		
-6127	Andrews, T. C. H.	a	-7120	Atkins, A. W.		
-8769	Angel, A. J. S.		-7606	Atkins, N. J.		
-8961	Angell, B. B.		-5153	Atkins, W. K. D.	a	
-8634	Angold, L. P.		-8265	Atkinson, G. A.		
-4867	Antill, T. T.	a, k 31/10/17	-0383	Atkinson, Cpl. R. G.	a	
-8600	Apps. A. R.		-5430	Atkinson T.		
904	Archbutt, S. L.		-6419	Atley, H. N.		
6245	Archer, C. T.	a	-7181	Atwell, E. A.	o	
-0325	Archer, C. B.	a	-8411	Attfield, L/Cpl. F.		
-3645	Archer, P. J.	d 23/3/19	-8722	Attree, L/Cpl. E.		
2868	Arkwright, G. R.	a	-4397	Attwood, T. H.		
-4971	Armes, F. W.	a, k 31/10/17	-7814	Aubepin, A. L.		
-3559	Armitage, J. F.		-3512	Auer, A.		
-3145	Armstrong, F.		-9275	Austin, L. N.		
2088	Armstrong, H.		2834	Austin, Sgt. M. G.	a, f	
-1078	Arnold, Cpl. A. F.		-6887	Averill, W. C.		
-6462	Arnold, A. J.	e	-8636	Ayres, L/Cpl. H. E.		
-0694	Arnold, F. J.		96	Babbage, W. F.		
-6339	Arnold, G. H.		-8022	Bacchus, Cpl. H. M.		
-2928	Arnold, Cpl. H. B.		-9508	Bache, H. N.		
-9179	Arnott, R. W. J.		2737	Back, Sgt. A. F.	a, f	
-9322	Arthur, C. H.		2739	Badley, J. E.	a, w 17/8/18	
-6273	Arup, A. S.		-7286	Bagel, J.		
5980	Ashburner, N.	a	1762	Bagley, Sgt. E. G.	a, f	
6967	Ashby, W. E.	a, k 31/10/17	-7101	Bagot, L/Cpl. C. W.	a, k 27/9/18	
8279	Ashdown, A. E.	a	-6676	Bailey, Cpl. C. W.	a, f	
1571	Ashford, R. E. C.	a, k 31/10/17	-5858	Bailey, G. H.		
-6041	Ashley-Emile, R. H.		6676	Bailey, H. S.		
-8721	Ashman, E. H.		6918	Bailey, J. A.	a, k 30/10/17	
-4110	Ashmead, Cpl. A. E.		-0162	Bailey, J. H. P.		
-5310	Ashton, E. L.	a, w 31/10/17	-3726	Bailey, J. K.		
-8683	Ashwin, L/Cpl. M. F.	d 19/2/18	-9123	Bailey, L. L.		
-8635	Ashworth, A. S.					

OTHER RANKS: ARTISTS' RIFLES.

−5261	Bailey, R. E.		*a*	−9698	Barclay, H. L. M.	
−7141	Baily, H. W.		*a, w* 30/9/18	5646	Barclay, R. H.	*a, k* 31/10/17
6247	Baines, H. M. S.		*a*	−9243	Bardswell, A. H.	
−6363	Baines, J. E.		*a*	−8867	Barfield, G. J.	
−7635	Baird, W.			−5431	Barfoot, W. P.	
−9608	Baker, A. E.			−2627	Barkas, H. W.	
−6677	Baker, A. G.		*a, k* 23/8/18	−4603	Barker, E.	*a, k* 30/10/17
−7687	Baker, C.		*a*	−9618	Barker, John Wm.	
7292	Baker, C. G. S.		*o*	−3724	Barker, Joseph Watson	*a*
−8109	Baker, L/Cpl. C. J.			887	Barker, Sgt. R. J.	*a, f*
−3560	Baker, E.		*a*	−6918	Barker, S. R.	
−7186	Baker, E. C.			−4082	Barker, L/Cpl. W. B.	
4236	Baker, E. G.		*a, w* 23/8/18	5675	Barker, W. G. St. B.	*a*
−3774	Baker, F. F.		*a, k* 31/10/17	−4529	Barlow, Cpl. A. H. H.	*a*
−7167	Baker, F. V.		*a, w* 3/9/18	−3905	Barlow, J. W.	
2282	Baker, G.		*o*	−5215	Barlow, Sgt. W. A.	
−8723	Baker, G. A.			1978	Barmiston, H. M.	
3258	Baker, G. F.			−5103	Barnacle, H. F.	*a, k* 30/10/17
−8962	Baker, V. S.		*d* 7/10/18	−8412	Barnes, L/Cpl. H. C.	
7033	Baker, W. J.		*a, w* 30/12/17	3622	Barnes, J. A.	*o*
−8866	Balding, J. W.			9141	Barnes, J. R.	
−8564	Baldock, F. R.			5889	Barnes, W.	
−6211	Baldwin, F. G.		*a, w* 27/8/18	6042	Barnett, C. S.	*a, w* 30/12/17
−6464	Bales, T. H.		*e*	−4594	Barnstable, S. J.	*a, p*
−4221	Ball, A. C.			−4305	Barr, A.	
−8110	Ball, E. H.			−6100	Barr, G. L.	
−4869	Ball, F. W.		*a*	2715	Barr, Bugler J. M.	*o*
−7663	Ball, H. M.			−7946	Barr, P. M.	
−8990	Ball, S. G.			−2970	Barr, L/Cpl. R.	*o*
8630	Ball, S. R.		*a*	−5646	Barraclough, A. E.	*a, w* 30/12/17, [31/3/18]
7775	Ballard, G. E.			−4679	Barraud, F. J.	*a*
−0721	Ballisat, L/Cpl. R.			−7490	Barrell, F. B.	
−1734	Balls, W. W.		*o*	6935	Barrett, B. T.	*a*
−7488	Baly, J. P.			−5077	Barrett, C. C.	
−4541	Bambridge, B. A.		*o*	−5822	Barrow, E. L.	
−6241	Banbury, Sgt. F. P.			−3915	Barrow, J. V.	
−6826	Bancroft, J. H.		*e*	−8684	Barrow, L. G.	
−8948	Banfield, P.			−8746	Barrs, Sgt. A. J. N.	
7020	Banfield, R. H. S.		*a*	−7790	Barry, H. C.	
−9436	Bangstaff, J. B.			−8311	Barry, J. S.	
−7145	Banks, J. B.			−8747	Bartholomew, J. H. C.	
−9632	Bannerman, J.			−6631	Bartlett, C. A.	
−8288	Bannister, H. J.			−6632	Bartlett, H. H.	*a*
−8462	Barber, L. C.			4837	Bartlett, L. A.	*o*
−2969	Barber, W. M.		*e*	−4938	Bartlett, R. H.	*a, w* 24/8/17
−4575	Barbour, W.		*a*	7393	Barton, H. M.	
−8500	Barclay, F. J. S.			−9203	Bason, G. D.	

For explanation of Abbreviations see p. 434.   437

−9224	Bassett-Smith, C. W.	
−9425	Bateman, W. L.	
4222	Bates, C. M.	
−8748	Bates, G. M.	
2382	Bathurst, Sgt. C. J.	a, f
−1369	Bathurst, F. V.	a, w 2/8/17
−8501	Batson, L. P.	
−4476	Battersby, G. A.	a
8503	Battersby, J. R.	a
−3018	Baugh, A. W.	a, k 30/10/17
1926	Bax, R-S-M W. M.	a, f M-S-M ℳ
−4680	Baxter, A. H.	
−8502	Baxter, R. W.	
−7868	Bayley, L/Cpl. G. H.	
4521	Baylis, T. F.	o
−7037	Bayne, R. M.	
6747	Beach, G. H. L.	o
8431	Beadle, H.	
−8119	Beal, L/Cpl. J. K.	
2364	Beale, W. P.	a
−3841	Bealey, D. P.	
−7216	Beanland, F. M.	a
2012	Bearne, A. D.	a, k 31/10/17
3213	Beatty, H. C.	o
−2989	Beaven, G. R.	e
−8053	Beazley, L/Cpl. R. U.	
4123	Bebby, G. H.	
−5104	Beck, Cpl. H. H.	
−6213	Beck, J.	d 9/1/18
−8565	Beckwith, L/Cpl. A. C. S.	
−9649	Beddow, B. J.	[w 27/3/18]
5566	Beddow, C-S-M F. M.	a, D-C-M]
9511	Bedell, G. F.	o
2600	Beesley, R. M.	a
6968	Beeby, W.	a
−3920	Beeson, G.	
−5028	Beeston, H.	a, w 9/11/18
−6546	Begley, L. J.	a, w 27/8/18
−6708	Belaieff, T. G.	a, w 30/12/17
−6961	Belcher, E. V.	
−8770	Bell, A. R.	
−4973	Bell, B.	e
7104	Bell, L/Cpl. F. A.	a
−9509	Bell, H. E.	
−9196	Bell, J. W.	
6093	Bell, S. F.	a, k 31/10/17
8653	Bell, W. E.	a

−6776	Belsom, F.	
−2711	Benbow, H. M. S.	a
−3146	Benbow, L/Cpl. J. H.	a, k 31/10/17
−8464	Benbow, J. J.	
−4747	Bennett, L/Cpl. C. J.	a, w 27/3/18
−7023	Bennett, E. O.	a
−9105	Bennett, H. W.	
7683	Bennett, P.	o
−2202	Bennett, Sgt. R.	
−8894	Bennett, W. G.	
−8503	Benson, K. L.	
−4179	Benthall, L/Cpl. G.	o
−3119	Berg, E. C.	a
6537	Bergman, S.	a
−3055	Berkeley, Cpl. S.	
−8637	Bernard, G. C.	
−8638	Bernays, Sgt. F. E. H.	
−9360	Berry, H. H.	
2037	Berry, P. H.	d 30/4/15
−5783	Berry, W.	o
5676	Berry, W. H.	
−8991	Berry, W. W.	
−6465	Berryman, Cpl. E. H.	
−4746	Beech, J. H.	a
8385	Bescoby, H. B.	a
−7076	Bestow, A. C.	a, w 21/8/18, 9/11/18
7058	Bestow, S. F.	a
3561	Bevan, C. R. G.	a
−2971	Bevan, T. D. T.	
6396	Bevington, C. E.	a
−4307	Bickerdyke, W.	a
−8811	Biggin, C.	
−0483	Biggs, J. H.	a, w 31/10/17
−7187	Bignall, W.	
−3842	Bignell, J.	a, w 20/8/17
−4010	Billing, A.	a
−6466	Billing, Sgt. B. L.	a
−4956	Billington, G.	a, k 30/10/17
−8465	Billson, F.	
−4871	Bingley, W. L.	
4914	Bird, A. J.	a
−6635	Birdsall, G.	a, k 17/6/18
−5831	Bishop, G. S.	
665	Bissett, L/Cpl. C. S.	
−1158	Bissett, T. L.	
7759	Bittles. L. V.	o
−7381	Black, D. A.	

OTHER RANKS: ARTISTS' RIFLES.

-8685	Black, E.			-9377	Boote, A. P.	
-6678	Black, H. W.			6442	Booth, A.	*a*
-7767	Blackburn, W. C.	*a, w* 27/8/18		3269	Booth, E.	*a*
1392	Blackford, A. G.			-7356	Booth, F. L.	
-7582	Blackhurst, F. H.			-9555	Booth, H.	
-8868	Blacklock, G. T.			-6731	Booth, L/Cpl. H. M.	*a*
-0330	Blackmore, R. G. S.	*a*		-0441	Booth, R. P.	*a, w* 2/8/17
-8812	Blackmore, Walter A.	[*w* 27/8/18]		-6679	Booty, E. J.	*e*
-7439	Blackmore, L/Cpl. William A.	*a,*		-5025	Borrer, C. D.	*o*
2903	Blaikley, Sgt. E.	*a*, M-S-M		3220	Borrow, C.	
-4224	Blair, Sgt. E. R.			-2773	Bossham, R. A.	*o, w*
-1518	Blair, R. G.	*a*		2346	Bossom, W. H.	*o, w* (*Palestine*)
3710	Blake, H. C.			-7964	Botting, L/Cpl. A. J.	
-8191	Blake, Cpl. L. E.			-8869	Boucher, L/Cpl. C. J. O.	
-9361	Blake, M. E. V.			-7024	Bouchette, E. M.	
-8145	Blake, Cpl. W. S.			-8466	Boulton, Sgt. F. A.	
-8112	Bland, G. A.			-3921	Bound, Sgt. M.	*a*
-4974	Bland, W. H.			-3445	Bourne, S.	*a*
4593	Blankley, R. M.	*o*		-4947	Bouts, W. E. M.	*a, w* 31/10/17
-2713	Blasdale, A. W.	*a*		-9579	Bovell, H. D.	
6680	Blenkinsop, I. E.	*a*		-6504	Bovington, T. P.	*a, w* 7/9/18, M-M,)
-0461	Bloice, A. J.			1014	Bowden, B. G.	[*k* 9/11/18]
-9400	Blomfield, R. McA.			8595	Bowen, E. S.	*a*
-0275	Bluhm, C S-M J.	M		-7549	Bowen, G.	
-0718	Bluhm, Cpl. R. C.			-8603	Bowen, G. F.	
-9058	Blundell, L.			-6547	Bowen, H.	*a*
-9554	Bly, H. J. B.			-9647	Bowen, R. F. J.	
-8178	Blyth, H. D. S.			-5642	Bowen-Rowlands, C. F. W.	*a, k*)
-7962	Boardman, H. W.			-8814	Bowers, T. A.	[30/10/17]
5677	Bobby, L. A.	*a, w* 4/7/18		-9106	Bowie, H.	
-5105	Boden, L. F.	*a*		-1735	Bowie, J. M.	
-5753	Bodger, W. T.	*e*		-4873	Bowman, W. H.	
-0239	Body, R. B.	*o*		-3686	Bowskill, J. B.	
-7574	Bolander, H.	*a, w* 27/8/18		-7550	Bowyer, F. W. S.	*a, k* 30/9/18
-3253	Bolingbroke, C-S-M-I-M H. W.			-8896	Boxall, R.	
-7355	Bolt, R. H.			-6330	Boxill, W. C.	*a, w* 1/6/18
-5341	Bolton, A.	*a*		-9225	Boyer, F.	
-3813	Bolton, Sgt. E. A.	*a*		-1138	Boyes, R.	
960	Bonacina, N. A. L.			-9342	Boyle, R. J.	
-8131	Bond, F. G.			5467	Bracher, W. V. A.	*d* 9/5/16
-9358	Bond, P. A. W.			-6637	Brackenridge, T.	*a*
-6805	Bond, S. E.	*a*		-4814	Bradbrook, C. J.	
-4183	Bone, F. T.	*a*		-5107	Bradbrook, G. H.	*e*
-6954	Bonewell, E. J.			-0872	Bradfield, W. L.	*a, k* 20/6/17
-7963	Bonthorne, R. B.			-7930	Bradford, H. St. J.	
1344	Boone, H. J.			3353	Bradshaw, Sgt. J. G.	*a*
-6375	Boot, J. S.			-6214	Braid, W. H.	*e*

For explanation of Abbreviations see p. 434.

-0853	Brambleby, F. C.	a		-9534	Brookman, H. G.	
-7537	Bramley, K. W.			668	Brooks, F. A.	
-0385	Brand, S. W.	a		-5528	Brooks, F. P.	e
-9124	Brandt, R. E.			-5172	Brooks, H. R.	
-4629	Brann, S. C.	a		-8687	Brooks, J. C.	
-4627	Branson, A. H.	a, k 17/8/17		-9037	Brooks, John Emanuel	
-9609	Branston, B. G.			-9362	Brooks, John Ernest	
5940	Brash, T.	a		-4011	Brooks, Sgt. J. H.	a, w 30/10/17
-7281	Brasier, C. R.			-8055	Brooks, R. L.	
-6777	Bray, W. C. L.	a		-8815	Brooks, W. T.	
-8566	Brazier, G.			5197	Broomfield, P. K.	o
3833	Brede, Sgt. C. R.	a, d 30/11/16		3912	Broughton, F. C.	a
1128	Breen, P. T.	a, w 25/3/18		-4285	Brown, A. E.	o
3059	Brett, A. E.	o		-4682	Brown, A. F.	
-9087	Bretherton, H.			-6377	Brown, A. H.	a, k 30/12/17
-7891	Brewer, L/Cpl. H. F.			-7770	Brown, A. M.	
-8435	Brewer, W. L.			-9038	Brown, A. W. I.	
1908	Brewster, T. W.	a, w 25/10/17,}		-7393	Brown, C. H.	
-7608	Brice, S.	[27/8/18]		-9197	Brown, C. T.	
-9343	Bridge, R. S.			-3515	Brown, D. M.	a
-9056	Bridger, A. G.			-8266	Brown, L/Cpl. E. C.	
-3815	Bridger, F. S. C.	o		-7551	Brown, E. M.	
-0786	Bridger, H. E.	a, w, p		2250	Brown, F. P.	
-0617	Bridgman, C-Q-M-S J. E.			-8467	Brown, F. S.	
-4630	Brierley W. B.			-4479	Brown, G. E.	a, w. 30/9/18
-6548	Briggs, C. V.			-8336	Brown, H.	
6150	Brightman, L/Cpl. F. S.	a		8415	Brown, H. B.	a, k 31/10/17
-7769	Brimelow, Cpl. S.	a, w 26/9/18		-3254	Brown, L/Cpl. H. D.	a, w 25/3/18
-7892	Brinkley, C. B.			3270	Brown, Henry George	a
-5745	Bristow, L. B.	e		7494	Brown, Howard Glanville	a
-6376	Britnor, L. E.	a		-9088	Brown, H. H.	
-7000	Broackes, C-S-M-I-M A. V.	o		-2745	Brown, H. J.	
-5649	Broad, J. C.	e		-8436	Brown, L/Cpl. J.	a
-6778	Brocklehurst, B.			-5579	Brown, J. D.	e
1814	Brocklehurst, C.	o		-7703	Brown, L. W.	
-8567	Brode, R. H.			-3922	Brown, Ralph	a
-6043	Brodie, D. H.			-8437	Brown, Ralph Noel	
-7941	Brodie, G. R.			-4631	Brown, Robert	a, M-M, M-S-M, p
-8291	Brodie, L. A.			-2798	Brown, Sgt. S.	
-8639	Brodie, W. T. J.			-7742	Brown, T.	
-8038	Bromley, R. R.			-8391	Brown, Rev. T. B.	
-7392	Brook, S.	a		-7854	Brown, L/Cpl. V. H.	
-9165	Brooke, E. J.			-6827	Brown, W. F.	a
-4130	Brooke, F. W.			-2265	Brown, W. R.	a, k 30/10/17
-5832	Brooke, Cpl. R.			3255	Brown, Sgt. W. T.	a, w
-3147	Brooker, L/Cpl. E. N.	a		-8771	Browne, C. A.	
-8686	Brookes, G. W.			-8640	Browne, F. D.	

OTHER RANKS: ARTISTS' RIFLES.

4314	Browne, L/Cpl. H. A.	3001	Burke, E. H. M. *a, o*
-8641	Browne, M. J. O'N.	-4683	Burkitt, S. M.
-8505	Brownhill, H.	-7966	Burleigh, L/Cpl. H.
5941	rowse, E. S. W. *a*	-3870	Burley, L/Cpl. H. *a, w 30/10/17*
-9580	Bruce, G. A.	1075	Burn, C. W.
-9276	Bruce, H. D.	-5921	Burn, S. E. *a, w 30/12/17*
2456	Brudenell, A. E. *a*	-6509	Burne, W. A. *a, k 5/7/18*
7764	Brunstron, W. *o*	-8506	Burnell, H. J.
-4530	Brunt, E. *a, k 31/10/17*	-5711	Burnell, R. S. *e*
-7771	Brunt, G. A.	-6747	Burnett, H. A. *a, w 23/3/18*
-6215	Brunyes, Cpl. N. *a, w 24/8/18*	-8749	Burney, C. E.
-8337	Bryan, L/Cpl. A. M.	-9689	Burnham, S. J.
-1398	Bryan, C. V. H. *o*	-4632	Burnup, B. J. W.
-8312	Bryan-Brown, V. F.	-9401	Burr, P. B. F.
-4188	Bryans, J. G. *o*	-1643	Burrage, A. McL. *a*
-7044	Bryant, G. K. *a*	2313	Burrow, Sgt. A. C. C. *a, f*
-8141	Bryce, Cpl. J. K. R. *a*	-8468	Burrows, C. R.
-2429	Buchanan, Sgt. F. C.	-5158	Burslem, R. H. *e*
-8247	Buchanan, L/Cpl. J.	-7077	Burt, H. C. *d 4/7/18*
-0471	Buck, Bandsman F.	-3517	Burton, E. C. *a, o*
-6507	Buckby F. *o*	2489	Burton, R. R. *a*
8685	Buckels, A. *a*	4610	Burton, W. E. B. *d 5/3/16*
-4877	Buckingham, E. *o*	-4085	Burtwell, G. J. *o*
-7965	Buckingham, L/Cpl. E. J. *a*	-0692	Bury, E.
4823	Bucknall, N. *a*	-6274	Bury, J. *a*
-9447	Buidon, G. S.	-8267	Bushby, H.
-3418	Bulcock, L/Cpl. C. J.	-7432	Bushell, L/Cpl. A. L.
-7772	Bulcock, E.	8487	Bussell, C. H. *a*
98	Bull, L/Cpl. F. H. *o*	-9479	Bussey, G.
-9426	Bullard, C.	-5219	Bussey, S. R. *a*
4952	Bullard, N. F. *a*	-9256	Butcher, H. G.
907	Bulleid, A.	-3021	Butler, Sgt. D. J. *a*
-4189	Bullock, A. S. *a, k 30/10/17*	-1658	Butler, Sgt. E. L. *a, f*
1258	Bullpitt, C. M.	-8469	Butler, E. W. C.
-4878	Bulman, C. G. *o*	-1541	Butler, R-Q-M-S F. *a. w 30/10/17*
-7121	Bultitude, R. G. *a, w 20/5/18*	-8225	Butler, J. S.
-6589	Bunce, E. E. *o*	-2930	Butler, O. H. S. *a, k 30/10/17*
-7275	Bunker, L/Cpl. F. R.	-2694	Butler, Sgt. V. M. *a, w 30/10/17*
-4480	Bunny, V. H. *a, k 20/2/18*	4949	Butler, W. W. *o*
-2214	Burchell, Sgt. J. R. R.	-8689	Buttar, I. D. W.
-8224	Burdock, C. B.	1850	Butterick, Sgt. F. *a, f*
1065	Burford, J.	-7051	Butters, J. H.
-0629	Burgess, Cpl. C. J.	-9699	Butterworth, E. M.
-8065	Burgess, G. L.	3271	Butterworth, W. *o*
-4227	Burgess, S. H. *a*	-8526	Byers, J. S.
-7830	Burgis, H. C.	1448	Byng, F. G. [25/3/18]
		-6963	Byrne, L/Cpl. A. *a, w 8/3/18,*

For explanation of Abbreviations see p. 434.

-9221	Byrne, G.		6892	Carter, Sgt. E. W.	*a, w* 30/10/17
-5712	Byrne, Sgt. H.		-7149	Carter, G. C.	*a, w* 17/5/18
5365	Byrne, P. S.	*a, k* 21/10/17	-7583	Carter, G. V.	
-8772	Byrt, E. W.		-9057	Carter, N. I.	
			-1709	Carter, V. G.	*a, w* 30/10/17
-3566	Cadman, S. J.	*a*	-7609	Carter, W. G.	
-2951	Cahill, A. J.	*a, w* 18/8/17, 7/8/18	6048	Cartland, A. B.	*o*
-0472	Caigur, H. A.		-7931	Cartledge, T. H. A.	
1292	Cain, H. N.		-8816	Cartwright, E. A.	
7336	Cairns, R. W.	*o*	-2267	Cartwright, F. E.	
-6935	Cake, W. V.		1635	Cartwright, G.	*o*
-0870	Calder, Cpl. G. J.	*a, k* 30/10/17	-3320	Cartwright, P.	
-7571	Calver, W.		-9010	Cash, A. C.	
-9427	Cameron, A. E.		-0023	Caslake, Sgt.-Drmr. A.	*a*
-5382	Cameron, A. W.	*o*	3437	Cassels, J. K.	*a*
-9693	Cameron, D. J.		-6378	Casson, H. G.	*a, k* 10/10/18
-9089	Cameron, R. B.		1592	Castello, M.	
-1603	Cammack, W. P.		-8023	Castle, H. P.	
-0596	Campbell, Sgt. A.	*Flt.-Sgt.*, R-A-F	-9428	Castle, N.	
-4815	Campbell, A. K.	*o*	-9491	Castledine, H. W G.	
3064	Campbell, D. R.		-7480	Castleton, L/Cpl. W. S.	*a*
-7230	Campbell, G. W. P.	*a*	-6964	Catchpoole, G. W.	*a*
-9180	Campbell, J. V. T.		2894	Catford, Sgt. J. A.	
-9402	Campbell, T. P. E.		5335	Cathcart, J. L. W.	*a, w* 27/9/18
3260	Canavan, P. J.		-6217	Caton, L/Cpl. F.	
-9490	Cannon, E. E.	*d* 4/11/18	-8527	Cattermull, Sgt. P. G. A.	
-3776	Cannon, H. M.	*a*	1671	Cattling, H. S.	*o*
-9619	Cant, H. H.		-7773	Cave, A. C.	
-9675	Capron, H. M.		-5758	Cave, D.	*e*
7106	Caradine, L. L. G.	*a*	-9181	Cave, E. W.	
-8162	Carbis, S.		-8413	Cave, P.	
-7330	Cariells, F.	*a*	-8314	Cawdle, H. W.	
-7380	Carling, L/Cpl. J. A.	*a*	-0595	Cee, Cpl. W.	
3589	Carlson, G. E.		-9378	Chaddock, L/Cpl. P. S.	
-4816	Carlton, Sgt. H.		-6639	Chadwick, L/Cpl. F. W.	
4429	Caro, M. S.	*o*	-6709	Chadwick, J. H.	*a, w* 27/9/18
-9451	Carpenter, H. G.		-4132	Chadwick, J. W.	*o*
2877	Carpenter, L.		-4750	Chadwick, P. G.	
2209	Carr, D. V.	*o, w* 14/10/16	5165	Chadwick, R. P.	
-6424	Carr, H. N.		-6467	Chadwick, S. E.	*a*
-9227	Carr, L.		-2516	Chaffey, L/Cpl. G. F.	*a, k* 25/4/17
-6844	Carr, S. R.	*o*	-9071	Chalmers, R. L.	
-9166	Carriss, L/Cpl. K. G.		-5922	Chambers, A. J.	*e*
-9142	Carroll, B. P.		-8415	Chambers, C. H.	
-5111	Carroll, Cpl. H. A.	*a*	5982	Chambers, F. H. J. C.	
-8507	Carson, J. S.		-9535	Champion, L. G.	
-4086	Carter, E. A. H.	*a, w* 27/3/18	2922	Champness, B.	*o*

2167	Channell, H. M. T.			−6965	Clarke, A. W.	a, w 30/9/18
−6683	Chapman, A. P.	a		−7231	Clarke, F. A.	
4315	Chapman, F. C.	a		−8227	Clarke, F. W.	
4451	Chapman, R. L.	a, k 31/10/17		−5924	Clarke, L/Cpl. H.	o
−9072	Charles, L. H.			−0109	Clarke, H. G.	
−6275	Charnley, H. K.			−4417	Clarke, L.	a
8885	Chaston, E.	a		6307	Clarke, R. J.	a, w 3/9/18
−8268	Chatfield, C. F.			−0381	Clarke, W.	
−2475	Chauncy, Sgt. M.			−3984	Clarke, Sgt. Walter	a
1226	Cheavin, G C. L.	a, w 25/3/18		1750	Clarke, W. H.	
−5725	Cheesman, D. G.	d 29/7/18		−4229	Clarkson, H.	a
−8690	Cheetham, A.			3315	Clay, D. A. C.	o
7107	Cheshire, V. M.	a		−2853	Clay-Thomas, C-S-M A. W.	
−8605	Chester, R. C.			−3520	Claydon, D. C.	a, k 18/8/17
5732	Chester, W. H.			1685	Clayton, Sgt. A. H.	a, f
−9650	Chettle, N.			−0371	Cleaver, R. F.	
−8082	Chetwynd, G. J.			−1447	Clegg, A. E.	a
1337	Chevalier, R.			5435	Cleland, A. I. H.	a, k 31/12/17
−9403	Chick, E. B.			−7317	Clement, A. R.	a
−9011	Chicken, E.			−4934	Clement, H. W.	
−9581	Child, P. F. A.			−6103	Clements, A. B.	o
−3257	Chipperfield, E. J.			4009	Clements, H. B.	
−6685	Chipperfield, P. A. W.	e		−0012	Clendinning, C-S-M H.	
−7572	Chipperfield, S.	a		−9379	Cleugh, E. A.	
−4686	Chisholm, D. W.	a, k 30/10/17		−9536	Cleus, H. H.	
−9296	Chisnell, C. T.			−3323	Cleveland, Sgt. K. F.	15/O-C-B
−5923	Chitty, A. C.	a, k 30/10/17		−6549	Clissitt, L/Cpl. W. C.	a, w 26/5/18
−9429	Chown, F. A.			−8571	Clitheroe, G. W.	
−0556	Christien, R. R.	a, w 31/12/17		−2037	Clode, F. A.	a
4697	Chuckerbutty, S. A. W. O.	o		−3780	Clunn, C. G.	
−8509	Church, A. E.			−9702	Coane, R. P.	
−7870	Church, L/Cpl. L.			−4634	Coates, B. N.	d 31/3/17
4438	Church, L/Cpl. R.	a		−5352	Coates, R. W.	o
−0898	Churcher, L. W.	a, w 30/12/17		−9687	Cobb, A. K.	
−4088	Churchill, H. C.	e		−9512	Cobbett, A. B.	
7200	Churchward, L.	o		−1351	Cock, E. M.	a, k 26/5/17
−9514	Cirfield, L. C.			−4312	Cocks, Cpl. F. E.	a, D-C-M, w
1845	Clack, A. E.			−7750	Cockram, L/Cpl. C. H.	[21/8/18]
−3567	Clapham, P. A.			−7774	Coghill, G. H.	
−2499	Clare, D. E.			−6591	Cohen, L/Cpl. A. H.	o
−9073	Clark, A.			−5112	Cohen, E. L.	
5616	Clark, C. F.	a, w 27/9/18		−3194	Cohen, M.	
4171	Clark, F. W.	o		−3096	Colborne, R.	a, k 30/10/17
5572	Clark, C-Q-M-S J. J.	a		−4056	Colbourne, G. E.	a, w 12/3/17
−9511	Clark, P. L.			−6013	Cole, C. H.	
−7634	Clarke, A. A.			2370	Cole, R-S-M G. H.	a
9054	Clarke, A. R. M.	a		−1174	Cole, H. M.	o

-8548	Cole, M. B.		6166	Cook, Sgt. H. C.	*a*
-6748	Cole, P. W.	*a, w* 21/8/18	4530	Cook, H. H. M.	
433	Coleman, D. J.		-7584	Cook, L. M.	
-4420	Coleman, E. R.	*a, w* 2/8/17	-9293	Cooke, L/Cpl. A. K. D.	
-9513	Coleman, H. A.		-6219	Cooke, H.	
-4752	Coles, C. C.		1139	Cooke, J. A.	
-4290	Coles, E.		-5465	Cooke, W. H. T.	
-8528	Coles, E. W.		-4963	Cooksey, G. B.	
-7968	Coles, L/Cpl. K.		-7448	Cookson, R.	*a*
5390	Coley, D. M.	*o*	7713	Cookson, R. T. C.	
-8338	Collen, P. H.		-9012	Coombes, D.	
-8228	Colley, H. J.		4919	Coombs, H. F. M.	*o*
-7496	Collier, L/Cpl. C. H.		-8470	Coombs, J. A. H.	
-7942	Collier, D. M.		-3964	Coombs, S. D.	
-9344	Collier, F. S.		-9040	Cooney, D. C.	
-6301	Collier, L.		-6379	Cooper, A.	
-4754	Collings, E. H. R.		-7382	Cooper, H. D.	
-1739	Collings, Sgt. H. J.		-6427	Cooper, R. B.	*o*
-1200	Collins, A. L.	*a, k* 24/7/17	-2045	Cooper, Sgt. T. H.	
-4399	Collins, A. S.		-7296	Cooper, W. E.	*a*
-6888	Collins, H. S.	*o*	2898	Cooper, W. F.	*a, w* 26/10/17
-6105	Collins, J. R. McD.	*e*	-3324	Cooper, W. S.	
-0314	Collins, L.	*a*	-6220	Cope, C-Q-M-S S. D.	
1597	Collins, P. H.		-8530	Copestake, C. J. W.	
-3489	Collins, S. H.		5988	Coplans, S. H.	*o*
-7394	Collins, S. T.	*a, k* 27/8/18	-8248	Corfield, A. H.	
-8897	Collins, W. H.		-3569	Cornes, C. G.	
5093	Collins, W. M. W.		-0884	Corney, Cpl. J. W.	
-0954	Collis, Sgt, A. B.	*a, k* 30/10/17	-6129	Cornford, F. J.	*a*
-8147	Collis, H. H.		-2348	Cornish, A. H.	
4874	Collman, F. G.	*o*	-6781	Cornwell, W. H. A.	*a, k* 6/4/18
-6806	Collopy, E. J.	*a, w* 27/9/18	3386	Cose, W. G.	*a*
-2169	Colquhoun, E. F. C.		-9168	Cosgrove, G. W.	
2322	Colson, F. C.	*a*	-9515	Costello, W. G.	
-0735	Commander, C. S.		-8817	Cottle, H. R.	
-2038	Common, L/Cpl. T.	*a, k* 30/10/17	-9059	Cotton, H. E.	
2888	Comper, J. S.		-9686	Coulson, J. N.	
-9701	Compertz, R. H. L.		-4133	Coulter, A.	
-4313	Compigne, A.		-7426	Couper, D.	
3507	Compton E.		-9144	Couper, W. S.	
-8416	Conisbee, L. R.		-7763	Coupland, K.	
-5436	Coningsby, H. A.	*a, k* 31/10/17	-3965	Court, C. E.	
-7025	Constantine, E.		-7689	Courtney, E. T.	
-2253	Cook, Sgt. A. C.		9712	Cousins, E. T.	*a*
-3637	Cook. A. S.		5737	Couves, S. E.	*a*
5617	Cook, E. H.	*a, w* 31/10/17	7801	Covey, D. F. J.	
-0399	Cook, G. W.		-7848	Cowan, L/Cpl. C. W. S.	

OTHER RANKS: ARTISTS' RIFLES.

-0964	Cowan, Sgt-Inst. M.	15/O-C-B	
-7871	Cowan, R. H. McD. G.		
-7872	Coward, N. R.		
1141	Cowlin, Sgt. S. D.	*a, w* 30/10/17	
7131	Cowlishaw, V. C. P.		*a*
-4057	Cowtan, J. G.		
-7102	Cox, A. P.		*a*
-7202	Cox, L/Cpl. E.		*a*
5243	Cox, L/Cpl. F. D.	*a, k* 26/10/16	
-3293	Cox, G.	*a, w* 30/12/17	
-4486	Cox, G. P. L.	*a, k* 30/10/17	
-7610	Cox, Cpl. J. G.		
-7553	Cox, P. A.		*a*
-6181	Cox, V. R.		
-8775	Coxwell, C.		
4648	Coyley, R. J.		
5618	Crabb, J. M.		*a*
-7776	Craig, G. A.		
-5420	Craig, J.		*a*
-9290	Cram, J.		
-9013	Cramb, J.		
-3229	Cramond, W.	*a, k* 31/10/17	
-8751	Crampton, C.		
-9481	Cranswick, R. L.		
-3738	Craster, V.		
-4881	Craven, P. O.		*a*
-3638	Crawford, E. G.	*a, k* 30/10/17	
-8471	Crawford, H. L.		
6538	Craze, W.		
-8179	Creasy, L/Cpl. F. J. R.		
1195	Creasy, L. E.		
-0768	Creighton, Cpl. H. R.		
5740	Crepin, L. E.		*a*
-4882	Crew, F. A.		*o*
7086	Crew, W. K.		*a*
1743	Crippin, A. E.		
7852	Crisp, W. B. F.		
-9610	Crockwell, C. H.		
-4230	Croft, A. C.		*a*
-7611	Croft, H. G.		
4750	Crompton, T. S.		*d*
-6711	Cronin, J. L.		*o*
3009	Cronin, M. J.	*a, w* 30/10/17	
-6889	Cronin, L/Cpl. N. W.		
-5160	Crooke, F. B.		*o*
-7538	Crosland, L/Cpl. A. C.		
-2777	Crosland, J. J.		
-6380	Cross, A. C.		
-0817	Cross, Sgt. A. V.	[*a, w* 30/10/17]	
1248	Cross, Sgt-Inst. H. C.	15/O-C-B	
-4316	Crossling, W. E.		*a*
-9694	Crossman, H. H.		
-5835	Croucher, H. V.		
-4756	Crowder, R. A.	*a, k* 30/10/17	
-9229	Crowe, H. A.		
-2017	Crowly, F. C.		
-4016	Crowther, C. W.		
-8819	Crowther, D.		
-3259	Croxford, H. H. R.		
-6248	Croxton, A. B.	*a, k* 27/9/18	
-7079	Cruickshank, L/Cpl. W. R.		
-3571	Cruikshank, R. J.		
-5161	Crump, G. F.		
-4605	Crutchley, S. E.		*a*
-8898	Cruttenden, P.		
-8607	Cryer, L/Cpl. H. G.		
-6856	Cuddy, L. B.		
-3688	Culley, S.		
-9108	Culling, V. J.	*d* 28/10/18	
-3572	Cullis, F. S.		
-7744	Cumack, F. H.		
7606	Cumming, P. A.		*o*
-2854	Cummings, A. G.	*a, k* 31/10/17	
-8691	Cummings, B. S. J.		
-5987	Cumper, H.		*o*
-8608	Cunnack, A. R.		
-4018	Cunningham, V. E. B.	*a, k* 30/10/17	
-5162	Cunnison, J.		
-9430	Curr, T. S.		
3404	Currie, P. M. H.		*o*
-9206	Currie, W. I.		
-4422	Curry, L/Cpl. F. S.	*a, w* 5/4/18	
-9537	Curtis, E. C.		
-4758	Curwen, J. E.		*a*
-0224	Cursons, R-Q-M-S F. J.		
-3295	Cutler, Cpl. H.	*a*, D·C·M	
-1425	Cruttenden, T.		*a*
8579	Cutts, Sgt. C.	*a, w* 15/O-C-B	
-8963	Cutts, C. W.		
6681	Dadswell, J. A.	*d* 6/4/17	
-9198	Dagg, L/Cpl. S.A.		
-4089	Dain, F. W. M.		*a*
-1890	Dakin, E.		

For explanation of Abbreviations see p. 434.   445

-4687	Dale, O. B.	a, k 24/8/17		-8692	Davies, H. B.	
-2931	Dalton, Cpl. E. E.			-3262	Davies, H. E. L.	a
8195	Dalton, E. N.	a		-7554	Davies, Cpl. H. S.	
-7414	Dalton, Cpl. J. H. P.			6970	Davies, I. M. R.	o
-0748	Daly, H.	a		-7054	Davies, John	a, k 31/8/18
-7257	Daly, J.	a, w 3/9/18		-8964	Davies, John Howard	
-6593	Dalziel, R.			-8938	Davies, John Hughes	
2803	Dalziel, Sgt. T.	a, k 31/10/17		3449	Davies, L. R.	a
8821	Danby, A.	a		-6686	Davies, R. A.	a
-4688	D'Andria, A.	a, w 30/12/17		2350	Davis, A. H.	d
349	Dangerfield, Sgt. R. J.	a, f		-7318	Davis, C. C.	
-8725	Daniel, C. J.			-1202	Davis, F. C. V.	a, w 9/7/17
-0848	Daniel, C-S-M J. B.	15/O-C-B		-1654	Davis, J. O.	a, k 31/10/17
-6160	Daniel, T. E.	o		-4426	Davis, L. D.	a
-3873	Daniels, M.	o		-4690	Davis, P. G.	o
-3263	Dansom, H. G. S.	a		-2952	Davis, P. J.	
-7430	Danson, J. N.			-3010	Davis, S. J. G.	a, k 30/12/17
-2267	Darley, C. T.	a		-8727	Davison, A. McP.	
-7539	Darley, J. H.			-9337	Davison, C.	
-8726	Dare, W. H.			2993	Davison, E.	
-7258	Darke, F. B.	a, w 27/3/18		-7959	Davison, W. F.	
-9329	Darr, R. H.			-4637	Davy, C. L.	o
-6595	Darwall, B.	a		-9634	Davys, G. G.	
7043	d'Ascanio, H. J.	a		2817	Dawbarn, K. R.	a
-9182	Davan, C. W.			-5931	Dawe, L. J.	o
-6222	Davenport, A. G.	a		-7585	Dawes, D. A.	
-7569	Davenport, J. E.			8352	Dawes, H. H.	a, k 30/10/17
-9292	Davenport, T. H.			-9582	Dawkins, I. M. E.	
-9230	Davey, F. H.			-5652	Dawkins, T. S.	e
-8269	Davey, V. E. McM.			3878	Dawn, H. C.	a
-8534	David, K. T.			1869	Daws, A.	a, k 31/10/17
-2864	Davidson, E. H. L.	a, k 27/8/18		-8438	Dawson, R. A.	a
-8572	Davidson, J.			-8510	Dawson, W. R.	
-7395	Davidson, L. A.			-5224	Day, A. C.	o
-6203	Davidson, L. F.			-3024	Day, C. R.	a, w 30/12/17
-9493	Davies, A.			-0353	Day, E. E.	a
-6513	Davies, A. B.			2251	Day, G. H. J.	a
-4571	Davies, C.	a		-8965	Day, R.	
-1161	Davies, Sgt. D. C.			-1880	Day, W. H.	
-6641	Davies, D. F.	o		2592	De Caen, E.	a
-4424	Davies, D. M.	a		-7408	de Chazal, G.	o
6789	Davies, D. S.	o		-8270	De Laubenque, L.	
-9556	Davies, E. S.			-3325	De Leon, H. M.	
-6857	Davies, G. A.	e		-6551	Dean, A. H.	a, k 30/12/17
-6858	Davies, G. E.	a		-2953	Dean, L. S.	a, k 30/12/17
5245	Davies, G. E. C.	a, k 25/3/18		-7831	Dean, V. E.	
-8417	Davies, G. M.			-3657	Dearlove, P. O.	

-3927	Defries, D.	a, w 30/10/17		-7933	Dixon, L/Cpl. S. T.	
8219	Denis-Marklaw, L. E.	a		-9611	Dixon, W. A.	
-5354	Denis, M.	e		2869	d'Ivernois, V. H. B.	a
-9404	Denison, H. I.			-8394	Dobinson, W.	
3742	Dennis, L. W.			3092	Dodd, J. F.	o
-7690	Dennis, W. H.			-3782	Dodds, N. G.	a
-8870	Dennison, J. A.			-9538	Dodds, W. D.	
-8610	Denrocks, J. G. H.			-0465	Dodgson, W.	a
-6583	Densem, N. W.			-7745	Dodington, S. P.	
-8643	Denton, L/Cpl. J. F. St. A.			3435	Dodsworth, E. F.	o
-4292	Denver, J. G.			-6919	Dodwell, C. E.	a, w 27/8/18
-7948	Denys, C. P.			-7843	Doherty, H. V.	
-9661	Derbyshire, J. G.			-0176	Doll, Sgt. P. J.	a, f
-8371	Derrington, V. W.			-9488	Donald, W. F.	
-5714	Desa, P. W. R.	o		-6710	Donaldson, Sgt. A. W. J.	
8220	De Sages, G. P.	a		-1730	Done, F. W.	a
-1754	Des Champs, L. B.			-8776	Donelly, W. P.	
-6015	Deslongrais, G. D.	[27/9/18]		-7677	Doody, A. C.	
-0609	Detroy, Sgt. L. G.	a, w 6/4/18,		-5786	Doody, J. McC.	o
-6161	De Veber, L. S.	o		34	Dorrington, R-Q-M-S F. G.	
-8644	Devereux, L/Cpl. W. A.			5399	Doswell, E. V.	a
-4134	De Ville, H. C.	a, w 30/10/17		-8821	Doubleday, L/Cpl. J. F.	
-3966	Devine, L. A. E.	o		-8385	Douglas, A. E.	
2532	Dew, Sgt. A. H. E.	a, f		-9516	Douglas, L/Cpl. A. H.	
-8339	Dew, M. T.			-7259	Douglas, R. C. G.	
-4358	Dew, Sgt. W. B.	a, f		-2696	Douglas-Powell, L.	
-7442	Dewberry, E. W.			-4759	Doust, S. E.	a
-3176	Dewey, F. C.	a, k 30/12/17		3431	Dovey, B. S.	
-9308	Dewey, L/Cpl. L. F.			-8611	Dowden, Cpl. A. P. A.	
-9423	Dewhurst, P. M.			976	Dowell, A. W.	
-8149	Dickens, A. F.			-0533	Downe, C. M.	
5438	Dickens, A. J. E.	d 3/6/16		5483	Downing, P. J.	
4587	Dickens, C. E.	o		-6711	Downing, R.	e
-5860	Dickenson, Richard Hay	e		-8645	Downs, L. H.	
-8005	Dickenson, L/Cpl. Richard Heath			4696	Drage, F.	a
-7232	Dickenson, T. R.	a		-9145	Drake, F. C. F.	
800	Dicksee, C. B.			-9431	Drake, G. L.	
-2386	Dickson, J.	a, k 8/8/17		7217	Drake, W.	o
-0394	Digby, A. E.	a		-9278	Draper, W. B.	
-8752	Dillon, L. J. F. P.			4922	Drew, E. H.	
-6130	Dillon, T. J.			-7375	Drew, J. P.	
-0979	Dimes, Cpl. P. E.	e		-5431	Drew, Cpl. V. L.	a
-7795	Dimmock, S. J.			-9366	Drewer, S. W.	
-1392	Dingley, A. C.	a, w 5/8/17		-0016	Drewry, Col.-Sgt. A. S.	15/O-C-B
-3846	Dixon, C. A.	a, k 31/10/17		-8871	Driver, C. H.	[M(2)]
-8573	Dixon, F. A.			5311	Dronsfield, S. W.	a
-4136	Dixon, J. S.			-7678	Druery, L/Cpl. G. M.	

For explanation of Abbreviations see p. 434.

-8536	Drummond, C. H.	*a*		1379	Eames, C. G.	
-8193	Dryden, L/Cpl. G. H.			1720	Eames, L. J.	
5749	Du Bern, T. E.	*o*		-5764	Earle, E.	*e*
-8952	Duchesne, C. S. C.			-4691	Earle, G. F. R.	*e*
-6516	Duck, F. E.			-8272	Earnshaw, L/Cpl. H. D. W.	
-3493	Duckworth, J.	*a, o*		-9539	East, P. V.	
3591	Duclos, R-Q-M-S H. F.	*a*		-6226	Eastaugh, L/Cpl. H. N.	
7370	Dudley, E. A.			1891	Easton, J.	
-7412	Duff, Sgt. C. L.			-9356	Eastwood, V. A.	
-8205	Duffus, H. W.			-1785	Eaton, A. H.	*a*
7195	Duggan, A. C.	*o*		-7906	Eatough, R. E.	
-2855	Duggan, E. W.			-7092	Ebbetts, F. T.	
-6470	Duggan, Sgt. V.			-6411	Eccles, E.	
5484	Duguid, G.	*o*		-8993	Ecklin, W. D.	
-8206	Duignan, J.			7420	Ede, C. B.	
-9128	Duke, S. M.			-2448	Eelsten, C. W.	
-5225	Dumbell, P. H.	*o*		-9257	Edgley, G. W.	
-2144	Dumbleton, G. G.	*a*		8795	Edlin, Cpl. A. J. B.	*a, w* 29/5/18
-6920	Duncan, A. C.	*a, w* 27/8/18		-0835	Edwards, Cpl. G. F.	*a*
-8951	Duncan, Sgt. W. G.	*a,* M-S-M		-2663	Edwards, H.	*a, k* 30/10/17
-5787	Dunham, G. H.	*e*		-4764	Edwards, O. W.	*a, w* 6/9/18, 27/9/18
-4760	Dunkley, C. F.	*a*		4515	Edwards, T. C.	*o*
-8872	Dunlop, I. W.			1082	Edwards, W. A.	
-7374	Dunn, E. H.			-4231	Ffford, T. Le-C.	*a, w* 29/10/17
-4293	Dunn, H. A.	*a, k* 24/7/17		-3967	Egerton, J. H.	*a, k* 31/10/17
-1482	Dunn, L.			5171	Egerton, Sgt. R. H.	*a, f*
-4060	Dunn, R.	*o*		-9309	Eginton, L. C.	
-3384	Dunning, H. P.	*a*		-1140	Elder-Duncan, Cpl. J. H.	
9492	Durant, W. B.	*o*		-4317	Eldred, H. T.	
8131	D'Ydevallee, L/Cpl. C. M. P. G. V. O.			8438	Eldridge, C. J. W.	
-0094	Dye, Sgt. E. W.	*a*		-6428	Eldridge, L/Cpl. J. W.	
-4762	Dyer, S. B.	*a*		-8134	Eley, J. R.	
7191	Dyke, E. C.	*a, w* 21/3/18		-6688	Elgie, R. L.	*a*
1404	Dykes, R. A.			5104	Elias, H. W.	*a*
-6808	Dykes, W.	*a, w* 27/8/18		5897	Ellen, P. H.	[*o, w*(2)]
-8804	Dyne, G. W.			-7709	Ellender, C-S-M G. E.	15/O-C-B
-1568	Dysart, C. H. G.	*a, w* 27/3/18		-3029	Ellerman, G. D'H.	*a*
-6949	Dyson, G.	*a, k* 30/12/17		-0722	Elliott, H. C.	
6444	Dyson, G. S.	*a, w* 22/9/17		6213	Elliott, E. W.	*a, w* 25/3/18
-6517	Dyson, P. L.	*a, w* 4/1/17		-7260	Elliott, H. J.	*a, k* 11/11/18
				-3574	Elliott, R. A.	*a*
-9557	Eadon, E. W.			-5677	Elliott, R. C.	*o*
-2894	Eager, L/Cpl. G.	*a*		-0723	Elliott, L/Cpl. S. G.	
-2698	Eagland, L. H.	*a*		-7613	Elliott, L/Cpl. T. G.	
-7827	Eaglesfield, T. L.			-5343	Elliott, W. B.	
-7348	Eales, R. E.			2932	Ellis, B. W.	
-9558	Eales, W. F.			-8873	Ellis, F. H. W.	

OTHER RANKS: ARTISTS' RIFLES.

-3877	Ellis, G. V. G.			-1216	Facey, Pioneer-Sgt. G. F. J.	
-8097	Ellis, L/Cpl. J. P. M.			-9382	Fahy, F. A. A.	
-7122	Ellis, N. T. H.		a	-7873	Fairclough, V.	
-4295	Ellis, Sgt. R. S.		15/O-C-B	-6429	Falby, R. L. S.	o
-6642	Ellis, L/Cpl. W. S.	a, w 25/3/18		-7081	Falkner, E. G.	
-8537	Ellison, J. M. R.			-9163	Fallon, J. J.	
8311	Elwood, C. B.		o	-5586	Fallow, J.	e
-8273	Elmhurst, L/Cpl. L. K.			-4489	Fanshawe, C.	
-7249	Elton, L/Cpl. A. B.	a, w 27/8/18		-7006	Faragher, F. C.	a, w 27/8/18
-9249	Elton, B. A.			-9164	Farmer, H. W. G.	
-5933	Elton, G. Y.		o	-8361	Farmer, J. L.	
-7026	Elvey, H. H. W.			-8208	Farmer, R. V.	
-4693	Elvin, G. E.	a, w 30/12/17		5116	Farmer, S. D. S.	a
-8431	Elvin, S. L. W.			-4427	Farr, F. J.	a, k 30/10/17
-8647	Eley, Cpl. T. G.			-8085	Farrand, W. B.	
-7934	Emanuel, H.			-5788	Farrar, T. S.	e
-6206	Emerson, A. H.	a, w 27/9/18		-7010	Farrow, H. T. C.	a
-8419	Emery, G. E.			-8012	Farthing, S.	
6698	Emms, S J.		o	-4983	Fawcett, J. H.	a
-0540	Emond, Sgt. J. O.	a, w 30/10/17		-9093	Fawkes, F. S. E.	
5401	Ennals, J. L.		a	-7069	Feather, R. H.	
4415	Ernst, R. S.		o	-6707	Feather, V. L.	
4955	Ernst, W. A.		o	3304	Featherstone, M. B.	a
-7080	Erskine, P. W.		a	5996	Fehr, A. H.	a
-8966	Esdale, E. W.			1191	Felgate, R. L.	
1561	Essex, R. A. Y.	a, k 30/10/17		-7007	Fell, K. G.	a, k 4/10/18
2410	Etheridge, S. G.		a	-0042	Fellows, Sgt. L. D.	a, f
-6936	Evans, C.		a	-6733	Felton, D. U.	
-8207	Evans, C. B.			-5361	Fennell, L. A. R.	d 14/4/17
-3267	Evans, E.		a	-7008	Fennell, L. R.	a
-7559	Evans, E. N.		o	-4233	Fenner, P. G.	a, k 31/10/17
-6983	Evans, G. K.			-3640	Ferguson, B. V.	a, w 26/10/17,
8375	Evans, H. W. A.		a	-9517	Ferguson, J. McN.	[k 8/3/18
7277	Evans, J. M.		o	-2546	Ferguson, R. H. C.	a, w 30/10/17
-4607	Evans, M. L.		a	-7422	Ferguson, Cpl. W. H.	a, w 30/5/18
-7005	Evans, O. I.			-4234	Fermo, L.	a
-4765	Evans, R. H.		a	-4235	Fermo, R.	
-7443	Evans, T. C.		a	-4695	Ferriday, G. C.	a
-2227	Evans, V. W. E.		o	-2479	Ferris, R. W.	o
-8612	Evans, Wilfred Morgan			670	Ficklin, Sgt. A. H.	a, f
3454	Evans, William Melbourne			-7027	Field, B.	
-4232	Everest, T. S.	a, w 24/8/17		-6950	Field, R. H.	a, k 29/6/18
-4061	Everett, S.	a, k 30/10/17		-2973	Field, L/Cpl. W. G. L.	
1250	Evershed, C. R.			3637	Fielding, P. A.	
1701	Evison, Cpl. E. C.			-7614	Fieldsend, A. F.	
-9297	Ewins, W. G.			2838	Fighiera, L/Cpl. G. C. C.	a
				-6108	Finch, G. D.	a

For explanation of Abbreviations see p. 434.   449

−5227	Finch, R. C.	*a*		−9405	Foggin, R. A.	
−8135	Findlay, L/Cpl. J. S.			−9146	Foley, P. G.	
−2115	Finill, W. F.	*a*		−6018	Folkard, C. J.	
−8274	Finlayson, J.			−8362	Fooks, L/Cpl. W. J.	
−7349	Finn, C-Q-M-S A.			−3522	Foote, L. W.	*a*
6759	Finn, L. R.			−5319	Forbes, R. B. G.	*o*
4266	Finnis, R. Q.			−3389	Forbes, W. D.	*a, p*
−5990	Firmin, L. A. L.			7179	Ford, O-R-S P. C.	
−6890	Firth, E.	*a, k* 1/6/18		−8777	Forde, A. M. A.	
−4400	Firth, F. R.			−2128	Forde, J. H.	*a, k* 31/10/17
1181	Fischel, S. W.			−3232	Fordham, R.	
6670	Fischer, H. J. W.			3746	Forrester, H.	*o*
2823	Fish, Bugler G. F. N.	*o*		7153	Formoy, R. R.	
−6713	Fisher, D. K.	*a*		−6966	Forster, N.	*a, w* 5/4/18
6798	Fisher, E. W.	*o*		1433	Foster, C.	
−3879	Fisher, H	*a, w* 31/10/17		−6750	Foster, C. L.	*a*
−2749	Fisher, J. G. B.	*a, w* 11/8/17		−7168	Foster, W. L.	*a, p*
−6069	Fisher, P.			−6690	Foulds, J.	
−0365	Fisher, R. E.	*a*		−7104	Fountain, T. O.	
−0277	Fisher, Sgt. W. H.			−5035	Fowle, H. S.	*a, w* 30/10/17
−3969	Fisk, H. H.	*a, k* 31/10/17		1172	Fowler, H. O.	
−7233	Fitch, Cpl. G. A.	*a, w*		−8648	Fowler, McD. G.	
−4641	Fitt, P. R. J.	*a*		−7714	Fowler, R.	
−4914	Fitton, A. E.			7409	Fowler, T. D.	*o*
−7308	Fitton, F.	*a, w* 8/10/17		6286	Fox, R-S-M E.	*a. w* 22/3/18 D-C-M
−8939	Fitts, A. H.			−0610	Fox, Sgt. F. H. B.	*a, w* 19/8/17
−4139	Fitzsimmons, C. H.	*a, k* 17/8/17		−8728	Fox, G. F.	
−8025	Flanigan, Cpl. J. L.			−4964	Fox, H.	*a*
7089	Flanigan, J. P.	*a*		−5165	Fox, H. B.	
−8275	Flavell, A. G. V.			−6967	Fox, W.	*a, w* 17/5/18
−5765	Flaxman, Sgt. J. R.			−9657	Fox, W. R. L.	
−7203	Fleet, C. A.			−5188	Foxcroft, J. A.	*o*
−2780	Fleet. F. J.	*a*		−3523	Fradd, F. H.	*e*
−6996	Fleischer, L/Cpl. L. C.			7036	Frampton, G. V. M.	*a*
−1066	Fleming, Cpl. E.	*a*		−8613	France, T. R.	
−8915	Fletcher, C. B.	*d* 4/11/18		−8341	Francis, B. S.	
944	Fletcher, C.			−8874	Francis, D. E.	
−8823	Fletcher, J.			−3328	Francis, Sgt. D. J.	*a*
−3970	Flinders, J. J.	*k* 31/10/17		2415	Francis, E. C.	
6977	Flint, O. J.	*a*		7180	Francis, J. W.	*o*
−9060	Flood, S. B.			−0332	Francis, T. C.	*o*
5173	Flooks, A.	*a*		285	Franck, C-S-M H. E.	*a, w* 30/12/17
−3388	Floyd, Cpl. W. E.			1894	Franghaidi, Sgt. G. P.	*a*
−8395	Flux, H. P.			−2538	Franken, W.	*a*
4202	Foard, B. H.	*a, k* 30/10/17		−7055	Franks, B.	
−5228	Foche, L/Cpl. F. J.	*a*		566	Franks, C. V.	
−5679	Foden, A.	*o*		−8150	Franks, Cpl. F. H.	

FF

91	Fraser, C-S-M A. J.	a	−7321	Gardiner, W. N.	a
−0984	Fraser, B.	a, p	−8824	Gardner, C. H.	
−7969	Fraser, C. C.		−2934	Gardner, F. W.	
−9406	Fraser, C. H.		−1331	Gardner, R. P.	a, k 24/5/17
−5167	Fraser, D. K.	a, w 31/10/17	−8136	Gardner, Cpl. W. J. L.	
−8994	Fraser, H.		8389	Gare, J. H.	a, k 30/12/17
6287	Fraser, Sgt. J. E.	a, w 30/10/17	−8539	Garforth, H.	
1198	Freaker, A. L.	a, k 31/10/17	−5931	Garland, T. W. D.	a
−8778	Freeman, L. W.		−6812	Garraway, M. L.	
8376	Freeman, P. E.	a	5686	Garraway, W. G.	a, o, k 17/8/17
−3575	Freiensener, H. J.		366	Garrett, G. G.	
−8779	French, A.		−8780	Garrie, S.	
−8574	French, A. D.		4365	Garside, J.	
−1892	French, D. A. G.		−9700	Gaskell, L.	
5842	French, H. C.		−9432	Gates, F.	
−6430	French, L/Cpl. T. C.	a	−8039	Gates, P. E.	
−3124	Fricker, R. F.		−4430	Gates, R. R.	
−2676	Friend, Cpl. W. K.		−6019	Gates, V.	
−0907	Frier, O-R-S H. E.		1729	Gattling, W. R.	
−8362	Frocks, W. J.		−6111	Gattrell, H. E.	
−8875	Froome, H. V.		−9453	Gavine, E.	
−6228	Frost, A.		−4927	Geake, R. A.	
−7152	Frost, D.	a, w 30/9/18	2680	Gedge, H. E.	o
−4237	Frost, J. R.	a	5688	Gee, E.	a
7229	Fullagar, Sgt. C. E.	a, k 5/4/18	−7153	Gee, E. A.	
−6229	Fuller, E. S.	e	5340	Geffen, L/Cpl. E.	o
−9199	Fuller, H. A.		−2782	Gelder, Cpl. S.	
−8650	Fullerton, J.		−8967	Gent, W. T.	
−6251	Furber, L/Cpl. J. E.	a	−8105	George, B.	a, w 28/6/18
−7320	Furmston, H. F.		1763	George, Sgt. C. H.	a
−7715	Fyson, E. G.	a, w 22/9/18	7472	George, L. S.	o
			5111	Gerard, F. W.	a, k 31/10/17
−7746	Gabriel, C. C.		−7376	Gerhardi, Sgt. A.	o
110	Gadsby, G. S.		−8269	Gerhardi, Sgt. T. E.	a, M-S-M
−9223	Gaffney, E.		−7413	Gerrard, W.	
−6691	Gains, C. G.		−3850	Gething, S.	a, k 28/10/17
−7431	Galbraith, A.	a, w 1/10/18	5844	Ghosley, H. S.	a
−9095	Galbraith, W. E.		−3683	Gibb, H. R.	
−9147	Gale, F. J.		−3762	Gibb, L/Cpl. S. W.	a, k
−5036	Gale, R. A. B.	o	−7229	Gibbon, A. C.	
−1353	Gall, L/Cpl. A.	o	−6412	Gibbon, F. C.	
−4092	Gallagher, D.	a	−1243	Gibbons, Sgt. C. S.	15/O-C-B
−8940	Galley, F. A.		5620	Gibbons, Sgt. J.	a, f
1851	Gallop, Sgt. P. C.	a, w 15/1/18 F/D	1657	Gibbons, James Fitz-Gerald	a
−4299	Gamlin, Sgt. H.	a	3154	Gibbons, Sgt. James Francis	a, f
−3576	Garbutt, J. H.	a, k 10/11/18	−7894	Gibbons, J. O. C.	
−8729	Gardener, L/Cpl. P. C.		−4093	Gibbs, A. E.	a, w 2/4/18

-8826	Gibbs, C. A.		-9668	Good, T. G.	
-8575	Gibbs, J. C.		6563	Goodall, N.	a, o
-8968	Gibbs, L/Cpl. P. V.		20	Goodchild, Armr.-Sgt. S. N.	
4894	Gibbs, P. W.	o	6700	Gooden, N.	o
4967	Gibson, J. D.		-7170	Gooding, L/Cpl. L. T.	
3230	Gibson, J. E.	o	-4402	Gooding, R. J.	a, k 31/10/17
-9148	Gibson, J. McK.		-7543	Goodman, F. R.	
1589	Gilbee, S. J.		-9042	Goodway, L/Cpl. L. R.	
5494	Gilbert, E. A.	a, k 25/4/17	2463	Goodwin, J.	o
-9540	Gilbert, H. S.		-9595	Goodwin, L.	
-8969	Gilbert, R.		-3928	Goodyear, C. J. C.	
-4698	Gilbert, W.	o	2984	Goodyear, W. E.	o
-3233	Gilby, C. J.	a	-9640	Gorbishley, H. R.	
1373	Giles, G.		8469	Gordon, M. B.	a
5904	Gilham, E. L.	o	-8753	Gordon, M. J.	
-8473	Gill, G. H. R.		-6693	Gordon, W. N.	
3606	Gill, J. H.		-7747	Gore-Clough, M.	
-6131	Gill, R.		-7262	Goreley, S. G.	a
-9651	Gillett, H. D.		6895	Goreman, G. P.	o
-1068	Gilley, Sgt. J.	a, f	3443	Gosling, C. L.	
6706	Gillgrass, Sgt. A.	a, f	-2302	Goss, S.	a, w 31/10/17
-8730	Gillison, K. H.		-5861	Gotelee, F.	a, p, k 10/10/18
-6047	Gillison, L/Cpl. S. N.	a, w 5/4/18	-5767	Gough, A. T.	e
2341	Gilmour, C. W.	o	-9043	Gould, C. N.	
-0392	Gilmour, Sgt. G. F.	a	-8995	Gould, K. J. G.	
-5937	Gits, R. W.		-9041	Gould, R. M.	
-4886	Gladding, R. H.	a	-8827	Gould, S. H.	
-7082	Glanfield, P.		-8828	Gould, W.	
5756	Glen, Sgt. V.	a, f, ⓌⒹ	-7748	Goulden, F. W. A.	
-0650	Glendell, L. G.		-0605	Gow, Sgt. A.	
-0138	Glibbery, R-Q-M-S H. E. 15/O-C-B, ⓌⒹ		-4113	Gow, D. R.	a, w 30/10/17
2423	Glossop, H. S.	o	1900	Gower, L. A.	a, w 23/3/18
7090	Goddard, A. P.		-5445	Gowlland, R.	
-8941	Goddard, L. J.		-9697	Gowring, H. J.	
3903	Goddard, Sgt. N. C.	a	-9167	Grace, F. W.	
-6859	Goddard, T. R.	a	-0497	Grace, W. H.	a, k 31/10/17
-7804	Godet, H. M.		-6432	Graham, C. M.	e
-3421	Godfrey, Cpl. E. H. S.		-8194	Graham, J.	
5012	Godson, S. F. T.	a, k 31/10/17	-5768	Graham, L. P.	o
-6472	Goggs, L/Cpl. G. A.	a	-9676	Graham, R.	
4544	Goldie, A.		-3690	Granlund, C. E.	
-6431	Golding, A. P.	a	-5004	Grant, F.	
3274	Goldspink, H. J.		-3708	Grant, K. McL.	
-6383	Goldup, A. E.	a	-0027	Grant, C-Q-M-S K. S.	
-3156	Gollcher, F. K.	a	-9258	Grant, R. B.	
-0574	Golle, Sgt. C. V.	a, k 20/12/17	-3823	Gray, A.	a
-2720	Golmick, P.		7190	Gray, D.	

OTHER RANKS: ARTISTS' RIFLES.

-6718	Gray, Cpl. G. E. K.	
-9583	Gray, H. J. B.	
-6891	Gray, L/Cpl. O.	a, k 27/8/18
8538	Gray, W. H.	a
3951	Graystone, Sgt. C.	a, w 1/10/18
-2804	Graystone, W. J.	a
-8694	Greaves, F. N.	
-6134	Greaves, H. B.	o
-5085	Green, Albert	a
-4023	Green, Archibald Bertram	a
-7043	Green, Arthur	a
-3579	Green, Arthur Bowden	a, k 30/10/17
-7865	Green, A. L. F.	
-2502	Green, C. C.	
3699	Green, C. H.	
9450	Green, Charles Herbert	a, w 30/12/17
-6113	Green, L/Cpl. C. W.	
5174	Green, G. G.	
-7849	Green, K. W.	
-3580	Green, L. S.	a, w 23/3/18
-8420	Green, R. E.	
7358	Green, R. K.	a
7820	Greenhough, G.	
-7083	Greenhough, R.	a
-2737	Greening, F. V.	a, M-M
-8195	Greenwood, N.	
-7544	Greenwood, W. E. W.	
9641	Greenwood, Sgt. W. J.	a, w
-0389	Gregory, Sgt. C. G.	a
-6207	Gregson, O.	
-8342	Greville, H. A. B.	
-5543	Grew, E. M.	e
-9518	Grey, A.	
-9109	Grey, W. C.	d 30/10/18
753	Grice, Sgt. A. N.	a, f, ℳ
-0238	Grice, c-Q-M-S O. H.	
6381	Grierson, Sgt. R. H. F.	a, f
1673	Griffin, H. M.	
-5544	Griffin, J. T.	
-6923	Griffiths, G.	a, k 2/10/18
-4240	Griffiths, E. T.	e
-3062	Griffiths, G. J.	e
-8876	Griffiths, H L.	
-8614	Griffiths, L/Cpl. J. L.	
6311	Griffiths, L. A.	a
-8943	Griffiths, P. D.	
-6861	Griffiths, T. A.	
-7204	Griffiths, T. D.	
-6984	Grigg, L. J.	
-8917	Griggs, K. B.	
-9061	Grime, S. L.	
-4770	Grimmer, R. P.	
-5656	Grimmer, Cpl. S. E.	
-3331	Grinsted, A. W.	a
-9231	Grisewood, J.	
1325	Grobbelaar, P. E.	
2583	Grogan, J. D.	a
-8916	Groom, J. W.	
200	Groom, W. O.	
-3225	Gross, H. A.	
-5121	Groves, F. L.	
-9247	Gudger, A. D.	
-3675	Guest, A.	a
1486	Gunn, B.	
6870	Gurley, A. L.	o
-5545	Gurteen, O.	o
-8953	Gwinn, A. G. S.	
1586	Gysin, H.	
3811	Gyssels, L.	
211	¶Hack, R-Q-M-S M. S.	a, M-S-M, ℳ
-9110	Hackforth, R.	
-7514	Hacquoil, F. W.	
-8829	Haddock, Sgt. T. P.	
-9324	Hadingham, H. R.	
-4572	Hadley, W. A.	
5908	Hager, Sgt. E. A. W.	
-8345	Haggie, L/Cpl. D. J.	
2569	Haggis, Sgt. B.	a, ℳ
5949	Hahn, B.	o
5950	Hahn, J.	o
-9041	Haig, L/Cpl. N. S.	
-3392	Haigh, B. S.	a
-6021	Haigh, F. C.	
-4363	Hailstone, A. E.	a, w 29/10/17
2252	Haines, A. K.	o
1714	Hale, H. E.	
-0431	Hale, J.	
5497	Hales, G. W.	a
-9219	Hales, S. J.	
-3661	Haley, Sgt. E. R.	
-6230	Halford, L/Cpl. E.	
5119	Hall, A. H.	
7156	Hall, C. J.	a

For explanation of Abbreviations see p. 434.   453

-5354	Hall, F. A.		*o*	4773	Harding, S. W.	*a, k* 30/3/18
813	Hall, G. H.			6461	Hardwick, S. H.	*a, k* 6/9/18
-9641	Hall, H. S.			-3824	¶Hardy, C-S-M H. H. C.	
-6862	Hall, L.			-6782	Hardy, W. E.	
-7396	Hall, L. C.			7924	Hare, P. Z.	
-9044	Hall, L/Cpl. N. H.			-6715	Hare, S.	
-8068	Hall, Cpl. R.			-9062	Hargraves, F.	
-5940	Hall, R. A. N.		*e*	-7322	Hargreaves, L/Cpl. R. J.	
-7125	Hall, L/Cpl. R. C.		*a*	-7084	Harland, M. L.	*a, k* 27/8/18
-8970	Hallett, E. H.			-8364	Harle, L/Cpl. W. S. B.	
2546	Hallett, G. H. W.		*o*	4090	Harlock, Sgt. E. R. B.	*a, w* 31/10/17
-9559	Halliday, G.			-5994	Harman, F. R.	*e*
5176	Halls, W. J.	*a, w* 12/3/18, }		-9232	Harman, R.	
-9045	Hallman, W. W.	[*k* 11/11/18 }		-8615	Harper, L/Cpl. A. H.	
6734	Ham, G.	*a, w* 2/4/18		3344	Harper, Ernest E.	*a*
-7925	Ham, H.			2132	Harper, Evelyn	*o, k* 8/12/17 *(Jerusalem)*
6004	Hambrough, D. B.		*o*	-5839	Harper, E. W. W.	*a*
-9454	Hamilton, C. F.			-0128	Harper, Q-M-S H. H.	*a, f*, M-S-M, 𝕸
-9455	Hamilton, G. D.			-4493	Harper, H. P.	*o*
-8363	Hamilton, J. O. A. E.			-6937	Harper, J. H.	
-9456	Hamilton, P. J.			-0458	Harper, Bandsman M. J.	
-7126	Hamilton, R. A.			-0514	Harries, E. D.	*a*
3318	Hamlen, P.	*d* 9/3/15		-8086	Harries, H. W.	
-6643	Hamlyn, Cpl. H.		*a*	-0444	Harrild, Cpl. A. G.	
-8971	Hamlyn, J. A.			-3884	Harrington, F. C.	*a*
4532	Hamlyn, R.			3232	Harris, C. E. L.	*a*
-9248	Hammelt, C.			-9620	Harris, C. H. R.	
-4492	Hammersley, A. H.	*a, w* 5/8/17		-6892	Harris, E. B.	*a, k* 23/8/18
-9408	Hammill, N. B. J.			-7010	Harris, E. W.	*e*
2390	Hammond, Sgt. C. C.	*a, w* 30/10/17		-3334	Harris, F. T.	
-8651	Hammond, E. C.			-6863	Harris, G. E.	
-4320	Hammond, L. G.	*a, k* 31/10/17		-9519	Harris, G. G. R.	
-7009	Hammonds, J. F.	*a, w* 6/9/18, }		-8365	Harris, G. I.	
-8422	Hampson, F. A.	[27/9/18 }		-6433	Harris, L/Cpl. H. A.	*a*
-6714	Hampton, G. S.	*a, w* 27/8/18		1672	Harris, J.	
5120	Hanchard, C.		*a*	-3527	Harris, J. G.	
-9249	Hancock, H. P.			-7749	Harris, M.	
-4643	Hand, J. W.	*a, k* 24/3/18		-4364	Harris, M. S.	*o*
1354	Handcock, A. J.			-9149	Harris, R. G.	
5846	Hane, A. H.			-9656	Harris, S.	
-8919	Hankinson, R. J.			6601	Harris, T. G. L.	*a*
-9015	Hannah, H. B.			-0158	Harris, Sgt. T. M.	*a, w* 8/10/18
-8781	Hannam, A. M.			6951	Harris, V. R.	*a*
-4888	Hanson, J. E.			-0630	Harris, W. G.	
-7875	Harbaugh, G.			2595	Harris, Wilfrid Henry	*o*
-7970	Harborne, G. St. L.			-6520	Harris, William Henry	
-9016	Hardaker, H.			2308	Harrison, Austen	*o*

OTHER RANKS: ARTISTS' RIFLES.

−5619	Harrison, Ainsley	a
−7220	Harrison, Cpl. A. C.	
−4956	Harrison, A. E.	a
5498	Harrison, Sgt. A. H.	a, w 30/10/17
−9457	Harrison, D. F.	
−7445	Harrison, H. B.	
5500	Harrison, J. C.	
−2152	Harrison, J. E. B.	
−7399	Harrison, L. A.	
−1393	Harrison, L/Cpl. T.	a, p
−9677	Harrison, W.	
−6813	Harrap, R. L.	a
−3264	Hart, S. L.	
−3971	Hartland, O. U.	a
−8830	Hartley, R. J.	
5580	Hartley, W. C.	a, k 31/10/17
3333	Hartsilver, L/Cpl. J.	o
−9017	Hartwell, L/Cpl. F. J.	
6165	Harty, F. S.	o
−6968	Harvey, A.	e
−6474	Harvey, A. L.	
−8296	Harvey, L/Cpl. G. H.	
1135	Harvey, C-S-M H. L.	a, w 30/10/17
−7363	Harvey, P. T.	
−8877	Harvey, R. I.	
−6645	Harwin, S.	a
−7562	Harwood, L/Cpl. V.	
1751	Haslam, John Alfred	
−0237	Haslehust, C-Q-M-S T. E.	
−5233	Hassall C. S.	
−4646	Hassall, J. D.	o
4910	Hassell, S. H.	
−8027	Hastings, Cpl. F. A.	
−5548	Haswell, C. W.	
6863	Haswell, G. D.	a
−3852	Hatcher, F. H.	a, p
−6716	Hatherly, R. E.	
−6829	Hatton, R. J.	
−7717	Hawden, J. B.	
−8169	Hawes, C. T.	
−8616	Hawes, E.	
−4533	Hawkes, H. F.	
−9018	Hawking, J. L.	
−6144	Hawkings, H. L.	
8472	Hawkings, J. W. C.	a
5204	Hawkins, D. E.	o
−8617	Hawkins, H. H.	
−4830	Hawkins, J. D.	o
−0463	Hawkins, S. H.	
−5415	Hay, J. M.	
8952	Hay, R. McD.	a, k 31/10/17
−5123	Haydon, F. W.	a, k 30/10/17
−5014	Hayes, A.	
−3454	Hayes, M. P.	
−7297	Hayes, R. G.	
−7563	Hayes, T. F.	a, k 16/7/18
−6694	Haylock, Sgt. E. M.	
−5124	Haymen, H. L.	o
−6969	Haynes, R. E.	e
−2332	Haynes, S. H.	a
−4890	Hayter, R. F. G.	a, w 31/10/17
−4495	Hayward, A. D.	
−8754	Hayward, H. C.	
−5346	Hayward, H. W.	a, w 30/12/17
−6783	Hayward, S. G.	a
−1545	Haywood, C. T.	a
−2004	Hazard, E. E.	
1193	Head, C-Q-M-S F. V.	a
−7859	Head, J. S. C.	
−3103	Heal, H. H.	
−8972	Heald, H.	
−0562	Healey, N.	a, w 31/10/17
−7190	Hearn, C B.	
−7323	Hearn, R. P.	
−2131	Hearson, J. O.	o
−3455	Heath, J.	a, w 26/7/17
−8271	Heaton, W. B.	
−0205	Hebden, Sgt. G. L.	a, w 24/7/17
−9495	Heberden, H. W.	
−0923	Hecht, Sgt. H. J.	
9297	Hedgecock, S.	d 27/11/16
3733	Heely, N.	
−4321	Heggs, P. J. D.	a, w 29/9/18
−7577	Hein, L. J. H.	a
−9259	Helcke, E. W.	
−8166	Hellings, D. R.	
−7616	Hemens, L. G.	a, w 31/10/17
2187	Hemingway, F. E.	a
−9433	Hemingway, R. L.	
−6384	Hemmings, W. H.	
−2805	Hemus, C. H.	
−4366	Henderson, C. R.	a
−3909	Henderson, E. S.	a, k 30/10/17
−9097	Henderson, H. J. C.	

For explanation of Abbreviations see p. 434.   455

−3987	Henderson, R.		869	Hill, S. A.	
−6164	Henderson, R. E.	o	−6646	Hill, T. St. Q.	
6980	Henley, F.	a, k 31/10/17	628	Hills, C-S-M P. C.	a, w 30/10/17
4886	Hennell, A.	a	−1204	Hilton, Sgt. J. B.	
−0228	Heppenstall, C-Q-M-S H. H.		−6051	Hilton, J. G.	o
−5038	Heppenstall, L/Cpl. R. A.	a, k 27/3/18	7037	Hilton, L/Cpl. J. L.	
−7409	Hepworth, F.	a	−7012	Hilton, W. A.	a
−7011	Herbert, J.	a	−6753	Hinde, C. A.	
3809	Herman, J.		−6948	Hinton, W. J.	a, p
40	Herold, C-Q-M-S E. F.	a	−5789	Hird, B. H.	o
−0014	Herold, Sgt. W. C.	a	8669	Hirons, W. J.	
−4647	Heron, V. H.	a, k 30/10/17	−5840	Hirst, L/Cpl. G. S.	a, w 27/8/18
3405	Herrman, E. R.	a	−7171	Hirst, H.	a, w 27/3/18
−8643	Heskett, E. A.		6498	Hislop, W. A.	a
−3787	Hetherington, H.	a, w 30/12/17	2109	Hitch, Cpl. J. O. B.	o
9691	Hewitt, A. H.	a, k 31/10/17	−8168	Hitch, R. A.	
−5770	Hewitt, G. A.	e	−4496	Hitchings, Cpl. T.	
−5271	Hewitt, G. S.	a, w 30/12/17, k 8/3/18	−8044	Hitchins, D. M. S.	
−9458	Hewitt, J. H.		−9434	Hitchins, J. F.	
8779	Hewitt, R. C.	a, w 30/4/17	−4403	Hoar, R. V.	
−6600	Hey, L/Cpl. E.	a	−0390	Hoare, C. K.	a
−9111	Heyhoe, H. A.		7497	Hoatson, J. R.	a
−9112	Heywood, H. W.		−7805	Hobbs, Cpl. A. R. B.	
−6476	Hibbard, C. J.	a, M-M	−6814	Hobbs, L/Cpl. B. T.	
−0420	Hibberd, Cpl. E.		−7750	Hobbs, L/Cpl. C. R.	
5122	Hickley, G.		−7589	Hobbs, Cpl. E.	
−4988	Hickox, E. H.	a	−5717	Hobbs, J. P.	e
−3886	Hicks, Sgt. E. J.		−9346	Hobson, M. C.	
−6938	Hicks, F.	a, p	−0493	Hoddinoth, H. C.	a, w 11/8/17,
−0635	Hicks, G.		−5790	Hodge, Cpl. A. D.	6/4/18
−3359	Hicks, G. C.	a, w 30/10/17, 30/12/17	6480	Hodge, E. E.	a
−6304	¶Hicks, Sgt. J. S.		−9325	Hodge, E. F. R.	
−7300	Hickson, S. A.		−8057	Hodge, Cpl. E. W.	
−3763	Higgins, T.		−7221	Hodges, L/Cpl. J. B.	a
−3424	Higgins, L/Cpl. W. L. G.	a	−2271	Hodgkins, W. A.	a
−3301	Higson, H.		7114	Hodgkinson, L/Cpl. E.	o
−3998	Higson, W.	a, w 30/10/17	−9597	Hodgson, S. R.	
−7324	Hilburn, Cpl. F. J.		−8920	Hoer, J. J.	
−0413	Hilder, B. R.		2530	Hogg, E.	
2846	Hill, C-S-M A. B.	a, R. VICT. MED.	−4367	Hogg, H. E.	a, w 23/3/18
−2806	Hill, C. C.	a	−5505	Hogg, Cpl. W. L.	a
−8833	Hill, F. G.		−8834	Hogge, R. P.	
−9113	Hill, L/Cpl. F. R.		−5125	Holden, L/Cpl. E. G. V. H.	
2883	Hill, G. E.	a	−8423	Hole, C. B.	
−4534	Hill, J. A.	a, k 31/10/17	−0061	Holgate, B.	
−2807	Hill, J. C.		−6276	Holgate, J. E.	
−4989	Hill, L. W.	o	7340	Holland, E. W.	o

OTHER RANKS: ARTISTS' RIFLES.

-9098	Holland, E. S.	
-8542	Holland, R.	
-7564	Hollands, C. B.	
-5126	Holloway, L/Cpl. T. J. M.	
-4067	Hollyman, W. H.	a, k 30/12/17
-3972	Holman, G. E.	a, w 2/8/17
1789	Holme, R.	
8303	Holmes, A. J.	a, w 31/8/18
3338	Holmes, Sgt. J. M.	a, f
-8731	Holmes, R. C.	
-7565	Holmes, S. W.	
-9063	Holstrom, E.	
-6997	Hood, Cpl. N. S.	
-7937	Hooker, T. A.	
-6950	Hooper, C. F.	a
-3302	Hopcroft, C. J.	a, w 30/12/17
8607	Hope, N. E.	a
-5127	Hope, R. E.	o
-4833	Hopkins, A.	o
1568	Hopkins, S. E.	
-5039	Hopper, A. C.	e
435	Hopper, J. R.	
5125	Hopson, A. W.	a
-5128	Hopwood, L/Cpl. A. W.	
-6050	Hore, S. H.	e
-2901	Horn, R.	
-4473	Horn, T. H.	a, p
-2723	Horn, W. H.	a
-5449	Hornby, R.	e
-7806	Horne, L/Cpl. D. C.	
-3528	Horne, F.	
3296	Horne, J. G.	a
6619	Horne, S. T. C.	o
-9383	Horner, D. S.	
-1737	Horner, F. R.	a
-9260	Hornibrook, C. E. B.	
-3237	Horrocks, J. G.	a, k 31/10/17
-4598	Horsfall, Cpl. W.	a
-6647	Horswill, P.	a
-6970	Horton, A. M.	a, k 27/8/18
-9347	Horton, C. A.	
-7222	Horton, D. B.	a, w 1/10/18
7133	Horton, E. G.	a
1268	Horton, J. E.	
-1115	Horwood, A. A.	a
-8397	Hoskins, E. A.	
-5594	Hoste, J. M. D.	o
-8755	Hounsfield, P. C.	
8539	Housden, A. T.	a, k 31/10/17
-8069	Housley, E.	
1228	Howard, C. F.	a
2741	Howard, Sgt. F. E.	
-0025	Howard, c-s-m G. E.	
-6269	Howard, L. P.	a, p
-9076	Howe, F. W. C.	
2799	Howell, L. J.	a
-1774	Howell, O. H.	
8393	Howells, G.	a
-6479	Howells, R. J.	a
-3336	Howgrave, A. A.	o
-6739	Howis, A. W. H.	a
-8901	Howitt, W. A.	
-6648	Hows, G.	
-5791	Howse, H. L.	o
-8805	Hoy, W. B.	
-7235	Hoyland, M. H.	
-7155	Hoyle, J. W.	a, k 5/4/18
-9669	Huband, K. G.	
-9496	Hudson, C. B.	
-6136	Hudson, G.	
-3127	Hudson, H. J.	
-7333	Hudson, J.	
-9541	Hudson, L. N.	
-7310	Hudson, W. A.	
-9130	Huggam, H.	
243	¶Huggins, Pioneer-Sgt. L. R.	a
362	Huggins, c-s-m W. A.	
-7287	Hughes-Bonsall, J. C.	
-8070	Hughes, A. T.	
-8954	Hughes, E. T.	
-7951	Hughes, H. R.	
-8424	Hughes, H. T.	
-9678	Hughes, J. E.	
-8782	Hughes, J. F. B.	
-8543	Hughes, R. R. E.	
-5129	Hughes, S. D.	o
-7156	Hughes, Sgt. T. R.	
-9497	Hulburd, R. J.	
-9498	Hulland, A. E.	
-7115	Hulcoop, R. W.	a, w 30/12/17
-3974	Hulme, F. W. P.	
-8835	Hulse, C. W.	d 2/11/18
-4832	Humpleby, E. S.	a, k 30/10/17
-3036	Humphrey, H. G.	a, k 30/10/17

For explanation of Abbreviations see p. 434.   457

-7263	Humphreys, A. B.	*a, k* 20/12/17		-2229	Ingram, L/Cpl. H. C.	
-4368	Humphreys, Cpl. J. R.	*a, w* 17/8/17		-5889	Ingram, Cpl. H. F.	
5058	Humphreys, L. C.			-7462	Inman, L/Cpl. J. L. J.	
-2724	Humphreys, Cpl. W. C.			-8212	Instrell, Sgt. A. W.	*a*
-8878	Humphries, A. R.			-1205	Irons, Sgt. G.	
-7642	Hunt, E. S.	*a, w* 21/8/18		-9670	Irvine, J. R.	
-4069	Hunt, G. A.	*a, k* 29/10/17		-0039	Irwin, C-S-M H. G.	*e*, 🎖
646	Hunt, H. V.			3564	Irwin, W. E.	*o*
-3719	Hunt, W. H.			6736	Isaac, W. J.	*a*
-8973	Hunter, F. D. P.			-6740	Isaac, W. J. P.	*a, w* 13/4/18
-7264	Hunter, G. W. L.			1707	Izard, G. W.	
-6385	Hunter, J. C.					
-2601	Hunter, L/Cpl. M. C. F.	*o*		-5552	Jackson, A. F.	*e*
-8251	Huntley, W. H. G.			2331	Jackson, Sgt. A. S.	*a*
-5771	Huntsman, C.			6856	Jackson, Sgt. C.	*a*
-2755	Hurd, Sgt. G. W.			-7890	Jackson, C. P.	*a*
-9635	Hurd, L.			-8322	Jackson, Cpl. G. B.	
-3105	Hurd, L. E.			-8544	Jackson, H.	
-4895	Hurlow, W. H.	*a*		-6951	Jackson, J. H.	*a, k* 27/3/18
5909	Hurn, L/Cpl. R. B.	*a*		1995	Jackson, K. S.	*a, k* 30/10/17
-4437	Hurrell, S. C.	*o*		-7311	Jackson, N. P.	*a*
-5015	Hustwit, Sgt. C. H.			-6985	Jackson, R. E.	*a, w* 26/8/18
-8783	Hutchings, S. A. R.			-5718	Jackson, S. J.	*o*
-8696	Hutchinson, F. L.			-9499	Jackson, W.	
-0318	Hutchinson, L/Cpl. G. L.	*a*		-7074	Jacob, C. H.	*o*
-8511	Hutchinson, L.			-4369	Jacob, E.	*a, k* 28/5/18
-7107	Hutchinson, W. L.	*a, k* 27/8/18		7971	Jacob, P. H.	*a*
-0674	Hutt, H. R.	*a, k* 30/10/17		-7378	Jacobs, A. G.	*a, w* 27/9/18
-3827	Hutter, W.	*a*		-6927	Jacobs, F. B.	*a*
-9046	Hyatt, Cpl. E. R.			-6755	Jacobs, G. A.	
-9183	Hyde, R. F. W.			-8974	Jacobs, H. S.	
-2168	Hyem, C. N. G.			7194	Jacques, L/Cpl. G.	*a*
-9222	Hyland, J. C.			-3499	Jaffe, S. A.	*o*
				990	Jakeman, J. A.	
300	Ibbetson, E.			4277	James, A. G.	
-7834	Idle, Cpl. C. W.			-4941	James, A. W.	*a*
-1684	Iles, D. E.			-6865	James, C. J.	*a*
1302	Illingworth, T. M.			-1884	James, F. C.	
-5622	Illingworth-Law, I.			-0427	James, H. B.	
5885	Imrie, D.	*a*		-4742	James, R. H.	
-6784	Ince, Cpl. H. W.			-6601	James, L/Cpl. T. G.	
-7428	Inch, G. F.			116	James, W. A.	
2101	Ingall, C. H. L.	*o*		-6137	James, Sgt. W. M.	
5507	Ingall, Cpl. E. M.	*a*, M-S-M, 🎖		-7059	Jamieson, A. F.	*a*
420	Ingall, H. E.			-6386	Jardine, J. B.	*e*
-3037	Ingham, J. L.	*o*		-6255	Jarman, Sgt. J. T.	
-6555	Ingram, E.	*a, w* 30/12/17		-1118	Jarman, Sgt. J. W.	

458   OTHER RANKS: ARTISTS' RIFLES.

−0361	Jarris, F. H.		*o*	−7797	Johnson, J. A.	*a, w* 22/8/18
−7172	Jarvis, C. B.		*a*	6515	Johnson, J. B.	*o*
−6557	Jarvis, D. F. C.	*a, k* 30/12/17		−6851	Johnson, P. H.	*e*
−0361	Jarvis, Sgt. F. H.		*a*	−7950	Johnson, R. A. C	
−9261	Jarvis, J. I. G.			2987	Johnson, S.	*o*
−4148	Jarvis, R.		*a*	−0455	Johnson, T.	
−8346	Jarvis, L/Cpl. V. R.			−4775	Johnson, W.	*a*
−9077	Jeeves, L/Cpl. L.			−4435	Johnston, D. C. B.	*a, k* 30/10/17
−4992	Jefferson, H.	*a, k* 31/10/17		−2902	Johnston, R. C.	
−9326	Jeffrey, J. W.			−4705	Johnston, W.	*a, k* 30/10/17
8611	Jeffreys, P. J.		*a*	−7718	Johnstone, J. D.	
1964	Jeffries, C-S-M C. S.		*a*	1892	Jollivet, A. E.	
−5947	Jeffries, Sgt. G. H.	*a, w* 30/10/17		−8253	Jones, A. T.	
1632	Jeffries, Sgt. L. M.			−9234	Jones, A. W.	
−6166	Jemmett, G. C.		*o*	−4706	Jones, B. A.	*a, p*
−8366	Jempson, F. J.			−7855	Jones, B. E.	*a*
3694	Jenkin, H. A. J.			−5623	Jones, D.	*e*
−3459	Jenkins, D. J.			−0945	Jones, D. B.	*o*
−5176	Jenkins, D. J.			−6928	Jones, D. C. F.	*a, w* 27/9/18
−8619	Jenkins, J.			−7878	Jones, D. H.	
1005	Jenkins, R.			1911	Jones, D. W.	
−6756	Jenkins, L/Cpl. W. J.		*a*	−4996	Jones, E.	*a*
−9114	Jenner, H. E. L.			−5719	Jones, F.	*e*
7476	Jennings, H.		*o*	−6558	Jones, F. H.	*a*
−6757	Jennings, Cpl. J. W.			−9598	Jones, G.	
−9435	Jennings, L. A.			−5890	Jones, George Arthur	
−3395	Jennings, W. L.		*o*	−6559	Jones, George Arthur	*a, w* 30/9/18
−4434	Jerem, H. E.		*a*	−8732	Jones, L/Cpl. G. L. C.	
6981	Jerrald-Nathan, S. P. R.		*a*	−8879	Jones, G. W.	
−7173	Jessett, Sgt. H. W.			2057	Jones, H. G.	*a*
−8252	Jessup, E. F.			−6986	Jones, Sgt. H. I.	
5955	Jessup, L. H.		*a*	−5322	Jones, H. I.	
4575	Jewell, J. B			5658	Jones, J. E. *a, w* 30/12/17, *k* 27/9/18	
1511	Jewers, F. S.			−8697	Jones, J. H.	[*k* 21/8/18]
6344	John, E. A. C. D.			−5996	Jones, J. H. E.	*a, w* 30/12/17
3217	John, S. C.		*a*	−9459	Jones, J. J.	*a*
−4031	Johns, T.	*a, k* 2/4/18		−7452	Jones, J. P.	
−2391	Johnson, L/Cpl. A. J. H.			−5780	Jones, L. H.	
−3853	Johnson, A.		*a*	−9460	Jones, L. H.	*o*
−3910	Johnson, Albert Eric	*a, w* 30/10/17		−1700	Jones, L. L.	
−5841	Johnson, Alfred Edwin		*e*	−8367	Jones, L. W.	
5207	Johnson, C. E.	*a, k* 30/10/17		−0771	Jones, Sgt. M. I.	15/O-C-B, m
1165	Johnson, Sgt. E. D.	15/O-C-B, *a*		−6193	Jones, P. R.	*e*
−0419	Johnson, E.		*a*	−9662	Jones, R. G.	
−7591	Johnson, E. C. R.			−8997	Jones, R. G.	
6897	Johnson, G. F.		*a*	−4326	Jones, S.	*e*
7925	Johnson, H. N.		*o*	−6976	Jones, Thomas	*a*

For explanation of Abbreviations see p. 434.

−1413	Jones, Thomas		*a*	−8442	Ker, E. H.	
−9131	Jones, T. H.			−8784	Ker, T. L.	
3379	Jones, William Alfred			−8369	Kerr, L/Cpl. J. H.	
−5624	Jones, William Arthur			7000	Kerr, P. M.	
−9560	Jorden, W. H.			−3932	Kerridge, C. D.	*a, k* 30/10/17
−1636	Josephs, S. S.		*a*	5585	Kettle, G. B.	*a*
−6801	Joynes, Sgt. G. W.			3249	Keys, A. J.	*a*
2959	Jukes, S. C.			8270	Kidd, A.	*a*
−4559	Jump, S.	*a, k* 30/12/17		−3988	Kiely, R. E.	*a, k* 30/10/17
−3337	Jupp, G. W.			−5588	Kilkenny, L.	*a*
1092	Juppa, Q-M-S-I C. L. W.	*a, f*		−7108	Killick, G. C.	*a*
				−8656	Kilner, R.	
−8902	Kahn, D. L.			−0194	Kilner, S. A.	*a*
−6024	Kane, J. St. G. S.			3539	Kimber, Sgt. W. E.	*a, w*
7477	Kapp, R. O.		*o*	−8999	King, A.	
−7341	Kavanagh, G. P.		*a*	421	King, c-s-m C. W. K.	*a,* F/D,
−9327	Kay, A.			−3791	King, E. C.	[*k* 30/10/17]
−8733	Kay, H. W.			2148	King, Cpl. F.	*o*
−9663	Kay, W. P. H.			6846	King, G. C. H.	*o*
−8756	Kay, W. S.			2573	King, G. H.	
−0391	Keast, H.		*a*	−7779	King, H.	
−6649	Keefe, P. A. F.			−2086	King, H. J.	
−9298	Keel, W. E.			−4896	King, J. W.	*a, k* 30/10/17
−6999	Keeler, L. J. W.		*a, p*	−9348	King, J. N.	
−5178	Keene, A. T.		*a*	−3500	King, Sgt. S. T.	
−8998	Keith, G. C.			−9078	King, W. H.	
−0400	Keith, R.		*a*	−7411	King, W. T.	*a*
−8474	Kellick, L/Cpl. A.			−0230	Kingsbury, Sgt. H.	
−3693	Kelly, C. U. F.	*a, k* 30/10/17		−6896	Kingsbury, L/Cpl. R. R.	
−6167	Kelly, J. D.		*o*	−7908	Kingston, E.	
−8059	Kelly, J. F.		*a*	−2506	Kirby, A. J.	*a*
−8512	Kelly, M. G.			5586	Kirby, H. A.	
−6436	Kelly, P. D.		*a*	−2171	Kirk, Sgt. E. C.	
−9384	Kelly, P. J.			−8475	Kirby, W. A.	
−9020	Kelly, W.			−9279	Kirkman, H. C.	
−9664	Kelly, W. D.			−9561	Kirkness, E. C.	
−4436	Kemble, C. S.	*a, k* 5/4/18		−8476	Kirkpatrick, L. B. D.	
8452	Kemp-Welch, A.		*o*	6403	Kirton, S.	
−7751	Kemp, J. W. J.			−4652	Kitchen, A.	*a, w* 16/2/18,
−9696	Kendall, R. G. G.			−8347	Kitchener, H. J.	[*k* 30/5/18]
−6277	Kendall, L/Cpl. S. T.			−4099	Kitson, J. H.	
−4777	Kendrick, L. D.			−6388	Knell, C. F.	*a*
−0279	Kennett, Sgt. C. F.			−7780	Knight, A. J.	*a*
5510	Kennett, P. W.	*a, k* 30/10/17		−4834	Knight, o-r-Col-Sgt. C. B.	
6898	Kent, H.		*o*	−9621	Knight, F. A.	
66	Kent, H. C.			−2409	Knight, J. H.	*a*
−6895	Kent, J. P.			−7473	Knight, J. L.	

2387	Knight, J. T.	a		-3161	Lang, E. G.	
-5347	Knight, T. H.			1263	Lang, E. W. S.	
-0494	Knight, W.			-1723	Lange, C.	o
5769	Knight, W. J.	a		-6696	Langford, W. H.	a
-8370	Knipe, P. R.			-7592	Langmead, Cpl. L.	
-1685	Knott, F. C. G.	a		-7015	Langstaff, B. P.	
3278	Knowles, A. B.	a		-0283	Langton, C.	a, w 1/7/16
-9562	Knowles, J. B.			-4998	Lankester, R. B.	a
-7029	Knowlton, L/Cpl. A. B.	a		1223	Lansdell, J. A. D.	
408	Knuth, Sgt. H. F. C.	a		-0624	Lara, Sgt. P. L.	15/O-C-B
4669	Konschel, P. H. V.	a		5061	Larg, A.	
-0602	Koppenhagen, H. M.	a, w 5/4/18		-7094	Large, L/Cpl. O. C.	
6916	Kyte, E. C.	a		-6602	Lascelles, G. A.	
-2602	Kyte, N. D.	o		-9099	Lascelles, P. St. G.	
				-4238	Lascelles, R. M.	a, k 16/9/17
-8922	Lack, W. T.			-9584	Latham, J. C.	
-9409	Lackland, D. G.			-1253	Lathey, Cpl. H. T.	a, 15/O-C-B
-6734	Ladd, S. E.	a, w 12/3/18		-9385	Laurie, C. A.	
2818	Lafford, Sgt. W. J.	a, k 30/10/17		-8836	Laurie, H. C.	a
-6054	La Hive, Cpl. L. C.			-9522	Lavender, J. C.	
-8757	Laine, R. L.			-8444	Laverack, D. A.	
-3428	Laing, J. G.			-6910	Lavers, A. E.	o
-6897	Laird, J. R.			-8579	Law, P. W.	
-9563	Laird, R. M.			-4329	Lawler, F. W.	a
-9116	Laister, E. H.			-3694	Lawn, W. J.	
-9410	Lake, F. J. C.			-7821	Lawrence, B. L.	
-4997	Lake, H. G.			-0316	Lawrence, Sgt. C. G.	
5060	Lake, N.	a, w 16/3/18		-8348	Lawrence, L/Cpl. D. S.	
6289	Lake, W. C.			10500	Lawrence, E. E.	d 10/2/17
2131	Laker, S. F. C.			-9047	Lawrie, J. A.	
-3201	Lamb, S. P.	a		-5459	Lawson, G. D.	o
-5949	Lambert, C. W.	o		4398	Lawson, P. S.	
-9469	Lambert, H. G.			2045	Lawson, S. R.	a, w 5/4/18
-7567	Lambeth, L/Cpl. O.			-6603	Lawson, T. M.	a
-6898	Lambirth, P. G.	e		-6899	Lawton, C-S-M D. H.	o
-3429	Lamont-Fisher, S.			-7476	Lawton, F. B.	
4135	Lampert, Cpl. T. H.	o, k		-5505	Lawton, W. E.	
-2582	Lamplough, R. E.			-7477	Layton, E. C.	
-8698	Lamplugh, F.			-4440	Lazarus, M. A.	a, w 30/12/17
-6741	Lancaster, C. B.	a, w 8/3/18, 6/4/18		-6115	Lea, H. E.	a, w 27/3/18
1173	Lance, F. P.			2859	Lea, W. E.	o
3643	Land, C-S-M L. F.	a, m		-8170	Leach, L. H.	
4957	Land, P. S.	a		-4032	Leach, W. L. de B.	
-5237	Lander, J. H.	d 21/3/17		-1738	Leader, Trans-Sgt. G. F.	
7315	Landless, F.	o		-1712	Leader, S. H. C.	o
6738	Lane, F. C.	o		2946	Leaker, R. M.	
-7385	Lane, J. W.	a		-3162	Lean, Cpl. D. J.	

For explanation of Abbreviations see p. 434.   461

−8734	Leaning, J. F.	
−7593	Learner, C. H.	
−6270	Le Bas, A. O.	a, k 4/5/18
8585	Leckie, J. A. G.	
4424	Ledbrook, A. B.	o
−3129	Lee, A. G.	
−8699	Lee, F. S.	
−8880	Lee, H. C.	
490	Lee, Sgt. J.	a, f
−6939	Lee, L. H.	
−8881	Lee, P.	
6463	Lee, Sgt. R. A.	a
6806	Lee, R. K.	
3808	Lee, W. H.	
−2500	Lee-Dunham, D.	a
−9313	Leeb, R. P.	
3907	Leech, E. Y. T.	o
6110	Leeding, Sgt. W. J.	a, f
−7451	Leembruggen, R. G.	
1579	Leeper, A.	
−9079	Lees, H. R. C.	
2885	Lees, J. R. D'O.	
−4898	Leete, A. A. C.	
−6350	Le Feuvre, M.	e
6111	Leftwich, C. A.	
−4441	Leigh, E. H.	
−4622	Leigh, S.	
−6076	Leigh, Sgt. W. D.	
2718	Leigh-Bennett, R. H.	
8204	Leighton, Sgt. W.	a, f
−2411	Leir, M. A. W.	o
−9280	Leivers, G. D.	
−7938	Leland, N. G.	
−7085	Lenthall, G. J.	
−8904	Lenz, G. W.	
−7068	Leslie, C. D.	e
−6038	Leslie, H. H.	a
−8151	Lever, J.	
−0127	Levick, L/Cpl. E. C.	
3512	Lewer, G. F.	a
−3854	Lewis, A. F.	a, w 1/6/18
−3792	Lewis, D.	a, k 28/7/18
−7157	Lewis, F. J.	a, w 24/3/18
−6868	Lewis, F. R.	a
−7927	Lewis, H. C.	
−3465	Lewis, Cpl. H. Y.	a
6481	Lewis, J. E. L.	o
−6604	Lewis, J. P.	a
−9299	Lewis, K. S. G.	
−6603	Lewis, R. T.	
−9599	Lewis, S. B.	
−6786	Lewis, S. F.	
−4608	Ley, J. W.	a, k 30/12/17
−6869	Leyland, A. J.	a
7216	Lichenstein, L.	o
−9411	Liddell, R. V.	
−7237	Liddle, A. W.	a, w 18/5/18
−9622	Lidsey, A. J.	
−8513	Lidstone, F. H.	
−9170	Lieberg, O. S.	
−7238	Lierneux, L/Cpl. R.	
−8785	Light, F. N. D.	
−7265	Light, Cpl. W. W.	
−0662	Limburg, Sgt. H.	a, w 21/8/18
−6759	Lincoln, Sgt. F.	
−9100	Lindsay, J. A.	
−9500	Lindsay, T.	
−3366	Lindsell, E.	a
5315	Linford, A.	o
−7781	Linley, Cpl. J. N.	
−8701	Linscott, L/Cpl. J. H. S.	
−7985	Linton, R. T.	
−4838	Lisle, H. T.	
−8548	Lisle, L/Cpl. J.	
−4837	List, G. H. P.	
−5132	Litchfield, C. N.	a, w 1/6/18
3887	Llewellin, C. E.	o
−1119	Llewellin, L. C. C.	o
−3202	Llewellyn, G. W. T.	a
6955	Llewellyn, L. G.	a
−2838	Llewellyn, Sgt. T. G.	a, k 30/10/17
−5950	Llewellyn, W. J.	
−9422	Lloyd, H.	
−0050	Lloyd, C-Q-M-S J. W.	a, 𝐌
−4330	Lloyd, J. W.	a, w 31/10/17
1783	Lloyd, Sgt. L. A.	a
−6196	Lloyd, M.	a
10099	Lloyd, O. O.	a, w 27/3/18, M-M
−8371	Lloyd, R. D.	a
−8735	Lloyd, W. J.	
−7472	Lloyd-Jones, H. H.	a, w 27/9/18
−6832	Lloyd-Jones, L/Cpl. R.	a
−7879	Lloyd-Smith, S.	
−3466	Lobb, W. G.	a

462 OTHER RANKS: ARTISTS' RIFLES.

−6523	Lockhead, Cpl. A. S.			−3164	Lumley, A. F. C.	
2491	Lock, B.			−6760	Lundie, F. L.	a
−7960	Lock, Cpl. R. H.			7656	Lundie, K. G.	
−6168	Locke, C. E.	o		−9501	Lungley, G.	
−8171	Locker, J. R.			6739	Lye, P.	a
−7504	Lockie, D. J. W.			−7206	Lynas, H. F. E.	
−0382	Locking, F. K.			3908	Lynch, B. E.	
−7283	Lockington, A. a, w 4/5/18, 15/8/18			8520	Lynch, C. J.	
−8837	Lockley, C. C.			−6833	Lynch, F.	a
−9185	Lockwood, G.			−4899	Lyne, F. S.	
−9021	Lockwood, J. P.			3222	Lyon, F. H.	a
2199	Lofting, F. B.			−6974	Lyon, Cpl. J.	a
−4780	Logette, B. a, w 30/12/17, 5/4/18			−8838	Lyons, L/Cpl. C. J. McM.	
−8626	Lomas, H. N.			−2981	Lyons, L/Cpl. M.	
−8088	London, E. H. C.			−0460	Lyons, Cpl. T.	
8444	Lonergan, R. S.	a		8569	Lythall, A. H.	a
−4442	Long, F. E.					
−8254	Long, J. R.			−8787	MacDermott, R.	
219	Long, J. V. T.			5110	MacGowan, J. J.	a
−4708	Longcroft, H. M.	a		−0421	MacKinnon, J.	
7235	Longland, F.	o		3503	MacLennan, E.	a
−8975	Longley, L/Cpl. A.			−4201	MacMillan, C. E. a, k 25/8/18	
−5183	Lonsdale, S. D.			−9679	Macadam, E. H.	
−0183	Lorenz, Sgt. R. E. a, 15/O-C-B			−2247	Macandrew, W. F. a, d 26/5/17	
5098	Lott, A. S.			−5042	Macaree, J. W. a, w 30/10/17	
−3619	Lott, E, R.			−8278	Macarther, N.	
2288	Lotz, L/Cpl. H. J. a, o, p 23/3/18			−5135	Macdonald, A. S.	
−9437	Loughrey, R. W. H. P.			−5660	Macdonald, J.	
2912	Loup, M. B.			−7182	Macdonald, R. F. K. d 25/12/17	
−7192	Lovegrove, L/Cpl. F. N.			−5844	Macfarlane, C-S-M I. A.	
−6973	Lovell, G. H.			−6761	Macfarlane, P. T.	a
1099	Low, H. St. J. d 21/9/17			−7881	Macgregor, F. G.	
−0397	Low, K. R. T.	a		−8479	Macgregor, L/Cpl. I. D.	
−3959	Low, C. A.			−9523	Macintosh, D.	
−3833	Lowes, C. H. a, w 17/8/17			−5661	Mackay, S. E.	
−9386	Lowes, H. S.			−8839	Mackean, D. R.	
1650	Lowman, P. W.			−5637	Mackean, P. K.	e
3370	Lowman, W. L. a, w 19/7/17			−5864	Mackelcken, Cpl. L. H.	
−0999	Lubbock, R-S-M H. L. 15/O-C-B			−5823	Mackenzie, A.	
7206	Lucas, G. T.	a		−3203	Mackenzie, A. G.	
1047	Lucas, H.			−4155	Mackenzie, J. A. A. a, w 30/10/17,}	
−6787	Lucas, H. V.	a		−9474	Mackie, J. B. [25/3/18}	
−9368	Lucas, W. E.			8780	Mackie, T. A.	a
−7415	Luckin, W. H.			−6698	Mackintosh, J.	
−4443	Ludlow, E. E.	e		−6951	Mackson, J. H.	
−5774	Luff, E. T.			−8514	Mackwood, G. G.	
−9132	Luiton, T. N.			−8351	Maclean, W. E.	

For explanation of Abbreviations see p. 434.   463

−8299	Madders, L.			−5909	Marryat, F. F.	*o*
−1432	Maddison, D.		*a*	−5279	Marsh, A. E.	*a, w* 30/10/17
−7252	Maddock, F. J.			−6439	Marsh, F. C. A.	*o*
−5136	Maddox, G.			−8117	Marsh, F. L.	
−1747	Maeer, W. H.			−4929	Marsh, J. L.	
5588	Magor, W. H.		*a*	−8199	Marsh, J. W.	
7046	Magson, W.	*a, k* 27/9/18		−7882	Marshall, A. W. S.	
−0879	Maguire, H. W.			−5078	Marshall, H. D.	*o*
−8173	Maidment, F. C.			7184	Marshall, H. R.	*o*
−5908	Maingot, C. E.		*o*	−7301	Marshall, J. J.	*a*
−6414	Maingot, E.	*a, k* 27/9/18		−6139	Marshall, L/Cpl. R. G.	
−2148	Maitland, W. G. B.			−3999	Marshall, T. W.	*a, w* 31/10/17
−7240	Makinson, G. R.		*a*	−6058	Marshall, W. J.	*e*
−9439	Mallett, K. J. W.			−5977	Martin, A. A.	
−8582	Mallin, P. F.			−3536	Martin, A. E.	*a, k* 30/12/17
−7478	Mallinson, E.			−8926	Martin, B. L.	
−4156	Malpass, W.			−0459	Martin, C. M.	
−3130	Malsom, F. G.	*a, k* 30/10/17		−5337	Martin, G. D.	*a, w* 19/7/17
−0015	Malyn, Sgt. A. S.			−7506	Martin, H. F. H.	*a*
5857	Manby, L/Cpl. C. J.	*a, k* 30/10/17		−7351	Martin, H. J.	*a*
−7836	Mander, L. C.			−9695	Martin, J. E.	
4462	Manfield, C. W.		*a*	−9542	Martin, K. A. T.	
−9624	Mangan, T. A.			−3830	Martin, M. E.	*a, w* 30/12/17
7167	Mann, J. E. H.		*o*	−5794	Martin, O. P.	
−6312	Mann, R. E.			−8427	Martin, T. J. F.	
−5307	Mann, R. F.			−9600	Martin, T. S.	
−6325	Manners, V. C.			7435	Martin, W. C.	*a*
−8585	Manning, J. J.			−8703	Martin, William John	
−6762	Mansfield, E.		*a*	−3072	Martin, William Joseph	
−0446	Mansfield, M.			−4503	Martindale, D.	*a*
−3720	Mansfield, P. H.			7610	Marton, R. H.	
−0454	Mapleson, J.			−1373	Marvin, C-Q-M-S E. D.	
1353	Mapliston, H. R.			3347	Marzetti, N.	*a*
−4901	Mapp, T. C.			−7911	Maskell, L/Cpl. G. N.	
−6608	March, J. N. F.		*a*	−4103	Maskray, H.	*a, k* 31/10/17
−8373	Marchant, F. J.			−6483	Mason, A.	*e*
−7387	Marchant, H. L.		*a*	−7998	Mason, L/Cpl. A.	
3309	Marchant, J. W.			1852	Mason, C.	
2254	Margetts, R. C.		*a*	−7720	Mason, F. A.	
−9526	Marigold H. L. H.			−8123	Mason, J. M.	
1526	Maris, L. G.	*a, w* 30/10/17		7888	Masson, A.	
−3709	Markheim, Sgt. P. G.	*a, w* 23/3/18		2191	Masters, C. J.	
−6975	Marler, Cpl. A. H. G.			6876	Masters, F.	*a*
−4902	Marquis, Cpl. V.	*w* 11/8/17		−0355	Math, A. E.	
1459	Marriott, A. E.			2421	Mathams, S. A.	*o*
−7986	Marriott, S. H.			−9349	Mather, R. K. S.	
−9525	Marrs, J.			−0567	Matheson, Sgt. C.	

-9440	Mathias, B. P.			-4248	McGuire, J.	*a, w* 30/10/17
-8581	Mator, A. J.			-8029	McGuire, T.	*a*
-2445	Matthew, A. C.	*a*		-7061	McHardy, D.	
-6699	Matthews, D. C.			-2861	McHugh, L/Cpl. A.	
4628	Matthews, G. C.	*o*		-6650	McIlroy, J.	*a, missing* 23/3/18
-6140	Matthews, H. B.			-8350	McIntosh, P. R.	
-2651	Matthews, H. G.			-9341	McJannett, H. G.	
-4839	Matthews, H. W. G.	*e*		-6351	McKean, Cpl. A.	*a*
-0612	Matthews, Sgt. J. W.			-8702	McKenzie, Cpl. D. S.	
2089	Mattingley, H.			-7247	McKenzie, W. P.	*a*
-7721	Maude, T. R.			-9564	McKinnelk, J. K.	
3282	Maudsley, Cpl. H. D.	*a, k* 30/10/17		-9357	McLaglan, Cpl. C. R.	
-7524	Maughan, R. G.			-4609	McLaren, A. C.	*a, k* 30/10/17
-6651	Mauldon, J. C.	*a*		-9502	McLaren, O. G.	
-9171	Mauley, W. H. B.			-9658	McLarnon, T. S.	
-3793	Maunders, W. J.	*o*		-8925	McLean, J. C.	
820	Maxwell, C-S-M E. K.	*a*		-9281	McLeod, J.	
-6561	Maxwell, J. H.	*a, k* 24/3/18		-8657	McLure, A.	
-3794	Maxwell, L/Cpl. W. G.	*a*		-9464	McMahon, E. J. R.	
3474	Maxwell, S.	*o, w*		-8658	McMillan, A. J.	
-7266	May, W. A.	*a*		3610	McMinn, C. A. G.	*a, w* 26/5/17
-8621	McAdam, G. M.			-9680	McMorran, R. A. C.	
-9652	McAdam, J. S.			-9489	McMullen, R.	
-9022	McAllen, J. E.			-6847	McPherson, J.	*a, w* 6/4/18
4958	McAnsh, E. J.	*a*		7375	McQueen, R. W.	*o*
-9671	McArthy, J. M.			-6674	McVeigh, A.	
1795	McAuley, Sgt. P. J. S.	*a,* 15/0-C-B		-8580	McVitie, W. H.	
-9064	McCann, J. C.			-7401	Mead, L. H. P.	*a*
-4560	McCarthy, C. E.	*a*		-9172	Meads, G.	
-8478	McCarthy, J. J.	*d* 20/12/18		-7812	Measor, C. W.	*a*
-8439	McCausland, J. A.			-9000	Mee, H. N.	
-1527	McCoy, H. W.	*a*		7478	Meek, H.	*o*
1246	McCloud, E. N.			5629	Meere, J. J.	*o*
-9438	McClure, E. L.			-8401	Meeson, C. M.	
-5898	McColl, T. L.			-7851	Meikle, A. M.	
5703	McCormick, C.	*o*		-7193	Meldrum, A. R.	*a, w* 29/3/18
4536	McCullagh, B. E.			-5315	Meldrum, R. A. J.	*a*
-8956	McCutchoon, F. S.			1912	Melhuish, Cpl. A. S.	*a*
-8198	McDavid, W. J. M.			-5848	Mellor, Cpl. G. R.	
-0498	McDiarmid, L/Cpl. D.			-7223	Melville, C.	
-9623	McDonald, A.			5157	Membury, B. J.	*o*
-8400	McDonald, T.			5348	Mendes, E. G.	*o*
-6311	McDougald, C. E.			-8905	Mercer, D. W.	
-9585	McFarland, B. A. T.			941	Mercier, R. F.	
-8137	McGaffin, R. C.			-4333	Mertens, E. H.	*a, k* 30/10/17
-8013	McGibbon, G. P.			-4787	Merry, F.	*a, w* 30/12/17
-9328	McGibbon, J.			-7620	Mery, L/Cpl. A. V.	

G. St.G. S. CATHER, V.C.   [pp. 44, 489.

THE LAST STAND OF THE 2ND DEVONS AT BOIS-DES-BUTTES, 27th May, 1918
(From the picture by Capt. W. B. Wollen, in the possession of the Officers of the Battalion. By permission.)

5858	Messervy, Sgt. E. S.	*a, k* 30/10/17		-6900	Milne, J. L.	
-8788	Metcalfe, F.			-4710	Milne, N.	*a, k* 30/10/17
-2652	Mew, R.	*a, k* 30/12/17		-8584	Milner, F. A.	
1686	Meyer, Sgt. C. G.	*o, w* 4/1/18		6317	Milnes, G.	*o*
-8906	Meylan, T.			-7464	Milward, H. A. H.	
-5560	Meynell, E. M. E. H.	*e*		-8550	Minson, W. N.	
-4841	Meyrick, F. E.	*e*		-5508	Mirams, D. V.	
8644	Michell, R. R.	*a*		1955	Mitcham, C. J.	*a*
-8138	Middleton, L/Cpl. C. E.			-8214	Mitchell, L/Cpl. D. D.	*d* 24/10/18
-8200	Middleton, L/Cpl. E.			-6116	Mitchell, D.	*e*
-9210	Middleton, G. F.			-8516	Mitchell, G. T.	
4594	Middleton, H.			-9370	Mitchell, H. S.	
-7666	Middleton, P. V.			-9636	Mitchell, H.	
6230	Middleton, V	*a*		-5358	Mitchell, H. A.	*d* 15/4/17
-3167	Milburn, E. L.	*a*		-9503	Mitchell, L. E. S.	
-9565	Mildred, W. D.			5785	Mitchell, W. A.	*o*
-8883	Miles, A. C.			-7961	Mobbs, G. F.	*a, w* 30/9/18
-6390	Miles, F. D.	*a, k* 27/8/18		-9412	Mogridge, H. T.	
-7031	Miles, Cpl. H.			8554	Mohan, E.	*a*
-9369	Miles, R. F			-7953	Mole, S. D.	
-8428	Milestone, J. H.			-9065	Molison, W. J.	
6423	Mi holland, A. W.	*a*		-9504	Molony, T. St. P.	
-8445	Millar, L/Cpl. A. L.			-9282	Money, C. P.	
-8704	Millar, Rev. B. E.			1933	Montefoire, F. E.	*d* 3/11/18
-8840	Millar, H. C.			-3678	Montgomery, Cpl. S. A.	
-7129	Millar, J. J.	*a, w* 27/7/18, 30/9/18		-5689	Moody, W. H.	*o*
-9688	Millar, R. E.			-4784	Moon, C. W.	*a*
-3470	Millar, S/Sgt. W. G.	*To Army Gym.*		-4711	Mooney, A. E.	
1235	Millard, B. A.	*[Staff]*		-9413	Moorcroft, G. H.	
5630	Miller, A. G.	*a*		-2000	Moore, Cpl. C. E.	*e*
-6701	Miller, F.	*a, o, k* 17/7/18		4366	Moore, E. V.	*[Gym. Staff]*
-8549	Miller, G. G.			2408	Moore, S/Sgt.-Ins. E. P.	*Army*
-9527	Miller, J. L.			-4903	Moore, E. T.	*a, w* 30/12/17, 27/8/18
-0433	Miller, P. G. H.			-7525	Moore, F. J. D.	
-4202	Miller, R.	*a*		-9528	Moore, I. E.	
-6609	Miller, S.	*a, w* 27/3/18		-2349	Moore, L/Cpl. J. F. S.	
2467	Miller, T. O.			-4334	Moore, J. A.	*a, k* 30/10/17
5024	Miller, W. J.	*o*		5185	Moore, L. A.	*o*
-3074	Miller, L/Cpl. W. E.	*a, k* 30/10/17		6518	Moore, Leslie Louis	*a*
3765	Millican, F. A. H.	*a, w* 31/10/17		-9151	Moore, Lionel Leopold	
-6353	Mills, B. N.			-2319	Moore, R.	
-4375	Mills, C. C.	*a*		-0449	Moore, R. F.	*a, k* 30/10/17
-0924	Mills, Cpl. F. G. N.			-6391	Moore, S. B.	*e*
-5019	Mills, H. T. V.	*o*		-9372	Moore, S. R.	
-4071	Mills, L. G. E.	*a, k* 30/10/17		-8958	Moore, S. S.	
-5578	Mills, P. E.			7401	Moore, T. S.	*o*
2872	Millwood, R.			3033	Moore, W. D.	

G G

-9672	Moore, W. S.			-8738	Mullett, Cpl. J.	
-6258	Moorehouse, A.	a, k 24/3/18		-4786	Mullings, E.	a
-5662	Moorhouse, Sgt. H. B.			-8185	Mullins, C.	
-5593	Moorhouse, W. D.	a		4126	Mumford, C. G.	
-8662	Moran, L/Cpl. W. A.			-3001	Mumford, S. G.	
-5484	Morant, B. L.			-0393	Mummery, Sgt. A. C. W.	
-4191	Morey, Sgt. F. L.			-8623	Munday-Castle, W. F.	
-7623	Morgan, A. T. H.			-7723	Mundy, T. K.	
-9211	Morgan, D.			-7465	Munro, Cpl. H. A.	a, w 27/9/18
-1184	Morgan, Sgt. I. I.			-9350	Murdock, K. McD.	
-6563	Morgan, J. R.	a, k 24/3/18		-6653	Mure, J. G. D.	
-6652	Morgan, L/Cpl. J. A.	a		-4713	Murgatroyd, F.	a
-8233	Morgan, L. R.			-4714	Murphy, G. M.	a, k 30/10/17
-7017	Morgan, M. H.			-3914	Murray, A. R.	
1149	Morgan, R. C.			-7302	Murray, B.	a
-1713	Morgan, S. W.	a, w 30/12/17		-3833	Murray, E. F.	a, k 30/10/17
-8446	Morgan, V. B.			-2868	Murray, E. S.	a, w 29/10/17
7514	Morgan, W. E.	o		-6416	Murray, H. R.	
-8841	Morley, S. K.			-1943	Murray, J. K.	
1797	Morris, C. L.			-8977	Murray, L. A.	
-1206	Morris, Cpl. F. E.			-9235	Murray, R. McN.	
-9152	Morris, G. W.			-8884	Musgrave, L/Cpl. F. C.	
6983	Morris, J. O.	a, k 30/10/17		-6393	Musgrave, F. P.	a, w 1/3/18
6652	Morris, J. T.	o		-1548	Musselwhite, W. H.	a
-7174	Morris, L. F.	a, w 27/8/18, 20/11/18		-6173	Musson, R. T.	o
5859	Morris, R. J. L.	a, w 30/10/17				
-8429	Morris, S. C. P.			-8885	Nall, J.	
-7722	Morris, W. P.			-9117	Nash-Leitranot, J. E.	
9933	Morris, W. T.			-2739	Nathan, Cpl. E.	
-8256	Morrison, A. E.			-0201	Nathan, o-r-Col-Sgt. J.	m
-8737	Morrison, R. T.			-9421	Naylor, C. H.	
-5002	Morter, A. G.	d 7/3/17		-8978	Neal, A. F.	
-9659	Morton, J. S.			2113	Neal, H.	
8645	Moscrop, H. A.	a		-6564	Neal, T.	
-9685	Moses, F. W.			-2008	Neale, Cpl. R. W.	
-9566	Moss, C. E. D.			-9283	Neave, R. F.	
-2908	Moss, M. A.	a, k 30/10/17		-6654	Neil, H. E.	o
7413	Moss, W. C.	o		-8929	Neill, D.	
-4712	Mott, A.	o		-4599	Neill, R.	a, k 30/12/17
-6077	Mott, Sgt. C.	a, k 22/5/18		-2103	Nell, L/Cpl. C. G.	
-8551	Mottram, Cpl. A. H.			-5999	Nelson, E. H.	
-8789	Mould, H. T.			-6816	Nelson, F. A. J.	a, k 22/8/18
-6028	Mould, P.	e		-9262	Nelson, R. A.	
-9251	Mounsdown, C. F.			-6394	Nelson, W. W.	a, k 1/9/18
-1528	Mountcastle, H. W.	a, k 30/10/17		-6442	Nettlefield, W. H.	o
2386	Moylan-Jones, Sgt. R. A. W.	a, f		-6279	Newbold, E. W.	
-9578	Muirhead, N.			-8483	Newborn, L. O.	

−4118	Newcombe, N.	a		−9263	Normand, L/Cpl. G. H.	
8365	Newell, H. B.	a, p		7765	Norris, R.	a, k 30/12/17
2761	Newham, R. E. F.	o		−0463	Norris, Bandmaster S.	
2625	Newham, T. N.	o		−0462	Norris, Band/Sgt. S. G.	a, ʀ/D
−8663	Newhouse, J. C.			6018	Norrish, R. S.	o
−9477	Newington, A.			−6612	North, C. E. P. J.	a, k 28/8/18
−9133	Newland, R. F.			−7929	Northcroft, J. F. S.	
−7809	Newling, E. V.			−8843	Norton, L.	
−0457	Newman, Cpl. A. C. T.			−2010	Norton, C-Q-M-S S. H.	15/O-C-B
−0367	Newman, H. J.	a, w 1/11/17		−7063	Nott, G. E.	
−7454	Newman, W. G.			3957	Nutt, A.	o
−3858	Newnes, E. C.	a		−5849	Nutt, H. C.	
−7681	Newsome, W. T. S.			−8664	Nye, T. F.	
3300	Newth, J.	o				
−4788	Newton, F. A.	a		4935	Oakeley, C. C.	o
−3400	Newton, H. M.			−4000	Oakes, Sgt. C. G.	15/O-C-B, a, }
−9024	Newton, H. R.			−8552	Oakes, L/Cpl. J. F. S.	[w 30/10/17]
−6611	Newton, J. H. C.	a		−9441	Oakeshott, B. F.	
6189	Newton, W. McI.			−7423	Oates, R. E.	
−6029	Nicholls, H. J.			−8447	O'Brien, D. J.	a
−7896	Nicholls, J. C.	a		−6988	O'Brien, V.	a, w 29/5/18
−6881	Nicholls, Sgt. W. E.			7209	Ochs, H. S.	o
−4376	Nichols, A. G.			7379	O'Clarey, E. W.	
−7109	Nichols, C. K.	a		−7096	O'Connor, J.	a
−7180	Nichols, L/Cpl. O. C.			−8844	O'Donnell, J. T.	
−9118	Nichols, W. B.			−0387	O'Donoghue, D. A.	a, k 30/10/17
−4405	Nichols, W. S.	e		−0388	O'Donoghue, R. C.	a, k 30/10/17
−4336	Nicklin, E. N.			−9193	Offegett, L. F.	
2492	Nicklinson, Sgt. H. E.	a		5527	Ogden, A.	a
−9315	Nicol, H. J.			−3860	Ogden, H. L.	
−9387	Nicoll, J. T. B.			−9388	O'Grady, H.	
−9567	Nicoll, R. N.			−9134	O'Grady, H. S.	
−2018	Niebergall, Sgt. J. F. A.			3553	Okey, W. E.	a
−7175	Nightingale, L.	a		−9465	Oldfield, A.	
−1004	Nind, Cpl. V.			−6059	Oldfield, F. J.	
−1223	Nobbs, S. W.			309	Oldham, Sgt. H. V.	
8646	Nodder, J. R. B.	a		−9135	Oldroyd, G. H. M.	
−5242	Noel, H. W. E.	a, k 30/10/17		−0052	Olive, C-Q-M-S G. F.	15/O-C-B
6899	Nolan, F. A.	o		−9025	Oliver, L. S.	
1348	Nolan, J. D.			−69 9	Oliver, L. M.	a
−8517	Nolan, W. J.			−8448	Oliver, P. G.	
−8015	Noonan, T. J.			−8430	Olivieri, F. J. R.	
−1687	Nops, J. H.	a, w 31/10/17		3140	O'Neill, D. Q.	a
−8759	Norden, W. A.	d 28/8/18		−8553	O'Neill, T. W.	
−5333	Norley, Cpl. F. W.			−3243	Ongley, R. D.	a, k 30/10/17
−5326	Norley, G. R.	a		4974	Oppenheim, H.	a
−4337	Norman, E. G.	a, k 28/8/18		−2790	O'Reilly, F. J.	

OTHER RANKS: ARTISTS' RIFLES.

-2762	Orme, Cpl. A. H.	*a*		-8846	Pape, G. W.	
-1821	Orpen, R. de V.			-5371	Paradise, L/Cpl. J.	*a, k* 30/10/17
-8705	Orr, L/Cpl. R. F.			4232	Parienté, J.	
-6742	Orton, L/Cpl. R. O.			-8125	Park, W.	
-9466	Orton, T. W.			-8449	Parker, A. J.	
-6487	Orton, Cpl. W. J.	*a*, M-M		-7334	Parker, C.	
-6444	Osborn, C. E.			3846	Parker, C. J.	
-7267	Osborne, Sgt. C.	*a*		-8376	Parker, L/Cpl. C. G. C.	
-9467	Osborne, G. W.			-8944	Parker, C. P.	
-5139	Osborne, W. N.			-7257	Parker, F.	
4936	Osborne, L/Cpl. W. E.	*a*		-9644	Parker, F. A.	
-3208	Osborne, W. W.			-3557	Parker, H. G.	*a, w* 26/9/17
-9155	Oscroft, J.			-8979	Parker, M. B.	
-7194	O'Sullivan, D. N.	*a*		6258	Parker, Sgt. S.	*a, w* 31/10/17
-9136	Oswald, W. C.			-1094	Parker, Cpl. S. H.	
-0376	Outlaw, A.	*a*		-8930	Parker, W.	
-4581	Ovastor, A. D.	*a, k* 30/12/17		6021	Parkes, C-Q-M-S N. E.	*a*, F/D
2816	Owen, E.			7186	Parkin, Sgt. J. A.	*a, f*
-1240	Owen, G.			9590	Parkinson, C. F.	*a*
-6743	Owen, J. F.	*a*		-6657	Parkinson, H.	
-6952	Owen, L/Cpl. P. H. A.	*a*		-7498	Parks, W. R.	
-8282	Owen, Cpl. R. P.			1229	Parkyn, Sgt. G. H.	*a*
-7340	Owen, W. E.	*a, k* 23/3/18		-7884	Parmeter, V. G.	
2653	Owens, F. H.	*o*		-0563	¶Parnall, C-Q-M-S J.	15/O-C-B
-7897	Oxenham, Cpl. I. L.			-9352	Parnham, L. N.	
				2813	Parris, J. W.	*a*
-9568	Packer, H. W. P.			-6395	Parrish, F. H.	*a, w* 27/8/18
-1006	Pacy, G. H.	*e*		-3274	Parry, L/Cpl. E. D.	*a*
2990	Padbury, Cpl. G. F.	*o*		-2351	Parry, R. M.	*a*
-2983	Padel, S. E. C.	*o*		-6396	Parson, R. M.	
1307	Page, E. C.	*o, k* 29/12/17		-6117	Parsons, B. W.	
-4790	Page, E.	*a, p* 23/3/18		-5349	Parsons, C. W.	*a, k* 4/1/18
177	Page, H. T.			-8666	Parsons, F. G.	
4271	Paget, B. L.	*o*		-0117	Parsons, Sgt. G. M.	*a, f*
-7530	Paget, L/Cpl. R. C. B.	*a*		-5377	Parsons, H. J.	
-6141	Pailthorpe, L. S.	*a, k* 3/6/18		-7304	Pass, J. H.	
7173	Pain, F. W. H.	*o*		-4204	Pasqua, U. A.	
-8845	Pain, G. C.			-5563	Paterson, A. E. W.	
-0381	Paine, J. H.	*a, k* 30/12/17		5597	Paterson, D. S.	*a*
622	Palmer, A. G.			-7177	Patterson, J.	*a, w* 27/5/18
5416	Palmer, E. D.	*a, k* 30/12/17		-9414	Paterson, J. H.	
-5626	Palmer, F. R.			-9317	Patterson, R. H. S.	
-9080	Palmer, H.			-6614	Pattie, J. W.	*a, w* 22/3/18
7724	Palser, H.	*o*		6446	Paul, A. A.	*a*
-8760	Pamment, S.			6672	Paul, A. H.	*a*
-3402	Pannell, T. S.	*a, w* 30/10/17		7221	Payne, A. F.	*o*
-3861	Panter, T. C.			-9543	Payne, W. G.	

-1229	Payton, H. G.	*o*		-7312	Perry, A. M.	*a, w* 31/3/18
-5641	Payton, L. T.			-6903	Perry, E.	
1374	Peacock, A. W. K.			-0369	Perry, F. B.	
-6940	Peacock, E.			-4379	Perry, J. S.	
6740	Peacock, H.	*a*		-0005	Perry, P. H.	
-0223	Pearce, Sgt. C. M.			-6995	Peters, A. G.	
-5777	Pearce, F. W.			-6527	Peters, S.	*a*
-8707	Pearce, L/Cpl. S. B. P.			3698	Petford, H. A.	
-8847	Pearman, C. H.	*d*		2937	Peto, C. A. F.	
-6702	Pearmund, A. S. W.			-7513	Petrie, Cpl. J.	
-0450	Pearse, Bandmaster A. J.	*a*		-8980	Petrie, L/Cpl. J. N.	
-8283	Pearse, H. L. S.			-4717	Petter, C. H.	*a, w*
-9200	Pearse, J. E.			-3367	Petters, Sgt. L. M.	
-0296	Pearse, W.	*a*		6190	Pettit, R. B.	
-7914	Pearsen, C. H.			-8887	Pexton, S.	
-1348	Pearson, L/Cpl. B.	*a*		-7093	Phelan, J.	
-6615	Pearson, K. H.	*a, k* 30/8/18		-8301	Pheby, H. J.	
-6260	Pearson, L.			2465	Phillips, A. E.	
3235	Peart, R. E.	*a, k* 27/10/17		-7305	Phillips, A. H.	
-9173	Peatfield, E. C.			-7337	Phillips, L/Cpl. E. P.	
-6281	Peatfield, Sgt. G. O.			-6528	Phillips, G. C.	
2692	Peck, N. A			-3593	Phillips, G. E.	*a, k* 30/12/17
6943	Peerless, Sgt. C. L.	*a, k* 30/10/17		-7744	Phillips, H. J. B.	*o*
-4158	Pegg, H. E.			-6488	Phillips, H. T.	*e*
3736	Pierce, E. F.			5793	Phillips, H. D.	*a*
-7988	Pellatt, Cpl. L. A.			-4205	Phillips, H. T.	*a, w* 24/7/17
-7087	Pelling, C. H.			532	Phillips, Sgt. N.	*a, k* 30/10/17
-8907	Pell-Smith, D. H.			-7159	Phillips, S.	*a, w* 27/8/18
3781	Pemberton, A. G.			8459	Phillips, S. T.	*a*
3595	Pemberton, L. G.			-4454	Phillips, W. H.	*a, k* 30/10/17
-9295	Penfold, M. E. H.			-1869	Phillips, Sgt. W. L.	
-9373	Penfold, T.			-7898	Phillipson, Cpl. L.	
-1058	Pengelly, C. R.	*a, w* 11/8/17		9592	Phillpot, A. J.	*o*
-9179	Penn, C. D.			8449	Philpott, W. H.	*a*
-9389	Penn, C. E.			-9026	Phimister, A. L.	
8379	Penna, V. G.	*a*		-8586	Phipps, C. E	
-6355	Penny, R. G.	*a*		-9415	Pick, R. N.	
-5873	Pentin, H. R.	*a, w* 27/9/18		-6529	Pickman, E. J.	*a*
-8377	Pepin, K.			3996	Picknell, L.	*a*
-6080	Pepper, S. M.			-0956	Pidgeon, F. A.	*a*
-8667	Percy, E. C.			-8486	Pierce, F.	*a*
-4662	Perfect, E. J.	*a*		7070	Pierson, H. S.	[1/6/18]
10158	Perkins, L/Cpl. S. W.	*a*		6389	Pierce, R.	*a, w* 30/10/17, 23/3/18
-1535	Perkins, W. E.	*a, k* 30/10/17		-6489	Piggott, Sgt. R. S. P.	
-1750	Perks, G. R.			-3558	Pilgrim, Cpl. E. A. E.	
-9353	Perram, H. E. L.			-8258	Pilkington, W. H.	
-8945	Perriam, R.			-8089	Pitty, W. C.	

−7241	Pincombe, A. J. F.	a, w 28/8/18	−7866	Powell, J.	a, f
−4160	Pinfield, B. F.	a, w 4/1/17	−3978	Powell, Sgt. J. H.	
−7753	Piper, D. N. C.		6119	Powell, J. M. H.	a
−6000	Pither, C. S.	o	−1051	Powell, P. G.	a, k 22/6/18
−9569	Pitt, B. A. R.		2361	Powell, R. W.	a, w 30/12/17
−0587	Plaice, A. J.	S/Sgt-Inst. Army	6358	Powell, W. H.	a
−7643	Plant, S. A. N.	[Gym. Staff]	−7915	Powell, W. J.	
2848	Platt, E. A.		6191	Power, B.	d
−8790	Platten, W. P. E.		5794	Poynton, A.	a
−9331	Playdon, W. S.	[1/6/18]	−6448	Prager, B.	
2513	Poley, Cpl. A. E.	a, w 30/12/17	−9390	Prance, F. A.	
−8302	Polglaze, L/Cpl. G. H. F.		−8017	Pratt, Sgt. C. B.	
−9601	Polkinhorne, A. L.		−8587	Pratt, L/Cpl. L. R.	
−8487	Pollard, G. H.		−8185	Preece, C. V. G.	
−3505	Pollard, J. T.	a, w 31/10/17	−9301	Prendergast, J. F.	
6195	Pollard, S. R.	a, w 11/8/17	−9505	Prendergast-Arnold, G. A.	
−3134	Pollock, H. E. F.	a, w 7/4/18	−3701	Presnell, C. E.	a, k 30/12/17
−3625	Pollock, J.	a, k 4/1/18	2675	Pressney, Drummer J. R.	
−8668	Polson, T. C.		−9530	Prestage, W. H.	
−8848	Polsue, A. E.		−2322	Preston, C. B.	
−7207	Pomphrey, L. T.		7774	Preston, H.	a
6318	Ponder, F. V.	a	−8554	Preston, H. L.	
6022	Pool, A. C.	a	5924	Preston, J. E.	o
−2940	Poole, A. E.	a, w 30/10/17	−3936	Preston, R. E.	a, w 5/3/18
−3040	Poole, F. H.	a	−6704	Price, A. L.	a
−7268	Poole, G.	a, w 30/9/18	−7039	Price, E. C.	
−4252	Poole, R. H.	a, w 16/1/18, 27/7/18	−6990	Price, R. A.	a
1332	Pope, A. J.	a	−7810	Prigmire, L. J.	
1214	Pope, C. J.		8541	Priestley, D. L.	a, k 30/10/17
10160	Pope, E. V.	a, w 16/3/18	−9703	Priestley, H. R. G.	
−2984	Popkin, R. G.	a, w 11/8/17, k 29/9/18	7197	Prince, L.	o
−8450	Porter, C. E.		−7371	Pring, H. F. D.	a, k 1/6/18
−8378	Porter, E. D. St. G. K. K.		6078	Pringle, A. J. E.	o
−4718	Porter, J. M.	a	−2912	Prior, A. E.	
−8739	Porter, J. P.		−8849	Pritchard, J. E.	
−8099	Porter, T. B.		−5287	Pritchard, K.	
−0913	Posso, G.	a	−7724	Privett, A. C.	
−0502	Potter, Sgt. F. T.		−6658	Protheroe, G. G.	a
6023	Potter, G. C.	o	6718	Proudfoot, Sgt. A.	a, f
−8451	Potter, H. C. N.		−6848	Prowse, T.	
6911	Potter, M. H.	o	3019	Pryke, Sgt. A. W.	a, f
8478	Potter, W. G.	a, w 8/10/18	2321	Pryke, N.	a
−9570	Potts, E. J.		−7810	Pugmire, Sgt. J. C.	
−9626	Poulton, W. G.		6329	Pulford, J. C.	a, k 4/1/18
−6356	Powel, E.	e	2032	Pullen, C-Q-M-S C. S.	a, M-S-M
−6491	Powel, W. E.	e	−6142	Pullen, E. A.	e
−5286	Powell, E. J.	a	−6834	Pullin, F. H.	a

5004	Purdon, S. E.			-8708	Read, L/Cpl. T. C.	
-9101	Purdy, A.			2446	Read, V. H.	a
-4163	Purnell, S.	a, k 30/10/17		-7032	Read, W. F.	a, w 23/8/18
-8488	Purves, H. W. R.			-5289	Read, L/Cpl. W. W.	
-5800	Purves, R. L.			-3473	Reaks, Sgt. G. L.	
-8850	Purvis, H.			-8931	Reaks, G. S.	
6259	Pycock, Sgt. H. R. H.	d 20/3/16		7800	Ream, N. S.	a, k 30/10/17
-8761	Pym, A. J. W.			-3864	Reardon, E.	a, w 30/12/17, 23/8/18
-1189	Pym, R. S. R			3189	Reavell, G. N.	o
-6284	Quantock, W.	e		-7599	Reckie, N. T.	
-6084	Quarmby, F. W.			5538	Redfern, C. J.	o
-6530	Quelch, L/Cpl. F. G.			-3244	Redman, C. S.	a, k 30/10/17
-8762	Quick, C. P.			-5664	Reece, E. T. B.	e
-1872	Quick, Sgt. S.	a, M		-9627	Reed, A. W.	
8498	Quicke, H. T.	a		-8187	Reed, L/Cpl. B. H. C.	
-6874	Quigley, W.	a		-9186	Reed, C. N.	
4020	Quinton, R. W.			-9391	Reed, H. F.	
-6357	Rabbeth, J. G. S.	a		-2566	Reed, L. H. B.	
-4341	Radcliffe, J.	a, w 30/10/17		5599	Rees, C. B.	a
2349	Radford, W. H.	a		-3405	Rees, C. D.	
2153	Radmall, J.	a		-6904	Rees, C. F.	a, p 24/3/18
-8518	Raffle, D. J.			-9213	Rees, L. R.	
7095	Rainforth, G. V.	a, d 16/3/16		-8959	Rees, W. F.	
-8624	Raker, H. H.			3504	Reeve, C. H.	a, k 23/8/18
496	Raleigh, W. R.			-6359	Reeve, J. L.	a
-8126	Ralli, P. S.			-8303	Reeve, J. R.	
-7867	Ralli, R. P.			5029	Reeve, M.	o
-1902	Ralph, L/Cpl. H. F.			-9001	Reid, A. P.	
-3863	Ramsden, S.	a		-9252	Reid, C.	
-5893	Ramsay, C. A.	o		-9571	Reid, H. S.	
-3041	Randell, A. E.	e		-8625	Reid, J. T.	
-9102	Rankin, L.			-7160	Reid, R. M. P.	o
3497	Rata, c-s-m S.	a, k 30/12/17		-8519	Reid, T. W.	
-7139	Ratcliffe, H.	a		-9303	Reid, W. D.	
-6174	Rattle, W. F.	o		-9544	Reiss, G. S.	
1028	Rawlins, G. E. C.	a, k 11/12/14		-6198	Reiss, Sgt. V.	
5000	Rawlins, S. G.	o		-4795	Relton, L/Cpl. L. S. S.	
-9614	Rawlinson, A. F.			-8981	Renison, C. H.	
-5190	Rawnsley, P.	a		-4847	Renshaw, E. G.	a, k 30/10/17
-9302	Rawson, F. E.			-8669	Resker, B. A.	
-7673	Rawstorne, N. A.			2929	Restall, B. G.	
-4260	Raymond, Cpl. A. J.	a, M-M		5798	Retford, H. H.	a, k 28/10/17
7255	Rayner, A. E	o		1382	Reuss, F. V.	
-9120	Read, F. S.			-9392	Revington-Jones, L/Cpl. T. M.	
-7372	Read, M. V. H.	a, p 20/5/18		-9236	Reynolds, R. W. G.	
-6875	Read, L/Cpl. N.			-9545	Reynolds, S. S.	
1295	Read, P. F.			-5565	Reynolds, T. J.	

OTHER RANKS: ARTISTS' RIFLES.

−6798	Reynolds, W. H.	a, k 27/9/18		−8851	Roberts, C. H.	
−9572	Rheam, H. L.	d 4/11/18		−7625	Roberts, E. O.	
−3474	Rhind, W. H.			8525	Roberts, F.	a
2019	Rhodes, C. A.	a		6941	Roberts, F. W.	a
−9506	Rhodes, C. W. F.			−6492	Roberts, George	
−8888	Rial, G. W.			−4383	Roberts, George	a, k 27/9/18
−6886	Rice, A. G.	a, k 3/9/18		−6876	Roberts, H.	e
−3702	Richards, A. H.	a		−3136	Roberts, H. N.	
2780	Richards, A. M.	a		−6199	Roberts, J. A.	
−9156	Richards, A. T.			−6061	Roberts, L. W.	a, k 27/5/18
−6449	Richards, F. J.	a		−8791	Roberts, O. P.	
4868	Richards, G. W.			−8489	Roberts, R. B.	
−8670	Richards, H. F.			−6620	Roberts, R. W.	a
−9157	Richards, John Haydn			−8960	Roberts, R. M.	
−4848	Richards, John Henry	a		−9304	Robertson, A. A.	
2175	Richards, R. W.	o		−8589	Robertson, A. C.	
−8588	Richardson, E. V.			−4796	Robertson, D. W.	a, k 5/4/18
−4259	Richardson, G. S.	a, w 24/3/18		−6568	Robertson, G. A.	
−7113	Richardson, K.	a, w 16/5/18		−9602	Robertson, J.	
8479	Riche, W. E.	a		−5140	Robertson, R. E.	a
−5866	Riches, H. H. C.			−8709	Robertson, R. S.	
−9214	Richmond, H. N.			−9267	Robertson, W.	
−6175	Rickard, R. H.	o		−5246	Robertson, W. A.	a
−7114	Rickard, W. C.	a, k 27/9/18		−7434	Robins, G. W.	
−7064	Ricketts, F. M.	a, w 30/9/18		−0652	Robins, Sgt. W. P.	
−5867	Riddell, A. McG.			−6569	Robinson, Sgt. A.	
4403	Riddell, G. S. St. E.	a		−9665	Robinson, B. S.	
−4931	Riddiford, J. E. J.	e		560	Robinson, C. E.	
7004	Ride, W. H.	a		6743	Robinson, C. R.	a
5138	Ridgwell, E. T.	a, w 30/12/17		−6722	Robinson, Cpl. C. M.	
−8671	Ridley, C. H. G.			−6621	Robinson, G. A.	
−8452	Ridley, J.			−7886	Robinson, G. M.	d 22/10/18
−4613	Rigby, L/Cpl. G.	a		−8889	Robinson, H. S.	
−3796	Rigg, Cpl. S.	a, w 30/12/17		−4455	Robinson, J. M.	a
−9681	Riley, A.			−6571	Robinson, W. G.	
−1485	Rimer, R. C.	o		−8284	Robson, G. W.	
5963	Rimington, W.	a, w 7/3/18, M-M		−8672	Roby, Cpl. W. W.	
−6675	Rippon, W.	a, w		−7646	Robyns, Sgt. E. G. H.	
1916	Risdon, C-S-M M. T.	a, M-M		7119	Rocca, J. D.	a
7201	Risley, P. R.	o		249	Rodgers, J. T.	
−4908	Ritchie, W. H.	a		−0627	Roger, Cpl. F. C. G.	a
−7292	Ritson, C. R.	a, k 27/8/18		5189	Rogers, L/Cpl. A. H.	a
8499	Roadhouse, J. C.	a		−0926	Rogers, F.	
−0726	Roan, Cpl. A. B.	15/O-C-B		−8673	Rogers, J. W.	
3266	Robbins, F.			−3541	Rogers, W. H.	a, w 30/12/17
−3475	Robert, A. J.	o		−4909	Rogerson, J. H.	a, w 30/10/17
−9639	Roberts, C.			−4258	Roloff, C.	o [30/9/18]

For explanation of Abbreviations see p. 434.   473

1157	Rolleston-Woods, A. V.			-6184	Russauw, I. J.	o
-6031	Ronvray, F. G.			3017	Russell, E. S.	
-9175	Roocroft, W. T.			-9334	Russell, F. A.	
-9029	Rook, E. B.			-8260	Russell, H. G.	
-0677	Room, F. B. C.	o		1370	Russell, J. C. W.	
2756	Rope, G. A.	a		5146	Russell, Sgt. J. J.	a
1649	Roper, Sgt. B. W.	a, f		-6176	Russell, J. T.	o
-8155	Roper, E. E.			-9445	Russell, L. J.	
2969	Roper-Pitman, A.			7143	Russell, M.	a
3847	Rose, J. F.	o		-9468	Russell, T. I.	
-5141	Rose, W. J.			-7115	Russell, V. H. D.	
-7755	Ross, A. E.	a		-7682	Russell, W. J. L.	
-6905	Ross, C. F.			-4344	Rutledge, E. A.	a
7771	Ross, C. M.			-4798	Rutter, E. V.	o
-4614	Ross, E. S.	a		-5629	Rutter, R. R.	e
-8792	Ross, L/Cpl. H. C.			6079	Ryan, J. A.	a
6591	Ross, H. H.			8059	Sabin, R. S.	
-8379	Ross, L/Cpl. R. W. D.			-3991	Sadler, F. V.	
-9201	Rossiter, R. G. C. W.			-5474	Sahl, L/Cpl. A. F.	a
-9311	Roundell, L. F.			-8127	Sainsbury, W. J.	
4937	Routh, F. R.	a, M-M		1514	Salisbury, H. G.	a
-6316	Roux, A. S.			-6849	Salmon, A. F.	
8381	Rowe, B.	a, w 31/10/17		-3346	Salter, W. G.	
5420	Rowe, J. S.	a		-7270	Sampson, E. W. E.	
-8236	Rowe, N. A.			-9682	Sams, G. E. R.	
-9002	Rowell, William			-0037	Samson, C-S-M A. J. a, f, M-S-M, 🎖
-6661	Rowell, William			1639	Samson, Sgt. C. A.	a, d 23/2/17
-7707	Rowland, F.			4136	Samson, Sgt. T. F.	a, o, f
4579	Rowland, S.	o		2558	Samuel, Cpl. H. B.	o
-6144	Rowland, Cpl. S. C.			-4169	Samuel, P.	a
5450	Rowlands, J. G. V.	o		-9628	Sandbach, J. C. H.	
4054	Rowley, J. de la M. C.			1342	Sanders, E. J.	a, w 3/6/18
674	Rowlinson, M.			1123	Sanderson, F. W.	
-9574	Roxburgh, C. M. W.			-4548	Sandford, P. H.	
-9354	Rozier, W. L.			-7863	Sang, F.	
-8590	Rubie, G. O.			-4043	Sargent, A. N.	
-9305	Ruck-Keene, E. H.			-8380	Sargent, G. F.	
-6705	Rudd, F.			-7403	Saul, L.	a, p 20/5/18
-7600	Rudd, H. A.			-8032	Saunders, Cpl. F. T. W.	
-5961	Rudd, R. H.	a, w 27/9/18		-8100	Saunders, L/Cpl. R. T.	
-0686	Ruddock, A. B.			4194	Saunders, W. H.	o
-4666	Rudge, E.	a, p 19/9/17		-7860	Savage, H. P.	
8758	Rudolf, G. R. A. de M.			1310	Savel, L/Cpl. V. N.	a
-2842	Rundle, J. L.	a, w 30/10/17		-7131	Savidge, H.	
7029	Rush, E. A.	a		-9588	Saxby, T. E.	
-2867	Rusling, B.	e		-7418	Saver, D. H.	
-6573	Rushworth, J. A.			1315	Schieckel, J. P. J.	o

-9121	Schlick, W. H.			-9340	Severs, W. F.	
6793	Schofield, A. H.		o	-3437	Sewell, C-Q-M-S P. E. H.	
1465	Schofield, E. W.			7618	Sewell, R. F.	o
-6574	Schofield, J. L.		a	-4910	Seymour, L/Cpl. E. E.	
3865	Schofield, R. S.			-2418	Seymour, L. J.	a
-6986	Schofield, L/Cpl. W. M.			-8521	Shackell, G. R.	
-7668	Schonfield, L.			-4384	Shackleton, W. B. D.	a, w 30/12/17
-7531	Schreyeck, F.			-7864	Shaddick, H. E.	
-6766	Scoble, W. H.			-7899	Shannon, Cpl. O.	
-8710	Scoker, J. N.			-7458	Shappie, H. V.	
-8102	Scolt, F. N.			3085	Sharman, A. P.	
-0554	Scorer, E. S.			-4458	Sharman, B. T.	a, k 30/10/17
-8710	Scorer, J. N.			-8327	Sharp, A. J.	
-3601	Scotcher, T. B.			-6978	Sharp, C.	a
-6662	Scott, A. W.	a, w 27/9/18		-9653	Sharp, G. E.	
-8101	Scott, C. H.			1032	Sharp, J. M.	a
-6177	Scott, C. M.		o	-7813	Sharp, J. T. J.	a
-2625	Scott, E. T.	a, w 24/3/18		2662	Sharpe, E.	o
-6744	Scott, H. G.			-7018	Sharpley, E. N.	a, w 6/9/18
-2536	Scott, Cpl. J. J.			-9176	Shaun, C. E.	
5712	Scott, Sgt. R. P.	a, f		-6706	Shave, L. S.	a
8908	Scott, V.		a	-6202	Shaw, A. C.	
-8763	Scully, V. W. T.			7222	Shaw, L. H.	o
-5630	Seager, G. L.			-9253	Shaw, W.	
-5666	Seager, Sgt. J. E.			-2766	Shea, W. D.	a, k 30/10/17
690	Seagrove, C.			-8982	Sheard, H.	
2856	Seale, A. E.			-3733	Shears, W. H.	
-9187	Seale, O. E.			-8007	Sheepshanks, H.	
-9589	Searle, E. W.			-7517	Sheldon, Cpl. G. J.	
-6532	Sears, C. H.		e	-8740	Shelton, S. B.	
-7601	Seaton, R. E.			-9019	Shepherd, F. W.	
-4002	Secker, Cpl. W. E.			-4207	Shepherd, G. J.	a
-9202	Seddon, S. P.			6193	Shepherd, J. E.	a
899	Segrave, J. H.			-3280	Sheridan, H.	a
-6906	Selby, M. G.	a, k 27/9/18		-9442	Sheridan, J. M. F.	
-0368	Selfe, Sgt. L. P.	a, f		4938	Sheridan, L. F.	
-5963	Selfe, V. E.		e	-3836	Sherry, J. A.	
-9691	Sellar, F. C.			-5900	Sherwood, S. W.	
3002	Sellers, G. E.	a, w 30/12/17		-8432	Sherwood, W. J.	
5544	Sellek, B. C.		o	-3371	Shewring, H. T.	
-7279	Selley, A. W.		a	-8626	Shields, D. G.	
-8216	Semple, F. B.			-3407	Shiers, A. T.	
-8156	Sen, M. P.			-7976	Shilling, L/Cpl. E. J.	
-6120	Senior, A. E.		e	-1317	Shipstone, F. E.	a, k 20/7/17
-1340	Sequiera, H.		a	-5803	Shipp, R. H. K.	
-5194	Settles, G. W. R.		e	2594	Shipway, G. F.	a
-7132	Sevier, R. H.			-8453	Shores, W. W.	

7055	Shrubb, J. F. H.		a	-8793	Sleigh, F.	
-6663	Shuck, G. A.			-9469	Sleigh, F. R.	
-9416	Shuffrey, S. J.			-9003	Sleight, R. S.	
-1702	Shurlock, C. P.			-2089	Sly, F. C.	a, w 27/8/18
5637	Shute, W. E.		o	-5050	Sly, L/Cpl. H. F.	a, M-M
991	Sibley, L. H. J.			-8403	Sly, J. W.	
-6992	Sibley, W. E.			2694	Small, C. P.	
-1449	Sidgwick, S.		a	-9138	Small, F. C.	
-9546	Silverman, J.			-5196	Smailes, G. I.	a, p 24/3/18
-9338	Silverster, V. M.			-3476	Smalley, F. W.	
-6624	Silverstone, N.			-0022	Smalley, C-Q-M-S W.	
-6877	Simm, A. G.		e	2505	Smart, L. T.	o
6626	Simcox, C. G.	a, d 23/4/16		-5080	Smart, W. J.	o
-8908	Simmons, A. D.			-7065	Smerdon, J. R.	a
-9654	Simmons, B. F.			497	Smith, Sgt. Alan Edward	
-7271	Simmons, E.	a, w 22/3/18		-4074	Smith, Albert	a
-8909	Simons, E. N.			-3409	Smith, Albert Edward	
-0396	Simnett, C. R.		a	-9067	Smith, Albert Henry	
1500	Simpson, A.			-4386	Smith, Alfred Henry	a, p 23/3/18
-6625	Simpson, A. C.		a	-8176	Smith, Andrew	
-8008	Simpson, C. H.			9703	Smith, A. J.	a
-4800	Simpson, G. E.		e	-2767	Smith, Sgt. A. V.	a, M
-9268	Simpson H. L.			-4044	Smith, B.	
-9194	Simpson, J.			-5316	Smith, C. D.	
-6451	Simpson, J. A.	a, k 30/12/17		-7306	Smith, C. G.	
5603	Simpson, J. R.			-0013	Smith, O-R-S C. H.	
5804	Simpson, R. A.		a	-8983	Smith, C. H. A.	
6028	Simpson, W.			-8711	Smith, C. J.	
-3646	Simpso, L/Cpl. W. D.	a, k 24/3/18		-0456	Smith, D.	
-1732	Sinclair, C.			-7066	Smith, D. E.	a
5290	Sinclair, W. K.	a, d 16/3/16		-3647	Smith, D. L.	
-4565	Singer, J. M. L.	a, k 31/10/17		-6792	Smith, E. D.	a, p 23/3/18
3007	Singleton, J. H. P. A.			4490	Smith, E. F.	
-6361	Sizer, L/Cpl. F. W.		a	6524	Smith, E. J. K.	o
-9137	Skelton, D. N.			-8808	Smith, E. M.	
-4799	Skelton, R.	a, w 21/3/18		6413	Smith, E. R.	o
-6907	Skerrett, A. C.			-9443	Smith, E. S.	
-9291	Skertchly, L/Cpl. E. W.			-3706	Smith, E. V.	a, w 31/10/17
-8009	Skinner, L/Cpl. F.			-6767	Smith, Cpl. F.	
-9216	Skinner, H. V.			-9476	Smith, F. E. V.	
-5195	Skinner, W. A.		a	-9335	Smith, F. G. H.	
7318	Skuce, E. E.		o	-8713	Smith, F. S.	
-9028	Sladen, H. E. H.			-5476	Smith, L/Cpl. G. E.	
-5049	Slater-Eggert, W. J.	a, w 31/10/17		-6452	Smith, G. H.	a, k 22/3/18
7552	Slater, R.			-8139	Smith, G. K.	
-8048	Slater, R. D.			31	Smith, Sgt. G. W.	
5546	Slatter, A. J.		o	-1765	Smith, Sgt. H. A.	

OTHER RANKS: ARTISTS' RIFLES.

−6399	Smith, L/Cpl. H. C.			−4669	Somerville, Sgt. M. T.	
−0008	Smith, Sgt-Shoemaker, H. G.			−3543	Sommerfield, V. D.	
73	Smith, H. J.			−5053	Sorrell, C. E.	a, k 30/10/17
−0220	Smith, Sgt. H. N.			−5198	Souray, L/Cpl. E. G.	
−6362	Smith, L/Cpl. Jabez	a		−8001	Souray, J. B.	
−9683	Smith, James			−7616	Soutar, W. D.	a
−4668	Smith, James			−7756	Southern, G. W. R.	
−4667	Smith, James			−6122	South, E. R.	
−5901	Smith, J H.	o		6822	Southwood, F.	a, w 17/9/17
−7326	Smith, C.pl. J. K. M.			−5519	Spafford, R. G.	a, w 30/10/17
7498	Smith, Sgt. J. P.	a, f		−4943	Spedding, L. A.	a, w 27/8/18
−6768	Smith, J. T.	a		−8104	Speller, Cpl. G.	
4595	Smith, K. P. O'B.	o		−8714	Spence, A. M.	
−5631	Smith, L. F.			−9637	Spencer, A. E.	
−8386	Smith, L. G.	a		−3438	Spencer, E. D.	a, k 31/10/17
−3969	Smith, M D.			−1038	Spencer, F. H. W.	
−9487	Smith, M K.			−2137	Spencer, H. G.	
−4268	Smith, L/ Cpl. N.			−7811	Spencer, J. V.	a
−5197	Smith, R. A. A.			−2917	Spiers, W. E.	o
−8852	Smith, R. C.			−6878	Spiller, L/Cpl. H. G.	a
−7390	Smith, R. L.	a, w 30/9/18		−8405	Spiller, R.	
−9103	Smith, S. A.			−9615	Spink, L/Cpl. D. O.	
−6205	Smith, Sgt. S. H.			−9507	Spink, S. T.	
−0845	Smith, S. R.			−4347	Spinks, S. M.	a, k 24/7/17
−0395	Smith, Cpl. V. W.			4501	Spittle, W. D.	o
−4459	Smith, W.	e		3127	Sprange, S. F.	o, M-M
−5695	Smith, W. A.			−1956	Spratt, A. C.	
−9646	Smith, W. E.			−4388	Springthorpe, W. F.	a, k 30/10/17
−8592	Smith, William James			1532	Sproat, D. C.	a, w 5/4/18
−9660	Smith, William John			−3544	Spurll, R.	a
−7067	Smith, William John	a		−9139	Spurr, F.	
−0409	Smith, Sgt. W. R.	a		5453	Spurrell, W. R.	a
−9319	Smitheman, D. F.			−9269	Spurrier, E. M.	
1811	Smyly, Sgt. C. F.	a, f		−6665	Squiers, V. H.	a
10345	Smyth, G. R.			−9270	Stables, J. G. I.	
3257	Smyth, S. C.	a		−7627	Stace, L/Cpl. H. E.	
−4585	Smythe, C. W.	a, w 17/1/18		−3080	Stafford-Badger, H. P.	a, k 29/5/18
−8404	Smythe, E. C.			−0806	Staines, W. J.	a, k 30/10/17
6298	Snape, T.			−5571	Stainland, W. F.	
−8491	Snare, J. E.			−7696	Stamer, W. A. J.	
2464	Snell, H. J.			7619	Stanier, C. H.	o
8574	Snoaden, E. A. B.	a, w 31/10/17		5291	Staniforth, J. S.	o
−2741	Snow, C. R.	a		−4350	Stansfield, L/Cpl. A.	
4507	Snow, P. S. H.			−9629	Stansfield, E. H.	
−4461	Snowden, F. W.	a, w 27/8/18		−0069	Stanton, Cpl. W. T.	
−4460	Snowsell, N. E.	a		2025	Stanway, Sgt. C.	a, w 31/10/17
−8786	Sockett, C.			1920	Stanway, Sgt. E. A.	a, f

1919	Stanway, Sgt. O.	*a*		−9004	Stiebel, L. L.	
2021	Staples, Sgt. H. W.	*a, f*		−0843	Stiles, S. H.	
−8715	Stapleton, O. C.			−9217	Stirling, A. C.	
−4670	Stapleton, W. R.	*a, k* 30/12/17		−9082	Stirling, G. A.	
−9284	Stark, A. G.			1937	Stock, Sgt. E. T.	*a, f*
−9444	Start, L. B. H.			−8716	Stocken, F. A.	
5	Startin, R-Q-M-S E. C.	*a*, M-S-M, 🎖		−8492	Stocks, F. A.	
7821	Startin, G.	*a*		−7404	Stocks, J.	
−7226	Stather, L/Cpl. S. P.	*a, p* 23/3/18		−9237	Stokes, C. W.	
−6123	Stead, R.			7083	Stokes, W. V.	*a*
−9630	Stear, L. R.			−7244	Stokoe, C. N.	
−7316	Steel, A.			−0633	Stone, Sgt. A. L.	*a, w* 31/10/17
−4586	Steel, Cpl. C. R.	*a*		−5059	Stone, H. E.	
−8794	Steer, G. J.			−5145	Stone, L.	
5003	Steiner, A. C.			2901	Stone, Sgt. P. R.	*a, f*
−7977	Stemp, G. R.			−4855	Stowe, L.	*a, p* 11/4/18
−0424	Stent, H.			−3993	Stowell, G. W.	*o*
−6363	Stephens, C. H.			−7227	Stoye, F.	*a, w* 2/4/18, 27/9/18
−7410	Stephens, C. H. B.	*a*		−9306	Strachan, E. E.	
−9189	Stephens, F. E.			−7728	Stranack, L/Cpl. C. J. L.	
−8219	Stephens, G.			−8471	Strand, A. H.	
−9603	Stephens, H. E.			−8853	Strang, H. F. E.	
6089	Stephens, R. H.			−3246	Strange, A. R. H.	
2373	Stephens, Col.-Sgt. W. J.	*a*, F/D		−7313	Stratton, L/Cpl. A. S.	
−5058	Stephenson, A. G.	*a, w* 27/7/17		−8049	Stratton, J. H.	
−9417	Stephenson, G.			−8286	Strawson, L/Cpl. H. G.	
−6063	Stephenson, P. J.	*o*		2342	Street, C. H. L.	
−0440	Steptoe, G. W.			−6883	Strickland, William Henry	*a*
3264	Steptoe, J. P.			7847	Strickson, J. T.	*a*
2846	Stern, A. M.			−6723	Stringer, T. C.	
−0496	Stevens, C. B.	*a*		1946	Strode, Sgt. J.	*a*, M-S-M, 🎖
−9543	Stevens, C. E.			−7800	Strode, V. L.	
−9255	Stevens, G. A.			−7757	Strong, C. J.	
−9394	Stevens, J. R. C. M.			−2963	Stross, A.	
−6364	Stevens, T.	*e*		−4390	Sroud, G.	*a, w* 31/10/17
−0428	Stevens, W. S.			−9684	Strover, H. K.	
−3895	Stevenson, E. E.	*a*		−0762	Strube, Sgt-Instr. S. C.	*a*, 15/O-C-B
−8091	Stevenson, Cpl. J. B. L.			−2523	Struth, M. le V.	*a*
−6575	Stewart, A. F. T.			−8461	Stuart, John Charles	
−5291	Stewart, G.	*e*		−6146	Stuart, John Charles	*a*
2785	Stewart, Sgt. J. D.	*a, f*, 🎖		−4913	Stuart, W. R.	*o*
−9470	Stewart, P. C.			6658	Stubbs, C. T.	*o*
−6455	Stewart, W. C. J.			−8742	Stubbs, K. A.	
−8795	Stewart, W. H.			8481	Stubbs, S. G. P.	*a, w* 31/10/17
7050	Stibbs, W. E.	*a*		1801	Sturgeon, G. V.	
−3710	Stich, Sgt. C. G. W.	*a, w* 21/8/18		6194	Sturgess, M. E.	*a, k* 30/10/17
1883	Stickland, O-R-S C. S.	*d* 25/10/18		−3047	Sturrock, G. H.	*a, k* 31/10/17

478   OTHER RANKS: ARTISTS' RIFLES.

3518	Styer, W. H.	a, k 27/10/16	-4936	Taylor, A. J.		o
-5966	Styles, E. L.	e	-7405	Taylor, B.		
-8381	Suines, B.		3645	Taylor, B. W.		
-8890	Sullivan, A. H.		3519	Taylor, C. S. M.		a
-7034	Sullivan, W. C.		6825	Taylor, D. C.	a, k 30/12/17	
-5607	Summers, A. J. H.		5876	Taylor, E. H.		
5091	Summers, L. W.	a	2302	Taylor, E. L. F.		o
-4351	Sumner, T.		5968	Taylor, E. O.		
4745	Sumption, J. C.		-5739	Taylor, F. L. V.	d 10/11/17	
-7212	Sutcliffe, N.	a	-6908	Taylor, F. V.		
-5483	Sutherland, Cpl. W. A.		-5968	Taylor, G. C. A.		
-4122	Sutherland, Cpl. W. J. C.	a,	-6993	Taylor, G. E. T.		
1331	Sutton, J. S.	[w 31/10/17	-5213	Taylor, Herbert Andrew		
-9604	Swanton, H. P.		1524	Taylor, Transpt-Sgt. H. J.		a
-5738	Swayne, A. D. C.		-4274	Taylor, Harold William		
-8628	Swayne, F. R.		-9418	Taylor, Hubert William		
-9031	Sweeting, E. H.		-4549	Taylor, J. C.		
-0542	Swetman, H. J.		-2047	Taylor, Lawrence		
-9218	Swift, E. R.		-8764	Taylor, L/Cpl. Leslie		
-1779	Swindells, F. E.	a	-5854	Taylor, N. S.		
-9083	Swoffer, F. E.		2006	Taylor, P. H.	a, k 30/10/17	
-3802	Swoffer, Sgt. G. G.		-1595	Taylor, L/Cpl. R.		a
-3282	Sworder, S. R. H.	a, w 17/9/17	-6536	Taylor, R. E. D.		
-9605	Sydenham, A. E. F.		-6941	Taylor, S.		
6881	Sykes, A. H.	a, w 23/9/17	-6770	Taylor, T. S.		a
-3940	Symonds, L/Cpl. C. W.	a,	7491	Taylor, Sgt. W. D.	a, w 30/10/17	
-9285	Symons, A. J. A.	[w 30/10/17	8410	Taylor, Cpl. W. J.	F/D. a,	
5814	Symons, R. G.		2795	Taylor, W. S.	[k 19/5/18	
-7578	Symington, J. A.		-7917	Taylor-Lowen, W.		
-8675	Tait, J. W.		4513	Tebbitt, C. L.		o
-9160	Talbot, C. R.		2085	Tegetmeier, A.	o, k 8/12/17	
-7956	Talbot, D. S.		-9575	Ternan, A. W. M.		
-7784	Tallemach, T.	a	4582	Terry, E. G.		a
-7989	Tandy, G.		-7568	Terry, F. C. A.		
-7251	Tannahill, F. F.	a	-9104	Terry, L/Cpl. H. S.		
-7650	Tanner, F. G.		2566	Terry, J. E. H.		
-4046	Tanner, Cpl. H. J.	a, w 30/12/17	-9606	Terry, N. W.		
1503	Tanner, R.		6581	Terry, S.		o
-9005	Taplin, T. J.		-7758	Thackara, F.		o
7498	Taplin, W. G.	a	-6034	Thacker, E. M. D.		
-9050	Tarbutt, G. C.		4942	Thackeray, L.		d
-5812	Targett, W. K.		6582	Thing, L/Cpl. J. E. H.		a
-6932	Tarrant, S. A.		2401	Thoday, S. A.		o
-9547	Tate, J. A.		-5426	Thomas, B.	O-B-E	
-8854	Tausley, F. J.		8382	Thomas, D. H.		a
-8891	Taylor, Arthur		-4511	Thomas, E. C. H.		
-6666	Taylor, Arthur	a	-6909	Thomas, E. H.		

For explanation of Abbreviations see p. 434.

-7979	Thomas, E. M.			-5632	Thornton, T. L.	
5715	Thomas, F. G.	o		-8329	Thornton, L/Cpl. W. J.	
-6290	Thomas, F. L.	a		-2869	Thorp, A. E.	a, k 30/12/17
2568	Thomas, G.			-6942	Thorp, A. H.	a
-9471	Thomas, G. S. P.			-3898	Thorp, C. A.	a
-5669	Thomas, H. C.	a, w 30/10/17		-7196	Thorp, F. E.	
-6365	Thomas, H. N. S.	a		-4728	Thorp, W. R.	
-7135	Thomas, L/Cpl. J.			-9032	Thrale, W.	
-8063	Thomas, M. D.	a		-2870	Thurgood, L/Cpl. L. A. W.	
1088	Thomas, Reginald			-8676	Thurley, L/Cpl. E. C.	
-0698	Thomas, Sgt. Reginald	d 10/11/18		-2848	Thurston, L/Cpl. H. F. W.	a,
-8984	Thomas, L/Cpl. R. H.			-8766	Thurston, J. N. D.	[w 4/1/18]
-4727	Thomas, R. J.	a, w 11/7/17,		-9033	Tickle, A. W.	
-9294	Thomas, R. W.	[k 31/10/17]		-8677	Tidmarsh, L/Cpl. E. A.	
-8392	Thomas, W.			3721	Tierney, Cpl. J. R.	a, w 30/10/17
-8157	Thomas, W. A.			-4124	Tilbrook, C. T.	a
-5741	Thompson, A. R.	e		6706	Tillard, P. L.	o
-5814	Thompson, E. E.			-6885	Tilley, D. C.	
-5060	Thompson, F. B.	a, w 10/1/18		6723	Tilley, H. B.	o
-7163	Thompson, F. G.	a, p 23/3/18		-8594	Tilsley, J. M.	
-1622	Thompson, H. S.	a		-9034	Timaeus, L. C.	
-8743	Thompson, H. Y.			-6626	Timms, W. F.	a, w 27/3/18, k 27/9/18
-8765	Thompson, J. K.			-6090	Tinckler, E. H.	a, k 24/3/18
-7852	Thompson, J. T.			-8559	Tinsley, L/Cpl. H.	
-5061	Thompson, Cpl. P. M.			-4517	Tippett, J.	
-7838	Thompson, L/Cpl. R. W.			-8767	Tipples, S. T.	
-0831	Thompson, S. R.	a, k 30/12/17		-8496	Tobin, F. J.	
-4076	Thompson, T. H.	a		-4729	Tobin, J.	
1629	Thompson, W. J.	a, k 27/11/14		-4513	Tobin, L/Cpl. R. J.	
-7255	Thomson, A.			-3215	Todd, C. F.	
-6200	Thomson, B.	d 20/11/18		2312	Todd, M. C. B.	o
-0545	Thomson, D. C.			7097	Tolefree, H.	a
-8933	Thomson, G.			-7697	Toll, P. E. S.	
-3049	Thomson, G. W. R.			-9548	Tomkins, E. S.	
-6125	Thomson, H. B.	a		-3247	Tomlinson, J. H.	
-9648	Thomson, J. S.			-7765	Toms, S. E.	
-1455	Thomson, W. E.	a		-8159	Tong, W. S.	
3646	Thorgood, E. L.			-3837	Toogood, R. C. L.	a, w 30/12/17
1262	Thorn, H. L.			8914	Topalian, H. D.	o
-9084	Thornber, G.			-2493	Torlot, S. A.	o
-4210	Thorne, Col.-Sgt. G. C.	a, M-S-M		-0731	Torres, Sgt. E. H. M.	o
-6737	Thornhill, G.	a, w 27/9/18		-3217	Torry, G. H.	
-5743	Thornhill, W. U.			-6884	Tory, R. N.	
-9271	Thornley, F. E.			-7070	Townend, H.	
-3082	Thornley, J.			-8629	Townend, T. E.	
-4857	Thorns, H.	a		-7528	Townsend, C. H. G.	
-3866	Thornton, Cpl. E. G.			-7990	Townsend, H. H.	

OTHER RANKS: ARTISTS' RIFLES.

−8797	Toyer, R. V.	
−7674	Tozer, A. R.	
5930	Travers, C. J.	a
−6294	Travis, C. H.	
−1887	Traviss, F. E.	
−6236	Trayner, F. E.	a, k 21/8/18
−6091	Trelawny-Ross, S. M.	a, p 23/3/18
−7002	Tremlett, E.	a
6860	Trenbath, F. T.	a, k 30/10/17
8174	Trench, A. H. D. de la P.	
−9122	Trenwith, F. W.	
−1052	Trestrail, E. M.	a, k 20/8/17
−6320	Trevarthen, J. M.	d 30/7/17
−4600	Trevenen, S.	a, k 30/12/17
−8630	Trevethan, H. C.	
−6366	Tricker, J. A.	a, w 30/12/17
7360	Trill, H. G.	
−0326	Trilsback, L/Cpl. L.	
−7957	Trimble, L/Cpl. C. J. A.	
−7652	Trinder, G. L.	
−3768	Troop, P. F. R.	
−8052	Trotman, L/Cpl. J.	
8197	Trotter, J. L.	a
1143	Trotter, Sgt. K. E.	
−7945	Trower, R. G.	
−5608	Truman, F. R.	
−7518	Truman, S. J.	
−6745	Truscott, E. P.	
1136	Truscott, L. G.	
1856	Truscott, L/Cpl. P. S.	a, w 30/12/17
−2118	Trusty, Drummer W. C.	
−8595	Tubb, L/Cpl. W. H.	
5296	Tucker, A.	o
−5964	Tucker, F. G.	
−8798	Tucker, F. L. O.	
5817	Tucker, J. D.	a, k 21/2/17
−0402	Tucker, R. S.	a
−6338	Tudor, A. de R.	a, k 19/5/18
8501	Tugham, V. C.	a, w 30/10/17
−4915	Tulk, J. A.	
5605	Tully, c-s-m P. J.	a, k 30/10/17
−4464	Tunks, Cpl. W. H.	
−7519	Turfitt, A. D.	
−8454	Turnbull, R.	
−6148	Turnbull, R. W. E.	a, w 30/9/18
−9272	Turner, A. F.	
−7576	Turner, A. R.	a, w 27/8/18
−9287	Turner, C. H.	
−5206	Turner, E. H.	
−4916	Turner, E. R.	d 14/12/17
8020	Turner, F. M.	o
−4005	Turner, F. W.	
−7712	Turner, G. W.	
−9666	Turner, H. F.	
−7630	Turner, L. J.	
3062	Turner, P. G.	a, o, k 8/10/16
−7391	Turner, St. J.	a
3685	Turpin, W. F.	a, k 30/12/17
−7900	Turton, R. W.	a
−3085	¶Tustin, E. H.	o
−8631	Tutt, L/Cpl. C. L.	
6128	Twiss, W.	a
−9478	Tyack, G. H.	
−9191	Tye, E. G.	
−1193	Tyerman, C. W.	
1118	Tyers, L/Cpl. K.	a, w 31/10/17
1538	Tyler, G. C.	
6138	Tyldesley, W. A. F.	
−9329	Tyndall, C. J.	
4259	Uhthoff, J. A.	a
−2439	Underhill, E. C.	
5643	Underwood, L. V.	
−6003	Unwin, E.	e
−0622	Upchurch, G.	
4475	Upsom, R. R.	o
−6799	Upton, S. H. F.	a
3559	Usher, R. G. P.	a
−7071	Vail, F.	a, w 27/9/18
−9549	Vaizey, G. de H.	
−0408	Vale, F. S.	a
−5744	Valentine, J.	e
7056	Vallange, L/Cpl. T.	a
7269	Van der Bergh, W. J.	a
−6368	Van der Linde, S.	
1326	Van der Spuy, Transpt-Sgt. D. C.	
1736	Van Dyke, E. A.	
−6822	Vann, W. A. B.	a
6129	Vantier, J. G.	a
6902	Vasey, Sgt. R. E.	a
−0260	Vasey, q-m-s W. H.	a
−5256	Vaughan, F. E.	a, w 16/7/18
2500	Vaughan, Sgt. H. F.	o
−9052	Venables, F. I.	
−4730	Venables, W. A.	a

Crown Copyright. By permission of the Imperial War Museum and Messrs. Judd.] [Sgt. JOHN NASH.
"OVER THE TOP": THE ARTISTS AT MARCOING: 30th December, 1917. (p. xxvi.)

TYPES DE L'ARMEE BRITANNIQUE EN BELGIQUE
dessins d'Album de Georges Scott.

TAMBOUR DU BATAILLON "ARTIST-RIFLES."
(By permission of the French Journal, "L'Illustration," *June 19th*, 1915.)

−8855	Venn, H.		−9321	Wallace, J. M.
3740	Venn, J. R.		−2692	Wallace, Sgt. J.
1466	Vernon, H.		−2568	Waller, M. S. *a, w* 30/10/17
−8856	Verrells, R. T.		−1796	Wallis, Sgt. A. O. S. ℳ
−6369	Viall, L/Cpl. R. *a*		5456	Wallis, C. F. *a, k* 29/8/18
6707	Viccars, A. J. *a, w* 31/10/17		6417	Wallis, N. H. *a*
−5367	Vickers, J. F. *e*		2589	Wallis, T. J. W.
−7176	Vinden, L/Cpl. F. R. *a*		5457	Wallis, W. C. *o*
217	Vincent, Sgt. C. S. *a*		−7272	Wallis, L/Cpl. W. H.
−8985	Vincent, H. F.		−1443	Walmsley, Sgt. H. *a*, M-M
5455	Vincent, J. *o*		−0815	Walsh, A. J.
−1551	Vivian, R. McL. *e*		−8160	Walsh, J. A.
−9336	Voigt, A. C.		−4217	Walsh, Sgt. W. H. St. J. *e*
4218	Voigt, F. R. *a*		167	Walters, A. E.
−6321	Vos, H.		−2425	Walters, A. H. *a*
−7844	Vowles, Cpl. C. J. F.		−4918	Walters, B. A. *o*
			2671	Walters, F. L. *a*
−0370	Wace, E. F.		−3916	Walters, H.
−8858	Waddington, C. R.		−4656	Walters, H. L. *a*
7040	Waddy, R. A. *a*		−0320	Walters, L/Cpl. H. W. *a*
−9238	Wade, A.		−6772	Walters, R. E. *a, k* 5/9/18
5226	Wade, J. A. *o*		−7889	Waltho, B. J.
−0894	Wade, R. A. *a*		−9532	Walton, A. E. H.
−8064	Wagstaff, W. A.		−3809	Walton, A. J.
−5071	Waighill, M. H.		−7501	Walton, E. R.
−4125	Waite, H. *a, w* 31/10/17		−5066	Walton, F.
−2872	Wakley, H. W. *o*		−9053	Walton, J. R.
7211	Waldeck, G. J. *o*		−8433	Walton. W.
−6725	Waley, L/Cpl. H. D.		−3769	Wand, S. J. G.
−8407	Walker, A.		−5317	Wanmer, L/Cpl. W. E. *a*,
−3248	Walker, A. J. W. *a*		8341	Ward, A. [*w* 30/10/17]
6832	Walker, L/Cpl. C. A. *a*		4348	Ward, A. B. *o*
−5334	Walker, D. G.		−2164	Ward, A. S.
−8799	Walker, E.		−9273	Ward, C. T.
−9254	Walker, E. J.		−7185	Ward, D. G. *a, k* 24/3/18
2892	Walker, F. W. *a*		4213	Ward, Frank
−7291	Walker, H.		−7655	Ward, Frank
−9069	Walker, I. C.		−3900	Ward, L. D. *a, w* 27/9/18
−9673	Walker, L.		1085	Ward, W.
−4355	Walker, J. T. *a, k* 16/7/18		−6851	Ward, W. W.
−4465	Walker, R. H.		−3315	Warden, J. N.
−4731	Walker, S. B. *a*		3727	Wardlaw, A. H. *a*
−1888	Walker, T. F. *a, k* 30/10/17		−8768	Warmoll. W. E. S.
−7021	Walker, W. D.		−7521	Warne, N. P.
−6539	Walker, W. G. *o*		−4859	Warner, A. *a*
−4805	Walker, W. J.		−7353	Warner, A. L.
−6577	Wallace, L/Cpl. A. M.		−8408	Warner, C. R. S.

H H

-7656	Warner, W. P.			-4358	Webster, P.	a
-8497	Warton, L/Cpl. T. A.			7496	Webster, Sgt. W. J.	a, f
-8190	Warren, Cpl. E. C.			-3511	Webster-Miller, C. C.	a
-7164	Warren, G. A.	a		-0751	Wedgwood, F.	a
1329	Warren, R. H.			-4466	Weeden, H. F.	a
294	Warren, W.	a, k 27/11/14		-7759	Weekes, R.	
-4356	Wasey, A. C.	o		-3712	Wehrle, Sgt. A. A.	a, d 4/11/18
-0273	Wasmuth, Cpl. H. R.			6991	Weigall, H. S.	a
-2704	Watchorn, F. P.	a, w 28/5/18		-0482	Welch, H. R.	
-4218	Waters, C. F.	a, w 30/10/17		-2658	Wellborne, Cpl. J. E. de M.	
-1170	Waters, F. B.			-9239	Wellby, P. S.	
-2922	Waters, L/Cpl. J. McA.	a		-5876	Wellings, A.	e
-8859	Waterhouse, C. H.			-7604	Wells, F. J.	a, w 27/8/18
-3140	Waterman, T. H.	a, w 30/10/17		-8678	Wells, J.	d 30/10/18
-8910	Waterson, C. W.			4765	Wendt, G. N.	o, k 26/9/16
3509	Watkins, C. E. L.	a		-9070	West, G. B.	
5327	Watkins, J. H.	a, o, k 2/12/16		-6322	West, G. H.	
-8596	Watson, D. C.			-8561	West, G. W.	
-4806	Watson, G.	a		1879	West, H. A.	o
8576	Watson, G. S.	a		-9398	West, J. V.	
-9533	Watson, G. V.			3373	Westlake, Sgt. A. M.	a, ℞
-1714	Watson, J. M.			4791	Weston, A. N.	
-7603	Watson, J. W. H.			1241	Weston, Sgt. D. G.	a, ℞
-8107	Watson, R. L.			-8598	Wetherell, T. A.	
-1278	Watson, W. H.	a		-9149	Whalley-Tooker, H. C.	
-7841	Watt, A. B.			-9054	Wharton, A. M.	
-7675	Watts, A. L. M.			-7760	Wharton, E. P.	a, k 6/9/18
-2314	Watts, E. G. E.			-6418	Wharton, R. A.	a
-6149	Watts, F. V. H.	e		-8719	Whate, D. L.	
-7793	Watts, H. A.	a, w 22/8/18		-2925	Whawell, J.	
2309	Watts, L/Cpl. R. A.	a		-3481	Wheatcroft, F.	a
-6910	Waugh, L/Cpl. H.	a		-1195	Wheatley, Sgt. J. L.	
-9674	Wavell, C. W. F.			-6541	Wheatley, L. F. P.	a
-4219	Wearing, J.	a, w 30/10/17		-3219	Wheawill, E. K.	a, k 30/10/17
-1129	Webb, D. U.			-4807	Wheeler, F. W.	a, w 30/9/17
1699	Webb, Sgt. E. O.	a, f		-9550	Wheeler, H.	
-9397	Webb, F. H.			-8801	Wheeler, H. J.	
2862	Webb, Francis Rands	a		6632	Wheeler, H. S.	a
-4617	Webb, Frederick Russell	a, w		-0063	Wheeler, L/Cpl. L. B.	a, w 27/8/18
-8718	Webb, G. S.			3227	Whidbourne, G. W.	d 6/3/17
-0347	Webber, W. K.	a, k 22/8/18		6130	Whitchurch, C. G.	
-1552	Weber, O-R-S A. C.	a		7041	White, B. L.	a
-8000	Webley, L/Cpl. R. C.			-5895	White, E.	
4065	Webster, B.			-2706	White, Sgt. F.	a, k 27/9/18
-8409	Webster, C. J.			-6795	White, F. J.	a, w 27/9/18
-2705	Webster, E. H.	a		-6657	White, G. McB.	
-4395	Webster, G.			-4524	White, Cpl. H. J.	

-0354	White, John Howlett		-9192	Wilkinson, L. T.	
2917	White, John Howard	a	-3352	Wilkinson, Cpl. N.	
-7072	White, Leslie Alex.	a, w 30/9/18	-3220	Wilkinson, R. C.	
6686	White, L/Cpl. Lewis Avory		-1421	Wilks, H. G.	a
2645	White, P. G.	o	-8498	Willan, C. E.	
7121	White, R. L. H.	o	-9177	Willans, K. W.	
-4601	White, T. L. V.		-8522	Willbourn, P. N.	
-6495	Whitehead, J. R.		-4174	Willcocks, R. W.	
-6004	Whiteley, R. R.		-9591	Willers, W. G.	
-1466	Whitelock, W. O.	a, w 21/3/18	-8562	William, E.	
-8239	Whiter, L/Cpl. F. S. S.		-9035	Williams, B. M.	
-8332	Whiter, V. R.		-3172	Williams, C. F.	
-9638	Whiteway, A. R.		-7314	Williams, D. T.	
-3316	Whitfield, H. J.		-5481	Williams, E. E.	o
-9577	Whiting, E. R. S. M.		-0500	Williams, F.	
-6726	Whitlock, L/Cpl. J. B.		-4738	Williams, F. F.	a
1979	Whitmore, H. R.		-6942	Williams, F. J.	a, p 23/3/18
-7406	Whitmore, J. P.		-3353	Williams, F. P.	
2956	Whitney, F. C.		-8523	Williams, G.	
778	Whittington, A. J.		-8599	Williams, Cpl. George Alfred	
3324	Whittome, G. I.		-8240	Williams, Gwyne Alan	
-2083	Whitton, C. A. V.		-9616	Williams, G. F.	
-6457	Whitton, J. S. H.		-8632	Williams, G. I. R.	
-8679	Whitworth, A.		8515	Williams, H.	a
-0799	Wichelow, T.	a, k 30/10/17	-4739	Williams, H. A.	a
-9006	Wicks, F. H.		-0517	Williams, H. B.	a, k 30/10/17
-5855	Wicks, Sgt. H. H.		-9551	Williams, H. E.	
1831	Wight, L. L.	a	-8524	Williams, H. H.	
-8357	Wightman, J.		-0676	Williams, H. P. G.	a, k 30/10/17
-9288	Wigg, L. G. T.		-6578	Williams, Cpl. H. W.	
-2708	Wilcox, H. L.	a	-3707	Williams, I.	e
-9375	Wilcoxson, L. S.		7122	Williams, J. C.	o
3428	Wild, Sgt. A.	a, w 30/10/17	-8861	Williams, J. L.	
-0800	Wild, o-r-s J.		-0582	Williams, Sgt. S. J.	
-8307	Wild, H. W.		-8021	Williams, L/Cpl. M.	
9670	Wildash, T. M.		-7633	Williams, M. J.	a, k 27/9/18
-4396	Wilde, C.	a, k 22/9/17	-2872	Williams, Cpl. R.	a, w 30/9/18
-3961	Wildsmith, G. F.	a, k 30/10/17	-5451	Williams, R. A.	
-4737	Wili, A. B.		4197	Williams, T. C.	o
-9590	Wilkes, S. H.		-5298	Williams, T. H.	a, k 30/10/17
4006	Wilkins, Bugler W. R.	o	-9289	Williams, W. D.	
-4526	Wilkins, S. E.	a, k 30/10/17	-3901	Williams, W. J.	a
-4861	Wilkins, T. A.	a	-8525	Williams, W. R.	
-4527	Wilkinson, L/Cpl. A. W.		-5214	Williamson, A. J.	
-5074	Wilkinson, D. O.	o	-8202	Williamson, D. I.	
-8860	Wilkinson, E. F.		-6824	Williamson, E. F.	a, w 27/8/18
-7901	Wilkinson, G. D.		-8241	Williamson, W.	

OTHER RANKS: ARTISTS' RIFLES.

-9161	Williamson, W. H.	
-8108	Williamson, W. W.	
-8455	Willing, J.	
1425	Willis, Sgt. A. B.	a, f
6322	Willis, T. B.	a
-4469	Willis, S.	
-1338	Willis, Walton Stanley	
3648	Willis, William Stephen	a
-0091	Willmore, F. P.	a
1060	Willmott, Drummer G. A.	a
-1733	Wills, C. H. C.	a, k 24/8/17
-5203	Wills, T. M.	e
-6126	Willson, E. A.	
-7847	Willson, L/Cpl. J. H.	
-2743	Willson, R. F.	
5359	Wilsher, A. G.	o
4049	Wilshire, R. S.	
-9007	Wilsmore, T. G.	
-6934	Wilson, A. J.	e
-5973	Wilson, C. E. C.	a
-4862	Wilson, C. T.	a, k 24/11/17
1474	Wilson, G. C.	
-0504	Wilson, H.	
-0308	Wilson, H. L.	a
-9472	Wilson, H. V.	
-6729	Wilson, J. C.	
-8456	Wilson, J. D.	
-3650	Wilson, James H.	a, k 2/11/17
-8862	Wilson, John Henderson	
-6578	Wilson, John Herbert	a
-5856	Wilson, J. M.	
-4741	Wilson, L. A.	e
-8287	Wilson, L. S.	
6484	Wilson, P. E.	a
-7435	Wilson, P. G.	a, k 1/10/18
-3354	Wilson, P. S.	
-6324	Wilson, R. E.	a
-6459	Wilson, L/Cpl. R. L.	a
7284	Wilson, W. P.	o
-7328	Wiltshire, S. E.	a
-5150	Wimpenny, L. H.	
-0452	Wimpory, A.	
-8892	Windridge, A.	
-6460	Wingrove, H. W.	a
-3186	Winn, H. W. J.	
-5634	Winney, Cpl. L.	
5671	Winstanley, H. J.	a
-5258	Winter, T.	
-8744	Winterbotham, R. J.	
-1740	Winterbourne, Sgt. H.	
-8475	Wisdom, R. P.	
-8457	Wise, F. J.	
7123	Wiseman, C.	a, d 16/3/16
3242	Witcombe, Cpl. S. F.	a, m
3599	Withers, W. E.	
-7801	Withnall, F.	
-7802	Withnall, R.	
1438	Witt, Sgt. C. T.	a, f
6726	Witty, W.	a
-6484	Wolfe, J.	
-9667	Wolfe, R. S.	
3292	Wollaston, W. H.	a
-4732	Wolsey, F.	a, w 30/10/17
7597	Wolstencroft, H. N. G.	o
-6409	Womersley, P. K.	
-3903	Wood, B.	a, w 27/9/18
-4528	Wood, C. A. T.	a
-4591	Wood, C. B.	a, k 30/10/17
-8633	Wood, C. E. G.	
1039	Wood, C. W.	
-6542	Wood, D. G.	a
2300	Wood, Sgt. F. R.	a, k 29 10/17
2997	Wood, G. D.	o
4023	Wood, G. G. B.	
-2771	Wood, H. W.	a
-7919	Wood, R. S.	
-6994	Wood, S.	a
-7734	Wood, Cpl. W. S.	
-9592	Woodcock, F. B.	
-8681	Woodcock, W. G.	
-7355	Woodforde, G. A.	a, k 27/8/18
-4810	Woodgate, P. S.	a
9482	Woodhead, F. G.	a, k 4/1/18
-8220	Woodman, A. B.	
-3441	Woodman, E. P.	
-7197	Woodroofe, P. E.	
-4592	Woods, A. E.	a, w 30/12/17
1157	Woods, Sgt. A. V. R.	a, f
-3415	Woodyard, H. C.	a, w 27/8/18
2891	Wooler, R.	
6597	Woolfe, W. S.	a
-0118	Woollett, C-Q-M-S L. W.	a
-1176	Woolley, L/Cpl. R. S.	a, w 20/7/17
-6672	Woolven, S. W.	a, w 20/5/18, 27/9/18

−9655	Wooral, G.		5331	Wyld, P.	*a*
−8563	Worfolk, J. B.		2258	Wyndham, C. E.	
2049	Worlidge, Sgt. R. L.	*a*			
−9086	Worrall, L. H.		−6543	Yates, D.	*a, w* 27/8/18
−8986	Worsley, L/Cpl. E.		−7243	Yeal, S.	
6727	Worth, S. A.	*o*	−1492	Yeldham, L/Cpl. H. E.	*a*
−8384	Worthington, K. H.		−6007	Yeldham, T. H.	*e*
−6405	Wray, Cpl. A. L. O.		−4471	Yeaman, F.	
−8410	Wright, C. C.		−9445	Yeats, C. W.	
−9552	Wright, E. D. M.		−3771	Yeo, H. A.	
8306	Wright, E. R.	*a*	−4281	Yewdall, M.	*a, d* 13/11/18
5308	Wright, E. W.	*a, k* 30/10/17	−9158	Youdan, A. de B.	
−9162	Wright, F. W.		4947	Youels, J. A.	
−9376	Wright, J.		−8936	Young, Alan	
−8803	Wright, Sgt. J. H.		−9307	Young, Alexander	
−6095	Wright, L.		−8499	Young, L/Cpl. A. W.	
−5857	Wright, Sgt. P. R.		−7789	Young, D. C. A.	
−1019	Wright, R. W.	*a*	−6627	Young, Cpl. F. N.	*e*
−9036	Wright, S. H.		−9355	Young, J. C.	
−1704	Wright, Cpl. S. W.		−9008	Young, J. S.	
−4856	Wright, T. A.	*a, k* 29/10/17	−3052	Young, Sgt. J. L.	
−8118	Wyatt, A.		−0362	Young, S. M.	*a, k* 30/8/18
5230	Wyatt, G. H.	*o*	−8802	Youngman, H. E.	
6551	Wyatt-Smith, H. H.	*d* 17/2/16	6132	Yendell, A. T.	
−8309	Wybrow, A. W.				
−4470	Wyes, G. H.		2991	Ziell, K.	
−7958	Wykes, L/Cpl. J. L.				

SECTION V.

SOME OLD MEMBERS

OF THE CORPS (RESIGNED BEFORE AUGUST 1914) WHO ARE KNOWN TO HAVE SERVED DURING THE WAR IN OTHER UNITS.

[Those who rejoined the Artists will be found in Section III. (by reference to the Index at end of Book) or in the alphabetical Section IV. ED.]

OLD MEMBERS.

Co.	Reg. No.	Name (and date of leaving).	Unit.
G	*867	Adams, H. F. (1914)	Lieut. R.A.M.C.
E	2498	Adams, H. P. (1885)	Cpl. 1/Hon. Artillery Company
Adjutant		Addison, A. J. B. (1906)	Lt.-Col. 9/York & Lancs. Killed in action 1/7/16
M	4973	Armitage, W. J. (1907)	Major 4/York & Lancaster
C	*679	Atherley, E. J. M. (1912)	Capt. 4/Manchester
B	*487	Atkin-Berry, H. C. (1912)	Major D.A.A.G. D-S-O ✠
F	¶4650	Austin, F. C. (1905)	Major 9/N. Stafford w. –/6/16
F	¶3297	Austin, J. M. C. (1901)	Capt. & Adjt. 6/Suffolk
A	4855	Baker, A. W. (1896)	Lieut. 5/Yorkshire L.I. Killed in action 28/7/16
C	*276	Bare, A. R. (1910)	Capt. 1/N. Lancs. Staff-Capt. 189/Inf. Bde. D-S-O ✠
A	*476	Barraud, C. H. (1912)	Lieut. 43/Canadians (Cameron Highldrs. of Canada)
D	*415	Basevi, J. (1912)	Major Canadian M.G.C.
M	*184	Bird, C. K. (1910)	Lieut. R.E.
D	4481	Beley, G. (1901)	Capt. R.A.M.C.
D	5397	Beley, W. (1901)	Pte. 73/Canadian Highldrs. Killed in action 28/4/15
M	6535	Bell, A. N. (1906)	Lieut. Canadians Killed in action
G	3087	Benn, I. H. (1890)	Commander R.N.V.R.
D	4554	Besant, P. E. (1894)	Major 1/R. Warwick
E	5907	Binns, H. W. (1904)	Capt. R.F.A.
H	2999	Blagden, B. H. (1892)	2/Lt. R.D.C.
G	3462	Blyth, C. F. T. (1908)	Lt.-Col. R.A.S.C. C-M-G
F	*252	Boot, H. P. (1909)	Capt. R.F.C.
H	3554	Booth, C. A. (1900)	Major 3/Manchester and 3/Wiltshire
D	2314	Bostock, R. A. (1886)	Surgeon-Capt. 2/Scots Guards
K	6248	Bowie, G. P. (1904)	Capt. 5/(Canadian) Western Cavalry Killed in action 7/7/15
L	6385	Braddell, T. A. D. (1903)	Lieut. R.N.V.R.
D	4390	Brakenridge, F. J. (1898)	Lt.-Col. R.A.M.C. C-M-G
A	*271	Brock, E. A. P. (1909)	Capt. R.A.M.C.
D	2628	Brook, H. D. (1908)	Colonel R.A.M.C.
D	2734	Brook, W. F. (1889)	Lt.-Col. R.A.M.C.
C	6403	Bruzaud, S. J. (1908)	Lieut. R.A.O.D.
D	3831	Bullar-Allan, E. (1892)	Major R.A.M.C. (Australian)
A	4744	Buller, W. A. H. (1900)	Lieut. R.N.V.R.
G	4565	Burt, A. (1893)	Brig.-Genl. (Colonel 3/Dragoon Gds.) C-M-G D-S-O A-M
F	1588	Bussell, H. J. (1908)	Sergt.-Major R.A.M.C.
G	*1175	Butcher, V. H. (1913)	Lieut. 4/Essex
D	*504	Buxton, St. J. D. (1913)	Major R.A.M.C. F/D
H	1932	Calderon, A. M. (1887)	Capt. 13/Canadian Infantry
F	314	Carey-Thomas, H. (1908)	Capt. R.E.
C	*401	Carpenter, J. H. (1912)	Capt. 6/Cavalry, Indian Army
G	*115	Caslake, A. J. (1912)	Sgt. 5/Canadian Highlanders Killed in action 25/5/15
G	4932	Castle-Smith, H. (1900)	Major Suffolk Regt. (attached Egyptian Army)
L	5483	Castle, W. H. (1902)	Lieut. R.A.S.C.

* Indicates Regimental Nos. in 28/London : all others are 20th Middlesex R.V.

H	*685	CATHER, G. St. G. S. (1911)	Lieut. 9/R. I. Fusiliers Killed in action 2/7/16 V.C.
C	6164	CATHIE, H. W. (1909	Lieut. W. African Frontier Force Killed in action in
C	3413	CHATER, A. G. (1889)	Lieut. R.N.V.R. [the Cameroons]
A	4018	CHEW, R. (1900)	Major 15/London
D	4371	CHILD, G. A. (1892)	Capt. R.A.M.C. O-B-E
H	4758	COCKE, T. D. (1909)	Major R.A.S.C. Staff-Officer Min. of Munitions O-B-E
F	*382	COLE, T. P. (1912)	Capt. R.A.M.C. (114/Bde., R.F.A.) Salonika
B	5795	COLLARD, R. D. (1908)	Capt. R.A.S.C.
B	6015	COLLIN, W. H. (1903)	Lieut. R.E.
F	2327	COLLINS, J. A. (1894)	Capt. 6/Essex
C	5655	CORK, R. P. (1902)	Capt. 22/London (H.Q. Staff, 47th Div.) ✠
G	1997	COUNSELL, H. E. (1882)	Major R.A.M.C.
D	3508	COURTNEY, G. B. (1889)	Capt. R.A.M.C.
D	*888	COURTNEY, J. M. (1911)	Capt. R.A.M.C.
G	5747	CRANMER, A. T. (1903)	Capt. 8/Middlesex
H	4048	CROCKFORD, P. T. (1899)	Capt. K.R.R.
H	¶4400	CROFT, Peter (1901)	Capt. S. African Forces
B	4653	CULVERWELL, W. (1906)	Capt. Essex Regt.
B	2786	CROSBY, J. G. (1886)	Lt.-Col. 7/Essex
G	5286	DARBISHIRE, C. W. (1899)	Capt. 6/R. Welch Fusiliers
F	3517	DAVIS, L. H. B. (1908)	Lieut. Labour Corps
B	*427	DAWSON, H. R. W. (1913)	Capt. & Adjt. 5/R. Sussex
A	6276	DETRAZ, F. F. (1906)	Capt. R.A.M.C.
D	*207	DE VILLE, E. A. J. (1912)	Lieut R.N.A.S.
H	2239	DICKSON, G. A. H. (1884)	Lt.-Col. S. African Forces
K	6062	DIXON, H. J. (1903)	Lieut. M.G.C.
G	3206	DIXON, S. W. (1896)	Major R.A.S.C.
E	6126	DORE, W. C. H. (1913)	Lt.-Col. Labour Corps ✠
H	*291	DOWDEN, A. E. (1909)	Capt. Railway Transport
E	6390	DOWN, A. J. (1908)	Major 8/Middlesex Died 28/11/18
G	*1097	EATON, J. E. C. (1914)	2/Lt. Special Employment
E	4163	EDIS, R. H. W. (1902)	Capt. T.F. Reserve Died May, 1916
B	6320	EDSALL, D. B. (1906)	Capt. 14/London
B	4913	EGERTON, V. C. (1901)	Major 16/London
F	5213	ELLIOTT, D. A. (1904)	Lieut. R.N.V.R.
C	*387	EVANS, H. W. (1913)	Capt. R.A.M.C. ✠
E	*232	EVANS, S. H. (1910)	Lieut. S. Staffs To R.E., I.W.T. Wounded
E	*429	FARADAY, M. S. (1909)	Lieut. R.F.A and R.F.C.
G	5898	FELTON, R. (1907)	Lieut. R.A.M.C.
A	6120	FINNIS, A. C. (1902)	Lieut. 6/S. Staffordshire
G	2855	FLEMING, A. D. (1889)	Major 17/R. Warwick
C	4571	FLOWER, V. A. (1895)	Lt.-Col. 1/22 London & 1/13 London D-S-O Killed
C	*39	FOWLER, A. C. O. (1910)	Lieut. 13/Worcester & M.G.C. [in action 15/8/17]
G	*1172	FOWLER, H. O. (1914)	Lieut. Singapore Rifles

OLD MEMBERS.

F	5941	FOX, R. H. (1902)	... ...	Capt. R.F.A. ✠
G	*381	GALE, H. M. (1910)	... ...	Staff-Capt. R.A.S.C. ✠
D	*798	GATEHOUSE, G. J. W. (1914)	... Capt.	1/Northumberland Fusiliers
H	2904	GAZZANA, C. J. (1888)	... ...	Sgt. 11/Canadians
G	1953	GILBERTSON, J. H. (1886) ...	... ...	Major 1/Hertford
G	*880	GODBER, H. G. (1913)	Capt. 15/Northumb. Fus.	Killed in action 18/7/16
C	*37	GRANT-DAVIES, H. (1913) ...	... ...	Capt. 7/R. Lancaster
B	2277	GRAVES, H. (1897)	... ...	Capt. 2/6 Suffolk
D	*146	GREGORY, M. S (1910)	Capt. 3/Sappers & Miners, Indian Army ✠
F	*627	GRIFFITH-JONES, M. P. (1913)	...	Capt. 2/Durham L.I. ✠
F	*511	GRIFFITH-JONES, W. L. P. (1910)	... Lieut.	Killed in action 12/7/16
B	6501	GURNEY, C. H. (1904)	... ... Lt.-Col.	12/E. Yorkshire D-S-O
D	*513	HALL, G. L. D. (1913)	... ...	Capt. 13/London
Staff	*237	HALL, H. F. (1912)	... Special Equipment Duties	M-B-E D-C-M
G	*212	HAMBLEY, R. J. H. (1911)	... ...	Lieut. R.G.A. ✠
E	5050	HARKNESS, G. F. J. (1903)	... Major	Indian Medical Service
A	4787	HARTON, W. H. (1898) ...	... Lieut.	5/Canadian Mounted Rifles
E	4409	HAYWARD, A. B. (1900)	... ... Lieut.	Guards M/G Regt.
F	6266	HELLARD, W. B. (1905) ...	... ...	... Capt. R.F.C.
C	6510	HEMSLEY, H. N. (1908) ...	... ...	Major 21/London ✠
F	*171	HENDERSON, G. W. (1909)	... ...	Major 9/London
F	2682	HENDREY, S. C. (1892)	... ...	R. Defence Corps
D	*352	HICHENS, J. B. (1910)	... Lieut. 16/K.R.R.C.	Killed in action 16/7/16
D	*726	HOGBEN, H. F. T. (1913)	Lieut. 10/Middlesex (2/Norfolk)	Killed in action 22/11/15
C	5530	HONNOR, T. (1901)	... Lieut. R.A.F.	
E	4812	HOPKINS, P. A. (1900)	... Lt.-Col. 13/London and 15/Worcester	O-B-E
D	1108	HORSLEY, Sir Victor (1880)	Colonel A.M.S. ⚕ C-B	Died in Mesopotamia
D	*890	HUGHES, H. L. G. (1914)	Capt. R.A.M.C. D-S-O ✠ F/D ⚕	[16/7/16
C	5906	HUNT, A. G. (1901)	2/Lt. 4/Guards M/G Regt.	Killed in action 4/11/18
E	*646	HUNT, H. V. (1914)	... ...	Capt. R.A.S.C.
E	4350	HYNDMAN, H. H. (1896)	... ...	... Lieut. R.G.A.
D	1996	JONES, S. Lloyd (1882)	... ...	Lt.-Col. R.A.M.C.
F	6084	KELSEY, P. A. Clive (1903)	Capt. 6/E. Kent	Died of wounds 26/7/15
D	3898	KITCAT, S. A. P. (1895) ...	... ...	Commr. R.N.V.R.
A	3004	KYSH, H. H. (1891)	... ... Lieut.	1/Staffordshire Yeomanry
F	*531	LACK, J. W. (1913)	Capt. 8/Suffolk	Died of wounds 26/7/16 ⚕
G	5899	LAWFORD, B. (1903)	... ... 2/Lt.	Base Censor, Boulogne
G	1399	LAWSON, G. L. L. (1882) ...	... ...	Major R.A.M.C.
D	*702	LEDGER, R. J. (1914)	... 2/Lt. 7/R. Sussex	Died of wounds 11/3/17
E	5651	LEE, J. S. (1902)	... ...	Capt. R.A.O.D.
Adjutant		LEES, E. H. H. (1912)	Capt. 2/Border Regt.	Killed in action 28/10/14
A	3762	LEWIS, F. B. (1906)	... 19/K.R R.C.	Died on active service 30/3/17
G	6018	LOCKETT, R. F. (1905)	... ...	... Major R.E.
C	5193	McCALL, C. W. H. (1901) ...	... ... Lieut.	Liverpool Scottish

The date in brackets is the year in which each member left the Corps.

M	6426	MACKENZIE, R. H. (1906) ...	Lt.-Col. R.E. (Brigadier) D-S-O ✠ F/D
G	4627	MANLEY, A. H. (1898) ...	Capt. 18/Rifle Brigade
F	4951	MARSHALL, C. de Z. (1902)	Capt. R.A.M.C.
B	5519	MARTIN, A. R. (1902)	Major R.F.C.
C	6458	MARTIN, G. E. (1907)	Capt. 11/Cheshire Killed in action 2/8/17
E	*1042	MARVIN, J. D. (1913)	Flt.-Lieut. R.N.A.S.
C	3473	MATHEWS, H. E. (1908)	Major 4/Royal Sussex Staff-Captain
G	2932	MATTHEWS, M. C. (1890)	Lt.-Col. General Staff D.I.M.
G	3673	MATTHEWS, V. (1898)	Sgt. 18/Rifle Brigade
F	5244	MAUNDE-THOMPSON, F. G. (1900)	Major R.A.O.D.
E	5820	MELLISH, Rev. E. N. (1901)	Army Chaplain V.C. ✠
H	5613	MILEHAM, C. A. (1906)	Lieut. R. Sussex To Indian Army
H	5111	MILEHAM, E. C. (1906)	Lieut. R.G.A.
A	*365	MILLWOOD, A. M. (1912)	Lieut. 1/55 Cookes Rifles, Indian Army ✠ ⊞
E	*161	MOORE, P. (1911)	Lieut. R.A.S.C.
C	5022	MORELAND, H. (1898)	Staff-Capt. Trench Warfare Dept. (W.O.)
A	4873	MURRAY, A. C. (1910)	Capt. R.A.S.C.
D	*179	NAYLOR, W. L. (1914)	Sgt. Grenadier Guards and R.E. M-S-M
B	*21	NEALE, P. (1913)	Lieut. 44/Canadians ✠
H	2869	NICHOLLS, J. E. (1891)	Major Southern Rhodesia Vols. & Capt.⎱
D	*552	NOEL, G. B. E. (1914)	Lieut. R.A.S.C. [2/Rifles Cav. Regt.⎰
E	*56	O'CONNELL, E. J. D. (1911)	Lieut. 3/London
G	4985	ODGERS, A. W. (1901)	Capt. 8/Worcester
H	5614	O'HALLORAN, S. N. E. (1902)	Lieut. 2/Essex
H	5843	OMMANEY, C. C. (1901)	Capt. Imperial Yeomanry & R.E.
H	5921	OMMANEY, L. M. (1902)	Capt. 10/E. Lancashire
H	5427	PARKER, A. S. (1906)	Capt. 5/Manchester Wounded (Gallipoli) 27/5/15
M	*82	PARKER, C. R. (1910)	Divl. Engnrs., R.N.D. Died of wounds (Gallipoli)⎱
G	5911	PARKER, R. F. (1903)	Capt. 21/Manchester ✠ Staff-Capt. [10/7/15]⎰
G	4637	PARSONS, A. C. (1898)	Major R.A.M.C.
F	1826	PARSONS, H. C. (1886)	Lt.-Col. R.A.M.C.
G	4762	PARSONS, W. J. (1901)	Capt. 12/Middlesex
C	5028	PASSMORE, A. (1903)	
C	6512	PILCHER, A. H. (1906)	Capt. Durham L.I.
B	3261	PILKINGTON, C. (1911)	Attached 2/Scots Guards
B	6479	PILKINGTON, G. (1909)	Lieut. R.F.C Died of wounds 18/10/17
D	3463	POTT, Frank (1903)	Capt. 10th Bn. Canadian Exped. Force Killed in action⎱
G	2468	POTT, Marcus (1903)	Capt. British Columbia Regt. [23/4/15 (nr. Ypres)⎰
G	3069	POTTON, E. (1882)	Lieut. R.N.V.R.
B	*26	POWELL, R. W. (1914)	2/Lt. 3/Worcester Killed in action 10/7/17
G	2468	PRALL, S. E. (1887)	Lt.-Col. Indian Medical Service
M	6711	PRETYMAN, M. W. (1909)	2/Lt. R.E. Killed in action 10/8/15
D	5480	PRIESTLEY, H. E. (1903)	Major R.A.M.C. C-M-G
C	*654	PRITCHARD, G. B. (1912)	Capt. R.A.M.C.

E	4703	PULLAR, E. J. (1902)	...	...	...	Capt. R.E.
D	*750	PURSER, P. A. (1913)	...	Lieut. R.A.S.C.	Died of wounds 30/4/16	
C	6491	QUEKETT, G. O. (1908)	...	...	...	Lieut. R.F.A.
C	*102	RHODES, W. C. (1912)	...	..	...	Lieut. Indian Army
E	4967	RICHARDS, F. (1909)	...	...	...	Sgt.-Major Roughriders
C	6452	RICHMOND, W. S. (1909)	...	...	Colonel R.E.	C·M·G F/D
D	3768	RIDSDALE, A. E. (1891)	...	...	...	Capt. R.A.M.C.
D	*735	ROBINSON, A. D. (1912)	...	...	Lieut. R.E.	[C·B C·M·G]
Adjutant		ROMER, C. F. (1902)	Chief of Staff	-/Canadian Division	Major-General	
F	*717	ROMER, G. F. (1910)		2/Lt.	13/Middlesex	Killed in action 12/5/16
H	2095	ROPER, H. (1901)	...	...	Major	Royal Guernsey L.I.
C	*260	RUSSELL, R. T. (1914)	...	...	Major	2/9 Gurkhas D-S-O
D	*346	RYDE, J. T. (1911)	...	2/Lt.	3/Bedford	Died of wounds 8/5/17
C	5378	SAFFELL, R. T. (1905)	...	...	...	Capt. R.F.A.
F	5408	DE STE. CROIX, G. (1901)	...	...	...	Capt. R.A.S.C.
A	4988	ST. JOHN-BEALE, A. (1898)			Lieut. Labour Corps	D-C-M
G	*865	SAW, N. H. W. (1914)	Capt. R.A.M.C.	✠	Killed in action 9/10/17	
D	3262	SAYRES, A. W. F. (1890)	...	...	...	Lt.-Col. R.A.M.C.
C	*797	SCOTT, P. D. (1914)	...	...	...	Capt. R.A.M.C.
H	*938	SEARCY, J. W. (1913)	...	..	Lieut. Australian I.F.	✠
G	3990	SEBASTIAN-SMITH, C. A. (1892)	...	Major	R.E.	Submarine Mining
F	6352	SHARPE, W. S. (1910)	...	...	...	Capt. 1/R. Fusiliers
D	4492	SHARPS, H. A. (1908)	...	...	...	Cpl. R.E.
M	6086	SHEPPARD, J. (1905)	Capt. 6/S. Stafford	Wounded in Dublin, Easter, 1916		
M	6678	SHEPPARD, R. M. (1908)	...	...	...	Capt. S. Staffordshire
D	3060	SIEVEKING, A. R. (1887)	...	...	...	Lieut. R.A.M.C.
	¶3411	SLEMAN, R. R. (1908)	Col. R.A.M.C.	A.D.M.S. (Malta)	C-B-E M·V·O	
A	3957	SMITH, S. J. (1897)	...	...	...	Capt. R.A.M.C.
D	4240	STALLARD, H. G. F. (1896)	...	...	...	Lt.-Col. R.A.M.C.
C	2145	STIRLING, T. (1903)	...	...	Capt. T.F. Reserve	D.I.M.
E	6298	SULMAN, A. E. (1905)	...	...	Lt.-Col.	11/R. Fusiliers ✠
D	*957	THOMAS, A. E. R. (1913)	Cpl. 18/Australian Infantry	Killed in action 27/8/15		
K	5493	THURSTON, J. W. (1904)	..	...	Capt.	Railway Traffic Officer
E	4667	TRAVERS, H. C. (1899)	...	...	Brigadier-Genl. R.A.O.D.	D-S-O
E	6263	TRAVERS, W. T. (1904)	...	...	...	Major R.E.
A	*275	TRIPP, H. E. H. (1913)	...	...	...	Lieut. R.A.S.C.
D	3876	TRUSTRAM, L. C. J. (1890)	...	...	Lieut.	3/Lincoln
F	3241	TURNER, Martin N. (1886)	Lt.-Col. 1/D.C.L.I.	Wounded (Aisne) 9/9/14		
		[C-B C-M-G C-B-E ☩(2) Brig-Genl. 15/Inf. Bde.]				
B	4972	UPTON, R. G. (1906)	Capt. 25/London	Staff Capt. 227/Inf. Brigade		
B	6395	UPTON, R. (1906)	...	...	...	Capt. 25/London
D	3067	VAUGHAN, H. S. (1888)	...	Lieut. R.F.A.	Killed in action 31/7/17	
F	5166	VAUGHAN, J. C. F. D. (1906)		Surgeon R.N.	(H.M.S. Carysfort)	
H	4199	WEBB, A. C. (1895)	...	...	...	Capt. 9/Shropshire L.I.

The date in brackets is the year in which each member left the Corps.

A	2215	WEBB, L. (1884)	Lt.-Col. 13/*London*
G	2852	WEIL, P. H. (1885)	T.F. Reserve *Capt. in Army*
G	3652	WEST, R. M. (1892)	Lt.-Col. R.A.M.C. Wounded (*Vermelles* 9/10/15
D	*308	WHIFFEN, S. W. (1911)	Capt. R.A.S.C.
A	5854	WHITLEY, H. S. B. (1906)	Capt. R.E.
F	5410	WICKHAM, J. A. (1901)	Brigadier-Genl. R.E.
H	6115	WILKS, P. W. (1905)	...Lieut. I.W.T.
F	3179	WILLIAMS, A. H. (1887) ... Capt. Attd. H.Q. *London District* O-B-E
G	6405	WISE, A. R. (1909)	47/*Canadians*
G	4152	DE WITT, H. M. (1896)	Capt. 4/*Wiltshire*
H	4015	WOOD, C. M. A. (1891)	Lt.-Col. A.A.G. *Southern Command* C-M-G D-S-C
Adjutant		WORSHIP, V. T. (1909) ...	Lt.-Col. 1/*R. Munster Fusiliers* D.S.O.
C	*107	WRIGHT, L. D. (1912)	Capt. R.A.M.C.

For ADDENDA.

For ADDENDA (Old Members).

SECTION VI.

THE ARTISTS' RIFLES V.A.D.

On the 31st January, 1911, at the suggestion of Colonel Walter Horsley, the then Commanding Officer, a small Provisional Committee was formed with a view to raising a Voluntary Aid Detachment in connection with the Battalion. The result was the formation of the 104th (Artists' Rifles) V.A.D., the original members of which were all relatives or friends of officers and men in the Regiment, and on the outbreak of the war there was immediately available a well-trained Detachment, numbering over 40, the whole of whom at once volunteered for service abroad or at home.

The primary idea of such an organisation was to look after the sick and wounded necessarily left behind a Territorial Army in action, for whom no provision had yet been made, and to pass them back to the Base Hospitals.

Owing to the Territorial Units being merged into the other fighting forces the V.A.D.s were not required for the purpose for which they were originally intended. Thereupon the 104th offered to equip and staff an Auxiliary Military Hospital. Their offer was accepted and the Hospital was opened on April 28th, 1915, at Egremont, Lyndhurst Gardens, Hampstead, as an auxiliary to the Hampstead Military Hospital, to receive 23 patients, soon increased to 25, and after a year to 32. The entire work of the Hospital—Superintending, Nursing, Cooking, and Cleaning was done by the members of the Detachment.

Before the Hospital was closed, on the 31st May 1919, nearly 1,000 patients had passed through the wards, two at least of whom were old members of the Regiment.

THE 104TH (ARTISTS' RIFLES) V.A.D.
LIST OF MEMBERS WHO SERVED IN THE HOSPITAL.

Dr. Lewis Glover	*Medical Officer.*
Miss A. S. Goodall	*Commandant.*
*Mrs. de Segundo	*Lady Superintendent.*
*Mrs. Herbert Shirley	*Lady Superintendent.*
Miss Ethel Allbutt	*Matron from April,* 1918.
Miss Janet Venables	*Quartermaster.*
Miss A. Sawtell	*Quartermaster.*
Miss M. Goodall, M.B.E.	*Secretary & Treasurer.*

Miss Ackers.	*Miss Greenwood.	Miss Showell.
*Mrs. Baines.	Miss D. Grinling.	Miss Cecil Smith.
Miss G. Barrett.	Miss Hammersley.	Mrs E. Stewart.
Miss Bodkin.	Mrs. Hammond.	*Miss J. Stewart.
Miss Brereton.	Miss Harris.	*Miss M. Stewart.
Miss Brown.	Miss Hodson.	Mrs. Sutcliffe.
*Miss M. Bruce.	Miss Hutchinson.	Miss Taylor.
Miss Burton.	Miss E. Jones.	Miss Travers.
Miss Coleman.	Miss J. Manley.	Miss Turner.
Miss Cowell.	Miss N. Manley.	Miss Turton.
Miss Carey Morgan.	*Miss Marvin.	Miss E. Wallis.
*Miss D. Davidson.	Mrs. Morewood.	Miss F. Wallis.
*Miss E. Davidson.	Miss Moir.	Miss H. Webb.
*Mrs. Edlmann.	Miss Moore.	Miss H. Welch.
Miss Edgell.	*Miss Neame.	Miss M. Welch.
Miss Fischel.	Miss Pepper.	Miss West.
Miss D. Ford.	Miss Patterson.	Miss Whitehead.
Miss Freer-Smith.	Miss Reaney.	Miss Wilkinson.
*Mrs. Fry.	Miss Richardson.	Miss M. Wilson.
Mrs. Gittens.	Miss Robinson.	Miss Whyte.
Miss Gordon.	*Miss Selfe.	

Major Arthur Davidson, V.D., *Chairman of Committee from October 20th,* 1916

LIST OF HONOURS AND AWARDS, 1914-1918.

Order of the British Empire.—Miss A. S. Goodall, M.B.E.
Order of St. John of Jerusalem.—Mrs. de Segundo, "Honorary Serving Sister."

BROUGHT TO NOTICE (Secretary of State's Mentions).

Dr. Lewis Glover.	Mrs. de Segundo.
Miss A. S. Goodall.	Miss O. M. Selfe.
Miss G. M. Goodall.	Mrs. Herbert Shirley.
Miss D. Grinling.	Miss W. Turton
Miss M. Neame.	Miss J. Venables
Miss A. Sawtell.	Miss M. Wilson.

* Original Members.

Index

TO

THE ROLL OF HONOUR

HONOURS AND DECORATIONS

AND

COMMISSIONS

THIS INDEX DOES NOT INCLUDE THE ALPHABETICAL SECTIONS "OTHER RANKS" (No. IV.) AND "OLD MEMBERS" (No. V.)

THE "*Addenda*" REFERRED TO WILL BE FOUND AT THE BEGINNING OF THE BOOK: THE "*Corrigenda*" AT THE END.

INDEX TO COMMISSIONS, HONOURS, and ROLL OF HONOUR.

NAME.	PAGE.	NAME.	PAGE.
Abbey, H. R. B.	366	Adams, T. J.	53, 258
Abbot, W.	322	Adams, T. W.	184
Abbot-Anderson, L. G.	149, 159, 309	Adams, W. A. C.	309
Abbott, K. D.	399	Adams, W. B.	215
Abbott, N.	371	Adams, W. C.	53, 224¶
†Abbott, T. W.	20, 165	Adams-Acton, G. M.	219
Abbott, W.	285	Adamson, C.	240
Abbott, W. F.	182	Adamson, C. P.	165
Abbott-Greenwood, W. E. W.	223	Adamson, J. W. E.	196
Abbreviations	162, 307, 434	Adcock, C. W.	225
†Abecasis, A.	13, 350¶	Adderley, C. J. H.	201
Abel, F. W. P.	289	†Addie, R. L.	26, 269
†Abel, J. E.	53, 263§	Addington, G.	235
Aberdein, A.	399	†Addis, D. M.	17, 246
†Ablett, L. W.	23, 333	Addison, C. R.	263
Ablitt, H.	213	Addison, R.	54, 152, 272
Abraham, E. E. U.	287	Addison, V.	311a
Abrahamson, H.	278	†Addy, K. J. B.	5, 265
Abrook, W. R. C.	422	Addy, L.	260
Abson, P.	201	Adkins, G.	412
†Aburn, E. M.	23	Adeney, E.	355
Acheson, J. F.	349	Adolph, W. E. L.	366
Ackermann, E. C.	299	†Affleck, B. P.	20
Ackermann, G	165	Agar, S. W.	396
Ackernley, R. C.	196	Agar, T. F. J.	185
Ackroyd, G. F.	403	Agnew, R. C.	405
Ackroyd, J. A.	366	Agnew, R. J.	233
Acton, G. R.	415	Ailles, H. C.	303
Acton, J. W. D.	302	Ainge, D. A. L.	54, 373
Acton, R.	201	Ainley, W. H. S.	379
†Adair, E. S. B.	41	†Ainsworth, H. G.	22, 316
Adam, W.	221	Ainsworth, S. J.	290
†Adams, A. C.	31, 313a	Aird, G. M.	355
†Adams, A. C. H.	29, 383	*Air Force Cross*	*147*
Adams, A. E. St. J.	245	*Air Force, Royal*	*182*
Adams, A. F.	427	Aiston, W.	276
Adams, A. G.	152, 234	Aitken, R.	201
Adams, A. G. C.	249	Aitken, W. J.	424
Adams, A. H.	409	Aitken, W. L. E.	424
Adams, A. J.	363	Aitken-Davies, E.	235
†Adams, A. M.	21, 53, 285	Aitkens, J. B.	289
Adams, B.	53, 333	Akehurst, C. H.	201
Adams, B. R. C.	224	†Akerman, R. P.	5, 298
†Adams, C. H.	21, 363	Akroyd, J. C.	342
†Adams, E. L.	39	Alanthwaite, S. V.	409
Adams, F.	355	Alberry, W. C.	165
†Adams, J. B. P.	12, 372	†Albury, N. H.	20, 165
Adams, K.	337	Aldous, A. J.	355
†Adams, L. R.	23	Aldous, G. J.	54, 152, 403
Adams, O. H.	53, 101	†Aldous, H. E.	23
†Adams, P. H.	39, 335	Alldred, S. D.	187
Adams, P. W.	165	†Aldrich, A.	33, 383
†Adams, R.	4, 327	Alexander, A. V.	412
Adams, R. B.	164	Alexander, C.	210
Adams, R. C.	196	Alexander, H. R.	340
Adams, R. G. H.	319	Alexander, N.	243
Adams, S.	398	Alexander, R. G.	246
Adams, S. A.	201	†Alexander, T. H.	23

† Killed in action or died. § See this name in *Addenda*.

ARMES

This Index does not include the Alphabetical Sections IV. and V. (Other Ranks and Old Members).

Name	Pages	Name	Pages
Alexander, W. W. W.	409	Anderson, C. A.	217
Alford, A. W.	409	†Anderson, D. W.	36, 54, 291
Alger, A. S.	409	Anderson, E. E.	54, 220
†Alington, G. W. S.	41, 149	Anderson, E. J.	258
Allan, K. E.	415	Anderson, F. St-K.	165
Allan, R. I.	383, 415	†Anderson, H. C.	23
Allan, W.	297	Anderson, H. I.	191
†Allanson, H. P.	8, 354	Anderson, J. L.	257
Allbeury, W.	54, 240	Anderson, J. W. F.	427
Allbutt, H. S.	163	Anderson, P. A.	165
†Allchin, S. M.	27, 263	Anderson, R.	385
Allden, W. L.	236	Anderson, R. T.	253
Allen, A. H.	399	Anderson, R. W.	286
†Allen, C.	29, 165	†Anderson, R. W. L.	17, 165
Allen, C. J.	152, 209	†Anderson, W. W.	11, 187
Allen, C. S.	280	Andrew, B. S.	359
Allen, D.	240	†Andrew, F. D.	32, 316
Allen, D. A. K.	217	Andrew, L. E.	311
Allen, D. G.	381	Andrew, R. B. W. G.	54, 152, 299
Allen, E.	195	Andrew, W. B. S.	191
Allen, E. R.	398	Andrews, A. E. C.	165
Allen, E. V.	230	Andrews, C. C. N.	412
Allen, F. E.	223	Andrews, L. R.	55, 278
†Allen, F. J.	5, 148¶, 152, 236	Andrews, P. C.	412
†Allen, G. A.	7, 241	†Andrews, R.	18, 268
Allen, G. J. B.	191	Andrews, R. C.	219
Allen, G. N.	310a	Andrews, S. A.	46, 55, 152¶, 366
Allen, G. W.	165	Andrews, T. E.	233, 415
Allen, G. W. L.	373	Andrews, W. T.	303
Allen, H. C.	54, 152, 195	Angas, R.	302
Allen, J. Gordon	213	Angel, R.	399
Allen, J. Gwyn	261	Angell, B. O.	149, 165
†Allen, L. E.	28	Angell, T. T.	412
†Allen, M. R.	9, 335	†Annand, A. Y.	12, 256
†Allen, M. R. W.	19, 328	Annesley, P. de Vere	412
†Allen, N.	33, 369	Annes, W. P.	355
Allen, S. W.	395	Anns, H. F.	159, 162, 306
Allen, T. W.	366	Anoni, A. F.	268
Allen, W. A.	187¶	†Anson-Jones, J. S.	42, 201
Allen, W. S. B.	320	†Antill, T. T.	23
Allengame, A. K.	385	Anwyl, R. J.	380
Allerton, A. R.	54, 286	†Apergis, T. S.	9, 297
Allison, G. H.	210	Appleton, J.	55, 389
†Allison, H.	37, 373	Appleyard, C. H.	278
Alliston, G.	159, 162, 359	Appleyard, V. H.	165
Allney, R. F.	316	†Apps, J. H. M.	26, 331
Allnut, E. F.	262	†Arbery, E. E.	17, 165
†Allum, J.	23	†Arbuthnot, J.	9, 217
Allwood, C.	327, 379	†Archer, H. C.	40, 325
Alston, W. G.	399	Archer, J.	153, 277
Aman, J. G.	208	†Archer, P. J.	42
Ambler, C.	152, 335	Arden, W. H.	399
Amery, T. F.	201	Arding, L. H.	359
Ames, H. E.	327	Arend, R. S.	344
†Amoore, R. H.	28	Arkwright, A. J.	359
Amor, E. H.	296	*Argyll and Sutherland Highlanders*	*221*
†Amos, A. R.	23	Arliss, E. W. H.	287
Amos, E. A.	291	†Armes, F. W.	23
†Ancell, H.	31	Armes, T. W.	327

¶ See reference to this name in *Corrigenda*.

ARMITAGE

INDEX TO COMMISSIONS, HONOURS, and ROLL OF HONOUR.

Name	Page	Name	Page
Armitage, J. W.	412	Astbury, A.	427§
Armitage, L. R.	266	Astill, F. H.	381
Armour, W. N. Mc-S.	159, 256	†Astington, T. J.	13, 359
Armsden, R.	186	Aston, A. J. G.	249
Armstrong, G. D.	194	Atchison, H. P. R.	152, 201
†Armstrong, L. W.	16, 228	Atchley, R. W.	165
Armstrong, M. D.	320	Atherley, S. H.	164
Armstrong, R. W.	268	Atherton, A. W.	276
Army Chaplains' Dept., Royal	*397*	Atherton, J.	165
Army Cyclists Corps	*397*	Athole, G. B. J.	201
Army Medical Corps, Royal	*398*	†Atholl, C. C.	...37, 313a, 415
Army Ordnance Corps, Royal	*398*	Atkin, H. D.	315
Army Service Corps, Royal	*403*	Atkin-Berry, H. G.	55, 216
Arnall, H.	187	Atkins, C. A.	273
†Arnold, B. M.	...6, 265	Atkins, G. L.	336
Arnold, D. H.	350	Atkins, H. E.	196
Arnold, E.	182	Atkinson, C. G.	213
Arnold, H.	165	†Atkinson, E. A.	55¶, 289§
†Arnold, H. G.	32, 368	Atkinson, G. H.	365
Arnold, J. K.	165	Atkinson, H.	399
Arnold, R. F.	191	Atkinson, J. F. V.	165
Arnold, R. T.	356	Atkinson, W.	152, 218
Arnold, R. W.	358	Atkinson, W. L.	361
†Arnold, T. S. D.	22, 359	Atter, W. G.	415
Arthrell, H. J.	388	Attfield, A. J.	399
Arthur, F. P.	55, 285	Attwooll, F. J.	262
Arthur, J. C. F.	295	Attwell, J. H.	422
Arthur, J. F.	246	Augustus, W.	377
Arthur, W. H.	325	Aulagnier, F. C.	242
Artillery, Royal	*187*	Austen, E. E.	46, 152, 307
Artists' Rifles (Officers)	*307*	Austin, C. B.	358
Arundel, T. H.	299	†Austin, C. F.	...2, 361
Asche, H. C. J.	201	Austin, H. E.	319
Ash, S. H.	152, 210	Austin, J. L.	405
Ashbourne, T. G. W.	201	Austin, M. G.	314
Ashbridge, J. P.	302	Aveling, N. H.	213
Ashbrooke, J. J.	415	Avins, W. W.	316
†Ashby, W. E.	23	Avison, F.	278
Ashcroft, H. H.	383	Aykroyd, T.	389
Ashdown, P. J.	389	†Ayles, F. P.	34, 217
Ashdowne, K.	55, 242	Ayres, F. E.	214
Ashenden, E. J.	322	Ayton, M. C.	312a
Ashfold, G. A.	362	Ayton, R. C.	165
Ashford, A. C.	322		
Ashford, F. M.	152, 396		
†Ashford, R. E.	24	Babbage, C. E.	415
Ashford, S. R.	312	Baber, J. M.	165
Ashleigh-Boddington, H. K.	152¶, 405	Baber, W. H.	358
Ashman, H. W.	305	Back, A. F.	314
Ashmore, J. W.	150, 196	†Backhouse, H. F.	37, 320
Ashplant, W. R.	236	Bacon, D. C.	56, 303
Ashton, A.	274	Bacon, F. C.	405
Ashton, C. H.	196	Bacon, P.	182
Ashton, P.	287	Bacon, R. H.	295
Ashton, W. R.	412	Bacon, S. F. W.	254
†Ashwin, M. F.	42	Bacon, W. G.	339
Ashworth, A. R. E.	409	Bacon, W. S.	353
†Askey, C. H. L.	32, 283	Baddeley, A. W.	322
Askwith, J. E.	386	Baden-Powell, C. L.	396

† Killed in action or died. § See this name in *Addenda*.

This Index does not include the Alphabetical Sections IV. and V. (Other Ranks and Old Members).

Bagenal, N. B. 356	†Balfour, A. S. 28, 191
Bagley, E. G. 313a	Balfour, C. G. C. 159, 218
Bagg, E. E. ... ... 342¶	Ball, A. C. 292
Baggallay, F. C. 220	†Ball, A. H. 23, 56, 201
†Baggallay, G. T. ... 313, 376, 415§	Ball, E. J. 297
Baggallay, W. R. 395	Ball, F. C. 371
†Bagot, C. W. 39	Ball, F. L. 56, 393
†Bailey, Arnold 30, 279	†Ball, G. H. 33, 56, 415
Bailey, Arthur 292	Ball, H. C. J. 237
Bailey, E. S. 191	Ball, H. T. S. 210
Bailey, G. 249	†Ball, L. A. 21, 320
Bailey, H. M. S. 358	Ball, R. T. 399
†Bailey, H. P. 18, 56, 359	Ball, S. C. 56, 152, 278
†Bailey, H. P. A. 26, 377	Ball, S. H. 218
†Bailey, J. A. 24	†Ball, T. H. 12, 56, 280
Bailey, J. V. M. 56, 399	Ball, W. A. 56, 282
†Bailey, L. J. 17, 165	Ball, W. B. 217
Bailey, S. H. 273	Ball, W. M. 227
Bailey, T. 182	Ballance, H. E. W. 399
Bailey, W. E. 201	Ballard, A. L. 165
Bailey-Churchill, J. L. A. ... 320	Ballard, F. C. 196
Baillie-Hamilton, G. 309	Ballard, J. C. 342
Bain, J. C. 392	†Ballard, M. A. 4, 305
Bainbridge, J. 240	†Ballard, R. F. C. 8, 222
Bainbridge, T. 268	†Balls, F. W. 35, 354
†Baines, E. E. 36, 398	Balmford, W. C. 165
Baines, K. C. 295	Bamber, D. W. B. 271
Baird, C. A. 350	Bampton, H. R. 318
Baird, R. 258	Bancks, H. A. 246
Baird, S. 315	Bancroft, P. L. 369
†Baker, A. G. 36	Bancroft, R. 348
†Baker, A. W. 8	Band, G. E. 249
Baker, B. G. 342	Baness, H. E. 220
Baker, C. B. 148, 150, 338	Bankart, P. G. 165
Baker, C. G. 210	Banks, D. C. 356
Baker, F. B. 165	Banks, J. W. 332
Baker, F. E. 297	Banks, L. G. 165
†Baker, F. F. 24	Bannatine, J. D. 345
†Baker, F. V. 30, 266	Banner, D. R. 287
Baker, G. 165	†Bannester, J. 39, 300
Baker, H. C. 399	Bannister, J. B. 274
†Baker, H. N. 20, 223	Banting, A. D. 57, 201
Baker, J. C. 333	Banwell, F. E. 261
Baker, L. W. 363	Barber, A. E. 187
Baker, P. A. 328	†Barber, B. K. B. ... 20, 152, 331
Baker, P. R. 322	Barber, E H. 279
Baker, R. C. W. P. 422	Barber, F. 405
†Baker, T. S. 14, 300	†Barber, H. M. 36, 359
Baker, V. E. 182	†Barber, J. 21, 242
†Baker, V. S. 40	Barber, J. H. 399
Baker, W. J. W. 380	Barber, P. H. 320
†Balderson, H. L. P. 8, 236	Barber, W. 185
Baldwin, A. C. 165	Barber, W. R. 295
Baldwin, A. E. 246	Barbour, G. B. 187
†Baldwin, A. P. 38, 356	Barbrook, J. O. 355
Baldwin, W. J. F. 322	Barckley, A. E. W. 187
Bale, F. S. 149, 404	Barclay, M. 201
Bale, H. M. 359	†Barclay, R. H. 24
†Bales, K. 3, 226	Bardsley, A. 57, 274

¶ See reference to this name in *Corrigenda*.

Name	Pages	Name	Pages
†Bare, A. E.	23, 148, 308	Barratt, A. J.	322
Bare, A. R.	46, 57, 152, 162, 304	Barratt, F. H.	165
†Barfoot, G. A.	4, 381	†Barratt, J. L.	21, 287
Barham, G. C. A.	233	†Barret, J. H. P.	41, 282
Barham, H.	399	†Barrett, A. E.	20, 266
Barkas Geoffrey de G.	57, 289	Barrett, F. F.	223
Barker, A.	150, 152, 196	Barrett, H.	249
Barker, A. W.	165	Barrett, W. M.	57, 298
Barker, B. J.	371	Barrington, W. O.	287
Barker, Eric	358	Barron, G. H. A.	186
†Barker, Ernest	24	Barrow, T. H.	57, 152¶, 304
Barker, E. W.	283	Barrowcliff, F.	391
Barker, F.	276	Barry, A. C.	259
†Barker, F. E.	23, 396	Barry, E.	152, 231
Barker, G. H	399	Barter, H. E.	191
†Barker, H. W.	33, 283	†Bartholomew, B. J.	11, 229
Barker, J. W.	284	Bartholomew, S. A.	245
Barker, L. I.	165	Bartlett, C. H.	165
Barker, Robert A.	422	Bartlett, F. H.	271
Barker, Ronald A.	246	Bartlett, H. F. W.	202
Barker, R. F.	57, 381	Bartlett, J. D.	302
Barker, R. J.	313a	Bartlett, K. R.	349
†Barker, T.	16, 318	†Bartlett, Leonard (4968)	39, 338
Barker, T. B.	239	Bartlett, Leonard (5981)	320
Barley, E. J.	356	Bartman, C.	296
Barley, G. W.	361	Bartman, W. A.	225
Barley, W. H.	184	Barton, A. L.	405
Barlow, H. M. D.	218	Barton, B. C.	148, 403
Barlow, I. A.	235	Barton, C. G.	404
Barlow, N. F.	358	†Barton, C. H.	23, 166
Barlow, W. G.	165	†Barton, E. W.	15, 268
†Barnacle, H. F.	24	†Barton, G. F.	13, 328
Barnard, A. G.	184	Barton, G. S.	58, 152, 372
Barnard, S. S.	399	Barton, M. M.	287
Barnes, A. D.	57, 305	Barton, S. F.	166
Barnes, A. F.	152, 201	Bartram, G. A.	316
†Barnes, A. R.	21, 350	†Bartrum, A. A.	10, 359
Barnes, J. E.	399	Barugh, W. H.	159, 332
Barnes, L. F.	338	Barwood, F. J.	328
Barnes, O. E.	405	Base, E. H.	152, 237
Barnes, Reginald Chas. (3383)	57, 385	†Baseley, A. L.	19, 152, 268
Barnes, Reginald Chas. (765493)	292	†Bassett, G. E.	29, 340, 404
Barnett, A.	386	Bassett, H. W.	287
†Barnett, D. O.	4, 282	Bassett, R. L.	405
Barnett, H. A.	152, 313a, 404	Bassham, R. A.	300
Barnett, H. F. W.	329	Bastable, F. J. N.	246
Barnett, R. A.	57, 309	†Batchelar, R. T.	30, 363
Barnett, R. O.	299	Batchelar, S. C.	363
†Barnett, W. A.	26, 165	†Batchelor, E.	21, 306
Barnett, W. D.	388	Batchelor, L. H.	217
Barns, H. M.	269	Bate, H. R.	58, 315
Baron, F. O.	57, 276	Bate, R. E.	58, 152, 385
Barr, C. B.	228	Bateman, A. J.	166
Barr, G.	317	Bateman, E. F.	234
Barr, L.	381	Bateman, J.	331
Barr, R. A.	325	Bateman, J. W.	315
Barraclough, J. G.	149, 246	Bateman, K. S. D.	237
Barraclough, T. H.	196	Bates, F. P.	58, 339
Barradell-Smith, W.	346	Bates, H.	422

† Killed in action or died.   § See this name in *Addenda*.

This Index does not include the Alphabetical Sections IV. and V. (Other Ranks and Old Members).

Bath, F. N.	... ...	313, 415
Bates, R. N.	... ...	... 300
Bath, Order of the	... ...	... *148*
†Bath, R. F.	... ...	10, 297
Bathurst, A.	... ...	... 268
Bathurst, C. J.	... ...	... 314
Batstone, R. K.	... ...	152, 424
Battersby, J. R.	... ...	... 399
Battersby, R. H.	... ...	302, 399
Battiscombe, H.	... ...	... 361
†Battock, T. W.	... ...	29, 268, 271
Batty, C.	... ...	... 386
Batzer, A. E.	... ...	... 210
Batzer, R. J.	... ...	58, 312
†Baugh, A. W.	... ...	... 24
Baugh, J.	... ...	... 381
Baumgartner, J. M. V.	...	152, 354
Bawtree, E.	... ...	... 301
Bax, E. G. G.	...	152¶, 313, 415
Bax, F. L.	... ...	... 187
Bax, W. M.	... ...	...149, 152, 313
Baxendale, T. J.	... ...	... 287
†Baxter, G. W.	... ...	22, 316
Baxter, H.	... ...	... 287
†Baxter, R. P.	... ...	10, 227
†Bayley, C. D. W.	... ...	... 165§
Bayley, J. R.	... ...	... 317
Baylis, R. H.	... ...	58, 363
†Bayne, E. G.	... ...	21, 357
Bayne, H. G.	... ...	... 309
Baynes, J. E.	... ...	... 277
Baynes, V.	... ...	... 333
Bayzand, G.	... ...	58, 218
Beach, T. S.	... ...	152, 210
†Beacham, C. J.	... ...	22, 382
Beacham, O. H.	... ...	... 202
Beachell, R. P.	... ...	... 202
†Beadell, A. G.	... ...	14, 249
Beadle, L. A.	... ...	150, 370
Beadnell, H. J. L.	... ...	152, 405
†Beak, F. L.	... ...	32, 187
Beal, L. F.	... ...	58, 222
Beale, M. C.	... ...	... 363
Beall, R. W.	... ...	... 412
Beall, W. C.	... ...	... 404
Beaman, G. B.	... ...	... 368
Beamish, A. S.	... ...	... 383
Bean, D. Mc. G.	... ...	... 405
Bean, H. L.	... ...	... 196
Beard, C. A.	... ...	... 230
Bearn, A. F.	... ...	... 187
†Bearne, A. D.	... ...	... 24
†Beaton, G. C.	... ...	39, 59, 196
Beaton, P. F.	... ...	... 331
Beattie, J. A. N.	... ...	... 337
Beaufort, P. S.	... ...	... 166
†Beaumont, C. L.	... ...	16, 166
Beaumont, E. E.	... ...	152, 166
Beaumont, P.	... ...	... 421
†Beaumont, W. N.	... ...	...5, 226
Beaumont-Edmonds, C. W. F.	...	399
Beausire, F. R.	... ...	... 310
Beauvais, C. J. C.	... ...	... 184
Beauvais, L.	... ...	152, 228
Beavan, J.	... ...	... 405
Beavan, R. W.	... ...	... 311a
†Beavon, D. J.	... ...	20, 249
Beavon, J. A.	... ...	... 249
Beazeley, G. E. A.	... ...	... 253
Beazley, T. F.	... ...	... 278
Bebington, J. A.	... ...	... 202
†Beck, J.	... ...	... 28
Beck, T. W.	... ...	... 286
Becke, H. R.	... ...	... 311
Beckett, C. J. R.	... ...	... 186
†Beckingsale, J. E.	...	20, 233
Bedford, E. R.	... ...	... 340
Bedfordshire Regt.	... ...	... *222*
Beddow, F. M.	... ...	... 149
Beeby, M. O.	... ...	... 196
Beeney, J. A.	... ...	...144, 166, 305
Beecroft, A.	... ...	... 399
Beer, G. T.	... ...	... 235
Beer, J. A.	... ...	... 399
Beer, J. T.	... ...	... 322
Beesley, C. J.	... ...	... 356
Beesley, H.	... ...	59, 268
Beeson, A. C.	... ...	... 249
Beeson, L. A.	... ...	... 196
Beetham, C. W.	... ...	... 385
Beetham, G. C.	... ...	59, 385
Beeton, E. C.	... ...	... 312a
†Begg, A.	... ...	29, 327
Beighton, J. D. K.	... ...	... 266
Belchamber, D. F.	... ...	313, 415
Belcher, A. E. I.	... ...	59, 390
Belcher, F.	... ...	... 166
Belfield, J. H.	... ...	... 196
Belham, A. S.	... ...	... 359
Bell, A. E.	... ...	... 358
†Bell, C. C.	... ...	26, 269
Bell, C. W.	... ...	... 166
Bell, D. C.	... ...	59, 150, 320, 321
Bell, F. A.	... ...	... 318
Bell, F. W.	... ...	... 291
†Bell, G. B.	... ...	15, 268
Bell, H. B.	... ...	... 322
Bell, H. L.	... ...	59, 289
Bell, J. H.	... ...	... 210
†Bell, O.	... ...	... 37, 152, 166
Bell, P. H.	... ...	... 424
Bell, P. M.	... ...	... 363
†Bell, R. J.	... ...	25, 330
Bell, R. O.	... ...	... 310
†Bell, S. F.	... ...	... 24
Bell, S. J.	... ...	... 246
Bell, T. F.	... ...	... 412
Bell, T. W.	... ...	... 374

¶ See reference to this name in *Corrigenda*.

BELL

INDEX TO COMMISSIONS, HONOURS, and ROLL OF HONOUR.

Bell, V. A.	390
Bell, W. G. A.	196
Bellamy, K. J. G.	164
Bellamy, S.	405
Bellhouse, D. J.	191
Bellis, A. W.	274
Belton, F. H.	291
†Benbow, J. H.	24
Benbow, L. J.	299
Benbow, O. B.	415
Bending, C. O.	415
Benedictus, J. H.	196
Benjafield, H. W.	297, 424
Benjamin, H. S.	370
Benn, A. N. M.	196
†Bennett, A. H.	11, 336
Bennett, C. S.	424
Bennett, E. H.	202
Bennett, E. P.	45, 59, 152, 381
†Bennett, G. A.	27, 369
Bennett, G. C.	213
Bennett, H. D.	275
Bennett, J.	259
Bennett, J. H. R.	382
Bennett, J. Henry	376
Bennett, J. Hadfield	369
†Bennett, J. N.	16, 202
Bennett, S. E.	152, 360
Bennett, T. H.	255
Bennett, W.	166
†Bennett, W. B. H.	14, 336
Bennett, W. G.	389
†Benningfield, M. V.	2, 381
Ben Oliel, J. B.	305
Benson, H. W.	340
Benson, L.	392
Benson, O.	152, 415
Benson, R. E.	152, 403
Benson, T. N.	59, 249
†Benstead, H. E.	14, 292
Benthall, G.	196
Bentley, A.	59, 327
Bentley, C. J.	191
Bentley, H. C.	202
Benton, A. S.	342
†Benton, J. W.	10
Benton, P. F.	424
†Benton, S.	23, 328
Benton, S. J.	350
Benwell, L. N.	305
Berdinner, C. R.	166
Berdee, J. S.	166
Beresford, J.	286
Bergh, V. E. D.	423
Beringer, B.	233
Berkeley, A. F. M.	415
†Berkeley, C.	42, 166, 218
Berkeley, G. S.	403
Berkeley, C. J. A.	182
Berkshire Regt., Royal	224
Berliner, P. B.	60, 291
Bernard, A. J.	371
Bernard, H. F. W.	263
Bernays, J. S. N.	60, 281
Bernhard, H. A.	191¶
Bernie, W. G.	166
Berry, A. E.	210
Berry, A. G.	365
Berry, B. O.	322
†Berry, J. A.	5, 252
Berry, J. W.	187
†Berry, P. H.	3
Berry, T. A.	196
Berry, W. R.	318
Bertie, A. W.	60, 152, 187
Bertrand, L.	166
Besch, R. C. F.	60, 310
Bessant, H. W.	213
Bessant, J. A.	60, 215
Best, C. E.	404
Best, G.	249
Best, G. H. T.	268
Bestow, S. F.	210
†Beswick, J. C.	14, 279
Betbeder, G. L.	297
Betts, A. J.	342
†Betts, T. W.	18, 337
Bevan, A. P.	383
†Bevan, T. W.	40, 213
Bevan, V. R.	412
†Bevan, W.	166§
Beveridge, D. A.	210
Beveridge, R. F.	260
Bevis, D. A.	216
Bevis, L. C.	153, 256
Bewsey, J. C.	259
Bickley, A.	249
Bickley, C. H.	227
Bickley, C. W.	249
Biddulph, P. V.	343
Bidwell, T. E. P.	217
Bigg, D.	399
Biggart, A. S.	310a
Bigger, I. W. E. L.	274
Bigger, T. H. L.	275
Biggs, F. G.	287
Biggs, J. H. C.	202
Biggs, J. H. E.	265
†Biggs, S.	42, 405
†Bilby, E. J.	19, 322
Billham, F. D.	373
Billing, A. W.	243
†Billington, G.	24, 196¶
Binder, A. E. L.	159, 382
Binder, E. S.	389
Bindon, G. S.	409
†Biner, F. A.	27, 166
†Bingham, M. H.	33, 388

† Killed in action or died.   § See this name in *Addenda*.

Binns, A. 202	Blake, H. M. 239
Binns, H. I. 187	Blake, L. G. 327
†Birch, A. ... 12, 225	Blake, S. G. 328
Birch, A. V. 249	Blanc, L. D. 216
Birch, H. 241	Blanc, L. G. 233
Birch, R. A. 166	Blanchard, H. C. A. ... 60, 312
Birch, W. K. ... 148, 153, 162	Bland, A. ... 149, 409
†Bird, A. L. ... 20, 370	Blanckensee, G. E. S. ... 259
Bird, A. W. ... 150, 225	Blanco-White, G. R. ... 202
†Bird, C. E. ... 12, 242	Blane, T. H. ... 196
Bird, C. L. 339	Blankley, C. H. ... 186
†Bird, E. J. ... 15, 381	Blanshard, C. J. ... 409
†Bird, E. S. ... 19, 258	Blaxill, A. D. ... 243
Bird, H. W. ... 391	Bleathman, W. E. P. ... 350
†Bird, J. W. ... 27, 184	Blenkin, F. ... 333
Bird, L. G. 289	Blenkin, J. A. ... 419
Bird, P. A. 328	Blight, W. ... 310a
Bird, R. T. 363	Blindell, C. W. ... 406
†Bird, S. T. ... 9, 265	Bliss, A. ... 363
†Birdsall, G. ... 35	†Bliss, F. K. ... 10, 187
Birkett, F. S. ... 310	Blomfield, C. J. ... 159, 311
Birks, H. A. ... 166	Bloomer, D. W. H. ... 166
Birnie, R. ... 209, 252	Blore, E. ... 367
Birse, A. H. ... 412	Blore, J. H. ... 409
†Birtles, R. P. ... 13, 153, 381	Blower, A. B. ... 349
Biscoe, C. H. ... 191	Blower, A. L. ... 415
Bishop, E. G. C. ... 406	Bloxham, L. W. ... 299
†Bishop, F. E. ... 18, 166	Bluck, G. E. ... 412
†Bishop, K. F. ... 9, 196	Blue, A. J. ... 399
Bishop, P. B. ... 303	Blundell, A. H. ... 159, 311
Bishop, T. C. ... 191	Blundell, D. R. ... 60, 303
Bispham, C. ... 209	Blunden, B. O. ... 399
†Bispham, D. C. ... 25, 166	Boak, C. B. ... 285
†Black, F. H. ... 3, 369	Boby, R. S. P. ... 150, 268
Black, F. K. ... 229	Boden, J. P. ... 363
Black, J. ... 60, 220	Bodilly, R. W. T. ... 233
Blackaller, C. D. ... 194	Bodimeade, E. J. ... 394
Blackborn, C. T. ... 328	Boggon, J. H. ... 223¶
†Blackburn, H. D. ... 13, 214	Boggon, N. G. ... 333
Blackhurst, S. ... 60, 292	Boileau, E. F. ... 420
Blackie, A. ... 216	Bolders, L. J. G. ... 380
Blacking, W. H. R. ... 295	Boles, R. P. ... 263
Blackler, E. F. ... 382	†Bolitho, V. A. ... 13, 184
Blackmore, O. W. ... 153, 406	†Bolland, F. W. H. ... 17, 245
Blacktin, T. S. ... 415	Bolter, A. E. ... 415
Blackwell, P. W. ... 329	Bolter, C. A. ... 33, 313a, 415
Blackwood, A. P. ... 46, 308	Bolton, A. ... 187
Blackwood, J. ... 165	Bolton, F. W. G. ... 419
Blackwood, N. F. ... 153, 162	†Bolton, G. B. ... 11, 352
Blagrove, H. C. ... 366	Bolton, H. S. ... 191
Blaiberg, A. M. ... 373	Bolton, J. H. ... 383
Blaiberg, H. E. ... 369	Bolton, P. ... 393
Blair, A. ... 210	Bolton, R. P. ... 351
Blair, J. M. ... 149, 153, 358	Bolton, T. A. ... 306
Blaikley, E. ... 149	Bolton, T. T. ... 317
Blake, A. E. ... 322	Bolus, L. ... 363
Blake, A. T. ... 387	Bolwell, H. C. ... 371
†Blake, C. E. N. ... 35, 60, 187	Bomford, H. J. P. ... 166, 310a
Blake, F. J. ... 223	Bonar, H. H. ... 406

¶ See reference to this name in *Corrigenda*.

BOND

INDEX TO COMMISSIONS, HONOURS, and ROLL OF HONOUR

Name	Pages	Name	Pages
Bond, C. H. C.	149, 405	Boyes, C. E. C.	409
Bond, F. E.	166	Bovet, F. F.	399
Bond, G. A.	61, 185	Bovet, V. C. A.	162, 380
Bond, S. A.	321	Bovington, T. P.	41¶ 149
Bond, V. P.	415	Bowden, G. J.	166
Bone, F. H.	61, 380	Bowden, J. L.	235
Bonner, S. A.	148, 153, 162	Bowden, J. P.	427
†Bonnet, E. C.	23, 418	Bowden, R. C.	235
Bonnett, F. W. L.	420	†Bowe, E. A.	34, 239
Bonnyman, G. A.	210	Bowen, C. G.	423
Bookless, T.	202	Bowen, C. R.	385
Boon, E. G. F.	61, 202	Bowen, E. E. W.	360
Boon, S. J. L.	283	Bowen, H. T.	373
Boosey, R.	166	Bowen, I. G. J.	374
Boot, M. W.	166	Bowen, V. A. P.	380
Booth, A. A.	182	†Bowen-Rowlands, C. F. W.	24
†Booth, E. A.	42, 162	Bower, B. C.	386
†Booth, F. A.	5, 260	Bower, G. R.	196
Booth, H. R.	348	Bower, G. S.	196
Booth, J.	196	†Bowermann, A. J.	9, 350
Booth, R. G. J.	289	Bowers, C. R. A.	365
Boothroyd, B. M.	409	Bowers, C. S.	286
Boothroyd, F.	392	†Bowie, A. S. H.	34, 196¶
Boothroyd, N.	233	Bowie, W. M.	383
Border Regt.	226	Bowler, W. J. B.	339
Bore, T. E.	339	Bowles, J. H.	369
Boret, J. A.	61, 147, 166, 362	†Bowling, A. H.	39, 196
Borrajo, S. A.	163	Bowling, T.	309
Borrer, A. C. H.	399	†Bowley, R. W.	34, 317
Borrie, P. J.	249	†Bowman, C. H.	19, 339
Borrowdale, W. G.	240	Bowman, J. H.	244
Borthwick, Hon. A. M.	217	Bowyer, C. T.	220
Borthwick, W. T.	344	†Bowyer, F. W. F.	39
Borwick, R. H.	227	Box, C. H.	355
Bostock-Wilson, E. L.	403	Box, E. H.	153, 162, 354
†Boswell, C. O.	22, 271	Box, K. J.	61, 388
Boswood, C. G. G.	309	Boxall, E. M.	394
†Boswood, L. J.	38, 166	Boxall, F. S.	153, 317
Bothamley, B. P.	301	Boxall, T. M.	415
Bott, D. A. L.	257	Boxer, E. M.	166
Bott, H. D.	399	Boyce, A. F.	427
Bott, H. E.	427	†Boycot, H. C.	29, 218
Bottomley, W. A.	396	Boyd, C. N.	166
Botterill, P. W.	383	Boyd, G.	344
Boughton, F. C.	163	†Boyer, E. A.	32, 292
Boughton, G.	196	Boyes, B.	392
†Bouie, J. A. A.	13, 166	Boyes, C. E. C.	409
Boullen, C. E.	370	Boyle, D. H.	221
†Boulting, S. E.	14, 355	Boyle, J. A.	196
Boulton, E. E.	399	Boys, J. C.	399
Bound, R. B.	246	†Boys, R. H.	11, 222
Bourchier, L. G. G.	202	Boyton, J. L.	61, 280
†Bourdillon, T. L.	20, 61, 265	Brace, J.	285
Bourhill, N. E.	409	Brace, L.	210
Bourne, H.	424	Bracey, G. J.	311a
Bourne, P. R.	235	†Bracewell, H.	21, 337
Bousfield, C.	166, 395	Bracewell, J. R.	202
Boustred, R. W.	289	†Bracher, W. V. A.	7
Boutflower, C.	228	Brachi, M.	61, 215

† Killed in action or died. § See this name in *Addenda*.

This Index does not include the Alphabetical Sections IV. and V. (Other Ranks and Old Members).

Name	Page(s)	Name	Page(s)
Brackett, F. J. N.	263	Brewer, F. H. J.	261
Bradfield, G. E.	404	Brewer, H. H.	336
†Bradfield, W. L.	17	Brewer, L. G. T.	202
Braden, W. E.	340	Brewster, J. A.	422
Bradley, A. J.	255	Brickell, A. M.	279
Bradley, A. T.	366	Brickell, D. F. H.	166
Bradley, F.	182	Bridell, L. T.	380
Bradley, W. C.	327	Bridge, A. J.	166
Bradley-Cooke, H. J.	399	†Bridge, D. G. C.	4, 224
Bradshaw, H. L.	298	Bridge, W. A.	244
Bradshaw, J.	310a	Bridges, C.	166, 406
Bradshaw, P. S.	342	Bridgett, H.	406
Bradshaw, W.	236	Bridson, E.	191
Braendle, H. A.	268	Brigenshaw, R. J.	322
Brain, P. G.	246	Briggs, C.	427
Braines, T. F.	166	†Briggs, E. F.	42, 420
Braithwaite, B. F.	166	Briggs, F.	166
Braithwaite, N.	166	Briggs, H. B.	315
Bramall, D. H.	215	Briggs, H. T.	322
Bramley, J. A.	166	†Briggs, W. L.	20, 279
Bramwell, J.	271	Brigham, W.	333
Bramwell, J. C.	244	Brindley, S. G.	153, 404
Branch, C. S.	281	Brine, G. E.	202
†Brand, P. A. E.	21, 342	†Brisley, C. E.	35, 164
Brandon, H.	355	Bristol, F. L.	166
Branford, J. G.	260	Bristol, L.	196
†Bransom, A. H.	19	British Empire, Order of	148
Brasher, W.	153, 299	Brittain, S. T.	187
Brassington, B. E.	371	Brittan, N. F.	321
Bray, C. F.	191	Brittenden, J. E.	210
Bray, F. D.	358	Britton, W.	382
†Bray, F. H.	34, 365	†Broad, J. E.	30, 223
Bray, J.	233	Broad, K. S.	153, 282
†Bray, S. H.	35, 395	†Broad, W. V. M.	30, 299
Bray, W.	244	Broadbent, C. F.	13, 187
†Brayden, K.	27, 301	Broadbent, E. G.	272
†Brazier, A. D. C.	13, 225	Broadbent, E. W.	187
Brazier, J. P.	394	Broadbent, T. E.	396
Brealy, S. G.	61, 246	Broadbridge, F. L.	254
Brearcy, A. D.	201	Broadbridge, M. C.	187
†Brede, C. R.	12	Broadbridge, M. O'B.	62, 153, 236
†Bregazzi, E.	41, 336	Broadhurst, H.	296
†Brenchley, J.	22, 61, 218	†Broadhurst, T. C.	21, 166
Brennan, F. K.	266	Broadley, A.	187
Brennand, E. W.	261	Broady, G. S.	318
Brereton, J. L.	202	Broatch, P.	62, 333
Brereton, V. F.	409	†Brock, A. B.	23, 236
Bretherton, C. H.	400	†Brock, C. H.	41, 236
Bretherton, F.	163	Brock, R. L.	263
Brett, B. L. W.	292	Brockhurst, A. H.	276
Brett, C. C.	196	Brocklebank, S. J.	196
Brett, F. A.	383	Brocklehurst, E. H.	404
Brett, J.	273	†Brocklehurst, T. P.	7, 361
Bretelle, L. M. C.	339	Brocklehurst, S. T.	415
Brewer, A. G.	240	Brockliss, A. A.	422
Brewer, C. E.	292	Brockliss, W. J.	185
Brewer, C. E. S.	361	Brockman, F. G.	167, 313
Brewer, C. H.	62, 166, 222	Broderick, M. J. A.	419
Brewer, E.	166	Brodie, C. F. C.	311a

¶ See reference to this name in *Corrigenda*.

Brodrick, P.	153, 291
Bromfield, F. L.	62, 271
†Bromham, C. A. R.	40, 235
Bromley, C. J. M.	240
Bromley, E. J.	202
Bromley, F. E.	421
†Bromley, H. F. G.	5, 365
Brook, C. H.	167, 298
Brook, L. T.	149, 282
Brook, W. S.	396
Brooke, A.	287
Brooke, A. C.	301
Brooke, A. W.	415
Brooke, C. B.	62, 415
Brooke, F.	278
Brooke, H.	184
Brooke, J. A. L.	378
†Brooke, L.	32, 62, 274
Brookes, A.	406
Brookes, A. W.	393
†Brookes, P.	26, 230
Brooks, A. G.	225
Brooks, C. B.	256
Brooks, D. C. J.	62, 374
Brooks, J. C.	363
Brooks, V.	386
Brooks, W. J.	321
Brooks-Hill, R.	383¶
Brooman, F. R.	234
Brooman, H. B.	234
Broomfield, H. F.	304
Brophy, C. J.	406
Brough, W. J.	320
†Broughton, T. D.	14, 389
Brouse, W. H. D.	409
Brown, A. F.	356
Brown, A. G.	262
†Brown, A. H.	28
Brown, A. J.	62, 365
†Brown, A. L.	5, 361
Brown, A. R.	328
Brown, A. T.	62, 153, 396
Brown, Alfred W.	286
Brown, Arthur W.	202
Brown, C. A.	427
Brown, C. E. G.	289
Brown, C. G.	362
Brown, C. K.	196
Brown, D. F.	236
Brown, D. L.	274
Brown, E.	196
Brown, E. A. J.	167
Brown, E. B.	62, 353
†Brown, E. J.	19¶, 167
Brown, E. W. W.	274
Brown, F.	210
†Brown, F. A. N.	8, 382
†Brown, Frederick C.	4, 337
Brown, Felix C.	274
Brown, Frank P.	167
Brown, Frederick P.	362
Brown, H.	386
†Brown, Harold A.	3, 280
†Brown, H. B.	24
Brown, H. C.	362
Brown, H. D.	406
Brown, Harold G.	63, 387
Brown, Horace G.	322
Brown, Humphrey G.	298
Brown, Harold, J.	427
†Brown, Herbert J.	25, 373
Brown, H. I.	368
Brown, H. V.	370
Brown, J. A.	279
Brown, J. H.	339
Brown, J. McI.	295
Brown, J. W.	167
Brown, L.	162¶, 182
Brown, L. S.	380
Brown, M. B.	298
Brown, M. F.	187
Brown, N. M.	286
Brown, P.	210
Brown, R.	149
Brown, R. H.	322
Brown, R. J. H.	289
Brown, R. L.	278
Brown, S.	63, 331
Brown, T. S.	182
Brown, U.	376
Brown, Wilfred	391
Brown, William	341
Brown, W. C.	260
Brown, W. E.	369
Brown, W. I.	228
Brown, Walter James (3669)	63, 276
Brown, Walter James (6046)	238
Brown, William J.	244, 421
Brown, W. J. C.	167
†Brown, W. R.	24
Browne, A. G.	63, 153, 327
Browne, A. G. D.	400
Browne, A. W.	395
Browne, A. W. C.	409
Browne, B. M.	195
Browne, H. N.	287
Browne, H. W.	325
†Browne, L. K.	13, 333
Browne, O. H. G.	263
Browne, S. N.	244
Browne, W. R.	248
Browne, W. S.	153, 210
Browning, A. J.	182
Browning, F.	191
Brownlie, J.	210
Brownlee, F.	263
Bruce, A. H.	310a
Bruce, R.	150, 210

† Killed in action or died. § See this name in *Addenda*.

This Index does not include the Alphabetical Sections IV. and V. (Other Ranks and Old Members).

Name	Pages	Name	Pages
Bruce, R. C.	256	Bullard, S.	424
Bruce, R. F.	167	Bullen, G.	262
Bruce, R. R. H.	167	Bullett, R. F.	365
Bruce, S. F.	246	†Bullman, H. R. H.	26, 262
Bruckman, R. T.	227	Bullock, A. B.	167
Brudenell, C. S.	261	Bullock, A. D.	366
Bruges, J. P.	210	†Bullock, A. S.	25
Brumwell, B. H.	153, 202	Bullock, W. H.	361
Brunsdon, A. F. E.	223	Bullpitt, J.	63, 153, 313a, 416
†Brunskill, J. J.	15, 383	Bulteel, W. G.	218
†Brunt, E.	24	Bunce, W. L.	148, 153, 285
Brunt, H. S.	202¶	Bundle, H. W.	196
Brunton, G.	148, 412	Bunford, J. H.	244
Bryan, L. J.	330	Bunker, H. E.	322
Bryan, R.	210	Bunn, R. F. I.	261
†Bryans, J.	23¶, 273	Bunn, R. W. E.	249
Bryant, A. L.	242	†Bunney, V. H.	29
Bryant, E. H.	242	†Bunning, R. J.	422
Bryant, G. E.	237	Burbridge, D. G.	333
Bryant, S. C.	383	Burbury, A. V.	63, 162, 164, 390
Bryant, S. G.	187	Burch, H. J.	423
Bryce, A. W.	196	Burch, J. C.	365
†Bryne, P. S.	24	Burchell, C. M.	244
Bryning, F. A.	281	Burd, W.	383
Bryson, G.	63, 229	Burder, C. V.	63, 320
Bryson, John (766947)	382	Burdett, B.	249
Bryson, John (7824)	167	Burdge, C. C.	253
Bryson, R. E.	63, 346	†Burfoot, W. M.	34, 238
†Buchanan, E. L.	427§	Burgess, F. J.	424
Buchanan, E. S.	167	Burgess, G. W.	167
Buchanan, L. G.	286	Burgess, H.	318
Buchanan, W.	256	Burke, F. W.	220
Buck, N. A.	374	†Burley, E. S.	42, 412
Buckingham, L. F.	246	Burman, H. S.	409
Buckland, F. W.	295	†Burmann, R. M.	40, 46, 63, 153, 162, 226, 308
Buckland, L. L. R.	409	Burn, H. F. J.	290
Buckle, F. D.	279	Burn, T. C.	218
Buckley, C. H. S.	234	Burnard, R. A.	395
Buckley, F.	348	Burnett, C. F. P.	246
Buckley, J.	379	†Burnett, C. G. A.	7, 331
†Buckley, J. M.	27, 341	Burnett, F. S.	327, 419
†Buckley, S. J.	30, 353	Burnett, T. R.	228
Bucknell, L. H.	210	Burns, D. B.	213
Buckton, C.	167	Burns, D. G.	269
Buddle, E. G.	350	Burns, H. C.	416
Budge, W. S.	196	†Burns, W. A.	35
Budgen, W. H.	196	Burns, W. J.	182
†Budibent, C.	5, 282	Burr, B.	283
Bulger, A. G.	326	Burr, E. H.	272
Bulgin, R.	246, 305	Burr, P. B.	370
†Bulkeley-Hughes, G. M. W.	13, 265	Burrell, J.	361
Bull, E. R.	387	Burroughs, P. W.	64, 305
Bull, G. H.	365	Burrow, A. C.	313a
†Bull, J. W.	10, 209, 271	Burrows, C. A. E.	406
Bull, L	223	Burrows, H. N.	186
†Bull, R. J. H.	18, 300	Burrows, W. F.	246
Bull, W.	362	Burslem, F. G.	167
Bull, W. G.	263	Burt, A. H.	329
Bull, W. R.	167	Burt, G. C.	217

¶ See reference to this name in *Corrigenda.*

BURT

INDEX TO COMMISSIONS, HONOURS, and ROLL OF HONOUR.

†Burt, H. C. ... 35	Bytheway, A. W. ... 231
Burt, W. G. ... 386	Bywater, W. E. ... 350
Burton, A. A. C. ... 196	
Burton, C. E. ... 230	
†Burton, C. H. ... 7, 336	Cabespine, E. W. H. ... 235
Burton, E. G. ... 412	†Cable, J. S. ... 38, 202
Burton, E. R. ... 427	Cable, L. ... 167
Burton, F. ... 406	Cackett, C. W. ... 286
Burton, F. J. ... 397	Caddy, W. L. ... 278
Burton, R. G. ... 216	Cadman, H. E. S. ... 427
Burton, R. W. ... 64, 357	Cadman, J. F. ... 306
†Burton, W. E. B. ... 6	Caesar, L. V. ... 261
Burwash, H. A. ... 187	Caffarey, B. J. ... 162, 208
Bury, W. G. ... 258	†Cahill, J. A. ... 19, 64, 153, 224¶
Bury, W. H. ... 274	Cahill, M. ... 239
Bush, M. H. ... 389	Caiger, F. E. ... 317, 393
Bush, R. E. ... 164	Cain, C. W. ... 227
Bushby, E. F. ... 286	Cain, D. W. T. ... 167
Bushnell, C. F. ... 371	Cain, R. H. ... 333
Buss, F. B. ... 383	Caine, C. V. ... 330
Bustard, F. ... 148, 153, 162, 278	Caithness, W. ... 150, 153, 191
Bustard, R. ... 278	†Calder, G. J. ... 24
Buswell, H. B. ... 336	Calder, R. C. ... 202
Butcher, D. J. ... 210	†Calder, W. P. ... 17, 266
Butcher, T. R. P. ... 388	Calderbank, P. ... 223
†Butland, G. ... 34, 385	Caldwell-Cook, E. A. ... 223
†Butland, W. H. ... 6, 240	Caldwell-Cook, F. ... 355
Butler, E. J. ... 333	Calhaem, R. L. ... 418
Butler, E. L. ... 314	†Calkin, J. E. ... 13, 333
Butler, F. W. ... 153, 403	†Callanan, M. ... 12, 326
Butler, H. A. R. ... 363	Callf, G. S. ... 427
Butler, H. C. ... 351	Calcott, H. N. H. ... 298
†Butler, O. H. S. ... 24	Callender, A. H. ... 343
Butler, S. A. V. ... 389	Callender, E. ... 240
Butler, S. J. ... 292	†Callender, G. W. ... 12, 383
†Butt, A. ... 28, 167, 223	Callingham, L. F. ... 420
Butt, C. F. ... 322	Calverley, E. ... 337
Butt, D. M. ... 244	Calvert, C. C. ... 416
Butt, H. ... 322	Calvert, R. D. ... 406
Buttemer, E. D. A. ... 153, 188, 419	Calvert, W. H. ... 318
Butterfield, J. ... 186	*Cambridgeshire Regt.* ... 229
Butters, P. P. ... 273	*Cameron Highlanders* ... 229
Butterworth, H. B. ... 237	Cameron, J. ... 148, 153, 210
†Buttery, R. A. ... 35, 340	Cameron, S. S. ... 229
†Buttery, W. ... 36, 392	Camp, A. F. ... 314, 423
Buttfield, L. F. ... 64, 339	Camp, H. M. ... 336
Buttrick, F. ... 313a	Campbell, Alan ... 365
Buxton, O. ... 150, 225	Campbell, Andrew ... 64, 153, 188
Buxton-Knight, A. ... 194	Campbell, C. J. ... 202
Buxton-Knight, O. ... 153, 404	Campbell, F. ... 295
Byerley, A. J. A. ... 388	†Campbell, G. ... 16¶, 149, 153, 332, 415
Byers, A. P. ... 245	Campbell, J. T. ... 321
Bygott, E. ... 348	Campbell, S. V. ... 64, 227
†Byles, A. B. ... 27, 335	Campbell, W. R. C. ... 186
Byles, W. H. ... 406	Campkin, D. J. ... 380
†Byng, H. ... 3, 226	†Campkin, R. E. ... 31, 290
Bynee, E. D. ... 409	Candler, A. P. ... 285
Byrne, A. W. ... 271, 309¶	Candy, R. G. ... 167, 399
†Byrne, T. E. ... 29, 220	Candy, R. E. ... 196

† Killed in action or died.   § See this name in *Addenda*.

This Index does not include the Alphabetical Sections IV. and V. (Other Ranks and Old Members).

Name	Pages	Name	Pages
Cannan, V. C.	302	Carr, M.	65, 150, 153, 344
†Canning, E. H.	39, 144, 248	Carr, R.	333
†Cannon, E. E.	41	Carr, R. S.	191
Cannon, G. M.	150, 399	Carr, W. F.	406
Cannon, H. C.	64, 153, 363	†Carre, E. M.	11, 283
Cannon, S. W. W.	369	Carrington, C. W.	46, 153, 217
Canter, F.	297	Carroll, J. A.	188
Canty, F. J.	188	Carroll, L. G.	299
Canty, H.	273	Carruthers, A. R.	272
Cape, H. J.	400	Carson, J. H. B.	420
Capes, G. A.	254	Carson, M. A.	342
Capon, R. S.	285	Carson, R. T.	385
Capp, E. H.	246	Carson, W. F.	167
Capp, R. W.	329	Carson, W. J.	188
Capper, A. H.	260	†Carter, A.	35, 167
†Capper, E. R.	27, 64, 244	Carter, A. B.	254
†Capper, H. K.	35	Carter, Arthur C.	376
Capper, W.	381	Carter, Alfred C.	150, 406
†Card, A. H.	10, 64, 322	Carter, A. E.	333
Card, L. H.	421	Carter, A. H.	196¶
Cardell, J. E.	153, 215	Carter, B. E.	427
Cardell-Oliver, J. E.	194	Carter, H. J.	254
†Carden, R .H.	2, 380	Carter, H. S.	159, 263
Carder, F. C.	424	Carter, H. W.	65, 153, 362
Carder, S. M.	383	Carter, M. J.	295
†Carefull, J. H.	29, 287	Carter, P.	370
†Carew, C. J. T.	3, 392	Carter, R. T.	357
Carey, C. M.	188	Carter, S. N.	383
Carey, R. B.	167	Carter, S. V.	202
Carey, R. M.	276	Carter, W. C.	167
Carlaw, H. W.	167	†Cartman, J. V.	35, 286
Carless, G. E.	399	Cartmell, R. J. G.	263
Carless, W. E.	422	Cartwright, S.	358
Carlton, G. F.	285	Cartwright, S. H.	188
Carlton, John (761808)	202	Case, F. M. B.	328
Carlton, John (760584)	202	†Case, G.	30, 276
Carmalt, H. E.	311a	Caslon, E. W.	327
Carmichael, E. W.	258	Cassell, H. E.	374
†Carmichael, G.	29, 316	Cassels, J. S.	65, 167, 366
Carmichael, H. M.	396	Casserly, J. H. G.	312a
†Carne, M. H.	12, 232	Cassidy, A. J.	167
Carnelley, H.	65, 210	†Cassidy, C. M.	4, 265
Carney, J. J.	240	†Casson, H. G.	40
Carnochan, T. M.	381	Castleman, F. B. G.	167
Carnon, J. S. M.	251	Cater, C. D.	333
†Care, J. P.	33, 301	†Cates, G. E.	13, 45, 341
Carolin, H. G.	326	Catford, W. A.	277, 35
Carpenter, A. E.	262, 313	Cathcart, W. C	318
Carpenter, A. H. D.	244	†Cather, G. St. G. S.	44
†Carpenter, H. G.	6, 306, 397	Catling, W. R.	194
Carr, A. C. E.	403	Catherall, C.	412
Carr, C. E.	266	Caton, E. P.	167
Carr, F. A.	228	Cattell, A. G.	65, 306
Carr, F. B.	320	†Catterall, A.	29, 336, 397
Carr, F. R.	427	Catterall, G.	318
Carr, J. B.	320	Cattle, A. P.	232
Carr, J. D.	383	Catton, E. D.	328
Carr, L.	228	Causton, D. K.	153, 162
†Carr, L. G.	33, 65, 289	Cavaghan, T.	228

¶ See reference to this name in *Corrigenda*.

CAVALRY

INDEX TO COMMISSIONS, HONOURS, and ROLL OF HONOUR.

Cavalry Regts. *184*	Chapman, J. F. 322
Cave, C. F. 167	Chapman, J. T. 406
†Cave, J. 21, 396	†Chapman, M. G. H. 19, 342
Cave, R. N. 330	†Chapman, R. L. 24
Cave, R. G. 359	Chapman, R. W. T. 302
Cavenagh, F. A. 188	Chapman, T. S. 327
Cavill, P. R. 295	Chapman, W. 317
Cawley, J. D. 65, 188	Chappell, W. 422
Cawse, A. W. 409	Chappell, W. J. 360
†Cawson, G. A. 26, 167	Chard, H. A. 298
Cawte, E. V. 255	Charles, C. W. C. 361
†Cayford, G. E. 18, 167	Charles, D. S. 202
Cayless, F. 387	Charles, N. H. 210
Cayley, P. J. 249	Charlesworth, M. P. 412
Chace, G. P. ... ... 153¶, 224	†Charlton, F. T. 39, 276
Chadwell, A. E. 235	Charlton, G. J. 270
Chadwick, C. H. 153, 167	Charlton, R. 362
Chadwick, J. B. 270	†Charman, J. E. 21, 365
Chadwick, J. H. 182	Charnaud, F. C. 149, 153, 162
Chadwick, W. 269	Chart, E. 266
†Chaffey, G. F. 15	Chartress, E. E. 400
Challis, C. L. 238	Chaston, W. A. 406
†Challis, I. J. 33, 270	Chater, A. D. 252
Challis, J. A. McD. 188	Chater, G. L. 327
Chamberlain, B. 196	†Chatfeild-Clarke, H. 15, 367, 419
Chamberlain, G. F. 237	Chatfeild-Clarke, H. C. 188
Chamberlain, H. R. M. 292	Chatfeild-Clarke, S. 153, 307
Chamberlain, J. E. 412	Chatham, R. F. 159, 339
Chamberlain, S. D. 393	Chatterton, R. 66, 153, 197
Chambers, M. T. 283	Chauncey, P. ... ... 167¶
†Chambers, P. C. 30, 416	Cheel, E. S. 66, 263
Chambers, S. 197	†Cheers, D. H. A. 33, 167
Champion, A. 167	†Cheesman, D. G. 35
Champion, J. B. 400	Cheesman, G. B. 246
†Champness, B. 8	Cheesewright, F. C. 327
Chance, G. P. 360	Cheetham, J. C. 251
Chandler, A. H. 380	Cheriton, W. G. L. 153, 279
Chandler, A. L. 65, 153, 404	Cheshire, L. S. 342
†Chandler, C. R. 5, 357	Chester, G. S. 167
†Chandler, C. W. 32, 65, 326	Chester, H. S. 312
Chandler, G. H. 311a	Chesterton, H. 341
Chandler, W. F. 311	Chesterton, S. J. 406
·Chandley, R. T. F. 188	†Chetwood, E. S. 23, 153, 309
Chantrey, L. H. 187, 365	Chetwood, H. J. 162, 163
Chantrill, H. H. 322	†Cheverton, T. B. ... ... 30 ,66, 195
Chaplin, F. P. 167	Chiazzari, H. W. 292
Chaplin, L. F. C. 312a	Chick, A. E. 329
†Chaplin, S. S. 29, 315	Chick, A. L. 147, 167
Chaplin, T. H. G. 322	Chignell, A. H. 163
†Chaplyn, C. E. 33, 244	Child, A. J ... 66, 148, 150, 153, 164, 309
Chapman, A. A. 167	Child, F. J. 304
Chapman, A. H. 332	Child, P. A. 202
Chapman, B. E. 65, 327	Childs, C. L. 227
Chapman, B. O. 319	Childs, L. 422
Chapman, D. J. 318	Chilton, A. E. 286
Chapman, E. C. 167	Chilvers, J. E. 66, 260
Chapman, G. W. 387	†Chippington, H. L. 36, 356
Chapman, H. E. S. 159, 400	†Chisholm, D. W. 24
†Chapman, H. R. 22, 317	Chiswell, R. M. F. 167

† Killed in action or died. § See this name in *Addenda*.

This Index does not include the Alphabetical Sections IV. and V. (Other Ranks and Old Members).

†Chitty, A. C.	24	Clarke, A. S.	266
Chiverall, L. C. H.	393	Clarke, D. B.	292
†Chowne, G. H. T.	15, 272	†Clarke, E. A.	10, 303
Chrisfield, D. F.	210	Clarke, F.	323
Christelow, J. W.	210¶, 395	Clarke, F. J.	400
Christian, A. M. C.	287	Clarke, F. V.	236
Christian, W. A.	366	Clarke, F. W. H.	281
Christie, H. J.	323	Clarke, G. M.	147, 167, 282
Christie, J. F.	66, 223	Clarke, H. E.	153, 202¶
†Christmas, B. L.	7, 290	Clarke, H. F.	197
†Christmas, D. V.	6, 162, 355	Clarke, H. G.	153, 249
†Christmas, E. C. R.	10, 266	Clarke, H. L.	337
Christopher, E. O.	386	Clarke, H. W.	182
Christophers, R. B.	355	Clarke, J. F.	389
Christopherson, H. C.	352	Clarke, J. M.	271
†Christy, J. G.	39, 281	Clarke, J. W. A.	153¶, 315
Church, C. T.	191	Clarke, R. C. L.	383
Church, E. H.	167	Clarke, S. E.	213
Church, T. E.	317	†Clarke, T. P.	10, 386
†Churchfield, S. P.	7, 319	†Clarke, V. C.	11, 240
Churchman, J. E. L.	409	Clarke, W. P.	255
Churchman, S.	246	Class, H. R.	66, 153, 370
Churchward, H. M.	361	Clausen, G. F.	153, 313, 416
Churchward, L.	263	Clay, R. R.	312a
†Chuter, H. A.	13, 246	†Claydon, D. C.	20¶
†Chutter, G. P.	35, 249	†Clayton, A. O.	30, 153, 380
Channel Islands Militia	*229*	Clayton, A. H.	314
Cheshire Regt.	*230*	Clayton, E. C. D.	197
Circuitt, C. M. L.	149, 153, 300	Clayton, E. G.	153, 300
Circuitt, G. F. L.	404	Clayton, J. S.	400
Clancy, J.	326	Clayton, S. L.	292
Clapham, A. W.	366	Clayton, S. W.	339
Clapham, T.	197	Cleave, S. W.	301
Clapton, W. T.	215, 289	Cleaver, G. L.	330
Claridge, C. G.	275	Cleaver, P. A.	250
Claridge, W. S.	263, 312	Clegg, C. H.	385
Clark, A. B.	412	Clegg, G. W.	167
Clark, A. G.	202	Clegg, J. A.	348
Clark, A. N.	373	Clegg, J. H.	396
Clark, E. C.	356	Clegg, W.	153, 370
Clark, F. Longman	228	†Cleland, A. I. H.	28
Clark, F. Leonard	359	Cleland-Hollamby, D. M.	263
Clark, F. S.	167	Cleland-Hollamby, L. K.	292
Clark, G. S.	243	Cleland-Hollamby, R. C.	263
Clark, J.	409	Clemens, C. J. S.	202
Clark, J. A.	289	Clement, G. P.	359
Clark, L. E. C.	225	Clements, H. M.	383
Clark, L. F.	167	Clements, J. E.	400
Clark, N. R.	342	Clementson, L. H.	168
Clark, P. L.	153¶, 366§	Clemmens, J. R.	371¶
Clark, R.	299	Clery, G. J.	325
Clark, R. B.	313, 403	Clery, L. L.	323
†Clark, R. H.	30, 342	Cleveland, J. T. E.	276
Clark, S. H.	333	Clews, L. C.	352
Clark, T. J. C.	369	Clifton, E. N.	164, 218
†Clark, W. L.	16, 164, 322	†Clifton, H. N.	2, 218
Clarke, A.	354	Clinckett, J. E.	371
†Clarke, A. L.	31, 268	Clisby, H. E.	303
Clarke, A. R.	360	†Clively, J. H.	15, 385

¶ See reference to this name in *Corrigenda*.

K K

Clively, R. C.	66, 153, 277, 415
Cloquet, J. S. N.	263
†Close, M. A.	2, 256
Close, R. L.	404
Clough, S. B.	388
Cloutee, H. J.	162¶
Clow, J. P.	292
Clowes, D.	400
Clowes, R.	168
Clutterbuck, N. S.	311a
Coakley, J.	270
Coates, A.	337
†Coates, B. N.	13
Coates, F. S.	168
Coates, G. T.	188
Coates, L. J. M.	427
Coates, P. H.	378
Coates, R. R.	250
†Coates, S.	16, 168
Coates, W. H. E.	290
†Coats, W. E.	26, 344
Cobb, P. H.	409
†Cobb, R.	11, 225
Cobb, R. L.	167
†Cock, E. M.	16
Cock, G. H.	66, 165, 168
†Cockburn, G. P.	30, 355
Cocke, P. M.	292
Cockell, D. H.	246
Cockell, E. H.	202
Cockerill, F. C.	329
Cockman, R. T.	246
Cockrell, P.	197
Cocks, F. E.	149
Cocup, C. H.	302
Codd, C. J. C.	66, 240
Codling, B. P.	351
Coe, E. W.	349
Coffin, T. A.	339
Cohen, R. C.	409
Coke, E.	67, 188
Coke, H. M.	317
†Colborne, R.	24
Coldstream Guards	*218*
Cole, A. E.	386
Cole, A. P.	187
†Cole, C. C.	23, 202
Cole, C. C. E.	323
Cole, F. W.	202
Cole, G. J.	67, 342
Cole, J. T.	234, 237
Cole, P. J. L.	153, 331
Cole, T. A.	363
†Cole, W. M.	35, 67, 281
Coleman, A. J. P.	246
Coleman, C. B.	338
Coleman, C. H.	188
Coleman, C. T.	255
Coleman, F. A.	427
Coleman, F. C.	163
Coleman, F. D.	168
Coleman, G. H.	67, 286
Coleman, G. W. J.	188
Coleman, R.	159, 309
Colepepper, F. E.	409
Coles, A. J.	225
Coles, E. L.	67, 362
Coles, F. E.	296
†Coles, H.	26, 342
Coles, R. V.	234
Colin, B. J.	182
Collander-Brown, W. H.	168
Collenette, C. L.	424
Collett, F. G.	159, 398
†Colley, A.	2, 232
†Colley, D. J.	12, 286
†Colley, E. V.	20, 246
Colley, R. H.	188
Collier, E. A.	236
Collier, E. C. F.	300
Collier, P. F.	255
Colling, G. C.	331
Collinge, F. J.	338
Collinge, J.	270
Collings, J. S.	184
†Collings, L. L.	39, 231
†Collins, A. D.	13, 168
Collins, A. H.	427
Collins, A. J.	159, 291, 323
†Collins, A. L.	18
Collins, F. D.	353
Collins, F. G.	280
Collins, C. T. W.	369
Collins, H. A.	321
Collins, J. E.	67, 304
Collins, S. T.	37¶, 315
Collins, W. L. F.	188
†Collis, A. B.	26
Collison, F. L.	168
Collyer, C. A. S.	251
Collyer, W. T.	238
Colman, C. W. T.	218
Colquhoun, J. C.	256
Colquhoun, R. W. S.	281
Colquhoun, W. H. C.	406
Colson, H. J. C.	254
†Colvill-Jones, T.	34, 168
Colvin, A.	67, 153, 242
Comber, H. C.	202
†Comber, T.	38, 67, 244
Comfort, H. W.	202
Commands and Staff	*162*
Commin, R. G.	396
Commissions, Analysis of	*430*
Commissions, Roll of	*161*
†Common, T.	24
Comper, G. Q.	392
Compston, P.	258, 265

† Killed in action or died. § See this name in *Addenda*.

This Index does not include the Alphabetical Sections IV. and V. (Other Ranks and Old Members).

Name	Pages	Name	Pages
Comyn, C. H. F.	202	Coop, R. W.	68, 191
Concanon, J. B.	301	Coope, T. E.	255
Conder, R. E.	168	Cooper, A. E.	312a, 422
Conibeer, R. W.	68, 360	Cooper, C. R.	333
†Coningsby, H. A.	24	Cooper, D. J.	159, 309
Connaught Rangers	*232*	Cooper, E. P.	68, 392
Connolly, S. M.	336	Cooper, F. A. L.	197
Connolly, F. J.	312	†Cooper, F. E.	42, 246
Conoley, T. S.	342	Cooper, F. S.	421
Conolly, F. G.	210	Cooper, G. J.	168
Conquest, G.	363	†Cooper, G. S.	12, 330
Conrad, A. G.	302	Cooper, J. E.	400
Conran, E. D.	68, 326	Cooper, J. F.	312
Conran, H. C. R.	422	Cooper, J. S.	418
Conroy, E. P.	278	Cooper, R. B.	202
Constable, A. B.	210	Cooper, Sidney (1199)	168
†Constance, W. E.	36, 292	Cooper, Sidney (766190)	168
Conway, F. H.	297, 312	Cooper, Stanley	371
†Conway, J. M.	8, 279	Cooper, S. W.	188, 313
Conyngham, D. P.	168	Cooper, T. C.	68, 279
Cook, A. H.	328	Cooper, T. F.	263
Cook, A. S.	292	Cooper, W. C.	250
Cook, C. A. B.	153, 319	Cooper, W. R. D.	325
Cook, C. S.	224	Coore, A.	391
Cook, E. J.	182	Cope, E. H.	292
Cook, F. E.	400	†Cope, G. Q.	16, 315
Cook, G. A.	377	Cope, H. S.	242
Cook, G. R.	197	Copeland, E. F.	323
Cook, H. H.	185¶	Copeland, W. T. C.	333
Cook, H. H. M.	266	Copeman, L.	422
†Cook, H. M.	30, 292	†Copland, D. C. J.	3, 335
Cook, H. W.	279	†Coppin, R. A.	14, 363
†Cook, P. M.	10, 266	†Coppock, H. S.	32, 153, 277
Cook, R. A.	245	Corbett, H. S.	188
Cook, W. S.	210	Corbin, G.	360
Cook, Wm. Tebbutt	329	Cordingley, T. R.	218
Cook, Wm. Tucker	241	Corfield, F. J. A.	153, 339
Cooke, A.	286	Corke, J. F.	191¶
Cooke, A. B.	301, 422	Corke, R. T.	389
Cooke, A. M.	330	Corkill, L. L.	191
Cooke, B. C.	289	Corlett, R. L.	272
Cooke, G. G.	426	Corlett, W. H.	422
Cooke, H. H.	197	Cormack, A. R.	68, 416
Cooke, L. A.	275	†Cornelius, H. W.	35, 222
Cooke, M. J.	68, 328	Cornelius, J. C.	191
Cooke, P. A.	68, 148, 265	Cornford, K. M. A.	168
Cooke, S. C. F.	246	Cornish, A. C.	209
Cooksey, P. T.	263	Cornish, G. M.	68, 217
Coombe, A. S. N.	168	Cornish, H. D.	197
Coombe, R. G. B.	186	Cornthwaite, J. W.	391
Coombes, C. H. J.	363	Cornwall, R. E.	251
Coombes, P. J.	374	†Cornwell, W. H. A.	32
Coombs, A. C.	320	Correll, C. E.	68, 390
Coombs, A. R.	254	†Corrie, W. R.	15, 392
†Coombs, C. S.	8, 263	†Corry, F. M.	27, 168, 336
Coombs, H. C.	427	Corry, J. E.	69, 361
Coombs, V. C.	168	Corser, F. G.	188
Coombs, W. K.	343	Cory, D. H. C.,	241
Coop, H. H.	374	Cory, R.	159, 197

¶ See reference to this name in *Corrigenda*.

COSGROVE

INDEX TO COMMISSIONS, HONOURS, and ROLL OF HONOUR.

Name	Page	Name	Page
Cosgrove, H. G.	326	†Cox, Lupton J.	33, 248
Cossar, C. T.	344	†Cox, N. J.	5, 365
†Cossar, N. T.	16, 342	Cox, R. J.	336
Coston, J. A. C.	168	Cox, R. W.	389
Cottam, A. E.	69, 153, 357	†Cox, W. G.	38, 210
Cotterill, R. T.	351	Coxhead, H. J.	69, 365
Cotterill, T. H.	383	†Coxon, W. B.	32, 333
†Cottle, W. E. W.	18, 217	Coxwell, L. L.	356
Cotton, E. N.	290	†Coy, A. R.	8, 394
Cotton, G.	291	Coyle, E.	400
Cotton, G. V.	404	Cozens, F. G.	400
Cotton, R.	272	Crabb, H. L.	274
Cottrell, L. W.	393	Crabb, J. B.	168
Coulson, C. S. L.	144, 153, 168	Crabtree, J.	379
Coulson, F. B.	409	Crabtree, M. B.	266
Coulson, G.	310a	Cracknell, J. S.	392
†Counsell, H. C.	34, 191	Craddock, P.	421
Coupland, A. J.	287	†Craddock, V.	40, 353
Courtauld, S. L.	69, 381	Craig, A. G.	370
Courtice, J. C.	168	Craig, J. H.	340
Courtney, C.	229	Craig, R. G.	406
Courtney, W. E. L.	168	†Cramond, W.	28
Cousins, H. F.	210	Crampton, H.	69, 315
Coutts, F.	168	Cran, C. R.	69, 268, 386
Covell, E. H.	168	†Crane, L.	29, 202
Coviello, A.	149, 310a	†Crane, L. F.	40, 383
Covington, R. L.	340	†Crane, R. H.	21, 393
Cowan, Alexander	188	†Cranmer, G. P.	22, 388
Cowan, Alfred	246	Cranna, A. P.	252
Cowan, J. A.	346	Crapper, C.	373
Coward, D. C.	366	†Crasten, J.	3, 262
Cowell, F. H.	404	Craven, C. E. P.	292
Cowell, H. C. H.	298	Craven, E. B.	292
Cowell, P. B.	332	Craven, S. C.	406
Cowell, P. S.	202	†Crawford, E. G.	24
Cowey, T. W.	287	Crawford, H.	406
Cowie, H. A.	343	Crawford, P.	236
Cowie, K. V.	406	Crawford, J. E. A. C. M.	256
Cowl, C. H. H.	241	Crawley, D. V.	168
†Cowley, A.	18, 336	Cray, H. F.	320
Cowley, J. N.	153, 194	Creak, W. A.	338
Cowley, R. H.	381	Crease, S. H.	275
Cowley, T. P.	382	Creasey, R. D.	310a
Cowlin, A. C.	168	Creed, T. P.	69, 280
Cowling, J. A.	159, 165	Creegan, E. W.	359
Cownie, I. T. W.	202	Creer, F. N.	406
Cownley, A. L.	291	Creese, S. H.	349
Cowper, A. L.	285	Cremetti, P. E.	148, 153, 162, 345
Cowper, C. F.	168	Cresswell-George, J. R.	218¶
†Cowper, L. H.	11, 333	Cribbett, W. C. G.	299
Cowper, R. H.	263	Crichton, A. C.	197
Cox, A. R. S.	229	Crick, T. H.	266
Cox, E. H. G.	191	Crick, W. E.	244
†Cox, F. D.	11	Crickmay, G. H.	363
Cox, G. Bernard	392	Crickmore, E. B.	168
†Cox, G. Beckett	19, 292	Crighton, J. S.	263
†Cox, G. P. L.	24	†Crisp, C. B.	19, 350
Cox, H. R. B.	261	†Crisp, F. E. F. J.	2, 217
Cox, Leonard J.	168	Crisp, G. W.	69, 305

† Killed in action or died. § See this name in *Addenda*.

Name	Pages	Name	Pages
†Croall, J. J.	21, 345	Cubitt, S. W.	395
†Crocker, J.	21, 379	Cuckney, E. J.	52, 163, 164
Crocker, J. F.	416	Cudd, W. A.	197
Crocker, W. C.	69, 237	Cuddon, P. B.	70, 253, 363
†Crockett, W. J.	38, 168	Cudworth, R.	240
†Croft, B.	41, 308	Cuff, A. S.	400
Croft, H. D.	330	Cuff, J.	292
†Croft-Smith, E. S.	3, 265	Cull, A. E. K.	197
Crofts, G. P. S.	318	Cullen, C. G.	356
†Croker, F. R.	15, 268	Cullen, J. M.	168
Crompton, A. A.	289	Cullen, P. H.	371¶
†Crompton, T. S.	6	Cullerne, A. B.	70, 275
Croneen, S.	69, 406	Culley, W. W. B.	153, 202
Cronin, W. F.	326	†Culling, H. W.	8, 379
Crook, D.	202	†Culling, V. J.	40
Crook, F. W.	265	Cullum, H. W.	275
†Crook, L. A.	21, 69, 361	Culpepper, B. A.	281
Crookes, N. R. D.	188	Culver, N. J.	265
†Crookston, W. J.	33, 346	Cumberhatch, H. C.	421
†Croom, W. C.	17, 297	Cumberledge, G. F. J.	47, 70, 150, 153, 246
Crosbie, W. G.	409	Cumming, B. D.	188
Crosfield, S.	427	Cumming, G. D.	416
†Crosier, V. S.	32, 292	Cumming, J.	168
Crosland, L.	70, 202	†Cummings, A. G.	24
†Crosland, W. P.	19, 394	Cummings, R. C. A.	397
Cross, A. V.	416	Cummings, S. R.	360
Cross, C. H.	391	†Cumner, C. W.	31, 289
Cross, J. G.	390	Cundall, H. A.	70, 352
Cross, J. R.	254	Cundy, C. W.	153, 336
Cross, L. B.	333	Cunningham, B. J.	341
Cross, L. W. A.	265	Cunningham, F. A. J.	341
Cross, R. J.	184	Cunningham, J. F.	296
Cross-Sheen, R.	322	Cunningham, J. J. I.	70, 298
†Crosse, M. E. B.	2, 390	Cunningham, L. C.	243
†Crouch, F. H.	30, 70, 268	Cunningham, P. J.	296
†Crouch, W. B.	14, 202	†Cunningham, V. E. B.	25
†Crow, A. A.	22, 273	†Curling, F. T.	37, 302
Crow, B. E.	202	Currall, R. T.	423
†Crowder, R. A.	24	Currall, W. J. R.	330
Crowdy, H. P.	289	Curran, C. R. P.	277
Crowdy, R. St. J.	380, 415	Curran, E. C.	404
Crowe, A. A. R.	250	†Currey, G. G.	4, 391
Crowe, F. M.	263	Currie, C.	318
Crowe, W. H.	400	Currie, C. H.	409
Crowther, C. C.	378	†Currie, J. A. V.	13, 297
Crowther, D	391	Cursley, N. S.	281
Crowther, J. E. M.	70, 359	Curties, T. S. P.	203
Crowther, F. H.	409	Curtis, B. E.	406
†Croxon, A. B.	39	Curtis, F.	71, 416
†Cruickshank, E.	38, 150, 187	Curtis, H.	312a
Cruickshank, H. W.	249	Curtis, H. J.	168
Crumpton, G. R.	360	†Curtis, H. N.	18, 168
Cruse, G. A.	244	Curtis, Harold T.	215
Cruttenden, R.	416	†Curtis, Henry T.	12, 306
Cruttenden, R. F.	191	Curtis, R. H.	255
Cryan, R.	210	Curtis, W.	355
†Cryer, H. I.	23, 168	Curtis, W. A.	182
Cubitt, C. N.	222	Curtis, W. H.	238
Cubitt, G. B.	356	Curtiss, W. J.	423

¶ See reference to this name in *Corrigenda*.

Name	Pages	Name	Pages
Curwen, J. P.	420	Darby, A. R.	394
Curwen, R.	261	Darby, E. H. W.	168
Cushing, E. C.	296	D'Arcy, N. C.	253
Cuthbertson, F. T.	226	D'Argenton, H.	265
Cutler, E. C.	71, 366	Dark, S. G.	256
Cutler, H.	149	Darley, C. F.	195
Cutler, W. H.	323	Darling, N.	333
Cutmore, H. E. V.	253	Darlington, H. L.	320
Cutting, C. G.	203	Darracott, J. S.	254
Cutting, R. H.	47, 71, 153, 234	†Darrell, A.	6, 357
Cuttle, E.	203	Davenport, C. R.	310a
†Cuttle, G.	2, 390	Davenport, H. S.	306
†Cuxson, B. P.	4, 343	Davenport, S. F.	203
		Davenport-Handley-Humphreys, J.	323
Dabell, N. V.	222	Davey, H. W.	363
Dadd, T. E.	263	Davey, G. L.	312a
Dade, H. D.	182	Davey, S.	240
Dade, J. F.	412	†Davidson, E. H. L.	37
Dadley, E. A.	281	Davidson, H. H.	197
Dadson, R. T.	148, 153, 301	Davidson, K. C.	71, 253
†Dadswell, J. A.	13	Davidson, T.	191
Dafforn, E. E.	168	Davidson, W. H.	230
Dainty, S.	287	Davidson, W. H. B.	292
Dakin, E. H.	362	Davies, A. C.	71, 242
Dalby, B. C.	379	Davies, A. W.	382
Dalby, F. B.	276	Davies, C. E.	220
Dale, A. F.	315	Davies, C. H.	339
Dale, F. A.	210	Davies, D. A.	220
Dale, F. J.	153, 253	Davies, D. B.	71, 220
†Dale, O. B.	20	†Davies, D. H.	41, 380
†Dale, R. J. N.	29, 315	Davies, D. K.	368
Dales, J. F.	197	Davies, E. B.	368
Dalpiaz, G.	168	Davies, Edward James	287
Dalton, J.	71, 222	Davies, Edward John	396
Dalton, T. F.	400	†Davies, Evan Jones	31, 220
Daly, A. J.	71, 153, 191¶	Davies, F. B.	196
Daly, O.	188	Davies, E. H.	72, 168
Daly, R. O.	197	†Davies, Geraint	33, 332
†Dalziel, T.	24	Davies, Gwylon	72, 332
D'Ambrumenil, W.	233	†Davies, G. E. C.	31
Dancer, L.	310a	Davies, G. V. F.	344
Dand, J. H.	149, 168	Davies, G. R.	182, 313
Danger, E. O	168	Davies, Harry	72, 373
Danger, H. G.	197	Davies, Henry	213
Dangerfield, R. J.	313a	Davies, H. C.	377
Dangerfield, P.	71, 150, 153, 260	†Davies, H. H.	25¶, 368
Daniel, A. F.	188	Davies, H. P.	376
†Daniel, A. M.	21, 262	Davies, H. R.	374
Daniel, F. C.	168	Davies, H. S.	255
Daniel, K. H.	262	Davies, H. T. W.	383
Daniel, W. L.	237	†Davies, J.	37
Daniell, C. H. P.	328	Davies, J. D. G.	169
Daniell, T. E. St. C.	71, 148, 163, 164¶	Davies, J. H. R.	333
Daniels, D. W. L.	379	Davies, J. L.	197
Daniels, H. A. W.	306	†Davies, J. R.	26, 305
†Dann, H. N. G.	20, 168	Davies, N. K.	418
†Dansey, F. R. A.	35, 292	Davies, R. L.	169
Danvers, C. H. D.	409	Davies, R. S.	169
		†Davies, R. W. M.	13, 332

† Killed in action or died. § See this name in *Addenda*.

DE LA COUR

This Index does not include the Alphabetical Sections IV. and V.(Other Ranks and Old Members). 519

Davies, T. ...	377	†Dawson, F. A. ... 36, 73, 360¶
Davies, T. H. ...	72, 216¶	Dawson, G. G. ... 191
Davies, T. J. M. ...	376	Dawson, G. J. C. ... 317
Davies, T. L. ...	188	Dawson, J. R. ... 396
Davies, T. T. ...	72, 377	Dawson, J. S. ... 236
Davies, V. K. N. ...	246	†Dawson, R. G. ... 38, 329
Davies, W. ...	376	Dawson, W. C. P. ... 194
Davies, W. Edgar ...	169	†Dawson, W. L. ... 27, 370
†Davies, W. Edward ...	6, 230	Dawson-Scott, C. E. ... 333
†Davies, W. L. ...	18, 374	Day, A. ... 356
Davies, W. T. ...	169	Day, A. P. ... 310a
D'Avigdor, G. H. ...	222	Day, E. F. ... 421
Davis, A. F. ...	208	Day, E. S. ... 406
†Davis, A. H. ...	2	Day, E. T. ... 301
Davis, B. O. ...	388	Day, E. V. G. ... 341
Davis, C. ...	423	Day, F. H. C. ... 203
Davis, C. H. ...	360	Day, G. H. J. ... 246, 313a
Davis, C. L. ...	323	Day, J. P. ... 73, 341
Davis, D. H. ...	150, 187¶	Day, J. W. ... 298
Davis, E. F. ...	400	†Day, M. ... 3, 224
Davis, E. M. ...	321	Day, M. I. R. ... 412
Davis, E. N. ...	356	Day, R. H. ... 197
Davis, F. ...	352	Day, T. G. ... 336
Davis, George ...	312	†Day, W. L. ... 13, 226
Davis, Gerald ...	366	Day-Lewis, A. K. ... 395
Davis, H. ...	312a	Dayton, W. R. ... 321
Davis, J. M. ...	242	Deacon, E. T. ... 153, 367
†Davis, J. O. ...	24	Deacon, R. S. ... 242
Davis, James W. ...	409	†Dean, A. H. ... 28
Davis, Joel W. ...	412	Dean, D. J. ... 45, 264
†Davis, M. A. D. ...	34¶, 72, 266	Dean, H. S. C. ... 153, 400
†Davis, P. H. H. ...	41, 315	†Dean, L. S. ... 28
†Davis, P. W. T. ...	13, 260	†Dean, R. E. ... 17, 297
Davis, R. ...	72, 337	Dean, W. T. ... 153, 242
Davis, R. A. ...	383	†Deane, A. R. ... 26, 365
Davis, R. H. ...	169	Dear, G. J. ... 333
Davis, R. H. L. ...	388	Dear, T. ... 356
Davis, R. K. ...	169	Dearden, J. R. B. ... 345
Davis, R. N. ...	72, 280	Dearlove, B. J. ... 169
†Davis, S. J. G. ...	28	Deaton, A. J. ... 73, 249
Davis, T. H. C. ...	73, 191	Debono, G. P. ... 73, 225
†Davis, U. P. ...	14, 297	De Buriatte, H, ... 222
Davison, H. W. ...	263	†De Buriatte, J. P. ... 2, 357
Davison, J. A. ...	383	†De Buriatte, W. H. ... 40, 201
Davison, P. M. ...	421	De Chazal, E. M. ... 409
Davison, T. ...	240	†Dedman, W. A. ... 29, 394
Davy, E. H. ...	406	Dee, J. ... 244
Davy, L. B. ...	194	†Deedes, H. P. ... 8, 265
Daw, E. E. W. ...	251	Deedes, R. ... 153, 349
Dawbarn, A. L. ...	406	Deer, J. H. ... 73, 246, 266
Dawe, E. M. ...	233	Deffee, C. F. ... 353
†Dawe, S. C. ...	29, 73, 283	De Fontenay, P. A. C. ... 169
Dawe, W. W. F. ...	244	De Fores, J. W. ... 410
†Dawes, H. H. ...	24	De Gersigny, N. ... 169
Dawkins, C. C. ...	328	De Gex, R. G. ... 410
Dawkins, J. R. ...	185	†Dehn, T. G. R. ... 14, 380
†Daws, A. ...	24	Deighton, R. H. ... 315
†Daws, H. ...	12, 240	De La Bere, S. B. ... 197
Dawson, A. D. ...	209	De La Cour, H. H. H. ... 186

¶ See reference to this name in *Corrigenda*.

De La Coze, F. M. H.	306
Delafield, F. H.	153, 278
†De Landre-Grogan, L. V. St. P.	40, 73, 287
De Laporte, A.	210
De Lemos, C.	382
Dell, C. J.	323
Dell, R. V. J.	400
Delmege, H. B. E.	185
Deltiel, E. L. R.	182
De Mattos, G. W.	203
Dempster, A. E.	358
Dempster, E. N.	358
Dench, B.	236
Denchar, V. H.	197
Denholm, W. H.	240
Denis-Browne, A. G.	399
Dennett, G. A.	366
Denney, O. L.	406
Dennis, A. S.	203
Dennis, B. W.	341
Dennis, L. V.	169
Dennison, C. H.	191
†Denny, E.	19, 300
Denny, R. L.	182
Denny, S. E.	243
†Dennys, K. R.	3, 326
Dent, H. B.	300
†Dent, R. T.	31, 341
Denton, L. A.	248
Depass, R. D.	153, 321
De Pinna, C. D.	290
De Pury, C. F. P.	162, 290
Derbyshire, F. C.	419
†De Rougemont, M. H.	3, 361
Derry, C.	233
Derry, C. J.	416
Derry, E. G.	412
De St. Croix, L. L.	149, 153, 229, 406
De St. Croix, P. E.	410
De St. Felix, P.	169
De Segundo, C. S.	308
†Deslandes, D. G.	11, 359
Deverall, E. P.	423
Devereux, R. H. F.	73, 341
Devereux, T.	203
Devereux, W.	246
Devonshire Regt.	*234*
Dew, A. H. E.	313a
Dew, E. A.	144, 169
Dew, P. R.	197
Dew, W. B.	314
Dewar, D.	410
Dewar, J. G. B.	424
†Dewes, B. O.	4, 319
†Dewey, F. C.	28
Dewey, L.	213
Dewson, L. J.	299
Diamond, A. G. H.	335
Diamond, I. J. A.	210
Diamond, W. E. de B.	169
Dibben, C. R.	148, 281
†Dick, G. F. G.	3, 335
Dick, G. R. A.	182
†Dickens, A. J. E.	7
Dickens, E. C.	169
Dickens, F.	330
†Dickinson, C. J. H.	8, 230
†Dickinson, G. S.	8, 283
†Dickinson, H.	23, 312a
†Dickinson, H. W.	36, 332
†Dickinson, L. St. C.	9, 289
Dickinson, S.	188
†Dickinson, W. S.	15, 284
Dickman, H. A.	73, 210
Dicks, H. V.	163
Dicksee, H. J. H.	169, 313
Dicks, A. J.	356
†Dickson, G. H. M.	40, 257
†Dickson, J.	19
Dickson, L. T.	182
Dickson, R. G.	410
Didcott, F. E.	169
Diemer, P. H.	369
Digby, F. N. D. D.	229
Digby, L.	237
Dillon, D. T.	389
Dillon, T. J.	203
Dimmock, E. L.	352
Dimmock, N. H.	147, 169
Dingle, W. W.	169
Dinham, G. A.	201
Dinsdale, C. A. M.	223
Diplock, R. M.	260
Disley, H. R.	230
D.C.M.	*149*
D.F.C.	*144*
D.S.C.	*52*
D.S.O.	*46*
Ditcham, V. A.	403
D'Ivernois, V. H. B.	366
†Dix, C. B.	19, 360
Dix, J. A.	188
Dix, J. W.	163
Dixie, W. L.	416
Dixon, A.	396
Dixon, A. C.	73, 424
†Dixon, C. A.	24
Dixon, D'A. B.	360
Dixon, G. L.	266
Dixon, J. G.	221
Dixon, S. F.	261
Dixon, W. E.	406
Dixon, Wm. Scarth	203
†Dixon, Wm. Swanston	33, 283
Dobb, B. F.	197
Dobb, W. C. N. F.	197
Dobson, F. O.	227
†Dobson, N. G.	42, 227

† Killed in action or died.   § See this name in *Addenda*.

This Index does not include the Alphabetical Sections IV. and V. (Other Ranks and Old Members).

Name	Pages	Name	Pages
Dobson, R.	400	Dowson, R. A.	416
†Dodd, A.	40, 169	Dowson, S. H.	74, 369
†Dodd, E. J.	18, 187	Dowson, S. T.	380
Dodd, H. E.	242	Doyle, A. G.	74, 215
Dodd, K. H.	374	Doyle, W. F.	268
Dodd, T. C.	331	*Dragoons*	*184*
Dodd, W.	377	Drake, D. B.	382
†Dodds, H. A.	7, 385	Drake, S. E.	186
Dodds, W. F.	364	Drakeford, H.	74, 285
Doe, C. V.	292	†Draper, M. D.	12, 169
Doherty, F.	248	Drapes, G. R.	337
Doherty, J. W.	423	Drew, W.	400
†Doherty, P.	19, 259	Drewry, A. S.	159
Dolbear, A.	210	Drey, R. F.	318
Doll, P. J.	313	Dreyfus, T. H.	194
†D'Ombrain, R. M.	6, 261	Driskell, J. A.	406
†Donaghy, R. A.	34, 197	Driver, E. T.	153, 169
Donald, T. H.	197	Driver, H. O.	312
Donaldson, A. J.	74, 263	Driver-Holloway, T. H.	203
†Donaldson, W.	17, 344	Drower, E. G.	398
Donaldson-Selby, T. T. G.	209	Druce, C. J.	251
Done, J. P. C.	153, 216	†Drummond, J. R.	38, 169
Done, R.	169	Dryland, L. G.	211
Donkin, C. D. G.	364	Drysdale, A. M.	188
Donne, A. C.	418	Drysdale, M. W.	334
Donne-Smith, L.	362	*Dublin Fusiliers, Royal*	*238*
Donovan, T. N.	224	Duce, W.	303
Doody, F. S.	231	Duckworth, J. E. H.	74, 153, 382
Doran, T. A.	315	†Duckworth, W. C.	40, 377
Dorman, R. B.	381	Dudbridge, M.	169
Dorn, J. S. G.	395	†Duddy, G. L. A.	32, 356
Dorrington, S. F.	74, 330	Duddy, J. F. E.	323
Dorsetshire Regt.	*237*	Dudley, A. T.	75, 391
Dottridge, H. R.	290	†Dudley, H. E.	20, 153, 350
Douche, W. H.	416	†Dudley, N. M. C.	11, 286
Doughty, J.	233	Duff, F. M.	344
Douglas, A. H.	313, 416	Duff, Gordon	150, 197
Douglas, F.	252	†Duff, J. C.	4, 252
Douglas, G. F.	74, 209	Duff, K. M.	252
Douglas, R. M.	276	Duffy, F.	169
Douglas, W. S.	398	Duffy, W. A.	320
Dove, H. V. B.	391	Duggan, L. B.	169
†Dove, S. E.	9, 263	Du Heaume, F. H.	153¶, 300
Dove, W. W.	223	*D.C.L.I.*	*232*
Dovey, A. G.	406	Duke, W. A.	416
Dowden, H. J.	74, 191	†Dulin, W. W. M.	35, 169
Dowdeswell, F.	209	Dulley, H. A.	400
Dowell, A. E.	318	Dun, A. L.	203¶
Dowler, E. H.	220	Dunand, A. M.	339
Down, H. H.	147, 169	Dunbar, Sir A. E. Bart.	75, 153, 395
Downer, F.	315	Duncan, A.	315
Downer, R. St. Q.	418	Duncan, C. P. H.	325
Downes, A.	353	†Duncan, J. A. G.	29, 169
Downey, F. N.	400	†Duncan, P. C.	23, 295
Downey, T. P.	197	Duncan, W. G.	149
Downie, G. A.	403	Dunell, A. G.	149, 153, 404
Downton, L. A.	406	Dunford, C. W.	169
†Dowsett, H. G.	35, 169	Dunkerton, E. L. H.	75, 385
Dowsing, S. H.	153, 400	Dunlop, G. A.	346

¶ See reference to this name in *Corrigenda*.

Name	Page(s)	Name	Page(s)
Dunmore, C. W.	323	East Surrey Regt.	*357*
Dunn, D. W.	364	East, W.	244
†Dunn, E. G.	17, 285	East Yorkshire Regt.	*392*
†Dunn, H. A.	18	Eastaugh, C. J.	182, 313a
Dunn, H. B.	37, 236	Eastcott, J. N.	169
Dunn, J. H.	233	†Easterbrook, H. G.	33, 296
Dunn, W. H.	286	Eastman, A. G.	208
Dunn, W. M.	239	Easton, P.	295
Dunnage, G. E.	215	Eastwood, R. G.	416
Dunston, G. H.	188	Eaton, G. E.	197
Dunt, L. A.	245	†Eaton, H.	18, 251
Dunwoody, J. O.	254	Eaton, J. E. C.	163, 423
Dupas, F. M.	406	Eatough, J. O.	270
Duplock, F. W. M.	386	Ebbles, J. K.	227
Dupont, A. N.	147, 169, 280	Ebdon, R. A.	197
Durham L.I.	*239*	Eddison, H.	364
Durand, E. D.	153, 398	Ede, C. W.	419
Durkin, F. V.	382	†Ede, E. W.	37, 75, 246
Durlacher, N. G.	242	Eden, W. G.	379
Durrant, J. R. G.	251	†Edey, W. J.	29, 242
Durrant, N.	406	†Edgar, B. R.	18, 416
Durrant, R. T.	75, 195	†Edge, E. H.	30, 295
†Durston, C. G.	10, 298	Edge, J. D.	169
Duruty, C. E.	75, 371	Edge, P. G.	148, 309
Duthie, D. J.	75, 370	†Edghill, A. G.	33, 76, 268
Dutt-Ross, F.	387	†Edinger, V.	36, 371
Dutton, A. B.	421	Edinow, S.	169
Dutton, C. E.	328	Edis, Sir R. W.	148, 307
Dutton, V. J.	271	Edlmann, E.	153, 283
Dutton, W. J.	75, 250	Edlmann, F. J. F.	47, 153, 332
Duval, C. A.	356	Edlmann, H. E.	154, 307
†Duxbury, A. M.	32, 75, 339	Edminson, H. C.	231
Duxfield, G. C.	427	Edminson, L. O.	76, 317
Dyall, A.	153, 412	Edmond, A. D.	203
Dyball, J. F.	404	†Edmonds, E. P. P.	39, 169
Dye, J. E.	340	Edmonds, W. B.	164, 350
Dyer, A. E.	197	Edmonds, W. H.	416
Dyer, F. E.	245	Edmunds, J.	76, 303
Dyer, W. S.	191	†Edwards, A. Edward	37, 373
†Dyke, C. J.	25, 306	Edwards, A. Ernest	393
Dykes, O.	75, 192	Edwards, C.	404
Dyne, F. L. P.	246	Edwards, Cecil G.	275
Dyne, H. E. L.	362	Edwards, Cyril George	47, 154, 395
Dyott, H. F.	412	Edwards, C. H.	416
Dysart, G. A. H.	362	Edwards, E. D.	268
Dyson, D. H.	410	Edwards, F. S.	203
†Dyson, G.	28¶	Edwards, George Cyril	159, 309
		Edwards, G. H.	287
Eagar, W. Mc. G.	192	†Edwards, G. O.	21, 76, 334
Eales, C.	255	Edwards, Harold	154, 236
†Eames, A. H.	8, 390, 392	†Edwards, Harry	24
Eames, F.	312	Edwards, H. C.	394
Earee, R. C. W.	292	Edwards, H. F.	405
Earl, C. C.	377	Edwards, H. P.	307
Earnshaw, P. H.	188	Edwards, H. T.	197
Earp, G. N.	203	Edwards, J. P.	169
Eason, W. S.	169	Edwards, R. O.	148, 150, 154, 265, 397
East Kent Regt.	*260*	†Edwards, W.	31, 404
East Lancashire Regt.	*271*	Edwards, W. B.	374

† Killed in action or died.   § See this name in *Addenda*.

This Index does not include the Alphabetical Sections IV. and V. (Other Ranks and Old Members).

Name	Pages	Name	Pages
Edwards, W. H.	76, 154, 374	Ellis, J.	77, 393
Edwards, W. T.	373	Ellis, J. E.	339
†Edwards-Trollip, J.	37, 292	Ellis, P. D.	400
Eeles, G. N.	266	Ellis, R.	77, 154, 397
Egerton, B. S.	154, 188, 404	Ellis, R. D.	77, 239
Egerton, F. C. C.	251	†Ellis, S. D.	6, 77, 209
†Egerton, J. H.	24	Ellis, T. M.	211
Egerton, R. H.	314	Ellison, A. M.	339
Eglington, D. C.	76, 257	Ellison, H.	317
Eilbeck, W. A.	270	Ells, F. C.	358
Eiloart, F. R.	76, 203	Elms, E. C.	386
†Elborough, A. C. E.	4, 365, 388	Elms, W. G.	387
Elder, A. A.	154, 348	Elmslie, N.	309
Elder, I. N.	228	Elphick, E. R.	337
†Eley, R. C.	31, 303	Elphick, H. G. T.	312
Elford, P. W. T.	231	Elphick, R.	238
†Elias, H. J.	17, 334	†Elsom, H.	15, 284
Elkington, C. G.	47, 154, 251	Elston, J.	387
Elkington, G. L.	153, 211	†Eltham, C. W.	11, 361
Elkington, G. W.	235, 354	Eltham, G.	371
Elkington, H. G.	76, 303	Eltoft, W. C.	275
Elkington, R. L.	395	Elton, C. B.	184
†Elkington, W. H.	30, 255	Elton, H. S.	77, 154, 289
Elkins, A. J.	311	†Elvin, A. G.	23, 355
Ellam, H. J.	338	Elvy, L. T.	77, 299
Ellams, G. E.	270	Elwell, B. L.	345
†Ellen, E. A.	12, 271	Elworthy, S. G.	251
Ellen, R. B.	386	Emberson, W. S.	244
Ellen, W. P.	76, 154, 366	Emerson, G. C.	369
Ellerby, H. F. St. G.	405	Emery, M. F.	332
Ellerker, W. T.	197	†Emery, W. H. V.	40, 272
Ellery, H. W. O.	203	Emlyn, O. A.	374
Ellett, H. P.	310a	Emmerson, E. N.	332
Ellingston, J. R.	416	Emmett, J. H.	396
†Elliot, N.	18, 329	†Emslie, P.	36, 149, 150
Elliott, A. E. T.	76, 312	Engelbach, R.	216
Elliott, A. G.	77, 217	*Engineers, Royal*	209
Elliott, E. E.	77, 363	England, H. F.	255
Elliott, F. T.	203	†English, A. C.	28, 149, 310a
Elliott, F. W.	323	English, F.	356
Elliott, H. E. D.	242	English, F. G.	231
Elliott, H. F.	162	Enguell, G. J.	169
†Elliott, H. J.	41	†Ennis, R. J.	19, 259
Elliott, H. P.	236	Ennor, F. H.	217
†Elliott, P. M.	7, 319	Epps, R. S. G.	306
Elliott, R. D.	349	Esam, E. S.	336
Elliott, W. C.	250	Esch, R. E.	287
Ellis, A. D.	310a	Eskdale, J. A.	334
Ellis, A. E.	169	Esmond, Jack J.	424
Ellis, A. G.	182	Essex, A. C.	251
Ellis, C. V.	159, 306	†Essex, P. C.	9, 269
Ellis, F. G.	337	*Essex Regt.*	*241*
Ellis, F. H.	278	†Essex, R. A. Y.	25
Ellis, F. P.	231	Etheridge, A. H.	301
†Ellis, F. W.	29, 299	Etheridge, D. H.	169
†Ellis, G. S.	18, 169	Evans, B. S.	77, 149, 362
Ellis, H.	192	Evans, C.	374
Ellis, H. C.	149, 406	Evans, C. F.	352
Ellis, H. F.	250	Evans, D. M.	377

¶ See reference to this name in *Corrigenda*.

EVANS

INDEX TO COMMISSIONS, HONOURS, and ROLL OF HONOUR.

Evans, D. T. ... 368
Evans, D. W. ... 77, 297
†Evans, F. B. ... 29, 169
Evans, F. T. ... 325
Evans, G. E. T. H. ... 246
†Evans, H. E. ... 31, 77, 390
Evans, H. K. ... 312a
†Evans, Hugh Robert ... 38, 377
Evans, Hugh Richmond ... 374
Evans, H. R. G. ... 323
Evans, H. W. C. ... 416
†Evans, Jenkin E. ... 38, 235
†Evans, John E. ... 36, 377¶
†Evans, P. L. ... 42, 169
Evans, R. B. ... 243
Evans, R. D. ... 265
Evans, Richard, R. ... 169
Evans, Robert R. ... 373
Evans, T. C. W. M. ... 197
Evans, T. E. ... 78, 374
Evans, T. H. ... 355
Evans, T. K. ... 78, 334
Evans, T. P. ... 416
Evans, T. W. ... 188
Evans, U. R. ... 358
Evans, V. H. ... 374
Evans, W. ... 218
Evans, W. E. ... 203
Evans, W. H. ... 373
Eve, R. M. ... 333
Eve, V. L. ... 312
Evelyn, A. F. ... 290
Evenett, P. M. ... 244
Everatt, E. ... 169¶
†Everett, S. ... 24
Evers, J. Mc E. S. ... 228
†Evershed, P. D. ... 36, 292
Evetts, R. C. T. ... 197
Evison, F. C. ... 283
Ewbank, C. H. P. ... 170
Ewels, C. ... 370
Ewen, A. J. C. ... 383
†Ewen, H. S. ... 32, 78, 305
Ewing, J. H. ... 269
Exley, F. H. ... 236
Eyles, W. G. ... 412
Eyre, A. B. B. ... 356
Eyre, F. T. ... 287

Faber, E. G. ... 274
Fabling, H. W. ... 154, 214
Facey, R. V. ... 170
Facey, W. E. ... 389
Fagan, H. A. ... 78¶, 390§
Fahy, C. P. J. ... 192
Fahy, D. F. ... 188
Fair, J. ... 239
Fairbairn, A. R. ... 144, 170
†Fairbairn, G. E. ... 4, 240

Fairbairn, G. H. ... 78, 341
†Fairbairn, M. ... 18, 279
Fairbairn, W. F. ... 78, 385
Fairbairns, C. P. ... 403
†Fairbairns, I. M. ... 20, 192
Fairbairns, R. H. ... 78, 405, 416
Fairchild, J. B. W. ... 154, 203
Fairclough, D. F. C. ... 334
Fairholme, H. W. ... 154, 398
Fairhurst, W. E. ... 159, 243
Fairney, L. ... 292
†Fairtlough, G. H. ...35, 78, 154, 214, 308
Fairtlough, L. W. ... 361
Fairweather, H. F. ... 412
Faith, A. ... 400
†Falby, E. F. ... 9, 274
Falck, L. L. ... 150, 170, 321
Falk, C. J. ... 79, 380
Falkner, W. B. ... 383
Falkner-Lee, F. ... 381
Fallon, J. R. ... 342
Fallow, H. F. ... 276
†Fanshawe, H. V. ... 22, 220
Faraday, L. B. ... 315
†Faraday, R. ... 17, 291, 416
Farey, P. N. M. ... 265
Farmborough, J. C. ... 214
Farmer, A. E. ... 225
Farmer, A. V. ... 356
Farmer, C. A. ... 278
Farmer, G. J. ... 300
Farmer, H. E. ... 163, 372
Farmilce, K. M. ... 341
Farmiloe, T. H. ... 296
Farnan, A. W. ... 266
Farnes, H. E. ... 241
Farnes, T. N. ... 339
Farnham, J. A. G. ... 406
Farnsworth, S. R. ... 277
Farquharson, A. G. ... 345
†Farquharson, H. J. ... 9, 327
†Farr, F. J. ... 24
†Farran, C. ... 9, 265
Farrant, V. T. ... 154, 276
Farrar, F. J. ... 243
Farrel, R. H. ... 229
Farrell, K. G. ... 170
Farrier, A. V. ... 159, 170, 233
Farrimond, W. ... 79, 154, 371
Farrington, F. V. ... 312
Farrington, R. L. ... 318
Farrington, W. B. ... 47, 150, 153, 335
Farrow, A. ... 271
Farrow, G. H. ... 313a, 416
Farrow, J. W. ... 159, 400
Farrow, R. J. R. ... 230
Farthing, A. ... 170
†Fattorini, T. ... 36, 170
Faucett, L. W. ... 170

† Killed in action or died.   § See this name in *Addenda*.

This Index does not include the Alphabetical Sections IV. and V. (Other Ranks and Old Members).

Name	Pages	Name	Pages
Faulkner, H. E.	306	Ficklin, A. H.	313
Faulkner, H. F.	170	Fiddaman, W. A. M.	387
Faulkner, J. B.	323	Field, A. J.	347
Faulkner, R.	272	Field, E.	154, 416§
†Faunch, E. A.	16, 203	Field, H. C. P.	393
Favell, W. R. A.	209	Field, H. F.	364
Fawcett, E. H.	340	Field, John	406
Fawcett, R. M.	406	Field, Joseph	211
†Fawcett, W.	30, 339	†Field, R. H.	35
Fawkes, F. H.	154, 197	Field, R. T.	306
†Fazan, R.	3, 365	Field, S.	170
†Fear, R. S.	29, 170	Field, V. M.	182
Fearn, C. A.	79, 388	Fielden, L.	196
†Fearn, H.	22, 360	Fielding, E. F.	350
Fearne, S.	316	Fielding, W. H.	148, 154, 215
Featherstone, H.	406	Figg, S. V.	79, 154, 369
Featherstone, J. E.	396	Fildes, G. P.	218, 296
Fehr, F. C.	388	†Filmer, V. R. R.	26, 185
Fehrman, A. A. F.	405	Filsell, G. V. P.	376
Feilden, G. St. Clair	393	Finch, A. W. B.	365
Felkin, S. D.	148, 150, 164	Finch, E. L. W. J.	183
Fell, A. L.	395	Findlay, J. W.	265
Fell, E.	337	Findlay, L. H.	244
†Fell, K. G.	39	Findlay, R. M.	427
†Fellowes, C. W.	30, 352	Findon, R. H.	383
Fellows, F. B.	150, 154, 304	Finke, R. F. G. B.	170
Fellows, L. D.	313	Finlay, G. L. K.	312a
Fells, S. F. J.	170	Finn, W.	243
†Feltham, A.	10, 227	†Finnemore, H. J.	31, 366
Felton, A. R.	170	Finnigan, E. A.	344
Felton, C. T.	170	Finnigan, F.	258
†Fennell, L. A. R.	14	Finnis, H. J.	395
†Fenner, A. T.	27, 352	Finnis, W. T.	154, 365, 406
Fenner, P. G.	24	Finn-Kelsey, W. J.	405
†Fenning, R. W.	215	†Firth, E.	34
Fenning, W. G.	203	Firth, F. G.	398
†Fenn-Smith, W. K.	28, 170	†Fischer, A. W.	7, 154¶, 234
Fenton, D.	197	†Fish, B. E.	9, 366
Fenton-Jones, D. W.	400	†Fish, B. L.	41, 323
Fentum, C. G.	333	Fisher, C. H.	40, 143, 358
Fenwick, B. A.	359	†Fisher, E. H.	4, 390
Fenwick, C. J.	320	Fisher, G. R. S.	247
Fenwick, H. E.	334	Fisher, H. C.	79, 154¶, 322
Ferguson, A. C. W.	275	Fisher, J. J.	410
†Ferguson, B. V.	29	Fisher, T. W.	383
†Ferguson, D. C.	12, 256	Fisher, W. E.	79, 405
Ferguson, D. G.	79, 154¶, 260	†Fisk, H. H.	24
Ferguson, J. C.	170	Fisk, W. E.	154, 276
Ferguson, J. S.	79, 347	Fitch, C. A.	217
Ferguson, M. G.	203	Fitch, I. F.	264
Ferguson, R. M. J.	292	Fitch, S. A.	379
Ferguson, T.	203	Fitz-Gibbon, F. C.	360
Ferguson, W. A.	344	Fitzgerald, C. T.	403
Fern, P.	424	Fitzgerald, G.	385
Ferraby, D.	392	Fitzgerald, K. G.	398
Ferraby, F.	400	Fitzgerald, R. E.	398
†Ferris, H. N.	22, 250	Fitzpatrick, J. T.	286
Fewkes, L.	170	†Fitzsimmons, C. H.	19
Ffoulkes-Jones, E. J.	170	Fixter, T.	302

¶ See reference to this name in *Corrigenda*.

FLANDERS

INDEX TO COMMISSIONS, HONOURS, and ROLL OF HONOUR.

Flanders, F. G. P. ... 423	Forrester, J. ... 154, 218
Flawn, N. G. ... 203	Forshaw, R. ... 424
Fleeming, W. H. ... 339	Forster, J. M. ... 197
†Fleet, W. A. ... 34, 217	Forster, H. ... 192
Fleming, A. D. ... 262	Forster-Knight, G. ... 197
Fleming, C. B. R. ... 412	Forsyth, J. ... 370
Fleming, D. M. ... 183	†Forsyth, J. C. ... 20, 381
Fleming, H. S. ... 79, 332	Forsyth, J. D. ... 333
†Fleming, J. A. ... 8, 262	Forsyth, T. T. ... 334
Fleming, J. S. ... 263	Fortune, G. E. ... 150, 396
Fleming, L. P. ... 255	†Fortune, S. W. ... 6, 341
Fleming, R. B. ... 251	Foskett, A. S. ... 313, 319
Fleming, S. H. ... 250	Foskett, H. H. ... 154, 314, 416
Fleming, S. W. ... 228	Foskett, N. ... 416
Fleming-Sandes, A. J. T. ... 44, 357	Foskett, R. F. J. ... 249
†Fletcher, C. B. ... 41	Foss, W. ... 188
Fletcher, C. H. ... 188	Foster, A. ... 334
Fletcher, H. ... 287	Foster, A. E. ... 376
Fletcher, M. R. ... 330	Foster, E. C. ... 311
Fletcher, P. ... 335	Foster, E. H. ... 301
Fletcher, R. B. ... 313, 416	†Foster, F. H. ... 17, 170
Fletcher, R. C. ... 313, 405	†Foster, F. J. ... 20, 170
Flight, B. P. ... 255	Foster, F. M. ... 223
†Flinders, J. J. ... 24	Foster, H. O. ... 215
Flinn, C. H. ... 183	Foster, R. F. ... 271
Flinn, H. E. ... 232	Foster, S. I. ... 183
Flint, A. W. ... 360	Foster, T. S. ... 400
†Flint, C. W. ... 8, 332	Foster, W. A. ... 316
Flint, G. H. ... 321	†Foulger, M. ... 4, 348
Flint, H. ... 79, 154	Foulkes, E. ... 80, 277
Flint, R. P. ... 318	Foulkes-Jones, G. G. ... 374
†Flower, A. C. ... 10, 217	Foulsham, C. S. ... 356
Flux, H. J. ... 203	Foulsham, E. C. ... 354
Flying Corps, Royal ... *164*	Foulsham, F. C. ... 203
Flynn, E. H. ... 239	Foulsham, R. ... 356
Foale, W. E. ... 197	Fountaine, A. C. ... 374
†Foard, B. H. ... 25	Fowden, B. L. ... 231
Fold, E. S. ... 339	Fowle, A. C. ... 342
Folkard, H. F. ... 412	Fowle, H. A. ... 371
Folkes, P. L. ... 247	†Fowler, F. A. ... 18, 203
Foord, B. A. ... 79, 292	Fox, A. W. ... 301
†Foot, D. V. ... 16, 170	Fox, D. ... 400
Foot Guards ... *217*	Fox, D. C. ... 331
†Forbes, A. ... 9, 154, 369	Fox, E. ... 149
†Forbes, A. S. ... 9, 347	Fox, E. C. ... 250
†Forbes, D. ... 31, 344	Fox, G. L. ... 321
Forbes, G. F. M. ... 80, 248	Fox, H. G. ... 260, 369
†Forbes, L. ... 18, 291, 321	Fox, Joseph ... 278
†Ford, C. W. ... 19, 278	Fox, John ... 389
Ford, E. V. ... 364	Fox, J. H. G. ... 203
Ford, F. B. ... 266	Foxon, S. W. ... 278
Ford, H. F. P. ... 260	Fradgley, A. D. ... 423
Ford, L. B. ... 150, 163¶, 309	†Frampton, J. R. ... 18, 251
Ford, L. C. ... 214	France, B. E. ... 203
†Ford, R. D. ... 2, 154, 259	Francis, C. W. ... 163
Ford, T. F. ... 416	Francis, E. L. ... 400
†Forde, J. H. ... 24	Francis, I. ... 154, 197
Foreign Orders, etc. ... *150*	†Francis, W. G. ... 29, 170
Forrer, L. ... 371	†Francis, W. J. ... 30, 247

† Killed in action or died.   § See this name in *Addenda*.

This Index does not include the Alphabetical Sections IV. and V. (Other Ranks and Old Members).

Name	Page	Name	Page
Francis-Hawkins, F. H. M.	... 170	Frost, A. St. J.	154, 366
Franghaidi, G. P.	... 314	Frost, E. A.	... 247
Frank, C. F.	144, 170	Frost, F. A.	... 290
Frank, H. E.	... 370	†Frost, K.	...2, 262
†Frankenstein, O. R.	13, 377	Frost, N. P. A.	... 286
Frankish, W. M.	... 309	Frost, W.	... 203
Frankland, C. H.	... 197	Frost, W. E.	... 371
Frankland, T. L.	... 362	Frost, W. F.	... 197
Franklin, A. T.	... 224	†Froud, H. W.	18, 239
Franklin, C.	... 211	Froy, W. A.	... 290
Franklin, H.	... 312a	Fry, A. J.	... 421
Franklin, K.	... 211	Fry, D. C.	... 277
Franklin, L.	80, 388	Fry, G. C. L.	... 162
Franklin-Adams, B. I.	310a, 154¶, 211	Fryer, R. E.	... 209
Franks, D. A.	... 370	Fryer, S. E.	149, 163
Fransham, W. H. E.	... 297	Fryer, T. J. H.	80, 266
Fraser, A.	80, 257	Fulbeck, C. E.	... 203
†Fraser, A. C.	37, 80, 292	Fulcher, W. J.	... 412
†Fraser, C. D.	30, 290	†Fullagar, C. E.	... 32
Fraser, C. G.	170, 280	†Fuller, E. P.	21, 362
Fraser, C. T.	... 326	Fuller, G. J. F. F.	... 306
Fraser, D.	... 412	Fuller, H. N.	... 410
Fraser, D. W.	... 410	Fuller, R. U.	... 170
Fraser, E. A.	154, 286	Fuller, T.	... 264
†Fraser, E. L.	26, 416	Funnell, T. H.	... 356
Fraser, G. T.	154, 416	Furmston, C. W.	... 377
Fraser, I. M.	... 292	Furrell, B.	... 291
Fraser, J. W.	... 412	Furze, C.	... 311a
Fraser, K.	... 300	Furze, C. G.	... 398
Fraser, R. D.	... 301	Furze, G.	80, 163, 218, 311
Fraser, W. A.	... 394	Fusiliers, Royal	... 245
Frater, A. H.	...154, 170, 232		
Fray, H.	... 410	Gabbott, E. P.	... 203
Frazier, F. W.	... 282	Gadd, C. A.	... 281
†Freaker, A. L.	... 24	Gadd, L. C.	... 362
Frecker, A. C.	... 323	Gage, T. W.	... 242
Free, S. C. H.	... 233	Gahan, J.	... 403
Freeman, C. J. A.	... 272	Gains, A. T.	... 264
Freeman, F. J. C.	... 356	Gale, G. A.	... 381
Freeman, G. H.	154, 197	Gale, H. F.	... 387
Freeman, P.	... 203	Gale-Hasleham, D. A.	... 170
Freeman, W. A.	... 412	Gall, W. S.	... 195
Freeth, C. E.	... 230	Gallagher, C. F.	... 315
Freeth, H. F.	... 338	Gallagher, J.	... 197
French, A. C.	... 255	Gallard, W. J. H.	... 170
French, D. H.	... 321	Gallichan, H. N.	... 224
French, R. H.	... 170	Gallienne, J. W. H.	... 368
French, S.	... 303	Gallop, A. J.	... 183
French, W. H.	... 192	Gallop, H. H.	... 250
Frew, J. G. H.	... 170	Gallop, P. C.	... 150
†Fricker, E.	10, 264	Galloway, L. D.	... 197
Friend, C. P.	80, 380	Galloway, V.	... 393
†Friend, F. H.	...5, 380	Gamble, D. B.	... 310a
Friend, R. A.	... 421	Gamble, P. A.	... 332
Fright, H. W.	80, 274	Gammon, A. K.	... 254
Frisby, E. C.	... 170	Gammon, K.	... 197
Frisley, H. R.	... 405	Gandy, F.	... 356
Frith, R. W.	... 223	Gane, A.	... 170
†Frost, A.	23, 309, 415	Gantlett, R. A. R.	... 383

¶ See reference to this name in *Corrigenda*.

Name	Pages	Name	Pages
†Garbutt, J. H.	41	Gedney, C. F. W.	400
Garbutt, J. R.	81, 264	Gedye, A. J.	251
Garden, J. A.	256	Gee, A. S.	318
Garden, J. B.	298	Gelsthorpe, A. M.	47, 154, 239, 415
Garden, W. E.	183	Gemmel, J. A. B. S.	159, 273
Gardiner, H. M.	170	General List	409
Gardiner, J. H.	273, 279	†Gent, G. E.	20, 192
Gardiner, P. E.	251	†George, A. L.	33, 371
Gardner, E. M.	312	George, E. B.	403
Gardner, G. H.	243, 419	George, J. R. C.	218
Gardner, H.	81, 154, 203	George, W. H.	81, 154, 162, 222
Gardner, H. E.	331	German, A. G.	286
Gardner, J. W.	312	†Gerhardi, C.	42, 427§
Gardner, O. J.	163	Gerhardi, T. E.	149
Gardner, R. D. C.	302	†Gerrard, F. W.	24
†Gardner, R. P.	16	Gerson, J. L.	412
Gardner, W. O.	293	†Gethin, P. F.	7, 235
†Gare, J. H.	28	Gething, S.	24
Garland, A. S. T.	237	Gianella, C. L.	227
Garmonsway, G. N.	188	Gibb, H. R.	293
Garner, A. E.	281	Gibb, R.	251
Garner, A. L. C.	355	Gibb, W. M.	424, 403
Garner, P. R.	159, 170	†Gibbon, F. W.	37, 334
Garnett, A. W.	170	Gibbon, H. M.	170
Garnett, J.	342	Gibbons, F. R.	283
Garrans, H. H.	211	Gibbons, H. V.	234
Garrard, C. P.	81, 365	Gibbons, J.	314
Garratt, H. W.	353	Gibbons, J. F. G.	81, 335
†Garraway, W. G.	19	Gibbons, J. F.	314
Garrett, A. W.	264	†Gibbins, R. B.	27, 370
†Garrett, M. H.	38, 300	Gibbons, W. E.	154, 353
Garrod, J. D. L.	170	Gibbs, E. N.	82, 312
Garside, W.	423	Gibbs, G. Y.	148, 154, 409
Garth, H. R.	215	†Gibbs, H. A.	15, 225
Gartly, W. H. A.	390	Gibbs, H. B. S.	195
Garvie, H. A.	256	Gibbs, J. E. A.	368
†Garvin, W. M.	21, 242	Gibbs, L. H.	82, 272
Gascoigne, H.	81, 163	Gibbs, T. H.	203
Gasson, S.	203	Gibbs, T. R.	82, 256
Gates, C. E.	198	Giblett, H. D.	182
†Gates, D. L.	5, 354	Gibson, A.	82, 343
Gates, P. H.	312a	Gibson, A. J.	263
Gates, W. C.	340	†Gibson, A. M.	10, 395
Gatheral, G. M.	287	Gibson, A. W.	227
Gathercole, E. H.	371	†Gibson, C. M.	16, 386
Gatty, D. I. V.	203	Gibson, D.	257
Gaulder, C. W. E.	81, 154, 388	Gibson, D. R.	82, 225
†Gaunt, B. W.	38, 387	Gibson, G. C.	242
Gaunt, H. N.	393	Gibson, G. W.	351
Gawler, H. S.	81, 387	Gibson, J. A.	154, 170
Gawley, R. J.	410	Gibson, J. R.	303, 336
Gawthrop, W. O.	266	Gibson, J. T.	410
Gay, F. G.	255	Gibson, J. W.	393
Gaynor, H. F.	299	Gibson, K. G.	287
Gaywood, C. H.	364	Gibson, R. B.	154, 222, 353
Gaywood, F. J.	81, 360	Gibson, R. J. C.	377
†Geary, R. F.	6, 303	Gibson, S. R.	203
Geddes, W. J.	148, 188	Gibson, T.	416
Gedge, L. S. V.	170	Gibson, W. O.	395

† Killed in action or died.   § See this name in *Addenda*.

This Index does not include the Alphabetical Sections IV. and V. (Other Ranks and Old Members).

Gibson, W. W.	... 374	†Girard, G. M. E. ... 26, 282
Giffard, D. G. C.	... 330	Girling, F. J. ... 309
Giffen, L. E.	... 306	Girling, R. O. ... 395
Gifford, R. P.	... 424	†Girling, S. E. ... 39, 233
Gifford, W. D. G.	82, 386	Girvan, C. ... 154, 286
Gigg, W. G.	... 383	Gits, E. J. ... 393
Giggins, R. C.	... 211	Gitsham, A. H. ... 279
†Gilbert, E. A.	... 15	†Gittings, C. ... 30, 272
Gilbert, G. H.	... 394	†Gittins, H. S. ... 170¶
Gilbert, M.	... 303	Givan, H. C. ... 371
Gilbert, S. P.	... 186	†Gjems, A. O. M. ... 19, 245
Gilby, A. J.	... 282	Gjertsen, R. ... 83, 150, 154¶, 243
Gilchrist, J.	82, 344	Gladman, C. W. ... 364
Gilding, E. B.	... 198	Gladwin, D. R. M. ... 198
Giles, A.	... 170	Glanley, S. A. ... 214
†Giles, G.	...7, 252	Glason, J. A. ... 268
Giles, J.	... 323	†Glass, L. G. ... 22, 268
Giles, M. H.	159, 276	Glassborow, J. E. R. L. ... 366
Gilkes, C. A.	... 356	Glazer, D. P. ... 170
Gilks, Harold L.	154, 319	Gledhill, A. C. ... 279
Gilks, Humphrey, L.	82, 154, 308	Glen, V. ... 154, 314
Gill, C. L.	... 287	Glencross, D. G. ... 233
Gill, G. G.	... 293	Glencross, L. H. ... 241
Gill, Henry S.	... 228	Glendening, A. G. ... 302
Gill, Hugh S.	83, 187	Glendining, W. C. ... 236
†Gill, J. W.	...6, 389	Glenfield, F. ... 403
Gill, R. R.	211, 313	Glenister, R. T. ... 365
†Gill, W. R.	20, 339	Glennie, G. H. ... 203
Gillard, S. H.	... 251	Glenton, F. ... 154, 293
Gillbard, G.	... 170	Glibbery, A. B. ... 383
Gillbee, S. J.	... 246	Glibbery, H. E. ... 159
Gillespie, A. H.	... 345	Glinister, A. C. ... 214
†Gillespie, G. W.	14¶, 321	*Gloucestershire Regt.* ... 248
Gillespie, I.	... 278	†Glover, C. J. ... 11, 297
Gillespie, J. W. M.	... 351	Glover, C. W. ... 154, 203
†Gillespie, L. H. G.	27, 164	Glover, H. ... 255
Gillespie, T. L.	83, 381	Glover, J. ... 389
Gillett, E. B.	... 356	Glover, M. C. ... 83, 370
Gillett, F. C. B.	... 293	Glover, N. ... 287
Gillett, H. V.	... 217	Glover, W. A'L. D. ... 182
Gillett, P. T. R.	... 198	†Gluckman, P. ... 11, 306
Gillett, S.	... 412	Gluckstein, L. H. ... 154, 355
Gillett, S. E.	... 233	Gluckstein, M. ... 214
Gilley, J.	... 314	†Glynn, A. H. ... 12, 300
Gilliard, L. P.	... 403	Goacher, F. ... 83, 310a
Gillgrass, A.	... 314	Goadby, A. W. ... 281
Gilliat, A.	... 228	Godber, L. ... 413
†Gilliat, R. V.	34, 317	Goddard, F. C. ... 182
Gilliatt, L.	... 328	Goddard, F. D. ... 410
Gillies, K.	... 256	†Goddard, G. C. ... 40, 360
Gillings, G. A.	... 170	Goddard, W. J. ... 83, 264
Gillon, G. S.	... 203	Godefroi, J. ... 400
Gillott, A.	... 362	Godfrey, E. G. ... 83, 291
Gillott, C.	83, 240	†Godfrey, H. ...9, 269
Gilmore, A. M.	... 188	Godfrey, S. C. ... 83, 149, 154, 344
Gilmour, R.	... 244	†Godfrey, S. M. ... 28, 309
Gilvray, G. F.	... 192	†Godfrey, V. ... 7, 154, 344
Ginger, A. H.	... 383	Godfrey, W. E. ... 353
Ginger, L. S.	... 321	Goding, R. R. ... 171

¶ See reference to this name in *Corrigenda*.

GODSON

INDEX TO COMMISSIONS, HONOURS, and ROLL OF HONOUR.

Name	Pages	Name	Pages
†Godson, S. F. T	24	Goodwin, B. M.	211
Godward, G.	332	Goodwin, J.	233
Godwin, C. R.	320	†Goodyear, F.	16, 244
Goering, E. F.	198	†Goolden, A. W.	42, 357
Goldburg, P.	323	Goossens, A. A.	328
Goldby, Frank L.	406	Gordon, A.	410
Goldby, Frederick L.	171	†Gordon, A. F.	33, 229
Goldie, B. C.	83, 297	Gordon, A. H.	154, 211
Goldie, J.	400	Gordon, E.	216
Goldie, M. F.	364	Gordon, H.	427
†Goldie, P.	5, 273	*Gordon Highlanders*	252
Goldie, R. G.	154, 273	Gordon, J. E.	221
Golding, C. T.	355	Gordon, S. R.	154, 419
†Golding, H. G. L.	277§¶	Gordon, W. P. L.	328
†Golding, H. W.	41, 154, 403	Gore, E. C.	385
Golding, J.	47, 150, 154, 398	Gore, W.	311a
Golding, J. A.	359	Goring, L. T.	185
Golding, O.	198	Gorman, A	239
Goldring, W. G.	366	Gornall, L. A.	272
†Golds, F.	10, 359	Gorrell, J. N.	273
†Golds, I. T.	26, 359	Goslett, R. G.	84, 150, 154, 403
Golds, R. L.	171	Gosnell, V. C.	311
Goldsbury, C. M.	84, 296	Gosney, H. W.	84, 341
Goldschmidt, H. H. A.	163, 298	Goss, W. A.	233
Goldsmith, G. L.	201	Gosse, R. W.	329
Goldsmith, W. L.	400	Gossey, L. S.	148, 159, 420
Goldstein, R. M.	400	Gossling, F. F.	254
Goldthorp, R. H.	47, 154¶, 311a	Gossling, H. F.	363
Gollan, A. L. D.	390	Gossling, R. E.	350
†Golle, C. V.	28	Gossling, T. B.	351
Good, C. F.	261	†Gotch, D. H.	2, 381
Good, J. W.	416	Gotch, D. I.	84, 154, 330
Good, R. W.	203	†Gotelee, F.	40
Good, T. S.	389	†Gotelee, G. H.	38, 367
†Goodale, A. W.	4, 348	Gothard, C. F.	203
Goodbody, F. W.	312a	Gouda, W. F.	323
Goodbody, J. B.	185	Goudie, N.	144, 165, 171
Goodbrook, P. H.	337	Gough, H. G.	163
†Goodchild, S. C.	7, 241	Gough, J. A.	317
†Goodchild, S. J.	31, 348	Gould, Alec.	244
Goodchild, S. T.	371	†Gould, Arthur	7, 230
Goode, G. H.	264	Gould, A. N.	84, 248
Goode, H. P.	406	Gould, C. E.	84, 194
Goodearle, F. R.	171	Gould, C. F.	416
Gooderham, G. H.	427	†Gould, J. R. S.	33, 154, 313, 416
Goodfellow, A. W.	360	Gould, L. C.	154, 416
Gooding, H. E.	315	Gould, R. M.	150, 321
†Gooding, R. J.	24	Gould, V. F.	392
Goodlass, C. W.	391	Gould, W. J. E.	186
†Goodman, J.	14, 278	Gould, W. S.	154, 299
Goodman, K. I.	170	Goulder, A. C.	309
†Goodman, R. M.	4, 154, 226	Gourlay, C. W.	192
Goodman, S.	350	Gowen, H. G.	227¶
Goodrich, E. E.	242	Gower, F. W.	325
Goodrich, H. B. V.	342	†Grace, A. A. G.	17, 171
Goodrick, M. G.	150, 198	†Grace, W. H.	24
Goodsall, R. H.	195	Graddon, W. D.	188
Goodway, H. W.	154, 301	Graham, A. G. N.	238
Goodwin, B. E.	182	Graham, E. A.	330

† Killed in action or died.   § See this name in *Addenda*.

This Index does not include the Alphabetical Sections IV. and V. (Other Ranks and Old Members).

Graham, H. J. ... 228	Green, A. J. ... 304
Graham, J. ... 163	Green, A. L. ... 211
Graham, K. ... 84, 255	Green, A. S. ... 359
Graham, P. ... 332	Green, A. V. ... 247
Graham, R. R. ... 424	Green, C. W. S. ... 330
†Graham, T. E. ... 31, 84, 346	Green, E. A. ... 240
Graham-White, R. ... 423	†Green, F. C. ... 4, 282
Grahame, K. M. ... 233	Green, F. D. H. ... 182
Grainger, J. C. ... 299	Green, F. J. ... 198
Grammont, R. T. ... 171	Green, G. R. ... 85, 217
Grange, F. ... 336	Green, Harold ... 396
†Granger, E. E. W. ... 19, 154, 268	Green, Harold J. ... 237
Grant, A. ... 374	Green, Harry ... 331
Grant, A. C. ... 368	Green, Henry J. ... 264
Grant, E. H. S. ... 297	Green, H. M. ... 312a
Grant, F. D. ... 171	†Green, J. G. A. ... 26, 416
Grant, G. D. ... 366	Green, J. H. ... 164, 171
Grant, John (6869) ... 159, 256	Green, N. J. ... 407
Grant, John (765938) ... 253	Green, O. H. ... 387
Grant, J. A. ... 275	Green, W. B. ... 171
Grant, J. L. ... 257	Green, W. C. ... 85, 150, 352, 392
Grant, R. ... 198	Greenacre, W. D. C. ... 220
Grant, T. H. ... 383	Greenaway, B. V. ... 171
†Grassick, W. H. ... 188§	Greenbank, J. R. ... 195
Grattan, D. A. ... 396	†Greene, D. W. ... 29, 421
†Gratwick, H. D. ... 42, 235	Greene, R. E. ... 171
Grave, F. J. ... 407	Greenfield, E. F. ... 247
Graves, A. G. ... 350	†Greenhill, F. W. R. ... 22, 217
Graves, E. ... 288	Greenhill, H. P. ... 171
Gray, C. G. ... 198	Greenidge, S. C. C. ... 301
Gray, C. G. D. ... 171	Greening, C. B. ... 349
†Gray, C. K. ... 14, 302	Greening, F. V. ... 149
Gray, C. R. ... 203	Greenman, J. E. ... 400
Gray, D. ... 304	Greenshields, L. W. ... 337
†Gray, E. B. ... 27, 208	Greenwall, E. B. ... 192
Gray, F. W. ... 288	†Greenwood, A. D. ... 37, 224
Gray, G. Sidney ... 266	Greenwood, C. ... 154, 211
Gray, G. Sinclair ... 271	Greenwood, C. F. H. ... 47, 154, 305, 307
†Gray, H. A. ... 35, 85, 262	Greenwood, C. H. ... 400
Gray, H. L. ... 188	Greenwood, D. S. ... 389
Gray, H. R. ... 243	Greenwood, F. T. ... 407
Gray, H. V. ... 84, 249	Greenwood, F. W. ... 261
Gray, James (2430) ... 85, 150, 362	Greenwood, J. E. ... 358
Gray, James (4237) ... 303	†Greenwood, J. H. ... 35, 85, 264
Gray, J. A. ... 317	Greenwood, J. S. ... 227
Gray, J. E. ... 203	Greer, A. ... 254
Gray, J. H. ... 192	†Greeves, A. F. W. ... 21, 352
†Gray, O. ... 37	Gregg, R. A. ... 316
Gray, S. A. ... 85, 305	Gregory, E. G. ... 353
Grayson, E. ... 171	Gregory, G. ... 400
Greasley, J. E. ... 281	Gregory, H. ... 413
Greaves, H. F. K. ... 171	Gregory, J. S. ... 198
Greaves, R. G. ... 366	†Gregory, P. J. ... 21, 334
†Green, Allen ... 20, 396	Gregory, R. J. ... 423
Green, Arthur (760934) ... 356	Gregory, W. J. I. D. ... 321
Green, Arthur (5495) ... 85, 233	†Greiffenhagen, N. ... 6, 260
†Green, A. B. ... 24	Greig, D. McN. ... 148, 354
†Green, A. F. ... 30, 351	Greig, H. G. ... 288
Green, A. G. N. ... 240	†Grellier, A. B. ... 31, 270

¶ See reference to this name in *Corrigenda*.

GRENADIER

INDEX TO COMMISSIONS, HONOURS, and ROLL OF HONOUR.

Grenadier Guards ... 217	†Growse, J. H. ... 31, 329
Grenside, H. C. ... 203	Grugeon, H. ... 348
Gresham, H. T. ... 367	Grundy, C. V. ... 204
Gretton, E. W. ... 289	Grundy, F. ... 297
Greville, W. ... 353	Grundy, G. F. ... 198
†Grew, W. E. ... 22, 371	Gruskin, C. ... 407
Grey, H. K. ... 288	Gubbins, A. B. G. ... 188
†Grey, W. C. ... 41	Guerrier, A. P. ... 204
Grice, A. N. ... 154, 133	Guinee, J. ... 225
†Grice, L. C. ... 14, 194	Guinness, R. C. ... 245
Grice, S. ... 288	Gulick, J. D. ... 285
Grice, S. W. ... 365	Gully, S. ... 371
Grice, W. S. ... 85, 203	†Gummer, B. A. ... 9, 285
Grierson, J. T. ... 345	†Gunn, E. A. ... 42, 204
Grierson, K. Mc. I. ...48, 85, 150, 154, 318	Gunn, H. J. ... 154, 346
Grierson, R. H. F. ... 314	Gunn, H. S. ... 192
†Griffen, H. S. ... 13, 349	Gunn, M. R. ... 221
Griffin, A. E. ... 85, 154, 209	Gunn, W. H. ... 253
†Griffin, E. W. ... 38, 250	Gunnell, D. A. ... 362
Griffin, S. W. ... 154, 162	Gunning, W. G. ... 171
Griffith, F. ... 171	Gurdon, F. ... 407
Griffith, F. S. ... 313, 416	Gurner, E. D. ... 272
Griffith, G. W. ... 374	†Gurney, K. G. ... 27, 250
Griffith, J. ... 334	Gurney, P. S. ... 204
Griffith, J. E. ... 237	Gurney, R. B. ... 407
Griffith, J. R. ... 286	Gurney, R. W. ... 251
Griffiths, A. ... 195	Gurton, W. H. ... 211
Griffiths, D. R. ... 171¶	Guthrie, L. R. ... 312a
Griffiths, F. V. ... 275	Guthrie, W. ... 413
†Griffiths, G. ... 39	†Gutteridge, R. H. ... 10, 296
Griffiths, H. O. ... 377	Guttridge, G. W. ... 373
Griffiths, H. P. ... 320, 322, 426	Guttridge, J. F. ... 86, 154, 391
Griffiths, H. P. J. ... 269	Guy, J. K. ... 209
Griffiths, S. A. ... 297	Guy, R. ... 323
Griffiths, T. V. ... 336	†Guy, R. C. ... 37, 225
Griffiths, W. H. ... 86, 371	Guyer, A. K. ... 349
Grigor, J. A. ... 410	Gwatkin, F. P. ... 424
†Grimsdell, R. E. ... 10, 290	Gwatkin, V. C. H. ... 342
Grimshaw, J. E. ... 272	Gwyn, A. G. ... 403
† Grimsley, W. H. ... 40, 391	Gwynn, E. J. C. ... 288
Grimwood, H. ... 317	Gwynne, T. H. ... 367
Grinter, T. G. ... 226	
†Grissell, F. ... 9, 218	Hack, M. S. ... 149, 154
Grist, A. P. ... 407	Hack, W. P. ... 86, 284
Groocock, A. D. ... 198	Hacker, T. H. S. ... 192
Groocock, G. H. ... 281	Hacklett, L. A. ... 333
†Groom, C. ... 28, 309	†Haddock, J. H. ... 31, 260
Groom, C. R. N. ... 260	Haddon, B. L. ... 154, 350
Groom, V. E. ... 145, 171¶	Haddon, H. ... 171
Groom, W. O. ... 313a	Haden, V. W. ... 198
Gros, H. S. ... 318	†Hadley, E. S. ... 20, 250
Grose, H. H. ... 250	Hadley, J. A. ... 192
Grout, M. H. ... 264	Hadrill, C. I. ... 86, 393
Grove, A. G. ... 231	Hadwick, W. ... 390
Grove-Price, W. F. ... 326	†Haeffner, F. W. ... 8, 191
Groves, H. F. ... 331	Haggart, D. D. ... 416
Grover, G. W. M. ... 418	Haggart, E. C. ... 171
Groves, F. ... 386	Haggart, J. G. F. G. T. ... 230
Groves, J. ... 171	Haggerjudd, W. ... 381

† Killed in action or died.   § See this name in *Addenda*.

This Index does not include the Alphabetical Sections IV. and V. (Other Ranks and Old Members).

Haggis, B.	154
Haggis, E. V.	325
Haggis, K. C.	360
Haigh, G. D. D.	407
Haigh, G. R.	171
Haines, L. W.	198
Hakewill, T. G.	6, 164, 352
†Halcrow, A. P.	15, 254
Halcrow, M. E.	305
Halcrow, O. H.	329
Halden, R. J.	423
Haldin-Davis	312a
Hale, C. F. W.	342
Hale, G. T.	154, 225, 416
Hale, H. M.	383
Hales, W. C.	198
Halford, R. C.	188
Halford-Adcock, H. H.	240
Halkett, G. W.	163, 185
†Hall, A. L.	32, 154, 360
Hall, A. R. C.	368
Hall, A. W.	86, 308
Hall, C. R.	323
Hall, E. T.	171
Hall, F. J.	366
Hall, F. W. G.	416
Hall, H. W.	318
Hall, J. E.	387
†Hall, J. S.	16, 393
Hall, L. E.	86, 154, 265
Hall, M.	188
†Hall, N. de H.	10, 354
Hall, P. H.	270
Hall, R. C.	251
Hall, S. E.	366
Hall, S. F.	192
Hall, T. F. B.	388
Hall, T. N.	304
Hall, V. O.	366
Hall, W. B. C.	262, 328
Hall, W. E.	171, 304
Hall, W. J.	305
Hall, W. T.	256
Hallam, F. V.	334
Hallam, H. J. B.	377
Hallet, C. J. S.	400
Hallett, L.	316
Hallewell, A. V.	350
Halliday, C. P.	86, 388
Halliday, H. E.	86, 382
Hallinan, C.	260
†Halliwell, Fred (764065)	33, 318
†Halliwell, Frederick (764241)	40, 318
†Hallmark, P. H.	38, 387
†Hallowes, R. P.	5, 44, 86, 154, 319
†Hallpike, C. G.	32, 204
Halls, J. L.	293
†Halls, W. J.	41
†Hallward, K. L.	7, 381
Halsall, H.	407
Halse, E. A.	154, 393
Halsey, E.	198
†Halsey, E. C.	17, 292
Hambley, R. L.	306
Hamel-Smith, A. H.	225
Hamer, W.	407
Hamill, J.	204
Hamilton, A. D.	256
Hamilton, C. R.	220
†Hamilton, Claude W.	25, 266
Hamilton, Cyril W.	171
†Hamilton, H. J.	35, 86, 171, 232¶
Hamilton, J. A.	221
Hamilton, J. G.	198
Hamilton, J. R.	347
Hamilton, M. M.	171
†Hamilton, N. C.	8, 330
Hamilton, R. B.	265
†Hamlen, P.	2
Hammersley, C.	171
Hammond, A. E.	223
Hammond, F.	230
†Hammond, H. J.	30, 251
†Hammond, K. L. C.	30, 334
Hammond, L. G.	24
Hammond, R. F.	204
Hammond, W.	399
Hampshire Regt.	253
†Hampshire, S.	22, 271
†Hanafy, S. R.	26, 171
Hanbury, F. C.	211, 310a
Hanbury, H. G.	186
Hancock, E.	87, 204
Hancock, W.	209
Hand, E. F.	211
Hand, H. G.	405
†Hand, J. W.	31
Handley-Read, E. H.	149, 416
Hands, J. G.	261
Hanford, S.	211
Hanger, A. C.	382
Hankin, F.	247
Hankins, H. W.	299, 309
Hankins, T. P.	405
Hanna, W. H.	154, 368
Hannaford, L. G.	392
†Hannaford, W. A.	26, 350
Hannah, T. R.	298
Hannam-Clark, G. F.	413
Hannan, T. G.	413
Hansford, J. S.	285
Hanson, H.	171
Hanson, J.	218
Hanson, J. S.	391
Hanton, P. K.	211
Harbottle, J. R.	410
Harcourt, G. E.	371
Hardie, N.	211

¶ See reference to this name in *Corrigenda*.

Name	Pages	Name	Pages
†Hardie, W.	14, 268	†Harris, E. B.	37
Hardie, W. J.	254	Harris, E. R.	285
Harding, D. A.	427	Harris, E. V.	209
Harding, G. H.	371	Harris, F.	247
Harding, G. P.	87, 330	Harris, G. G. H. W.	340
Harding, H. R.	427	Harris, G. L.	255
Harding, P. H.	211	Harris, H. A.	270
†Harding, S. W.	32	†Harris, H. J. L.	11
Harding, V. R.	264	Harris, H. M.	17, 186
Hardman, D.	171	Harris, H. V.	416
†Hardman, K.	40, 256	Harris, J. A. L.	182
Hardman, L.	230	Harris, J. L.	154, 407
†Hardman, W. F. K.	23, 87, 211	Harris, L.	233
Hardwick, C.	236	Harris, P. E.	171
Hardwick, D.	379	†Harris, S. E.	34, 275
Hardwick, G. H. J.	396	Harris, W.	363
Hardy, C. E.	265	Harris, W. C.	286
Hardy, L. C.	171	Harris, W. H.	407
Hardy, W. J. R.	418	Harrison, A. C.	218
Hare, A. W.	355	Harrison, C. E.	328
†Hare, B. V.	5, 154, 319	†Harrison, C. G.	26, 385
†Hare, E. A. A.	2, 319	Harrison, C. L. R.	424
Hare, H. R.	198	Harrison, E. C.	171
Hare, J. T.	321	Harrison, Edward H.	87, 209
Hare, L. H. E.	323	Harrison, Ernest H.	336
Hare, P. V.	336	Harrison, E. L.	323
†Harel, L. O.	20, 171	Harrison, Frank (537)	87, 148, 326
†Harger, E. O.	38, 211	Harrison, Frank (765270)	171
Hargest, H. L.	350	Harrison, F. C.	413
†Hargreaves, C. A.	19, 171	Harrison, F. C. S.	240
†Hargreaves, E. B.	335	Harrison, F. N.	171
Hargreaves, R.	317	Harrison, F. O. P.	403
†Hargreaves, W. F.	29, 171	Harrison, F. S.	281
Hargreaves, W. J.	274	Harrison, G.	288
Harker, C. P.	359	Harrison, H.	427
†Harland, M. L.	37	Harrison, J. G.	87, 283
†Harland, R.	35, 198	Harrison, N.	277
Harle, N. H.	337, 390	Harrison, S. P.	311
†Harley, J.	4, 383	Harrison, W. R. E.	154, 261
Harley, M. R.	258	†Harrison, W. S. B.	8, 275
Harley, N. F.	317	Harrison, W. T.	284
Harness, J.	354	Harrower, A. B.	403
Harper, E. E.		†Harry, F. C.	40, 421
Harper, E. R.	87, 325, 407	Hart, A. H.	359
Harper, H.	371	Hart, B. L.	359
Harper, H. H.	149, 154, 313, 407	Hart, E. J.	155, 274
Harper, J. R.	374	Hart, G. R.	410
Harper, S. W.	374	Hart, J. A.	87, 155, 358
Harrap, B. C.	150, 198	Hart, T. E.	273
Harries, W. T.	376	Hart, W.	337, 342
Harington, J.	311a	Harteg, W. G.	423
†Harrington, W.	17, 377	†Hartley, Alfred	40, 204
Harris, A.	407	Hartley, Allan	171
Harris, A. A.	211	Hartley, A. S.	171
Harris, A. S.	171	Hartley, G. C.	293
Harris, C. A.	250	†Hartley, W. C.	24
Harris, C. R.	154, 321	Hartley, W. E.	5, 230
Harris, D. C. A.	262	†Hartman, C. H.	35, 262
Harris, D. R.	195	Hartnett, D. P.	237

† Killed in action or died. § See this name in *Addenda*.

HEATLEY 535

This Index does not include the Alphabetical Sections IV. and V. (Other Ranks and Old Members).

Hartnup, F. V.	374
Hartopp, C. W. E. C.	155, 162, 211
†Hartree, C.	34, 204
Hartung, C. F. A.	398
†Harty, W.	39, 349
Harvey, A.	48, 87, 155, 286
Harvey, A. F.	328
†Harvey, D.	31, 217
Harvey, E. B.	164, 309
†Harvey, E. H.	39, 88, 249
Harvey, F. B.	344
Harvey, F. E. E.	288
Harvey, G. W.	356
Harvey, H. A.	304
Harvey, J. W.	305
Harvey, M.	284
Harvey, R.	283
†Harvey, R. G. B.	27, 283
Harvey, W. H.	40, 188
Harvey, Walter R.	360
Harvey, Wilfred R.	374
Harvey, W. S.	211
†Harvey-James, A. K.	14, 155, 162, 261
Harwood, A. C.	369
Harwood, A. W.	155, 369
Harwood, E. H.	369
Harwood, G. W.	221
Haselden, E. F.	171
Haskins, L. J.	155, 187
Haslam, H. T.	387
†Haslam, J.	23, 309
Haslehust, G. B.	214
Hassall, J. E. G.	172
Hasslacher, A. J. E.	88, 293
Hastie, P. D.	288
Hastings, A. R.	361
Hastings, N. W.	172
Hastings, V. P.	318
Haswell, H. L.	424
Haswell, R. M.	235
Hatfield, F. E.	271
Hatfield, S.	211
Hatton, D. L.	358
Hattersley, G.	378
Hatfield-Wright, M.	349
Haw, E. A.	227
Hawes, E. M.	266
Hawes, J. W.	244
Hawke, H.	424
Hawken, B. R. P.	332
Hawken, G. H.	222
Hawken, T. W.	424
Hawker, S. W. A.	247
Hawkes, E.	416
Hawkes, P. J.	349
Hawkes, T. W. P.	339
Hawkins, B. L.	316
Hawkins, Charles Frederick (764096)	423
Hawkins, Charles Frederick (10095)	149
Hawkins, C. N.	413
Hawkins, D. M. C.	266
Hawkins, G.	306
Hawkins, H. A.	410
Hawkins, J.	373
Hawksford, F. H.	148, 159, 172
Hawksley, E. B.	220
Hawksley, T. E.	217
†Hawksworth, H. C. H.	30, 88, 244
Hawley, L. H.	295
Haworth, L.	274
Haworth, P.	145, 172
Haworth, S.	387
Hawthorne, F. M.	172
†Hawtrey, R.	9, 211, 330
Hay, H. J.	290
Hay, Robert (5695)	275
Hay, Robert (4036)	363
†Hay, R. M.	24
Haycock, H.	208
Haydock-Wilson, H.	316
†Haydon, F. W.	24
Haydon, P. M.	395
Haydon, R. A.	204
Hayes, A. P.	155, 304
Hayes, F. C.	247
†Hayes, M. F.	15, 393
Hayes, N.	295
†Hayes, T. F.	35
Hayhurst, C.	266
Haylett, F. E.	328
Haylock, S. W.	302
Hayne, R. L.	264
Haynes, C. G.	88, 265
Haynes, F. C. G.	347
Haynes, F. H.	172
Haynes, L.	410
Haynes, R. J.	293
Hayward, A. L.	198
Hayward, A. R.	198
Haywood, H. W.	410
†Hazel, D. D. F.	15, 379
Hazelden, W. A.	374
Heady, H.	192
Heald, F.	416
Heald, H. C.	188
Heald, W. M.	355, 399
Healey, A. J.	284
Healey, H. A. H.	416
Heap, H. S.	387
Heap, N. R.	334
†Hearn, L. W.	23, 233
Hearnshaw, H.	293
Heath, C. R. G.	336
†Heath, G. B.	34, 219
Heath, P. S.	330
Heath, W. F.	272
Heathcote, N. H. de V.	172
†Heatley, C. F.	33, 374

¶ See reference to this name in *Corrigenda*.

Heaton, C. S.	332
Heaton, F.	277
Heaton, L. H.	389
Heaton, R.	351
Heavans-Trewman, R. F. P.	192
†Hebden, G. S.	15, 281
Hedgecock, A. T.	220
†Hedgecock, S.	12
Hedgecock, S. D.	377
Hedgecock, S. E.	377
Hedges, N. H.	88, 385
Hedges, R. B. T.	172
Hedges, W. F.	273
Hedley, H. T.	366
Hedley, R. R.	368
Hedley, W. T.	398
†Hellicar, G. T.	8, 303
Helm, C.	311a
Hellmers, A.	3, 259
†Hemming, J. C.	20, 382
Heming, P.	310a
Hemphill, R. D.	235
Hemphill, H. H.	88, 280
Hempson, O. A.	189
Hemsworth, N. E. C.	327, 382
Henderson, A.	228
Henderson, C. E.	48, 155, 297
Henderson, C. K.	204
Henderson, C. R.	155
†Henderson, E.	17, 295
Henderson, E. J.	48, 88, 155, 271
Henderson, E. M.	172
†Henderson, E. S.	24
Henderson, K. R.	88, 390
Henderson, L. E.	352
Henderson, R. E.	189
Henderson, R. G.	339
Henderson, R. L. S.	353
†Hendry, C. A.	31, 247
Hendry, H. D.	155, 216
Hendy, G. F.	305
Heney, J. H. W.	88, 219
Henham, R. J.	400
Henley, A. E.	225
†Henley, F. J.	24
Henley, W. G.	248
†Henna, J. R.	9, 259
Hennessy, J. J.	270
Henri, A. W.	231
Henri, C.	400
Henry, C. N.	334
Henry, G. A.	285
Henry, J. H. W.	410
Henson, A. E.	253
Henson, E. D.	316
Hepburn, A.	145, 172
Hepburn, D. F.	303
†Heppell, H. D.	13, 225
†Heppenstall, R. A.	34
Herbage, P. F. W.	369
Herbert, L. A.	318
Herbert, S. H.	339
Herbert, S. M.	334
Herd, G. G.	257
Herdman, T. A.	332
Herkomer, S. H.	362
Hermelin, A.	312
Herman, R.	393
†Heron, V. H.	24
Herratt, J.	305
Herrera, J. A.	172
Herring, D. D.	251
Herringshaw, E. A.	413
Herron, R. W. C.	155, 407
Hertfordshire Regt.	*223*
Hertslet, H. R. E.	214
Hervey, A. F.	365
Hervey, E. G.	355
Hervey, G. A. K.	162
†Heskett, J.	33, 378
Heslop, E. C.	318
Heslop, G. E.	259
Heslop, J. C.	240
Hesse, E. T.	340
Hetherington, E. C.	155, 359
Hetherington, H. W.	185
Hetherton, J.	395
Hewat, F. A.	389
†Hewat, R. A.	37, 172
Hewett, F. S.	256
Hewett, W. G.	293
†Hewitson, J.	26, 334
Hewitt, A. E.	88, 304
†Hewitt, A. H.	24
Hewitt, A. R.	417
Hewitt, F. M.	321
†Hewitt, G. S.	29
Hewitt, H. J.	391
Hewitt, L. W.	427
Hewitt, M. B.	155, 309
Hewkley, N. T.	244
†Hewlett, H. A. T.	36, 290
Hewson, S. B.	311a
Hey, P.	198§
Hey, R.	392
Heyes, L.	159, 361
†Heynes, D. H.	34, 192¶
†Heywood, A. B.	21, 389
Heywood, E. P.	209
Heywood, F.	204
Heywood, H.	270
Hibbard, C. J.	149
Hibbard, H. E.	89, 311a
†Hibbert, A. J.	19, 192
Hibbert, J. G.	89, 155, 399
Hitchens, B. S.	155, 194
Hickey, H. G.	393
Hicks, A. M.	198

† Killed in action or died.   § See this name in *Addenda*.

This Index does not include the Alphabetical Sections IV. and V. (Other Ranks and Old Members).

†Hicks, C. H.	...	...	...	35, 336	Hillas-Drake, R. F. H.	...	...	...	266
Hicks, G. A.	...	...	...	... 243	†Hillyer, W. H.	...	...	7, 90, 155, 215
Hicks, G. R.	...	...	...	145, 172	Hilton, J. H.	...	...	...	277
†Hicks, H. R.	...	...	...	22, 172	Hilton, R. B.	...	...	...	267
Hicks, J. S.	...	...	...	... 379	Hinckley, G. P.	...	...	...	417
Hicks, S. V.	...	...	...	... 211	Hind, H. C. D.	...	...	...	342
†Hickson, R. D.	...	...	... 15, 89, 243	Hind, I. F.	...	...	...	172
Hide, J. B.	...	...	... 89, 155, 204	Hind, W. M.	...	...	...	240
Hield, H.	...	...	...	... 275	Hinde, G. N.	...	...	...	185
Higgins, C. A.	...	...	...	... 341	Hinde, W. B.	...	...	...	198
Higgins, D. A.	...	...	...	... 192	Hindle, E. V.	...	...	...	389
Higgins, E.	...	...	...	... 317	Hindle, J. W.	...	...	...	423
Higgins, G. J.	...	...	...	... 386	Hindmarsh, C.	...	...	90, 275
†Higgins, H. E. P.	...	...	...4, 279	Hindmarsh, F.	...	...	...	356
†Higginson, J. V.	...	...	89, 372§	Hine, A. J.	...	...	...	374
Higgs, H. L.	...	...	...	... 311a	Hine, F. L.	...	...	...	184
†Higgs, R. F.	...	...	...	38, 361	Hine, H. J. K.	...	...	...	225
Higham, E. E.	...	...	...	... 291	†Hines, A.	...	...	...6, 240
Higham, J. A.	...	...	...150, 155, 172	Hingley, A. N.	...	48, 90, 155, 322
Higham, L.	...	...	...	... 242	Hinshalwood, R. K.	...	...	211
Higham, R. L.	...	...	...	... 204	Hirst, F. E.	...	...	...	413
Higham, S. S.	...	...	...	... 307	Hiscocks, C. E.	...	...	...	198
Higham, W. P.	...	...	...	... 385	Hislop, D. H.	...	...	...	221
Highland L.I.	...	...	...	... *256*	Hislop, W. A.	...	...	... 227¶
Highlanders, Royal	...	...	... *257*	†Hitchcock, C. A.	...	...	...6, 348
Highmore, C. B.	...	...	...	... 417	Hitchcock, L.	...	...	155, 254
Higlett, G. W.	...	...	...	89, 339	Hitchen, D.	...	...	...	382
Hilder, E. C. L.	...	...	...	... 231	Hitching, A. S.	...	...	...	172
Hildersley, S. H. H.	...	...	... 427§	Hitchings, D. B.	...	...	...	368
†Hill, A.	...	...	...	20, 352	Hitchings, F. A.	...	...	...	304
†Hilditch, C. H.	...	...	...	... 427§	Hitchman, J. W. C.	...	...	410
Hill, A. A.	...	...	...	... 337	Hoal, E. G.	...	...	90, 316
Hill, A. B.	...	...	...	... 149	Hoare, J. H.	...	...	...	353
Hill, A. D.	...	...	... 89, 155, 319	†Hoare, W. J. G.	...	11, 48, 155, 246
Hill, A. G.	...	...	...	... 183	Hoather, W. H.	...	...	... 310a
†Hill, A. L.	...	...	...	...5, 319	Hobbes, H. H.	...	...	...	261
Hill, B. A.	...	...	...	... 330	†Hobbs, G. H. C.	...	...	10, 238
†Hill, C. D.	...	...	...	6¶, 366	Hobbs, W.	...	...	90, 155, 222
Hill, C. E.	...	...	...	... 424	Hobbs, W. C.	...	...	...	233
Hill, C. H.	...	...	...	... 301	Hoblyn, R. A.	...	...	...	398
Hill, C. J. K.	...	...	...	... 189	†Hoblyn, W. F.	...	...	...5, 218
Hill, C. V.	...	...	...	89, 339	Hobrough, F. R.	...	...	...	316
Hill, C. W.	...	...	...	... 424	†Hobson, G. H.	...	...	14, 253
Hill, E. V.	...	...	...	... 209	Hobson, H. R.	...	48, 155, 163, 403
Hill, G. F. B.	...	...	...	... 215	Hobson, J. C.	...	...	...	379
†Hill, J. A.	...	...	...	... 24	†Hobson, R. C.	...	...	41, 90, 332
Hill, J. E. V.	...	...	...	... 388	Hockey, A. L.	...	...	90, 303
Hill, J. S.	...	...	...	90, 192	Hocking, W. S.	...	...	...	364
Hill, K. H.	...	...	...	... 418	Hodding, W. M.	...	...	...	418
Hill, P. H.	...	...	...	... 366	Hodge, F. E.	...	...	...	189
Hill, P. J.	...	...	...	... 262	†Hodge, F. G.	...	...	25, 303
Hill, S.	...	...	...	... 407	†Hodge, L. C.	...	...	26, 263
Hill, T. G.	...	...	...	155, 204	Hodge, W. E.	...	...	...	233
Hill, W. P.	...	...	...	... 325	Hodge, W. R. C.	...	...	...	397
†Hilliar, G. E.	...	...	...	...5, 276	Hodges, A. E. H.	...	...	...	198
†Hillier, S. N.	...	...	...	31, 368	Hodges, C. E.	...	...	...	427
Hillis, J.	...	...	...	... 256	Hodges, C. W. R.	...	...	...	327
Hills, E. A. R.	...	...	...	... 172	Hodges, H. P.	...	...	...	183
†Hills, M. A.	...	...	...	...9, 260	Hodgins, A. W. M.	...	...	...	196

¶ See reference to this name in *Corrigenda*.

Hodgkins, A.	... 172
Hodgkins, A. E.	90, 189
Hodgkinson, H. D.	148, 403
Hodgkinson, R. J.	... 265
Hodgshon, F. W.	... 298
Hodgson, A. T.	... 394
Hodgson, D. C.	... 283
Hodgson, G.	... 334
Hodgson, J. V.	... 400
Hodgson, R.	... 275
Hodgson, S. G.	... 238
Hodson, F. C. M.	... 244
Hodson, P.	... 231
Hoffgaard, G. A.	... 220
Hogarth, G. W.	... 198
Hogarth-Swann, A. L.	91, 328
Hogg, G. A.	... 358
Hoggarth, A. H. G.	... 228
Holbeche, C. G.	... 172
Holdaway, N. A.	91, 316
Holden, A.	... 391
Holden, E. C.	... 409
Holden, G. H.	... 424
Holden, G. M.	... 424
Holden, H. S.	... 274
Holden, J. W.	... 413
Holden, W. C.	... 211
Holderness, L. C.	... 185
Holdsworth, H.	91, 271
Holgate, B.	... 314
Holgate, L. G.	91, 270
Hollamby, H. J.	... 230
Holland, A. L.	91, 310a
†Holland, B. T.	...2, 257
Holland, D. H.	... 281
Holland, F. R.	... 304
Holland, H.	... 373
Holland, R. H.	... 323
Hollick, G.	... 356
Hollidge, A.	...149, 397, 407
Hollingdale, G. F.	... 407
Hollingsworth, C. R.	... 250
Hollinrake, J. C.	... 354
Hollins, C. B.	... 217
Hollinworth, E.	... 277¶
†Hollis, A. R.	38, 234
Hollis, H. L.	163, 390
Holloway, H. J.	... 204
†Holloway, L.	13, 333
Holloway, N. E.	... 369
Holloway, R. J.	... 286
†Hollyman, W. H.	... 28
†Holm, F. D.	16, 209
Holman, H. G.	... 172
Holman, W. M.	... 204
Holmes, A.	... 413
Holmes, E. J.	... 249
Holmes, F.	... 305
Holmes, F. C. V.	... 333
Holmes, F. W.	... 272
Holmes, G. R.	... 204
Holmes, H. C.	... 418
Holmes, J. K. W.	... 417
Holmes, J. M.	... 314
Holmes, K. E. M.	... 198
Holmes, M.	... 264
Holmes, R.	... 350
Holmes, W.	... 387
Holmes, W. E.	... 413
Holroyd, R. E.	...
Holroyd, V. H.	155, 263
Holt, G. G.	... 323
Holt, H. F. G.	... 355
Holtham, E. J.	... 306
Holton, J. R.	... 388
Holton, W. H.	... 183
†Holwill, W. B.	34, 417
Hombrow, V. P.	... 303
Home, A. E.	... 332
Home, G. W.	... 198
Homewood, T. S	159, 204
Hone, R. A.	... 254
Honey, G.	... 407
Honey, W. J.	... 278
Honour, F. L.	... 208
Hood, B. T.	... 346
Hood, F. W.	... 327
Hood, J. E.	... 198
†Hood, O.	...9, 366
Hood, R.	... 172
†Hood, R. P.	21, 172
Hooke, A. H.	... 323
Hooker, J. T.	... 410
Hooker, M. W.	... 293
Hoole, D. R.	... 236
†Hoole, G.	...9, 300
Hoole, W.	... 407
Hooper, F.	... 286
Hooper, G. W. E.	... 192
Hooper, H. R.	... 225
Hooper, L. A.	... 413
Hooper, V. A.	... 204
Hooson, D. J. S.	... 318
Hope, B.	... 231
Hope, H. J.	155, 219
Hope, O. W.	... 228
Hope, W. E. C.	... 208
Hopgood, F. J.	... 172
Hopkins, C. A.	... 182
Hopkins, C. E.	... 293
†Hopkins, G. H. S.	313, 417§
Hopkins, H. G.	... 334
Hopkins, J. H.	... 283¶
Hopkins, J. L.	... 185
Hopkins, P. A.	...
Hopkinson, C. O. J.	... 186
Hopley, W. A.	91, 371
Hopper, G.	149, 247

† Killed in action or died. § See this name in *Addenda*.

HUGGINS

This Index does not include the Alphabetical Sections IV. and V. (Other Ranks and Old Members). 539

Hopps, F. L.	... ...	147, 172	Howard, H. L.	... ...	92, 155, 209
Hopson, M. G. S.	... ...	... 405	Howard, H. W.	... ...	... 424
Hopwood, J.	... ...	91, 155, 195	Howard, S. B.	... ...	... 274
Horabin, T. L.	... ...	... 229	†Howard, W. A.	... ...	15, 345
Hordle, S. L.	... ...	... 367	Howard, W. E.	... ...	315, 415
Horley, C. R.	... ...	91, 155, 338	Howarth, R.	... ...	... 223
Horn, C. R.	... ...	... 378	Howcroft, S. M.	... ...	92, 361
Horn, F. W.	... ...	... 189	Howden, J. B.	... ...	... 400
Horn, M. L.	... ...	150, 165	†Howe, A. E.	... ...	23, 310a
Hornabrook, A. W.	... ...	... 316	Howe, C. A.	... ...	26, 374
Hornabrook, E. M.	... ...	... 317	†Howe, C. K.	... ...	...7, 225
Hornby, J. A.	... ...	... 407	Howe, E. G.	... ...	... 254
Horne, A. W.	... ...	... 350	Howe, G. H.	... ...	198, 291
Horne, G. S.	... ...	... 290	Howe, J. A.	... ...	... 410
†Horne, J. A.	... ...	...8, 300	Howe, P. P.	... ...	... 198
Horne, J. C.	... ...	... 257	Howe, R. E.	... ...	... 396
Horne, J. G.	... ...	... 319	Howe, S. G.	... ...	... 352
Horne, O. W.	... ...	92, 241	Howe, V. A.	... ...	92, 328
Hornsby, P. R.	... ...	... 403	Howe, W. L.	... ...	... 401
Horrax, C. B.	... ...	... 328	Howell, C. R.	... ...	... 284
Horrobin, S. L.	... ...	... 413	Howell, H.	... ...	... 417
†Horrocks, J. G.	... ...	... 24	Howell, H. D.	... ...	... 323
Horsburgh, A. L.	... ...	159, 289	†Howell, H. E.	... ...	...3, 271
Horsburgh, L. G.	... ...	... 214	†Howell, J.	... ...	...5, 266
†Horsey, C. J.	... ...	11, 277	Howells, F. W.	... ...	... 198
†Horsfall, A. M.	... ...	3, 155, 326	†Howells, G. D.	... ...	29, 325
†Horsley, O.	... ...	...36, 92, 155, 172, 252	Howells, G. J.	... ...	26, 172
Horsley, S. M.	... ...	... 252	Howes, E.	... ...	... 355
Horsley, V.	... ...	... 333	Howgill, R. J. F.	... ...	... 331
Horsley, W. C.	... ...	159, 311	Howgrave-Graham, H. M.	... ...	... 254
Horsman, E. W. F.	... ...	... 350	Howkins, F.	... ...	... 211
†Horsnell, A. G.	... ...	...7, 355	Howse, H. A. G.	... ...	... 293
Horth, F. J.	... ...	... 285	Howse, T. F.	... ...	... 364
†Horton, A. M.	... ...	... 37	Howson, J. H.	... ...	... 334
Horwood, E. B.	... ...	... 185	Hoy, J. N. R.	... ...	... 413
†Hosken, H. R.	... ...	19, 417	†Hoyle, J. W.	... ...	... 32
Hosking, J. C.	... ...	92, 234	Hubbard, N. F. S.	... ...	... 172
Hoskyns-Abrahall, T.	... ...	... 304	Hubble, W. G.	... ...	... 277
Hotchkiss, A.	... ...	... 184	†Huckle, H. W.	... ...	38, 229
Houghton, A. L.	... ...	... 186	Hucklebridge, E. C.	... ...	... 172
Houghton, A. S.	... ...	... 364	Hucklebridge, P. A.	... ...	... 268
†Houghton, G.	... ...	37, 396	Huddle, L. W.	... ...	... 426
Houghton, N. D.	... ...	... 249	Hudgell, E. W. G.	... ...	... 339
Houlder, A. C.	... ...	... 363	†Hudson, C. H.	... ...	...3, 285
Houlston, F. H.	... ...	... 192	Hudson, E. B.	... ...	... 204
Hounsell, F. W.	... ...	... 300	Hudson, E. H.	... ...	... 364
†Housden, A. T.	... ...	... 24	Hudson, E. P.	... ...	92, 192
Household Battalion	... ...	*184*	Hudson, F. E.	... ...	... 423
Hussars	... ...	*184*	Hudson, H. J.	... ...	... 172
Houston, T.	... ...	... 211	Hudson, H. S.	... ...	... 317
How, F. R.	... ...	... 298	Hudson, John W.	... ...	... 396
Howard, A.	... ...	155, 172	Hudson, Joseph W.	... ...	... 231
†Howard, A. L.	... ...	38, 275	Hudson, R. C.	... ...	... 189
Howard, B. F.	... ...	... 309	Hudson, R. G.	... ...	... 369
Howard, E. H.	... ...	155, 374	Hudson, T.	... ...	... 211
Howard, F. C.	... ...	313a, 417	Huggill, H. P.	... ...	... 230
†Howard, G. G.	... ...	40, 249	Huggill, S. C. C.	... ...	... 417
Howard, G. V.	... ...	... 145	†Huggins, D. F.	... ...	37, 289
Howard, H. H. W.	... ...	... 269	Huggins, H. H.	... ...	... 410

¶ See reference to this name in *Corrigenda*.

HUGGINS

Huggins, N. L.	... ...	403
Huggins, R. H.	... ...	247
Huggins, W. L.	... ...	413
†Hugh-Jones, K. H.	... ...	21, 342
Hughes, A.	... ...	221
Hughes, A. P.	... ...	258
Hughes, A. V.	... ...	243
Hughes, B. V.	... ...	331
Hughes, C. E. C.	... ...	233
Hughes, E.	... ...	410
Hughes, F.	... ...	401
Hughes, F. A.	... ...	204
Hughes, G. C.	... ...	172
Hughes, G. E.	... ...	362
†Hughes, G. W. V.	... ...	26, 389
Hughes, H.	... ...	371
Hughes, H. A. M.	... ...	155, 354
Hughes, H. O.	... ...	349
Hughes, H. L. G.	... 48, 92, 150, 155
Hughes, J. B. W.	... ...	251
Hughes, K. E. A.	... ...	417
†Hughes, R. B.	... ...	17, 172
Hughes, R. G.	... ...	339
Hughes, T. H.	... ...	211, 309
†Hughes, T. McK.	... 29¶, 155, 164, 265
†Hughes, W.	... ...	35, 224
Hughes, Walter Owen (6871)	...	374
Hughes, Walter Owen (6314)	...	423
Hughes-Davies, H. E.	... ...	374
†Hughesdon, A. H.	... ...	38, 192
Hughesdon, R. H.	... ...	92, 232
Hugo, R. G.	... ...	31, 256
Hulbert, B. W.	... ...	192
Hull, G. V.	... ...	317
Hull, H. C.	... ...	172
Hullcoop, E. F.	... ...	364
†Hulm, W. O.	... ...	5¶, 236
†Hulse, C. W.	... ...	41
Hume, W. D.	... ...	410
Humpherson, S. F.	... ...	189
Hummerstone, L. G.	... ...	311a
Humphrey, G. M.	... ...	352
†Humphrey, H. G.	... ...	28
Humphrey, R. W.	... ...	364
†Humphreys, A. B.	... ...	§
Humphreys, B.	... ...	386
†Humphreys, D. F.	... ...	3, 361
Humphreys, J. C.	... ...	346
Humphries, G. R.	... ...	375
†Humphries, L. G.	... ...	20, 172
†Humpleby, E. S.	... ...	24
†Hunstone, G. N.	... ...	17, 172
Hunt, A.	... ...	255
Hunt, A. H.	... ...	93, 303
Hunt, A. T.	... ...	387
†Hunt, A. W.	... ...	33, 242
†Hunt, C. F.	... ...	42, 172
Hunt, E. G.	... ...	264
Hunt, F.	... ...	224

†Hunt, G. A.	... ...	23
Hunt, H. F.	... ...	401
Hunter, A.	... ...	336
†Hunter, A. F.	... ...	7, 304
Hunter, A. P.	... ...	155, 162
†Hunter, C. J.	... ...	41, 222
Hunter, E.	... ...	...
Hunter, G. F.	... ...	172
Hunter, G. T. F.	... ...	172
†Hunter, H.	... ...	25, 172
Hunter, J. D.	... ...	204
Hunter, J. E.	... ...	186
†Hunter, J. W.	... ...	8, 330
Hunter, R. M.	... ...	222
Hunter, R. Y.	... ...	204
Hurley, A. V.	... ...	172
Hurley, W. M. M.	... ...	172
Hurn, F. L.	... ...	334
Hurndall, C. F.	... ...	93, 194
Hurnell, H. F.	... ...	238
Hurrell, L. H. M.	... ...	221
Hurst, V. d. la M.	... ...	366
Hurst, W. M.	... ...	172
Hurt, W. G.	... ... 155, 322, 426
Husband, C. T. M.	... ...	209
Huskinson, A. W.	... ...	204
Hussey, T. McD.	... ...	255¶
Huston, A. R.	... ...	318
Hutcheson, C. R.	... ...	257
Hutchins, A. T. G.	... ...	336
Hutchinson, G. H.	... ...	278
Hutchinson, N. W.	... 159, 229
Hutchinson, N. W. H.	...	401
Hutchinson, S.	... ...	392
†Hutchinson, W. L.	... ...	37
†Hutchinson-Innes, O.	... 6, 257
Hutson, A. B.	... ...	231
†Hutt, H. R.	... ...	24
†Hutt, H. V.	... ...	2, 365
Hutton, A. M.	... ...	403
†Hutton, L. de H.	... ...	30, 417
Hutton, P. G.	... ...	300
Hutton, W. S.	... ...	286
Hyams, G.	... ... 155, 247, 279
Hyams, H. D.	... ...	93, 305
Hyatt, J. B.	... ...	364
Hyde, H. C.	... ...	280
Hyde, S.	... ...	318
Hyde-Parker, A. C.	... ...	383
Ibbotson, C. C.	... ...	322
†Ikin, A. E.	... ...	29, 172
Ilett, J. J.	... ...	317
Illingworth, J. R.	... ...	380
Imrie, D. P. C.	... ...	93, 289
†Imroth, L.	... ...	42, 254
im Thurn, A. McK.	... ...	256
Inch, T. A. D'L.	... ...	369
Indian Army R.O.	... ...	*421*

† Killed in action or died. § See this name in *Addenda*.

This Index does not include the Alphabetical Sections IV. and V. (Other Ranks and Old Members)

Infantry Regts.	221
Ingall, E. F.	149, 155
Ingall, H. E.	313a
Ingham, C. R.	392
†Ingleton, H. J.	41, 268
Inglis, T. G.	204
Ingram, J. T.	211
Ingrey, S. A.	401
Inland Water Transport	213
Inman, G. H. M.	420
Inman, J. J. T.	219
Inman, R. K.	407
Innes, C. G. D.	307
Innes, E. R.	412
Innes, F. I.	389
Inniskilling Fusiliers, Royal	258
Inns of Court O.T.C.	412
Inwood, C.	401
Iredale, J. T.	323
Ireland, A.	417
Ireland, D. W. S.	183
Ireland, E. P.	93, 424
Ireland, J. W.	247, 311
Irish Fusiliers, Royal	258
Irish Guards	220
Irish Regiment, Royal	259
Irish Rifles, Royal	259
Irving, G. G. H.	93, 341
Irwin, H.	231
Irwin, H. G.	314§¶
Irwin, R. W.	211
Irwin, W. G.	293
†Isaac, F. P.	4, 348
Isaacs, F. H.	304
†Isaacs, H. R.	13, 355
Isaacs, M. S.	228
†Isaacs, V. H.	38, 247
Isbell, H.	281
Itter, A.	360
Ivens, F. B.	155, 219
Ivers, W. E.	421
Ives, E. D. K.	172
Iveson, C. C.	300
Ivison, T.	173
Ivory, H. F.	148, 155, 405
Jack, J. F. S.	211
Jackes, A. E.	334
Jackman, R. J.	316
Jacks, R. N.	217
Jacks, W. G. C.	218
†Jackson, A.	12, 173
Jackson, A. F.	312
Jackson, A. G.	313a
Jackson, A. R. F.	365
Jackson, C. E.	371
Jackson, F. H.	240
Jackson, H. G.	173
Jackson, J. A.	275
†Jackson, James H.	31
†Jackson, John H.	9, 269
†Jackson, K. S.	24
Jackson, M. K.	93, 370
†Jackson, S. S.	30, 93, 381
Jackson, W.	219
Jackson, W. A.	224
Jackson, W. A. F.	173
Jackson, W. A. L.	417
Jackson, W. L.	274
Jacob, A. F.	305
Jacob, C. G.	269
†Jacob, C. O. R.	26, 234
Jacob, E.	34
†Jacobs, T. W.	198
Jacques, H. W.	390, 395
†Jacques, W. G.	40, 336
Jaques, W. H.	282
Jagger, C. S.	93, 383
Jago, E. G.	290
James, A. C.	173
James, C. G.	306
James, C. H.	275
James, E. A.	173
James, E. L.	267
James, E. W. H.	198
James, G.	155, 399
James, G. P. L.	356
James, H. G.	40
†James, H. S.	15, 227
James, H. W.	239
James, J. S.	413
†James, J. S. H.	3, 265
James, J. V.	420
James, L.	367
James, L. E.	94, 292
†James, M. C. C.	11, 381
James, P. L. S.	298
James, P. S.	198
James, R. S.	393
James, R. W.	337
†James, S. F.	11, 251
James, S. T.	272
James, W. E.	285
James, W. H.	383
James, W. T.	94, 289
James, W. T. B.	349
Jameson, R. H.	155, 392
†Jamieson, J.	32, 270
Jamieson, R. K.	413
Janson, F. E.	149, 229
Jaques, T. A.	211
Jarchow, C. J. F.	336
Jarry, M.	254
Jarvis, A.	94, 251
Jarvis, A. H.	173
†Jarvis, D. F. C.	28
†Jarvis, E. C.	9, 277
Jarvis, F. J.	255

¶ See reference to this name in *Corrigenda.*

JARVIS

INDEX TO COMMISSIONS, HONOURS, and ROLL OF HONOUR.

Jarvis, M. F.	300
Jarvis, P. W. L.	173
Jasper, R. F. T.	241
Jay, C. G.	356
Jeff, R. N. W.	173
†Jeffcock, R. S.	7, 353
Jefferies, S. S.	427
†Jefferson, H.	24
†Jeffery, G. J.	198
Jeffery, J. E.	394
Jefferys, C. J. M.	427
Jefferys, D. E.	350
Jeffree, H.	422
Jeffreys, A. H.	94, 155, 321
Jeffreys, J. R.	272
Jelks, W. M.	318
Jenkin, A. M.	228
Jenkins, A. C.	322
Jenkins, F. A.	392
Jenkins, G. R.	211
Jenkins, H. J. B.	211
Jenkins, I. C.	427
Jenkins, J. C.	220
Jenkins, J. L.	247
Jenkins, W. V.	262
Jenkinson, F. C.	274
Jenkinson, J. M.	386
Jennings, C. B.	356
Jennings, E. D.	173
Jennings, J.	211
Jennings, J. W.	159, 173
Jennings, P. H.	391
Jennings, P. J.	410
Jennings, S. H.	419
†Jensen, C. T.	7, 318
†Jephson, C. M. W.	27, 362
Jepson, L. R.	192
Jermyn, C. H.	370
Jermyn, O. R.	150, 163
Jerwood, E. L.	94, 155, 173, 224
†Jerwood, J. H.	30, 94, 240
Jevons, B.	284¶
Jewell, C. F. H.	163
Jewers, S. F.	278
Joad, S. F.	242
†Job, E. D.	8, 309, 415
John, A. H.	362
John, A. S.	375
Johns, G. G.	360
Johns, R. C.	358
†Johns, T.	32
Johnson, A.	356
Johnson, A. Dineen	334
Johnson, A. Dunphy	320
Johnson, A. F.	94, 204
Johnson, A. H.	204
Johnson, A. R.	189
Johnson, A. W.	382
Johnson, C.	214
Johnson, C. B.	94, 155, 227
†Johnson, C. E.	24
Johnson, D. D.	323
†Johnson, F. B.	17, 342
†Johnson, Francis H.	9, 302
Johnson, Frank H.	173
Johnson, F. L.	276
Johnson, F. S. B.	311a
Johnson, G.	312
Johnson, G. S.	
Johnson, H. S. V.	264
Johnson, J. F. F.	198
Johnson, J. H.	228
Johnson, L. O.	389
Johnson, R.	392
Johnson, R. C. B.	280
Johnson, R. F.	351
Johnson, R. N.	295
Johnson, R. W. S.	289
†Johnson, S. M.	16, 173
Johnson, T. A.	332
Johnson, W.	427
Johnson, W. F. L.	394
†Johnson, W. L.	6, 226
Johnson, W. Spencer	204
†Johnson, W. Stanley	13, 204, 360
†Johnston, A.	6, 348
Johnston, A. A.	240
†Johnston, D. C. B.	24
Johnston, E. J. C.	242, 371
Johnston, J. A.	321
Johnston, J. D.	94, 249
†Johnston, William (767984)	198
†Johnston, William (764705)	24
Johnstone, C. M.	413
Johnstone, F.	350
Johnstone, J. B.	238
Johnstone, R.	95, 173, 290
Joint, P. J.	236
Jolivet, A. E.	350
Jolley, J.	293
Jonas, L. N.	364
Jones, A.	373
Jones, A. A.	247
Jones, A. E.	330
Jones, A. G.	380
Jones, A. G. N.	173
Jones, A. I. M.	173
Jones, A. R.	378
Jones, A. T.	198
Jones, Cecil	259
Jones, Cecil Edmund	401
Jones, Cecil Greenstreet	304
†Jones, Clifford	19, 375
Jones, Clifford Ernest	268
†Jones, Cyril Gordon	26, 328
†Jones, C. T.	5, 155, 361
Jones, D.	198
Jones, D. H.	173

† Killed in action or died. § See this name in *Addenda*.

This Index does not include the Alphabetical Sections IV. and V. (Other Ranks and Old Members).

Name	Pages	Name	Pages
Jones, D. R.	367	Jones, W. E. F.	145, 173
Jones, D. W. C.	308	Jones, W. H.	155, 204
Jones, E.	336	Jones, W. H. L.	323
Jones, E. D.	293	Jones, W. R.	246
Jones, E. K.	173	Jones, W. S.	189
Jones, E. M.	377	Jordan, L. C. E.	247
Jones, E. O.	323	Jorgenson, E. S. L.	298
Jones, E. R.	417	Jose, E. S.	401
Jones, E. W.	366	†Joseph, J. R.	15, 173
Jones, F. B.	173	Joseph, M. B.	173
Jones, F. C.	211	Josephs, E. A. W.	95, 250
Jones, G.	286	Joslin, H. A.	368
Jones, G. A.	204	Josling, H. W.	189
Jones, George L.	374	Jubb, N.	316
Jones, Godfrey L.	395	Judd, C. E.	301
Jones, G. M.	376	†Judd, F. G.	4, 238, 313
†Jones, Harry (3137)	34, 290	Judge, L. J.	281
Jones, Harry (765314)	329	Jukes, S. C.	313a
Jones, H. C. B.	427	Jull, R. C.	95, 155, 198
Jones, H. F. N.	318	†Jump, S.	28
†Jones, H. J.	32¶, 259	Jump, W. B.	407
Jones, H. L.		Jungius, E. J. T.	95, 222, 313, 417
Jones, H. M.	399	Jupp, E. P.	227
Jones, Harold N.	275	Jupp, J. M. S.	95, 155, 316
Jones, Herbert N.	155, 374	Juppa, C. L. W.	313
Jones, H. R.	407	†Jurgens, S. G.	4, 279
Jones, H. V.	173	Jurjans, A.	337
Jones, J. D. W.	372	Jury, R. A.	373
†Jones, J. H. E.	37	Justice, H. M.	304
Jones, J. J.	330	Justice, W. B.	155, 204
Jones, J. L.		Kane, J. J.	220
Jones, J. P.	375¶	†Karslake, H. H.	15, 236
Jones, J. W.	427	Kassell, L. C.	204
†Jones, K. C.	7, 271	†Kay, G. A.	4, 335
†Jones, Lawrence	21, 358	Kay, J. du P.	335
†Jones, Leonard	3, 372	Kay, T. K.	219
Jones, Llewellyn	397	Kay, W. G.	321
Jones, L. O.	298	Kaye, H. G.	224
†Jones, L. P.	21, 378	Keable, B.	271
Jones, M. B.	288	Kear, B. M.	381
Jones, O. E.	310a	Kearton, A. S.	375
Jones, P. H.	95, 155, 209	Kearton, R.	173
Jones, P. L.	374	Keates, B.	264
Jones, R. E.	317	Keates, B. C.	405
Jones, R. H.	247	Keay, C. F. M.	281
Jones, R. L.	95, 296	Keay, W. H.	204
Jones, R. M.	288	Keddie, G. D. F.	291
†Jones, R. R.	20, 49, 155, 220	Keeble, G. H.	335
Jones, R. T.	261	Keech, F. S.	407
Jones, S. A. M.	304	Keefe, F. J. M.	389
Jones, Stanley G.	311a	Keeling, E. A.	410
Jones, Sydney G.	192	Keen, F. F.	173
Jones, T.	332	Keenahan, J. E. A.	173
Jones, T. J. W.	306	Keenan, F. W.	228
Jones, T. P.	264	Keene, A. V.	307
Jones, V.	341	Keene, G. G.	159, 401
Jones, V. E.	424	Keene, R. F.	295
Jones, W. B.	173	Keep, A. R.	95, 361
Jones, W. E. C.	282		

¶ See reference to this name in *Corrigenda*.

KEEPING

INDEX TO COMMISSIONS, HONOURS, and ROLL OF HONOUR.

Name	Pages	Name	Pages
†Keeping, C. J.	37, 321	Kenward, A. H. W.	306
Keeping, H. B.	149, 405	Kenyon, Reginald	211
Keeves, J. H.	424	Kenyon, Robert	379
Keevil, R. H.	407	Kenyon, S.	204
Keey, C. W.	95, 293	Kerckhove, H. V.	96, 358
†Kiely, R. E.	24	Kerr, J. V.	96, 293
†Keighley, L. R.	27, 278	†Kerr, R. T.	11, 386
Keites, W. L.	189	Kerr, T. H.	257
Keizer, M.	345	†Kerridge, C. D.	24
Kekewich, S. B.	95, 189	Kershaw, H.	286
†Kelland, R. S.	34, 421	Kessels, S. H.	247
Kellaway, G. L.	238	Kethro, G. G.	250
†Keller, F. F.	16, 291	Kew, E.	330
†Kellie, E. L.	3, 222	Keyes, F.	350
Kelly, B. R.	204	Keys, F. S.	366
Kelly, C. L.	275	Kibble, A. W.	155, 405
†Kelly, C. U. F.	24	Kibble, H. J.	173
Kelly, E. H. F.	326	Kidd, A. L.	173
Kelly, J. D.	256	†Kidd, C. B.	31, 96, 230
Kelly, P. H.	424	Kidd, J. C.	417
Kelly, W.	204	Kidd, N.	256
Kelsey, L. B.	218, 309	Kidd, R. C.	417
Kelsey, P. G.	173¶	Kidd, R. J.	221
Kelty, S. W.	96, 286	Kidner, C. H.	423
Kemball, S. J.	407	Kilbourn, W. G.	369
†Kemble, C. S.	32	Kilburn, J. E.	397
Kemble, J. A. E.	198	Kilham, F. L.	247
Kemp, A. F.	173	Killick, S. G.	323
Kemp, E. A.	366	†Kilner, C. U.	11, 354
Kemp, G.	211	Kilner, S. A.	313a
†Kemp, G. H.	34, 240	†Kilsby, G. A.	38, 329
Kemp, W. J.	293	†Kilvert, H.	19¶, 375
Kemp-Gee, P. N.	184	Kimber, D. V.	198
Kempson, H. L.	260	Kimber, E. D.	293
Kendall, F. J.	267	Kimber, J. A.	321
Kendall, S.	173	Kimberley, H. C.	218
Kendon, D. G.	155¶, 204	Kindell, A. O. W.	339
Kendrick, M. T.	391	King, B. E.	96, 155, 328
Kennard, G. V.	410	King, C. B. E.	352
Kennard, H. H. A.	420	†King, C. W. W.	23, 150
Kennedy, C. A. R.	96, 192	King, D. H.	204
Kennedy, F. C. de B.	401	King, E. C.	293
Kennedy, J.	274	King, E. F.	339
†Kennedy, John Gilbert	9, 280	King, E. G.	236
Kennedy, John Gordon	389	†King, E. G. L.	18, 217
†Kennedy, S. L. R. A. E.	9, 295	King, G.	244
Kennett, A. C. H.	305	King, G. A.	413
†Kennett, P. W.	24	King, G. B.	384
Kenney, D. G.	185	King, Guy Standish	198
Kensett, P. F.	251	King, Guy Stuart	417
Kent, C. W. T.	424	†King, H. G.	33, 244
†Kent, H.	19, 367	King, H. J.	297
Kent, J.	198	King, H. N.	96, 273
Kent, J. C.	403	King, H. W.	312
†Kent, L. V.	19, 367	King, J. B.	342
Kent, P. E. A.	315	King, J. M.	284
Kent Regt., East	260	King, J. T.	267
Kent Regt., Royal West	262	†King, J. W.	24
Kentsbeer, H. R.	264	King, K. V.	35, 173

† Killed in action or died. § See this name in *Addenda*.

This Index does not include the Alphabetical Sections IV. and V. (Other Ranks and Old Members).

Name	Page(s)
King, L. J. R.	279
King, Mark	49, 155, 218
King, Maurice	393
King, R.	230
King, Thomas Charles	319
King, Thomas Claude	403
King, Thomas Clifford	354
King, W.	204
King, W. C. C.	184
King, W. F.	234
Kingdon, F. D.	96, 192
Kingdon, R.	216
K.R.R.C.	265
Kingsley, H. T.	384
†King-Stevens, L. E.	12, 336
Kingston, H. F.	389
Kingswell, C. W.	192
Kinnear, A.	221
Kinnear, G. A.	221
Kinnel, B.	422
Kinniburgh, T. F.	346
Kinsey, H. W.	407
Kipping, S. D.	189
Kirby, F.	421
Kirby, G. T.	333
Kirby, H. G.	336
Kirby, N. F.	325
Kirby, R. W.	348
Kirby, W. H.	291
†Kirch, C. S.	3, 222
Kirchner, B. J.	352
Kirchner, L. G.	268
Kirk, A. W.	218
Kirk, H. W.	401
Kirk, J.	386
Kirk, K. L.	269
Kirk, L. D.	347
†Kirk, R. L.	38
†Kirkaldy, C. H.	2, 347
Kirkbride, G. H.	334
Kirkbride, H. J.	186
Kirkby, N. W.	251, 390
Kirkpatrick, J.	221
Kirkpatrick, K. J.	204
†Kirkus, C. H.	19, 204
Kirton, H. H.	278
Kirton, S.	401
Kissane, R.	284
Kitcat, A. J.	380
Kitcat, E. N.	394
†Kitchin, A.	34¶
Kitching, G. C.	311a
Klein, A. B. L.	148, 150, 327
Klingner, F. V.	195
Klugman, J. V.	318
Knapman, T. B.	401
Knee, H. J.	223
Knevitt, E. B.	410
Knight, A. E.	235
Knight, A. G.	173
Knight, A. O.	97, 274
Knight, D. J.	217
†Knight, E. J.	16, 269
Knight, F. W.	296
Knight, H.	189
Knight, H. de B.	255
Knight, H. F.	150, 163
Knight, H. J.	356
Knight, H. W.	336
Knight, R.	173
Knock, N. H.	173
Knott, C. D.	283
Knott, H. P.	311
Knowles, A. R.	173
Knowles, C. G.	173
Knowles, P.	199
Knowles, R. E.	97, 204
Knowles, S. A.	318
Knowles-Brown, A. W.	183
Knowles-Brown, F. H.	267
Knox, H. H.	293
Knox, J.	410
Knox, P. J.	173
†Knox, T. C.	36, 286
Knuth, C. H. L.	215
†Koch, M. A.	5, 348
Kowin, J.	350
†Krohn, N. A.	3, 226
Kruse, E. C.	235
Kruse, H. S.	199
Kyle, J.	309
Labatt, W. H. E.	394
Labour Corps	412
Labrow, L.	173
Lacey, E. A.	286
Lacey, N.	410
Lacy, A. O.	173
Ladefoged, E. L. N.	192
Ladefoged, N. N.	187
Ladell, C. S.	155, 413
†Lafford, W. J.	24
Lagesee, C. H. R.	145, 150, 155, 173
La Hive, B.	401
Laidlaw, G. A.	257
†Laidlaw, J. C.	25, 346
†Laily, E. L.	6, 233
Lailey, G. B. P.	233
Laing, D. M.	345
†Laing, I.	27, 97, 218
†Laing, J. G.	39, 309, 415
Laing, W.	218
Laing, W. D.	244
Laithwaite, A.	155, 301
Lake, H. C. E.	291
Lake, M. B. C.	364
†Lakeman, H. L.	36, 407
Laker, J. C.	401

¶ See reference to this name in *Corrigenda*.

LAMB

INDEX TO COMMISSIONS, HONOURS, and ROLL OF HONOUR.

Name	Page(s)	Name	Page(s)
Lamb, A. L.	318	Larkman, R.	304
Lamb, H.	413	Larlham, P. E.	246
Lamb, J. E.	173	†Lascelles, R. M.	21
Lamb, T. S.	204	Lasker, R. S.	174
†Lambdin, J. R.	38, 97, 395	†Last, E. R.	31, 97, 155, 285
Lambert, C. O.	155, 269, 290	Latham, H.	322
Lambert, E. C.	276	Latham, L. S.	174
Lambert, F. P.	97, 173	Latham, W. G.	174
†Lambert, P. F.	15, 378	Lathbury, R. J.	291
Lambert, R.	267	Lathom, F. W. F.	311a
Lambert, S. A.	238	La Touche, A. P. D.	155¶, 297
Lambert, W.	275	Latour, A. F.	384
Lambert, W. H.	248	Lauder, D. M.	316
Lamble, A. H.	228	Lauderdale, T. M.	378
Lamigeon, R. O.	223	Laughland, D. S.	204
Laming, H. E.	401	Laughlin, G. E.	225
Lampshire, L. F.	391	†Laughton, G.	27¶, 334
Lancashire Fusiliers	*268*	†Laughton, J. T.	39, 222
Lancashire Regt., East	*271*	Laurent, H. F.	310a
Lancashire Regt., Loyal North	*273*	Laurie, A. M.	215
Lancashire Regt., South	*276*	Laver, B. L.	187
Lancaster, J. H. L.	373	Laver, C. H.	187
Lancaster, J. W. C.	195	Lavers, F. G.	255
Lancaster Regt., Royal	*278*	Laverton, W. K.	186
Lance, F. P.	313a	Lavoipierre, M. J. M. L.	293
Lancers	*184*	†Law, C. L. G.	5, 354
Land, L. F.	155, 424	Law, E. R.	174
†Lander, J. H.	13	Law, H. R.	424
Landless, M.	173	Law, K. K.	227
Lane, F. S.	260	Lawless, A. P.	220
Lane, G. B.	264	Lawless, P. H.	97, 155, 163¶, 322
Lane, H. A.	247	Lawrence, B. L.	352
Lane, H. C. J.	383	†Lawrence, E. E.	12
Lane, J. R. C.	327	Lawrence, Francis C.	298
Lane, R. B.	174	Lawrence, Frederick C.	391
Lane-Claypon, J. C.	283	Lawrence, G.	397
Laney, E. C.	199	Lawrence, H. A.	422
Lang, A. H.	384	Lawrence, H. P.	297
Lang, E. G.	419	Lawrence, H. W.	273
Lang, R. S.	231	Lawrence, J. H.	148, 155, 403
Langdon, E. M.	247	Lawrence, J. N.	375
Langford, J. C.	174	Lawrence, L.	424
†Langford, J. J.	9, 266	Lawrence, S. B.	289
Langford, T. H.	211	Lawrence, S. G.	192
†Langford, W. G.	7, 266	Lawrie, T.	269
Langhorne, A. J.	204	†Lawson, A. C.	18, 341
†Langley, F. J.	37, 217	Lawson, G. L. L.	312a
Langley, R. K.	293	Lawson, J. P.	396
Langley, W. R.	321	Lawson, P. H.	204
Langton, E. S. W.	298	Lawson, V. W.	174
Langston, H. P.	267	Laxton, E. W. H.	405¶
Lant, A. E.	215	Layborn, T. A. E.	159, 174
†Larcombe, H. R. R.	20, 247	†Laycock, J. H.	10, 266
Larcombe, M. A.	401	Layman, A. T.	330
Lardelli, M. S.	189	Lazarus, G. M.	205
Lardner, R. S.	222	Lazarus, J. P.	301
†Larken, J. S.	38, 186	Lazenby, B. W.	262
Larkin, J.	275	Lazenby, H.	293
Larkins, G. J.	427	Lazzari, R.	174

† Killed in action or died.   § See this name in *Addenda*.

LEWIS

This Index does not include the Alphabetical Sections IV. and V. (Other Ranks and Old Members). 547

Lea, G. H. ... 359	†Leftwich, N. G. ... 33, 155, 230
Leach, J. ... 272	Legg, A. H. ... 337
Leach, T. H. du B. ... 417	Legg, J. F. ... 311a
Leadbeater, A. J. O. ... 413	Legg, W. ... 215
Leader, C. ... 186	Legg, W. G. ... 393
Leahy, E. ... 199	Legge, L. ... 174
Leahy, J. M. ... 359	Leggett, G. W. ... 299
†Leake, G. E. A. ... 17, 49, 155, 290	Leggett, S. J. ... 192
Leake, R. ... 174	Legh-Jones, G. ... 415
Leal, J. H. ... 255	Leicester, J. ... 230
†Leaning, R. W. ... 34, 286	*Leicestershire Regt.* ... 280
Lear, E. C. R. ... 306	Leigh, H. G. ... 267
Lear, F. H. ... 370	Leigh-Bennett, E. P. ... 311
†Learoyd, E. S. ... 26, 323	Leigh-Breeze, P. L. ... 390
†Leatherdale, D. R. ... 8, 262	Leighton, K. A. W. ... 174
†Leaver, S. H. ... 32, 323	Leighton, N. ... 313
†Le Bas, A. O. ... 28	Leighton, W. J. C. ... 312
†Le Chene, H. P. ... 304	*Leinster Regt.* ... 282
†Lechertier, J. A. ... 41, 192	Leishman, W. G. ... 262
Ledger, A. P. ... 264	Leith, G. H. ... 98, 155, 417
Ledger, G. ... 189	Leivers, F. A. ... 350
Ledger, H. G. ... 339	Le Maistre, F. W. ... 214
Ledger, R. ... 174	Le Mare, Ralph ... 258
Ledward, C. H. ... 205	Le Mare, Reginald ... 258
Lee, A. F. ... 424	Lemon, K. C. ... 251
Lee, A. H. ... 281	†Lemon, L. T. ... 14, 238
Lee, C. F. ... 255	Lemon, M. M. S. ... 250
Lee, D. M. ... 277	Lemon, R. H. ... 362
Lee, E. C. ... 301	Lennard, W. D. ... 225
Lee, E. J. ... 159, 269	Leonard, G. C. ... 323
Lee, F. R. M. ... 341	Leonard, J. J. ... 232
†Lee, F. S. ... 30, 342	Leonard, T. J. ... 405
Lee, J. ... 313	Lepine, R. D ... 283
Lee, J. R. L. ... 293	Lepingwell, G. B. ... 309
†Lee, P. W. ... 13, 349	Leppard, P. H. ... 225
Lee, R. W. ... 97, 242	Leslie, A. D. ... 279
†Lee, W. N. O. ... 5, 352	Leslie-Smith, J. ... 163
†Leech, A. W. ... 33, 97, 331	Lester, R. M. ... 323
Leech, N. H. ... 174	Lett, W. T. C. ... 259
†Leech, R. E. H. ... 39, 349	Letts, A. P. ... 332
Leech, S. F. ... 261	Lever, E. H. ... 150, 155, 205
Leech-Porter, J. E. ... 418	Leverett, J. I. ... 186
Leeding, W. J. ... 314	Leverson, D. L. F. ... 295, 309
Leefe, J. F. F. ... 321¶	Leveson, A. H. ... 323
Lee-Hankey, W. ... 309	Levett, S. C. B. ... 205
Leek, F. W. ... 395	†Levick, C. ... 35, 174
Leek, P. A. ... 375	Levien, C. H. ... 305
Lees, A. A. ... 396	Levy, B. H. ... 417
Lees, Geoffry ... 215	Levy, F. W. ... 410
Lees, H. W. ... 379	Levy, G. ... 279
Lees, J. H. ... 296	Levy, O. C. ... 199
Leese, L. E. S. ... 405	Lewin, H. J. ... 355
Lee-Smith, D. L. ... 401	Lewin, W. E. ... 290
Lee-Smith, G. ... 296	Lewington, C. ... 313a, 417
Lee-Smith, K. ... 250	Lewis, A. G. ... 174
Leete, B. M. T. S. ... 174	Lewis, A. H. ... 340
Leete, F. B. ... 300	Lewis, A. T. ... 367
Le Fevre, F. E. ... 98, 283	Lewis, C. A. ... 174
†Lefroy, T. E. ... 27, 155, 311, 370	Lewis, C. J. B. ... 305

¶ See reference to this name in *Corrigenda.*

Lewis, C. M.	208
Lewis, C. W.	174
†Lewis, D.	20
Lewis, D. I.	317
Lewis, D. R. T.	278
Lewis, E. F.	375
Lewis, F.	189
Lewis, F. A.	98, 277
Lewis, F. T.	228
Lewis, Gerald	214
Lewis, Grafton	407
Lewis, G. P.	192
Lewis, G. W.	423
†Lewis, H. L.	23, 334
Lewis, H. S.	274
Lewis, James	199
Lewis, John	223
Lewis, J. P.	375
Lewis, L. A.	174
Lewis, M.	311
Lewis, N. C.	227
Lewis, O. B.	373
Lewis, R. P.	189
Lewis, T. F.	375
Lewis, T. H. L.	174
†Lewis, T. W.	23, 375
Lewis, William	205
†Ley, J. W.	28
†Leybourne, P. E.	38, 98, 254
Libby, W. N.	325
Lichfield, G. F.	244
Liddell, A. R.	155, 333
Liddiard, T. G.	293
Liddington, H. V.	189
Liddle, A. R.	413
Liddle, D. M. P.	155¶, 403
†Lidgett, J. C.	30, 277
Liebert, A. J.	405
Liell, K.	195, 403
Liffen, G. T. T.	394
Light, F. R.	309
Lightbourn, F. G.	192
†Lightfoot, F. B.	28, 310a
Lightley, E.	199
Lilley, E. S.	253
Lilley, J. L.	260
Lima, W.	401
Lincolnshire Regt.	282
Lindars, L. H.	189
Lindbergh, W. H.	410
Linden, G. H.	276
Linder, H.	401
Lindley, G. W.	224
Lindop, R. A. E.	258
†Lindrea, W. G.	32, 250
Lindsay, G. P.	98, 226
Lindsay, J.	345
Lindsay, J. G.	279
Line, J. P.	289
Lines, A. J.	277
Linford, B. O. M.	174
Ling, G. A.	355
Lingard, H.	332
Linter, F. C.	323
Lintern, L. E.	249
Linton, W. E.	350
†Lintott, H. C.	30, 291, 311a
Lipschitz, J. M.	192
Lipscombe, D. de B.	336
Lissack, M. S.	299
Lisser, H. C. J.	293
Lister, A. W.	98, 192
†Lister, J. C.	16, 187, 359
Little, H. R.	174
†Littleboy, V. H.	27, 164
Littler, A. E.	286
†Littler, F.	18, 277
†Littler, T.	18, 174
†Livermore, E. B.	10, 306
Liverpool Regt.	285
Livesey, J. W.	337
Livingstone, F. M.	174
†Livock, E. S.	25, 174, 362
Livock, R. P.	214
†Llarena, E. F.	4, 354
Llewellyn, A. H.	350
Llewellyn, J. T.	331
†Llewellyn, T. G.	24
†Llewellyn, V.	41, 375
Lloyd, C. T. J.	375
Lloyd, D. H.	325
†Lloyd, E. C.	39, 367
†Lloyd, F. B.	10, 234
Lloyd, G. L.	155, 192
Lloyd, G. Y. L.	199
Lloyd, H. S. J.	377, 415
Lloyd, O. O.	149
Lloyd, R. J.	389
Lloyd, S. C.	274
Lloyd, T. R.	291
†Lloyd-Jones, J.	6, 98, 155, 390
Loader, G. S.	199
Lobb, A. J.	421
Lock, H.	159
†Lock, J. A.	10, 334
†Lock, J. P.	29, 189
Lock, P.	323
Lockett, C. C.	199
Lockett, M. V.	410
†Lockhart, R. F.	18, 299
Lockie, L. P. D.	267
Lockier, A. E.	423
Lockwood, E. J.	98, 243
Lockwood, G. K.	392
Lockwood, R.	413
Lodder, W. C.	413
Lodge, A. P. D.	363, 426
Lodge, D. R.	219

† Killed in action or died. § See this name in *Addenda*.

This Index does not include the Alphabetical Sections IV. and V. (Other Ranks and Old Members).

Lofthouse, C. T.	... 317	Lowe, E. 272
†Lofting, C. E.	12, 334	Lowe, G. M. ... 228
Lofting, H. J.	... 220	Lowe, J. L. 155, 192
Lofts, F.	... 319	Lowe, S. T. ... 317
Logan, W. W.	... 189	Lowe, T. H. ... 410
Lomas, L. F.	... 174	Lowe, W. C. ... 288
Lomax, G. C.	... 209	Lowick, J. S. ... 272
London Regt.	*289*	Lowles, H. ... 338
Long, A. W.	... 174	†Lowrie, J. E. ... 184§
Long, B. E.	... 263	Lowrie, W. A. ... 267
Long, E. B.	... 372	†Lowry, V. C. 32, 358
Long, F. C.	... 303	Lowther, W. J. 194, 298
Long, F. W.	... 214	*Loyal North Lancs. Regt.* *273*
†Long, J. T.	22, 174	Loynes, J. H. ... 185
Long, O. A.	... 228	Luard, S. D'A. ... 384
Long, S. H.	... 183	Lubbock, H. T. ... 310
Long, T. D.	155, 271	Lucas, A. W. T. ... 205
Long, W. B.	... 340	Lucas, C. J. 99, 293
Long, W. H.	... 260	Lucas, E. H. A. ... 386
Longbotham, C .B.	98, 333	Lucas, H. D. ... 304
Longden, G.	... 174	Lucas, J. K. ... 268
Longley, P. R. H.	... 256	Lucas, L. M. ... 419
†Longstaff, J. C.	...8, 385	Lucas, L. W. ... 356
Longstaff, R.	99, 393	Lucas, T. M. ... 199
Longstaff, R. F.	... 337	Lucke, D. H. ... 261
†Longthorpe, F.	38, 424	Lucke, F. W. ... 401
†Longuet-Higgins, K.	...3, 418	†Luckhurst, W. H. 15, 390
Lonsdale, P. H.	... 385	Ludbrook, P. ... 291
†Looker, A. D.	40, 356	†Ludlow, L. 11, 296
Looms, A.	... 250	Ludski, J. C. ... 174
Looseley, C. A.	... 199	Luke, A. W. G. ... 174
Lord, C. G.	... 199	†Lumb, H. ...5, 187
†Lord, F. S.	...2, 234	Lumby, R. E. A. ... 424
Lord, G. H.	99, 279	Lumsden, F. ... 205
Lord, H.	... 363	Lund, P. A. ... 427
Lorimer, J. S.	99, 327	Lunn, A. R. ... 282
Lort, R. G.	... 378	Lunn, B. H. ... 257
Lort, W. V.	99, 293	Lunn, P. R. ... 376
Lott, F. A.	99, 376	Lupton, L. ...155, 268, 278
Loudon, R. M. W.	... 174	Luscombe, D. A. ... 427
Loudon, W. F.	... 346	Luscombe, R. A. ... 233
†Loudoun, T.	35, 257	Luscombe, V. ... 227
Loup, L. A.	... 335	Luscombe, V. C ... 199
Love, G. R. S.	... 399	Lusty, R. A. ... 366
Love, R. N.	... 364	Lyal, D. H. ... 298
Loveless, R. B.	155, 298	Lye, P. ... 205
Loveless, R. E.	... 254	Lyford, E. ... 199
Lovell, A. H.	... 362	Lyford, J. ... 428¶
Lovell, B.	99, 424	Lyle, A. H. ... 249
†Lovell, E. C.	26, 269	Lyle, A. M. A. ... 349
Lovell, G. H.	163, 401	Lynam, E. W. O'F. ... 259
Lovell, P. T.	... 189	Lynch, G. A. ... 389
Lovell, P. W.	... 331	Lynch, J. F. A. ... 407
Loveridge, J. L.	99, 225	Lynch, M. G. L. ... 410
Lovett, F. J.	... 251	Lyne, H. W. 99, 388
†Low, H. St. J.	... 21	Lynes, J. A. ... 305
Low, H. V.	... 174	Lynn, D. L. ... 174
†Lowder, N. R.	15, 369	Lynn, H. ... 407
Lowe, A. E.	... 396	Lynn, S. ... 205

¶ See reference to this name in *Corrigenda*.

LYON

INDEX TO COMMISSIONS, HONOURS, and ROLL OF HONOUR.

Name	Pages
Lyon, F. T. B.	155, 286
Lyon, W. W.	... 251
Lyons, E. F.	100, 236
†Lyons, E. T.	22, 272
Lyons-Campbell, A.	... 189

In determining alphabetical order the prefix "MC" is treated in this Index as if spelt "MAC."

Name	Pages
Mabe, H. P.	... 284
Mabey, C. D.	... 263
†Mabey, J. H.	26, 305
†McAdam, A. C.	38, 418
McAlester, C. J.	... 239
McAllister, A.	... 233
†MacAndrew, W. F.	... 16
MacArthur, R.	... 362
†Macarthy, J. J.	... 42
Macaulay, D. I.	... 253
Macaulay, J.	... 174
Macaulay, W. H.	... 242
McAvoy, D. G.	... 244
McBain, H.	100, 241
Macbean, C. A.	... 337
Macbeth, B. J. G.	... 205
†McCall, A.	20, 100, 345
McCall, E. B.	... 221
McCann, W. J.	155, 326
McCarraher, C.	... 385
†McCarthy, T. F.	33, 100, 274
†McClarence, S.	14, 334
McClellan, J. F. M.	... 225
McClellan, R. J.	... 413
McConachy, J. L.	... 267
McConnel, J. E. G.	... 292
McCormick, A. E.	... 302
†McCormick, H.	16, 271
McCorquodale, G. M.	155, 273
McCubbin, B. A.	... 175
†MacCullock, A. G.	... 391
McCullock, A. G.	... 391
MacDonald, A.	... 413
MacDonald, A. L.	16, 316
MacDonald, C. A.	... 211
McDonald, D. C.	... 175
MacDonald, E. A. G.	... 240
Macdonald, E. N.	145, 174
Macdonald, E. P.	... 186
MacDonald, J.	150, 174
McDonald, John (765660)	... 205
McDonald, John (764502)	... 231
Macdonald, K.	100, 347
MacDonald, R.	... 228
†MacDonald, R. F. K.	... 27
McDonogh, B. M.	... 375
MacDougall, P. A.	100, 174
McDowall, R. A.	155, 378
Mace, A.	... 250
Mace, A. C.	... 407

Name	Pages
Mace, E. R.	102, 285
Mace, H. K.	... 298
McEwan, H. H.	... 238
†Macey, C. J.	...4, 237
McFadyen, J. C.	17, 189
Macfarlane, D. M.	100, 270
McGhee, G. D.	... 428
†McGibbon, W. P.	21, 239
†McGibney, F. G.	15, 258
McGorrery, C. M.	175, 403
MacGrath, M. R.	... 220
MacGregor, C. S.	... 174
McGregor, Evan	... 410
MacGregor, G. G.	... 189
MacGregor, H. J.	... 205
MacGregor, J.	... 423
MacGregor, J. E. M.	... 365
MacGregor, J. S.	... 344
McGregor, N. M.	52, 164
McGregor, R. T.	... 413
McHale, J. E.	... 205
†McHardy, S. J.	33, 293
Machin, N. F.	102, 218
Machine Gun Corps	... 415
Machine Gun School	... 313
†McIlroy, J.	... 30
McIlwraith, T. F.	... 345
McIlwraith, W. L.	... 175
MacInnes, W. A.	100, 256
McIntyre, E.	229, 403
McIntyre, N.	... 403
McIver, C. D.	... 362
Mack, E. H.	... 328
†Mackain, H. F.	13, 165
Mackay, D. J. E.	101, 212
†Mackay, G.	19, 417
Mackay, J. W.	... 392
Mackay, R. L.	... 189
Mackay, S. T.	... 423
McKechnie, W.	... 286
McKeever, G. N.	155, 321
McKelvey, G. F.	... 205
Mackendrick, B.	... 212
Mackenzie, A.	... 347
Mackenzie, E. C. F.	... 253
†Mackenzie, F. B.	35, 196
Mackenzie, K.	... 345
McKenzie, L.	... 227
Mackenzie, R. S.	227, 328
McKenzie-Fowler, F. L.	... 261
McKeown, F. Q.	101, 205
McKerrow, H. D.	... 345
†McKie, D. H.	14, 333
†McKie, E.	31, 267¶
Mackie, J. H.	... 228
McKie, R. D. M.	155¶, 199
Mackie, W. G.	101, 379
McKim, W. R.	... 212
McKinley, C.	101, 312

† Killed in action or died. § See this name in *Addenda*.

This Index does not include the Alphabetical Sections IV. and V. (Other Ranks and Old Members).

Name	Pages	Name	Pages
McKinty, H. B.	101, 192	Madge, H. E.	231
Mackinley, D. M.	266	Maggs, L. E.	342
Mackinnon, G. W.	192	†Magson, W.	39
Mackinnon, N. L.	185	Mahon, J. F.	192
Mackintosh, C. S.	410	†Mahony, J.	13, 363
†Mackintosh, H. L.	2, 155, 352	†Maiden, A. A.	10, 389
Mackintosh, J. M.	214	Maidlow, G.	348
Mackintosh, P. R.	424	Maidment, C. V.	298
†Macklin, D. H.	31, 223	Maile, W. S.	155, 403
McKnight, C. H.	420	†Maingot, E.	39
Mackrell, H. R.	185	Maingot, J. H.	102, 174, 426
MacLachlan, R.	245	Maingot, J. P. L.	355
†McLaren, A. C.	24	Maingot, L. F.	410
Maclaren, D.	174	Maingot, P. S.	102, 155, 275
McLaren, E.	386	Maingot, R. J.	245
McLaren, R. A.	175	Maingot, V. J.	426
McLean, A. J.	276	Mainwaring, E. C.	310a
McLellan, C. D.	205	Maitland, N. E.	423
McLellan, R. B.	286	Maitland-Edwards, R. S.	218
MacLennan, J. C.	174	Makalua, M. J. M.	148, 150, 163, 366
McLeod, E. D.	407	Makin, L. S. L.	424
Macleod, E. L. H.	384	Malabar, R. F.	174
McManus, A.	195	Malan, J. G. M.	212
†MacMillan, C. E.	37	†Malcham, E. H.	32, 385¶
McMillan, E. A.	101, 229	Malcolm, E. A.	333
MacMillan, R. J.	323	†Malcolm, K. J.	29, 303
McMillan, W.	340	Male, S. J.	102, 266
McMullen, J. R.	225	†Mallalieu, J.	25, 379
McNair, F. R.	363	Mallen, A.	413
McNair, W. L.	253, 371	Mallett, A. W.	249
McNally, I.	330	Mallett, E. A.	342
McNally, R. J. C.	330	†Mallett, E. S.	7, 271
'Macnamara, G. E.	302	Mallett, N.	205
McNamara, J. P.	410	Mallinson, B.	285
McNaught, J. M.	362	†Mallock, D.	9, 209
MacNaughton, A.	312	Malpass, C. E.	102, 312
MacNaughton, R.	174	†Malsom, F. G.	24
McNeil, A. A.	186	Maltby, R. A. L.	312a
MacNichol, D.	410	†Manby, C. J.	24
McNiel, R.	410	*Manchester Regt.*	*315*
McNiell, J. D.	217	Manley, G. D.	220
McNulty, G. H.	407	Manley, H. C.	355
McNulty, M. S.	279	Manlove, J. E. D.	279
†Macouat, J.	14, 344	Mann, C. C.	372
Macpherson, Mc. G.	253	Mann, D.	103, 361
MacQueen, A. J.	183	Mann, D. B. U.	103, 350
McQueen, J. F. F.	380	Mann, E. H.	410
McSweeney, E. A.	401	†Mann, F. C.	2, 351
McTurk, E.	183	Mann, F. R.	103, 155, 255
McWalter, T. B.	101, 359	Mann, J. G.	301
McWilliam, E. C.	276	Mann, J. W.	410
McWilliam, W. R.	323	Mann, P. J.	247
Madan, A. G.	245	Mann, P. R.	148, 155, 298
†Madan, N. C.	6, 279	†Mann, R. L.	11
Madden, C. R.	102, 283	†Mann, W. G.	26¶, 174
†Maddock, O. L.	10, 296	Manners, C.	192
Maddock, R. H.	102, 155, 361	Manning, A. R. O.	277
†Maddocks, J. A.	7, 371	Manning, J. W. G.	224
†Maddox, L. G.	37, 102, 304	†Mansel-Howe, C. I.	36, 305

¶ See reference to this name in *Corrigenda*.

INDEX TO COMMISSIONS, HONOURS, and ROLL OF HONOUR.

Name	Pages
Mansfield, F. A.	262
Mansfield, F. T.	103, 212, 262, 319
Manson, A. M.	289
Mantegazza, R.	174
Manvell, F. G.	323
March, B. D.	403
Marchant, A. R.	407
†Marchant, C. V.	27, 300
Marchant, H. H.	330
Marchant, S. G.	261
Marcus, L. J.	356
Mares, A. F.	421
Mares, F. G.	407
Margetson, A. C.	383
Margetson, E.	103, 310
†Margetson, E. A.	17, 175
†Margoliouth, A. H.	13, 175
Margoliouth, J. F.	297
Margrett, G. M.	300
Marines, Royal	418
Mark, J.	192
Markham, L. A.	300
Markham, R. C. S.	428
Marks, A. E.	175
Marks, E. G.	236
†Marks, J.	40, 241
Marks, L.	365
†Marlor, E.	15, 379
†Marlow, C. D.	19, 239
Marrable, C. G.	156, 325
Marriott, C.	413
Marriott, C. L.	428
Marriott, D. W.	175
Marriott, H. B.	267
Marriott, J. R.	428
Marriott, J. S.	272
Marryat, H. P.	270
Marsden, D. H.	191
Marsden, G. R.	175
Marsden, W.	103, 274
Marsh, C. H.	263
Marsh, C. J. M.	225
Marsh, W. E.	306
†Marshall, A. de la P.	3, 271
Marshall, C. M.	378
Marshall, F.	103, 192
†Marshall, H.	41, 413
†Marshall, J. H.	11, 271
Marshall, J. W.	310
Marshall, L. G.	244
Marshall, O. F. B.	156, 313, 388
Martin, A.	205
Martin, A. D.	175
†Martin, Alfred Edgar	28
Martin, Alfred Ernest	253
Martin, A. G.	301
Martin, A. S.	247
Martin, A. W. D.	103, 257
†Martin, C. B.	32, 304
Martin, C. F.	199
†Martin, C. S.	22, 281
Martin, D. R.	342
Martin, E. A.	156, 389
†Martin, E. J.	38, 289
Martin, E. L.	378
†Martin, E. W.	8, 327
Martin, E. W. L.	104, 405
†Martin, F. A.	5, 335
Martin, G. B.	104, 297
Martin, H. A.	297
Martin, L.	391
Martin, L. N.	236
Martin, O. S.	349
Martin, R.	254
Martin, Reginald D.	104, 156, 330
Martin, Richard D.	232
Martin, R. I.	163
Martin, R. J.	297
Martin, T. G.	234
Martin, V. C.	163, 338
†Martin, W. H.	19, 341, 375
Martin-Smith, F. A.	342
Martindale, D. P.	370
Martinez, H. E. N.	297
Martyn, A. N.	175
Martyn, R. N.	189
Martyr, A. G.	397
Martyr, H. A. C.	175
†Marvin, D.	3, 347
Marvin, D. W.	163
†Marvin, H. L.	23, 175
Marzetti, C.	362
Marzetti, L.	362
Mascall, V. C.	274
Masding, S. H. P.	325
Mash, J. L.	340
Maskall, R. G.	175
Maskell, H. P.	104, 380
†Maskray, H.	24¶
Mason, A. H.	348
Mason, C. A.	175
Mason, C. J. M.	255
Mason, D. C.	384
Mason, D. H.	238
Mason, F.	156, 354
†Mason, George (764004)	33, 352
†Mason, George (763073)	16, 175
Mason, G. B.	252
Mason, H.	300
Mason, H. G.	254
Mason, H. J.	104, 244
Mason, K. S.	104, 223
Mason, L. R.	163
Mason, W. T.	238
Massey, A. E.	185
Massey, H.	199
Massey, R.	175
Massey, W. G.	396

† Killed in action or died. § See this name in *Addenda*.

MENTIONS

This Index does not include the Alphabetical Sections IV. and V. (Other Ranks and Old Members).

Name	Pages	Name	Pages
†Massie, S. E.	16, 349	May, H. A. R.	148, 156, 307
Massing, G. C.	339	May, H. R. D.	105, 370
Massingham, G.	240	May, R. H.	249
Massy-Burnside, G. E.	156, 418	May, R. R.	199
Masterman-Smith, P. A.	417	May, Samuel	407
†Masters, C. W.	20, 245	May, Stuart	189
Masters, E. H.	151, 175	Maybin, J. A.	189
Masters, F. J. J.	340	†Maybrook, W. R.	7, 380
Matcham, J. N. L.	293	Maycock, S. H.	205
Mather, H. G.	267	Mayer, J. J.	212
†Mather, V.	19, 274	Mayes, R. B.	330
Matheson, D. W. M.	228	Maylin, B. H.	286
†Matheson, H.	31, 299	Maynard, F. G.	159, 284
Mathias, D. E.	156, 368	Mayne, W. E.	175
Mathias, E. J.	377	Mayo, A. H.	105, 393
Matson, R. C.	398	Mayo, B. A. J.	338
Matthew, A. J.	379, 395	Mayo, C. D.	343
Matthew, C. F.	175	Mayo, S. H.	225
Matthew, D.	104, 312a	Mayoh, T.	396
Matthew, J. R.	209	Mayor, B. R.	205
Matthews, B. F. S.	241	Maywood, R. A. J.	279
Matthews, C. C.	175	Meachem, F. R.	105, 205
Matthews, E. F.	149, 156, 348	†Meacock, R. H.	11, 240
†Matthews, E. P.	10, 341	†Mead, B. W.	4, 245
Matthews, F. N.	305	Mead, C. E.	410
Matthews, G. H.	104, 393	Mead, C. J. H.	418
Matthews, G. J. J.	183	Mead, J. R.	214
Matthews, H. E.	148	Mead, J. T.	350
Matthews, J. A.	175	†Meade, C.	13, 250
Matthews, J. C.	175	Meadon, E. E.	424
†Matthews, J. H.	31, 225	Meadows, C. S.	105, 193
†Matthews, R. M.	21, 391	Meadows, R. M.	428
Matthews, R. P.	385	Meakins, A. T.	340
Matthews, S. E.	275	Meakins, J. B.	306
†Matthews, T.	35, 149, 205	Meany, W.	326
Matthews, W. H.	104, 358	Mears, S. S.	244
Matthyssens, F. A.	401	†Measures, P.	28, 280
Mattocks, C. F.	250	Mcates, G. M.	263
Mattocks, W. T. E.	382	Meatyard, G. W.	254
†Maudsley, H. D.	24	Meddings, E. S.	425
Maudsley, H. P.	270	†Medland, J. E. P.	30, 212
Maughan, M. L.	413	Medlicott, G. P.	419
†Maule-Ffinch, E. J. H.	37, 293	Medlicott, S. J. E.	422
Maule-Ffinch, K. H. O.	293	Medlock, C. H.	398
Maurice, F. J.	285	Meek, G. A.	253
Mauritzen, R. W.	175	Meeson, A.	421
Mavor, H. R.	242	Meggitt, A.	377
Mawson, J. H.	413	Melhado, C.	296
Mawson, P. S. de M.	405	Melhuish, P.	428
Mawson, S.	318	Melles, R. E.	199
Maxey, P.	263	Mellish, E. N.	44
Maxted, C. B.	105, 291	†Mellish, R. C.	5, 320
Maxwell, G. B.	105, 417	Mellor, A.	240
Maxwell, H. A.	350, 397	Mellor, B. F.	247
Maxwell, J. C.	347	Melvin, J. W.	342
†Maxwell, J. H.	31	Membrey, R. H.	343
†Maxwell, W.	10, 303	Menhinick, J. S.	362
May, F.	384	Mennell, E. D.	413
May, G. T. C.	175	*Mentions*	*152*

¶ See reference to this name in *Corrigenda*.

MENZIES

INDEX TO COMMISSIONS, HONOURS, and ROLL OF HONOUR.

Name	Page(s)
Menzies, C. D.	293
Meo, I. L.	366
Mercer, R. R.	363
†Merchant, A. D.	16, 175
Meredith, A. C.	105, 341, 415
Meredith, H. R.	413
Meredith, R. S.	159, 401
Merefield, B.	367
Merfield, S. H.	156, 321
†Merrett, A. E.	12, 255
†Merrett, H. E.	36, 338
Merriman, E. C. B.	219
†Mertens, E. H.	24
Messenger, A. L.	147, 175
†Messervy, E. S.	24
†Messom, H.	4, 105, 156, 361
Messulam, R.	175
Metcalf, A.	364
Metcalfe, C. P.	239
†Metcalfe, G	33, 344
Metcalfe, P. H. G.	185
Methuen, Hon. A. P.	219¶
Mew, G. M.	259
†Mew, R.	28
Miall, E. J.	300
Michael, C. A.	401
†Michell, A. C.	22, 264
†Michelsen, A. C.	23, 189
Micklem, C.	49, 156, 418
Micklethwaite, T. D. A.	270
†Middleditch, A. M.	7, 242
Middlesex Regt.	*310*
Middleton, A. G.	175
Middleton, J.	407
Middleton, R. E.	193
Middleton, S.	156, 199, 419
Middleton, T. H.	105, 212
Midwinter, W. H.	405
Mieville, A. M.	151, 156, 392
Mieville, L. C.	323
Mieville, W. S.	106, 156, 310
Milbank, H. R.	365
†Miles, A. C. V.	5, 376
†Miles, F. D.	38¶
†Miles, H. E.	9, 345
†Miles, H. G.	9, 234
Miles, L. G.	49, 156, 257
Miles, M. H.	395, 407
Milford, C. A.	379
M.C.	53
M.V.O.	*148*
Military Medal	*149*
M.S.M.	*149*
Millar, E. F.	335
Millar, H. F.	275
Millar, L. P.	219
Millar, M. A.	175
†Millard, A. G.	19, 360
Millard, R. V.	411
Millen, A. D.	313, 397
Miller, A. H.	293
Miller, C.	195
†Miller, Frank	35
Miller, Frederick	189
†Miller, F. C.	33, 250
Miller, G. L.	411
Miller, G. W.	293
Miller, H. C.	411
Miller, H. D.	411
Miller, James	270
Miller, Joseph	221
Miller, J. A.	156, 205
Miller, J. B.	270
Miller, J. G. R.	156, 339
†Miller, J. L.	7, 295
Miller, J. M.	401
Miller, J. S.	423
Miller, Ronald A.	156, 280
Miller, Russell A.	384
Miller, S. H.	420
Miller, S. J. H.	219
Miller, T. S.	156, 214
Miller, W. D. B.	425
†Miller, W. E.	24
Miller, W. H.	215
Millian, J. C.	205
Milligan, A.	106, 156, 394
Millman, F. W.	234
Mills, B. R.	375
Mills, D. H.	368
Mills, E. T.	199
Mills, F. O.	199
Mills, H.	366
Mills, H. G. H.	214
†Mills, H. J.	34, 313, 319, 417
Mills, J. E.	375
†Mills, K. Le G.	26, 175
†Mills, L. G. E.	24
†Mills, R. C. L.	42, 330
Mills, W. V.	212
†Milne, J. A. D.	22, 219
†Milne, N.	24
Milne, O. P.	403
Milne-Robertson, W. M. M.	316
Milnes, W. A.	382
Milton, S. F.	380
Mimmack, S. C.	175
†Minors, R. T.	42, 382
Minors, W. J.	384
†Minshull, J. L.	13, 156, 290
Minter, L. J.	175
Miscellaneous Establishments	*419*
Misick, F. C.	214
Mitchell, Alan	106, 385
Mitchell, Alfred	362
†Mitchell, D. D.	40
Mitchell, E.	396
Mitchell, E. T.	175

† Killed in action or died.   § See this name in *Addenda*.

This Index does not include the Alphabetical Sections IV. and V. (Other Ranks and Old Members).

Mitchell, F. C.	... 296	Moore, E. A.	... 356
Mitchell, G. R.	... 300	Moore, E. G.	... 311a
†Mitchell, H. A.	... 14	Moore, F. H.	... 361
†Mitchell, J. L.	17, 302	Moore, F. L.	106, 325
Mitchell, J. M.	...148, 159, 175	Moore, F. S.	... 315
Mitchell, R. G.	... 293	†Moore, F. W.	... 15, 106, 236
Mitchell, T. P.	... 312	†Moore, G. A.	34, 372
Mitton, G. C.	... 330	Moore, G. G.	... 257
Mitton, P. D.	... 274	Moore, H. E.	49, 107, 156, 214
Mitzakis, A. V. M.	...151, 156, 299	†Moore, J. A.	... 24
Mix, A. E.	... 212	†Moore, J. G.	32, 175
Mobbs, G. W.	... 339	Moore, J. H.	... 403
Mochrie, D. R.	... 189	Moore, J. L. M.	107, 156, 163, 209
Modlen, C. L.	... 343	†Moore, K. H.	...8, 238
Modlen, S. E.	... 323	†Moore, K. W. J.	20, 242
Moffat, G. R.	... 189	Moore, L. P.	159, 311
Moffett, T. H.	... 199	Moore, L. T.	107, 212
Mogg, L. H.	... 350	Moore, M. B. H.	... 375
Moir, E. W. C.	... 244	Moore, P.	... 240
Moir, G. T.	... 411	Moore, R. C.	... 315
Moir, K. M.	106, 358	Moore, R. E. M.	... 325
Moir, L. J. A.	... 358	†Moore, Reginald F.	... 24
Moir, S. E.	... 411	†Moore, Robert F.	...34, 49, 107, 156, 335
Moir, T. N.	... 411	Moore, W. J.	156, 298
Mokler, L. W.	... 212	Moore, W. R.	107, 392
Moller, A. A.	106, 217	†Moorhouse, A.	... 31
Mollett, F. N.	... 325	Moorhouse, H.	... 384¶
Mollett, W. B.	... 384	Moors, B. R.	... 342
Molliar-Smith, H.	... 205	Moran, P. F.	... 252
†Molyneux, E. S.	... 27, 156, 381	Morant, J. G.	... 267
Molyneux, G. W.	... 275	Mordecai, L. R.	156, 269
†Molyneux, J. H.	19, 267	Morden, C. S.	... 193
†Monaghan, D. L	... 26, 260, 415	Morden, H. W.	... 225
Monckton, I. P.	... 185	†Moreton, N. H.	34, 175
Money, D. F.	...106, 156, 308	Morewood, T. C.	... 273
†Monk, G. B.	...2, 369	Morgan, D. E.	... 428
Monkman, E. A.	... 290	†Morgan, D. P.	21, 381
Monkman, F. H.	... 392	Morgan, D. R.	... 367
Monkton, A. R.	... 291	Morgan, E. L.	107, 187
Monmouthshire Regt.	... *325*	Morgan, E. R.	... 189
Montague, J. C.	... 363	Morgan, F. R. H.	... 428
Montague-Smith, V. M.	... 353	Morgan, G. E.	... 378
Monteath, D. T.	148, 421	Morgan, H.	... 199
Montgomerie, H. S.	... 175	Morgan, H. G.	... 368
Montgomery, L. H.	... 346	Morgan, H. J.	... 234
†Montgomery, N. S.	...7, 218	Morgan, H. T.	... 417
Moody, B. C.	... 297	Morgan, J. G.	... 425
Moody, J. C.	... 247	Morgan, J. J.	... 297
Moody, P.	...106, 156, 372	†Morgan, J. R.	... 31
Moolenaar, F. A.	... 193	Morgan, L. D.	... 205
Moon, J.	... 407	Morgan, M. H.	... 428
Moor, F. H.	... 417	Morgan, R. S. L.	312, 368
Moorcroft, W.	... 262	Morgan, S. C.	... 189
Moore, A. J.	... 377	†Morgan, W. H.	32, 368
Moore, A. M.	... 328	Morgan, W. Lawrence	... 297
†Moore, A. R.	14, 394	Morgan, W. Llewellyn	... 272
Moore, A. W.	... 413	Morison, R. H.	...310a
Moore, C. A.	... 387	†Morland, L. M.	...7, 395
Moore, C. C.	106, 269	Morley, B. J.	... 244

¶ See reference to this name in *Corrigenda*.

Name	Pages	Name	Pages
Morley, F. S.	396	†Moss, W. T. G.	18, 175
Morley, J. A.	401	†Mosse, P. G.	6, 371
†Morrall, J. B.	30, 372	Mosse, S. H.	199
Morrell, C.	164, 326	†Mossman, H. A.	33, 108, 224
Morrell, P. F. A.	270	†Mott, C.	34
†Morris, A. A. T.	40, 107, 324	Mott, G.	407
Morris, A. J.	366	†Mottershall, H. S.	22, 318
Morris, C. G.	423	Mottershead, R. F.	212
Morris, C. L.	395	Mottram, C. E.	275
†Morris, C. W.	3, 265	Mould, R.	314, 417
Morris, D. W.	330	Mouldey, W. E.	156, 269
Morris, E. G.	175	Moulding, E. P.	189
Morris, F. B.	156, 353	Moule, A. J. C.	199
Morris, F. L.	183	†Mountcastle, H. W.	24
Morris, J. E.	376	Mountford, F. G.	281
Morris, J. H.	311a	Mousley, N. L.	372
†Morris, J. O.	24	Mower, E. E.	306
Morris, J. T.	428	Moxon, G. H.	199
†Morris, T. B.	18, 156, 175, 373	Moylan-Jones, R. A. W.	314
Morris, Walter A.	359	Mozley, F. W.	212
Morris, William A.	272	Muckle, R.	332
Morris, W. B.	247	Muckleston, H. P.	274
Morris, W. F.	233	Mucklow, S. L.	269
Morris, W. G.	377	Mudge, J.	253
†Morrish, D. B.	9, 389	Muff-Ford, J. W. D.	303
Morrison, J.	379	Muir, R. G.	215
Morrison, R. A.	205	Mules, J. C. G.	255
Morrison, R. W. G.	359	Mull, E.	175
Morrison, T. H.	205	Mullan, D. R.	336
Morrison, W.	205	†Mullane, B. P.	32, 247
Morrow, A.	300	Mullen, J. W.	175
Morrow, F.	107, 212	Mulligan, A. W. P.	386
†Morse, G. E.	25, 175	Mullins, C. W.	401
Morse, W. E.	401	Mullins, G. T.	212¶
Mort, F.	344	Mullins, R. M.	175
†Morten, G.	4, 285	†Mulock, E. R.	2, 252
Morten, H. M.	327	Mumford, G.	330
†Morter, A. G.	13	Mumford, T. J. C.	247
Mortimer, A. B.	107, 395	Mummery, H. H.	321
Mortimer, L.	175	†Mummery, H. N. S.	36¶, 256
Mortimer, O. W.	332	Muncey, F. T.	176
Mortimore, E. A.	217	Munday, J.	343
Mortishead, J. W	349	Mundy, W. F.	159, 256
Morton, C. F.	293	Munro, D. A. J.	176
Morton, G. C.	300	Munro, H.	376
Morton, H. M.	411	Munro, J. G.	320
†Morton, W. Cattell	18, 107, 156, 194	Munro, R.	208
Morton, W. Chamberlain	108, 289	†Munro, R. G.	10, 220, 301
†Moses, F. S.	37, 205	Munro, S. H.	235
Moses, L. F. C.	272	†Munro, W. P.	38, 193
Mosley, E. B.	219	†Munsey, W. F.	19, 267
Moss, E. N.	275	*Munster Fusiliers, Royal*	326
†Moss, G. A.	36, 318	Munt, E.	108, 156, 187
Moss, G. O.	270	Murch, A. H.	108, 374
†Moss, H. S.	36, 184	Murch, L. C.	250
†Moss, M. A.	24	Murdo, G.	236
†Moss, R. B. N.	10, 261	Murdock, H. S.	176
Moss, R. E.	297	Murly, C. J.	411
Moss, V. N.	108, 260	Murphy, C. E.	413

† Killed in action or died. § See this name in *Addenda*.

This Index does not include the Alphabetical Sections IV. and V. (Other Ranks and Old Members)

Name	Pages	Name	Pages
†Murphy, G. M.	24	Neal, J. E.	337
†Murphy, J.	37, 332	Neal, L.	156, 318
Murphy, T. J.	306	Neale, A. W.	366
Murrane, H. D.	108, 279	Neale, B. P.	189
†Murray, A.	36, 366	Neale, C. D.	381
Murray, A. S.	283	Neale, G. B.	156, 176, 313
†Murray, E. D.	8, 257	Neame, A. J.	308
†Murray, E. F.	24	Neden, H. G.	320
Murray, G.	108, 176	Neech, W. P.	324¶
Murray, G. V.	151, 273	Needham, L. W.	108, 303
Murray, H. R.	368	†Neely, H. B.	3¶, 354
Murray, J. B.	216	Neighbour, G. M.	199
Murray, J. C.	401	Neighbour, S. W.	148, 151, 156, 308
Murray, M.	293	†Neill, R.	28
Murray, P.	225	Nelson, E. M.	228
†Murray, R. M.	41	†Nelson, F. A. J.	36
Murray, S. Mc. P.	411	†Nelson, H.	10, 303
Murrell, H. F.	216	Nelson, Jesse	338
Musgrave, J.	186	Nelson, Joseph	407
†Musgrove, G. H. S.	7, 359	Nelson, J. P.	324
Mussared, W. J.	176	Nelson, L. A.	109, 280
Musselwhite, D. W.	428	Nelson, R.	199
Musselwhite, F. J.	176, 398	Nelson, W. P.	143, 312*a*
Myers, D.	156, 403	†Nelson, W. W.	37
Myers, M. F.	304	Neobard, H. J. C.	148, 151, 156, 225
Myers, W.	312a	Nesling, R. E.	243, 266
		Nethercot, R. P.	109, 394
Nadin, W. E. F.	183	Nethery, W. C. E.	205
Nailer, R. C. F.	176	Nettleton, J.	156, 341
Naimby, W.	283¶	Nevill, E.	271
Napier, C. W. S.	235	Neville, H. M.	373
Napier, J. S.	401	New, J. W.	428
Napier, M.	254	Newberry, G. H.	199
Napier, R. W.	183	Newberry, T. F.	109, 417
Napier, W. F.	193	Newbery, H. S.	311
Nash, A. B.	419	Newby, F. W.	214
Nash, E. A.	428	†Newcombe, C. C. U.	20, 382
†Nash, H. A.	34, 176	Newcombe, F. V.	288
Nash, H. M.	205	†Newcombe, J. C.	30, 212
Nash, J. N.	428	†Newcombe, P. C.	241
Nash, P.	255	†Newcombe, R. C. D.	7, 271
†Nash, P. G.	22, 318	Newell, A.	356
Nash, W. H.	176	†Newell, A. F.	32, 343
Nathan, C.	151, 380	Newell, F. A.	311a
Nathan, C. H.	176, 399	Newitt, N. J.	364
Nathan, J.	159	Newland, A. M.	109, 218
Nathan, M.	375	Newman, A. J.	109, 193
Naughton, J. J.	262	Newman, C. S.	324
Naval Air Service, Royal	*164*	Newman, C. E. S.	156, 413
Naval Reserve, Royal	*420*	Newman, E. M.	176
Naval Volunteer Reserve, Royal	*420*	Newman, G. L.	176
Navy, Royal	*420*	Newman, H. J.	356
Nayler, E. B.	183	Newman, R. N.	425
Naylor, G. E.	396	Newman, S.	407
Naylor, T.	375	Newman, W. A.	255
Naylor, T. H.	156, 277	Newport, H.	312a
Naylor, W. L.		Newport-Gwilt, R. J.	230
Neal, C. T. D.	375	Newsom, R. A.	370
Neal, H.	165	Newth, R. C.	316

¶ See reference to this name in *Corrigenda.*

NEWTON

INDEX TO COMMISSIONS, HONOURS, and ROLL OF HONOUR.

Name	Pages	Name	Pages
Newton, A. R.	159, 234	Nixon, L. G.	176
Newton, C. E.	159, 310	†Nixon, T. W.	40, 387
Newton, C. F.	300	Nixon, W.	205
Newton, C. R.	316	Noad, C. K.	162, 320
Newton, C. V.	109, 156, 366	Noad, F. M.	320, 426
Newton, E. L.	420	†Noakes, H. T.	18, 176
Newton, G. B.	302	Nobbs, G. F. P.	356
Newton, H. E.	394	Noble, A. V.	355
Newton, H. M.	230	Noble, G. A.	193
†Newton, M. E.	17, 301	Noble, J. M.	156, 212
Newton, S. B.	423	Noble, L. R.	287
†Newton, W. C.	18, 273	Noble, R.	340
Newton, W. G.	109, 305, 310	Noel, G. B. E.	403
Newton-Clare, H. J.	148, 176, 399	Noel, G. H.	311
Neyroud, R. C. E.	420	†Noel, H. W. E.	24
Nicholas, E. O.	368	Nokes, W.	245
Nicholas, G. B.	145, 176	Norbury, V.	176
Nicholas, T. U. J.	176	Norcombe, T. P.	205
Nicholas, W. E.	314	Norden, R. W.	185
Nicholls, E. H. R.	373	†Norden, W. A.	42
Nicholls, E. J.	109, 370	*Norfolk Regt.*	*327*
†Nicholls, H. K.	32, 358	Norfolk, W. J. A.	312
Nicholls, J. E.	287	Norman, A. S.	385
Nicholls, N. C.	283	Norman, C. P.	428
Nicholls, W.	216	†Norman, E. W.	37
†Nichols, H.	36¶, 358	Norman, M.	247
Nichols, H. W.	189	Norman, R. C.	312
Nichols, W. A.	218	Norman, R. E.	339
†Nicholson, B. G. M.	40, 333	Norman, R. F. H.	176, 281
Nicholson, C. A. J.	220, 386	Norman, S. O.	110, 337
Nicholson, C. H.	388	Normandale, L.	236
Nicholson, E. D.	401	Norris, A.	247
Nicholson, F. H.	193	Norris, C. A.	189
Nicholson, H. A.	247	Norris, F. C.	189
Nicholson, J. A.	287	Norris, G. S.	428
Nicholson, J. F. W.	176	†Norris, R.	28
†Nicholson, P. C.	33, 389	Norris, S. G.	151
Nicholson, R. L.	193	Norris, V. L.	324
Nicholson, T.	317	†Norris, W. F.	5, 327, 397
Nicholson-Lailey, J. R.	189	Norrish, G.	176
Nickalls, B. A.	236	†North, C. E. J. P.	37
Nicks, A. E.	236	North, E. B.	401
Nickson, G. B.	109, 205	North, P.	425
Nicol, G. G.	267	North, W. L.	311
Nicol, I. S.	109, 189	*Northamptonshire Regt.*	*329*
Nicol, R. J.	212¶	*Northumberland Fusiliers*	*331*
Nicol, W. A.	340¶	†Norton, A. G.	3, 271
Nicoll, G. S.	193	Norton, E.	293
Nicoll, W. J.	360	†Norton, G.	42, 176
Nield, H. M.	375	Norton, H. S. M.	293
Nightingale, C. T.	299	Norton, K. S. M.	293
Nightingale, F. B.	428	Norton, R. H.	219
Nimmo, A. A.	276	Norwak, C. F.	328
Nimmo, W. W.	110, 191	†Notley, A. C.	34, 279
Nisbet, E. C.	205	Nott, C. A.	225
†Niven, A. S.	25, 279	Nott, D. G.	310a
Nivet, E. L. A.	233	Nott, G. E.	212
†Nivison, R. B.	10, 266	Nott, L. H.	381
Nix, S.	312a	Nott, P. J.	263

† Killed in action or died.   § See this name in *Addenda*.

Notts. and Derby Regt.	...	...	...	335	Oliver, E. A. C. ...	...	...	...	350
Nowell, C.	...	...	...	304	Oliver, Herbert Wm. ...	...	...	...	316
†Nowell, W. J.	...	...	...	13, 191	Oliver, Hubert Wm.	...	...	...	176
Nuding, E. G.	...	...	...	176	Oliver, I. M. L. ...	...	...	...	353
Nunn, E. R.	...	...	...	407	Oliver, S. H.	...	...	...	425
Nurse, W. I.	...	...	...	262	Oliver, T. F.	...	...	...	284
†Nutcombe, T. A.	...	...	...	35, 272	Oliver, T. S.	...	...	...	199
Nuthall, S.	...	...	...	205	Olivier, B. C. C.	...	...	...	339
					Olley, J. F.	...	...	...	199
Oakden, G. E.	...	...	...	417	Olney, J. K.	...	...	...	362
Oakden, G. F.	...	...	...	392	†Olver, J. D. C. ...	...	...	15¶, 111, 191
†Oakenfall, H. J.	...	...	...	11, 297	†O'Meara, L. A.	...	...	...	12, 271
Oakeshott, H. A.	...	...	...	313, 417	†O'Neill, D. Q.	...	...	...	33, 372
Oakey, J. M.	...	...	...	110, 156, 341	O'Neill, G. L.	...	...	...	176
Oakley, E. R.	...	...	...	231	†Ongley, R. D.	...	...	...	25
Oakley, W. G.	...	...	...	224	Onslow, O. L.	...	...	...	255
†Oates, H. P.	...	...	...	21, 287	†Oppenheimer, L. J.	...	...	...	11, 305
O'Brien, James (1523)	...	...	...	110, 156, 232	Oram, H. ...	...	...	...	401
O'Brien, James (6548)	...	...	...	326	Oram, R. G.	...	...	...	159, 296
O'Brien, John	...	...	...	232	Orchard, A.	...	...	...	411
O'Brien, J. A.	...	...	...	164, 310	Orchard, C. H.	...	...	...	284
O'Brien-Moore, F. A.	...	...	...	411	Orchard, O.	...	...	...	328
O'Byrne, M.	...	...	...	302	Ord, B.	...	...	...	176
O'Callaghan, J. P.	...	...	...	401	Ord, E. M.	...	...	...	156¶, 407
†O'Connor, B. J.	...	...	...	39, 245	Ordish, B. W. A.	...	...	...	176
O'Connor, C. A.	...	...	...	326	Ordish, F. J.	...	...	...	242
O'Connor, D	...	...	...	419	O'Regan, A. J.	...	...	...	314, 417
O'Connor, D. R.	...	...	...	362	Ormerod, T. L.	...	...	...	363
O'Connor, J. L.	...	...	...	318	Ormiston, W. H.	...	...	...	111, 299
O'Dell, E. S.	...	...	...	351	Orr, C. W. L.	...	...	...	218
Oddy, D. C.	...	...	...	199	†Orrell, J. T.	...	...	...	27, 176
†O'Donnell, A. P.	...	...	...	17, 386	Orrett, H. E.	...	...	...	230
†O'Donoghue, D. A.	...	...	...	24	†Orton, E. H.	...	...	...	3, 313, 346
†O'Donoghue, R. C.	...	...	...	25	Orton, W. J.	...	...	...	149
O'Donohoe, M. W.	...	...	...	247	Osborn, L.	...	...	...	396
O'Donovan, R. A.	...	...	...	110, 381	Osborn, M.	...	...	...	301
O'Dowd, E. M.	...	...	...	411	†Osborne, E. B.	...	...	...	32, 272
Oelrichs, R. V.	...	...	...	208	Osborne, F. J.	...	...	...	250
Offiler, H. C.	...	...	...	336	Osborne, F. W.	...	...	...	298
O'Flaherty, H. F. R. L.	...	...	...	343	Osborne, H. W. S.	...	...	...	372
O'Flynn, G.	...	...	...	259	Osborne, J.	...	...	...	232
O'Garr, J. W.	...	...	...	270	Osborne, P. A.	...	...	...	250
Ogden, F. W.	...	...	...	316	O'Shane, C.	...	...	...	223
Ogden, G. S.	...	...	...	270	O'Shaughnessy-Levy, R. P.	...	...	316
Ogden, W. E.	...	...	...	110, 316	O'Shea, F. J.	...	...	...	176
Ogle, H. R.	...	...	...	217	Osman, L. W.	...	...	...	342
†Okey, W. E.	...	...	...	6, 232	Osmond, F. E.	...	...	...	362
Oldbury, A. E.	...	...	...	401	Osmond, W. H.	...	...	...	324
Oldbury, H. E.	...	...	...	288	Ostle, H. K. E.	...	...	111, 156, 226, 308
Oldfield, A. A.	...	...	...	418	†O'Sullivan, H. A.	...	...	...	15, 205
Oldfield, A. E.	...	...	...	334	Oswald, H. R.	...	...	...	111, 377
Oldfield, C. C.	...	...	...	328	†Ottey, R. G.	...	...	...	18, 280
Oldfield, R. T.	...	...	...	110, 156, 222	Outlaw, W. H.	...	...	...	163, 237
Oldham, Edward H.	...	...	...	199	†Ovastor, A. D.	...	...	...	28¶
Oldham, Ernest H.	...	...	...	349	Overton-Jones, E.	...	...	...	111, 218
Oldham, M. A.	...	...	...	231	Owen, A. E.	...	...	...	247
Oldham, T. J. F.	...	...	...	368	Owen, A. J.	...	...	...	288
†Oliphant, M. F.	...	...	...	4, 327	Owen, B. C.	...	...	...	212
Oliver, A. A.	...	...	...	302	Owen, C. H.	...	...	...	373

¶ See reference to this name in *Corrigenda*.

Owen, E. T.	411
Owen, F. D.	298
Owen, G. A.	264
Owen, G. L.	208
†Owen, H. E. M.	18, 176
†Owen, H. J.	37, 375
Owen, H. W.	375
†Owen, J. M.	15, 372
Owen, L. A.	255
†Owen, M. de B.	41, 111, 223
Owen, P. H. A.	310a
Owen, P. R. T.	260
Owen, R. O.	378
Owen, S. J.	318
Owen, V. E. O. N.	319
†Owen, W. E.	30
†Owen, W. E. S.	41, 111, 316
Owens, H. H.	343
Owens, J.	212
Owers, F. T.	111, 299
Owles, S. G.	356
Owrid, T.	318
Oxenford, A. H.	386
Oxenford, D.	415
Oxford and Bucks. L.I.	*338*
Oxley, G. L.	183
Oxley-Boyle, E. H.	176
Pace, A.	199
Paddle, K. C. L.	111, 199
Paddle, L. H.	176
Paddon, C. E.	235
Padfield, F. H.	148, 310
Padfield, F. J.	397
Pafford, H. J.	255
Page, C. C.	398
Page, F. J.	267
†Page, F. T.	3, 326
Page, F. W. R.	324
Page, G. F.	189
Page, H.	255
Page, H. A.	249
Page, H. T.	313
†Page, J. C.	11, 328
Page, J. O.	233
Page, M. J. I.	411
Page, P. P.	219
Page, P. S.	235
Page, S. C. M.	189
†Page, T. S.	11, 329
Page, W. I. G.	156, 371
Paget, B. K.	411
Paget, L. R.	351
Paget-Cooke, O. D. P.	217, 403
Paice, E. B.	189
†Pailthorpe, L. S.	35
Pain, C. H. S.	176
Paine, G. A.	408
†Paine, G. G.	31, 111, 156, 224
†Paine, J. H.	28
Paine, R. S.	205
Painter, H. T. H.	250
Palfreyman, F. J.	205
Pallett, L. C.	301
†Palmer, A. B. B.	36, 322
Palmer, C. B. W.	355
Palmer, C. J.	401
†Palmer, E. D.	25
Palmer, E. L.	408
Palmer, F. N.	242
Palmer, F. S.	302
Palmer, C. W.	341
Palmer, H. G.	327
†Palmer, H. J.	32, 233
Palmer, H. W. S.	225
†Palmer, J. S.	11, 239, 419
Palmer, L.	236
Palmer, L. C. G.	366
Palmer, L. W.	356
Palmer, M. C.	381
Palmer, P. R.	111, 374
Palmer, P. S.	214
Palmer, W.	313, 417
†Palmer, W. S. H.	20, 176
Palmer, W. W.	156, 267
Panter, G.	319
Pantlin, L. A.	193
†Papworth, A. W.	13, 212
Papworth, R.	289
†Paradise, J.	25
Parfitt, A. J.	243
Parish, W. E.	254
Park, A.	189
Park, A. B.	279
Park, C. A. R.	310a
†Park, H. S.	23, 228
Park, J. L.	205
Park, R. H. M.	112, 220
Park, R. S.	147, 176
Parker, A. A. F.	156, 405
Parker, A. H.	270
Parker, D. H.	336
†Parker, E. T.	4, 268, 395
Parker, F. G.	156, 320
†Parker, F. N.	3, 265
Parker, F. P.	235
†Parker, G.	14, 274
Parker, H. H.	293
Parker, J. A.	112, 209
†Parker, L. R.	39, 368
Parker, M. G.	413
Parker, R.	408
Parker, T. Cecil	264
Parker, T. Cornwall	393
Parker, T. R.	329
Parker, W. B.	364
†Parker, W. H.	3, 326
Parkes, A.	319

† Killed in action or died.   § See this name in *Addenda*.

This Index does not include the Alphabetical Sections IV. and V. (Other Ranks and Old Members).

Parkes, G. H.	112, 184	
†Parkes, H. F.	2, 156, 372	
Parkes, H. P.	259	
Parkes, J. W.	364	
Parkes, N. E.	151, 314	
†Parkes, P. R.	32, 302	
†Parkes, T. D.	22, 352	
†Parkhurst, G. H.	35, 315	
Parkin, J.	112, 205	
Parkin, J. A.	314	
Parkinson, L.	336	
Parkinson, N.	176	
Parks, G. C.	282	
Parkyn, H. S.	236	
Parminter, P. D.	350	
Parrish, E. P.	324	
Parrott, L. K.	360	
Parry, G. O.	275	
Parry, J. W. G.	261	
†Parry, S.	34, 209	
Parry, S. A.	425	
Parry, S. H.	413	
Parry, S. H. A.	270	
Parry, W. S.	368	
Parry-Jones, R. J. S.	234	
Parsloe, J. A. E.	199	
†Parslow, Albert J.	11, 296	
Parslow, Archibald J.	334	
Parslow, J. W.	234	
Parson, H. A.	421	
Parsons, A. F.	237	
†Parsons, C. W.	28	
Parsons, G. E.	388	
Parsons, G. M.	313a	
†Partington, L.	31, 151, 156, 331	
Partridge, G. W.	353	
†Passingham, E. G.	15, 112, 331	
†Passmore, A. W.	6, 363	
Paterson, C. R.	425	
Paterson, F. J.	112, 290	
Paterson, G.	310a	
Paterson, J. S.	279	
Paterson, R. F.	156, 193	
Paterson, R. W.	419	
Paton, A. J.	190	
Paton, E. C.	324	
†Paton, E. K.	15¶, 417	
Paton, J. A.	367	
Paton, J. H.	417	
Paton, T. H. M	241	
Patrick, C. W.	289	
Patrick, F. A. P.	224	
Patten, H. T.	289	
Patterson, H. M.	235	
Pattison, E. E. L.	199	
Pattison, J. E.	386	
†Pattison, R.	27, 156, 297	
Pattison, S. P.	303	
Patton, E.	413	
†Paul, A. R.	29, 176	
†Paul, E. N.	27, 265	
†Paul, H. J.	26	
Paul, R. B.	276	
Paul, R. W.	193	
Paul, V. C.	190	
Paulsen, P. H.	319	
Paulton, H. F.	176	
Pavey, P. R. V.	312	
Pawsey, A. M.	273	
Pawson, F. G.	288	
Payne, C. C.	327	
†Payne, C. G. C.	2, 256	
Payne, J. A.	176	
Payne, J. G.	348	
†Payne, J. O.	3, 369	
Payton, S.	112, 425	
Payton, W. T.	149	
Peach, C. S.	312a	
Peachey, G. F.	262	
Peacock, C. R.	212	
†Peacock, E. G.	8, 246	
Peacock, G.	277	
Peacock, S. C.	298	
†Peake, J. T.	3, 329	
Peal, F. A. H.	112, 386	
Pearce, C.	193	
Pearce, G. H.	176	
Pearce, G. O.	316	
†Pearce, G. V.	2, 369	
Pearce, G. W.	225	
Pearce, H. E.	394	
†Pearce, N.	22, 279	
Pearce, W. L.	423	
†Pearkes, A. M.	4, 395	
†Pearman, C. H.	41	
Pearn, C. L.	388	
†Pears, N.	15, 250	
Pease, D.	343	
Pearson, A. M. W.	156, 417	
Pearson, B. J.	375	
Pearson, E. L.	413	
†Pearson, K. H.	37	
Pearson, L. M.	421	
†Pearson, R.	36, 391	
†Pearson, R. O.	4, 156, 282	
Pearson, W. D.	247	
Pearson, W. G. F.	113, 367	
Pearsons, L. M. J.	282	
†Peart, R. E.	11	
Peckston, J. G.	240	
Peckover, J. E.	373	
Peddar, H. S.	357	
Peebles, A. J. D.	147, 176¶	
†Peebles, P. N.	14, 298	
†Peer, E. F.	15, 393	
†Peerless, C. L.	25	
Peers, V. A.	372	
Pegg, H. G.	221	

¶ See reference to this name in *Corrigenda*.

INDEX TO COMMISSIONS, HONOURS, and ROLL OF HONOUR.

Name	Pages	Name	Pages
†Pegram, C. E.	41, 113, 342	Perry, W.	385
Peirce, A.	205	Pertwee, J. W.	277
Peirce, A. R.	190	Pertwee, L.	234
†Pells, C. E.	34, 235	Peter, G.	190
Pells, H. H.	408	Peters, M. W.	295
Pemberton, A. L.	176	Peters, T.	293
†Pemberton, A. G.	4	Pether, W. G.	243
Pemberton, W. G. T.	362	Petherbridge, C. A.	113, 156, 343
Pembroke, W. A.	217	†Petley, H.	10, 289
Penaluna, W.	234	Petley, R. E.	311a
†Penderel-Brodhurst, B. R.	39, 212	Petrie, P. C.	199
Pendleton, W.	351	Petry, A. McN.	212
Pendred, W. A.	267	Petter, C. H.	401
Pennick, H. W. F.	176	Pettitt, H. B.	297
Pennington, H. E.	382	Pettitt, L. C.	258
†Penny, B. W.	20, 245	Pettitt, L. H.	269
Penny, F.	199	Petts, G. A.	401
†Penny, G.	9, 394	Phelps, F. W.	299
Penny, W. N.	208	Pheysey, J. E.	113, 190
†Penrose, G. A.	14, 156, 363	Philcox, A. R.	177
Penrose, J.	413	Philip, J. B.	411
Penrose, L.	393	Philip, T. V. R.	257
†Pentecost, C. G.	31, 176	Philip, W. Y.	411
Pentreath, H. L.	401	Phillipowski, I. R.	316
Penty, N.	267	Phillips, A.	293
Penty, W. S.	319	Phillips, C. L.	425
Penwill, L. C. B.	244	Phillips, C. S.	247
†Pepper, A. T.	41, 212	Phillips, E.	250
Pepper, E. G.	366	Phillips, E. L.	205
Pepper, W. A.	156, 408	Phillips, E. T. A.	149, 205
Peppiatt, C. F.	247	†Phillips, F. E. S.	11, 113, 235
Percival, E. J.	185	Phillips, G. A.	288
Percival, F. G.	199	†Phillips, G. E.	28
Percival, G.	284	Phillips, G. H.	241
Percival, H. A. B.	357	Phillips, H. C.	375
Percival, J. B.	401	Phillips, J. F. M.	183
Percy, A. F.	176	Phillips, J. Reginald	375
Percy, A. J.	423	Phillips, J. Robert	264
Perkes, A. R.	413	Phillips, L. E.	417
Perkins, J.	215	Phillips, L. J.	305
Perkins, L.	156, 273, 329	Phillips, Malcolm, H.	381
Perkins, S.	354	†Phillips, Mark H.	22, 353
†Perkins, W. E.	25	Phillips, M. McG.	186
Perks, H.	321	†Phillips, N.	25
Perl, B. H.	113, 278, 310	Phillips, P. A.	271
Pern, C.	147, 176	Phillips, P. J.	280
†Perrin, A. J.	22, 389	†Phillips, R.	15, 368
†Perring, C. R.	36, 177	†Phillips, R. G.	12, 260
Perring, R. B.	177	Phillips, R. L.	428
Perris, L. R.	367	†Phillips, S. V.	9, 281
Perrott, E. S.	113, 312	†Phillips, T. M.	183
Perry, A. E. C.	35, 205	Phillips, W. H.	25
Perry, A. F.	302	Phinn, C. W.	428
Perry, G. M.	156, 218, 310	Phipps, J. D. B.	190
Perry, J.	401	Phipps, P.	156, 405
Perry, J. L.	365	Pick, N.	190
†Perry, K. G.	11, 367	Pickard, F. R.	401
Perry, P. R. W.	156, 306	Pickbourne, M.	279
Perry, R. W.	293	†Pickering, G. A. R.	25, 330

† Killed in action or died. § See this name in *Addenda*.

This Index does not include the Alphabetical Sections IV. and V. (Other Ranks and Old Members).

Name	Pages	Name	Pages
Pickersgill, E.	332	Plummer, W. G.	296
Pickett, W. F.	411	†Plumpton, R.	42¶, 391
†Pickles, H.	14, 227	Plunkett, D. W.	261
Pickrell, L. J.	428	Plunkett, J. R.	296
†Pickup, A. J.	5, 390	Pocock, G. C.	219
Picton, C. J.	378	†Pocock, R. L. A.	20, 272
Picton, T.	413	Pocock, R. W.	114, 190
Pierce, Alfred	113	Podd, J. K.	114, 394
Pierrepont, A. D.	281	Podmore, G. C.	205
Pierson, V. M.	199	Podmore, J. D.	164
Pieterson, E. S.	375	Pogson, D. P.	146, 177
Piggott, J.	311a	Pogue, C. W.	425
Piggott, M. W.	428	Pogue, R. T.	114, 238
Pignatel, E. C.	408	Polgreen, J. C. V.	341
Pike, C. W.	310	Poll, D. E.	114, 306
Pike, G. B.	151, 177	Pollard, A. H.	401, 405
Pilcher, W.	264	Pollard, C. A.	422
Pile, G. H.	401	Pollard, C. L.	364
Pile, S. J. H.	113, 324	Pollard, J.	227
†Pilgrim, H. B.	7, 299	Pollard, J. L.	156, 404
Pilling, S. H.	177	Polley, N. G. F.	247
Pinching, C. L.	420	Polley, W. S.	294
Pinder, A. G.	219	Pollock, H.	389
Pinder, L.	272	†Pollock, J.	28
Pinder-Brown, H.	163, 310	Pontet, H.	425
Pine, A. W.	243	Ponting, P. W.	398
Pineger, G. F. R.	408	Pool, M. L.	237
†Ping, A. R.	18, 381	†Poole, L. S. R.	42, 177
Pink, P.	327	Pooley, J. E. N.	296
Pinney, F. S.	242	†Pooley, R. M.	9, 285
Piper, E. H.	177	Pope, D. H.	389
Piper, N.	156, 268	Pope, F. J.	252
Piperno, J. H.	339	Pope, F. W.	193
Pitcher, H. B.	214	Pope, W. J. C.	195
Pitcher, W. H. B.	113, 218	Popham, A. E.	151, 156, 164
Pitchford, A. N.	177	†Popkin, R. G.	39
Pitel, A. P.	419	Popplewell, H. M. S.	177
Pitman, A. T.	388	Porritt, C. H.	388
Pitman, R. O.	184	Port, F. J.	205
Pitt, B. O.	316	Porteous, F. J.	428
Pitt, G.	417	Porteous, J. D.	395
Pittard, R. S. R.	373	Porteous, R. A.	294
Pitten, W. H.	312	Porter, B. A.	206
Pitts, A. W.	114, 404	Porter, F. S.	334
Pitts, S. E.	330	Porter, J.	206
Piveteau, J. G. L.	273	Porter, N. K. F.	310
Place, H. M.	357	Porter, O. J.	206
Plackett, H. W.	428	Porter, S.	380
†Plant, F. G.	5, 361	Porters, R. H.	151, 163
Plant, H. M.	379	Poston, L. I.	414
Plant, H. N.	156, 199	Pothecary, H. M. R.	114, 394
Platt, A. G.	177	Potter, A. F.	294
†Platt, C. L. F.	34, 193	Potter, A. L.	234
Platt, H. C.	387	Potter, C. V.	231
Platt, O. G.	114, 388	†Potter, F. J.	7, 295
†Plested, H. G.	8, 318	Potter, H. A.	177
Plowman-Brown, C. H.	361	Potter, J. E.	357
Plummer, A. A.	294	Potter, L. C.	284
Plummer, A. J.	319	Potts, F. S.	163

¶ See reference to this name in *Corrigenda*.

INDEX TO COMMISSIONS, HONOURS, and ROLL OF HONOUR.

Name	Pages	Name	Pages
Potts, J. H.	114, 305	Price, G. H.	193
Potts, J. P.	300	Price, H.	254
Poulson, S.	401	Price, H. L.	224
Powe, G. H.	337	†Price, H. S.	4, 245
Powell, C. A.	384	Price, K. D.	243, 266
Powell, C. S.	194, 229	Price, R. H.	277
Powell, E. A.	177	Price, W. L.	244
Powell, G. R.	183	Priday, A. K.	156, 252
Powell, H. J.	368, 419	Prideaux, J. B. L. C.	236
Powell, J. Henry	314	Priest, C. E.	311a
Powell, J. Hirst	296	Priest, W. H.	223
Powell, L.	114, 191	†Priestley, D. L.	25
Powell, M.	193	Priestley, H.	316
†Powell, P. G.	32	Priestley, L. S.	156, 206
Powell, R. T.	273	Priestman, A.	256
Powell, W.	368	Priestman, C. C.	241
Powell, W. G.	212	†Prime, A.	30, 315
Powell, W. P.	151, 156, 339	Pring, A. L.	206
†Power, B.	41	†Pring, H. F. D.	34¶
Power, C. M.	114, 346	Pringle, G. C. W.	334
Power, F. W.	384	Prior, E. G.	267
Power, H. T.	301	†Probert, A. J.	14, 331
Power, P.	360	†Procter, G. H. V.	20, 269
Power, R. V.	164	Proctor, Rev. T. H.	397
Powl, S. R.	296	†Prosser, A. E.	41, 115, 156, 381
Pownall, C. H.	164	†Prosser, D. R.	325
Pownall, N. L. S.	330	Protheroe, P. E.	378
Poynton, A.	324	Proudfoot, A.	314
Pozzi, F. W.	374	Provis, E. J.	199
Prada, L. E.	272	Provis, H.	247
Pratt, H. B.	420	Prowse, C. H.	338
Pratt, H. D.	115, 294	Pryce, H. E.	177
Pratt, H. E.	349	Pryce-Jones, J.	177
Pratt, P. D.	183	Pryke, A. W.	314
†Preedy, L. J.	32, 370	†Pryke, E.	27, 177
Preen, A. F.	190	Prynne, G. M. F.	226
Prentice, C. N.	177	Puckle, O. S.	301
Prentice, J. F.	337	Puddephatt, N. H. G. O.	382
Prentis, J. E.	310	Puddicombe, F. C.	428
†Prescott, R. J.	14, 270	Pugh, T. P.	290
Prescott, W.	322	†Pulford, J. C.	28
Preshous, W. R.	349	Pulford, J. F.	294
†Pressnell, C. E.	28	Pulford, R. G.	190
Preston, B. F.	280	Pullen, C. S.	149
Preston, E. W.	362	Pullen, E. W.	297
Preston, H.	177	Pullen, F. J.	177, 376
Preston, I. K.	199	Pullen, G. F.	248
Preston, J. F.	115, 294	Pullen, L. E.	411
Preston, K.	428	Pulley, E.	294
Preston, W. F. A.	193	Pulleyn, J.	220
Prestwich, H. W.	241	Pullinger, C. E.	115, 267
Price, A. P.	396	Pullman, H. J.	115, 339
Price, B. P.	156, 214	Pulpher, H. H.	274
Price, C. A.	369	Pulsford, B. F.	382
Price, D.	159, 177	†Pulverman, O. P.	5, 354
Price, E. H.	327	Pumfrey, M. A. V. K.	177
Price, F.	280	Punnett, A. H.	261
†Price, F. M.	17, 156, 283	Purchase, W. H.	199
Price, F. N.	250	Purkiss, S. H.	294

† Killed in action or died. § See this name in *Addenda*.

This Index does not include the Alphabetical Sections IV. and V. (Other Ranks and Old Members).

Name	Page	Name	Page
Purkiss-Ginn, S.	242	Raikes, A. F. M.	156, 385
Purnell, A. J.	258	*Railway Traffic Officers*	163
†Purnell, S.	25	Rainford, R.	177
†Purser, N. F.	29, 177	†Rainforth, G. V.	6
Purser, P. W.	405	Rainsford, G.	148, 364
Pursey, H. S.	212	Raisin, F. S.	234
Purton, T. D.	252	Raleigh, R. A.	306
†Purver, B. A.	10, 263, 359	Ralph, J. L.	116, 375
Purver, T. G.	247	Ralston, K. B.	230
Purves, J. M.	190, 115	Ram, H.	428
†Purvis, J. E.	40, 420	Ramage, L. G. E.	339
Purvis, J. L. F.	185	Ramsay, A. C.	402
Purvis, T.	294	Ramsay, A. F.	402
Putt, J.	199	Ramsay, D.	363
Puttick, H. C.	250	Ramsay, H. O.	327
Pybus, J. W.	285	Ramsay, W.	222
†Pycock, H. R. H.	6	Ramsay, W. Mc. A.	200
Pye, F. E. E.	280	Ranalow, A. V.	243, 266
Pye, H. A.	247	Randall, E.	343
Pyke, A. C.	386	Randall, E. J. J.	185
Pyke, E. J.	195	Randall, E. L.	193
Pykett, G. F.	115, 156, 370	Randall, G. E.	146, 177
Pym-Mannock, F. L. A.	230¶, 373	Randall, J. E.	116, 227
Pyne, P.	177, 290	Randall, L. J. A.	364
		†Randall, R. W. S.	3, 329
†Quail, H. C.	29, 212	Randall, S. H.	227
Quainton, A. J.	357	Randall, W. H.	380
Quare, H. A. B.	115, 156, 326	Randell, D. M.	156, 212
Quarmby, R. L.	200	Ranken, J. S.	193
†Quarrell, C. H.	17, 334	Rankin, C. R.	177
†Quarterman, P. H.	22, 305	Ranson, D. F.	336
Quartermaine, C. G.	185	†Rapley, W. G.	21, 320
Quartermaine, H. L.	261	†Rata, S.	28
Quelch, L. M.	177	Ratcliff, J. H.	177
Quesnel, R. E.	275	†Ratcliff, S. A.	13, 190
Quick, S.	156	Ratcliffe, C.	238
Quigley, F.	294	Ratcliffe, C. St-A.	304
Quin, D. H.	428	Ratcliffe, H. C.	231
Quin-Harkin, A.	384	Ratcliffe, J. W.	177
†Quinn, J. E.	39, 287	Rathbone, L.	315
		†Rathbone, T. E.	21, 352
Rabbage, P.	243	Rattigan, G. E.	402
Rabie, E. L.	411	Raven, F. P.	341
Rabino, F. A.	115, 238	Ravenscroft, G. E.	375
†Rabone, M.	5, 326	†Ravenscroft, R. B.	19, 223
Rackett, H. W.	394	†Rawbone, C. R.	27, 177
Rackham, A. C.	425	†Rawe, C. H.	33, 190
Ractivand, D.	116, 348	Rawes, A. N.	190
Radcliffe, C. N.	116, 302	Rawes, V. N.	355
Radcliffe, E. A.	288	Rawlings, F. R.	250
†Radcliffe, E. J.	6, 165	†Rawlins, G. E. C.	2
Radford, J. A.	116, 156, 351	†Rawlins, G. V. C.	42, 209
Radiey, H. C.	391	Rawlins, H. W. B.	354
†Rae, J.	22, 347	Rawlinson, H.	319
Rae, L. M.	357	Rawnsley, C.	396
Raeburn, F. C.	185	Rawnsley, P.	177
Raeside, D.	428	Rawson, E. S.	396
Ragg, C. W.	275	Rawsthorne, H. C.	209
Raggett, E. L.	250	Ray, A. G.	408

¶ See reference to this name in *Corrigenda*.

Ray, P. C.	492
Raybould, C.	349
Rayment, C. G.	320
Raymond, A. F.	417
Raymond, A. J.	149
Raymond-Barker, C. L.	5, 341
Rayner, A. H.	177
Rayner, G. H.	369
Rayner, R. S.	156, 274
Raynes, H. B.	377
Rayward, C. C.	363
†Reacher, S. W.	8, 341, 371
Read, A. B. H.	310a
Read, A. H.	177
Read, E. C.	261
Read, H. C.	190
†Read, L. St. C.	12, 244
Read, M. R.	363
Read, O. H.	328
Read, S.	206
Read, V. S.	236
Reader, W.	177
Reading, A. A.	206
†Reading, J. F.	7, 382
Reading, S. J.	379
†Reading, V. J.	31, 177
Reading, W.	296
Reah, H. W.	116, 212
†Ream, N. S.	25
Reardon, W. R.	231
Reaside, D.	212
Reason, D. J.	177
Reckin, G.	310a
Reckitt, C. E. H.	392
Reddall, H. C.	290
†Reddick, G. A.	11, 421
Reddick, H.	421
Redding, R. W.	177
†Redler, H. B.	35, 116, 177
†Redman, C. S.	25
Redman, E. D.	327
Redpath, W. H.	206
Redwood, E.	409
Reece, F. W.	190
Reed, A. E.	275
Reed, C.	235
Reed, D. L.	156, 335
Reed, J. P.	116, 391
Reed, P. S. V.	283
Reed, R. G.	414
Reed, W.	117, 156, 209
Reed, W. A.	252
†Reeder, R.	28, 317
Reekie, J.	177
Rees, D. W.	375
Rees, J. F.	411
†Rees, J. T.	2, 375
Rees, R. F. W.	378
†Reeve, C. H.	37
Reeve, F.	232
†Reeve, G. N. B.	38, 316
Reeve, G. R.	311a
Reeve, J.	206
Reeve, L. St. J.	339
Reeves, H. C.	177
Reeves, R. S.	280
Reeves-Moore, R.	296
†Reid, A. D.	19, 320
Reid, Algernon Frederick (764177)	247
Reid, Algernon Frederick (10/Lon.)	312
Reid, C. R.	190, 241
Reid, D.	322
Reid, D. D.	257
Reid, R. E.	294
Reid, W.	345
Reidinger, S. L. J.	324
Reilly, M. L. P.	177
Reinecke, A. J.	298
Relph, C. W.	391
Remnant, E. A.	190
Remington, W.	325
Rendell, F. C.	419
Rendle, H. B.	414
†Renshaw, E. G.	25
Rerrie, H. G.	117, 385
Reserve of Officers	421
†Retford, H. H.	23
Revill, L. E. H.	283
†Rew, D. J.	18, 243
†Reynard, H. C.	5, 352
Reynolds, A. W.	402
Reynolds, C. W.	254
Reynolds, C. M. W.	411
Reynolds, D.	271
Reynolds, Francis	177
†Reynolds, Frank	9, 335
Reynolds, H. C.	402
Reynolds, H. N.	117, 151, 370
Reynolds, L.	333
Reynolds, L. A.	190
†Reynolds, Wm. Halliday	39
Reynolds, Wm. Henry	281
†Rheam, H. L.	41
Rhind, P. J.	417
Rhodes, C. W.	284
Rhodes, D.	117, 156, 201, 206
Rhodes, F. M.	231
Rhodes, H.	156, 405
Rhodes, O. N.	414
Rhodes, W.	379
Rhodes, W. F.	329
Rhys, G.	395
Ribbans, E.	355
Riccomini, J. A.	212
Rich, C. A.	288
Rich, C. O.	117, 425
Richard, S.	417§
†Richards, A.	17, 325

† Killed in action or died. § See this name in *Addenda*.

This Index does not include the Alphabetical Sections IV. and V.(Other Ranks and Old Members).

Name	Pages	Name	Pages
Richards, C. A. F.	324	Rivers, F. W.	200
†Richards, C. W.	10, 285	Rivington, K. A. S.	299
†Richards, E. H.	13, 319	†Rix, L. G.	12, 156, 290
Richards, F. A.	193	Road-Night, C.	294
Richards, L. J.	428	†Robbins, A. H.	30, 258
Richards, L. W.	117, 283	Robbins, K. A.	357
Richards, W. A.	372	Roberts, A. H.	320
Richards, W. H.	372	Roberts, C. H.	209, 385
Richardson, A.	373	Roberts, C. St-J. C.	408
Richardson, A. B.	264	Roberts, D. J.	250
Richardson, A. G.	311a	Roberts, D. M.	360
Richardson, C.	335	Roberts, D. R.	368
Richardson, C. A.	212	Roberts, Edward G.	177
Richardson, F. A.	408	Roberts, Ernest G.	425
Richardson, F. S.	235	Roberts, E. L.	387
Richardson, H. B.	156, 332	Roberts, E. R.	159, 302
Richardson, J. E.	212	Roberts, Frank A.	284
†Richardson, R. H.	25, 302	†Roberts, Francklin A.	36, 294
Richardson, S. J.	294	Roberts, F. A. D.	270
Richardson, T. H.	324	†Roberts, G.	39
†Richens, R. I.	14, 302	†Roberts, G. B.	21, 177
Richer, R. A.	422	Roberts, H.	118, 395
†Richmond, H. B.	27, 304	Roberts, H. L.	402
Richmond, O. L.	423	Roberts, H. P.	215
†Rickard, W. C.	39	†Roberts, J.	41, 118, 156, 190
Rickards, C. G.	177	†Roberts, L. P.	29, 177
Rickards, L. J.	393	†Roberts, L. W.	34
Rickatson, H. C.	118¶, 222, 308	Roberts, O. D.	241
Ricketts, A.	312a	Roberts, O. P.	338
Rickwood, J. E.	118, 226	Roberts, R. O.	378
Riddall, G.	408	Roberts, T. L.	280
Riddett, B. P.	206	†Roberts, T. W.	10, 264
†Ridgway, H. C.	10, 202	Roberts, W. C. L.	193
Ridgway, I.	287	Roberts, W. H.	195
†Ridgway, W.	10, 243, 266	Roberts, W. S. H.	353
Riding, G. E.	274	Robertshaw, W. L.	212
Ridley, B. H. W.	333	Robertson, A.	119, 349
Ridley, J. W. B.	425	Robertson, A. G.	417
Ridlington, A. C.	118, 425	Robertson, C. B.	156, 404
†Ridpath, F. C. L.	27, 362	Robertson, D.	206
Rifle Brigade	*341*	†Robertson, D. W.	32
Rigby, A.	206	Robertson, F. B.	119, 280
Rigby, B. C.	355	Robertson, F. K.	241
Rigby, D. F.	270	†Robertson, J.	39, 303
Rigby, H. J.	395	Robertson, L. G.	253
Riggs, H. S.	402	Robertson, R. J.	156, 408
Rigold, E. E.	118, 196	Robertson, T. S.	186
Riley, A. I.	147, 177	Robey, A. E. L.	157, 232
Riley, L.	270	Robin, C. C.	212
†Riley, P.	22, 270	Robin, N. O.	321
Rimington, W.	149	Robins, A. H.	242
Rippengal, A. H.	200	Robins, P. D.	178
Ripper, F. S.	243	Robins, R. T.	310
†Ripperger, H. T. A.	40, 118, 250	Robinson, A.	428
Risdon, M. T.	149	Robinson, A. C.	294
Rissik, G. H.	212	Robinson, A. D.	209
Rist, W. K.	364	Robinson, A. G.	247
Ritchie, D. R.	294	†Robinson, A. H.	3, 315
†Ritson, C. R.	38	Robinson, A. K.	215

¶ See reference to this name in *Corrigenda*.

Robinson, A. R. T.	...	...	...	296	Rogers, Cecil E.	...	...	...	206
Robinson, A. V.	...	...	...	231	Rogers, Charles E.	...	...	...	178
Robinson, B. C.	...	...	...	312a	Rogers, C. M.	...	...	157, 305
Robinson, C. C.	...	...	...	324	†Rogers, Cecil W.	...	...	27, 364
†Robinson, C. C. E.	...	...	33, 178	Rogers, Clive W.	...	...	...	371
Robinson, C. F.	...	...	...	227	Rogers, G. R.	...	...	313, 417
Robinson, C. H. M.	...	...	...	361	Rogers, G. T. H.	...	...	...	267
Robinson, D. G.	...	...	...	178	Rogers, H. B.	...	...	...	281
Robinson, D. H.	...	...	...	190	Rogers, H. M.	...	...	...	411
Robinson, E. A. K.	...	...	157, 355	Rogers, J. W.	...	...	...	178
Robinson, F. W.	...	...	157, 377	Rogers, L.	...	...	...	367
†Robinson, G. M.	...	...	...	40	Rogers, L. E.	...	...	...	379
Robinson, Harry	...	...	119, 332	Rogers, O. L.	...	...	...	178
Robinson, Herbert	...	...	...	255	†Rogers, R. M.	...	...	...8, 266
Robinson, H. D.	...	...	...	391	Rogers, W. R.	...	...	...	178
Robinson, H. S.	...	...	...	304	Rogerson, H.	...	...	...	324
Robinson, J. C.	...	...	209, 353	Rolfe, C. H.	...	...	...	294
Robinson, J. L.	...	...	...	336	†Rolfe, R. H.	...	...	33, 217
Robinson, L.	...	...	...	324	Rolinson, F.	...	...	...	178
Robinson, L. T. A.	...	...	...	178	*Roll of Honour*	...	...	...	2
Robinson, M. F.	...	...	...	384	Rolles, N.	...	...	119, 372
Robinson, N. S.	...	...	119, 206	Rollinson, E. H.	...	...	...	329
Robinson, R. A.	...	...	...	178	Rolph, J. G.	...	...	...	178
Robinson, T.	...	...	...	425	Rolston, J. L.	...	...	...	183
Robinson, V. L.	...	...	...	294	Romanes, J.	...	...	...	228
Robinson, V. O.	...	...	...	237	Roocroft, E. T.	...	...	...	319
Robinson, W.	...	...	...	377	Rooks, F. O.	...	...	...	372
Robinson, W. A. B.	...	...	...	200	†Roots, P. W.	...	...	17, 294
Robinson, W. P.	...	...	157, 187	Roper, B. W.	...	...	...	313a
Robinson, W. S.	...	...	...	178	Roper, E. W.	...	...	...	237
Robison, D. L.	...	...	...	219	Roper, F. H.	...	...	...	255
Robothan, G. P.	...	...	...	402	†Roper, W. H. S.	...	...	22, 217
Robson, C. H.	...	...	...	428	Roper-Nunn, C. D. E.	...	...	333
Robson, E. S	...	...	...	178	Roscoe, W.	...	...	...119, 157, 276
Robson, F. J.	...	...	...	317	Roscow, R. E.	...	...	...	393
Robson, J.	...	...	...	390	Rose, A.	...	...	...	414
Robson, Leonard (760696)	...	...	408	Rose, A. E.	...	...	...	411
Robson, Leonard (763627)	...	...	414	Rose, A. St-J.	...	...	...	294
Robson, L. D. H.	...	...	...	178	Rose, C.	...	...	...	186
Robson, L. H.	...	...	...	268	†Rose, E. W.	...	...	32, 119, 270
Robson, N. G. F.	...	...	...	384	Rose, F. C.	...	...	...	190
Robson, W.	...	...	...	178	Rose, G. A.	...	...	...	428
†Roch-Austin, S. L.	...	...	41, 379	Rose, M. H.	...	...	120, 318
Rochat, R. R.	...	...	...	264	†Rose, S. A.	...	...	31, 331
Roche, J. A. E.	...	...	...	280	Rose, W. H. S.	...	...	...	249
Rochelle, W. A.	...	...	...	178	Rosher, J. B.	...	...	49, 120, 157, 240
Rochester, W. K.	...	...	...	408	Roskilly, S. T. H.	...	...	284, 353
Rochford, C.	...	...	...	244	Rosmallcocq, G. A.	...	...	206
Rochford, J. R.	...	...	119, 372	Ross, A. F.	...	...	...	330
Rock-West, O. G.	...	...	...	414	Ross, C.	...	...	...146, 151, 178
Roden, H. J.	...	...	...	384	Ross, C. G.	...	...	...	334
Rodger, F. C. G.	...	...	...	340	Ross, F. W.	...	...	...	329
Rodgers, J.	...	...	...	290	Ross, G. A.	...	...	...	178
†Rodney, B. W.	...	...	14, 264	Ross, Harold	...	...	...	294
Roe, A.	...	...	119, 269	Ross. Hunt	...	...	...	294
†Roeber, D. A.	...	...	...9, 222	Ross, J. A.	...	...	...	359
Roeber, O.	...	...	...	222	†Ross, J. K.	...	...	14, 178
Roffey, N. J.	...	...	...	241	Ross, N. H.	...	...	...	399
†Rogers, A. F.	...	...	35, 178	†Ross, P. C.	...	...	17, 178

† Killed in action or died.   § See this name in *Addenda*.

This Index does not include the Alphabetical Sections IV. and V. (Other Ranks and Old Members).

Ross, R. J.	... ...	294
Ross, R. O.	... ...	324
Ross, W. J. E.	... ...	157, 380
Rosselli, J. E.	... ...	178, 404
Rosselloty, G. A. C.	... ...	305
Rossiter, R. J.	... ...	234
Rostron, S. R.	... ...	288
Rothera, J.	... ...	183
Rothfield, J.	... ...	423
Rothwell, S.	... ...	277
†Rought, C. G.	... ...	42, 361
Rought, P.	... ...	120, 209
Roughton, H.	... ...	206
Roughton, W.	... ...	294
Roulston, R. P.	... ...	384
Round, F. H.	... ...	364
Rouse, G. N.	... ...	310
Rouse, R. P. Y.	... ...	294
Roussiano, T.	... ...	157, 423
Routh, F. R.	... ...	149
Routh, R. P.	... ...	241
Rouvray, F. G.	... ...	228
Row, G. K.	... ...	294
Rowden, E. J.	... ...	249
Rowe, C. B.	... ...	200
†Rowe, G. J. B.	... ...	33, 226
Rowe, G. L.	... ...	238, 417
Rowe, H. A.	... ...	234
Rowe, H. C.	... ...	200
Rowe, H. M.	... ...	351
Rowe, S.	... ...	394
Rowe, S. T.	... ...	178
Rowland, D. M.	... ...	209
Rowland, F. S.	... ...	120, 336
Rowland, G. M.	... ...	282
Rowland H. E.	... ...	324
†Rowland, M.	... ...	22, 389
Rowland, T.	... ...	373
†Rowland, W. R.	... ...	17, 301
Rowlands, Edward	... ...	368
Rowlands, Ernest	... ...	408
Rowlands, J. W.	... ...	269
Rowley, S. S.	... ...	236
Rowntree, D. W.	... ...	324
†Rowson, T. H.	... ...	10, 302
Roxburgh, J. A.	... ...	157, 408
R.A.	... ...	187
R.A.C.D.	... ...	397
R.A.F.	... ...	182
R.A.M.C.	... ...	398
R.A.O.D.	... ...	398
R.A.S.C.	... ...	403
R.E.	... ...	209
R.F.A.	... ...	187, 191
R.F.C.	... ...	164
R.G.A.	... ...	196, 201
R.H.A.	... ...	187
R.N.A.S.	... ...	164
R.N.R.	... ...	420
R.N.V.R.	... ...	420
R.T.O.	... ...	163
Roycroft, J. H.	... ...	231
Royden, T. W. E.	... ...	329
Royds, A. F.	... ...	308
†Royds, J. I.	... ...	30, 310
Rubenstein, R. F.	... ...	249
†Ruck, J. A.	... ...	7, 165, 178
Rudall, W. L.	... ...	283
Rudd, R. G.	... ...	283
Rudderham, J. E.	... ...	329
†Rudge, A. E.	... ...	178§
Rudkin, H. C.	... ...	402
Rudling, E. R.	... ...	362
Rudolf, G. R.	... ...	223
Rumford W. A.	... ...	190
†Rumilly, A. H. R.	... ...	18, 382
†Rundell, L. E.	... ...	27, 120, 157, 291
†Runnels-Moss, C. G. V.	... ...	27, 178
Rushbridge, W. G.	... ...	348
†Rushmore, E. R.	... ...	20, 268
†Rushton, F. G.	... ...	7, 380
Rushworth, N.	... ...	178
Russ, O. H.	... ...	310a
Russell, A. V.	... ...	331
Russell, H.	... ...	357
Russell, H. G.	... ...	253
Russell, J. C. W.	... ...	428
Russell, J. D.	... ...	236
Russell, J. F.	... ...	335
Russell, J. F. R. V.	... ...	294
Russell, L. M.	... ...	267
Russell, R. T.	... ...	50
Russell, S. H.	... ...	341
Rust, P.	... ...	149, 310
Rutherford, S.	... ...	120, 360
Rutherford, W. F.	... ...	243, 266
Ruxton, J.	... ...	291
Ryan, C. H.	... ...	238
Rycroft, G. J.	... ...	425
Rycroft, Sir R. N., Bart.	... ...	311
Ryder, C. T. W.	... ...	411
Rydings, D. G.	... ...	339
Rylands, E. C.	... ...	178, 314
Sackett, A. A.	... ...	261
Sadler, A. K.	... ...	227
Sadler, H. A.	... ...	324
Sadler, N. G.	... ...	289
Sadler, P. H.	... ...	178
Sadler, W. R.	... ...	244
Sagar, A. L.	... ...	50, 157, 272
†Sage, D. M.	... ...	27, 178
Sainsbury, P. C.	... ...	330
Saint, H.	... ...	195
St. Clair-Fowles, M. F.	... ...	179
†St. George, A. R.	... ...	276
St. Michael and St. George, Order of	...	148
St. Noble, G.	... ...	397

¶ See reference to this name in *Corrigenda*.

St. Quintin, R. G.	 376	Savage, J. P. 120, 299
Salisbury, F. R. ...	 423	Savage, W. A. 281
†Salisbury, W. F	... ... 28, 310a	†Savage, W. L. 17, 178
Salisbury, W. L.	 193	Saville, A. H. 364
Salmon, F. A. ...	 358	Savory, K. S. ... ... 50¶, 157, 164§
Salmon, M. W. ...	... ... 157, 209	Savours, E. W. 375
Salmon, S. A. ...	 178	Savours, H. J. 121, 247
Salsbury, A. F. ...	 423	Sawbridge, R. J. W. 178
Salt, C. H. ...	 402	Sawney, L. T. 121, 396
Salter, C. R. C. ...	... ... 120, 303	†Sawyer, R. H. 39, 178
Salter, J. F. ...	 281	Saxelbye, C. H. 393
Salter, L. E. ...	 316	Saxon, V. D. J. 157, 397
Salusbury, J. T. ...	 206	Sayer, C. E. 428
Salway, J. P. ...	... ,... ... 414	†Sayers, H. G. D. 17, 305
Salwey, D. E. L. ...	 288	Scaife, A. J. 243
Sams, R. A. ...	 279	Scantlebury, C. W. O. 303
Samson, A. J. ...	... ... 149, 313a	Scantlebury, J. E. 267
†Samson, Clyde A. ...	 12	Scarlett, L. S. 178
Samson, H. F. ...	 226	†Scattergood, T. V. 17, 334
Samson, I. A. C. ...	 193	†Schell, F. S. 36, 206
Samson, T. F. ...	... ... 312a	Schofield, C. 304
†Sampson, Charles A. ...	... ... 36, 306	Schofield, C. E. 324
Sampson, H. W. ...	... ... 311a	Schofield, C. G. 387
†Samuel, G. S. ...	... ...8, 393	Schofield, H. 212
Samuels, L. ...	 235	†Schofield, J. L. 28
Sandell, C. M. ...	 255	Schofield, J. W. 178
Sandeman, R. J. ...	 428	Schofield, R. S. 333
Sanders, J. N. ...	 369	Scholes, J. 178
Sanderson, A. B. ...	 186	Schooley, N. V. 178
Sanderson, A. F	 347	Schrader, F. J. 235
†Sanderson, G. S. ...	... ...8, 298	Schuler, W. E. D. 335
Sanderson, H. F. ...	... ... 157, 162	Sciama, A. 279
Sanderson, R. W. ...	 360	Scofield, E. W. 359
†Sanderson, S. C. ...	... ... 11, 302	†Scolding, G. H. 31, 328
†Sandford, C. J. V. ...	... ... 16, 321	Scoones, T. C. 121, 157, 252
Sandhurst Cadets ...	... ... *104*	Scotcher, A. E. 367
Sandland, K. ...	... ... 151, 162	Scotcher, H. G. 193
†Sandoe, M. W. A. ...	... ... 16, 236	Scothorne, J. P. 292
Sands, G. F. ...	... ... 157, 363	*Scots, Royal* *343*
Sandy, B. F. ...	... ... 178¶	*Scots Fusiliers, Royal* *344*
Sandys, A. F. ...	 261	*Scots Guards* *219*
†Sanger, H. K. ...	... ... 33, 393	†Scott, Alexander 15, 256
Sangster, A. W. ...	 261	Scott, Arthur 230
Sankey, H. ...	 250	Scott, A. A. 331
Sant, R. ...	 315	Scott, A. W. 428
Saqui, L. V. H. ...	... ... 328, 415	†Scott, C. 19, 243
Sargeant, W. ...	 229	Scott, C. E. 121, 157, 266
Sargent, E. V. ...	... ... 34¶, 332	Scott, D. N. 232
Sargent, F. H. St. C. ...	...146, 159, 178	Scott, E. D. 178
Sargent, J. H. ...	 206	Scott, E. R. 228
Sargood, H. T. ...	 324	Scott, F. M. 121, 287
Sartin, G. E. ...	 373	Scott, I. J. 193
†Saull, H. T. ...	... ... 39, 288	†Scott, J. F. 15, 343
Saunders, C. J. ...	...120, 151, 157, 305	Scott, J. J. 294
Saunders, G. W. ...	 343	Scott, J. L. 221
Saunders, H. A. ...	 272	Scott, R. 295
Saunders, J. A. ...	... ... 157, 404	Scott, R. F. C. 121, 282
†Saunders, L. D. ...	... ...5, 367	Scott, R. J. L. 257
Saunders, W. L. ...	 163	Scott, R. P. 314

† Killed in action or died.   § See this name in *Addenda*.

SHAW

This Index does not include the Alphabetical Sections IV. and V. (Other Ranks and Old Members). 571

Scott, T. G. 121, 328	Semple, W. J. 363
Scott, W. ... ... 206¶	Sendell, C. H. ... ... 190¶, 404
Scott, W. D. 206	Senior, W. E. 332
Scott-Eames, G. 425	Sennett, R. H. 281, 352
Scottish Borderers *345*	Sennett, R. L. 337
Scottish Rifles *346*	Sergeant, J. P. 206
Scott-James, R. A. 121, 206	Servante, S. Q. 243
Scott-Nicholson, E. 228	†Service, G. B. ... ... 32¶, 417
Scougall, J. M. 190	†Sessions, D. H. 35, 122, 178
Scourfield, D. P. 375	Sessions, R. V. 178
Screaton, E. 338	Seth-Smith, G. 405
Scrimgeour, J. M. 206	Settle, R. H. 206
Scriven, D. A. 408	Sevenoaks, P. L. 422
Scriven, S. A. 183	Seward, J. R. 342
Scrivener, E. R. 364	Seward, W. J. 178
Scrivener, W. E. R. 226	†Sewell, E. J. 32, 200
Scruby, R. K. F. 183	Sewell, J. ... ... 183¶
Scrutton, A. E. 122, 157, 310	Sewill, R. W. 404
Scrutton, J. A. 122, 157, 214	Sexton, A. A. 414
Scudamore, C. G. 121, 292	Seymour, B. G. 272
Scudamore, Stanley 292	Seymour, J. 157, 310
Scudamore, Stephen 242	Shaddick, H. E. 378
Sculthorpe, A. 178	Shadwell, L. C. 404
Scurlock, S. J. 122, 269	Shankey, E. W. 258
Seabrook, A. D. 310a	Shanks, E. B. 277
Seabrook, A. L. 305	Shanks, M. H. 122, 157, 354
Seabrooke, G. S. 409	Shann, C. E. 402
Seabrooke, J. 248	Shannaw, C. J. F. 343
Seaforth Highlanders *347*	Sharland, C. N. A. 355
Seale, B. 230	†Sharman, B. T. 25
Seale, C. S. St. B. 242	Sharp, C. G. 364
Seale, J. H. 261	Sharp, C. S. 200
Searcy, J. H. 324	Sharp, E. G. 241
Searle, G. D. 395	Sharp, E. R. 365
Searle, F. H. 379	Sharp, F. B. 338
Searle, R. S. 372	Sharp, F. G. 183
Searle, W. D. W. 157, 369	Sharp, J. F. 200
Searson, A. M. 195	†Sharp, M. 29, 122, 294
†Seath, D. A. 15, 346	Sharp, R. 321
Seaton, J. W. 294	Sharp, R. H. 425
Seaton, J. W. S. 360	Sharp, T. H. 267
Seccombe, J. H. 325	†Sharp, W. D. C. 22, 327
Seddon, A. L. 304	Sharpe, C. B. 369
†Sedgley, H. F. 38, 296	†Sharpe, C. L. A. 3, 320
Sedgwick, D. W. 178	†Sharpe, G. N. 8, 385
Seed, C. W. S. 299	Sharpe, H. E. 325
Seeman, F. H. 157, 195	†Sharpe, H. N. 12, 178
Sefi, C. R. R. 178	Sharpe, J. S. 280
Selby, E. W. 274	Sharpe, P. 282
†Selby, M. G. 39	Sharpe, P. B. 206
Selby-Bigge, J. A. 404	Sharvell, G. W. C. 310a
Selfe, A. E. F. 122, 218, 222, 311	Shaul, P. J. 200
†Selfe, E. D. 36, 157, 328	†Shave, L. H. 14, 238
Selfe, L. P. 313a	Shaw, A. E. 288
Seligsohn, H. L. 122, 290	Shaw, A. T. 428
Sell, A. E. 183	†Shaw, B. L. 15, 374
Selven, W. A. 305	Shaw, C. N. 244
Selway, E. J. 163	Shaw, E. B. 302
Semmens, J. J. 414	Shaw, E. L. 354

¶ See reference to this name in *Corrigenda*.

Shaw, E. St. L.	159, 312a
Shaw, E. W.	316
Shaw, F. R.	294
Shaw, L. B.	391
Shaw, L. G.	227
Shaw, L. H.	333, 393
†Shaw, P.	23, 331
†Shaw, W. D.	41, 123, 246
Shaylor, H.	414
†Shea, R. T.	41, 200
†Shea, W. D.	25
Shearman, H. H.	235
Sheehan, F. G. E.	313a, 415
Sheehan, J. J.	193
†Sheen, C.	16, 355
Sheffington, H. E.	419
Sheldon, G. H.	183
Sheldon, H. J.	402
Sheldon, H. P.	382
Sheldrick, R. H.	179
Shelley, P. N.	352
Shelton, F. N.	236
Shephard, E. F.	185
Shepheard, S. J.	230
Shepherd, E.	306
Shepherd, G. W. B.	227
Shepherd, L. G.	240
Shepherd, M. W.	324
Shepherd, P. T.	179
Shepherd, T. D.	187
Shepherd, T. J. N.	357
Shepherd, W. S.	123, 151, 157, 380
Sheppard, H. J. G.	226
Sheppard, R. J.	348
Sheppee, H. V.	244
Shepperd, H. E.	179
Sheridan, C. W.	200
Sheridan, R.	302
Sheringham, A. I.	184
Sherlock, A. F.	123, 329
Sherlock, C. C.	123, 157, 321
†Sherlock, G.	313a, 417§
Sherlock, T. P.	382
Sherman, R. K.	395
Sherrard, L. H.	324
Sherriff, R. C.	360
Sherry, J.	183
Sherwin, H. C.	157, 190
Shiel, S.	423
†Shield, W. J.	13, 286
Shilcock, H. G.	123, 294
Shillinglaw, E. C.	360
Shillito, G.	302
Shilston, A. C.	367
Shilstone, A. B.	179
Shiner, F. W.	250
Shiner, L. A. D.	212
†Shinner, W. G. B.	28¶, 310
†Shipstone, F. E.	18
Shipton, J. E.	361
Shirley, H. J.	159, 268, 307
Shirley, W.	148, 159, 311
Shore, B. A. R.	341
Short, F. P.	235
Short, H.	123, 275
Short, H. C.	179
Short, J. R.	123, 157, 386
Short, S. C. T.	224
Shott, P.	223
Shovel, E. G.	236
Shread, A. C.	402
Shropshire L.I.	*348*
Shuffrey, G.	277
†Shute, G. F.	23, 250
Shutt, D. B.	280
Sibree, H. J. H.	123, 327
†Siddall, T. A.	14, 306
†Sidey, W. H.	22, 200
Sidgwick, F.	163
Siems, F. W. M.	294
Siemssen, G. H.	379
Sieveking, G. E.	344
Sieveking, L. de G.	52, 164
Sievey, V. C.	297
Silcock, A.	352
†Silcock, B. B.	4, 157, 420
Silcock, F. H.	310a
Siles, S. H.	250
Silk, E.	157, 377
Silley, H. A. J.	212
Sillery, W.	206
†Silmon, W. O. de Weld	13, 394
Silver, G. J.	428
†Silvester, R.	17, 303
†Sim, L. G. E.	9, 217
†Simcox, C. G.	6
Sime, W. E. B.	345
Simeon, C. B.	157, 214
Simeons, W. R.	184
Siminson, B. D. N.	261
Simkin, R. I.	179
†Simmonds, A. G.	17, 190
Simmonds, D. G. H.	364
Simmons, F. K.	123, 151, 157, 162, 308
Simmons, F. L.	363
†Simmons, R. D.	38, 294
Simmons, S. J. R. B.	294
Simmons, W. A.	179
Simner, S. A.	348
Simnett, R. F.	392
Simon, A. F. S.	352
Simon, H. J. B.	290
Simon, J. M.	343
Simonds, S. F.	301
Simpkin, J. W.	414
†Simpkin, R. J. H.	8, 370
Simpson, C.	190
Simpson, Cecil, H.	179

† Killed in action or died.   § See this name in *Addenda*.

This Index does not include the Alphabetical Sections IV. and V. (Other Ranks and Old Members).

Name	Pages	Name	Pages
Simpson, Charles H	... 396	Sly, H. F.	... 149
Simpson, G. G.	52, 164	Sly, W.	... 228
Simpson, G. M. F.	... 294	Small, D. F.	... 231
†Simpson, H. G.	4, 233, 258	Small, E. V.	... 311
†Simpson, J. A.	... 28	Small, H. L.	... 408
Simpson, J. G.	124, 367	Small, V.	...149, 157, 346
Simpson, J. R.	... 276	Smallman, C. S.	... 289
Simpson, J. S. M.	... 190	Smallpage, F. H.	... 206
Simpson, M. B.	... 208	†Smallwood, W. S.	29, 179
†Simpson, R.	16, 267	Smart, A. R.	... 354
Simpson, S. E. M.	... 179	Smart, C. A.	... 300
†Simpson, W. D.	... 31	†Smart, E. H.	27, 291
†Simpson, W. R. C.	...4, 226	Smart, H. W.	... 319
Sims, A. J. F.	... 244	Smart, J. L.	125, 394
Sims, B. W.	... 375	Smart, N. H.	... 425
Sims, N. W.	151, 206	Smart, R. B.	... 306
Simson, J. H.	157, 212	Smart, W. P.	125, 287
†Sinclair, E. R.	40, 124, 221	Smeardon, E. N.	... 270
Sinclair, J.	... 221	Smedley, W. H.	... 277
Sinclair, P. J.	... 411	Smellie, B.	... 179
†Sinclair, W. K.	... 6	Smerdon, H. E.	... 265
†Singer, J. M. L.	... 25	Smiles, A. R.	... 402
Singleton, J. H.	... 342	Smirke, E. A.	125, 269
Sisson, J. A.	... 286	Smith, A. B.	... 343
Sizen, R.	124, 248	Smith, A. D.	... 404
Skeats, L. F.	... 200	Smith, A. D. N.	... 214
Skeet, C. H. L.	... 246	Smith, A. E.	157, 414
Skeete, C. de C.	... 411	Smith, A. H.	... 288
†Skelton, H.	39, 270	Smith, A. J.	... 386
Skene, G. A.	... 163	Smith, A. T. S.	... 292
†Skerry, J. B.	...7, 322	Smith, A. V.	... 159
Skevington, A. P.	...124, 157, 394	Smith, Alfred W.	... 375
Skey, L. G.	... 249	Smith, Arthur W.	... 165
Skiller, F. H.	... 428	Smith, A. W. G.	125, 224
Skingley, T. G.	... 274	Smith, B. de B.	... 414
Skinner, E. H. D.	... 414	Smith, B. K.	.. 193
Skinner, W. W.	... 379	Smith, Campbell	... 375
Skippon, D. L.	124, 425	Smith, Clement	... 425
Skull, A.	295, 320	†Smith, Colin	13, 179
Slade, K. R.	... 364	Smith, Carl A.	... 179
Slaney, A. J. R.	124, 301	Smith, Cecil A.	... 408
Slater, G. E. H.	124, 226	Smith, C. A. B.	... 422
†Slater, H.	34, 353	Smith, C. B.	... 272
Slater, H. E.	... 294	Smith, C. D.	... 311a
†Slater, J. E.	16, 272	Smith, C. E. B. McF.	149, 335
Slater, S. A.	... 179	†Smith, C. F.	32, 357
Slatter, A. W.	... 206	Smith, C. H. C.	... 190
†Slattery, F. J.	42, 157, 209	Smith, C. H. K.	... 367
Slaughter, V.	... 306	Smith, C. L.	... 179
Sleap, J. W.	... 250	Smith, Charles R. (1766)	... 408
Slee, W. A.	... 236	Smith, Charles R. (7319)	... 361
Sleep, C. F.	... 345	Smith, Cecil V.	... 397
Sleigh, R. P.	... 421	Smith, Cyril V.	... 351
Sleigh, W. R.	... 278	Smith, C. W.	... 280
Slingsby, H. V.	265, 417	Smith, D. C.	... 357
Sloan, C. H.	... 313a	†Smith, D. R. McC.	34, 315
Sloan, J. W. J.	313a, 417	Smith, Edward (4206)	... 304
Sloane, W. H. St. J.	... 417	Smith, Edward (765736)	... 294
Sloot, J. N. C.	... 237	Smith, E. B.	... 212

¶ See reference to this name in *Corrigenda*.

SMITH

INDEX TO COMMISSIONS, HONOURS, and ROLL OF HONOUR.

Smith, E. E. 411	Smith, L. G. 193
Smith, Edgar H. 294	Smith, L. H. 126, 418
†Smith, E. K. 6, 260	Smith, L. P. 226
Smith, Edward L. 281	†Smith, L. W. 33, 233
Smith, Esmond L. 244	Smith, M. C. 126
Smith, E. R. 125, 418	Smith, M. G. 273
Smith, E. S. 408	Smith, M. P. 208
Smith, E. W. 333	Smith, M. S. C. 411
Smith, F. 396	Smith, N. 226
Smith, F. A. 241	†Smith, N. H. 30, 303
Smith, F. E. C. D. 125, 241	Smith, N. L. 404
Smith, F. G. 206	Smith, N. R. 206
Smith, Frank H. 411	Smith, P. 414
Smith, Frederick H. 402	Smith, P. D. 245
†Smith, F. H. C. D. ... ... 27, 200¶	Smith, P. L. 126, 372
Smith, F. I. 384	Smith, Robert A. 321
Smith, F. L. 179	Smith, Rowland A. 316
Smith, F. T. 306	Smith, R. I. D. 425
Smith, G. 425	Smith, R. McK. ... ... 157¶, 256
Smith, G. E. 125, 151, 200	Smith, R. N. 183
Smith, G. G. 184	Smith, R. S. 420
†Smith, Geoffrey Harold ... 18, 330	Smith, Seymour 200
†Smith, Geoffrey Hubert ... 40, 125, 218	Smith, Sidney 200
†Smith, George Herbert 32	Smith, S. A. 338
†Smith, Gordon Hamilton ... 16, 237	Smith, Sidney B. 126, 275
Smith, G. K. 186	Smith, Stanley B. 263
Smith, G. N. 286	Smith, S. C. 190
Smith, G. R. 125, 378	Smith, S. F. C. 428
†Smith, G. W. 31, 280	†Smith, S. N. 19, 357
Smith, H. 331	Smith, S. P. 276
Smith, H. A. 279	Smith, T. 217
†Smith, H. B. 16, 292	†Smith, T. E. 18, 179
Smith, Harrison C. 157, 418	Smith, V. C. C. 200
Smith, Henry C. 179	Smith, V. St. G. 367
Smith, Herbert C. 298	Smith, W. 275
†Smith, H. D. 29, 270	Smith, W. A. N. 216
Smith, H. E. 363	Smith, W. B. 317
Smith, H. G. 402	Smith, W. C. ... 126, 143, 157, 310
Smith, H. H. 393	Smith, W. D. 193
Smith, Herbert Leslie 267	Smith, W. H. 219
Smith, Hubert Lionel 337	†Smith, W. L. 33, 126, 381
Smith, H. N. 340	Smith, W. M. 421
Smith, H. R. 126, 163, 415	Smith, W. P. 317
Smith, I. C. 303	†Smith, W. T. 26, 157, 369
Smith, J. A. 308	Smither, A. W. 358
Smith, John C. 277	Smither, B. 193
Smith, Joseph C. 294	Smither, S. T. 126, 297
Smith, J. H. 350	Smyly, C. F. 313a
Smith, J. L. 411	Smyth, C. St. J. 261
Smith, J. M. 344	Smyth, L. C. 248
Smith, J. Palmer 179	Smyth, M. 421
Smith, J. Percy 314	Smythe, L. L. W. 179
Smith, J. Poole 190, 314	Snalam, F. R. ... ... 193¶
Smith, J. R. 270	Snead, H. M. 304
†Smith, J. R. G. 12, 333	Sneddon, J. 375
Smith, J. S. 414	Snelling, L. C. 351
Smith, K. A. 428	Snelling, L. M. 305
Smith, K. T. 264	Snelling, W. J. 238
Smith, L. C. 338	Snow, G. M. 235

† Killed in action or died. § See this name in *Addenda*.

This Index does not include the Alphabetical Sections IV. and V. (Other Ranks and Old Members).

Name	Pages	Name	Pages
†Snow, R. A.	...6, 385	†Spencer, G.	27, 310
†Snowden, R. W.	...8, 353	Spencer, J. C. A.	... 283
Snowden, W. C.	157, 179	Spencer, J. G.	... 261
†Snyder, L.	15, 253	Spencer, J. T.	127, 296
Solley, S. W.	... 360	Spencer, J. W.	... 414
Sollom, V. P.	... 408	Spencer, R. A.	... 315
Solomon, C. S.	... 294	Spencer, S.	... 200
Solomon, J. B.	127, 151, 157, 162, 164, 338	Spencer, T. D.	... 218
Solsbury, G. H.	... 357	Spencer, W.	... 315
Solven, W. A.	... 428	Spenle, H. E.	... 298
Soman, C. D.	... 332	Spens, A. H.	... 311
Somerset, J. H.	212, 331	Spicer, E. M.	127, 271
Somersetshire L.I.	... 349	†Spicer, R. W.	13, 362
Somerville, T. T.	... 419	Spiess, W. F.	... 238
Sondheim, A.	... 194	†Spink, E. W.	40, 269
Sone, T. E.	... 386¶	Spink, L. R.	... 316
†Sorrell, C. E.	... 25	†Spinks, S. M.	... 18
Sorrell, F. G.	... 324	†Spinney, F.	10, 343
Souchon, A. M.	... 284	†Spinney, R. H.	...8, 218
Souchon, H. G.	... 183	Spinney, W. S.	... 335
Soul, C. F.	... 212	Spooner, H. G.	... 224
Soulby, A. C.	... 259	Spratt, N. N.	... 242
Soulsby, E. D.	... 316	Sprawson, E. C.	...127, 157, 398
Souper, C. A.	... 325	Spreadbury, H. V.	... 317
Souster, S. R.	... 245	Sprigings, R. H.	... 287
South Lancashire Regt.	... 276	Springbett, S. A.	... 269
South Wales Borderers	... 367	†Springthorpe, W. F.	... 25
Southam, A. W.	157, 421	†Spurgeon, D. F. P.	38, 303
Southan, R.	382, 415	Spurgeon, V. F.	... 275
Southern, A. J.	... 200	Spurrell, R. K.	127, 233
Southwell, S. A.	... 310a	Squibbs, C. F.	... 288
Soutten, A. C.	127, 298	Squire, A. M.	... 402
Soward, F.	127, 233	Squire, E. R.	127, 283
Sowden, P. J.	... 224	Stabler, A. W. E.	... 269
†Sowerby, V. H.	19, 282	Stables, W. W. G.	... 335
Spackman, R.	... 350	Stace, J. A.	157, 340
Spafford, A. V.	...127, 157, 379	Stacey, M. R.	... 324
Spalding, F.	... 179	Stacy, H. C.	... 329
Spanton, W. B.	... 206	Stadden-Lee, C. J.	... 255
Sparke, L. F.	... 267	Stafford, L. H. G.	159, 297
Sparling, P. S.	... 190	†Stafford-Badger, H. P.	... 34
Sparrow, A. C. G.	... 185	*Staffordshire Regt., North*	... *351*
Sparrow, F. P.	... 414	*Staffordshire Regt., South*	... *352*
†Spatz, W. R.	7¶, 320	Stahl, A.	128, 151, 157, 195
Spaul, E. A.	... 296	Staines, J. S.	... 193
†Speakman, A. E.	38¶, 248	Staines, T. F.	... 241
Spearing, C. H.	... 408	†Staines, W. J.	... 25
Spearing, J. R.	... 179	†Stainton, E.	42, 382
Special List	... *422*	Staley, H.	... 337
†Speight, J. L.	22, 394	Stalman, A. C.	128, 379
Speight, R. H.	... 179	Stammers, F. A. R.	... 206
Spiers, J.	... 404	Stamp, L. D.	... 212
Spence, W. B.	... 200	Stamper, C.	... 414
Spence-Layh, V. C. H.	... 381	Stancliff, R.	128, 290
Spencer, A.	... 428	Standen, L. R.	... 275
Spencer, A. F.	... 393	Standing, J. S. H.	... 193¶
Spencer, D.	... 402	†Standring, B. A.	...2, 369
†Spencer, Edwin D.	... 25	Standring, G. L.	... 364
Spencer, Eric D.	... 335	Stanesby, R. W. J.	157, 214¶, 386

¶ See reference to this name in *Corrigenda*.

Name	Pages	Name	Pages
Stanford, G. W.	355	Stephenson, A. C. P.	179
Staniland, W. F.	179	Stephenson, C.	310a
Stanistreet, C. R.	294	Stephenson, G. L.	310a
†Stanley, S. E.	23, 179	†Stephenson, H. V.	16, 232
Stanley, T. H.	264	†Stephenson, K. L.	5, 157, 222
Stansbury, G.	284	Stephenson, W. S.	208
Stansbury, W. B.	379	Sterndale-Bennett, T. C.	179
Stansfield, H.	149, 157, 179	†Sterndale-Bennett, W.	25, 50, 420
Stanton, R.	408	Stevens, A.	157, 212
Stanton, S. J. B.	331	Stevens, C.	303
Stanway, E. A.	313a	Stevens, C. P.	129, 232
†Stanwell, W. A.	4, 268	Stevens, C. W.	346
Staples, H. W.	313a	†Stevens, D. H.	36, 261
Stapleton, R. W.	387	Stevens, F. A.	200
†Stapleton, W. H.	37, 224	†Stevens, G. V.	28, 283
†Stapleton, W. R.	28	Stevens, H. J. H.	157, 209
†Stark, J. D.	38, 157, 345	Stevens, J. J. C.	353
Stark, M. A. N.	349	Stevens, J. L.	232
Startuck, J. W. S.	428	Stevens, J. M.	337
Starling, J. E.	194	Stevens, L. H.	179
Starling, M. C.	295, 362	Stevens, P. L.	213
Startin, E. C.	149	Stevens, R. H.	210
Startin, G.	235	Stevens, W. C.	129, 151, 381
Startin, H.	428	Stevenson, A. F.	157, 421
Staton, W. E.	128, 146, 179	Stevenson, J. C.	279
Staveley, W.	200	Stevenson, J. H.	429
†Stead, H. S.	30, 270	Stevenson, J. S.	404
†Stearns, E. G.	4, 245	†Stevenson, R. T.	37, 179
Steavenson, H. V.	248	Steward, D. H.	213
Stebbing, P. E.	254	Stewart, F. J.	206
Steckley, H. B.	290	Stewart, Jack	148, 344
Stedman, A. H. D.	254	Stewart, James (762095)	357
†Stedman, W. W. T.	11, 302	Stewart, James (765809)	402
Steel, E. G.	128, 303	Stewart, J. D.	157, 313a
Steel, J.	334	Stewart, O.	129, 147, 179, 321
Steel, J. W.	402	Stewart, W.	258
†Steel, N.	19, 250	Stewart, W. H.	129, 206
Steen, G. A.	420	†Stickland, C. S.	40
Steen, J. D.	311	Stiff, C. R.	248
Steer, J. S.	280	Stilgoe, N. G.	213
Steer, W.	179, 313a	Stilwell, C. F.	277
Steger, B. M.	364	Stilwell, S.	364
Stein, H. K.	428	Stilwell, W. M. F.	402
Stennett, J. N.	179	Stirling, A. C.	206
Stentiford, R. H.	128, 281	Stirzaker, R.	352
Stephany, M.	342	†Stiven, A.	12, 345
Stephens, A.	360, 418	Stisted, J. L. H.	347
Stephens, B. L.	206	Stobbs, H. L.	343
†Stephens, C. H.	40, 193	Stock, C. A.	429
Stephens, F. J.	370	Stock, E. T.	313a
Stephens, G.	128, 250	†Stock, J. L. W.	16, 237
Stephens, J. H.	288	Stock, R.	355
Stephens, K. T.	128, 382	Stocken, C. A.	254
†Stephens, L.	17, 179	Stocken, H.	340
Stephens, R. C.	287	Stocken, H. C. V.	294
†Stephens, R. M.	39, 262	Stockins, W. J.	304
Stephens, W. J.	151, 157	Stockman, G. D.	299
Stephens, W. T.	129, 336	Stockwin, G. H.	337
Stephenson, A.	272	Stodel, J. H.	425

† Killed in action or died. § See this name in *Addenda*.

This Index does not include the Alphabetical Sections IV. and V. (Other Ranks and Old Members).

Stogdon, R. H. A. 384	Streets, A. W. 250
Stoker, F. R. 414	†Stribling, F. G. 8, 335
Stokes, C. W. 206	Strick, R. B. K. 206
Stokes, G. C. 186	Strickland, J. A. 200
Stokes, J. H. 408	Stride, H. J. 245
Stokes, W. R. F. 179	Strode, J. 149, 157
Stokoe, E. 402	Strode, M. 130, 151, 361
Stone, A. 303	Strohm, E. C. 259
Stone, E. J. 298	Strong, H. V. 235
†Stone, H. 17, 305	Strongitharm, A. D. 384
Stone, H. C. 362	Stronner, R. C. 213
Stone, H. M. 397	Strother, F. W. 185
Stone, H. W. 317	Stuart, E. C. 193
†Stone, O. J. 10, 195	†Stuart, H. G. 42, 290
Stone, M. T. B. 249	Stuart, H. L. 193
Stone, P. M. 335	†Stuart, W. E. M. 10, 262
Stone, P. R. 314	Stuart-Cook, H. 322
Stone, R. H. 206	Stubbs, G. P. 372
Stone, W. B. 206	Stubington, R. E. 328
Stone, W. H. 129, 372	†Sturgess, M. E. 25
Stoneham, E. W. 206	Sturrock, G. H. 26
Stoneham, G. T. 263	†Sturt, G. C. N. 383
Stonehouse, A. D. 208	†Sturt, H. M. 28, 269
†Stonehouse, R. A. 15, 274	Sturton, H. C. 297
Stones, D. H. 299	†Styer, W. H. 11
†Stonier, W. J. 15, 222	Suckling, P. H. 157, 418
†Stoodley, P. B. 11, 380	Suffolk, F. F. 335
Stooke, H. N. 384	*Suffolk Regt.* *354*
Stops, J. F. 219	Sugars, A. M. S. 425
Storey, H. E. 179	Sugden, F. E. 206
Storey, J. 287	Sugden, J. R. 267
Storey, K. 129, 157, 239	Sugden, W. H. 210
Storey, R. 414	Suggate, W. A. 313a, 418
†Storm, W. G. 22, 129, 386	Suiter, C. R. 157, 227
Storry, E. R. 429	Sullivan, S. F. 130, 251
Stotesbury, R. K. 408	Summerfield, A. B. 157, 206
Stott, F. 238	Summerfield, G. 371
†Stott, W. G. 38, 315	Summers, A. R. 213
Stout, F. M. 130, 184	Summers, G. D. 329
Stout, J. M. 227	Summersell, J. G. 157, 206
Strachan, C. 418	Summerskill, J. H. 395
Strachan, H. K. 411	Summerton, F. G. 200
Stradling, F. B. 179	Sumner, J. A. 360
Strafford, C. A. S. 316	Surfleet, J. 179
Straight, R. M. 242	*Surgeons, R.N.* *420*
Strand, A. C. 306	*Surrey Regt., East* *357*
Strang, William (5224) ... 157, 281	*Surrey Regt., Royal West* ... *361*
Strang, William (5324) 370	*Sussex Regt., Royal* *365*
Stratton, G. K. 384	Sutcliffe, A. C. 179
Stratton, G. L. 130, 157, 193	Sutcliffe, A. L. 179
Strawbridge, R. 258	Sutcliffe, F. 130, 157, 254
Strawson, F. M. 380	Sutcliffe, J. H. 382
Strawson, P. C. 297	Suter, E. J. 319
†Streater, J. W. 35, 372	Sutherin, V. O. 248
Streather, C. T. 193	Sutherland, A. 402
Stredder, C. A. E. 248	Sutherland, D. C. 179
†Street, E. A. 7, 318	Sutherland, G. K. 206
Street, H. W. 200	†Sutherland, J. A. 27, 306
Streeter, S. A. 264	Sutherland-Hawes, H. V. 422

¶ See reference to this name in *Corrigenda*.

Suttill, R.	420
Sutton, A. A.	341
†Sutton, G. A.	26, 258, 260
Sutton, G. F.	404
Sutton, K. H. M.	217
Sutton, R. B.	338
Sutton, W. D.	324
†Sutton, W. H.	40, 376
Swabey, K.	257
Swaby, J. W.	179
Swaffield, F.	226
Swain, T. E.	362
Swainson, C. G. D'O.	261
Swainson, W. C. G.	361
Swales, E.	342
Swales, J. S.	179
Swallow, H.	414
Swan, K. T.	324
Swan, T. A.	213
Swann, F. T.	411
Swann, P. B.	231
Swann, P. W.	253
Swanton, E. F. W.	190
Swanston, C. B.	337
Swanwick, E. D.	338
Swash, F. C.	325
Swatman, C. M.	288
Sweeney, R. L.	269
†Sweeting, A. E.	35, 179
Swift, A. D.	207
Swift, F.	305
Swindell, J.	402
Swindell, J. F.	230
Swindley, E. J.	414
Swinney, L. A. E.	214
Swinnock, W. E.	355
Swinstead, N. H.	429
Sykes, H. V.	391
Sykes, I.	252
Symes, B. G.	238
Symington, P. K.	220
†Symonds, S. L. H.	26, 179
Symons, J. R.	157, 394
†Syrett, A. M.	16, 375
Syrett, R. M.	210
Taaffe, L. C.	190
Tackley, R. C.	254
Tafft, J. R.	404
Tait, A. A. D.	252
Tait, D. C.	207
Tait, N.	193
Talbot, J. A.	341
Talbot, J. H. G.	219
Talbot, L. H.	213
Talbot, S. G.	375
†Tall, J. J.	29, 235
†Tallentire, A. T.	6, 164, 310
Tamblyn, H. W.	130, 210
Tamlyn, J. R.	357
Tank Corps	*424*
Tanner, A. R.	404
Tanner, E. J.	404
Tanser, H. A.	348
Tapley, C. M.	294
Taplin, G. A.	130, 157, 196
Tapper, G. H.	235
Tapper, M. J.	130¶, 158, 310
Tapply, M.	130, 328
Tapson, A. G. E.	411
†Tarbet, V.	22, 235
†Tardugno, R.	18, 375
Targett, A. E.	396
†Tarrant, H. G. N.	19, 130, 226
Tarrant, R. W.	299
Tarver, A. A.	418
Tasker, E. C.	219
Tasker, R.	373
Tate, A. F.	159, 414
Tate, E. D.	217
Tate, W. E.	338
Tatham, R. P.	408
Tatlow, W. B.	337
Tautz, P. H.	402
Tautz, R. H.	131, 317
Taverner, E. S.	369
Taylor, A. C. J.	357
Taylor, A. E.	220
Taylor, A. H. S.	200
Taylor, A. R.	231
Taylor, B. F.	299
†Taylor, B. M.	25, 50, 131, 157, 232
Taylor, C.	255
Taylor, C. A.	213
Taylor, C. H.	248
Taylor, C. W. B.	317
†Taylor, D. C.	28
Taylor, D. H.	265
Taylor, E. A.	396
Taylor, E. C.	291
Taylor, E. G. L.	311a
Taylor, E. M.	397
Taylor, E. Raymond	402
Taylor, E. Richard	180
†Taylor, E. Reginald	36, 131, 243
Taylor, E. V.	411
†Taylor, F. L. V.	25
Taylor, F. P.	340
Taylor, F. V.	183
Taylor, G. A.	131, 279
Taylor, G. H.	368
†Taylor, G. T.	25, 245
Taylor, G. W.	180
Taylor, H. St. G.	217
Taylor, Harold S.	254
*Taylor, Herbert S.	15, 339
Taylor, I. M.	261
Taylor, James	421

† Killed in action or died. § See this name in *Addenda*.

THOMPSON

This Index does not include the Alphabetical Sections IV. and V. (Other Ranks and Old Members).

Taylor, John	... 264	†Theak, H. L.	16, 243
Taylor, Joseph	... 338	Theak, L. F.	... 405
†Taylor, J. Birley	27, 272	Theak, W. E.	... 180
Taylor, J. Burton	... 387	Thear, A. W.	... 296
Taylor, J. D.	... 354	Theobald, G. St. John	... 329
Taylor, J. F.	157, 186	Theobald, I. St. John	... 329
Taylor, J. J.	... 360	Thevenard, C .W.	... 277
Taylor, L. E.	... 365	Thiele, W. C.	... 245
†Taylor, Leonard F.	13, 353	†Thierry, F. G.	12, 180
†Taylor, Leslie F.	34, 131, 265	†Thirlby, S. L.	30, 281
Taylor, L. M.	... 360	Thistleton, J. F.	322, 394
Taylor, L. R.	... 284	Thomas, A. H.	... 193
Taylor, N. J.	... 180	Thomas, A. J.	... 310a
†Taylor, N. S.	151, 180§	†Thomas, A. L.	33, 329
†Taylor, P.	... 338	Thomas, Alban M.	163, 191
Taylor, P. C.	... 304	Thomas, Alroy M.	... 402
†Taylor, P. H.	... 25	†Thomas, C. R.	36, 368
Taylor, Percy S.	... 337	Thomas, D. E. J.	... 377
Taylor, Phillip S.	151, 157, 414§	Thomas, E.	... 180
Taylor, Robert	... 241	Thomas, E. T.	... 375
Taylor, Reginald	... 186	Thomas, George	... 334
Taylor, R. A.	... 408	Thomas, G. H.	... 243
Taylor, R. C.	... 240	Thomas, H. G. R.	... 414
Taylor, R. F.	... 222	Thomas, Hector W. M.	... 256
Taylor, R. G.	... 364	Thomas, Heinrich, W. M.	7, 271§
Taylor, S.	... 271	Thomas, I. G.	... 375
Taylor, S. A.	... 343	Thomas, L. A. S.	... 332
Taylor, S. G.	... 334	†Thomas, L. G. T.	21, 377
Taylor, T. M.	... 429	Thomas, L. J.	131, 377
†Taylor, W. A.	... 282	Thomas, P.	... 414
Taylor, W. H.	... 267	Thomas, Percy E.	...213, 148, 157
Taylor, W. J.	... 151	†Thomas, Phillip E.	14, 207
Taylor, W. R.	... 180	Thomas, P. V.	... 379
Tayton, W. E.	... 330	Thomas, Reginald (5556)	... 340
Teasdale, E. G.	... 353	†Thomas, Reginald (760698)	... 41
Teather, R. H.	... 213	Thomas, Rowland	... 374
Tebb, J. B.	... 251	Thomas, Rudolph	... 289
Tebbs, C. E.	... 180	†Thomas, R. I. V. C.	26, 367
Tebbutt, H. C.	... 207	†Thomas, R. J.	... 26
†Tedder, O. S.	33, 284	Thomas, Robt. Wm.	131, 292
†Tee, C. V.	36, 200	Thomas, S. S. L. St. G.	... 256
Teede, J. E.	... 402	Thomas, Thomas	...131, 151, 207
Temple, A.	151, 405	†Thomas, Tudor	26, 375
Tennant, B. V. A.	... 223	Thomas, T. P.	... 378
Tennant, G. M. C.	... 207	Thomas, W.	... 375
Terrell, W. C.	... 412	†Thomas, W. B.	40, 382
Terry, A. F.	... 234	†Thomas, W. H.	32, 281
Terry, E. F.	... 306	Thomas, W. S.	... 190
†Terry, J. N.	10, 291	Thomasson, W. J. M.	... 213
†Terry, S. F.	31, 131, 380	Thompson, A. E.	... 207
Terry, T. E. R.	... 263	Thompson, A. J.	50, 131, 157, 163, 219¶
†Tetley, J. C. D.	22, 217, 310	Thompson, Alexander R.	... 372
Tett, H.	... 350	Thompson, Arthur R.	... 308
Tew, A. H.	... 291	Thompson, C. E.	50, 132, 157, 276
Tew, W.	... 353	†Thompson, C. H.	...7, 239
Thacker, G. D. D. W.	... 357	†Thompson, Cecil V.	12, 157, 272
†Thackeray, L.	... 9	Thompson Clarence V.	... 310
Thackeray-Turner, E.	... 267	Thompson, E. R.	... 264
Thatcher, W. A. N.	... 351	Thompson, F.	... 280

¶ *See reference to this name in Corrigenda.*

THOMPSON

INDEX TO COMMISSIONS, HONOURS, and ROLL OF HONOUR

†Thompson, F. D.	12, 300
Thompson, F. H.	180
Thompson, F. R. T.	200
Thompson, F. W.	357
Thompson, G. K.	132, 271
Thompson, Harry	288
Thompson, Herbert	384
Thompson, H. T.	226, 419
†Thompson, H. V.	21, 180
Thompson, J. B.	148, 159, 227
Thompson, J. C.	271
†Thompson, J. C. C.	2, 219
Thompson, J. E.	284
Thompson, J. E. B.	402
Thompson, J. G.	382
Thompson, J. W.	193
Thompson, Leonard (4770)	387
†Thompson, Leonard (765742)	36, 180
Thompson, R.	393
Thompson, R. C.	291
‡Thompson, R. Seward	12¶, 302
Thompson, R. Sidney	200
Thompson, R. T.	241
†Thompson, R. W.	33, 325
†Thompson, S. R.	28
Thompson, Rev. William (8763)	397
Thompson, William (762282)	200
Thompson, W. D. H.	414
†Thompson, W. J.	2
Thompson, W. L.	338
Thomson, A.	425
Thomson, A. C. G.	227¶
Thomson, A. M.	346
†Thomson, B.	42
Thomson, B. W.	243
Thomson, G. D.	404
Thomson, G. G.	132, 252
†Thomson, G. V. B.	30, 344
Thomson, H. D.	273
Thomson, I. T.	186
Thomson, J. M.	180
Thomson, N.	278
Thomson, R. F.	193
Thomson, R. H. G.	420
Thorburn, J.	227
Thorburn, J. Mc.C.	207
Thoresby-Jones, M.	187
†Thorley, H. W.	36, 184
Thorley, W. B.	352
Thorn, A. P.	246
Thorn, F. C.	246
Thorn, F. J. W.	294
Thorn, P. E.	364
Thorn, R. N.	370
Thorn, S. A.	394
Thorn, W. M. W.	404
Thorn-Drury, J. G.	429
Thorne, A. J. P.	132, 215§
Thorne, F. C.	207
Thorne, G. C.	149
Thorne, P. H.	132, 157, 215
Thornewaite, A.	348
Thornewill, A. S.	351
Thorneycroft, E. C.	361
Thornhill, B. W.	394
Thornton, C. W.	225
Thornton, H.	379
†Thornton, H. B.	18, 296
Thornton, H. C.	233, 322
Thornton, R. A.	316
†Thorogood, E. L.	38, 269, 316
†Thorp, A. E.	28
†Thorp, C. E.	37, 180, 418
Thorp, P. P.	367
†Thorpe, A. E.	42, 391
Thorpe, J. H.	180
Thrippleton, H.	157, 388
Thrower, S. W.	300
†Thrupp, M.	19, 217
Thrupp, R. M.	335
†Thuell, W. J.	17, 180
Thurgood, W. J.	239
Thwaites, G. L.	425
Tibbenham, D. C.	329
Tibbotts, A. H.	388
Tibbles, J. C.	183
Tice, S. A.	327
Ticehurst, A. G.	277
Tichborne, W.	232
Tiddy, E. W. L.	132, 251
Tiddy, J. L.	193
Tidmarsh, F. E. V.	232
Tidy, J. O.	157, 408
Tidy, W. E.	132, 318
Tierney, J. P.	402
Tierney, T. J.	248
Tigar, A. A.	180
†Tigar, G. H.	23, 226
†Tigar, H. W.	3, 320
Tilbrook, R. H.	234
†Tilbury, R. W.	29, 180
Till, W. P.	190
Tilley, E. H.	200¶
Tilley, J. E.	132, 157, 255
Tilley, P. F.	281
Timms, A.	317
†Timms, W. F.	39
Timson, F. A.	270
†Tinckler, E. H.	31
Tindal-Atkinson, C. P.	275
†Tinniswood, A.	39, 213
†Tippett, A. A.	4, 348
Tippetts, J. B.	373
Tippetts, R. A. F.	200
Tipping, S.	207¶
Titchmarsh, C. H.	408
Titley, R. K.	255
Tizard, E. R. C.	184

† Killed in action or died. § See this name in *Addenda*.

This Index does not include the Alphabetical Sections IV. and V. (Other Ranks and Old Members).

Name	Pages	Name	Pages
Tobutt, R. L. W.	190	†Treadway, H. L.	16, 372
Tocque, F. A. C.	213	Treatt, C. C.	157, 163, 164, 273
Todd, C. K.	325	Tredgold, R. C.	411
†Todd, C. L. M.	9, 276	Tredinnick, G. H.	284
Todd, J.	344	Tregaskis, G.	370
Todd, J. W.	180	Tregenza, E. L.	359
Todd, L. W. C.	287	Tregenza, N. K.	234
Todhunter, A. J.	226	Treifus, A.	194
Tolerton, W.	200	Trelease, R. H.	180
Tolhurst, G.	283	Treliving, H.	384
Tolkien, C.	334	Treloar, G. D.	50, 133, 157, 218
Toller, W. G.	157, 408	†Trenbath, F. T.	25
Tollett, G. W.	316	Trench, F. C.	207
Tomkins, S. E.	207	Trery, N. H.	133, 213
Tomling, G. G.	132, 180	Tress, G. C.	255
Tomlinson, F. C.	284	Trestrail, C.	270
Tomlinson, G. C.	337	†Trestrail, E. M.	20
Tomlinson, J. E.	272	†Trevarthen, J. M.	18
Tomlinson, N. B.	164	Trevelyan, D. J.	248
Tomkins, R. W.	330	†Trevenen, S.	28
†Toms, S. M.	27, 302	Trevissick, W. J.	408
Tomson, H. G.	149, 354	Trew, S. T.	367
Tonks, A. E.	370	Trewby, J. F.	398
Tonks, H. H.	180	Tricker, R.	357
Tonnochy, A. B.	299	Trickett, J. M.	372
Tooley, F. W.	220	Tricks, D. N. F.	282
Tooley, R. F.	157, 248	Triebner, F. H.	425
Toonjan, J. G.	411	Trier, B. M.	392
Toop, A. G.	207	Trier, H. A. T.	164
Toothill, J. C. P.	213, 313a	†Trier, N. E.	5, 392
Topham, G. R. G.	302	Triggs, H. La R.	354
Topham, P. J. R.	338	Trimm, C. A.	133, 193
Topley, A. F.	358	†Trinder, A. J.	4, 331
Totton, A. K.	133, 232	Tritton, F. J.	418
Tourle, A. J.	429	Trohear, T.	133, 335
Tout, H. S.	375	Trollope, T. C. S.	388
Toward, G. W.	388	Trotman, E. W.	252
Towell, H. W.	200	Trotman, L. W.	231
Tower, H. G. E.	133, 327	Trotter, J. B.	228
Towers, G. L.	378	Trotter, S. E.	300
†Towers, W. G.	13, 315	Trounce, W. R.	252
Towerzey, A. R.	402	Trowbridge, B. B.	187
Townsend, C. A.	229	Trubshawe, W. V.	180, 285¶
Townsend, E.	230	Truesdale, R.	269
Townsend, P. P.	324	Truman, E. D.	157, 210
†Townsend, T.	7, 392	Truran, W. F. J.	264
†Towse, W. N.	10, 290	Truscott, C. M.	359
Tozer, M. C.	240	Truscott, G. H. C.	227
Tracey, B. D.	207	Truscott, M. J.	157, 207
Trafford, F. N.	213	Trussell, H. P.	180
Trafford, W. C. S.	304	Tubb, S. W. A.	248
Trangmar, H. E.	324	Tubbs, C. L.	245
†Tratman, L. W. D.	42, 180	Tubbs, E. H.	248
Travell, N. E.	331	Tubbs, W. E.	314, 425
Travers, E. W.	200	Tuck, N. J.	312a
Traviss, A.	180	Tucker, C.	291
†Traynor, F. E.	36	Tucker, D. G. S.	276
Treacher, H.	133, 366	Tucker, H. R.	358
Treadgold, J. R. W.	195	Tucker, J. D.	237

¶ See reference to this name in *Corrigenda*.

TUCKER

INDEX TO COMMISSIONS, HONOURS, and ROLL OF HONOUR.

Name	Pages	Name	Pages
†Tucker, J. d'A.	12	Tye, Frederick (762965)	408
Tucker, J. M.	232	Tyer, A. A.	148, 151¶, 158, 308¶
Tucker, N. P.	157, 229, 313a	Tyer, E.	272
Tucker, S. W.	299	Tyldsley, F.	380
Tucker, W. L.	380	Tyler, A. T.	200
Tucket, D. J.	235	Tyler, B.	388
†Tudor, A. de R.	34	†Tyler, G. C.	36, 327
Tudor, C. E. H.	387	Tyler, G. L.	340
Tue, G. A.	387	Tyler, H. S.	351
†Tuft, G. H.	15, 336	Tyler, L.	219
†Tully, P. J.	25	Tyler, N. F.	255
Tully, W.	421	†Tyler, W. A.	37, 294
Tunnicliffe, W.	180	†Tyndall, J.	17, 303
Tunstall, Rev. J. T.	133, 397	Tyrer, C. K.	389
Tupholme, G.	284	†Tyrrell, L. C.	22, 395
Turnbull, Matthew	158, 389	Tyson, A. W.	408
†Turnbull, Maxwell	40, 134, 158, 228	†Tyson, C. R.	20, 340
Turnbull, R. F.	159, 310	Tyson, H. C.	302
Turner, A.	272		
Turner, A. H.	134, 358		
Turner, A. J.	266	Udall, C. H.	302
Turner, C. E.	234	Umbers, J. L.	134, 332
Turner, C. P.	200	Underhay, G. F.	164
Turner, C. W.	311	†Underwood, C. C.	12, 383
Turner, C. C. T.	147, 180	†Underwood, C. H.	34, 301, 312a
Turner, E. E.	429	†Underwood, J.	14, 281
†Turner, E. R.	12	Underwood, J. E.	408
Turner, G. H.	276	Underwood, J. H.	180
Turner, H. J.	374	†Underwood, R. G.	38, 180
Turner, H. K.	134, 158, 348	Unger, F. D.	269
Turner, H. M.	234	Uniacke, R. H. F. G.	258
Turner, H. R.	341	Unwin, A. C.	351
Turner, J.	337	Unwin, R. B.	358
Turner, M. S.	429	†Upton, R. M.	17, 239
†Turner, P. G.	11	Urie, W. A. E.	316
†Turner, R.	9, 242	Urquhart, A. M.	193
Turner, R. A.	321	Urquhart, J. K.	408
Turner, S. B.	360	Urry, A. C.	226
†Turner, W. E.	20, 382	Urry, R. T.	342
Turner, W. J.	200	Usher, C. W.	180
Turner, W. P.	418	Uwins, C. C. G.	364
†Turpin, W. F.	28	Uzielli, E. N.	326
Turton, H. R.	418		
Tussaud, B. A.	251		
Tuthill, F. V.	340	Vale, R. E.	180
Tutte, A. E. V.	200	Valentine, H.	183
Tweddle, R.	207	Valentine, W. M.	399
†Tweddle, W. J.	14, 243	†Valiant, J.	23, 373
Tweedie, C. W.	419	Van Beek, T. H.	429
†Tweedie-Smith, A.	6¶, 158, 361	Van Coller, L.	311a
†Tweedy, C. F.	22, 269	Van der Noot, H. E.	158, 220
†Tweedy, G. V.	14, 228	Vanderplank, H. C.	301
Twine, C. E.	229	Vandervell, F.	277
Twist, W. N.	382	Vandyke, P. R.	163, 223
Tworney, G. W.	377	Van Eeden, F.	411
Twyman, C. E.	364	Van Essen, E. C.	207
Tyack, R.	180	Van Lessen, D. M.	408
Tyas, M.	386	†Vann, A. H. A.	5, 396
Tye, Frederick (6542)	110, 324	†Vann, B. W.	39, 45, 134, 151, 158, 336

† Killed in action or died. § See this name in *Addenda*.

This Index does not include the Alphabetical Sections IV. and V. (Other Ranks and Old Members).

Name	Page(s)	Name	Page(s)
Vanner, W. A.	360	†Wade, G. E. A.	16, 342
Varah, G. L.	274	Wade, J. B.	255
Varge, E. H.	261	Wade, J. T.	295
Vaughan, E. S. C.	134, 370	Wade, R.	263
†Vaughan, F. S.	29, 158, 262	Wadham, S. M.	239
Vaughan, M. F.	251	Wadlow, B. V.	429
†Vaughan, R. C.	14, 263	Wadie, V. H.	248
Vause, F.	414	Wadsworth, A.	135, 324
Vaux, E. E.	388	†Wager, W. S.	18, 334
Vawdrey, R. H.	254	Waggett, A. C.	237
V.C.	44	†Wagner, C. H. G.	11, 421
Veale, L. P. V.	200	Wagner, D. P.	135, 239
Veats, S. H.	386	Waight, G.	359, 397
Vellenoweth, A. C. A.	289¶	Wailes, F. G.	158, 207
Venmore, J. A. J.	252	Wainwright, J. N.	355
Venables, A.	296	Wainwright, N. S.	375
Venables, A. L.	311a	Waite, F. J.	190
Vergette, G.	134, 194	Wakefield, A. B.	408
Vermont, J.	388	Wakefield, A. J.	349
Vernham, J. R.	213	Wakefield, C. H.	411
Vernon, C. H.	134, 377	Wakeford, A. J.	207
†Vernon, F. L.	11, 274	Wakeham, R. D.	180
Vernon, H. R.	158, 207	Wakely, A. D.	135, 277
Vernon, R. D.	294	†Wakeley, J. E. S.	9, 158, 248
Veysey, H. G.	311	†Wakeman, F. T.	23, 180, 370
Viall, J.	364	Walby, H. C.	51, 135, 158, 351
Viccars, A. E.	340	†Walch, J. B. M.	...5, 361
Vicker, R. C. G.	264	Walford, J. O.	135, 382
Vickers, A. N.	414	Wales, H. G.	207¶
Vickers, V. R. S.	402	Walker, A.	370
Victorian Order, Royal	*148*	Walker, A. F. C.	159, 310
Vile, T. H.	190	Walker, A. L.	207
Villiers, A. H.	267	Walker, A. S.	268
Vincent, A. F.	425	Walker, C.	287
Vincent, B. B.	8, 252	Walker, C. V.	267
†Vincent, C. I. F.	40, 219	Walker, D. M. J.	214
Vincent, C. R. C.	134, 302	Walker, D. R. A.	253
Vincent, E. S.	158, 279	Walker, E. A. H.	276, 277
Vincent, J.	158, 284	Walker, E. H.	399
Vincent, R. D. C.	180	Walker, F. B.	270
Vincent, W. J.	305	Walker, George H.	351
Vine, C. C.	337	†Walker, Gordon H.	25, 330
Vine, E.	389	Walker, G. W.	195
Viner, C.	387	Walker, H.	200
Viner, C. C.	429	Walker, H. E.	136, 146, 180
Vinnicombe, T. H.	264	Walker, H. F.	149, 163
Vipond, F. R.	274	Walker, H. G.	367
Viret, A. W.	399	Walker, H. S.	340
Virgo, C. P.	180	Walker, J. H.	425
Visser, G. F.	336	†Walker, J. T.	35
Vivian, G. H. E.	411	Walker, N. H. E.	317
†Vivian, V.	429, 228§	†Walker, R.	9, 269
Vizard, H. C.	180	Walker, R. H.	149, 158, 209
†Vokes, B.	12, 340	Walker, S.	370
†Vokins, K. E.	8, 371	†Walker, T. F.	25
Vos, J.	337	Walker, T. G.	304
Vos-Üterlimmege, G. H.	240	†Walker, V. L.	16, 272
Voss, G. P.	135, 313a, 415	Walker, W. D.	421
Voysey, F. W.	286	†Walker, W. F.	32, 331

¶ See reference to this name in *Corrigenda*.

Walker, W. H.	207
Walker, W. L.	183
Wall, A. M.	278
Wall, C. C.	300
Wall, R. B. St. Q.	217
Wall, T.	402
Wallace, A. C.	245
Wallace, C. l'E.	295
Wallace, D. C.	226
†Wallace, G. D.	23, 319
Wallace, J. H.	180
Wallace, J. McG.	288
†Wallace, J. R.	3, 344
Wallace, W.	190
Wallace, W. E.	418
Waller, H. de W.	180
Waller, J. C.	360
Waller, J. G.	414
Waller, L. J.	200
Waller, T. A. R.	200
†Walley, J. C.	30, 281
Wallich, C. C. N.	194, 235
Wallingford, S.	343
Wallis, A. O. S.	158
Wallis, B. N.	421
†Wallis, C. F.	37
Wallis, E. P.	360
Wallis, G. P. D.	219
Wallis, L. P.	159, 180
Wallis, W. H. St. J.	421
Wallis, W. M.	266
Wallis, W. R.	295
Walls, F. H.	209
Wallwork, J. W.	136, 180
Walmisley, S. E.	290
Walmsley, A. A.	301
Walmsley, H.	149
Walsh, A.	319
Walsh, A. D.	274
Walsh, J. E.	326
Walsh, V. M.	398
Walsh, W. E.	370
Walter, A. K.	251
Walter, C.	200
Walter, G. L.	408
Walter, J. B.	429
Walter, R. K.	376
Walter, V. L.	351
Walters, I. G.	220
Walters, J. D.	377
†Walters, R. E.	38¶
Walters, R. S.	262
Walters, S. E.	136, 425
Walters, T. G.	220
Waltho, S.	180
Walton, G. K.	319
†Walton, I. M.	11, 274
Walton, L. R.	404
Walton, S.	136, 241
Walton, T. E. L.	311
Walwin, R. E.	248
Wand, S. J. G.	200
Wanostrocht, D. V.	310a
Warburton, C. M.	207
Warburton, E.	337
Warburton, H.	180
Ward, A.	277
Ward, A. E.	398
Ward, A. L.	213
Ward, C. H.	237
Ward, C. R. F.	190
†Ward, D. G.	31
Ward, D. H.	277
Ward, D. R.	429
†Ward, D. T.	21, 291
†Ward, E.	429§
Ward, F.	180
Ward, F. N.	208
Ward, F. V. C.	288
Ward, F. W.	298
Ward, G. M.	248
Ward, H.	396
Ward, H. E.	273
†Ward, H. F.	26, 136, 358
Ward, L. J.	242
Ward, N. G.	158, 195
†Ward, N. J.	9, 371
Ward, R.	379
Ward, S. L.	180
Ward, T. L.	386
Ward, W. H.	267
Wardall, H.	429
Warden, W. N. H.	180
Wardlow-Ramsey, E.	213
Ware, A. F.	331
Ware, D. H. S.	342
Ware, V.	194
†Warham, J.	16, 267
†Waring, F.	9, 386
Warland, L. G.	337
Warmington, S. J.	218
†Warner, A.	8, 291
†Warner, B. O.	16, 242
Warner, E. T. H.	306
Warner, F. B.	301
Warner, F. E.	261
†Warner, H. J.	17, 330
Warner, T. H.	213
†Warr, T. E.	23, 238
Warren, A. N.	158, 342
†Warren, A. R.	11, 296
Warren, E. D.	251
Warren, G. L.	418
Warren, H.	190
Warren, H. G.	213
Warren, H. S.	207
Warren, H. St. J. P.	201
†Warren, I. J.	29, 249

† Killed in action or died. § See this name in *Addenda*.

This Index does not include the Alphabetical Sections IV. and V. (Other Ranks and Old Members).

Warren, S. T.	...	...	...	357
†Warren, W.	...	...	...	2
†Warry, J. I.	...	...	...	15, 336
Warton, A. H.	...	...	...	181
Warwick, W. G.	...	...	...	181
Warwickshire Regt., Royal		...	...	369
†Waterhouse, G. W.	...	...	14, 264
Waters, E. G. R.	...	...	...	363
Waters, H. E.	...	...	...	181
†Waterson, F. P.	...	...	...	19, 338
Waterworth, G. W.	...	...	...	387
Wates, S. B.	...	...	...	252
Watkin, E. W.	...	...	...	269
Watkin, F. T. H.	...	...	...	395
Watkins, H. J.	...	...	...	383
†Watkins, J. H.	...	...	...	12
Watkins, L. F.	...	...	...	389
Watkins, P. M. C.	...	...	...	408
Watkins, W. H. E.	...	...	136, 392
Watkinson, J. G. B.	...	...	...	379
Watson, A. S. F.	...	...	...	402
Watson, A. V. C.	...	...	136, 418
Watson, B.	...	...	...	331
Watson, C.	...	...	...	391
Watson, C. H.	...	...	...	281
Watson, Clifford T. (2033)	...	...	335
†Watson, Clifford Thomas (6596)		27, 292
Watson, D. J.	...	...	...	213
Watson, F. A.	...	...	...	181
Watson, F. G.	...	...	...	243
Watson, G. F. T.	...	...	...	221
Watson, H. B.	...	...	...	408
Watson, H. T.	...	...	...	376
†Watson, H. J. A.	...	...	36, 223
Watson, J. B.	...	...	...	423
Watson, J. D.	...	...	...	181
Watson, R. A.	...	...	...	227
Watson, S. C.	...	...	...	402
Watson, T. B.	...	...	...	220
Watson, T. W.	...	...	136, 158, 195
Watson, W. F.	...	...	...	190
Watson, W. H.	...	...	...	346
Watson, W. M.	...	...	...	364
Watson, W. P.	...	...	...	304
Watt, A. L. I. W.	...	...	...	274
Watt, C. F.	...	...	...	194
Watt, C. H.	...	...	...	364
†Watt, H. B. C.	...	...	37, 137, 240
Watt, J. D.	...	...	...	358
Watt, J. J.	...	...	...	214
Watt, James McD.	...	...	158, 344
Watt, John M.	...	...	...	243
Watts, A. H.	...	...	...	251
Watts, A. K.	...	...	...	360
Watts, E. J.	...	...	...	418
Watts, G. H.	...	...	...	304
Watts, H. C.	...	...	159, 306
Watts, H. L.	...	...	158, 298
Watts, J. G.	...	...	...	284
Watts, James H.	...	...	...	252
Watts, Joseph H.	...	...	...	398
Watts, J. N.	...	...	...	248
Watts, L. D.	...	...	...	371
Watts, P. E.	...	...	...	262
Watts, W. E.	...	...	...	181
Watts-Russell, J. C.	...	...	326
†Wattson, C. B.	...	...	22, 181
Waud, F. C.	...	...	...	391
Waud, L. R.	...	...	...	353
Way, G. C.	...	...	...	379
†Way, R. E. A.	...	...	16, 275
Waydelin, F. J.	...	...	...	201
Waye, W. B.	...	...	...	274
Weale, W. W. C.	...	...	158, 236
Weatherhead, H. D.	...	...	426
†Weatherley, L. E. M.	...	...	29, 303
Weaver, C. F.	...	...	...	181
Weaver, F.	...	...	137, 158, 304
Weaver, H. L.	...	...	...	364
Weaver, S. M.	...	...	...	395
Weaver, W. A.	...	...	...	383
†Weawill, E. K.	...	...	...	25¶
Webb, A. P.	...	...	14, 349
Webb, B. H.	...	...	...	324
†Webb, C. F.	...	...	...5, 390
Webb, C. H.	...	...	137, 329
Webb, C. R.	...	...	...	295
Webb, D. D.	...	...	...	411
Webb, D. E.	...	...	...	181
Webb, E. C. H.	...	...	...	373
Webb, E. O.	...	...	314, 429
Webb, G. F.	...	...	...	201
Webb, G. H.	...	...	...	379
Webb, H. F.	...	...	158, 367
Webb, H. V. C.	...	...	180, 373
Webb, J. R.	...	...	...	418
†Webb, J. T.	...	...	...3, 291
Webb, N. D.	...	...	...	384
Webb, P. H.	...	...	...	241
Webb, R.	...	...	...	376
Webb, R. A.	...	...	...	421
Webb, R. D. C.	...	...	158¶,404
Webb, W. J.	...	...	...151, 158, 209
Webber, W. J.	...	...	158, 241
†Webber, W. K.	...	...	...	36
Webberley, J. W.	...	...	...	181
†Webberley, R. S.	...	...	21, 352
Weber-Brown, A. W.	...	...	158¶, 404
Webster, J. H.	...	...	...	304
Webster, T. M.	...	...	...	181
Webster, W. B.	...	...	...	429
Webster, W. J.	...	...	...	314
Weeden, W. A.	...	...	...	305
Weedon, V. C.	...	...	...	330
Weeks, C. H.	...	...	...	223
Weeks, W. E.	...	...	137, 367
Weeks, W. S.	...	...	...	181

¶ See reference to this name in *Corrigenda*.

INDEX TO COMMISSIONS, HONOURS, and ROLL OF HONOUR.

Name	Pages	Name	Pages
†Wehrle, A.	41	†West, M. S.	26, 181
Weighall, M. H.	396	West, R. G.	138, 217
Weight, A. F.	201	*West Riding Regt.*	*378*
Weight, S. L.	201	*West Surrey Regt., Royal*	*361*
Weir, C. H.	343	West, S. E.	253
Weir, J.	137, 345	West, S. H.	201
Weir, T. B.	425	West, W. G.	149, 307
†Weiss, H. F.	38, 296	Westbury, J.	340
Weiss, R. A.	190	Westcombe, A. B.	291
†Welby, D.	40, 207	Westcott, A.	306
Welch, H. A.	213	Westcott, E. J.	264
Welch, J. F. W.	213	Westendarp, H. E. A.	186
Welch, L. A.	388	Western, J. G.	149, 164
Welch, R. H.	418	Westgarth, G. W.	353
Welch, S. T.	137, 425	Westlake, A. M.	158
†Weld, H. E.	2, 219	Westlake, M. E. K.	332
Weldon, E. J.	287	Weston, A. T.	226
Weldon, H. A. C.	269	Weston, D. G.	158
Wellborne, H. H. G.	137, 408	Weston, M.	418
Welldon, J. C.	181	Weston, R. E.	281
Wellman, G. M.	324	†Weston, W. J.	5, 386
Weller, H. J.	224	*West Yorkshire Regt.*	*394*
Wells, A. J.	186	Wetenhall, J. P.	425
†Wells, A. L.	22, 220	†Wetherall, E. F. C.	42, 414
Wells, B. N.	402	Wettone, H. F.	306
Wells, D. G.	414	Whadcoat, C. J.	324
Wells, E. I.	341	Whall, L. G.	429
†Wells, H. E.	340	Whamond, J.	257
†Wells, J.	41	Wharton, A.	220
†Wells, M. C.	31, 194	Wharton, A. C.	288
Wells, R.	276	†Wharton, E. P.	§
Wells, S. A.	267	Wharton, L. E.	284
Wellsman, E. S.	298	Wharton, T. R. L. J.	264
Wellsman, F.	389	†Wheate, A.	6, 271
†Welsh, A. T.	16, 373	Wheate, T. E.	138, 194
Welsh, R.	137, 253	Wheatley, E. H.	317
Welsh Fusiliers, Royal	*372*	Wheatley, F. M.	291
Welsh Guards	*220*	†Wheatley, J. C.	39, 338
Welsh Regiment	*376*	Wheeldon, A. L.	402
Welte, E. J.	137, 194	Wheeler, A. G.	314, 429
†Welter, L. D.	17, 267	Wheeler, E. B.	310
Wenger, T. L.	138, 405	Wheeler, E. N.	300
Wenn, R. A.	340	Wheeler, E. V.	181
Wenyon, H. J.	51, 158, 263	Wheeler, P. H.	357
Wernham, H. F.	271	Wheeler, P. V.	317
Wessel, W. M.	378	Wheeler, S. A.	359
West African Regts.	*426*	Wheeler, T. B.	194
West, A.	181	Wheeler, W. R.	138, 151, 306
West, C. J. de la W.	237	Wheeler, W. S.	181
West, E. G.	414	Whibley, S. N.	194
West, F.	138, 158, 234	Whicher, C. T.	201
West, F. A.	365	†Whidbourne, G. W.	13
West, F. J.	273	Whiddington, W. A.	305
West, G. M. W.	201	Whinney, C. T.	138, 159, 322
West, H.	252	Whitaker, B. J. G.	313a, 378
West Indies (British) Regt.	*426*	Whitaker, B. T.	248
West Kent Regt.	*262*	Whitaker, D. N.	138, 255, 279
West, K.	216	†Whitaker, F.	16, 221
West, L. C.	267	Whitaker, G. M.	158, 207

† Killed in action or died.   § See this name in *Addenda*.

This Index does not include the Alphabetical Sections IV. and V. (Other Ranks and Old Members).

Name	Pages	Name	Pages
Whitaker, H. V.	181	Whittaker, C. J.	201
Whitby, C.	213	Whittaker, F.	429
White, A. J.	330	Whittaker, G. W.	201
White, B. G.	149, 159, 214	Whittall, V.	419
White, C. A. B.	241	Whittett, R. M.	352
White, C. D.	251	Whittington-Lowe, E. H. R.	411
White, C. F. T.	380	Whittle, W. G. A.	365
White, C. V.	414	†Whittle, W. V. P. C.	3, 381
White, D. A.	429	Whittles, E. D.	372
White, D .C.	328	Whittles, T.	319
White, E. E. J.	185	Whittome, J. E.	404
†White, E. R. B.	6, 331	Whitton, W. E.	287
†White, F.	39	†Whitworth, A. G. R.	32, 334
White, F. C.	297	Whitworth, A. S.	251
White, Francis E.	181	Whitworth, E. C.	279
White, Frank E.	223	Whitworth, F.	186
White, F. R.	295	Whitworth, J. C.	319
White, F. S.	379	Whitworth, S.	319
White, G. Fenwick	287	†Whitworth, W. H.	38, 269
White, G. Frederick	213	Whyte, A. McI.	139, 418
White, H.	396	†Whyte, G. H.	27, 181
White, H. B.	277	†Whyte, M. G.	36, 248
White, H. D.	279	Whyte, R.	347
White, H. R.	190	Whytehead, H. L.	191
White, J. B.	138, 295	Wichelow, T.	25
White, J. D.	312a	Wicht, J. D.	411
White, L. A.	429§	Wickett, C. W. M.	425
White, L. E.	226	†Wickett, T. P.	26, 226
†White, L. S.	3, 262	Wickham-Legg, G. P.	353
White, N. E.	414	Wickman, F. T.	408
White, N. S.	201	†Wicks, F. H.	41
White, P. F.	284	Widdecombe, A. J.	289
White, R. H.	350	Widderson, A. J.	148, 163
White, R. P.	357	†Widdop, A. N.	39, 261
White, R. S.	181	Widgery, F. W.	397
White, S. C.	278	Wiggins, S.	365
White, S. W.	201	Wiggins, T.	390
†White, T. H.	42, 138, 272	Wight, L. L.	139, 358
White, W. G. B.	186	†Wightman, J. F.	20, 181
White, W. L .C.	181	Wightwick, C. F.	381
Whiteaway, E. G. L.	138, 158, 388	Wigzell, H. E.	286
Whitehead, C.	183	Wilby, J. F.	393
†Whitehead, E. J. W.	42, 207	Wilcock, H.	315
†Whitehead, E. W.	29, 181	Wilcock, W. C.	317
Whitehead, F. W.	139, 194	Wilcox, B. S.	181
†Whitehead, H. M.	3, 358	Willcox, M. W.	254
Whitehouse, H. H.	286	Wild, F. N.	264
Whitehouse, S. W.	190	Wild, G.	402
Whitehouse, T. H. I.	237	Wild, H.	277
Whitelaw, W.	256	Wild, W.	181
†Whiteley, C. T.	35, 370	†Wilde, C.	21
†Whiteside, M. B. D.	35, 256, 404	Wilde, W. H.	207
Whiteside, W.	275	Wilders, C. A.	207
†Whitfield, F. A. H.	3, 320	Wilding, L. S.	267
Whiting, P. E.	384	†Wildsmith, G. F.	25
Whitlock, F. W.	414	Wiles, E. E.	186
Whitmore, A.	280	Wiles, O. D.	139, 349
Whitmore, E. W.	190	Wiley, W.	390
Whittaker, B. K.	317	Wilhelm, P. M.	295

¶ See reference to this name in *Corrigenda*.

WILKES

INDEX TO COMMISSIONS, HONOURS, and ROLL OF HONOUR.

Wilkes, B. C.	295
†Wilkes, G. L.	33, 295
Wilkes, G. T.	139, 359
Wilkie, J.	139, 275
Wilkin, L. J.	425
Wilkins, A. T. A.	340
Wilkins, C. G.	223
Wilkins, E. M.	256
Wilkins, F. B.	181
†Wilkins, G.	5¶, 331
Wilkins, N. J.	364
Wilkins, R.	148, 158, 399
†Wilkins, S. E.	25
Wilkinson, A. B.	139, 194
†Wilkinson, A. J.	10, 320
Wilkinson, C. N.	279
Wilkinson, C. T. A.	295
Wilkinson, D. F.	296
Wilkinson, D. H.	277
†Wilkinson, E. A.	5, 280
Wilkinson, E. G.	164
Wilkinson, E. P.	207
Wilkinson, F.	393
Wilkinson, H. G.	311a
Wilkinson, J.	425
Wilkinson, W.	191
†Wilkinson, W. D.	11, 243
Wilkinson, W. R.	389
Wilks, E. C.	411
Wilks, T. N. B.	264
Willans, H.	51, 139, 158, 222
Willcock, A.	429
Willcock, C. L.	283
†Willcox, A. O.	25
Willcox, C. J.	183
Willcox, G. H.	207
Willes, E. J.	354
Willett, F. W.	139, 281
Williams, A.	317
†Williams, A. J.	25, 378
Williams, A. T.	325
Williams, B. A.	270
Williams, B. M.	376
Williams, C. H.	377
Williams, C. P.	234
Williams, C. St. M.	269
†Williams, D. M.	6, 371
Williams, D. W.	349
Williams, E.	277
Williams, E. A. M.	320
Williams, F. J.	306
†Williams, F. S.	21, 336
Williams, George	181
Williams, Gilbert	264
†Williams, Gordon	23, 149, 310
Williams, G. D.	310a
Williams, G. E.	351
Williams, G. G.	181
Williams, Harold (6506)	213
Williams, Harold (7053)	139, 319
Williams, Hopkin	299
†Williams, H. B.	25
Williams, H. D.	181
†Williams, H. E.	10, 289
Williams, H. E. B.	429
†Williams, H. E. V.	16, 289
Williams, H. J. M.	290
Williams, H. M.	320
†Williams, H. O.	12, 324
†Williams, H. P. G.	25¶
Williams, H. W.	295
Williams, H. W. M.	368
Williams, J.	277
Williams, J. A. A.	245
Williams, James H.	423
Williams, John H.	429
Williams, K. H.	288, 368
Williams, L. D.	322
Williams, L. E.	158, 213
†Williams, M. H.	21, 301
†Williams, M. J.	39
Williams, M. L.	423
Williams, M. R.	376
Williams, N. V.	139, 239, 418
Williams, R.	213
Williams, R. P.	207
Williams, Reginald S.	201
Williams, Robert S.	376
Williams, R. T.	389
†Williams, R. V.	17, 181
Williams, S. F.	384
Williams, S. H.	353
Williams, Thomas (762873)	213
Williams, Thomas (766006)	201
Williams, T. B.	325
†Williams, T. E.	4, 349
†Williams, T. H.	25
Williams, T. J.	368
Williams, T. S.	372
Williams, W. G.	231
Williams, V. G.	194
†Williams, W. H.	41, 207
†Williams, W. James	21, 376
Williams, W. Jones	139, 337
Williams, W. T.	140, 158, 260
Williamson, A. F.	295
Williamson, F.	311a
†Williamson, G. C.	22, 243
†Williamson, G. D.	28, 181
Williamson, H.	184
Williamson, J. A.	313a
Williamson, J. C.	181
†Williamson, J. M.	4, 252
†Williamson, K. H.	14, 267
Williamson, W. H. R.	140, 151, 158, 201, 404
Williamson-Jones, C. E.	146, 315
Willis, A. B.	313a
Willis, A. E.	372

† Killed in action or died.   § See this name in *Addenda*.

WOOD

This Index does not include the Alphabetical Sections IV. and V. (Other Ranks and Old Members)

Willis, C. H. S.	...149, 159, 310
†Willis, C. L.	11, 299
Willis, C. R.	...140, 158, 187
Willis, D. H.	140, 369
†Willis, E. F.	31, 310
Willis, F. K.	418
Willis, G. H.	267
Willis, G. W.	340
Willis, N. S.	275
Willis, W. E.	357
Willmer, C. H.	219
Willmott, E. C. N.	213
Willmott, S. J.	333
Willoughby-Davis, V.	324
Wills, A. R.	140, 364
†Wills, C. H. C.	20
Wills, G.	296
Wills, W. A.	291
Willson, A.	201
Willson, H. G.	151, 158¶, 305
Wilmot, D. A. T.	340
Wilmot, W. L.	420
Wilshire, H. B.	210
Wilson, Arthur	389
Wilson, Andrew	334
Wilson, A. F.	181
†Wilson, Alexander G.	37, 258
Wilson, Alfred G.	357
Wilson, C. C.	221
†Wilson, C. E.	14, 181
†Wilson, C. G. G.	14, 346
†Wilson, C. T.	26
Wilson, D. M.	215
Wilson, E. W.	363
Wilson, F. W.	219
†Wilson, G. A. G.	19, 365
†Wilson, H. Algar	...6, 348
Wilson, H. Armstrong	207
†Wilson, H. B.	13, 302
Wilson, H. Cecil	302
Wilson, H. Christopher	234
Willson, H. G.	240
†Wilson, H. H.	29, 181
Wilson, I. Mc. L. T.	251
†Wilson, J.	...8, 320
Wilson, J. Baxenden	140, 332
Wilson, J. Blackburn	221
Wilson, J. C.	287
†Wilson, J. H.	25
Wilson, L. A.	316
Wilson, P.	151, 181
†Wilson, P. G.	39
Wilson, P. M.	201
Wilson, R. J.	374
†Wilson, R. P.	...9, 393
Wilson, R. T.	252
†Wilson, W. Clement	...5, 381
Wilson, W. Cronin	254
Wilson, W. L.	207
Wilson, W. W.	303
Wilson-Haffenden, J. R.	181
Wilton, R. A.	140, 371
Wiltshire Regt.	*380*
Wimbush, N. N.	278
Wimpenny, R. S.	181
Wincer, A.	254
Wincer, G. L.	429
†Winch, E. N.	40, 262
Winckworth, S. H.	310
Winder, W.	201
Windross, H. L.	338
Windsor, D. R.	368
†Windsor, L. St. L.	...4, 354
†Windsor, M. G.	...2, 234
†Windus, C. E.	...3, 259
Wing, E. B.	376
Wingrove, W. E.	270
Winkle, W. N.	384
Winks, A.	397
Winkworth, S. R.	158¶, 181
Winn, E. G. C.	365
†Winser, F. E.	20, 181
Winship, E. R.	140, 321
Winsor, A. W.	181
Winstanley, W. L.	226
Winter, D. W.	181
Winter, P. A.	414
†Winter, R. R.	29, 164
Winterbottom, A. G.	390
Winters, J. W.	372
Wintle, H. G.	140, 251
†Wiseman, C.	6
Witcomb, C. E.	140, 248
Witcomb, S. F.	158
With, A. W.	402
Withan, J. W.	382
Wither, A. McC.	243
Witney, J. H.	149, 402
Witt, C. T.	313a
Witt, G. B.	408
Wix, E. H.	251
Wolff, J. D.	149, 207
Wolsey, F.	388
†Wolstenholme, J. B. W.	36, 162
Wolton, R.	208
Womack, B.	141, 364
Wonnacott, J. P.	237
Wood, B. D.	195
Wood, B. G.	232
Wood, C.	295
†Wood, C. B.	25
Wood, C. K.	408
Wood, D.	225
†Wood, D. C.	...8, 252
Wood, E. J.	358
†Wood, E. L.	21, 345
Wood, E. M.	411
Wood, F. C.	421

¶ See reference to this name in *Corrigenda*.

WOOD

INDEX TO COMMISSIONS, HONOURS, and ROLL OF HONOUR.

Name	Page(s)	Name	Page(s)
†Wood, F. R.	23	Woollard, F. G.	360
Wood, G.	353	Woollcombe, L. A. W.	354
Wood, G. A.	181	Woolley, A.	295
Wood, H.	321	Woolley, E. C.	275
Wood, H. McG.	181	Woolley, W. J.	408
Wood, John (761663)	402	Woolliams, F. H.	182
Wood, John (764954)	181	Woolner, H. C.	295
Wood, John (767842)	241	†Woolnough, F. U.	30, 238
Wood, J. E.	181	Woolveridge, C. L.	158, 373
Wood, J. I.	357	*Woolwich Cadets*	419
†Wood, J. P. H.	12, 318	Woolveridge, C. S.	414
Wood, J. S.	182	Wootton, K. E.	141, 297, 425
Wood, J. W.	345	*Worcestershire Regt.*	381
†Wood, M. B.	26¶, 141, 182, 254	Worden, E. H. G.	142, 224
Wood, N.	296	Worlock, H. T.	422
Wood, N. C.	343	Wormald, H.	277
Wood, N. J.	373	Wornum, G. G.	239
Wood, N. P.	231	Wornum, T. H.	256
Wood, P. N.	158, 159, 187	Wornum, W. E.	142, 207
Wood, R. H.	402	Worrall, S.	142, 158, 207
Wood, T. L. C.	291	Worseldine, S. C. H.	207
Wood, S. G.	141, 263	Worsnam, C. A.	148¶, 399
Wood, T.	353	†Worstenholm, J.	21, 182
Wood, W. R.	418	Worth, H. I. S. J.	245
Woodbridge, D. S.	220	Worth, S.	267¶
Woodbury, E. B. C.	219	Worthington, C. E.	182
Woodcock, C. W.	328	Worthington, G.	231
Woodcock, H. N. H.	141, 263	Worthington, J.	269
†Woodforde, G. A.	41	Wray, L. H.	231
Woodhams, J. P.	367	Wray, W. J. O.	207
†Woodhead, F. G.	28	Wren, B. F.	423
Woodhouse, C.	378	Wren, L. R.	385
†Woodhouse, P. W.	31¶, 182	Wrench, E. L.	411
Woodhouse, W. J.	267	Wrenn, C.	300
Woodifield, F.	338	Wrentmore, J. H.	163
Woodman, C. G.	182	Wright, A.	194
Woodman, W. L.	182	Wright, A. A.	201, 374
Woodroffe, A. G.	249	†Wright, A. K. T.	27, 300
Woodroffe, B. C.	331	†Wright, A. S.	36, 393
Woodroffe, G. E.	310a	Wright, C. C. G.	239, 331
Woodroffe, K. D.	331	†Wright, C. L.	18, 207
Woodrow, A. B.	141, 367	Wright, D. R. M.	181
Woodruff, F. G.	275	†Wright, E. F. M.	13, 332
Woods, A. V. R.	313a	†Wright, E. S.	8, 356
Woods, C.	321	†Wright, E. W.	25
Woods, C. A.	276	Wright, F. S.	384
†Woods, E. E.	34, 288	Wright, G. E.	142, 404
Woods, F. H.	389	Wright, G. St. J.	270
Woods, J. A.	337	Wright, H. A.	142
Woods, W. A.	377	Wright, H. J. L.	423
Woodward, A. W. H.	351	Wright, John (8330)	228
Woodward, E. G.	237	Wright, John (769376)	310a
Woodward, G. de M.	191	Wright, J. W.	354
Woodward, W. J.	332	Wright, R. G. S.	302
Woodyear, R. P.	141, 151, 264	Wright, S. M.	377
Woodyear, S. J. D.	358	Wright, T.	295
Woolf, E.	191	†Wright, T. A.	23
Woolfe, W. S.	225	†Wright, W. W.	20, 207
Woollam, H. M.	319	Wrighton, E.	51, 158, 332

† Killed in action or died. § See this name in *Addenda*.

This Index does not include the Alphabetical Sections IV. and V. (Other Ranks and Old Members).

Wrightson, L.	... 352	York and Lancaster Regt. ... 385
†Wrigley, P. B.	30, 215	York, T. J. P. ... 343
Wrixon, M. P. B.	142, 217	York, W. A. ... 264
Wurr, A. H.	... 324	Yorke, R. C. ... 230
Wyatt, C. P.	... 373	*Yorkshire L.I.* ... *388*
Wyatt, R.	... 185	*Yorkshire Regiment* ... *390*
Wyatt, V. W.	... 423	*Yorkshire Regt., East* ... *392*
†Wyatt, W. H.	...7, 392	*Yorkshire Regt., West* ... *394*
†Wyatt-Smith, H. H.	... 6	Young, A. C. ... 311a
†Wykes, E. A. I.	27, 226	Young, A. L. G. ... 299
Wykes, R. A.	159, 234	Young, B. ... 213
Wynn, J.	... 182	Young, C. A. ... 273
Wynn-Wernick, F. C.	... 163	Young, C. O. ... 214
Wynne, E. S.	... 227	Young, E. V. ... 385
Wynne, G. W. L.	... 241	Young, F. F. ... 310
Wynne, R. B.	158, 372	Young, G. E. R. ... 257
Wyrall, E.	158, 408	Young, H. ... 343
		Young, H. F. ... 269
Yarrow, D.	... 381	†Young, H. H. ... 4, 245, 313a
Yateman, F. W.	... 266	†Young, J. C. ... 33, 248
†Yates, A. G. V.	8, 300¶	†Young, J. E. R. ... 18, 181
†Yates, F.	27, 253	Young, J. H. ... 301
Yates, G. A.	... 396	†Young, L. D. ... 22, 317
Yates, H. G.	142, 195	Young, L. G. ... 338
Yates, H. R.	... 352	†Young, L. G. B. ... 7, 231¶
Yates, J.	... 210	Young, O. ... 142, 332
Yates, S.	... 182	†Young, S. M. ... 37
Yates, V. J.	... 182	Young, T. ... 231
Yates, W.	142, 231	Young, V. C. H. ... 243
Yates, W. F.	... 201	Young, W. ... 330
Yeabsley, G. V.	... 312	Young, W. A. G. ... 147, 181
†Yeates, S. C.	14, 300	Young, W. C. ... 213
Yeatman, M. B.	... 364	Youngman, C. F. ... 357
Yendall, R. B.	... 325	Youngman, R. ... 248
Yeld, G. G.	... 414	Yuill, H. H. ... 51, 143, 151, 158, 209
Yeoman, E. W.	... 286	Yule, J. G. ... 386
Yeomanry	... *185*	
Yerbury, E. O.	... 418	Zaradi, D. ... 285
†Yewdall, M.	... 41	Zeylmans, P. C. ... 295
Yiend, D. A.	... 252	Zink, E. ... 356

¶ See reference to this name in *Corrigenda*.

CORRIGENDA.

The following corrections were received too late for insertion in the printed sheets on which they occur. The bulk of them are, however, noted in the foregoing Index. ED.

Page 3. April. 25. *For* NEELEY *read* NEELY.
" 5. Sept. 25. HULM. *For* Odverne *read* Odyerne.
" " 30. LAW. *For* Gwyder *read* Gwydyr.
" Oct 4. WILKINS. *Add* Battle of Loos.
" 6. " 13. TWEEDIE-SMITH. *Add* Loos.
" " Feb. 14. HILL. *For* Douglas Charles *read* Charles Douglas.
" 7. July 1. SPATZ. *Add* Carl (after Rudolph).
" 15. April 23. *For* CHATFIELD *read* CHATFEILD.
" " " 29. OLVER. *For* 29th *read* 27th.
" " May 2. PATON. *Add* Near Arras.
" 16. " 26. CAMPBELL. *For* Died *read* Accidentally Killed.
" 17. June 6. *For* MACFAYDEN *read* MACFADYEN.
" 19. Aug. 1. KILVERT. *Add* Passchendaele Ridge.
" " " 17. BROWN. *Add* Near Hoograaf.
" 23. Oct. 28. BRYANS. *Add* Near Poelcappelle.
" 24. Oct. 30. *For* MASKREY *read* MASKRAY.
" 25. " " " WEAVILL *read* WEAWILL.
" " " " WILLIAMS, H. P. G. *For* Garrons *read* Garnons.
" " Nov. 10. DAVIES. *Add* Passchendaele.
" 26. " 11. WOOD. *Add* ✠ ✠
" " " 28. MANN. *Add* Moorslede, Belgium.
" 27. Dec. 2. GILLESPIE. *For* Guy *read* Gray.
" " " 5. LAUGHTON. *Add* Battle of Cambrai.
" 28. " 30. SHINNER. *For* (Nov. 2) *read* (Jan. 2/18).
" " " " DYSON. *For* Gamm *read* Gavin.
" " " " *For* O'VASTON *read* O'VASTOR.
" 29. Feb. 5. HUGHES. *For* McKinney *read* McKenney.
" " Mar. 11. *Delete* KITCHEN, Arthur (*vide* p. 34 : May 20).
" 30. " 23. AREND. *Add* At Nurlu.
" 31. " 27. MACKLIN. *Add* Near Albert.
" " " 28. WOODHOUSE. *Add* Near Bucquoy.
" 32. " 29. JONES. *For* Joaquim *read* Joaquin.
" " " " *For* MALEHAM *read* MALCHAM.
" " April 5. " FULLAGER " FULLAGAR.
" 34. May 27. SARGENT. *For* Malcolm *read* Vernon.
" " " 29. *For* DAVIES *read* DAVIS.
" " June 1. " PRINGLE *read* PRING.
" 35. July 5. *Delete* WALTERS, R. E. (*vide* p. 38 : Sept. 5).
" 36. Aug. 6. MUMMERY. *Add* At Pforzheim, Baden.
" " " 7. *For* NICHOLLS *read* NICHOLS.
" " " 8. *Delete* CLAYDON, D. C. (*vide* p. 20 : Aug. 18).
" 37. " 27. COLLINS. *For* Arthur Leslie *read* Sydney Thomas.
" " " " *Delete* MILES, F. D. (*vide* p. 38 : Sept. 20).
" 38. Sept. 5. SPEAKMAN. *Add* Near Ploegsteert.

CORRIGENDA.

Page 41. Nov. 11. *For* BEVINGTON *read* BOVINGTON.
    42. Dec. 12. PLUMPTON. *Add* Murmansk, N. Russia.
    43. *For* SERVICES *read* SERVICE.
    55. ATKINSON, Lieut. Edward Arthur. *Delete* this Military Cross. (The recipient is not 2827 Edward Arthur Atkinson who obtained a Commission from the Artists and was killed in action 4/10/18).
   110. *For* NYE *read* TYE.
   148. (O.B.E.) *Delete* ALLEN, F. J.
    ,, *For* WORSSAM *read* WORSNAM.
   151. *Add* TYER, Capt. A. A., 1/Artists, *Croix de Guerre*, France.
    ,, *For* WILSON H. G. *read* WILLSON.
   152. *Delete* ALLEN, F. J.
    ,, *For* ASHLEIGH *read* ASHLEIGH-BODDINGTON.
    ,, ,, ANDREW (S.A.) *read* ANDREWS.
    ,, BARROW. *Initials are* T. H.
    ,, *For* BASE (E. G. G.) *read* BAX
   153. ,, CHASE *read* CHACE.
    ,, ,, 3172 CLARKE (P. L.) *read* 3712 CLARK.
    ,, ,, CLARKE (H. E.) *read* CLARK.
    ,, CLARKE, J. W. (7589). *Initials are* J. W. A.
    ,, *For* DU HENUME *read* DU HEAUME.
   154. ,, FERGUSSON, ,, FERGUSON.
    ,, ,, FISHER (A. W.) *read* FISCHER.
    ,, ,, FISCHER (H. C.) ,, FISHER.
    ,, FRANKLIN-ADAMS. *Initials are* B. I.
    ,, *For* GJERTSON *read* GJERTSEN
    ,, GOLDTHORP. *Initials are* R. H.
   155. KENDON. ,, ,, D. G.
    ,, LA TOUCHE. ,, ,, A. P. D.
    ,, LIDDLE. *For* D., M.P., *read* D. M. P.
    ,, MCKIE. *Initials are* R. D. M.
   156. ORD. *Initials are* E. M.
   157. *Add* 2256 SAVORY, Sqdn.-Commdr. K. S.
    ,, SMITH (6320). *Initials are* R. McK.
    ,, TAPPER. ,, ,, M. J.
   158. WEBB (2902) ,, ,, R. D. C.
    ,, WEBER-BROWN. ,, ,, A. W.
    ,, WINKWORTH. ,, ,, S. R.
    ,, *For* WILSON *read* WILLSON.
   162. BROWN. *For* 63610 *read* 763610.
    ,, CLOUTTE. ,, 64950 ,, 764950.
    ,, WOLSTENHOLME. *For* John Bernard *read* James Benjamin Wallace: *Add*:—To R A.F; Killed flying 20th August, 1918.
   163. DANIELL. ,, 8168 ,, 1868.
    ,, LAWLESS ,, 14447 ,, 1443.
    ,, FORD. *Add* F/D.
   167. *For* CHANCEY *read* CHAUNCEY.
   169. ,, EVERETT ,, EVERATT.

CORRIGENDA.

Page 170. *For* GITTINGS *read* GITTINS.
171. GRIFFITHS. *For* D. R. *read* David Rudolph
173. *For* KELSLY *read* KELSEY.
176. PEEBLES. *For* Zenda *read* John Douglas.
178. *For* SAWDY *read* SANDY.
179. *Add* 4138 SONE, Thomas Eric From 5/York & Lancaster.
180. TRUBSHAWE. *For* Walston *read* Wolstan.
182. *Delete* BAKER, Albert George.
  „   *Add to* BROWN (Lionel). Capt. M.B.E.
183. SEWELL. *For* Pte. *read* Sgt.
185. *Delete* COOK, Herbert Henry.
187. DAVIS, D. F. *Add* F/D.
  „   *Delete* ALLEN, William Alfred
189. *For* MCFADYON *read* MCFADYEN.
190. „   SENDALL   „   SENDELL.
191. „   BERNARD   „   BERNHARD.
  „   „   CORK   „   CORKE.
  „   „   DAY   „   DALY.
192. „   HAYNES   „   HEYNES.
193. „   SNALLAM   „   SNALAM.
  „   „   STANDRING „   STANDING.
196. *Delete* BILLINGTON, George.
  „   BOWIE. *Add* Died of wounds 8/5/18.
200. SMITH, Frederick H. C. D. *Add* Lieut.
  „   *For* TILLY *read* TILLEY.
202. BRUNT. *For* Stanley Herbert *read* Herbert Stanley.
203. *For* DUNN *read* DUN.
204. „   HOLMAN 6/4/18 *read* 21/3/18.
206. „   SCHOTT   „   SCOTT.
207. „   TOPPING   „   TIPPING.
  „   „   WAILES   „   WALES.
210. „   CHRISTLOW „   CHRISTELOW.
212. „   MULLENS   „   MULLINS.
  „   NICOL. *For* Thomas *read* James.
214. STANESBY. *Add* ℳ
216. DAVIES. *For* Yuab *read* Huab.
218. *Add to Coldstream Guards*
  RICKATSON, Capt. Hugh Cecil, from 5/Bedford, wounded 15/12/17 ✠
  „   *For* CRESSWELL, George *read* CRESSWELL-GEORGE.
219. THOMPSON, A. J. *Add* D.S.O. ✠ ℳ(3).
223. *For* BOGGEN *read* BOGGON.
224. *Add to* ADAMS, W. C. ✠
  „   „   „ CAHILL. ✠
227. HISLOP. *For* Archer *read* Archie.
  „   *For* GOWAN, George Henry *read* GOWEN, Henry George.
227. „   THOMPSON (A. C. G.)   „   THOMSON.
230. PYM-MANNOCK. *For* Louis A. *read* Lucius Aloysius.
231. YOUNG, L. G. B. *Add* Killed in action 19/5/16.

CORRIGENDA.

Page 232. HAMILTON, H. J. *Add* To R.F.C.
  240. BREWER. *For* Alexander *read* Alec.
  251. *Delete* CARTER, Albert Harry.
  255. HUSSEY. *For* Archibald *read* McDonald.
  267. *For* McKING *read* McKIE.
  267. *For* WORTHY *read* WORTH.
  271. THOMAS. *For* W. M. *read* William Max.
  277. *For* HOLLINGSWORTH *read* HOLLINWORTH.
  ,,   GOLDING. *Add* 8 Bn. w. -/7/17 (16/Devon) To 35/Sikhs d. 3/12/20 in
  283. *For* NAINBY *read* NAIMBY. [Palestine General Hospital, Ludd]
  ,,   ,, HOPKINSON ,, HOPKINS, John (Harold).
  284. ,, JERONS ,, JEVONS.
  ,,   ,, NABE ,, MABE.
  285. TRUBSHAWE. *For* Walston Vivian *read* Wolstan Vyvyan.
  289. *For* VILLENOWETH *read* VELLENOWETH.
  300. ,, YEATES ,, YATES.
  302. THOMPSON, Richard Seward. *For* 16/6/17 *read* 16/1/17.
  304. *For* BARRON *read* BARROW.
  308. TYER. *Add* M.V.O.
  309. BYRNE. *For* L/Cpl. *read* Sgt.
  313. GLEN. ,, Vuran ,, Vivian.
  314. *Add date* 21/11/15 to ADAMS, FOSKETT, FRANGHAIDI, MOULD, O'REGAN, RYLANDS, STONE and WHEELER.
  ,,   *Add date* 7/12/15 to GIBBONS, HOLMES, PRYKE and WEBB.
  ,,   ,, ,, 2/1/16 to AUSTIN, CLAYTON, DEW and MOYLAN-JONES.
  ,,   ,, ,, 3/9/16 to remaining names on page 314.
  ,,   IRWIN, A. G. *Add* ₥
  320. SPATZ. *Add* Rudolf Carl (after Walter).
  321. *For* LEESE *read* LEEFE.
  340. ,, NICHOL ,, NICOL.
  342. ,, BAGGS ,, BAGG.
  360. DAWSON *Add* Capt. ✠ ₥
  371. *For* CLEMMINGS *read* CLEMMENS.
  ,,   ,, CULLEN ,, CULLIN.
  375. *Delete* JONES, James Powell.
  377. ,, EVANS, Jenkin Evan.
  383. BROOKS-HILL. *Add* Capt.
  384. *For* MOOHOUSE *read* MOORHOUSE.
  385. ,, MALEHAM ,, MALCHAM.
  386. SONE. *Add* To R.A.F.
  390. FAGAN. *Add* To 9/Gurkha Rifles D.S.O.
  405. LAXTON. *Insert date* 15/5/16.
  491. PASSMORE. *Add* Major, H-Q Staff (Horse Guards).
  550. *Delete* " † MACCULLOCK, A. G."
  ,,   *Add* † to MACDONALD, A. L.
  567. ,, ,, RICHARDSON, A. B.
In Index. *Add* † and § to names of officers on first page of Addenda.
In Section IV. *Add* k and date of death to remaining names on that page.

www.ingramcontent.com/pod-product-compliance
Lightning Source LLC
Chambersburg PA
CBHW060357230426
43663CB00008B/1300